MASTER WINDOWS® 98

VISUALLY™

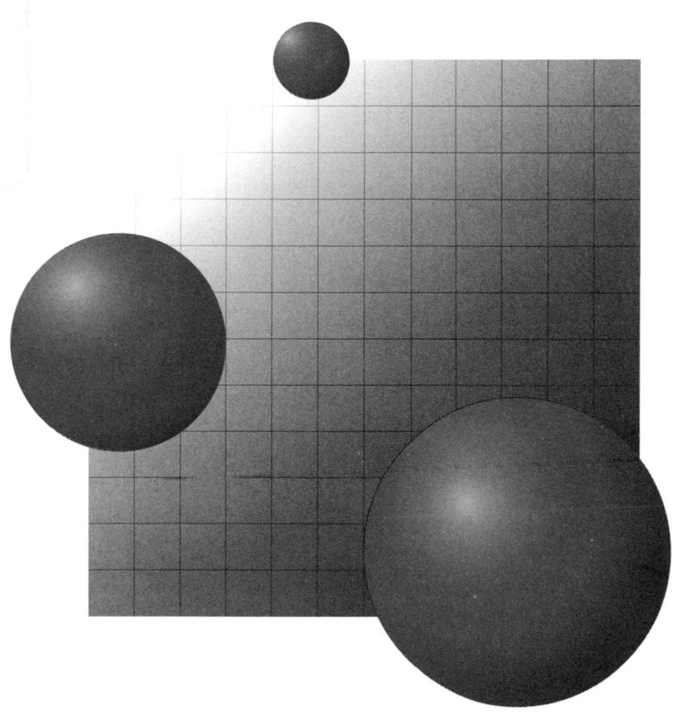

IDG's 3-D Visual™ Series

From

maranGraphics™

IDG Books Worldwide, Inc.
An International Data Group Company
Foster City, CA • Indianapolis • Chicago • Southlake, TX

Master Windows® 98 VISUALLY™

Published by
IDG Books Worldwide, Inc.
An International Data Group Company
919 E. Hillsdale Blvd., Suite 400
Foster City, CA 94404

Library of Congress Catalog Card No.: 98-84747

ISBN: 0-7645-6034-4

Printed in the United States of America
10 9 8 7

XX/XX/XX/XX/XX

Distributed in the United States by IDG Books Worldwide, Inc.

Distributed by Transworld Publishers Limited in the United Kingdom; by IDG Norge Books for Norway; by IDG Sweden Books for Sweden; by Woodslane Pty. Ltd. for Australia; by Woodslane Enterprises Ltd. for New Zealand; by Longman Singapore Publishers Ltd. for Singapore, Malaysia, Thailand, and Indonesia; by Simron Pty. Ltd. for South Africa; by Toppan Company Ltd. for Japan; by Distribuidora Cuspide for Argentina; by Livraria Cultura for Brazil; by Ediciencia S.A. for Ecuador; by Addison-Wesley Publishing Company for Korea; by Ediciones ZETA S.C.R. Ltda. for Peru; by WS Computer Publishing Corporation, Inc., for the Philippines; by Unalis Corporation for Taiwan; by Contemporanea de Ediciones for Venezuela; by Computer Book & Magazine Store for Puerto Rico; by Express Computer Distributors for the Caribbean and West Indies. Authorized Sales Agent: Anthony Rudkin Associates for the Middle East and North Africa.

For corporate orders, please call maranGraphics at 800-469-6616.
For general information on IDG Books Worldwide's books in the U.S., please call our Consumer Customer Service department at 800-762-2974.
For reseller information, including discounts and premium sales, please call our Reseller Customer Service department at 800-434-3422.
For information on where to purchase IDG Books Worldwide's books outside the U.S., please contact our International Sales department at 650-655-3200 or fax 650-655-3295.
For information on foreign language translations, please contact our Foreign & Subsidiary Rights department at 650-655-3021 or fax 650-655-3281.
For sales inquiries and special prices for bulk quantities, please contact our Sales department at 650-655-3200.
For information on using IDG Books Worldwide's books in the classroom or for ordering examination copies, please contact our Educational Sales department at 800-434-2086 or fax 817-251-8174.
For press review copies, author interviews, or other publicity information, please contact our Public Relations department at 650-655-3000 or fax 650-655-3299.
For authorization to photocopy items for corporate, personal, or educational use, please contact maranGraphics at 800-469-6616.
Screen shots displayed in this book are based on pre-release software and are subject to change.

Trademark Acknowledgments

Permissions

U.S. Corporate Sales
Contact maranGraphics at (800) 469-6616 or fax (905) 890-9434.

U.S. Trade Sales
Contact IDG Books at (800) 434-3422 or (650) 655-3000.

Welcome to the world of IDG Books Worldwide.

IDG Books Worldwide, Inc., is a subsidiary of International Data Group, the world's largest publisher of computer-related information and the leading global provider of information services on information technology. IDG was founded more than 25 years ago and now employs more than 8,500 people worldwide. IDG publishes more than 270 computer publications in over 75 countries (see listing below). More than 90 million people read one or more IDG publications each month.

Launched in 1990, IDG Books Worldwide is today the #1 publisher of best-selling computer books in the United States. We are proud to have received eight awards from the Computer Press Association in recognition of editorial excellence and three from Computer Currents' First Annual Readers' Choice Awards. Our best-selling ...For Dummies® series has more than 25 million copies in print with translations in 30 languages. IDG Books Worldwide, through a joint venture with IDG's Hi-Tech Beijing, became the first U.S. publisher to publish a computer book in the People's Republic of China. In record time, IDG Books Worldwide has become the first choice for millions of readers around the world who want to learn how to better manage their businesses.

Our mission is simple: Every one of our books is designed to bring extra value and skill-building instructions to the reader. Our books are written by experts who understand and care about our readers. The knowledge base of our editorial staff comes from years of experience in publishing, education, and journalism - experience which we use to produce books for the '90s. In short, we care about books, so we attract the best people. We devote special attention to details such as audience, interior design, use of icons, and illustrations. And because we use an efficient process of authoring, editing, and desktop publishing our books electronically, we can spend more time ensuring superior content and spend less time on the technicalities of making books.

You can count on our commitment to deliver high-quality books at competitive prices on topics you want to read about. At IDG Books Worldwide, we continue in the IDG tradition of delivering quality for more than 25 years. You'll find no better book on a subject than one from IDG Books Worldwide.

John Kilcullen
President and CEO
IDG Books Worldwide, Inc.

IDG Books Worldwide, Inc., is a subsidiary of International Data Group, the world's largest publisher of computer-related information and the leading global provider of information services on information technology. International Data Group publishes over 276 computer publications in over 75 countries. Ninety million people read one or more International Data Group publications each month. International Data Group's publications include: Argentina: Annuario de Informatica, Computerworld Argentina, PC World Argentina; Australia: Australian Macworld, Client/Server Journal, Computer Living, Computerworld, Computerworld 100, Digital News, IT Casebook, Network World, On-line World Australia, PC World, Publishing Essentials, Reseller, WebMaster; Austria: Computerwelt Osterreich, Networks Austria, PC Tip; Belarus: PC World Belarus; Belgium: Data News; Brazil: Annuário de Informática, Computerworld Brazil, Connections, Super Game Power, Macworld, PC Player, PC World Brazil, Publish Brazil, Reseller News; Bulgaria: Computerworld Bulgaria, Networkworld/Bulgaria, PC & MacWorld Bulgaria; Canada: CIO Canada, Client/Server World, ComputerWorld Canada, InfoCanada, Network World Canada; Chile: Computerworld Chile, PC World Chile; Colombia: Computerworld Colombia, PC World Colombia; Costa Rica: PC World Centro America; The Czech and Slovak Republics: Computerworld Czechoslovakia, Elektronika Czechoslovakia, Macworld Czech Republic, PC World Czechoslovakia; Denmark: Communications World, Computerworld Danmark, Macworld Danmark, PC Privat Danmark, PC World Danmark, PC World Danmark Supplements, TECH World; Dominican Republic: PC World Republica Dominicana; Ecuador: PC World Ecuador; Egypt: Computerworld Middle East, PC World Middle East; El Salvador: PC World Centro America; Finland: MikroPC, Tietoverkko, Tietoviikko; France: Distributique, Golden, Hebdo-Distributique, Info PC, Le Guide du Monde Informatique, Le Monde Informatique, Reseaux & Telecoms; Germany: Computer Partner, Computerwoche, Computerwoche Extra, Computerwoche Focus, I/M Information Management, Macwelt, PC Welt; Greece: GamePro, Multimedia World; Guatemala: PC World Centro America; Honduras: PC World Centro America; Hong Kong: Computerworld Hong Kong, PCWorld Hong Kong, Publish in Asia; Hungary: ABCD CD-ROM, Computerworld Szamitastechnika, PC & Mac World Hungary, PC-X Magazine; Iceland: Tolvuheimur/PC World Island; India: Information Systems Computerworld, PC World India, Publish in Asia; Indonesia: InfoKomputer PC World, Komputek Computerworld, Publish in Asia; Ireland: ComputerScope, PC Live!; Israel: People & Computers; Italy: Computerworld Italia, Computerworld Italia Special Editions, Macworld Italia, Networking Italia, PC Shopping, PC World Italia, PC World/Walt Disney; Japan: DTP World, HP Open World Japan, Macworld Japan, Nikkei Personal Computing, Open World Japan, OS/2 World Japan, SunWorld Japan, Windows World Japan; Kenya: East African Computer News; Korea: Hi-Tech Information/Computerworld, Macworld Korea, PC World Korea; Macedonia: PC World Macedonia; Malaysia: Computerworld Malaysia, PC World Malaysia, Publish in Asia; Mexico: Computerworld Mexico, Macworld, PC World Mexico; Myanmar: PC World Myanmar; Netherlands: Computer! Totaal, LAN Magazine, LanWorld Buyers Guide, Macworld, Net Magazine, Totaal! Beurskrant; New Zealand: Absolute Beginner's Guide, Computer Buyer, Computer Industry Directory, Computerworld New Zealand, MTB, Network World, PC World New Zealand; Nicaragua: PC World Centro America; Nigeria: PC World Nigeria; Norway: Computerworld Norge, Computerworld Privat (Datamagasinet), CW Rapport Norge, IDG's KURSGUIDE, Macworld Norge, Multimediaworld, PC World Ekspress, PC World Nettverk, PC World Norge, PC World's Produktguide, Windows World Spesial; Pakistan: Computerworld Pakistan, PC World Pakistan; Panama: PC World Panama; P. R. of China: China Computer Users, China Computerworld, China Infoworld, China Telecom World Weekly, Computer & Communication, Electronic Design China, Electronics Today, Electronics Weekly, Game Camp, Game Soft, Network World China, PC World China, Popular Computer Weekly, Software Weekly, Software World, Telecom World; Peru: Computerworld Peru, PC World Profesional Peru, PC World Peru; Poland: Computerworld Poland, Computerworld Special Report, Macworld, Networld, PC World Komputer; Philippines: Computerworld Philippines, PC World Philippines, Publish in Asia; Portugal: Cerebro/PC World, Computerworld/Correio Informático, Dealer World Portugal, Mac*In/PC*In, Multimedia World Portugal; Puerto Rico: PC World Puerto Rico; Romania: Computerworld Romania, PC World Romania, Telecom Romania; Russia: Computerworld Russia, Mir PK, Sety; Singapore: Computerworld Singapore, PC World Singapore, Publish in Asia; Slovenia: MONITOR; South Africa: Computing S.A., InfoWorld S.A., Network World S.A., Software World; Spain: Computerworld Espa-a, COMUNICACIONES WORLD, Dealer World, Macworld Espa-a, PC World Espa-a; Sweden: CAP&Design, Computer Sweden, Corporate Computing, MacWorld, Maxi Data, MikroDatorn, Nätverk & Kommunikation, PC/Aktiv, PC World, Windows World; Switzerland: Computerworld Schweiz, Macworld Schweiz, PCtip; Taiwan: Computerworld Taiwan, Macworld Taiwan, PC World Taiwan, Publish Taiwan, Windows World; Thailand: Thai Computerworld, Publish in Asia; Turkey: Computerworld Turkiye, MACWORLD Turkiye, PC WORLD Turkiye; Ukraine: Computerworld Kiev, Computers & Software, Multimedia World Ukraine, PC World Ukraine; United Kingdom: Acorn User, Amiga Action, Amiga Computing, Appletalk, Computing, GamePro, Macworld, Network News, Parents and Computers, PC Advisor, PC Home, PSX Pro UK, The WEB; United States: Cable in the Classroom, CD Review, CIO Magazine, Computerworld, Computerworld Client/Server Journal, Digital Video Magazine, DOS World, Federal Computer Week, GamePro, InfoWorld, I-Way, JavaWorld, Macworld, Multimedia World, Netscape World Online, Network World, PC Entertainment, PC World, Publish, SunWorld Online, SWATPro Magazine, Video Event, WebMaster; Uruguay: PC World Uruguay; Venezuela: Computerworld Venezuela, PC World Venezuela; and Vietnam: PC World Vietnam.

Every maranGraphics book represents
the extraordinary vision and commitment of a unique family:
the Maran family of Toronto, Canada.

Back Row (from left to right): *Sherry Maran, Rob Maran, Richard Maran, Maxine Maran, Jill Maran.*

Front Row (from left to right): *Judy Maran, Ruth Maran.*

Richard Maran is the company founder and its inspirational leader. He developed maranGraphics' proprietary communication technology called "visual grammar." This book is built on that technology—empowering readers with the easiest and quickest way to learn about computers.

Ruth Maran is the Author and Architect—a role Richard established that now bears Ruth's distinctive touch. She creates the words and visual structure that are the basis for the books.

Judy Maran is the Project Manager. She works with Ruth, Richard and the highly talented maranGraphics illustrators, designers and editors to transform Ruth's material into its final form.

Rob Maran is the Technical and Production Specialist. He makes sure the state-of-the-art technology used to create these books always performs as it should.

Sherry Maran manages the Reception, Order Desk and any number of areas that require immediate attention and a helping hand.

Jill Maran is a jack-of-all-trades who works in the Accounting and Human Resources department.

Maxine Maran is the Business Manager and family sage. She maintains order in the business and family—and keeps everything running smoothly.

CREDITS

Authors:
Ruth Maran, Paul Whitehead
and Maarten Heilbron

Director of Editing & Indexer:
Kelleigh Wing

Project Manager:
Judy Maran

Copy Development, Editing & Screen Captures:
Wanda Lawrie
Roxanne Van Damme
Jason M. Brown

Editing & Screen Captures:
Raquel Scott
Janice Boyer
Cathy Benn
Michelle Kirchner

Layout Designer:
Treena Lees

Layout & Illustrations:
Jamie Bell

Illustrators & Screen Artists:
Russ Marini
Jeff Jones
Peter Grecco

Post Production & Screen Captures:
Robert Maran

Editorial Support:
Michael Roney

ACKNOWLEDGMENTS

The goal of this book is similar to the goal of Windows itself: to take something powerful and make it simple. I hope that this book will make it easier to accomplish the tasks you bring to your computer.

I am deeply indebted to Ruth Maran for her patience and understanding, and her ability to synthesize complex tasks into clear and easy-to-follow steps. She made my work simple, and our collaboration efficient and harmonious.

I thank the entire staff of maranGraphics for their tireless pursuit of excellence. They have checked every detail and questioned every assertion, and made the book better at every turn.

Finally, I thank my wife Kim, and my children Kieran and Calla for their help and cooperation. This book would not be possible without them.

Maarten Heilbron

Thanks to the dedicated staff of maranGraphics, including Jamie Bell, Cathy Benn, Janice Boyer, Jason M. Brown, Francisco Ferreira, Peter Grecco, Vicki Harford, Jeff Jones, Michelle Kirchner, Wanda Lawrie, Treena Lees, Frances LoPresti, Michael W. MacDonald, Jill Maran, Judy Maran, Maxine Maran, Robert Maran, Sherry Maran, Russ Marini, James Menzies, Raquel Scott, Roxanne Van Damme, Paul Whitehead and Kelleigh Wing.

Finally, to Richard Maran who originated the easy-to-use graphic format of this guide. Thank you for your inspiration and guidance.

Ruth Maran

WINDOWS® 98

I GETTING STARTED

II WINDOWS 98 ACCESSORIES

III CUSTOMIZE WINDOWS 98

WHAT'S INSIDE

IV WORK WITH DISKS

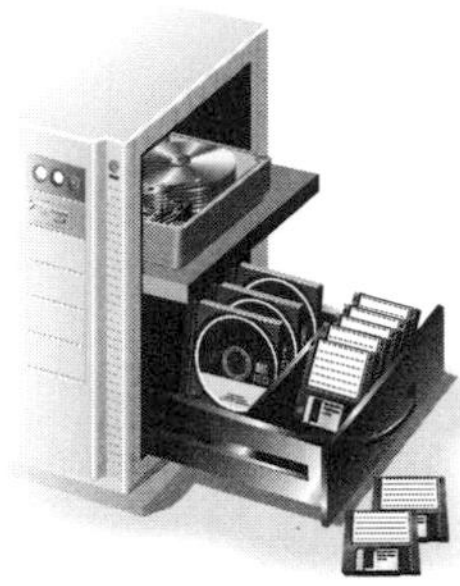

V CONNECT TO OTHER COMPUTERS

VI NETWORKING

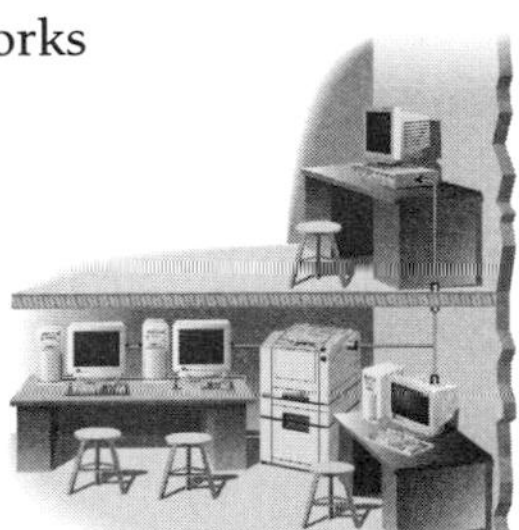

VII WINDOWS 98 AND THE INTERNET

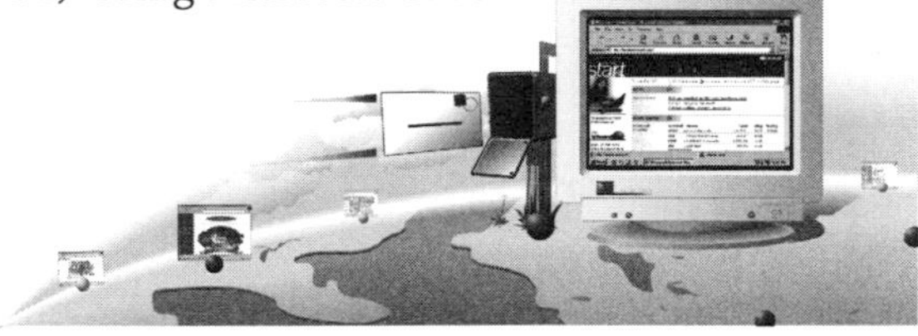

VIII INSTALLING AND TROUBLESHOOTING

1

GETTING STARTED

1) WINDOWS BASICS

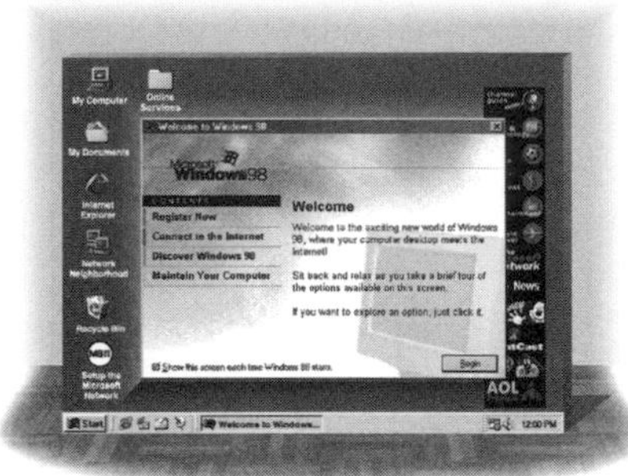

2) VIEWING FILES

TABLE OF CONTENTS

3) WORK WITH FILES

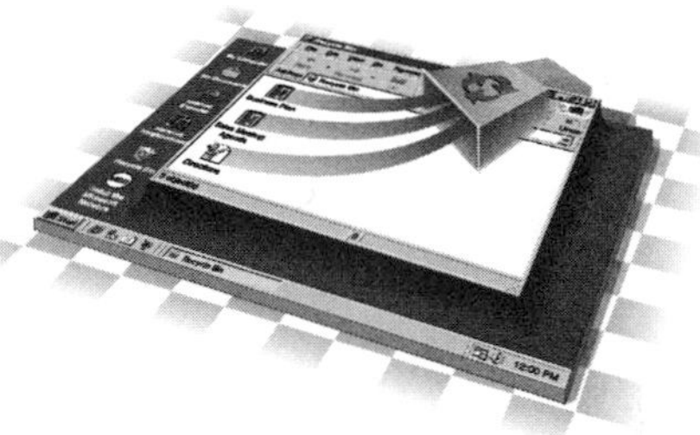

4) PRINTING

2 WINDOWS 98 ACCESSORIES

TABLE OF CONTENTS

8) USING PAINT

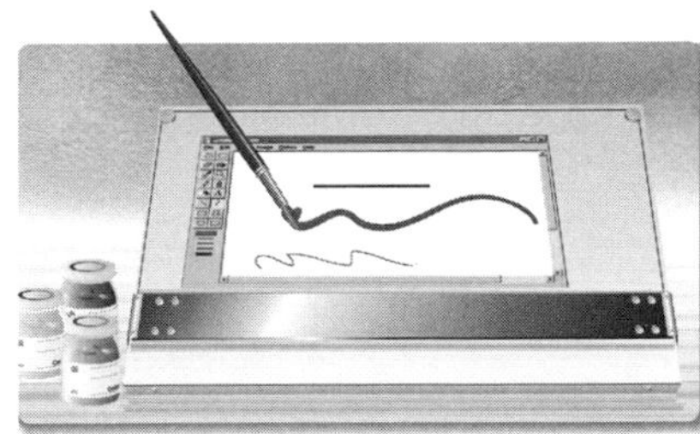

9) MORE ACCESSORIES

3 *CUSTOMIZE WINDOWS 98*

10) CUSTOMIZE YOUR COMPUTER

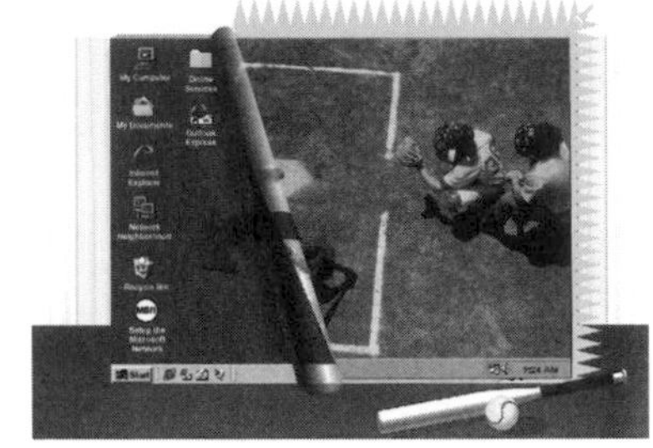

11) USING ACCESSIBILITY FEATURES

12) CUSTOMIZE THE START MENU

TABLE OF CONTENTS

13) MULTIMEDIA

4 WORK WITH DISKS

14) DISK MANAGEMENT

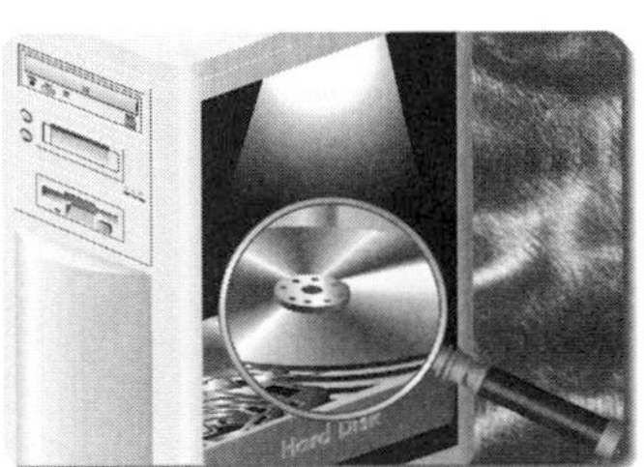

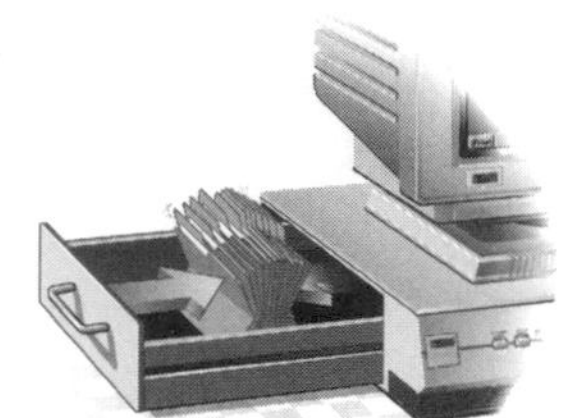

5 CONNECT TO OTHER COMPUTERS

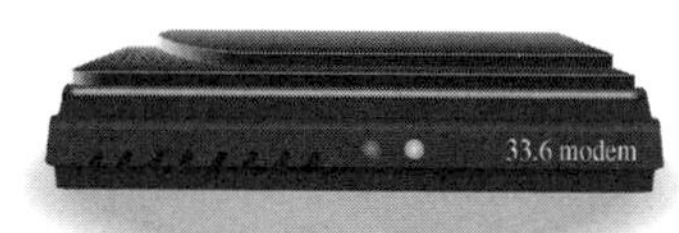

TABLE OF CONTENTS

19) HYPERTERMINAL

20) WORK WITH PORTABLE COMPUTERS

6 NETWORKING

21) INTRODUCTION TO NETWORKS

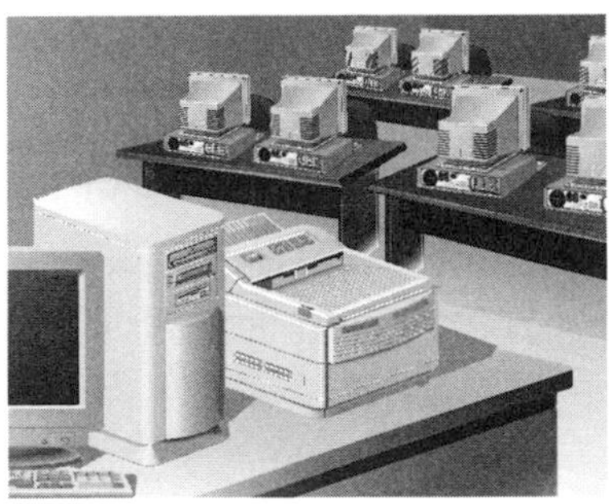

TABLE OF CONTENTS

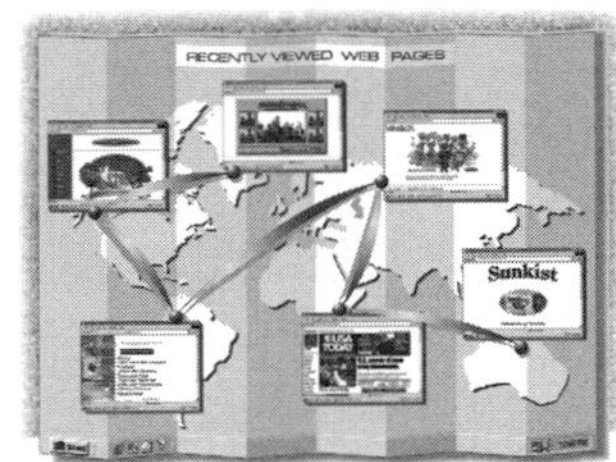

26) EXCHANGE E-MAIL MESSAGES

27) READING NEWSGROUP MESSAGES

28) VIEWING CHANNELS

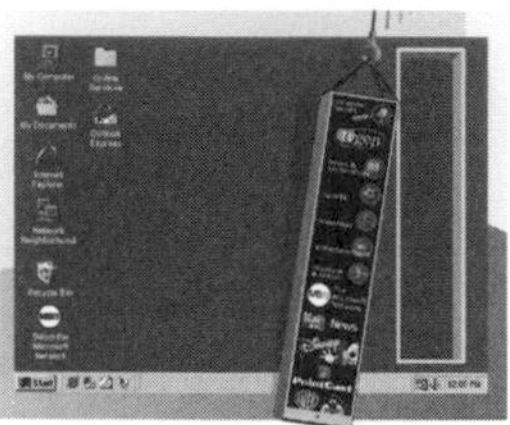

29) CREATING WEB PAGES

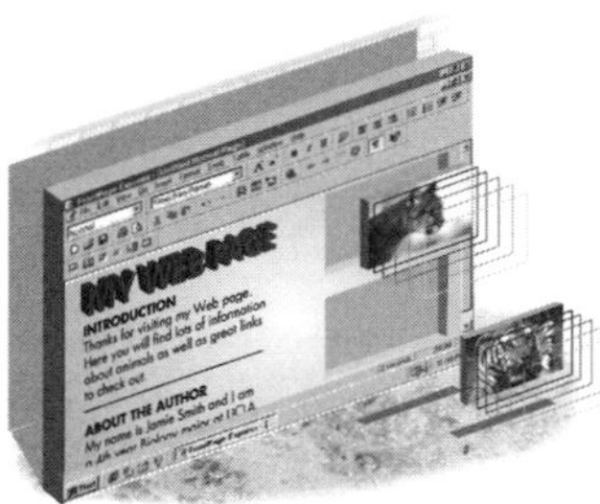

30) USING MICROSOFT NETMEETING

31) USING MICROSOFT CHAT

TABLE OF CONTENTS

8 INSTALLING AND TROUBLESHOOTING

32) INSTALL HARDWARE AND SOFTWARE

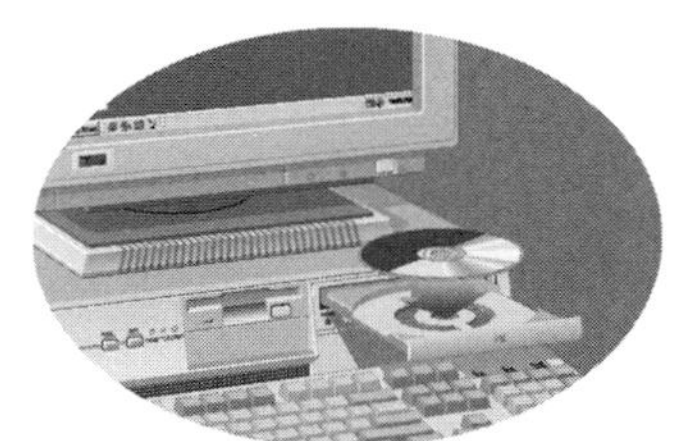

33) INSTALL AND ENHANCE WINDOWS 98

34) TROUBLESHOOTING

SECTION I

1) WINDOWS BASICS

2) VIEWING FILES

3) WORK WITH FILES

4) PRINTING

5) EXCHANGING DATA

6) MS-DOS PROGRAMS

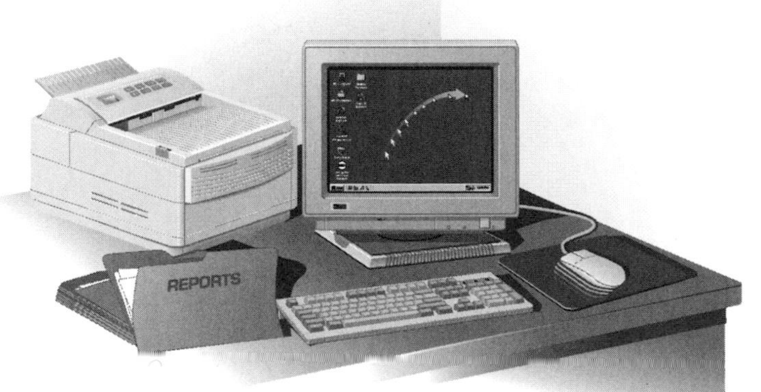

INTRODUCING WINDOWS 98

Windows 98 is an operating system which ensures that all parts of your computer work together smoothly and efficiently. Windows 98 controls the hardware on your computer and starts and operates your programs. Windows 98 makes it easy to use your computer for work or play.

Files and Folders

When you create and save a document, Windows stores the document in a file. You can open, move, copy, rename, print and delete your files. If you accidentally delete a file, you can usually restore the file from the Recycle Bin. You can create folders to organize your files. You can also use advanced cut and paste techniques, like object linking and embedding, to share information between your files and programs. Placing shortcuts on your desktop helps you easily access your favorite files and folders.

Fun Features

When you need a break from your work, you can play games such as Solitaire, Hearts or Minesweeper. You can also play video and sound files. Assigning sounds to program events, such as closing a program, can make Windows more enjoyable to use.

Accessory Programs

Windows includes several programs you can use to perform tasks. You can use WordPad to compose simple documents. You can create graphic images using Paint. You can perform calculations using the on-screen Calculator. Character Map allows you to use symbols that do not appear on your keyboard. The Imaging program lets you work with electronic versions of paper documents such as scanned newspaper clippings.

Customization and Personalization

You can change the appearance and behavior of Windows to suit your needs. You can place the taskbar in a more convenient location on the screen. You can display a picture on your desktop or change the color and font size used to display screen elements such as title bars. Changing the resolution allows you to display more or less information on the screen. You can also have a screen saver appear when you are not using your computer.

The Accessibility options may help make using the computer easier for people with special needs. You can also have a program start automatically each time you start Windows and add items you frequently use to the Start menu.

Disk Management

Windows 98 makes it easy to keep your computer performing at its best. You can view the amount of used and free space on your hard drive. If you are running out of free space, there are many ways you can create more free space. You can use ScanDisk to check your hard drive for errors and repair any errors that are found. Disk Defragmenter organizes the files on your hard drive and makes sure your programs start as quickly as possible. You can also tell Windows how you normally use your computer so Windows can use your hard drive more efficiently. To safeguard your work, you can use Microsoft Backup to create backup copies of your work.

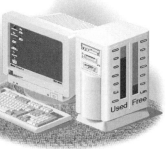

Connecting to Other Computers

There are many ways you can connect to other computers. You can use a dial-up connection to connect to your computer at work when you are traveling. You can use HyperTerminal to connect to local Bulletin Board Systems (BBS). A direct cable connection allows you to use a special cable to connect two computers to share information. The Briefcase feature allows you to work on your files when you are away from the office. When you return to the office, Briefcase can automatically update the files on your office computer.

Networking

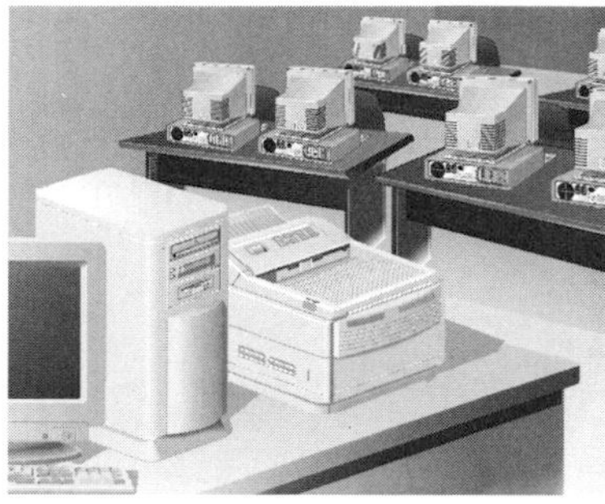

You can share your files and printer with individuals on your network. You can also determine the type of access that others will have to your shared resources. Network Neighborhood allows you to view the shared resources on your network. WinPopup allows you to exchange short messages with other people on your network.

Hardware and Software

Windows provides many ways for you to view information about your computer and modify your computer's settings. You can use the wizards included with Windows to make installing a new program or hardware device easy. The wizards guide you step-by-step through the installation process. Windows also provides Troubleshooters to assist you when your programs and hardware do not work properly.

INTRODUCING WINDOWS 98

What's New in Windows 98

Windows 98 is a new version of Microsoft's operating system. It is similar to Windows 95 and Windows NT 4.0 but includes several new features. If you are upgrading from Windows 3.1, you will discover a new interface that makes it easier for you to manage the parts of your computer and use your programs. If you are upgrading from Windows 95, you will already be familiar with the way Windows 98 looks and works, but you will discover many improvements and new capabilities.

Ease of Use

Windows 98 is easier to use than previous versions of Windows. You can access the same commands whether you are browsing the World Wide Web or looking through files stored on your computer. The ability to display your Windows desktop on multiple monitors makes working with several open documents or programs easier. The Task Scheduler feature allows you to schedule tasks that Windows will perform automatically for you at a specific date and time.

Customizing

Windows 98 offers the features that were included in Microsoft Plus! for Windows 95. You will find a selection of visual effects and desktop themes you can use to customize the way Windows looks. You can customize the appearance of folders by adding a picture to the folder's background. Windows 98 also allows you to view your desktop as a Web page and display active Web content on your desktop.

Internet Access

Windows 98 includes Internet Explorer 4.0, which allows you to browse through information on the World Wide Web. Internet Explorer also allows you to view channels of information. A channel is a specially designed Web site that Windows can automatically deliver to your computer.

Windows 98 also includes Outlook Express. This Internet mail program allows you to exchange e-mail messages with people around the world and read newsgroup messages.

You can use FrontPage Express to create and edit your own Web pages. Microsoft NetMeeting allows you to collaborate on projects with colleagues anywhere in the world. Microsoft Chat allows you to chat with people on the Internet in a comic strip setting.

Television

Windows 98 makes your computer more entertaining by including a WebTV program. You can use WebTV to watch your favorite television shows on your computer. The WebTV's program guide allows you to view all the current TV listings for your area on the screen and select the show you want to watch.

Computer Maintenance

Windows 98 is more reliable than Windows 95 and has improved computer maintenance capabilities. You can use the Maintenance Wizard to perform maintenance tasks, such as removing unneeded files from your computer. You can use Microsoft System Information to view details about your computer and how it is set up. Microsoft System Information includes many tools you can use to find and fix problems with your computer. For example, the Windows Report Tool lets you send information about your computer problems over the Internet to Microsoft. The System File Checker can notify you of errors in the system files stored on your computer. If these files have been damaged, Windows 98 may not run properly.

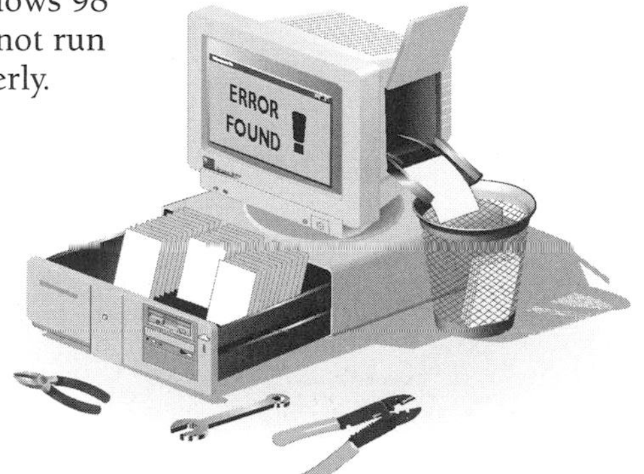

Computer Optimization

Windows 98 includes many improved features to help you optimize your computer's performance. FAT32 is a file system that better manages data on large hard drives to reduce wasted space. Windows 98 can convert your drives to FAT32 without disrupting your current programs and documents. Windows 98 also offers advanced compression capabilities that may help you double the amount of information your hard drive can store.

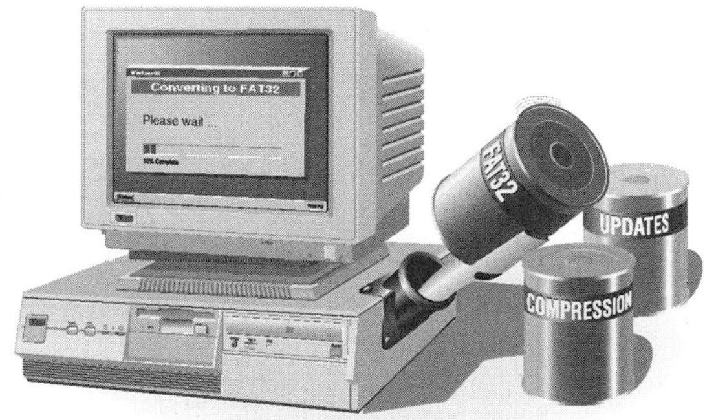

The Windows Update feature lets you check the Windows Update page on the World Wide Web for software updates, bug fixes and new features. You can also use the Windows Update feature to access technical support information available from Microsoft's Web site. Both portable and desktop computer users will find new power management capabilities that reduce energy consumption.

PARTS OF THE WINDOWS 98 SCREEN

The Windows 98 screen uses icons to display the items and information on your computer. Each icon is used to access a specific item. The available items depend on how your computer is set up.

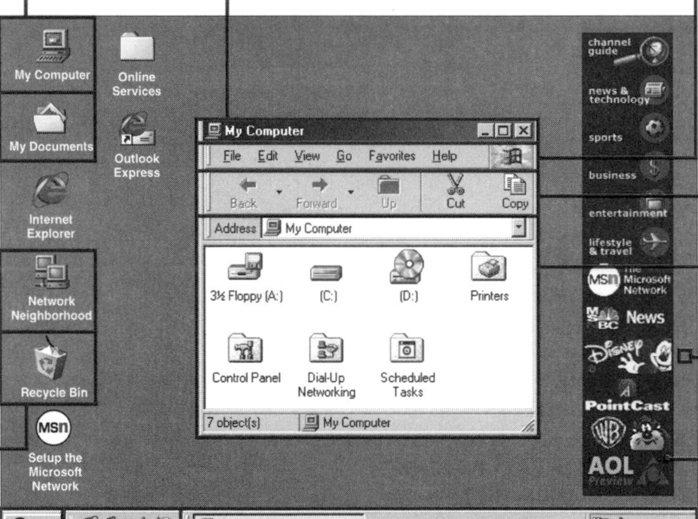

My Computer

Lets you view all the folders and files stored on your computer.

My Documents

Provides a convenient place to store your documents.

Network Neighborhood

Lets you view all the folders and files available on your local network.

Recycle Bin

Stores deleted files and lets you recover them later.

Start Button

Gives you quick access to programs, files, Windows Help and the settings on your computer.

Quick Launch Toolbar

Gives you quick access to commonly used features, including Internet Explorer, Outlook Express, the desktop and channels.

Taskbar

Displays a button for each open window on your screen. You can use these buttons to switch between the open windows.

Title Bar

Displays the name of an open window. The title bar of the window you are currently using is a different color than other open windows.

Menu Bar

Provides access to lists of commands available in a window.

Toolbar

Contains buttons that provide quick access to frequently used menu commands.

Window

A rectangle on your screen that displays information. A window can be moved and sized.

Desktop

The background area of your screen.

Channel Bar

Displays specially designed Web sites you can have Windows automatically deliver to your computer.

USING THE MOUSE

A mouse is a hand-held device that lets you select and move items on your screen. When you move the mouse on your desk, the mouse pointer on your screen moves in the same direction.

The mouse pointer assumes different shapes, such as ↖ or I, depending on its location on the screen and the task you are performing.

Click

Press and release the left mouse button. A click is used to select an item on the screen.

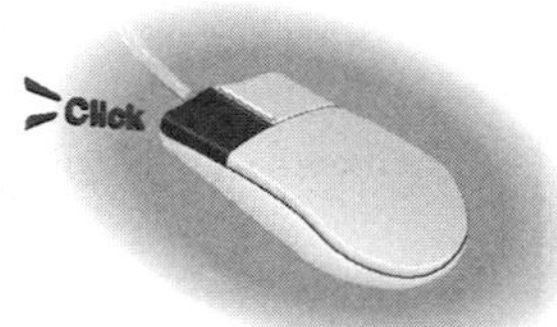

Double-Click

Quickly press and release the left mouse button twice. A double-click is used to open a document or start a program.

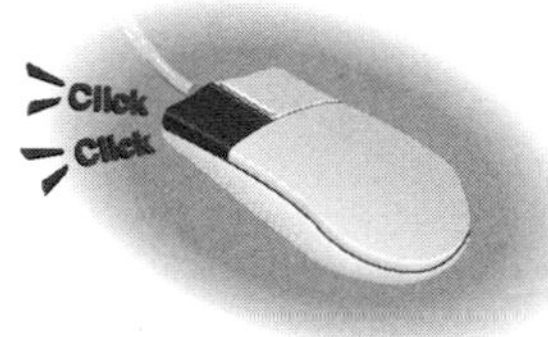

Right-Click

Press and release the right mouse button. A right-click is used to display a list of commands you can use to work with an item.

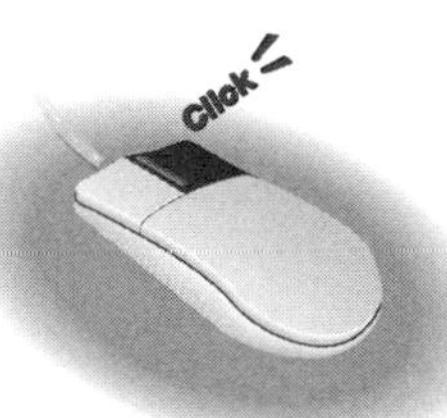

Drag and Drop

Position the mouse pointer over an item on the screen and then press and hold down the left mouse button. Still holding down the button, move the mouse to where you want to place the item and then release the button. Dragging and dropping makes it easy to move an item to a new location.

Cleaning the Mouse

You should occasionally remove the small cover on the bottom of the mouse and clean the ball inside the mouse. Make sure you also remove dust and dirt from the inside of the mouse to help ensure smooth motion.

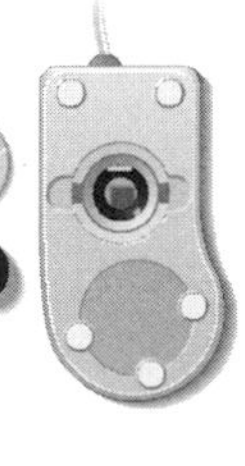

Mouse Pads

A mouse pad provides a smooth, non-slip surface for moving the mouse. A mouse pad also reduces the amount of dirt that enters the mouse and protects your desk from scratches. Hard plastic mouse pads attract less dirt and provide a smoother surface than fabric mouse pads.

START WINDOWS

Windows automatically starts when you turn on your computer. If your computer is connected to a network, you may need to enter a user name and password. Your user name and password identify you to the network and verify that you have permission to access and use network services. You may also need to enter a user name and password if you share your computer with other people. A unique user name and password enables each person to have a personalized working environment.

When your computer starts, you may be asked to choose which hardware setup you are using. Portable computers often use more than one hardware setup.

If your computer was not shut down properly the last time it was used, Windows automatically runs ScanDisk to check your hard drive for errors. For information on ScanDisk, see page 312.

The Welcome to Windows 98 dialog box appears when you start Windows. You can have this dialog box appear each time you start Windows.

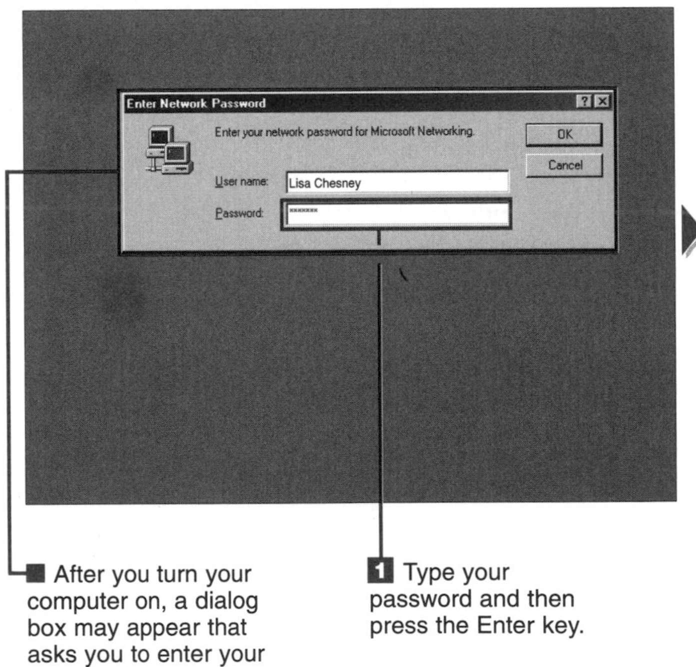

■ After you turn your computer on, a dialog box may appear that asks you to enter your password.

1 Type your password and then press the Enter key.

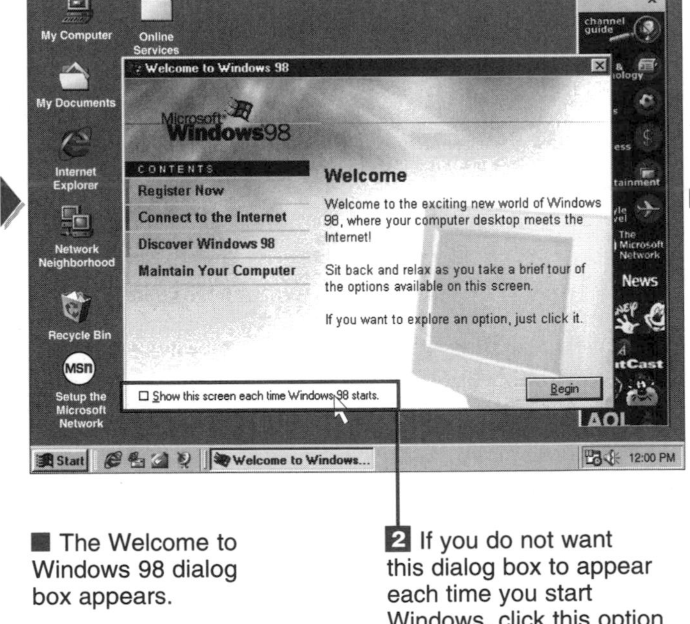

■ The Welcome to Windows 98 dialog box appears.

2 If you do not want this dialog box to appear each time you start Windows, click this option (☑ changes to ☐).

Can I redisplay the Welcome to Windows 98 dialog box?

To display the Welcome to Windows 98 dialog box at any time, click the Start button, select Programs and then click Accessories. Select System Tools and then click Welcome To Windows.

How do I remove the Channel Bar from my desktop?

The Channel Bar allows you to quickly access specially designed Web sites called channels. To remove the Channel Bar, position the mouse at the top of the Channel Bar until a gray area appears and then click ☒. To redisplay the Channel Bar, see page 560.

What options are available in the Welcome to Windows 98 dialog box?

The Register Now option allows you to register your copy of Windows 98 with Microsoft over the Internet. Registering allows you to receive Windows 98 updates and technical support. The Connect to the Internet option starts the Internet Connection Wizard. For information, see page 498. The Discover Windows 98 option allows you to learn more about how to use Windows 98. You can also choose the Maintain Your Computer option to run the Maintenance Wizard and improve the performance of your computer. For information, see page 328.

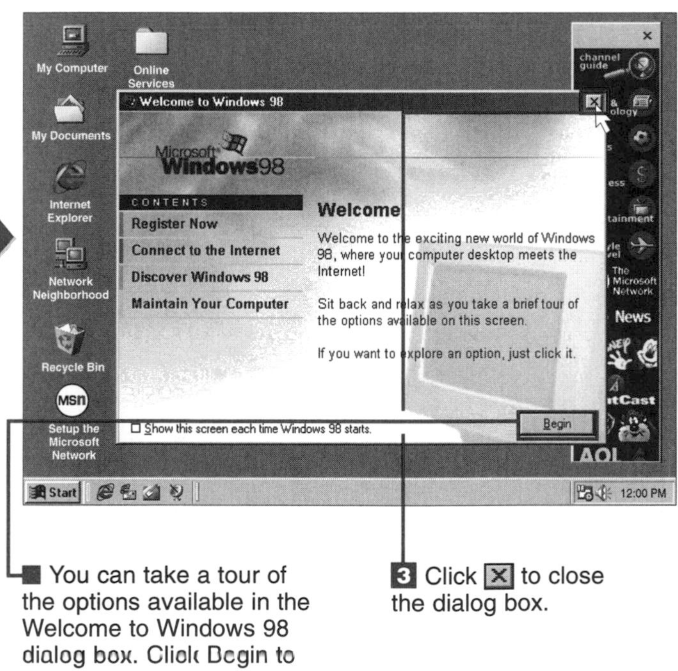

■ You can take a tour of the options available in the Welcome to Windows 98 dialog box. Click Begin to start the tour.

3 Click ☒ to close the dialog box.

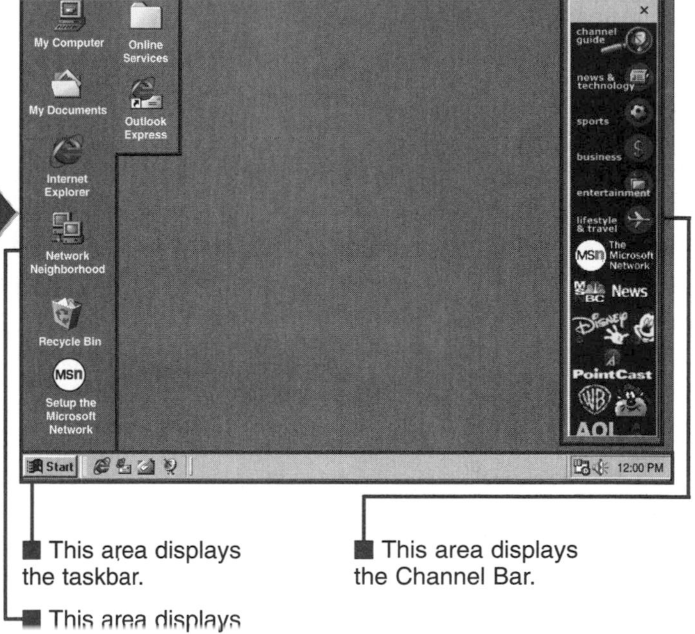

■ This area displays the taskbar.

■ This area displays your desktop icons.

■ This area displays the Channel Bar.

SHUT DOWN WINDOWS

You should always shut down Windows before turning off your computer. Shutting down properly allows Windows to save and close your documents, disconnect from the network and warn you about users who may be accessing your files. Turning off your computer without shutting down properly may cause you to lose data.

There are several shut down options you can choose from. The Stand by option places the computer in a low-power mode. Stand by mode is useful if you do not need your computer for a period of time. You should save all of your open documents before choosing Stand by mode.

The Shut down option shuts down your computer so you can turn off the power.

The Restart option restarts your computer to give the memory and resources a fresh start. Restarting is useful if your computer is not operating properly.

The Restart in MS-DOS mode option shuts down Windows and restarts your computer in MS-DOS mode. Many computer programs, particularly games, require MS-DOS mode to run.

You can also log off your computer so someone else can use it. Windows will restart so another person can log on to the computer.

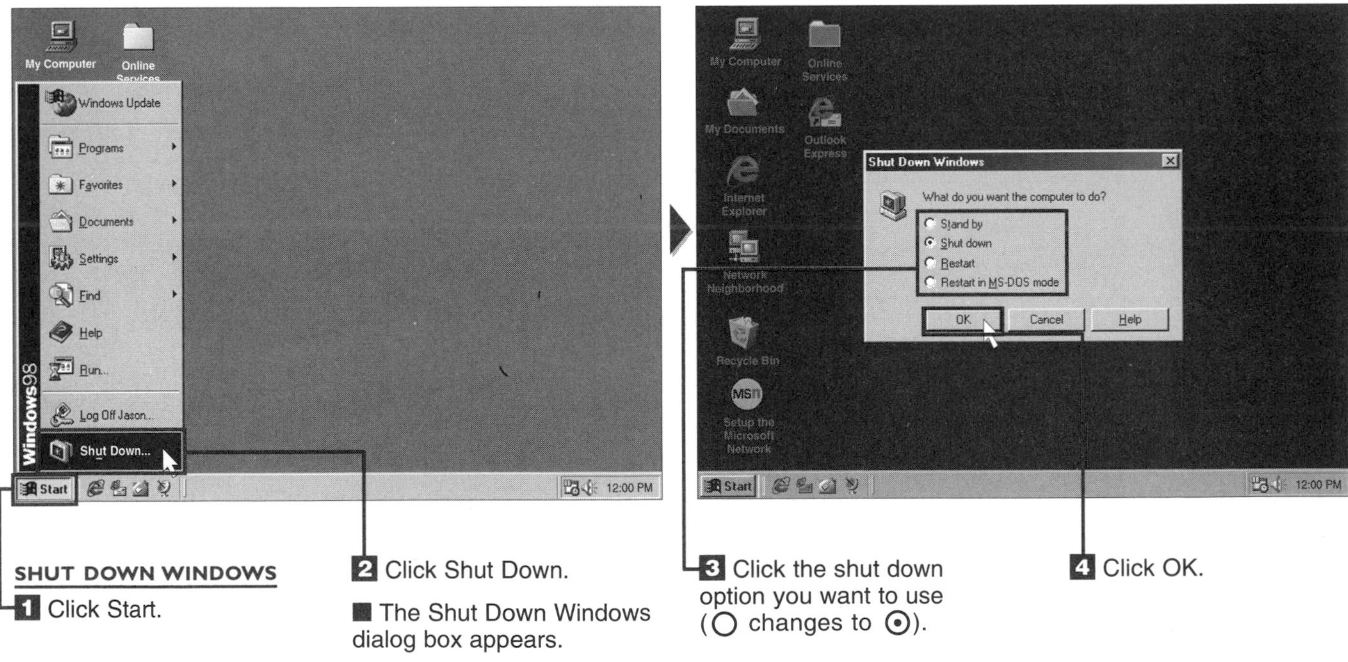

SHUT DOWN WINDOWS

1 Click Start.

2 Click Shut Down.

■ The Shut Down Windows dialog box appears.

3 Click the shut down option you want to use (○ changes to ⊙).

4 Click OK.

TIPS

Why isn't the Stand by option available on my computer?

Your computer may not support Advanced Power Management. For information about Advanced Power Management, see page 340.

How can I resume using my computer when it is in Stand by mode?

When you are ready to use your computer, move the mouse or press a key on your keyboard.

Can I quickly restart Windows without restarting my computer?

Yes. Select the Restart option in the Shut Down Windows dialog box. Then press and hold down the Shift key as you click OK.

Can I change the appearance of the screen that appears when it is safe to turn off my computer?

Yes. In Paint, display the Open dialog box, click the Files of type area and select All Files. Open the Logos.sys file located in the Windows folder. You can then use the tools available in Paint to change the message that appears or add a graphic.

Note: You may need to display hidden system files to find the Logos.sys file. See page 56.

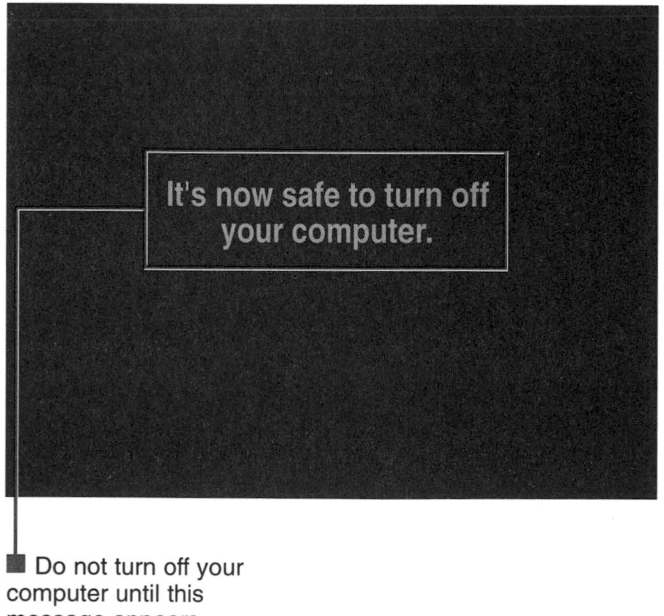

■ Do not turn off your computer until this message appears.

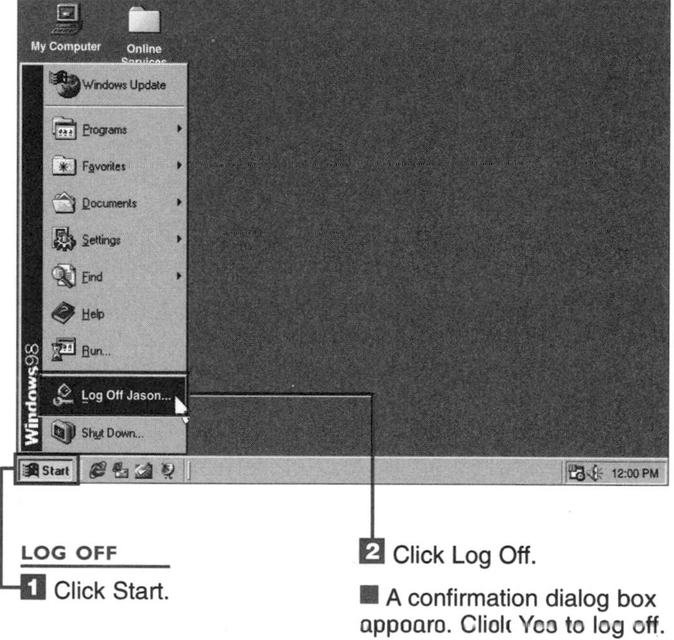

LOG OFF

1 Click Start.

2 Click Log Off.

■ A confirmation dialog box appears. Click Yes to log off.

START A PROGRAM

You can start a program by using the Start button. The Start button appears on the taskbar and is a good starting place for you to find and start your programs.

When you click the Start button, the Start menu appears, providing quick access to your programs. You can also use this menu to find documents, get help and shut down Windows.

You can use the Start button while you are working in any program. The Start button allows you to quickly start a new program without having to close or minimize the current program.

You can access the Start menu using the mouse or the keyboard.

When you start a program, a button for the program appears on the taskbar.

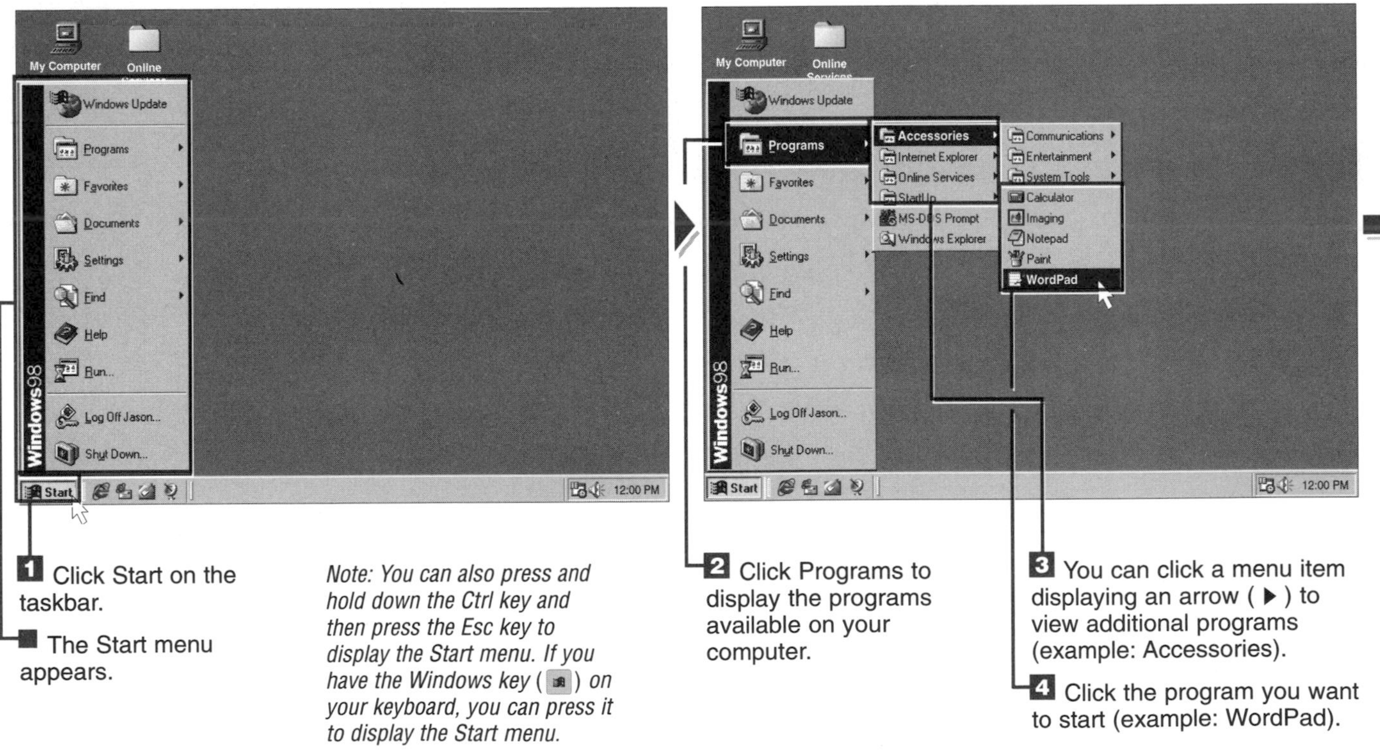

1 Click Start on the taskbar.

■ The Start menu appears.

Note: You can also press and hold down the Ctrl key and then press the Esc key to display the Start menu. If you have the Windows key ( ) on your keyboard, you can press it to display the Start menu.

2 Click Programs to display the programs available on your computer.

3 You can click a menu item displaying an arrow (▶) to view additional programs (example: Accessories).

4 Click the program you want to start (example: WordPad).

TIPS

When I clicked on a program in the Start menu, it did not start. What is wrong?

The program may start as a minimized button on the taskbar. Look for the button on the taskbar and then click the button to display the program's window.

How do I close the Start menu?

To close the Start menu, press the Esc key or click outside the menu area.

How can I find a program not on the Start menu?

You can try to locate the program using either My Computer, Windows Explorer or the Find feature on the Start menu. For information on the Find feature, see page 78.

Can I rearrange the items in the Start menu?

You might want to rearrange the Start menu so you can more easily access the programs you use most often. You can move any item on the Documents or Programs menu by dragging the item to a new location. For information on rearranging the Start menu, see page 266.

Can I add an item to the Start menu?

You can add any program or file to the Start menu. Find the item you want to add and drag it to the Start button. Do not release the mouse button and the Start menu will appear. You can then drag the program or file to the location you want on the Start menu or any submenu.

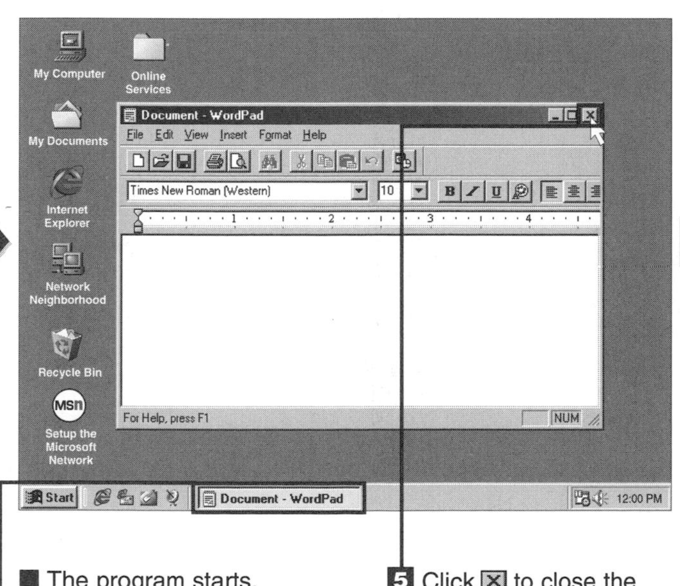

■ The program starts.

■ A button for the program appears on the taskbar.

5 Click ☒ to close the window.

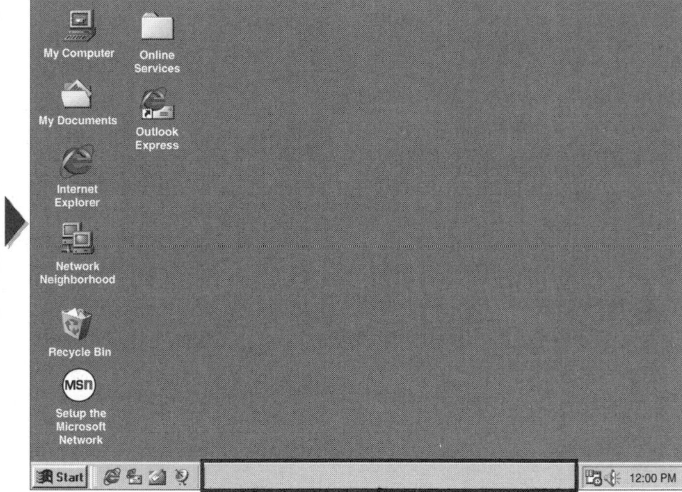

■ The window disappears from your screen.

■ The button for the window disappears from the taskbar.

USING RUN TO START A PROGRAM

You can use the Run command to start a program that does not appear on the Start menu.

There are many programs that Windows does not display on the Start menu, such as programs that can be used to change the settings on your computer. This helps to avoid the accidental misuse of these programs.

There are several utility programs included with Windows 98 that are not displayed on the Start menu.

You may have MS-DOS and older Windows programs on your computer, such as games, that are also not displayed on the Start menu. You can use the Run command to access these types of programs.

You can also display a list of programs you have recently started using the Run command and then choose a program from the list.

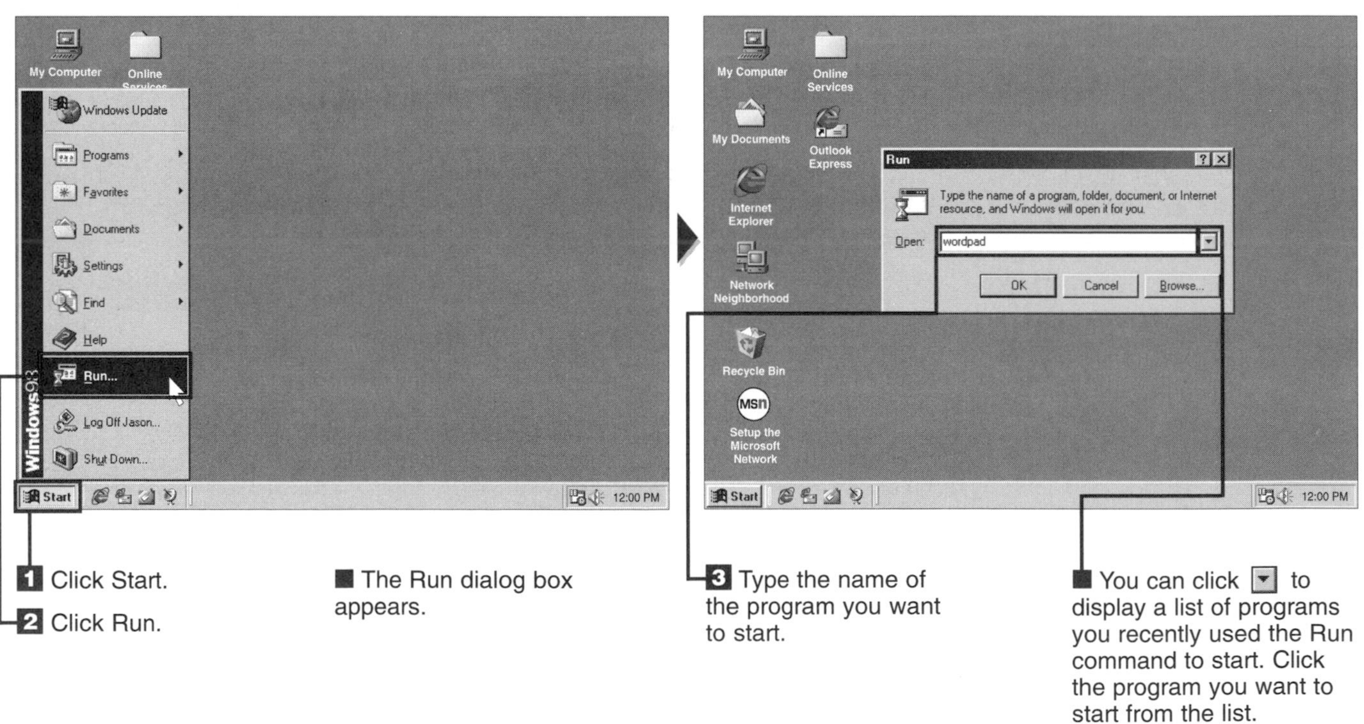

1 Click Start.

2 Click Run.

■ The Run dialog box appears.

3 Type the name of the program you want to start.

■ You can click ▼ to display a list of programs you recently used the Run command to start. Click the program you want to start from the list.

TIPS

What if I do not know the name of the program I want to open?

You can click the Browse button in the Run dialog box to find a program you want to open.

Is there another way to quickly start a program?

You can drag a program, folder or file from your desktop or an open window to the Start button. When you want to start the program, click the Start button and then select the program.

Can I use the Run command to open items other than programs?

The Run command can open many types of items. For example, if you type the address of a page on the World Wide Web, Windows will connect to the Internet, open your Web browser and display the Web page. You can also type the name and path of a folder, such as **c:\my documents\notes**, to display the contents of the folder on your screen.

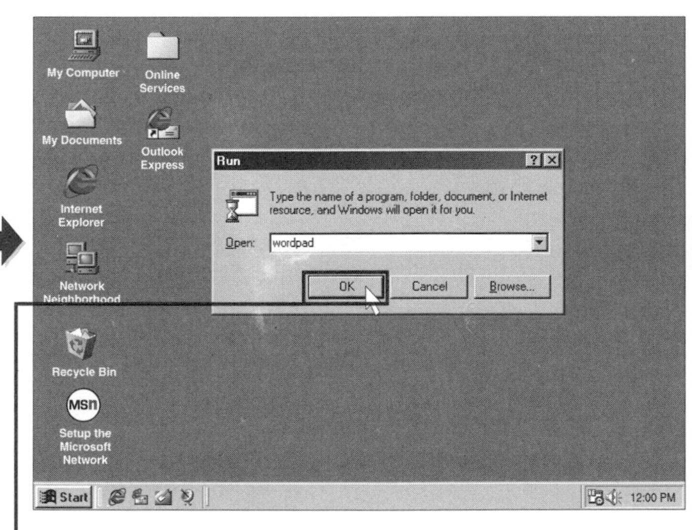

4 Click OK to start the program.

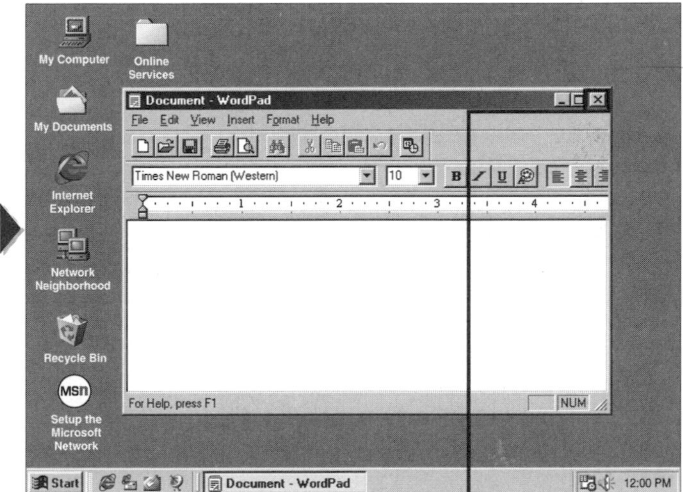

■ The program starts.

■ Click ☒ to close the program.

MAXIMIZE OR MINIMIZE A WINDOW

You may want to enlarge a window to fill your screen so you can see more information, or you can put the window aside while you concentrate on another task.

When you maximize a window, you enlarge the window to fill your screen. This allows you to view more of the contents of the window.

When you are not using a window, you can minimize the window to remove it from your screen. When you minimize a window, the window reduces to a button on your taskbar. When you once again display the window, the window will appear in its original location and in the same size it was displayed before you minimized the window.

If you have a lot of open windows on your screen, you can save time by minimizing all of the windows at once.

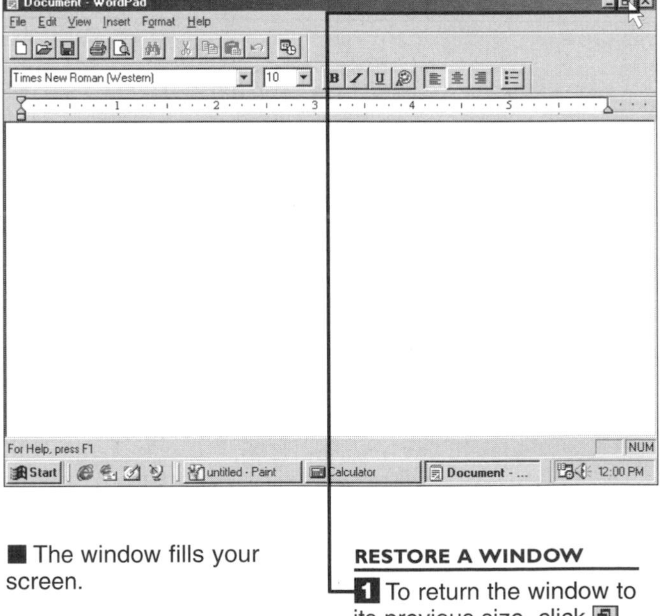

MAXIMIZE A WINDOW

1 Click □ in the window you want to maximize.

■ The window fills your screen.

RESTORE A WINDOW

1 To return the window to its previous size, click 🗗.

I keep clicking the wrong button when I try to maximize a window. Is there an easier way to maximize a window?

If you double-click the title bar of a window, the window fills your screen. Double-clicking the title bar again will return the window to its original size. You can also increase the size of the buttons at the top right corner of a window by using the Appearance tab in the Display Properties dialog box. See page 208.

How can I read the name of a button on the taskbar if the whole name is not displayed?

Position the mouse pointer over the button. After a few seconds, a box appears, displaying the full name of the button.

How do I close a minimized window?

If you no longer need a window that is minimized on your screen, you can close the window. To close a minimized window, right-click its button on the taskbar and then select Close.

Can I make the taskbar disappear so it does not cover the bottom of a maximized window?

You can change the way the taskbar behaves. For more information, see page 198.

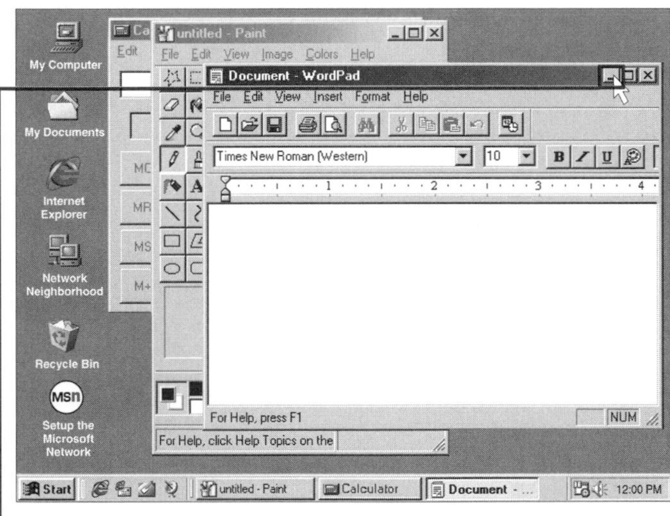

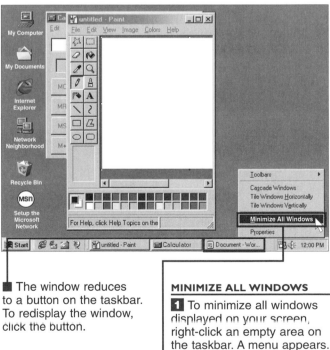

MINIMIZE A WINDOW

1 Click ▁ in the window you want to minimize.

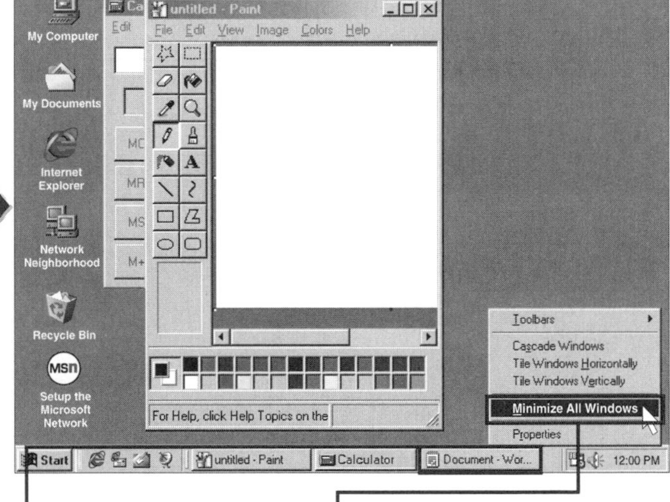

■ The window reduces to a button on the taskbar. To redisplay the window, click the button.

MINIMIZE ALL WINDOWS

1 To minimize all windows displayed on your screen, right-click an empty area on the taskbar. A menu appears.

2 Click Minimize All Windows.

MOVE OR SIZE A WINDOW

You can have many windows open on your desktop at one time. Adjusting the location and size of windows can help you work with their contents more easily.

You can move a window to a new location if it covers important items on your screen. If you have more than one window open, you can adjust the position of the windows to ensure that you can view the contents of each window. You can click on any open window to bring it to the front.

You can increase the size of a window to see more of its contents. You can reduce the size of a window to view more of the items it covers.

Just as you can move and size windows on your desktop, you can also move and size windows in open programs.

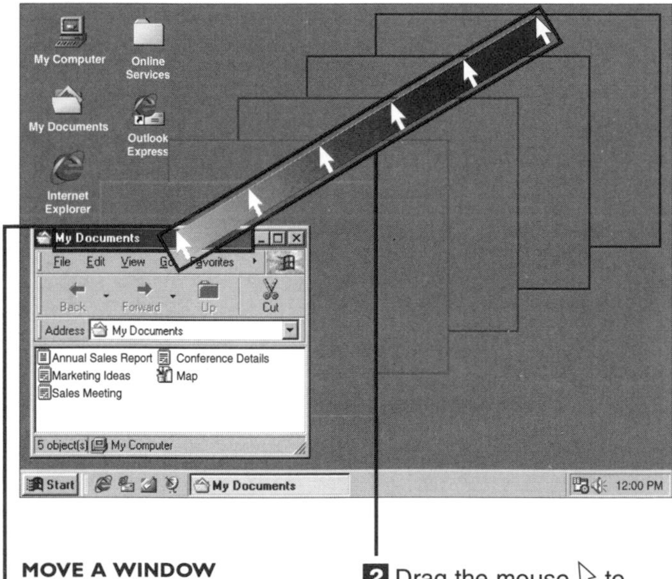

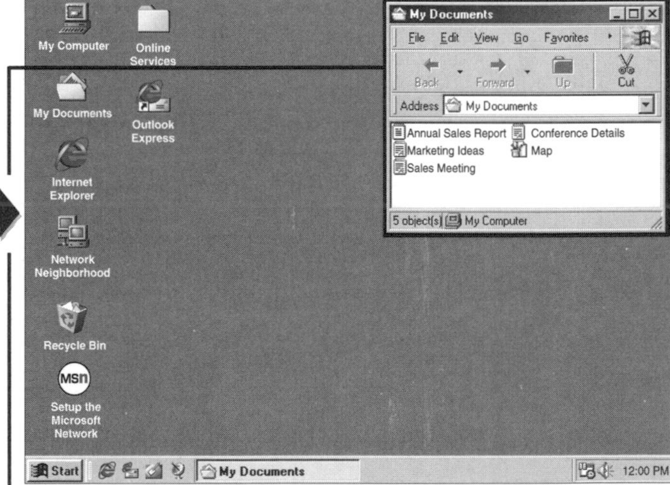

MOVE A WINDOW

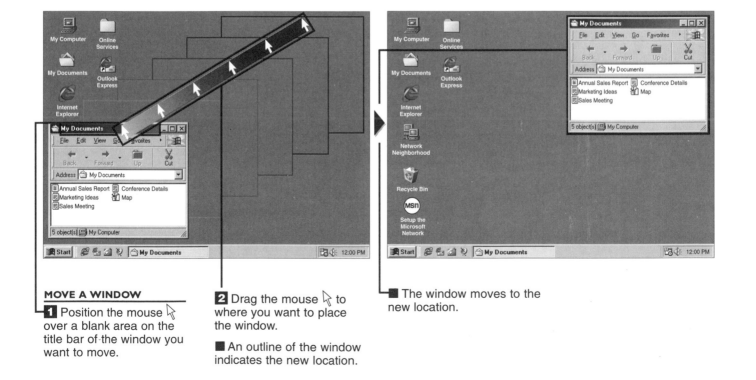

1 Position the mouse over a blank area on the title bar of the window you want to move.

2 Drag the mouse to where you want to place the window.

■ An outline of the window indicates the new location.

■ The window moves to the new location.

TIPS

How can I see the contents of a window I am moving or sizing?

Right-click a blank area on your desktop. On the menu that appears, select Properties. Click the Effects tab and then select the Show window contents while dragging option (☐ changes to ☑).

Can I move or size a maximized window?

You will not be able to move or size a window that has been maximized. Restore the window first and then move or size it. To restore a window, see page 18.

Can I move an entire window off the screen?

You can move most of a window off the screen but some of the window will still be visible. This allows you to put a document aside, as you might on a real desk.

Can all programs be sized?

Some programs, like Calculator, cannot be sized.

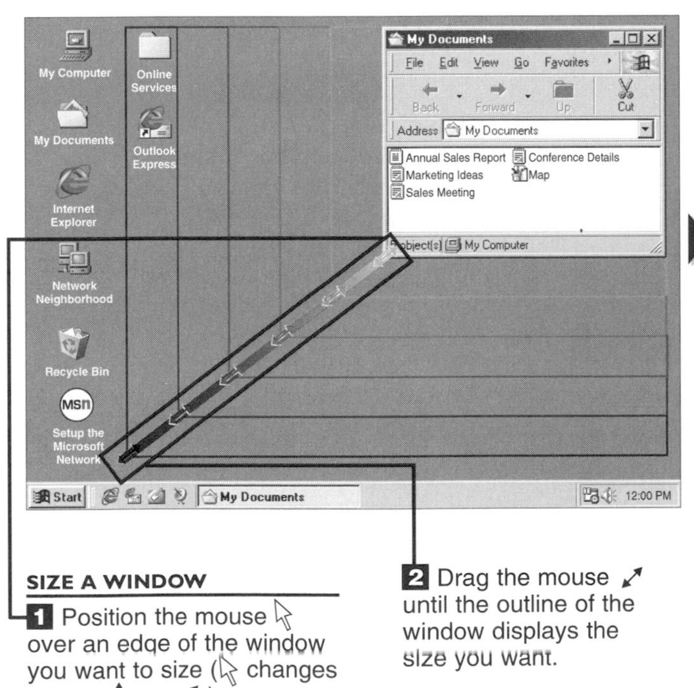

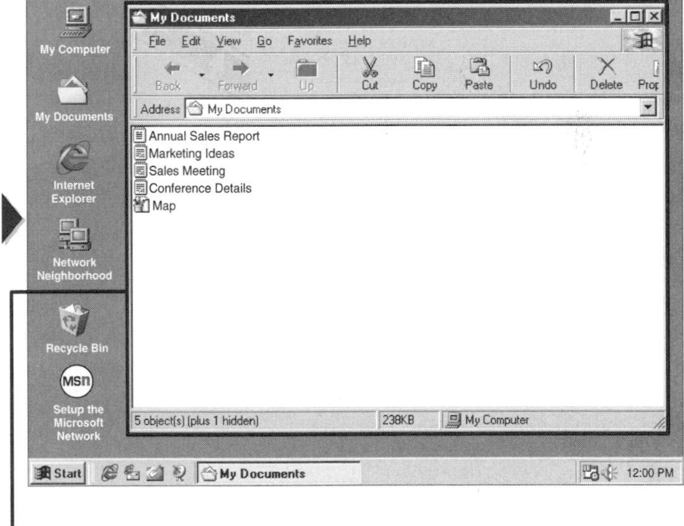

SIZE A WINDOW

1 Position the mouse over an edge of the window you want to size (pointer changes to ↔, ↕ or ⤢).

2 Drag the mouse ⤢ until the outline of the window displays the size you want.

■ The window changes to the new size.

SWITCH BETWEEN WINDOWS

When you have more than one window open, you can switch between all of the open windows.

Although you are able to have several windows open, you can only work in one window at a time. This window is called the active window. The active window appears in front of all the other windows. The title bar of the active window is a different color than the title bar of the other open windows.

The taskbar displays a button for each open window on your screen. Each taskbar button displays all or part of the name of the window it represents.

You can make a window active by clicking its button on the taskbar. You can also use your keyboard to switch between open windows.

The ability to have multiple windows open and switch between them is very useful. Switching between windows allows you to consult a report while you answer your e-mail, or verify a budget when you are preparing a presentation.

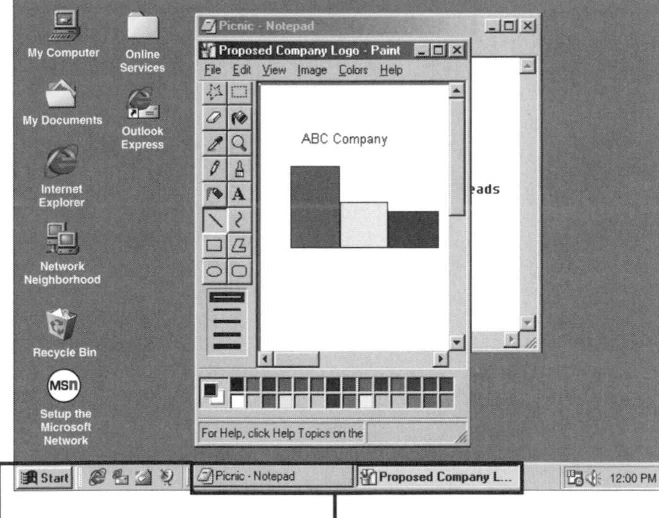

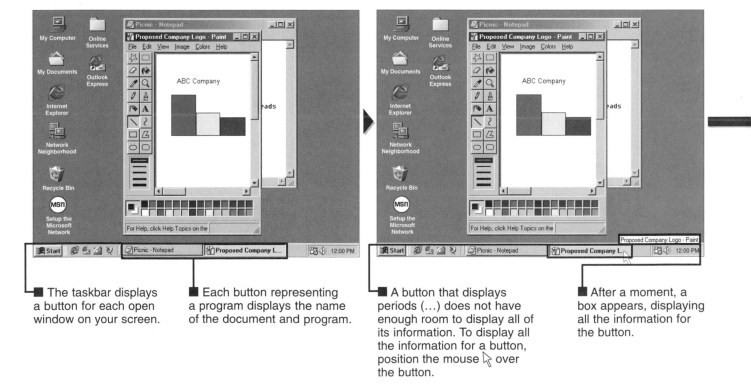

■ The taskbar displays a button for each open window on your screen.

■ Each button representing a program displays the name of the document and program.

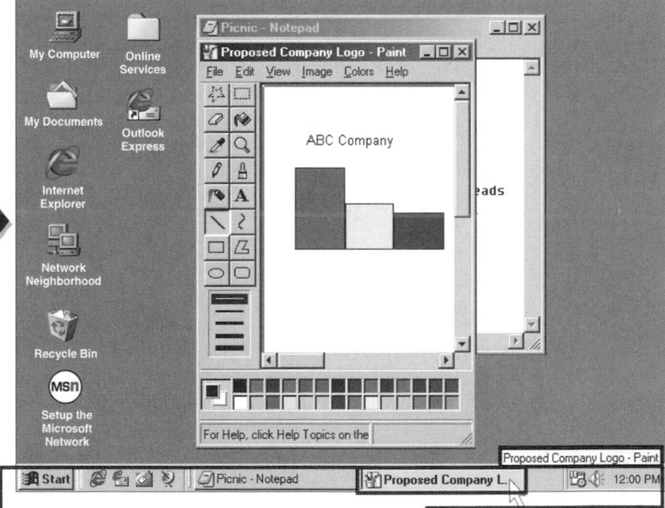

■ A button that displays periods (...) does not have enough room to display all of its information. To display all the information for a button, position the mouse over the button.

■ After a moment, a box appears, displaying all the information for the button.

TIPS

The taskbar is not displayed on my screen. How do I get the taskbar to appear?

If you have turned on Auto hide, move your mouse pointer to where the taskbar was last seen to display the taskbar. You can also press and hold down the Ctrl key and then press the Esc key to display the taskbar.

What can I do if my taskbar will not reappear?

Your taskbar may have been resized. Move the mouse pointer to the edge of the screen where the taskbar was last seen. When the pointer changes to a double-headed arrow (↕), drag the taskbar back onto the screen.

Is there another way to make an open window active?

You can click any part of an open window to make it the active window. If you have several windows on your screen, you can use your keyboard to switch between them. Press and hold down the Alt key and then press the Esc key until you see the window you want to work with.

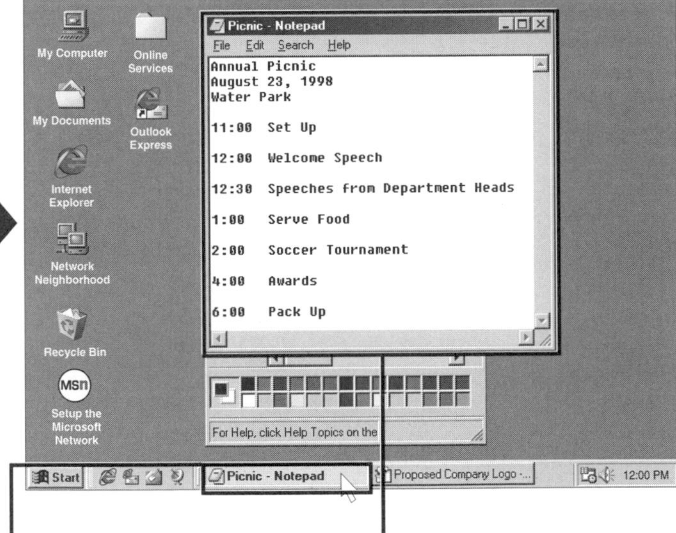

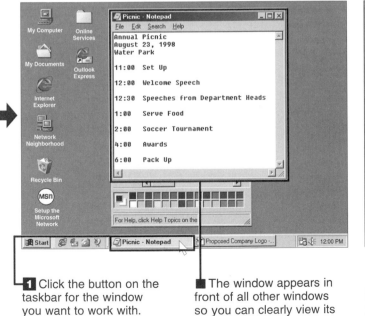

1 Click the button on the taskbar for the window you want to work with.

■ The window appears in front of all other windows so you can clearly view its contents.

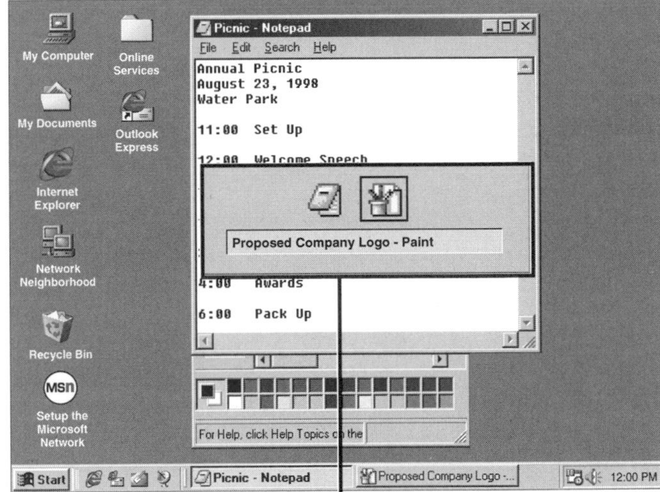

USING THE KEYBOARD

1 Press and hold down the Alt key.

2 Still holding down Alt, press the Tab key.

■ A box appears, displaying an icon for each open program.

3 Still holding down Alt, press the Tab key until the box displays the name of the window you want to work with. Then release Alt.

ARRANGE WINDOWS

You can arrange your open windows to make them easier to use or display more of their contents.

You can have several windows open at the same time. Similar to a real desk, you can have many items, such as an agenda, a letter and a budget, all open on your desktop at once. Windows allows you to arrange and organize these items so they are easier to use.

You can choose to cascade your open windows. Cascade displays windows one on top of the other so that you can see the title bar of each window. This is useful if you are working with My Computer and have many windows open. You can move between the open windows by clicking the title bar of the window you want to view.

You can use the Tile commands to see two or more windows side by side or one above the other. Tiling allows you to compare the contents of your windows and drag information from one window to another.

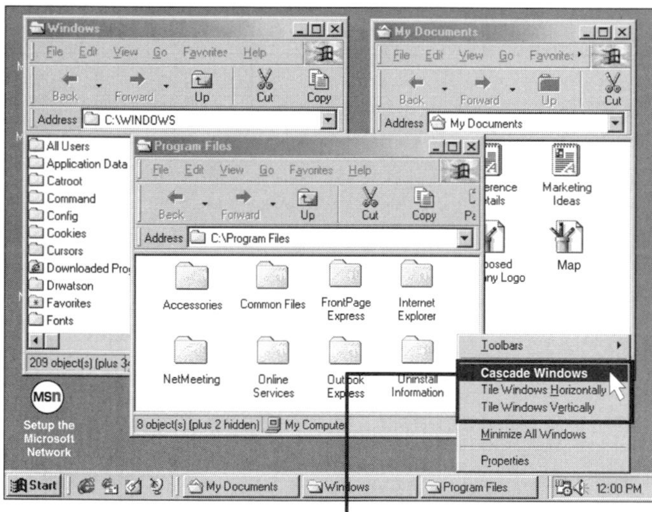

1 Right-click an empty area on the taskbar. A menu appears.

2 Click the way you want to arrange the windows.

CASCADE

■ The windows neatly overlap each other. You can clearly see the title bar of each window.

■ You can click the title bar of the window you want to work with. The window will appear in front of all other windows.

How do I make a window appear in front of all other windows?

Click any part of the window. You can also click the window's button on the taskbar.

How do I change back to the previous window arrangement?

To immediately change back to the previous window arrangement, right-click an empty area on the taskbar and then select Undo.

Why are some of my programs not tiling correctly?

Some programs with a fixed window size, like Calculator, cannot be tiled.

Why can't I see a difference between Tile Vertically and Tile Horizontally?

Tiled windows are displayed the same way on your screen when there are four or more windows open.

How do I tile or cascade only some of the windows I have open?

Minimize the windows you do not want included before you use the Tile or Cascade commands.

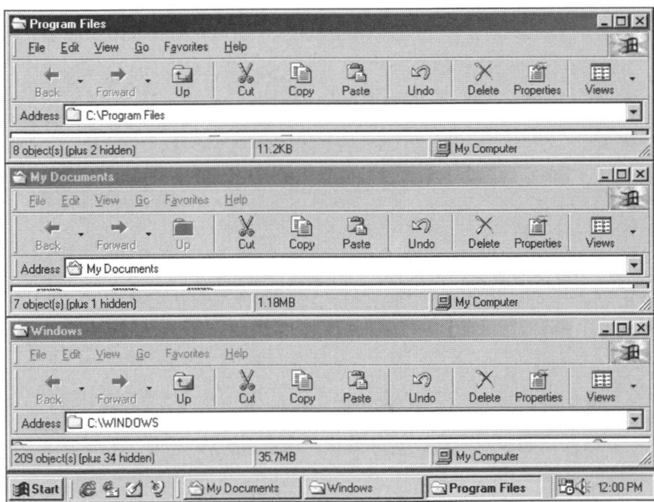

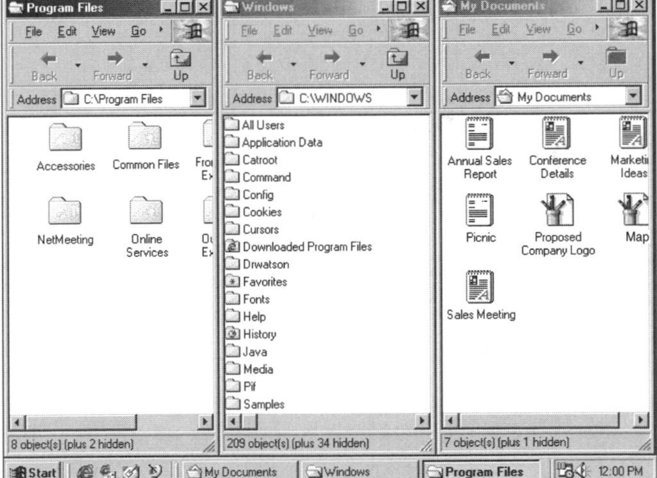

TILE HORIZONTALLY

■ The windows appear one above the other. You can view the contents of each window.

■ You can compare the contents of the windows and easily exchange information between the windows.

■ You can click anywhere in the window you want to work with to make that window active.

TILE VERTICALLY

■ The windows appear side by side. You can view the contents of each window.

■ You can compare the contents of the windows and easily exchange information between the windows.

■ You can click anywhere in the window you want to work with to make that window active.

SHOW THE DESKTOP

You can use the Show Desktop button to minimize all the open windows on your screen so you can clearly view the desktop. This allows you to quickly access the items on your desktop, such as My Computer, the Recycle Bin and shortcuts to programs and documents you frequently use.

Windows allows you to perform many tasks at once, so you may find that you often have several windows open on your screen at the same time. When you want to perform another task, like starting a program or opening a My Computer window, you may have to close or move several windows before you can access the items on your desktop.

The Show Desktop button does not close any of the open windows. The windows are minimized to buttons on the taskbar. You can return the windows to your screen one at a time by using the taskbar buttons or return the windows to the screen all at once by using the Show Desktop button.

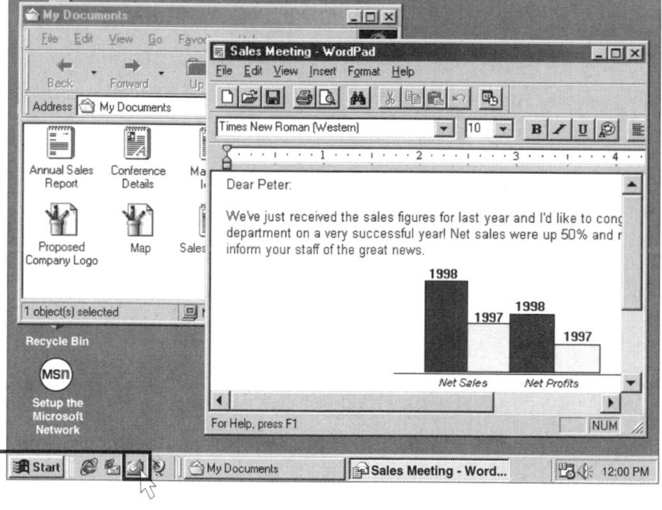

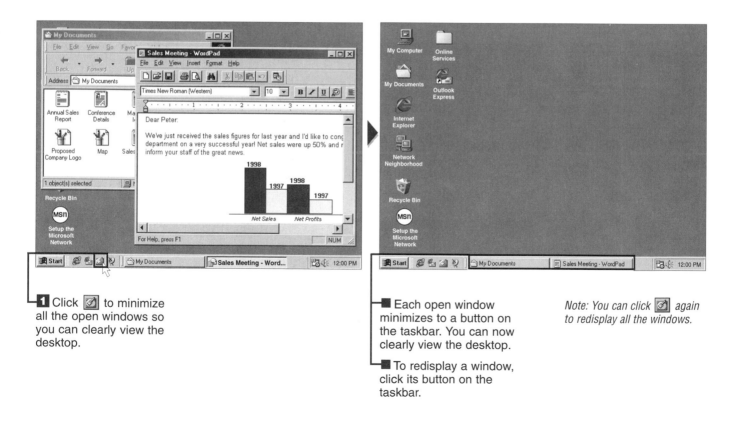

1 Click to minimize all the open windows so you can clearly view the desktop.

■ Each open window minimizes to a button on the taskbar. You can now clearly view the desktop.

■ To redisplay a window, click its button on the taskbar.

Note: You can click again to redisplay all the windows.

SHORTCUT MENUS

Most items in Windows have a shortcut menu that appears when you right-click the item. The shortcut menu includes actions and commands appropriate for the item. You can display a shortcut menu for any item on the screen, as well as for the desktop and the taskbar.

The shortcut menu for a file includes commands to Cut, Copy, Delete and Rename the file. Some programs may add additional commands to the shortcut menu.

On the shortcut menu, the default action for the item is listed in bold. The default action is performed when you double-click an item. For example, if the Open command is bold on a file's shortcut menu, double-clicking the file will open the file. The default action for a sound or movie file is Play. For a screen saver file, the default action is Test.

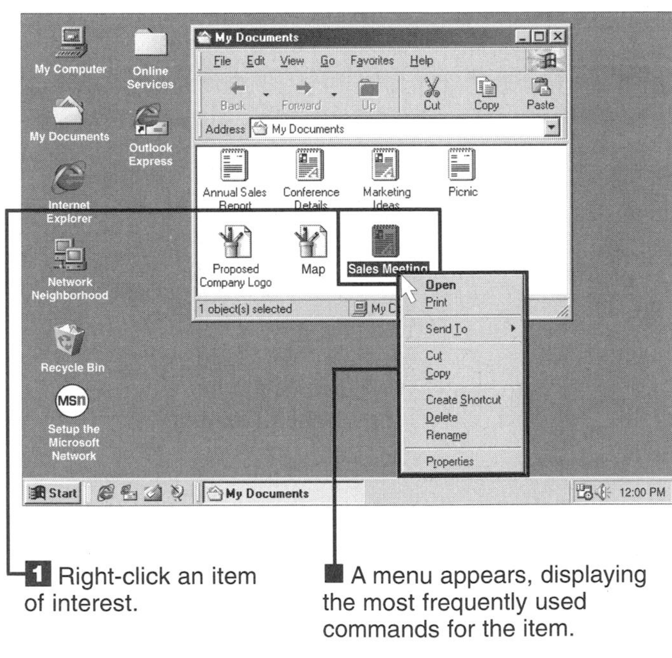

1 Right-click an item of interest.

■ A menu appears, displaying the most frequently used commands for the item.

Note: If you want to view all of the available commands for the item, press and hold down the Shift key as you perform step 1.

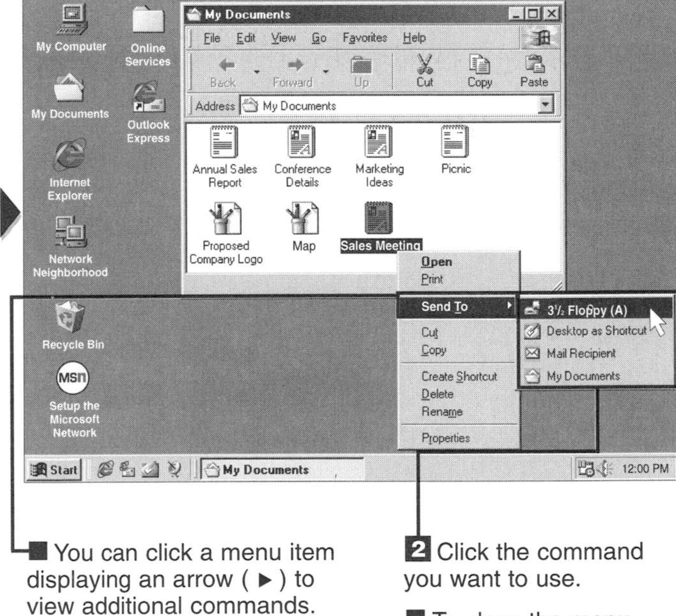

■ You can click a menu item displaying an arrow (▶) to view additional commands.

2 Click the command you want to use.

■ To close the menu without selecting a command, click outside the menu or press the Alt key.

SELECT COMMANDS

Windows programs provide menus and dialog boxes so you can access their commands and features. Most Windows programs share similar commands, which makes the programs easier to learn and use. You can use your mouse or the keyboard to select commands.

Each menu contains a group of related commands. Some menu commands, like Save or Undo, perform an action when they are selected.

Some menu commands, like Open and Print, open a dialog box. These commands are usually followed by three dots (...). A dialog box appears when a program needs more information to perform an action. Dialog boxes have areas where you can enter text or select options from a list.

You can use some menu commands to turn an option on or off. If an option is on, a check mark (✔) or a bullet (●) appears to the left of the command.

If a small arrow (▶) appears to the right of a menu command, the command will open another menu with more commands.

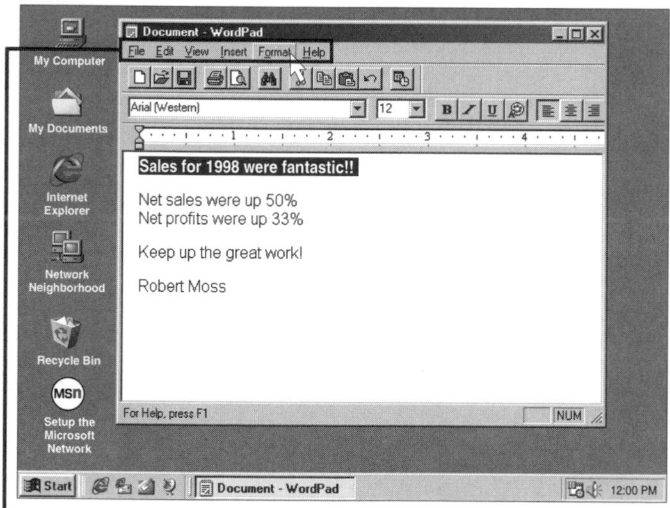

1 Click the name of the menu you want to display.

■ To select a menu with the keyboard, press the Alt key followed by the underlined letter in the menu name (example: o for F<u>o</u>rmat).

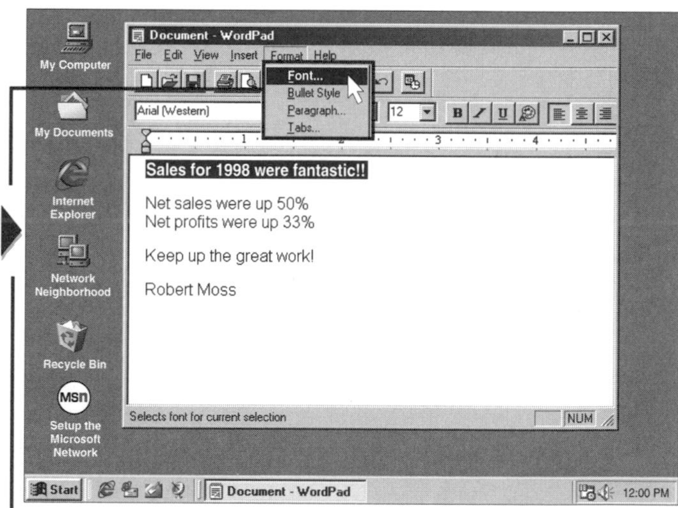

2 Click the name of the command you want to select.

■ To select a command with the keyboard, press the underlined letter in the command name (example: F for <u>F</u>ont).

■ To close a menu without selecting a command, click outside the menu or press the Alt key.

TIPS

Why do some menu commands have a dimmed appearance?

Commands that have a dimmed appearance are currently not available. You must perform a specific task before you can access the commands. For example, you must select text to make the Cut and Copy commands in the Edit menu available.

Are there shortcut keys for menu commands?

Many menu commands offer keyboard shortcuts you can use to quickly select the commands. For example, Ctrl+S saves the current document. If a keyboard shortcut is available, it appears beside the command in the menu.

What is the difference between an option button (○) and a check box (☐)?

When a list of choices displays round option buttons (○), you can select only one option. The selected option displays a dark center (⦿). When a list of choices displays check boxes (☐), you can select as many options as you want. Selected options display a check mark (☑).

Are there shortcuts I can use in dialog boxes?

In some dialog boxes, double-clicking an item selects both the item and the OK button. For example, you can double-click a file in an Open dialog box to quickly open the file.

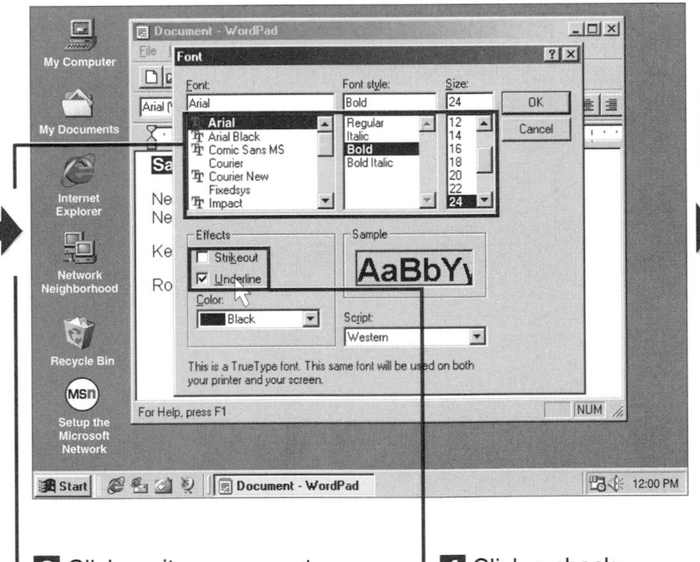

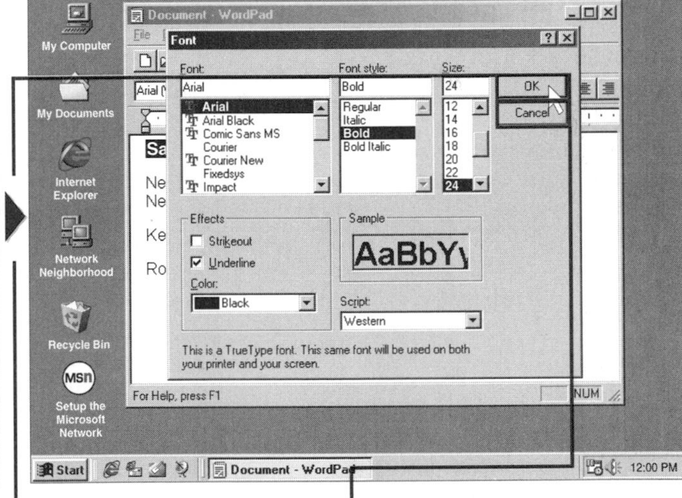

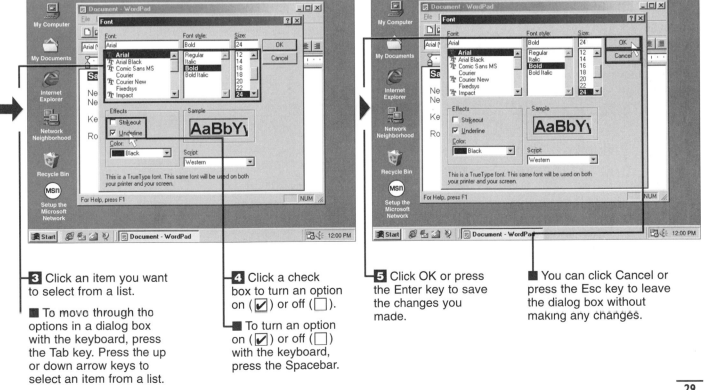

3 Click an item you want to select from a list.

■ To move through the options in a dialog box with the keyboard, press the Tab key. Press the up or down arrow keys to select an item from a list.

4 Click a check box to turn an option on (☑) or off (☐).

■ To turn an option on (☑) or off (☐) with the keyboard, press the Spacebar.

5 Click OK or press the Enter key to save the changes you made.

■ You can click Cancel or press the Esc key to leave the dialog box without making any changes.

SAVE DOCUMENTS

You can save a document you have created to keep a permanent copy of the document. Your document is saved as a file on your hard drive.

To save a document, you must name the document. In Windows 98, you can use up to 255 characters to name a document, including spaces and special characters. The only characters you cannot use to name a document are the \ / : * ? " < > or | characters. If you will be sharing the document with people who do not use Windows 95 or 98, the document name should use no more than 8 letters, with no spaces and no special characters.

You can use the Save As dialog box to move through folders and drives on your computer and store the document exactly where you want. You can use folders to organize your work so it is easier to find a document when you need it again. You can also view information about your saved documents, such as the date and time the documents were last changed.

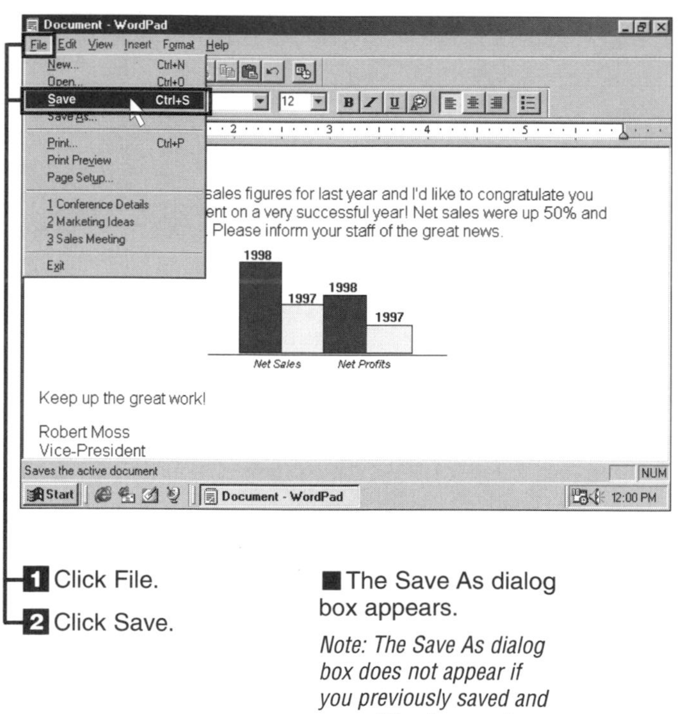

1 Click File.

2 Click Save.

■ The Save As dialog box appears.

Note: The Save As dialog box does not appear if you previously saved and named the document.

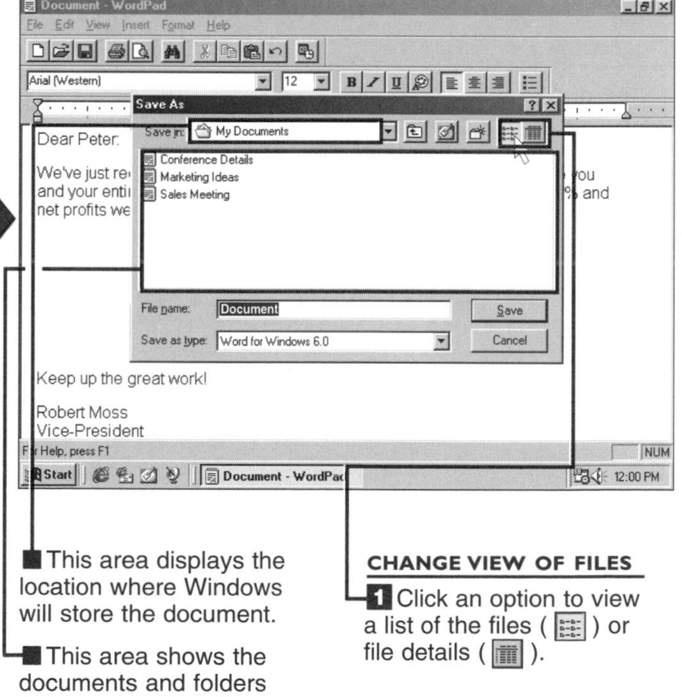

■ This area displays the location where Windows will store the document.

■ This area shows the documents and folders in the current location.

CHANGE VIEW OF FILES

1 Click an option to view a list of the files ( ) or file details ( ).

How often should I save the document I am working on?

You should save the document frequently. This will ensure that all the changes you make to the document are saved. Frequent saving also reduces the amount of work that could be lost in the event of a power loss or computer failure.

Can I make changes to a saved document without losing the original copy?

When you want to make major changes to a document, save the document with a different name before you begin. This gives you two copies of the document–the original document and a document with all the changes.

Can I open a saved document with an older program?

You may need to save a file in a different format if you want to access the document with an older program. In the Save As dialog box, click the area next to Save as type. Select the format you want from the list that appears. Click Save to save the document in the new format.

Can I manage files from the Save As dialog box?

You can right-click any file in the Save As dialog box. A menu appears containing commands, such as Delete and Rename.

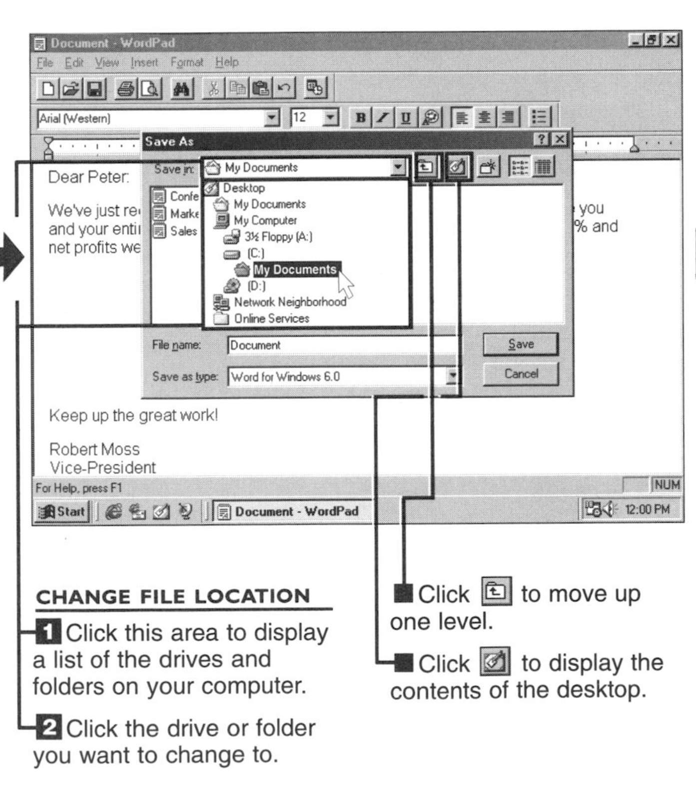

CHANGE FILE LOCATION

1 Click this area to display a list of the drives and folders on your computer.

2 Click the drive or folder you want to change to.

■ Click to move up one level.

■ Click to display the contents of the desktop.

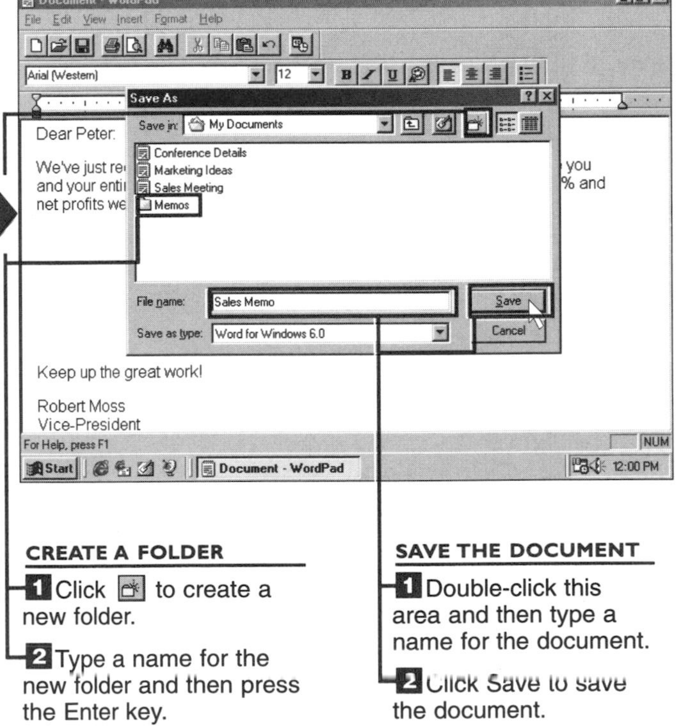

CREATE A FOLDER

1 Click to create a new folder.

2 Type a name for the new folder and then press the Enter key.

■ You can double-click the new folder to save the document in the folder.

SAVE THE DOCUMENT

1 Double-click this area and then type a name for the document.

2 Click Save to save the document.

GETTING HELP

Where to Get Help

If you have a problem using Windows, there are many sources of help available. You can refer to Windows Help, Microsoft Technical Support Knowledge Base and Internet newsgroups to find help. If you prefer more personal help, you can use help options such as telephone support, friends and professional consultants.

Windows Help

When you are using Windows, the most convenient source of help is Windows Help. The Windows Help feature is automatically installed with Windows and is free to use.

There are several ways you can use Windows Help to find the information you are looking for. You can browse through help topics by category, search Windows Help files for the information you need or use the alphabetical index of help topics.

Windows Help is available for the operating system and all Windows programs. Windows Help works the same way in all programs, so it is easy to learn and use. Windows Help is a good source of general information and can answer most of your questions.

Windows Help does not include information about problems, or bugs, that were identified after Windows 98 was released.

Newsgroups

You can use Internet newsgroups as a source of information and help.

Deja News maintains a list of messages posted to newsgroups. You can search through these messages to find the answers you need. You may have to spend a great deal of time reading messages to find one that answers your question. Deja News can be found on the Internet at www.dejanews.com

If you cannot find the information you need with Deja News, you can post a message to an appropriate newsgroup asking a specific question. Other readers may read your question and e-mail you the answer or post it in the newsgroup.

Keep in mind that the information you receive from Internet newsgroups may not always be reliable or may not work with the setup of your computer.

Microsoft Technical Support

You can use Microsoft Technical Support to obtain information about Windows. Microsoft Technical Support can be found on the Internet at support.microsoft.com

This Web site contains known problems and solutions to the problems that have been identified by Windows users and the Microsoft technical support staff. This Web site is constantly updated with new problems and solutions.

If you have a question or problem, you can search Microsoft's Technical Support Web site for the information you need. Microsoft's Technical Support Web site is not comprehensive and you may have to read many pages before you find the information you want.

Telephone Support

You can speak to a Microsoft support technician who will try to solve your problem over the phone. Depending upon your location, and how and when you purchased Windows, the Microsoft telephone support may be free.

Microsoft has many fee-based telephone support options that are explained to you when you call the appropriate number for your region. The number for your region is usually included with your license information.

If you purchased Windows pre-installed on a new computer, your manufacturer or vendor may provide telephone support.

Telephone support can sometimes be a frustrating experience. You may spend a long time on hold and if you are paying long-distance charges, it can be expensive.

Friends and Colleagues

When you have a problem, you can use friends and colleagues as a source of help.

Every office or neighborhood has a computer guru who can provide information and help less experienced users solve problems.

Friends and colleagues may not always be able to help solve your computer problems. Your friends and colleagues are usually not experts and may not understand how the setup of your computer differs from their own. A procedure that worked on your friend's computer may create more problems on your computer.

Consultants

Consultants are experienced professionals who provide expert, on-location help and advice. Consultants are trained in specific areas of computer hardware or software. You can have a consultant come to your home or office to solve your problem.

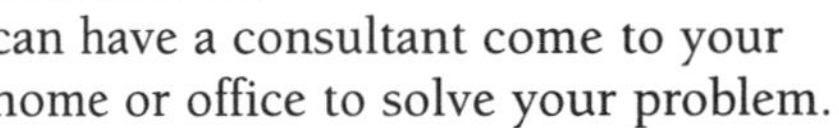

You should ask for recommendations from your friends, colleagues or other knowledgeable computer users when looking for a consultant.

Before you hire a consultant, make sure the consultant's area of expertise is in the area where you need help. For example, a consultant experienced in accounting software may not be able to help you with your Windows 98 problems.

GETTING HELP

Using the Contents Tab

You can use the Contents tab to browse through Windows help topics by subject.

The Contents tab contains categories of help topics arranged into books. The books contain general help, specialized information, tips and problem solving techniques on a wide range of Windows topics. Even experienced users will find useful information on the Contents tab.

The Introducing Windows 98 book is useful if you are using Windows 98 for the first time or if you are upgrading from a previous version of Windows.

The Exploring Your Computer book contains step-by-step procedures to help you work with your programs, folders and files. You can also find information on how to customize Windows 98.

The Managing Hardware and Software book contains useful information about installing new hardware and software, using a portable computer and working with more than one monitor.

The Troubleshooting book contains a list of troubleshooters you can use to help identify and resolve a problem with a device or a task you want to perform.

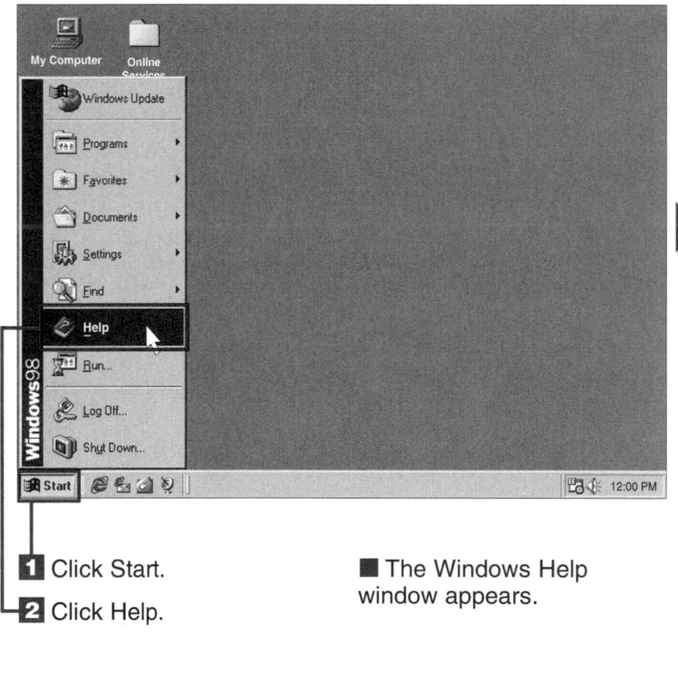

1 Click Start.

2 Click Help.

■ The Windows Help window appears.

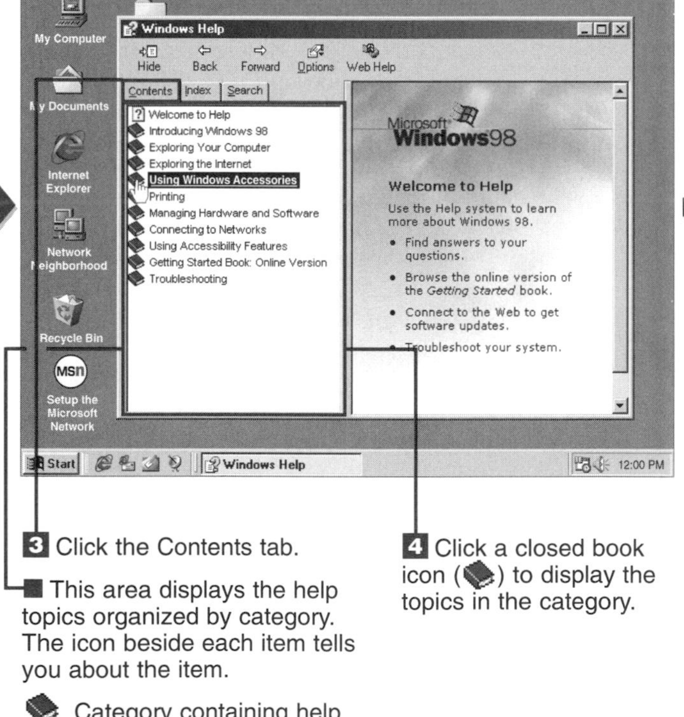

3 Click the Contents tab.

■ This area displays the help topics organized by category. The icon beside each item tells you about the item.

Category containing help topics

Help topic

4 Click a closed book icon ( ) to display the topics in the category.

TIPS

Is there a shortcut to Help?

Pressing the F1 key will open the Help feature in Windows and in nearly every Windows program.

Can I reduce the size of the Windows Help window?

You can hide part of the Windows Help window to more clearly view the desktop. This is helpful if you are using help to learn how to perform a task and need access to your desktop. Click the Hide button to hide the left pane of the window. Click the Show button to once again display the full window.

Can I print a help topic from the Contents tab?

Yes. To print the displayed help topic, right-click the topic in the left pane of the Windows Help window and then select Print. In the Print dialog box, you can choose to print the current topic, all the topics for the current heading or every topic in the Contents tab. For information on printing a help topic, see page 40.

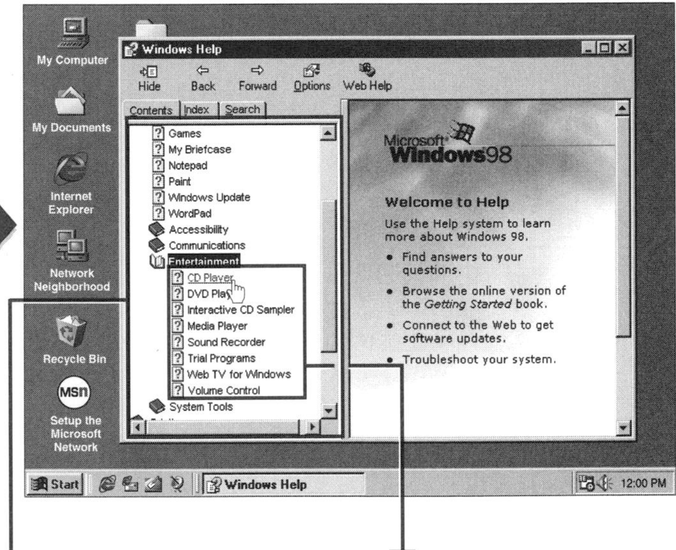

■ The topics in the category appear.

Note: You can click an open book icon (📖) to hide its topics.

5 Repeat step 4 until the topic of interest appears.

6 Click the topic you want information about.

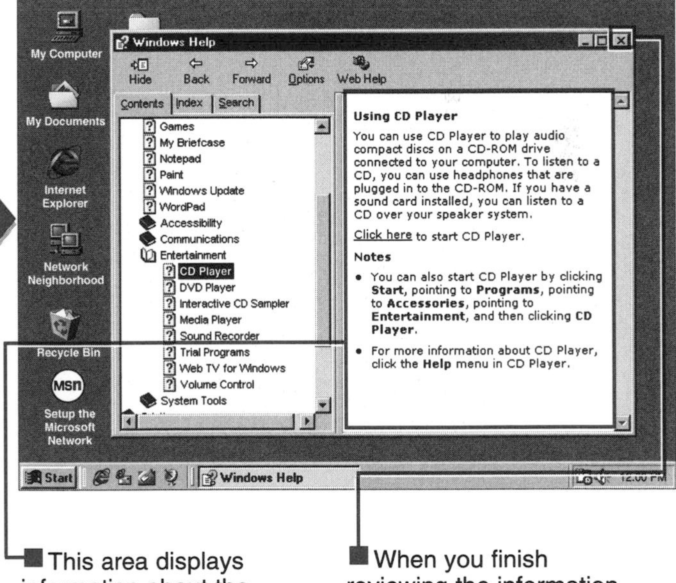

■ This area displays information about the topic you selected.

■ When you finish reviewing the information, click ☒ to close the Windows Help window.

GETTING HELP

Using the Index Tab

The Index tab contains an alphabetical listing of all the Windows help topics.

You can use the Index tab to find information the same way you would use the index in a book.

When you type the first few characters of the help topic you want to find, Windows will take you to the topic's location in the index.

Windows categorizes topics so you can quickly find the information you need. For example, if you want to add an item to your computer, you can type the word **adding**.

Listed under "adding," you will find help topics for adding programs, fonts, printers and hardware to your computer.

After you find the help topic you want, you can display the help information for the topic.

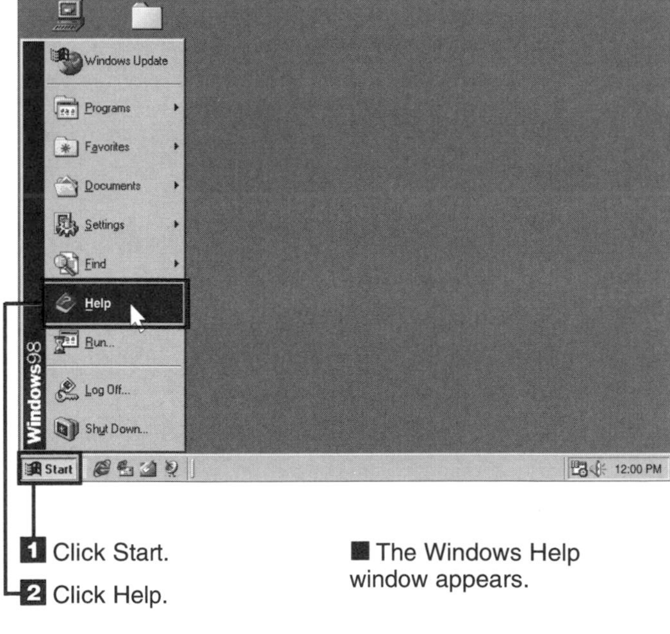

1 Click Start.

2 Click Help.

■ The Windows Help window appears.

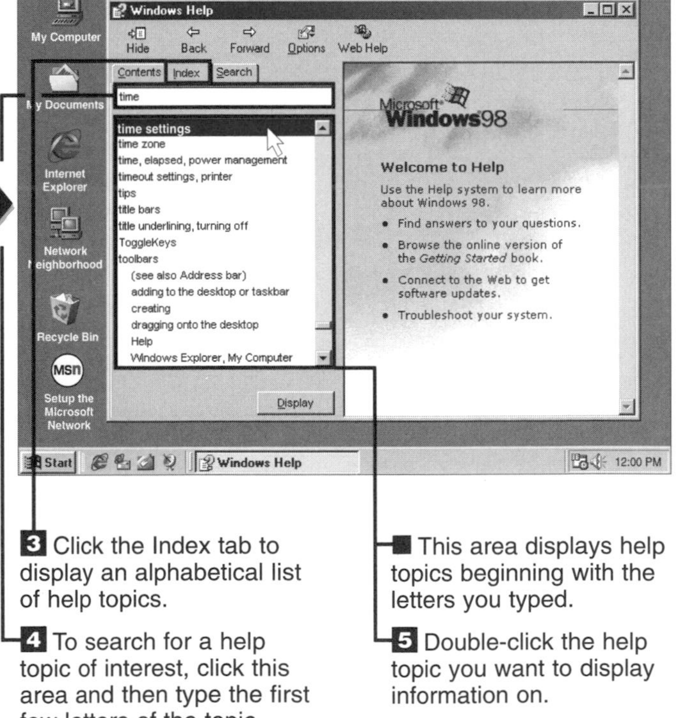

3 Click the Index tab to display an alphabetical list of help topics.

4 To search for a help topic of interest, click this area and then type the first few letters of the topic.

■ This area displays help topics beginning with the letters you typed.

5 Double-click the help topic you want to display information on.

TIPS

Can I make the Windows Help window any smaller?

To change the size of the window, position the mouse pointer over an edge of the window (↖ changes to ↕ or ↔). Drag the mouse until the outline of the window displays the size you want.

How do I return to a help topic I have already viewed?

You can click the Back or Forward buttons in the Windows Help window to move through the help topics you have viewed.

Can I copy help information into a document?

You can create your own help documents by copying Windows help information. In the Windows Help window, drag the mouse over the text you want to copy to a document to select the text. Right-click the selected text and then click Copy. Open the document you want to receive a copy of the information. Click the Edit menu and then select Paste.

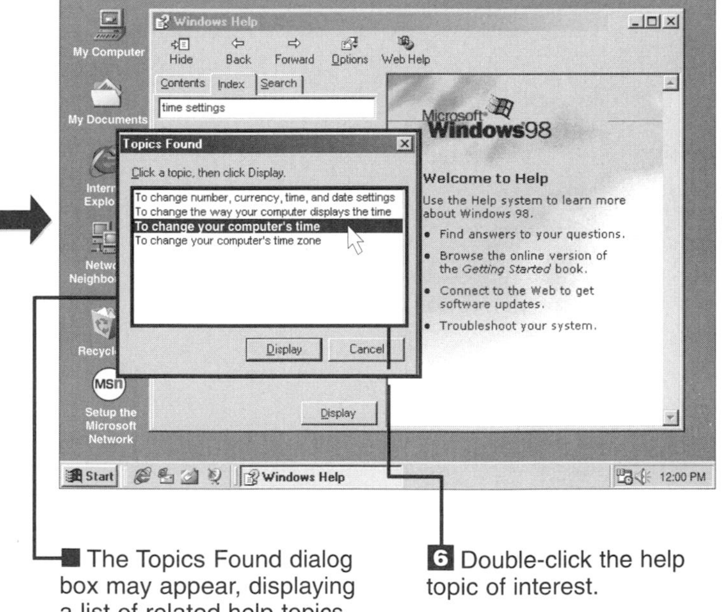

■ The Topics Found dialog box may appear, displaying a list of related help topics.

6 Double-click the help topic of interest.

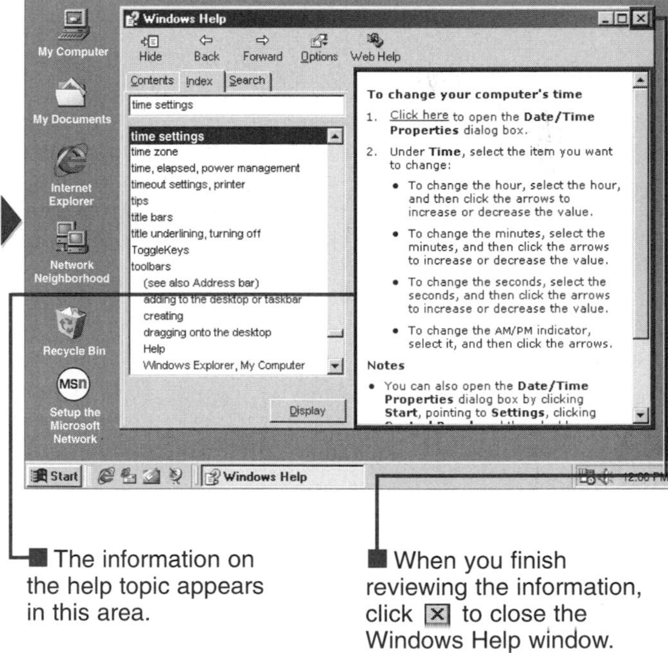

■ The information on the help topic appears in this area.

■ When you finish reviewing the information, click ☒ to close the Windows Help window.

GETTING HELP

Using the Search Tab

You can use the Search tab to search all of the words contained in Windows help topics.

You can type one or more words and have Windows search the help topics to find matches for the words.

When the search is complete, Windows displays a list of the matching help topics. If a lot of help topics are displayed, you can narrow your search by adding another word or searching for a more specific word.

Windows displays the help topics containing all of the words you typed, regardless of the order of the words.

After you find the help topic you want, you can display the help information for the topic.

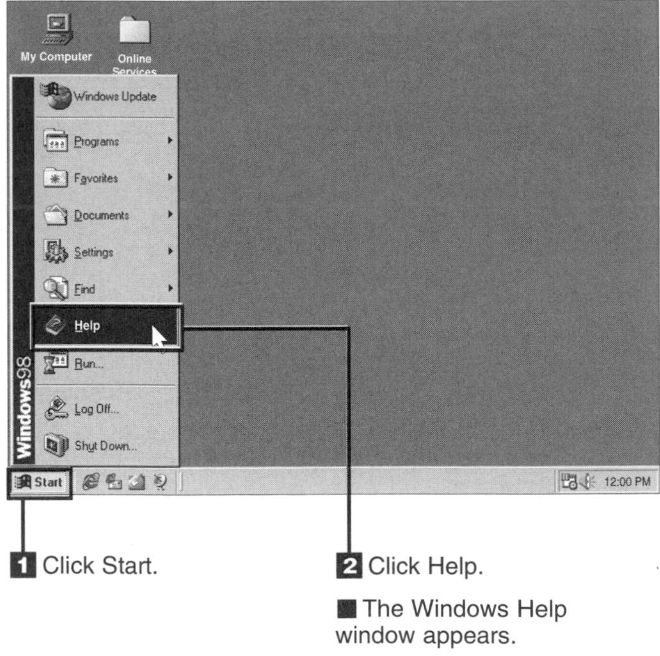

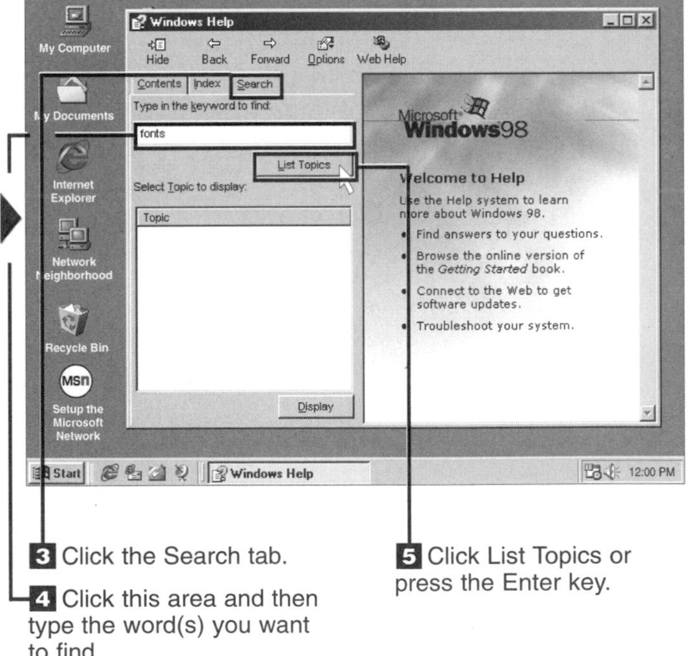

1 Click Start.

2 Click Help.

■ The Windows Help window appears.

3 Click the Search tab.

4 Click this area and then type the word(s) you want to find.

Note: If you want to find more than one word, separate the words with a space.

5 Click List Topics or press the Enter key.

Is there an easy way to find a topic related to the topic that is currently displayed?

Many help topics display the Related Topics option in the right pane of the Windows Help window. Click Related Topics to view a list of similar help topics. Then select the topic you want to display.

Can I search for help information on the Internet?

If you have registered with Microsoft, you can connect to Microsoft's Web site to access the most up-to-date help information about Windows 98. In the Windows Help window, click the Web Help button. Then click the Click here link to open Internet Explorer and display the Windows Update Web site. For information on registering, see page 11.

Can I search using only parts of words?

Windows allows you to search for help using parts of words combined with wildcard characters. The most common wildcard character is the asterisk (*), which allows you to search for any number of characters. For example, if you type **dis***, Windows will display help topics containing words such as "disk" and "display."

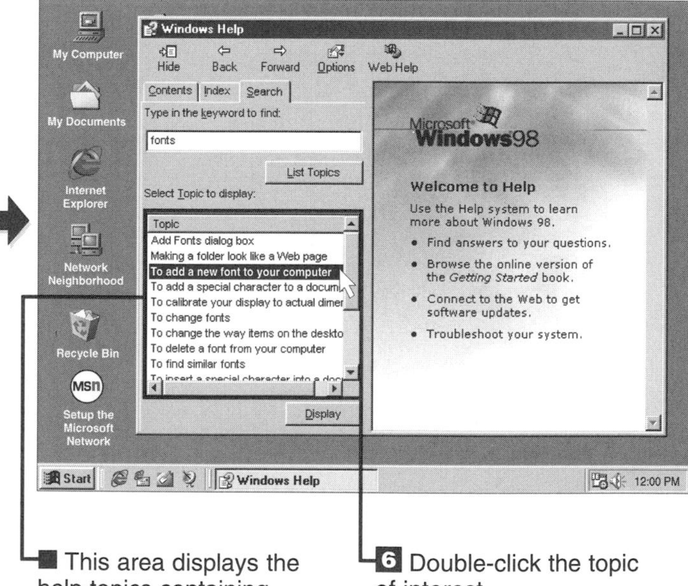

■ This area displays the help topics containing the word(s) you specified.

6 Double-click the topic of interest.

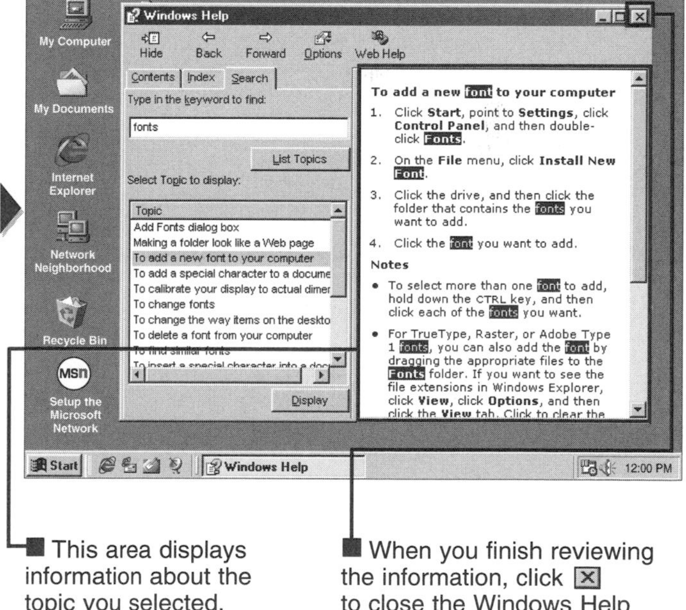

■ This area displays information about the topic you selected.

■ When you finish reviewing the information, click ☒ to close the Windows Help window.

GETTING HELP

Print a Help Topic

You can print a paper copy of the help topic displayed on your screen. Printing a help topic can be very useful because it is often difficult to remember all of the information in a Help window.

A printed copy of a help topic allows you to review a procedure from beginning to end before you start a task. You can also use a printed copy when you want to refer to other sources about a specific help topic.

It is not always possible to view the information in a Help window. If you are completing a task that requires you to restart your computer, you will not be able to refer to the help information while the computer is turned off. A printed copy of the topic will help you complete the task.

A printed reference of a help topic can also help you learn about Windows features more easily. For example, although it can take a long time to become familiar with all of the Windows shortcut keys, a printed reference can help you memorize them.

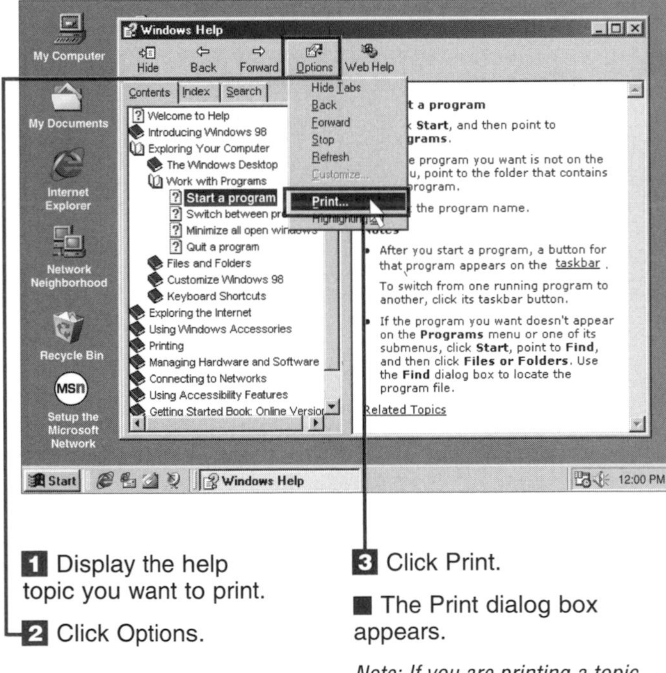

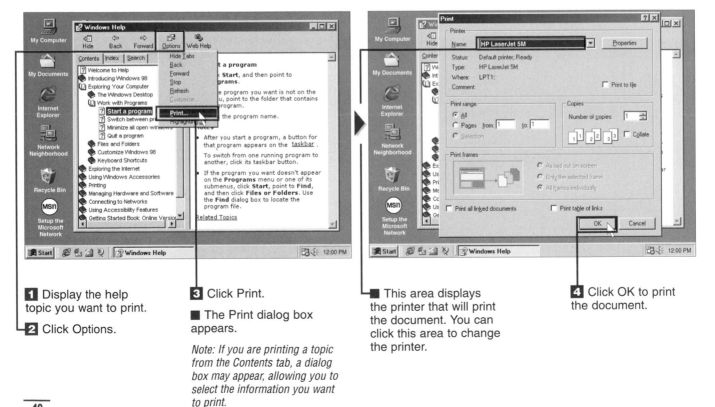

1 Display the help topic you want to print.

2 Click Options.

3 Click Print.

■ The Print dialog box appears.

Note: If you are printing a topic from the Contents tab, a dialog box may appear, allowing you to select the information you want to print.

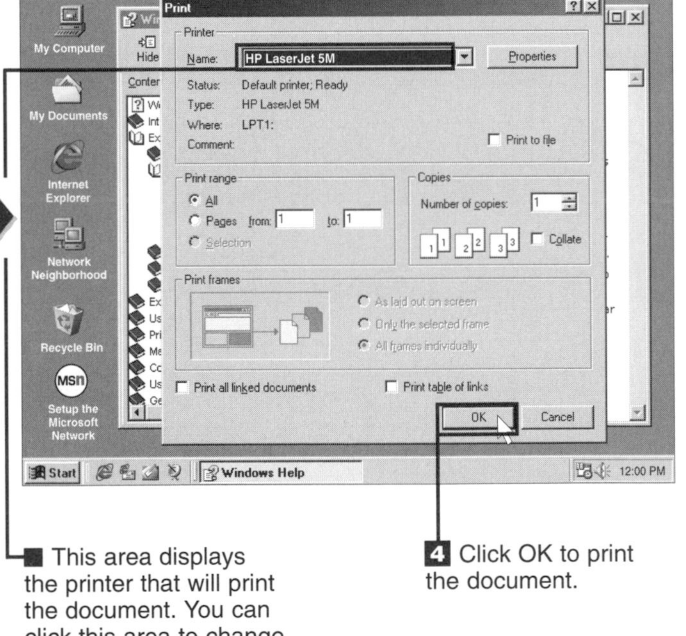

■ This area displays the printer that will print the document. You can click this area to change the printer.

4 Click OK to print the document.

GETTING HELP

Getting Help in a Dialog Box

You can find help information about a dialog box you are using.

If you are unfamiliar with a dialog box, you can use the Help button (?) to display Windows help information. The Help button provides you with details concerning the items in a dialog box.

When you click the Help button and then click an item in a dialog box, a box containing Windows help information appears. The help information explains what the item you selected does and how you can use the item. The help information stays on the screen while you learn about the item.

You must click the Help button each time you want to display help information for an item.

If the Help button is not available in the dialog box, you can press the F1 key to display help information. You can also right-click an item and then click What's This? to display help information.

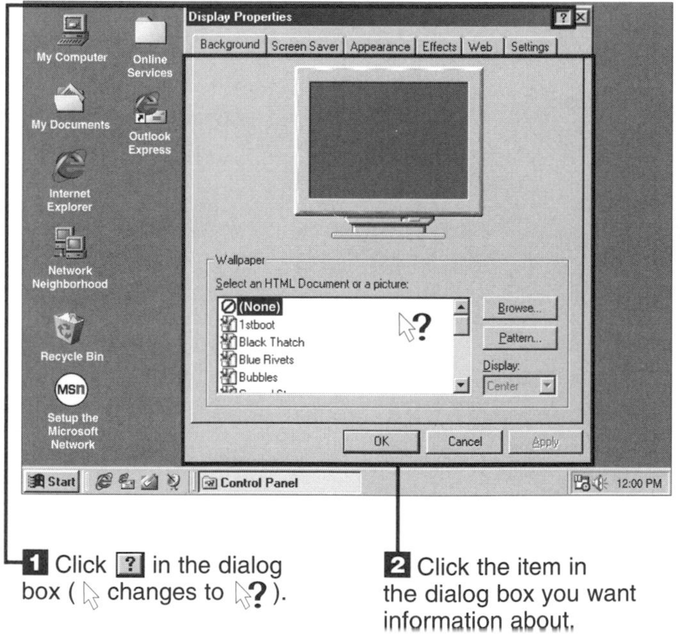

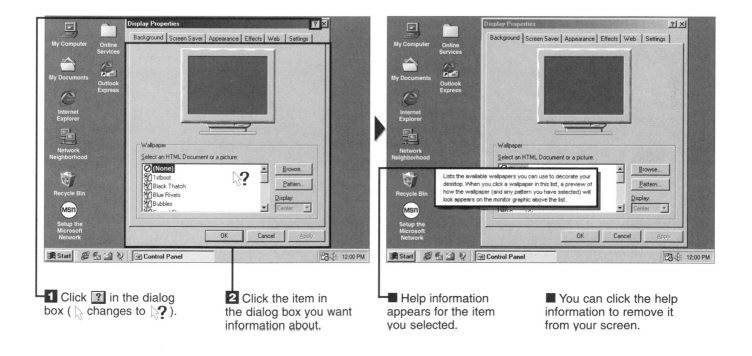

1 Click ? in the dialog box (pointer changes to ?).

2 Click the item in the dialog box you want information about.

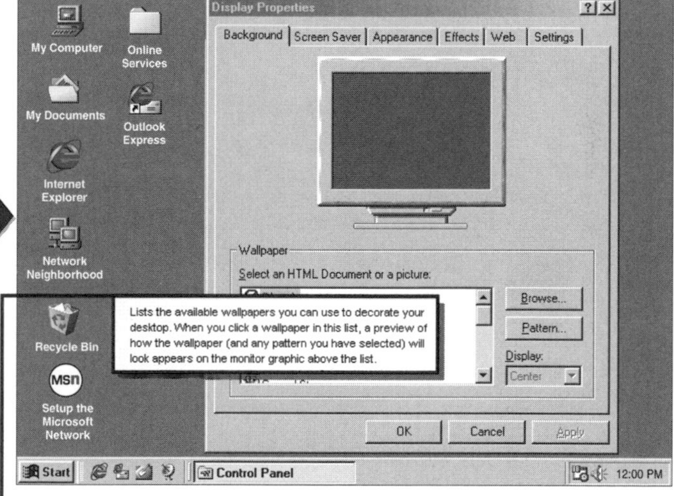

■ Help information appears for the item you selected.

■ You can click the help information to remove it from your screen.

COMPUTER HARDWARE

Devices You Attach to a Computer

Keyboard

A keyboard is used to enter information and instructions into a computer.

Speakers and Headphones

Speakers and headphones are used to listen to sounds created by a sound card. Headphones let you listen to sounds privately. Computer speakers must be shielded to prevent the magnets inside the speakers from distorting the image on a monitor. Most computer speakers include an amplifier and run on batteries or other power sources.

Video Camera

A video camera is used for videoconferencing or to create video files.

Mouse

A mouse is a hand-held device that lets you select and move items on your screen. There are many different types of mouse alternatives, including trackballs, touch-sensitive pads and tablets that use pens. Some mice have a wheel between the buttons to simplify the task of scrolling up and down through information in a window.

Monitor

A monitor displays text and images generated by the computer. The size of a monitor is measured diagonally across the screen. Common monitor sizes range from 14 to 21 inches.

Microphone

A microphone is used with a sound card to record speech and other sounds. Not all sound cards are compatible with all types of microphones.

Printer

A printer produces a paper copy of documents created on the computer. Laser printers produce high-quality pages. Inkjet printers make color printing affordable. Dot matrix printers are often used to print multi-part forms.

Removable Drive

A removable drive is a combination of a hard drive and floppy drive. The disks you use with a removable drive can contain from 100 MB to 1.5 GB of information. You can use a removable hard drive to transfer large amounts of information between computers.

Modem

A modem lets computers exchange information through telephone lines. You can use a modem to connect to the Internet. There are two types of modems. Internal modems are circuit boards that fit inside your computer. External modems plug into the back of your computer.

The speed of a modem determines how fast it can send and receive information through telephone lines. The most common modem speed is 33.6 Kbps.

You can use an Integrated Services Digital Network (ISDN) terminal adapter instead of a modem for connecting to the Internet using ISDN phone lines.

Scanner

A scanner converts graphics and text into a format your computer can use. Scanners range in size from small hand-held scanners to large flatbed scanners that can scan full pages.

Scan Convertors

Scan convertors are used to convert computer images so they can be displayed on a television. Scan convertors are sometimes built into a video card.

Tape Drive

A tape drive stores and retrieves information on tape cartridges. You can use a tape drive to back up files, archive old or rarely used files or transfer large amounts of information. There are many types of tape drives available, including the Travan drive, the QIC (Quarter-Inch Cartridge) drive and the DAT (Digital Audio Tape) drive.

Port

A port is a connector at the back of a computer where you plug in an external device, such as a printer or modem. This allows instructions and data to flow between the computer and the device. A parallel port has 25 holes and connects a printer, removable drive or tape drive. The computer uses the letters LPT to identify a parallel port. A serial port has either 9 or 25 pins and is used to connect many devices, such as a mouse or modem. The computer uses the letters COM to identify a serial port. Your system also has additional ports to connect devices like your monitor, joystick, speakers and a phone line. Universal Serial Bus (USB) and FireWire ports provide a way to connect several devices using only one port. Infrared ports let a computer communicate with devices by using infrared light instead of cables.

CONTINUED

COMPUTER HARDWARE

Inside a Computer

Floppy Drive

A floppy drive stores and retrieves information on floppy disks. A double-density (DD) floppy disk can store 720 K of information. This disk has only one hole at the top of the disk. A high-density (HD) floppy disk can store 1.44 MB of information. This disk has two holes at the top of the disk. You can prevent the erasure of information on a floppy disk by sliding the tab to the write-protected position.

CD-ROM Drive

A CD-ROM drive reads information stored on compact discs. You can use a CD-ROM drive to install programs, play games on CD-ROM discs and listen to music CDs. Some CD-ROM drives can hold several discs at once. CD-ROM discs can store up to 720 MB of information. You cannot record on a CD-ROM drive. CD-Recordable (CD-R) drives are available if you want to store your own information on a disc. You can also use the CD-R drive to play CD-ROM discs. Digital Versatile Disc (DVD) is a type of CD-ROM disc that can store up to 17 GB of information.

Expansion Slot

An expansion slot is a socket where you plug in an expansion card to add a new feature to your computer. The number of expansion slots your computer has indicates how many features you can add to the computer.

Hard Drive

A hard drive is the primary device that a computer uses to store information. Most computers have one hard drive, named drive C. Most hard drives have 1 GB or more of storage space.

Bytes

Bytes are used to measure the amount of information a device can store.

One byte is one character.

One kilobyte (K) is 1,024 characters. This is approximately equal to one page of double-spaced text.

One megabyte (MB) is 1,048,576 characters. This is approximately equal to one novel.

One gigabyte (GB) is 1,073,741,824 characters. This is approximately equal to 1,000 novels.

Motherboard

A motherboard is the main circuit board of a computer. All of the computer's electronic components plug into the motherboard.

TV and Radio Tuner Cards

TV tuner cards are used to listen to or watch television on your computer. The TV image appears in a window on the desktop. You can listen to the radio on your computer with the radio tuner card.

Central Processing Unit (CPU)

The Central Processing Unit (CPU) is the main chip in a computer. The CPU processes instructions, performs calculations and manages the flow of information through a computer system. Intel CPU chips are the most popular. Each new generation of CPUs is more powerful than the one before. Intel CPU generations include Intel486™, Pentium®, Pentium® Pro and Pentium® II processors.

Each CPU generation is available in several speeds, which are measured in megahertz (MHz). The faster the speed, the faster the computer operates. CPUs with MMX™ technology have additional capabilities to process large data types like photographic images, audio and video. Programs must be specially designed to take advantage of MMX™ technology capabilities.

Bus

The bus is the electronic pathway in a computer that carries information between devices. Common bus structures include ISA (Industry Standard Architecture), SCSI (Small Computer Systems Interface) and PCI (Peripheral Component Interconnect). AGP (Accelerated Graphics Port) is a new bus structure used to provide faster video speeds.

Memory

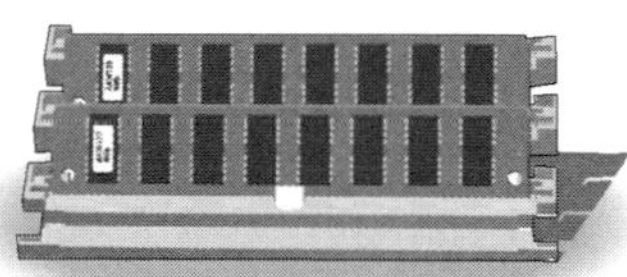

Memory, also known as Random Access Memory (RAM), temporarily stores information inside a computer. The information stored in RAM is lost when you turn off the computer. The amount of memory a computer has determines the number of programs a computer can run at once and how fast programs will operate. Most new computers have 32 MB of RAM.

Network Interface Card

A network interface card physically connects each computer to a network. This card controls the flow of information between the network and the computer. A network is a group of connected computers that allows people to share information and devices like printers and modems.

Video Capture Card

A video capture card is used to transform video from a video camera or a VCR into files that can be used by a computer.

Sound Card

A sound card lets a computer play and record sounds. A sound card allows you to record from a microphone or other audio device. Sound cards are also used to play music CDs and MIDI files as well as narration, music and effects during games. Some computers have sound capabilities included on the motherboard.

Video Card

A video card translates instructions from the computer into a form the monitor can understand. Some computers have video capabilities included on the motherboard.

USING MY COMPUTER

My Computer provides access to all of the drives, files and folders on your computer. It also contains all of the tools you need to set up, manage and control your computer, printer and connections to other computers. Each item in a My Computer window is represented by an icon.

You can use My Computer to browse through the files and folders on your computer. You can double-click a file or folder to open it and display its contents. A folder can contain items such as documents, programs and other folders. Folders keep items organized and easy to find and use.

My Computer can help you manage and organize your files and folders. You can create, rename, copy, move or delete files and folders in a My Computer window.

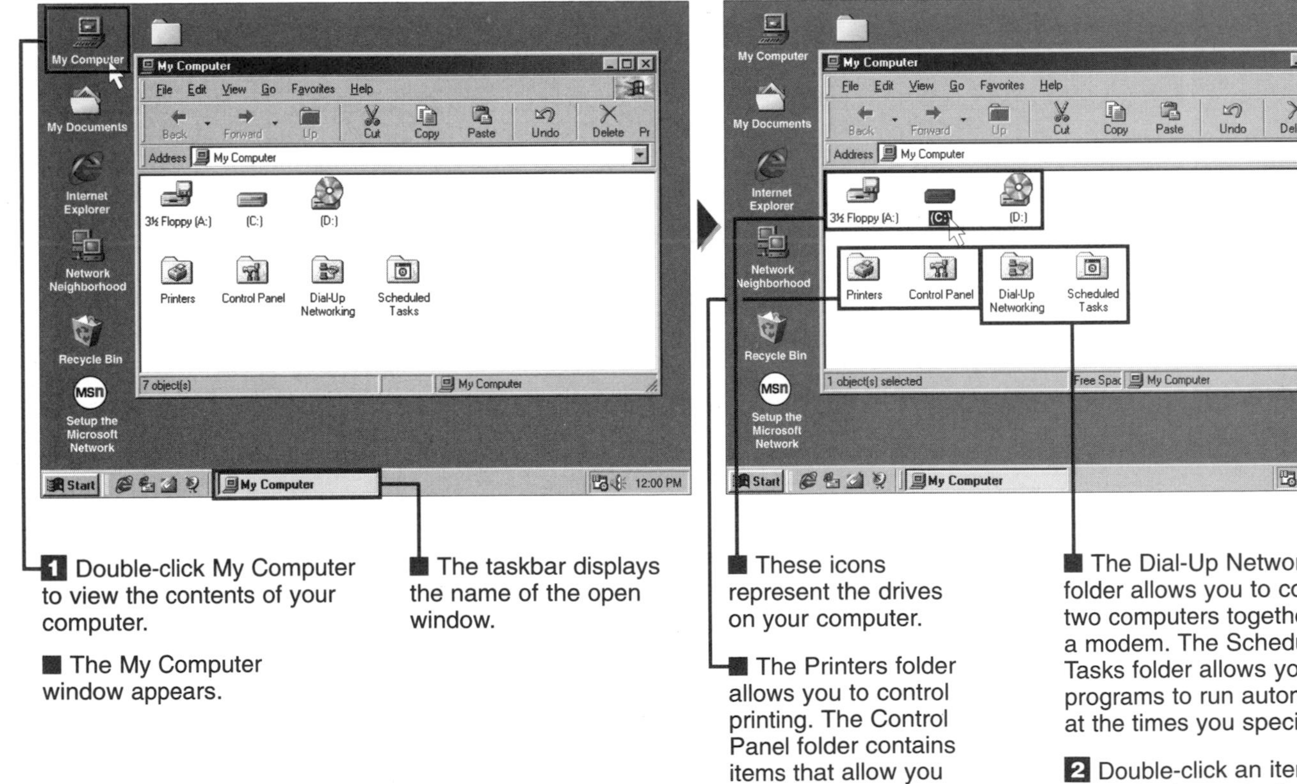

1 Double-click My Computer to view the contents of your computer.

■ The My Computer window appears.

■ The taskbar displays the name of the open window.

■ These icons represent the drives on your computer.

■ The Printers folder allows you to control printing. The Control Panel folder contains items that allow you to change computer settings.

■ The Dial-Up Networking folder allows you to connect two computers together using a modem. The Scheduled Tasks folder allows you to set programs to run automatically at the times you specify.

2 Double-click an item to display its contents.

TIPS

How can I open an item if I have trouble double-clicking?

Right-click the drive, file or folder and then select Open from the menu that appears.

Can Windows 98 display the contents of each folder I open in its own window?

Yes. You can use the custom folder options settings to have each folder open in its own window. For information, see page 224.

Can I change the way items look in a My Computer window?

You can change the appearance of items to make them easier to view and work with. See page 48.

Is there another way to display the contents of a drive or folder on my computer?

Click ▼ beside the Address area in the My Computer window to display a list of the drives and folders on your computer. Then click the drive or folder you want to view. The contents of the drive or folder you selected appear in the window.

How can I quickly move through the drives and folders?

You can click the Back or Forward buttons to move through the drives and folders you have previously viewed. You can also click the Up button to move up one level in the list of drives and folders on your computer.

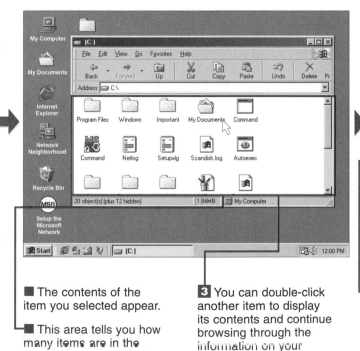

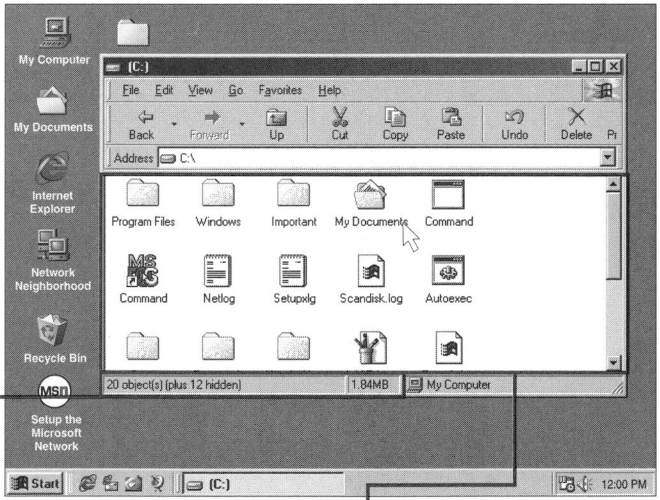

■ The contents of the item you selected appear.

■ This area tells you how many items are in the window and the size of the items.

3 You can double-click another item to display its contents and continue browsing through the information on your computer.

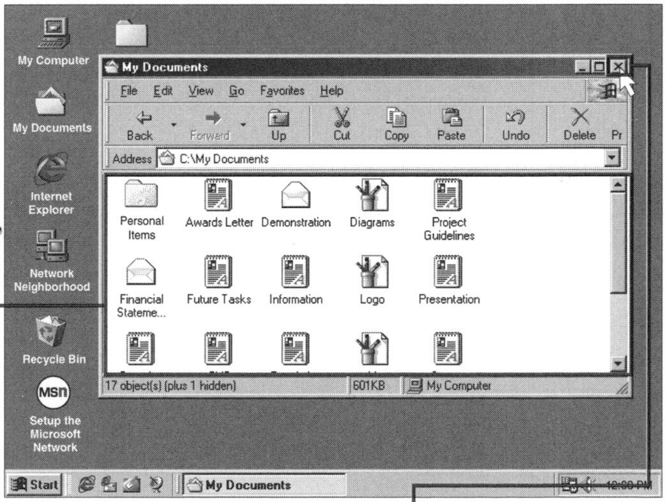

■ The contents of the item you selected appear.

4 Click ☒ to close the window.

CHANGE VIEW OF ITEMS

You can change the view of items in a window. The view you select depends on the information you want to see in the window.

Windows displays a picture, or icon, to represent each type of item in a window. For example, the icon indicates the item is a folder. Documents created in WordPad display the icon. Pictures created with the Paint program display the icon.

When you first use Windows, items are displayed as large icons. The Large Icons view makes it easy to see the types of items available in the window.

You can choose the Small Icons view or List view to see more items in a window.

The Details view displays information such as the file name and size in columns. You can change the width of the columns in the Details view to make the information easier to view.

Changing the view of items affects only the open window. Each window remembers the view you selected and displays the items in that view the next time you open the window.

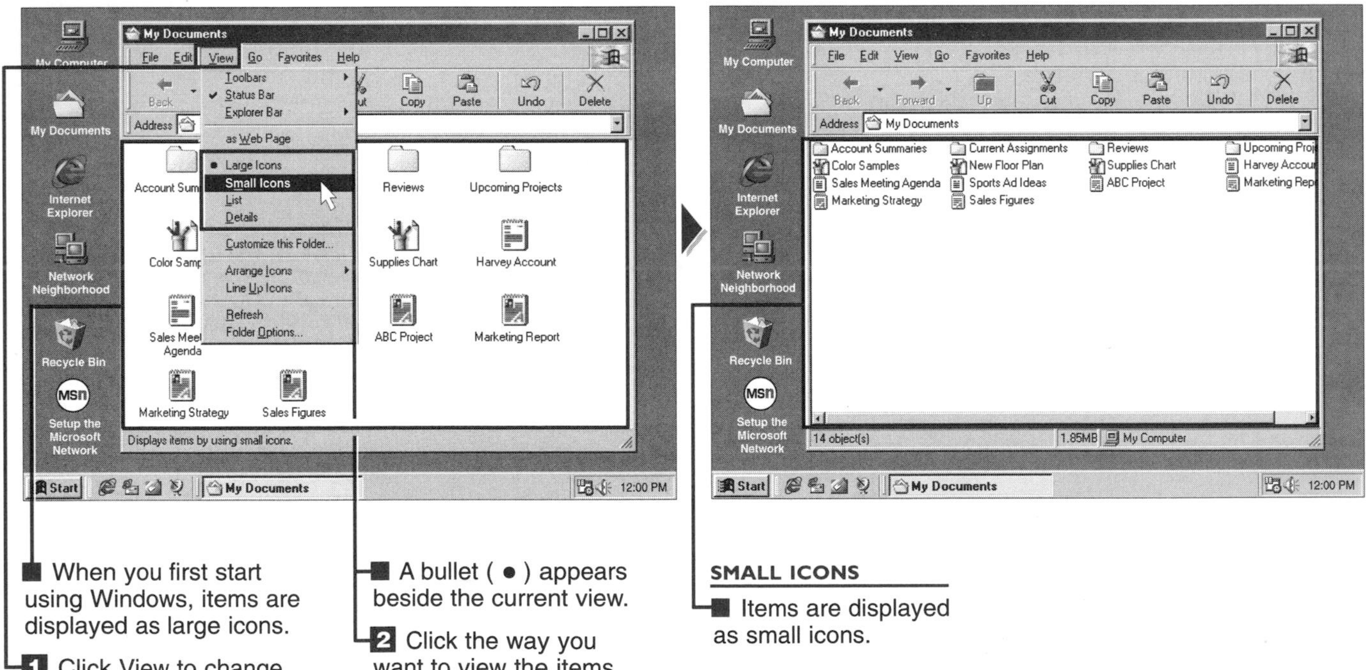

■ When you first start using Windows, items are displayed as large icons.

1 Click View to change the view of items.

■ A bullet (●) appears beside the current view.

2 Click the way you want to view the items.

SMALL ICONS

■ Items are displayed as small icons.

What is the difference between the Small Icons and List views?

The Small Icons view displays items from left to right in a window. You can arrange the items any way you like in the Small Icons view. The List view displays items from top to bottom in a window. You cannot arrange the items in the List view.

Can I refresh the items displayed in a window?

You can press the F5 key to update the items displayed in a window. This is useful if you are viewing the contents of floppy disks. When you switch disks, you can press F5 to display the contents of the second disk.

Is there a shortcut for changing views?

You can click the Views button in a window to quickly change the appearance of items. Repeat this step until the items in the window appear the way you want. If you cannot see the Views button, you may have to increase the size of the window. To size a window, see page 21.

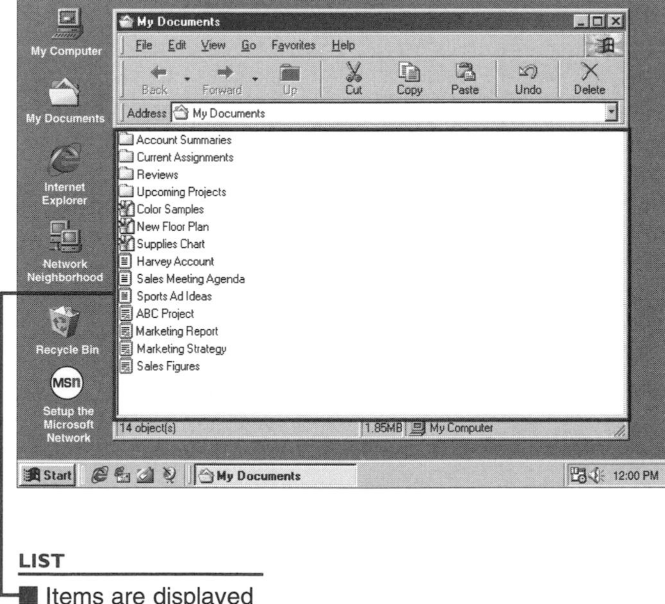

LIST

■ Items are displayed as small icons in a list.

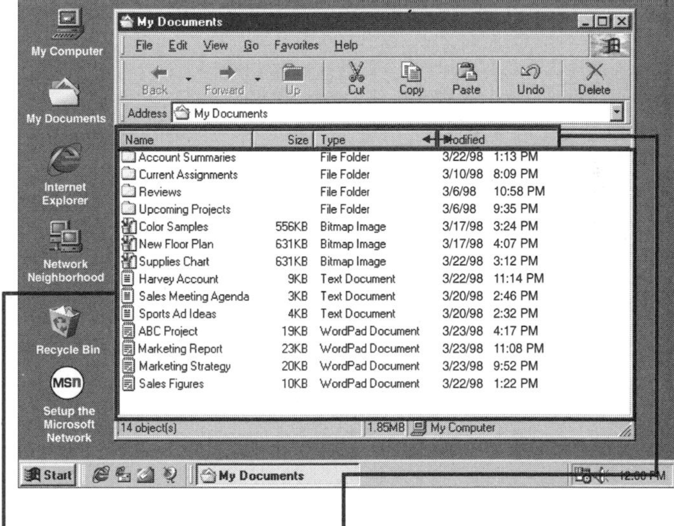

DETAILS

■ Information about each item is displayed, such as the name, type and size.

■ To change the width of a column, position the mouse over the right edge of a column heading (changes to ↔) and then drag the column to a new width.

Note: To resize a column to fit the longest item, double-click the right edge of the column heading.

ARRANGE ICONS AUTOMATICALLY

You can have Windows automatically arrange icons to fit neatly in a window. If your icons are scattered or piled one on top of another, arranging your icons will make the contents of your window easier to view.

The Auto Arrange feature places your icons at a fixed distance from one another in neat rows and columns. The icons will remain neatly arranged even if you resize the window or add and remove icons.

When the Auto Arrange feature is on, you can move an icon to a new location in a window. The other icons will shift to make space for the icon but will remain neatly arranged. You cannot move an icon to a blank area of the window when the Auto Arrange feature is on.

Just as you can arrange the icons in a window, you can also arrange icons on your desktop. Windows will arrange all the icons on your desktop in columns, starting at the left edge of your screen.

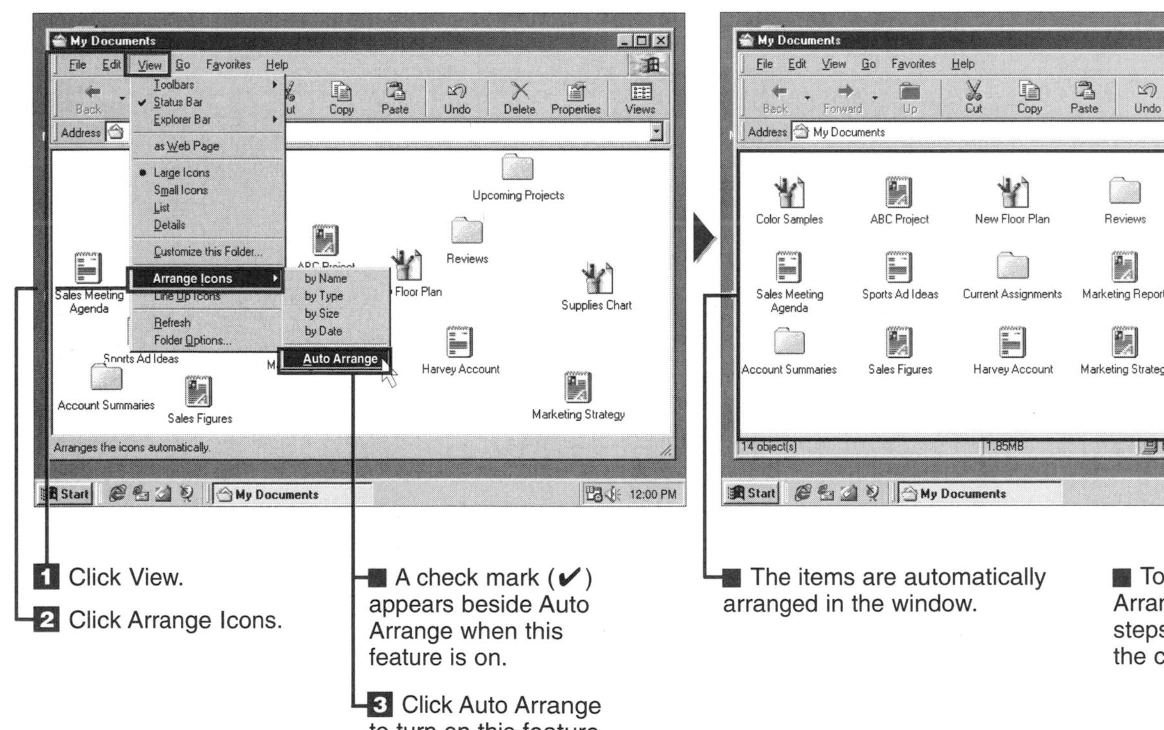

1 Click View.

2 Click Arrange Icons.

■ A check mark (✔) appears beside Auto Arrange when this feature is on.

3 Click Auto Arrange to turn on this feature.

■ The items are automatically arranged in the window.

■ To turn off the Auto Arrange feature, repeat steps 1 to 3 to remove the check mark (✔).

Why is the Auto Arrange feature not available?

The Auto Arrange feature is not available when your icons are displayed in the List or Details view. For information on changing the view, see page 48.

How can I move icons closer together or farther apart?

You can change the horizontal and vertical spacing of icons. In the Display Properties dialog box, choose the Appearance tab. Click the Item area and then select Icon Spacing (Horizontal) or Icon Spacing (Vertical). To increase or decrease the spacing between icons, double-click the Size area and then type a new number. For information on the Appearance settings, see page 208.

Is there another way to neatly line up the icons in a window?

Choose the View menu and then select Line Up Icons to have Windows move the icons to the nearest row or column. Unlike Auto Arrange, the icons will not shift if other icons are added or removed in the window.

I placed a folder icon on top of another folder icon and it disappeared. Why?

Windows thought you wanted to store one folder inside the other. From the Edit menu, select the Undo Move command to restore the folder that disappeared.

If you place a document icon on top of a program icon, the program starts and opens the document.

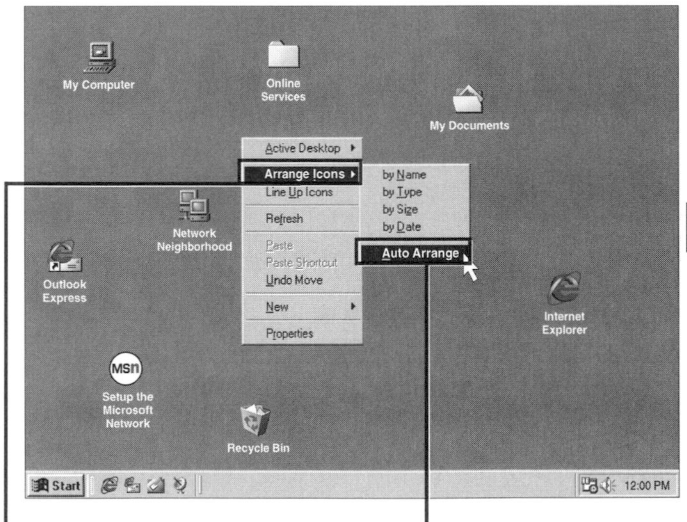

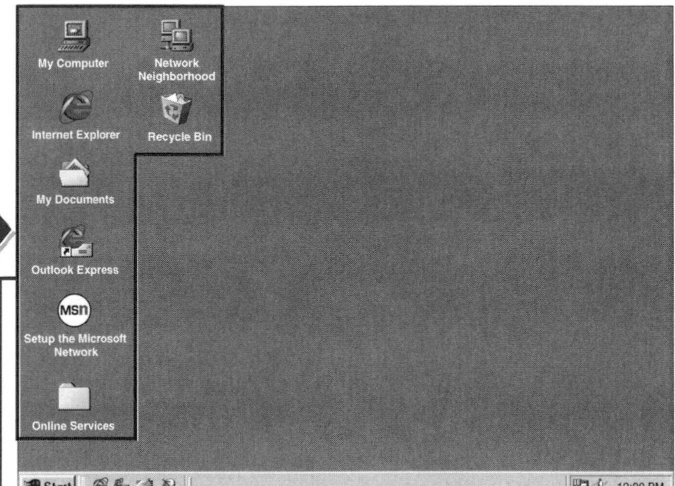

ARRANGE DESKTOP ITEMS

1 Right-click an empty area on the desktop. A menu appears.

2 Click Arrange Icons.

3 Click Auto Arrange.

■ The items are automatically arranged on the desktop.

SORT ITEMS

You can sort the items displayed in a window. This can help you find files and folders more easily.

Windows allows you to sort items by name, type, size or date.

Name sorts items alphabetically, from A to Z. If you know the name of the item you want to find, try sorting by name.

Type sorts items alphabetically according to the file type. If you are looking for a file of a specific type, try sorting by type.

Size sorts items by their size, from smallest to largest. To find a large file, try sorting by size.

Date sorts items according to the date they were last saved, from newest to oldest. If you know when the file you want to find was last saved, try sorting by date.

Regardless of how you sort items, Windows sorts files and folders separately and displays the folders before the files.

If a window displays column headings, you can use the column headings to sort items.

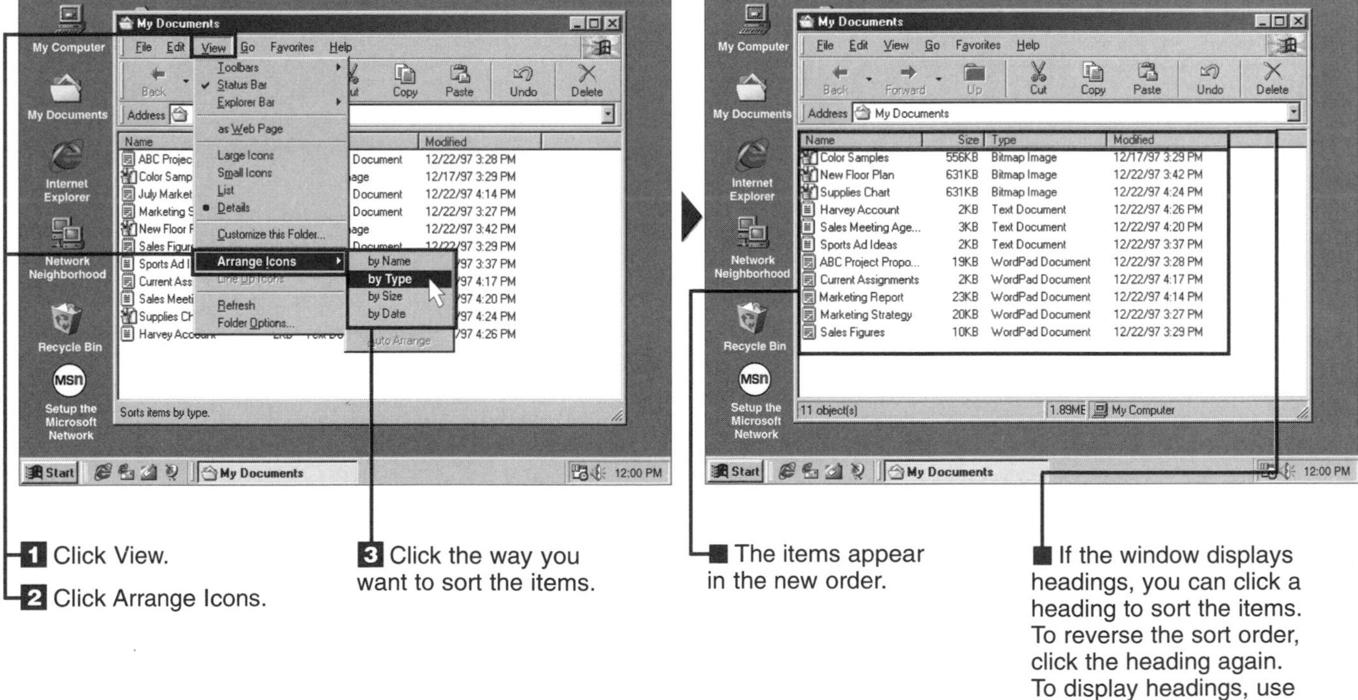

1 Click View.

2 Click Arrange Icons.

3 Click the way you want to sort the items.

■ The items appear in the new order.

■ If the window displays headings, you can click a heading to sort the items. To reverse the sort order, click the heading again. To display headings, use the Details display option. See page 48.

SCROLL THROUGH INFORMATION

A scroll bar lets you browse through information in a window. This is useful when a window is not large enough to display all the information it contains. Some dialog boxes also display scroll bars that you can use to view all of the items in a list.

The location of the scroll box on the scroll bar indicates which part of the window you are viewing. For example, when the scroll box is halfway down the scroll bar, you are viewing information from the middle of the window. The size of the scroll box varies, depending on the amount of information the window contains.

Some programs show new information as you drag the scroll box. Other programs display new information only when you release the scroll box.

The Microsoft IntelliMouse has a wheel between the left and right mouse buttons. Moving this wheel allows you to scroll through information in the most recent versions of some Microsoft programs.

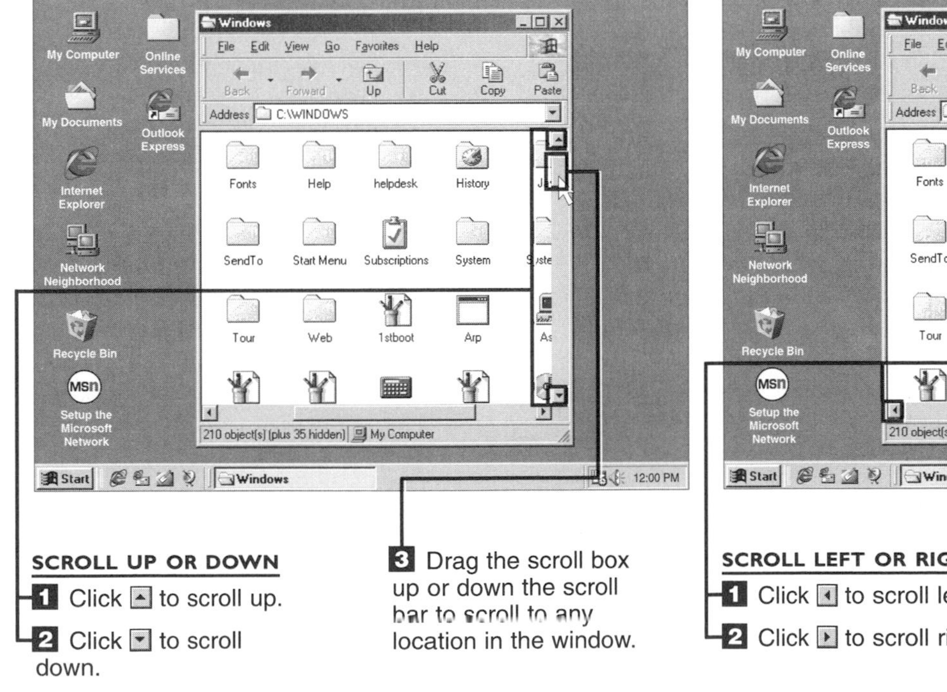

SCROLL UP OR DOWN

1 Click ▲ to scroll up.

2 Click ▼ to scroll down.

3 Drag the scroll box up or down the scroll bar to scroll to any location in the window.

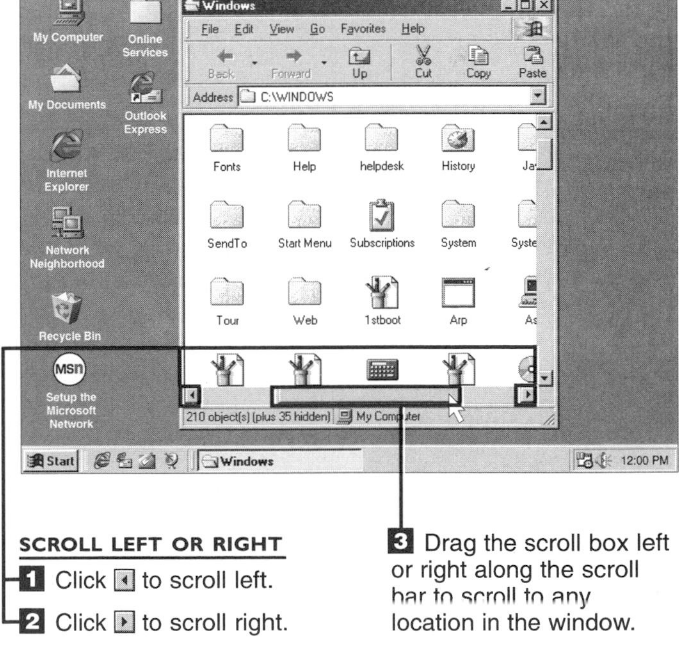

SCROLL LEFT OR RIGHT

1 Click ◄ to scroll left.

2 Click ► to scroll right.

3 Drag the scroll box left or right along the scroll bar to scroll to any location in the window.

DISPLAY OR HIDE TOOLBARS AND STATUS BAR

Toolbars allow you to quickly access commonly used commands and features. The status bar provides information about the items displayed in a window. You can display or hide these bars to suit your needs.

The toolbars appear at the top of a window. The Standard Buttons toolbar contains buttons that allow you to quickly select commonly used menu commands, such as Copy, Paste, Undo and Delete. You can use the Address Bar toolbar to view a list of the drives and folders on your computer. You can also type a Web page address in the Address Bar toolbar to access the Web without first starting your Web browser program. The Links toolbar contains links you can select to quickly access useful Web sites.

The status bar, which appears at the bottom of a window, displays information about the items in the window or the selected item. For example, when you select a drive, the status bar displays the free space on the drive and total capacity of the drive.

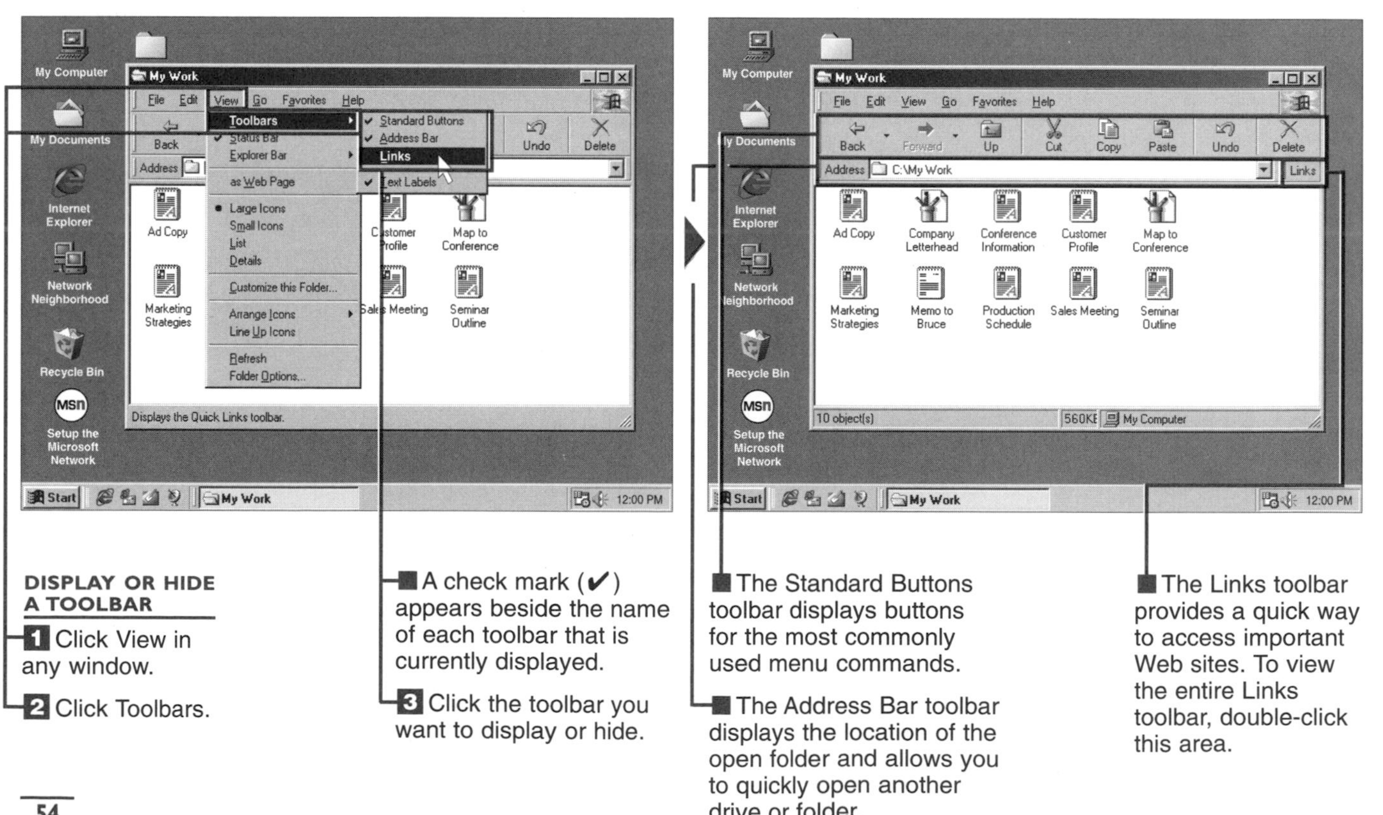

DISPLAY OR HIDE A TOOLBAR

1 Click View in any window.

2 Click Toolbars.

■ A check mark (✔) appears beside the name of each toolbar that is currently displayed.

3 Click the toolbar you want to display or hide.

■ The Standard Buttons toolbar displays buttons for the most commonly used menu commands.

■ The Address Bar toolbar displays the location of the open folder and allows you to quickly open another drive or folder.

■ The Links toolbar provides a quick way to access important Web sites. To view the entire Links toolbar, double-click this area.

TIPS

The Standard Buttons toolbar takes up too much room on my screen. How can I make it smaller?

You can remove the text labels from the buttons on the toolbar. From the View menu, select Toolbars and then click Text Labels.

Can I resize the toolbars?

Yes. Position the mouse over the bottom of the toolbars (↖ changes to ↕). Drag the bottom of the toolbars up or down until the toolbars appear the way you want.

How can I move a toolbar?

Position the mouse over the raised line on the toolbar you want to move (↖ changes to ↔). Drag the toolbar to a new location. You can place more than one toolbar on a single line.

When two toolbars are on the same line, how can I change their width?

When more than one toolbar is on a single line, a raised line appears between the toolbars. Position the mouse over the raised line (↖ changes to ↔). Drag the raised line to the right or left until the toolbars display the width you want.

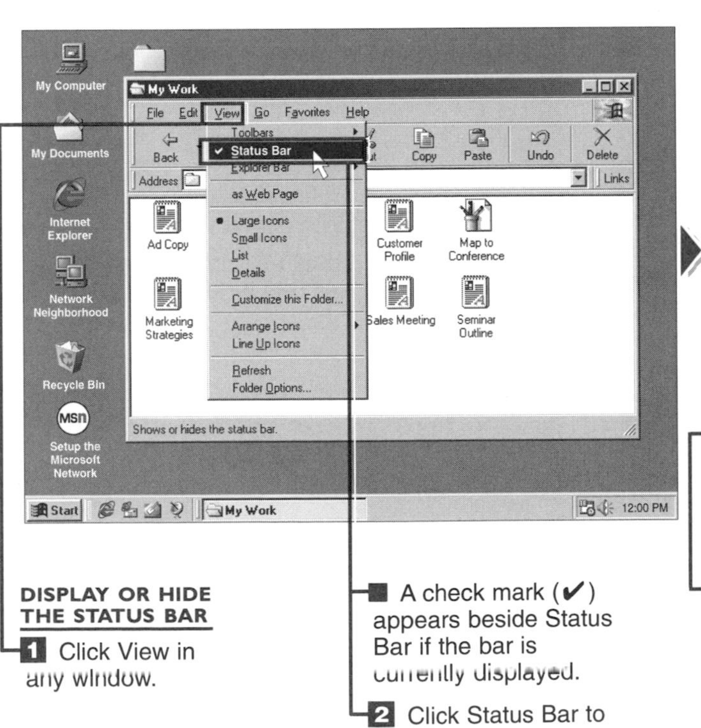

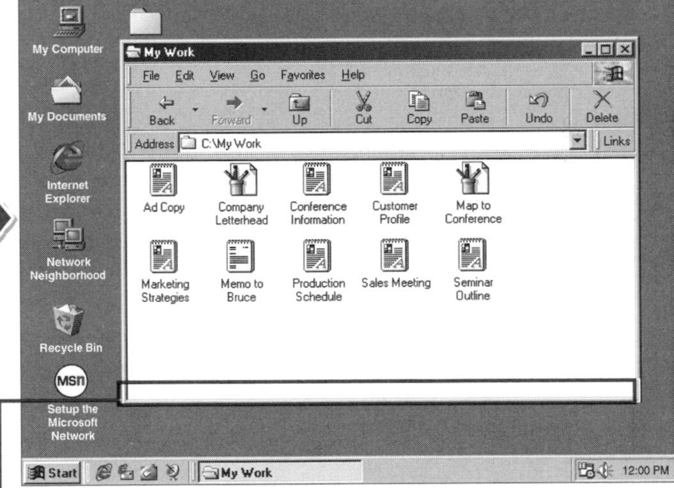

DISPLAY OR HIDE THE STATUS BAR

1 Click View in any window.

■ A check mark (✔) appears beside Status Bar if the bar is currently displayed.

2 Click Status Bar to display or hide the bar.

■ In this example, the status bar disappears.

■ The status bar tells you how many items are in the window and the size of the items.

CHANGE FOLDER VIEW OPTIONS

You can customize the way Windows displays the contents of folders.

You can have Windows remember which settings you select for each folder you open and redisplay the folder with the same settings the next time you open the folder. This is useful if you prefer to display the contents of one folder in the Details view and another folder as large icons.

When you open a folder, you can have Windows display the location of the folder in the title bar of the window. You can display the three-letter file extension for certain file types to view additional information about your files.

Windows lets you add buttons to the toolbar displayed in each window to help you work with network drives. If you use the Details view when displaying the contents of a folder, you can show the attributes of the files. You can also have Windows display a description of desktop items and folders in a small box.

When displaying folders in the Windows Explorer window, you can display certain file and folder names in uppercase letters. You can also have Windows hide or display hidden and system files in any folder.

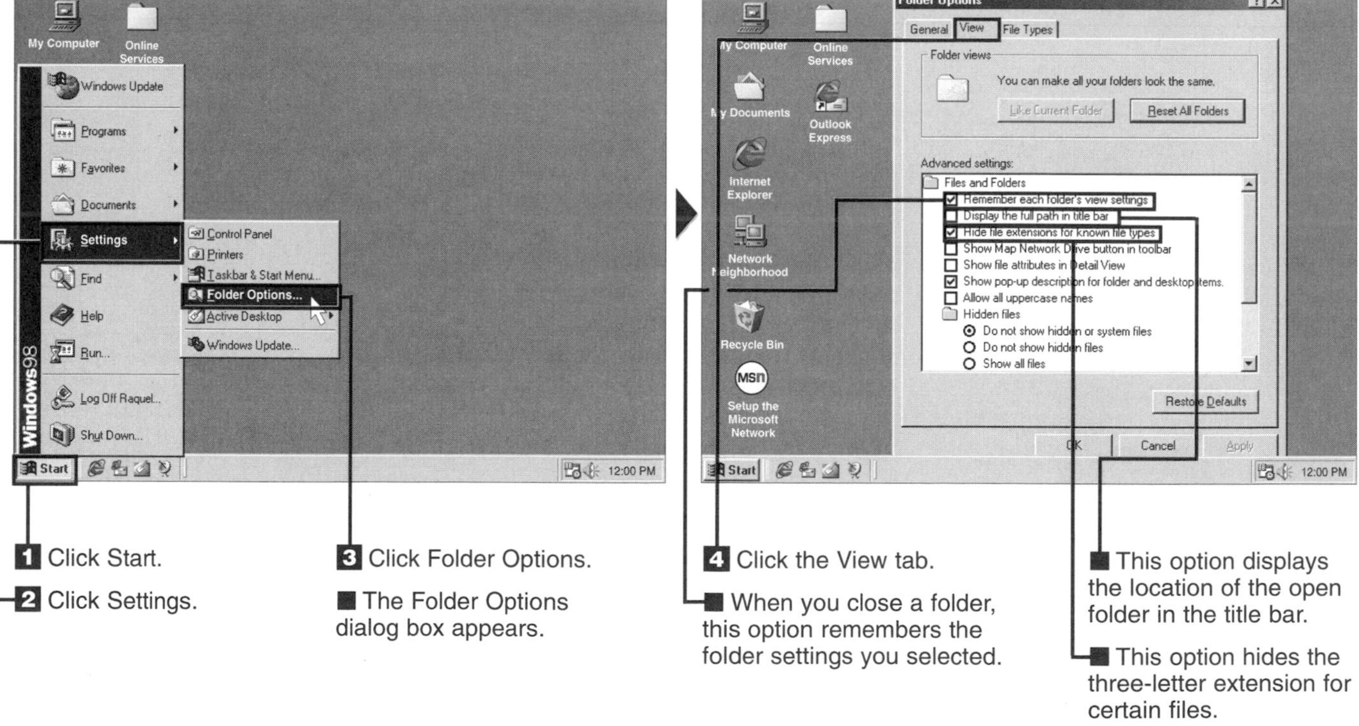

1 Click Start.

2 Click Settings.

3 Click Folder Options.

■ The Folder Options dialog box appears.

4 Click the View tab.

■ When you close a folder, this option remembers the folder settings you selected.

■ This option displays the location of the open folder in the title bar.

■ This option hides the three-letter extension for certain files.

TIPS

Can I use a previous set of folder view options?

You cannot save a set of folder view options, but you can return to Windows' default settings by clicking the Restore Defaults button on the View tab in the Folder Options dialog box.

How can I use the settings that I have customized for one folder when I open other folders?

Open the folder that displays the settings you want to use for all your folders. On the View menu, click Folder Options. On the View tab, click the Like Current Folder button.

Should I display extensions for my files?

File extensions can help you identify the types of files you are viewing. For example, viewing the file extensions would help you realize that the Notepad file you thought was named "read.me" is actually saved as "read.me.txt".

Why would I want to hide the hidden and system files?

Hidden and system files are files that Windows and your programs need to run. They cannot usually be opened. If you change or remove hidden or system files, your computer may no longer operate properly.

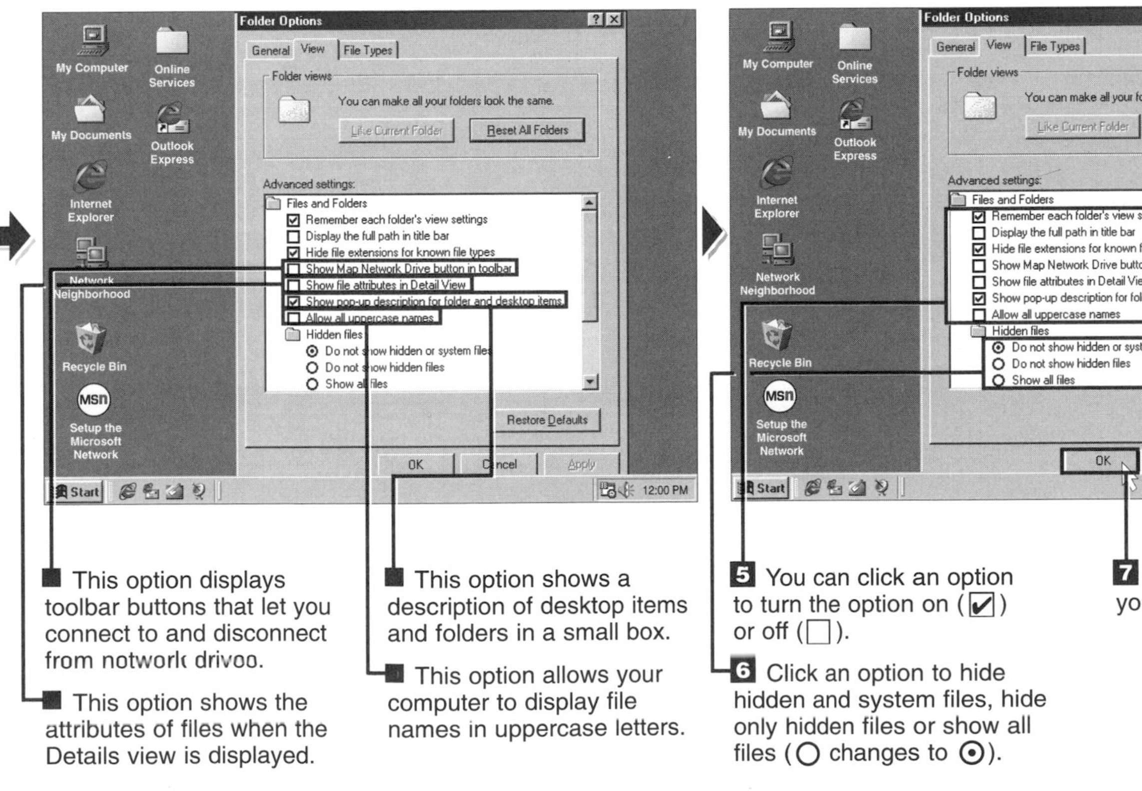

■ This option displays toolbar buttons that let you connect to and disconnect from network drives.

■ This option shows the attributes of files when the Details view is displayed.

■ This option shows a description of desktop items and folders in a small box.

■ This option allows your computer to display file names in uppercase letters.

5 You can click an option to turn the option on (☑) or off (☐).

6 Click an option to hide hidden and system files, hide only hidden files or show all files (○ changes to ⦿).

7 Click OK to confirm your changes.

PRINT CONTENTS OF A FOLDER

You can create, edit and print a list of the files stored in a folder on your computer. This can include a folder on your hard drive, a removable drive, a floppy disk or a CD-ROM disc. You cannot create a list for the My Documents folder on the desktop.

A printed list can help you organize information on your computer. You can create a printed index of the contents of your hard, floppy or removable disks.

A list of files is helpful when you are trying to create more free disk space. You can see which files you no longer need and which files are duplicated in several folders.

Although the ability to print the contents of a folder is not included in either My Computer or Explorer, you can use the MS-DOS directory (dir) command. This command displays a list of files on your screen. Additional commands are used to save the list in a file that you can open, edit and print.

MS-DOS commands require strict attention to detail. Carefully note the spelling, punctuation and spaces that are used or the command will not work.

When you double-click the file containing the list, it will open as a Notepad document. If the list is large, you will be able to use WordPad instead.

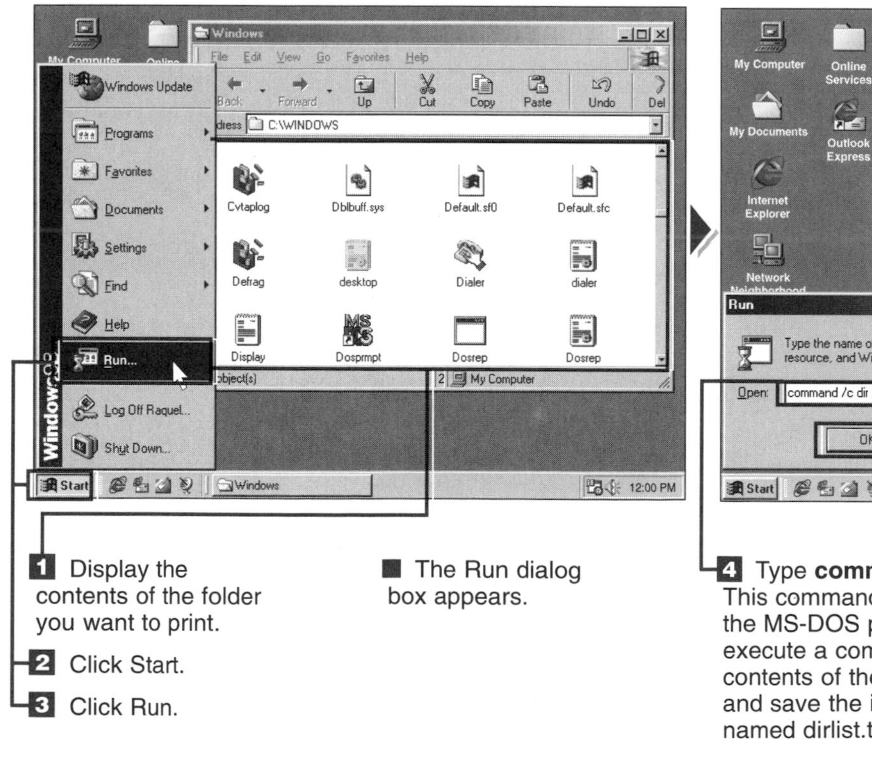

1 Display the contents of the folder you want to print.

2 Click Start.

3 Click Run.

■ The Run dialog box appears.

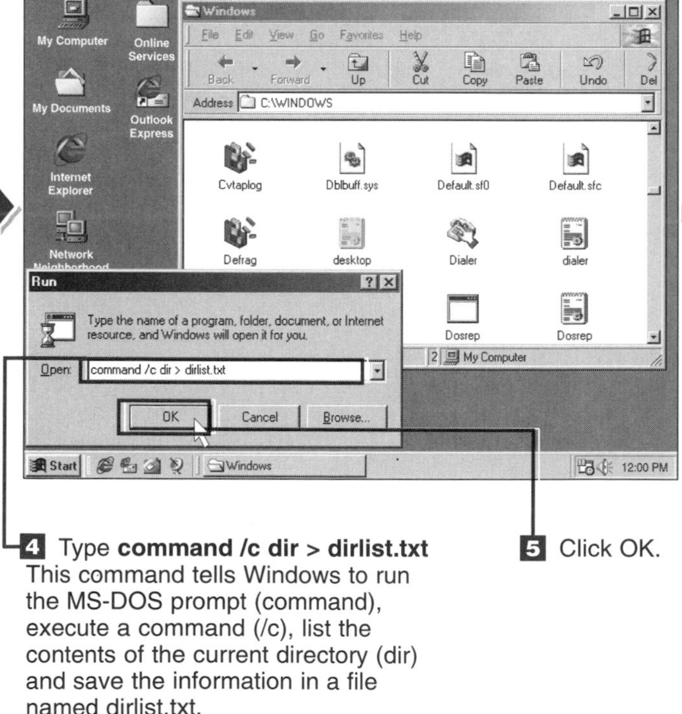

4 Type **command /c dir > dirlist.txt** This command tells Windows to run the MS-DOS prompt (command), execute a command (/c), list the contents of the current directory (dir) and save the information in a file named dirlist.txt.

5 Click OK.

TIPS

How can I create a list of all the files in the current folder and all the subfolders?

Use the /s command. For example, type **command /c dir /s > dirlist.txt**

Can I save the list with a different name?

Instead of typing **dirlist.txt**, type the name of the file you want. For example, type **command /c dir > files.doc**

How do I create a list of all the folders and files on my hard drive?

Type **command /c dir c:\ /s > dirlist.txt** You can replace c: with any drive letter.

Can I print the list without saving it?

In the Run dialog box, type **command /c dir > lpt1** This command will only work if you have a printer directly connected to your computer and the printer can print plain text.

Is it possible to sort the list?

To sort by name, type the **/on** command. To sort by date, type the **/od** command. For example, type **command /c dir /od > dirlist.txt** You can type **command /k dir /?** in the Run dialog box to view all the options you can use with the dir command.

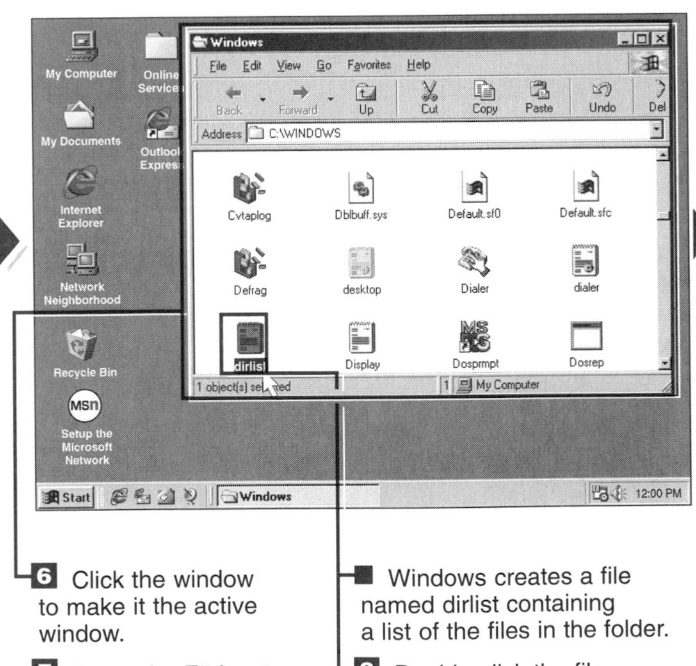

6 Click the window to make it the active window.

7 Press the F5 key to refresh the display of the files in the window.

■ Windows creates a file named dirlist containing a list of the files in the folder.

8 Double-click the file to display its contents.

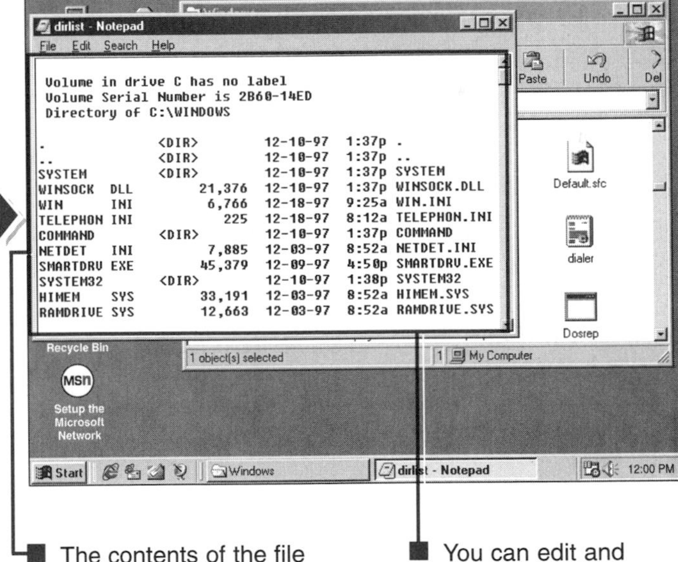

■ The contents of the file appear. Windows displays information about each file, including the MS-DOS file name, size, date last modified and the full file name.

■ You can edit and print the file as you would any document stored on your computer.

USING WINDOWS EXPLORER

Like a map, Windows Explorer shows you the location of every file and folder on your computer. The Exploring window helps you understand the relationship between files and folders on your computer. You can use Windows Explorer to find and view drives and folders on your computer, including the Control Panel, Printers, Dial-Up Networking and Scheduled Tasks.

The Exploring window has two panes. The left pane shows the structure of your drives and folders. The right pane shows the contents of the drive or folder selected in the left pane. You can expand the information available in the left pane to show some or all of the drives and folders available on your computer. You can also reduce the information in the left pane to provide an overview of the items available on your computer.

You can use Windows Explorer to manage and organize files, start programs and open documents.

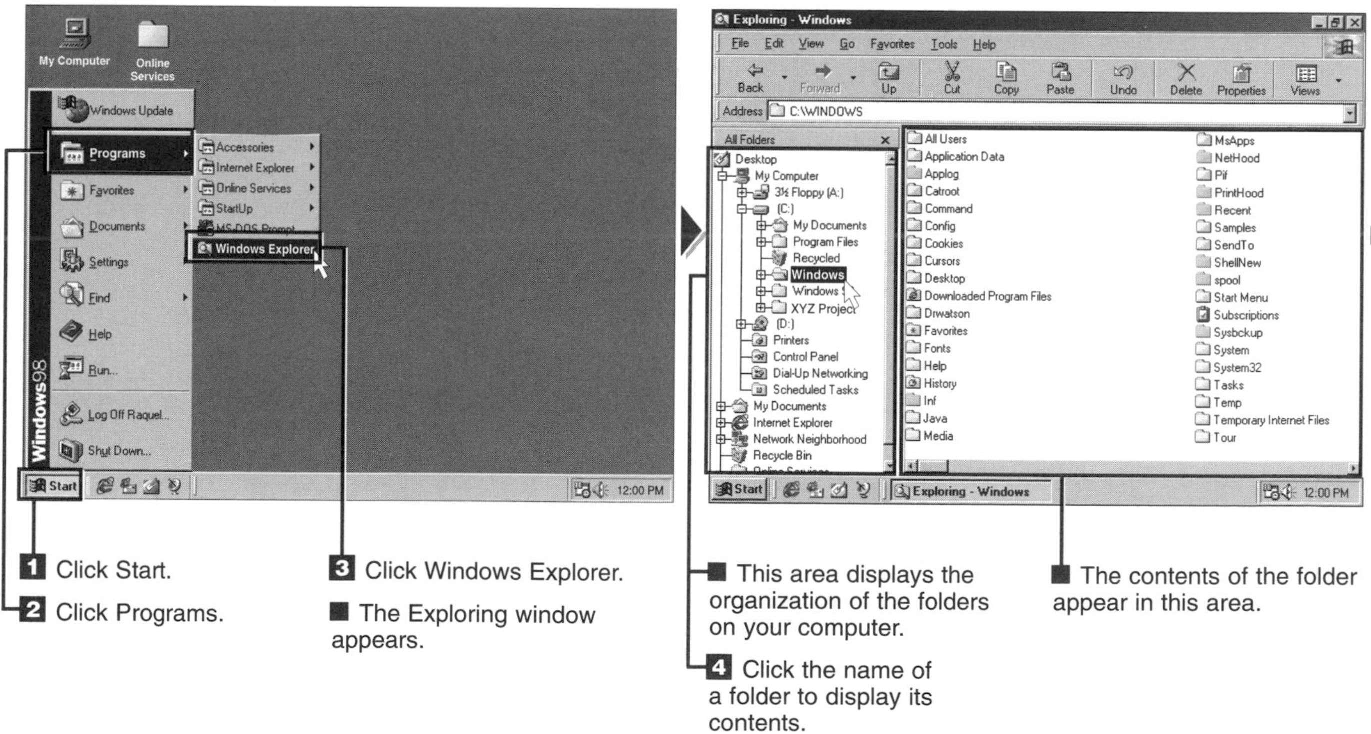

1 Click Start.

2 Click Programs.

3 Click Windows Explorer.

■ The Exploring window appears.

■ This area displays the organization of the folders on your computer.

4 Click the name of a folder to display its contents.

■ The contents of the folder appear in this area.

TIPS

Can I start Windows Explorer without using the Start menu?

Right-click My Computer or the Start button and then select Explore.

How do I open a file or folder using Windows Explorer?

You can double-click a file or folder in the right pane.

How can I quickly find information about a folder in the Exploring window?

You can display the status bar to view information about a selected folder, such as the number of items in the folder and the disk space used by the folder. To display the status bar, see page 55.

How do I list all the drives and folders without clicking each plus sign (⊞)?

To list all the drives and folders, select My Computer in the left pane. Then hold down the Alt key and press the * key on the numeric keypad. You can list all the items within a folder by selecting a folder and then pressing the * key on the numeric keypad. To again display only the main folder, click the minus sign (⊟) beside the top folder and then press the F5 key.

Can I see how much disk space is available on my drives?

Select My Computer in the left pane. Choose the View menu and then click Details. The column headings will change to display the Total Size and Free Space on each drive.

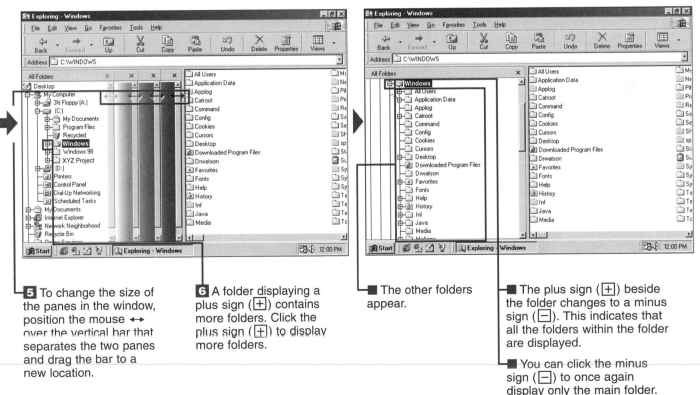

5 To change the size of the panes in the window, position the mouse ↔ over the vertical bar that separates the two panes and drag the bar to a new location.

6 A folder displaying a plus sign (⊞) contains more folders. Click the plus sign (⊞) to display more folders.

■ The other folders appear.

■ The plus sign (⊞) beside the folder changes to a minus sign (⊟). This indicates that all the folders within the folder are displayed.

■ You can click the minus sign (⊟) to once again display only the main folder.

SELECT FILES

Before you can work with a file or folder, you must select the item. For example, you can copy, move, delete or open a file or folder you select. When you select a file or folder, Windows highlights the item.

You can select and work with multiple files and folders. This lets you perform the same procedure on several files and folders at the same time. Working with multiple files and folders saves you from repeating the same tasks over and over.

You can select files and folders using different techniques. The best way to select a group of files will depend on which view you use to display the items. For example, when you are working in the Large or Small Icons view, you can drag the mouse to form a rectangle around the group of files you want to select. For information on the ways to view items, see page 48.

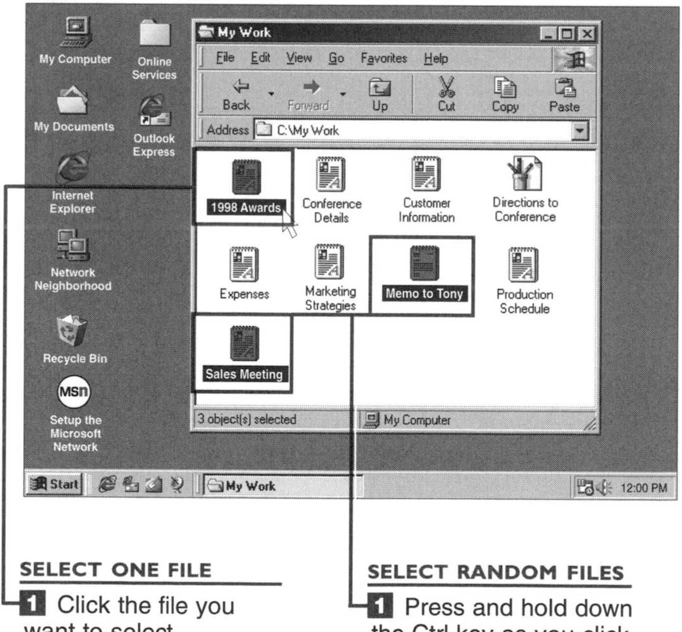

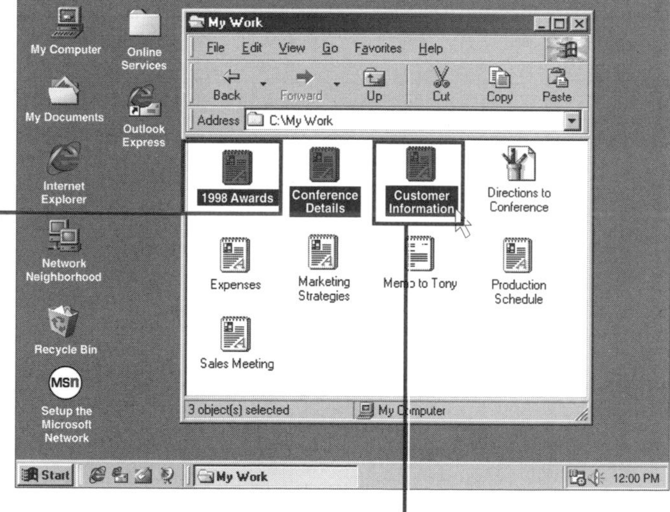

SELECT ONE FILE

1 Click the file you want to select.

■ The file is highlighted.

SELECT RANDOM FILES

1 Press and hold down the Ctrl key as you click each file you want to select.

SELECT GROUP OF FILES

1 Click the first file you want to select.

2 Press and hold down the Shift key.

3 Still holding down the Shift key, click the last file you want to select.

TIPS

How do I deselect files or folders and start over?

Click a blank area on your screen.

How do I deselect one file or folder from a group I have selected?

Hold down the Ctrl key while you click on the file or folder you want to deselect.

Is there an easy way to select all but a few files in a folder?

Select all the files in a folder and then hold down the Ctrl key while you click the files you do not want to select. You can also select the files you do not want and then choose the Edit menu and select Invert Selection.

How do I select a file or folder when the single-click option is turned on?

When the single-click option is turned on, you can open a file or folder with a single-click, instead of a double-click. You can select a file or folder just by moving the mouse over the file. To turn on the single-click option, see page 224.

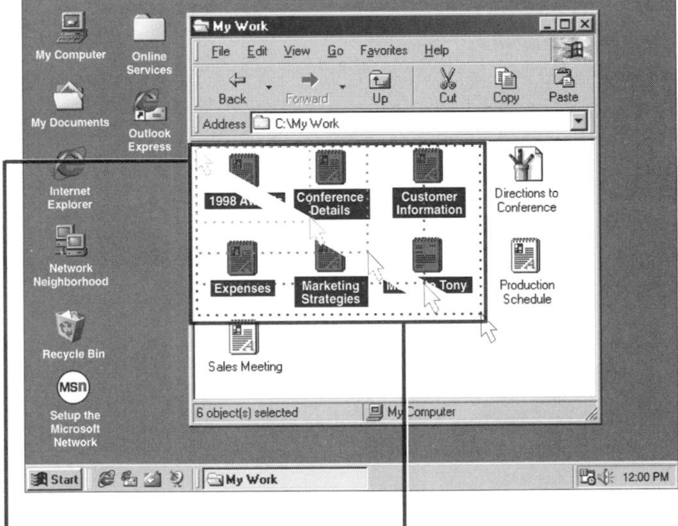

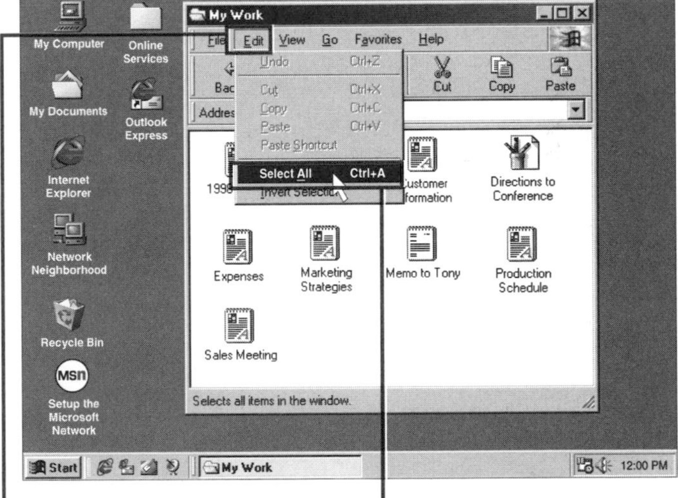

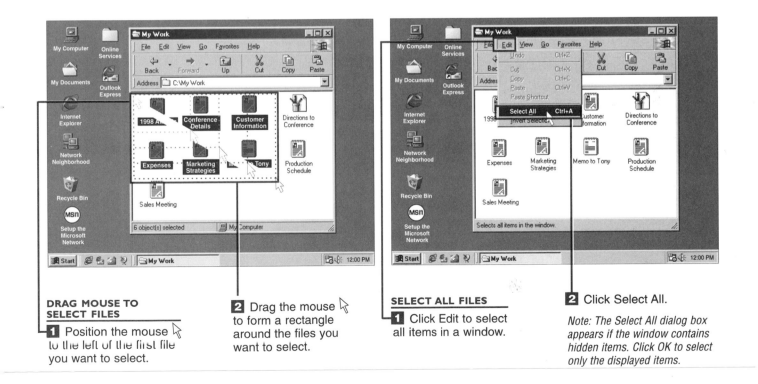

DRAG MOUSE TO SELECT FILES

1 Position the mouse to the left of the first file you want to select.

2 Drag the mouse to form a rectangle around the files you want to select.

SELECT ALL FILES

1 Click Edit to select all items in a window.

2 Click Select All.

Note: The Select All dialog box appears if the window contains hidden items. Click OK to select only the displayed items.

OPEN FILES

You can open a file directly from My Computer or Windows Explorer to display its contents on your screen.

Each file on your computer is associated with a program. When you open a file, the associated program starts automatically. For example, bitmap files with the extension .bmp are usually associated with the Paint program. When you open a file with the .bmp extension, the Paint program starts and the file is opened.

If Windows does not know which program to start, the Open With dialog box appears. You can then choose which program you want to use to display the file. For example, a software company may include an information file named readme.1st on an installation disk. Although readme.1st is a text file, the extension (.1st) is not associated with any Windows program. Windows does not know which program to start to open the file. You can use the Open With dialog box to specify the program you want to start to display the file.

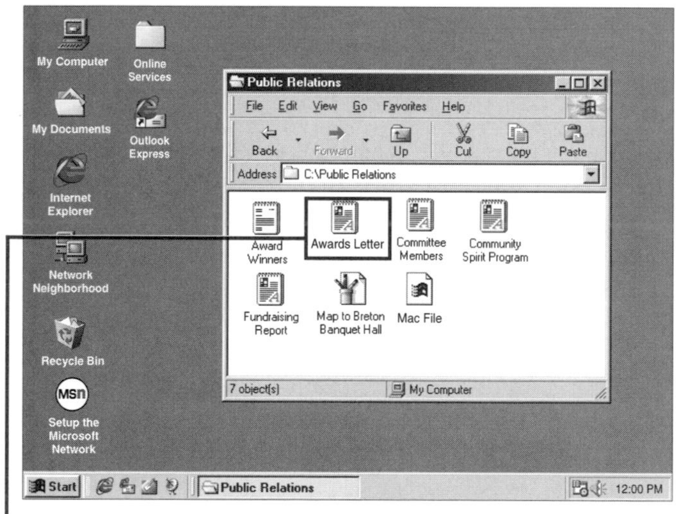

1 Locate the file you want to open.

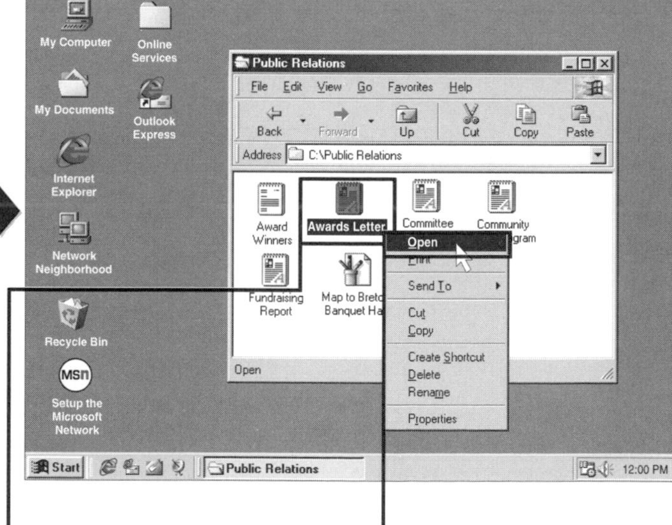

2 Right-click the file you want to open. A menu appears.

3 Click Open.

Note: You can double-click the file instead of performing steps 2 and 3.

TIPS

How do I find a file I want to open?

You can use My Computer or Windows Explorer to browse through the contents of your computer. The Find feature also allows you to locate a file. See page 78.

How can I find all the files created in a specific program?

From the Start menu, click Find and then select Files or Folders. Use the Advanced tab to set the Of type option to the program type you are looking for.

Can I verify a file is the one I want before I open the file?

You can right-click the file and select Quick View to preview the file without opening the program. See page 82.

How do I change which program always opens a file?

Click the file you want to change. Press and hold down the Shift key and then right-click the file. Click Open with and then select the program you want to open the file. Then click the Always use this program to open this type of file option (☐ changes to ☑).

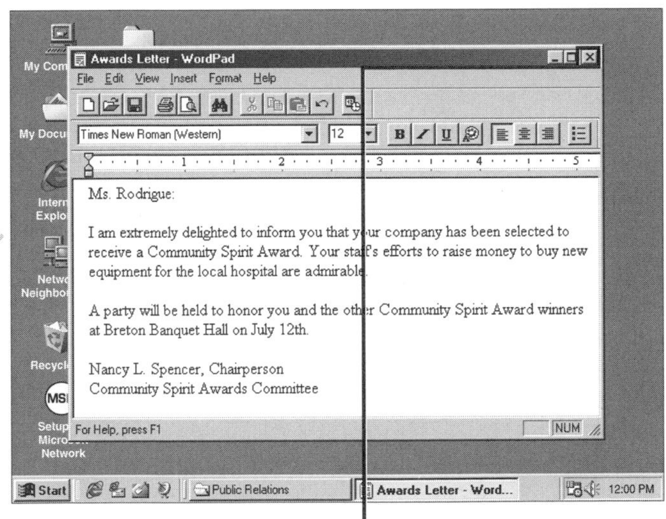

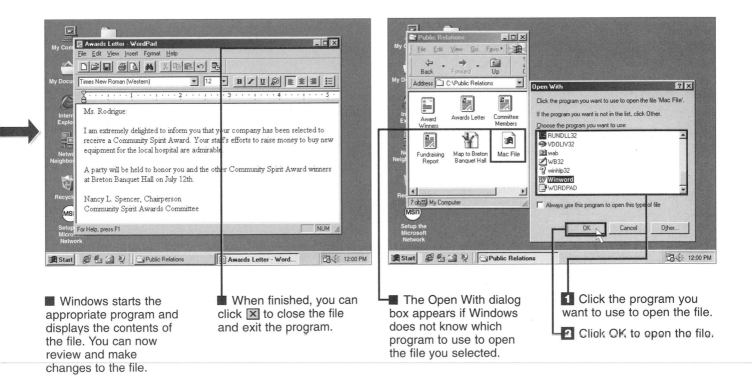

■ Windows starts the appropriate program and displays the contents of the file. You can now review and make changes to the file.

■ When finished, you can click ☒ to close the file and exit the program.

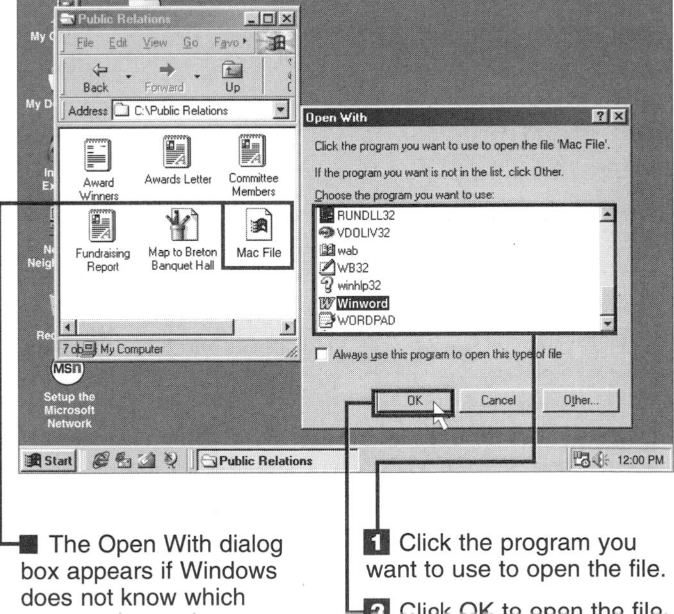

■ The Open With dialog box appears if Windows does not know which program to use to open the file you selected.

1 Click the program you want to use to open the file.

2 Click OK to open the file.

OPEN RECENTLY USED FILES

Windows helps you quickly find and open a file you recently worked with.

Windows remembers the last files you opened or saved and displays the names of the files in a list on the Start menu. You can quickly open any of these files to review or make changes to the files.

When you select a file from the list in the Start menu, the program starts and the file opens. Selecting a file from the list saves you from searching through folders on your computer to find the file you want to open.

Windows displays the files in the Start menu in alphabetical order to make it easier to find the file you are looking for. A small icon appears beside each file to indicate which program was used to create the file.

The Start menu also includes a shortcut to the My Documents folder to help you quickly access the files in the folder.

You can clear the list of recently used files at any time. Clearing the list is useful when the list becomes cluttered or contains many files you no longer need to work with. Clearing the list of recently used files will not remove the files in the My Documents folder.

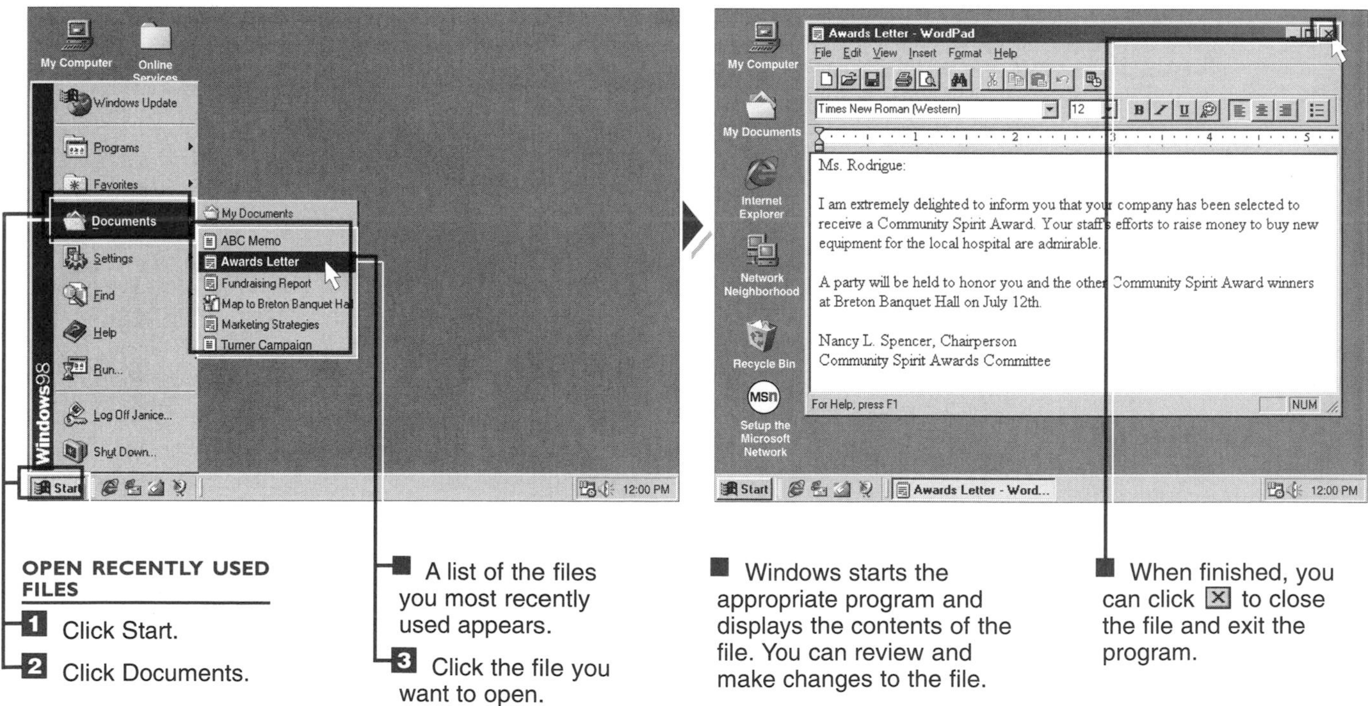

OPEN RECENTLY USED FILES

1 Click Start.

2 Click Documents.

■ A list of the files you most recently used appears.

3 Click the file you want to open.

■ Windows starts the appropriate program and displays the contents of the file. You can review and make changes to the file.

■ When finished, you can click ☒ to close the file and exit the program.

TIPS

How can I add files to the list of recently used files?

You can add a file to the list in the Start menu by opening the file. To open a file, see page 64.

How do I find a file that is not on the list of recently used files?

If the file you want to open is not on the list of recently used files, you can have Windows search for the file. To find files, see page 78.

Why is a file not listed in the Start menu?

A file will not appear in the list of recently used files if you use a program that was not designed for Windows 95 or 98. If you open a file in an e-mail message, the file will also not appear in the list.

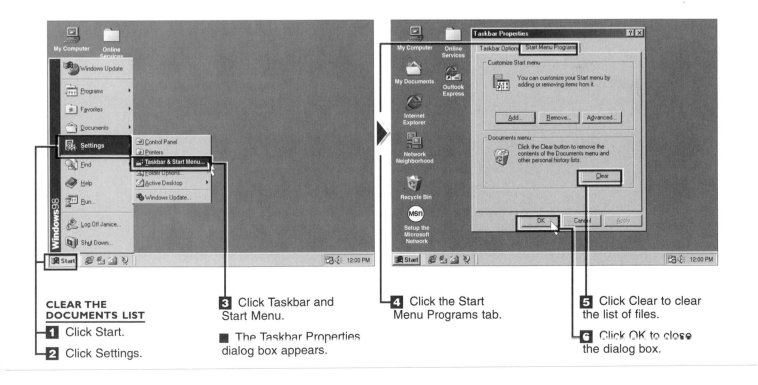

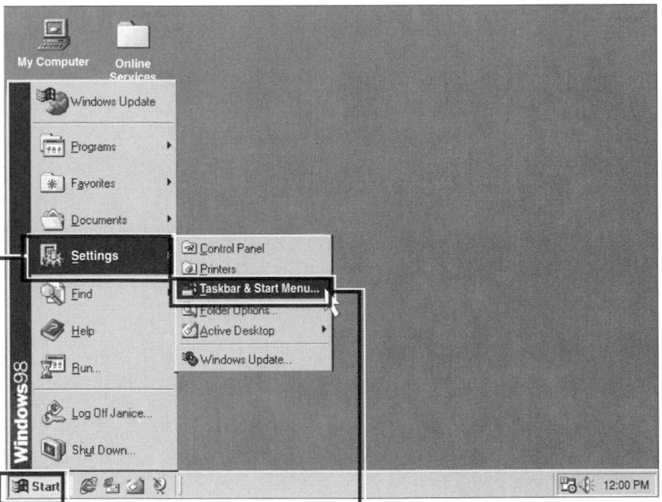

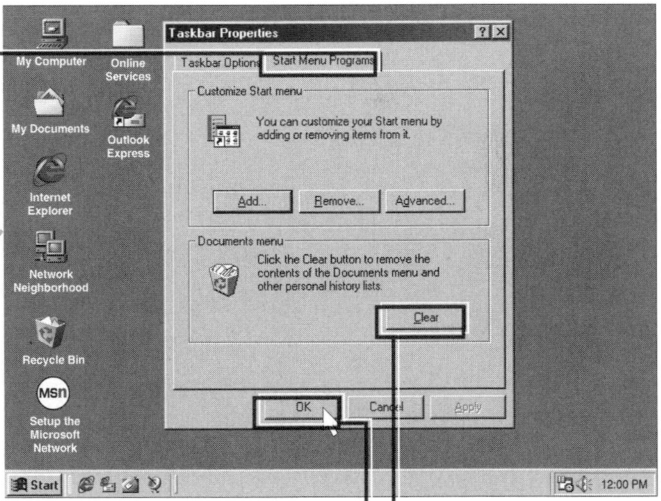

CLEAR THE DOCUMENTS LIST

1 Click Start.

2 Click Settings.

3 Click Taskbar and Start Menu.

■ The Taskbar Properties dialog box appears.

4 Click the Start Menu Programs tab.

5 Click Clear to clear the list of files.

6 Click OK to close the dialog box.

RENAME FILES

You can change the name of a file to better describe its contents. This makes it easier for you to find the file later. When naming your files, use a keyword that will identify the file, such as the name of a client, a project or an event.

In Windows 98, you can use up to 255 characters to name a file. You can also include spaces and periods. The only characters you cannot use to name a file are the symbols \ / : * ? | " < or >. If you use periods in the file name, the letters after the last period should be the file's extension.

An MS-DOS name has eight characters and a three-character extension. To shorten the name, Windows takes the first six letters, inserts the tilde (~) character and a number. You can see the shortened name used by older programs in a file's Properties dialog box.

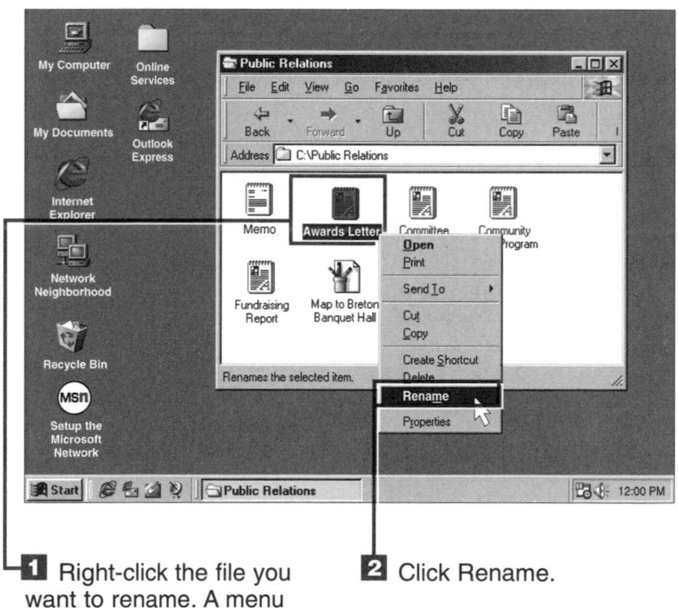

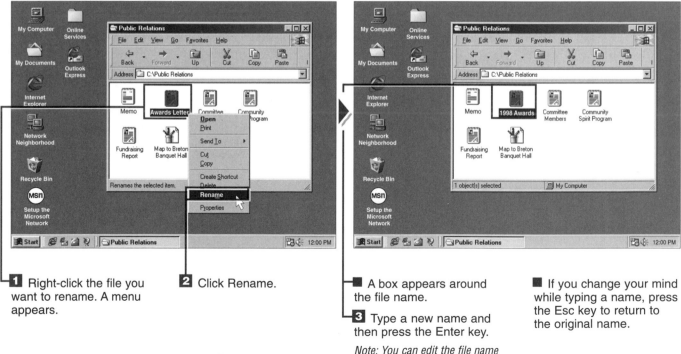

1 Right-click the file you want to rename. A menu appears.

2 Click Rename.

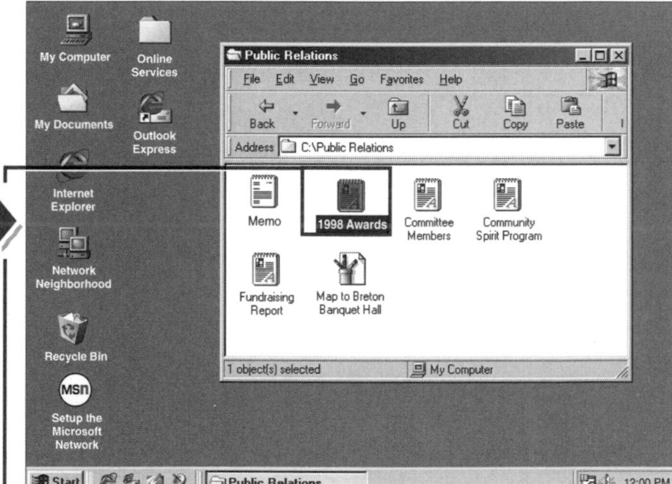

■ A box appears around the file name.

3 Type a new name and then press the Enter key.

Note: You can edit the file name instead of replacing the entire name. Click the file name where you want to make the change.

■ If you change your mind while typing a name, press the Esc key to return to the original name.

Can I rename folders?

You can rename folders, but make sure you only change the names of folders that you created. If you change the names of program or system folders, Windows will not be able to find the files it needs to operate.

Can I use both upper and lower case letters to name a file?

You can type upper and lower case letters to make file names easier to read, but Windows does not recognize the difference between upper and lower case letters. For example, Windows sees ReadMe.txt, README.TXT and readme.txt as identical names.

Can I use the same file name for two different files?

You can use the same file name for two different files if the files are located in different folders.

Are long file names compatible with all programs?

Some programs, such as older backup programs and other disk utility programs, do not support long file names. If you use these programs, you must save all your files with an MS-DOS file name.

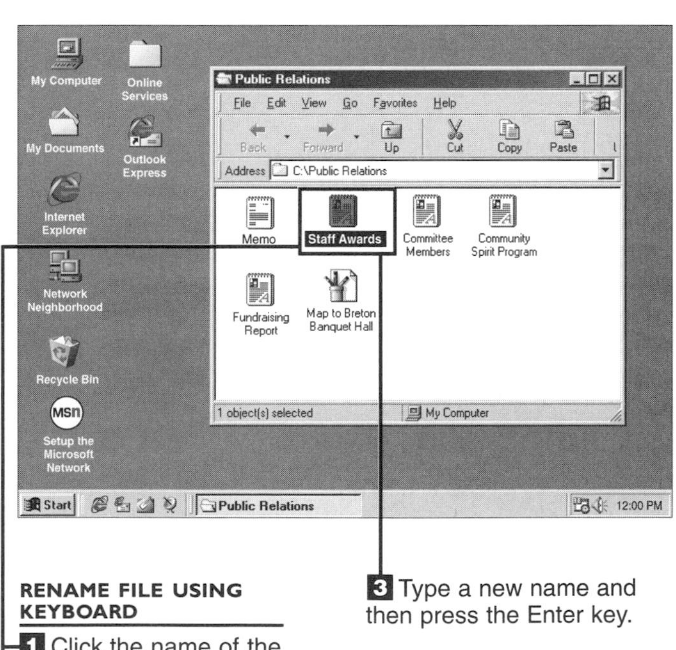

RENAME FILE USING KEYBOARD

1. Click the name of the file you want to rename.
2. Press the F2 key to select the current name.
3. Type a new name and then press the Enter key.

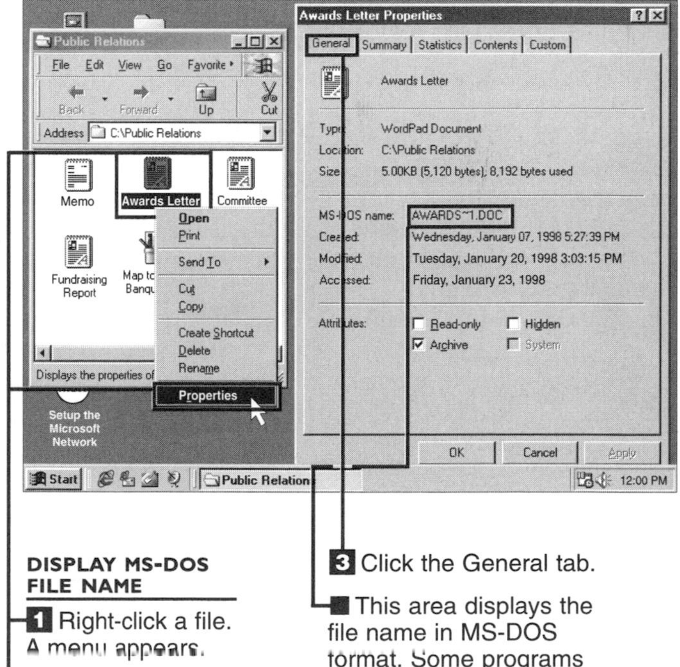

DISPLAY MS-DOS FILE NAME

1. Right-click a file. A menu appears.
2. Click Properties.

■ The Properties dialog box appears.

3. Click the General tab.

■ This area displays the file name in MS-DOS format. Some programs use this information for opening and closing files.

MOVE AND COPY FILES

You can move or copy your files when you want to take work home, share documents with a colleague or reorganize files on your hard drive. Copying files is also useful for making backup copies.

When you move a file, you delete the file from its original location.

When you copy a file, you create a second file that is exactly the same as the first. You can place the copy in another folder on your computer, on a network drive, on a floppy disk or on a removable disk. If you create a copy in the same folder, Windows will add "Copy of" to the file name.

You can also move and copy folders. When you move or copy a folder, all files in the folder are also moved or copied.

When you drag and drop a file, the result depends on the file's destination. When you drag a file to a new location on the same drive, Windows moves the file. When you drag a file onto a different drive, Windows copies the file.

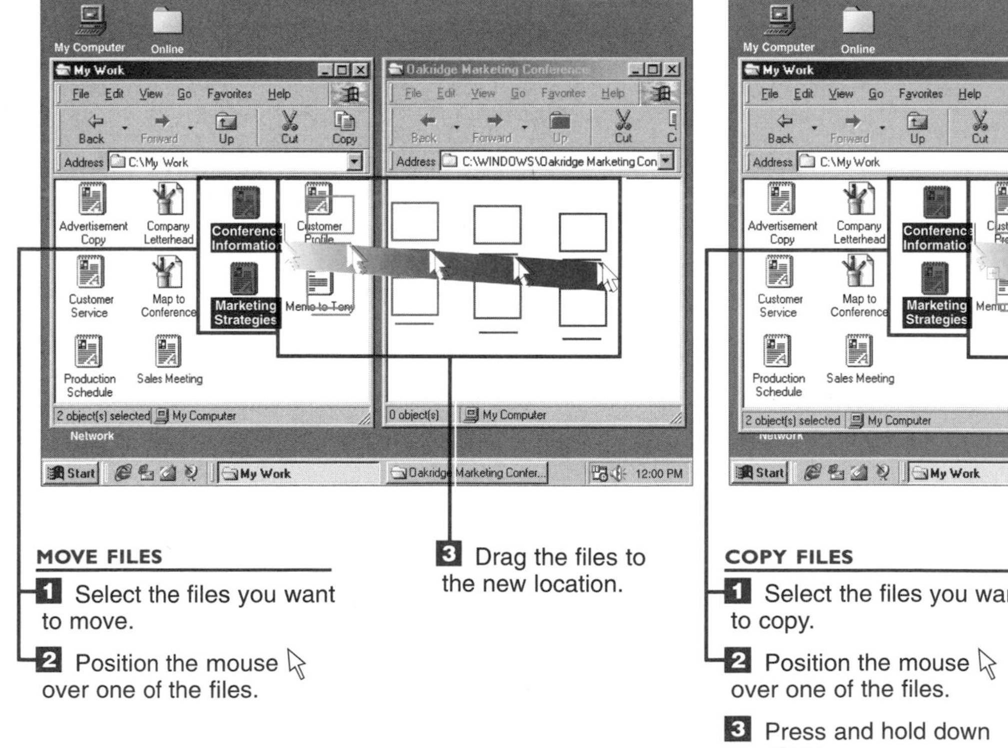

MOVE FILES

1 Select the files you want to move.

2 Position the mouse over one of the files.

3 Drag the files to the new location.

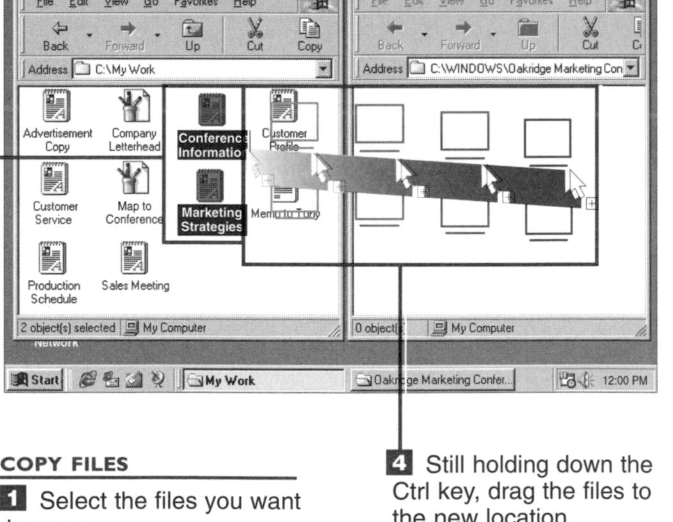

COPY FILES

1 Select the files you want to copy.

2 Position the mouse over one of the files.

3 Press and hold down the Ctrl key.

4 Still holding down the Ctrl key, drag the files to the new location.

■ When copying files, a plus sign (⊞) appears under the mouse pointer.

How do I move a file to a different drive?

When you drag a file to a different drive, a plus sign (⊞) appears under the mouse pointer, indicating that Windows will make a copy. To move the file, hold down the Shift key.

I tried to move an application, but Windows created a shortcut instead. What should I do?

To move an application, hold down the Shift key as you drag the application. To copy an application, hold down the Ctrl key as you drag the application. If you move applications from the directory where they were created, they may not function properly.

I frequently move files to the same folder. How can I simplify this procedure?

Add the folder you frequently use to the Send To menu. See page 232. You can also place a shortcut to the folder on your desktop. See page 90.

My computer screen is crowded when I try to view the contents of two folders. How else can I move and copy files?

Select the files you want to move or copy. Right-click one of the files. To move the files, click Cut. To copy the files, click Copy. Open the folder where you want the files to appear. Right-click a blank area in the folder and then click Paste.

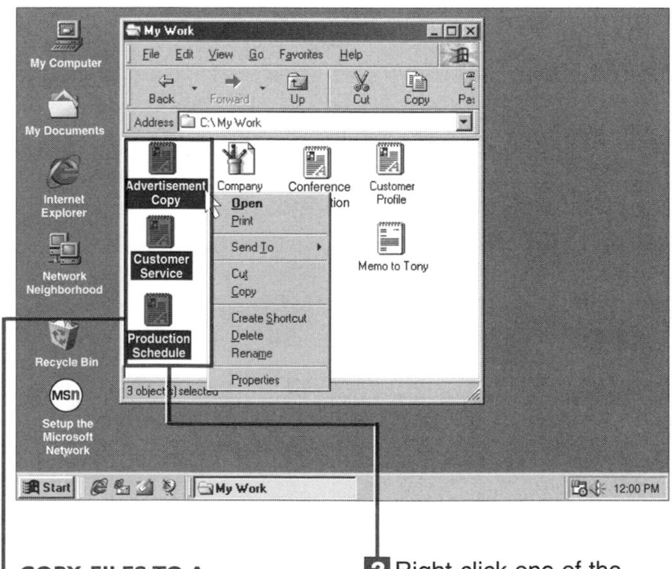

COPY FILES TO A FLOPPY DISK

1 Select the files you want to copy to a floppy disk.

2 Right-click one of the files. A menu appears.

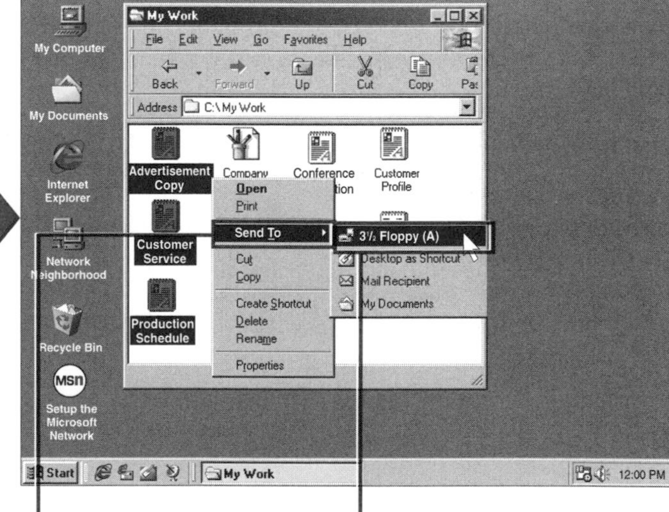

3 Click Send To.

4 Click the drive you want to receive a copy of the files.

DELETE FILES

You can remove documents, folders and programs you no longer need to free up space on your computer. If you delete a folder, Windows erases all the files and folders inside the folder. To protect you from accidentally erasing files, Windows stores deleted files in the Recycle Bin.

As a precaution, Windows asks you to confirm the files you are erasing. Make sure you do not delete system files required to run Windows or files required by programs you still use. Do not delete any file unless you are certain you no longer need the file.

Before you delete documents, consider the value of the documents. You may want to save a copy on a floppy disk or a backup tape. The cost of disks and tapes is small compared to the cost of recreating a document.

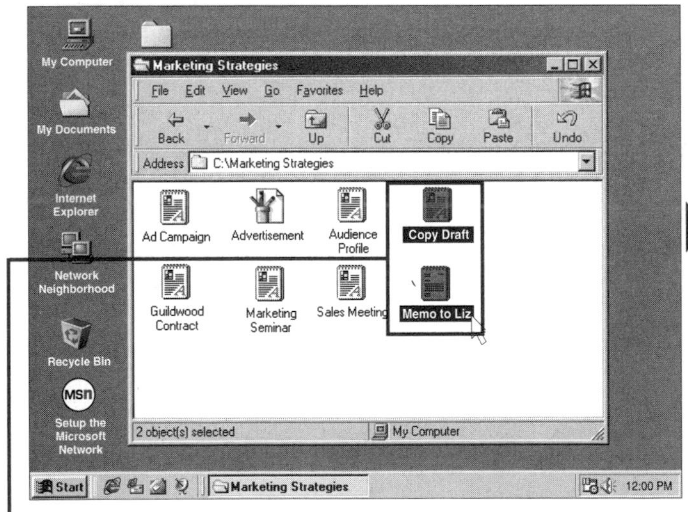

1 Select the files you want to delete. To select multiple files, see page 62.

2 Press the Delete key.

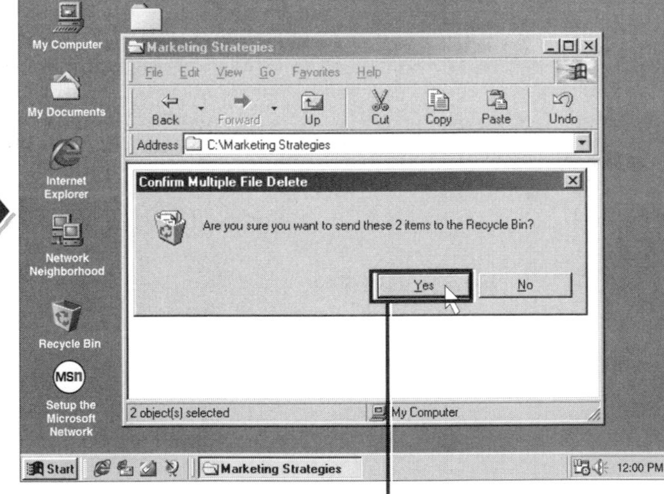

■ A dialog box appears confirming the deletion.

3 Click Yes to delete the files.

TIPS

How do I delete a confidential file so it cannot be recovered?

Select the file and then press the Shift and Delete keys. The file will be deleted from your computer and will not appear in the Recycle Bin.

Can I delete any file on my computer?

It is best to delete only the documents that you have created. If you want to delete other files or programs to free up space on your hard drive, you can use the Disk Cleanup tool. See page 310.

Can I turn off the Confirm File Delete dialog box that appears when I delete a file?

The Recycle Bin provides many options, including turning off the confirmation message. See page 76.

Is there another way to delete a file?

You can drag and drop a file to the Recycle Bin to delete the file.

Are all deleted files placed in the Recycle Bin?

Files deleted from floppy disks or other removable disks are not placed in the Recycle Bin and cannot be recovered.

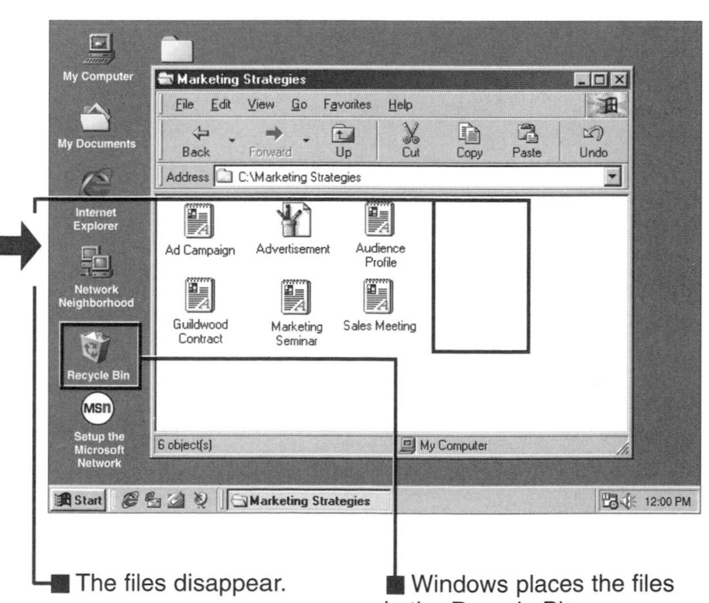

■ The files disappear.

■ Windows places the files in the Recycle Bin.

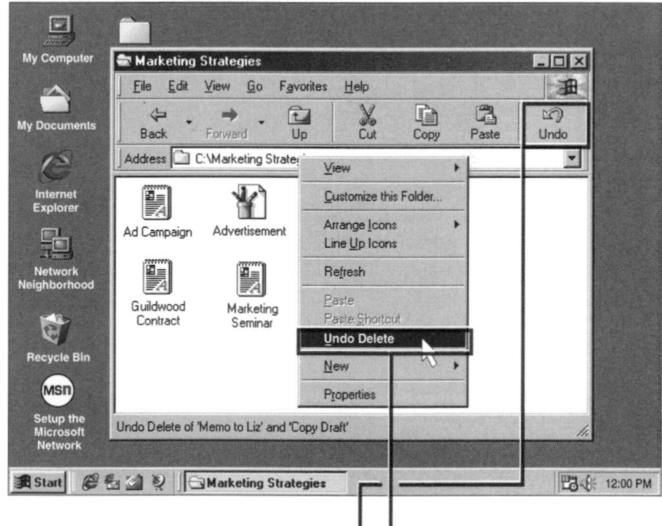

■ You can immediately restore files you just deleted.

1 Right-click a blank area in the window or on the desktop. A menu appears.

2 Click Undo Delete.

■ Instead of performing steps 1 and 2, you can also click the Undo button in the window.

RESTORE DELETED FILES

The Recycle Bin is a special folder that stores the files you have deleted. If you have accidentally deleted a file, you will probably find it in the Recycle Bin. You can then restore the file to its original location on your computer. You cannot restore files deleted from a floppy disk, removable disk or network drive. Files deleted from these items are not stored in the Recycle Bin.

When you are certain that you no longer need the files in the Recycle Bin, you can use the Empty Recycle Bin command to remove all the deleted files and increase the available disk space on your computer. When you empty the Recycle Bin, all the files are permanently removed from your computer.

When the Recycle Bin fills up with deleted files, Windows will permanently remove older and larger files without warning you.

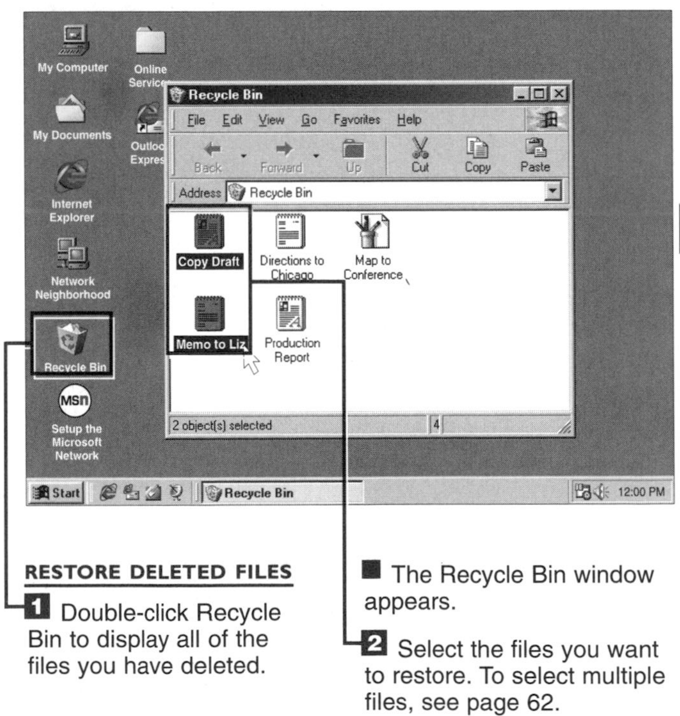

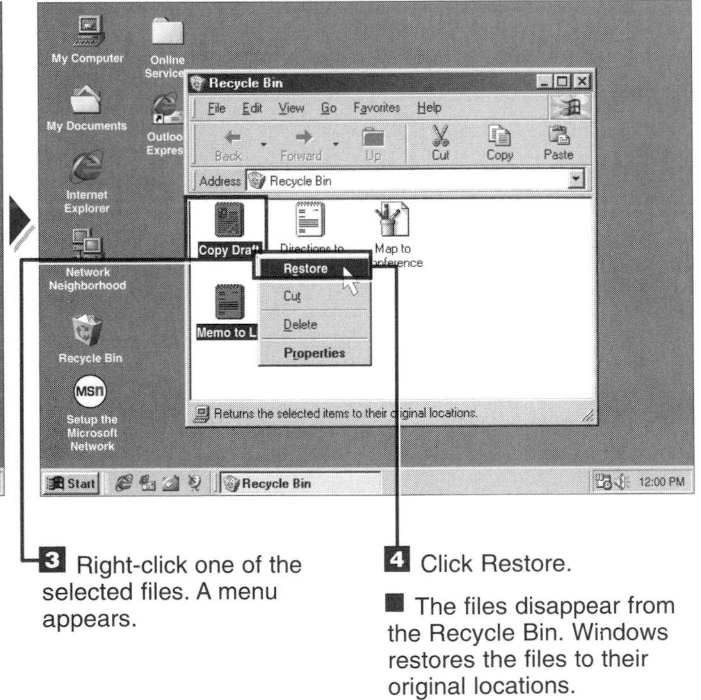

RESTORE DELETED FILES

1 Double-click Recycle Bin to display all of the files you have deleted.

■ The Recycle Bin window appears.

2 Select the files you want to restore. To select multiple files, see page 62.

3 Right-click one of the selected files. A menu appears.

4 Click Restore.

■ The files disappear from the Recycle Bin. Windows restores the files to their original locations.

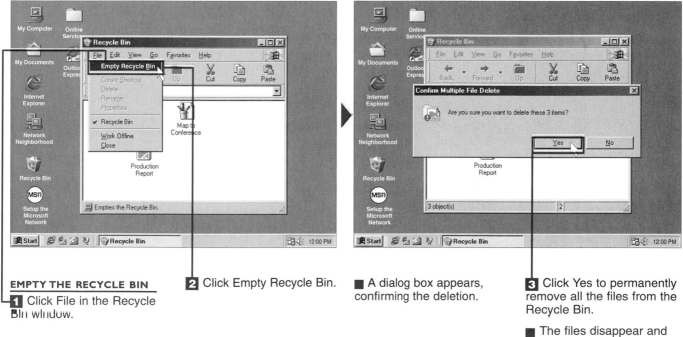

TIPS

How can I see the original location of the files in the Recycle Bin?

You can display information about Recycle Bin files by choosing the View menu in the Recycle Bin window and then selecting Details. The Original Location column shows where the deleted files came from.

How do I restore a deleted folder?

You can restore a deleted folder the same way you restore a deleted file.

How do I restore a file to a different folder?

Use My Computer or Windows Explorer to open the folder where you want to place the file. Then drag the file from the Recycle Bin to the open folder.

I deleted a file that does not appear in the Recycle Bin. What happened to my file?

If you delete a large file or many files at once, the files may bypass the Recycle Bin and be permanently deleted. Files deleted at the DOS prompt are also not placed in the Recycle Bin.

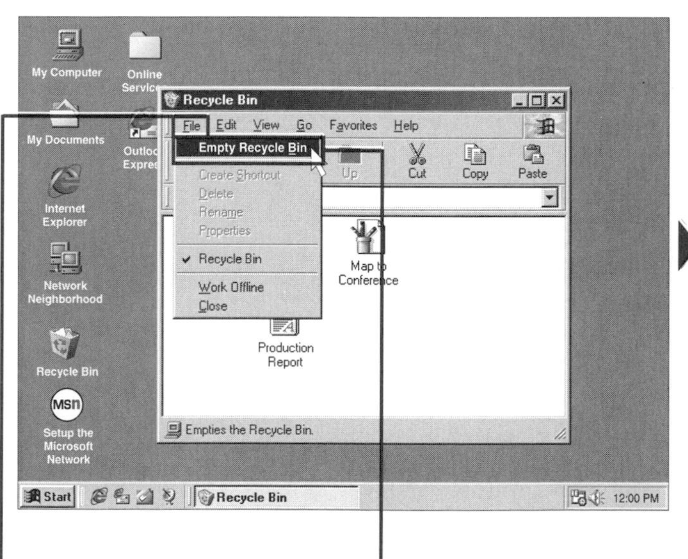

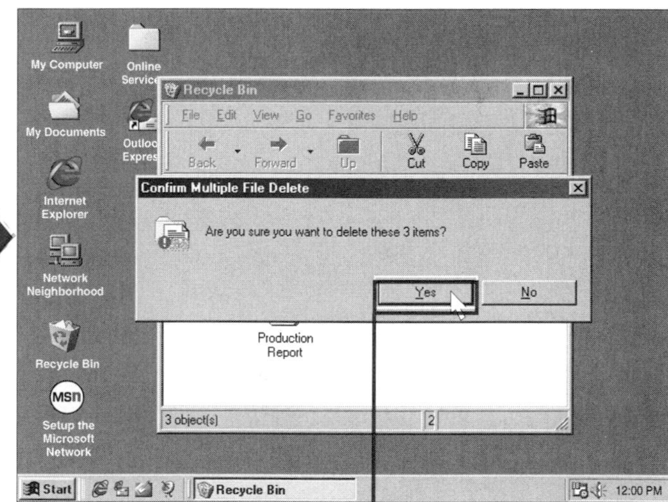

EMPTY THE RECYCLE BIN

1 Click File in the Recycle Bin window.

2 Click Empty Recycle Bin.

■ A dialog box appears, confirming the deletion.

3 Click Yes to permanently remove all the files from the Recycle Bin.

■ The files disappear and are permanently removed from your computer.

CHANGE RECYCLE BIN PROPERTIES

The Recycle Bin protects your files from accidents by temporarily saving the files you delete. Files cannot be saved in the Recycle Bin forever. You can change the properties of the Recycle Bin to give you the kind of protection you want.

The Recycle Bin normally uses up to 10% of your hard drive's space to store deleted files. On a 1 GB drive this means as much as 100 MB may be used by the Recycle Bin. By checking the status of files in the Recycle Bin for a week or two, you can estimate how much space is needed to safeguard a day's, week's or month's worth of work. You can then adjust the settings accordingly.

If you have more than one drive on your computer, each drive can have its own Recycle Bin settings. If you use one drive to store your applications and the other for documents, you may want to use a larger setting for the document drive and a smaller setting for the application drive.

Windows normally displays a confirmation dialog box when you delete a file. To delete files more quickly, you can change the Recycle Bin properties so the dialog box will no longer appear.

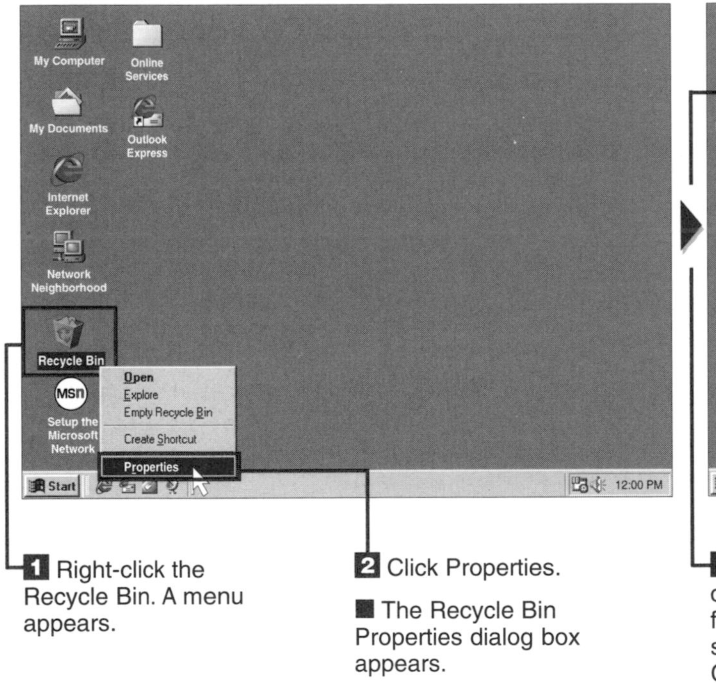

1 Right-click the Recycle Bin. A menu appears.

2 Click Properties.

■ The Recycle Bin Properties dialog box appears.

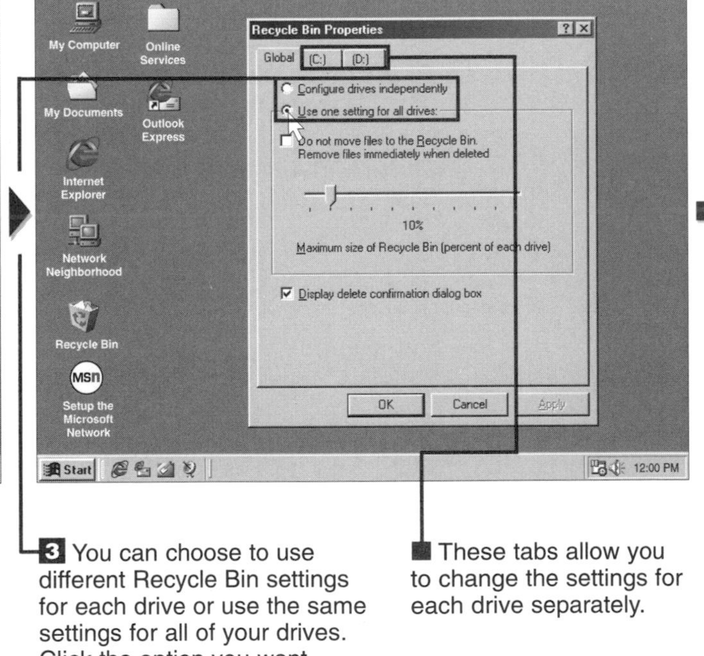

3 You can choose to use different Recycle Bin settings for each drive or use the same settings for all of your drives. Click the option you want to use (○ changes to ⊙).

■ These tabs allow you to change the settings for each drive separately.

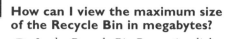

TIPS

How can I view the maximum size of the Recycle Bin in megabytes?

In the Recycle Bin Properties dialog box, click the Configure drives independently option. Then select the tab for the drive whose Recycle Bin properties you want to view. Windows displays the maximum space reserved on the drive for the Recycle Bin in megabytes (MB).

How do I adjust the size of the Recycle Bin for drives that do not have a tab, like my removable hard drive?

The Recycle Bin does not store files you delete from these types of drives.

How can I bypass the Recycle Bin and delete a sensitive or private document immediately without changing the settings for all files?

To delete a selected file or group of files permanently, hold down the Shift key while you press the Delete key. A dialog box will confirm your deletion. If the file is already in the Recycle Bin, just delete the file as you would delete any file.

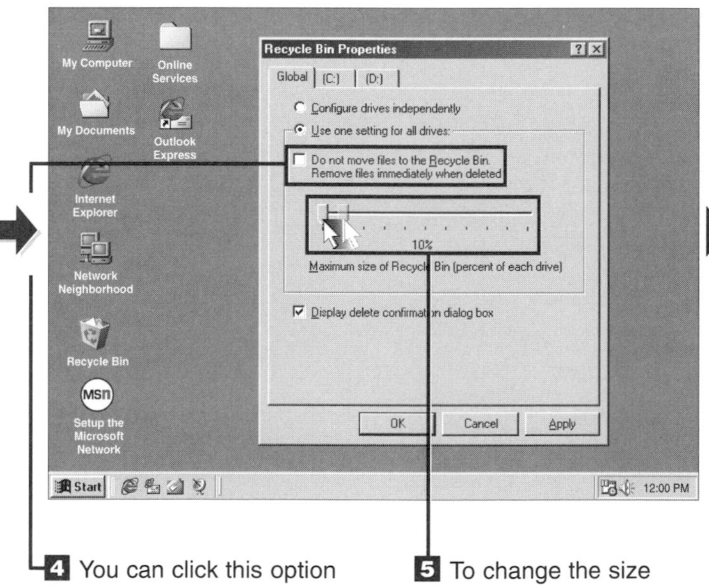

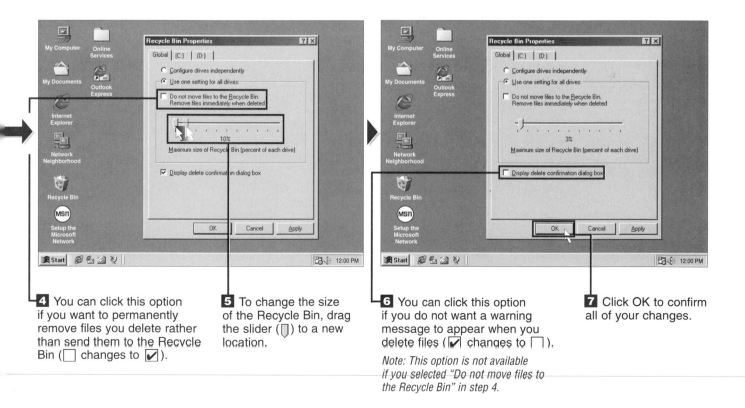

4 You can click this option if you want to permanently remove files you delete rather than send them to the Recycle Bin (☐ changes to ☑).

5 To change the size of the Recycle Bin, drag the slider (▯) to a new location.

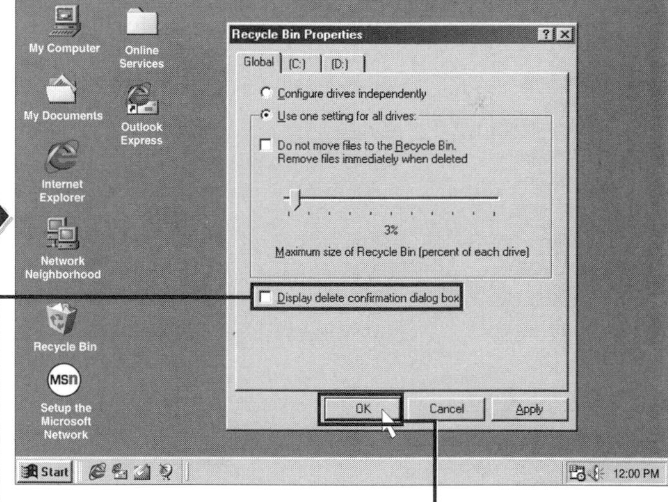

6 You can click this option if you do not want a warning message to appear when you delete files (☑ changes to ☐).

Note: This option is not available if you selected "Do not move files to the Recycle Bin" in step 4.

7 Click OK to confirm all of your changes.

FIND FILES

If you cannot remember the name or location of a file you want to work with, you can have Windows search for the file.

You can have Windows search for a file with a specific name. For example, a search for a file named "report" will find every file or folder that contains the word "report" in its name. This is useful if you know all or part of the name of the file.

If you know a word or phrase that the file contains, you can have Windows search for this information. Searching by file content slows down the search.

You can specify which area of your computer you want Windows to search for a file. If you select My Computer, Windows will search all of the drives and folders on your computer. This is useful if you cannot remember where the file is located.

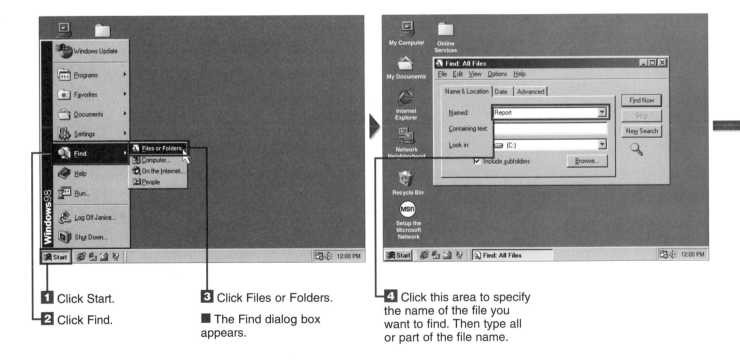

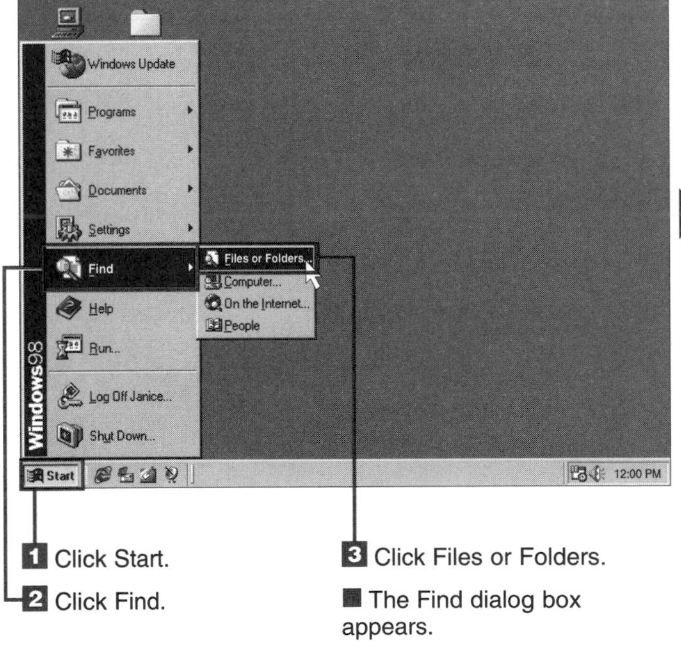

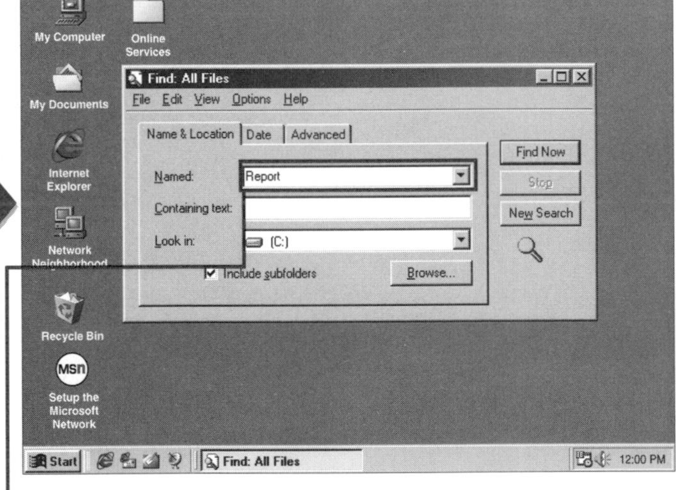

1 Click Start.

2 Click Find.

3 Click Files or Folders.

■ The Find dialog box appears.

4 Click this area to specify the name of the file you want to find. Then type all or part of the file name.

TIPS

Can I use wildcards to find files with specific characters in their names?

You can use the asterisk (*) or a question mark (?) to find files. The asterisk (*) represents many characters. The question mark (?) represents a single character. For example, type **d*.xls** to find all Microsoft Excel files with names beginning with the letter d.

Can I enter two words in the Named field?

If you enter two words in the Named field, Windows will locate every file that has at least one of the words in its name.

How can I have Windows only find files where the word "Report" is capitalized in the document?

From the Options menu, select Case Sensitive. Windows will only find documents that contain the word exactly as you typed it.

Can I list all the files on my drive?

To see a list of all the files on a drive, select the drive you want in the area beside Look in. Then click Find Now without specifying any other information in the Find dialog box.

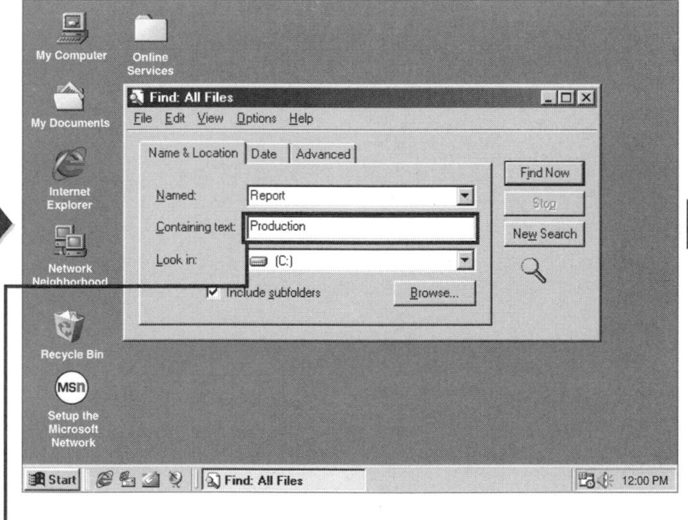

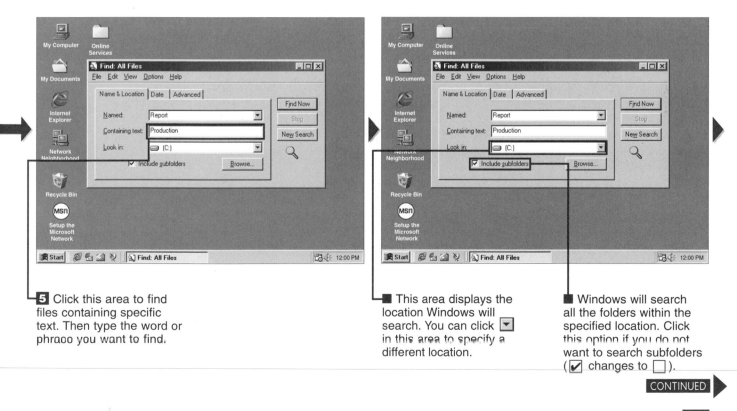

5 Click this area to find files containing specific text. Then type the word or phrase you want to find.

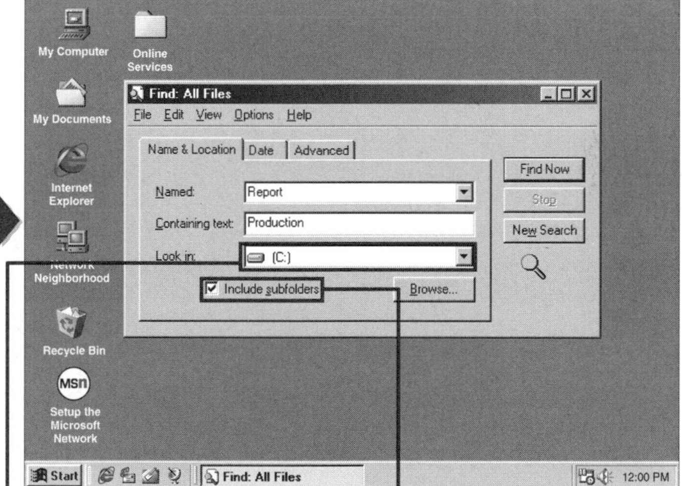

■ This area displays the location Windows will search. You can click ▼ in this area to specify a different location.

■ Windows will search all the folders within the specified location. Click this option if you do not want to search subfolders (☑ changes to ☐).

CONTINUED

FIND FILES CONTINUED

Windows allows you to narrow your search to find the file you want.

You can search for files based on the date the file was last changed. This is useful if you know the file was worked on during a specific time period.

You can also search for a specific type of file. This is useful if you want to locate a file such as an application or screen saver.

Windows can search for a file based on size. This is helpful if you want to find large files that are taking up a lot of drive space. You can search for files that are larger or smaller than the size you specify.

Windows displays all the matching files and information about each file, such as its name, location, size and type. You can open and work with any file Windows finds just as you would open and work with a file in a My Computer or Windows Explorer window.

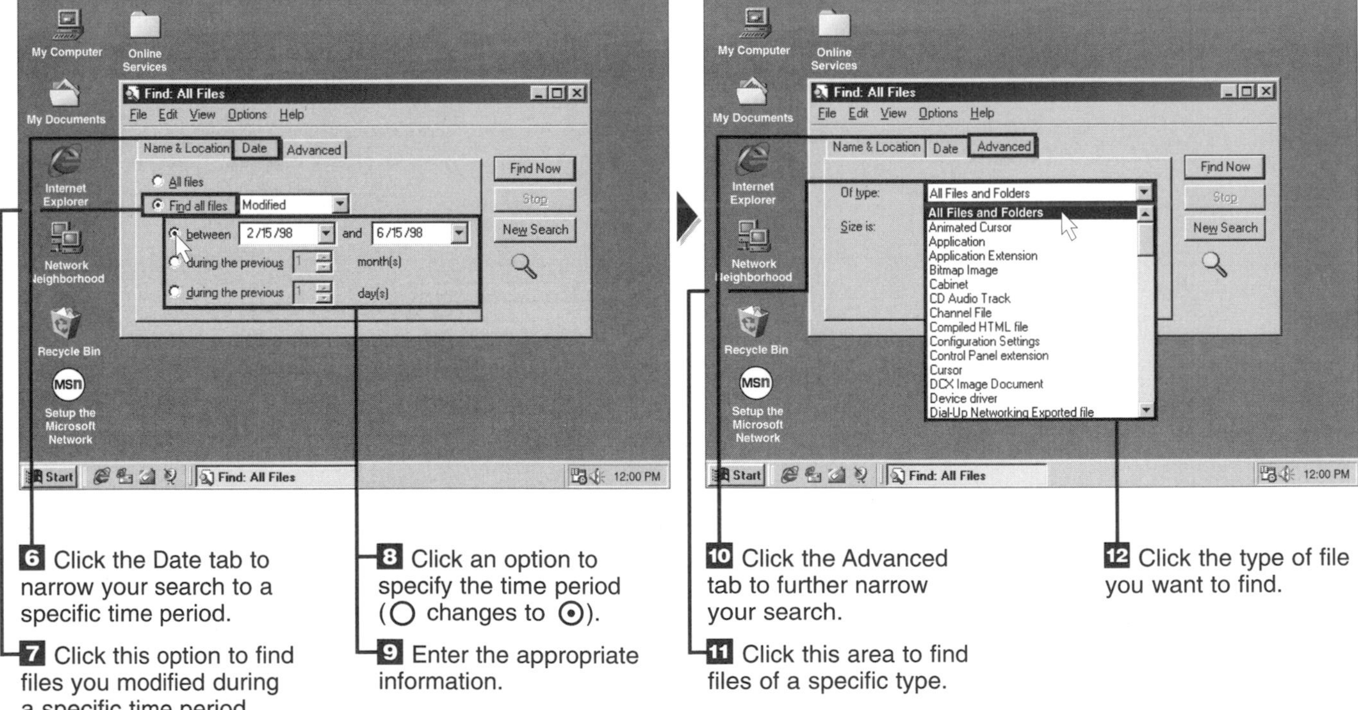

6 Click the Date tab to narrow your search to a specific time period.

7 Click this option to find files you modified during a specific time period (○ changes to ⊙).

8 Click an option to specify the time period (○ changes to ⊙).

9 Enter the appropriate information.

10 Click the Advanced tab to further narrow your search.

11 Click this area to find files of a specific type.

12 Click the type of file you want to find.

TIPS

Can I search for files I created or last accessed on a specific date?

Yes. To search for files based on the date they were created or last accessed, perform steps 1 to 7 starting on page 78. Click the area beside Find all files and on the drop-down list that appears, click the action you want to base the search on. Then continue specifying the information for the search.

Can I stop Find once it has found the file I am looking for?

You can click the Stop button at any time to end the search.

Can I save a search so I can use the same settings again?

From the File menu, select Save Search. The search appears as an icon on your desktop. Double-click the icon to display the Find dialog box with your saved search settings. You can also save the results of the search along with the settings. Before starting the search, choose the Options menu and select Save Results.

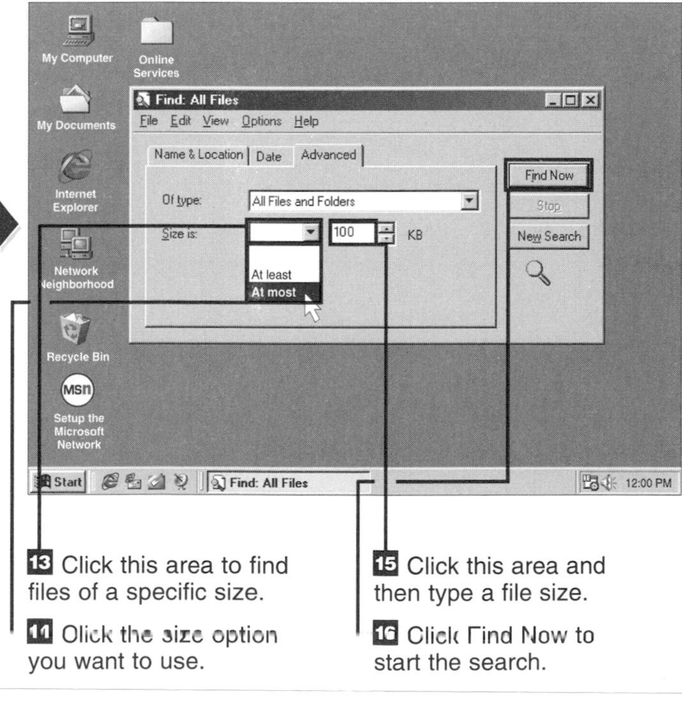

13 Click this area to find files of a specific size.

14 Click the size option you want to use.

15 Click this area and then type a file size.

16 Click Find Now to start the search.

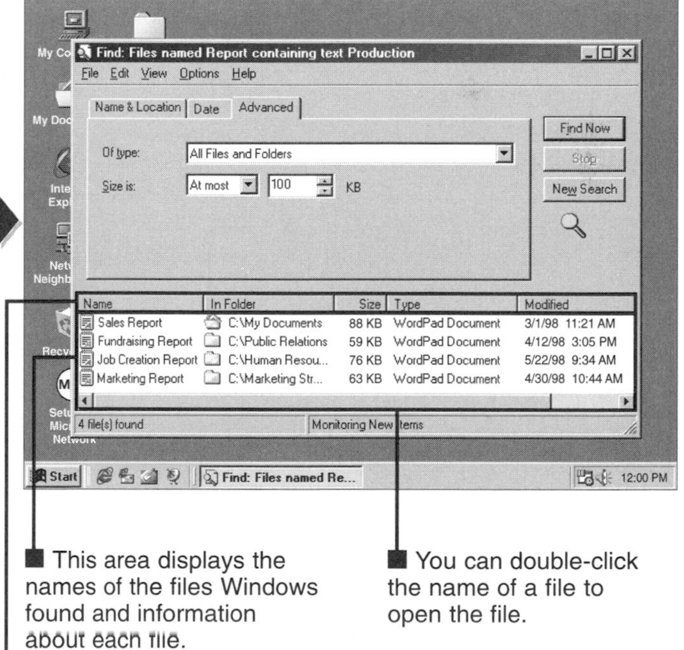

■ This area displays the names of the files Windows found and information about each file.

■ If Windows found several files, you can click a heading to sort the files.

■ You can double-click the name of a file to open the file.

PREVIEW A FILE

You can use the Quick View feature to view the contents of a file without starting the program that created the file. Quick View helps you quickly decide whether the file you selected is the one you want to work with.

You cannot use Quick View to edit a file. Once you have found the file you are looking for, you can use Quick View to start the application and open the file so you can make changes.

When you are viewing a text document, you can change the font size in Quick View to make the text easier to read. Changing the font size of your document in Quick View does not change the font size of the original file.

You can select the Page View mode to see a full page of your image or document in the Quick View window. The Page View mode simulates what the document will look like. For an accurate view of the document, you must open the document.

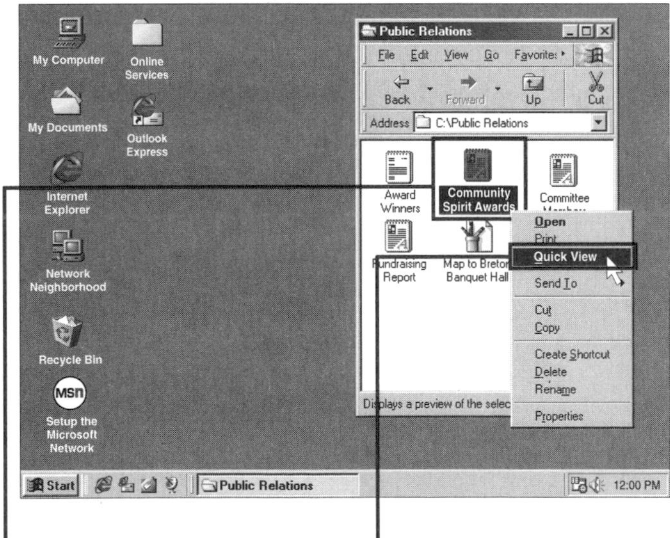

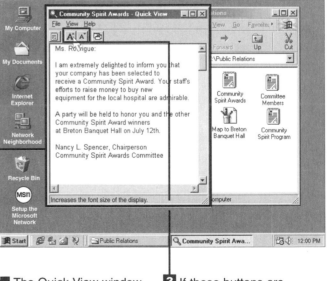

1 Right-click the file you want to preview. A menu appears.

2 Click Quick View.

■ The Quick View window opens, displaying the contents of the file. You cannot make changes to the file.

3 If these buttons are available, you can change the size of the displayed font to more easily view the information. Click (A↑) to increase the font or (A↓) to decrease the font.

TIPS 

Why is Quick View not an option on my right-click menu?

If Quick View is not available, either you cannot preview the type of file you selected or you must install Quick View from the Accessories component. To add Windows components, see page 610.

How can I preview more types of files?

You can purchase a utility called Quick View Plus, created by the same developers, to view more types of files. Quick View Plus can be found on the Internet at www.inso.com

My image is upside-down. How can I fix it?

If your images are upside-down when you preview them, choose the View menu and select Rotate to turn the images right-side up. This command is not available when Page View is selected.

How can I view my documents in a single window?

If you are previewing many files, each file will appear in a different Quick View window. To preview files in a single Quick View window and reduce the clutter on your screen, click [button]. Each file you preview will replace the current file in the Quick View window.

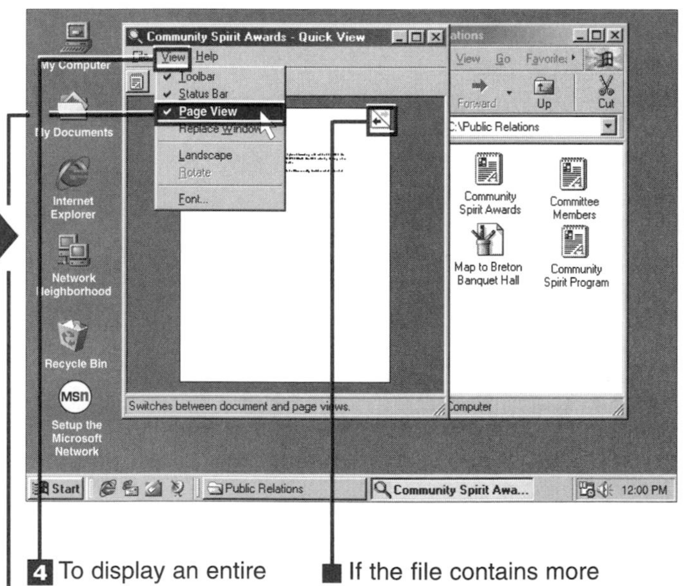

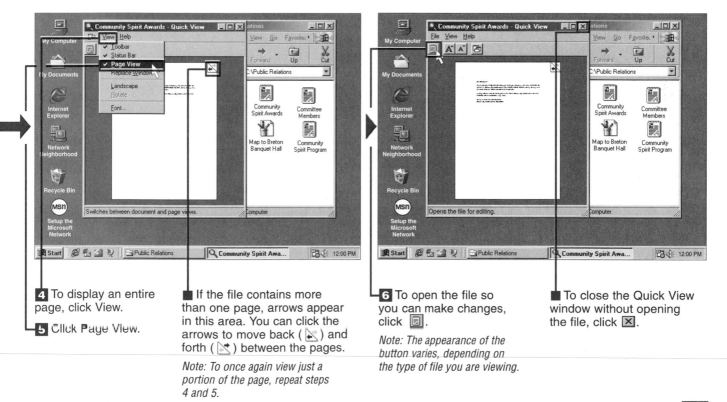

4 To display an entire page, click View.

5 Click Page View.

■ If the file contains more than one page, arrows appear in this area. You can click the arrows to move back ([back]) and forth ([forth]) between the pages.

Note: To once again view just a portion of the page, repeat steps 4 and 5.

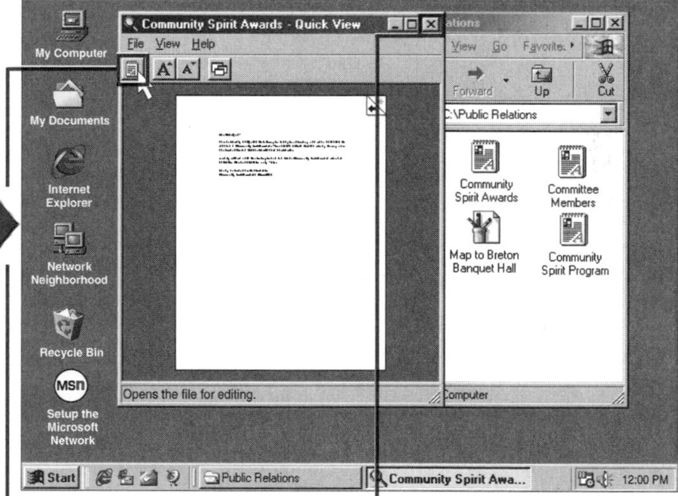

6 To open the file so you can make changes, click [button].

Note: The appearance of the button varies, depending on the type of file you are viewing.

■ To close the Quick View window without opening the file, click [X].

UNDO YOUR LAST ACTION

When you change your mind or make a mistake, Windows can help you undo your last action.

You can undo commands, such as delete and rename, from your desktop, a My Computer window or Windows Explorer. You can also undo dragging and dropping you performed to move or copy an item. The Undo command indicates which action is available to undo. You may be able to undo up to the last 10 actions.

You cannot undo all actions. For example, you cannot undo a delete command after you empty the Recycle Bin. You also cannot undo an undo or a save command. If you move a document to a folder that already has a document with the same name, Windows asks if you want to replace the original document. If you replace the document, you will not be able to undo the command to restore the original document.

Many programs also offer the Undo command.

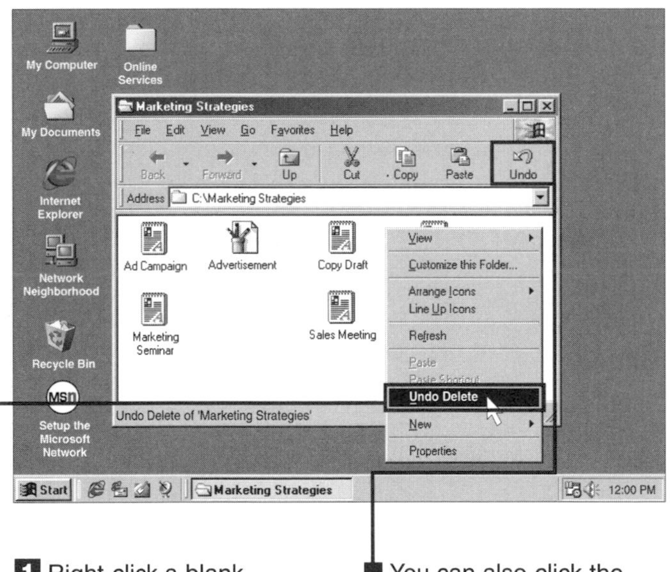

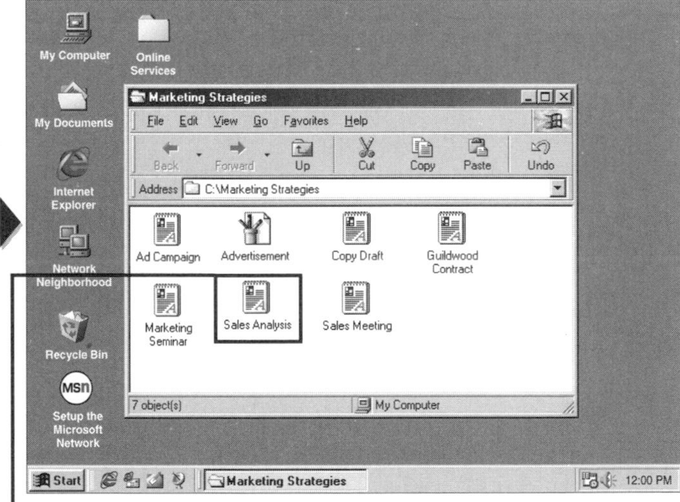

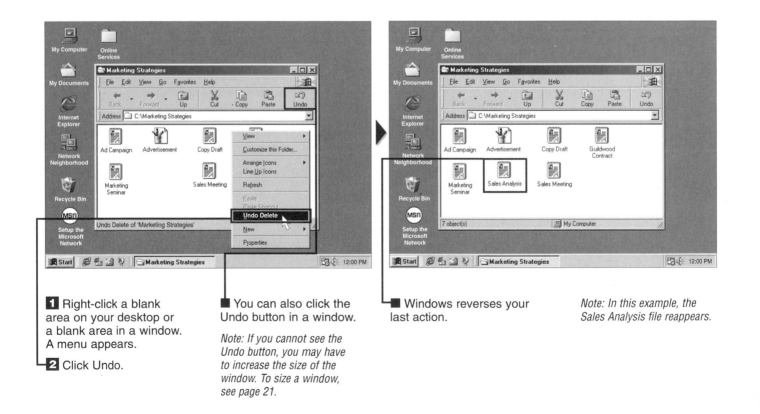

1 Right-click a blank area on your desktop or a blank area in a window. A menu appears.

2 Click Undo.

■ You can also click the Undo button in a window.

Note: If you cannot see the Undo button, you may have to increase the size of the window. To size a window, see page 21.

■ Windows reverses your last action.

Note: In this example, the Sales Analysis file reappears.

CLOSE MISBEHAVING PROGRAMS

You can close a program that is no longer working properly without closing Windows. You can close a program even when you do not have access to the program's menus or commands.

You can stop any active task on your computer. An active task can be a program, a utility or the software that controls your mouse.

When a program fails to check for mouse or keyboard commands, Windows identifies the program as not responding. Windows may detect that a program is not responding before you do and display a warning message. You may also discover, while using a program, that it is not behaving as it should.

When you close a program that is not responding, you lose all the unsaved information in the program. Closing a misbehaving program should not affect your other open programs or Windows.

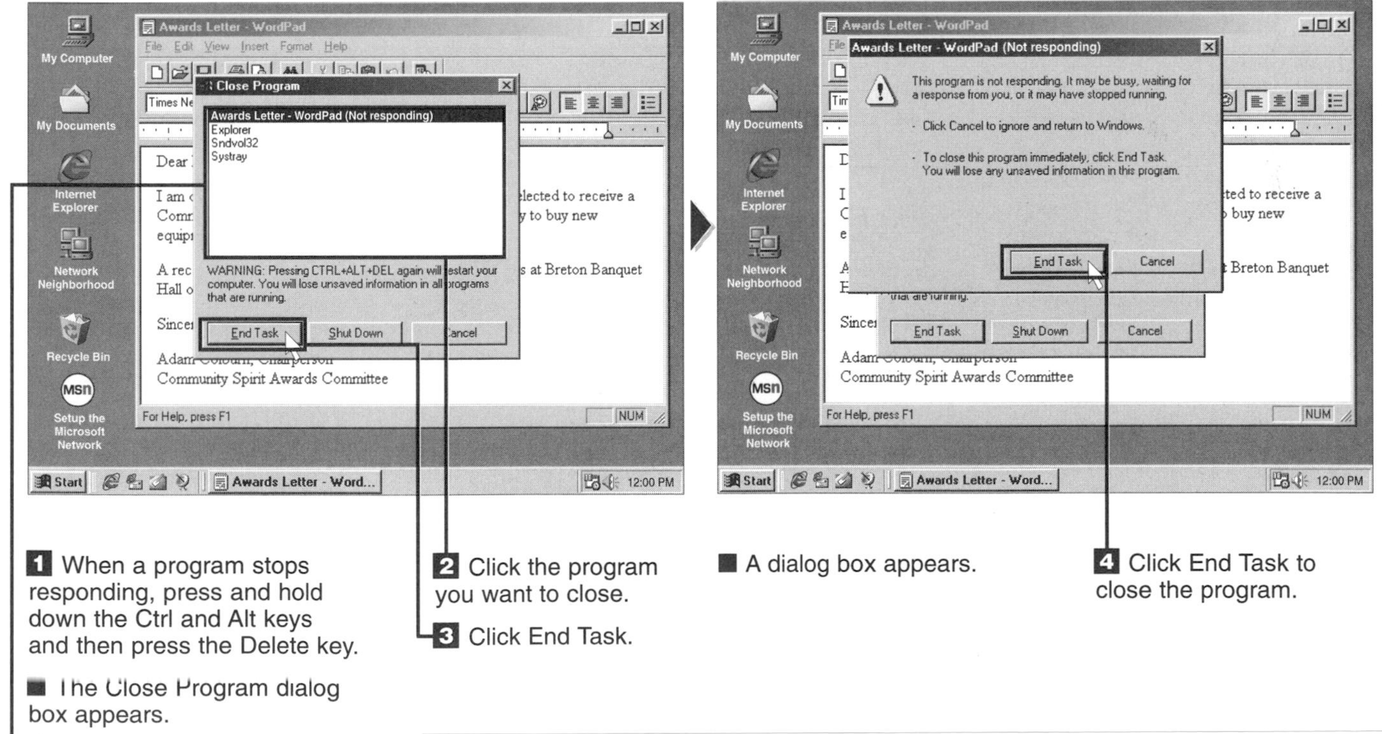

1 When a program stops responding, press and hold down the Ctrl and Alt keys and then press the Delete key.

■ The Close Program dialog box appears.

■ This area lists the programs that are currently running.

2 Click the program you want to close.

3 Click End Task.

■ A dialog box appears.

4 Click End Task to close the program.

CREATE A NEW FOLDER

You can create a new folder to better organize the information stored on your computer. Creating a new folder is like placing a new folder in a filing cabinet.

When you begin using your computer, you should create new folders to store your work. Storing documents in personalized folders will help you quickly locate your documents.

You can create folders inside other folders to help further organize information. For example, you can create a folder named "letters." This folder can store other folders named "clients," "colleagues" and "personal." You can also create folders on your desktop to organize your shortcuts.

You can create as many folders as you need to organize your documents by date, project or type. Use a system that makes sense to you and will help you find your documents.

A folder name can use up to 255 characters and can include spaces. Folder names cannot contain the \ / : * ? " < > or | characters.

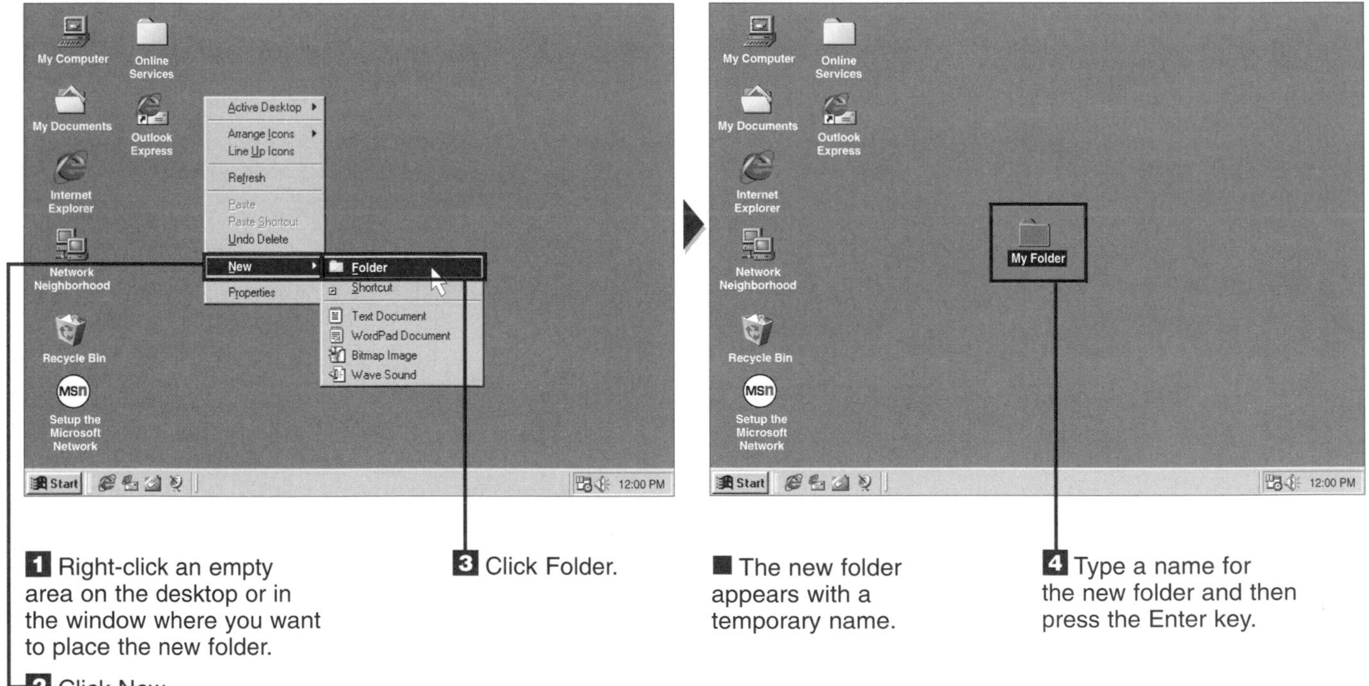

1 Right-click an empty area on the desktop or in the window where you want to place the new folder.

2 Click New.

3 Click Folder.

■ The new folder appears with a temporary name.

4 Type a name for the new folder and then press the Enter key.

CREATE A NEW FILE

You can create, name and store a new file in the appropriate folder without having to start any programs. This allows you to focus on your work, rather than the programs you need to accomplish your tasks.

Before writing a letter or creating a new spreadsheet, you can first determine where you want to store the new file. By selecting the location of the file you can organize your work and later find the file more easily.

Once you decide on the location of a new file, you can give the file a name. A file name can use up to 255 characters and can include spaces. File names cannot contain the \ / : * ?"< > or | characters.

The types of new files you can create depend on the programs installed on your computer. Programs not designed for Windows 95 or Windows 98 may require you to start the program before you can create a new file.

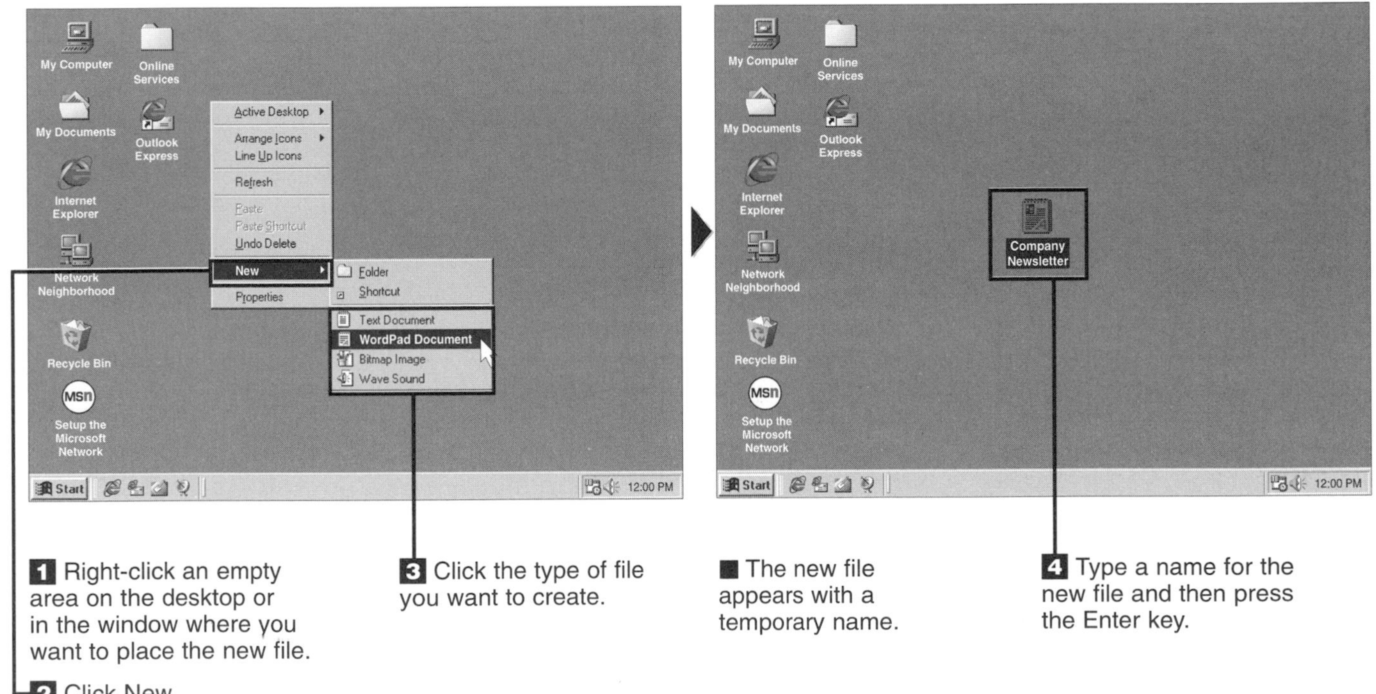

1 Right-click an empty area on the desktop or in the window where you want to place the new file.

2 Click New.

3 Click the type of file you want to create.

■ The new file appears with a temporary name.

4 Type a name for the new file and then press the Enter key.

DISPLAY AND CHANGE FILE PROPERTIES

You can find information about a file or folder by reviewing its properties. In addition to the file's name in both Windows 98 and MS-DOS format, you can find information about the file's type, location and size. You can also find the date the file was created, last changed and last opened.

A file has attributes which you can verify or change. The Read-only attribute prevents you from saving changes to the file. The Archive attribute is used to determine if the file has changed since the last backup. Windows uses the Hidden and System attributes to identify, hide and protect files it needs to operate.

When the Properties dialog box displays additional tabs, you can find even more information about a file. For example, when you view the properties for a sound file, you can use the additional tabs to view the copyright information or play the sound.

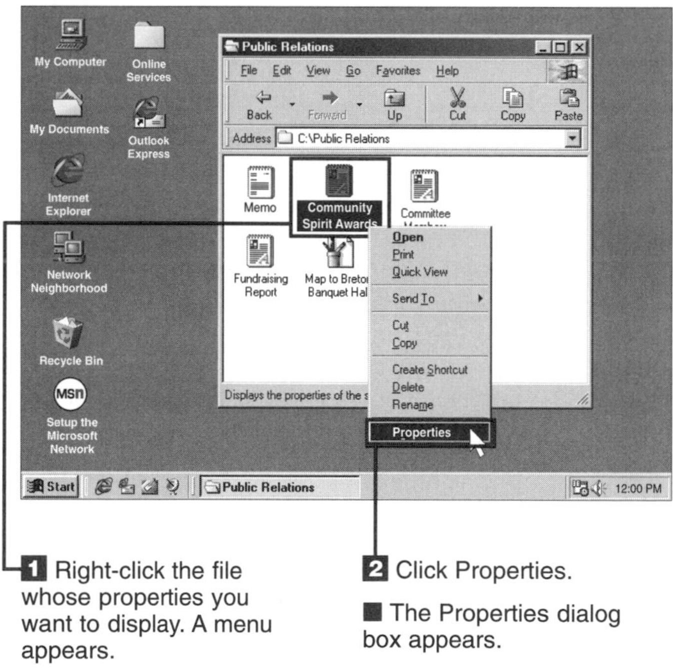

1 Right-click the file whose properties you want to display. A menu appears.

2 Click Properties.

■ The Properties dialog box appears.

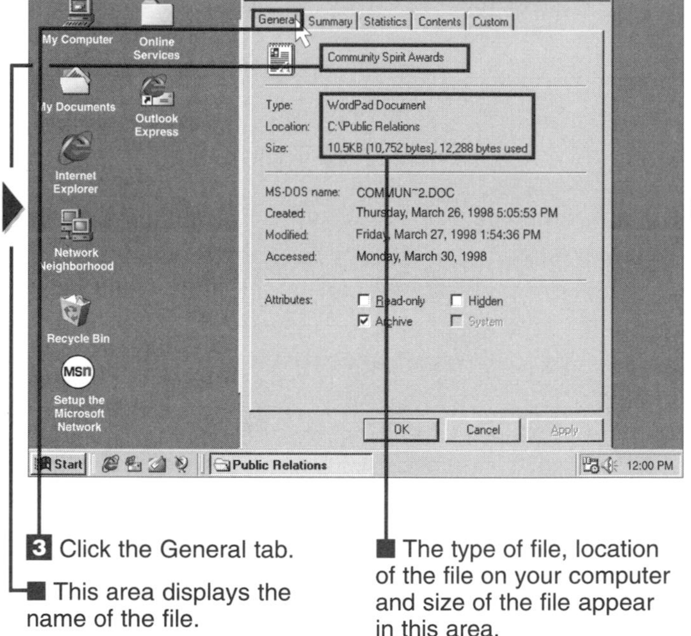

3 Click the General tab.

■ This area displays the name of the file.

■ The type of file, location of the file on your computer and size of the file appear in this area.

I turned the Hidden attribute on. Why is the file still visible?

There is another setting which determines whether hidden files are displayed or not. To change this setting, see page 56.

Is there another way I can display the properties of a file or folder?

You can click the file or folder and then click the Properties button in the window to display the properties. If you cannot see the Properties button, you may have to increase the size of the window. To size a window, see page 21.

What does the Read-only attribute do?

The Read-only attribute prevents a file from being changed. You can open a Read-only file, but if you change it you must save the file with a new name. This is useful for files such as letterhead or blank forms that you do not want altered.

Why does the Properties dialog box show two different numbers for the file size?

The Properties dialog box shows the size of the file in both kilobytes (KB) and bytes, followed by the amount of disk space required to store the file, in bytes. 1024 bytes are equal to 1 KB.

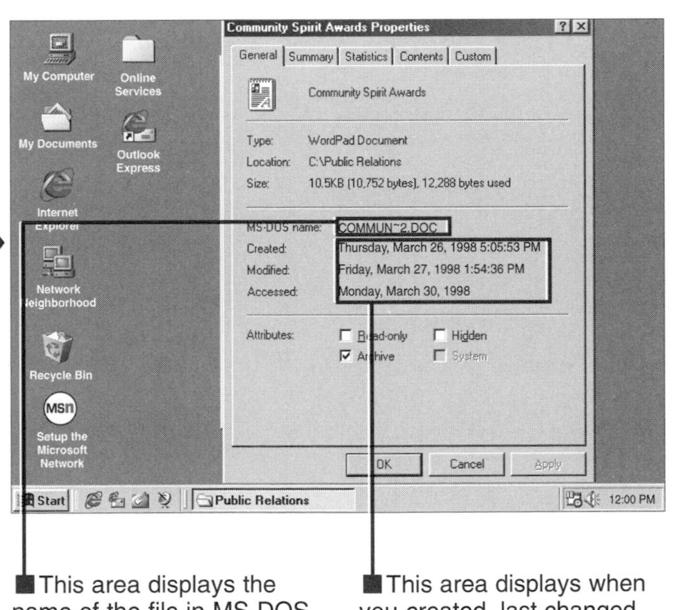

■ This area displays the name of the file in MS-DOS format. Some programs use this information for opening and closing files.

■ This area displays when you created, last changed and last opened the file.

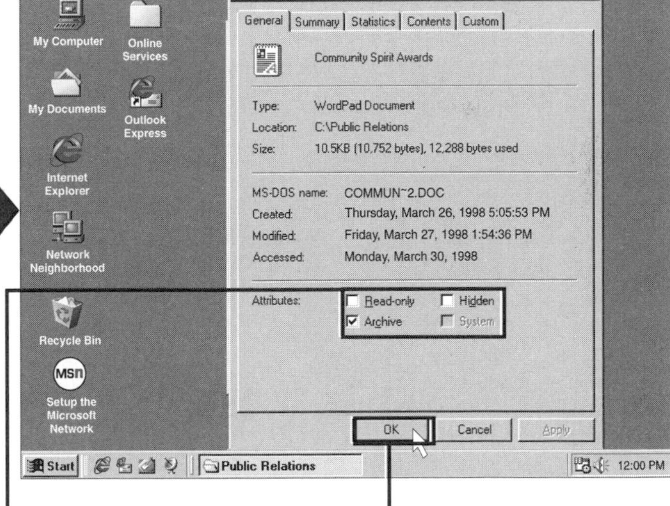

■ This area displays the attributes for the file.

4 Click an attribute to turn the attribute on (☑) or off (☐).

5 Click OK to confirm your changes.

CREATE A SHORTCUT

You can create a shortcut to provide a quick way of opening an item you use regularly.

A shortcut icon resembles the original item, but displays an arrow ( ) in the bottom left corner. A shortcut is a link to the original item.

You can place a shortcut icon on the desktop, inside a folder or on the Start menu. A shortcut icon on the desktop provides quick access to a program, document, folder or drive you use frequently.

Shortcuts make working with files easier. For example, you can use shortcuts to place all of the documents for a project in one folder, instead of moving all the documents and later returning them when the project is complete. This is particularly useful if some of the files are stored on other computers on a network.

You can create shortcuts for files, folders and other items, such as Dial-Up Networking connections, Control Panel icons and printers.

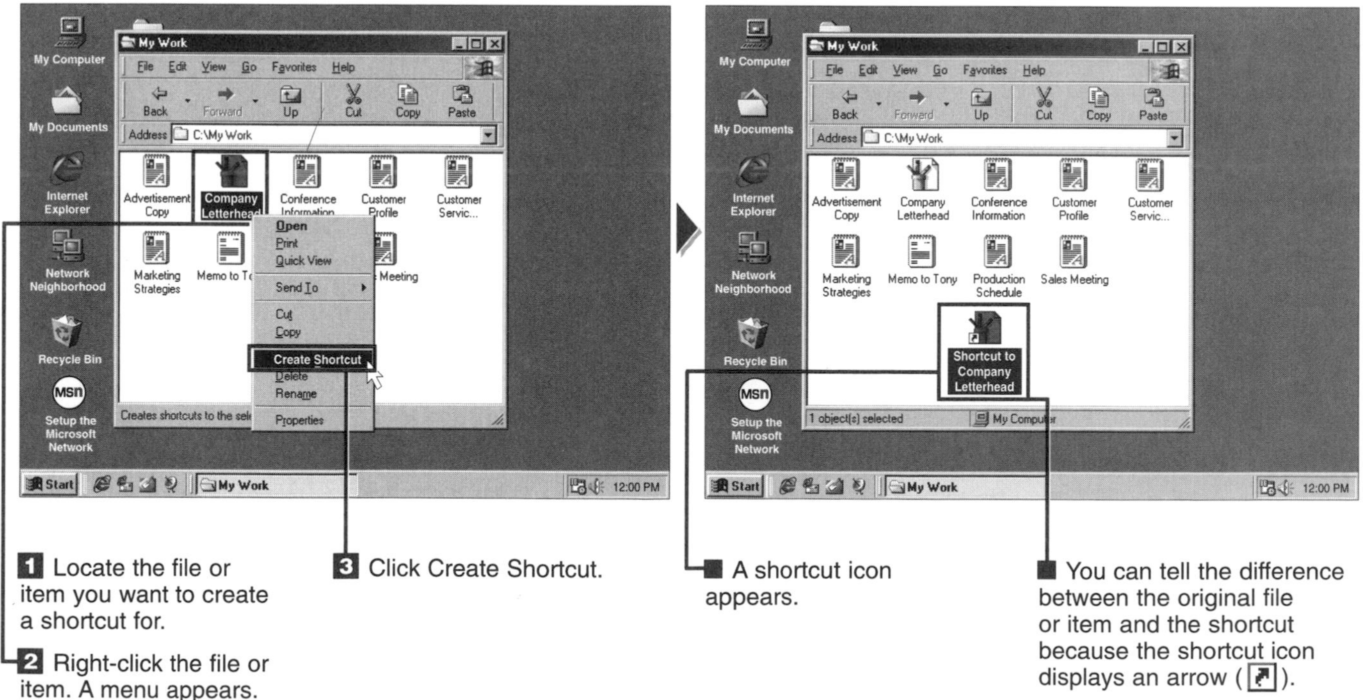

1 Locate the file or item you want to create a shortcut for.

2 Right-click the file or item. A menu appears.

3 Click Create Shortcut.

■ A shortcut icon appears.

■ You can tell the difference between the original file or item and the shortcut because the shortcut icon displays an arrow ( ).

TIPS

Can I rename a shortcut?

The name of a shortcut usually starts with "Shortcut to." To rename a shortcut, click the shortcut name and press the F2 key. Type a new name for the shortcut and then press the Enter key.

If I delete a shortcut, will the original file also be deleted?

A shortcut contains the information needed to find the file, but it does not contain the information from the file itself. If you delete a shortcut icon, the file remains on your computer.

What happens if I try to use a shortcut to a file that has been moved or deleted?

If Windows cannot find the file a shortcut refers to, a message appears, telling you there is a problem with the shortcut. Windows will try to help you find the file the shortcut icon refers to.

Is there a faster way to create a shortcut?

Using the right mouse button, drag the item to the location where you want to place a shortcut for the item. From the menu that appears, select Create Shortcut(s) Here.

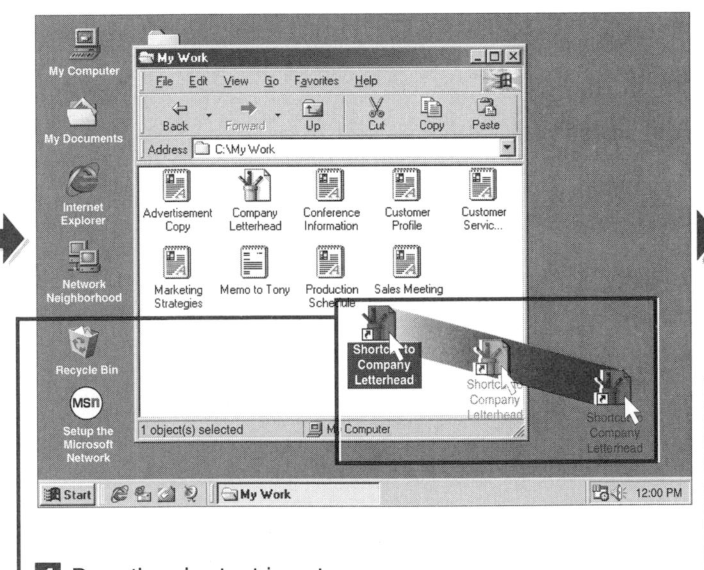

4 Drag the shortcut icon to the location where you want the shortcut to appear.

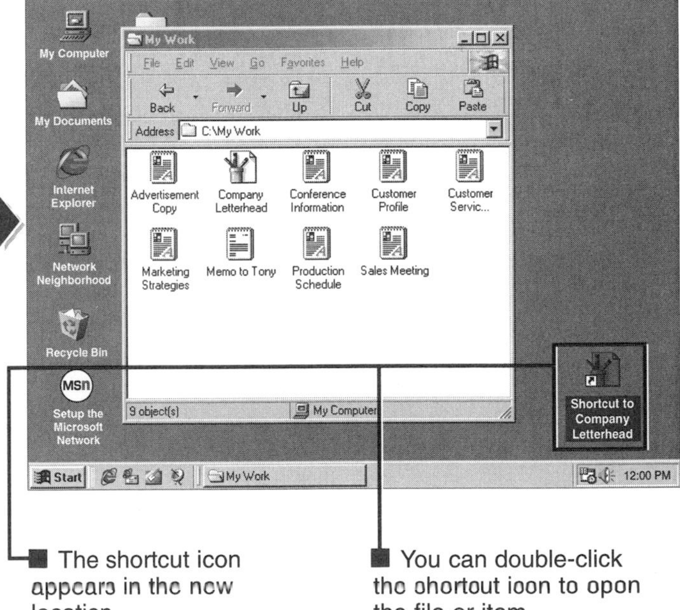

■ The shortcut icon appears in the new location.

■ You can double-click the shortcut icon to open the file or item.

CHANGE SHORTCUT PROPERTIES

You can view and change the properties of a shortcut. As with most Windows items, you can find information about a shortcut in the Properties dialog box. You can see where the shortcut is stored, its size and when it was created.

When viewing shortcut properties, you can find the location of the item that the shortcut opens. You can also use the Properties dialog box to change the way the shortcut works.

You can choose where you would like to save files related to the specific program. The location you choose to save files is the location that automatically appears when you use the Open or Save commands.

You can specify a shortcut key that allows you to press a single key or combination of keys to open the program or file the shortcut points to.

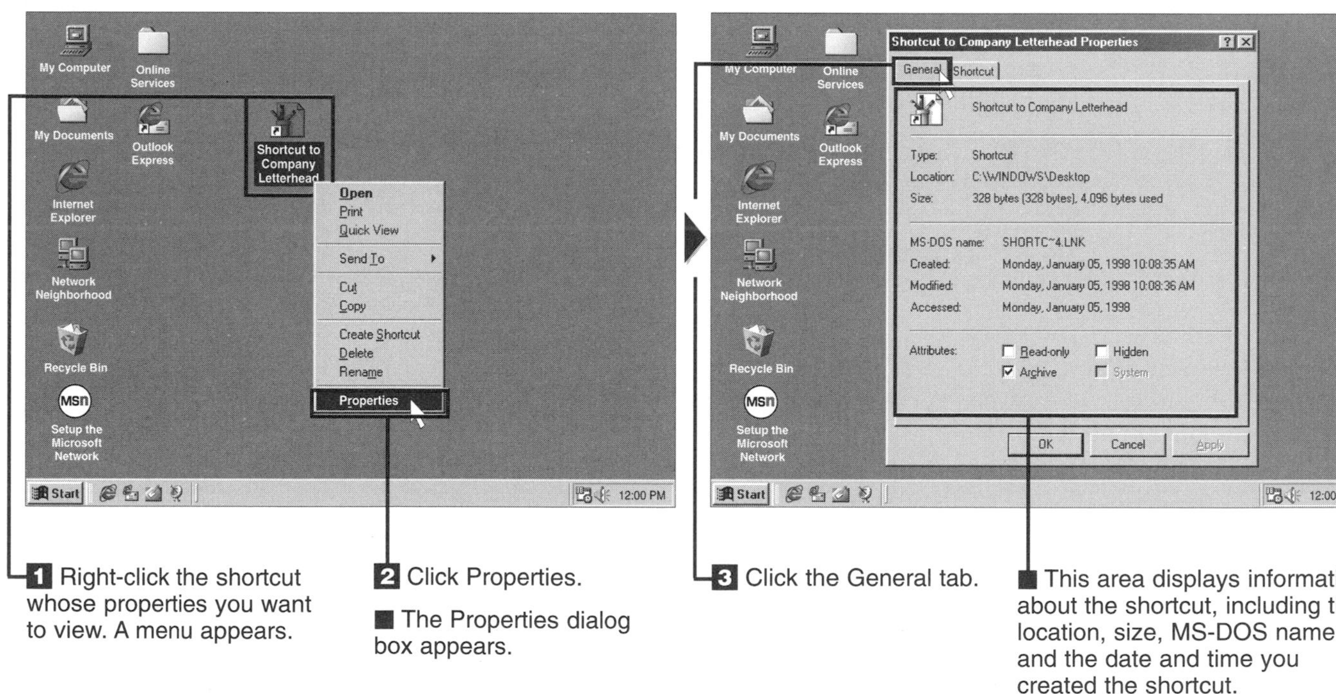

1 Right-click the shortcut whose properties you want to view. A menu appears.

2 Click Properties.

■ The Properties dialog box appears.

3 Click the General tab.

■ This area displays information about the shortcut, including the location, size, MS-DOS name and the date and time you created the shortcut.

TIPS

Can I use a shortcut key to open a program or file?

You can create a shortcut key to open any program or file that has a shortcut. A shortcut key only works if the shortcut is on the Start menu or the desktop. For example, if you create a shortcut on your desktop to a screen saver (.scr) file, you can create a shortcut key that will instantly activate the screen saver.

How can I quickly find the original file a shortcut points to?

In the Properties dialog box, select the Shortcut tab and click the Find Target button. The folder containing the original file opens and the file is selected.

Which are good shortcut keys to use?

The best shortcut keys are any combination of the Ctrl and Alt keys and a letter, such as Ctrl+Alt+Y. You can also use some of the function keys, like F9 through F12. When you select a function key for a shortcut, the shortcut cancels whatever function the key had. For example, if you use the F2 key as a shortcut key, you will no longer be able to use F2 to rename files.

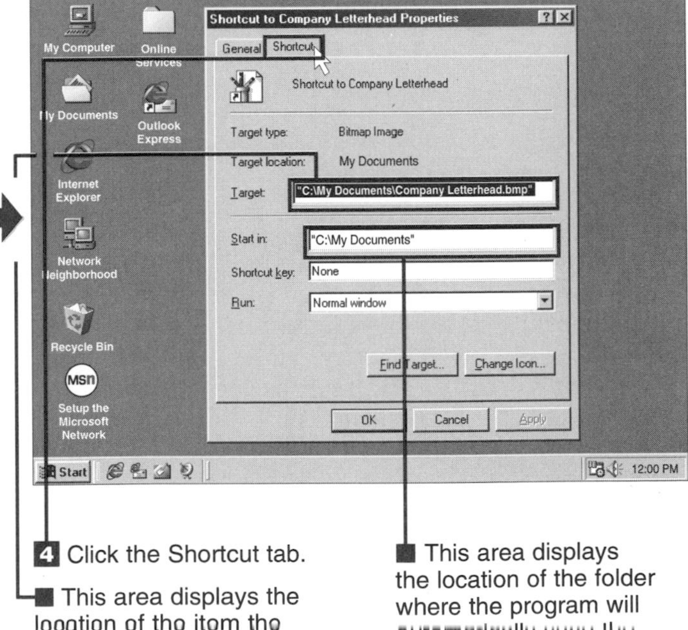

4 Click the Shortcut tab.

■ This area displays the location of the item the shortcut points to. You can change this information.

■ This area displays the location of the folder where the program will automatically save the files. You can change this information.

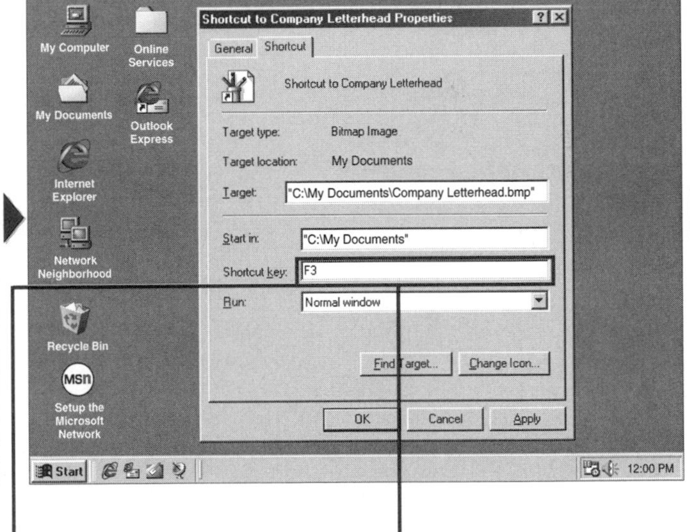

5 Click this area if you want to create a keyboard shortcut that will instantly activate the shortcut.

6 Press the keyboard key(s) you want to assign to the shortcut.

CONTINUED

CHANGE SHORTCUT PROPERTIES CONTINUED

You can change the appearance of a shortcut icon to better indicate the purpose of the program or file the shortcut opens. Windows provides a selection of icons you can choose from. When you change a shortcut icon, the appearance of the original item's icon does not change.

You can change the properties for a program's shortcut to choose how you want the program to appear when it starts. You can have the program open in a normal window, maximized to fill your screen or minimized as a button on the taskbar.

If a program requires the full screen area, you may want to display the program as a maximized window. If you have a program that opens automatically every time you start Windows, you may want to display the program minimized as a button on the taskbar so you can choose to display the window only when needed.

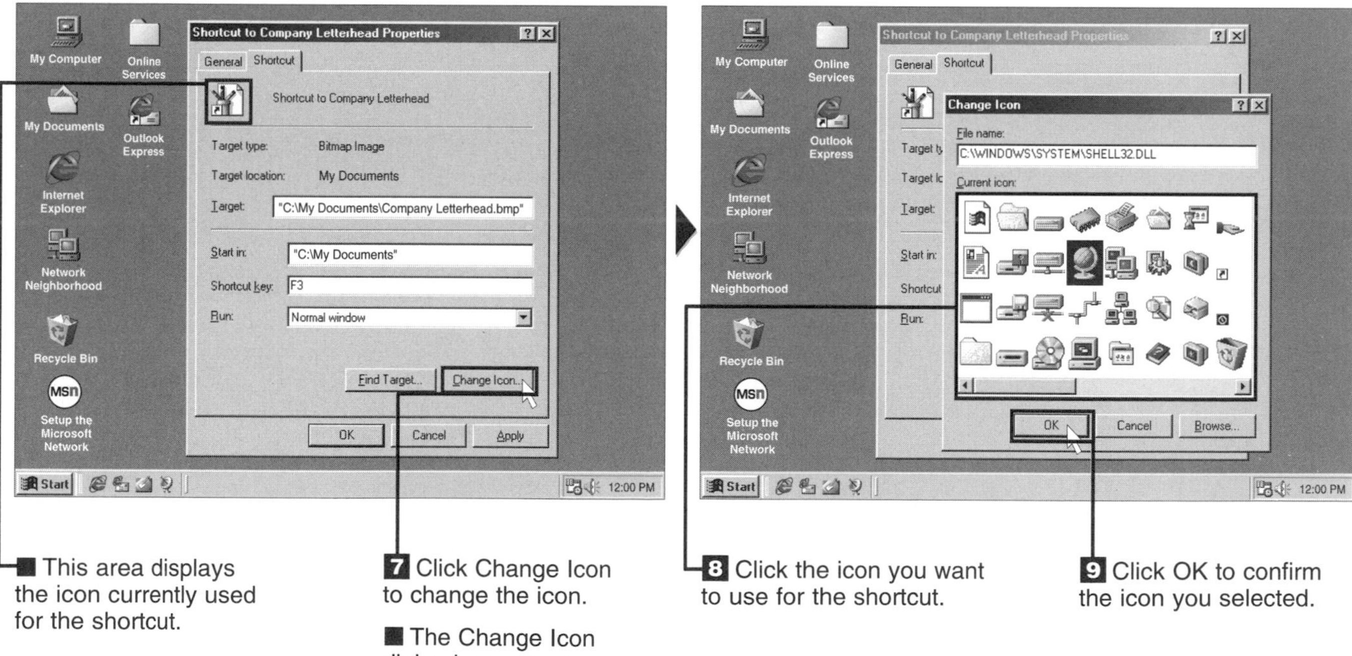

■ This area displays the icon currently used for the shortcut.

7 Click Change Icon to change the icon.

■ The Change Icon dialog box appears.

8 Click the icon you want to use for the shortcut.

9 Click OK to confirm the icon you selected.

TIPS

Can I change the default icon used for a specific type of file?

You can change the default icon used for a specific type of file by modifying the file type. See page 238.

Where can I find more icons for my shortcuts?

In the File Name area in the Change Icon dialog box, type **c:\windows\moricons.dll** and then press the Enter key to display more icons. You can also use the Browse button to find more icons on your computer. Most program files also contain more than one icon that you can use. Program files usually have the .exe, .com or .dll extensions.

I wanted a program to open maximized when I double-click the shortcut, but it is not working. What is wrong?

Not all programs are capable of opening in a different window size. This may be a result of the program's design. The program may also not be able to work with these settings if the program was created to work with a version of Windows prior to Windows 95.

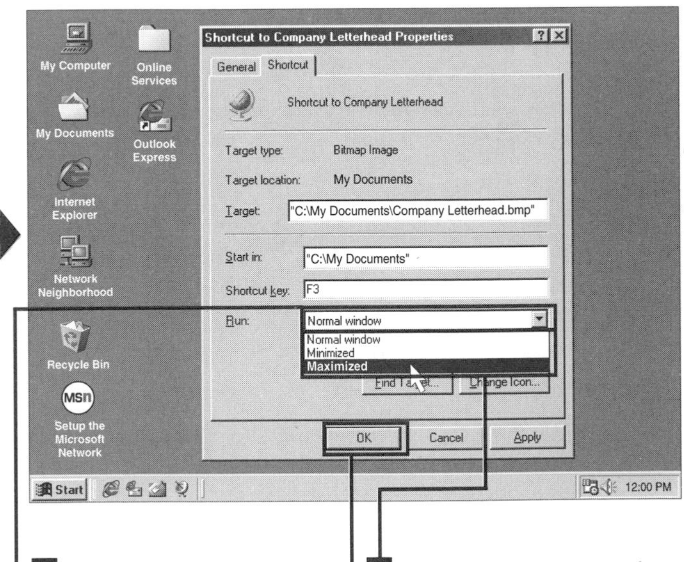

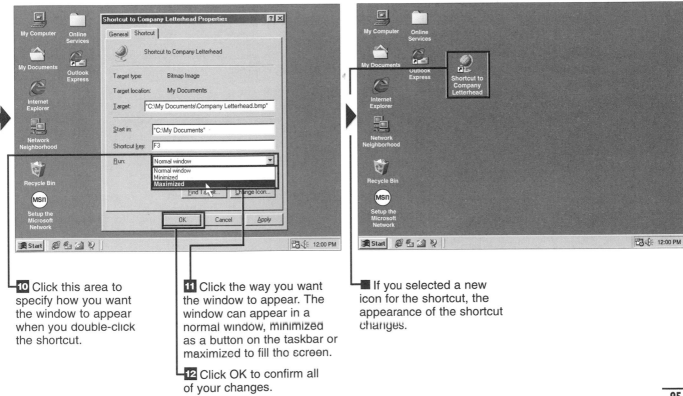

10 Click this area to specify how you want the window to appear when you double-click the shortcut.

11 Click the way you want the window to appear. The window can appear in a normal window, minimized as a button on the taskbar or maximized to fill the screen.

12 Click OK to confirm all of your changes.

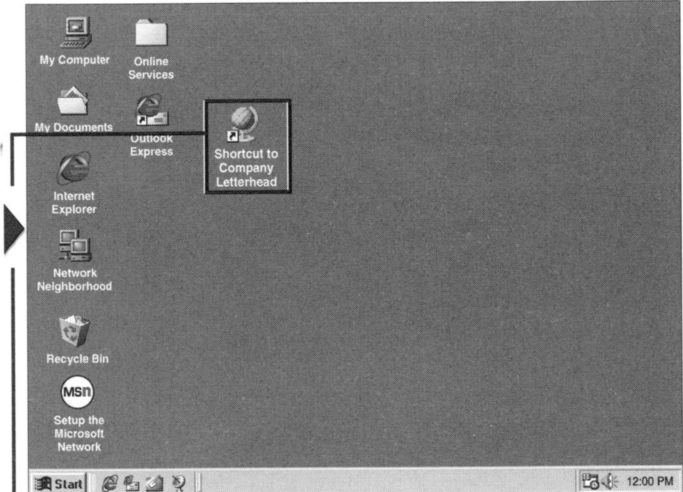

■ If you selected a new icon for the shortcut, the appearance of the shortcut changes.

PRINT FILES

You can produce a paper copy of a file even if the program that created the file is not open. This lets you quickly print a file from a My Computer or Windows Explorer window.

Windows can print most types of files. You can select many different types of files and print them all at the same time.

When you print a file, Windows starts the program associated with the file and displays the program on your screen. Windows may also display the file on your screen. Windows closes the program when the file has been sent to the printer.

You can also create a shortcut to a printer on your desktop. A shortcut lets you quickly print by dragging a file onto the shortcut icon.

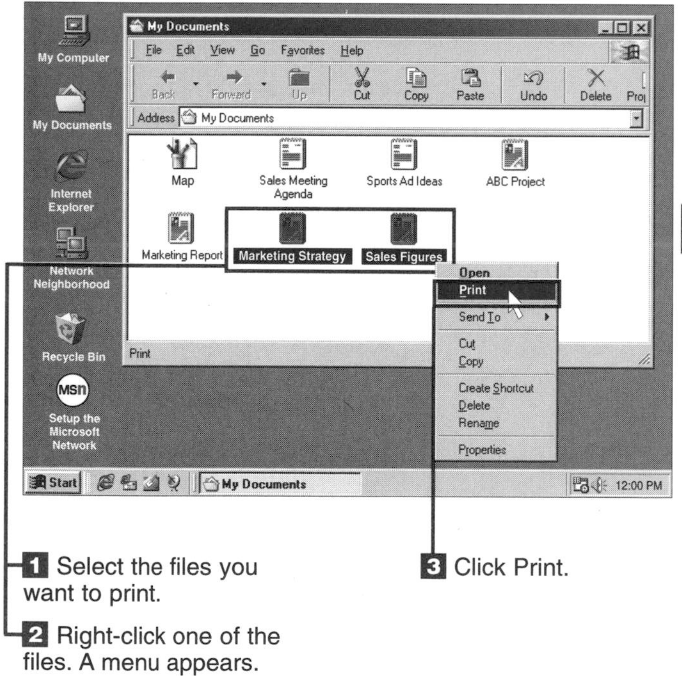

1 Select the files you want to print.

2 Right-click one of the files. A menu appears.

3 Click Print.

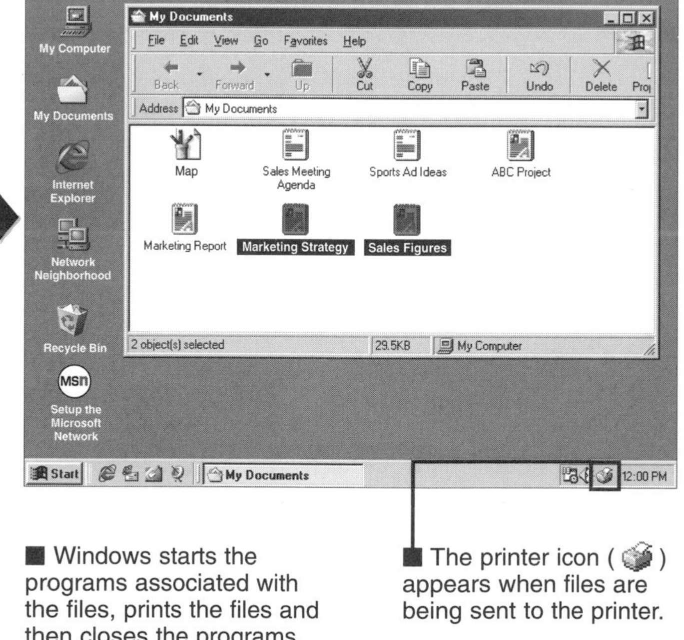

■ Windows starts the programs associated with the files, prints the files and then closes the programs.

■ The printer icon ( ) appears when files are being sent to the printer.

TIPS

Which printer will print my file?

When you use the Print command, Windows sends the file to your default printer. The default printer displays a check mark (✓). If you are using printer shortcuts, you can drag the file to the shortcut icon for the printer you want to print the file.

Why does a message appear, telling me to create an association when I drag a file to my printer's shortcut icon?

Windows does not recognize the file type and does not know which program to open to print the file. To tell Windows which program to use to always open this type of file, see the top of page 65.

If I delete a printer's shortcut icon, can I still use the printer?

You can still use the printer even if you delete the shortcut icon for the printer. The shortcut contains only the information needed to quickly access the printer. When you delete the shortcut icon, the printer is not removed from your computer.

How do I select multiple files for printing?

Click the first file you want to select. Hold down the Ctrl key and then click the other files you want to select.

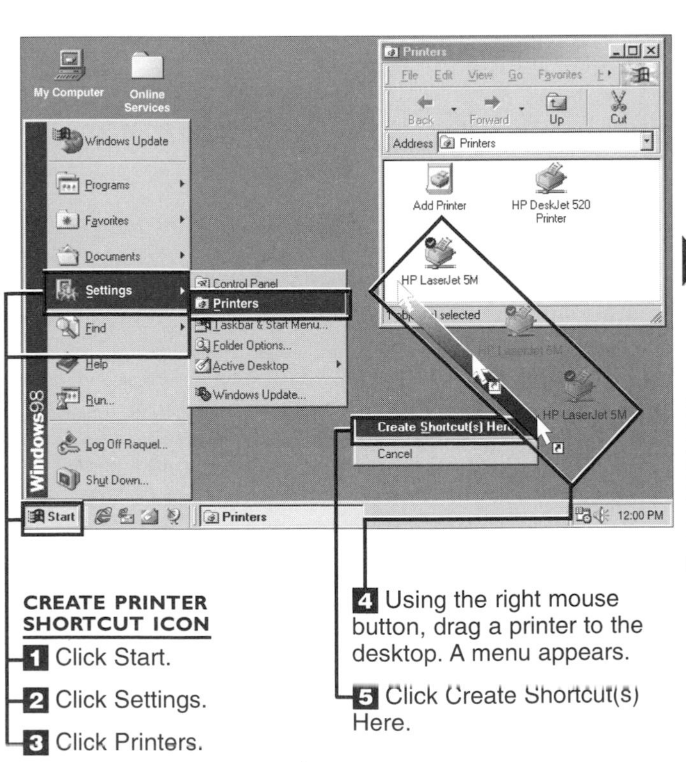

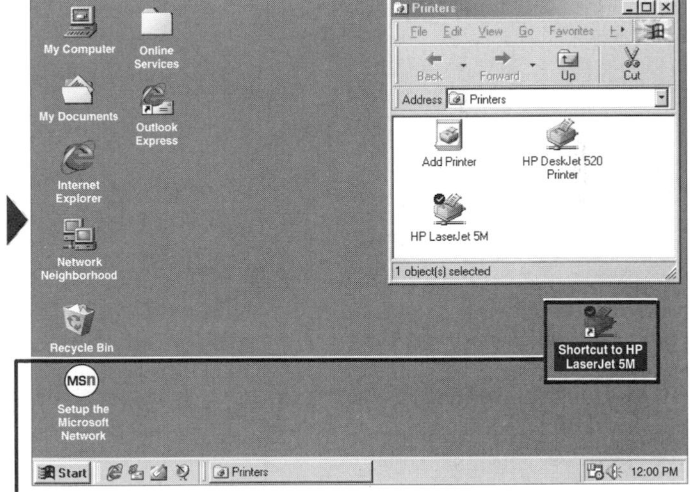

CREATE PRINTER SHORTCUT ICON

1 Click Start.

2 Click Settings.

3 Click Printers.

■ The Printers window appears.

4 Using the right mouse button, drag a printer to the desktop. A menu appears.

5 Click Create Shortcut(s) Here.

■ A shortcut icon for the printer appears.

■ You can now drag files to the printer's shortcut icon to print files.

VIEW PRINTING STATUS

You can view information about a printer and the files sent to the printer.

Each of your printers has its own print queue window. A print queue window displays information about the current status of the printer and the documents waiting to print. The title bar for a print queue window displays the name of the printer.

Each document that is printing or waiting to print is listed in the print queue window. Each column in the window lists information about the document, including the name, the status and which network station sent the document.

The Progress column indicates the size of the print job. While the document is printing, the Progress column keeps track of how much of the document has been sent to the printer.

The Started At column tells you the date and time a file was sent to the printer. This information is useful if you have a long list of print jobs.

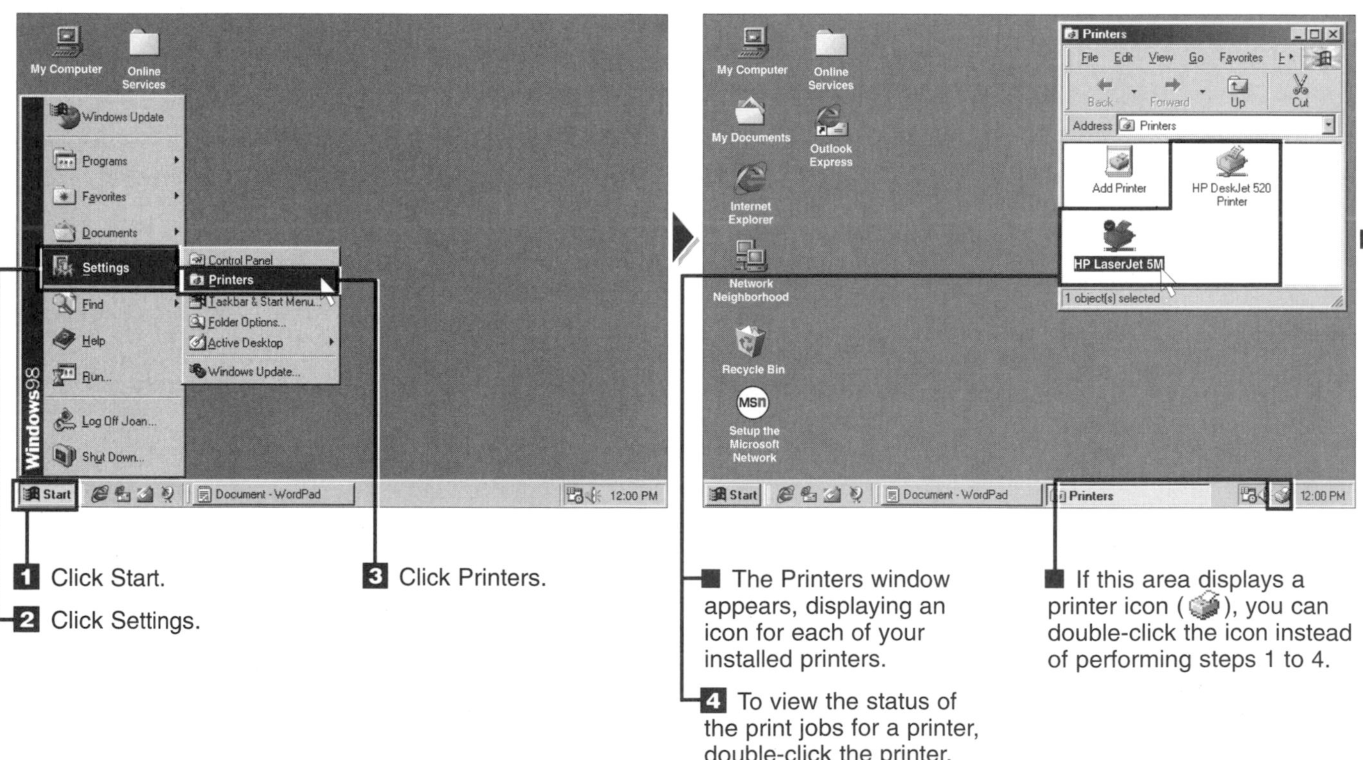

1 Click Start.

2 Click Settings.

3 Click Printers.

■ The Printers window appears, displaying an icon for each of your installed printers.

4 To view the status of the print jobs for a printer, double-click the printer.

■ If this area displays a printer icon ( ), you can double-click the icon instead of performing steps 1 to 4.

Can I sort the print jobs by clicking the column headings in the print queue window?

Windows does not support sorting in the print queue window. Print jobs are listed in the order they will print.

How can I view information about all available printers at once?

In the Printers window, choose the View menu and then select Details. Windows will display information about the status and number of documents printing on each printer. Viewing information on all the printers at once enables you to decide which printer to use.

How can I change the order of print jobs?

Open the print queue window and then drag a file to a new location in the list of print jobs. You cannot change the order of files other people have sent to a network printer.

What happens when I close the print queue window?

Closing the print queue window will not affect the files you send to the printer. The printer icon ( ) remains on the taskbar until the files are finished printing.

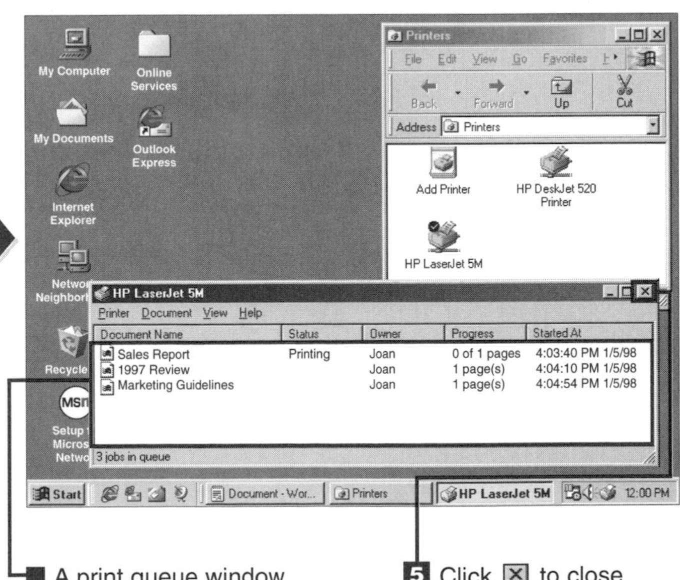

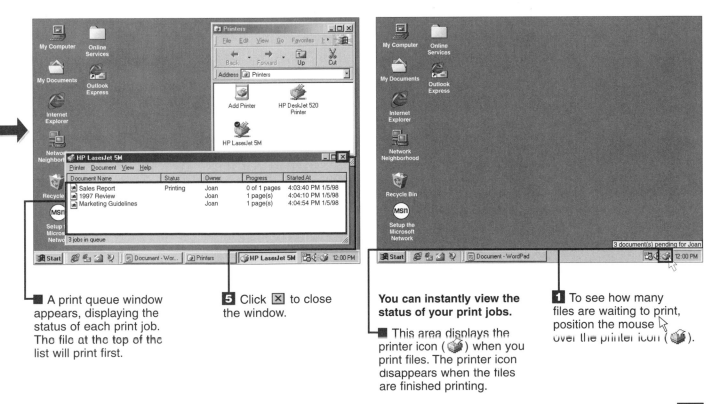

■ A print queue window appears, displaying the status of each print job. The file at the top of the list will print first.

5 Click ☒ to close the window.

You can instantly view the status of your print jobs.

■ This area displays the printer icon ( ) when you print files. The printer icon disappears when the files are finished printing.

1 To see how many files are waiting to print, position the mouse over the printer icon ( ).

PAUSE PRINTING

You can pause the printer to temporarily hold all print jobs. Pausing the printer is useful when you want to change the toner or add more paper to the printer. You can also pause the printer until all of your files are ready so you can pick all the files up from the printer at one time.

You can also use the Pause Printing command to pause the printing of a specific file. Pausing a file is useful to hold the file so more important documents can print first.

When you print a document, Windows creates a file and sends it to the printer. Pausing a file intercepts the file. The length of time allowed for you to pause the document depends on the number and size of files waiting to print and the speed of the printer.

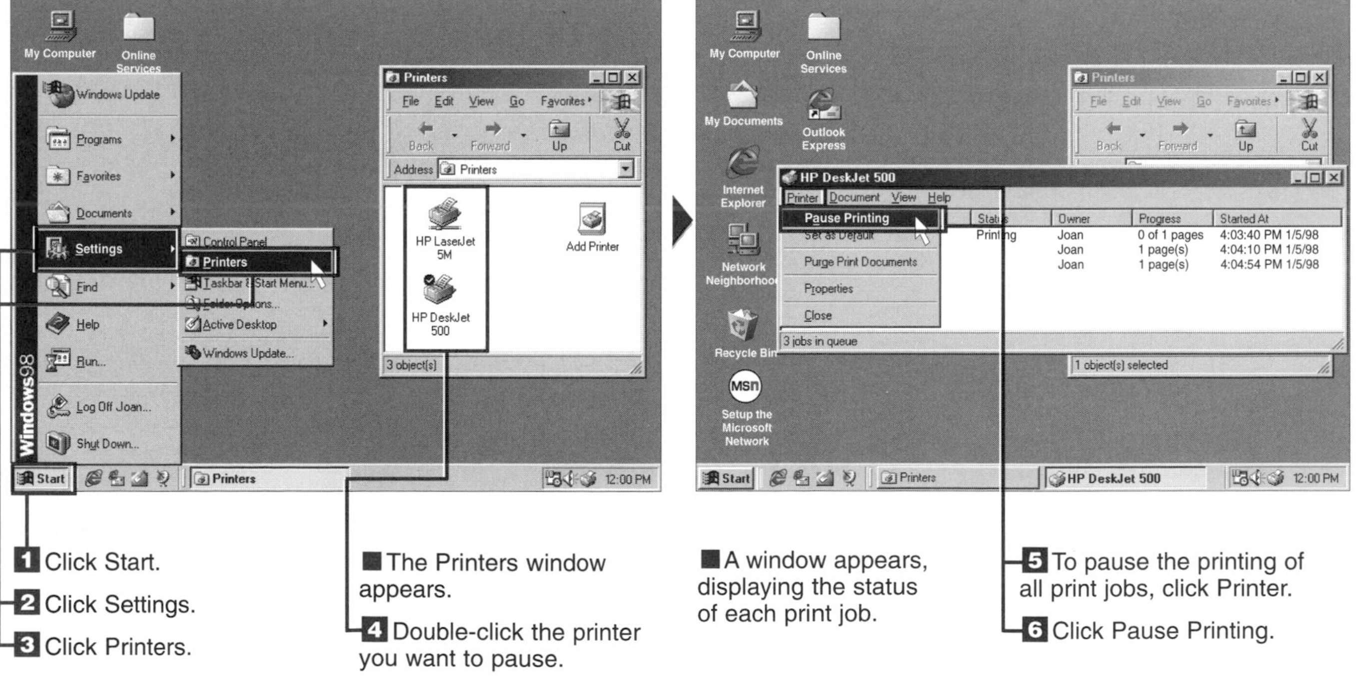

1 Click Start.

2 Click Settings.

3 Click Printers.

■ The Printers window appears.

4 Double-click the printer you want to pause.

■ A window appears, displaying the status of each print job.

5 To pause the printing of all print jobs, click Printer.

6 Click Pause Printing.

TIPS

If I unpause a file, when will it print?

When you pause a file, it keeps its place in the print queue. When you unpause a file, the file will print according to its location in the print queue. The print queue is the order in which documents are printed.

What happens if I pause the document that is currently printing?

If you pause a document while it is printing, there may be problems with the next print job or the printer may freeze. The printer will not print other jobs until the paused job is unpaused or canceled.

Can I pause the files of others on a network?

You cannot pause files printed by other people on a network unless you are the network administrator.

Can I pause the printer while files are printing?

You should not pause the printer while it is printing. If you need to pause the printer, you should first pause all the jobs in the queue except the one currently printing or wait until there are no print jobs in the queue.

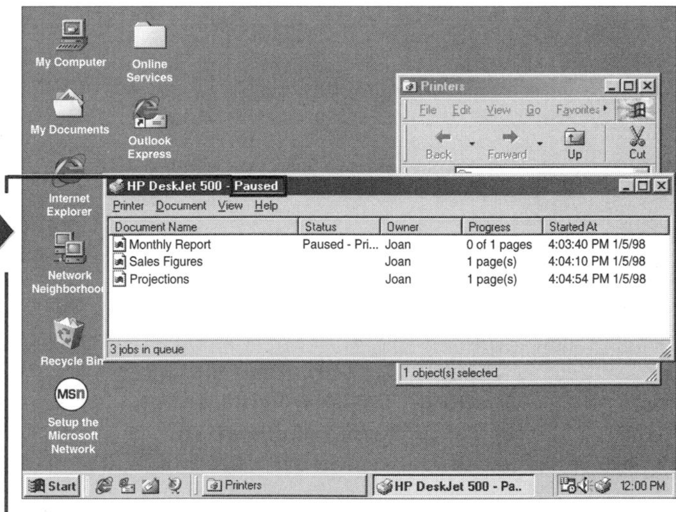

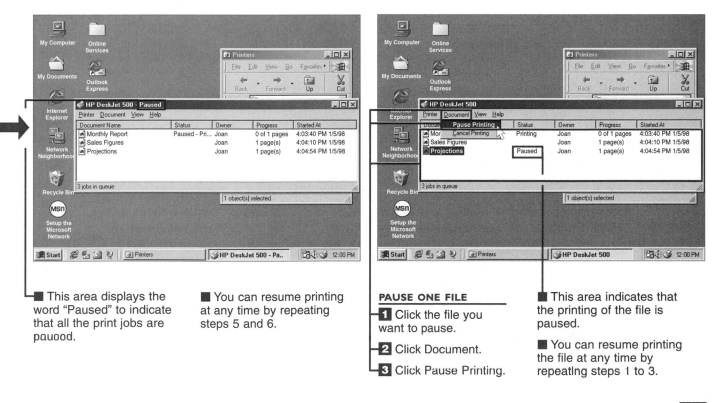

■ This area displays the word "Paused" to indicate that all the print jobs are paused.

■ You can resume printing at any time by repeating steps 5 and 6.

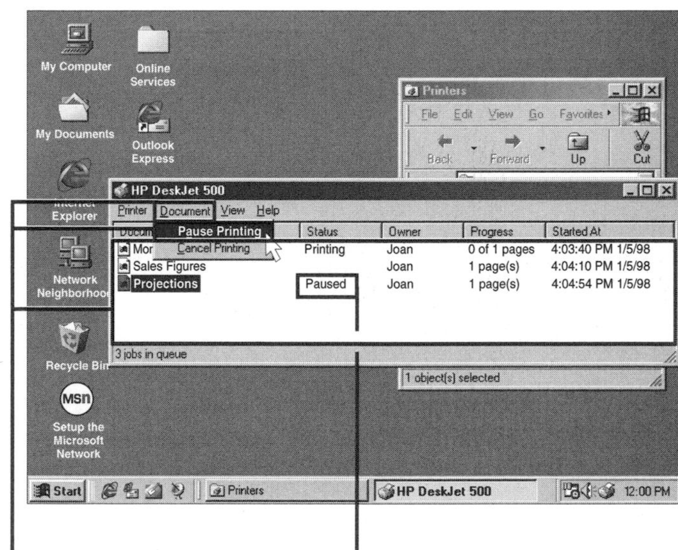

PAUSE ONE FILE

1 Click the file you want to pause.

2 Click Document.

3 Click Pause Printing.

■ This area indicates that the printing of the file is paused.

■ You can resume printing the file at any time by repeating steps 1 to 3.

CANCEL PRINTING

You can stop a document from printing if you have made a mistake and need to make a correction. The Cancel Printing command is available even if a document has already started to print.

Windows allows you to cancel a single print job or cancel the entire print queue. A print queue is a list of documents waiting to be printed. When using a network printer, you can only cancel your own print jobs.

When you stop printing a document or cancel all print jobs, Windows will not offer you a warning or an undelete option. Do not cancel any print jobs unless you are sure you do not want to print the documents. It may be wise to pause the printer first and then decide if you want to cancel the print jobs.

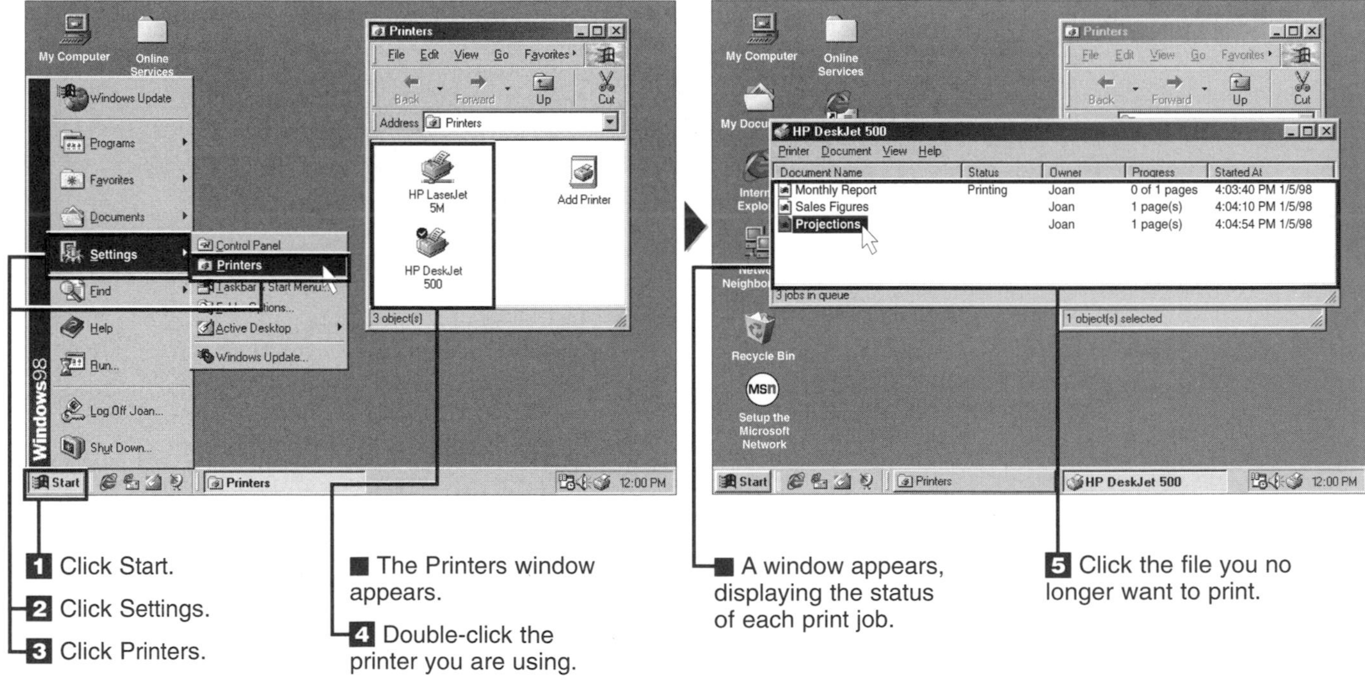

1 Click Start.

2 Click Settings.

3 Click Printers.

■ The Printers window appears.

4 Double-click the printer you are using.

■ A window appears, displaying the status of each print job.

5 Click the file you no longer want to print.

TIPS

How can I get quick access to a printer?

Using the right mouse button, drag the icon for the printer from the Printers window to your desktop. Select Create Shortcut(s) Here from the menu that appears. You can now double-click the shortcut icon to quickly access the printer at any time.

When you are printing a file, you can also double-click the printer icon that appears on the taskbar to access the printer.

Can I cancel all jobs while the printer is printing?

You can cancel all print jobs while documents are printing, but this may cause problems with some older printers. In some cases, the printer may have to be reset.

Can I cancel a document while it is printing?

You can cancel a document if the file has already started printing, but this can cause problems with the next print job. If you are using an older printer, the printer may have to be reset.

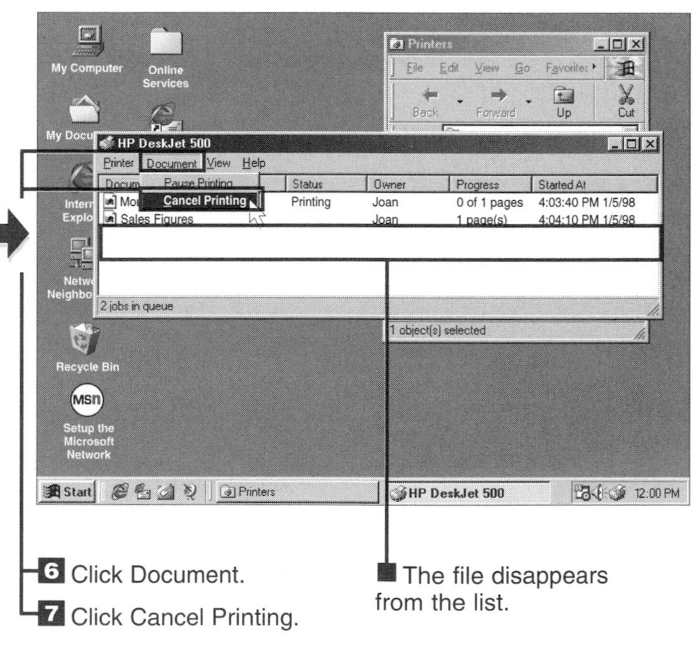

6 Click Document.

7 Click Cancel Printing.

■ The file disappears from the list.

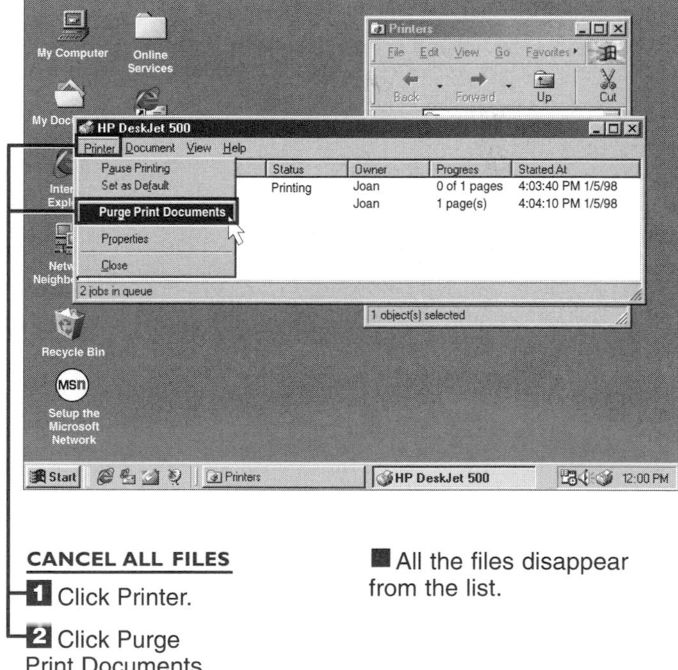

CANCEL ALL FILES

1 Click Printer.

2 Click Purge Print Documents.

■ All the files disappear from the list.

SET THE DEFAULT PRINTER

If you have access to more than one printer, you can choose which one you want to print your documents. You should choose the printer you use most often. The printer you choose is referred to as the default printer. Windows will automatically use the default printer to print your files unless you specify otherwise.

You may occasionally want to print a document on another printer. In programs such as WordPad, you must use the program's Print dialog box to select a different printer.

Some programs, such as Notepad, do not provide a Print dialog box and send your document directly to the default printer. A Print dialog box is also not available when you right-click a file and select the Print command. In these cases, changing the default printer is the only way you can choose a different printer.

You can change the default printer as often as you need.

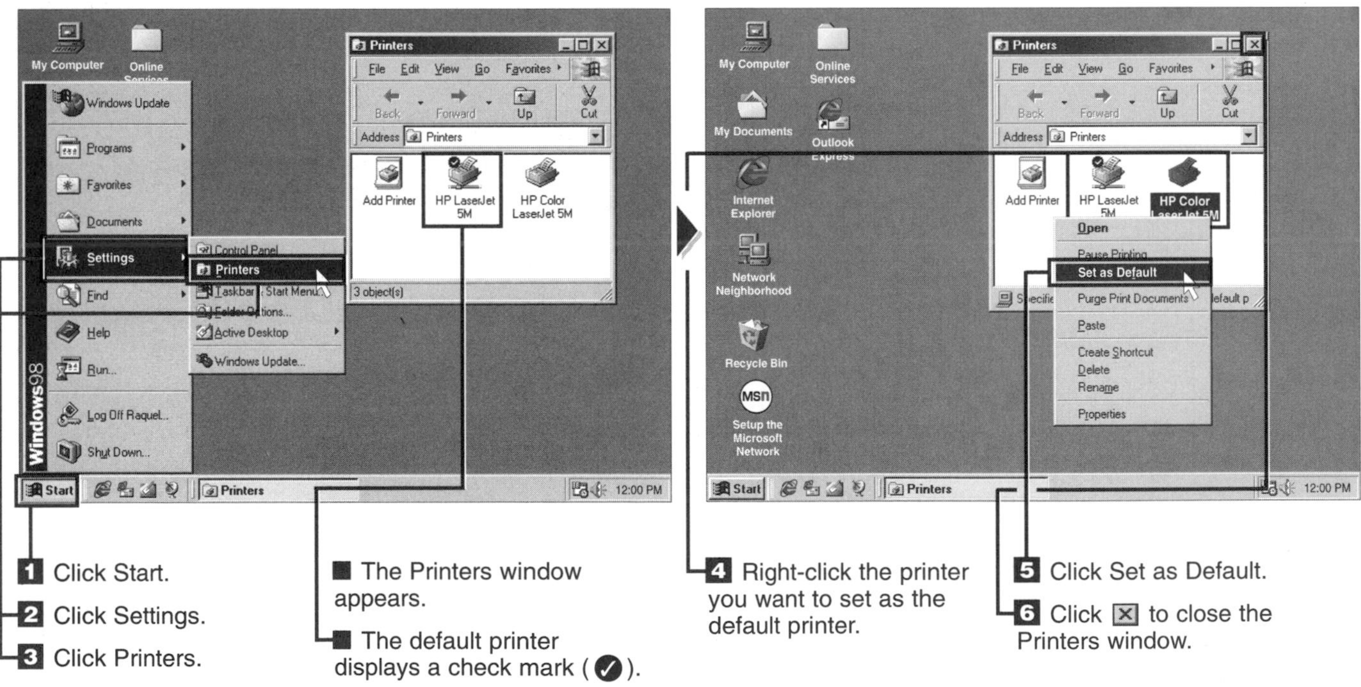

1 Click Start.

2 Click Settings.

3 Click Printers.

■ The Printers window appears.

■ The default printer displays a check mark (✓).

4 Right-click the printer you want to set as the default printer.

5 Click Set as Default.

6 Click ☒ to close the Printers window.

WORK OFFLINE

You can tell Windows that you are working offline. This will allow you to save your print jobs and print them later. Working offline is useful when you are not connected to a printer.

You can work offline when you are traveling and your portable computer is not connected to the network or when a network printer is unavailable because it needs paper, toner or maintenance. In both cases, Windows will save your print jobs until you are back in the office or the problem is fixed. Your documents will be sent to the printer as soon as you tell Windows you are no longer working offline.

By working offline, you save the time of having to reopen documents and print them later. You also eliminate the chance that you will forget which documents you wanted to print.

Working offline is only available for portable computers or for computers using a network printer. This feature is also called deferred printing.

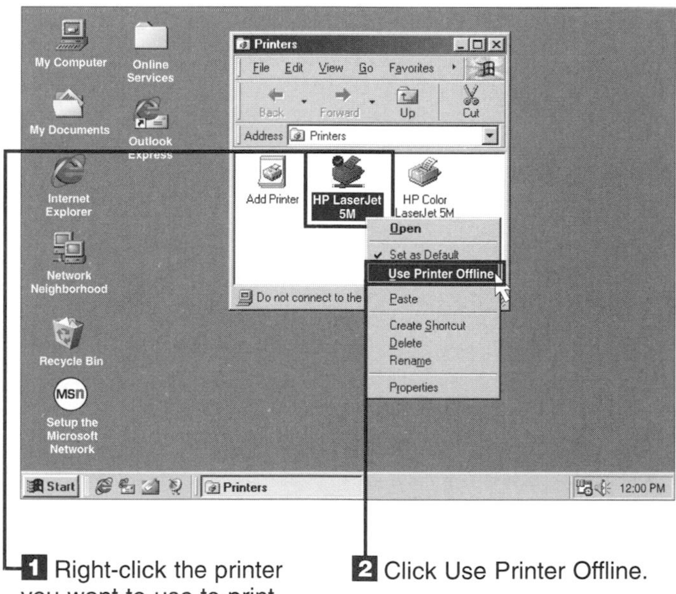

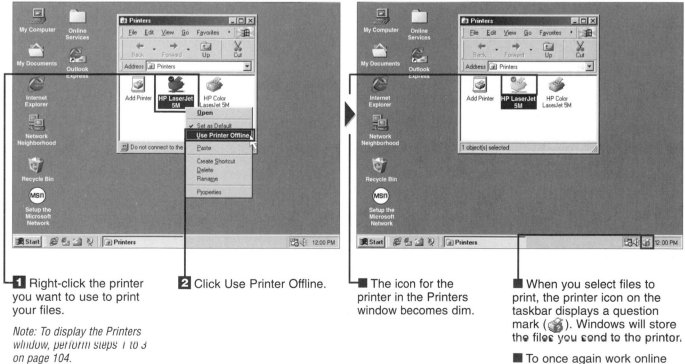

1 Right-click the printer you want to use to print your files.

Note: To display the Printers window, perform steps 1 to 3 on page 104.

2 Click Use Printer Offline.

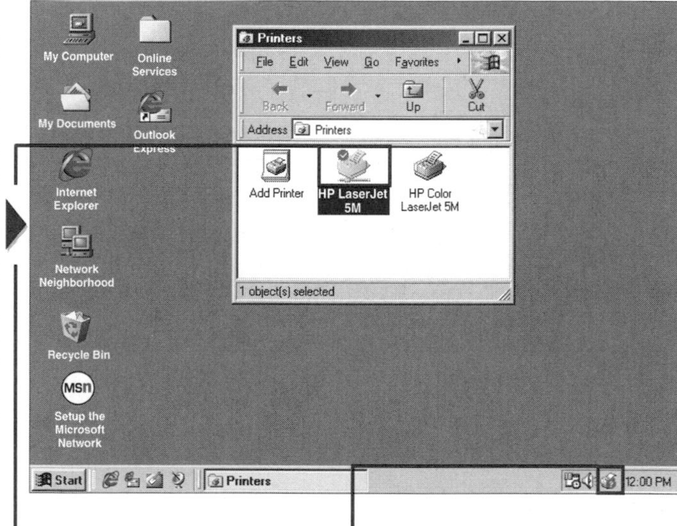

■ The icon for the printer in the Printers window becomes dim.

■ When you select files to print, the printer icon on the taskbar displays a question mark (). Windows will store the files you send to the printer.

■ To once again work online and print the files, repeat steps 1 and 2.

RENAME A PRINTER

You can change the name of a printer to help you identify its type and location.

Printer names can be up to 31 characters long, including letters, numbers and special characters. Long, descriptive printer names make it easier to choose the right printer and locate your printed documents.

For example, a printer named "Kim's color printer in room 204" is much easier to identify than a printer named "Printer 2."

When you rename your printer, the new name will appear in the Print dialog boxes in all of your programs. This helps you select the correct printer when printing a document.

Renaming the printer will not have any effect on documents currently waiting to print.

The Printers window displays an icon for each printer you currently have access to, with the name of the printer below each icon.

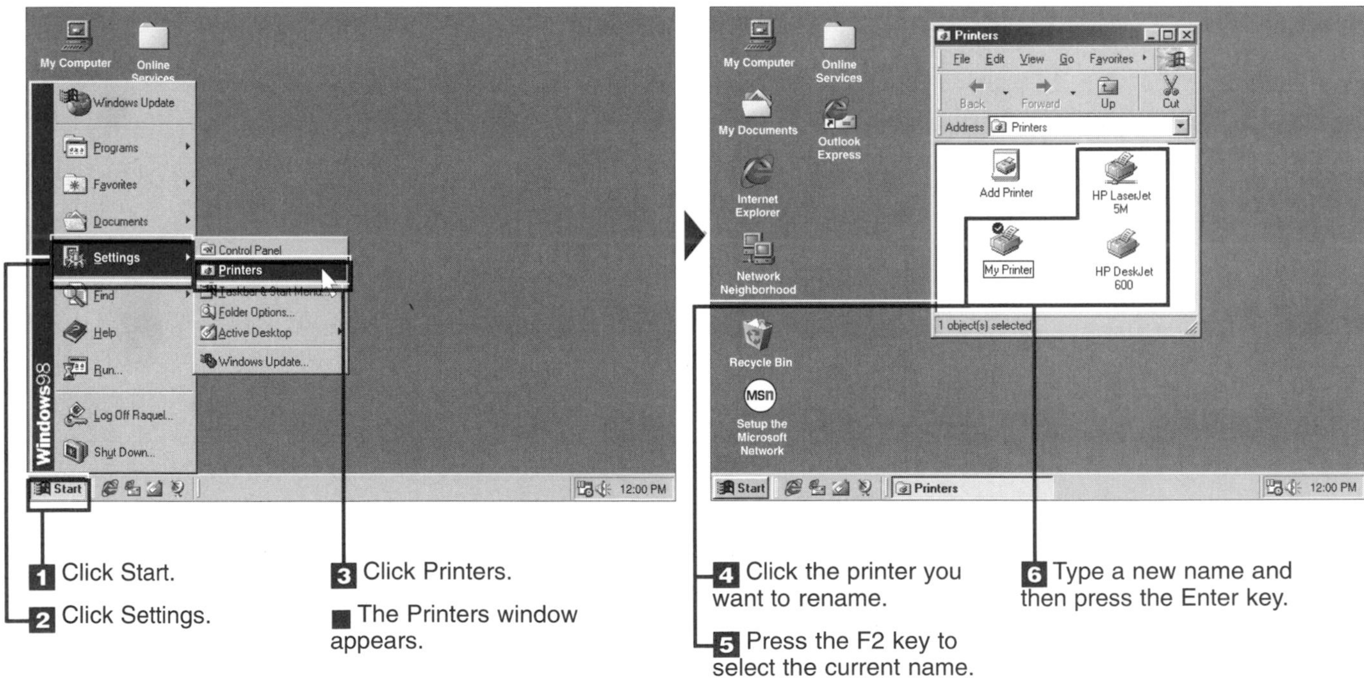

1 Click Start.

2 Click Settings.

3 Click Printers.

■ The Printers window appears.

4 Click the printer you want to rename.

5 Press the F2 key to select the current name.

6 Type a new name and then press the Enter key.

DELETE A PRINTER

If you no longer use a printer, you should delete the printer and disconnect the printer from your computer.

When you delete a printer, you remove the printer's settings from your computer. Windows will no longer display the printer in the Print dialog boxes of your programs.

If Windows detects that it no longer needs the files it used to communicate with the printer, Windows offers to remove the files for you. If you are removing the printer permanently, you should delete the old printer files to free up storage space on your computer. If you intend to reconnect the printer later, you should keep the files, especially if they were provided on a floppy disk or CD-ROM disc with the printer, or downloaded from the Internet.

When you are replacing an old printer with a new one, problems can occur if the commands and instructions designed for the old printer are sent to your new printer. Deleting the files used by the old printer from your computer will eliminate these problems.

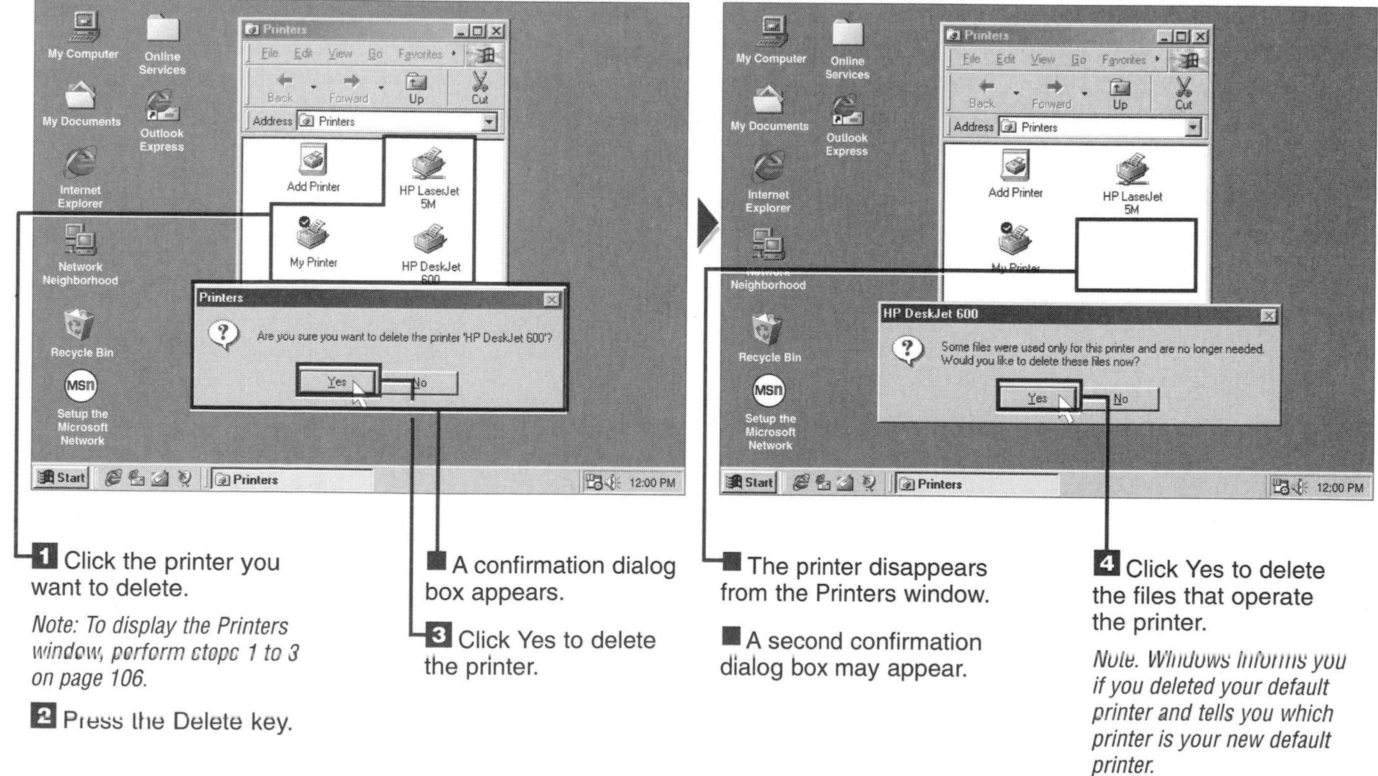

1 Click the printer you want to delete.

Note: To display the Printers window, perform steps 1 to 3 on page 106.

2 Press the Delete key.

■ A confirmation dialog box appears.

3 Click Yes to delete the printer.

■ The printer disappears from the Printers window.

■ A second confirmation dialog box may appear.

4 Click Yes to delete the files that operate the printer.

Note: Windows informs you if you deleted your default printer and tells you which printer is your new default printer.

CHANGE PRINTER OPTIONS

You can change your printer's settings to suit your needs. Changing a printer's settings will affect all the documents it prints. The printer you are using determines the available settings.

Changing your printer's general settings can be useful when the printer is shared with other people on a network. You can add a comment about your printer that can be seen by other people on the network when they install the printer and view its properties.

If your printer is used by many people, you can have the printer insert a separator page between each printed document. The separator page prints before the document and helps identify who printed the document. The Full separator page uses a large font and displays graphics. The Simple separator page uses the printer's default font and contains only text. You can only change the Separator page setting if the printer is attached to your computer. If you are using a printer connected to a network, you cannot change this setting.

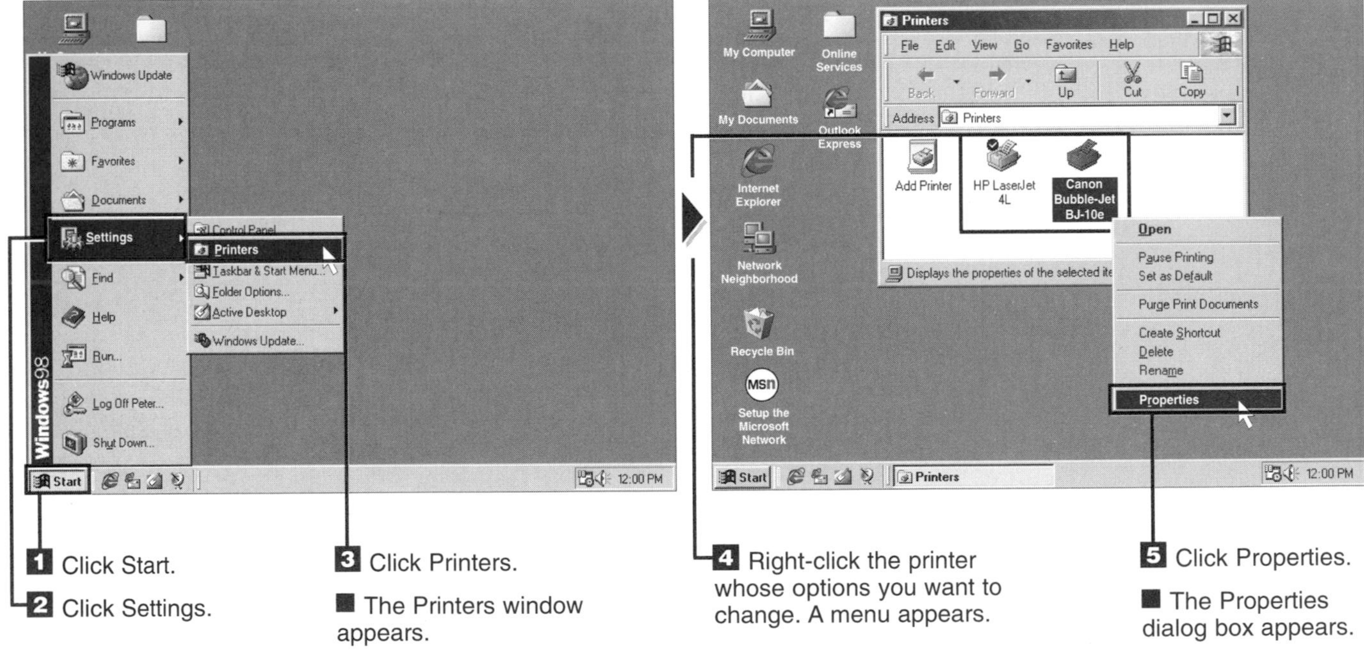

1 Click Start.

2 Click Settings.

3 Click Printers.

■ The Printers window appears.

4 Right-click the printer whose options you want to change. A menu appears.

5 Click Properties.

■ The Properties dialog box appears.

TIPS

Should I print a test page?

The printer test page confirms that the printer is working properly and provides information about the printer's driver. You can use this information if you want to check for an updated printer driver at the manufacturer's Web site.

My printer is not working. Can Windows help me find the cause of the problem?

Click the Start button and then select Help. Click the Contents tab and then select the Troubleshooting book. Click the Windows 98 Troubleshooters book and then select Print. Answer the questions that appear in the right pane to determine the cause of the problem.

Can I create my own separator page?

You can use files in Windows metafile (.wmf) format as a separator page. Advanced graphics programs, like CorelDRAW, can save files in the .wmf format. When you use your own separator page, Windows does not print the name of the user on the page. Use the Browse button in the Properties dialog box to find the .wmf file you want to use.

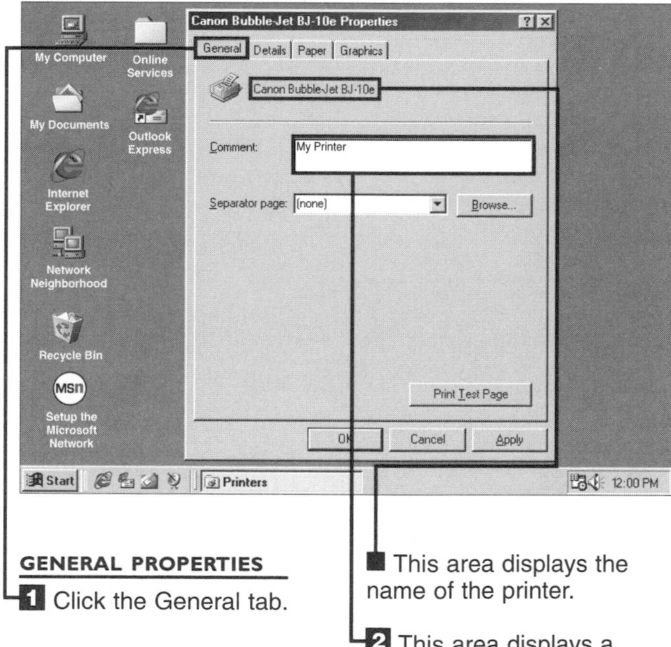

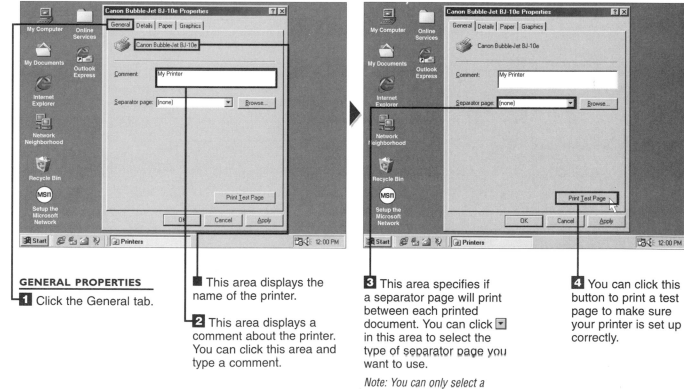

GENERAL PROPERTIES

1 Click the General tab.

■ This area displays the name of the printer.

2 This area displays a comment about the printer. You can click this area and type a comment.

3 This area specifies if a separator page will print between each printed document. You can click ▼ in this area to select the type of separator page you want to use.

Note: You can only select a separator page if the printer is attached to your computer.

4 You can click this button to print a test page to make sure your printer is set up correctly.

CONTINUED

CHANGE PRINTER OPTIONS
CONTINUED

You can specify how your computer works with your printer. Your printer must be attached to your computer to adjust some of the Details settings.

You can view which port is used to connect the printer to your computer. You can also view the printer driver. A driver is a program that helps your computer communicate with the printer. The driver also determines which settings are available for your printer.

The spool settings control how and when information is sent to the printer. When you print a document, the program you are working in creates a file on your hard drive to store the document until the printer is ready. When the program has finished creating the file, you can resume working with your computer. When the printer is ready, Windows sends the file from your hard drive to the printer. This process is called spooling and means that you do not have to wait for the printer to print your documents before using your computer to perform another task.

If your printer is capable of communicating with your computer in both directions, you should leave the bi-directional option enabled. This feature will allow Windows to provide additional information about your print jobs.

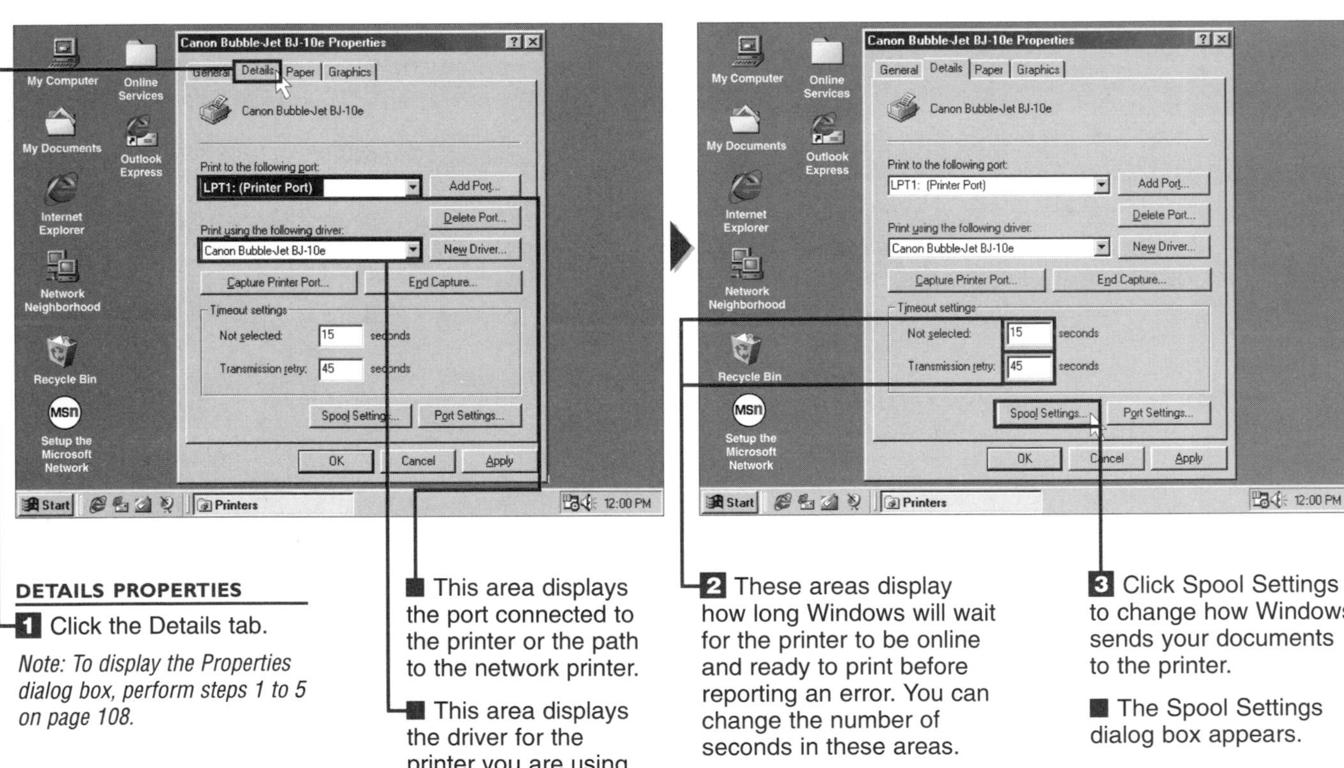

DETAILS PROPERTIES

1 Click the Details tab.

Note: To display the Properties dialog box, perform steps 1 to 5 on page 108.

■ This area displays the port connected to the printer or the path to the network printer.

■ This area displays the driver for the printer you are using.

2 These areas display how long Windows will wait for the printer to be online and ready to print before reporting an error. You can change the number of seconds in these areas.

3 Click Spool Settings to change how Windows sends your documents to the printer.

■ The Spool Settings dialog box appears.

TIPS

What are the Timeout settings used for?

The Not selected setting indicates the amount of time it takes your printer to be ready to print after you turn it on. The Transmission retry time reflects how long Windows will wait before sending your printer more data. This setting may need to be increased for printers using Postscript.

Which spool settings should I choose?

If you want your documents printed quickly, select the Print directly to the printer setting. If you want to be able to use your computer quickly, select the Spool print jobs so program finishes printing faster setting, the Start printing after last page is spooled setting and the EMF format setting.

What are spool data formats?

Spool data formats control the way information waiting to be printed is saved on your hard drive. EMF is the most efficient format for spooling data, but some printers cannot use this format. If you are having problems printing, try using the RAW format.

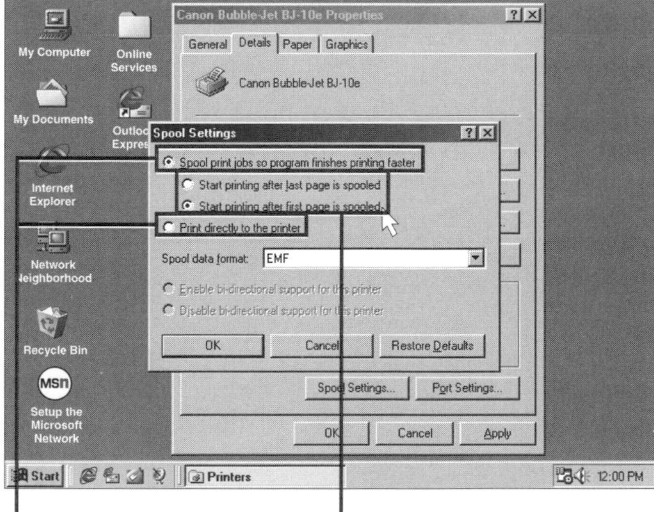

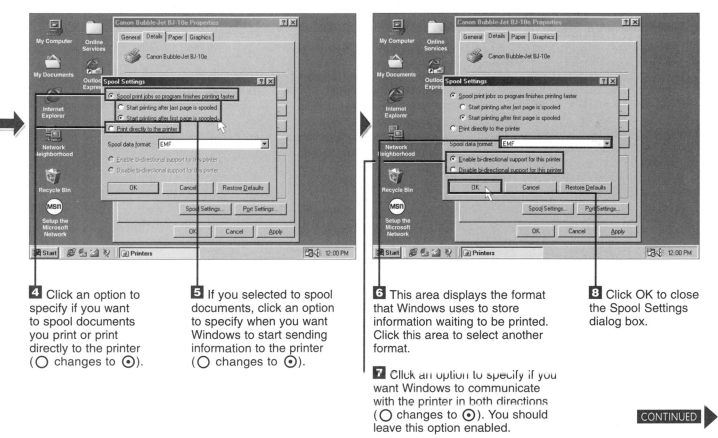

4 Click an option to specify if you want to spool documents you print or print directly to the printer (○ changes to ⦿).

5 If you selected to spool documents, click an option to specify when you want Windows to start sending information to the printer (○ changes to ⦿).

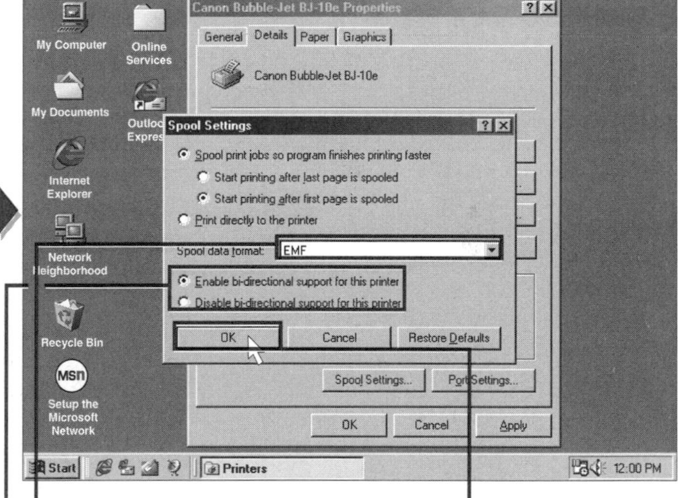

6 This area displays the format that Windows uses to store information waiting to be printed. Click this area to select another format.

7 Click an option to specify if you want Windows to communicate with the printer in both directions (○ changes to ⦿). You should leave this option enabled.

8 Click OK to close the Spool Settings dialog box.

CONTINUED

CHANGE PRINTER OPTIONS

CONTINUED

You can use different sizes of paper to print your documents. You can print on legal size paper, envelopes or custom paper, such as letterhead. The available paper settings depend on the printer you are using.

You can also change the orientation of the pages you print. Portrait is the standard orientation. Landscape is the orientation often used to print certificates and tables.

The Paper source setting allows you to specify where the paper you want to use is located in your printer.

Because the paper settings you choose will affect all the documents you send to the printer, you may find it better to change the paper settings in the program you are printing from. Changing the paper settings in the program allows you to leave the printer's settings at the settings you use most often.

You may also have settings that control how graphics are printed. You can change the resolution and method used to produce graphics. You can also have a graphic print lighter or darker on a page.

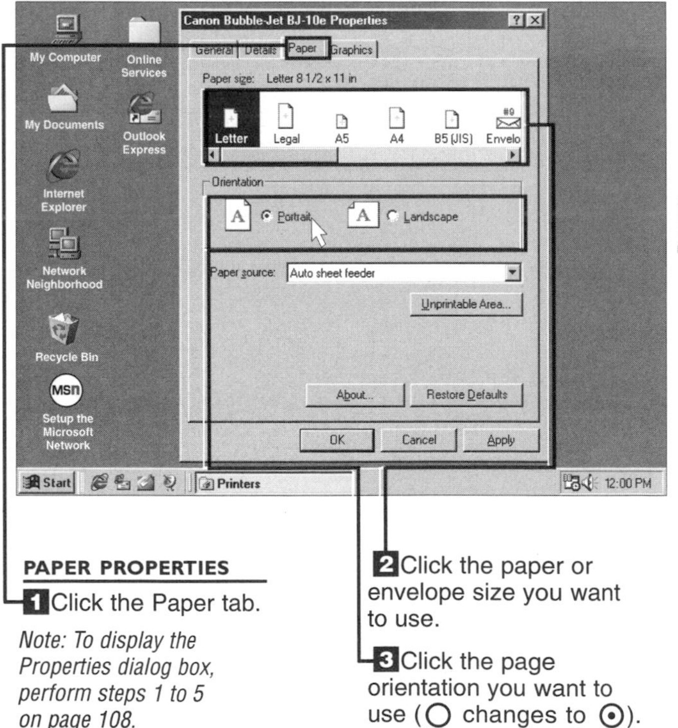

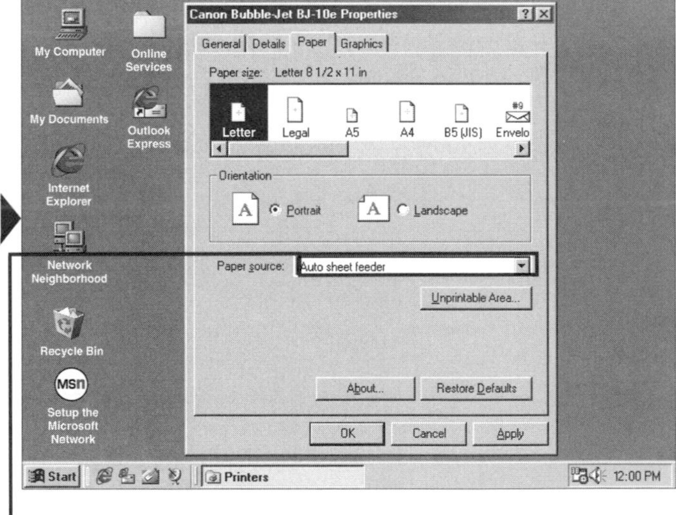

PAPER PROPERTIES

1 Click the Paper tab.

Note: To display the Properties dialog box, perform steps 1 to 5 on page 108.

2 Click the paper or envelope size you want to use.

3 Click the page orientation you want to use (○ changes to ⊙).

4 This area displays the location in the printer of the paper you want to use. You can click this area to change the paper source.

TIPS

I print envelopes frequently. How can I avoid changing my printer's settings each time?

You can install another copy of your printer and name the copy "envelopes." Specify the settings required to print envelopes on the new printer and then select the envelopes printer whenever you want to print an envelope. To install a printer, see page 114.

How many copies of my printer can I install?

You can install as many copies of your printer, or virtual printers, as you need. You may want to create one virtual printer to print high-resolution graphics and another to print using the letterhead tray. To install a printer, see page 114.

What is resolution?

Resolution is the number of dots printed per inch. A high-resolution setting produces better quality images, but documents take longer to print.

What is dithering?

Dithering is the technique of using dots to create the illusion of a wide range of grey tones or colors. This technique is used by most kinds of printers to enhance image quality.

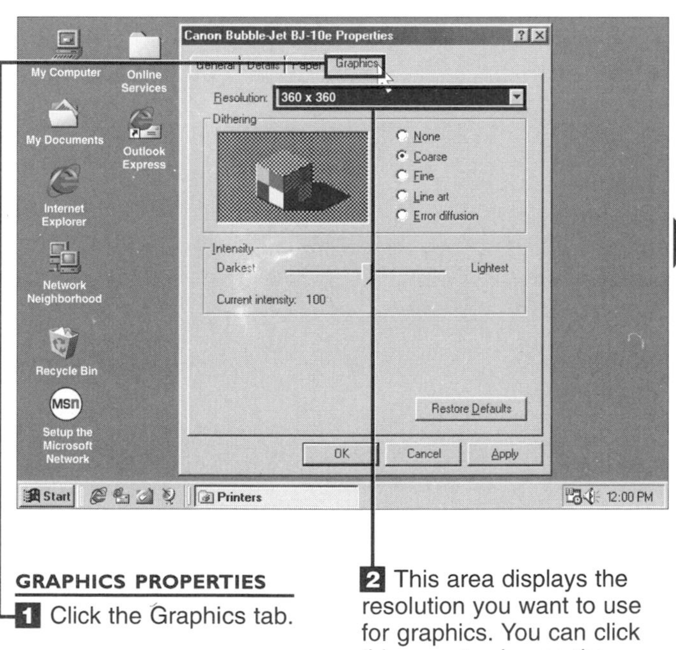

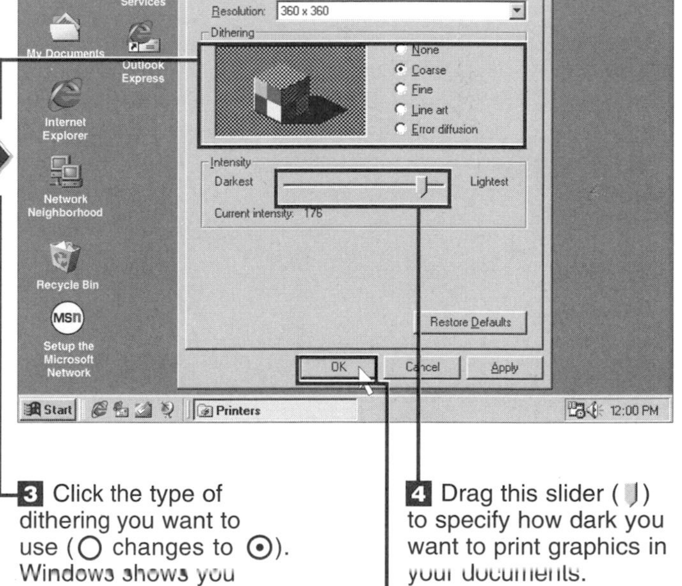

GRAPHICS PROPERTIES

1 Click the Graphics tab.

2 This area displays the resolution you want to use for graphics. You can click this area to change the resolution.

3 Click the type of dithering you want to use (○ changes to ⊙). Windows shows you how graphics will print.

4 Drag this slider ( ) to specify how dark you want to print graphics in your documents.

5 Click OK to confirm all of your changes.

INSTALL A PRINTER

You can install a new printer on your computer. The Add Printer Wizard helps ensure that your new printer is installed correctly and works properly. The wizard asks a series of questions and then sets up the printer according to the information you provide.

Windows includes a driver for most printer models. A driver is a program that helps your computer communicate with the printer. You may need to use your Windows 98 CD-ROM disc to add the correct driver for the printer you are installing.

Although Windows supports hundreds of models from over 50 different manufacturers, including Hewlett-Packard, Epson and Panasonic, your printer may not be on Windows' list of manufacturers and models. The documentation that came with your printer should contain information indicating that your printer is compatible with a similar model.

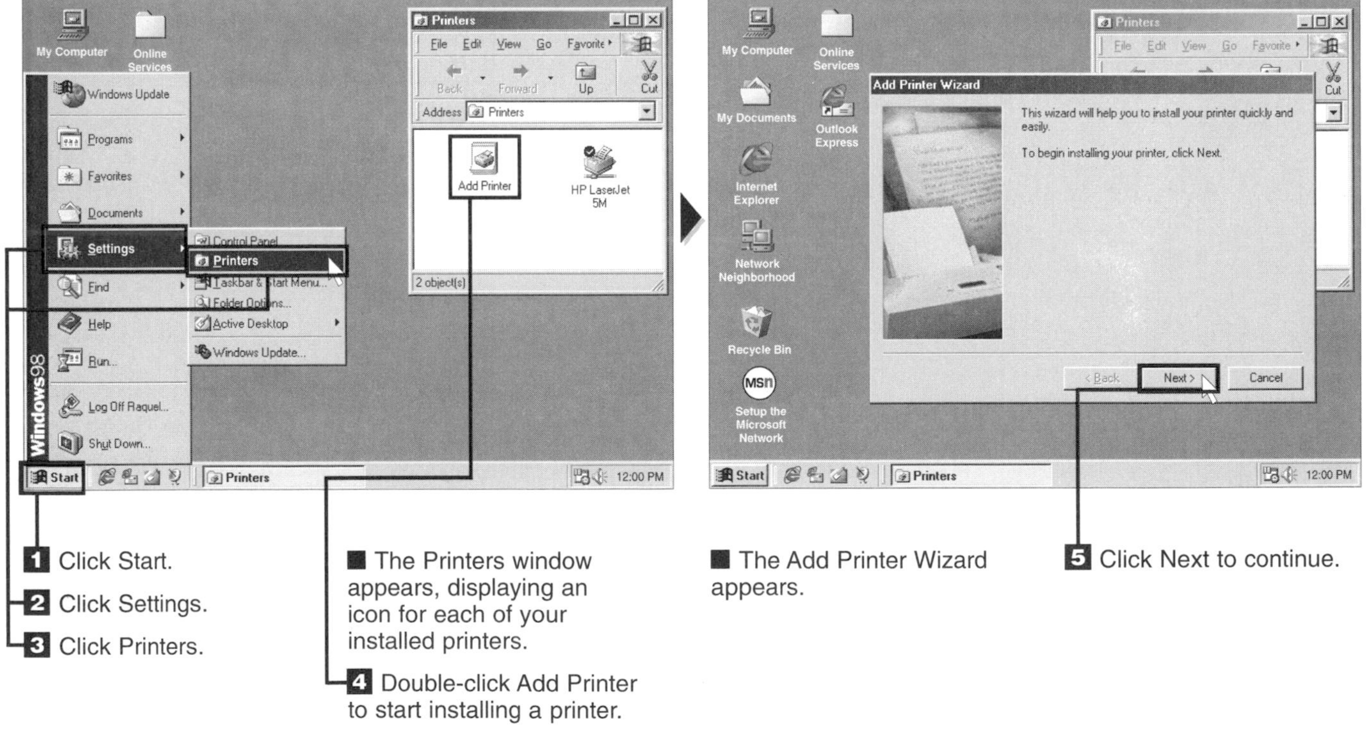

1 Click Start.

2 Click Settings.

3 Click Printers.

■ The Printers window appears, displaying an icon for each of your installed printers.

4 Double-click Add Printer to start installing a printer.

■ The Add Printer Wizard appears.

5 Click Next to continue.

TIPS

Which driver should I use if no documentation or disk was supplied with the printer?

You can use the Generic driver, but this driver is very limited. To install a laser printer, try the HP LaserJet IIIP. For a dot matrix printer, try the Panasonic KX-P1124.

My printer came with an installation disk. Should I use the disk to install the printer?

If you purchased the printer after the release of Windows 98, the driver on the disk may be more up-to-date than the driver included with Windows 98. Insert the installation disk and then click the Have Disk button. Windows will find all the necessary information on the disk.

What will happen when I install a printer with Plug and Play capabilities?

Windows will identify a printer with Plug and Play capabilities as soon as you plug in the printer and restart the computer. Windows will then prompt you to insert the disks supplied with the printer and will install the driver for you.

My printer can print both Postscript and PCL pages. Do I need two drivers?

Yes. Postscript and PCL are printer languages used to describe the information that will appear on a page. For printers that support both languages, you must install one driver for each language.

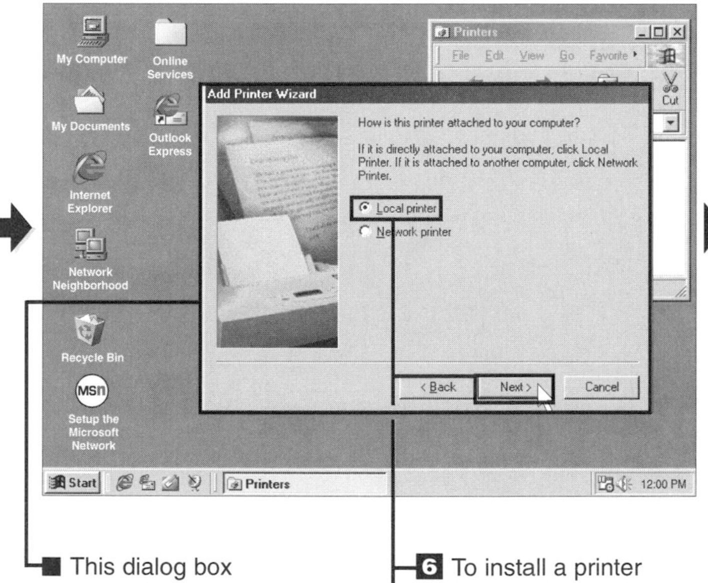

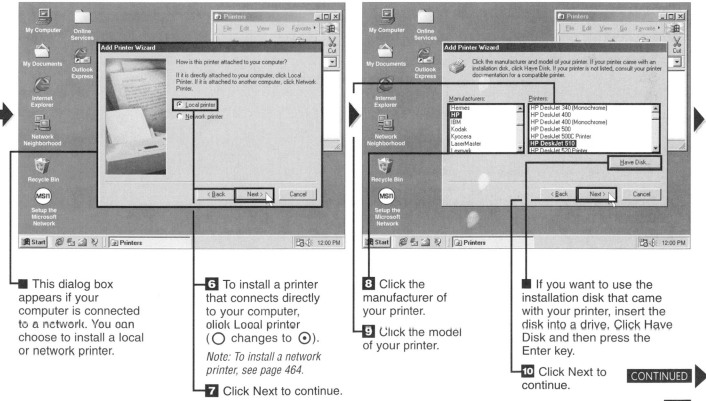

■ This dialog box appears if your computer is connected to a network. You can choose to install a local or network printer.

6 To install a printer that connects directly to your computer, click Local printer (○ changes to ⊙).

Note: To install a network printer, see page 464.

7 Click Next to continue.

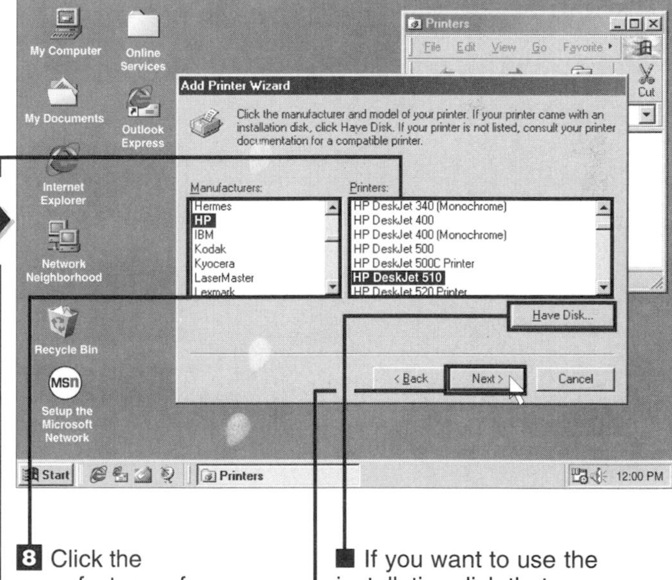

8 Click the manufacturer of your printer.

9 Click the model of your printer.

■ If you want to use the installation disk that came with your printer, insert the disk into a drive. Click Have Disk and then press the Enter key.

10 Click Next to continue.

CONTINUED

INSTALL A PRINTER

CONTINUED

You must tell Windows how the printer you are installing is connected to your computer. In nearly all cases, the printer is attached to the computer's parallel port, called LPT1.

The wizard allows you to type a name for your printer, which can be up to 31 characters long. This option is useful if you will be sharing the printer. Using a descriptive name helps other people on a network easily identify the printer's type, location and owner.

If you have only one printer, it will be the default printer. If you have several printers, you must select one to be your default printer. All of your programs will use the default printer unless you select a different printer.

Windows allows you to print a test page to confirm the printer is working properly. The test page contains information about the printer. You may want to keep the page for future reference.

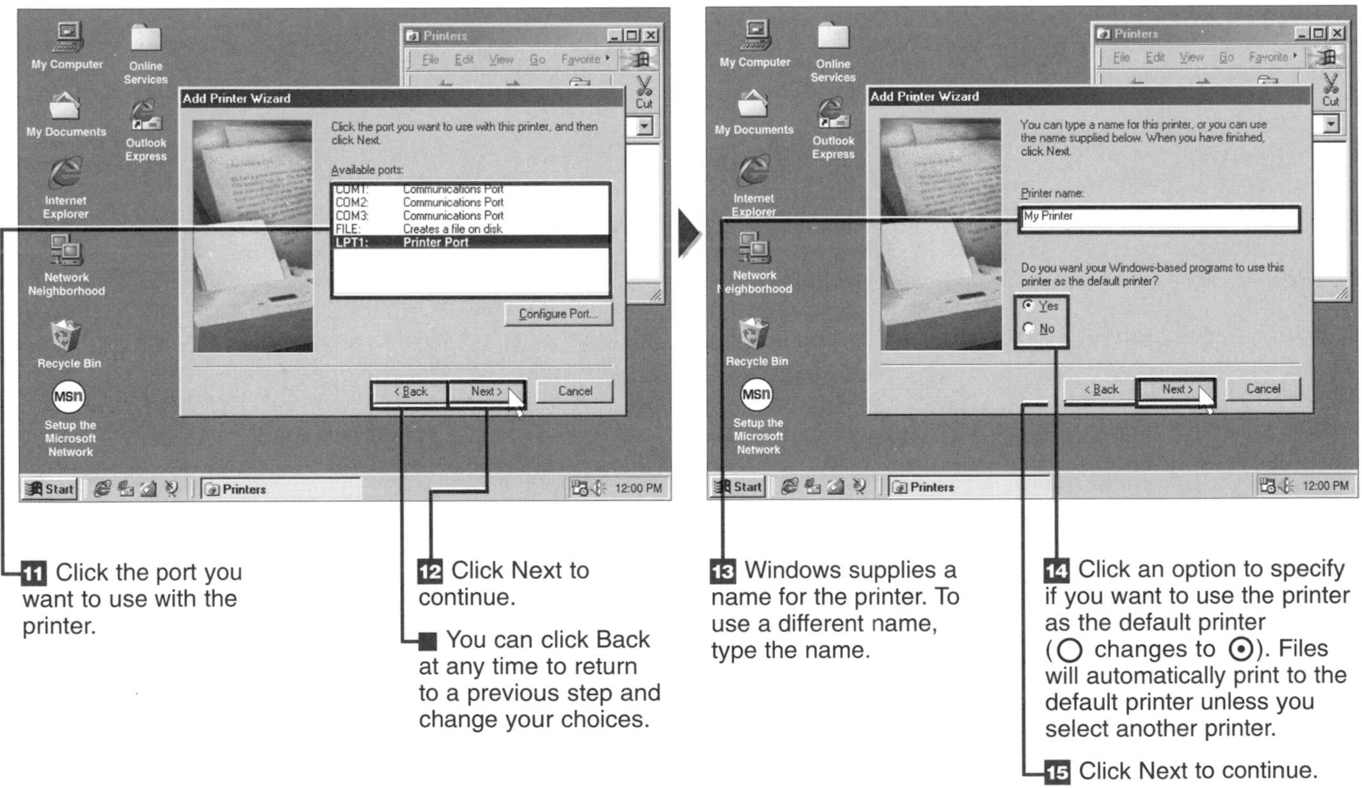

11 Click the port you want to use with the printer.

12 Click Next to continue.

■ You can click Back at any time to return to a previous step and change your choices.

13 Windows supplies a name for the printer. To use a different name, type the name.

14 Click an option to specify if you want to use the printer as the default printer (○ changes to ⊙). Files will automatically print to the default printer unless you select another printer.

15 Click Next to continue.

TIPS

Will I be able to use my printer with MS-DOS programs?

You will be able to use your printer with MS-DOS programs. However, each MS-DOS program that accesses the printer must have the correct printer driver to be able to communicate with your printer.

How do I change the default printer after installing a printer?

In the Printers window, right-click the printer you want to use as the default printer and then click Set as Default.

How do I rename a printer after I install it?

In the Printers window, click the printer you want to rename and then press the F2 key. Type the new name and then press the Enter key.

How can I print another test page?

In the Printers window, right-click the printer and then click Properties. Click the Print Test Page button.

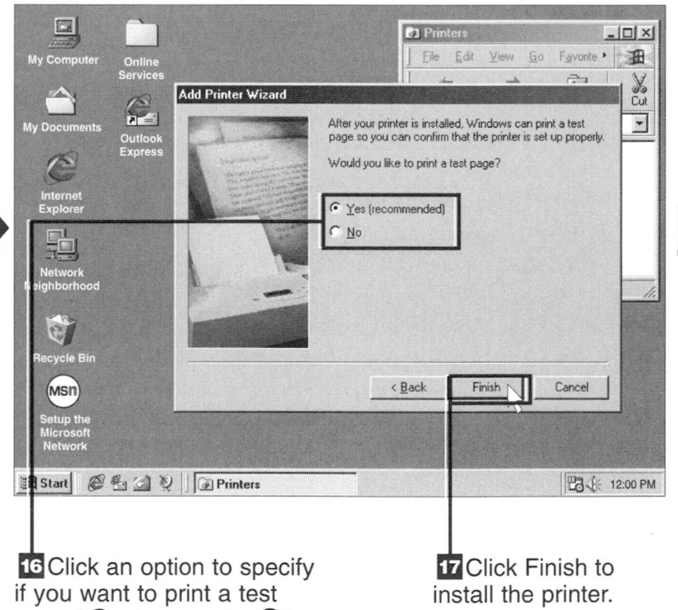

16 Click an option to specify if you want to print a test page (○ changes to ⊙). A test page will confirm your printer is set up properly.

17 Click Finish to install the printer.

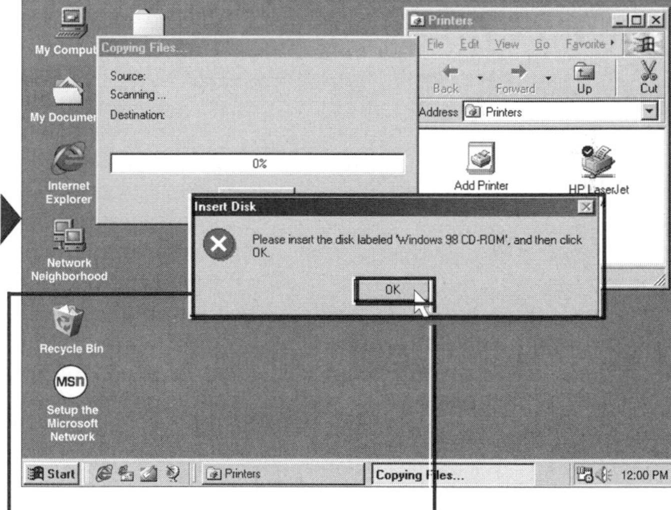

■ A dialog box appears, asking you to insert the Windows installation CD-ROM disc.

18 Insert the CD-ROM disc into a drive.

19 Click OK.

■ Windows copies the necessary information to your computer.

■ An icon for the printer appears in the Printers window.

MOVE OR COPY DATA

You can move or copy data to a different place in a document or from one document to another.

You can select text, numbers or images in a document and share the data with other documents, without having to retype or recreate the data. You can also share data between programs. For example, you can move an image created in Paint to a WordPad document.

The Clipboard is a temporary storage area for data you are moving or copying.

When you move data, Windows removes the data from the original document and places the data in the Clipboard. The data disappears from the original document.

When you copy data, Windows makes a copy of the data and places the copy in the Clipboard. The data remains in its place in the original document.

When you paste data into a document, Windows places the data from the Clipboard into the document. The data appears in the document where you positioned the insertion point.

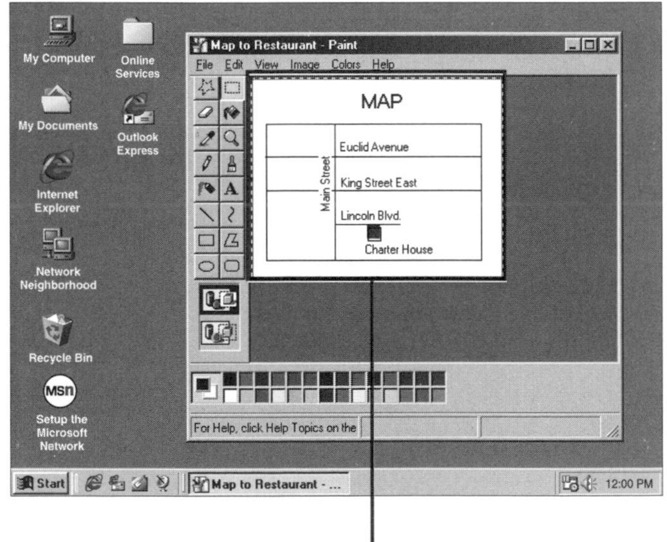

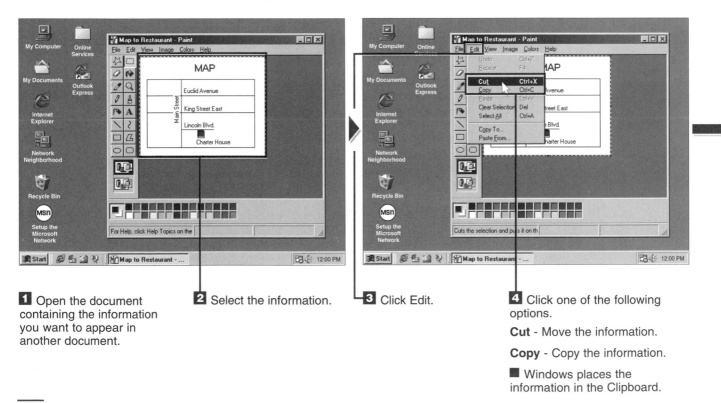

1 Open the document containing the information you want to appear in another document.

2 Select the information.

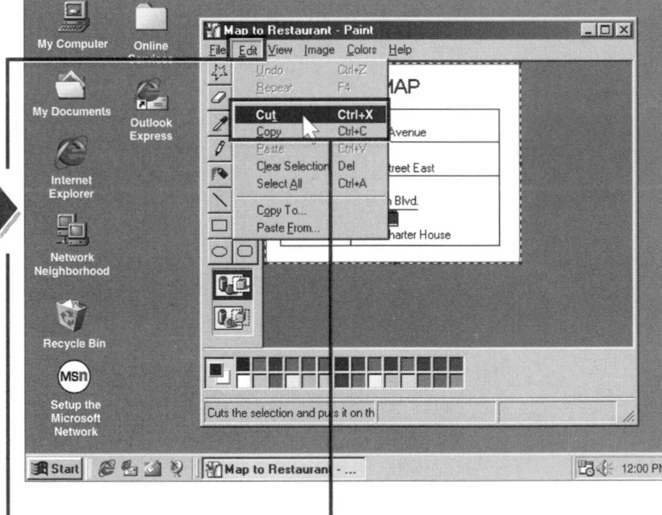

3 Click Edit.

4 Click one of the following options.

Cut - Move the information.

Copy - Copy the information.

■ Windows places the information in the Clipboard.

TIPS

How do I select the data I want to move or copy?

In most programs, you can drag the mouse over the data you want to select. Selected data usually appears highlighted on your screen.

Is there a faster way to move or copy data?

Many programs provide toolbar buttons you can use to quickly cut, copy and paste data.

Can I put several items in the Clipboard and then paste them all at the same time?

The Clipboard can hold only one item at a time. When you place a new item in the Clipboard, the previous item is replaced.

Can I move or copy data in a dialog box?

Most Windows programs allow you to use the keyboard to move or copy data whenever you do not have access to menus or toolbars. To move data, select the data and then press Ctrl+X on your keyboard. To copy data, select the data and then press Ctrl+C on your keyboard. To paste data, position the insertion point where you want the data to appear and then press Ctrl+V on your keyboard.

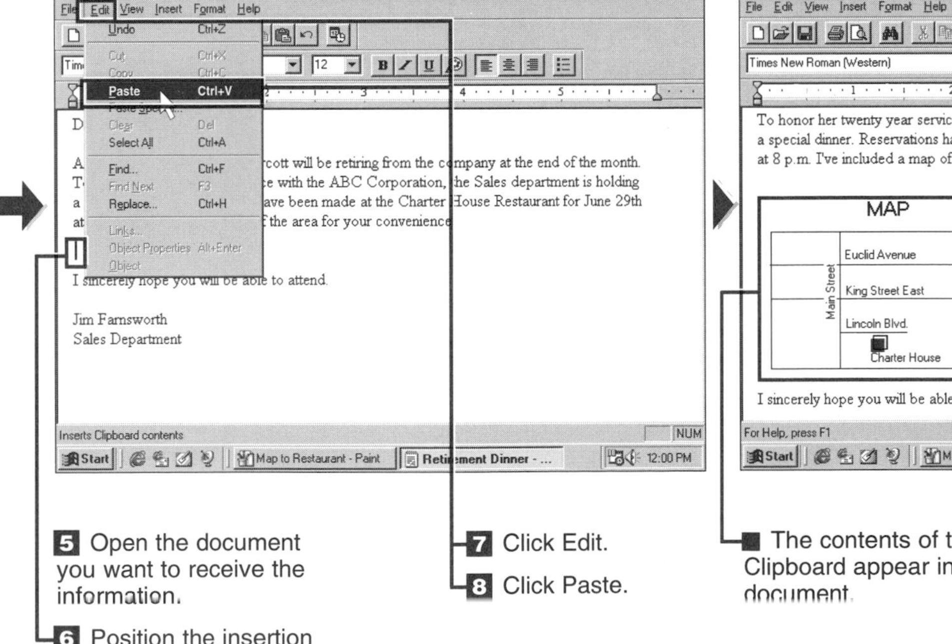

5 Open the document you want to receive the information.

6 Position the insertion point where you want the information to appear.

7 Click Edit.

8 Click Paste.

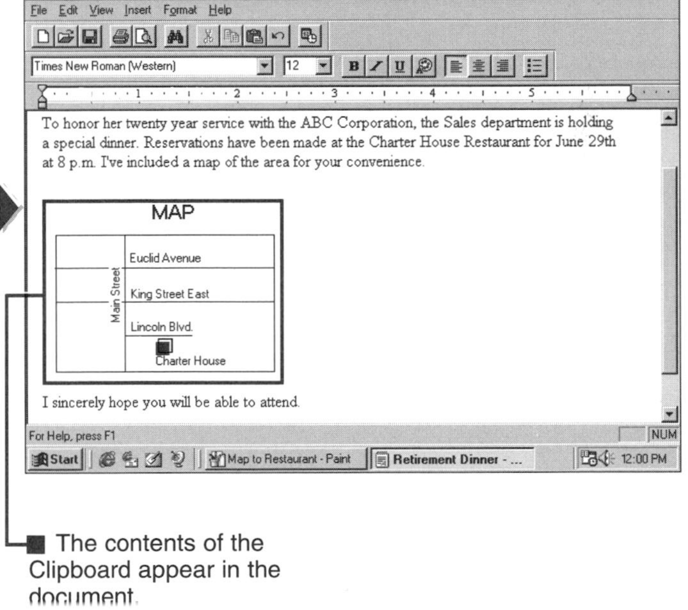

■ The contents of the Clipboard appear in the document.

USING DRAG AND DROP TO EXCHANGE DATA

You can use the mouse to drag information from its current location to a new location.

You can drag and drop information within a document or between two documents.

If both documents are displayed on the screen, you can select the information you want and drag it to the new location.

If you want to move or copy information to a program that is minimized on the taskbar, you can select the information and drag it to the program's button on the taskbar. Continue holding down the mouse button until the program window opens and then drag the information to where you want it to appear.

If you see a black circle with a slash through it (⃠) when you try to drag and drop information, you cannot place the information where the mouse pointer is. For example, you cannot drag text from a document into a Paint window.

Drag and drop will not work for all programs. If you are having trouble dragging and dropping, you can check your program's manual or Help information to see if the program supports the feature.

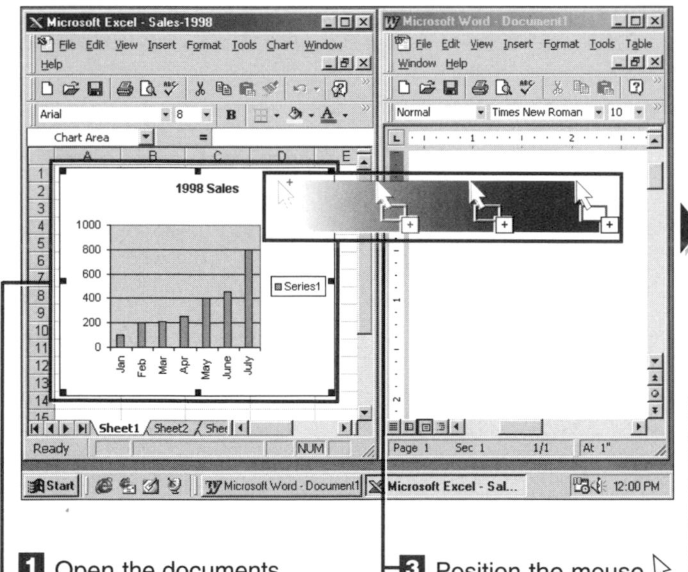

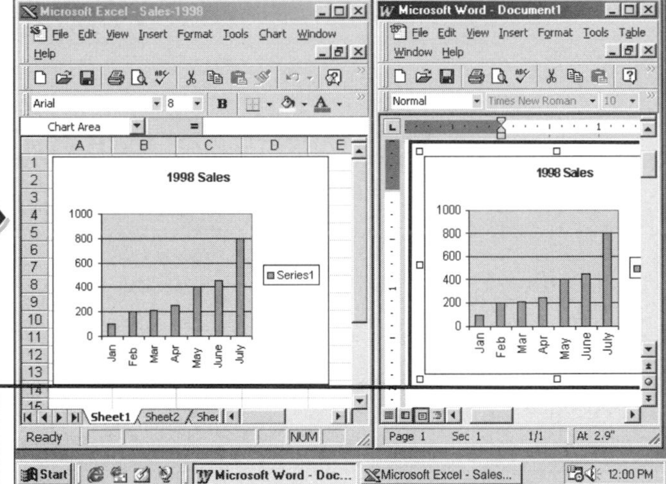

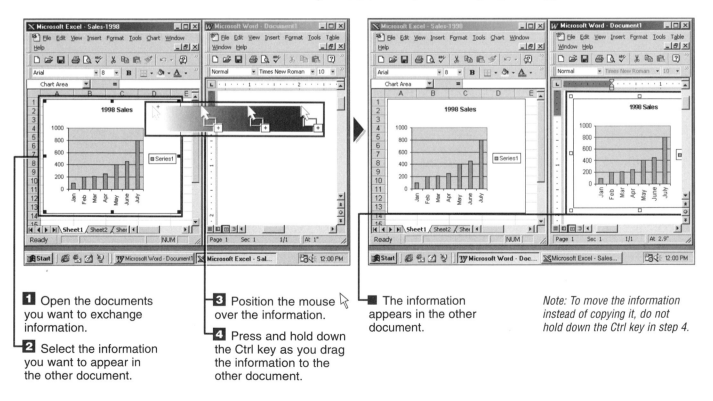

1 Open the documents you want to exchange information.

2 Select the information you want to appear in the other document.

3 Position the mouse over the information.

4 Press and hold down the Ctrl key as you drag the information to the other document.

■ The information appears in the other document.

Note: To move the information instead of copying it, do not hold down the Ctrl key in step 4.

COPY SCREEN OR WINDOW CONTENTS

You can take a picture of the entire desktop or just the active window. This is useful if you are trying to explain a computer problem or procedure and you need a visual example of what you are explaining.

When you copy the desktop or active window, the image is stored in the Clipboard. You can then place the image in a program like Paint or WordPad.

You can open the Clipboard Viewer to verify that the image is the one you want before pasting it into a program. You can also use the Clipboard Viewer to save your pictures. For information, see page 122.

You can buy programs that provide options the Print Scrn key does not offer. For example, some programs can include the mouse pointer in the image. There are also programs like Lotus ScreenCam and Microsoft Camcorder that can record a series of movements on your screen and save them as a movie.

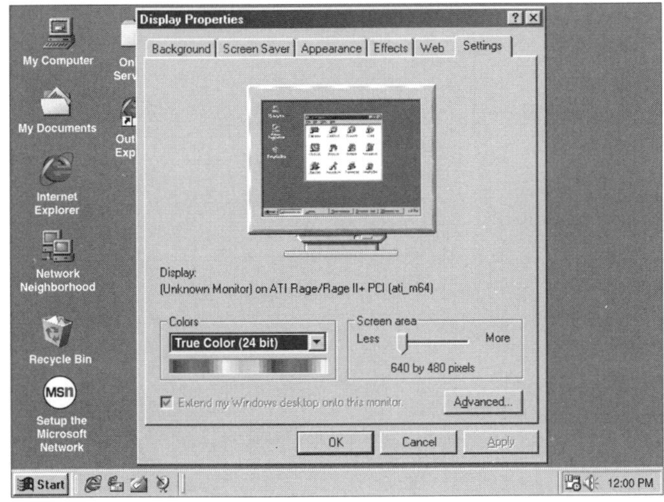

1 Press the Print Scrn key to copy the entire screen.

■ To copy just the active window or dialog box, press and hold down the Alt key as you press the Print Scrn key.

■ Windows places a copy of the image in the Clipboard.

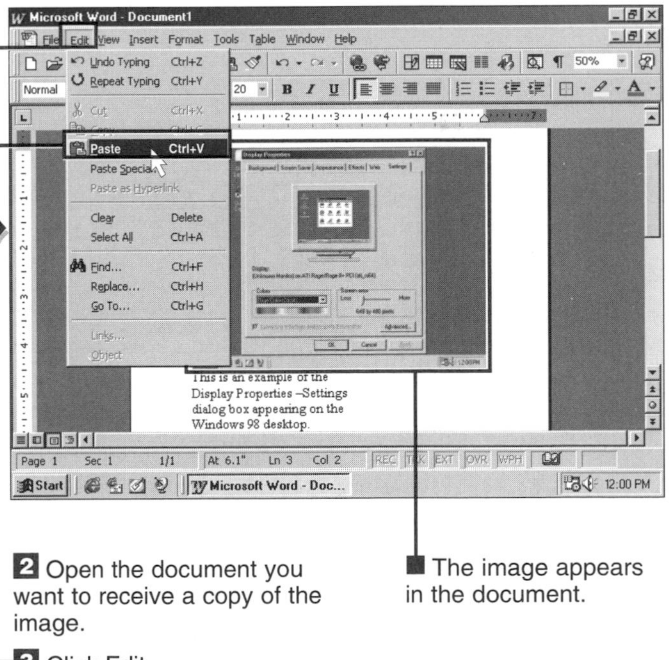

2 Open the document you want to receive a copy of the image.

3 Click Edit.

4 Click Paste.

■ The image appears in the document.

VIEW CONTENTS OF CLIPBOARD

You can use the Clipboard Viewer to view and save the text, image or other item currently stored in the Clipboard.

The Clipboard is an area of your computer's memory that temporarily stores information. Many different types of programs can access and use the information stored in the Clipboard.

What you see in the Clipboard Viewer depends on the type of item you placed in the Clipboard. When you place an item such as an image or text in the Clipboard, you can view the entire item. When you place an item such as a file or folder in the Clipboard, you can only view the path of the item. The contents of the item are not displayed.

When you place part of a sound file in the Clipboard, you can only view the icon that represents the item. When you place part of a video file in the Clipboard, you may be able to view a frame from the video.

You can save information stored in the Clipboard and reuse the information later. The information you save in the Clipboard will be saved in a file with the .clp extension.

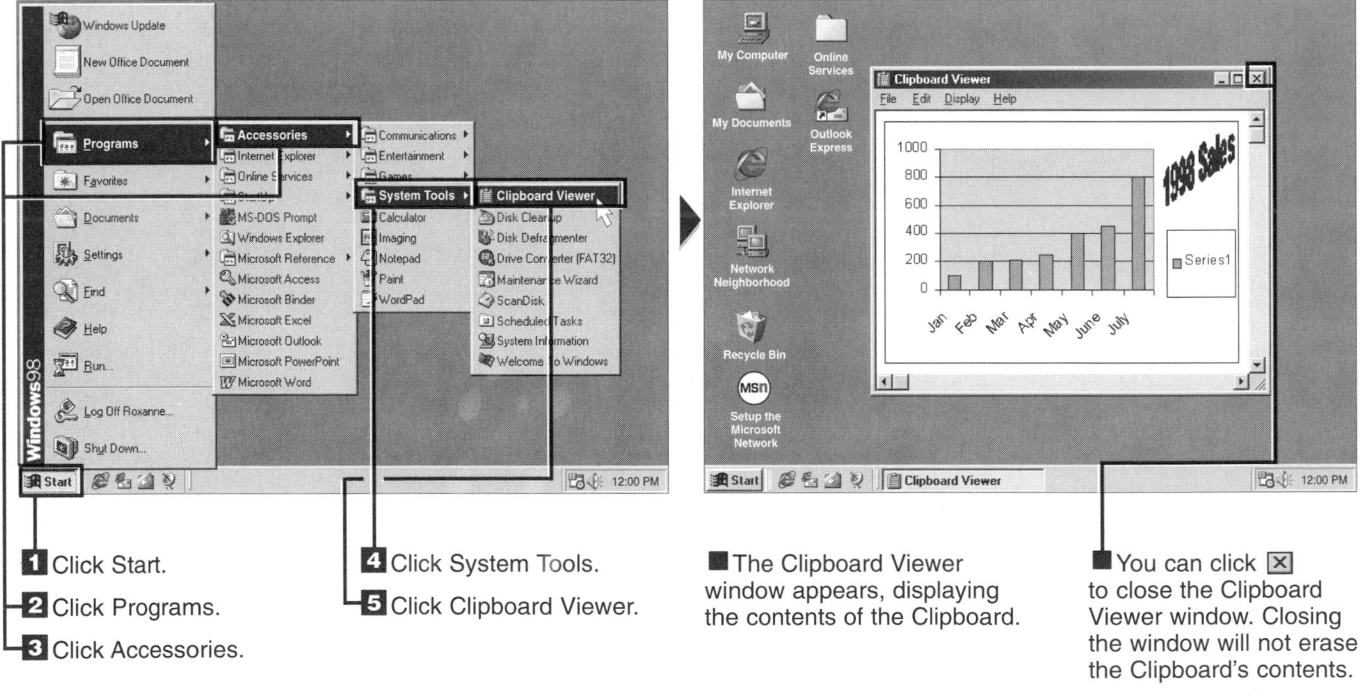

1 Click Start.

2 Click Programs.

3 Click Accessories.

4 Click System Tools.

5 Click Clipboard Viewer.

■ The Clipboard Viewer window appears, displaying the contents of the Clipboard.

■ You can click ☒ to close the Clipboard Viewer window. Closing the window will not erase the Clipboard's contents.

TIPS

Why can't I find the Clipboard Viewer on my computer?

The Clipboard Viewer may not be installed. The Clipboard Viewer is located in the System Tools component. See page 610 to add Windows components.

Why does the image appear distorted in the Clipboard Viewer?

The Clipboard Viewer automatically sizes items to fit the window. In some cases, you can choose the Display menu and then select the DIB Bitmap or Bitmap command to display the image at the original size. You can also resize the window.

How long does information stay in the Clipboard?

The Clipboard stores one item at a time. You can paste the item as many times as you want. As soon as you move or copy a new item, the new item replaces the item currently stored in the Clipboard. When you shut down Windows, the item in the Clipboard is deleted.

How do I open a Clipboard file I saved?

You can open a Clipboard file you saved by choosing the File menu and then selecting the Open command.

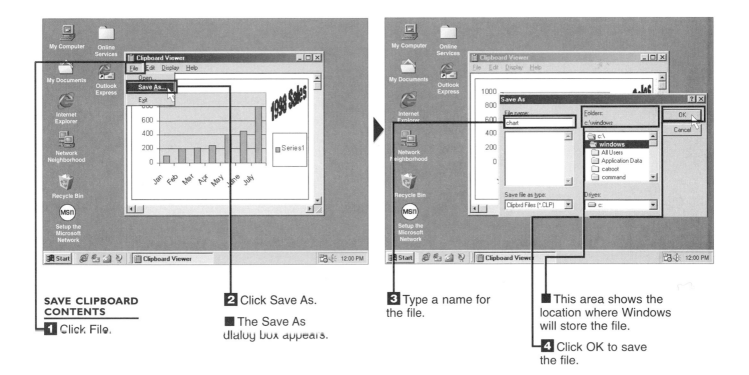

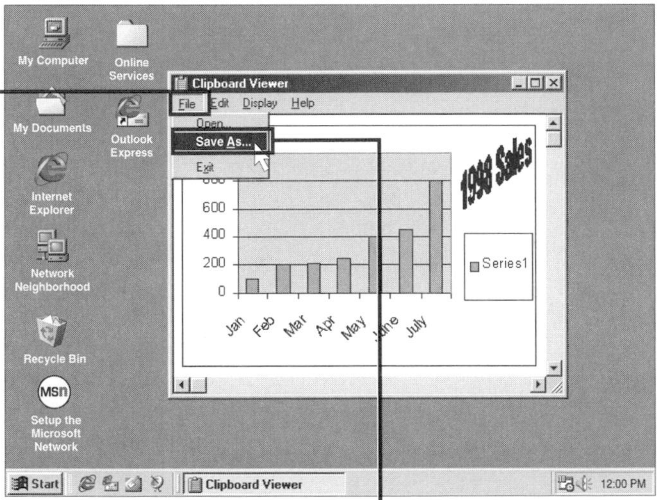

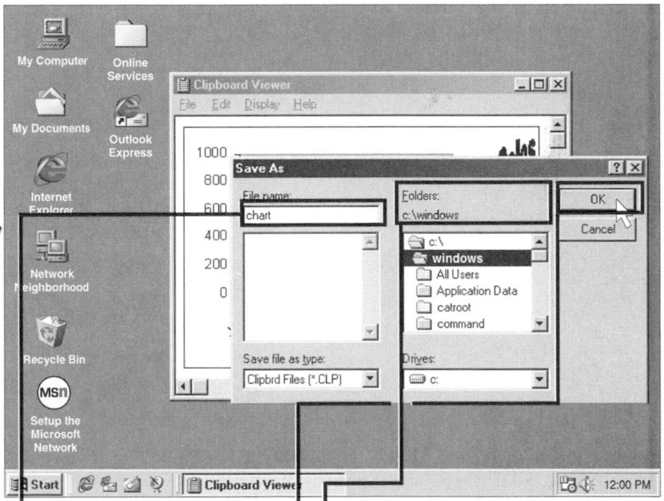

SAVE CLIPBOARD CONTENTS

1 Click File.

2 Click Save As.

■ The Save As dialog box appears.

3 Type a name for the file.

■ This area shows the location where Windows will store the file.

4 Click OK to save the file.

PUT PART OF DOCUMENT ON THE DESKTOP

You can place frequently used information on your desktop. This gives you quick access to the information. Information you place on the desktop is called a scrap.

Document scraps save you time since you do not have to retype the information over and over. For example, you can create a scrap containing your name, address and phone number. You can then drag the scrap into a document whenever you need the information.

You can also create a scrap for images, like your company logo. A scrap can also be a sound file that plays a message.

Using scraps is the easiest way to add frequently used information to your new documents.

Scraps are usually available for programs that allow you to drag and drop information and that support Object Linking and Embedding (OLE). For information on OLE, see page 126.

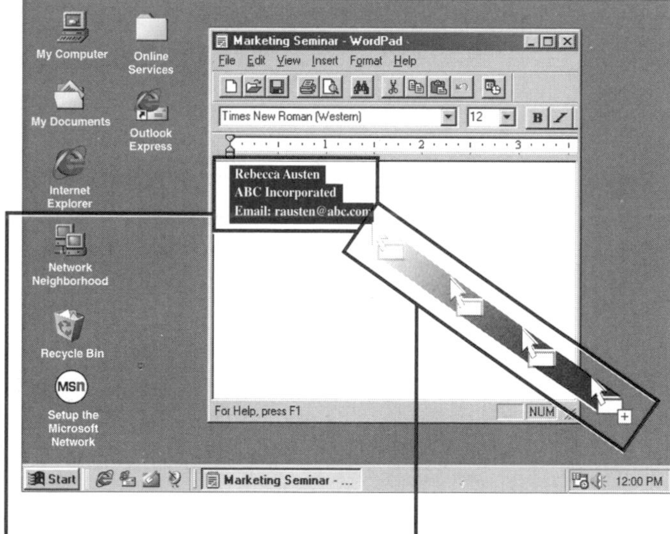

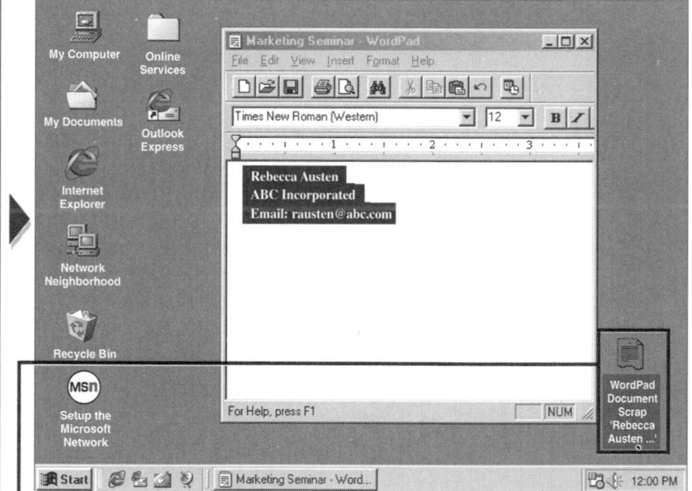

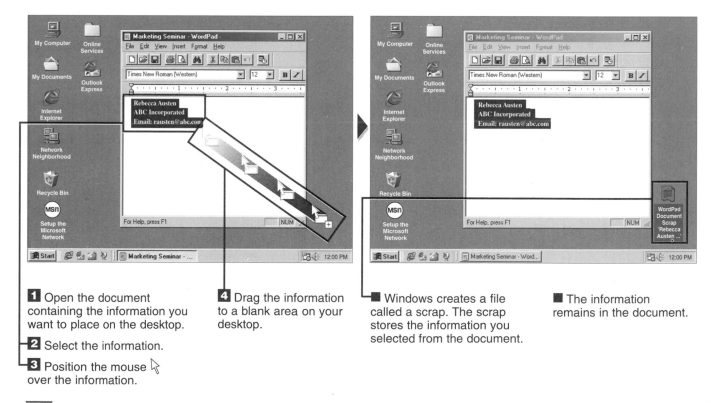

1 Open the document containing the information you want to place on the desktop.

2 Select the information.

3 Position the mouse over the information.

4 Drag the information to a blank area on your desktop.

■ Windows creates a file called a scrap. The scrap stores the information you selected from the document.

■ The information remains in the document.

TIPS

How can I remove a scrap I no longer need?

You can work with a scrap as you would work with any file on your desktop. To remove a scrap you no longer need, drag the scrap to the Recycle Bin.

Can I view or edit the contents of a scrap?

When you double-click a scrap, the program you used to create the scrap opens and displays the scrap. You can edit the scrap as you would any document.

How do I create a scrap from a program that does not support drag and drop or Object Linking and Embedding (OLE)?

You can often copy information from a program and then paste it on the desktop. For example, to create a scrap from a Paint image, select the image. Click the Edit menu and select Copy. Right-click the desktop and then select Paste to create the scrap.

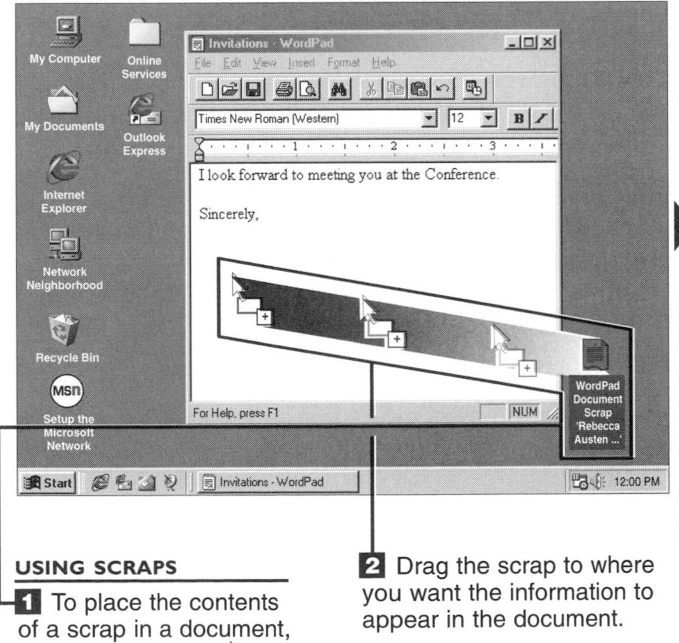

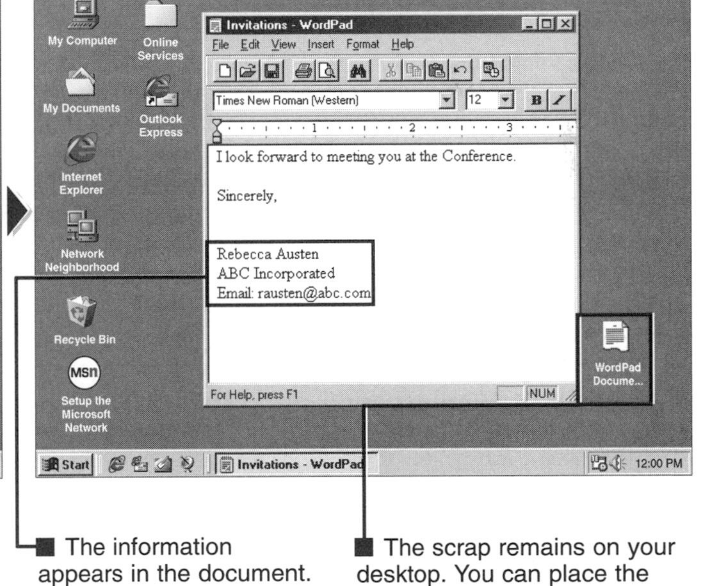

USING SCRAPS

1 To place the contents of a scrap in a document, position the mouse over the scrap.

2 Drag the scrap to where you want the information to appear in the document.

■ The information appears in the document.

■ The scrap remains on your desktop. You can place the information in as many documents as you wish.

EMBED INFORMATION

You can use Object Linking and Embedding (OLE, pronounced oh-lay) to create a document that contains information from several programs. This type of document is called a compound document.

Each piece of information used to create a compound document is called an object. You can use objects such as text, charts, graphs, images, sounds and video clips.

Each program on your computer is designed to work with a specific type of object. You can use specific programs to create objects and then embed all the objects you create in a compound document. For example, you can use a spreadsheet program to create a graph and a painting program to create an image. You can then embed these objects in a report created in a word processor.

When you embed objects, the objects become part of the compound document. The objects are not connected to the document they were created in.

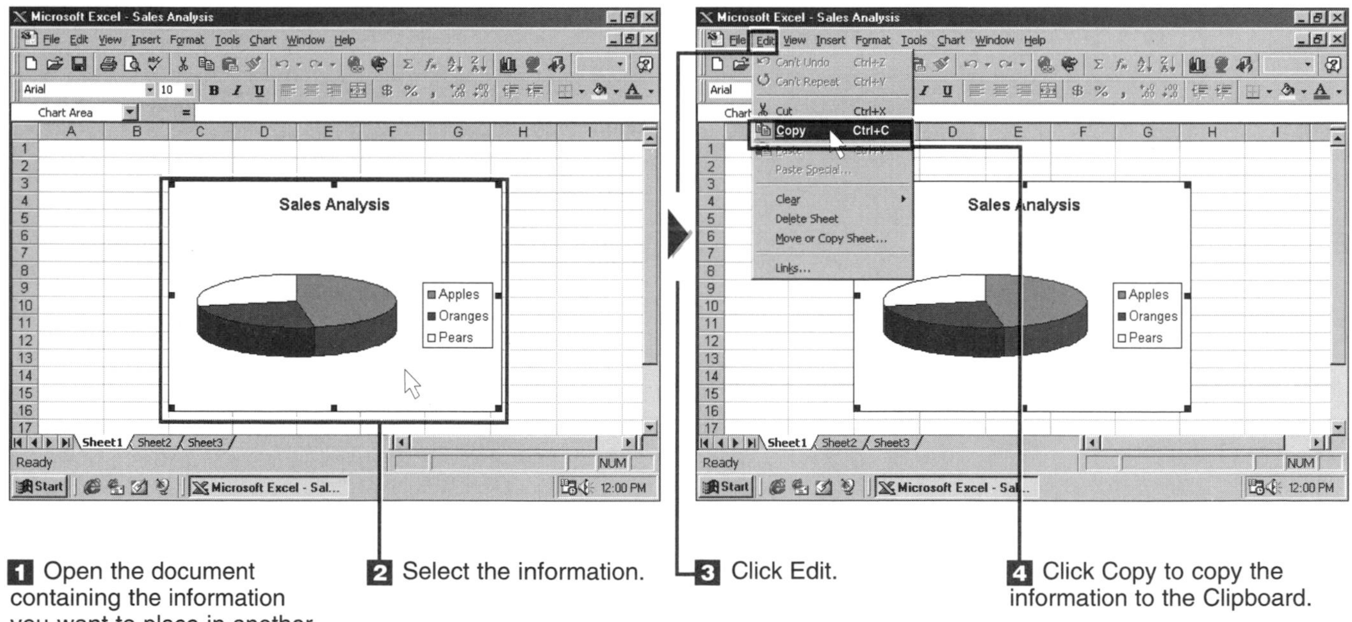

1 Open the document containing the information you want to place in another document.

2 Select the information.

3 Click Edit.

4 Click Copy to copy the information to the Clipboard.

TIPS

How can I tell if a program supports OLE?

If a program has the Paste Special command in the Edit menu, the program supports OLE.

Can I create a new object without first starting the program I want to use?

In the document you want to add an object to, choose the Insert or Create menu and then select the Object command. Select Create New and then click the type of object you want to create. You can use this procedure in the Microsoft, Lotus and Corel Office suites.

Can I use drag and drop to embed objects?

In programs that support drag and drop, you can drag and drop objects to embed them in another document. If you want to copy an object instead of moving it, hold down the Ctrl key as you drag and drop the object.

Can I embed an entire file in a document?

Yes. Choose the Insert or Create menu and then select the Object command. Select Create from File and then click the Browse button to find the document you want to embed. You can use this procedure in the Microsoft, Lotus and Corel Office suites.

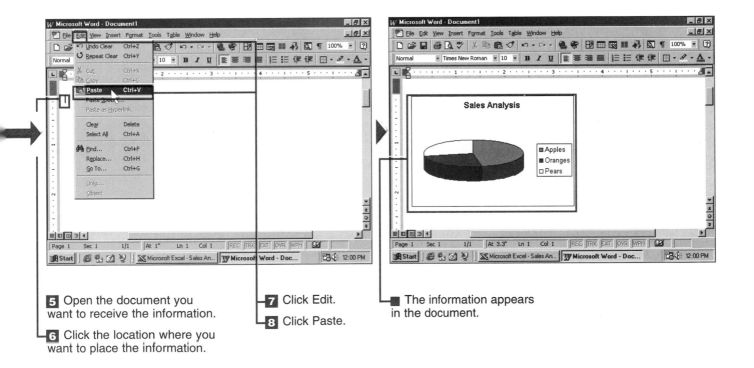

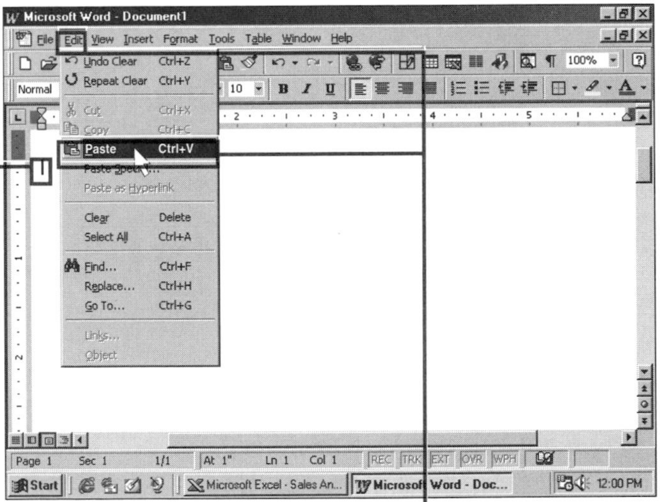

5 Open the document you want to receive the information.

6 Click the location where you want to place the information.

7 Click Edit.

8 Click Paste.

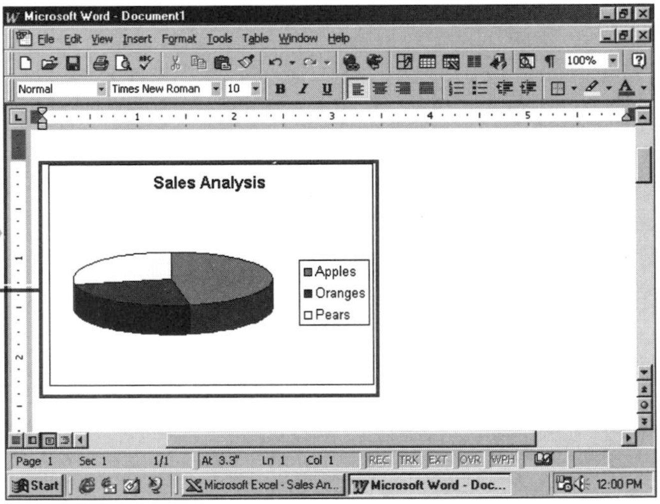

■ The information appears in the document.

EDIT EMBEDDED INFORMATION

You can change an embedded object in a compound document. You can edit the object using the same tools you used to create the object, without leaving the compound document.

An embedded object is part of the compound document. When you change an embedded object, the object in the original document does not change.

When you double-click an embedded object, the menus and toolbars of the program you used to create the object appear on your screen. In some circumstances, the embedded object may be displayed in a window and take on the appearance of the original program.

When you finish editing the object, the menus and toolbars from the original program are replaced by the menus and toolbars from the program used to create the compound document. You can then continue working with the compound document.

A compound document file is often large because it stores information about each embedded object and the program the object was created in.

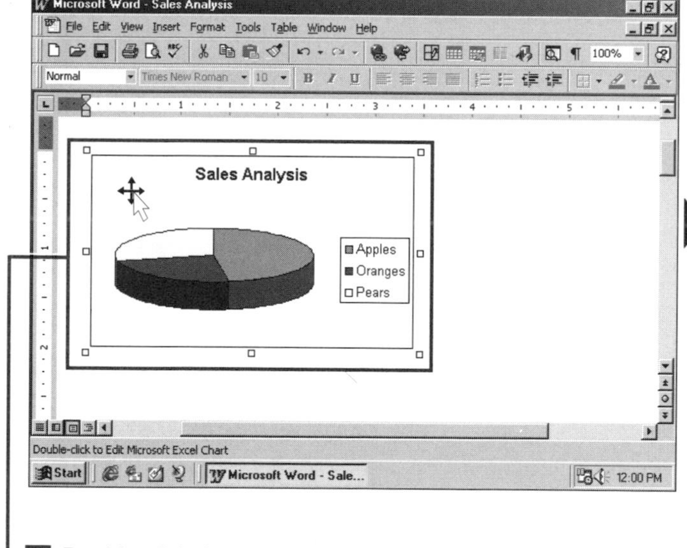

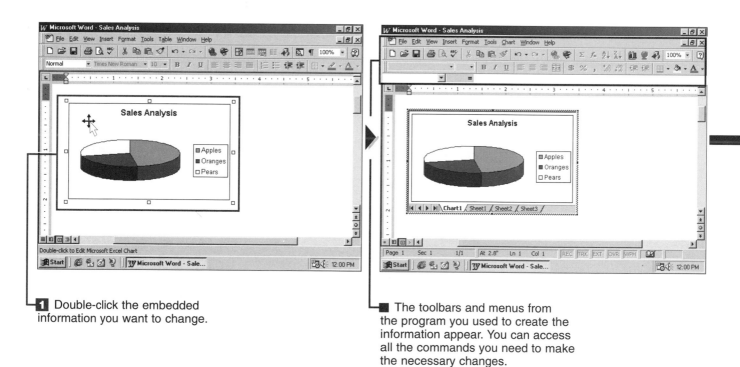

1 Double-click the embedded information you want to change.

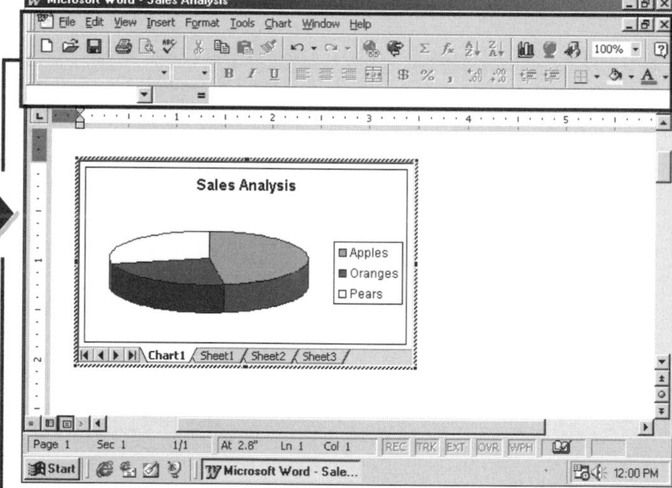

■ The toolbars and menus from the program you used to create the information appear. You can access all the commands you need to make the necessary changes.

TIPS

Why isn't an object I copied and pasted responding to my double-click?

When you copy and paste an object, the object may be only placed in the document, not embedded. You may need to paste the object again using a different procedure. Copy the object and then open the document where you want to embed the object. Choose the Edit menu and then select the Paste Special command. In the Paste Special dialog box, select Paste to embed the object.

Can I edit the objects in a document that someone else has created?

If you have the programs installed on your computer that were used to create the objects in the document, you can edit the objects. You will not be able to edit an object if you do not have the program used to create the object installed. You may not even be able to see the object.

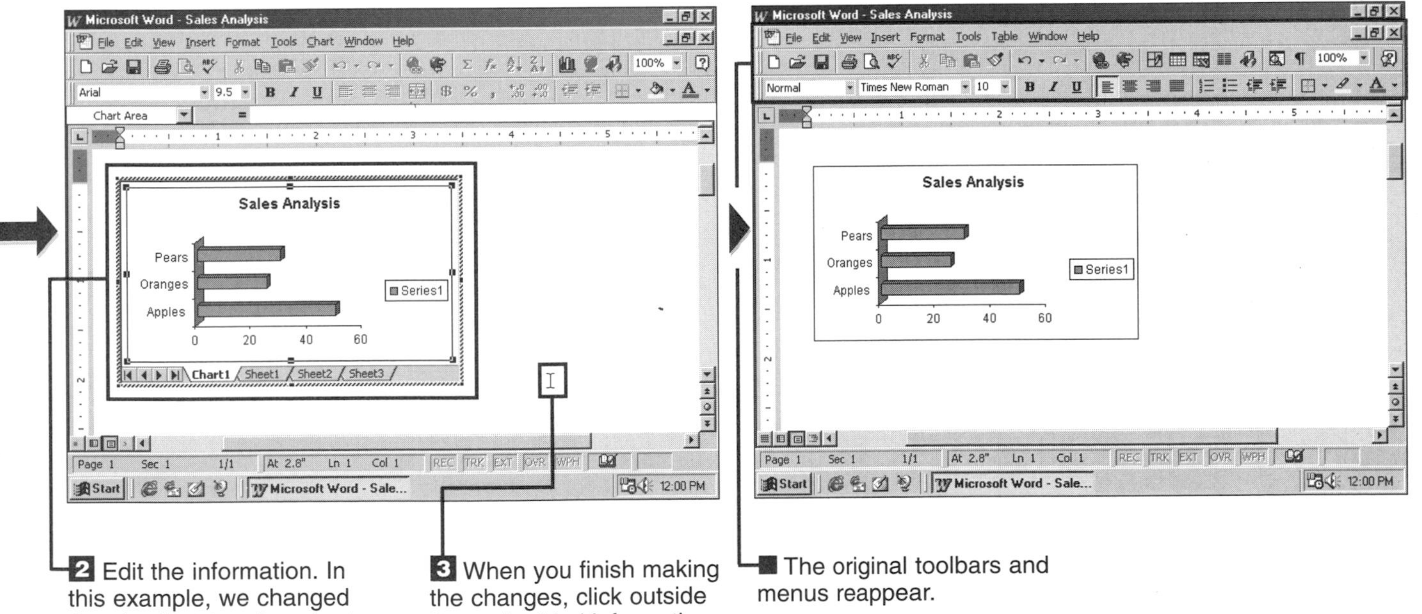

2 Edit the information. In this example, we changed the pie chart to a bar chart.

3 When you finish making the changes, click outside the embedded information.

■ The original toolbars and menus reappear.

LINK INFORMATION

You can use Object Linking and Embedding (OLE) to link the information in one document to one or more compound documents. A compound document can contain information from several sources.

The information you place in a compound document from another document is called an object and can include items such as text, pictures, charts, spreadsheets and slides. You can link an object between documents in the same program or in different programs. For example, you can link a chart in your spreadsheet to a report, a presentation and a newsletter.

When you link an object, the compound document displays the object but does not contain the object itself. The object remains in the original document. A connection, or link, exists between the original and compound documents. Since the linked object is always part of the original document, you should not delete, move or rename the original document.

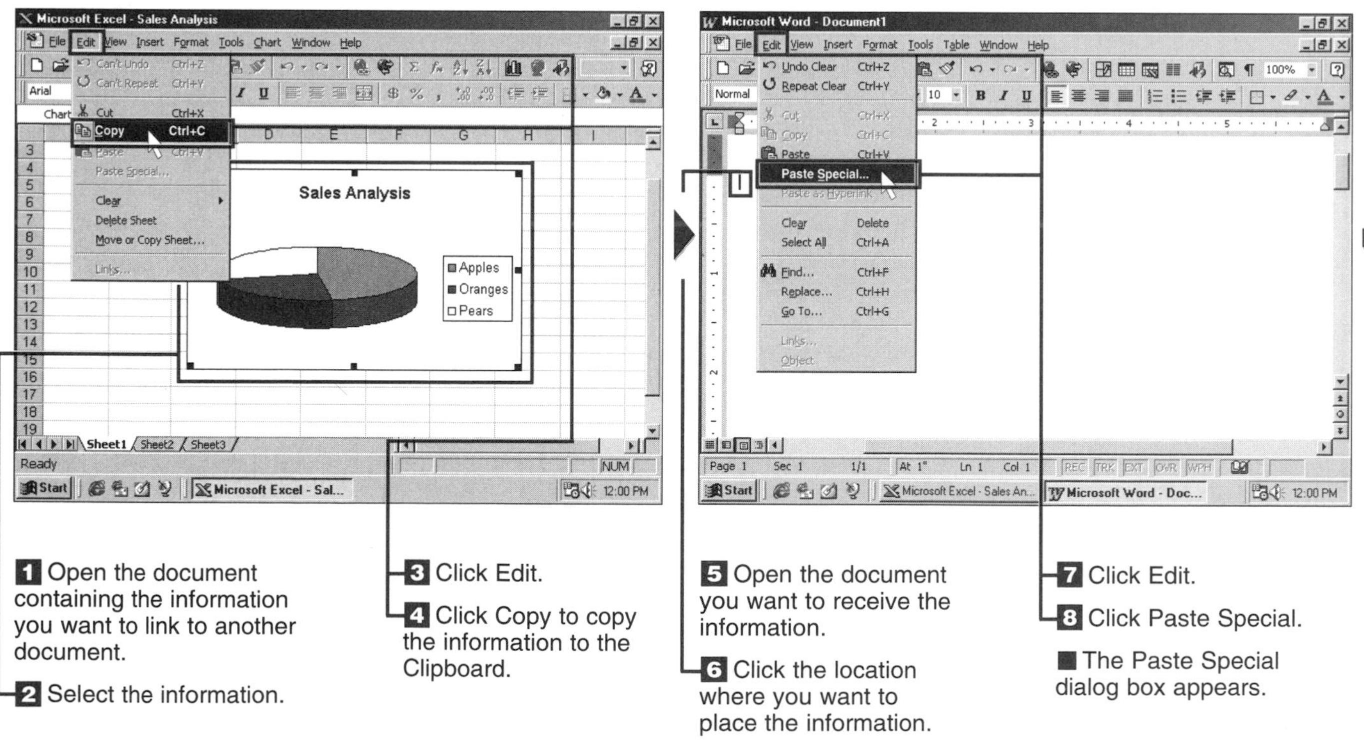

1 Open the document containing the information you want to link to another document.

2 Select the information.

3 Click Edit.

4 Click Copy to copy the information to the Clipboard.

5 Open the document you want to receive the information.

6 Click the location where you want to place the information.

7 Click Edit.

8 Click Paste Special.

■ The Paste Special dialog box appears.

TIPS

What is the difference between linking and embedding?

When you link an object, the object remains as a separate file that can be opened, changed and saved on its own. An embedded object becomes a part of the compound document and is not saved independently. For information on embedding, see page 126.

How can I tell if a program supports OLE?

If the program you are pasting an object into has the Paste Special command in the Edit menu, the program supports OLE. If the Paste link command is not available in the Paste Special dialog box, the program where you created the object may not fully support OLE.

Can I use drag and drop to link objects?

When you drag and drop an object, the object is embedded in the new document, not linked. For information on embedding, see page 126.

The information I linked between two documents created in the same program does not work properly. How can I fix this?

For many programs, the most reliable way to link information in the same program is to insert the information as an Object in the Paste Special dialog box.

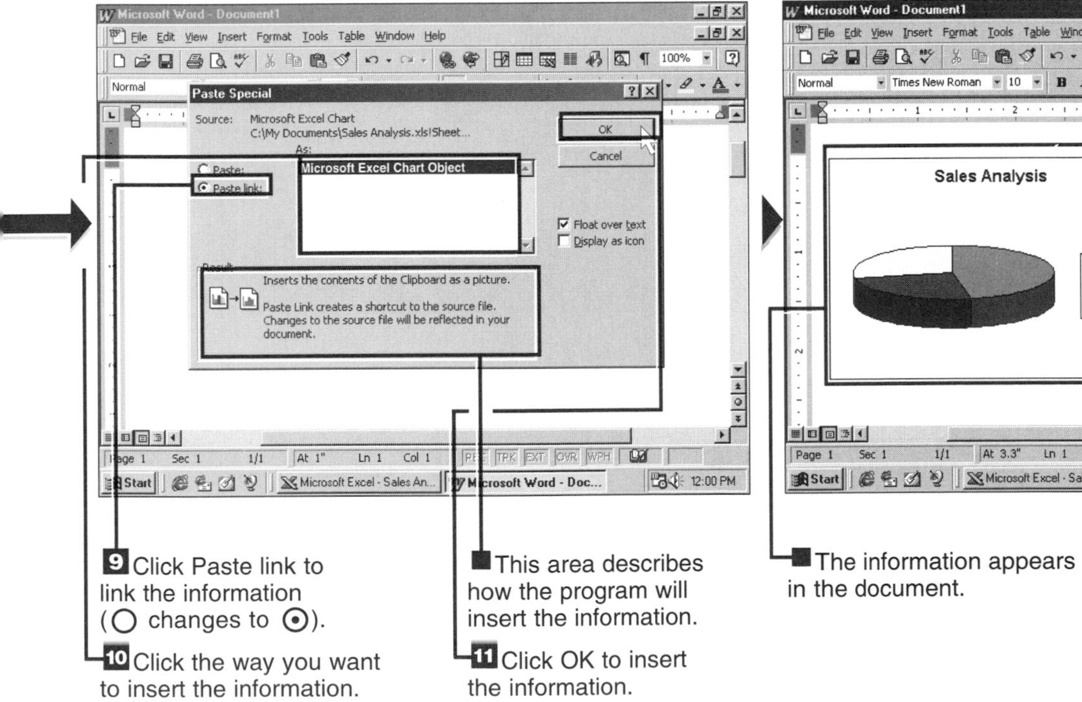

9 Click Paste link to link the information (○ changes to ⦿).

10 Click the way you want to insert the information.

■ This area describes how the program will insert the information.

11 Click OK to insert the information.

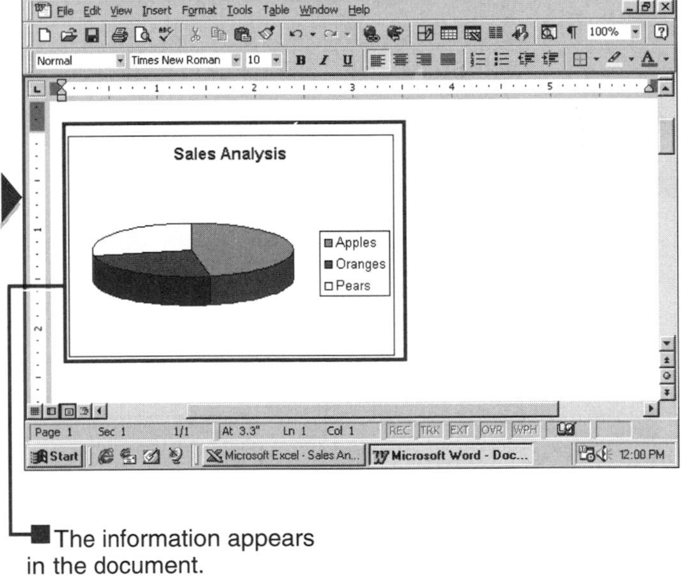

■ The information appears in the document.

EDIT LINKED INFORMATION

When you change a linked object, the original and compound documents both display the changes. If you have linked the same object to several documents, editing the linked object allows you to update all of the compound documents at the same time.

A compound document displays the object but does not contain the object itself. To edit the linked object, the original document must be available on your computer or network and the program used to create the object must be installed on your computer.

When you double-click a linked object in a compound document, the program used to create the object opens and displays the object in the original document. You can also go directly to the program to open the original document and display the object. You can then edit the linked object as you would edit any other object. All of the changes you make to the linked object appear in the compound documents.

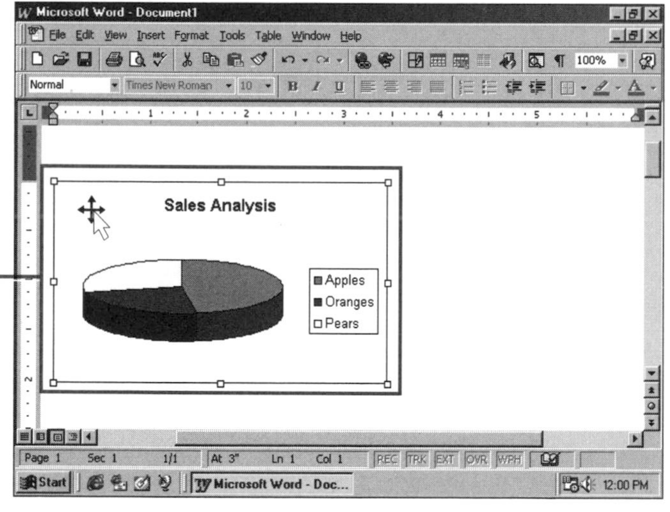

1 Double-click the linked information you want to change.

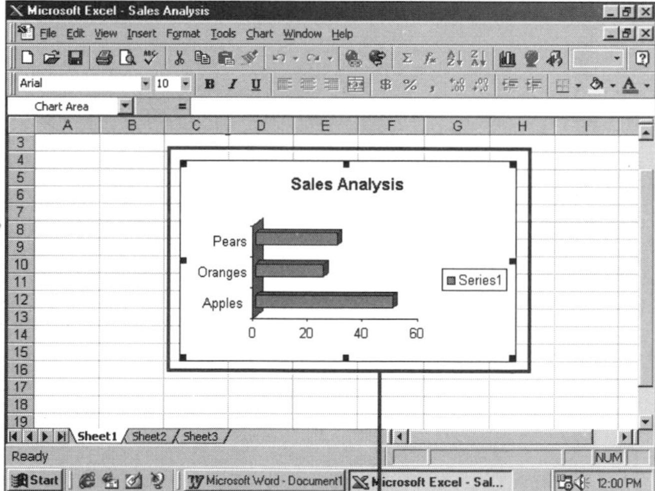

■ The program you used to create the information opens. You can access all the commands you need to make the necessary changes.

2 Edit the information. In this example, we changed the pie chart to a bar chart.

TIPS

How long does it take to update a linked object?

After you edit an object, the linked object will update within a few seconds in an open compound document. If a compound document is not open, you may be asked to update the linked object the next time you open the document.

How can I make sure the linked objects are up-to-date before I print a document?

You can choose the Edit menu and then select the Links command to view and update the links.

Can I e-mail a document that contains linked objects?

Yes, but if you e-mail the document to someone who does not have access to the original document, they will not be able to receive updates when you change the linked object. If the recipient does not have the program the object was created in, they will not be able to edit the compound document.

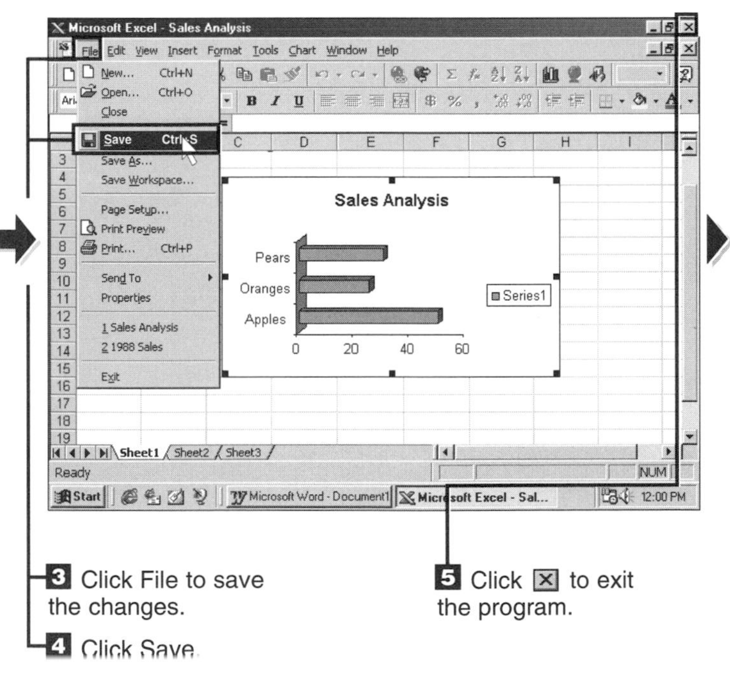

3 Click File to save the changes.

4 Click Save.

5 Click ☒ to exit the program.

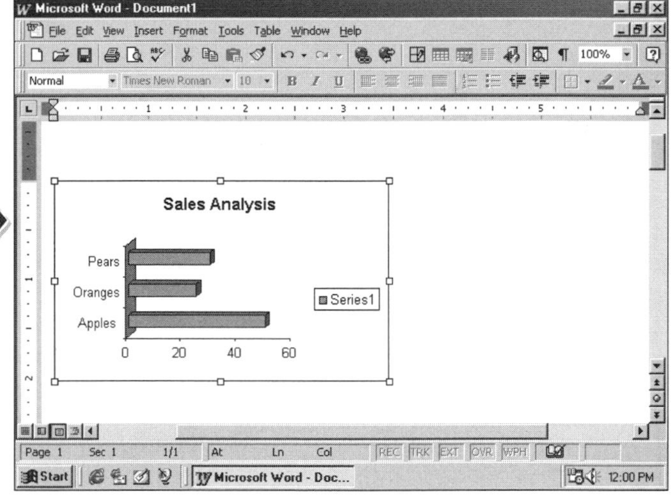

■ The linked document reappears, displaying the changes.

START AN MS-DOS PROMPT WINDOW

You can use the MS-DOS command prompt to work with MS-DOS programs and commands in Windows.

Windows can run almost all MS-DOS games and programs without any problem. Some MS-DOS utilities, such as backup programs, may not run properly in Windows. If you want to use these utility programs in Windows, a message may appear indicating that the program is not suitable for use with Windows or that the program cannot run while other programs are running.

To make the MS-DOS Prompt window easier to use, you can enlarge the window to fill your entire screen. You can also display text in the window in a different font.

Although you can have several MS-DOS Prompt windows open at the same time, they require some of your computer's resources. Having many MS-DOS windows open may slow down your computer's performance or prevent you from starting other MS-DOS or Windows programs.

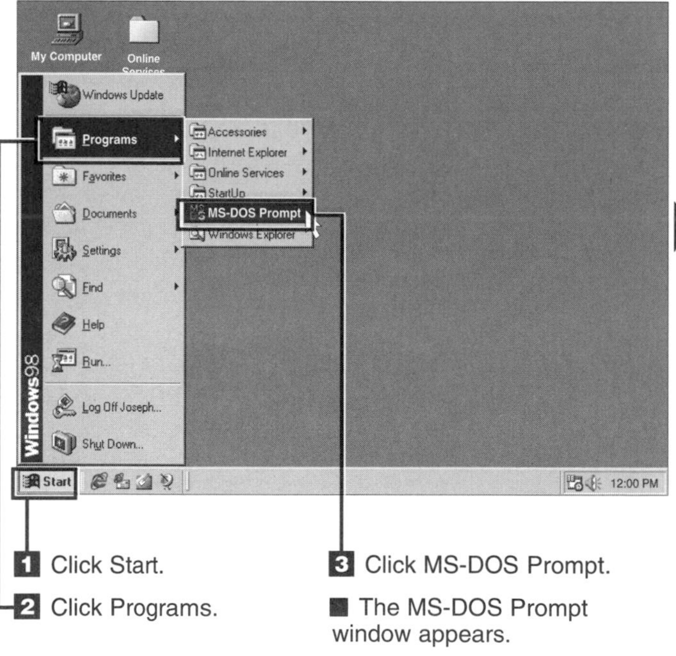

1 Click Start.

2 Click Programs.

3 Click MS-DOS Prompt.

■ The MS-DOS Prompt window appears.

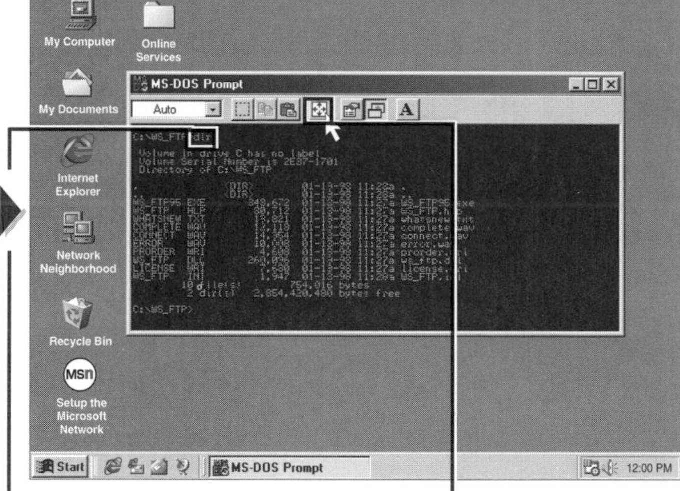

■ You can enter MS-DOS commands and start MS-DOS programs in the window. In this example, we enter the **dir** command to list the contents of the current directory.

4 Click to fill the entire screen with the MS-DOS Prompt window.

Note: You can also hold down the Alt key and then press the Enter key.

How do I change the size of the MS-DOS Prompt window?

When you choose a new font size, the size of the MS-DOS Prompt window also changes to accommodate the new font size. You can drag the edges of an MS-DOS window, but the window may not adjust to the new size properly.

Is there another way to close an MS-DOS Prompt window?

You can click ☒ to close the window, but a message may appear warning that you will lose any unsaved information.

How can I find out what commands MS-DOS uses?

In the MS-DOS window, type **cd c:\windows\command** to open the folder that contains the MS-DOS commands included with Windows. Then type **dir** to list the commands.

How can I find out what each MS-DOS command does?

Type the name of a command followed by /? For example, you can type **move/?** to find out what the move command does.

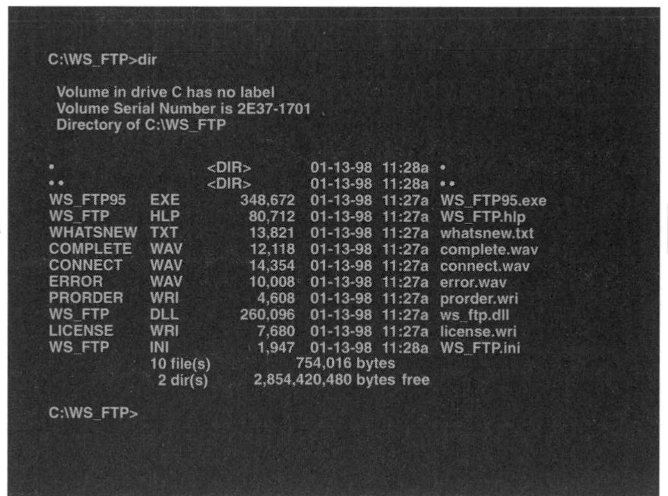

C:\WS_FTP>dir
Volume in drive C has no label
Volume Serial Number is 2E37-1701
Directory of C:\WS_FTP
. <DIR> 01-13-98 11:28a .
.. <DIR> 01-13-98 11:28a ..
WS_FTP95 EXE 348,672 01-13-98 11:27a WS_FTP95.exe
WS_FTP HLP 80,712 01-13-98 11:27a WS_FTP.hlp
WHATSNEW TXT 13,821 01-13-98 11:27a whatsnew.txt
COMPLETE WAV 12,118 01-13-98 11:27a complete.wav
CONNECT WAV 14,354 01-13-98 11:27a connect.wav
ERROR WAV 10,008 01-13-98 11:27a error.wav
PRORDER WRI 4,608 01-13-98 11:27a prorder.wri
WS_FTP DLL 260,096 01-13-98 11:27a ws_ftp.dll
LICENSE WRI 7,680 01-13-98 11:27a license.wri
WS_FTP INI 1,947 01-13-98 11:28a WS_FTP.ini
10 file(s) 754,016 bytes
2 dir(s) 2,854,420,480 bytes free
C:\WS_FTP>

■ The MS-DOS Prompt window fills the entire screen.

5 Hold down the Alt key and then press the Enter key to return the MS-DOS screen to a window.

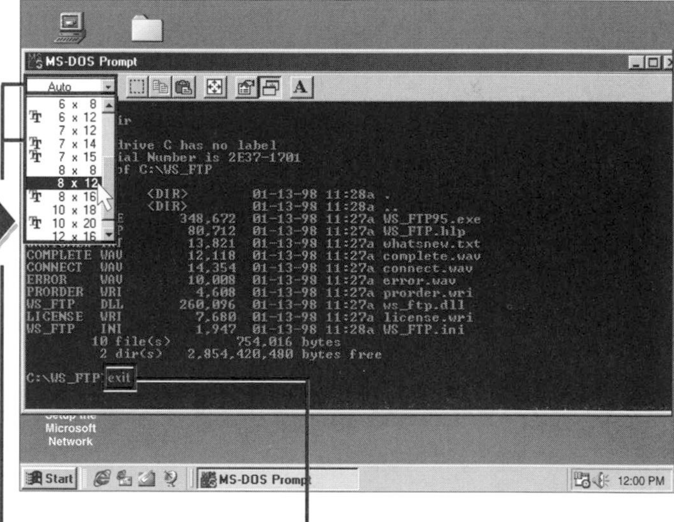

6 Click this area to change the font of the text.

7 Click the font you want to use.

■ The window displays the new font.

8 When you finish using the MS-DOS Prompt window, type **exit** and then press the Enter key to close the window.

COPY DATA BETWEEN MS-DOS AND WINDOWS PROGRAMS

You can copy and paste information from MS-DOS programs to Windows programs.

When you begin using Windows, you do not need to abandon your old MS-DOS programs or files. If your new Windows programs cannot open your old MS-DOS files, you can still use your older files by opening them in the MS-DOS program. You can then copy the information you need from the old documents and paste it into a document in a Windows program. Copying and pasting information from MS-DOS is not as efficient as in Windows programs, but it is better than having to find a paper copy of the document and then retyping it into a Windows program.

When you copy information from an MS-DOS program, you lose the format of the text and the word wrap. Any pasted text is displayed in the default font of the program you are copying to and a paragraph break is inserted at the end of every line.

You can also copy and paste MS-DOS commands and their results. For example, you can copy the directory listing created using the dir command and paste it into a text document.

1 Click ⬚ to turn on the marking mode.

Note: To display the MS-DOS Prompt window, see page 134.

■ A flashing cursor appears at the top of the window.

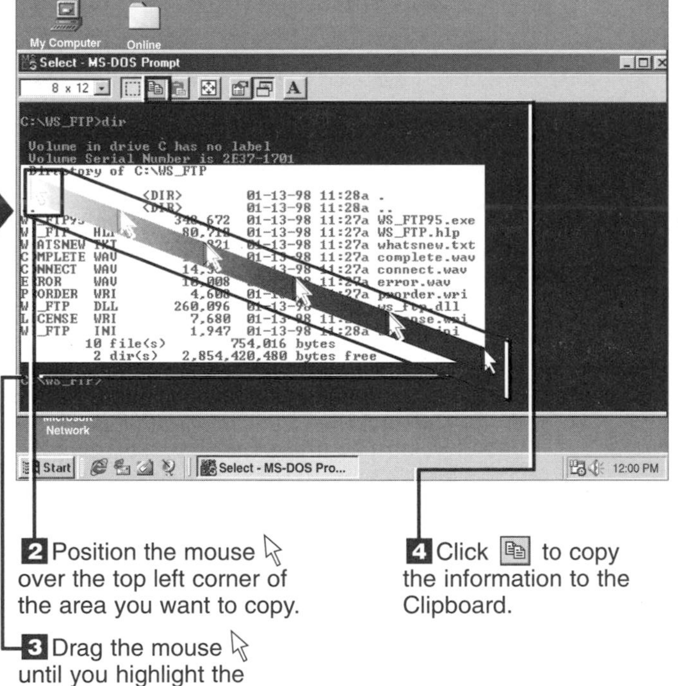

2 Position the mouse over the top left corner of the area you want to copy.

3 Drag the mouse until you highlight the area you want to copy.

4 Click to copy the information to the Clipboard.

Can I take a picture of the MS-DOS window?

To take a picture of the MS-DOS window, click anywhere in the window and then press Alt+Print Scrn. You can then paste the picture of the MS-DOS window in a document.

Can I copy text from an MS-DOS program displayed in full screen mode?

You cannot copy specific text if an MS-DOS program is displayed in full screen mode. You can copy all the text from the screen at once by pressing the Print Scrn key. You can then paste the text into a document.

Is there an easier way to select the text I want to copy?

You can use the QuickEdit mode instead of having to turn on the marking mode each time you want to select text. To turn on the QuickEdit mode, click to open the Properties dialog box. Select the Misc tab and click QuickEdit (☐ changes to ☑). In the QuickEdit mode, the mouse is used to highlight text at all times. You cannot use the mouse as a pointing device in the MS-DOS program when the QuickEdit mode is on.

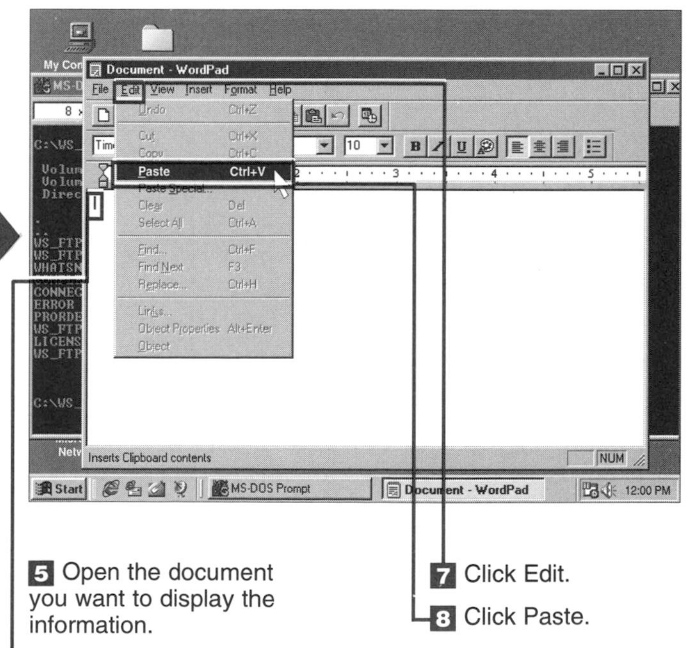

5 Open the document you want to display the information.

6 Click the location where you want to place the information.

7 Click Edit.

8 Click Paste.

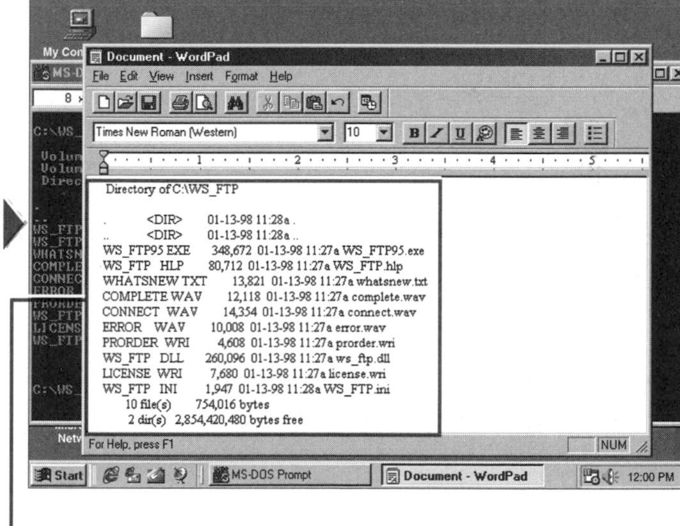

■ The information from the MS-DOS window appears in the document.

INSTALL AND RUN MS-DOS PROGRAMS

Programs designed to work with MS-DOS can be installed and used in Windows 98.

Before you can use an MS-DOS program, you must locate and run the installation program. Many programs provide a file with documentation to help you install the program. These files often have names such as "readme.txt" or "install.txt". You should read these files before installing any programs.

If a documentation file does not exist or does not contain specific installation information, look for the file you need to install the program on your computer. This file may start with the word install, setup or go, and may also have the .bat extension.

When you install an MS-DOS game, the program will often ask questions about the devices on your computer, such as a joystick or sound card. The program will then set itself up to work with your computer.

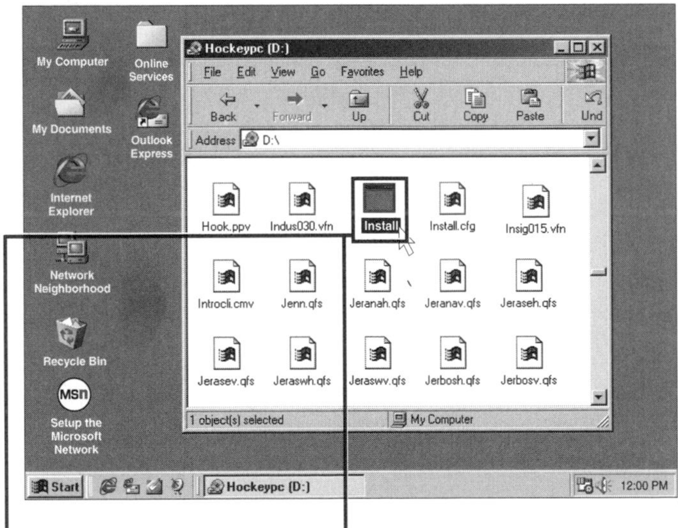

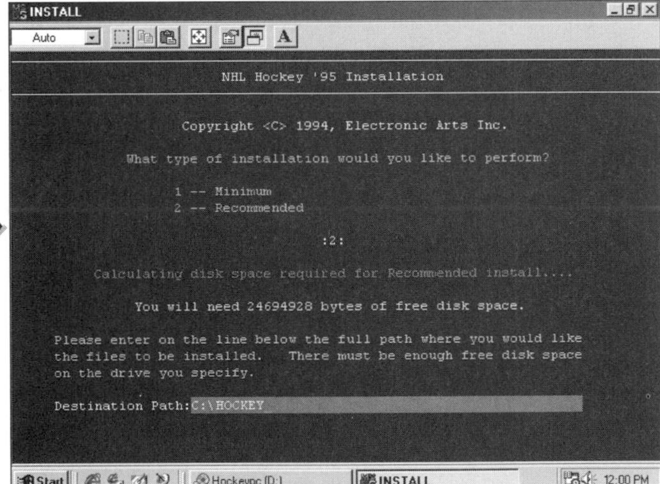

INSTALL A PROGRAM

1 Locate the installation file for the program you want to install.

Note: If you downloaded the program from the Internet, look for the file on your computer. If you bought the program at a store, look for the file on a floppy disk or CD-ROM disc.

2 Double-click the installation file.

■ The installation program starts.

3 Follow the instructions on your screen. Every program will install differently. In this example, we are installing a game named NHL Hockey '95.

Can I place the program on the Start menu?

MS-DOS programs you install do not appear on the Start menu. To add a program to the Start menu, you can drag the file you use to start the program onto the Start menu. See page 260 for more information.

How can I delete an MS-DOS program?

To delete an MS-DOS program, drag the folder that contains the program files to the Recycle Bin. Make sure the folder does not contain any documents you still need. You should also remove any shortcuts to the program on the desktop and the Start menu.

What can I do if there is no installation program provided?

Create a new folder on your computer and copy all the program's files into the folder. Use the program file to start the program. If you are not sure which is the program file, look for a file with a .bat, .com or .exe extension.

Why does my MS-DOS program indicate that there is no room left on my hard drive?

Some MS-DOS programs may be incompatible with FAT32 on drives larger than 2 GB. Contact the manufacturer of your MS-DOS program to see if an updated version of the program is available.

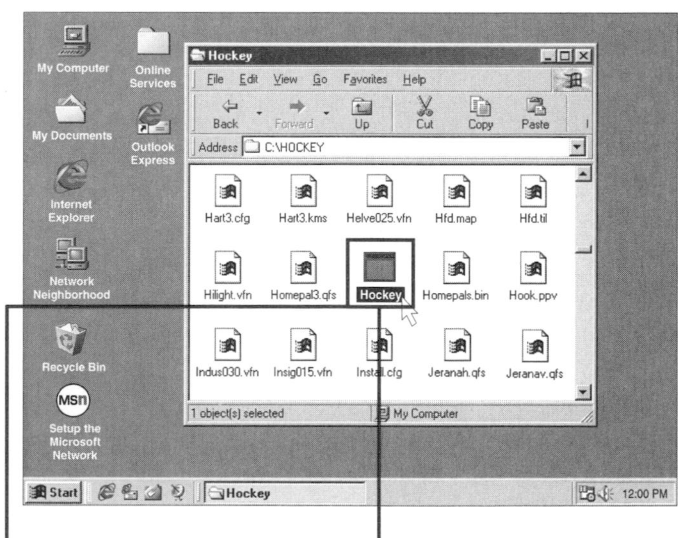

RUN A PROGRAM

1 Locate the file that runs the program.

Note: The file name often contains the name of the program.

2 Double-click the file.

■ The program starts.

OPTIMIZE MS-DOS PROGRAMS

General and Font Settings

You can view the General settings for an MS-DOS program to see additional information about the program. The General tab displays information about a program, including the size, the MS-DOS name and the date and time the file was created. You can also check the attributes for a file. Attributes include Read-only, Archive, Hidden and System. You should not have to change the attributes that Windows sets for the program.

You can use the Font settings in the Properties dialog box to select the font type and size you want to use for a program. The font you select determines the size of the window displaying the program. You can see a preview of the font and the way the program will appear on your screen. Changing the Font settings can make the program easier to view and use.

If you make changes to the Font settings, the new settings are saved and used when you run the program again.

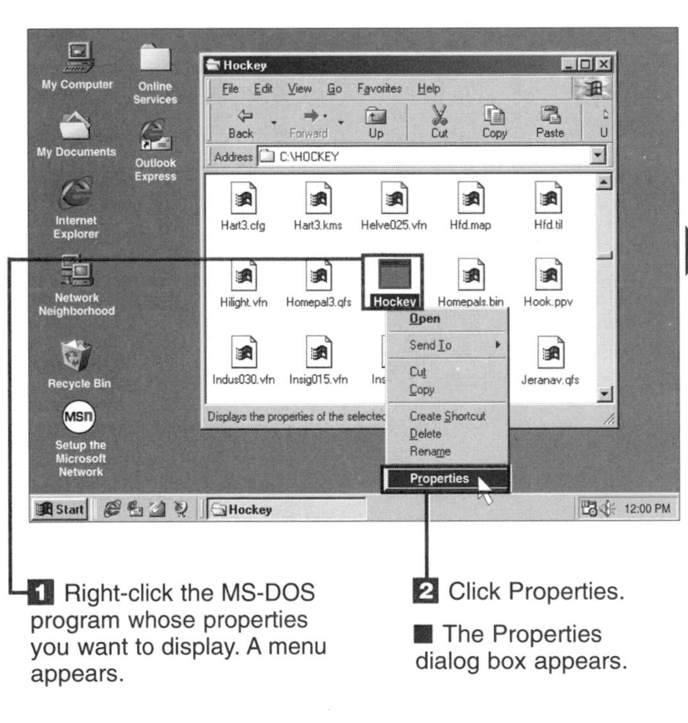

1 Right-click the MS-DOS program whose properties you want to display. A menu appears.

2 Click Properties.

■ The Properties dialog box appears.

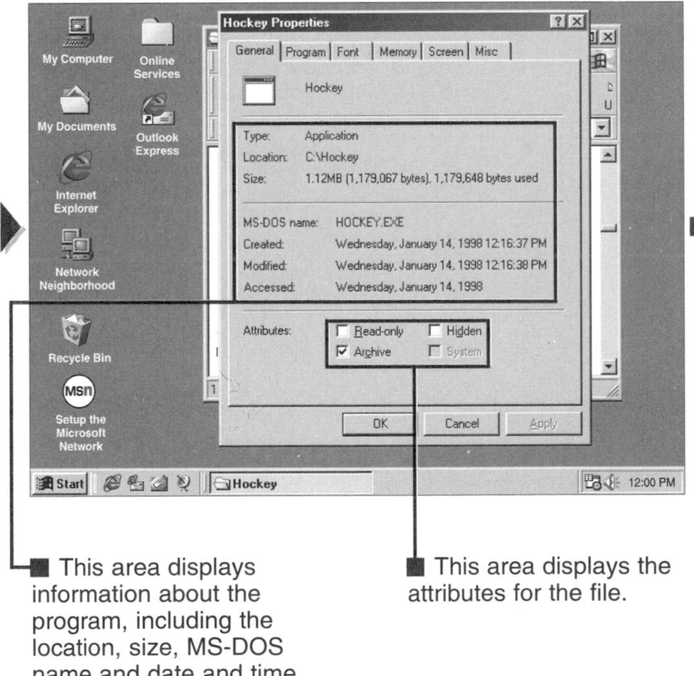

■ This area displays information about the program, including the location, size, MS-DOS name and date and time the file was created.

■ This area displays the attributes for the file.

TIPS

Why isn't the General tab shown in the Properties dialog box?

If you are displaying the Properties dialog box for a program that is currently running, the General tab is not available.

I selected a different font size. Why doesn't the font change in full screen MS-DOS mode?

Changing the font size will not affect the way text appears when a program is displayed in full screen mode.

Which font should I use?

Each font creates a window of a different size. You may find some font sizes and types easier to read than others. If you leave the font setting at Auto, Windows will use the appropriate font for the window size you use.

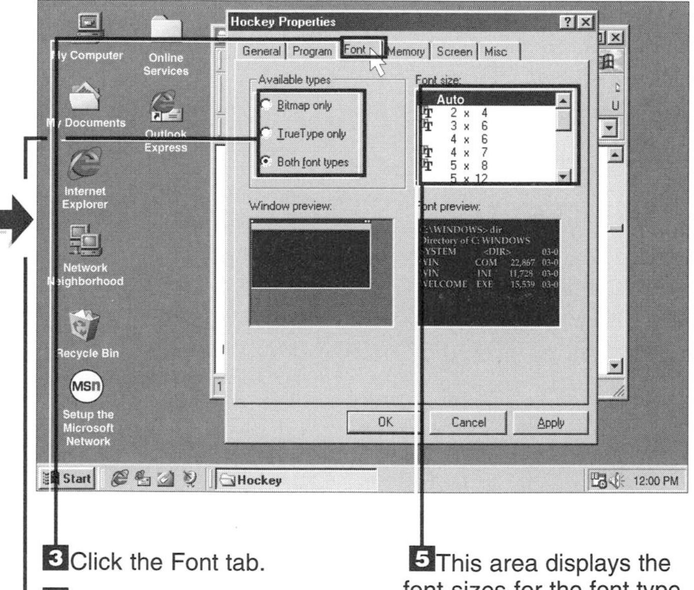

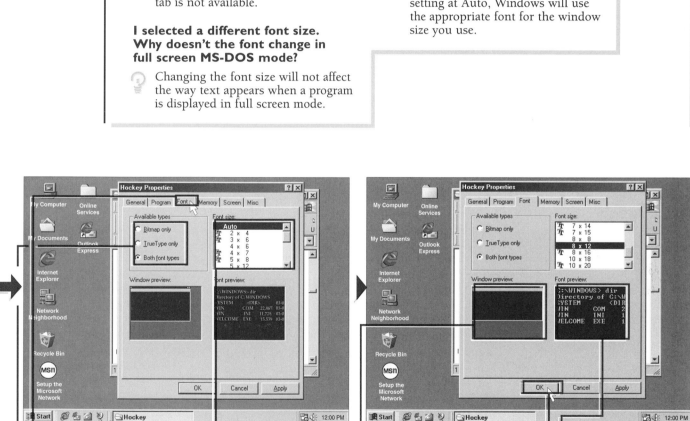

3 Click the Font tab.

4 This area displays the types of fonts available for the program. Click the type of font you want to use (○ changes to ⊙).

5 This area displays the font sizes for the font type you selected. Click the font size you want to use.

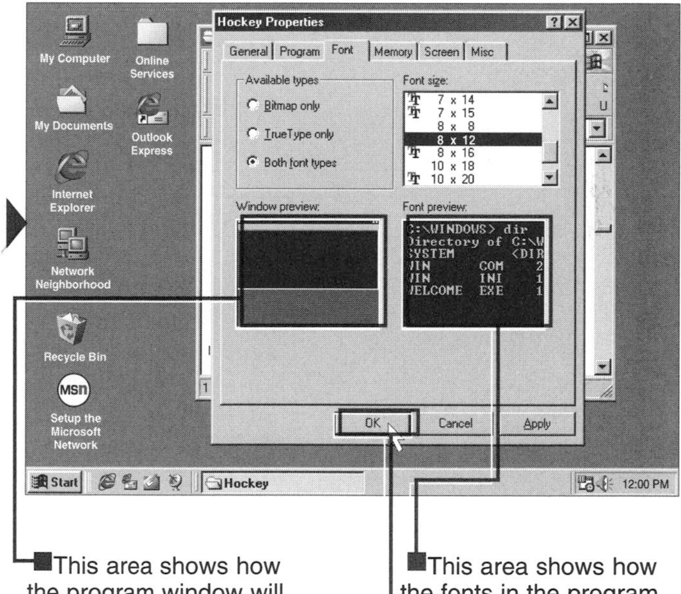

■ This area shows how the program window will appear on your screen.

■ This area shows how the fonts in the program window will appear.

6 Click OK to confirm your changes.

OPTIMIZE MS-DOS PROGRAMS

Change Program Settings

You can adjust the Program settings to control the way an MS-DOS program starts.

You can view the program name and icon, as well as the command that starts the program. There are additional icons you can choose from to represent the program.

You can specify the folder where you want the program to open and save files.

If the program needs to run a batch file, you can specify the name of the batch file. A batch file is a text file that contains commands your computer requires to run the program properly.

If you use the program regularly, you may want to give the program a keyboard shortcut so you can start the program using the keyboard.

When you start the program, you can have the program appear as a window, minimized as a button on the taskbar or as a maximized window on your screen.

You can have the MS-DOS window close automatically or stay open after you close the program.

After you change the Program settings, you must restart your computer for the new settings to take effect.

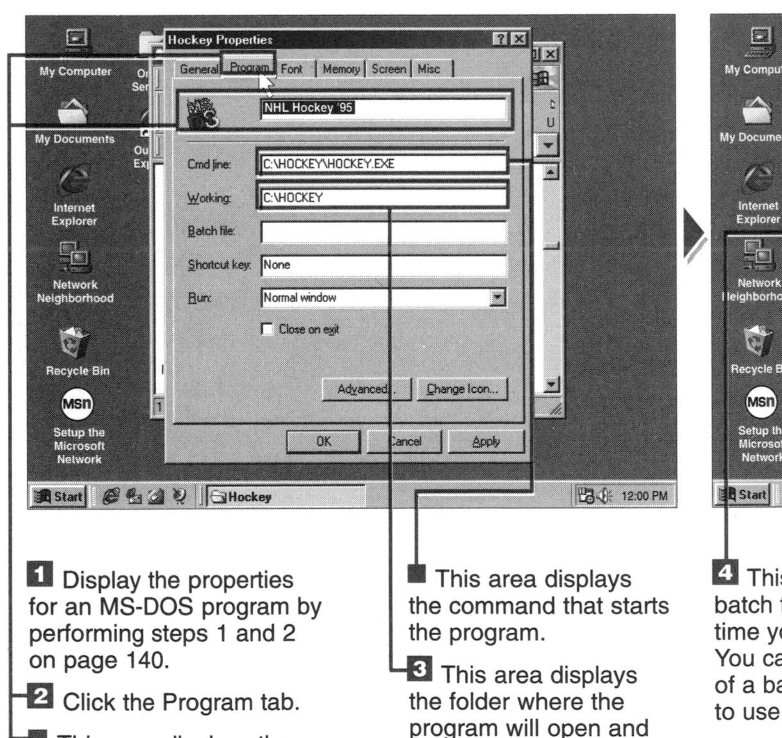

1 Display the properties for an MS-DOS program by performing steps 1 and 2 on page 140.

2 Click the Program tab.

■ This area displays the program icon and name.

■ This area displays the command that starts the program.

3 This area displays the folder where the program will open and save files. You can change this information.

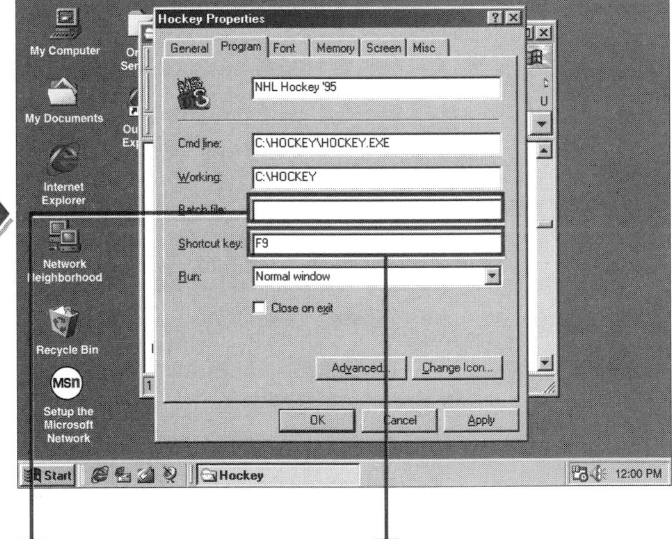

4 This area displays the batch file that runs each time you start the program. You can enter the name of a batch file you want to use.

5 This area displays the keyboard shortcut that will activate the program. You can click this area and then press the keyboard key(s) you want to use.

TIPS

How do I know if a program needs to run a batch file?

You can consult the program's manual or look for a readme file included with the program for more information about a batch file the program may need.

What shortcut key combination should I use?

You should use a combination made up of Ctrl or Alt and another key, such as Ctrl+Y. You may also use a function key that is not assigned to another task.

Why won't my shortcut key start the program?

A shortcut key will only start the program if the program is on the desktop or on the Start menu. Your shortcut key will also not work if it is assigned to another task in Windows.

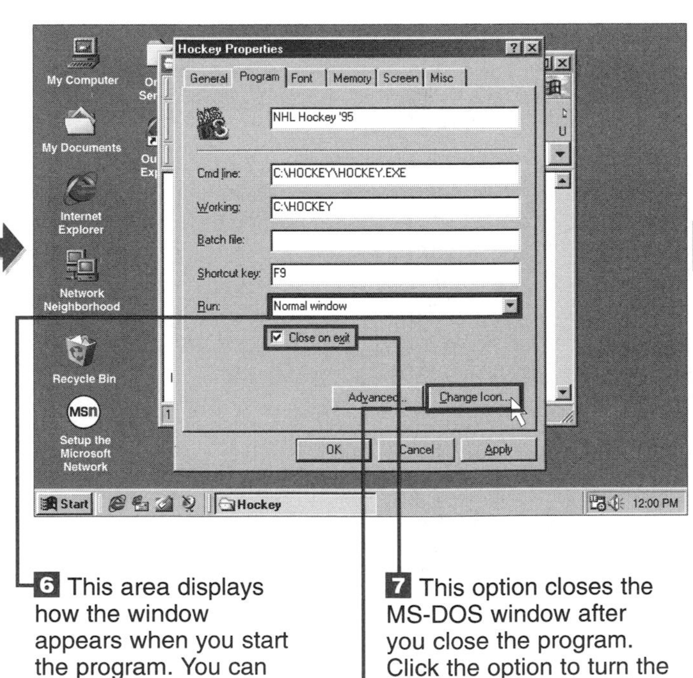

6 This area displays how the window appears when you start the program. You can click ▼ in this area to change the way the window appears.

7 This option closes the MS-DOS window after you close the program. Click the option to turn the option on (☑) or off (☐).

8 Click Change Icon to change the icon for the program.

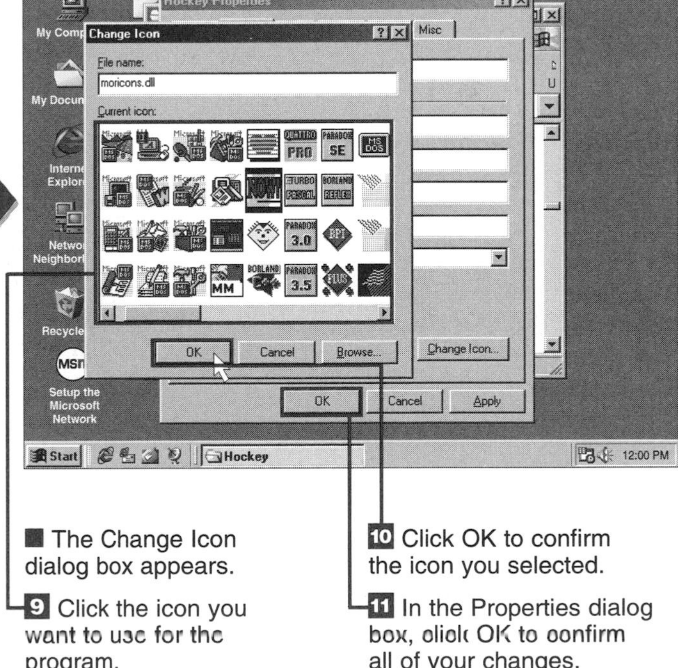

■ The Change Icon dialog box appears.

9 Click the icon you want to use for the program.

10 Click OK to confirm the icon you selected.

11 In the Properties dialog box, click OK to confirm all of your changes.

OPTIMIZE MS-DOS PROGRAMS

Change Advanced Program Settings

When you encounter problems with an MS-DOS program, adjusting the Advanced Program settings may help the program operate properly.

Some programs may not run properly or not run at all if they detect that Windows is running on the computer at the same time. You can choose to prevent the MS-DOS program from detecting Windows.

Some programs must be in MS-DOS mode to run properly. MS-DOS mode allows the program to shut down Windows and take complete control of your computer. You can have Windows determine whether the program requires MS-DOS mode or you can set the program to automatically use MS-DOS mode each time it runs.

When running a program in MS-DOS mode, you can have a warning appear before your other programs are shut down.

In MS-DOS mode, a program can use its own personalized set of startup configuration files. These files enable the program to run properly.

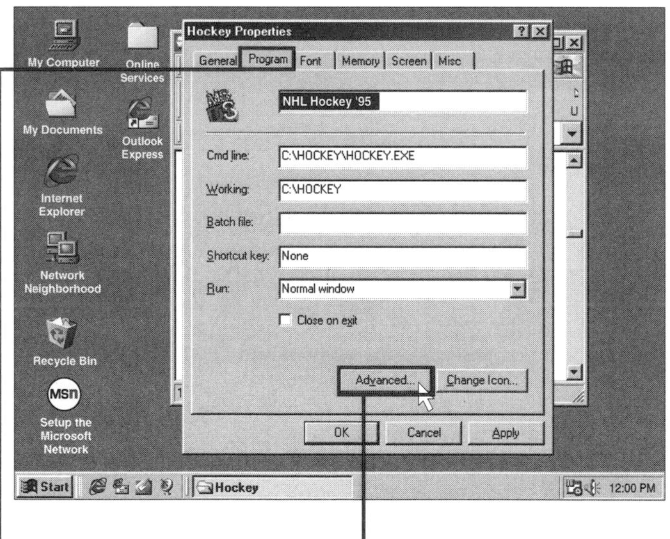

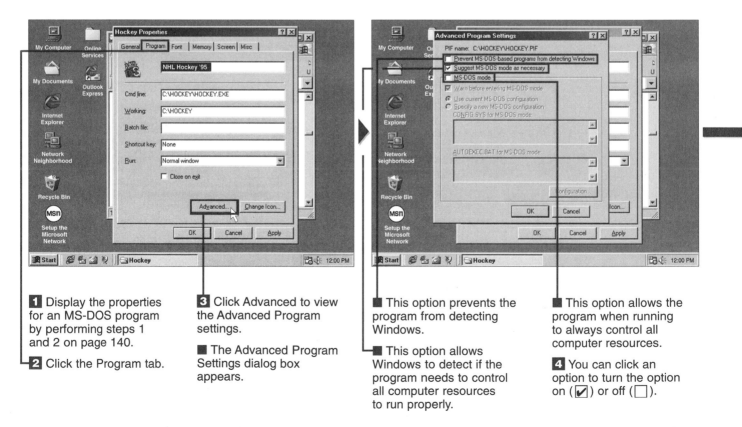

1 Display the properties for an MS-DOS program by performing steps 1 and 2 on page 140.

2 Click the Program tab.

3 Click Advanced to view the Advanced Program settings.

■ The Advanced Program Settings dialog box appears.

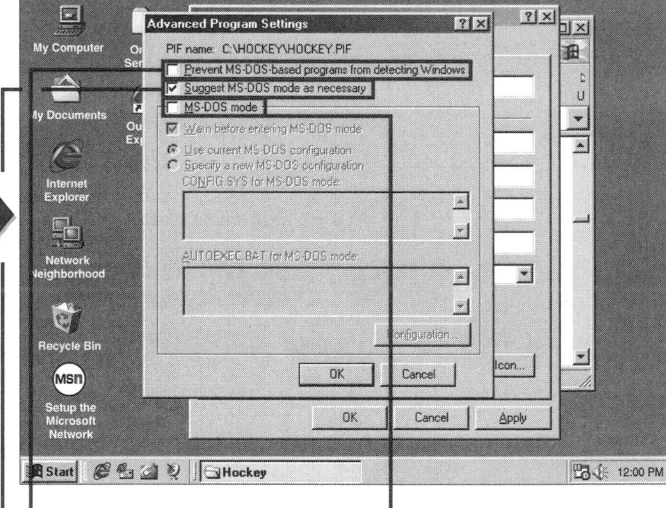

■ This option prevents the program from detecting Windows.

■ This option allows Windows to detect if the program needs to control all computer resources to run properly.

■ This option allows the program when running to always control all computer resources.

4 You can click an option to turn the option on (☑) or off (☐).

TIPS

When should I change the Advanced Program settings?

You should change the Advanced Program settings only as the last resort for programs that will not run properly.

What settings should I use in the Config.sys and Autoexec.bat files?

You can usually find details on the best settings for the configuration files in the MS-DOS program's manual. Help files or other instruction files on the program's disk or CD-ROM disc may also contain configuration information.

How do I set up the mouse in an MS-DOS program?

In the Advanced Program Settings dialog box, click the Configuration button to display the Select MS-DOS Configuration Options dialog box. If a warning dialog box appears, click Yes to continue. Select Mouse from the list (☐ changes to ☑) and then click OK. The mouse is not available for all programs.

Note: You may have to select MS-DOS mode and Specify a new MS-DOS configuration for the Configuration button to be available.

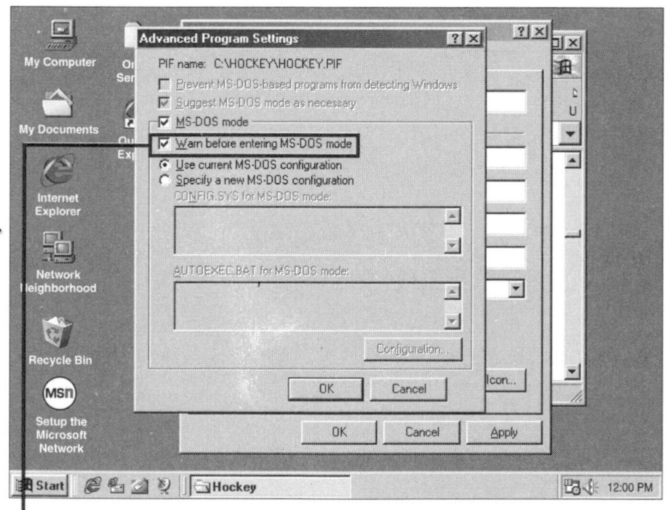

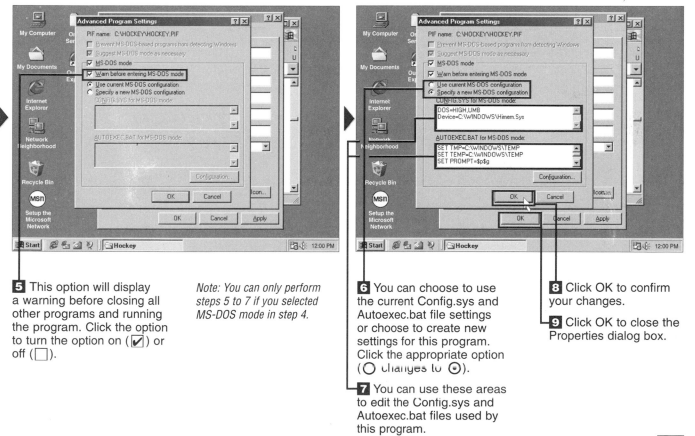

5 This option will display a warning before closing all other programs and running the program. Click the option to turn the option on (☑) or off (☐).

Note: You can only perform steps 5 to 7 if you selected MS-DOS mode in step 4.

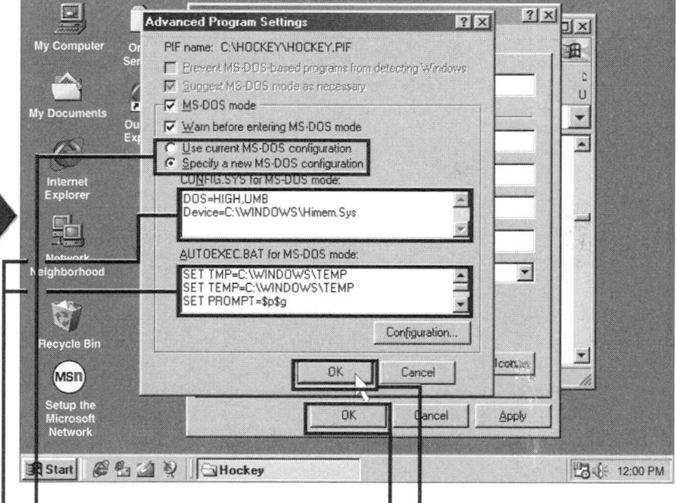

6 You can choose to use the current Config.sys and Autoexec.bat file settings or choose to create new settings for this program. Click the appropriate option (○ changes to ◉).

7 You can use these areas to edit the Config.sys and Autoexec.bat files used by this program.

8 Click OK to confirm your changes.

9 Click OK to close the Properties dialog box.

OPTIMIZE MS-DOS PROGRAMS

Change Memory Settings

You can manage the memory requirements of an MS-DOS program. You should leave the memory requirements set at Auto unless the program is not working properly. Before changing any memory settings, you should consult the program's manual or readme file to find the specific settings the program requires. Memory settings are saved and used each time you start the program.

If the amount of conventional memory for the program needs to be adjusted, you can specify a new amount in kilobytes (K). You can also protect other programs in memory from being affected by errors in the MS-DOS program. The MS-DOS program may run slower when you protect other programs in memory.

You can specify the maximum amount of expanded and extended memory for the program in kilobytes (K). You can also specify if the program can use the High Memory Area (HMA).

Windows chooses an amount of MS-DOS protected-mode memory for the program based on the setup of your computer. You can choose a different amount.

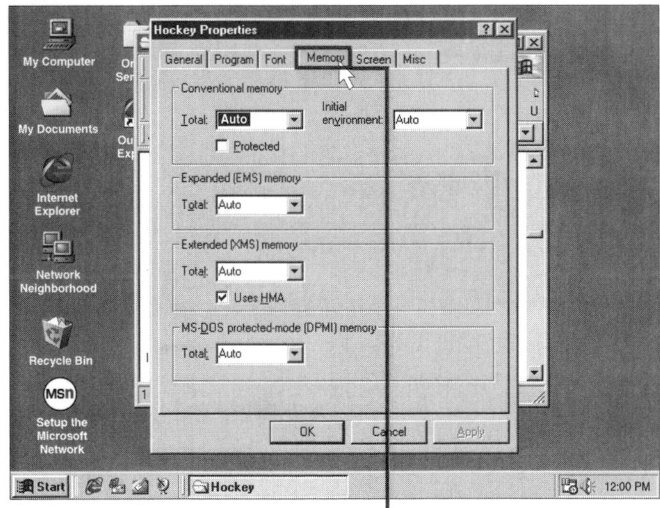

1 Display the properties for an MS-DOS program by performing steps 1 and 2 on page 140.

2 Click the Memory tab.

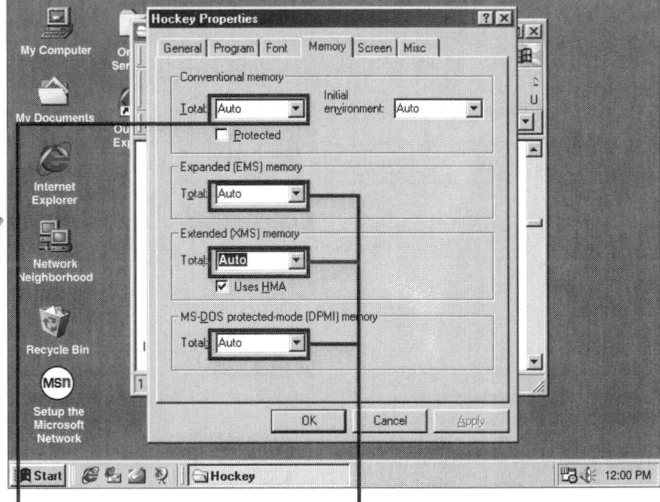

■ This area displays the amount of conventional memory required by the program.

■ These areas display the maximum amount of expanded, extended and MS-DOS protected-mode memory assigned to the program.

3 You can click ▼ beside a memory type to change the amount of memory assigned to the program.

TIPS

How can I view the amount of conventional memory available for MS-DOS programs?

Click Start and then select Programs. Click MS-DOS Prompt to open an MS-DOS Prompt window. Type **mem** and then press the Enter key. In most circumstances, there should be about 600 K of conventional memory available.

Why are there no settings on the Memory tab?

The program may be set to run in MS-DOS mode. See page 144. When a program runs in MS-DOS mode, Windows has no control over the memory settings.

My program is not running properly. How can I fix this?

Some MS-DOS programs do not perform well with access to an unlimited amount of expanded and extended memory. Try setting the amount of expanded and extended memory to 8192 K.

Why does the Memory tab indicate that my computer is not set up to use expanded memory?

You may not be able to use expanded memory if your computer's Config.sys file contains the emm386.exe command with the "noems" setting. To view the Config.sys file, see page 654.

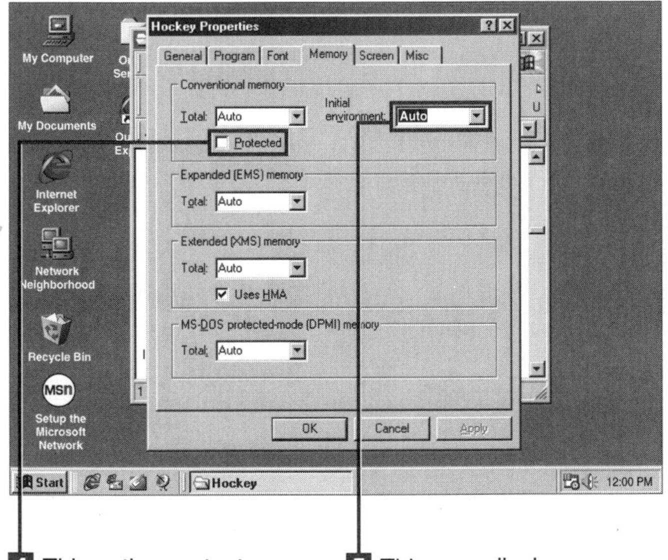

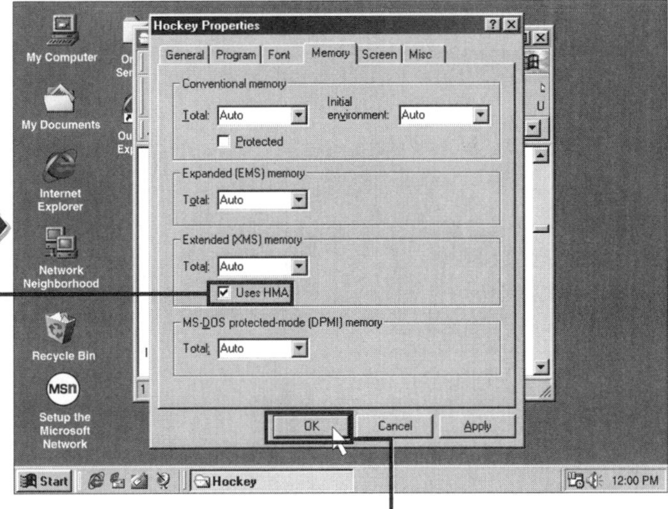

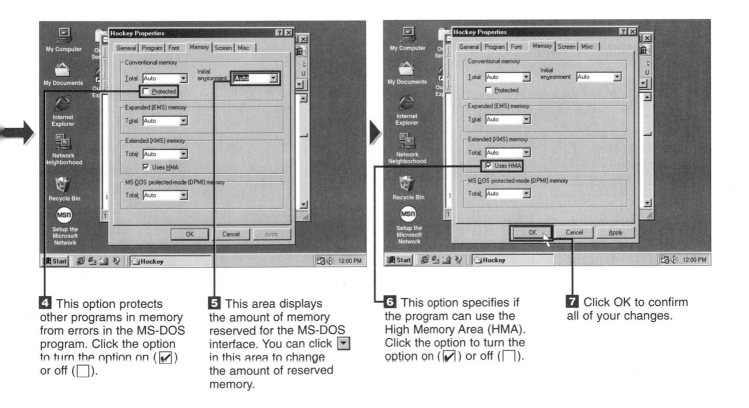

4 This option protects other programs in memory from errors in the MS-DOS program. Click the option to turn the option on (✔) or off (☐).

5 This area displays the amount of memory reserved for the MS-DOS interface. You can click ▼ in this area to change the amount of reserved memory.

6 This option specifies if the program can use the High Memory Area (HMA). Click the option to turn the option on (✔) or off (☐).

7 Click OK to confirm all of your changes.

OPTIMIZE MS-DOS PROGRAMS

Change Screen Settings

You can control the way an MS-DOS program appears on your screen. You should only change the Screen settings if the MS-DOS program is not appearing properly.

Most text-based MS-DOS programs appear in a window. This allows you to easily share information with other programs. MS-DOS programs that contain graphics usually fill your entire screen.

You can have the MS-DOS toolbar appear every time you start the program in a window. The toolbar provides buttons that allow you to quickly perform tasks such as copying text or changing the font of text.

You can have the window settings that are displayed when you close a program appear the next time you start the program. The settings you can restore include window size, font and position. This option is not available when the program fills your entire screen.

You can also adjust the performance settings if the program is not appearing properly on your screen.

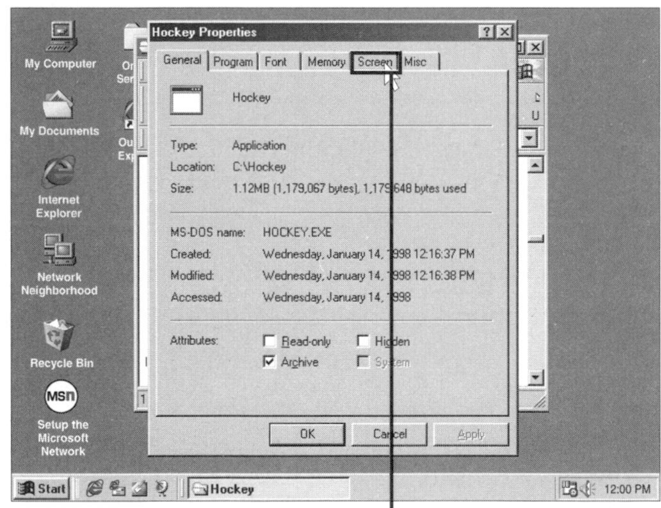

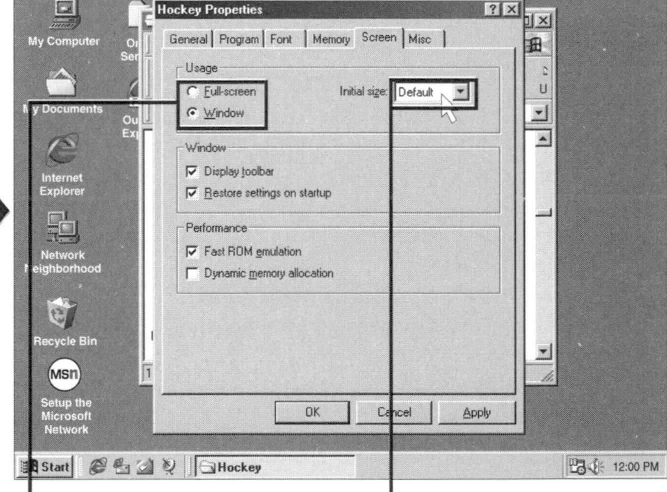

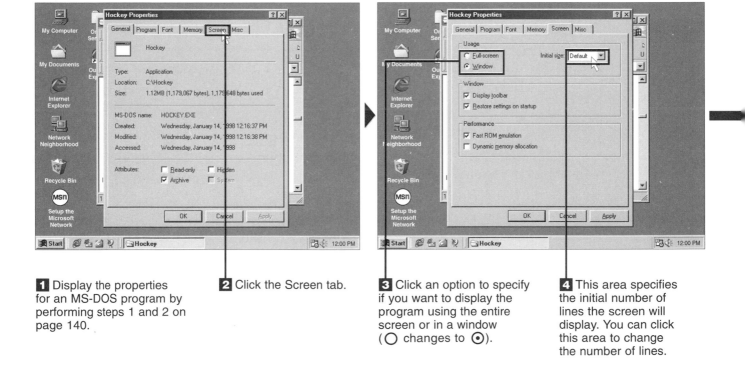

1 Display the properties for an MS-DOS program by performing steps 1 and 2 on page 140.

2 Click the Screen tab.

3 Click an option to specify if you want to display the program using the entire screen or in a window (○ changes to ⊙).

4 This area specifies the initial number of lines the screen will display. You can click this area to change the number of lines.

TIPS

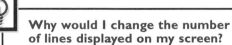

Why would I change the number of lines displayed on my screen?

Changing the number of lines allows you to display more information on your screen. For example, you can view 50 lines of a directory listing instead of 25 lines. You cannot change the number of lines displayed for some MS-DOS programs.

How do I switch between displaying the program in a window and using the entire screen?

You can use Alt+Enter to switch back and forth between displaying a program in a window and using the entire screen. If the program can only run using the entire screen, the program will not operate when you switch to a window.

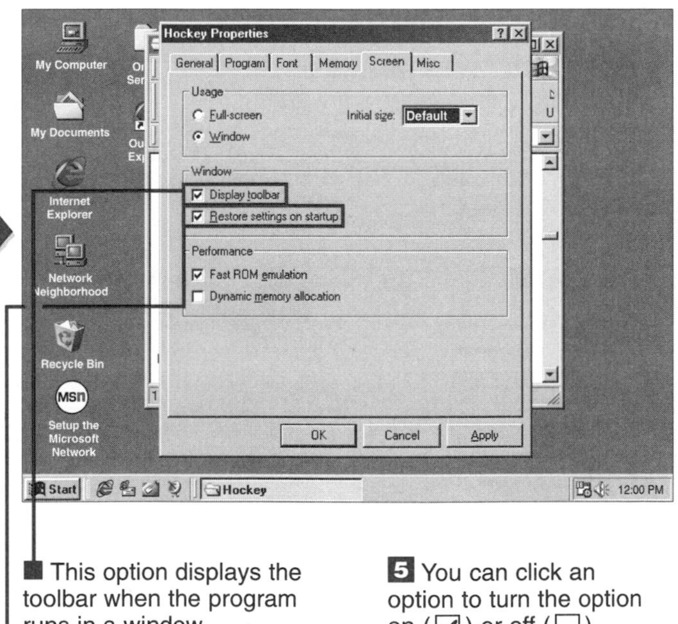

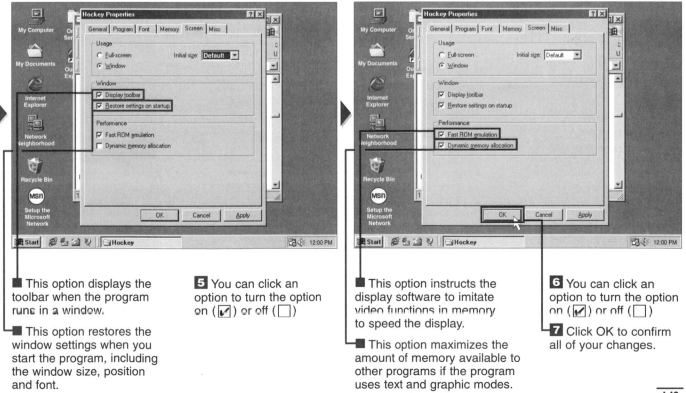

■ This option displays the toolbar when the program runs in a window.

■ This option restores the window settings when you start the program, including the window size, position and font.

5 You can click an option to turn the option on (☑) or off (☐).

■ This option instructs the display software to imitate video functions in memory to speed the display.

■ This option maximizes the amount of memory available to other programs if the program uses text and graphic modes.

6 You can click an option to turn the option on (☑) or off (☐).

7 Click OK to confirm all of your changes.

OPTIMIZE MS-DOS PROGRAMS

Change Miscellaneous Settings

You can control the way an MS-DOS program works with Windows. If a program is not working properly, it may help to adjust the settings on the Misc tab.

The Idle sensitivity option indicates how long the program can be idle before Windows reduces computer resources to the program. Low idle sensitivity lets the program run longer before computer resources to the program are reduced.

You can also use the Always suspend option to prevent the program from accessing any computer resources when the program is not active.

The Allow screen saver option lets the screen saver start even when the program is the active program. You may want to turn this option off if your screen saver interferes with the operation of your program.

The Warn if still active option displays a message on your screen when you try to close the program window while the program is running.

The MS-DOS program may use shortcut keys that you can also use in Windows. You can turn off the shortcut keys in Windows so you can use the shortcut keys in the MS-DOS program.

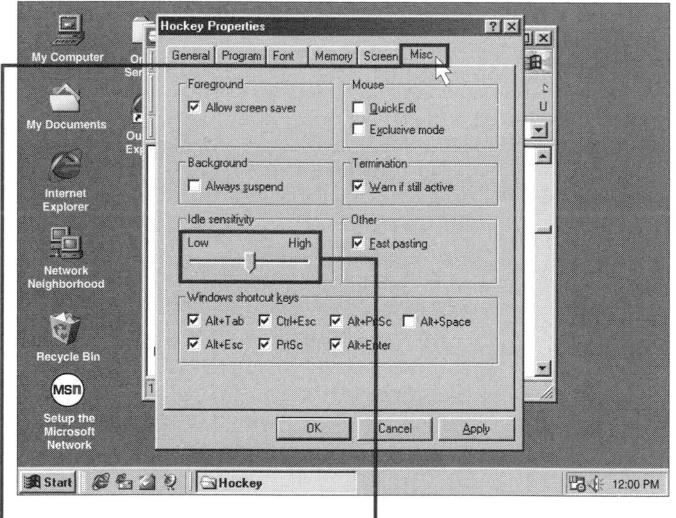

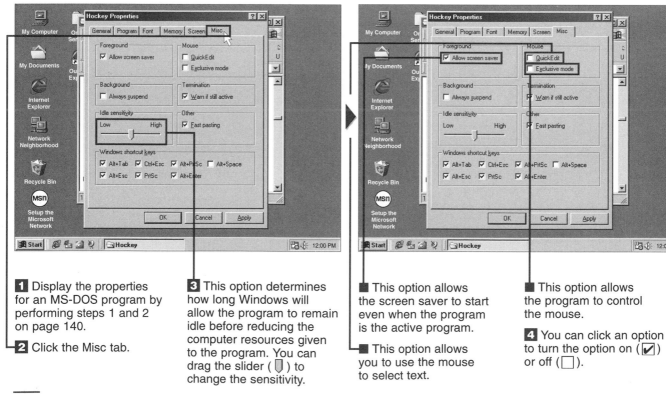

1 Display the properties for an MS-DOS program by performing steps 1 and 2 on page 140.

2 Click the Misc tab.

3 This option determines how long Windows will allow the program to remain idle before reducing the computer resources given to the program. You can drag the slider ( ) to change the sensitivity.

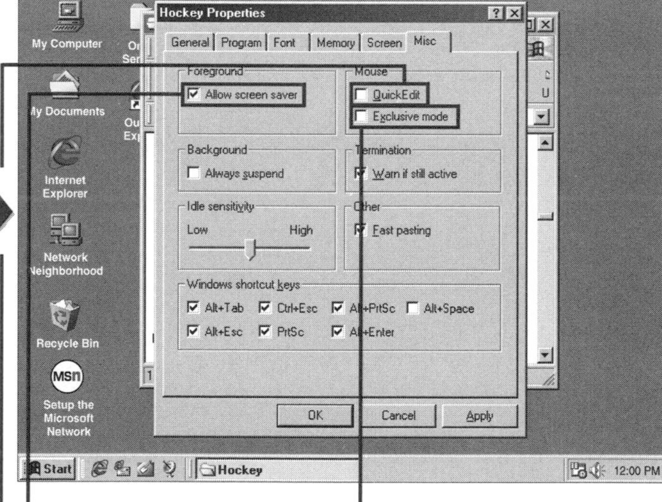

■ This option allows the screen saver to start even when the program is the active program.

■ This option allows you to use the mouse to select text.

■ This option allows the program to control the mouse.

4 You can click an option to turn the option on (✔) or off (☐).

Why isn't my mouse working properly?

When you set the mouse to Exclusive mode, you give control of the mouse to the MS-DOS program and you cannot use the mouse as a standard Windows pointer.

How can I display the Properties dialog box when the program fills my screen?

When the program fills your screen, use Alt+Spacebar+P to open the Properties dialog box.

How much of my computer's resources does an MS-DOS window use?

An open MS-DOS window, even when idle, uses 1-2 percent of your computer's resources and 2-3 percent of your processor's time.

The information I paste into the program does not appear properly. How can I fix this?

You can turn off the Fast pasting option. This will slow down the rate that Windows transfers pasted information to the MS-DOS program.

Where should I set the Idle sensitivity?

You can set the Idle sensitivity to high if the program waits for you to enter information. You should set the Idle sensitivity to low if the program performs a regular action or waits for a specific time to perform an action.

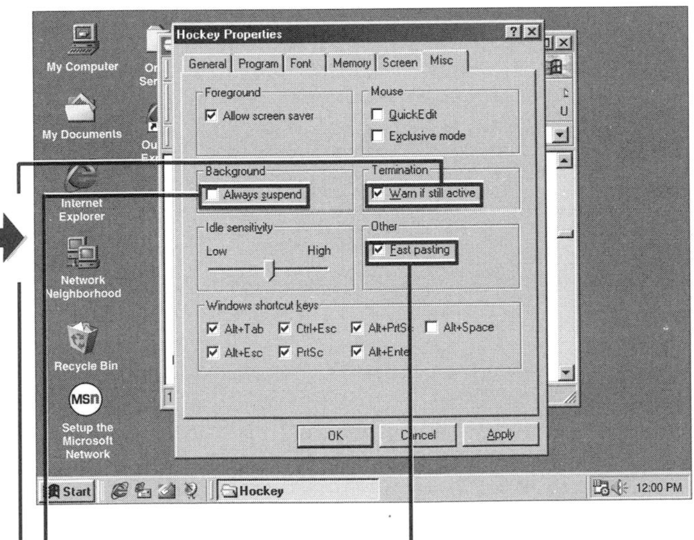

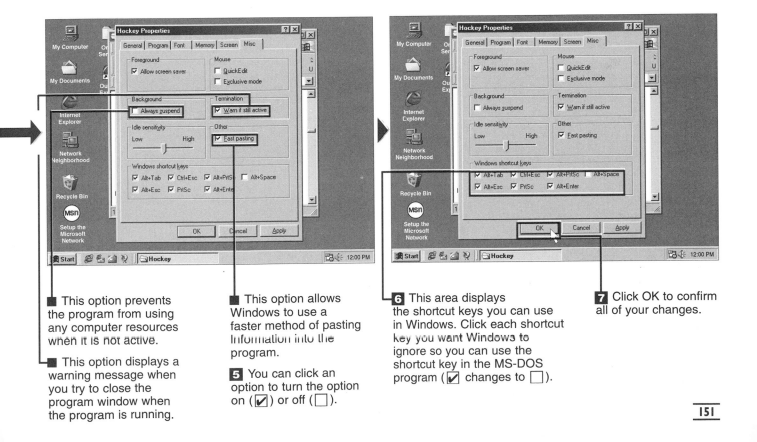

■ This option prevents the program from using any computer resources when it is not active.

■ This option displays a warning message when you try to close the program window when the program is running.

■ This option allows Windows to use a faster method of pasting information into the program.

5 You can click an option to turn the option on (☑) or off (☐).

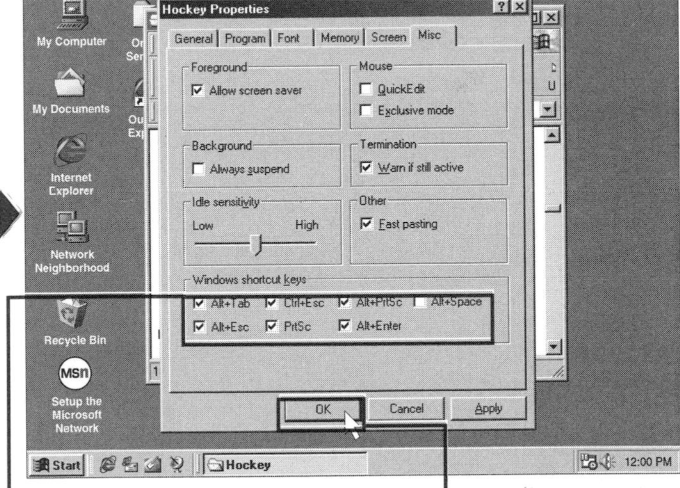

6 This area displays the shortcut keys you can use in Windows. Click each shortcut key you want Windows to ignore so you can use the shortcut key in the MS-DOS program (☑ changes to ☐).

7 Click OK to confirm all of your changes.

SECTION II

7) USING WORDPAD

8) USING PAINT

9) MORE ACCESSORIES

WINDOWS 98 ACCESSORIES

START WORDPAD

WordPad is a word processing program included with Windows 98. You can use WordPad to create simple documents, such as letters and memos.

WordPad uses many of the same commands and procedures used in more powerful programs, such as Microsoft Word. For example, you can use WordPad to review and edit files created with other word processing programs.

Word processing is similar to using a typewriter. You use some special keyboard keys, such as the Tab key, just as you do when using a typewriter. One of the advantages of using a word processor such as WordPad is that when you are typing text in a document, you do not need to press the Enter key at the end of each line. The text automatically moves to the next line.

Entering text in a document is only the beginning of word processing. When you finish typing the text, you can make changes to the content and appearance of your document.

Before performing many tasks in WordPad, you must select the text you want to work with. Selected text appears highlighted on your screen.

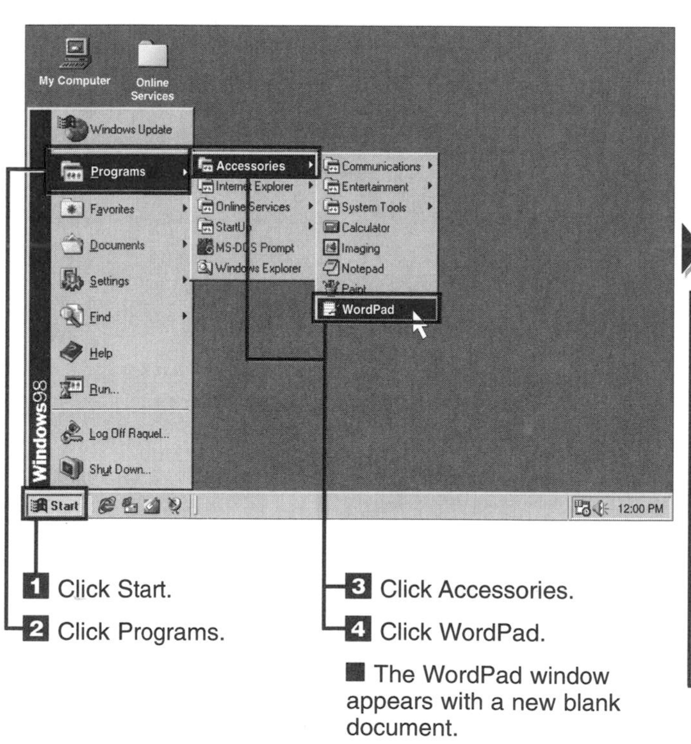

1 Click Start.

2 Click Programs.

3 Click Accessories.

4 Click WordPad.

■ The WordPad window appears with a new blank document.

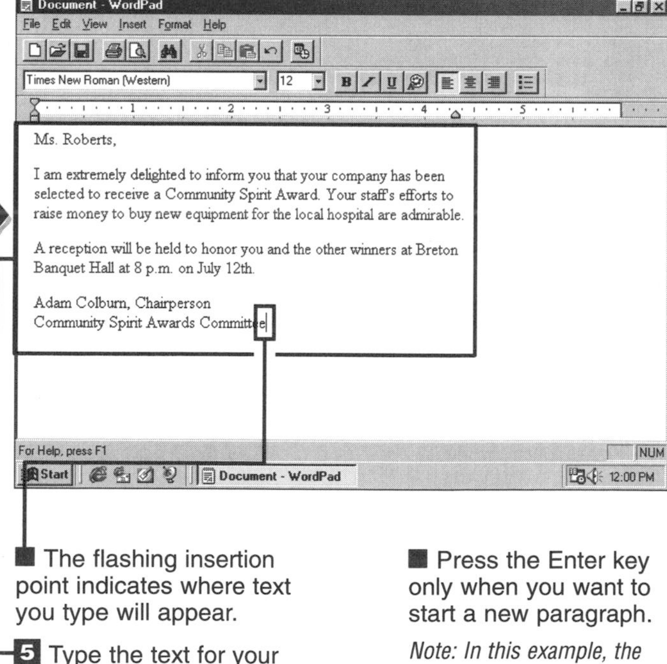

■ The flashing insertion point indicates where text you type will appear.

5 Type the text for your document.

■ Press the Enter key only when you want to start a new paragraph.

Note: In this example, the size of text was changed to make the text easier to read. To change the font size, see page 162.

TIPS

How can I select text using the keyboard?

Position the cursor at the start or end of the text you want to select. Hold down the Shift key while you use the arrow keys to select the text.

Why does WordPad sometimes select more text than I want?

When you are selecting part of a word and you include the space before or after the word, WordPad automatically selects the entire word. If you want to select parts of words, choose the View menu and then click the Options command. Select the Options tab and then click the Automatic word selection option (☑ changes to ☐).

Is there a fast way to select text?

To select a word, double-click the word. To select one line of text, click in the left margin beside the line you want to select. To select a paragraph, double-click in the left margin beside the paragraph you want to select. You can also triple-click any word in a paragraph to select the entire paragraph. To select all the text in the document, triple-click anywhere in the left margin of the document. When clicking in the left margin, the mouse I changes to ↗.

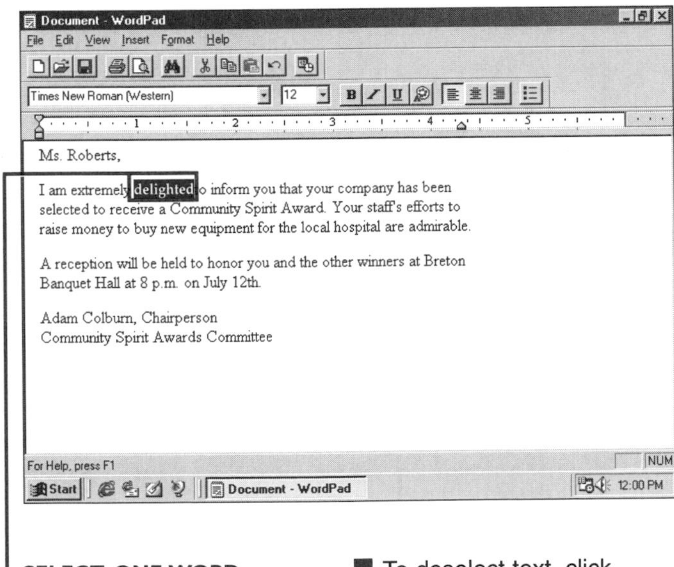

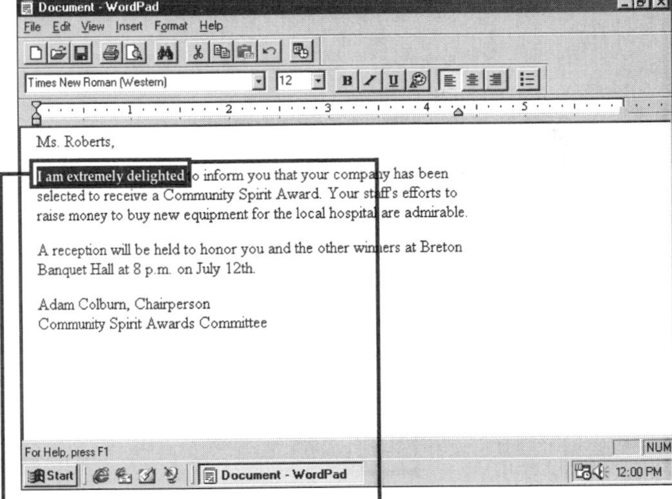

SELECT ONE WORD

1 To select one word, double-click the word.

■ To deselect text, click outside the selected area.

SELECT ANY AMOUNT OF TEXT

1 Position the mouse I over the first word you want to select.

2 Drag the mouse I until you highlight all the words you want to select. The text is highlighted.

Note: To select all the text in your document, press Ctrl+A on your keyboard.

EDIT TEXT

The ability to edit a document by changing or adding text makes a word processor a more powerful tool than a typewriter. You can insert, delete and reorganize the text in your document without having to retype the entire document.

You can add new text to a document. The existing text will shift to make room for the text you add.

You can delete text you no longer need from a document. The remaining text will shift to fill any empty spaces.

Moving text lets you try out different ways of organizing the text in a document. You can find the most effective structure for a document by experimenting with different placements of sentences and paragraphs.

You can also place a copy of text in a different location in your document. This will save you time since you do not have to retype the text.

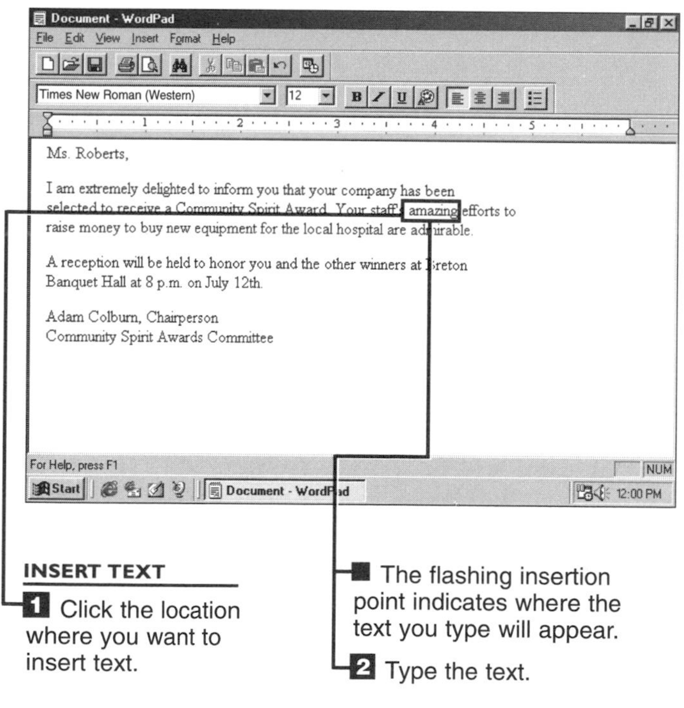

INSERT TEXT

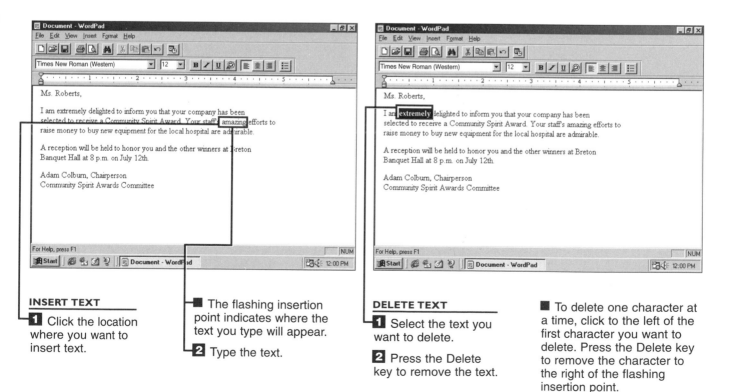

1 Click the location where you want to insert text.

■ The flashing insertion point indicates where the text you type will appear.

2 Type the text.

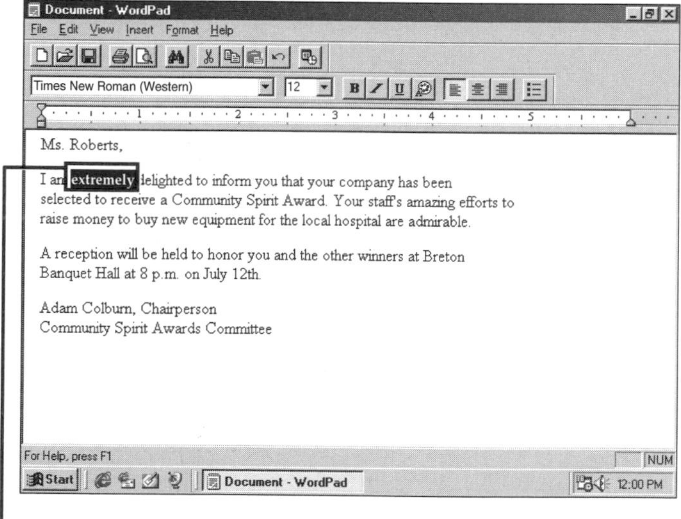

DELETE TEXT

1 Select the text you want to delete.

2 Press the Delete key to remove the text.

■ To delete one character at a time, click to the left of the first character you want to delete. Press the Delete key to remove the character to the right of the flashing insertion point.

TIPS

Can I cancel a change I made?

WordPad remembers the last change you made. From the Edit menu, select the Undo command to cancel the last change you made. You can also click the Undo button ( ) on the toolbar to cancel a change.

How can copying text help me edit my document?

If you plan to make major changes to a paragraph, you may want to copy the paragraph before you begin. This gives you two copies of the paragraph–the original paragraph and a paragraph with the changes.

Can I find or change every occurrence of a word in a document?

To locate every occurrence of a word or phrase in your document, click the Edit menu and then select the Find command. The Replace feature is also useful if you have misspelled a word or name throughout your document. To use the Replace feature, click the Edit menu and then choose the Replace command.

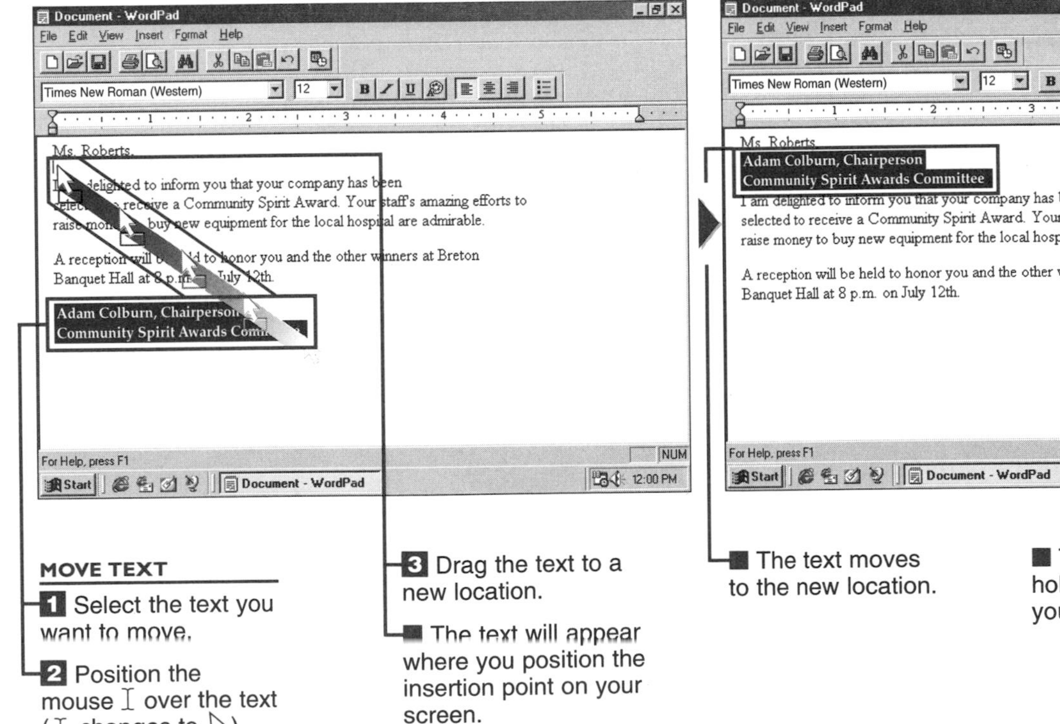

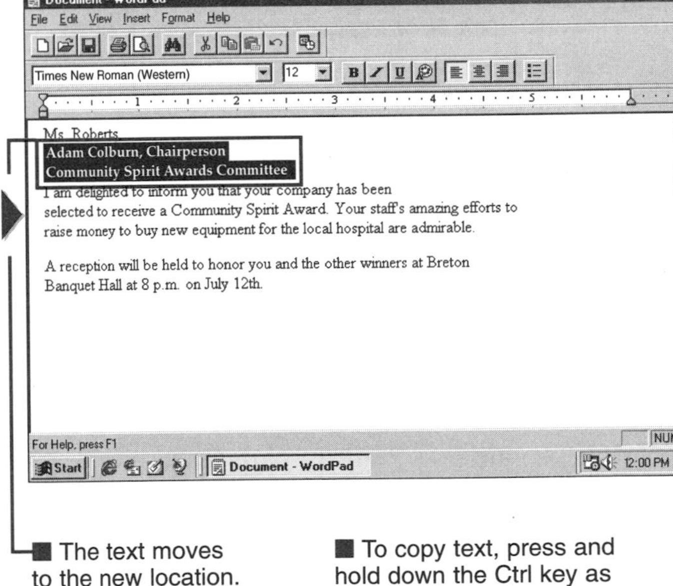

MOVE TEXT

1 Select the text you want to move.

2 Position the mouse I over the text (I changes to).

3 Drag the text to a new location.

■ The text will appear where you position the insertion point on your screen.

■ The text moves to the new location.

■ To copy text, press and hold down the Ctrl key as you perform step 3.

SAVE AND PRINT A DOCUMENT

You should save your document to store it for future use. This lets you later retrieve the document for reviewing or editing. When you save a document, you give the document a name.

You may want to save a document as soon as it has been created. If there is an equipment failure or power loss before you save your document, you will lose your work.

You should periodically save your document while you are working. This will ensure that all the changes you make to the document are saved. You can decide how often you want to save your changes. For example, if you are prepared to lose an hour of work, save every hour.

If you do not want to lose more than five minutes of work, save every five minutes.

You can produce a paper copy of a document. When you print your document, you can print the entire document, a range of pages or the text you have selected.

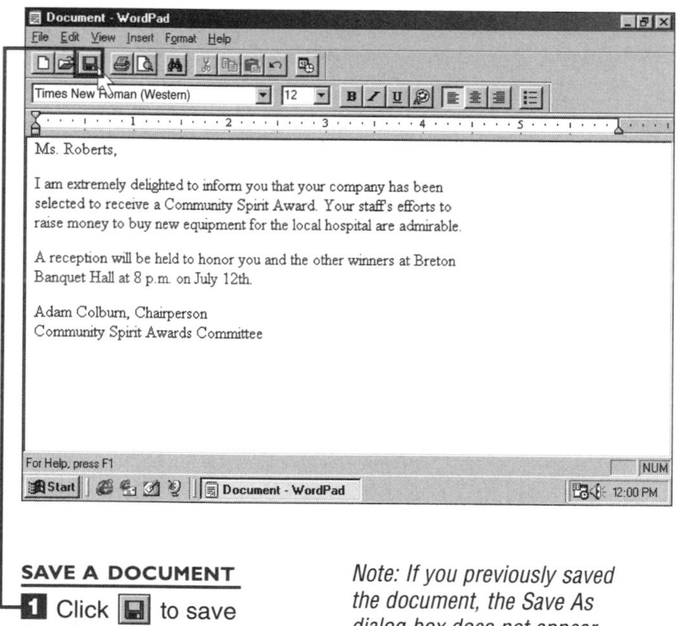

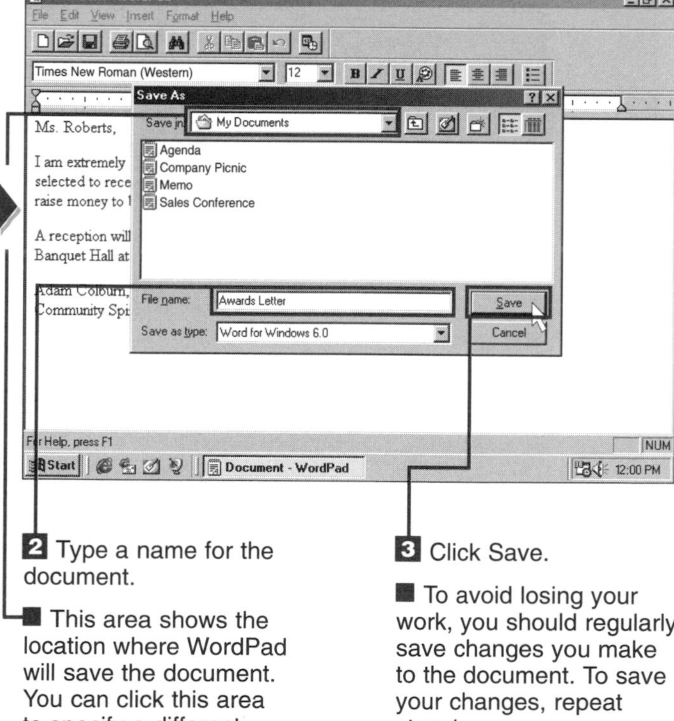

SAVE A DOCUMENT

1 Click [save icon] to save the document.

■ The Save As dialog box appears.

Note: If you previously saved the document, the Save As dialog box does not appear since you have already named the document.

2 Type a name for the document.

■ This area shows the location where WordPad will save the document. You can click this area to specify a different location.

3 Click Save.

■ To avoid losing your work, you should regularly save changes you make to the document. To save your changes, repeat step 1.

TIPS

WordPad wants to store all my documents in the My Documents folder. How can I automatically save them in a different folder?

By default, Windows saves documents you create in most applications in the My Documents folder. To change the default location, right-click My Documents on your desktop and then click Properties. Use the Browse button to specify the folder where you want to automatically save your documents.

How can I tell if my document is printing?

A printer icon (🖨) appears on the right side of the taskbar. You can double-click the printer icon for information about your print job. The printer icon disappears from the taskbar when your document has been sent to the printer.

Can I see how my document looks before I print it?

Yes. Click the File menu and then select the Print Preview command.

If I want to give my document to a friend who does not use WordPad, how should I save the file?

You should save your document as a different file type. In the Save As dialog box, click the Save as type area to display the file types you can use. To keep the document's formatting, such as bold or underline, select Rich Text Format. To save the document without formatting, select Text Document.

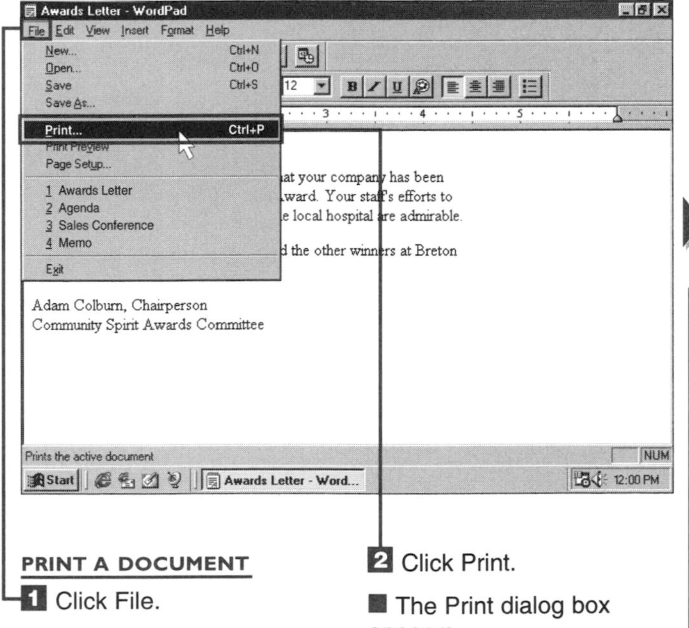

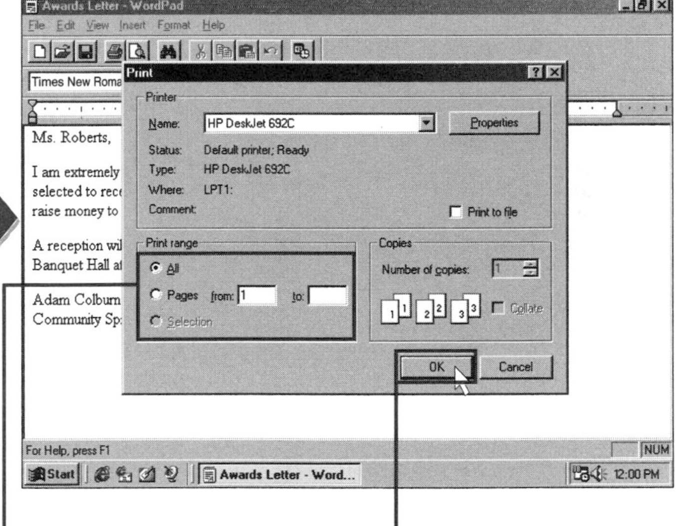

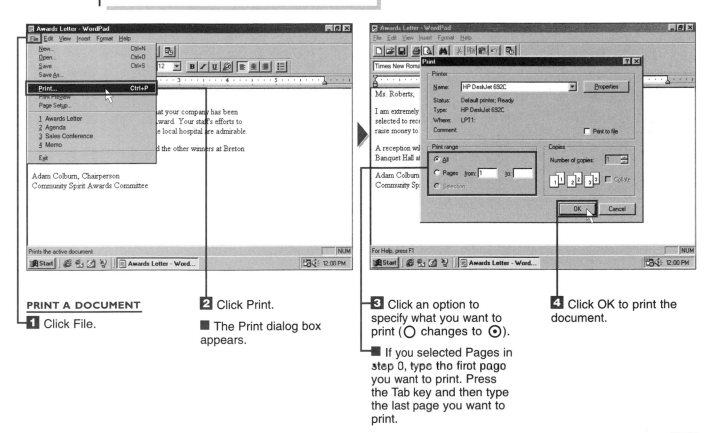

PRINT A DOCUMENT

1 Click File.

2 Click Print.

■ The Print dialog box appears.

3 Click an option to specify what you want to print (○ changes to ⊙).

■ If you selected Pages in step 0, typo tho firot pago you want to print. Press the Tab key and then type the last page you want to print.

4 Click OK to print the document.

OPEN A DOCUMENT

You can open a new document in WordPad to start writing a letter, memo or report.

When you open a new document in WordPad, you must choose the type of document you want to create. The Word 6 Document type is the standard type used for WordPad. You should select this type if you want people who use Microsoft Word for Windows 6.0 or later to be able to work with the document.

You can also create a document that people who do not use Word for Windows 6.0 can work with. The Rich Text Document type can be used by most word processors, including word processors for Macintosh computers. Rich text can contain formatting, such as bold or underline. The Text Document type can also be used by most word processors but contains no formatting.

The Unicode Text Document type lets you create documents using characters from different languages, such as Greek and Chinese.

You can open a saved document and display it on your screen. This allows you to review and make changes to the document.

WordPad only lets you work with one document at a time. If you are working with a document, save the document before opening another.

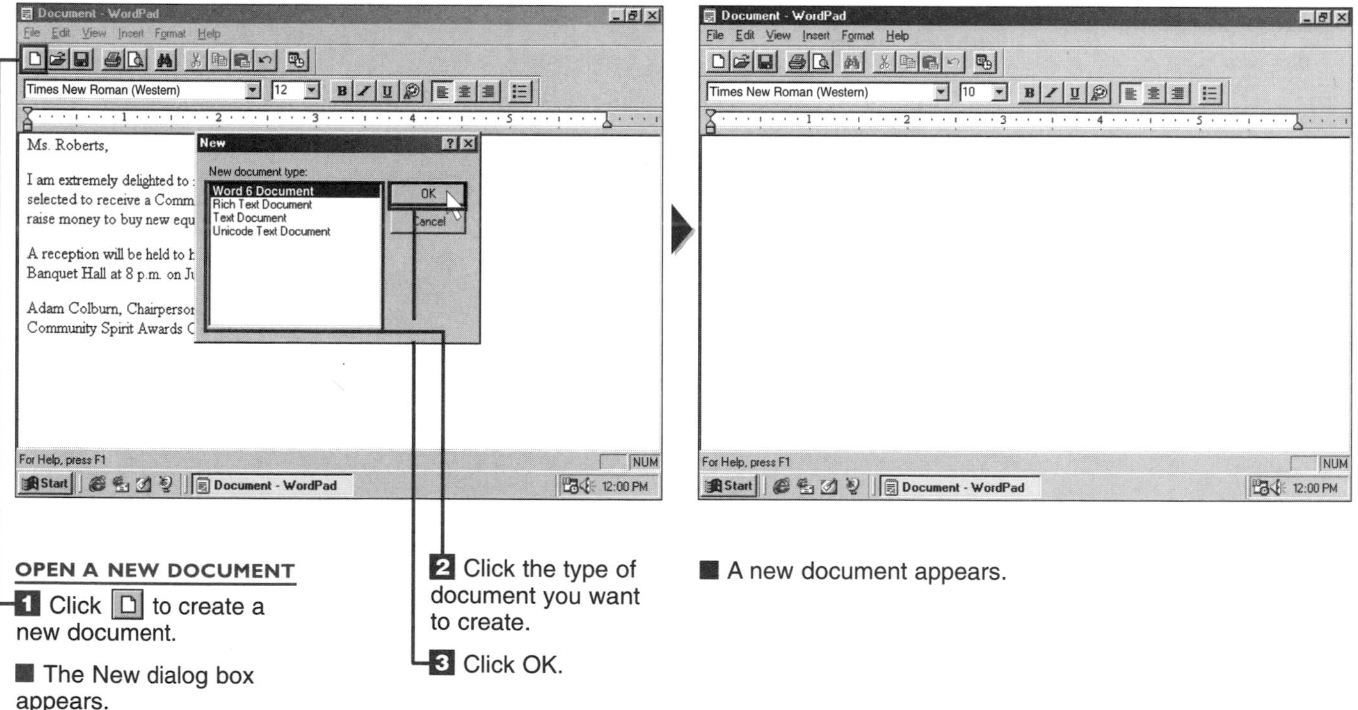

OPEN A NEW DOCUMENT

1 Click [new] to create a new document.

■ The New dialog box appears.

2 Click the type of document you want to create.

3 Click OK.

■ A new document appears.

TIPS

Is there a faster way to open a saved document?

The last four documents you worked with appear on the File menu. You can click any of these documents to open them. Also, the last 15 documents you worked with on your computer appear in the Documents folder on the Start menu. To open a document from the Start menu, see page 66.

Why can't I see the file I want to open?

If the file you want to open is not listed in the Open dialog box, the file may have been saved as a different file type. To view all the files in the current location, click the Files of type area and then select All Documents.

Can I use WordPad to open documents I created in Microsoft Word?

Yes, but some features may not display properly. WordPad does not support all of the features available in Microsoft Word.

Is there any way to work with two WordPad documents at the same time?

You can start WordPad multiple times to have several documents open at once. Having several documents open at the same time allows you to cut and paste information between documents. You can use the Start menu to start WordPad again. You can also double-click a WordPad document in a My Computer or Windows Explorer window to open another document.

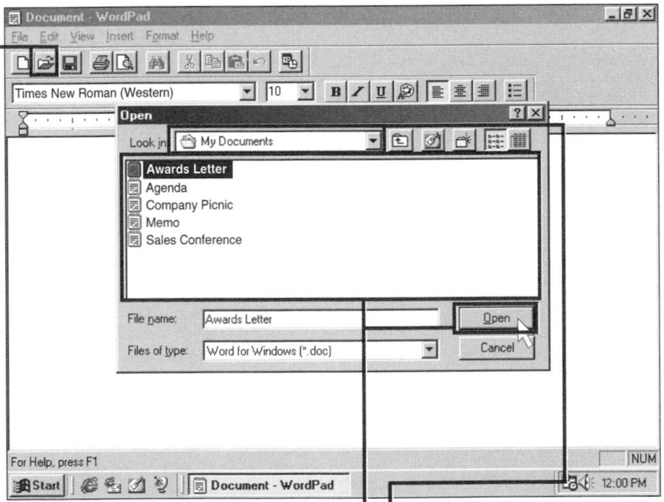

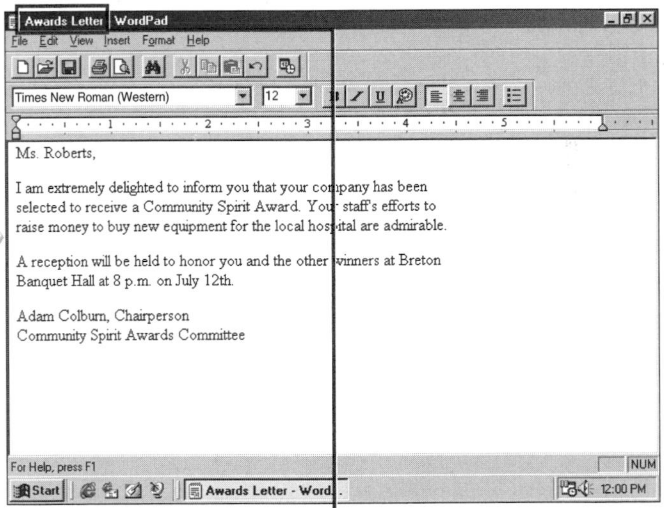

OPEN A SAVED DOCUMENT

1 Click [open icon] to open a document.

■ The Open dialog box appears.

■ This area shows the location of the displayed documents. You can click this area to change the location.

2 Click the document you want to open.

3 Click Open.

■ The contents of the document appear on your screen.

■ This area displays the name of the document.

FORMAT CHARACTERS

You can make text in your document look more attractive by using various fonts, sizes, styles and colors.

When you start WordPad, the text appears in the Times New Roman font. The default size for text is 10 points and the default color is black.

When you install Windows, some other fonts are also installed, including Arial and Courier New. The rest of the available fonts depend on your printer and the setup of your computer.

WordPad measures the size of a character in points. There are 72 points in one inch. Due to differences in design, two fonts may appear to be different sizes even though they are displayed using the same point size.

You can change the style of text using the Bold, Italic and Underline features. These features are used mainly for emphasis, or to set apart different types of text, such as titles.

You can change the color of text to draw attention to headings or important information in your document.

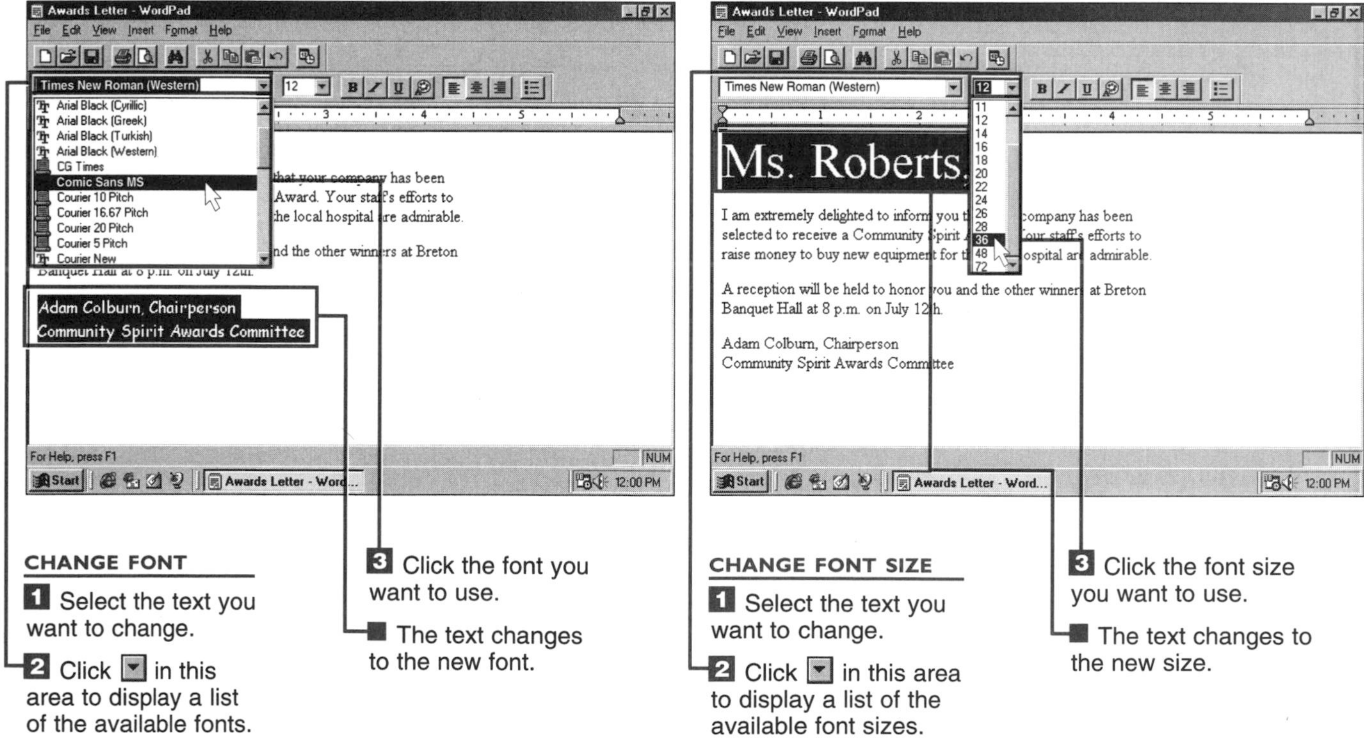

CHANGE FONT

1 Select the text you want to change.

2 Click ▼ in this area to display a list of the available fonts.

3 Click the font you want to use.

■ The text changes to the new font.

CHANGE FONT SIZE

1 Select the text you want to change.

2 Click ▼ in this area to display a list of the available font sizes.

3 Click the font size you want to use.

■ The text changes to the new size.

TIPS

How can I change the format of all the new text that I type?

Before you begin typing the text you want to format differently, change to the format you want to use. Any new text you type will display the new format.

How can I preview a font?

In the Format menu, select Font. The Font dialog box opens and allows you to change the formatting of your text. The dialog box displays an area where you can preview the font settings you choose.

Can I add fonts to my computer?

You can purchase fonts at most computer stores. To install fonts, see page 606. If you have installed other programs on your computer, WordPad can use the fonts provided with these programs.

Can I use colored text if I do not have a color printer?

You can use colors for your text, but they will appear as shades of gray when printed on a black-and-white printer. You can use color effectively in documents that will only be viewed on-screen.

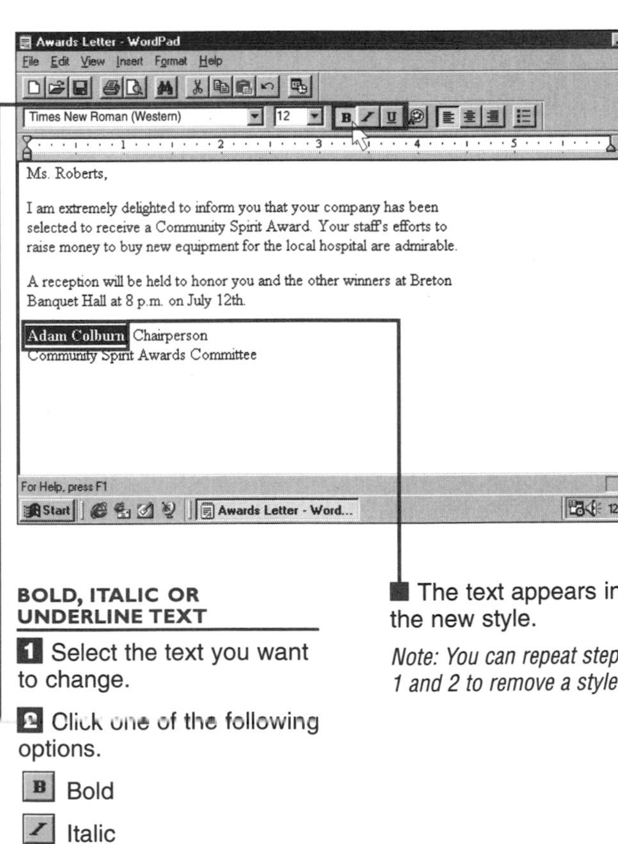

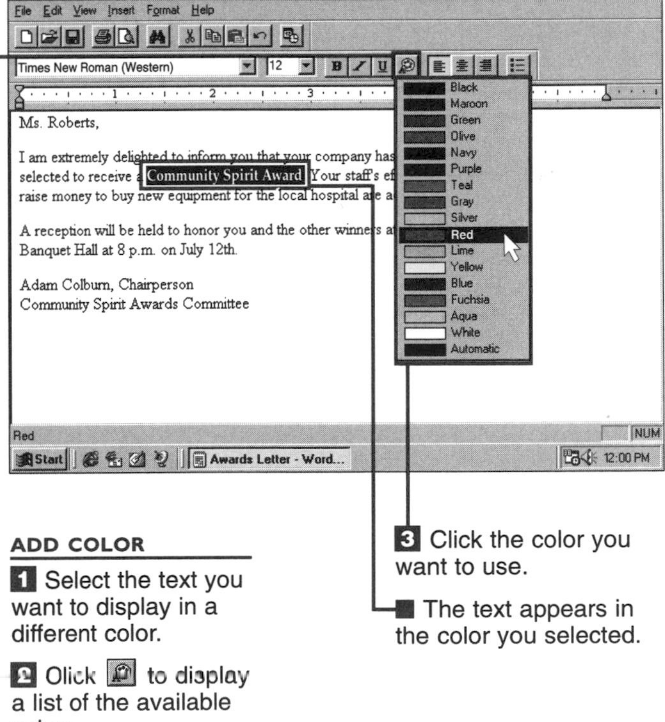

BOLD, ITALIC OR UNDERLINE TEXT

1 Select the text you want to change.

2 Click one of the following options.

- B Bold
- I Italic
- U Underline

■ The text appears in the new style.

Note: You can repeat steps 1 and 2 to remove a style.

ADD COLOR

1 Select the text you want to display in a different color.

2 Click the color button to display a list of the available colors.

3 Click the color you want to use.

■ The text appears in the color you selected.

FORMAT PARAGRAPHS

You can format the paragraphs in a WordPad document to help organize the document.

Aligning text allows you to line up the edge of a paragraph along a margin. Most documents are left aligned so the edges of the paragraphs line up along the left margin. Right alignment is often used to line up dates or return addresses along the right margin. You can also center paragraphs between the left and right margins. Centering paragraphs is most effective for headings and titles.

You can change the tabs in your document. This is useful for lining up columns of information. By default, WordPad sets a tab every 0.5 inches.

You can indent a paragraph from the left, right or both margins. Indenting paragraphs is often used to identify and set apart quotations. You can indent just the first line of a paragraph so you do not need to press the Tab key at the beginning of every new paragraph.

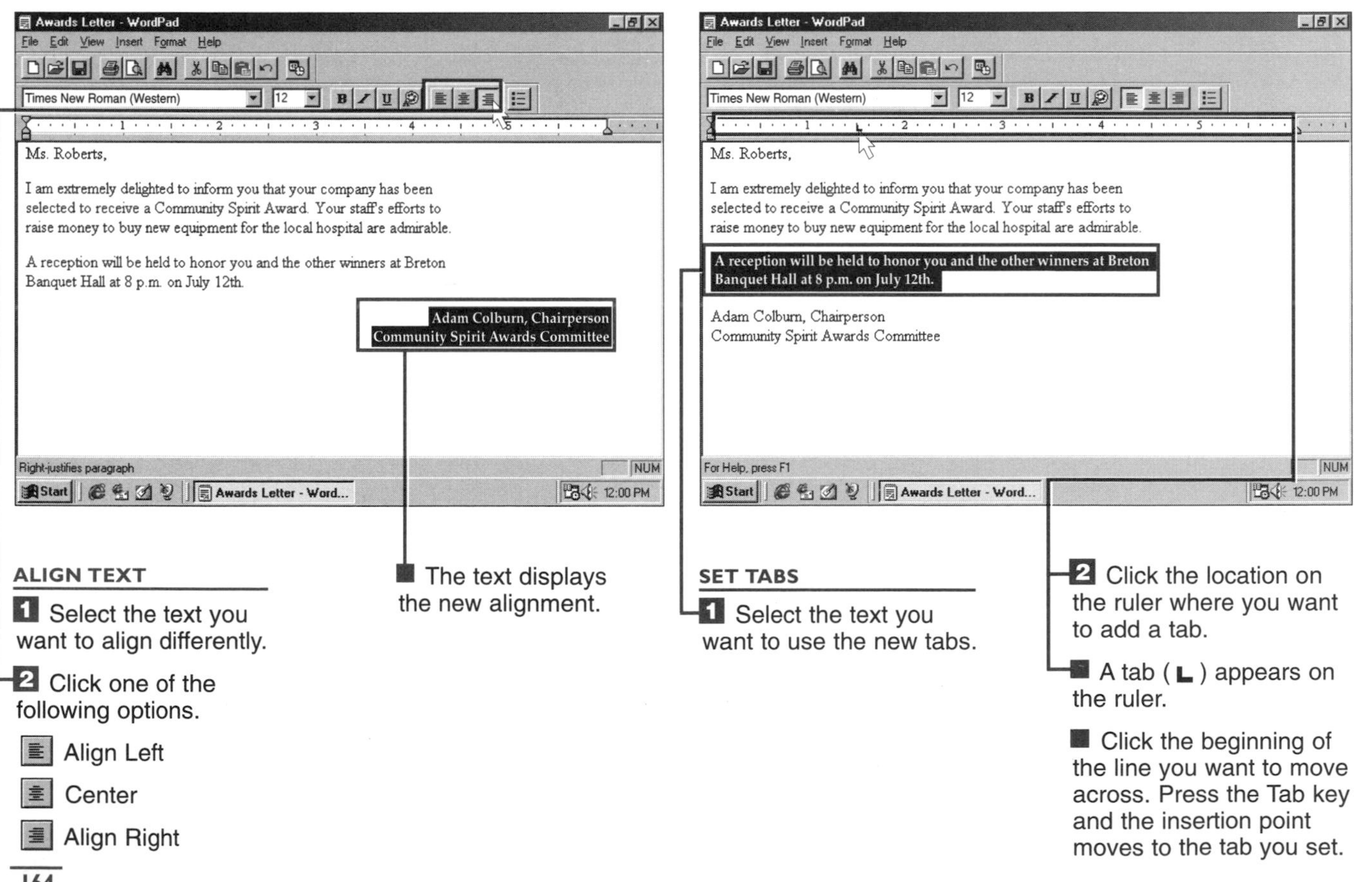

ALIGN TEXT

1 Select the text you want to align differently.

2 Click one of the following options.

- Align Left
- Center
- Align Right

■ The text displays the new alignment.

SET TABS

1 Select the text you want to use the new tabs.

2 Click the location on the ruler where you want to add a tab.

■ A tab (L) appears on the ruler.

■ Click the beginning of the line you want to move across. Press the Tab key and the insertion point moves to the tab you set.

TIPS

How do I display the ruler on my screen?

From the View menu, select Ruler to display or hide the ruler. When the ruler is displayed, a check mark appears beside Ruler in the menu.

How can I move a tab?

You can drag a tab (L) to a new location on the ruler. You can also drag a tab off the ruler to remove the tab. Only tabs in the currently selected paragraphs are changed.

How can I clear all the tabs?

From the Format menu, select Tabs to display the Tabs dialog box. Then click the Clear All button. You can also use this dialog box to set tabs.

Can I format more than one paragraph at a time?

You can format as many paragraphs as you want. WordPad applies your formatting changes to any paragraphs that are currently selected.

Can I align my text along both the left and right margins?

No. WordPad does not include a full justification feature.

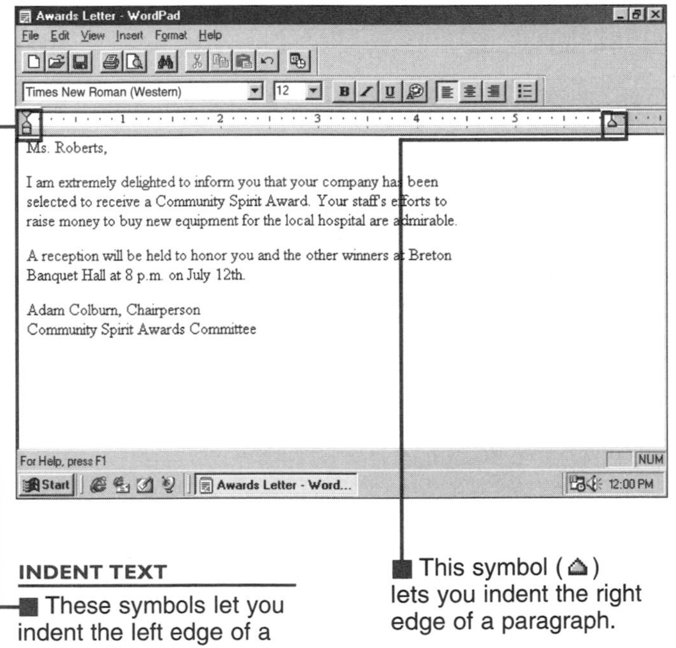

INDENT TEXT

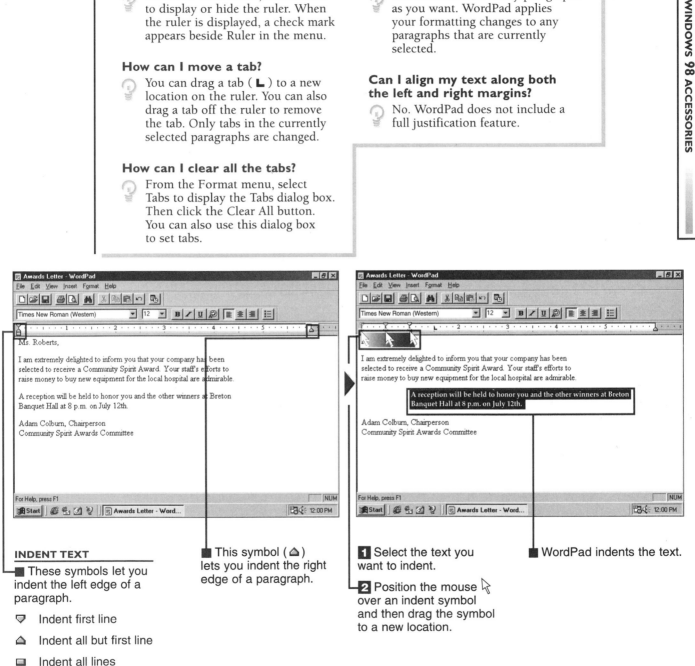

■ These symbols let you indent the left edge of a paragraph.

- Indent first line
- Indent all but first line
- Indent all lines

■ This symbol ( ) lets you indent the right edge of a paragraph.

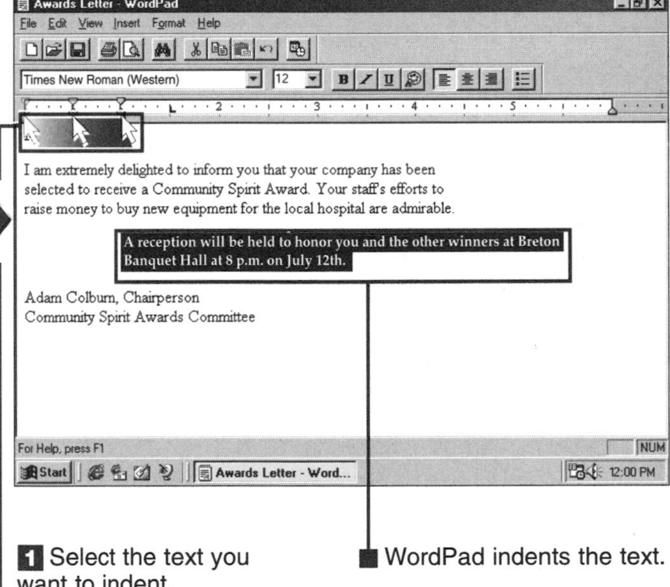

1 Select the text you want to indent.

2 Position the mouse over an indent symbol and then drag the symbol to a new location.

■ WordPad indents the text.

FORMAT PAGES

You can adjust the appearance of the pages in your document to suit your needs.

WordPad sets each page in your document to print on letter-sized paper. If you want to use a different paper size, you can change this setting. The available paper sizes depend on the printer you are using.

You can change the orientation of pages in your document. The Portrait orientation prints across the short side of a page and is used for most documents. The Landscape orientation prints across the long side of a page and is often used for certificates and tables.

A margin is the amount of space between text and the edge of your paper. You can change the margins to suit your document. Changing margins lets you accommodate letterhead and other specialty paper.

The Page Setup dialog box displays a sample of how your document will appear when printed.

The changes you make affect the entire document.

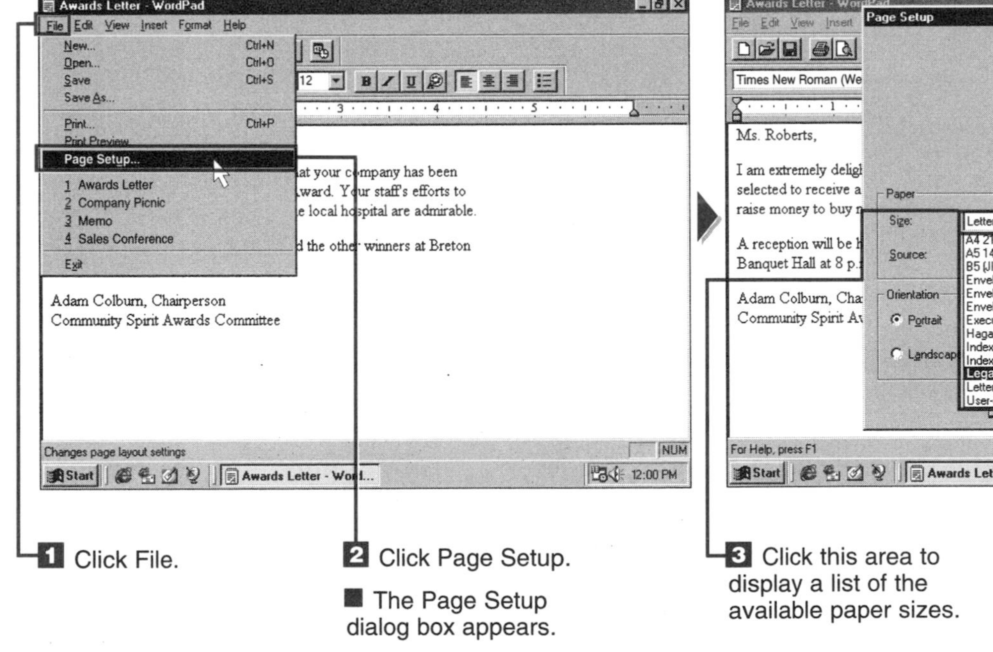

1 Click File.

2 Click Page Setup.

■ The Page Setup dialog box appears.

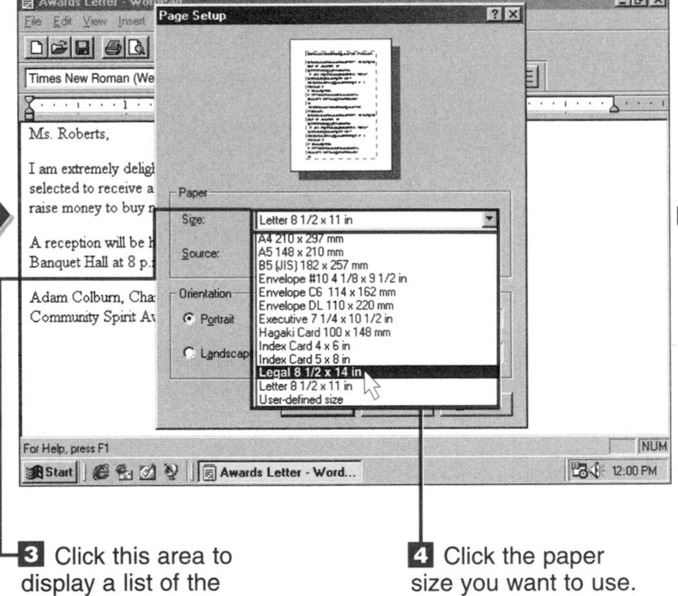

3 Click this area to display a list of the available paper sizes.

4 Click the paper size you want to use.

TIPS

How can I change the units a page is measured in?

From the View menu, select the Options command. Click the Options tab and select your preferred unit of measure. You can choose from inches, centimeters, points and picas. There are 72 points in one inch and 6 picas in one inch.

How do I change the margins for only part of my document?

If you want to change the left and right margins for only part of your document, you must change the indentation of the paragraphs. See page 165. You cannot change the top and bottom margins for only part of your document.

How can I see what my pages will look like before I print the document?

From the File menu, select the Print Preview command to preview your document before it is printed.

My printer stores letterhead in one location and plain paper in another. How can I tell WordPad which paper to use?

In the Page Setup dialog box, click the area beside Source and then select the location of the paper you want to use to print the document.

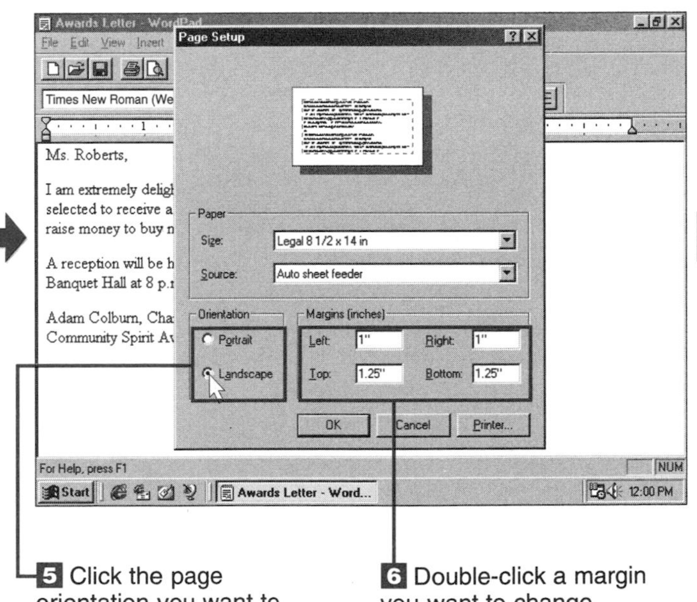

5 Click the page orientation you want to use (○ changes to ⊙).

6 Double-click a margin you want to change. Then type the new margin.

7 Repeat step 6 for each margin you want to change.

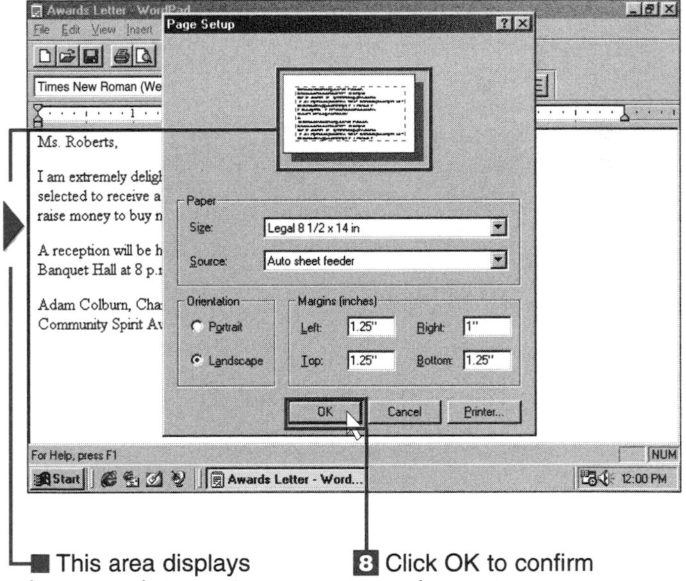

■ This area displays how your document will appear.

8 Click OK to confirm your changes.

START PAINT

Paint is a simple graphics program included with Windows 98. You can use Paint to create and edit images. Images you create in Paint can be inserted into other programs, printed and displayed as wallpaper on your desktop.

A Paint image is made up of a grid of tiny colored dots, called pixels. Paint uses the number of pixels from the top and left of the painting to indicate the position of the mouse on your screen. You can use these numbers to help line up objects in your painting.

Although Paint offers many features to help you create paintings, you may find you need a more sophisticated image editing program. To open and work with high-quality photo image files, you need a program like Corel PHOTO-PAINT or Adobe Photoshop. There are also programs such as CorelDRAW, Adobe Illustrator and Micrografx Designer that you can use to create drawings.

TIP 

How can I find out what each tool does?

To display a description of a tool, move the mouse pointer over the tool. After a few seconds, the name of the tool appears.

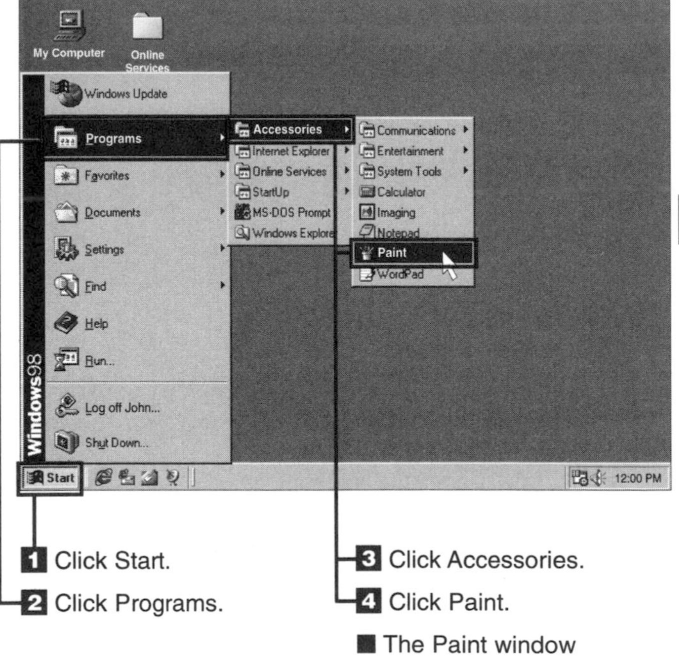

1 Click Start.

2 Click Programs.

3 Click Accessories.

4 Click Paint.

■ The Paint window appears.

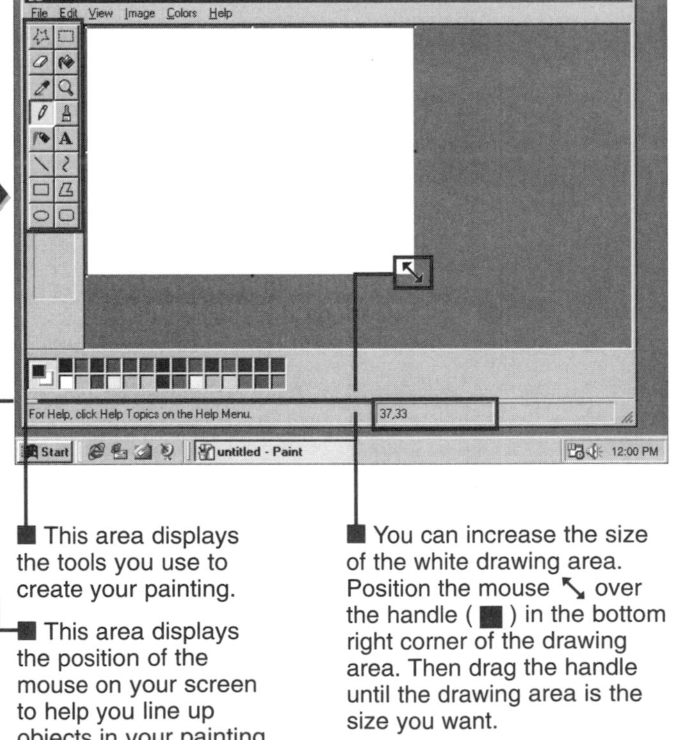

■ This area displays the tools you use to create your painting.

■ This area displays the position of the mouse on your screen to help you line up objects in your painting.

■ You can increase the size of the white drawing area. Position the mouse ↘ over the handle (■) in the bottom right corner of the drawing area. Then drag the handle until the drawing area is the size you want.

DRAW SHAPES

You can use Paint's tools to draw shapes such as rectangles, rounded rectangles, ellipses and polygons. You can use the Polygon tool to draw many different kinds of multi-sided shapes, ranging from simple triangles to complex objects.

Before you draw a shape, you can specify whether you want to outline the shape, fill the shape with a color or do both. You can also specify the colors you want to use for the outline and the inside of the shape.

TIP

How do I draw a circle or a square?

Press and hold down the Shift key as you drag the mouse to draw the shape. To draw a circle, select the Ellipse tool (⬭). To draw a square, select the Rectangle tool (▭).

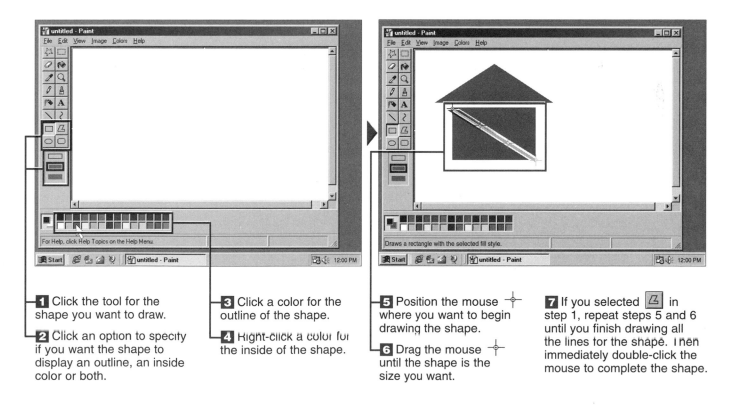

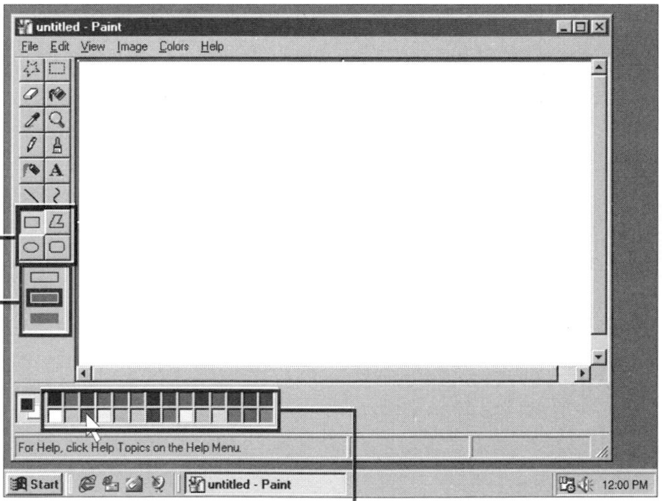

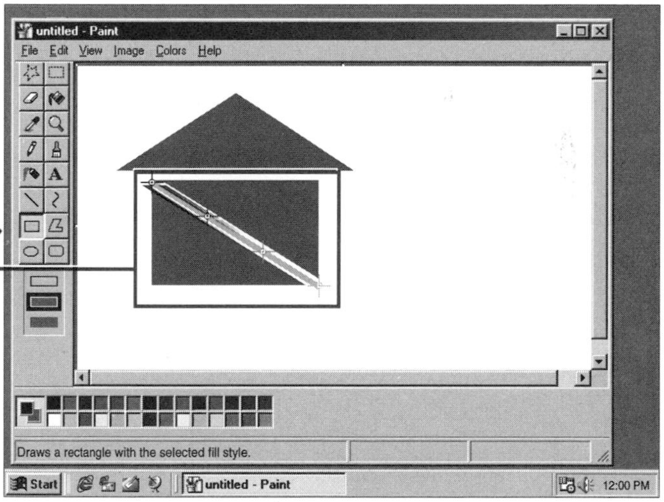

1 Click the tool for the shape you want to draw.

2 Click an option to specify if you want the shape to display an outline, an inside color or both.

3 Click a color for the outline of the shape.

4 Right-click a color for the inside of the shape.

5 Position the mouse where you want to begin drawing the shape.

6 Drag the mouse until the shape is the size you want.

7 If you selected ▱ in step 1, repeat steps 5 and 6 until you finish drawing all the lines for the shape. Then immediately double-click the mouse to complete the shape.

8

DRAW LINES AND USE BRUSHES

Paint can create three different types of lines in your paintings. You can draw straight lines, curved lines and pencil lines. You can also use brushes to create lines or spray areas of the painting.

The Line tool allows you to draw a perfectly straight line when you drag the mouse from one point to another.

When you use the Curve tool, the line begins as a perfectly straight line. You can then bend or twist the line to create the curve you want.

The Pencil tool allows you more freedom when drawing lines and curves.

The Brush tool is similar to the Pencil tool, but it has many different brush styles that you can choose from, including some that work like a calligraphy pen.

You can use the Airbrush tool to spray areas of color onto a painting and create shading effects. When using the Airbrush tool, the slower you drag the mouse, the darker the color appears in your painting.

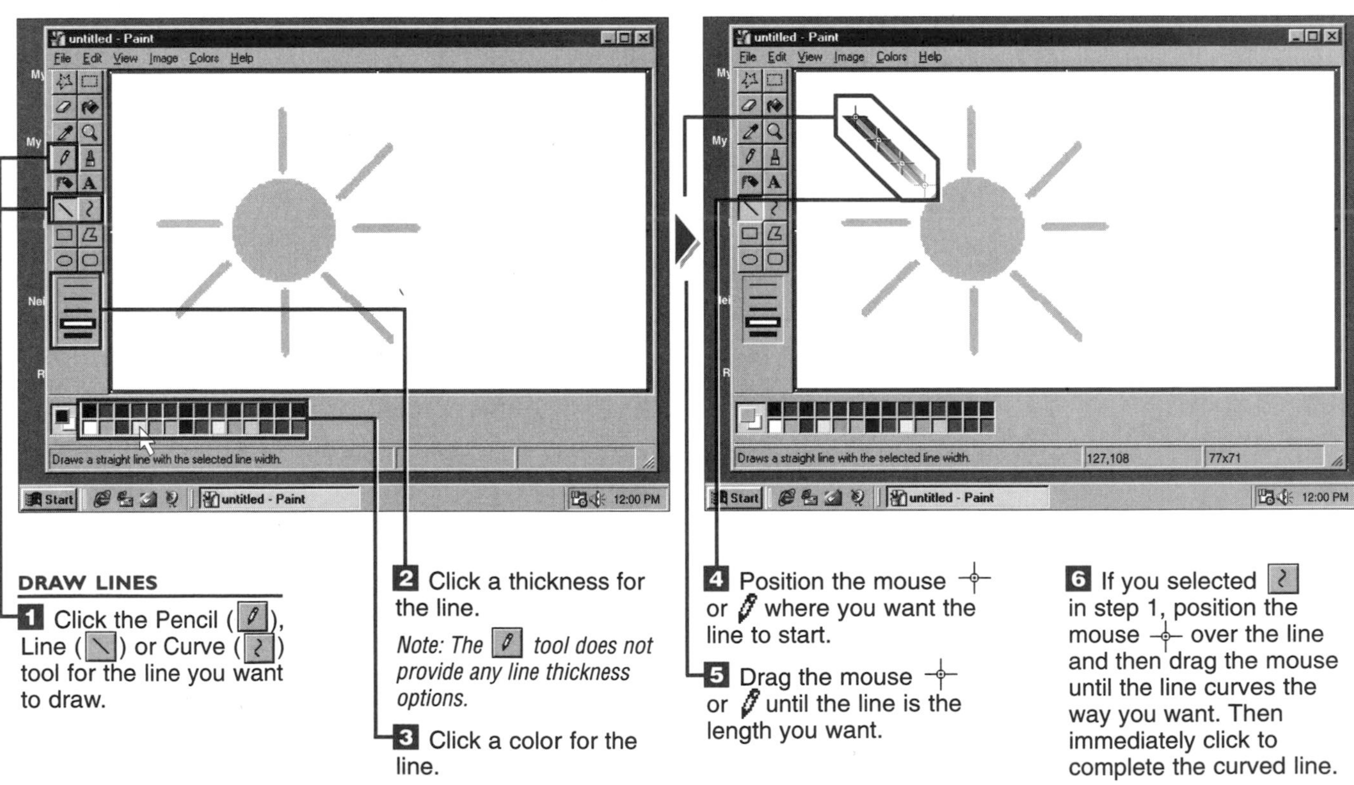

DRAW LINES

1 Click the Pencil (✎), Line (\) or Curve (≀) tool for the line you want to draw.

2 Click a thickness for the line.

Note: The ✎ tool does not provide any line thickness options.

3 Click a color for the line.

4 Position the mouse ⌖ or ✎ where you want the line to start.

5 Drag the mouse ⌖ or ✎ until the line is the length you want.

6 If you selected ≀ in step 1, position the mouse ⌖ over the line and then drag the mouse until the line curves the way you want. Then immediately click to complete the curved line.

TIPS

How do I draw a line that is exactly horizontal?

You can draw perfectly horizontal, vertical or diagonal lines by holding down the Shift key while you draw the line. This works for the Line, Curve and Pencil tools, but not the Brush or Airbrush.

Can I change the line width of the Pencil tool?

You cannot change the line width of the Pencil tool. Because of its thin line width, the Pencil tool is best used for editing detail when you are zoomed in on your painting.

How do I zoom in to draw precise lines?

To zoom in on your painting to draw precise lines, click the View menu. Select Zoom and then select Large Size. To view your painting at different zoom levels, click the View menu, choose Zoom and then select Custom. When you are finished, you can return to the normal zoom level by clicking the View menu and then selecting Normal Size.

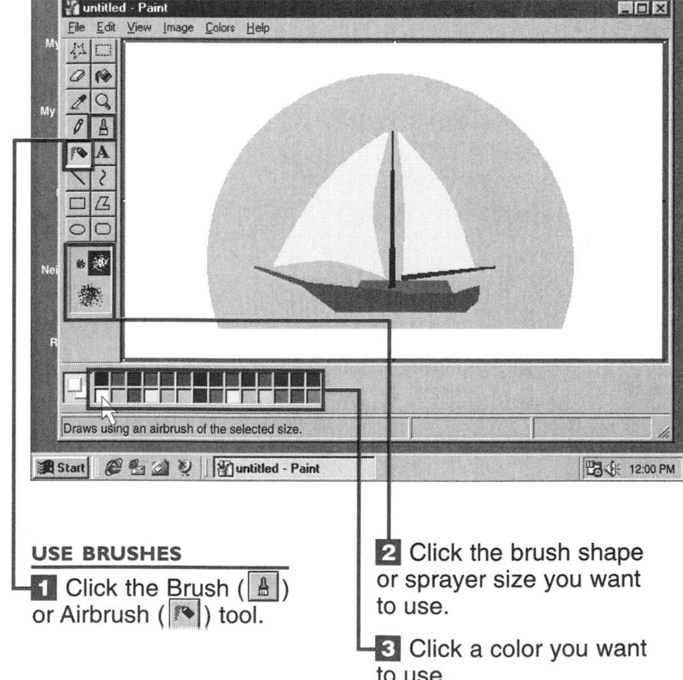

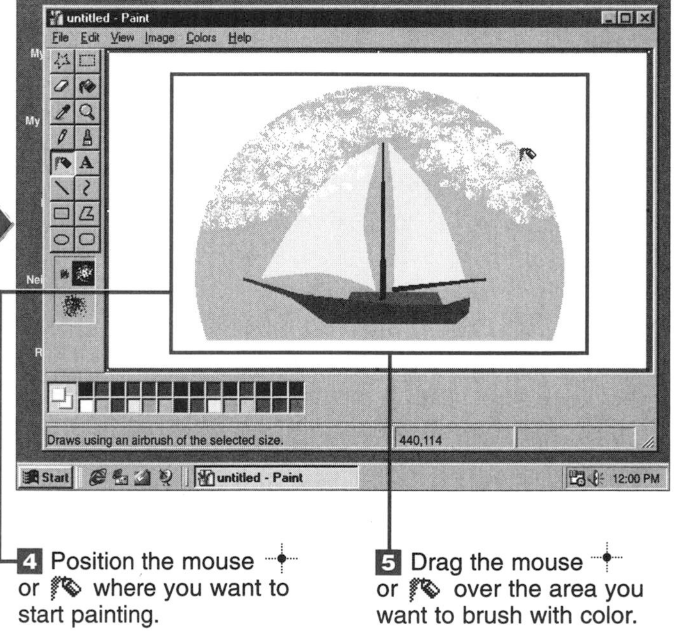

USE BRUSHES

1 Click the Brush ( ) or Airbrush ( ) tool.

2 Click the brush shape or sprayer size you want to use.

3 Click a color you want to use.

4 Position the mouse or where you want to start painting.

5 Drag the mouse or over the area you want to brush with color.

ADD TEXT

You can add text to your painting to provide written information or explanations. Adding text to a painting is useful for adding a title to a painting or street names to a map.

When you create a text box, the Text Toolbar appears. You can use the options on the toolbar to change the size and appearance of the text. You cannot change the text in a text box after you select another tool or click outside the text box.

Paint does not have a spell-checker, so you must make sure the text is correct before you continue creating your painting.

TIPS

Can I use text I have already typed in a document?

Select and copy the text you want to use in the original program. Display the Paint window and create a text box large enough to fit the text. Press Ctrl+V to paste the text into the text box.

How do I display the Text Toolbar?

If the Text Toolbar does not appear automatically, click the View menu and select Text Toolbar.

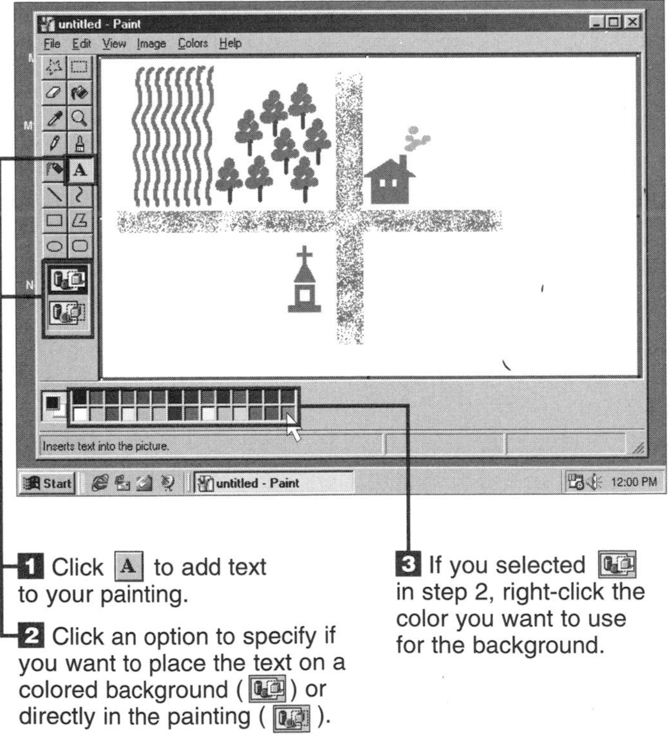

1 Click A to add text to your painting.

2 Click an option to specify if you want to place the text on a colored background ( ) or directly in the painting ( ).

3 If you selected in step 2, right-click the color you want to use for the background.

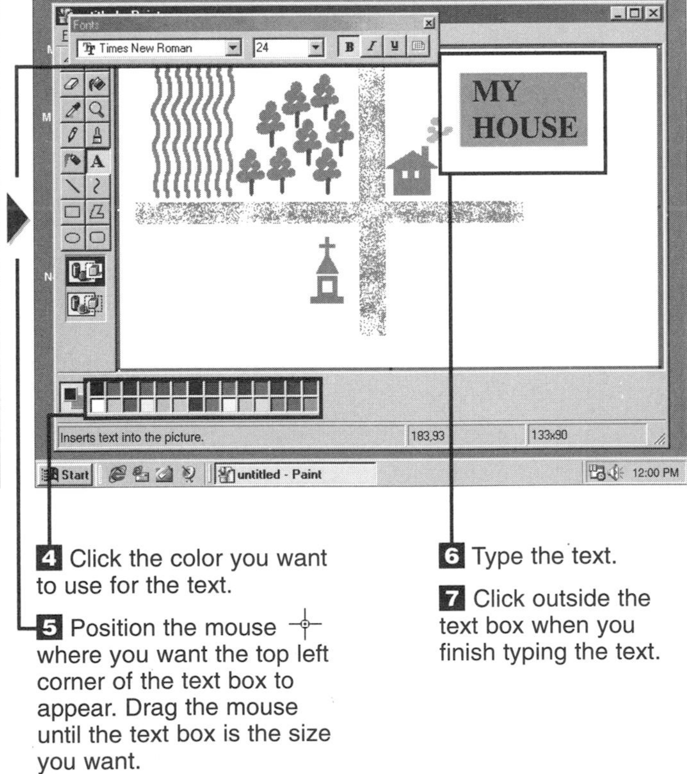

4 Click the color you want to use for the text.

5 Position the mouse where you want the top left corner of the text box to appear. Drag the mouse until the text box is the size you want.

6 Type the text.

7 Click outside the text box when you finish typing the text.

FILL AREA WITH COLOR

You can change the color of any solid object or any area in the painting that has a solid border.

If there are breaks or holes in the border of the area you are filling with color, the color will leak out into the surrounding area. Make sure you fix the holes in the object's border before you try filling the area with color.

Filling an area with color is useful if you want to color an entire item, recolor text letter by letter, or create a pattern of colors using lines drawn inside a circle.

You can also change the color of the entire background of your painting by clicking a blank area of your painting.

TIP

How do I copy a color from one area of my painting to another area?

If you want several areas to display the same color, click and then click the area displaying the color you want to copy. Then select the tool and click the area you want to display the color.

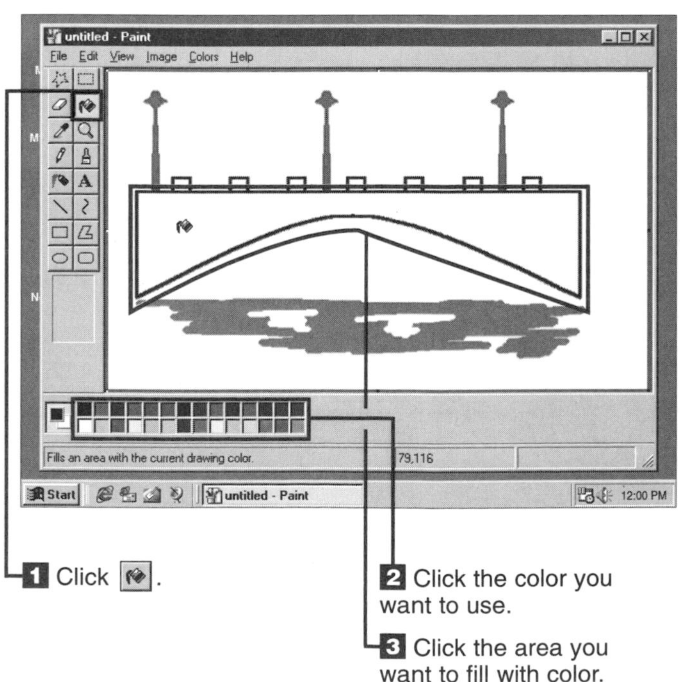

1 Click .

2 Click the color you want to use.

3 Click the area you want to fill with color.

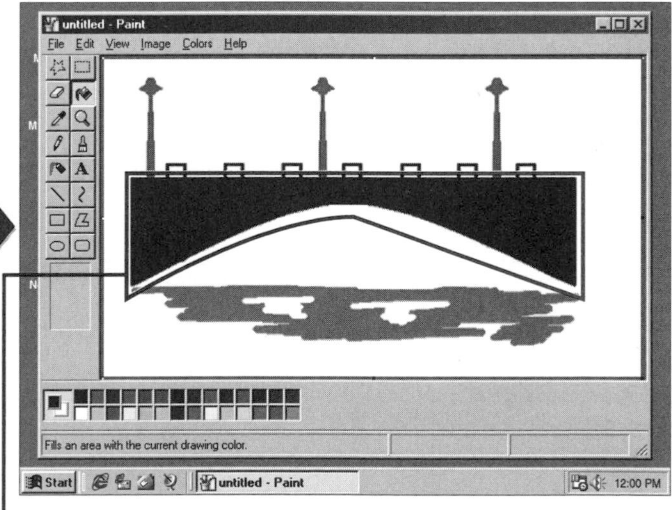

■ The area fills with color.

Note: You can click Edit and then click Undo to immediately cancel the change.

MOVE PART OF A PAINTING

You can rearrange the items in a painting. You can move items with or without their background. The empty space left by the moved item will be filled with a color you specify.

If you are planning to make several changes to a painting, you may want to save the original painting with a new name first. This will give you two copies of the painting–the original and one with all the changes. This is useful in case your changes do not work out the way you expect.

TIP 

Can I move an item back to its original location?

From the Edit menu, select the Undo command to move an item back to its original location. Paint can undo the last three changes you made.

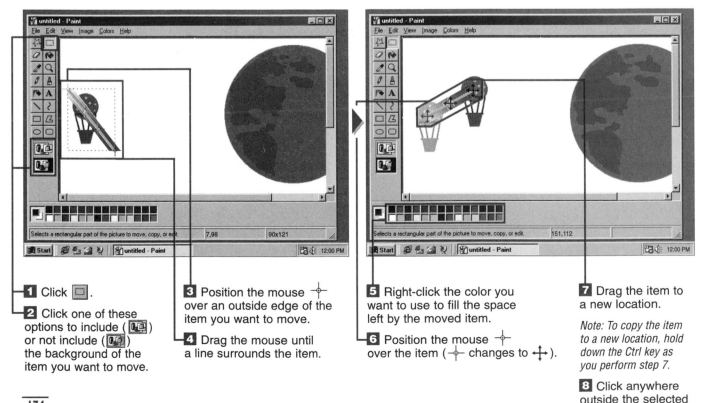

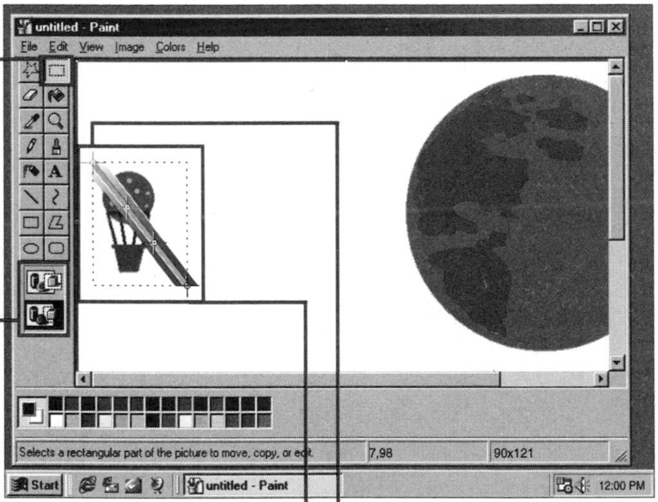

1 Click .

2 Click one of these options to include ( ) or not include ( ) the background of the item you want to move.

3 Position the mouse over an outside edge of the item you want to move.

4 Drag the mouse until a line surrounds the item.

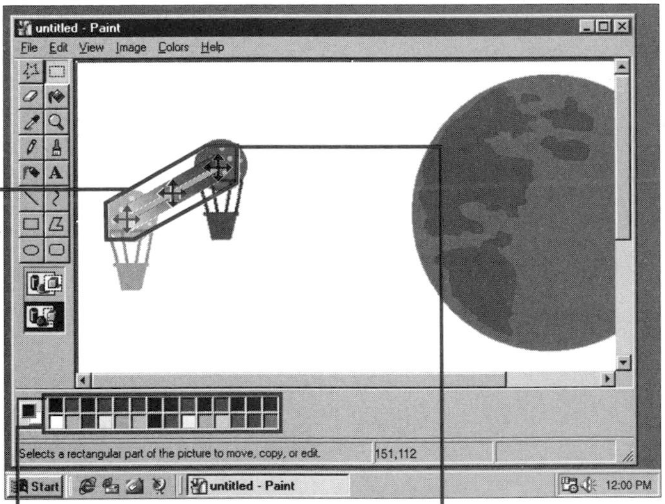

5 Right-click the color you want to use to fill the space left by the moved item.

6 Position the mouse over the item (changes to).

7 Drag the item to a new location.

Note: To copy the item to a new location, hold down the Ctrl key as you perform step 7.

8 Click anywhere outside the selected item.

ERASE PART OF A PAINTING

You can remove an area from your painting. Paint offers four different eraser sizes for you to choose from. Choose the small eraser when you want to be precise in your erasing. Choose the large eraser when you want to erase a large area of your painting.

You can use any color to erase an area of your painting. Use a white eraser when the area you want to erase has a white background. Use a colored eraser when the area you want to erase has a colored background.

TIP

Is there an easier way to erase a large area of my painting?

To select the area you want to erase, perform steps 1 to 4 on page 174. Right-click the color you want to use to fill the area and then press the Delete key.

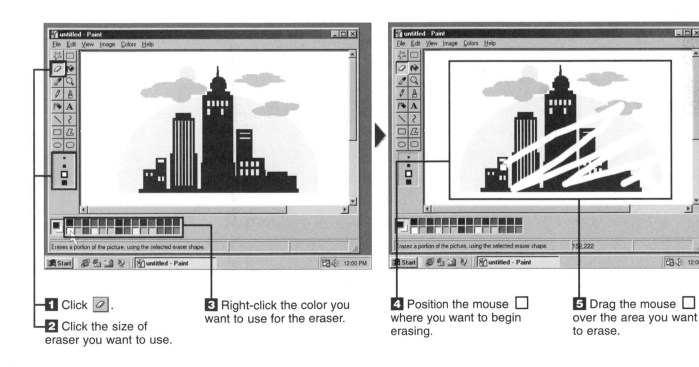

1 Click .

2 Click the size of eraser you want to use.

3 Right-click the color you want to use for the eraser.

4 Position the mouse where you want to begin erasing.

5 Drag the mouse over the area you want to erase.

SAVE AND OPEN A PAINTING

You can save your painting to store it for future use. This lets you later review and make changes to the painting.

By default, Paint stores paintings only in the bitmap (.bmp) format. If you have other applications installed on your computer, you may be able to save paint files in other formats than .bmp.

Store your paintings in a folder on your computer where you will be able to easily find them again. If you plan on using your painting as wallpaper on your desktop, store it in the Windows folder.

You should regularly save your painting while you are working. This will ensure that all the changes you make to the painting are saved, in case of a computer problem or power failure.

You can open a saved painting and display it on your screen. This allows you to view or make changes to the painting.

You can use Paint to modify image files saved in the .bmp format on your computer.

Paint lets you work with only one painting at a time. If you are currently working with a painting, save the painting before opening another.

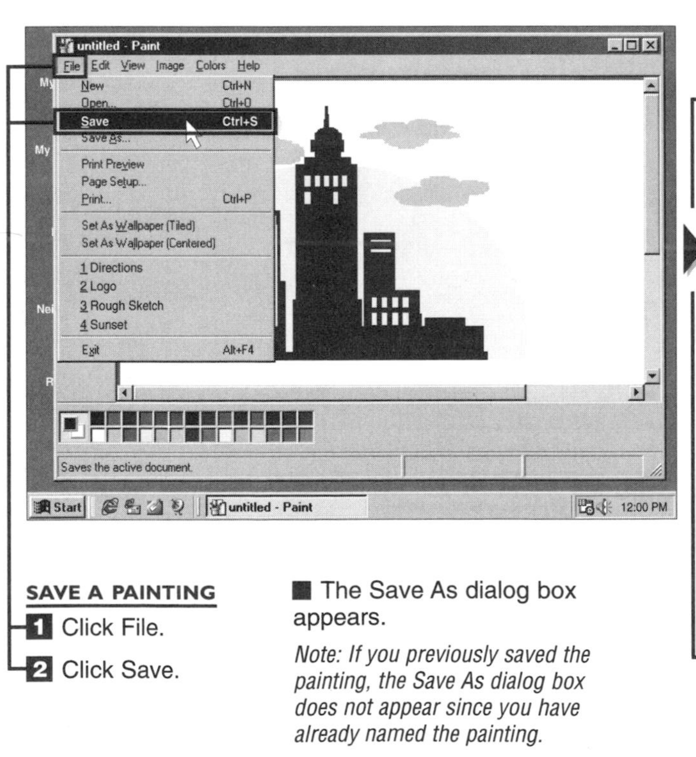

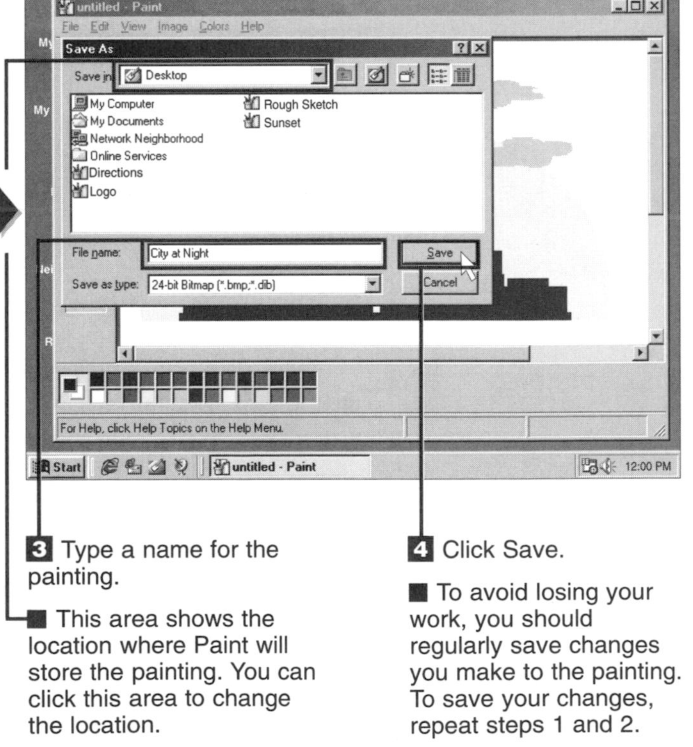

SAVE A PAINTING

1 Click File.

2 Click Save.

■ The Save As dialog box appears.

Note: If you previously saved the painting, the Save As dialog box does not appear since you have already named the painting.

3 Type a name for the painting.

■ This area shows the location where Paint will store the painting. You can click this area to change the location.

4 Click Save.

■ To avoid losing your work, you should regularly save changes you make to the painting. To save your changes, repeat steps 1 and 2.

TIPS

Can I work with two paintings at the same time?

You can start Paint several times to have several paintings open at once. To start Paint, you can use the Start menu or double-click a Paint file in a My Computer or Windows Explorer window.

Is there a faster way to open a painting?

The last four paintings you worked with in Paint appear on the File menu. You can click any of these paintings to open them.

Can I change the number of colors that are used to save the painting?

You can select the number of colors used to save your painting from the Save as type area in the Save As dialog box. Saving fewer colors results in a smaller file size. If your system can only display 256 colors, there may be no advantage in saving the painting using more colors.

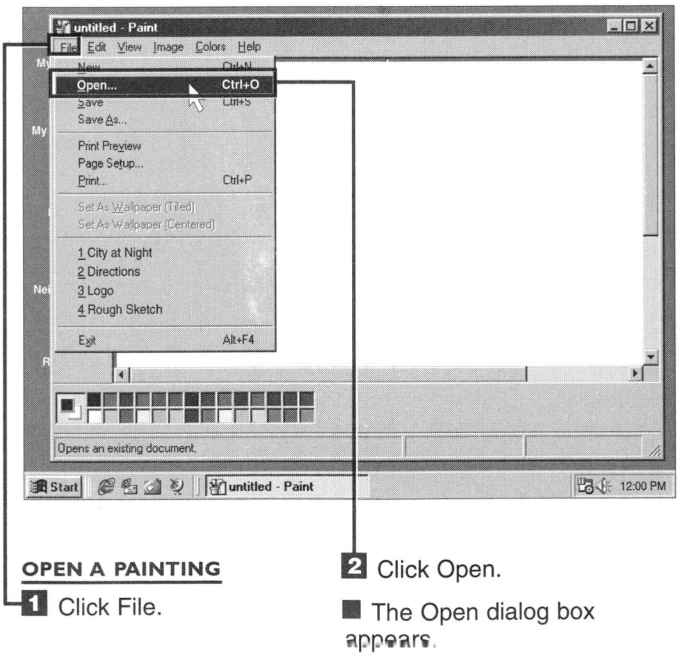

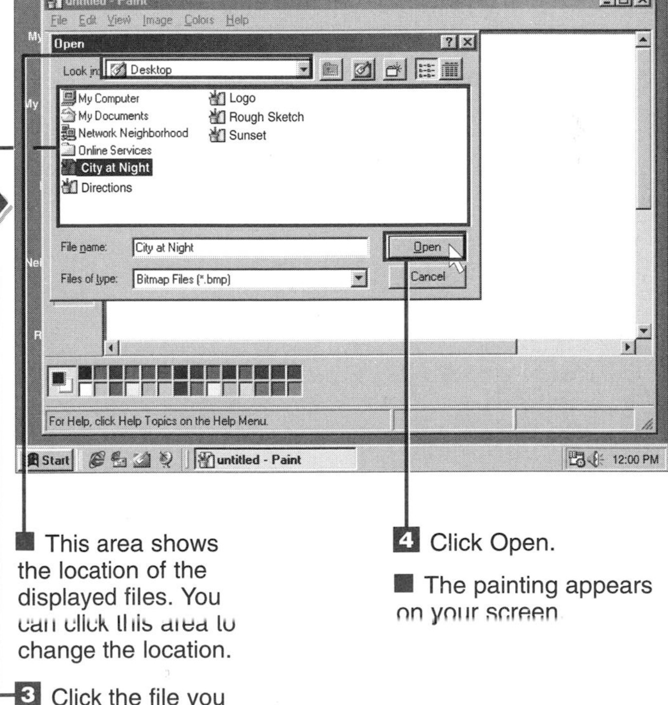

OPEN A PAINTING

1 Click File.

2 Click Open.

■ The Open dialog box appears.

■ This area shows the location of the displayed files. You can click this area to change the location.

3 Click the file you want to open.

4 Click Open.

■ The painting appears on your screen.

PRINT A PAINTING

When you finish creating a painting, you can print a copy of your work.

A color printer prints a copy of your painting in color. If you print your painting using a black-and-white printer, colors appear as shades of gray.

If your painting is too large to fit on one page, it will print on multiple pages. You can choose to print one page, a range of pages or all the pages.

How do I e-mail a painting to a friend?

You can send the painting as a file attached to an e-mail message. To attach a file to a message, see page 534.

How do I preview a painting before I print it?

From the File menu, select Print Preview to preview a painting.

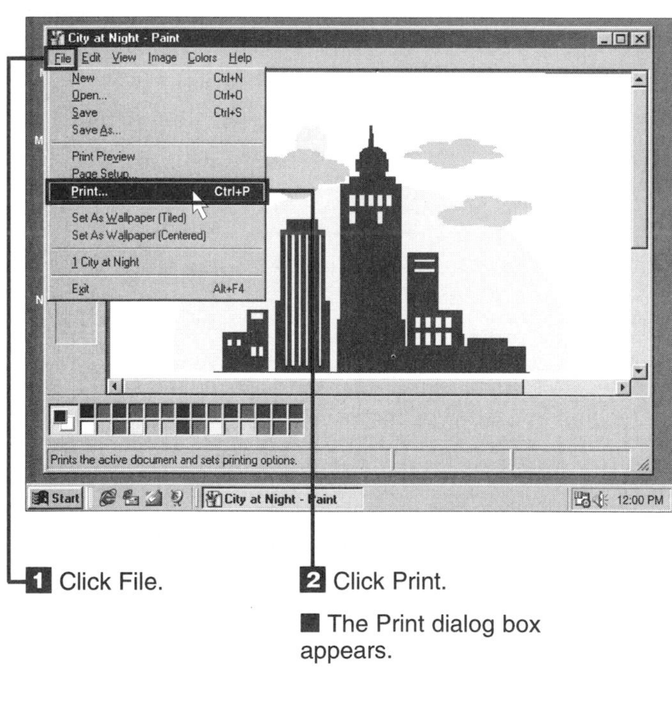

1 Click File.

2 Click Print.

■ The Print dialog box appears.

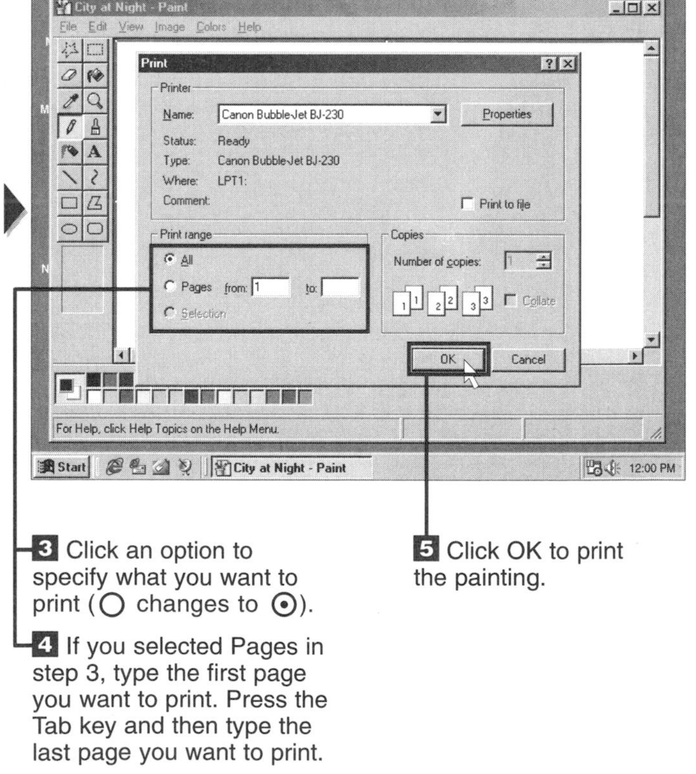

3 Click an option to specify what you want to print (○ changes to ⊙).

4 If you selected Pages in step 3, type the first page you want to print. Press the Tab key and then type the last page you want to print.

5 Click OK to print the painting.

USE A PAINTING AS DESKTOP BACKGROUND

You can use any painting created in Paint as a background for your desktop. This is an easy way to customize your desktop.

Your painting will be the same size on the desktop as it appears in the Paint window.

A painting can be centered on your desktop or tiled to cover the entire screen.

TIPS 

How do I make a painting smaller?

From the Image menu, select Stretch/Skew to shrink a painting that you already created. To change the size of a new painting and all your future paintings, click the Image menu and then select Attributes.

How can I remove a painting from my desktop background?

You can use the Display Properties dialog box to change your desktop background. See page 206.

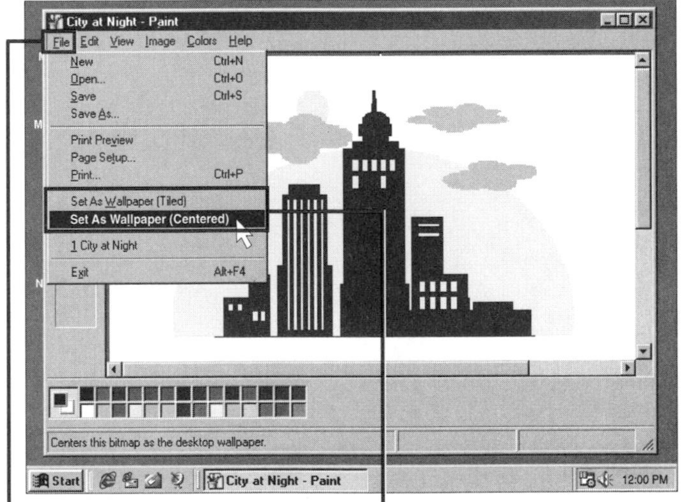

■ You must save a painting before you can use the painting as your desktop background. To save a painting, refer to page 176.

1 Click File.

2 Click the wallpaper option you want to use.

Tiled - Repeats painting to cover desktop.

Centered - Displays painting centered on the desktop.

■ The painting appears on your desktop.

Note: If a centered image does not fill your entire screen you can stretch it to fill your screen. See page 206.

USING THE CALCULATOR

Windows provides a calculator to help you perform calculations. You can work with the Calculator in either the Standard or Scientific view.

The Calculator's Standard view allows you to perform basic mathematical calculations. In this view, the Calculator resembles a small hand-held calculator.

You can use the Scientific view to perform more complex mathematical calculations. This view lets you calculate averages, exponents, sines, cosines, tangents and much more.

You can enter information into the Calculator by using your mouse to click the Calculator buttons or by pressing the keys on the numeric keypad on your keyboard. The result of a calculation appears in the Calculator window.

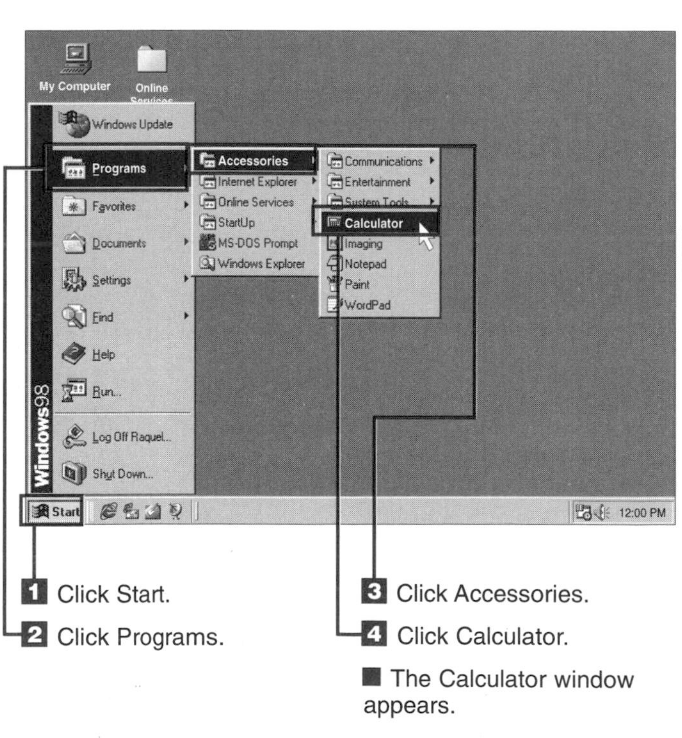

1 Click Start.

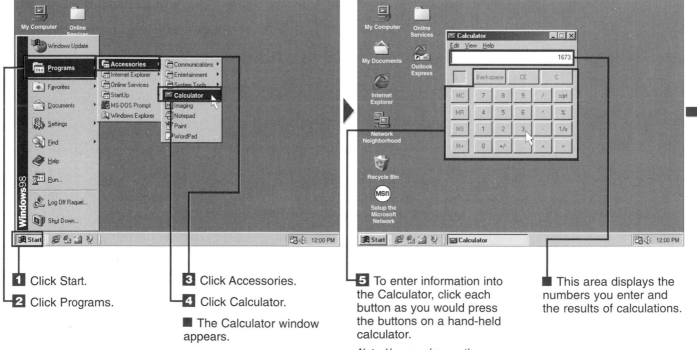

2 Click Programs.

3 Click Accessories.

4 Click Calculator.

■ The Calculator window appears.

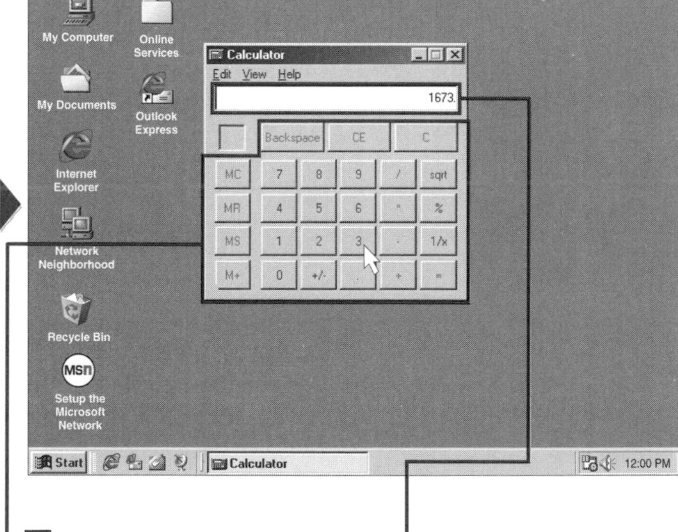

5 To enter information into the Calculator, click each button as you would press the buttons on a hand-held calculator.

Note: You can also use the numeric keypad on your keyboard to enter information.

■ This area displays the numbers you enter and the results of calculations.

TIPS

How can I copy the result of a calculation to another program?

To copy the result of a calculation, press Ctrl+C on your keyboard. Switch to the other program and then paste the result by pressing Ctrl+V on your keyboard. You can also use this technique to copy a selected number into the Calculator.

How can I find out what the Calculator buttons do?

Right-click a button of interest. A box containing the text "What's This?" appears. Click this box to display information about the button.

Why are the number keys on the numeric keypad not working?

Num Lock must be on in order for the numeric keypad to work. To turn this setting on, press the Num Lock key on your keyboard. A status light on your keyboard indicates this setting is on.

Can I keep the Calculator on the screen all the time?

Yes. You can also minimize the Calculator on the taskbar. To have the Calculator open each time you turn on your computer, place a shortcut to the Calculator in the StartUp folder. See page 268.

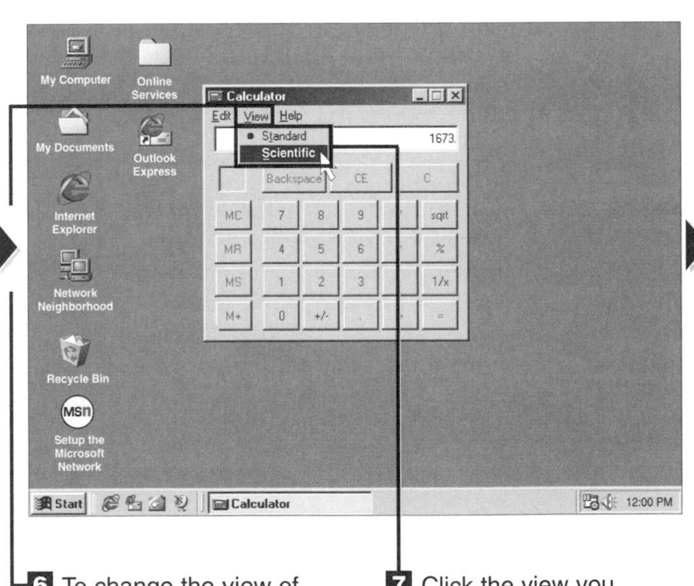

6 To change the view of the Calculator, click View.

7 Click the view you want to display.

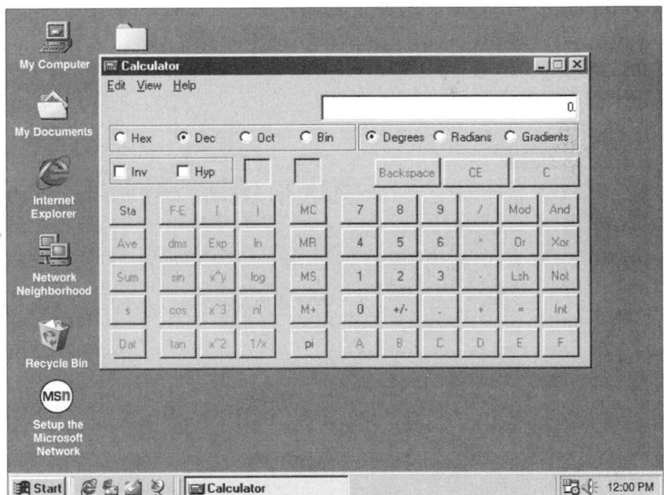

■ In this example, the Scientific view of the Calculator appears.

USING NOTEPAD

Notepad is a fast and easy-to-use text processor that can help you accomplish many tasks.

Notepad is a small Windows program that does not require a lot of your computer's resources to run.

You can use Notepad to take notes or create simple documents. Notepad files are small and can be opened by most word processors and publishing programs.

Notepad can be used to create and edit Web pages, MS-DOS batch files and to view .log and .ini files.

Notepad displays each paragraph of a document on one line. To read an entire line, you have to scroll from left to right in the window. You can use Notepad's Word Wrap feature to wrap the text within the width of the window. Wrapping text can make the document easier to read.

You can have Notepad enter the current date and time in your documents. This is useful if you use Notepad to take phone messages and want the messages time stamped.

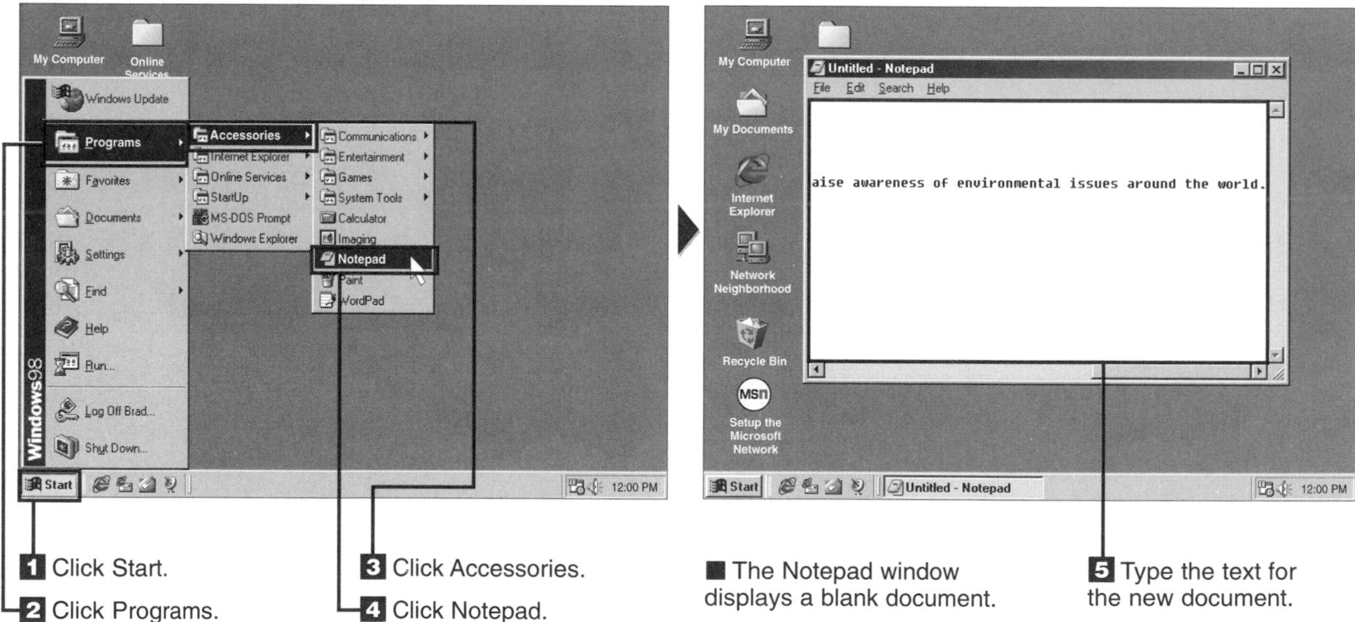

1 Click Start.

2 Click Programs.

3 Click Accessories.

4 Click Notepad.

■ The Notepad window displays a blank document.

5 Type the text for the new document.

TIPS

How do I open a document I previously created in Notepad?

You can open a Notepad document by choosing the File menu and then selecting the Open command. Notepad lets you work with only one document at a time. If you are currently working with a document, save the document before opening another.

Is there a way to have Notepad automatically enter the time and date in my document?

You can have Notepad display the current time and date at the end of a document each time you open the document. To do so, type .LOG on the first line of the document.

Can I change the font Notepad displays?

You can have Notepad display a different font to make the text easier to read. Click the Edit menu and then select Set Font. All the files you open in Notepad will display the new font.

How can I find a word in a Notepad document?

From the Search menu, select the Find command to search for a specific word in a document.

How do I save a document I created in Notepad?

You can save a Notepad document by choosing the File menu and then selecting the Save command.

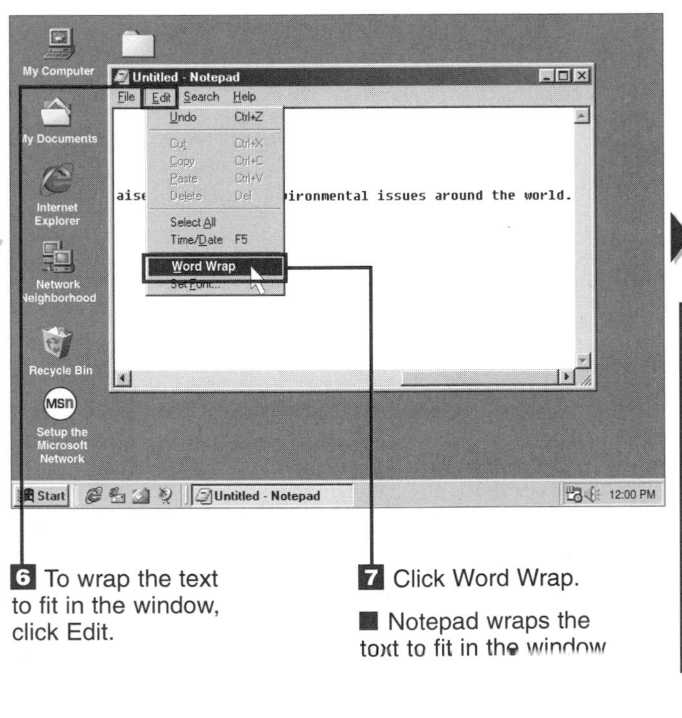

6 To wrap the text to fit in the window, click Edit.

7 Click Word Wrap.

■ Notepad wraps the text to fit in the window.

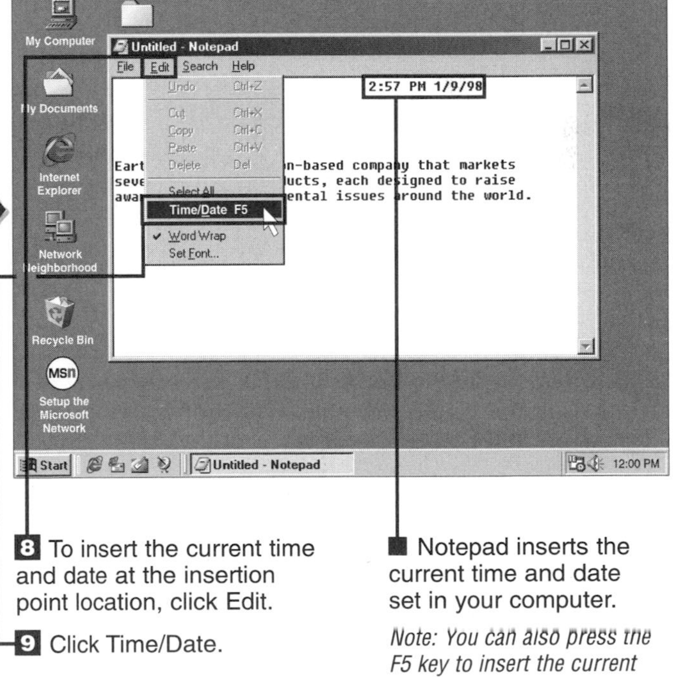

8 To insert the current time and date at the insertion point location, click Edit.

9 Click Time/Date.

■ Notepad inserts the current time and date set in your computer.

Note: You can also press the F5 key to insert the current time and date.

INSERT SPECIAL CHARACTERS

You can use Character Map to include special characters in your documents which are not available on the keyboard.

Your computer has many sets of characters, or fonts, for you to choose from. Most fonts have a selection of up to 255 characters, which can include upper and lower case accented letters such as è, one character fractions such as ¼ and symbols such as the copyright mark ©.

The Character Map window displays all of the characters for each font. You can view an enlarged version of each character a font offers.

Some fonts, such as Symbol and Wingdings, contain only special characters. The Symbol font primarily contains symbols used in mathematical equations. The Wingdings font contains bullet characters and arrows.

You can copy the special characters from Character Map and paste them into your documents.

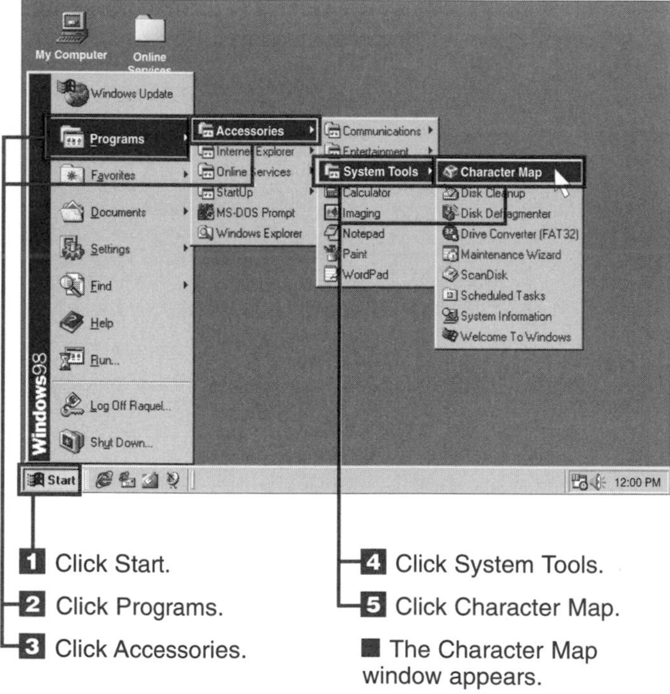

1 Click Start.

2 Click Programs.

3 Click Accessories.

4 Click System Tools.

5 Click Character Map.

■ The Character Map window appears.

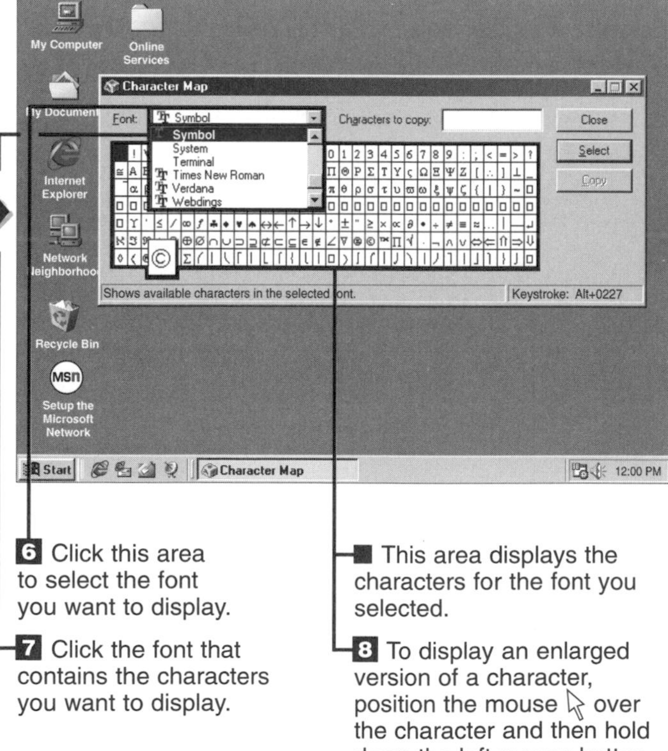

6 Click this area to select the font you want to display.

7 Click the font that contains the characters you want to display.

■ This area displays the characters for the font you selected.

8 To display an enlarged version of a character, position the mouse over the character and then hold down the left mouse button.

TIPS

Why isn't Character Map displayed on the Start menu?

You may need to install Character Map on your computer. Character Map is found in the System Tools component. To add Windows components, see page 610.

Can I use special characters without opening Character Map each time?

Each special character has a keystroke combination that appears in the Character Map window. When you enter the keystroke combination, the character appears in your document. For example, to enter the symbol for the English pound (£), choose the Arial font in your document. Then press and hold down the Alt key as you enter 0163 using the numeric keypad.

Some of the characters I copy and paste do not appear properly. How can I fix them?

Select the characters that appear incorrectly in the document and change them to the same font you selected in the Character Map window.

How can I make Character Map easier to access?

If you use Character Map regularly, you can leave it open on the desktop or minimize it on the taskbar. You can also place a shortcut to Character Map in the StartUp folder so Character Map will open each time you start Windows. See page 268.

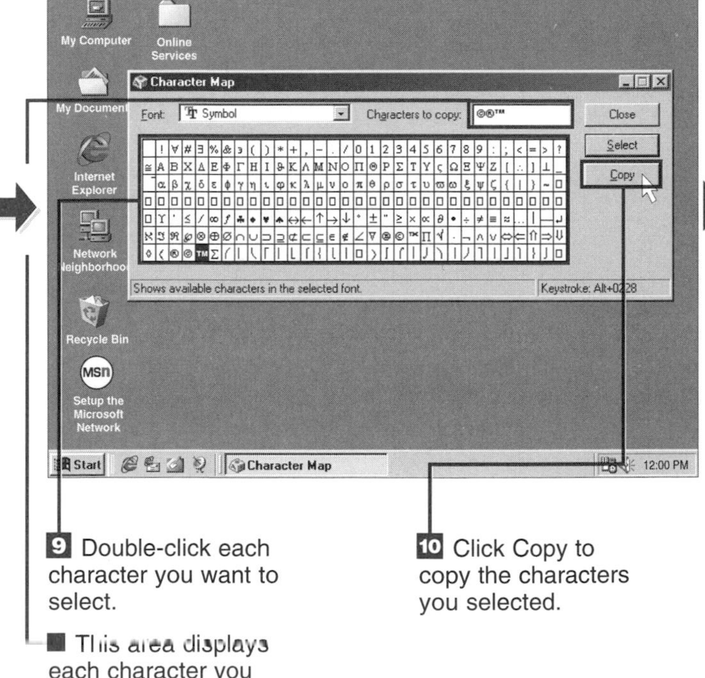

9 Double-click each character you want to select.

■ This area displays each character you select.

10 Click Copy to copy the characters you selected.

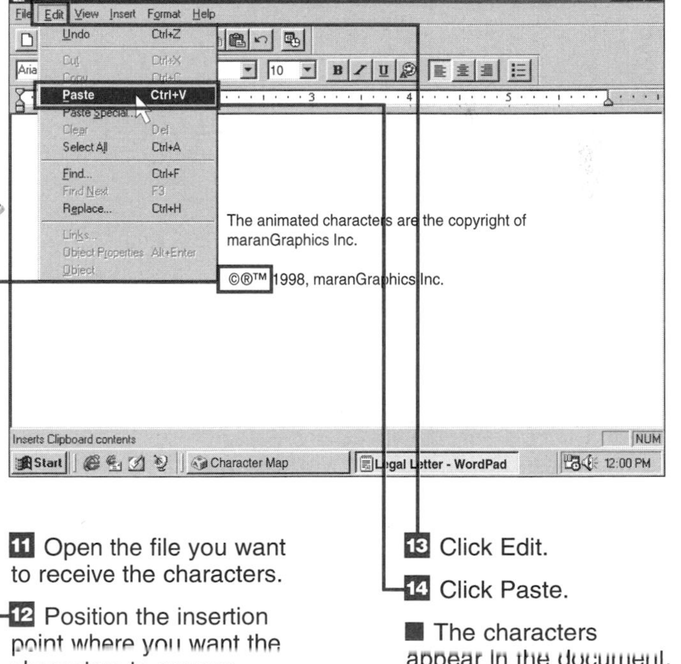

11 Open the file you want to receive the characters.

12 Position the insertion point where you want the characters to appear.

13 Click Edit.

14 Click Paste.

■ The characters appear in the document.

USING PHONE DIALER

If your computer has a modem installed, you can connect a telephone to the modem and use Phone Dialer to make telephone calls.

Phone Dialer allows you to enter a phone number in several different ways.

You can enter the phone number using the number keys in the numeric keypad on your keyboard. You can also use the mouse to click the numbers on the dial pad on your screen. The speed-dial buttons let you select a phone number you dial frequently.

You can have other programs that use the telephone line open at the same time you use Phone Dialer, but only one program can use the telephone line at a time.

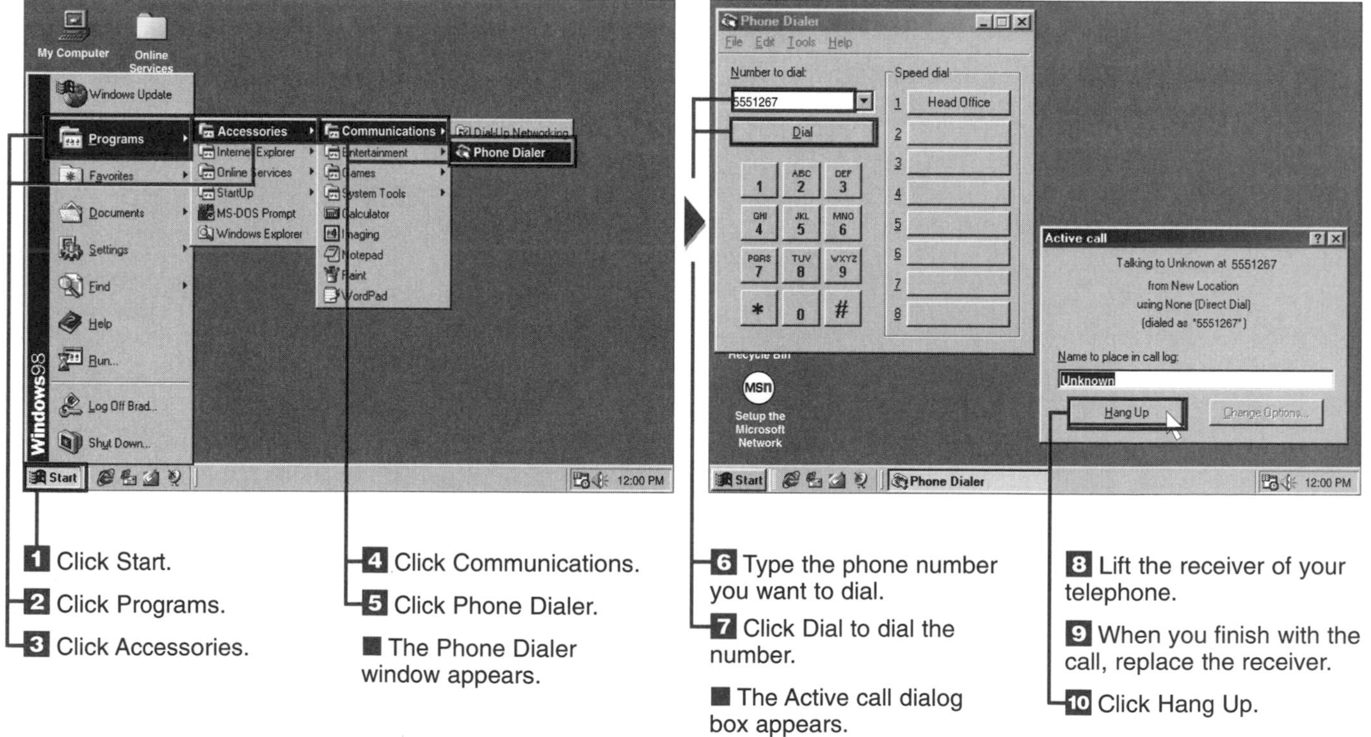

1 Click Start.

2 Click Programs.

3 Click Accessories.

4 Click Communications.

5 Click Phone Dialer.

■ The Phone Dialer window appears.

6 Type the phone number you want to dial.

7 Click Dial to dial the number.

■ The Active call dialog box appears.

8 Lift the receiver of your telephone.

9 When you finish with the call, replace the receiver.

10 Click Hang Up.

TIPS

How can I view a list of all my phone calls?

From the Tools menu, select Show Log to display a list of all your phone calls. The Call Log displays information about each call you have made. You can call any number listed in the log by double-clicking the phone number.

Is there a quick way to dial a phone number I recently used?

Phone Dialer stores a list of the phone numbers you recently used. Click ▼ in the Number to dial area in the Phone Dialer window and then select the number you want to dial from the list.

How can I stop Phone Dialer from treating a local call as a long-distance call?

Phone Dialer will automatically dial a 1 before any area codes that differ from yours. Click the Tools menu and then select Dialing Properties. Click the Area Code Rules button and then click the New button beside Do not dial 1 for numbers with the following area codes. Then enter the area code you want to treat as a local call.

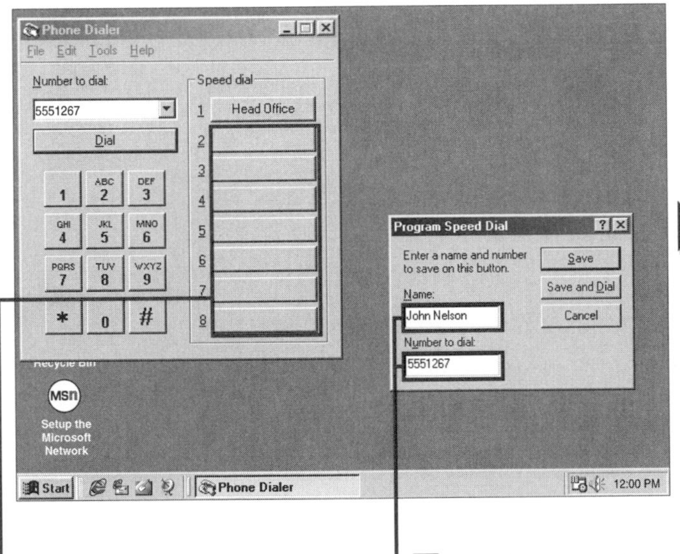

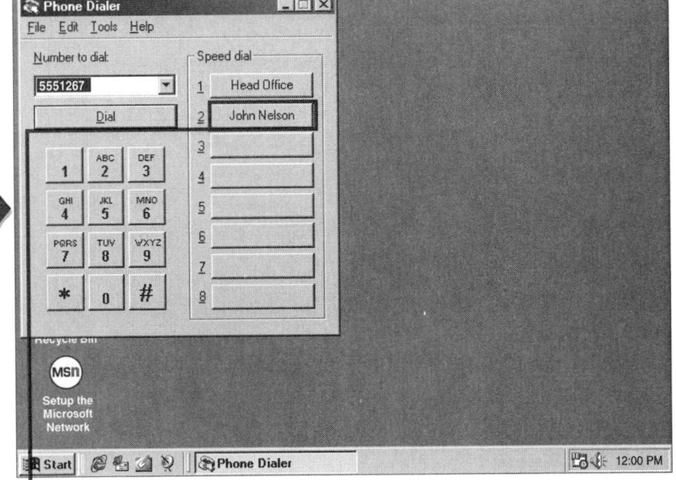

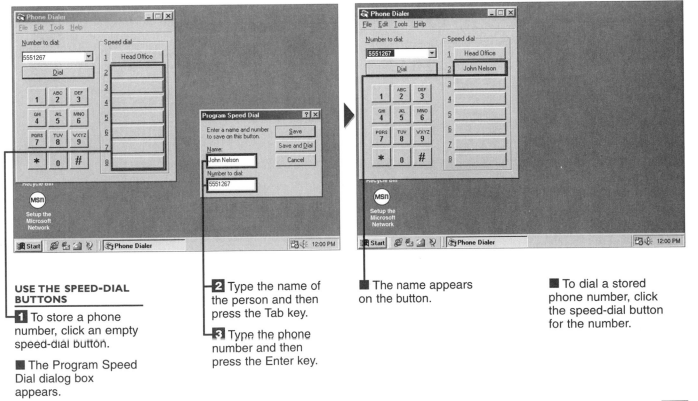

USE THE SPEED-DIAL BUTTONS

1 To store a phone number, click an empty speed-dial button.

■ The Program Speed Dial dialog box appears.

2 Type the name of the person and then press the Tab key.

3 Type the phone number and then press the Enter key.

■ The name appears on the button.

■ To dial a stored phone number, click the speed-dial button for the number.

USING IMAGING

You can use Imaging to turn paper documents such as forms, receipts, pictures and newspaper clippings into documents that can be used on your computer. This is useful if you want to store documents that clutter your desk and filing cabinet in your computer for quick access.

Once a paper document is an Imaging document, you can save, print and share the document as you would any document on your computer.

You can use a scanner to read a paper document into your computer.

You can change the way an Imaging document appears on your screen. You can magnify or reduce the size of the document and rotate the document to the left or right. Rotating the document is useful if the document appears upside down in the window.

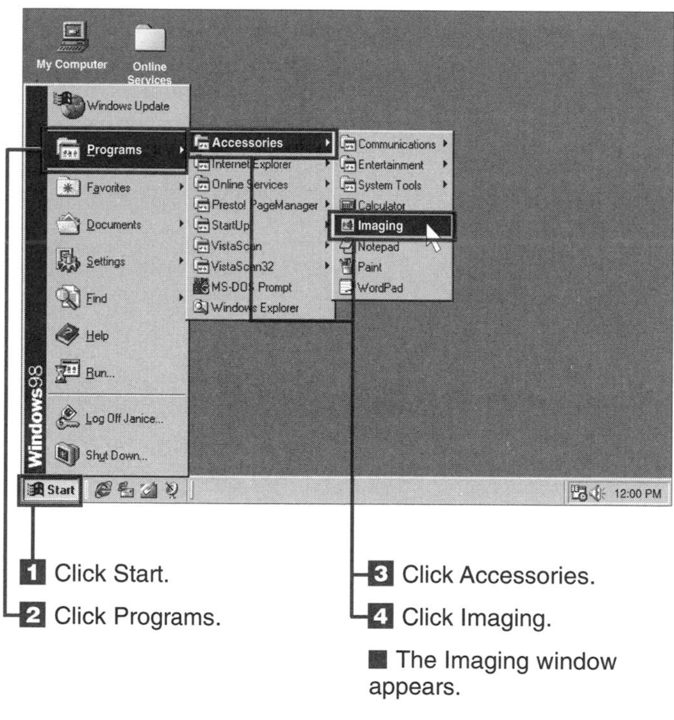

1 Click Start.

2 Click Programs.

3 Click Accessories.

4 Click Imaging.

■ The Imaging window appears.

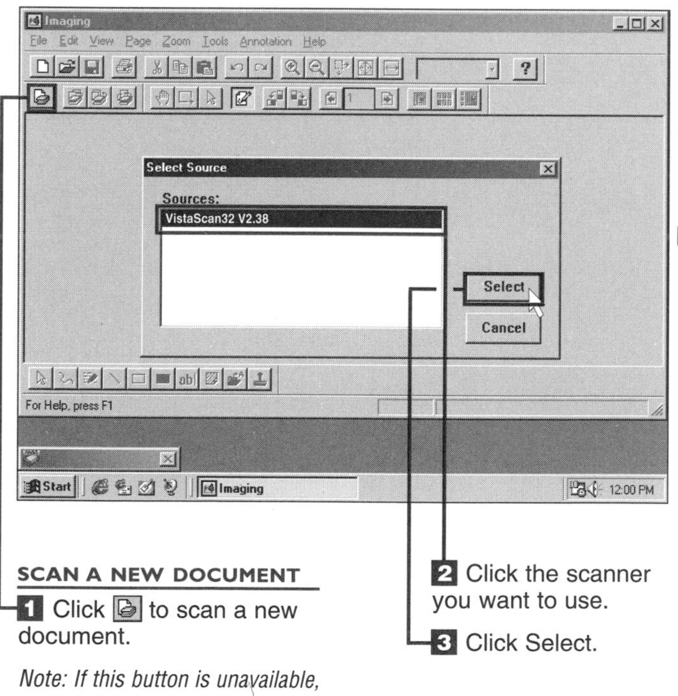

SCAN A NEW DOCUMENT

1 Click [scan button] to scan a new document.

Note: If this button is unavailable, consult the documentation included with your scanner.

■ The Select Source dialog box appears the first time you scan a document.

2 Click the scanner you want to use.

3 Click Select.

TIPS

How do I size a document to fit on my screen?

You can click [icon] to view the entire document on your screen. You can click [icon] to make the document fit your screen from side to side.

Can I view all the pages in my Imaging document at once?

You can click [icon] to display a small version of each page in the document. You can also click [icon] to view a small version of each page in the document on the left side of your screen and one full page of the document on the right side of your screen. You can click [icon] to again view only one page at a time.

Can I open other types of files in Imaging?

Imaging can open most image formats, including .jpg, .gif and .tif. This makes Imaging an effective tool for converting picture files to the Windows bitmap (.bmp) format.

Can I add pages to my document?

You can click [icon] to insert a new scanned page before the current page. You can click [icon] to add a new scanned page at the end of the document. You cannot add pages to a document saved with the .bmp extension.

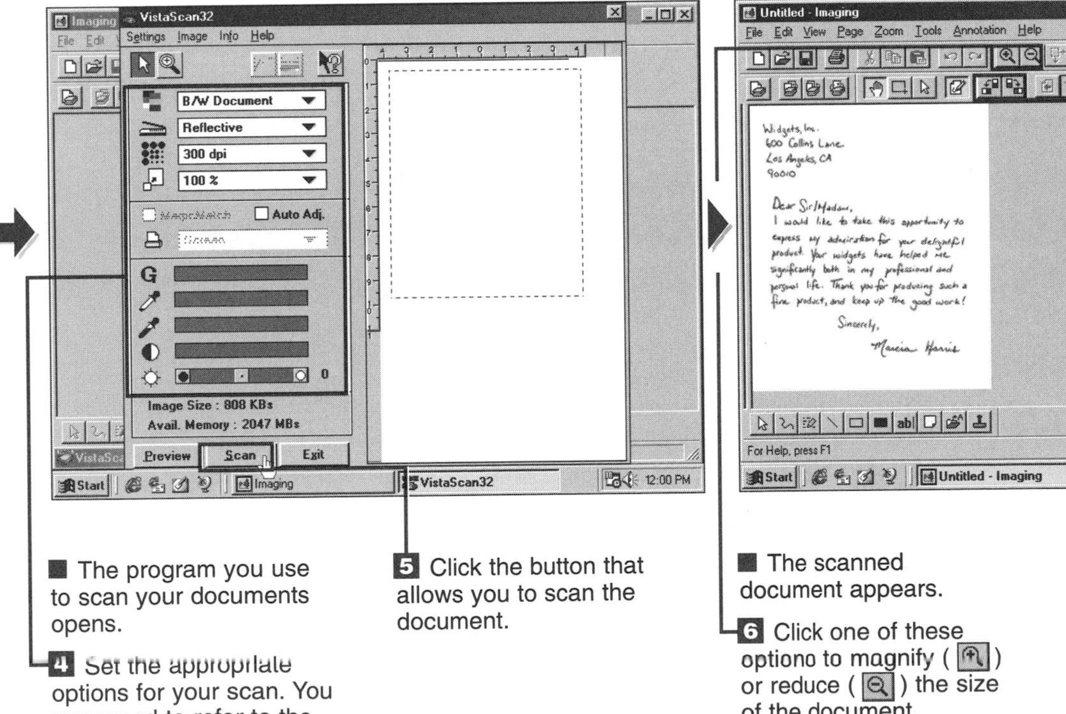

■ The program you use to scan your documents opens.

4 Set the appropriate options for your scan. You may need to refer to the documentation that came with your scanner.

5 Click the button that allows you to scan the document.

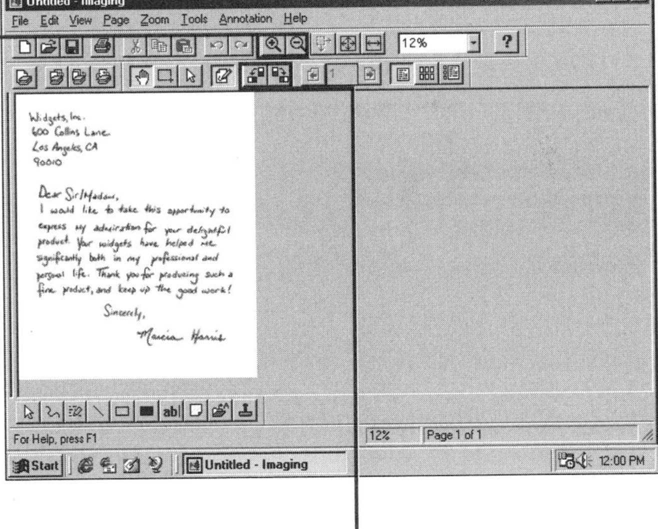

■ The scanned document appears.

6 Click one of these options to magnify ([icon]) or reduce ([icon]) the size of the document.

7 Click one of these options to rotate the document to the left ([icon]) or to the right ([icon]).

CONTINUED

USING IMAGING CONTINUED

You can work with an Imaging document as you would work with any paper document. You can fill in a form, add details to a receipt or put a message on a magazine clipping.

You can add a note or text to an Imaging document. Information you add to an Imaging document is called an annotation. Adding annotations is useful when you want a document to contain your remarks and comments. For example, you can scan the minutes of a meeting, use annotations to add your notes and then distribute the document to people who missed the meeting.

Imaging also includes a tool that you can use to rubber stamp a document. You can use a stamp to show the date you approved, received or rejected a document. You can also use a stamp to indicate that a document is a draft copy.

You can save an annotation with a document. You can also print a document that contains annotations.

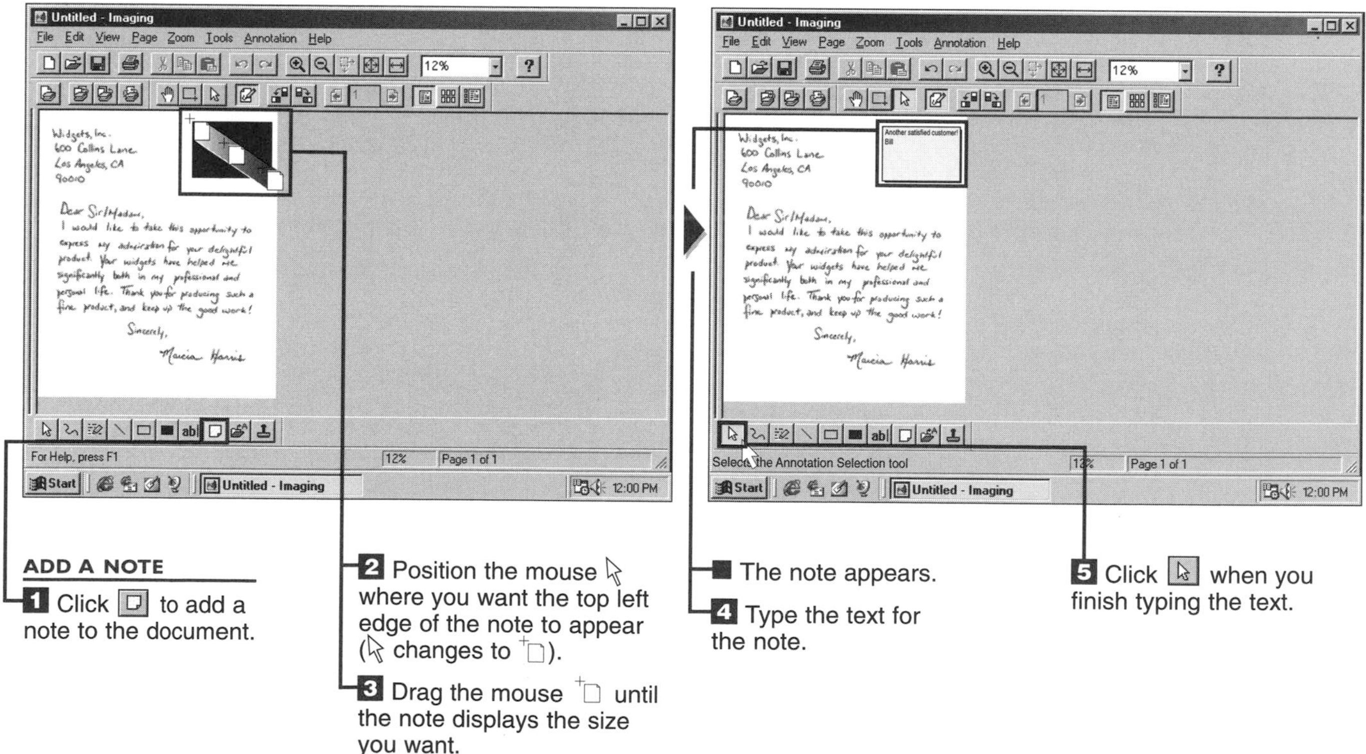

ADD A NOTE

1 Click [note tool] to add a note to the document.

2 Position the mouse where you want the top left edge of the note to appear (changes to [note cursor]).

3 Drag the mouse until the note displays the size you want.

■ The note appears.

4 Type the text for the note.

5 Click [selection tool] when you finish typing the text.

TIPS

Can I move or delete an annotation?

Click the Annotation Selection tool (). To move an annotation, drag the annotation to a new position. To delete an annotation, click the annotation and then press the Delete key.

How do I change the appearance of an annotation?

Click the Annotation Selection tool (). Right-click the annotation you want to change and then select Properties. The Properties dialog box appears, displaying the options you can change.

Can I print a document without the annotations?

In the File menu, click Print. In the Print dialog box, click the Options button. Then select whether you want to print the annotations with your document.

Why can't I move or delete the annotations after I save the document?

When you save a document with the .bmp extension, the annotations become a permanent part of the document. When you save a document with the .tif extension, the annotations remain separate. To make annotations a permanent part of a .tif document, click the Annotation menu and then click Make Annotations Permanent.

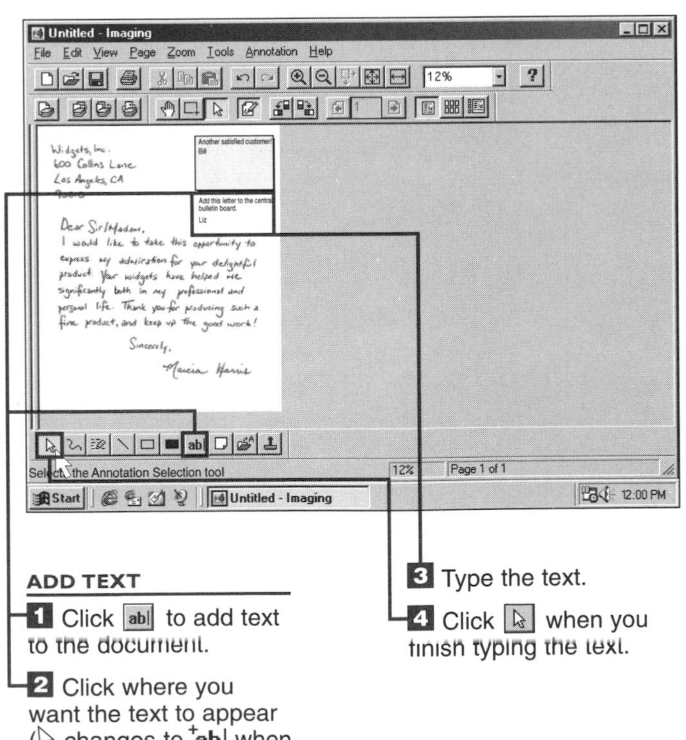

ADD TEXT

1 Click to add text to the document.

2 Click where you want the text to appear (changes to ab| when over the document).

3 Type the text.

4 Click when you finish typing the text.

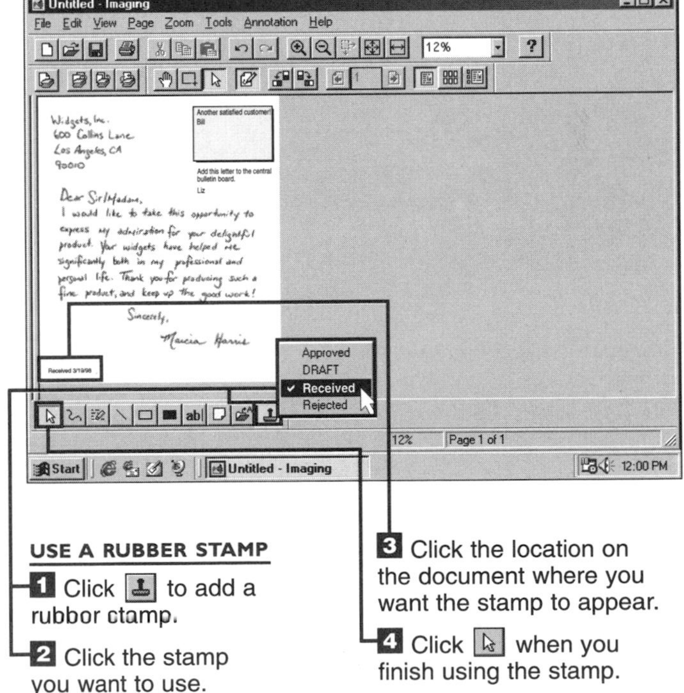

USE A RUBBER STAMP

1 Click to add a rubber stamp.

2 Click the stamp you want to use.

3 Click the location on the document where you want the stamp to appear.

4 Click when you finish using the stamp.

PLAY GAMES

Windows includes several games you can play when you need a break from your work. Games are also a fun way to improve your mouse skills and hand-eye coordination.

Windows 98 comes with three card games. Solitaire and FreeCell are single-player card games. If you are on a network with other Windows 98 users, up to four people can join in a game of Hearts. You can also play Hearts by yourself, with Windows playing the other three hands.

Minesweeper is a strategy game in which you try to avoid being blown up by mines.

If these games are not available on your computer, Games may not be installed. Games is located in the Accessories component. To add Windows components, see page 610.

The games included with Windows 98 are an introduction to the types of games you can play using Windows 98. You can buy additional games at computer stores or on the Internet.

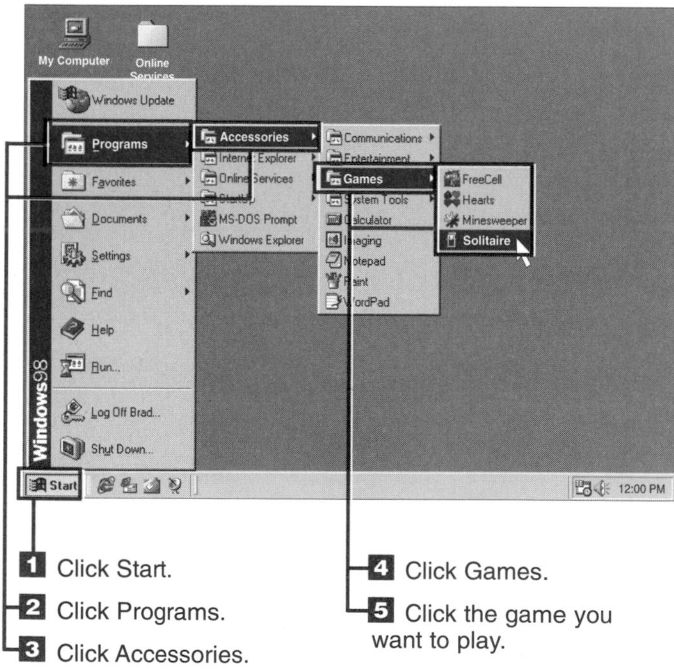

1 Click Start.

2 Click Programs.

3 Click Accessories.

4 Click Games.

5 Click the game you want to play.

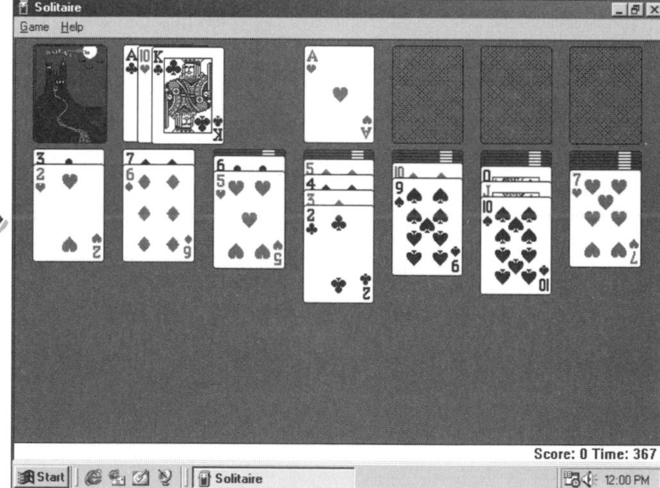

SOLITAIRE

Solitaire is a classic card game that you play on your own. You try to put all the cards in order from ace to king in four stacks, one stack for each suit.

How do I play a game of Hearts on the network?

To connect to a game of Hearts that someone else has started, click the I want to connect to another game option in The Microsoft Hearts Network dialog box and then click OK. Type the name of the dealer's computer in the dialog box that appears.

To start a new game of Hearts on the network, type your computer's name and then click the I want to be dealer option.

How do I play a game of Hearts by myself?

Type the name of your computer and then click the I want to be dealer option in The Microsoft Hearts Network dialog box. When The Microsoft Hearts Network window appears, press the F2 key.

How can I improve my score?

The Help information included in each game can help you improve your score. To display Help information, select the Help menu in the game window and then click Help Topics.

Does Windows include any other games?

The Windows 98 CD-ROM includes trial versions of games such as Golf 3.0 and Return of Arcade. To install these games, insert the Windows 98 CD-ROM into a drive. From the Start menu, select Programs and then click Accessories. Click Entertainment, select Trial Programs and then follow the instructions on your screen.

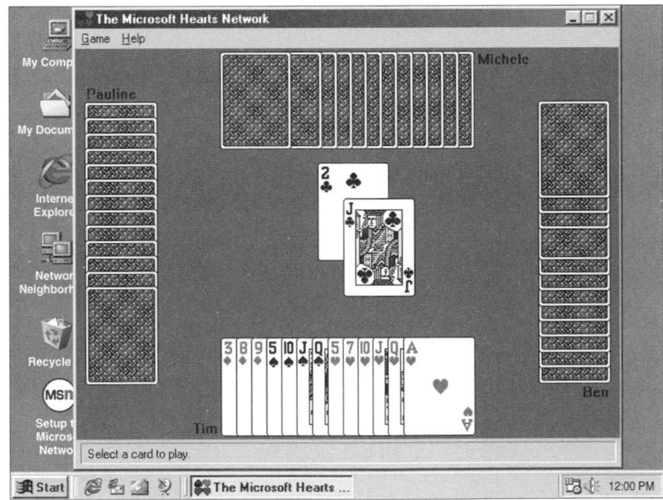

HEARTS

In Hearts, you try to avoid taking hands containing hearts or the queen of spades. The player with the lowest score at the end of the game wins.

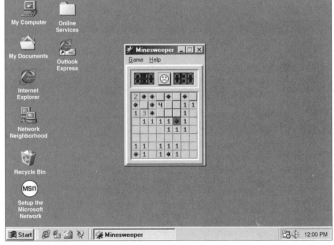

MINESWEEPER

In Minesweeper, you try to locate all of the mines without actually uncovering them.

SECTION III

10) CUSTOMIZE YOUR COMPUTER

11) USING ACCESSIBILITY FEATURES

CUSTOMIZE WINDOWS 98

12) CUSTOMIZE THE START MENU

13) MULTIMEDIA

MOVE AND SIZE THE TASKBAR

You can move and size the taskbar to accommodate your preferences. The taskbar is the starting point for most of the tasks you perform in Windows. The taskbar contains the Start button and displays the name of each open window on your screen as well as the current time. The Quick Launch toolbar appears beside the Start button on the taskbar and contains shortcut icons to Internet Explorer, Outlook Express, the desktop and channels.

Windows initially displays the taskbar at the bottom of your screen. You may want to display the taskbar in a different location on the screen. Windows allows you to move the taskbar to any side of your screen. Since other software programs display their menus at the top of the screen, you may prefer to have the taskbar appear there as well.

You can adjust the size of the taskbar. Increasing the size of the taskbar provides more space to display information about open windows.

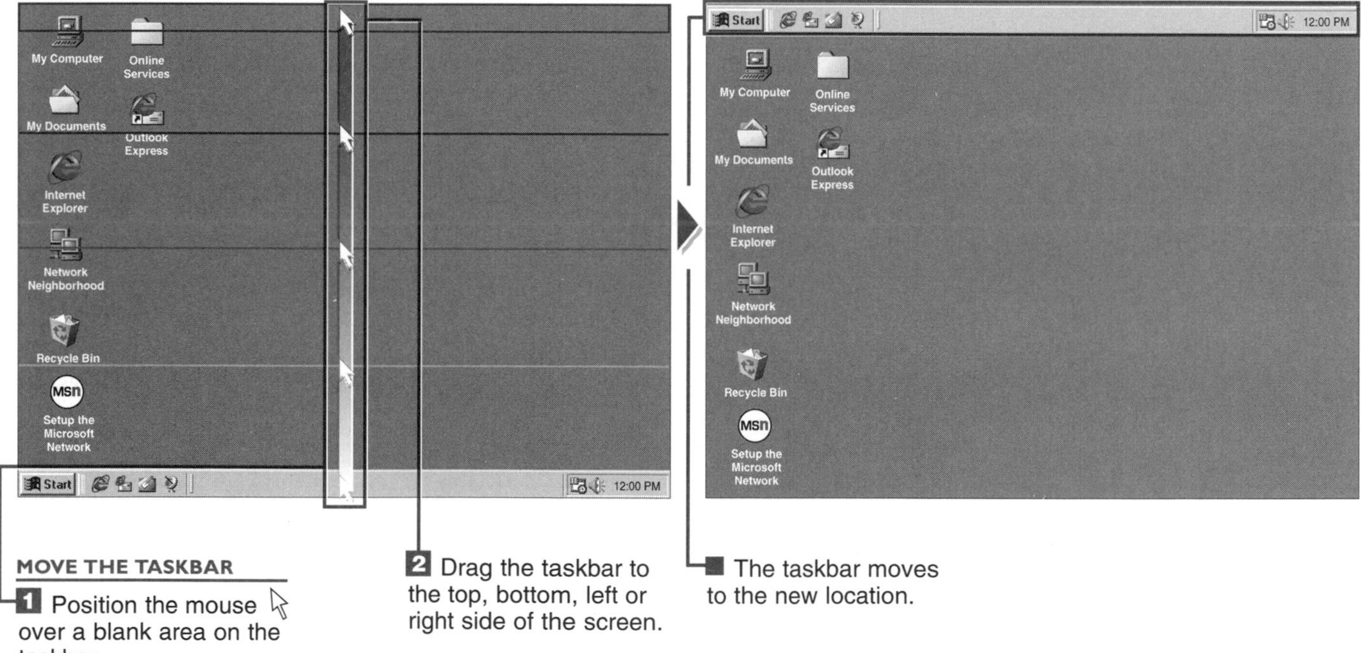

MOVE THE TASKBAR

1 Position the mouse over a blank area on the taskbar.

2 Drag the taskbar to the top, bottom, left or right side of the screen.

■ The taskbar moves to the new location.

TIPS

Why has my taskbar disappeared?

You may have accidentally sized the taskbar. Position the mouse pointer over the edge of the screen where the taskbar was last seen. When ↖ changes to ↕, you can drag the mouse to increase the size of your taskbar.

How can I see more information about a small button on the taskbar?

Position the mouse pointer over the button. After a few seconds, a box appears displaying the full name of the window the button represents.

How can I use the taskbar to display the current date?

Position the mouse pointer over the time. After a few seconds, Windows displays the current date.

How do I correct the time displayed on the taskbar?

Double-click the time to open the Date/Time Properties dialog box. This dialog box allows you to change the date and time on your computer. See page 200.

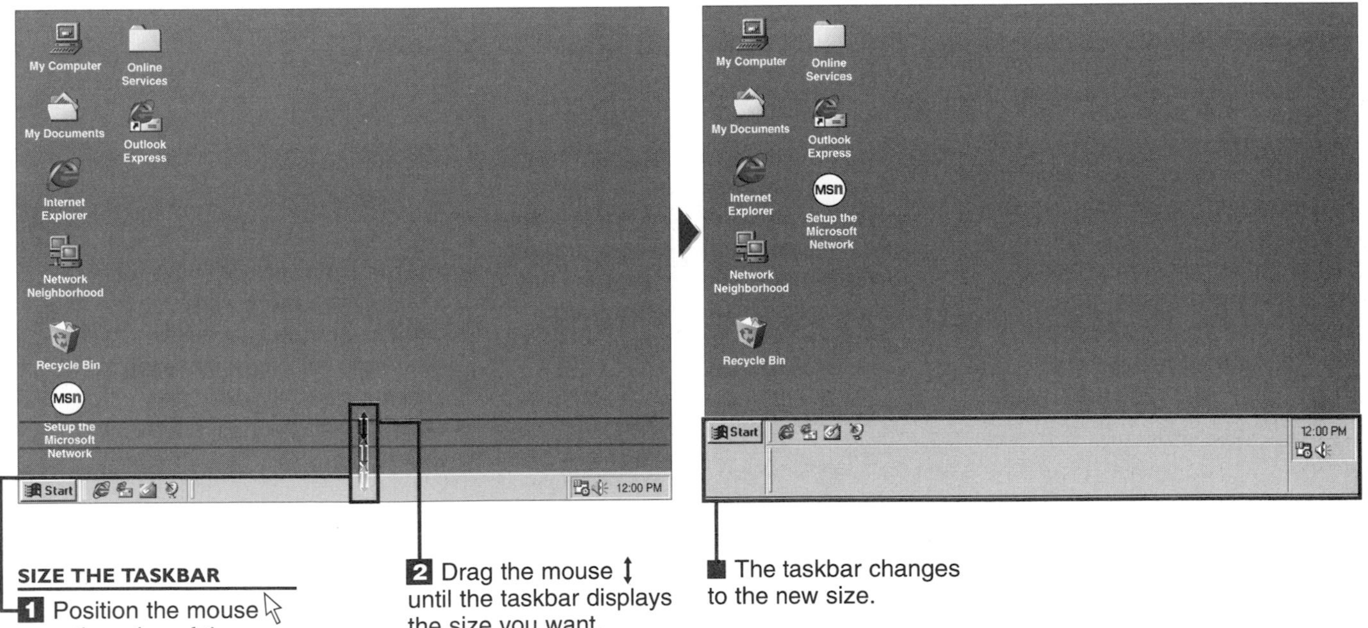

SIZE THE TASKBAR

1 Position the mouse ↖ over the edge of the taskbar (↖ changes to ↕).

2 Drag the mouse ↕ until the taskbar displays the size you want.

■ The taskbar changes to the new size.

CUSTOMIZE THE TASKBAR

You can modify the taskbar to suit your needs and make it easier to use.

Software programs designed for Windows 95 and Windows 98 leave space on the screen to show the taskbar. When you use older programs, the taskbar may cover important parts of the screen.

You can turn off the Always on top option while using older programs so you can see the entire screen.

You can use the Auto hide option to hide the taskbar when you are not using it. Hiding the taskbar provides more working area on your desktop.

The Show small icons in Start menu option reduces the size of the Start menu and the amount of space the menu takes up when displayed.

The Show clock option displays or hides the clock on the taskbar.

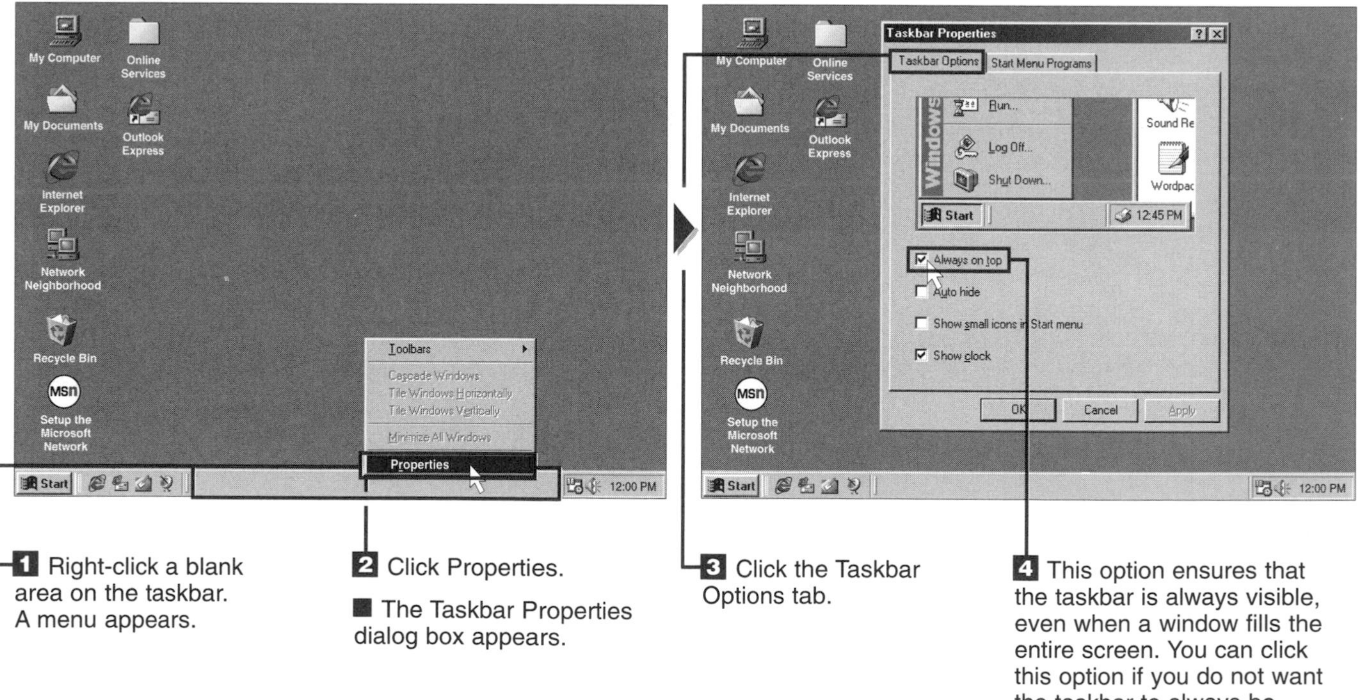

1 Right-click a blank area on the taskbar. A menu appears.

2 Click Properties.

■ The Taskbar Properties dialog box appears.

3 Click the Taskbar Options tab.

4 This option ensures that the taskbar is always visible, even when a window fills the entire screen. You can click this option if you do not want the taskbar to always be visible (☑ changes to ☐).

TIPS

How can I make the taskbar appear when the Auto hide option is on?

Position the mouse over the area where you last saw the taskbar. You can also hold down the Ctrl key and then press the Esc key to display the taskbar and the Start menu.

Can I size an individual taskbar button or remove a button from the taskbar?

Taskbar buttons cannot be sized. To remove a button from the taskbar, you must close the window the button represents.

Are all of my active programs displayed on the taskbar?

Windows may run programs that do not display a button on the taskbar. You can see a complete listing of your active programs in the Close Program dialog box. See page 85.

What happens when the number of buttons on the taskbar exceeds the available space?

Two small arrows appear to the right of the taskbar buttons. You can click these arrows to scroll through buttons not currently displayed on the taskbar.

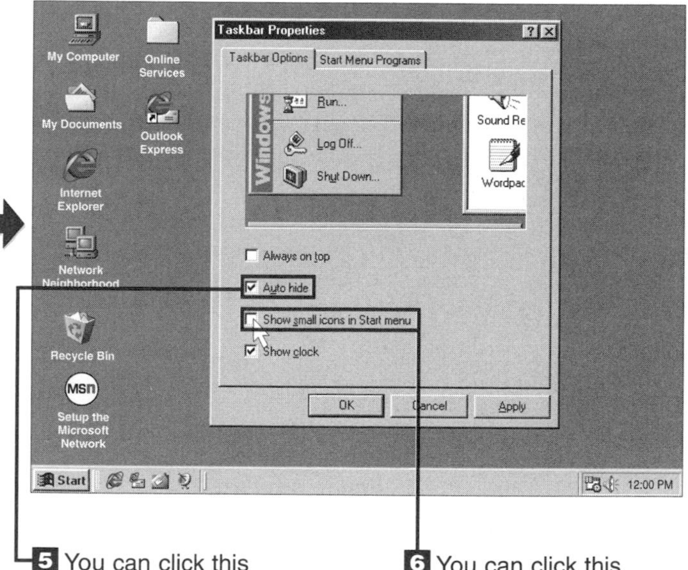

5 You can click this option to hide the taskbar when you are not using the taskbar (☐ changes to ☑).

6 You can click this option to reduce the size of the Start menu (☐ changes to ☑).

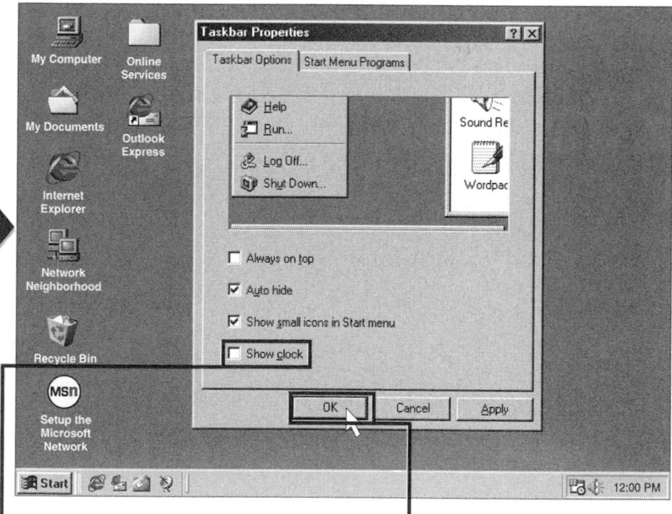

7 This option displays a clock on the right side of the taskbar. You can click this option to hide the clock (☑ changes to ☐).

8 Click OK to confirm all of your changes.

SET THE DATE AND TIME

You can set the correct date and time in your computer. Setting the correct date and time is important because Windows uses this information to identify when documents are created and updated. If your computer's calendar and clock are accurate, you will be able to find your files more easily.

Your computer maintains the date and time even when you turn off your computer.

Windows adjusts the date and time automatically to compensate for daylight savings time. When you turn on the computer after a time change, Windows will tell you that your date and time settings have been updated.

If complete accuracy of your computer's clock is important to you, there are programs available that will synchronize your computer's clock with one of the very precise clocks on the Internet.

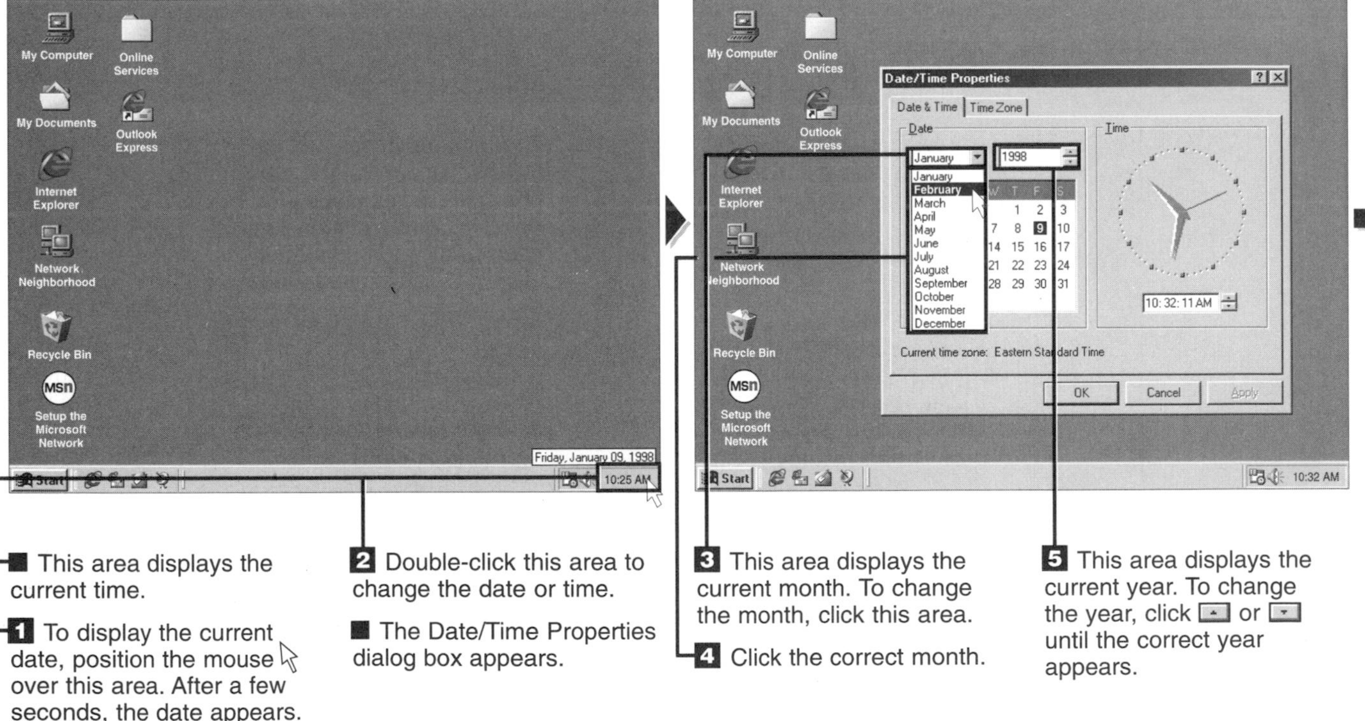

■ This area displays the current time.

1 To display the current date, position the mouse over this area. After a few seconds, the date appears.

2 Double-click this area to change the date or time.

■ The Date/Time Properties dialog box appears.

3 This area displays the current month. To change the month, click this area.

4 Click the correct month.

5 This area displays the current year. To change the year, click ▲ or ▼ until the correct year appears.

TIPS

How can I remove the clock from my taskbar?

In the Taskbar Properties dialog box, turn off the Show clock feature. See page 198.

How can Windows help me get to my appointments on time?

There are many calendar and time management programs, like Microsoft Outlook and Lotus Organizer, that use the date and time set in your computer to remind you of your appointments. These programs usually provide audio and visual warnings in advance of your scheduled appointments.

I use my laptop in two time zones. Can Windows automatically maintain both times like my watch can?

No, but you can switch back and forth between the time zones as often as you need to.

Will my computer's clock still work in the year 2000?

Some older programs might have difficulty making date calculations that span across both centuries, but Windows is designed to work with dates in the year 2000.

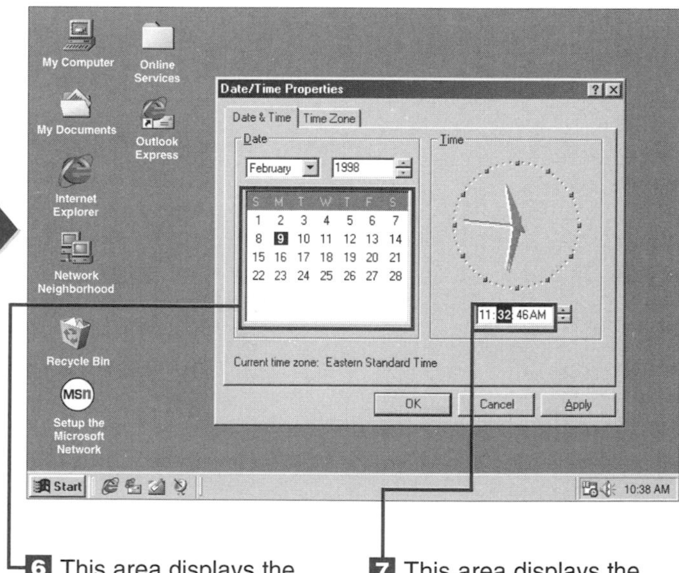

6 This area displays the days in the month. The current day is highlighted. To change the day, click the correct day.

7 This area displays the current time. To change the time, double-click the part of the time you want to change. Then type the correct information.

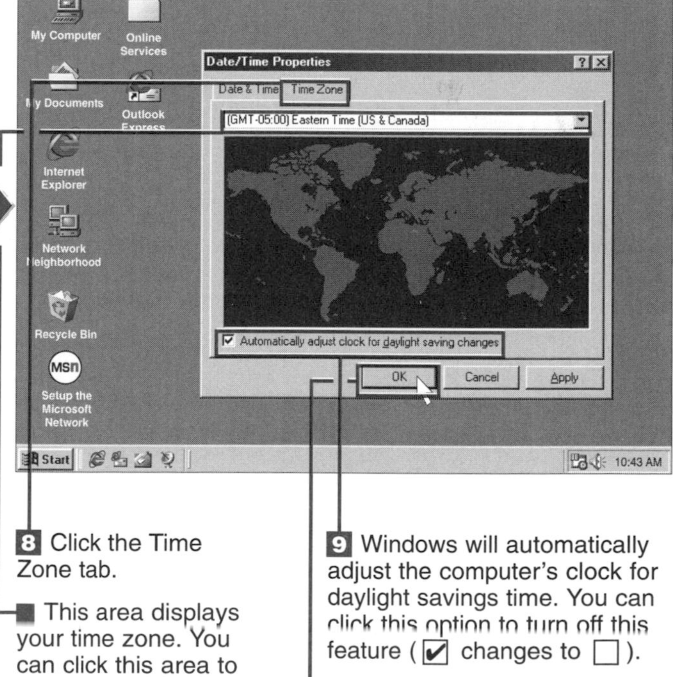

8 Click the Time Zone tab.

■ This area displays your time zone. You can click this area to select another time zone.

9 Windows will automatically adjust the computer's clock for daylight savings time. You can click this option to turn off this feature (☑ changes to ☐).

10 Click OK to confirm your changes.

CHANGE REGIONAL SETTINGS

You can change the way numbers, currency, dates and times are displayed on your computer. This allows you to use the settings common to your region of the world.

Most North Americans use a period (.) to indicate the decimal point and a comma (,) to separate larger numbers. These settings are not universal. In fact, in many regions, these settings are reversed.

When you select a new region for your computer, Windows changes the settings for all numbers, currency, times and dates.

Each region has its own settings, but you can adjust these settings to your own personal preference. For example, although most North Americans prefer to use a 12-hour clock, some people may prefer to use a 24-hour clock.

When you send a document to a computer in a different region, Windows changes the settings used in the document. Each person sees the document with the settings they have selected.

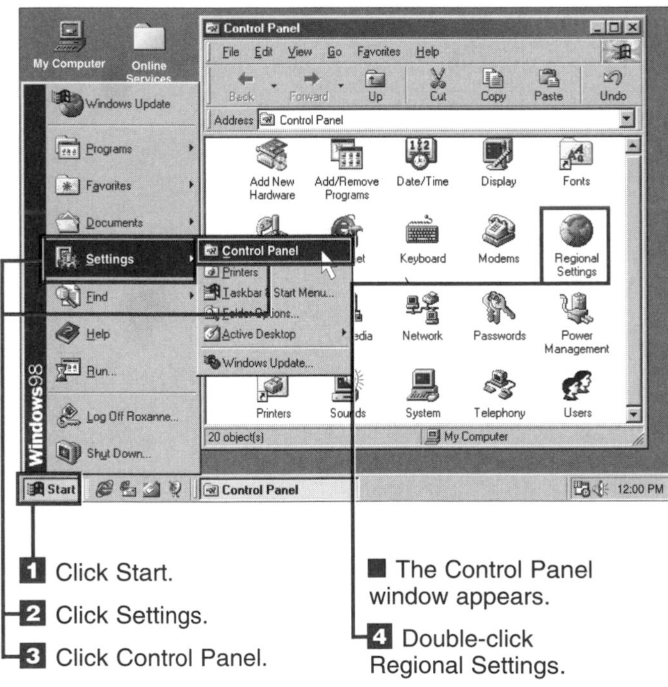

1 Click Start.

2 Click Settings.

3 Click Control Panel.

■ The Control Panel window appears.

4 Double-click Regional Settings.

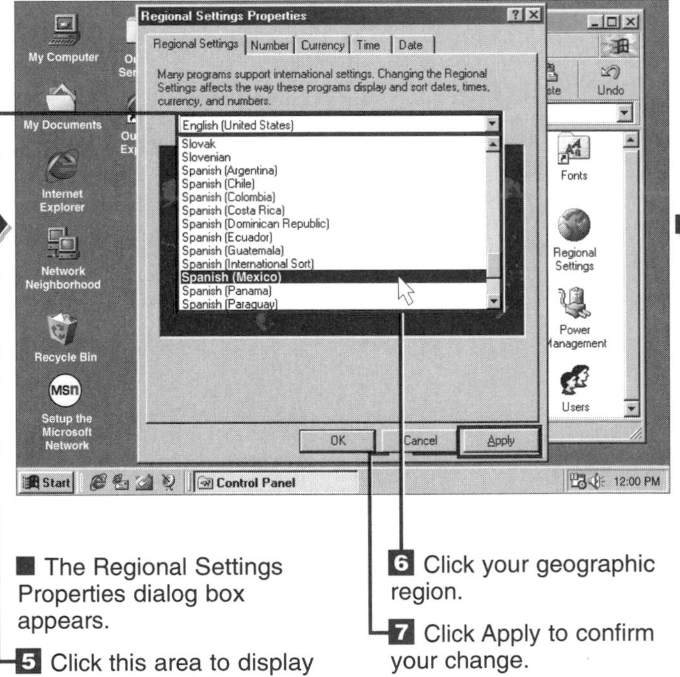

■ The Regional Settings Properties dialog box appears.

5 Click this area to display a list of geographic regions.

6 Click your geographic region.

7 Click Apply to confirm your change.

TIPS

How do I change to a 24-hour clock display?

In the Regional Settings Properties dialog box, click the Time tab. Then select a time style where the hours are represented by the capital letter H.

How do I install the files I need to display documents in a foreign alphabet?

To install files needed for a foreign alphabet, you should install the Multilanguage Support component. Multilanguage Support installs the files needed to work with and create documents in several alphabets including Greek, Polish and Ukrainian. To install Windows components, see page 610.

How do I change the language used in the Windows menus?

Changing the regional settings only affects numerical, financial, date and time-related options. To change the language displayed in items such as menus and the Help feature, you must buy a copy of Windows in the language you want to use.

Can I use my keyboard to enter text in another language?

If you need to type special characters and symbols used in another language that are not available on the standard keyboard, you can change your keyboard language settings. In the Control Panel, select Keyboard. In the Keyboard Properties dialog box, select the Language tab.

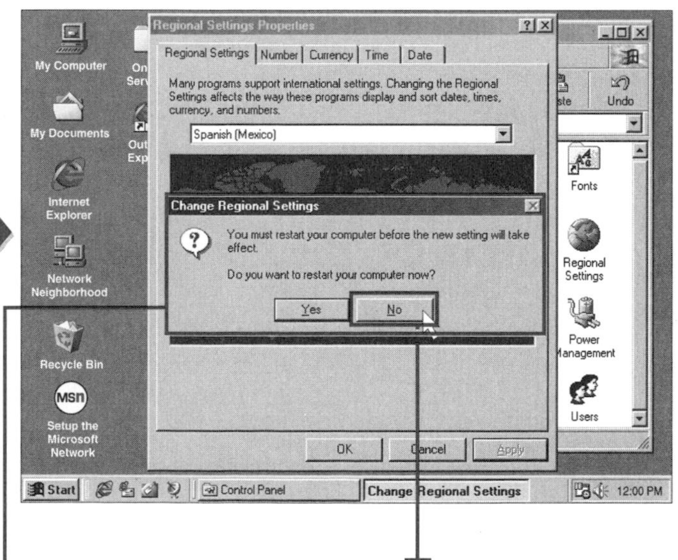

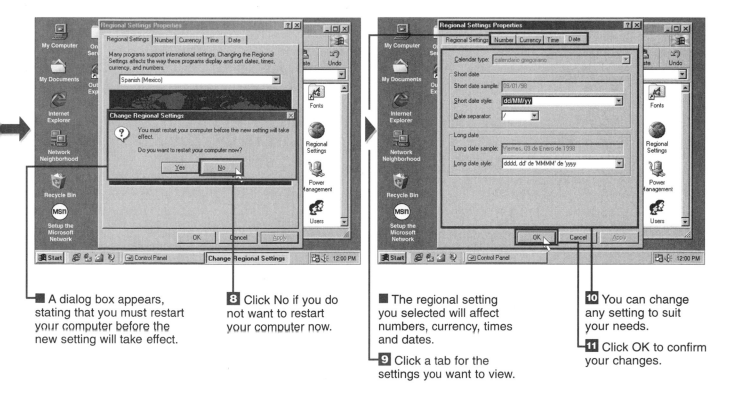

■ A dialog box appears, stating that you must restart your computer before the new setting will take effect.

8 Click No if you do not want to restart your computer now.

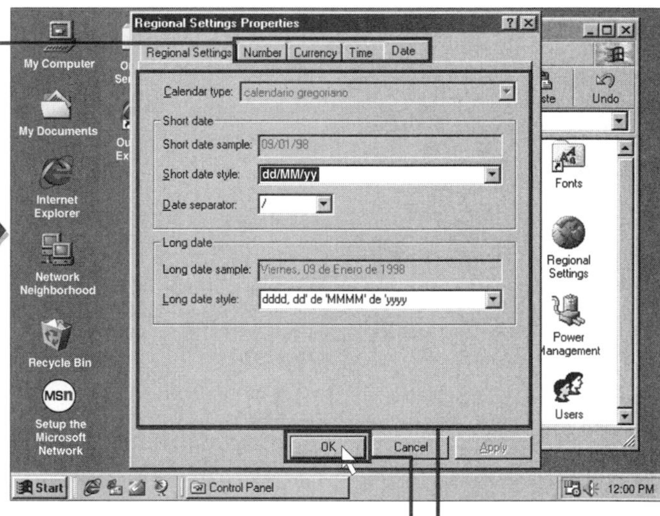

■ The regional setting you selected will affect numbers, currency, times and dates.

9 Click a tab for the settings you want to view.

10 You can change any setting to suit your needs.

11 Click OK to confirm your changes.

CREATE A NEW TOOLBAR

You can create a new toolbar on your desktop or add a toolbar to the taskbar. Toolbars contain buttons to provide easy access to commands and features.

You can create a toolbar from any folder on your computer. For example, you can create toolbars from the Control Panel, Printers and Dial-Up Networking folders. These new toolbars will allow you to quickly access the items in the folders. If all the documents you frequently use are stored in one folder, you can create a toolbar from the folder and then use the toolbar to quickly open the documents.

Windows includes several ready-made toolbars you can add to the taskbar. The Address and Links toolbars allow you to access the Web without first starting your Web browser program. You can type a Web page address in the Address toolbar to access the Web page from your desktop. You can click a link in the Links toolbar to access a useful Web site. The Desktop toolbar contains all the items on your desktop. The Quick Launch toolbar allows you to quickly access Internet Explorer, Outlook Express, your desktop and channels.

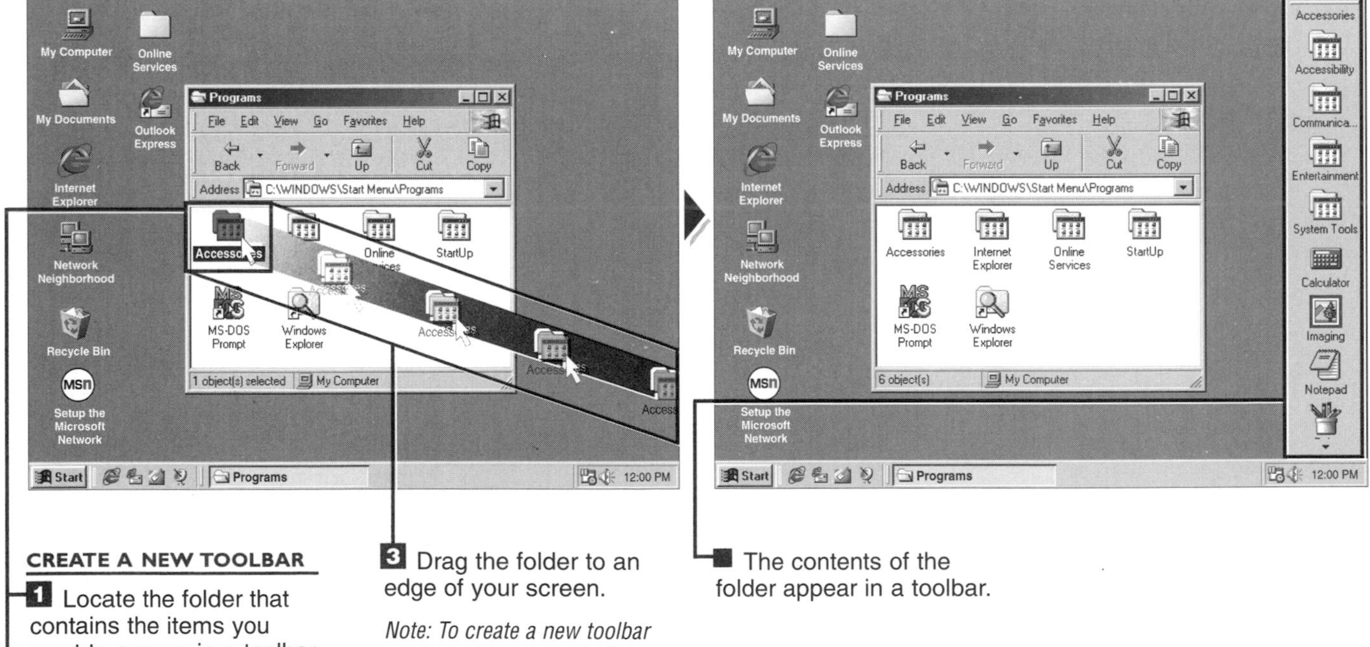

CREATE A NEW TOOLBAR

1. Locate the folder that contains the items you want to appear in a toolbar.
2. Position the mouse over the folder.
3. Drag the folder to an edge of your screen.

Note: To create a new toolbar on the taskbar, drag the folder to a blank area on the taskbar.

■ The contents of the folder appear in a toolbar.

TIPS

Why doesn't the toolbar display all the items in the folder?

When there are more items in a folder than will fit on the toolbar, a small black arrow (▼) appears at the bottom of the toolbar. Click this arrow to view the items that are not displayed.

Can I move a toolbar?

Position the mouse over the name of the toolbar and then drag the toolbar to any edge of your screen.

How do I remove a toolbar?

Right-click a blank area of the toolbar and then select Close.

Can I size a toolbar on the taskbar?

Position the mouse over the raised line on the toolbar you want to size (↖ changes to ↔). Drag the raised line to the left or right until the toolbar displays the size you want.

Can I add an item to the Quick Launch toolbar?

You can place a shortcut to an item such as a program, document or folder on the Quick Launch toolbar. To do so, drag the item to the Quick Launch toolbar.

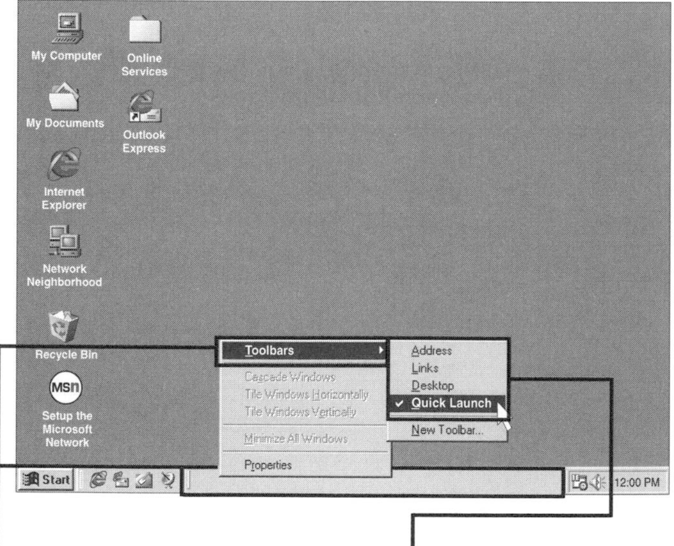

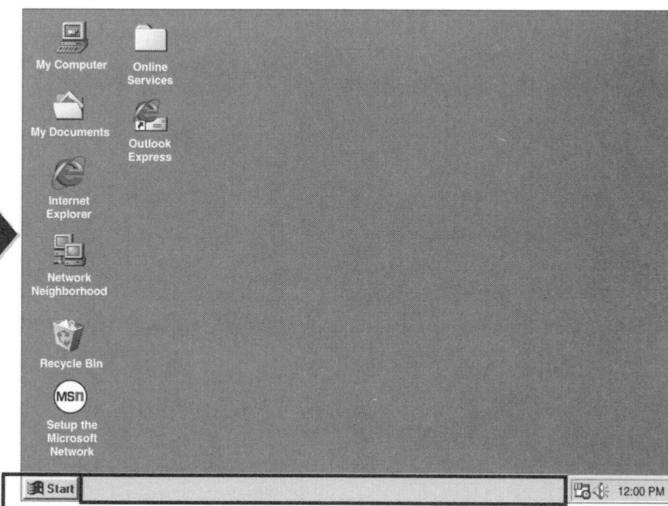

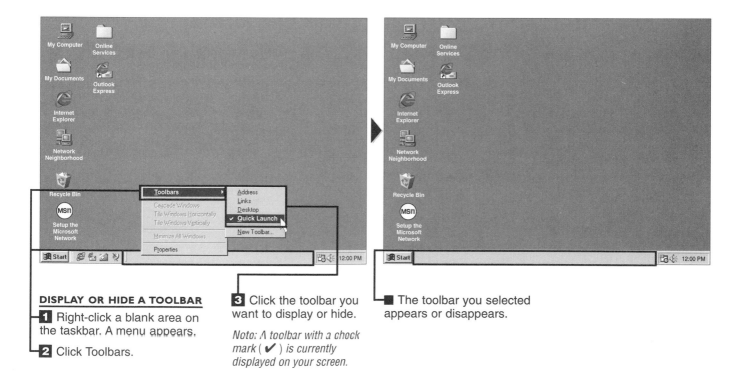

DISPLAY OR HIDE A TOOLBAR

1 Right-click a blank area on the taskbar. A menu appears.

2 Click Toolbars.

3 Click the toolbar you want to display or hide.

Note: A toolbar with a check mark (✔) is currently displayed on your screen.

■ The toolbar you selected appears or disappears.

CHANGE YOUR DESKTOP BACKGROUND

Like hanging posters on your walls or placing pictures on your desk, you can customize the Windows desktop to create a friendly and personalized working environment.

You can use wallpaper to customize your desktop. Wallpaper is an image you display on your desktop. You can center a large image on the desktop or tile a small image to repeat it over the entire desktop. You can also stretch a small image to cover your desktop.

Windows includes many different wallpaper designs. There is also additional wallpaper available on the Windows 98 CD-ROM disc.

You can search the Internet for sites providing free wallpaper. Collections of clip art and photographs found in computer stores can be used to create wallpaper. You can also use your scanner to create personal wallpaper from photographs or your own artwork.

You can create or modify wallpaper using Paint or another program that can save images in the .bmp format.

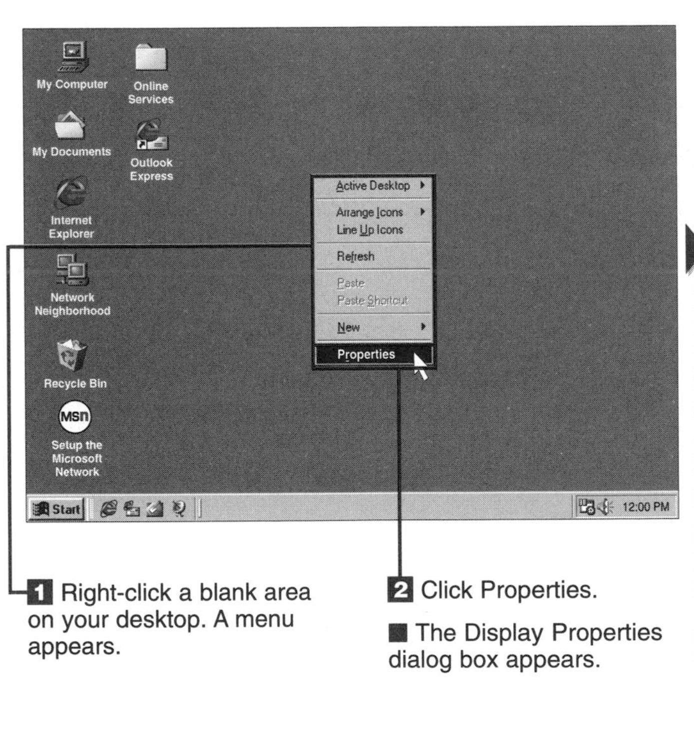

1 Right-click a blank area on your desktop. A menu appears.

2 Click Properties.

■ The Display Properties dialog box appears.

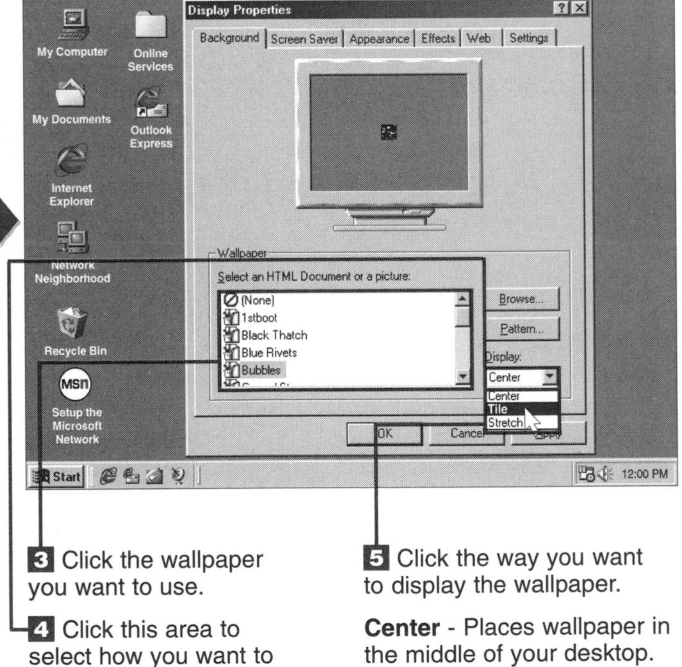

3 Click the wallpaper you want to use.

4 Click this area to select how you want to display the wallpaper on your desktop.

5 Click the way you want to display the wallpaper.

Center - Places wallpaper in the middle of your desktop.

Tile - Repeats wallpaper until it fills your entire desktop.

Stretch - Stretches wallpaper to fill your desktop.

How do I use clip art, scanned photographs or images I find on the Internet as my wallpaper?

Save the image in the .bmp format and place the image in the C:\Windows folder. The image will appear on the list of available wallpaper. If you have saved the image in another folder, you can use the Browse button to locate the image.

Can I display patterns on my desktop?

You can use patterns to add designs to your desktop. A pattern is a simple design made up of dots that alternate between black and the color of the background. In the Display Properties dialog box, click the Pattern button and then select the pattern you want to use.

Why do the colors in the image I am using look odd?

To display photographic-quality images, your color setting should be greater than 256. For information on color settings, see page 212.

Does using wallpaper have any effect on my computer's performance?

Some of the computer's resources must be devoted to keeping the wallpaper information in memory. On systems with less than 16 MB of memory, using wallpaper may affect the computer's ability to work with and switch between multiple programs. You may want to use a pattern instead, as patterns use fewer resources than wallpaper.

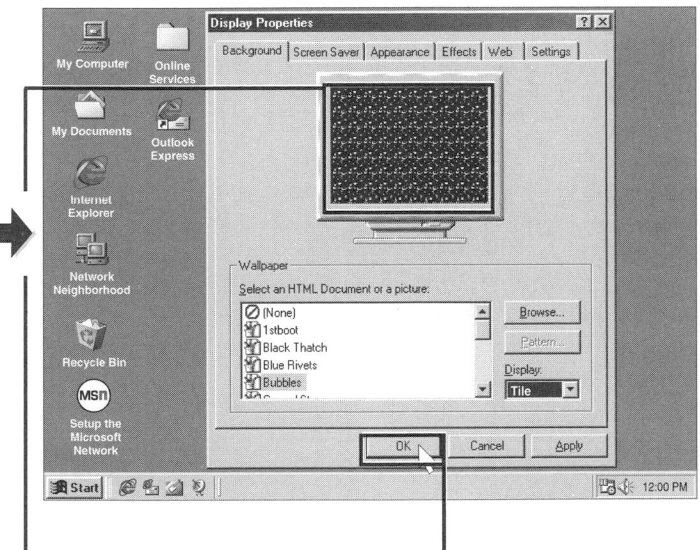

■ This area displays how the wallpaper you selected will look on your desktop.

6 Click OK to confirm your changes.

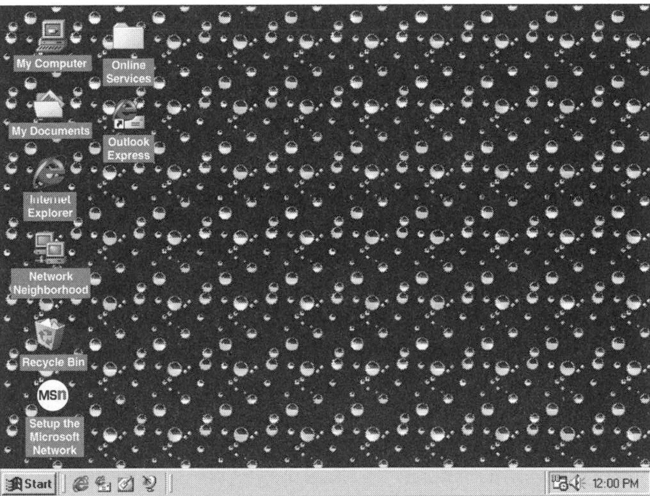

■ Your desktop displays the wallpaper you selected.

■ To remove wallpaper from your desktop, perform steps 1 to 3, selecting (None) in step 3. Then perform step 6.

CHANGE SCREEN COLORS

You can change the Windows screen to personalize and enhance your working environment.

Windows offers several schemes you can choose from. A scheme is a pre-defined screen appearance, including colors, text sizes and styles. Choosing a scheme allows you to make multiple adjustments with one choice.

High Contrast schemes are designed for people with vision impairments. High color schemes are designed for use on computers displaying more than 256 colors. VGA schemes are designed for use on computers limited to 16 colors.

If you find the text on menus and under icons too small to read or have trouble clicking on small buttons, you can change individual items to suit your needs and preferences. You can also change the font, color and size of individual items to create your own unique scheme.

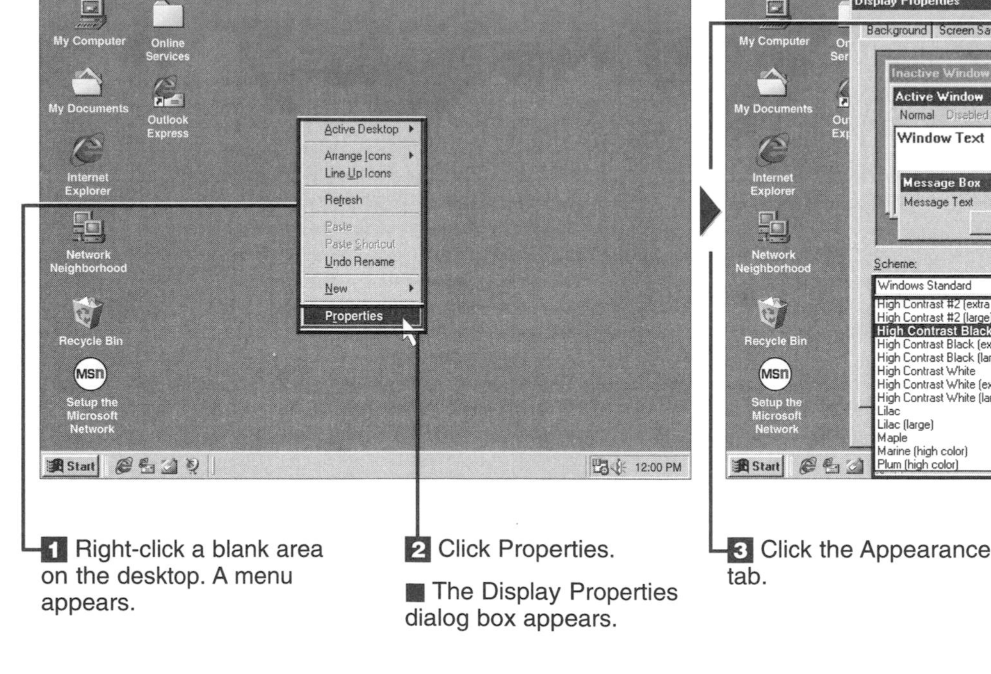

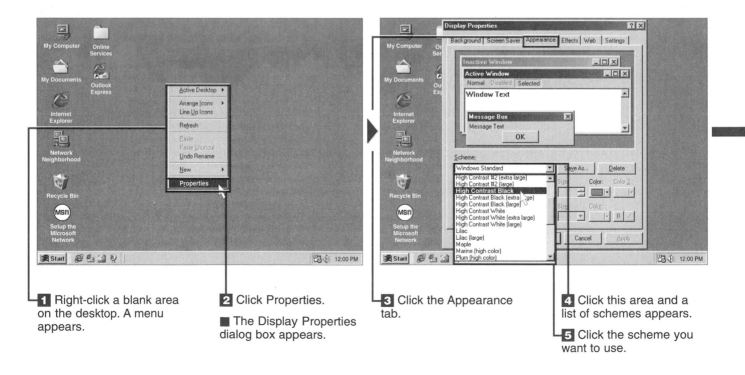

1 Right-click a blank area on the desktop. A menu appears.

2 Click Properties.

■ The Display Properties dialog box appears.

3 Click the Appearance tab.

4 Click this area and a list of schemes appears.

5 Click the scheme you want to use.

How can I save the changes I have made to a scheme?

Click Save As to save your scheme with a new name. Windows will not display a warning if this procedure will replace a scheme that already exists.

Why are some settings in the Display Properties dialog box unavailable?

The item you are adjusting may not require all of the settings. For example, if an item does not display text, then the Font settings are likely not available. The number of colors your screen displays may also affect which settings are available.

How else can I change my screen appearance?

You can also change the screen appearance by changing the desktop background. For information on changing the desktop background, see page 206.

How do I change my screen back to the way it was?

Select the original scheme for Windows, called Windows Standard.

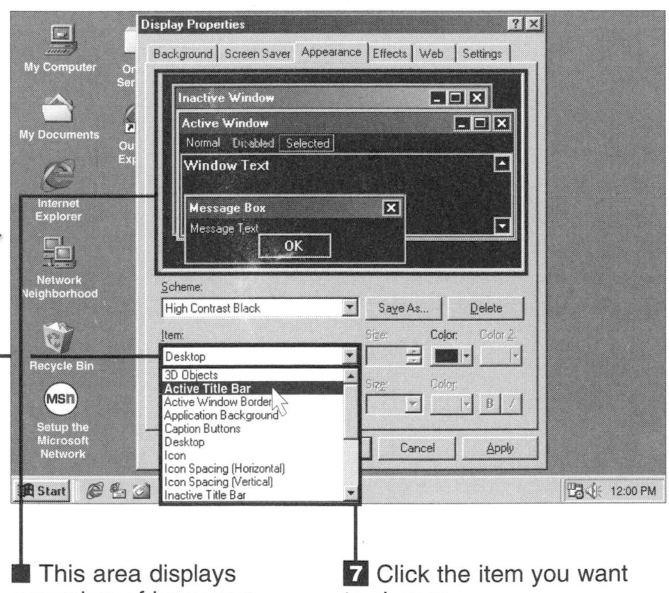

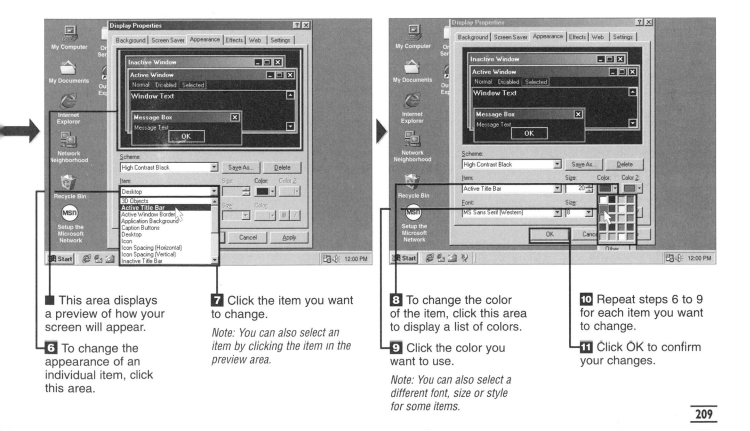

■ This area displays a preview of how your screen will appear.

6 To change the appearance of an individual item, click this area.

7 Click the item you want to change.

Note: You can also select an item by clicking the item in the preview area.

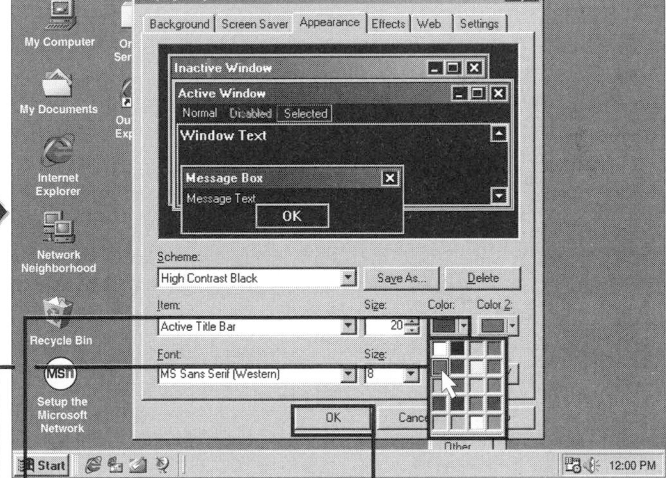

8 To change the color of the item, click this area to display a list of colors.

9 Click the color you want to use.

Note: You can also select a different font, size or style for some items.

10 Repeat steps 6 to 9 for each item you want to change.

11 Click OK to confirm your changes.

CHANGE THE SCREEN RESOLUTION

You can change the screen resolution to adjust the size of the image displayed on your screen. Your monitor and video card determine if you can change your screen resolution.

Resolution is measured by the number of horizontal and vertical pixels. A pixel is the smallest element on a screen. The standard screen resolution is 640x480, but most monitors can display resolutions up to 1024x768.

Lower resolutions display larger images so you can see the information on your screen more clearly. Some games are designed to run at a specific screen resolution. You may need to use a lower resolution to have the game fill your entire screen.

Higher resolutions display smaller images so you can view more information on your screen at once. A higher resolution allows you to see more of a word processing document or more cells in a spreadsheet without scrolling. In a graphics program, a higher resolution allows you to see more detail without zooming in or out.

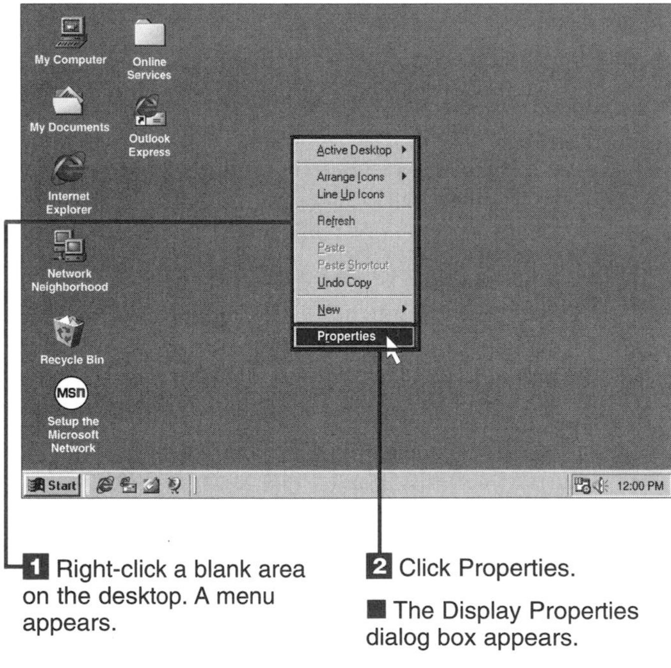

1 Right-click a blank area on the desktop. A menu appears.

2 Click Properties.

■ The Display Properties dialog box appears.

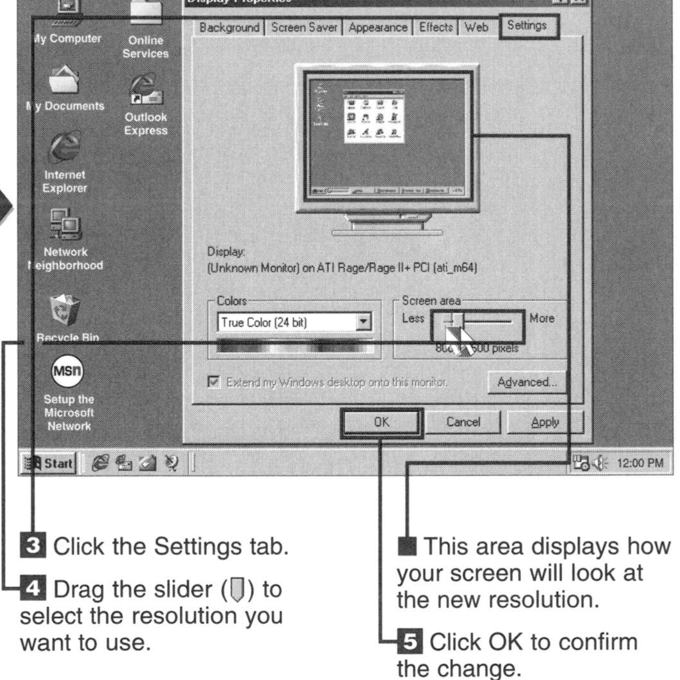

3 Click the Settings tab.

4 Drag the slider (▯) to select the resolution you want to use.

■ This area displays how your screen will look at the new resolution.

5 Click OK to confirm the change.

TIPS

Why do I have wide black borders around the edge of my screen or lose part of the desktop when I change the resolution?

You may need to make adjustments to your monitor after changing the resolution. Use the manual that comes with your monitor to find the horizontal and vertical size and position controls and then make the necessary adjustments.

Menus and other screen items are too small to read when I change to a higher resolution. What can I do?

You can increase the size of text in menus and other screen items to make the text easier to read. In the Display Properties dialog box, click the Settings tab and then click Advanced. Click the General tab and in the Font Size area, select Large Fonts.

Is there an easier way to change the resolution?

In the Display Properties dialog box, click the Settings tab and then click the Advanced button. You can then select the Show settings icon on task bar option to display the monitor icon on the taskbar. You can then click the monitor icon to display a list of all the available resolutions.

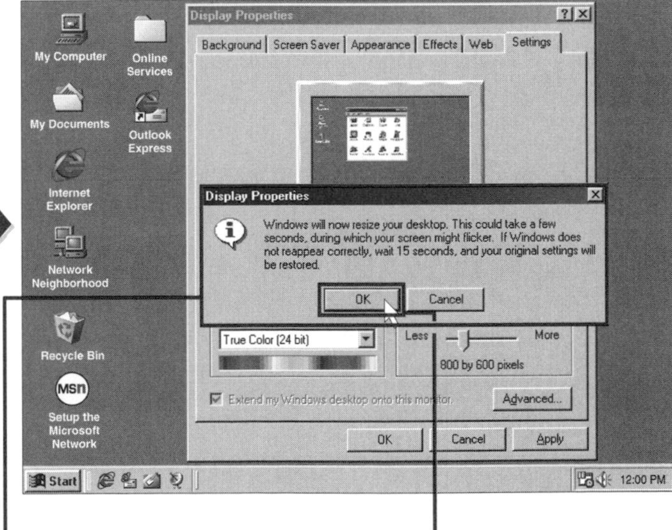

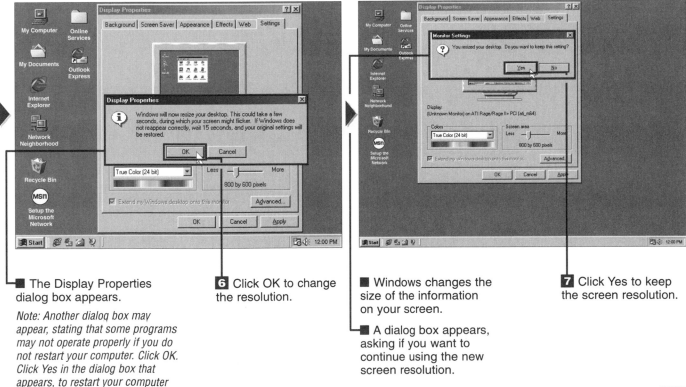

■ The Display Properties dialog box appears.

Note: Another dialog box may appear, stating that some programs may not operate properly if you do not restart your computer. Click OK. Click Yes in the dialog box that appears, to restart your computer and apply the new screen resolution.

6 Click OK to change the resolution.

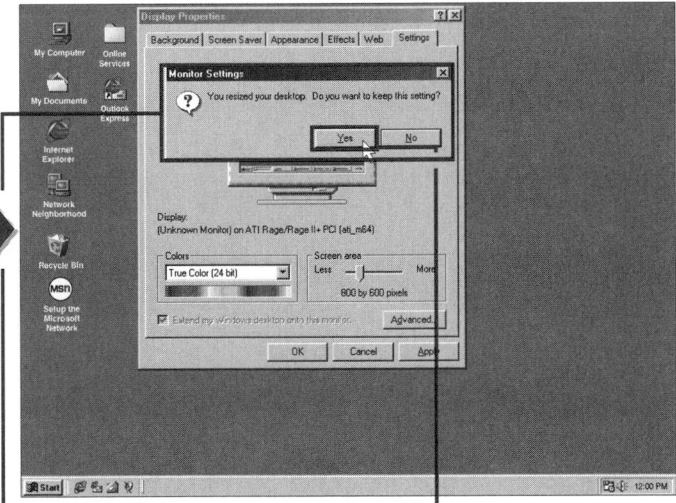

■ Windows changes the size of the information on your screen.

■ A dialog box appears, asking if you want to continue using the new screen resolution.

7 Click Yes to keep the screen resolution.

CHANGE COLOR DEPTH

Color depth refers to the number of colors your screen displays. You can increase the number of colors your screen displays to improve the quality of images and the general appearance of your screen.

Windows offers several different color settings. The 16 Color setting displays low-resolution images. The 256 Color setting is suitable for most home, business and game applications. The High Color setting (16 bit) is suitable for video and desktop publishing. The True Color settings are suitable for high-end graphics programs and photo-retouching.

With 256 or more colors you will be able to use some advanced Windows features including the 3-D and animated mouse cursors as well as font smoothing. Some multimedia programs also work better on computers that display 256 or more colors.

The number of colors your screen can display is directly related to the amount of memory on your computer's video card. A smaller video card memory means you must use a lower color setting.

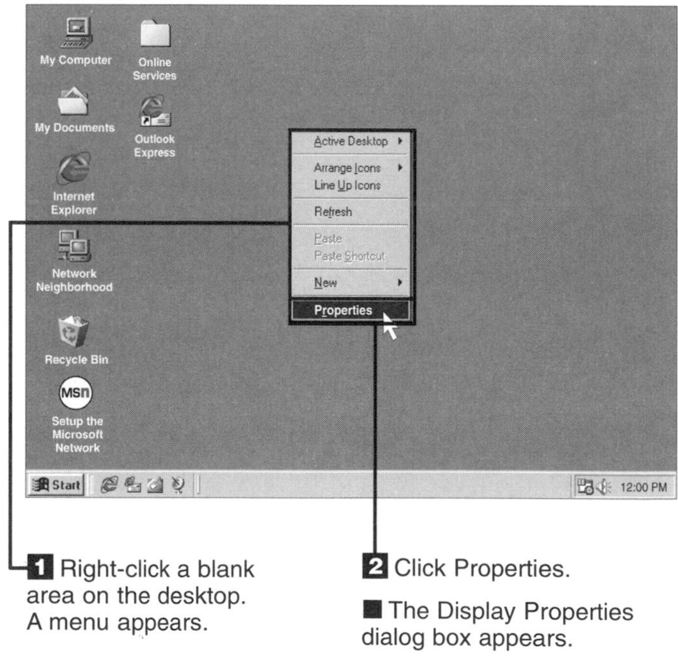

1 Right-click a blank area on the desktop. A menu appears.

2 Click Properties.

■ The Display Properties dialog box appears.

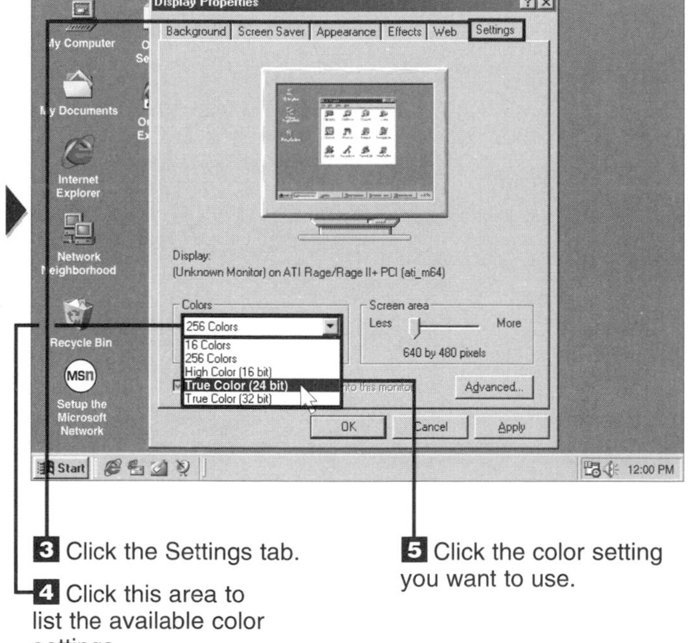

3 Click the Settings tab.

4 Click this area to list the available color settings.

5 Click the color setting you want to use.

TIPS

What is font smoothing?

Font smoothing softens the edges of letters with gray to make them appear to be higher quality than normal letters. Font smoothing makes it easier to read text on your screen for a long period of time. Font smoothing can only be used with a High Color (16 bit) or better setting. In the Display Properties dialog box, choose the Effects tab and then click the Smooth edges of screen fonts option to turn on font smoothing.

Can all monitors use the True Color settings?

All modern monitors are capable of using the True Color settings to display millions of colors.

Will a higher color setting affect my computer's performance?

Your computer's performance should not be affected. Although lower color settings are slightly faster than higher color settings, there is only a minor speed difference.

How can I control whether or not Windows will restart when I change the color setting?

In the Display Properties dialog box, choose the Settings tab. Then click the Advanced button and select the General tab. You can now tell Windows what you want to happen when the color setting is changed. This allows you to make changes without having to restart Windows.

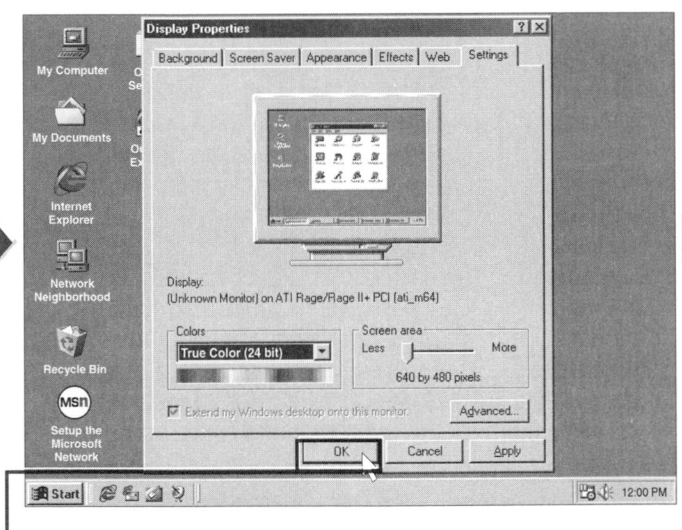

6 Click OK to confirm your change.

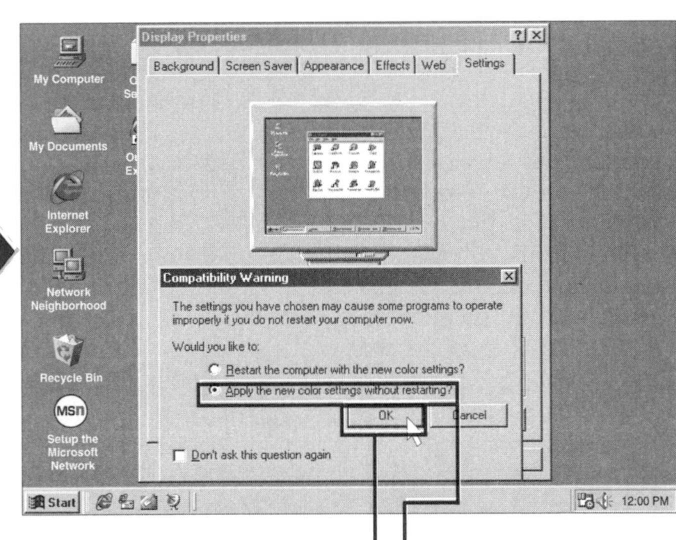

■ The Compatibility Warning dialog box appears. Some programs may not operate properly if you do not restart your computer.

7 Click this option to apply the setting without restarting your computer (○ changes to ⦿).

8 Click OK to change to the new color setting.

CHANGE DESKTOP ICONS

You can customize your desktop by changing the appearance of the icons.

Windows lets you change the icons for My Computer, My Documents, Network Neighborhood and both the full and empty Recycle Bin. Windows includes many different icons for you to choose from.

You can use the Visual effects settings to improve the way Windows displays items on your desktop. You can choose to hide all the desktop icons when you view your desktop as a Web page. To view your desktop as a Web page, see page 224.

The Use large icons effect is designed for a screen with a resolution of 1024x768 or higher. This effect makes icons appear approximately the same size at a resolution of 1024x768 as when the standard icons are displayed at a resolution of 640x480.

You can also use the Show icons using all possible colors effect to display icons using all the colors your computer can display.

The Use menu animations effect controls the way menus appear on your screen.

The text in your word processor and other programs will be easier to read if you use the Smooth edges of screen fonts effect.

The Show window contents while dragging effect allows you to see the contents of a window while you are moving and resizing the window.

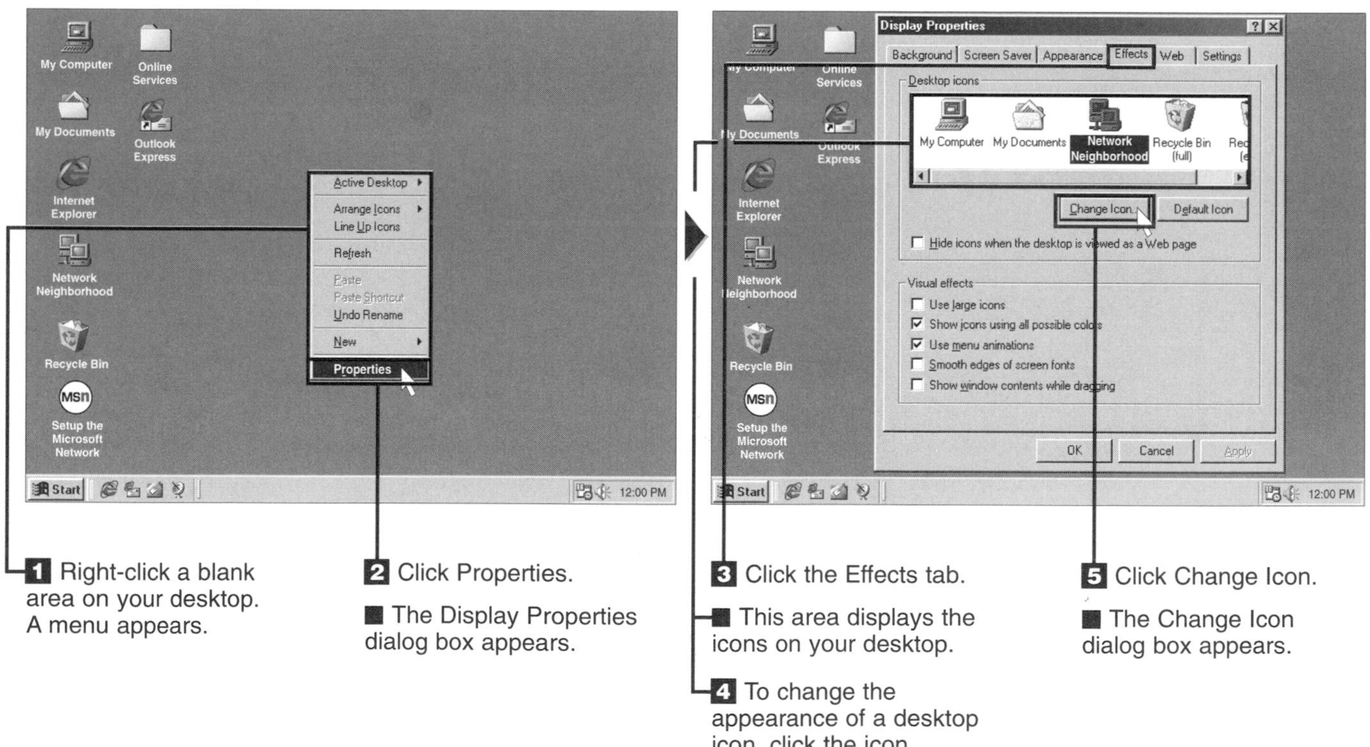

1 Right-click a blank area on your desktop. A menu appears.

2 Click Properties.

■ The Display Properties dialog box appears.

3 Click the Effects tab.

■ This area displays the icons on your desktop.

4 To change the appearance of a desktop icon, click the icon.

5 Click Change Icon.

■ The Change Icon dialog box appears.

Can I change the appearance of all the icons on my desktop at once?

Yes. You can change the appearance of all icons by applying a theme to your desktop. See page 216. Each desktop theme includes coordinated items such as icons, wallpaper, sounds and mouse pointers.

How can I change an icon on my desktop back to its original icon?

In the Display Properties dialog box, click the icon you want to change back to the default icon and then click the Default Icon button.

Will the Use large icons, Show icons using all possible colors and Use menu animations effects make my computer operate slower?

These effects may affect your computer's performance if the computer only meets or just exceeds the minimum system requirements for Windows 98. You may be able to improve the computer's performance by turning off these effects.

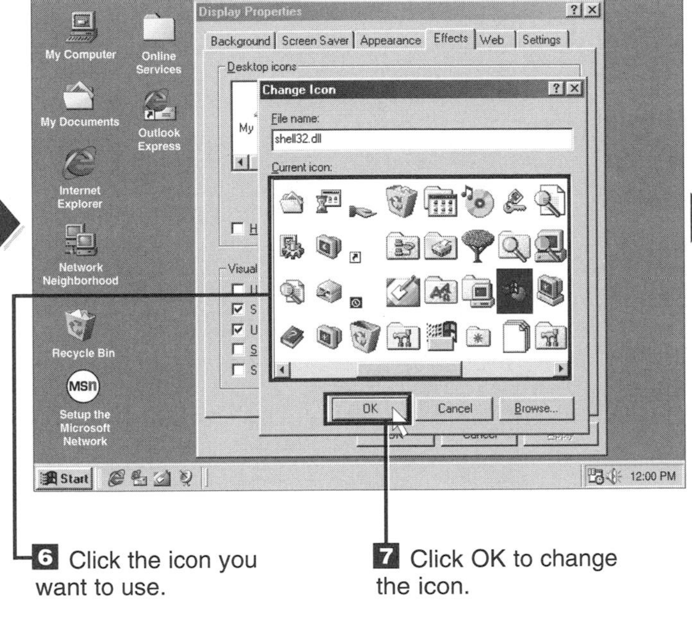

6 Click the icon you want to use.

7 Click OK to change the icon.

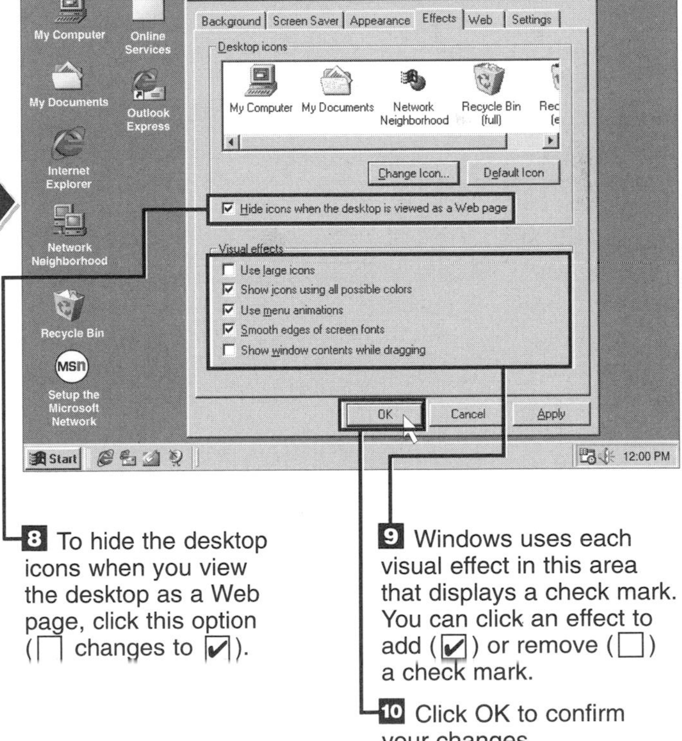

8 To hide the desktop icons when you view the desktop as a Web page, click this option (☐ changes to ☑).

9 Windows uses each visual effect in this area that displays a check mark. You can click an effect to add (☑) or remove (☐) a check mark.

10 Click OK to confirm your changes.

CHOOSE A DESKTOP THEME

You can choose a desktop theme to change the appearance of your desktop. Each desktop theme contains several coordinated items including wallpaper, a screen saver, a color scheme, sounds, mouse pointers, icons and fonts. You can select themes such as Dangerous Creatures, Baseball and Space.

The themes you should use depend on the number of colors your screen displays. If your screen displays 256 colors, you should only use the 256 color themes. If your screen displays more than 256 colors, you can use both the 256 and high color themes. Although you can select a high color theme when your screen displays 256 colors, you may experience odd color effects and mouse pointers may not appear to be three-dimensional. You also may not be able to see highlighted selections.

You can personalize a desktop theme by selecting only the theme settings you want to use. Some computer resources are required to store the wallpaper, screen saver, mouse pointers, sounds and other elements of a desktop theme. Even more resources are used when you choose a high color theme. This use of your computer's resources can affect your computer's performance. If you need to increase the performance of your computer, return to the Windows Default theme.

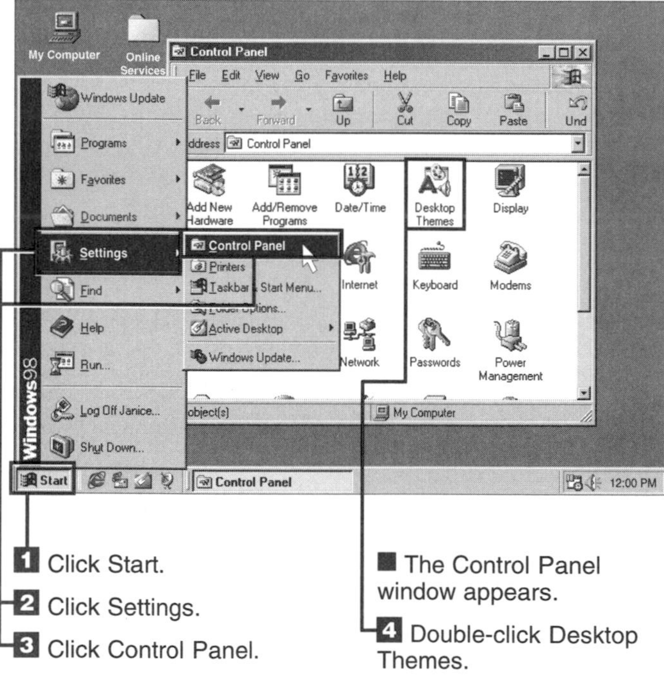

1 Click Start.

2 Click Settings.

3 Click Control Panel.

■ The Control Panel window appears.

4 Double-click Desktop Themes.

■ The Desktop Themes window appears.

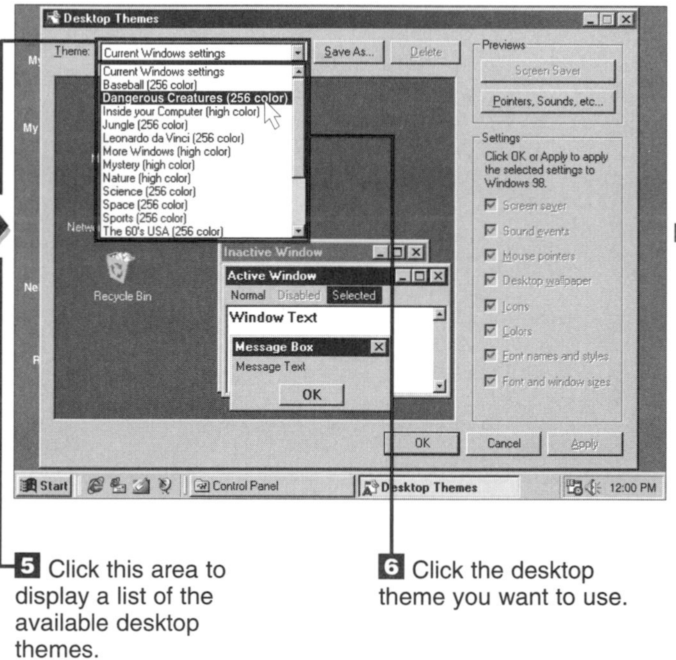

5 Click this area to display a list of the available desktop themes.

6 Click the desktop theme you want to use.

TIPS

Why don't I have the Desktop Themes icon in my Control Panel?

The Desktop Themes component may not be installed on your computer. To add Windows components, see page 610.

Can I save my personalized desktop theme?

After you confirm your changes, you can use the Save As button in the Desktop Themes window to name and save a theme with the settings you have chosen.

How can I change back to my original desktop?

To display the original desktop, select Windows Default from the list of available themes.

The fonts in the theme I want to use are hard to read. Can I use the fonts from the Windows Default theme instead?

Yes. Select the Windows Default theme in step 6 below and then make sure all of the settings are selected in step 7. Click OK to apply the theme. Then return to the Desktop Themes window and select the desktop theme you want to use. Click the Font names and styles setting, as well as the Font and window sizes setting (☑ changes to ☐). When you apply the new desktop theme, the Windows default font settings will be displayed.

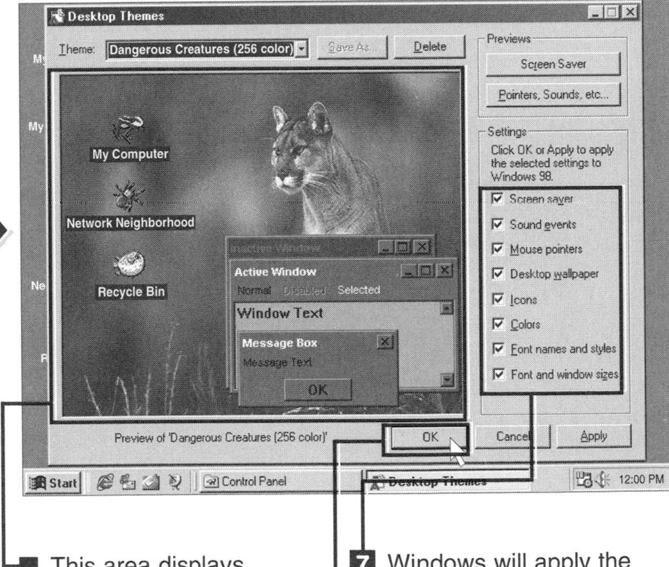

■ This area displays a preview of the theme you selected.

7 Windows will apply the theme to each setting that displays a check mark. You can click a setting to add (☑) or remove (☐) a check mark.

8 Click OK to confirm your changes.

■ The desktop theme you selected appears.

SET UP A SCREEN SAVER

A screen saver is a moving picture or pattern that appears on your screen when you do not use your computer for a period of time. You can use a screen saver to keep your work private while you are away from your desk.

There are many screen savers available that display interesting patterns, personal messages or entertaining images from popular cartoons, movies and television programs.

When you do not use your computer for a certain period of time, Windows starts the screen saver. You can select the amount of time the computer must be idle before the screen saver appears. Adjusting the time period is useful to prevent the screen saver from disrupting your work while you are reviewing material on your screen.

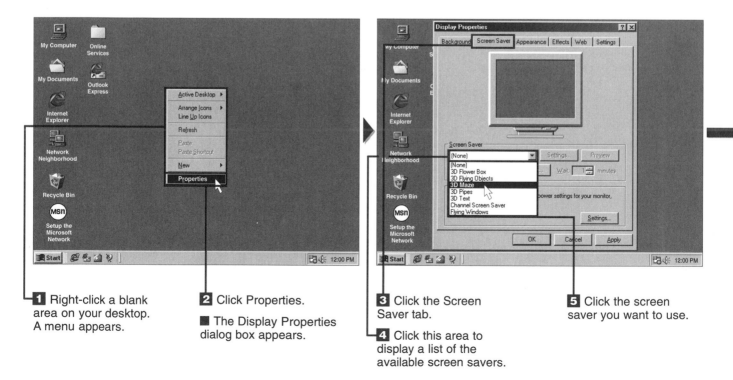

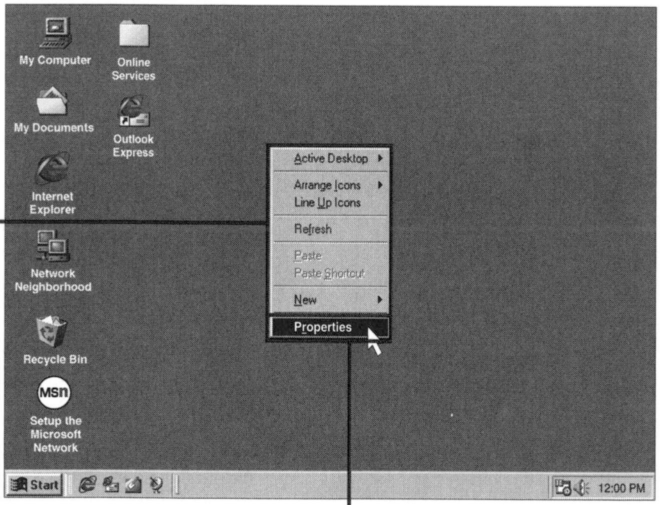

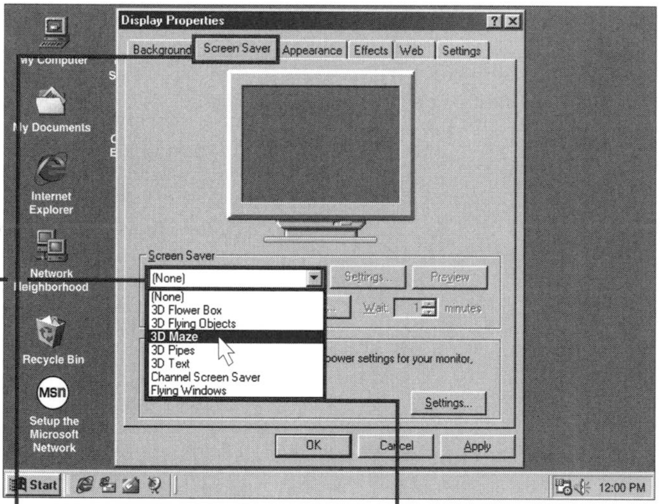

1 Right-click a blank area on your desktop. A menu appears.

2 Click Properties.

■ The Display Properties dialog box appears.

3 Click the Screen Saver tab.

4 Click this area to display a list of the available screen savers.

5 Click the screen saver you want to use.

TIPS

What do screen savers do?

Screen savers were originally designed to prevent screen burn, which occurs when an image appears in a fixed position on the screen for a long period of time. Today's monitors are designed to prevent screen burn, but people still use screen savers for entertainment.

Can I use a channel as a screen saver?

Yes. Perform steps 1 to 5 below, selecting Channel Screen Saver in step 5. Click the Settings button. A check mark (☑) beside a channel indicates the channel will be used as the screen saver. You must be subscribed to a channel to use it as a screen saver. To subscribe to a channel, see page 564.

Can I customize my screen savers?

You can click the Settings button to customize your screen savers. Each screen saver offers different options you can change.

Where can I get more screen savers?

The Windows 98 CD-ROM disc includes additional screen savers. These screen savers are found in the Accessories component. To add Windows components, see page 610. Double-click the Screen Savers component to display the Additional Screen Savers. You can also buy screen savers from stores and download screen savers from the Internet.

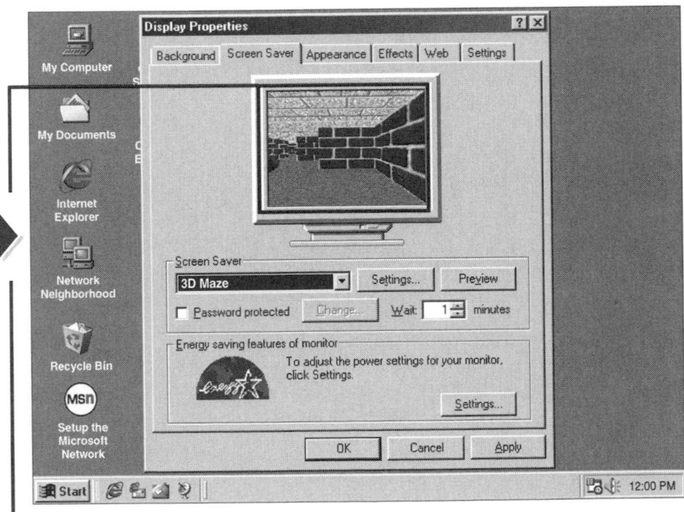

■ This area displays how the screen saver will look on your screen.

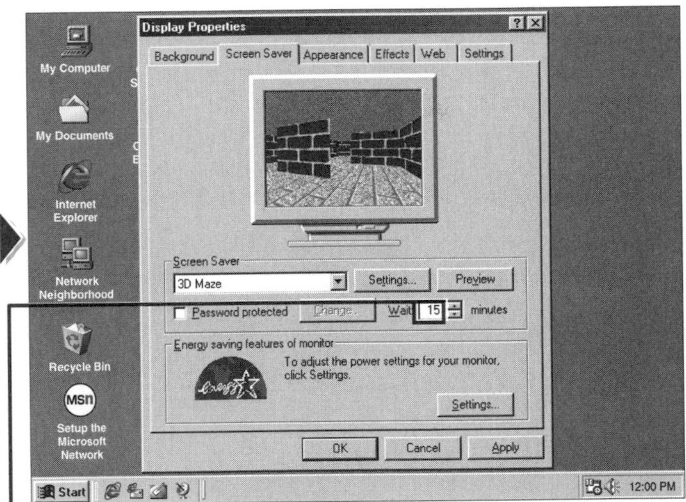

6 To change the length of time the computer must be inactive before the screen saver will appear, double click this area. Then type a new number.

CONTINUED

SET UP A SCREEN SAVER CONTINUED

Most screen savers can add a level of security and privacy to your work.

You can use the screen saver password feature to prevent other people from using your computer when you are not at your desk. This protects your work from unauthorized changes and keeps your documents private.

If you assign a password for your screen saver, you must enter the password correctly to remove the screen saver and use your computer. This makes it difficult for people to use your computer without your permission.

When you choose a password, do not use words that people can associate with you, such as your name or favorite sport. The most effective passwords connect two words or numbers with a special character (example: blue@123). To keep your password secure, do not write down your password in an area where people can find it. You may also want to change your password every few weeks.

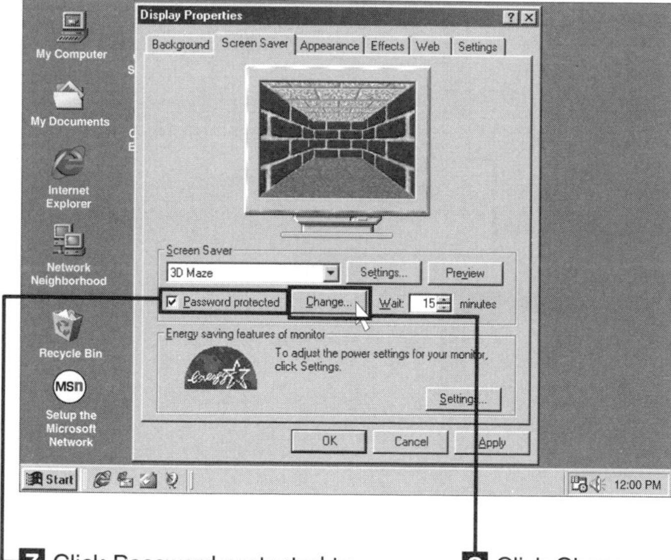

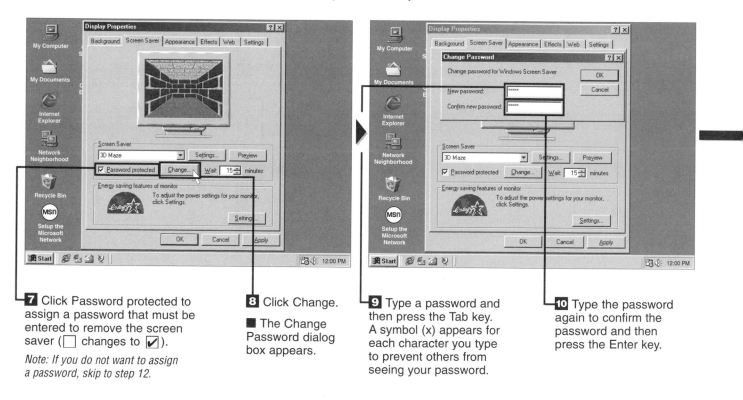

7 Click Password protected to assign a password that must be entered to remove the screen saver (☐ changes to ☑).

Note: If you do not want to assign a password, skip to step 12.

8 Click Change.

■ The Change Password dialog box appears.

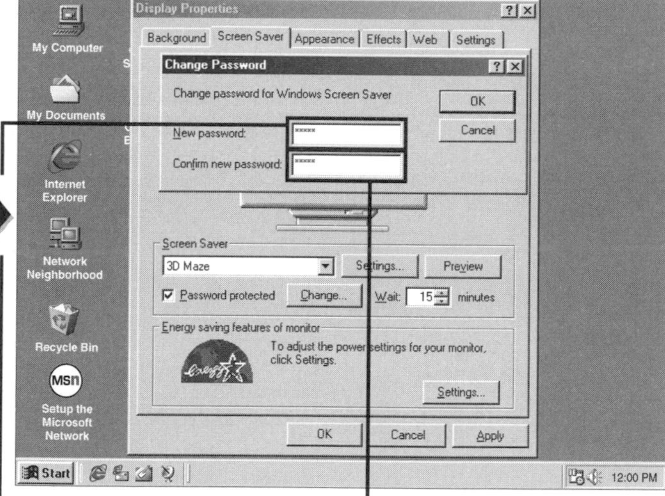

9 Type a password and then press the Tab key. A symbol (x) appears for each character you type to prevent others from seeing your password.

10 Type the password again to confirm the password and then press the Enter key.

TIPS

How do I stop the screen saver?

Press the Shift key or move your mouse to stop the screen saver. While the screen saver is on, you may have open programs on your computer. If you press a different key, you might affect an open program. If you use a password, you need to enter the password to turn off the screen saver.

What impact do screen savers have on my computer?

Screen savers can cause your computer to operate slower because they constantly monitor the activity of your computer. You may also have to wait while the computer switches from the screen saver back to your work.

How secure is the screen saver password feature?

Your screen saver password is not very secure. Other people can access your computer simply by restarting it. You can buy commercial screen savers that are more secure and do not allow access by restarting the computer.

How do I stop a screen saver from appearing?

If you no longer want to display a screen saver when your computer is idle, you can turn off the screen saver. Perform steps 1 to 5 on page 218, selecting (None) in step 5. Then perform step 12 below.

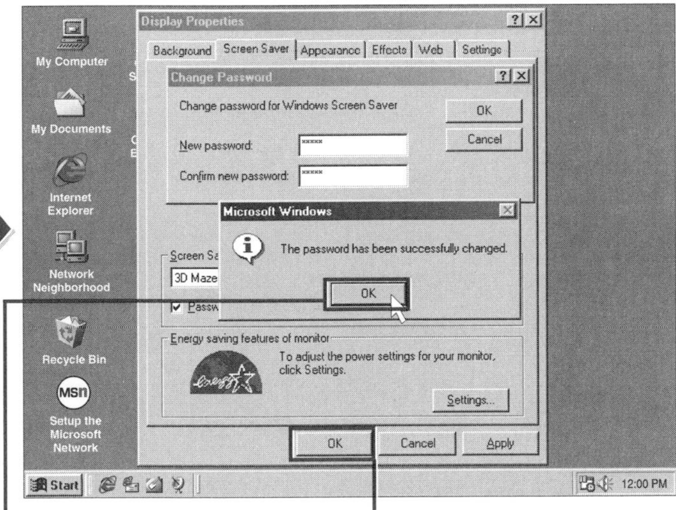

■ A dialog box appears, indicating that the password was successfully changed.

11 Click OK to close the dialog box.

12 Click OK to close the Display Properties dialog box.

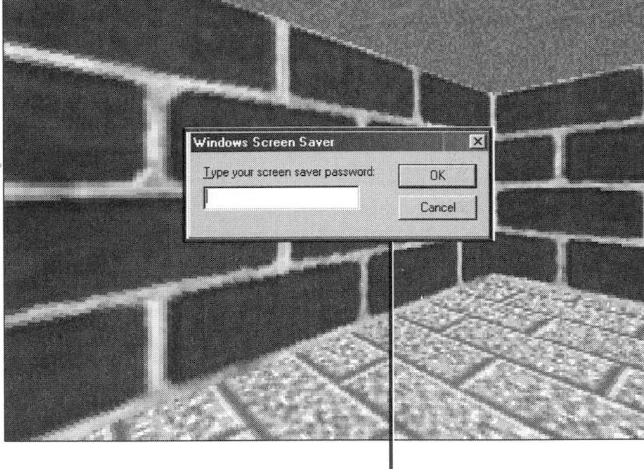

■ The screen saver appears when you do not use your computer for the amount of time you specified.

■ You can move the mouse or press a key on the keyboard to remove the screen saver.

■ If you assigned a password, the Windows Screen Saver dialog box appears, asking for your password. Type your password and then press the Enter key.

CUSTOMIZE FOLDER APPEARANCE

You can change the appearance of a folder by adding a picture to the folder's background. When you display the contents of the folder in a window, you will be able to view the background picture. The changes you make are saved with the folder and will be seen by everyone who opens the folder, including individuals on your network.

You can give each folder on your computer a distinctive look by adding a different picture. You can use the background pictures included with Windows, pictures you have created or pictures you have saved from the Internet. The picture you select must be in the .bmp, .gif or .jpg format. Windows tiles, or repeats the picture to fill the folder's window, regardless of the size of the picture.

You cannot customize the appearance of some folders on your computer. Folders you cannot customize include the My Computer folder, the Control Panel folder, the Printers folder, the Dial-Up Networking folder, the Fonts folder and the Scheduled Tasks folder.

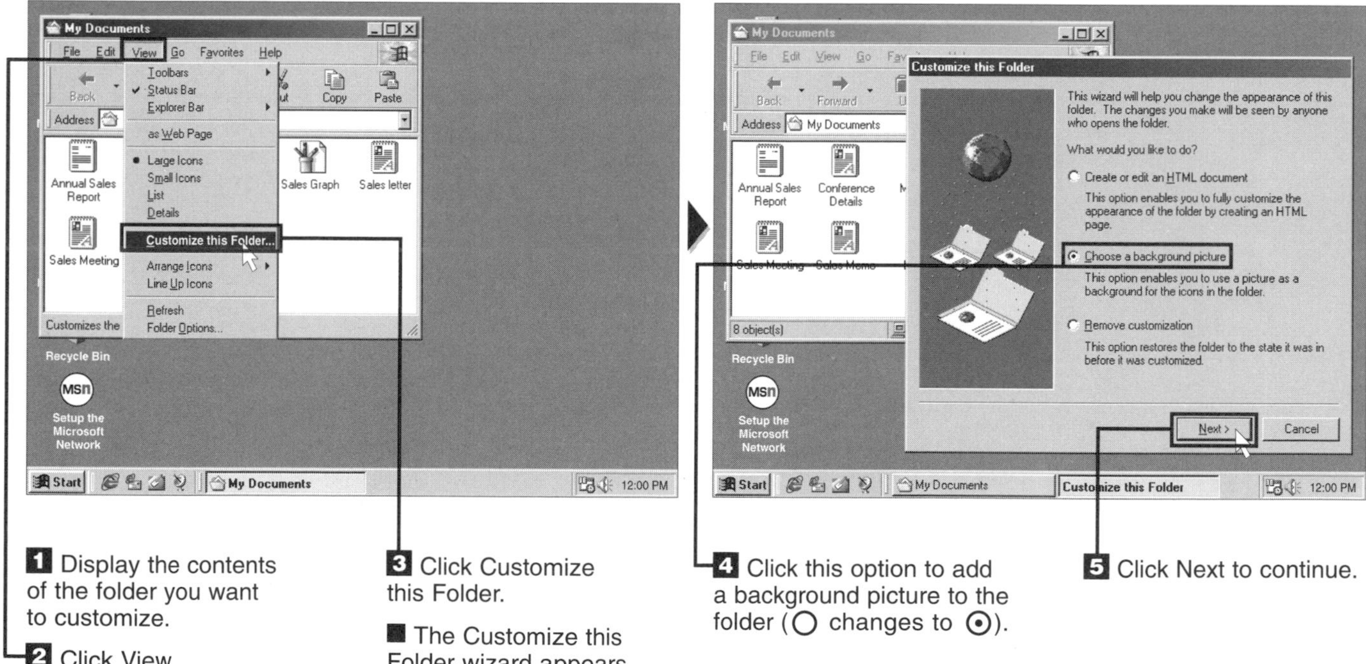

1 Display the contents of the folder you want to customize.

2 Click View.

3 Click Customize this Folder.

■ The Customize this Folder wizard appears.

4 Click this option to add a background picture to the folder (○ changes to ⊙).

5 Click Next to continue.

TIPS

When I add a picture to the background of my folder, the names of the icons become hard to read. How can I fix this?

You can change the color of the text, the background of the text or both. Perform steps 1 to 6 below and then use the buttons in the Icon caption colors area to select new colors for the text and for the background of the text.

What if the wizard does not display the name of the picture I want to use?

You can click the Browse button to find the picture you want to use. In the Open dialog box, select the type of picture you want to find in the Files of type area.

What is the Create or edit an HTML document option?

You can use this option to display the folder and its contents as a Web page or HTML (HyperText Markup Language) document. This option allows you to use HTML codes to specify exactly how you want the folder to look.

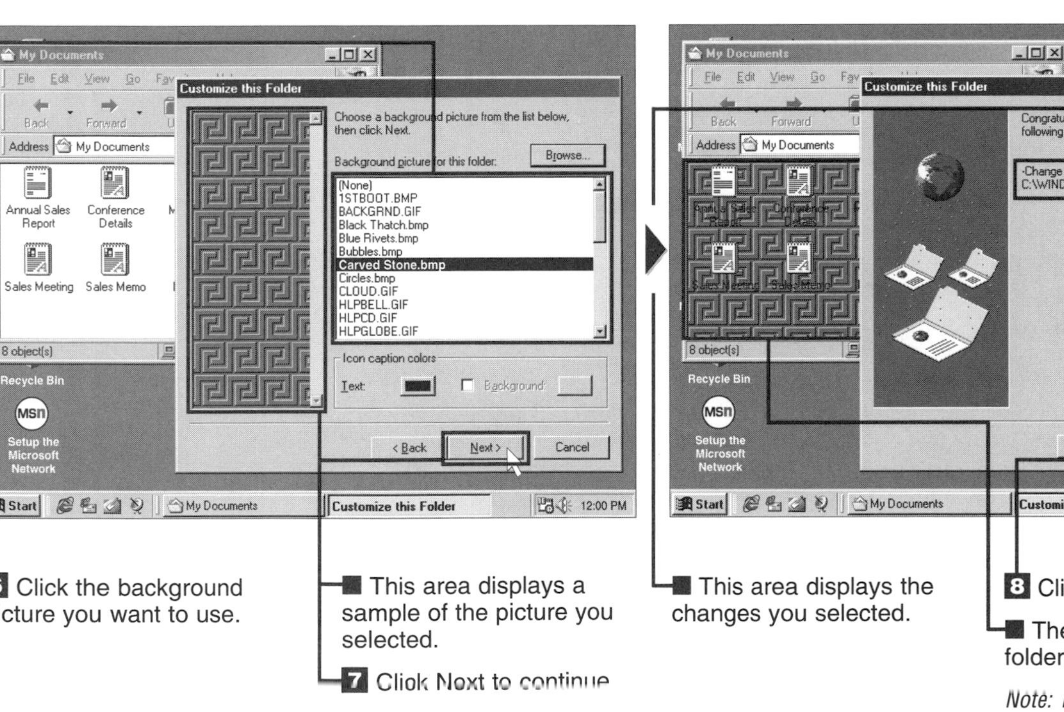

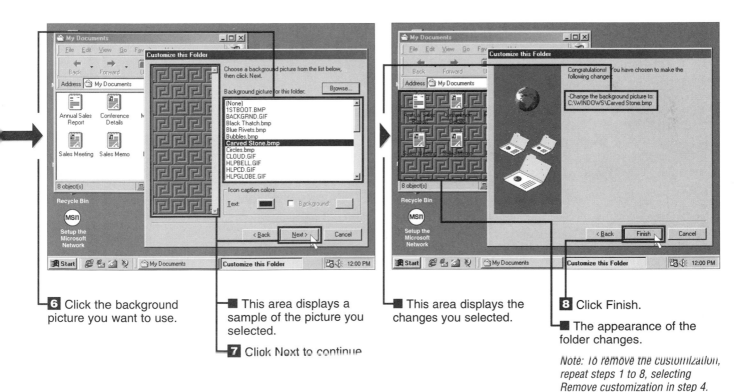

6 Click the background picture you want to use.

■ This area displays a sample of the picture you selected.

7 Click Next to continue.

■ This area displays the changes you selected.

8 Click Finish.

■ The appearance of the folder changes.

Note: To remove the customization, repeat steps 1 to 8, selecting Remove customization in step 4.

CHANGE THE WAY YOUR COMPUTER BEHAVES

You can choose the way you want the items on your screen to look and act. There are two styles you can choose from–Web style and Classic style.

When you select the Web style, your screen looks and acts like a Web page. Your folders are displayed as Web pages and the names of items on your screen are underlined. You can open or start an item by clicking it once, just as you would select a link on a Web page.

When you select the Classic style, the items on your screen look and act the same way items did in previous versions of Windows. Each folder you open appears in its own window and you must double-click an item to open or start it.

You can also create a custom style by combining your favorite settings from the Web and Classic styles. For example, you can have each folder appear in its own window and have the names of items appear underlined.

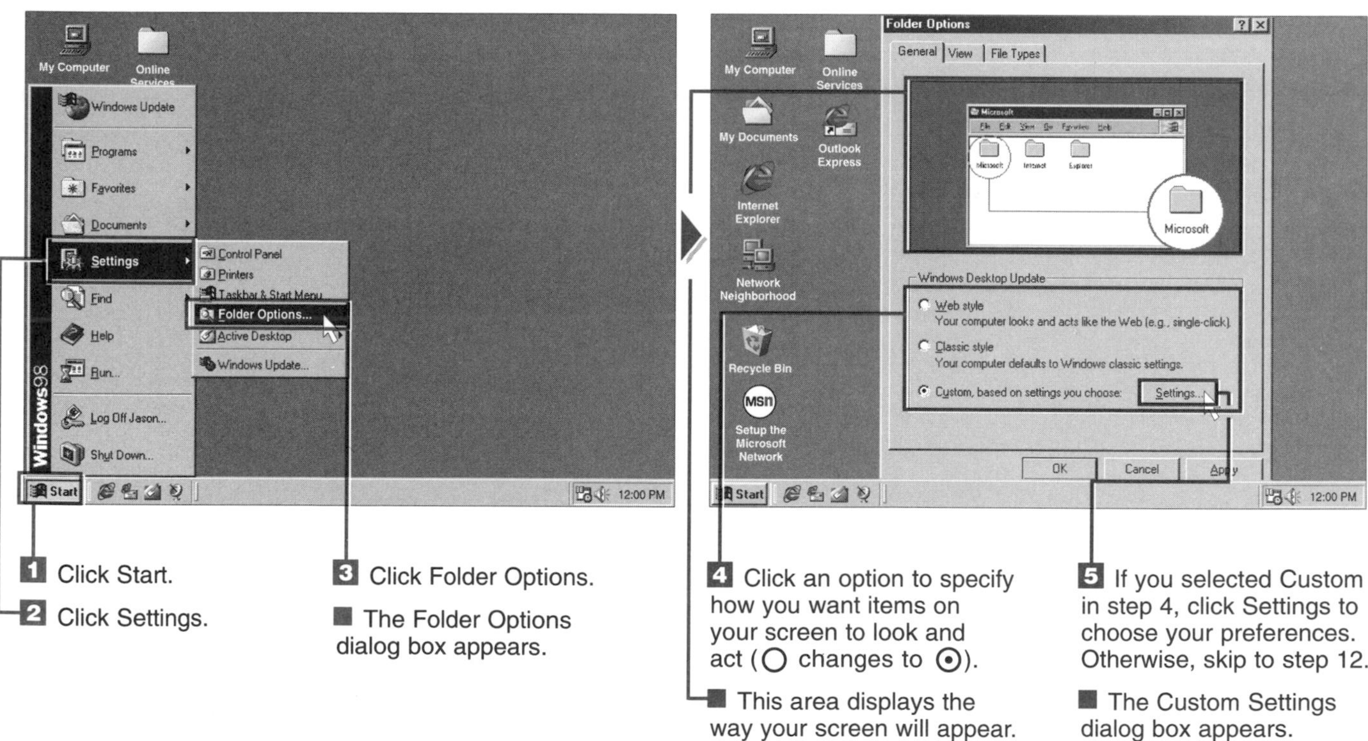

1 Click Start.

2 Click Settings.

3 Click Folder Options.

■ The Folder Options dialog box appears.

4 Click an option to specify how you want items on your screen to look and act (○ changes to ⊙).

■ This area displays the way your screen will appear.

5 If you selected Custom in step 4, click Settings to choose your preferences. Otherwise, skip to step 12.

■ The Custom Settings dialog box appears.

TIPS

I prefer the Classic style, but I want to display some of my folders as Web pages. How can I do this?

Double-click the folder you want to display as a Web page. From the View menu, select the as Web Page command.

Why did the Single-click dialog box appear when I chose the Web style?

The first time you choose the Web style, the Single-click dialog box appears, confirming that you want to single-click items to open or start them. Click OK to close the dialog box.

How do I select items when using the Web style?

You can select an item by positioning the mouse pointer over the item. To select a group of items, position the mouse pointer over the first item. Hold down the Shift key and then position the mouse pointer over the last item. To select random items, hold down the Ctrl key and position the mouse pointer over each item you want to select.

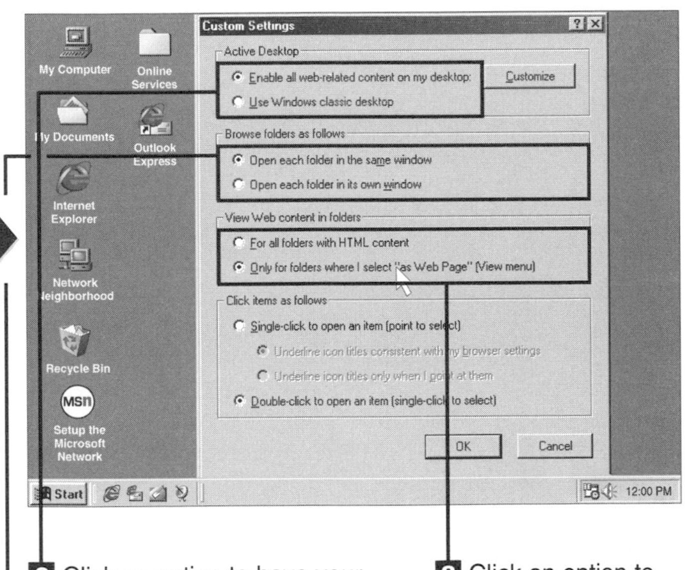

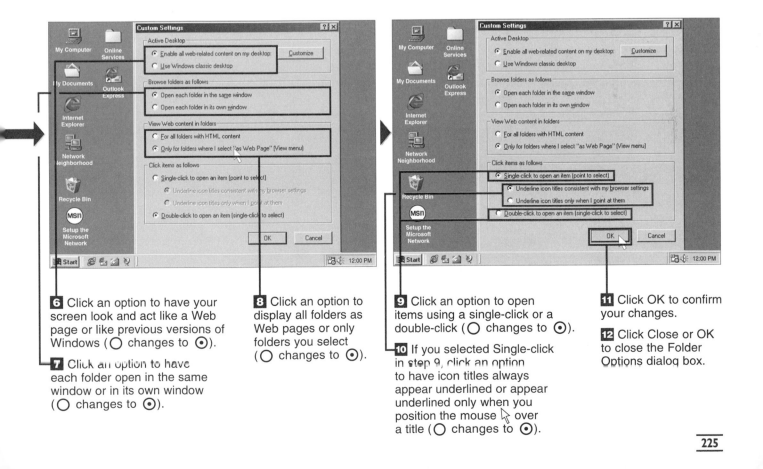

6 Click an option to have your screen look and act like a Web page or like previous versions of Windows (○ changes to ⦿).

7 Click an option to have each folder open in the same window or in its own window (○ changes to ⦿).

8 Click an option to display all folders as Web pages or only folders you select (○ changes to ⦿).

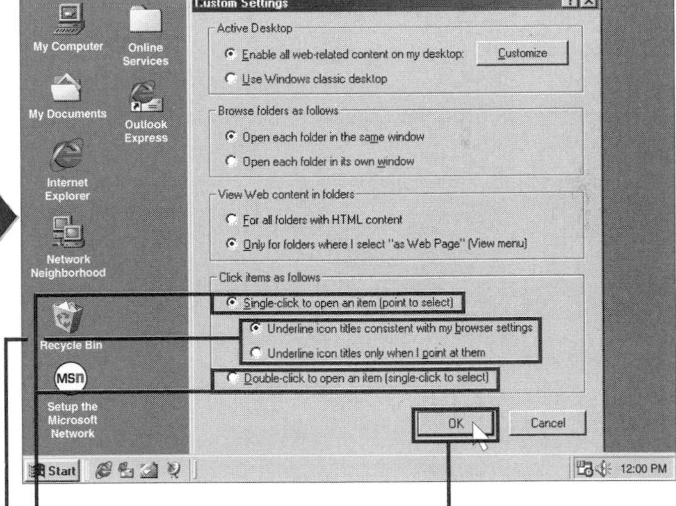

9 Click an option to open items using a single-click or a double-click (○ changes to ⦿).

10 If you selected Single-click in step 9, click an option to have icon titles always appear underlined or appear underlined only when you position the mouse over a title (○ changes to ⦿).

11 Click OK to confirm your changes.

12 Click Close or OK to close the Folder Options dialog box.

CHANGE MOUSE SETTINGS

You can change the way your mouse works to make it easier to use. The Mouse Properties dialog box offers many options you can adjust to suit your needs.

The left mouse button is used to select or drag items and click buttons. The right mouse button is used to display a list of commands for a selected item. If you are left-handed, you can switch the functions of the left and right mouse buttons to make the mouse easier for you to use.

Double-clicking is most often used to open an item. You can change the amount of time that can pass between two clicks of the mouse button for Windows to recognize a double-click. If you are a new mouse user or you have difficulty double-clicking, you may find a slower speed easier to use. You can try out the double-click speed to find the setting you prefer.

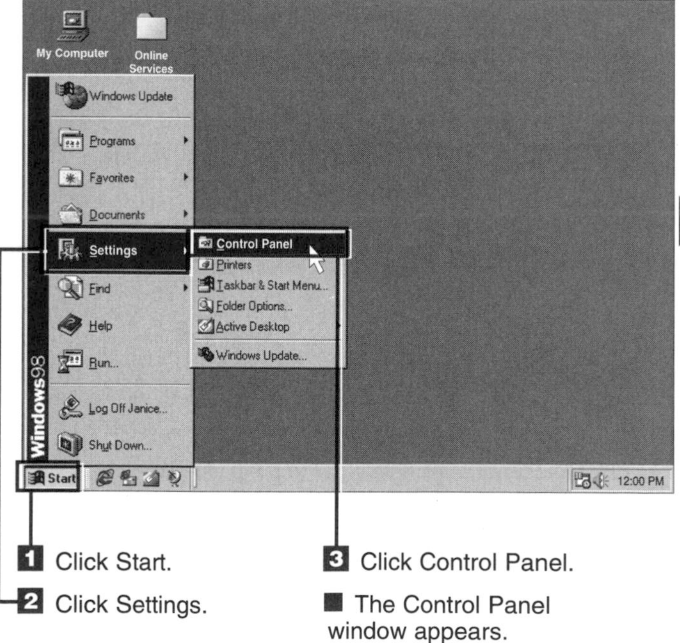

1 Click Start.

2 Click Settings.

3 Click Control Panel.

■ The Control Panel window appears.

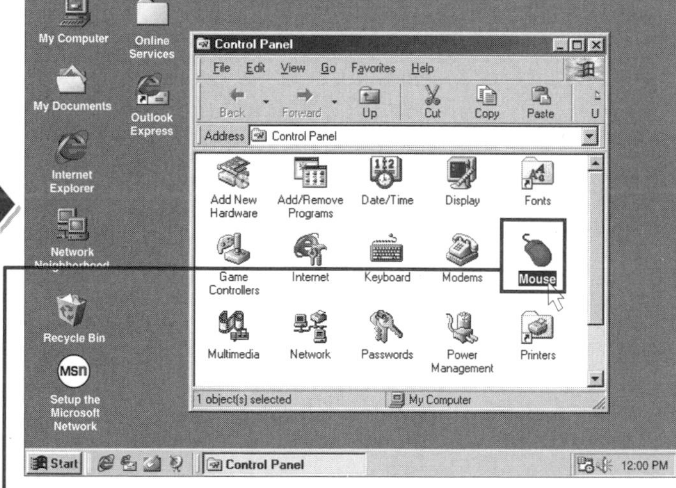

4 Double-click Mouse to change the settings for your mouse.

■ The Mouse Properties dialog box appears.

TIPS

My mouse pointer jumps around or gets stuck on the screen. What can I do?

Your mouse may need to be cleaned. Turn the mouse over and remove and clean the roller ball. Use a cotton swab to remove the dirt from the rollers inside the mouse. You can refer to the manual that came with your mouse for further instructions.

Why should I use a mouse pad?

A mouse pad provides a smooth surface for moving the mouse on your desk. You should choose a mouse pad with a hard plastic surface that is easy to keep clean. Fabric covered mouse pads collect dirt, which may stick to the roller ball of the mouse.

Are there any alternatives to double-clicking?

After you click an item, you can press the Enter key to perform the same action as double-clicking. You can also right-click an item and then click the first option in the menu that appears. Windows also offers a single-click mode so you can use one click to perform an action. See page 224 for information on the single-click mode.

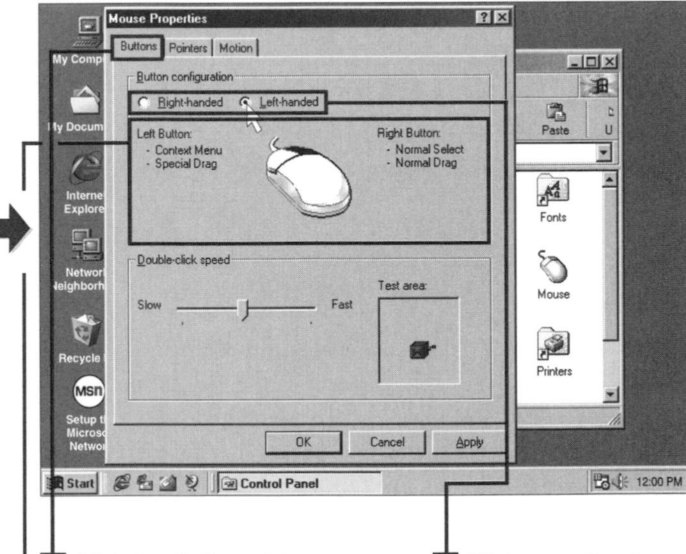

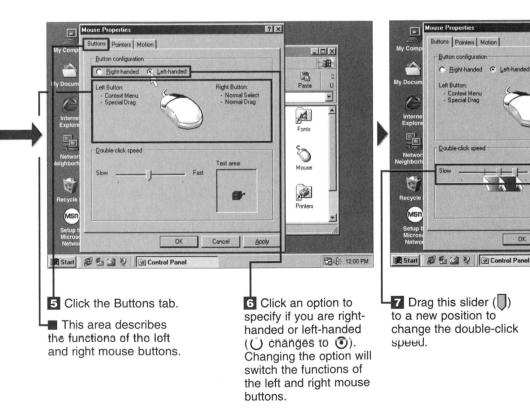

5 Click the Buttons tab.

■ This area describes the functions of the left and right mouse buttons.

6 Click an option to specify if you are right-handed or left-handed (○ changes to ◉). Changing the option will switch the functions of the left and right mouse buttons.

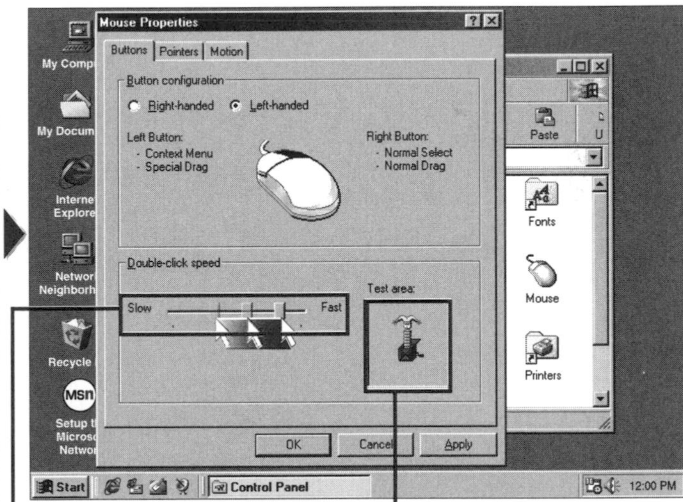

7 Drag this slider (▯) to a new position to change the double-click speed.

8 Double-click this area to test the double-click speed. A jack-in-the-box appears if you double-click at the correct speed.

CONTINUED

CHANGE MOUSE SETTINGS
CONTINUED

You can personalize your mouse by changing the look of the pointers and the way the pointer moves on your screen.

The mouse pointer assumes different shapes, depending on its location on your screen and the task you are performing. For example, the standard mouse pointer turns into an hourglass when the computer is busy, or a double-headed arrow when you are adjusting the size of a window.

Windows includes several sets of pointers including animated, three-dimensional and large pointers. You can choose to display a different set of mouse pointers.

You can also make the mouse pointer on your screen move faster or slower.

You can leave a trail of mouse pointers as you move the mouse around your screen. Displaying mouse trails can help you follow the movement of the mouse pointer. This is especially useful on portable computer screens, where the mouse pointer can be difficult to follow.

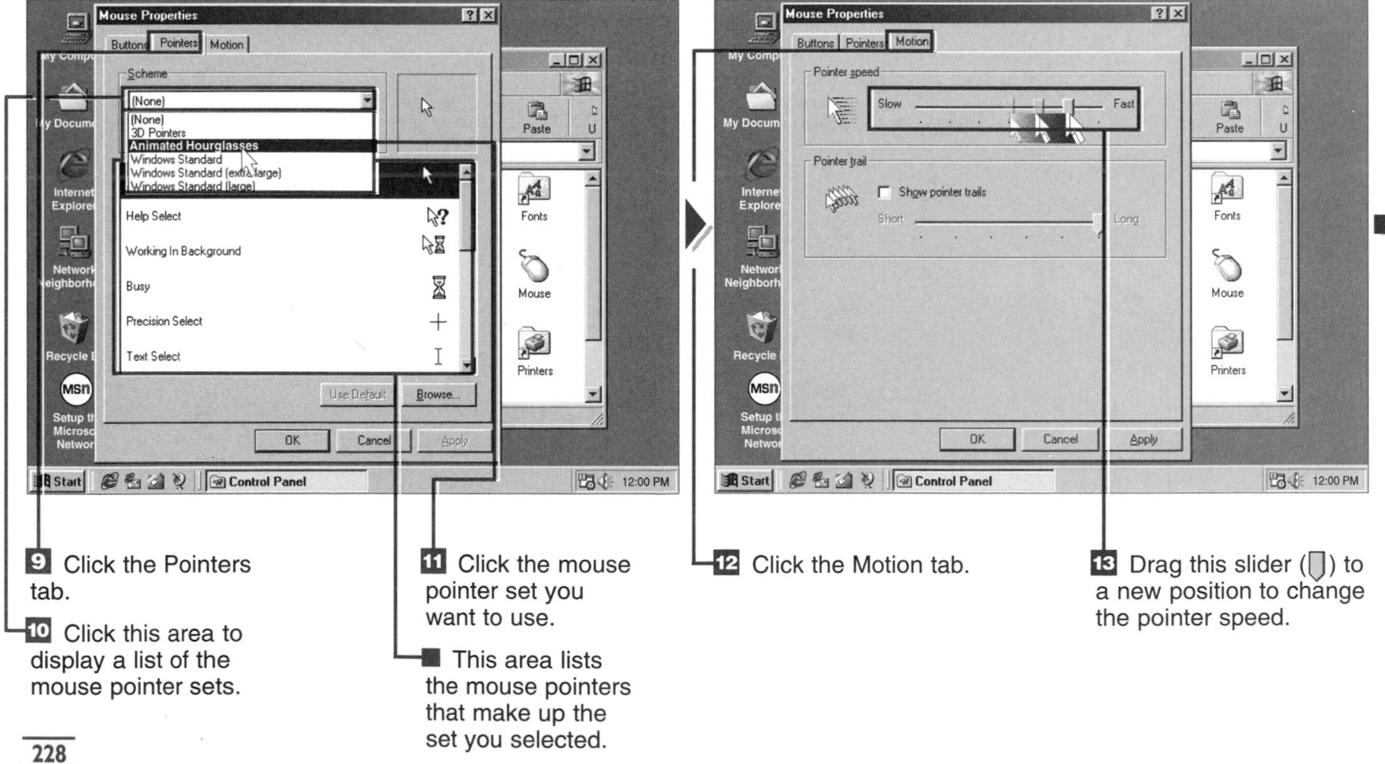

9 Click the Pointers tab.

10 Click this area to display a list of the mouse pointer sets.

11 Click the mouse pointer set you want to use.

■ This area lists the mouse pointers that make up the set you selected.

12 Click the Motion tab.

13 Drag this slider (▯) to a new position to change the pointer speed.

TIPS

Does Windows 98 provide any additional mouse pointer sets?

Windows includes some additional mouse pointer sets, which are found in the Accessories component. See page 610 to add Windows components.

Why does my Mouse Properties dialog box have additional options?

If you installed software that came with your mouse, you may find additional options in the Mouse Properties dialog box.

How can I change the appearance of individual pointers in a set of mouse pointers?

In the Mouse Properties dialog box, display the Pointers tab. Select the mouse pointer set you want to use and then double-click the mouse pointer you want to change. The Browse dialog box appears, displaying the available mouse pointers. Click the pointer you want to use and then click the Open button. After you have customized a set of mouse pointers, you can click the Save As button to name and save the set.

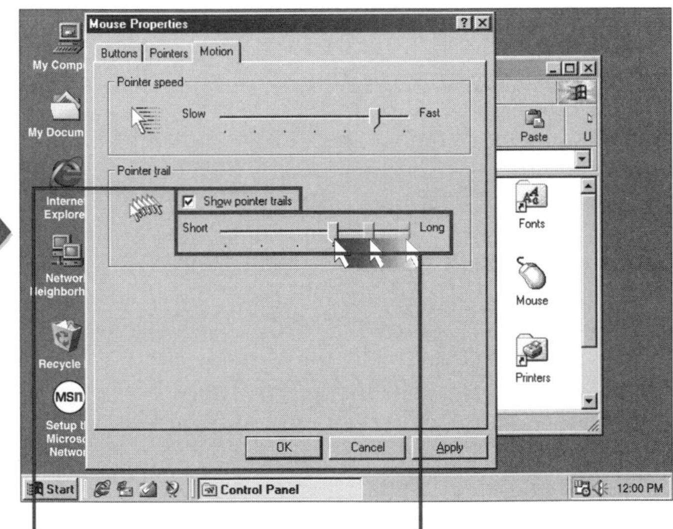

14 Click this option to leave a trail of mouse pointers when you move the mouse (☐ changes to ☑).

15 Drag this slider (▯) to a new position to change the length of the pointer trail.

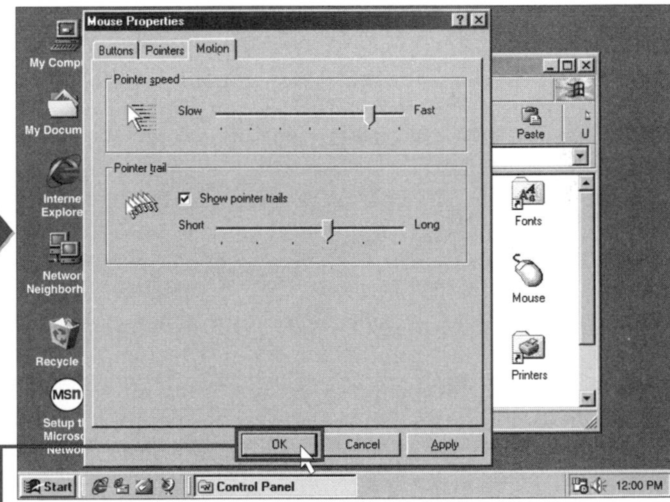

16 Click OK to confirm all of your changes.

CHANGE KEYBOARD SETTINGS

You can change the way your keyboard responds to your commands.

Repeated characters appear on your screen when you hold down a key on your keyboard. If you use repeated characters to underline, separate or emphasize text, you may want to adjust the Repeat delay and Repeat rate settings.

The Repeat delay setting adjusts the length of time a key must be held down before it starts to repeat.

The Repeat rate determines how quickly characters appear on your screen when a key is held down. You can test the settings while making adjustments.

You can also change the speed at which the cursor blinks. The cursor, or insertion point, indicates where the text you type will appear. The cursor should blink fast enough so it is easy to find, but slow enough so it is not distracting. You can preview your Cursor blink rate to find a setting you prefer.

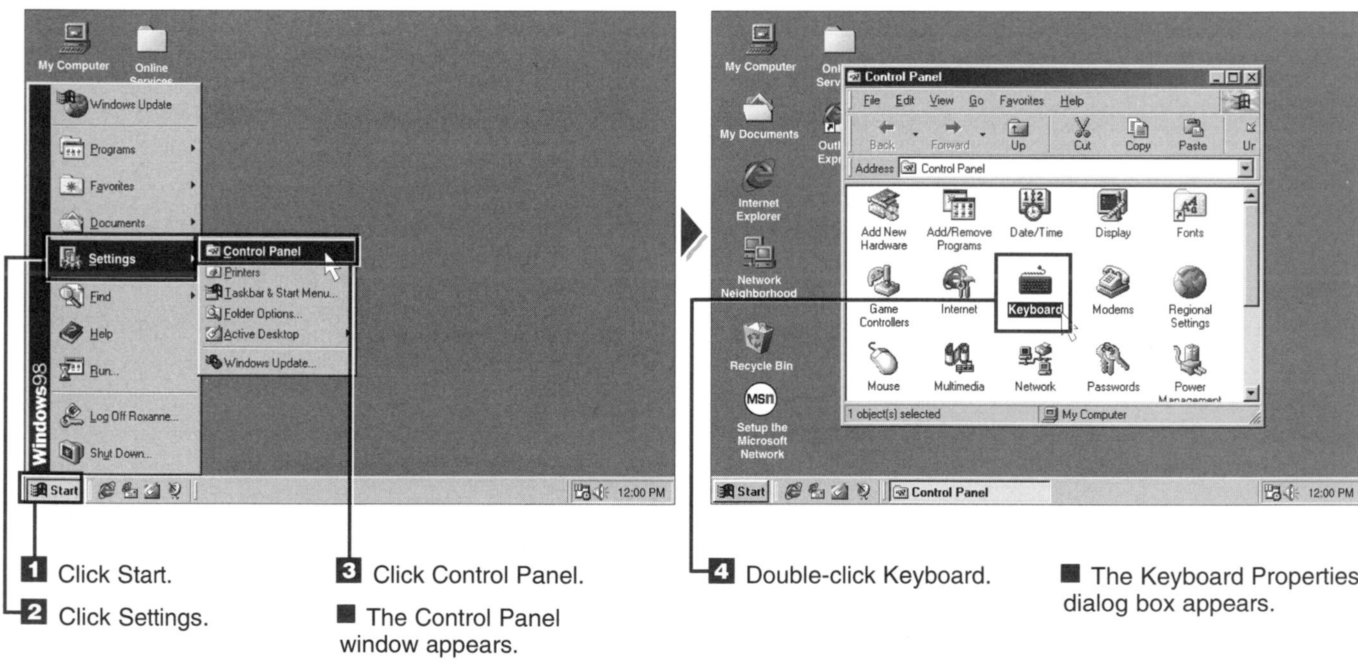

1 Click Start.

2 Click Settings.

3 Click Control Panel.

■ The Control Panel window appears.

4 Double-click Keyboard.

■ The Keyboard Properties dialog box appears.

TIPS

What is the correct typing position to help avoid wrist strain?

You should keep your elbows level with the keyboard. Always keep your wrists straight and higher than your fingers while working on the keyboard. You can use a wrist rest to elevate your wrists and ensure they remain straight at all times. If you start to experience any pain, tingling or numbness while working, take a break. If the sensation continues, you should see a doctor.

I find it difficult to hold down two keys and then press a third key. Can I make my keyboard easier to use?

The Accessibility options can make your keyboard easier to use. To adjust the Accessibility options, see page 252.

How do I clean my keyboard?

To remove dust, use a small paintbrush. To clean away dirt, use a cloth dampened with soapy water or a window-cleaning solution.

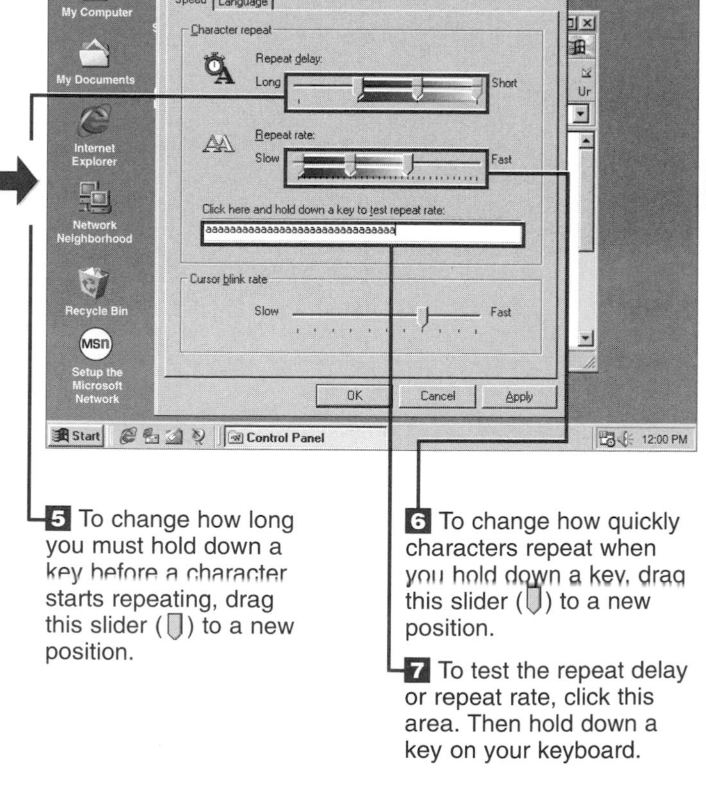

5 To change how long you must hold down a key before a character starts repeating, drag this slider (▯) to a new position.

6 To change how quickly characters repeat when you hold down a key, drag this slider (▯) to a new position.

7 To test the repeat delay or repeat rate, click this area. Then hold down a key on your keyboard.

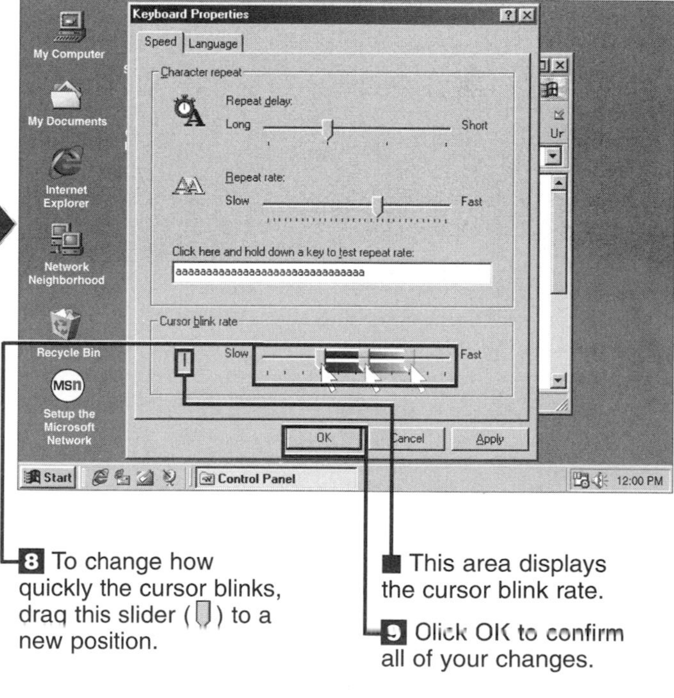

8 To change how quickly the cursor blinks, drag this slider (▯) to a new position.

■ This area displays the cursor blink rate.

9 Click OK to confirm all of your changes.

ADD DESTINATIONS TO SEND TO MENU

The Send To menu allows you to send files to another location. You can customize the Send To menu to include the folders, programs and devices you use most often. Your floppy and removable drives are already on the Send To menu.

You can place shortcuts to folders, programs and devices in the SendTo folder. Any item in the SendTo folder appears on the Send To menu.

You can use the Send To menu to open files in a specific program or quickly move files to a folder. Windows automatically places the My Documents folder in the Send To menu for you. You can also e-mail a file using the Send To menu.

Using the Send To menu simplifies many procedures. For example, if you frequently need to use WordPad to open files created in other programs, you can place a shortcut to the WordPad program in the SendTo folder. You can then use the Send To menu to quickly open the files without first opening the WordPad program. This is especially useful for files that do not have standard extensions, such as readme.1st.

You can also place a shortcut for a device, such as a printer, in the Send To menu. This allows you to send a selected file directly to the printer.

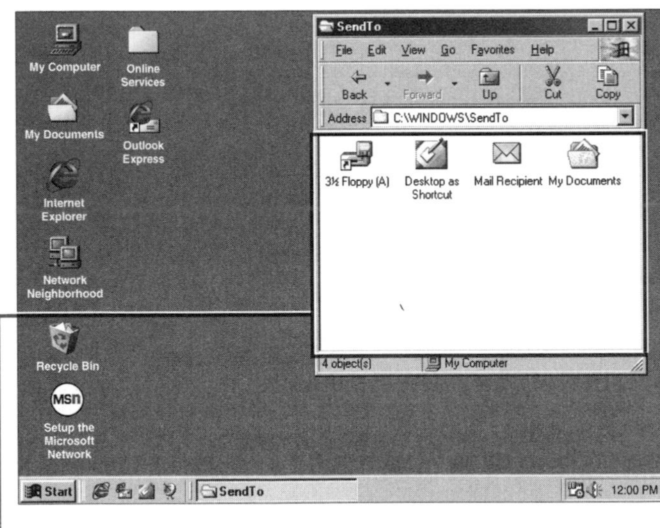

1 Display the contents of the SendTo folder. The SendTo folder contains all the items that appear on the Send To menu.

■ You will find the SendTo folder on your hard drive (C:), in the Windows folder.

Note: To search for the SendTo folder, see page 78.

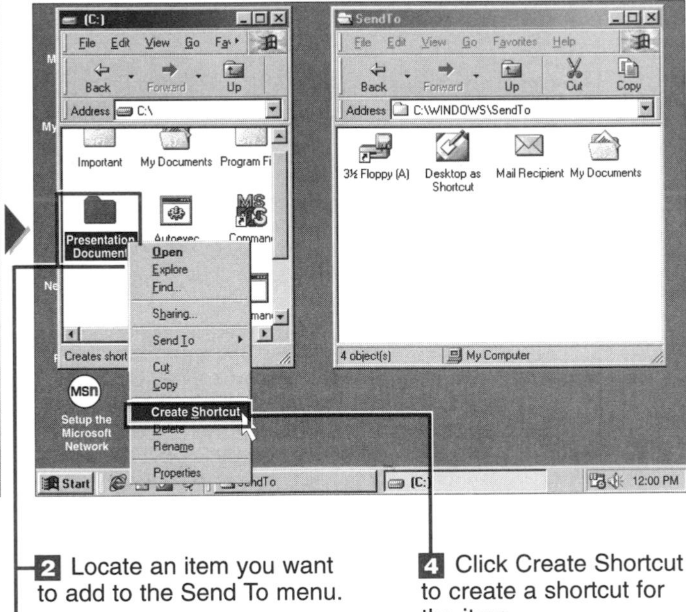

2 Locate an item you want to add to the Send To menu.

3 Right-click the item. A menu appears.

4 Click Create Shortcut to create a shortcut for the item.

Can I add shared folders on the network to my Send To menu?

Adding shared folders to the Send To menu is useful if you frequently send files to another person on the network. In Network Neighborhood, find the folder you want to add to the SendTo folder. Place a shortcut to the shared folder in the SendTo folder on your computer.

Can I use folders to organize the information on the Send To menu?

You can create a folder in the SendTo folder to better organize the items. See page 86 to create a folder. The folder will appear at the top of the Send To menu with an arrow (▶) indicating there are more choices. You can click the folder to display more choices.

When I send a file to a folder, how do I know if the file will be moved or copied?

If the folder and file are on the same drive, Windows moves the file. If the folder and file are on different drives, Windows copies the file. If you are sending a program to a folder, Windows places a shortcut to the program in the folder. The program remains in the original location.

How can I quickly open the SendTo folder?

To quickly open the SendTo folder, click the Start button and then click Run. Type **SendTo** and then press the Enter key.

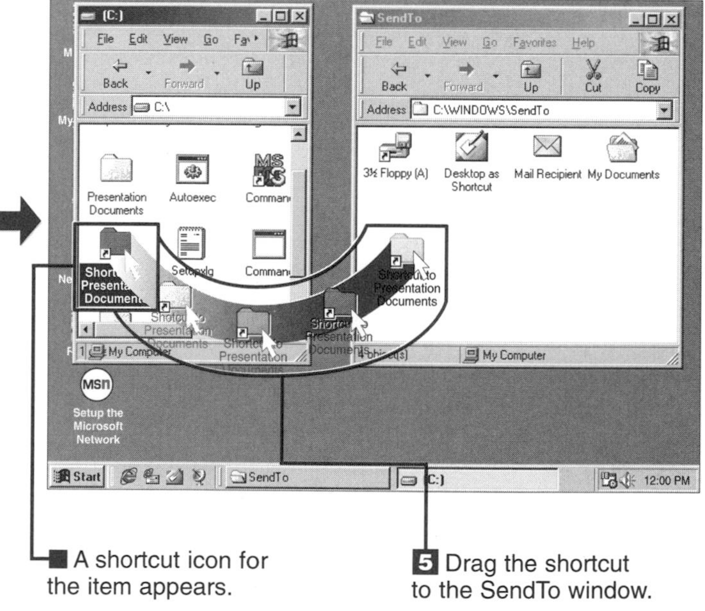

■ A shortcut icon for the item appears.

5 Drag the shortcut to the SendTo window.

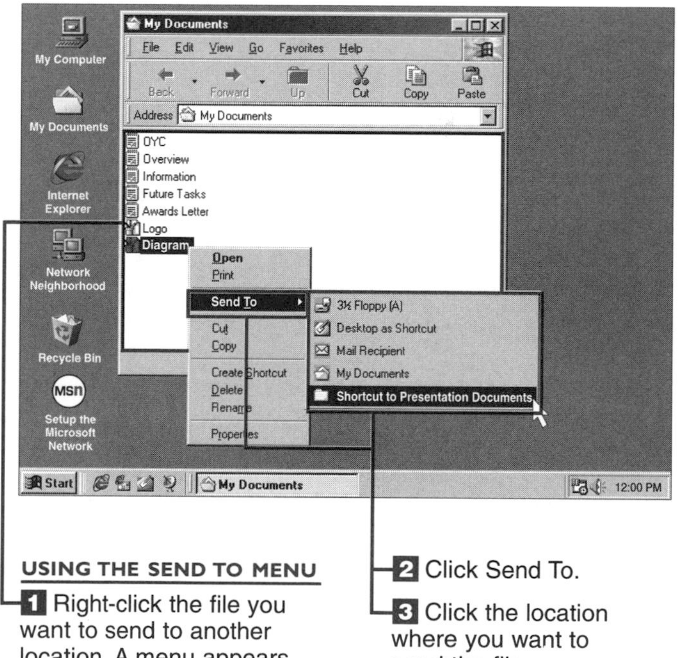

USING THE SEND TO MENU

1 Right-click the file you want to send to another location. A menu appears.

2 Click Send To.

3 Click the location where you want to send the file.

CREATE A NEW FILE TYPE

You can create a new file type to tell Windows how you want to work with certain types of files. When you create a new file type, you create an association between the file type and a specific program.

You can give your file type a description so you can identify it later.

You must give the new file type an extension. Windows uses extensions to associate a file type with a program. For example, you can create a file type for all of your letters with the .let extension. You can tell Windows to always open files of this type with the WordPad program. Every time you double-click a file with the .let extension, WordPad will open and display the file.

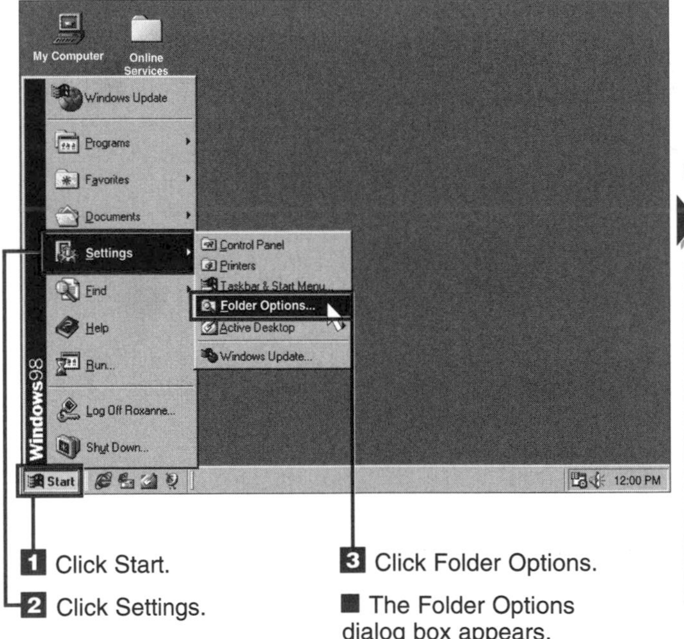

1 Click Start.

2 Click Settings.

3 Click Folder Options.

■ The Folder Options dialog box appears.

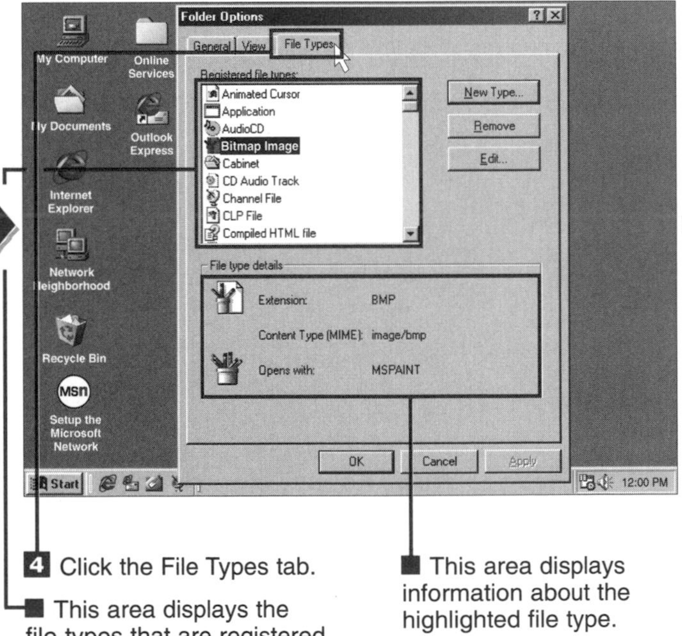

4 Click the File Types tab.

■ This area displays the file types that are registered with Windows.

■ This area displays information about the highlighted file type.

Note: You can click another file type to display information about the file type.

TIPS

Is there a faster way to register a new file type?

When you double-click a file that is not associated with a program, the Open With dialog box appears. You can use the dialog box to quickly register a file type. To specify the program you want to use, click the program. Then click the Always use this program to open this type of file option (☐ changes to ☑). For information on the Open With dialog box, see page 64.

Can I remove a file type I created?

Click the file type you want to remove in the Registered file types list. Click the Remove button and then click Yes to remove the file type. Keep in mind that when you remove a registered file type, you will not be able to open a file of that type by double-clicking the file.

Can I use more than three letters in a file type extension?

You can create longer extensions, such as .budget. Extensions cannot contain any spaces or periods. Longer extensions may not display fully in some dialog boxes. If you share files with people who do not use Windows 95 or 98, longer extensions may not work correctly.

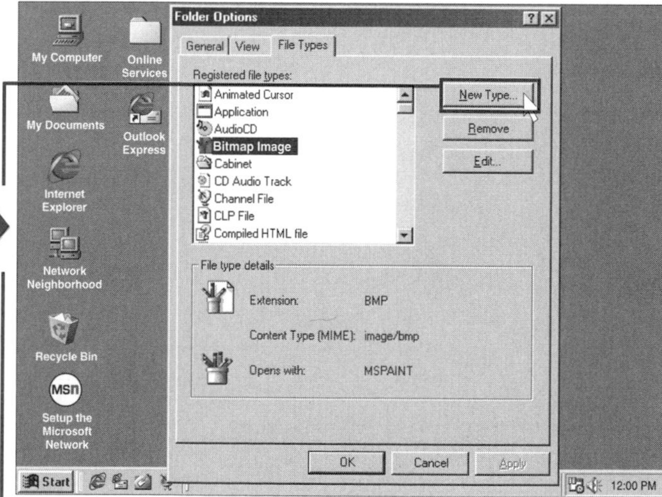

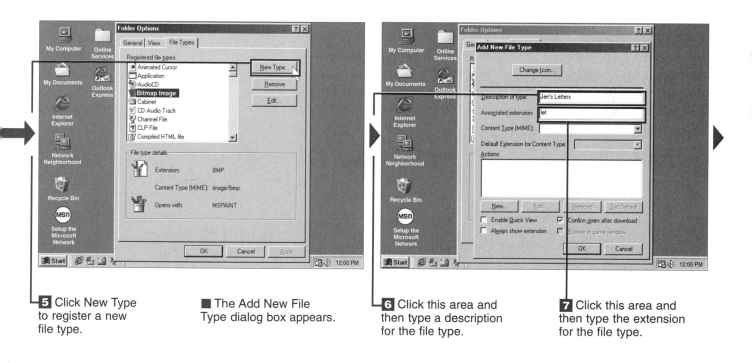

5 Click New Type to register a new file type.

■ The Add New File Type dialog box appears.

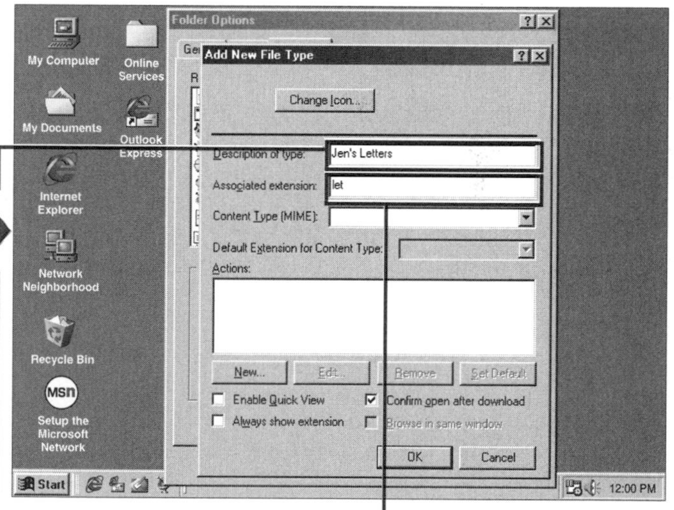

6 Click this area and then type a description for the file type.

7 Click this area and then type the extension for the file type.

CONTINUED

CREATE A NEW FILE TYPE CONTINUED

You can add an action to a file type you create. You can also specify what will happen when the action is selected.

For every file type you create, you should add the Open action. The Open action lets you start a program and open the selected file in one step.

When you right-click a file, Windows displays the available actions for the file in a menu. You can choose the name you want to appear for the action in the menu. An action name is usually one word that describes the action, such as Open or Edit.

You must then select the program you want to use to perform the action.

You may also want to add the Quick View command to the menu that appears when you right-click a file. Quick View allows you to view a file without opening the file. Quick View cannot display all file types. For information on Quick View, see page 82.

You can also choose to hide or display the extension for the file type.

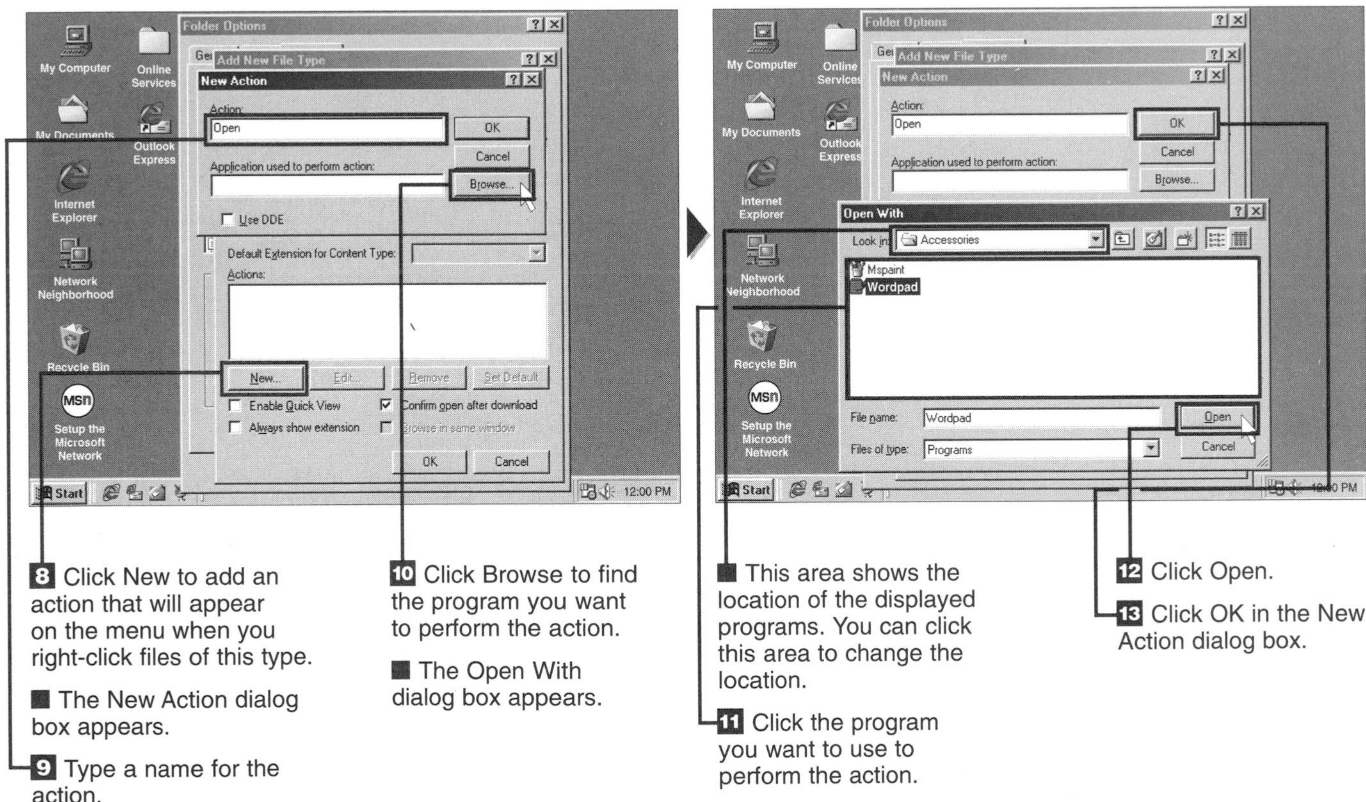

8 Click New to add an action that will appear on the menu when you right-click files of this type.

■ The New Action dialog box appears.

9 Type a name for the action.

10 Click Browse to find the program you want to perform the action.

■ The Open With dialog box appears.

■ This area shows the location of the displayed programs. You can click this area to change the location.

11 Click the program you want to use to perform the action.

12 Click Open.

13 Click OK in the New Action dialog box.

I used Browse to select a program, but Windows states that it cannot find the program. Why?

You may have selected the program's shortcut. Shortcuts only contain the information needed to find a program. When you create a file type, you must select the original program file. Program files have the .exe extension.

After creating a file type with the extension .let, I named a document report.let. Windows renamed it report.let.doc. Why?

Some programs make it very difficult to save using a non-standard extension. Type the name of the file inside quotation marks ("") to use a non-standard extension. For example, type "**report.let**" as the file name.

Can I create two actions for one file type?

You can create several actions for one file type. For example, you can have one action to open the file and another action to edit the file. Name the first action Open and select a program to open the file. Name the second action Edit and select a program to edit the file.

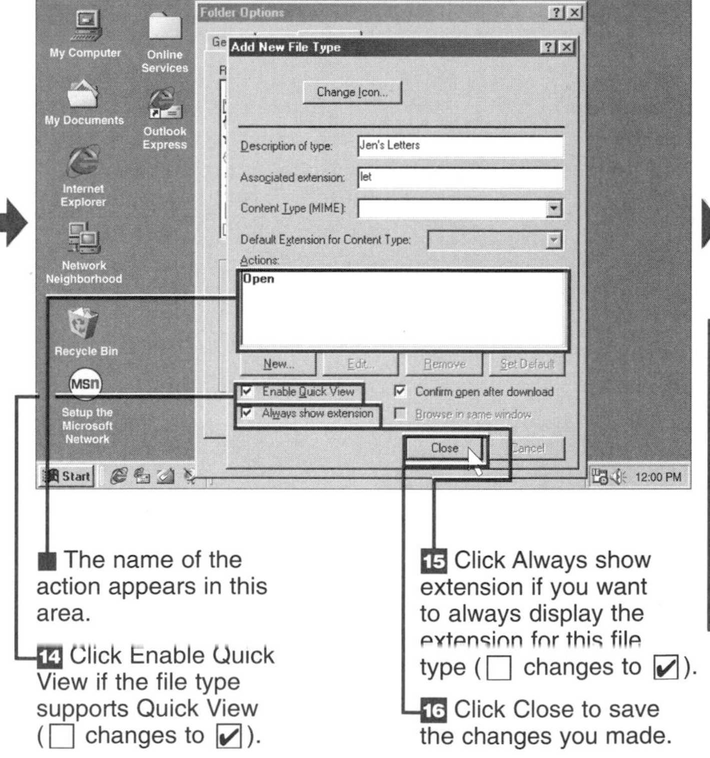

■ The name of the action appears in this area.

14 Click Enable Quick View if the file type supports Quick View (☐ changes to ☑).

15 Click Always show extension if you want to always display the extension for this file type (☐ changes to ☑).

16 Click Close to save the changes you made.

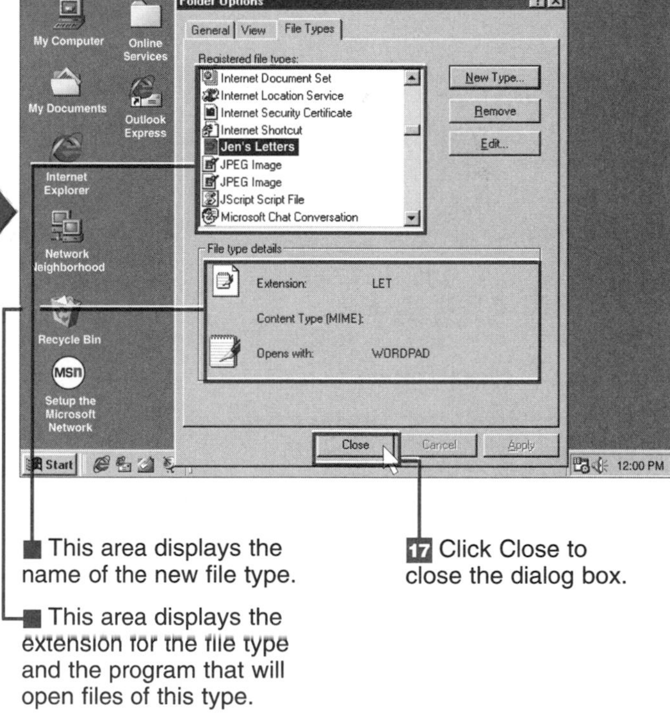

■ This area displays the name of the new file type.

■ This area displays the extension for the file type and the program that will open files of this type.

17 Click Close to close the dialog box.

CHANGE ICON FOR A FILE TYPE

Each type of file on your computer is represented by a specific icon. Icons help you identify each file and the type of information a file contains. You can change the icon Windows displays for a file type. Windows provides a list of icons you can choose from.

In addition to identifying the contents of a file, the icon beside the file name normally indicates the program that will be used to open the file. For example, if WordPad opens a file, Windows will display the WordPad icon beside the name of the file. If you create your own file type, you may want to change the icon to one that better represents the file type.

Make sure you only change the icons for file types you have created. Changing a file type Windows created can cause problems.

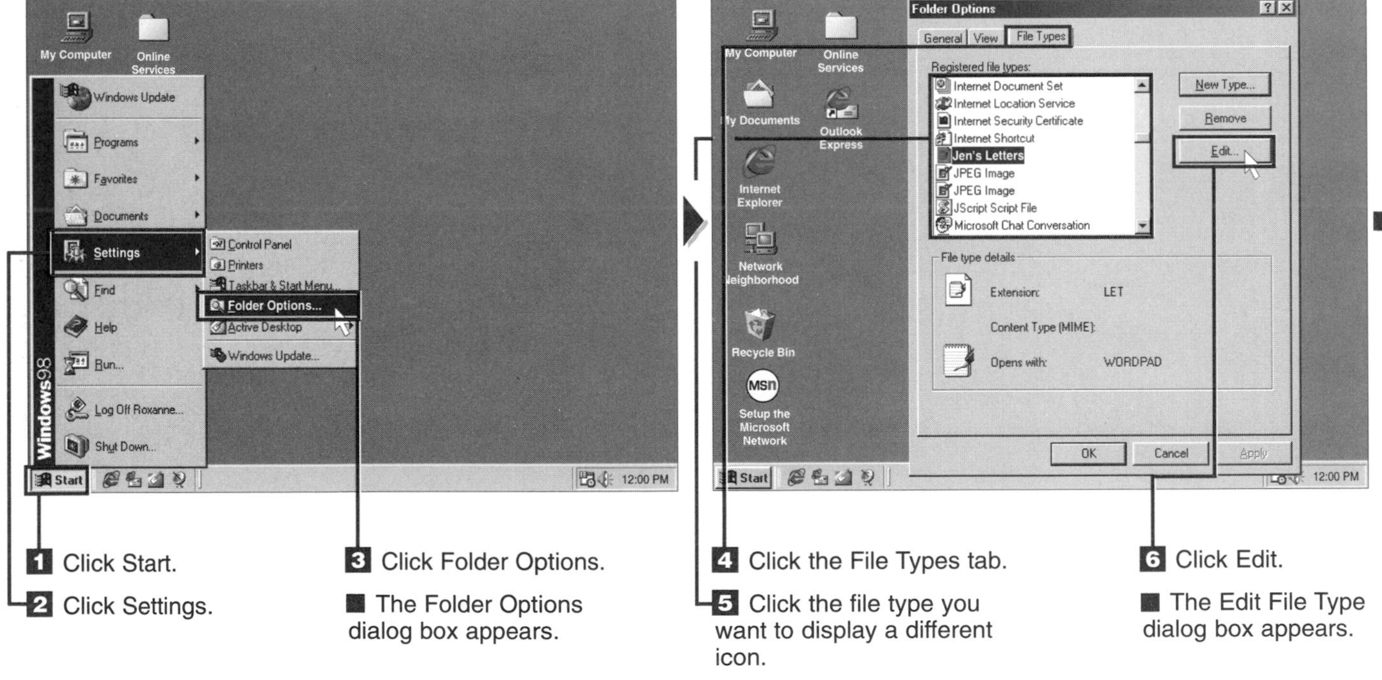

1 Click Start.

2 Click Settings.

3 Click Folder Options.

■ The Folder Options dialog box appears.

4 Click the File Types tab.

5 Click the file type you want to display a different icon.

6 Click Edit.

■ The Edit File Type dialog box appears.

Are there more icons available on my computer?

You can use the Browse button in the Change Icon dialog box to find files containing icons on your computer. Additional Windows icons are located in the C:\Windows\Moricons.dll file. You may first need to display hidden files. See page 56.

Files that contain icons often have the .dll or .exe extension. A file that contains a single icon often has the .ico extension.

Can I change the appearance of the icons displayed on my desktop?

Windows lets you change the appearance of the My Computer, My Documents, Network Neighborhood and Recycle Bin icons on your desktop. See page 214.

Can I create my own icons?

There are several programs available to create your own icons. Microangelo from Impact Software (www.impactsoft.com) and Icon Editor from NeoSoft (www.testware.co.uk/neosoft/ni.html) are both available as shareware programs and can be downloaded from the Internet.

Why isn't the Edit button available when I select the Application or MS-DOS Application file types?

These file types cannot be modified. You cannot change their icons.

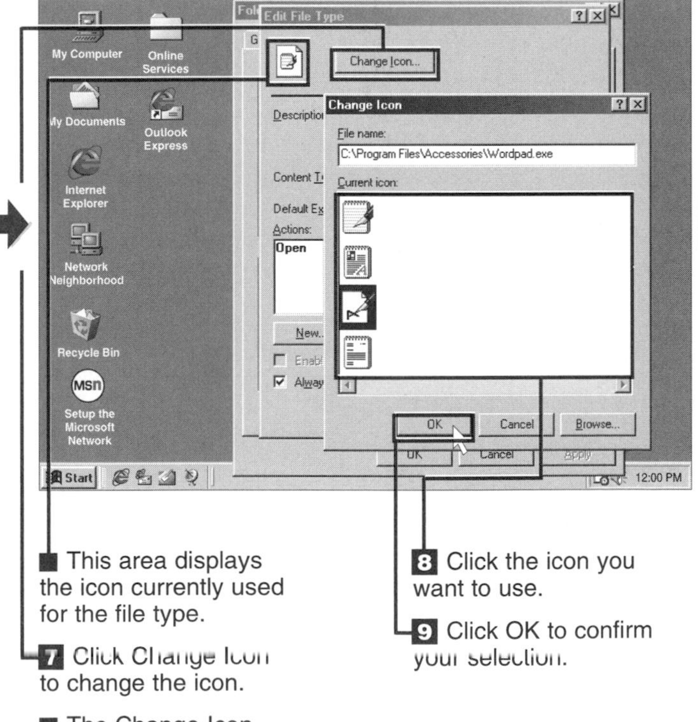

■ This area displays the icon currently used for the file type.

7 Click Change Icon to change the icon.

■ The Change Icon dialog box appears.

8 Click the icon you want to use.

9 Click OK to confirm your selection.

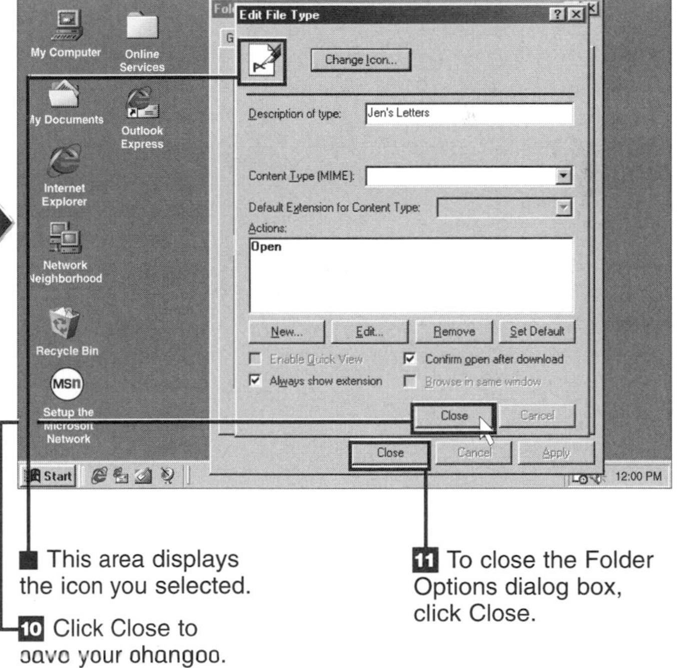

■ This area displays the icon you selected.

10 Click Close to save your changes.

11 To close the Folder Options dialog box, click Close.

EDIT A FILE TYPE

You can make changes to a file type. You should only edit the file types that you have created.

You can change the program that opens a file when you double-click the file. For example, if a file type is currently opened by Notepad, you can choose another program, such as WordPad, to open files of that type.

You can also add new actions to a file type. For example, besides Open, you may want to add actions such as Edit or Print to a file type.

You can change the description of your file type to one that better suits your file type. For example, you may want to change the description of a file type from Letters to Business Letters to make it easier to identify the file type.

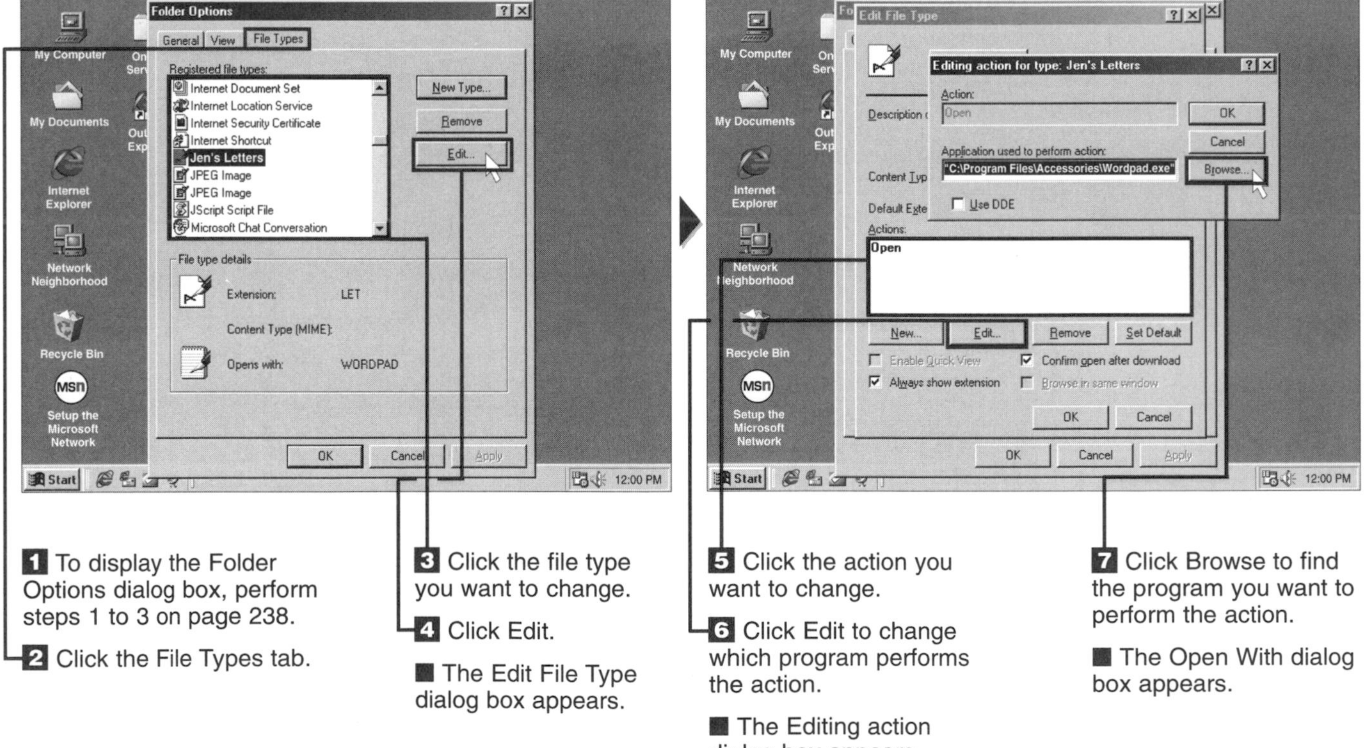

1 To display the Folder Options dialog box, perform steps 1 to 3 on page 238.

2 Click the File Types tab.

3 Click the file type you want to change.

4 Click Edit.

■ The Edit File Type dialog box appears.

5 Click the action you want to change.

6 Click Edit to change which program performs the action.

■ The Editing action dialog box appears.

7 Click Browse to find the program you want to perform the action.

■ The Open With dialog box appears.

TIPS

How do I add an action like Print to a file type?

In the Folder Options dialog box, you can click an existing file type and then select the Edit button to see how the file type performs an action you want to add. This is especially useful for actions such as Print, that need special instructions added to the program name. For example, if you want to include an action that prints a file using WordPad, click the Print action for the WordPad file type and then click the Edit button. You can use keyboard shortcuts to copy the highlighted information to a new file type. To copy information, use Ctrl+C. To paste information, use Ctrl+V.

How do I remove an action that I no longer want a file type to use?

Select the action you want to remove in the Edit File Type dialog box. Click the Remove button and then click Yes in the confirmation dialog box.

How do I change the extension for a file type?

You cannot change the extension for a file type. You can remove the file type and then create a new file type with the extension you want to use.

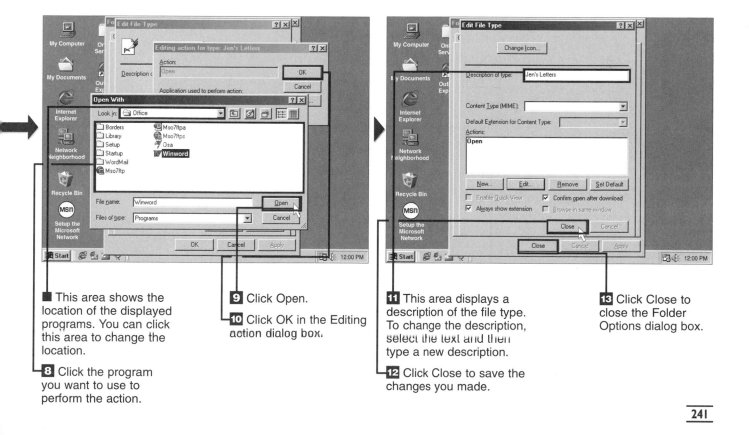

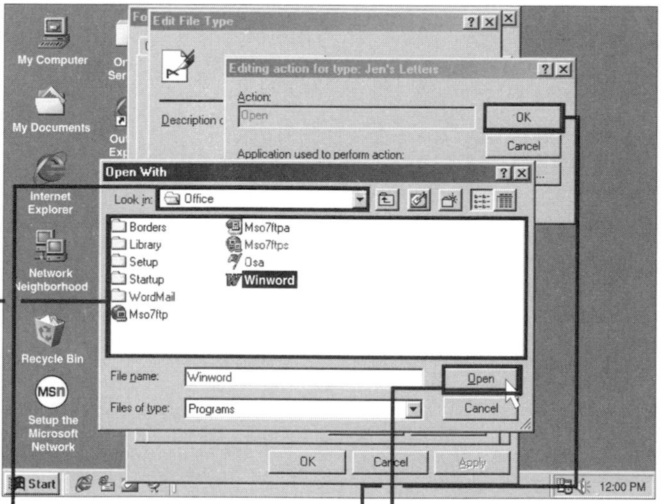

■ This area shows the location of the displayed programs. You can click this area to change the location.

8 Click the program you want to use to perform the action.

9 Click Open.

10 Click OK in the Editing action dialog box.

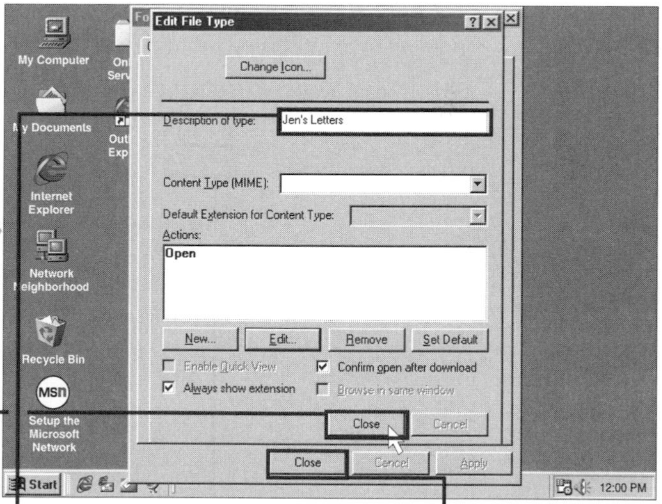

11 This area displays a description of the file type. To change the description, select the text and then type a new description.

12 Click Close to save the changes you made.

13 Click Close to close the Folder Options dialog box.

SET UP A GAME CONTROLLER

A game controller is a device, such as a joystick, that allows you to interact with a game. After installing a game controller on your computer, you can set up the controller to adjust and fine-tune the settings.

A game controller allows you to easily control the direction of movement in a game, such as forward, backward or at an angle. You can use a mouse instead of a game controller in many games, but the greater control that a game controller offers can enhance games such as flight simulators.

Most game controllers are equipped with at least one button that usually acts as a trigger in a game. Many controllers have several buttons that offer additional features and make the game more exciting.

Many games are designed to operate with specific types of game controllers. Each controller is different and may require you to adjust different settings before it works properly with the game you are playing.

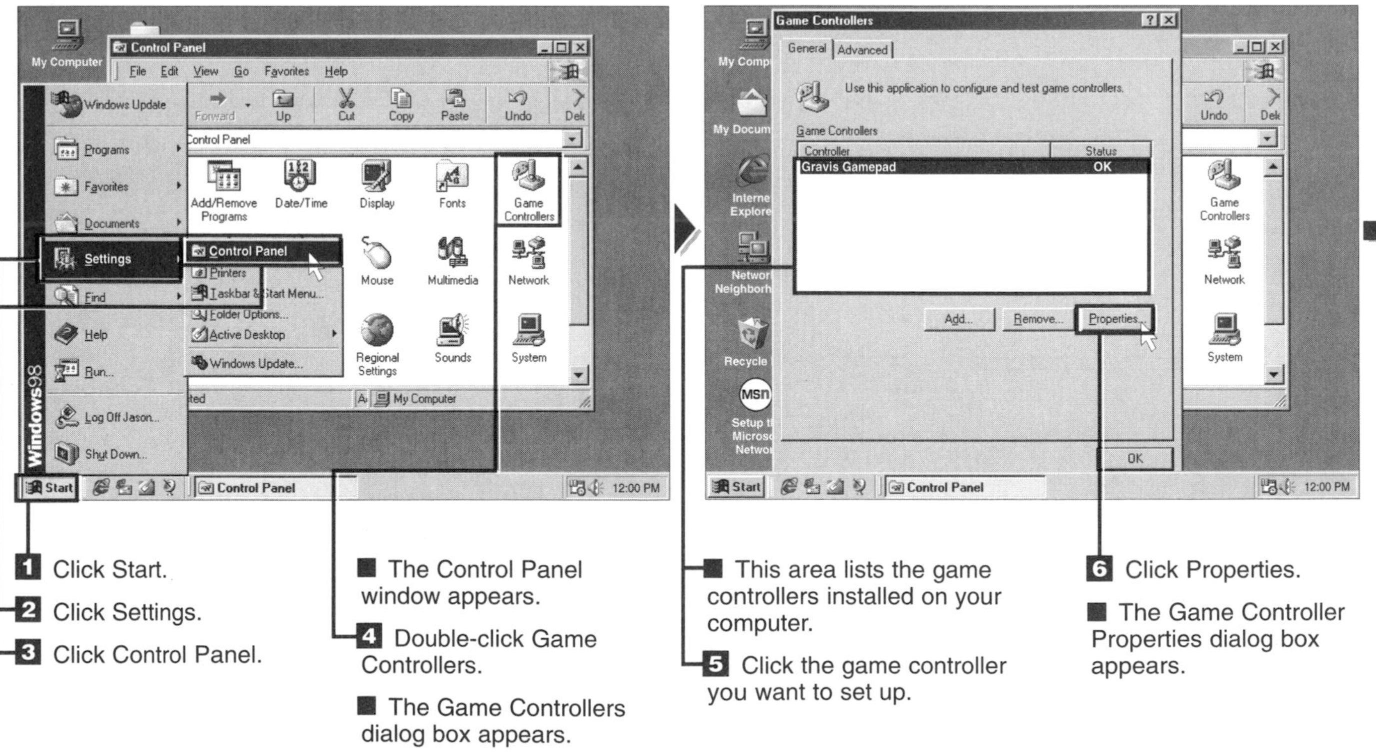

1 Click Start.

2 Click Settings.

3 Click Control Panel.

■ The Control Panel window appears.

4 Double-click Game Controllers.

■ The Game Controllers dialog box appears.

■ This area lists the game controllers installed on your computer.

5 Click the game controller you want to set up.

6 Click Properties.

■ The Game Controller Properties dialog box appears.

TIPS

How can I test my game controller?

After you finish setting up your game controller, perform steps 1 to 6 below and then click the Test tab. Windows lets you test certain features of the game controller to make sure the controller is working the way you want.

Why do some features of my game controller not work?

Some game controllers offer advanced features and are more complicated to set up. You may have to use the software that came with the controller to set it up. Check the game controller's documentation to find out how to properly set up the controller.

What is a rudder?

A rudder is a device you can attach to some game controllers to add more features to the controller. Some rudders work like the gas and brake pedals in a car. Other rudders work like the steering controls of a plane. To set up a rudder, perform steps 1 to 7 below and then click the Rudder/Pedals option.

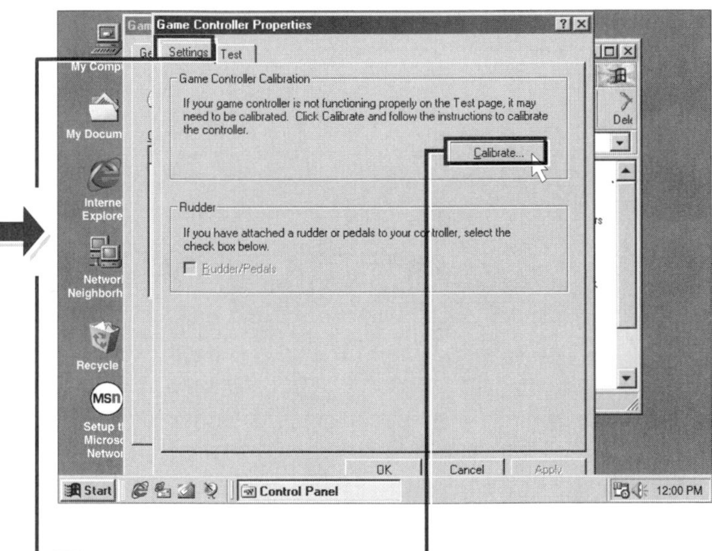

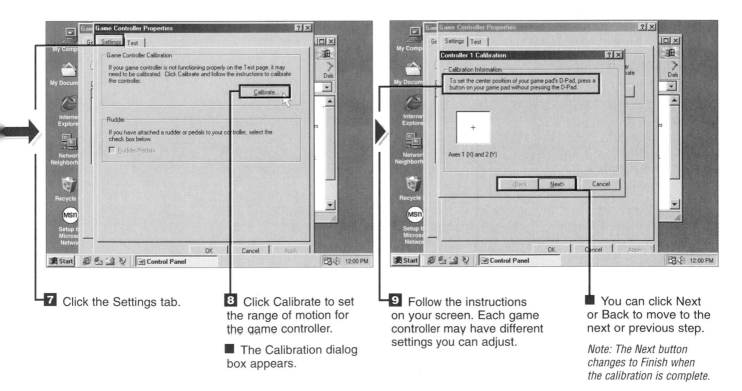

7 Click the Settings tab.

8 Click Calibrate to set the range of motion for the game controller.

■ The Calibration dialog box appears.

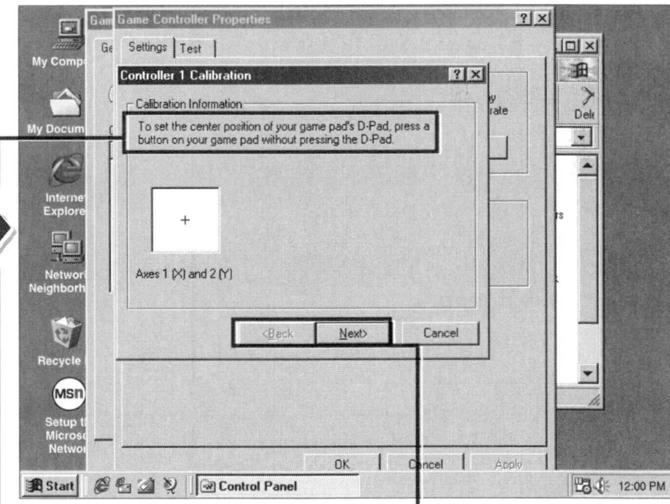

9 Follow the instructions on your screen. Each game controller may have different settings you can adjust.

■ You can click Next or Back to move to the next or previous step.

Note: The Next button changes to Finish when the calibration is complete.

USING MULTIPLE MONITORS

Windows 98 allows you to use more than one monitor. Using multiple monitors enables you to expand your desktop area. For example, graphic artists and desktop publishers often find it useful to display the image or page they are working with on one monitor and display their tools on another monitor. Multiple monitors can also be used to display several documents at once, read e-mail messages and browse the Web at the same time, or drag and drop items between applications. Using multiple monitors is also useful for games such as Flight Simulator, which allow you to display multiple views simultaneously.

Each monitor you use must have its own video adapter. The multiple monitor capability only supports certain types of video adapters.

When using multiple monitors, one monitor will be the primary monitor. The primary monitor displays the Windows taskbar and the Start menu. Although all the monitors display the same background and screen saver, the monitors do not need to be the same size or display the same color depth and resolution.

You can stack the monitors one above another or place the monitors side-by-side.

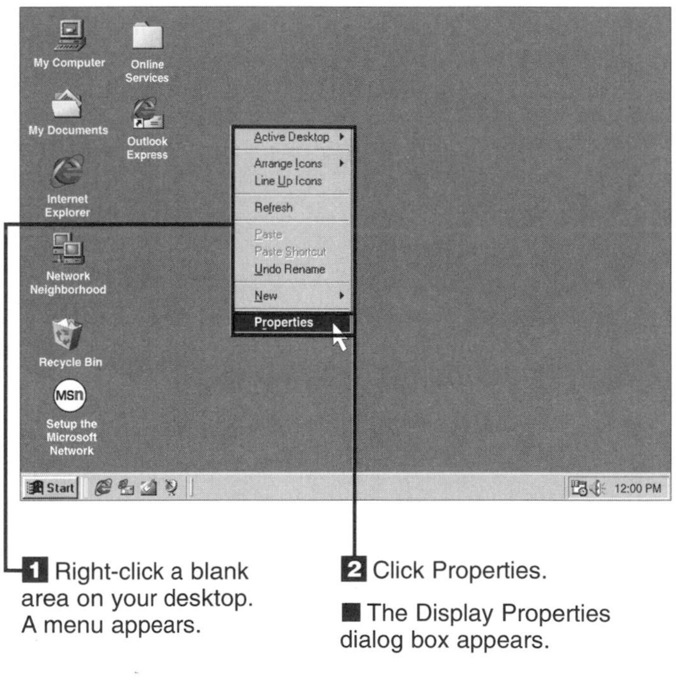

1 Right-click a blank area on your desktop. A menu appears.

2 Click Properties.

■ The Display Properties dialog box appears.

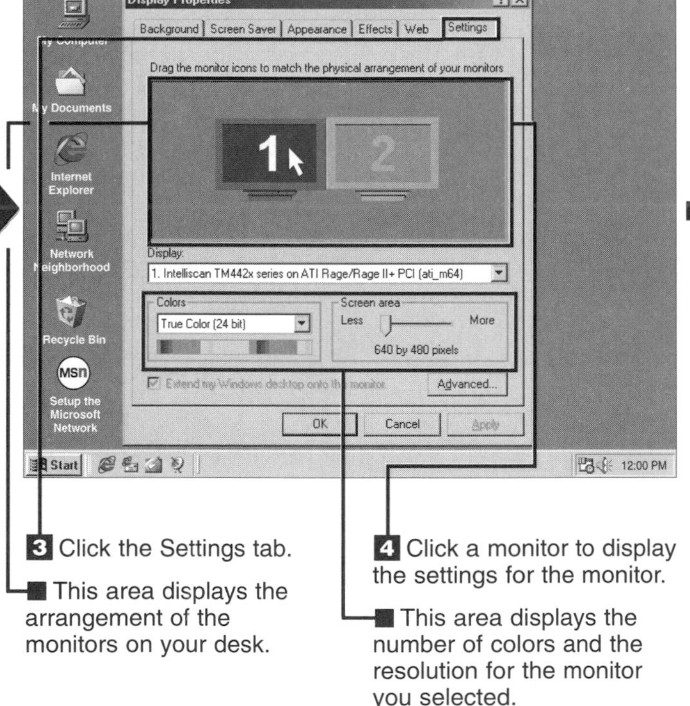

3 Click the Settings tab.

■ This area displays the arrangement of the monitors on your desk.

4 Click a monitor to display the settings for the monitor.

■ This area displays the number of colors and the resolution for the monitor you selected.

TIPS

How do I install a second monitor?

Install a second video adapter for the monitor by following the manufacturer's instructions. When you restart your computer, Windows will detect the new video adapter and automatically install the appropriate software.

How does my computer determine which monitor will be the primary monitor?

The primary monitor is the monitor that is plugged into the primary video adapter. Your computer determines the primary video adapter based on the configuration of the video adapters installed in the computer.

Will all my programs work on a secondary monitor?

No. You will not be able to watch television, play certain types of games or use a full-screen MS-DOS window on a secondary monitor.

How do I stop using a secondary monitor?

On the Settings tab of the Display Properties dialog box, click the monitor you want to stop using. Then click the Extend my Windows desktop onto this monitor option (☑ changes to ☐).

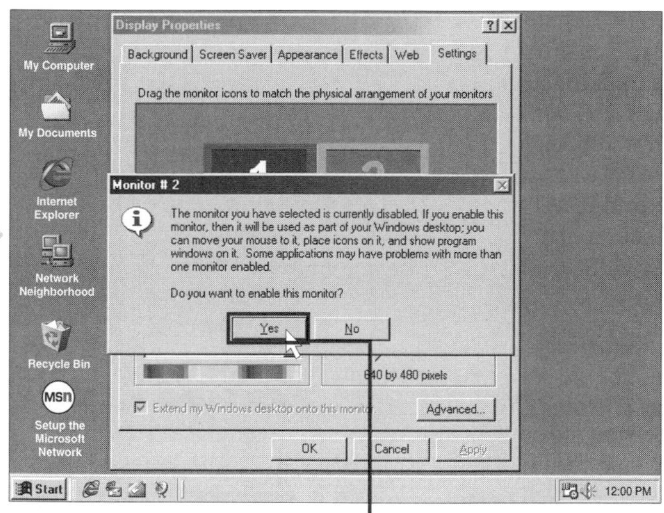

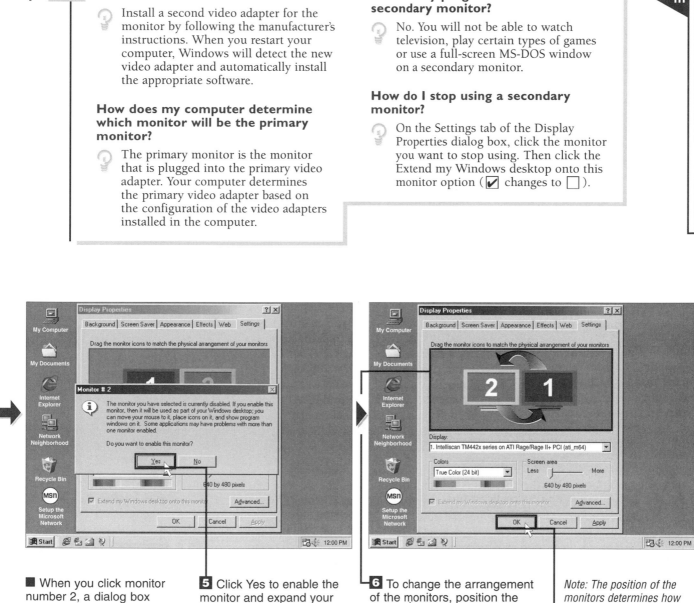

■ When you click monitor number 2, a dialog box appears.

5 Click Yes to enable the monitor and expand your desktop area.

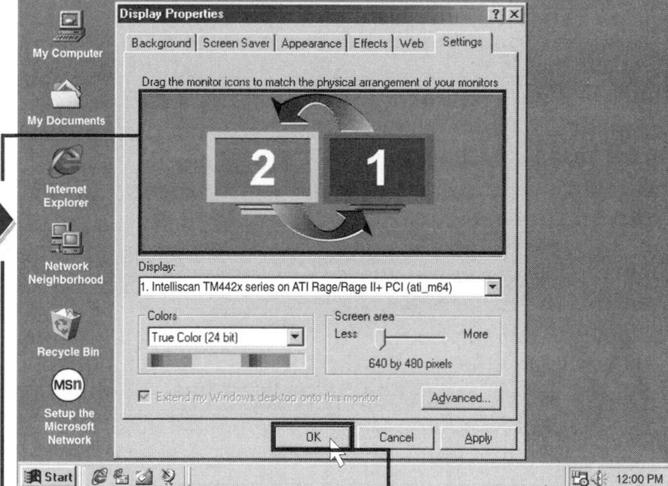

6 To change the arrangement of the monitors, position the mouse ↖ over a monitor and then drag the monitor to the new location.

Note: The position of the monitors determines how you move items between the monitors.

7 Click OK to confirm your changes.

SET UP MULTIPLE USERS

If you share your computer with one or more people, you can set up the computer so each person can use their own personalized settings.

Setting up your computer for more than one person allows you to meet the needs of specific users. For example, if children will be using your computer, you can personalize the settings so their favorite programs are on the Start menu.

Setting up a computer for multiple users is also useful when one person requires two or more custom settings. For example, if you use your computer to perform demonstrations, you can display the Windows default settings during demonstrations. When you are finished, you can go back to using your own personalized settings.

Windows asks you to specify a user name and password for each person. If you are currently using a user name and password to start Windows, use your current user name to set yourself up as the first user.

Windows stores the personalized settings for each person with their user name and password. When a person enters their user name and password to log on to Windows, their personalized settings are displayed.

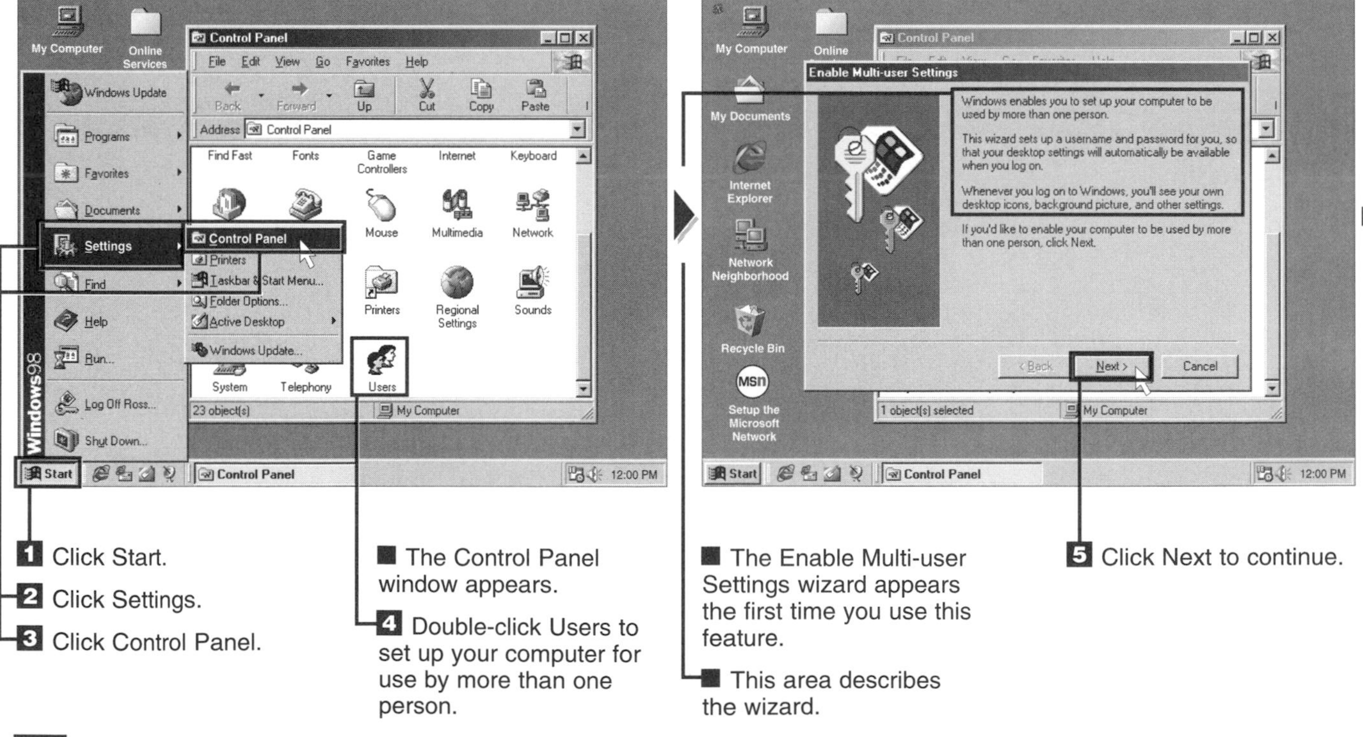

1 Click Start.

2 Click Settings.

3 Click Control Panel.

■ The Control Panel window appears.

4 Double-click Users to set up your computer for use by more than one person.

■ The Enable Multi-user Settings wizard appears the first time you use this feature.

■ This area describes the wizard.

5 Click Next to continue.

TIPS

Does a password prevent other people from reading my files?

No. When prompted for a user name and password, anyone can click the Cancel button to use Windows with the default settings. The person will be able to access all the programs and files on your computer, but they will not be able to access the network or your Internet account.

If one user installs a program, can we all use it?

Yes. Once a program has been installed on the computer, everyone who uses the computer will be able to use the program.

Once new users are set up, how do we switch from one user to another?

The current user must log off so another person can log on and use the computer with their personalized settings. Click the Start button and then click Log Off. Click Yes in the Log Off Windows dialog box. Windows restarts and displays a dialog box that enables another person to log on using their user name and password.

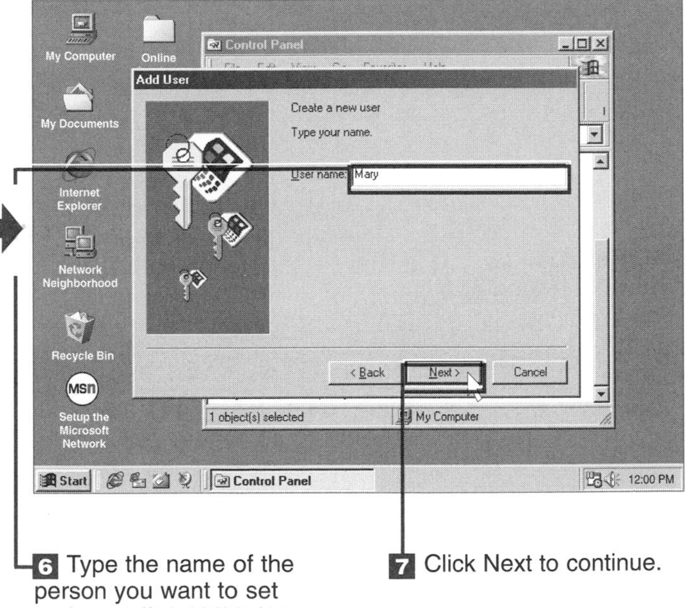

6 Type the name of the person you want to set up to use this computer.

7 Click Next to continue.

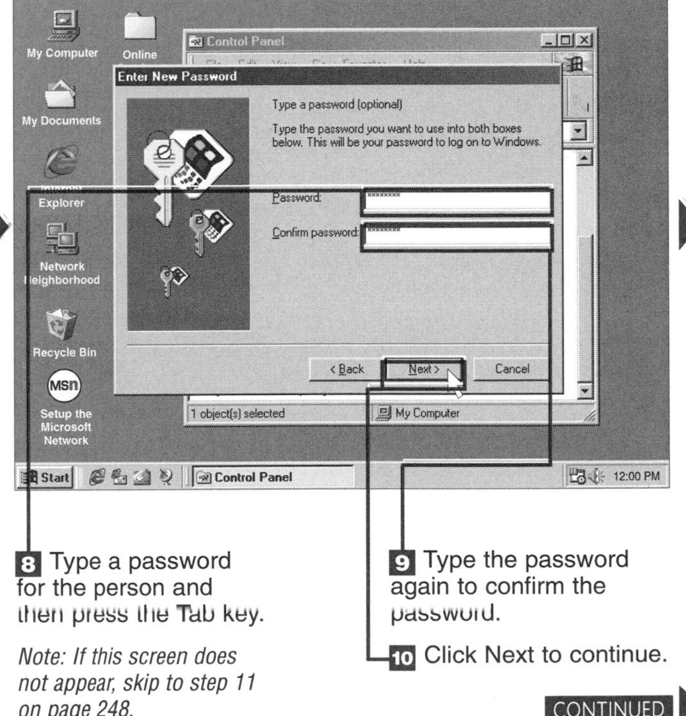

8 Type a password for the person and then press the Tab key.

Note: If this screen does not appear, skip to step 11 on page 248.

9 Type the password again to confirm the password.

10 Click Next to continue.

CONTINUED

SET UP MULTIPLE USERS CONTINUED

When setting up your computer for multiple users, Windows lets you specify which items each person can customize.

You can allow each person to customize the appearance of the desktop. Users can select wallpaper, create folders and add shortcuts to the desktop to suit their needs.

Each person can also customize the Start and Documents menus. This allows a user to organize the items on the Start menu and view a list of their recently opened documents.

You may want each user to have their own Favorites folder. This is useful if one person frequently visits Web pages other users are not interested in. Allowing each user to have a customized list of Web pages they have downloaded is also convenient. This ensures that each user's History folder will display only the Web pages they have visited.

You can also let each person customize the contents of the My Documents folder.

Windows lets you specify how you want to create the items. You can have Windows use the current set up of the computer to create the items or create new items using Windows' default settings.

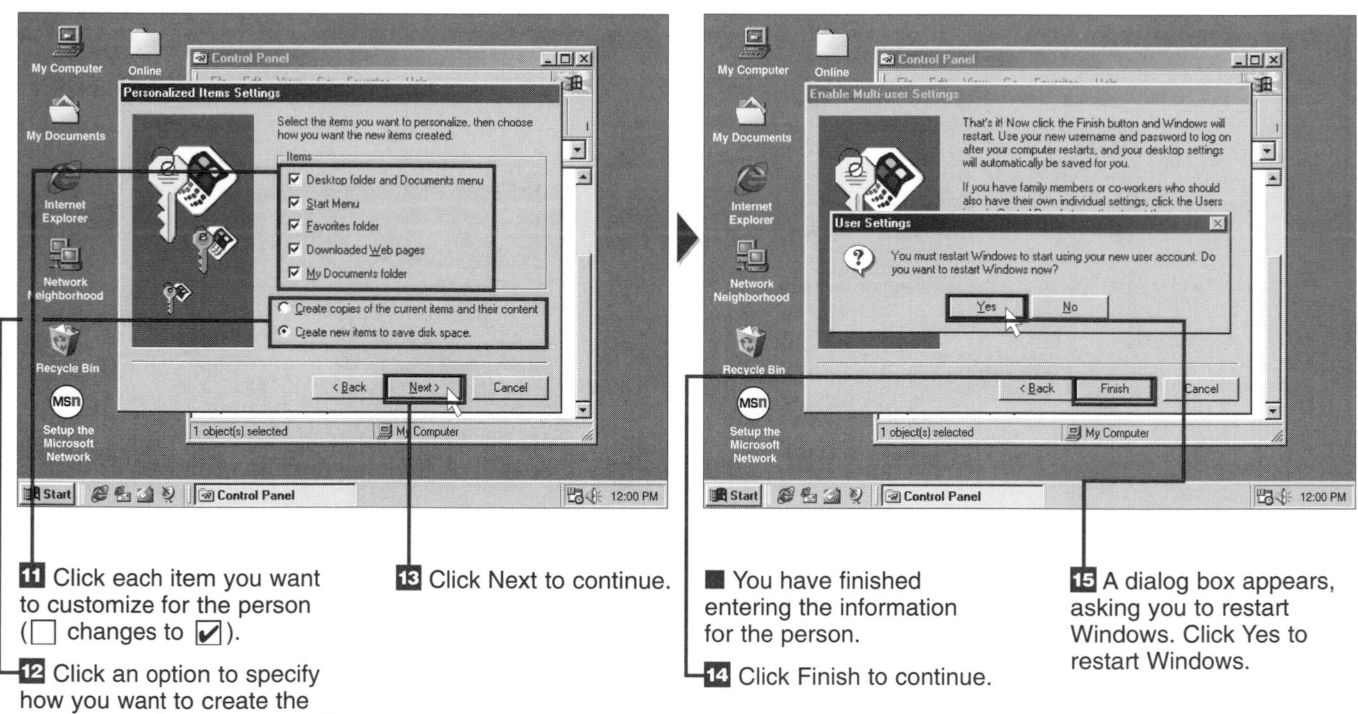

11 Click each item you want to customize for the person (☐ changes to ☑).

12 Click an option to specify how you want to create the new items (○ changes to ⊙).

13 Click Next to continue.

■ You have finished entering the information for the person.

14 Click Finish to continue.

15 A dialog box appears, asking you to restart Windows. Click Yes to restart Windows.

TIPS

How do I add another user?

Perform steps 1 to 4 on page 246. Click the New User button and then enter the information for the new user.

A new user can also be created each time Windows is started. Double-click the User name area and type a name for the new user. Press the Tab key and then enter a password. Click OK and then click Yes in the dialog box that appears.

How do I change the password for a user?

Perform steps 1 to 4 on page 246. Click the name of the person whose password you want to change. Click the Set Password button and then specify a new password. You must know the user's original password.

How do I remove users from my computer?

To remove a single user, perform steps 1 to 4 on page 246. Click the name of the person you want to remove and then click the Delete button.

How do I return my computer to a single-user system?

Display the Control Panel window and double-click the Passwords icon. Click the User Profiles tab and then select the All users of this computer use the same preferences and desktop settings option (○ changes to ⊙).

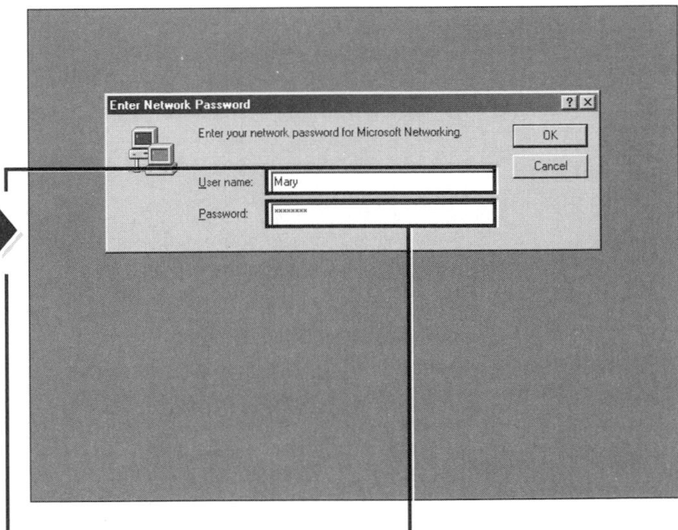

■ Each time Windows starts, a dialog box appears, asking you to enter a user name and password.

16 Double-click this area and then type your user name.

17 Click this area and type your password. Then press the Enter key.

■ Windows starts the computer using your customized settings.

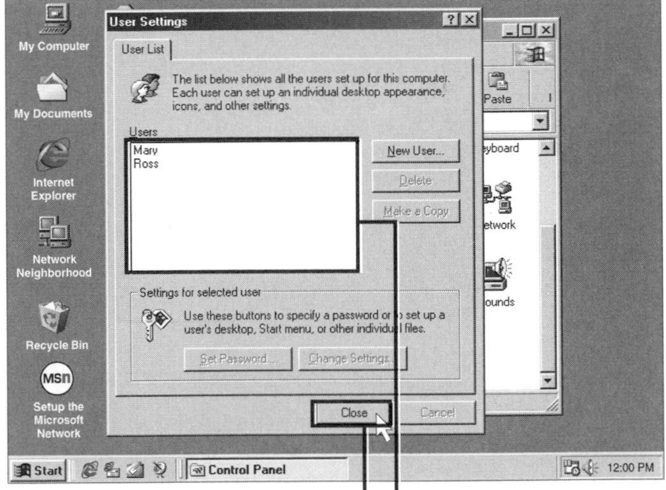

DISPLAY LIST OF USERS

1 Perform steps 1 to 4 on page 246.

■ The User Settings dialog box appears.

■ This area displays a list of users who have customized settings set up on the computer.

2 Click Close to close the dialog box.

USING MICROSOFT MAGNIFIER

If you have difficulty reading the information displayed on your screen, you can use Microsoft Magnifier to enlarge an area of the screen. The enlarged view appears in a window at the top of your screen.

You can customize Magnifier's settings to suit your needs. Magnifier is normally set to double the size of the area displayed in the magnifier window. You can increase or decrease the magnification level.

By default, Magnifier displays an enlarged view of the area surrounding the mouse pointer. If you find the continual movement in the magnifier window distracting, you may want to have Magnifier follow keyboard commands instead. This setting changes the area displayed in the magnifier window when you use keyboard commands such as the Tab or arrow keys.

You can also have Magnifier follow the insertion point when you are typing and editing text.

You can invert the colors displayed in the magnifier window. This changes the colors to their complementary colors. For example, blue changes to yellow and white changes to black. You can also have your entire screen display a high contrast color scheme.

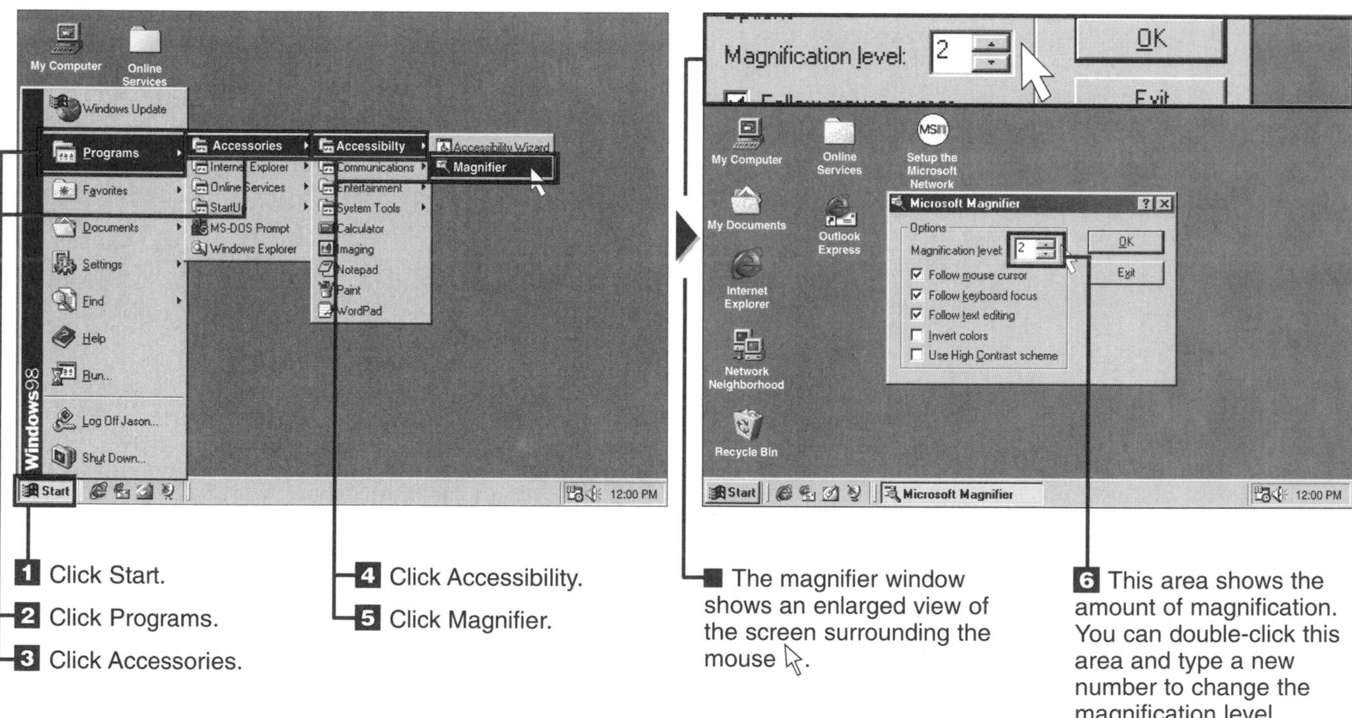

1 Click Start.

2 Click Programs.

3 Click Accessories.

4 Click Accessibility.

5 Click Magnifier.

■ The magnifier window shows an enlarged view of the screen surrounding the mouse ↖.

6 This area shows the amount of magnification. You can double-click this area and type a new number to change the magnification level.

TIPS

Why is Accessibility not available on my Accessories menu?

You may need to install the Accessibility component. To add Windows components, see page 610. When you install the Accessibility component, Microsoft Magnifier will also be installed.

Can I use the keyboard to change Magnifier's settings?

To change the magnification level, hold down the Windows logo key (⊞) and then press the up or down arrow keys to increase or decrease the magnification level. To turn the Follow mouse cursor setting on or off, press and hold down the Windows logo key (⊞) while you press the Page Down key. To turn the Invert colors setting on or off, press and hold down the Windows logo key (⊞) while you press the Page Up key.

How can I move the magnifier window?

Position the mouse pointer inside the window (↖ changes to ☝). Drag the window to any edge of your screen. You can create a floating window by dragging the window into the middle of your screen.

How can I size the magnifier window?

Position the mouse pointer over the bottom edge of the window (↖ changes to ↕). Drag the edge of the window until the window displays the size you want.

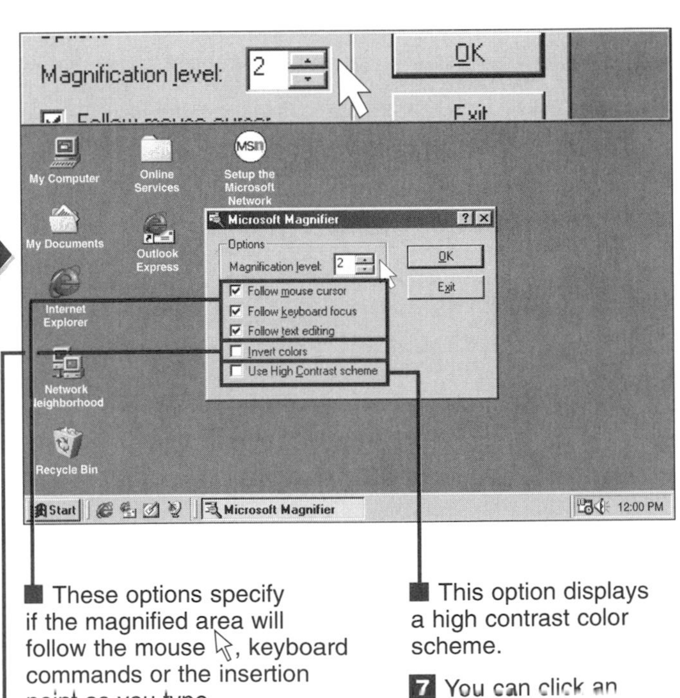

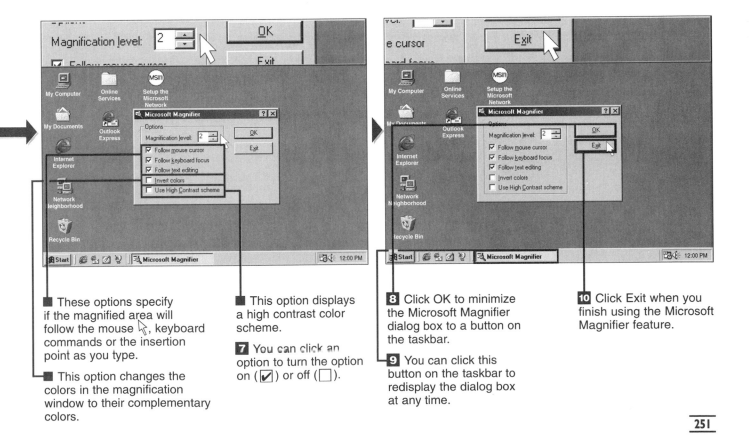

■ These options specify if the magnified area will follow the mouse ↖, keyboard commands or the insertion point as you type.

■ This option changes the colors in the magnification window to their complementary colors.

■ This option displays a high contrast color scheme.

7 You can click an option to turn the option on (☑) or off (☐).

8 Click OK to minimize the Microsoft Magnifier dialog box to a button on the taskbar.

9 You can click this button on the taskbar to redisplay the dialog box at any time.

10 Click Exit when you finish using the Microsoft Magnifier feature.

ACCESSIBILITY OPTIONS

The operation of your computer can be adjusted to accommodate special needs and situations. The Windows accessibility options allow you to make a computer easier to use if you have physical restrictions or when using a mouse is not practical.

Windows offers several options designed to make your keyboard easier to use.

StickyKeys helps users who have difficulty pressing two keys at the same time. When you press Shift, Ctrl or Alt on your keyboard, the key will remain active while you press the second key.

FilterKeys reduces the keyboard's sensitivity to repeated keystrokes and plays a tone every time you press a key.

ToggleKeys allows you to hear tones when the Caps Lock, Num Lock or Scroll Lock keys are pressed.

Many programs provide additional Help information about using the keyboard with the program. You can have your programs display the extra Help information when it is available.

Windows also allows you to replace sound cues with visual ones. SoundSentry flashes parts of your screen as a visual signal. ShowSounds provides on-screen captions for some speech and sound events.

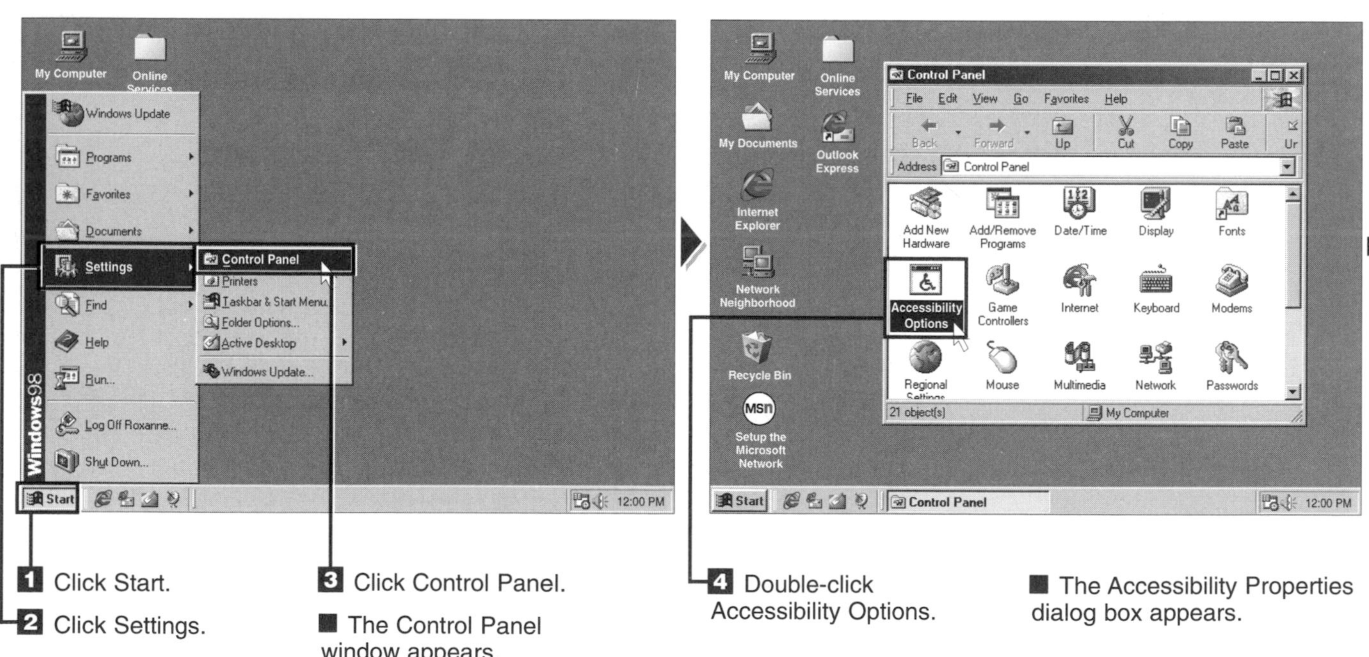

1 Click Start.

2 Click Settings.

3 Click Control Panel.

■ The Control Panel window appears.

4 Double-click Accessibility Options.

■ The Accessibility Properties dialog box appears.

TIPS

There is no Accessibility Options icon in my Control Panel window. How can I add this feature?

You must install the Accessibility Options component. To add Windows components, see page 610.

Are there keyboard shortcuts I can use to turn on the keyboard options?

Yes. To use a keyboard shortcut to turn on a keyboard option, click the Settings button beside the option. In the Settings dialog box, click Use shortcut (☐ changes to ☑). You can then turn on StickyKeys by pressing the Shift key five times. You can turn on FilterKeys by holding down the right Shift key for eight seconds. You can activate ToggleKeys by holding down the Num Lock key for five seconds.

How do I know if a feature is turned on?

Some features, like StickyKeys, display an icon on the right side of your taskbar to indicate they are turned on.

My keyboard is still too sensitive, even with FilterKeys turned on. What should I do?

Use the Settings button beside FilterKeys to adjust and test the FilterKeys option.

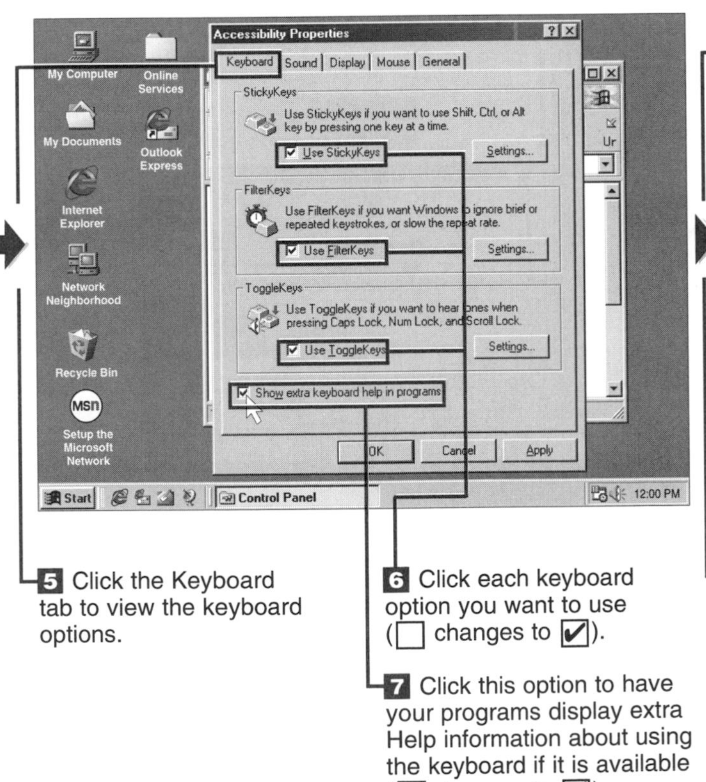

5 Click the Keyboard tab to view the keyboard options.

6 Click each keyboard option you want to use (☐ changes to ☑).

7 Click this option to have your programs display extra Help information about using the keyboard if it is available (☐ changes to ☑).

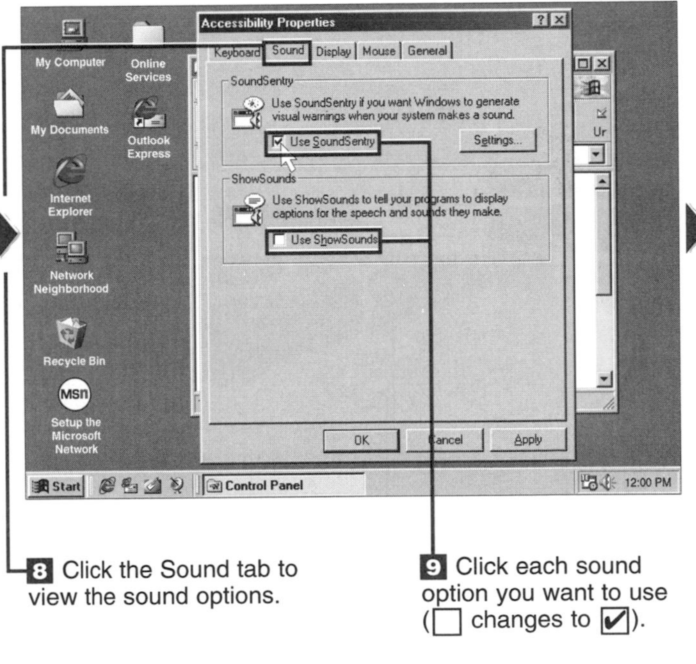

8 Click the Sound tab to view the sound options.

9 Click each sound option you want to use (☐ changes to ☑).

CONTINUED

ACCESSIBILITY OPTIONS
CONTINUED

The accessibility options can make your screen easier to read and allow you to perform mouse actions using your keyboard.

If you find the screen difficult to read, you can change to the High Contrast screen display. Windows will change the color and size of text and other items to increase the contrast and make the screen easier to read. This option is especially useful for people with vision impairments.

MouseKeys allows you to control the mouse pointer using the numeric keypad instead of the mouse. This can be useful in situations where a mouse is difficult to use, such as when using a laptop. Graphic artists who need finer and more accurate control of mouse pointer movements may also want to use MouseKeys.

If you share a computer with several users who do not all want to use the accessibility options, you can have Windows turn off these features automatically when they are not in use. You can use optional warnings to let you know when Windows turns an option on or off.

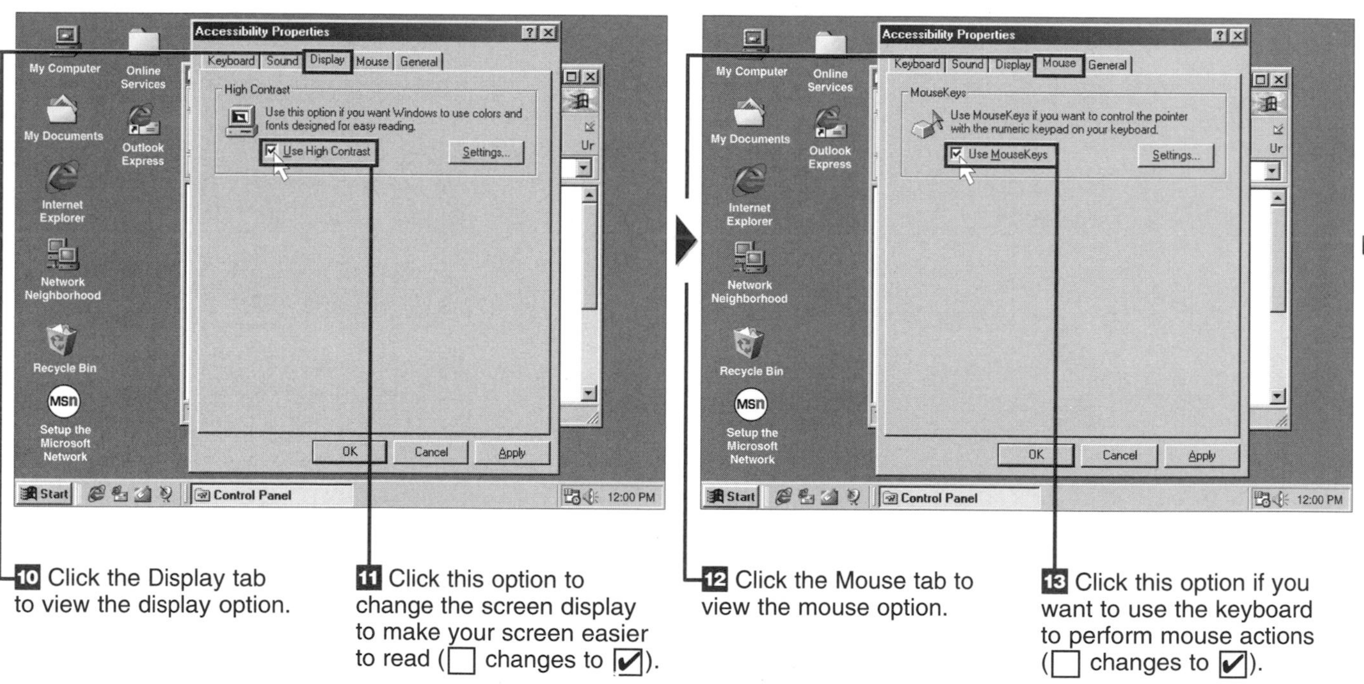

10 Click the Display tab to view the display option.

11 Click this option to change the screen display to make your screen easier to read (☐ changes to ☑).

12 Click the Mouse tab to view the mouse option.

13 Click this option if you want to use the keyboard to perform mouse actions (☐ changes to ☑).

After I turn on the MouseKeys feature, what keys can I use to control the mouse pointer?

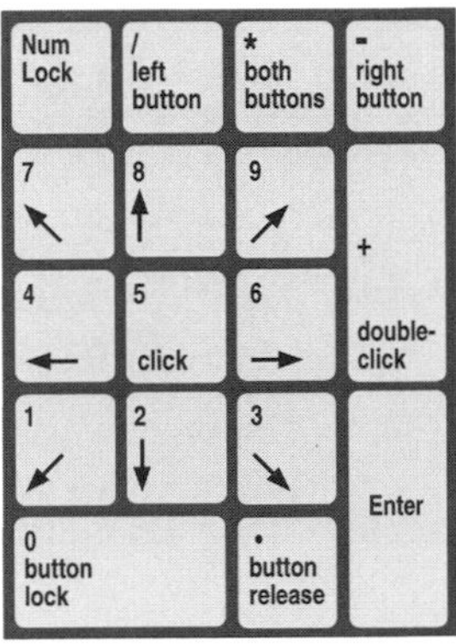

Why is the MouseKeys feature not working?

The Num Lock key must be on to use the MouseKeys feature. A light on your keyboard indicates the status of the Num Lock key.

Can I use shortcut keys to change the screen display?

On the Display tab, click the Settings button and then click Use shortcut. You can then press the left Alt key, the left Shift key and the Print Screen key at the same time to activate the High Contrast display. Pressing the same keys resets the screen to its previous settings.

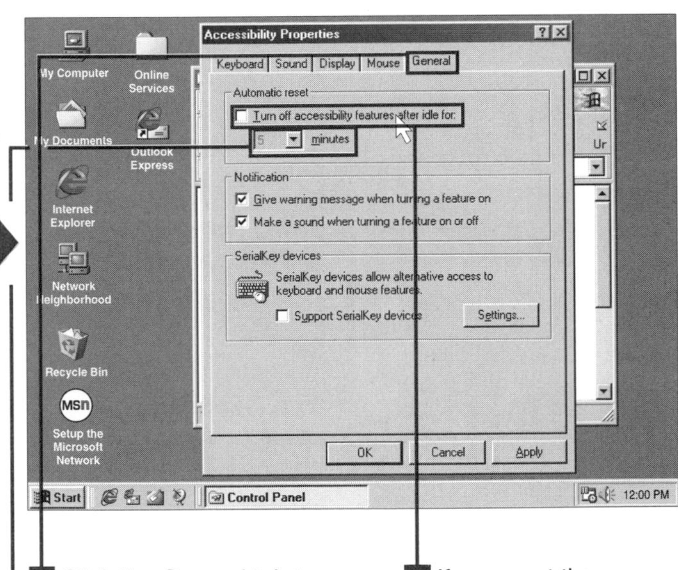

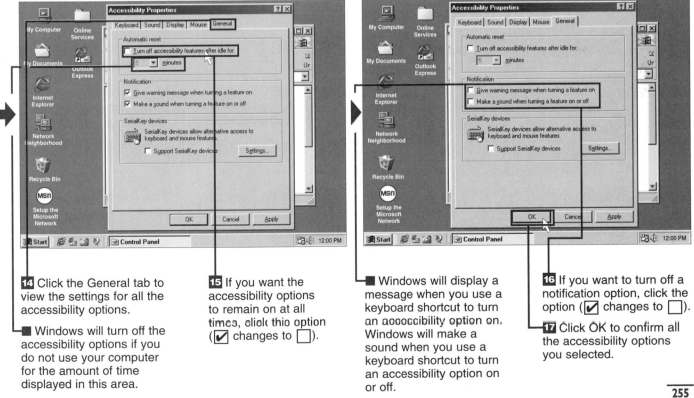

14 Click the General tab to view the settings for all the accessibility options.

■ Windows will turn off the accessibility options if you do not use your computer for the amount of time displayed in this area.

15 If you want the accessibility options to remain on at all times, click this option (☑ changes to ☐).

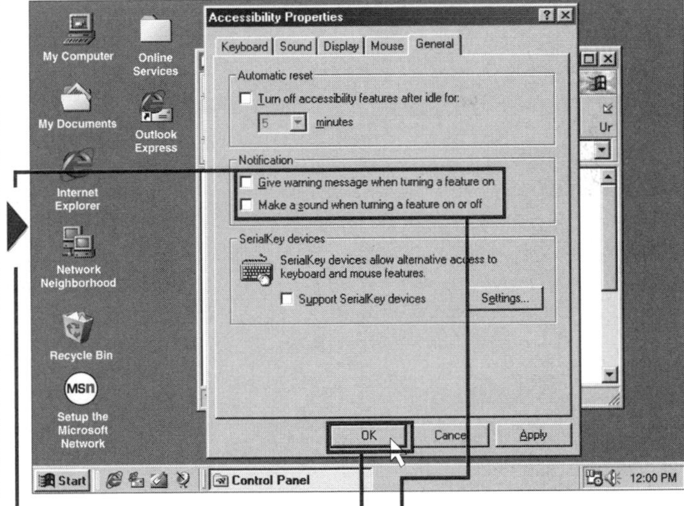

■ Windows will display a message when you use a keyboard shortcut to turn an accessibility option on. Windows will make a sound when you use a keyboard shortcut to turn an accessibility option on or off.

16 If you want to turn off a notification option, click the option (☑ changes to ☐).

17 Click OK to confirm all the accessibility options you selected.

USING THE ACCESSIBILITY WIZARD

The Accessibility Wizard can help you set up Windows to meet your vision, hearing and mobility needs. Although the accessibility options were designed to make it easier for people with special needs to operate a computer, there are some options which may be of interest to all users.

The wizard asks you to select the smallest text you can read. The selection you make helps Windows choose the next options for you. The text size options take effect immediately.

If you selected the largest text, Windows will automatically start Microsoft Magnifier. When Magnifier is turned on, the top of your screen displays an enlarged view of the area surrounding the mouse pointer.

The wizard displays a list of statements and asks you to select the ones that apply to you. The wizard will then offer you options that are appropriate for the statements you selected.

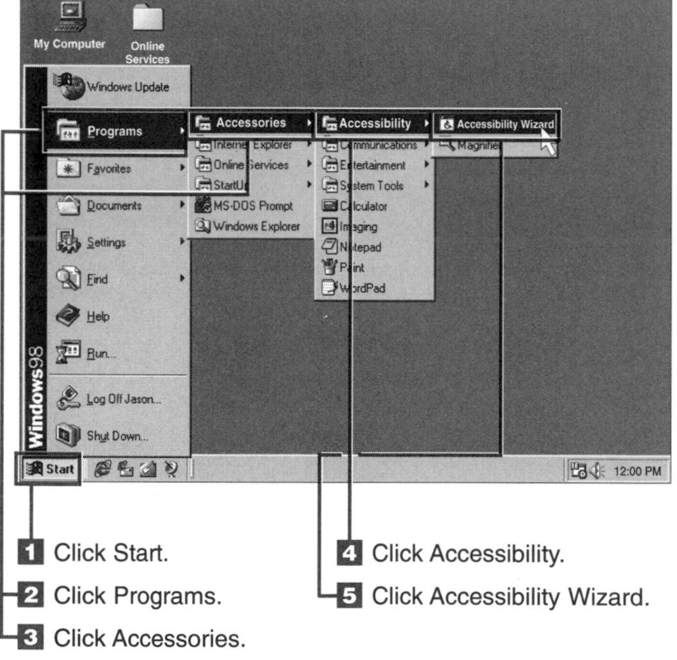

1 Click Start.

2 Click Programs.

3 Click Accessories.

4 Click Accessibility.

5 Click Accessibility Wizard.

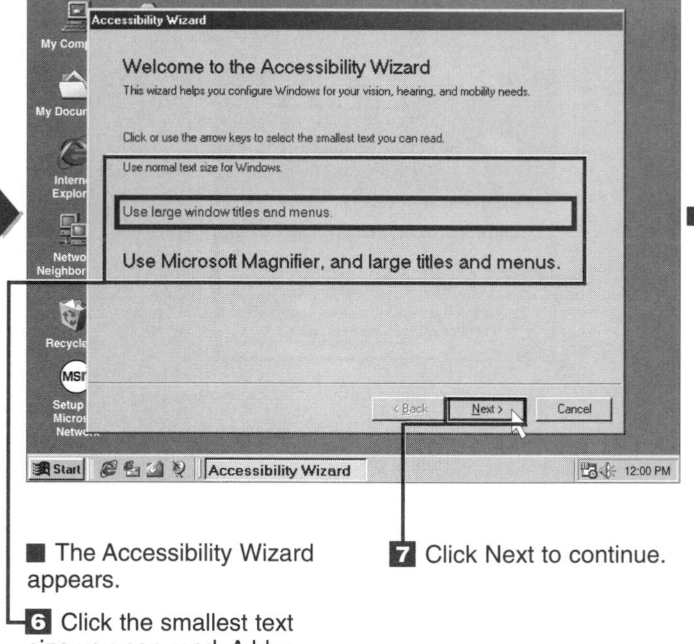

■ The Accessibility Wizard appears.

6 Click the smallest text size you can read. A blue border appears around your selection.

7 Click Next to continue.

Why is Accessibility not available on my Accessories menu?

You may need to install the Accessibility component. To add Windows components, see page 610.

Is there another way to make the text on my screen easier to read?

You can select the Switch to a lower screen resolution option in step 8 below. A lower screen resolution displays larger text and items so you can see the information on your screen more clearly. This option is not available if your screen currently displays a resolution lower than 1024x768. For information on changing your screen resolution, see page 210.

Can I turn on Microsoft Magnifier without starting the wizard?

Click the Start button, select Programs, click Accessories, click Accessibility and then select Magnifier. For information on Magnifier, see page 250. If you use Magnifier regularly, you can place a shortcut to the program on your desktop. Drag the Magnify.exe file from the C:\Windows\System folder to your desktop.

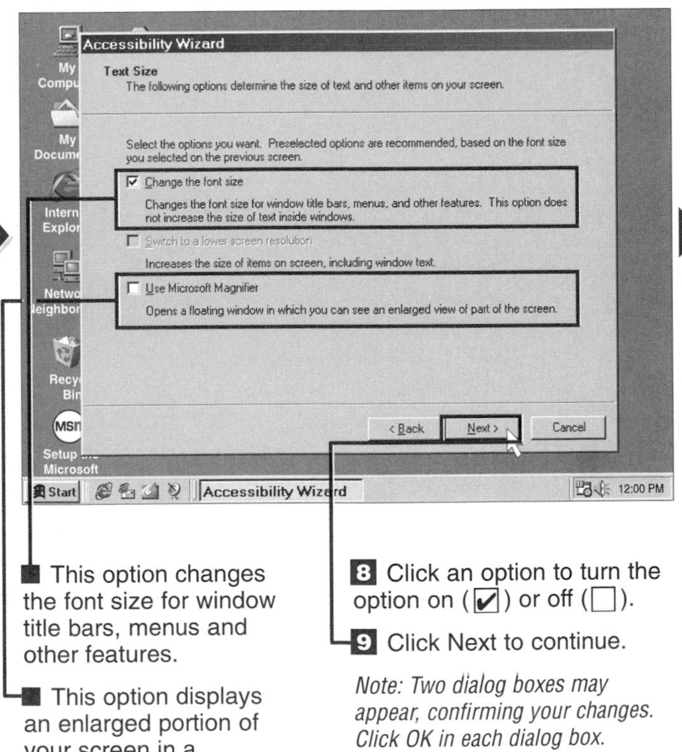

■ This option changes the font size for window title bars, menus and other features.

■ This option displays an enlarged portion of your screen in a separate window.

8 Click an option to turn the option on (☑) or off (☐).

9 Click Next to continue.

Note: Two dialog boxes may appear, confirming your changes. Click OK in each dialog box.

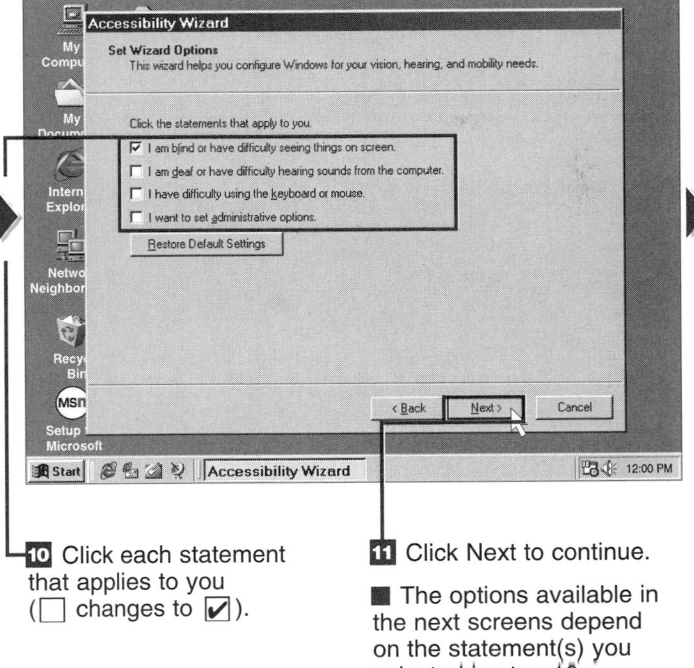

10 Click each statement that applies to you (☐ changes to ☑).

11 Click Next to continue.

■ The options available in the next screens depend on the statement(s) you selected in step 10.

CONTINUED

USING THE ACCESSIBILITY WIZARD
CONTINUED

The Accessibility Wizard helps you choose the accessibility options that will benefit you the most when using Windows. The options the wizard displays depend on the selections you have already made.

If you have difficulty seeing, you can set specific options to make viewing information on your screen easier. You can increase the size of scroll bars, window borders and icons. You can also choose to display a high contrast color scheme.

If you have difficulty hearing, you can have Windows display visual warnings when events occur on your computer. Windows can also display captions for spoken text whenever possible.

There are many options you can select to make the keyboard and mouse easier to use. You can have Windows ignore repeated keystrokes or use the numeric keypad instead of the mouse to move the pointer on your screen. You can also specify the size of the mouse pointer and how the pointer moves on your screen.

The administrative options allow you to turn the accessibility options on or off and customize the accessibility options for several users who may have different or conflicting needs.

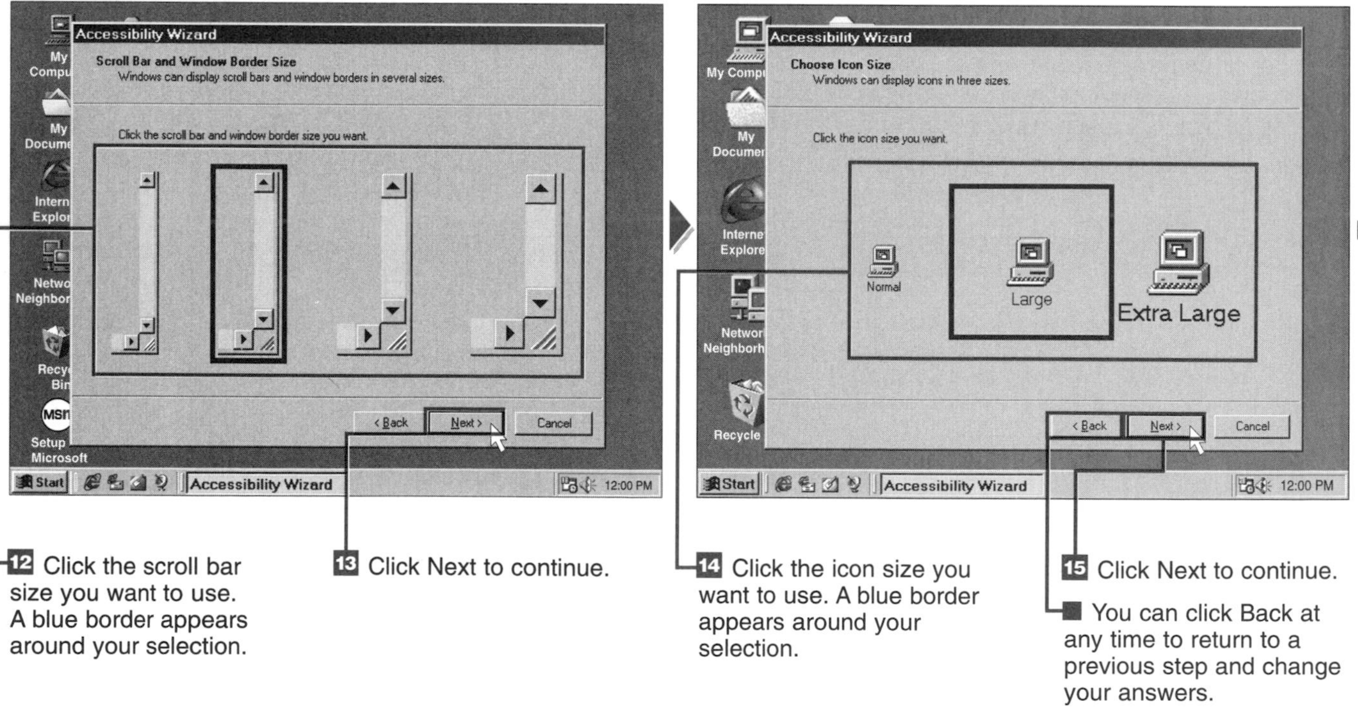

12 Click the scroll bar size you want to use. A blue border appears around your selection.

13 Click Next to continue.

14 Click the icon size you want to use. A blue border appears around your selection.

15 Click Next to continue.

■ You can click Back at any time to return to a previous step and change your answers.

TIPS

Where can I find more resources to assist users with special needs?

Microsoft's Accessibility Home Page contains accessibility-related information, resources and links. You can find the Accessibility Home Page on the World Wide Web at www.microsoft.com/enable

How can I return to my previous screen settings?

To return to your previous screen settings, you must start the wizard again and select the settings you want to use. If the wizard changed your screen resolution, right-click the desktop and select Properties. Use the Settings tab to adjust your screen resolution. For information, see page 210.

Is there another way to turn on accessibility options?

There are several icons in the Control Panel which you can use to turn on accessibility options. The Accessibility Options icon includes many of the same options available in the wizard. The Mouse and Keyboard icons allow you to specify how you want to use the mouse and keyboard. The Display icon allows you to adjust your screen resolution and color settings.

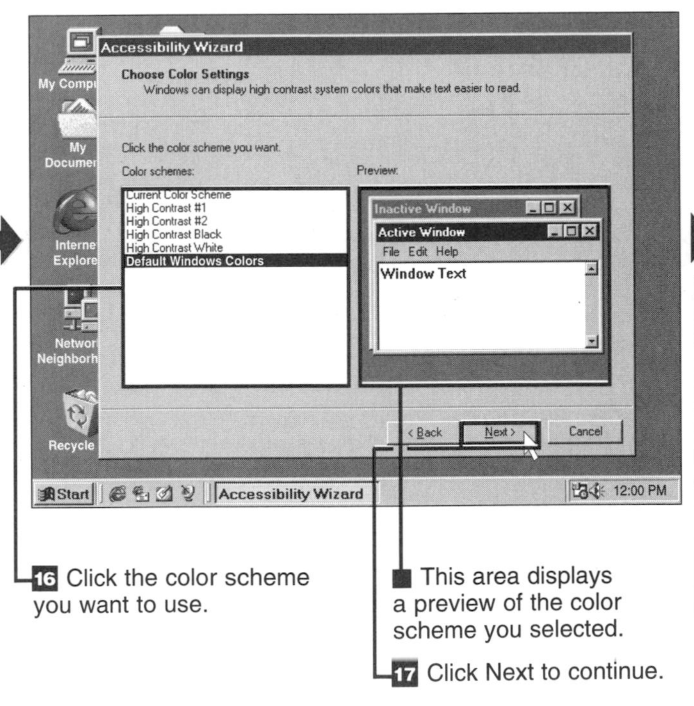

16 Click the color scheme you want to use.

■ This area displays a preview of the color scheme you selected.

17 Click Next to continue.

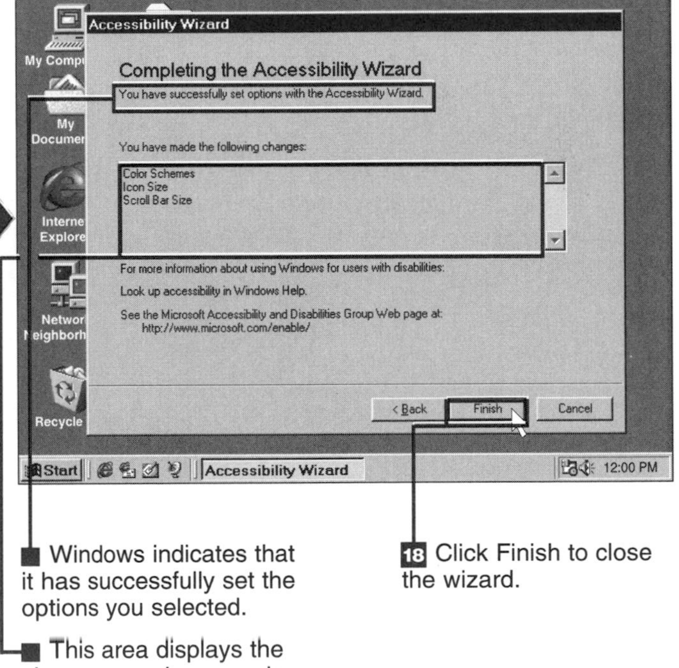

■ Windows indicates that it has successfully set the options you selected.

■ This area displays the changes you have made.

18 Click Finish to close the wizard.

ADD PROGRAM TO THE START MENU

You can add your favorite programs to the Start menu so you can quickly open them. You can also add files you frequently use to the Start menu for quick access. Having items you frequently use on the Start menu saves you the time of having to look for them on your computer.

Most programs designed for Windows will place a shortcut on the Start menu while they are being installed.

Windows does not add all of the programs and utilities available on your computer to the Start menu. If Windows does not add an item you want to access, you must manually add the item to the Start menu.

When you add an item to the Start menu, Windows creates a shortcut to the program or file. The original program or file stays in the same place on your computer.

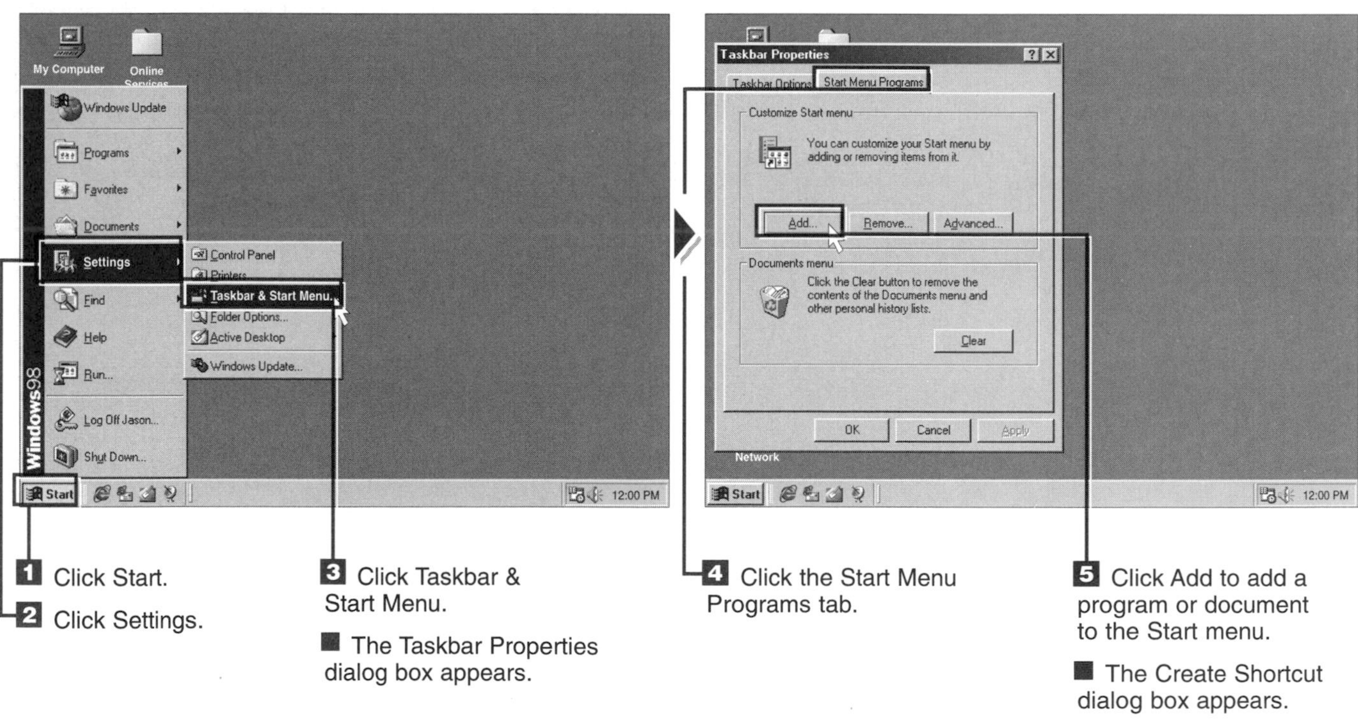

1 Click Start.

2 Click Settings.

3 Click Taskbar & Start Menu.

■ The Taskbar Properties dialog box appears.

4 Click the Start Menu Programs tab.

5 Click Add to add a program or document to the Start menu.

■ The Create Shortcut dialog box appears.

TIPS

How do I add a printer to the Start menu?

From the Start menu, select Settings and then click Printers. Drag the printer you want to add from the Printers window to the Start button. The printer will appear on the first level of the Start menu.

Can I add items on the network to the Start menu?

In the Browse dialog box, click the area beside Look In. Click Network Neighborhood in the list that appears and display the items on the network. You can then add network items to the Start menu.

Can I add an item to the Start menu from a My Computer window, Windows Explorer window or the desktop?

To add an item from any window or the desktop, simply drag the item to the Start button. The item will appear on the first level of the Start menu.

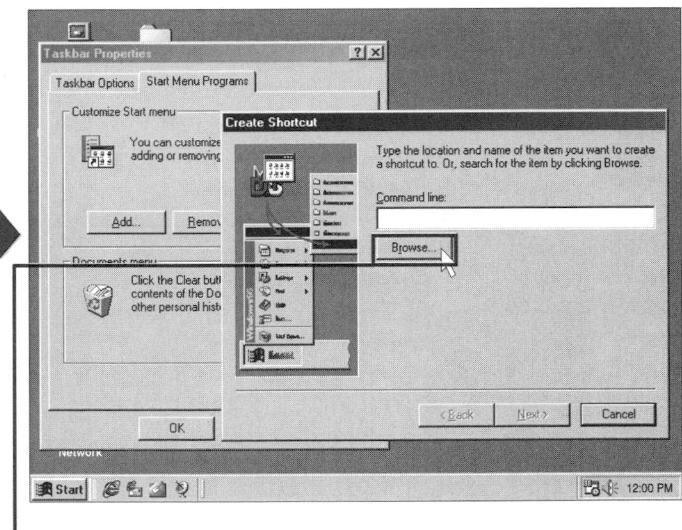

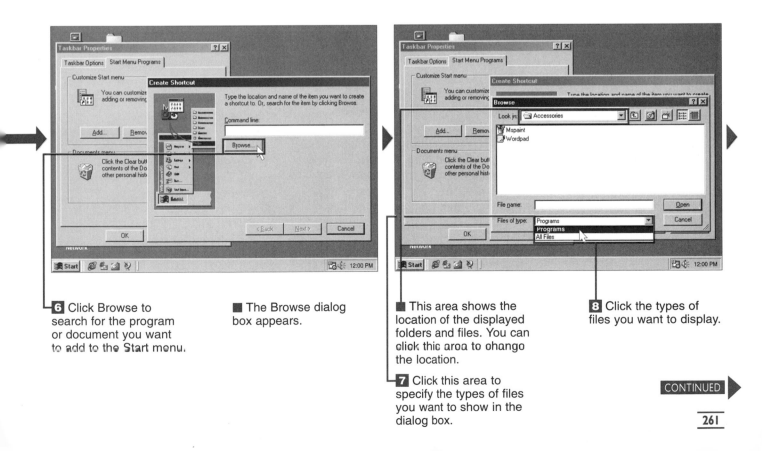

6 Click Browse to search for the program or document you want to add to the Start menu.

■ The Browse dialog box appears.

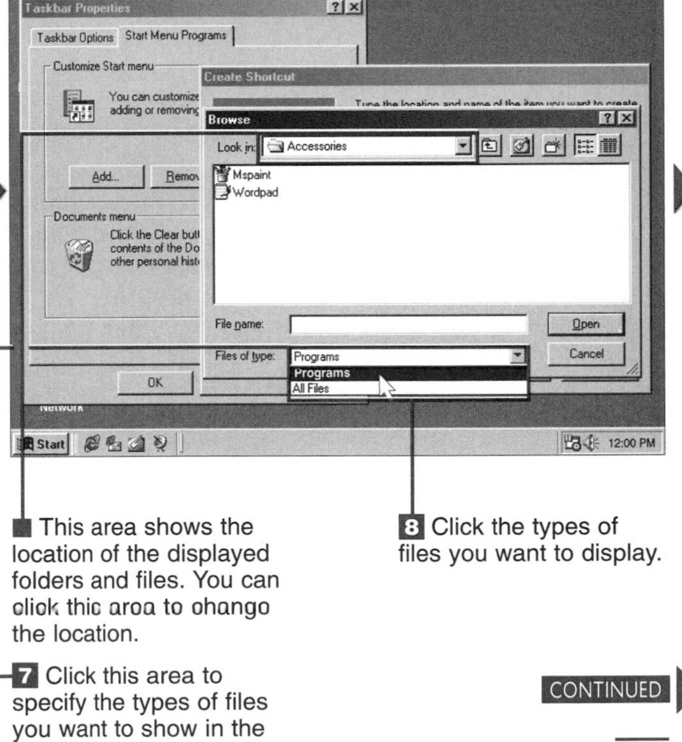

■ This area shows the location of the displayed folders and files. You can click this area to change the location.

7 Click this area to specify the types of files you want to show in the dialog box.

8 Click the types of files you want to display.

CONTINUED

ADD PROGRAM TO THE START MENU CONTINUED

You can choose which Start menu folder you want to contain a program or file.

The Start menu contains several levels and folders. You can place an item on the first level of the Start menu or inside one of the many folders. If you want an item to open automatically when Windows is started, you can place the item in the StartUp folder.

You can also give the program or file a descriptive name. Windows will suggest a name for the item based on the name of the original program or file. The name you choose will only appear on the Start menu item and will not affect the name of the original program or file.

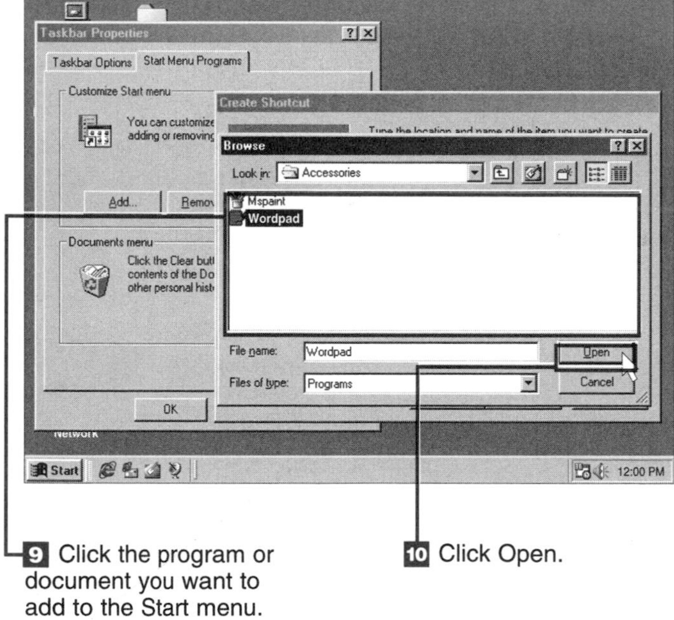

9 Click the program or document you want to add to the Start menu.

10 Click Open.

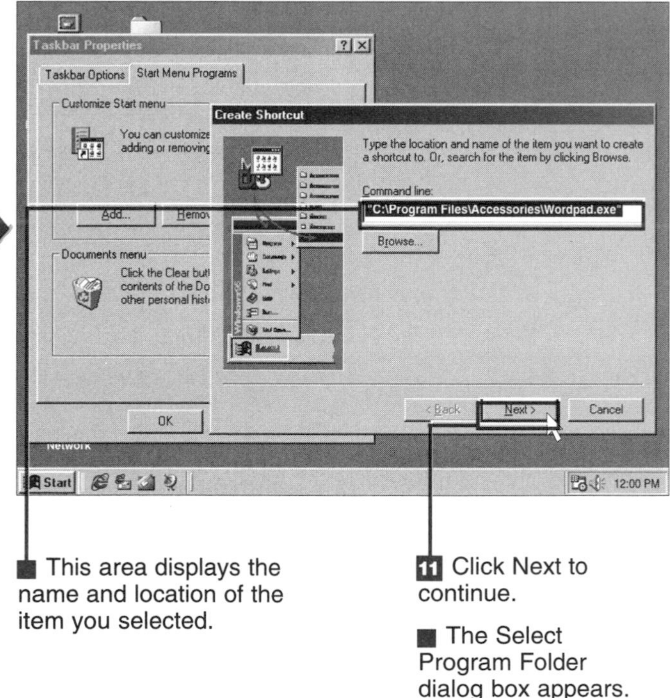

■ This area displays the name and location of the item you selected.

11 Click Next to continue.

■ The Select Program Folder dialog box appears.

Can I add another folder to the Start menu?

If you cannot find an appropriate folder on the Start menu, you can create a new folder. In the Select Program Folder dialog box, click the folder you want to contain the new folder and then select the New Folder button.

Can I change the order that items appear in the Start menu?

You can change the order of some of the items in the Start menu. Display the Start menu and then drag and drop the item you want to display in a new location. A black line indicates where the item will appear.

Are there any limitations on what I name a program or file?

Windows has several rules you must obey when naming an item. A name can contain up to 255 characters, including spaces. A name cannot contain the \ / : * ? " < > or | characters. Use a short name so the Start menu will not take up too much space when displayed on your screen.

Why does Windows ask me to choose an icon for the program?

If you are adding an MS-DOS program that Windows does not recognize, Windows asks you to select the icon you want to use to represent the program.

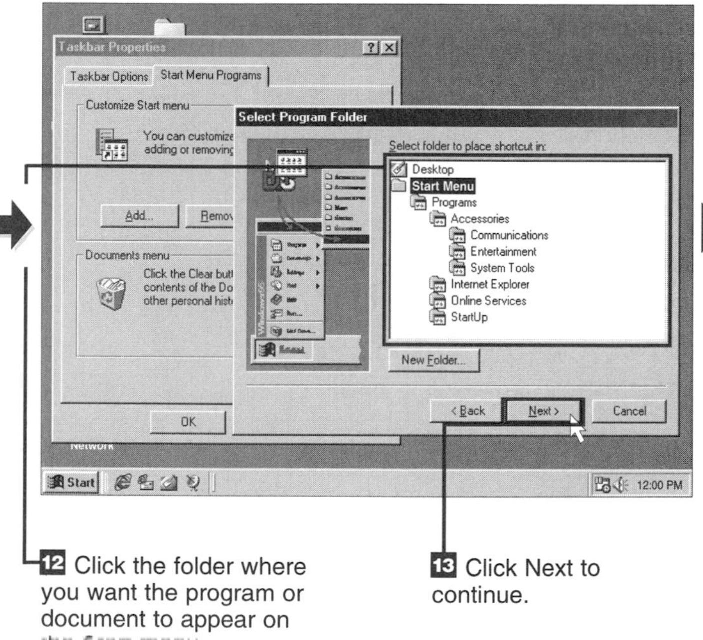

12 Click the folder where you want the program or document to appear on the Start menu.

Note: For example, click the Programs folder if you want a program to appear on the Programs menu.

13 Click Next to continue.

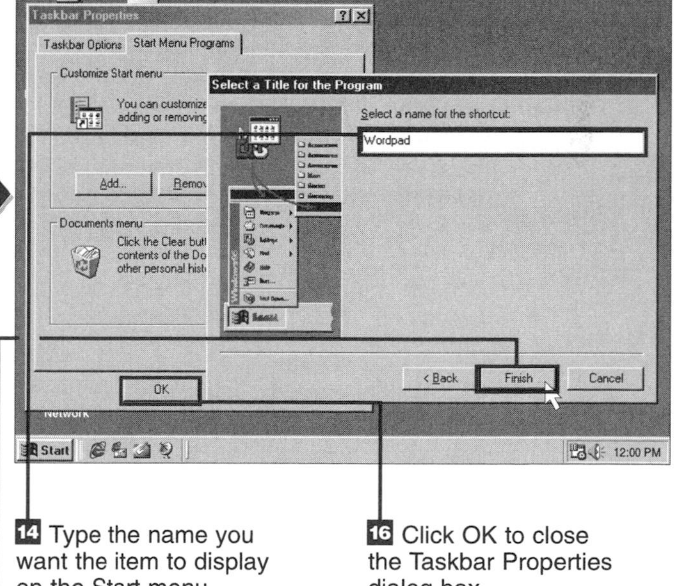

14 Type the name you want the item to display on the Start menu.

15 Click Finish to add the item to the Start menu.

16 Click OK to close the Taskbar Properties dialog box.

■ The program or document will now appear on the Start menu.

REMOVE PROGRAM FROM THE START MENU

You can remove a program you no longer want to appear on the Start menu. Removing items you do not need reduces clutter on the Start menu.

Most programs designed for Windows will place a shortcut on the Start menu while they are being installed. Even after you delete the program from your computer, the Start menu may still display the program. You can make the Start menu easier to use by removing programs no longer on your computer or programs you only use once in a while.

You can also remove files or folders from the Start menu.

When you remove a folder from the Start menu, all of the items in the folder are removed as well. Before removing a folder from the Start menu, you should view the contents of the folder to make sure you will not remove items you frequently work with.

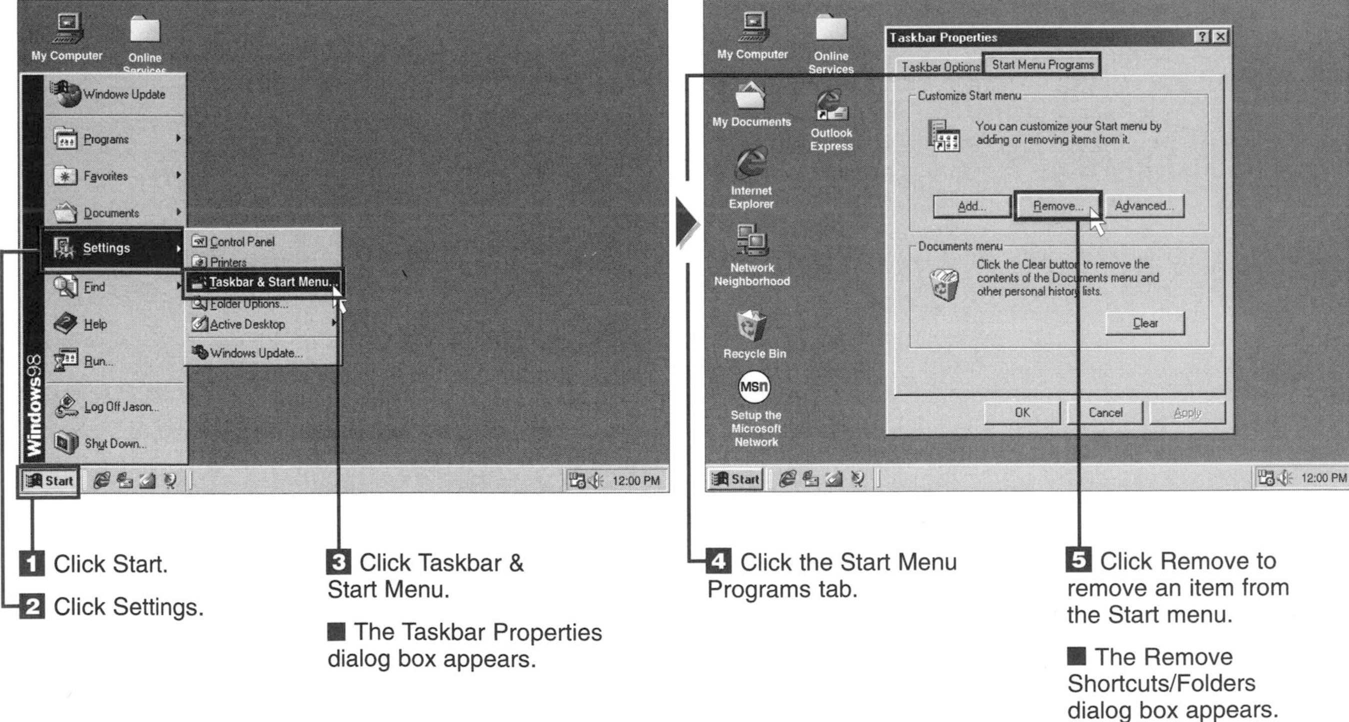

1 Click Start.

2 Click Settings.

3 Click Taskbar & Start Menu.

■ The Taskbar Properties dialog box appears.

4 Click the Start Menu Programs tab.

5 Click Remove to remove an item from the Start menu.

■ The Remove Shortcuts/Folders dialog box appears.

TIPS

Can I organize my items into folders on the Start menu?

You can organize items into folders to reduce the clutter on the Start menu without removing any items. In the Taskbar Properties dialog box, choose the Start Menu Programs tab and then click the Advanced button to organize items into folders. See page 266.

How can I bring back an item I accidentally removed from the Start menu?

You can use the Recycle Bin to restore any items you accidentally removed from the Start menu. See page 74. If the item is not available from the Recycle Bin, you can add the item to the Start menu again. See page 260.

Does removing a program from the Start menu delete the program from my computer?

Removing a program from the Start menu does not delete the program from your computer. The Start menu only displays shortcuts to the programs, not the programs themselves. You can delete a program from your computer by choosing the Control Panel and then selecting the Add/Remove Programs icon. See page 616.

Is there a faster way to delete an item from the Start menu?

On the Start menu, right-click the item you want to delete and then select Delete from the menu that appears.

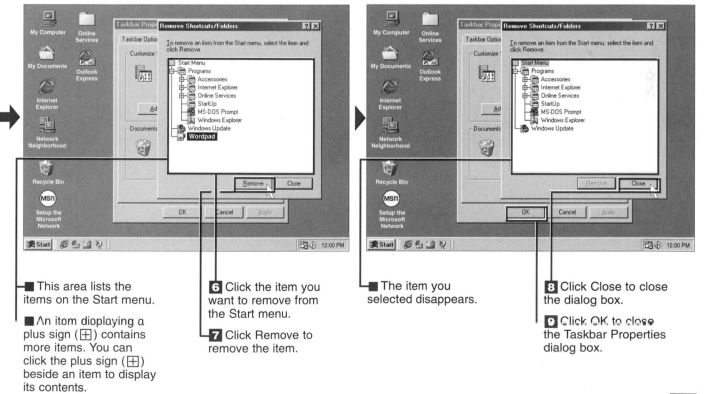

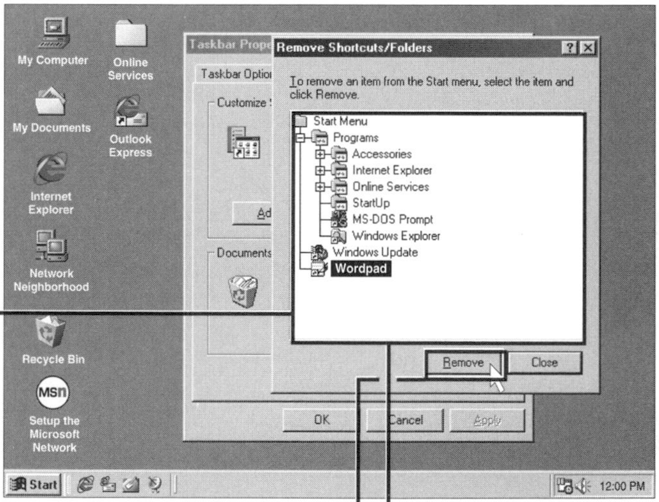

■ This area lists the items on the Start menu.

■ An item displaying a plus sign (⊞) contains more items. You can click the plus sign (⊞) beside an item to display its contents.

6 Click the item you want to remove from the Start menu.

7 Click Remove to remove the item.

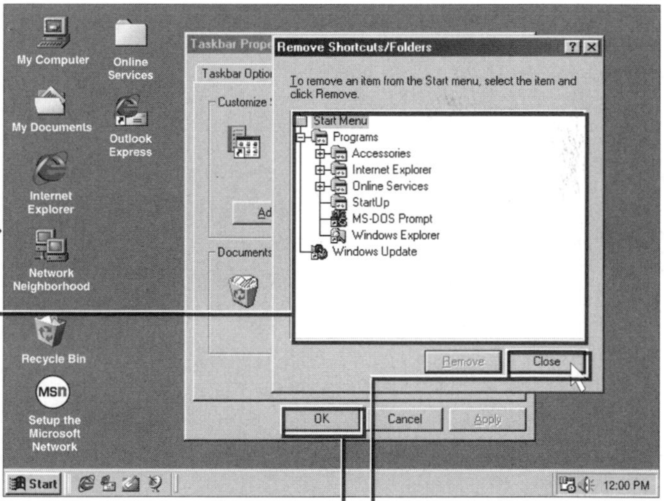

■ The item you selected disappears.

8 Click Close to close the dialog box.

9 Click OK to close the Taskbar Properties dialog box.

ORGANIZE THE START MENU

You can create folders to organize and store items on the Start menu. Each new folder will appear as a submenu on the Start menu.

When you install a new program, the name of the program appears on the Start menu. When you drag an item such as a document to the Start button, the name of the item appears on the first level of the menu. Eventually, the Start menu may become cluttered.

You can create folders to organize the programs and other items into logical groups. Items organized into folders are easier to find. For example, you can create a new folder named Utilities that will list the utility programs you frequently use. You can also create a folder named Reports to list your reports.

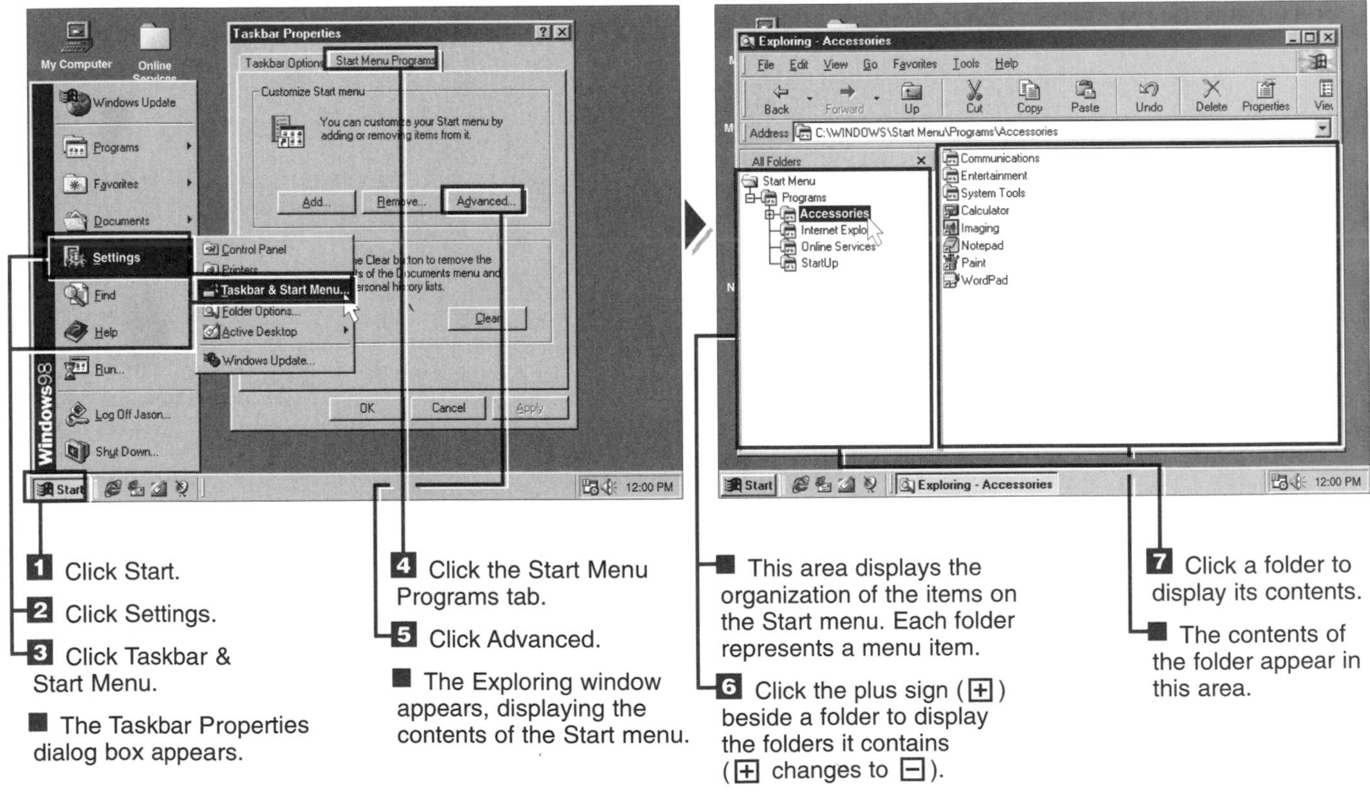

1 Click Start.

2 Click Settings.

3 Click Taskbar & Start Menu.

■ The Taskbar Properties dialog box appears.

4 Click the Start Menu Programs tab.

5 Click Advanced.

■ The Exploring window appears, displaying the contents of the Start menu.

■ This area displays the organization of the items on the Start menu. Each folder represents a menu item.

6 Click the plus sign (⊞) beside a folder to display the folders it contains (⊞ changes to ⊟).

7 Click a folder to display its contents.

■ The contents of the folder appear in this area.

Can I create a menu item that lists the contents of the Control Panel?

Creating a menu item for the Control Panel allows you to select an item without having to open the Control Panel window. Create a folder named **Control Panel.**{21EC2020-3AEA-1069-A2DD-08002B30309D}

You can create a menu item for Dial-Up Networking by naming the new folder **Dial Up Net.**{992CFFA0-F557-101A-88EC-00DD010CCC48} You can also create a menu item for the Printers folder by naming the new folder **Printers.**{2227A280-3AEA-1069-A2DE-08002B30309D}

How do I move an item to a different menu?

Drag the item from the right pane of the Exploring window to the folder in the left pane where you want to place the item.

How can I delete items I no longer want to appear on the Start menu?

Click the item you want to remove and then press the Delete key. This does not remove the item from your computer, but you can no longer access the item using the Start menu.

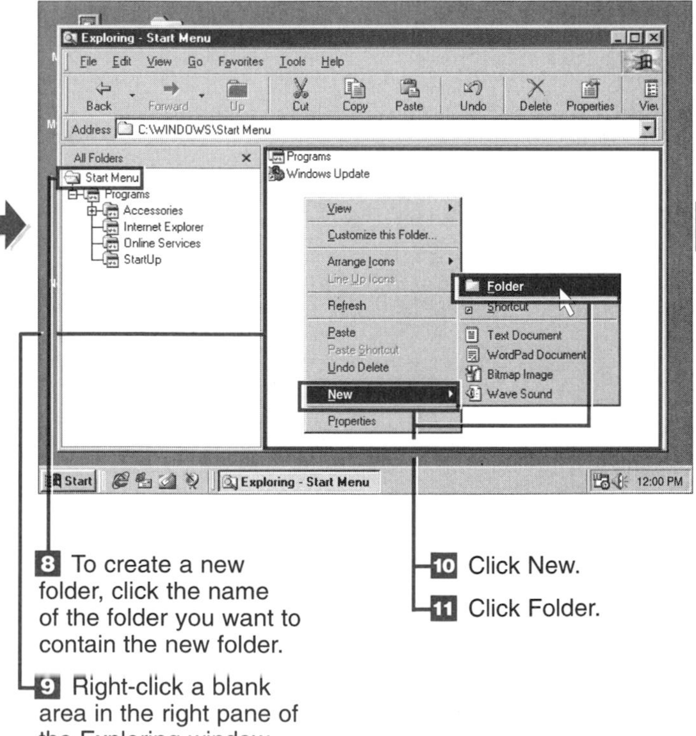

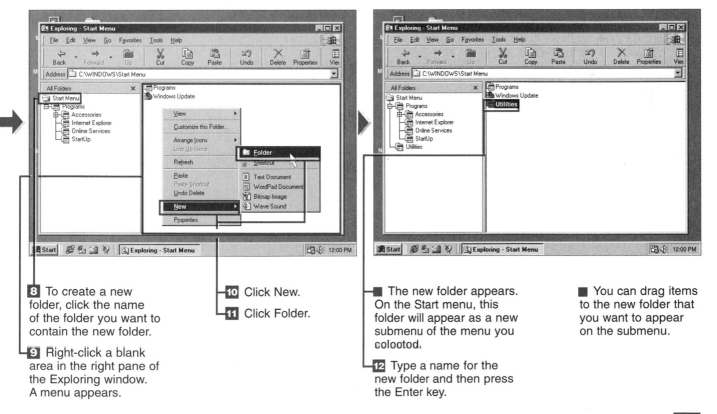

8 To create a new folder, click the name of the folder you want to contain the new folder.

9 Right-click a blank area in the right pane of the Exploring window. A menu appears.

10 Click New.

11 Click Folder.

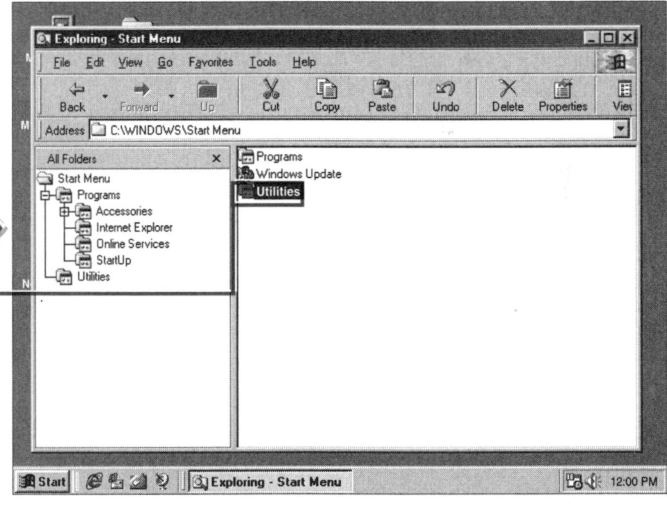

■ The new folder appears. On the Start menu, this folder will appear as a new submenu of the menu you selected.

12 Type a name for the new folder and then press the Enter key.

■ You can drag items to the new folder that you want to appear on the submenu.

START PROGRAM AUTOMATICALLY

You can have Windows automatically start programs each time you turn on your computer.

Having a program start automatically is useful for frequently used applications, such as Outlook Express, and for items you want to be able to access immediately, like a daily organizer or the Calculator.

You can also have documents you work with daily open automatically when you start Windows. This is useful for documents such as order forms.

Having a program start automatically saves the time required for you to locate and start the program.

Your StartUp folder may already contain several programs. Some programs are automatically added to the StartUp folder when you install them. Examples of programs that automatically add themselves to the StartUp folder include utility programs that speed up file access or check your computer for viruses.

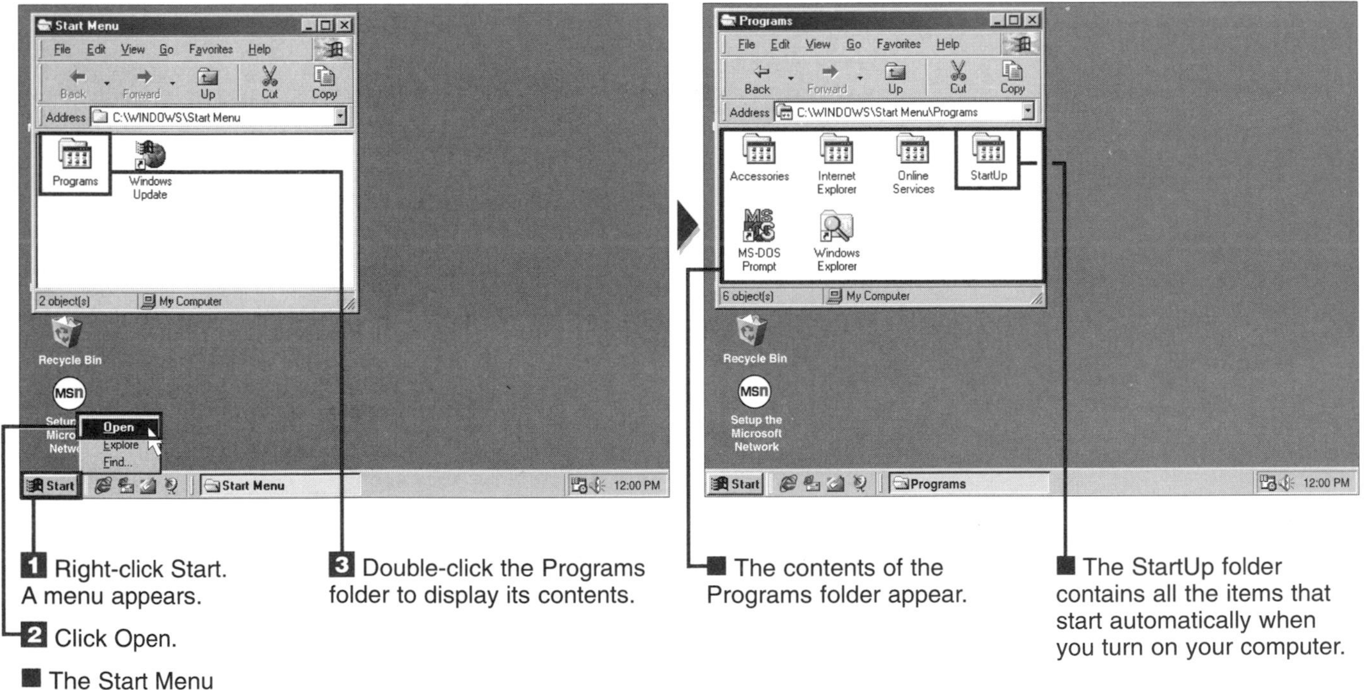

1 Right-click Start. A menu appears.

2 Click Open.

■ The Start Menu window appears.

3 Double-click the Programs folder to display its contents.

■ The contents of the Programs folder appear.

■ The StartUp folder contains all the items that start automatically when you turn on your computer.

TIPS

How do I stop a program from starting automatically?

If you no longer want a program to start automatically, delete the shortcut for the program from the StartUp folder. You can delete a shortcut the same way you would delete a program from the Start menu. For information, see page 264. Deleting a shortcut from the StartUp folder will not remove the program from your computer.

How do I find applications on my computer?

In the Find window, select the Advanced tab to search for applications. To use the Find feature, see page 78.

Can I stop the program from opening on the desktop and have it appear as a button on the taskbar?

Right-click the shortcut for the program in the StartUp window. On the menu that appears, click Properties. On the Shortcut tab, select Run: Minimized.

Should I add all my favorite programs to the StartUp folder?

Loading too many programs will cause your computer to slow down and place a strain on the computer's resources. You should only add frequently used programs to the StartUp folder.

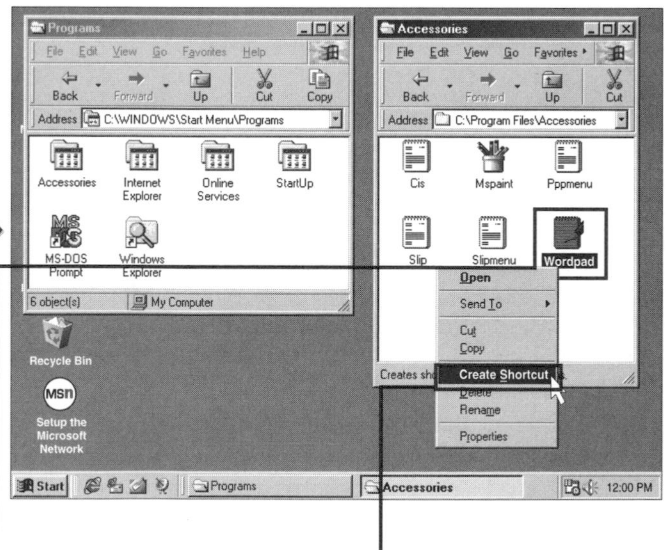

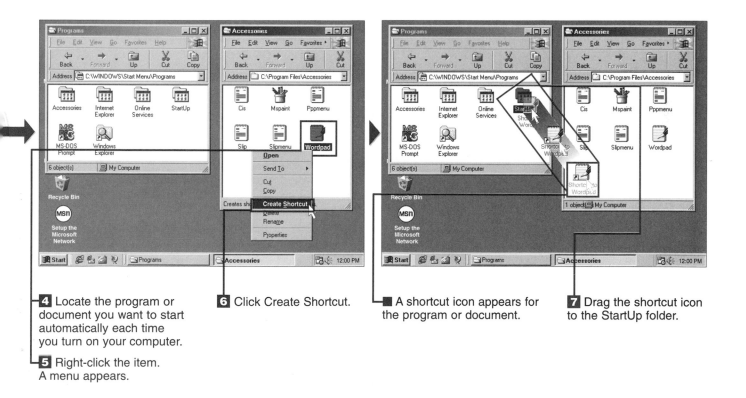

4 Locate the program or document you want to start automatically each time you turn on your computer.

5 Right-click the item. A menu appears.

6 Click Create Shortcut.

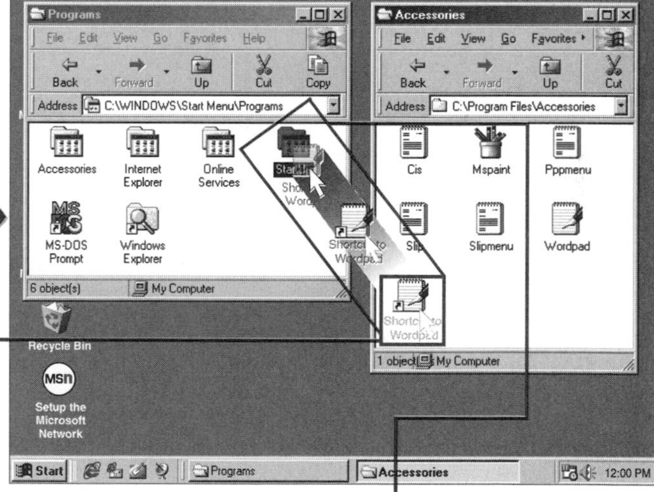

■ A shortcut icon appears for the program or document.

7 Drag the shortcut icon to the StartUp folder.

ASSIGN SOUNDS TO PROGRAM EVENTS

You can have Windows play sounds when you perform certain tasks on your computer. Assigning sounds can make Windows more fun and interesting.

You need a sound card and speakers on your computer to hear sounds. If your sound card and speakers are set up properly, you will hear a short musical introduction each time Windows starts.

The sounds on your computer can provide information about what Windows is doing, alert you to the appearance of a dialog box or let you know that e-mail has arrived.

You can add or change many sounds at once on your computer by choosing a sound scheme. A sound scheme is a set of related sounds that usually have a theme, such as jungle sounds, musical instruments or sounds from a favorite cartoon or movie.

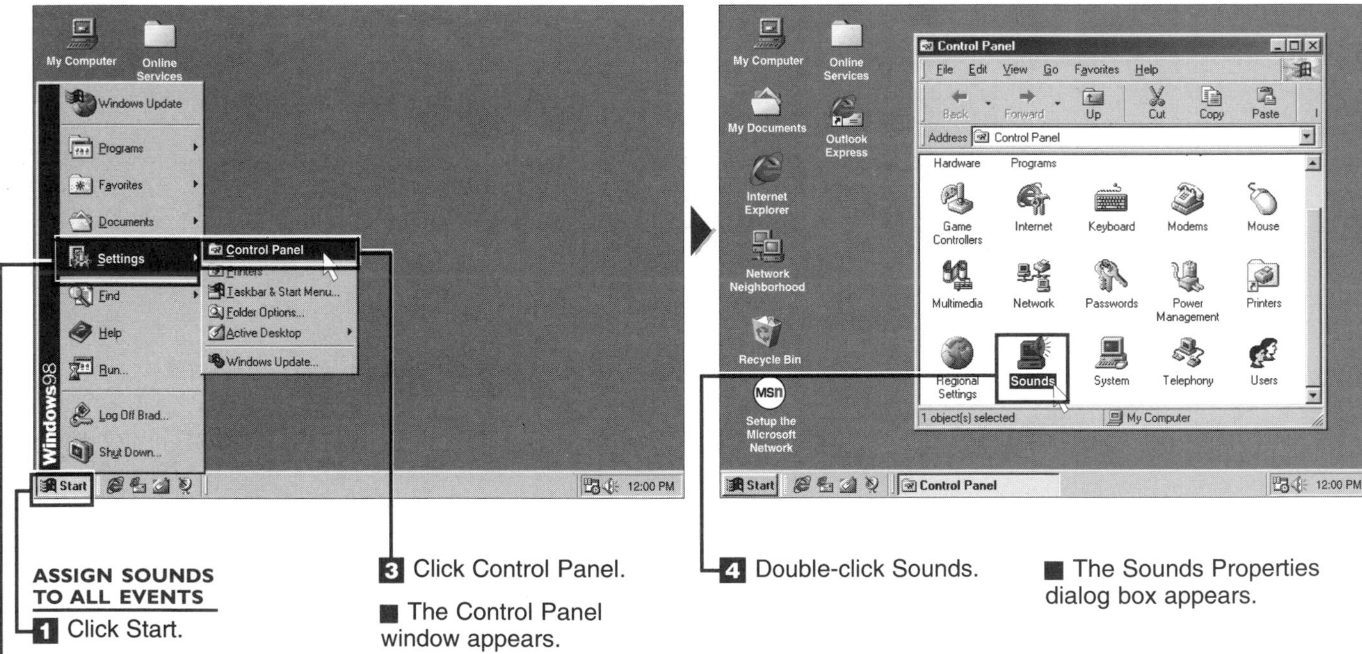

ASSIGN SOUNDS TO ALL EVENTS

1 Click Start.

2 Click Settings.

3 Click Control Panel.

■ The Control Panel window appears.

4 Double-click Sounds.

■ The Sounds Properties dialog box appears.

TIPS

Does Windows provide additional sound schemes?

You can add animal, new age and other sound schemes to your computer. These schemes are included on the Windows 98 CD-ROM disc. You can add these additional sound schemes from the Multimedia component. The Desktop Themes component also includes sounds. To add Windows components, see page 610.

Where can I get other sound schemes?

You can purchase sound scheme collections from computer stores. Many Web sites also provide sound schemes that you can download and install on your computer.

How do I adjust the volume of the sounds?

You can adjust the volume of the sounds by clicking on the speaker icon on the taskbar. A volume control box will appear. If you want additional volume controls, double-click the speaker icon on the taskbar. For more information, see page 274.

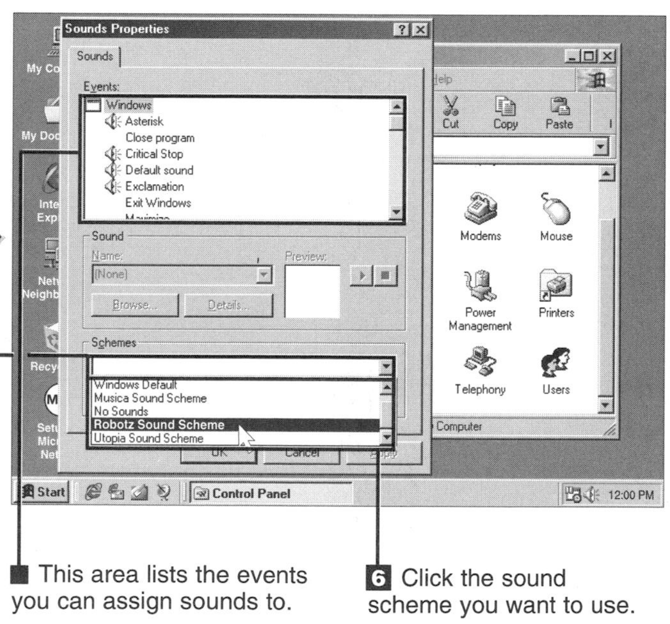

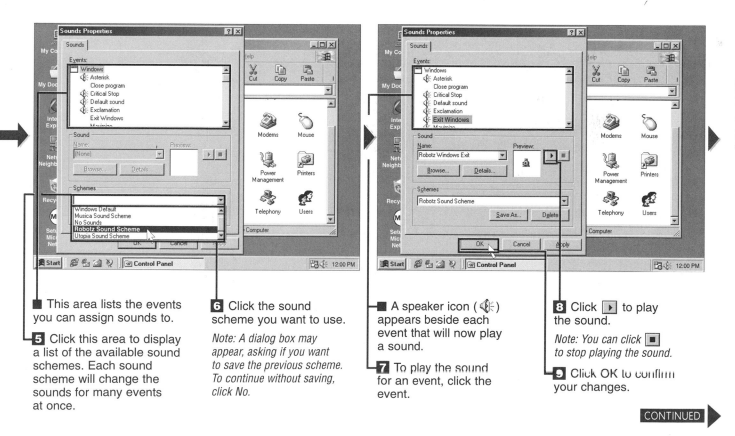

■ This area lists the events you can assign sounds to.

5 Click this area to display a list of the available sound schemes. Each sound scheme will change the sounds for many events at once.

6 Click the sound scheme you want to use.

Note: A dialog box may appear, asking if you want to save the previous scheme. To continue without saving, click No.

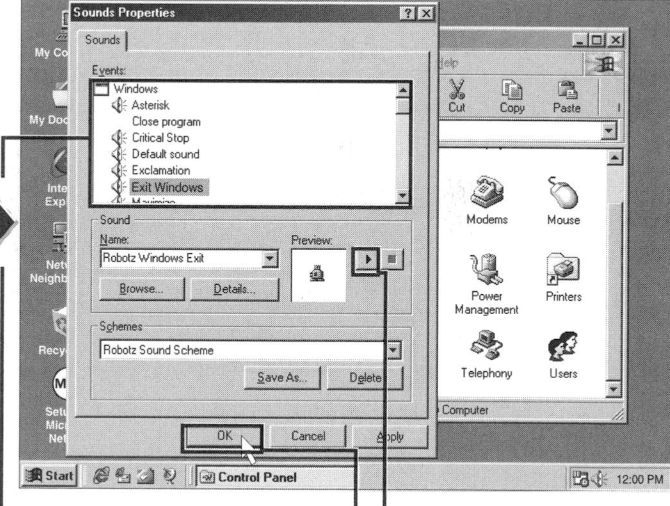

■ A speaker icon (🔊) appears beside each event that will now play a sound.

7 To play the sound for an event, click the event.

8 Click ▶ to play the sound.

Note: You can click ■ to stop playing the sound.

9 Click OK to confirm your changes.

CONTINUED

ASSIGN SOUNDS TO PROGRAM EVENTS CONTINUED

You can assign a sound to a specific event. You may like to play familiar music from the end of a cartoon when Windows closes or hear a sigh of relief when you restore a window. You can mix and match sound files to create a personalized scheme for your computer.

You can use sound files you have purchased, files included on the Windows 98 CD-ROM disc or files you downloaded from the Internet. You can also use sound files you created yourself. The sound files you use must be saved in the .wav format.

Windows 98 does not include a tool that lets you convert other types of sound files into the .wav format.

When you assign a sound to an event, you can listen to a preview of the sound.

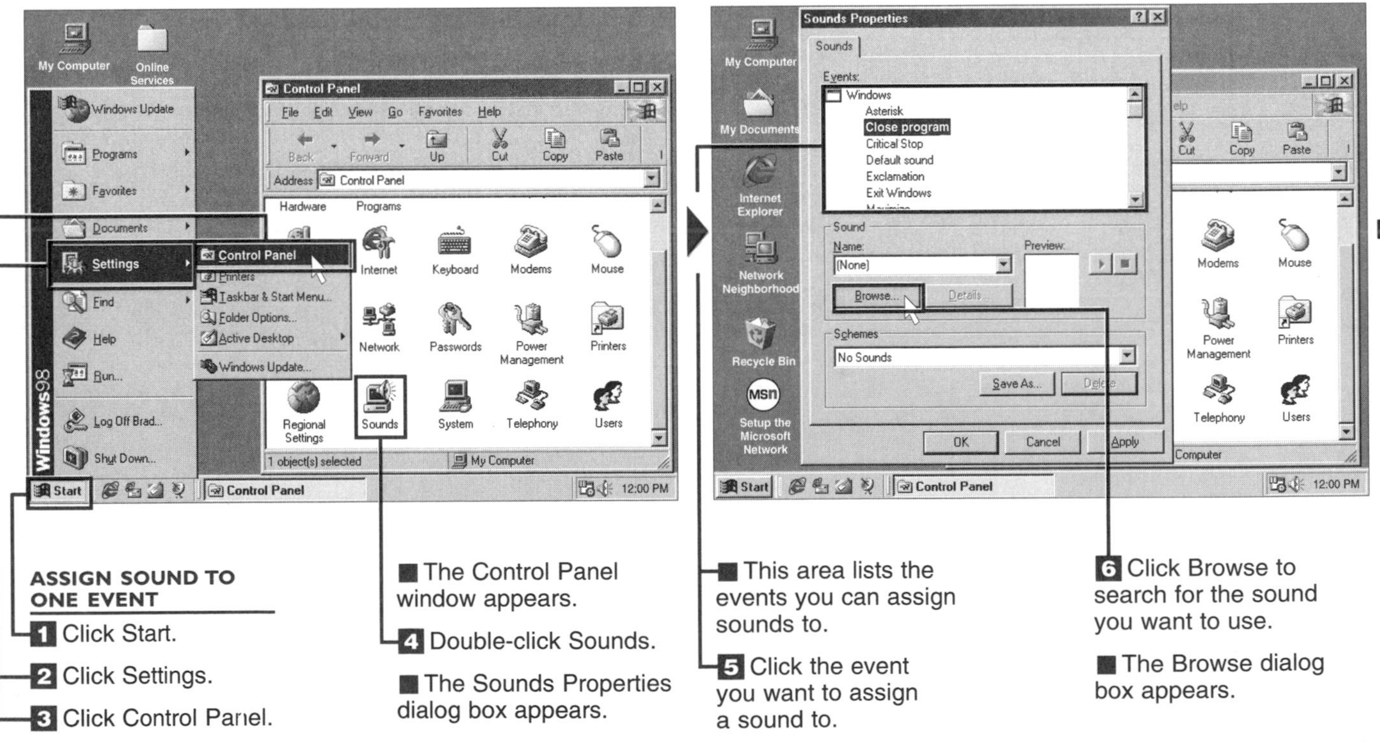

ASSIGN SOUND TO ONE EVENT

1 Click Start.

2 Click Settings.

3 Click Control Panel.

■ The Control Panel window appears.

4 Double-click Sounds.

■ The Sounds Properties dialog box appears.

■ This area lists the events you can assign sounds to.

5 Click the event you want to assign a sound to.

6 Click Browse to search for the sound you want to use.

■ The Browse dialog box appears.

TIPS

Can I save the sound scheme I have created?

Yes. Saving a scheme enables you to use other schemes and return to your personalized scheme. From the Sounds Properties dialog box, click the Save As button. Type a name for the scheme and then click OK.

Is there another way to add a sound to an event?

To assign a sound to an event, you can drag and drop a sound file from a folder on your computer onto an event in the Sounds Properties dialog box.

Where are sound files saved?

The sound files that come with Windows 98 are stored in the C:\Windows\Media folder.

How can I create my own sound files?

There are many different ways to create sound files. You can connect a microphone, a CD player or a cassette recorder to your sound card to create sound files. You can use the Sound Recorder to record sounds from any of these devices. See page 286 for information on using Sound Recorder.

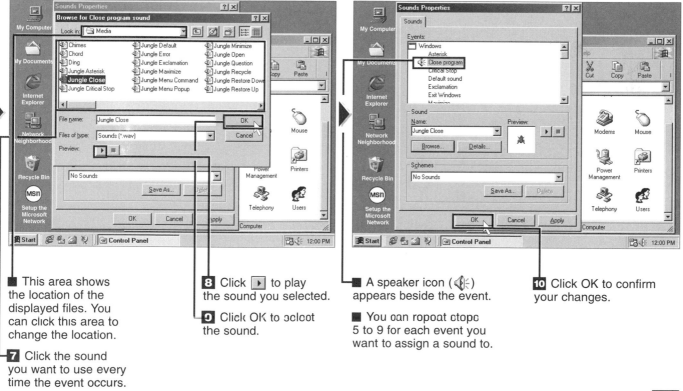

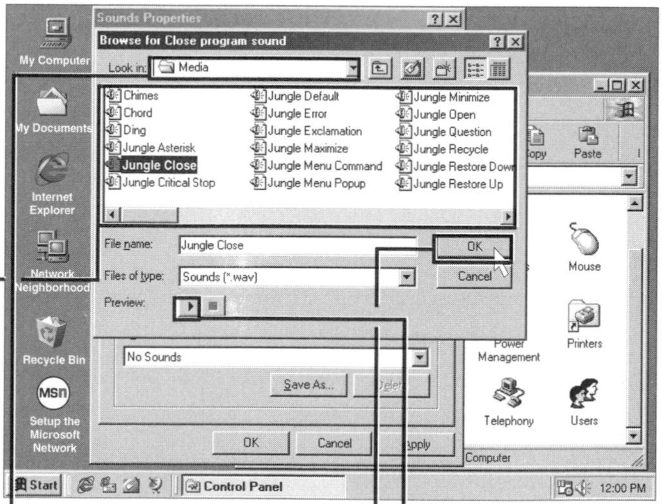

■ This area shows the location of the displayed files. You can click this area to change the location.

7 Click the sound you want to use every time the event occurs.

8 Click ▶ to play the sound you selected.

9 Click OK to select the sound.

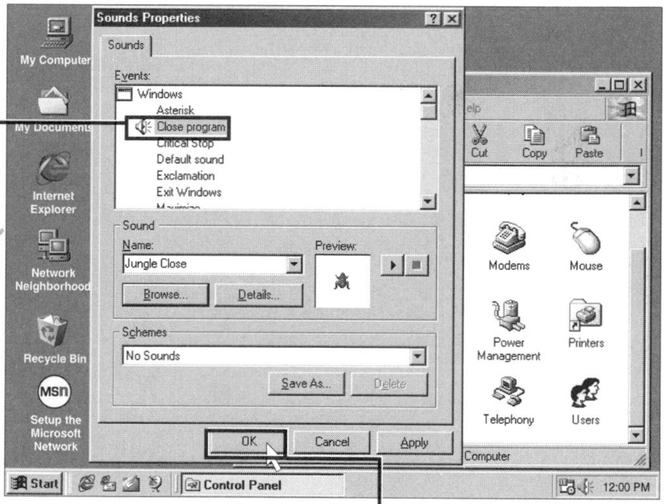

■ A speaker icon (🔊) appears beside the event.

■ You can repeat steps 5 to 9 for each event you want to assign a sound to.

10 Click OK to confirm your changes.

USING VOLUME CONTROL

You can adjust the volume of sound coming from your speakers.

You can use the volume control box to adjust the overall volume on your computer or mute all the sound.

You can use the Master Volume window to change the volume of specific items on your computer. For example, if your CD player is too loud, you can lower the volume of the CD player without affecting the volume of other items.

You can also make adjustments to the balance. Adjusting the balance makes one speaker louder than the other. If one speaker is further away from your preferred listening position, you can make that speaker louder.

You can have the Master Volume window display controls to adjust the balance and volume for either playing back or recording sounds.

You can also specify which devices you want to appear in the Master Volume window, such as the microphone or CD player. This window may look different depending on your sound card.

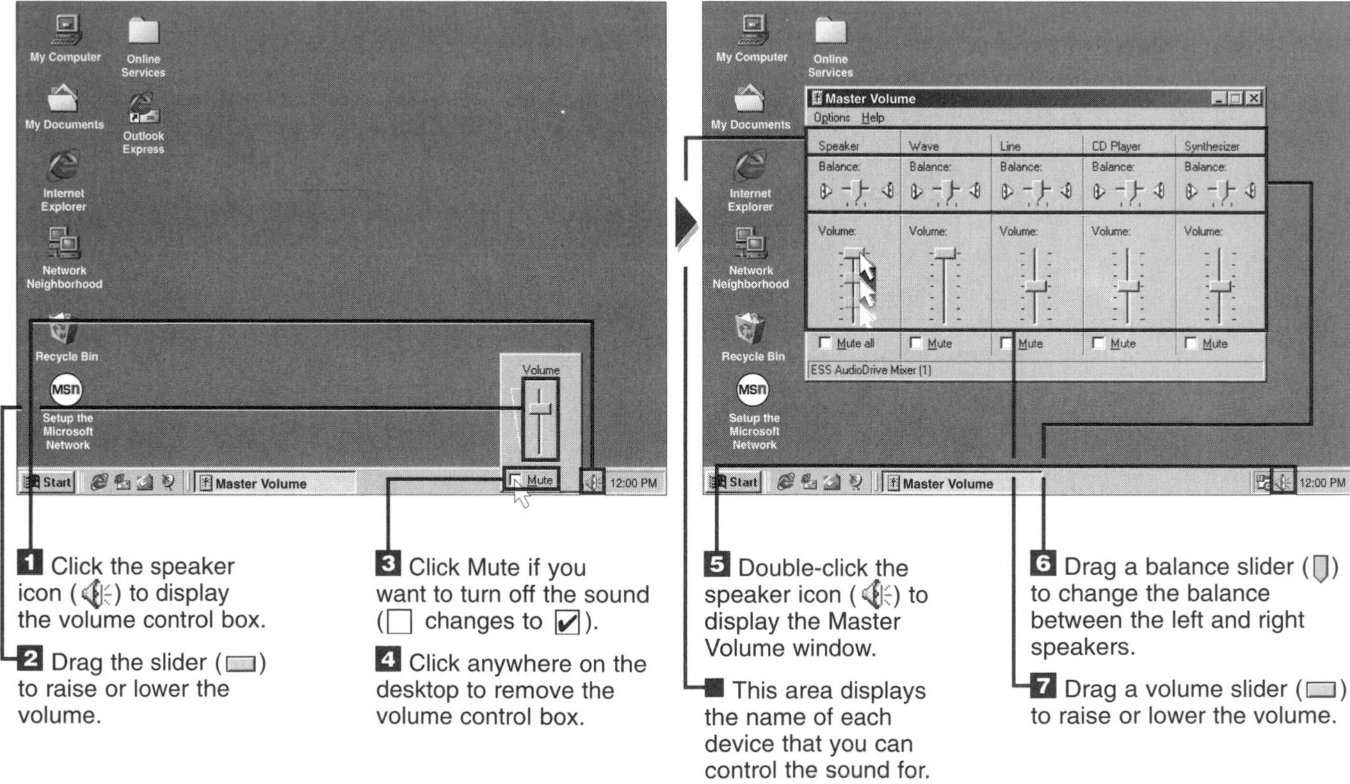

1 Click the speaker icon to display the volume control box.

2 Drag the slider to raise or lower the volume.

3 Click Mute if you want to turn off the sound (☐ changes to ☑).

4 Click anywhere on the desktop to remove the volume control box.

5 Double-click the speaker icon to display the Master Volume window.

■ This area displays the name of each device that you can control the sound for.

6 Drag a balance slider to change the balance between the left and right speakers.

7 Drag a volume slider to raise or lower the volume.

There is no speaker icon on my taskbar. How can I display the icon?

Display the Control Panel window and then double-click Multimedia. On the Audio tab, select the Show volume control on the taskbar option (☐ changes to ☑).

I adjusted the volume, but Windows did not make the change. What is wrong?

With some older sound cards, you cannot adjust the volume using Windows. These older sound cards have a control that lets you manually adjust the volume.

Why does my computer make beeping sounds even after I have muted the sound?

The beeping sounds are coming from the computer's internal speaker. Windows cannot control this speaker. You may have to physically disconnect the internal speaker if you want it muted.

Can I mute the volume using the keyboard?

You can press the Windows (⊞) +V keys on your keyboard to mute the sound.

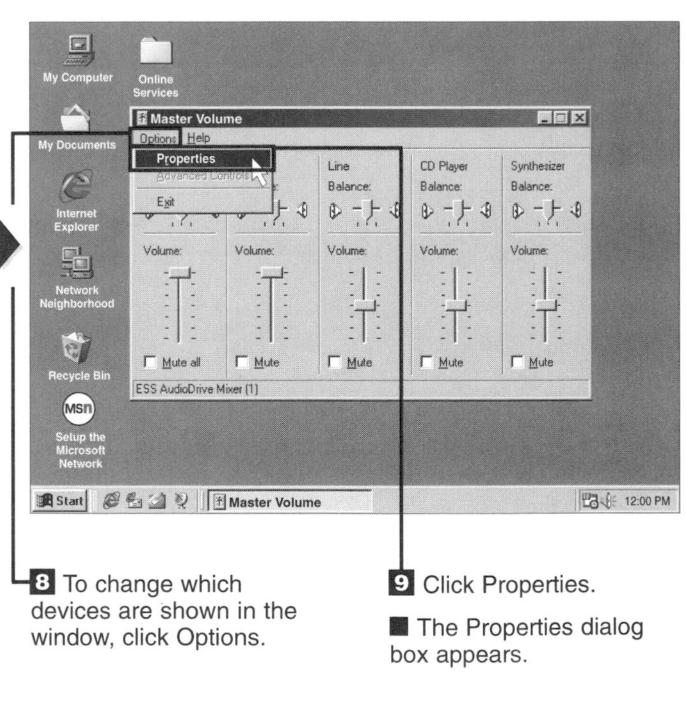

8 To change which devices are shown in the window, click Options.

9 Click Properties.

■ The Properties dialog box appears.

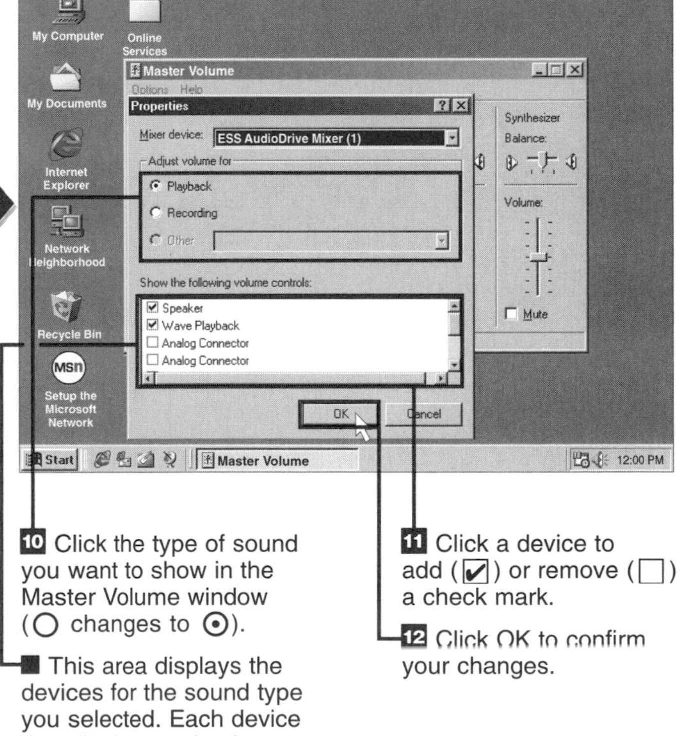

10 Click the type of sound you want to show in the Master Volume window (○ changes to ⦿).

■ This area displays the devices for the sound type you selected. Each device that displays a check mark (☑) will appear in the Master Volume window.

11 Click a device to add (☑) or remove (☐) a check mark.

12 Click OK to confirm your changes.

USING CD PLAYER

You can use your computer's CD-ROM drive to play audio CDs while you work.

You need a CD-ROM drive, a sound card and speakers to play audio CDs.

CD Player has many of the same controls as a standard CD player and can be used in the same way.

CD Player has controls to stop, start and pause a disc. Other buttons are used to skip backwards and forwards from selection to selection. You can also move forwards or backwards to other parts of the same selection. CD Player also has an option to play the selections on your CD in random order.

Once a CD has started playing, you can continue to work on your computer. CD Player uses only a small amount of resources and should have no effect on the speed of your programs.

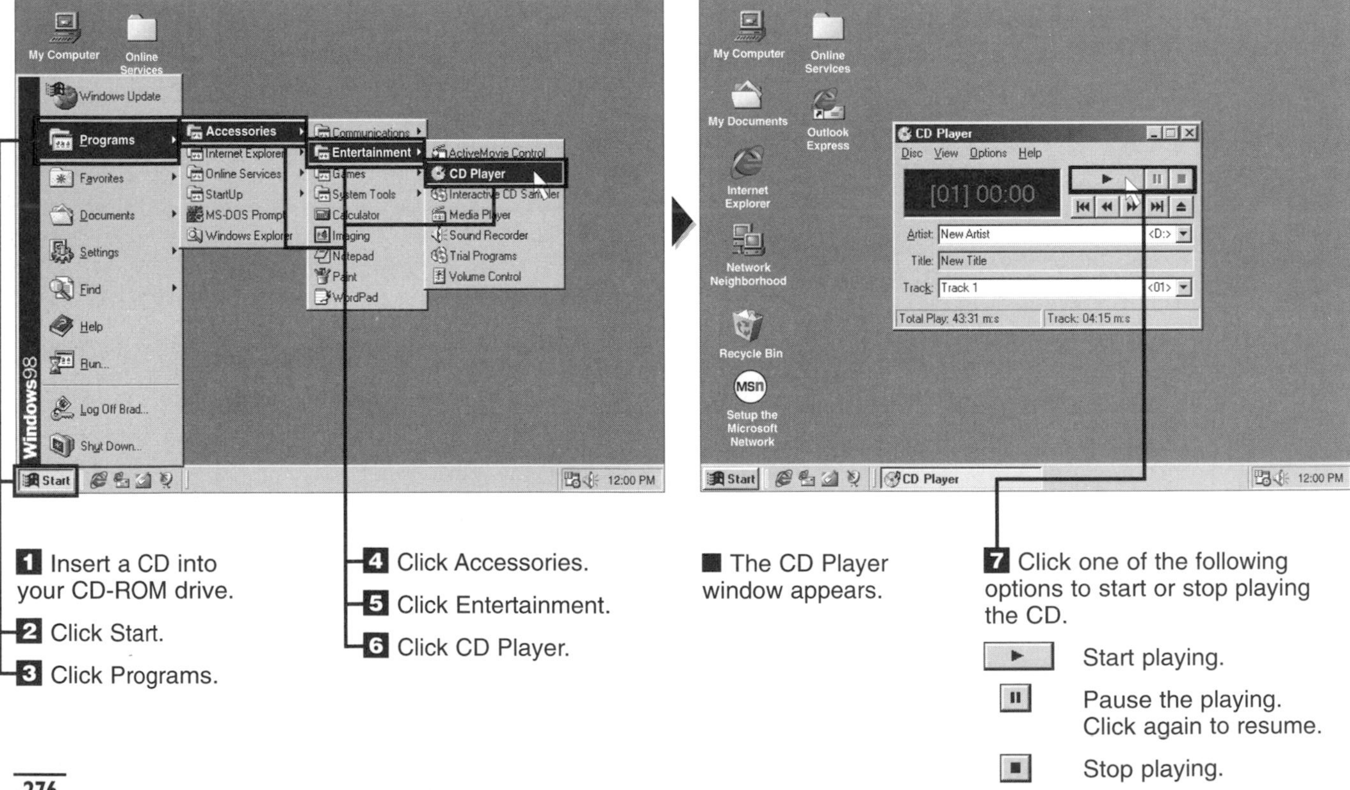

1 Insert a CD into your CD-ROM drive.

2 Click Start.

3 Click Programs.

4 Click Accessories.

5 Click Entertainment.

6 Click CD Player.

■ The CD Player window appears.

7 Click one of the following options to start or stop playing the CD.

▶	Start playing.
II	Pause the playing. Click again to resume.
■	Stop playing.

TIPS

Why does CD Player start automatically when I put in a CD?

Windows is set to automatically open CD Player and start playing a CD when you insert a CD in the CD-ROM drive.

How can I listen to a CD with headphones?

You can plug headphones into the CD-ROM drive's headphone jack. If the CD-ROM drive does not have a headphone jack, you can plug the headphones into the back of the computer, where the speakers plug in.

How can I adjust the volume?

To adjust your computer's master volume, click the speaker icon on the taskbar. See page 274.
If you are using headphones that are plugged into your CD-ROM drive, you can adjust the volume using the volume control on the front of the CD-ROM drive.

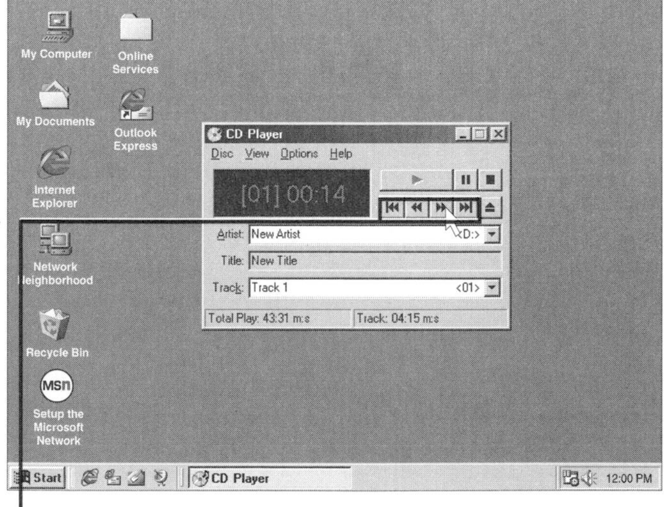

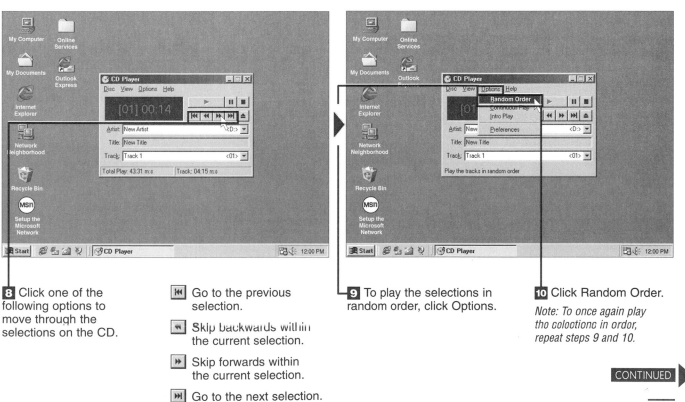

8 Click one of the following options to move through the selections on the CD.

- ⏮ Go to the previous selection.
- ⏪ Skip backwards within the current selection.
- ⏩ Skip forwards within the current selection.
- ⏭ Go to the next selection.

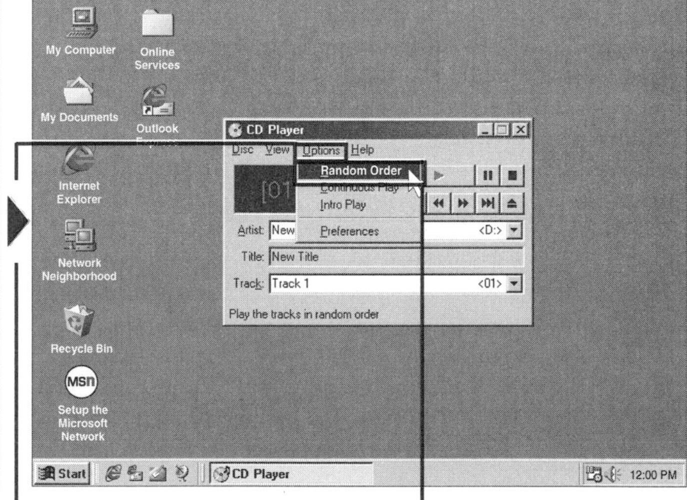

9 To play the selections in random order, click Options.

10 Click Random Order.

Note: To once again play the selections in order, repeat steps 9 and 10.

CONTINUED

USING CD PLAYER CONTINUED

You can enter the title of a CD, the name of the artist and the title of each selection on the CD.

When you have entered the information for a CD, Windows will recognize the disc each time it is inserted and display the information for the disc.

The information you enter for a CD will help you when you want to create a play list for the disc. A play list tells the CD Player which selections you would like to listen to and in what order. Creating a play list is useful because you can eliminate the selections that you dislike and rearrange the order of the selections you want to hear.

When you create or edit the play list, the CD Player saves your changes and recalls them the next time you insert the disc.

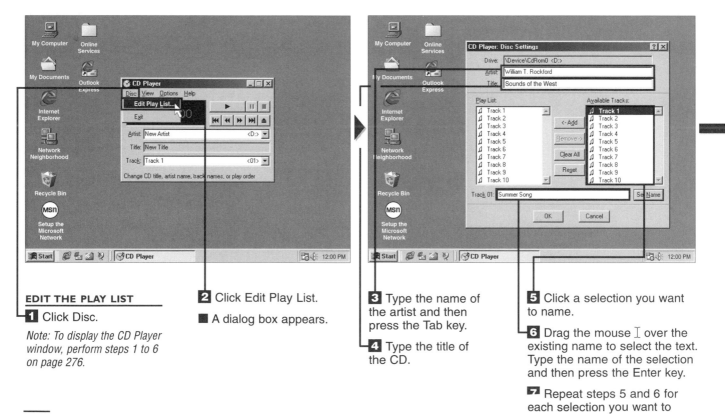

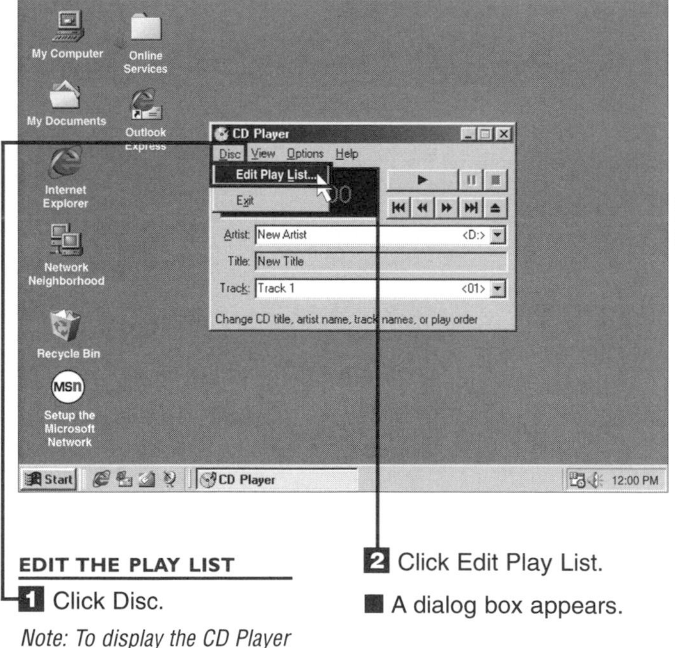

EDIT THE PLAY LIST

1 Click Disc.

Note: To display the CD Player window, perform steps 1 to 6 on page 276.

2 Click Edit Play List.

■ A dialog box appears.

3 Type the name of the artist and then press the Tab key.

4 Type the title of the CD.

5 Click a selection you want to name.

6 Drag the mouse I over the existing name to select the text. Type the name of the selection and then press the Enter key.

7 Repeat steps 5 and 6 for each selection you want to name.

TIPS

Is there an easier way to enter the information for my CD?

The Notify CD Player allows you to instantly connect to a database on the Internet that stores information for thousands of CDs. Notify CD Player will then automatically enter the information for the CD for you. You can get the Notify CD Player and the Internet database plug-in on the Web at: www.artech.se/~mlt/software/index.html

How can I reset the play list so that the entire CD plays?

You can click the Reset button to return the play list to its original order and listen to the entire CD.

Can I access the information for a CD in another program?

You can display the information for a CD in any word processor, including WordPad. This is useful if you want to print a listing of all the selections on your CDs. The information is saved in the Windows folder as a text file named cdplayer.ini

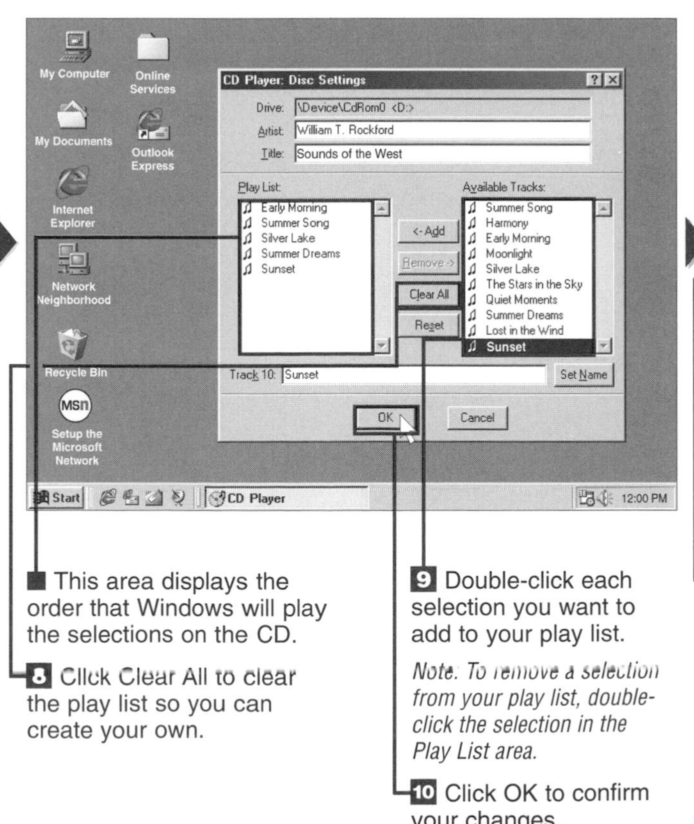

■ This area displays the order that Windows will play the selections on the CD.

8 Click Clear All to clear the play list so you can create your own.

9 Double-click each selection you want to add to your play list.

Note: To remove a selection from your play list, double-click the selection in the Play List area.

10 Click OK to confirm your changes.

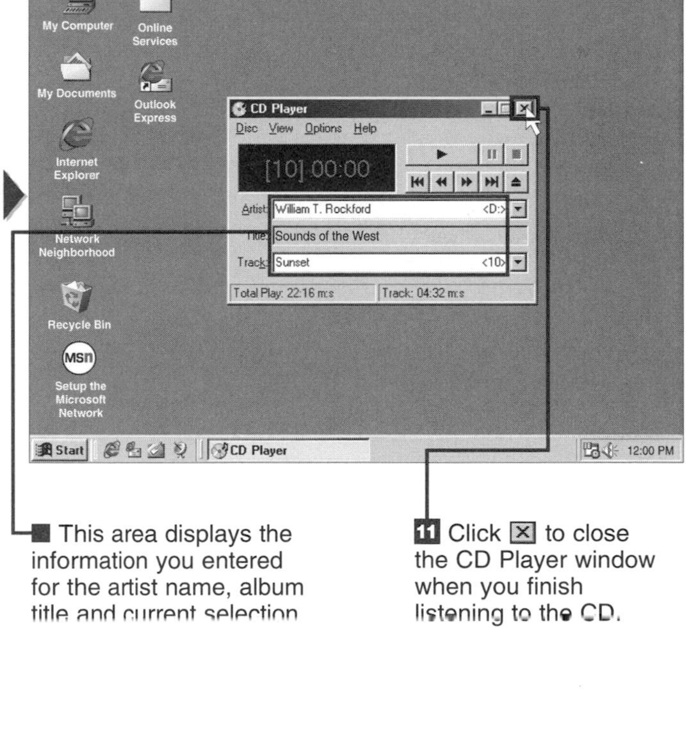

■ This area displays the information you entered for the artist name, album title and current selection.

11 Click ☒ to close the CD Player window when you finish listening to the CD.

CHANGE PROPERTIES OF A CD-ROM DRIVE

You can change the way Windows works with your CDs and CD-ROM drive.

The Auto insert notification option allows Windows to automatically detect a CD you place in your computer's CD-ROM drive. If the CD is a Windows 95 or 98 program CD with AutoPlay capabilities, the opening screen will appear. If the CD is a music CD, the music will start to play. When Windows detects a CD you have inserted, Windows displays the name of the CD below the CD-ROM drive icon in the My Computer window. You can turn off the Auto insert notification option if you do not want Windows to automatically detect your CDs.

On most computers, the CD-ROM drive is assigned the letter "D". The CD-ROM drive letter may change if you add other devices to your computer. A program that uses the CD-ROM drive may not be able to find the files it needs when the CD-ROM drive letter changes. To eliminate this problem, you can reserve a drive letter so the CD-ROM drive will always use the same drive letter.

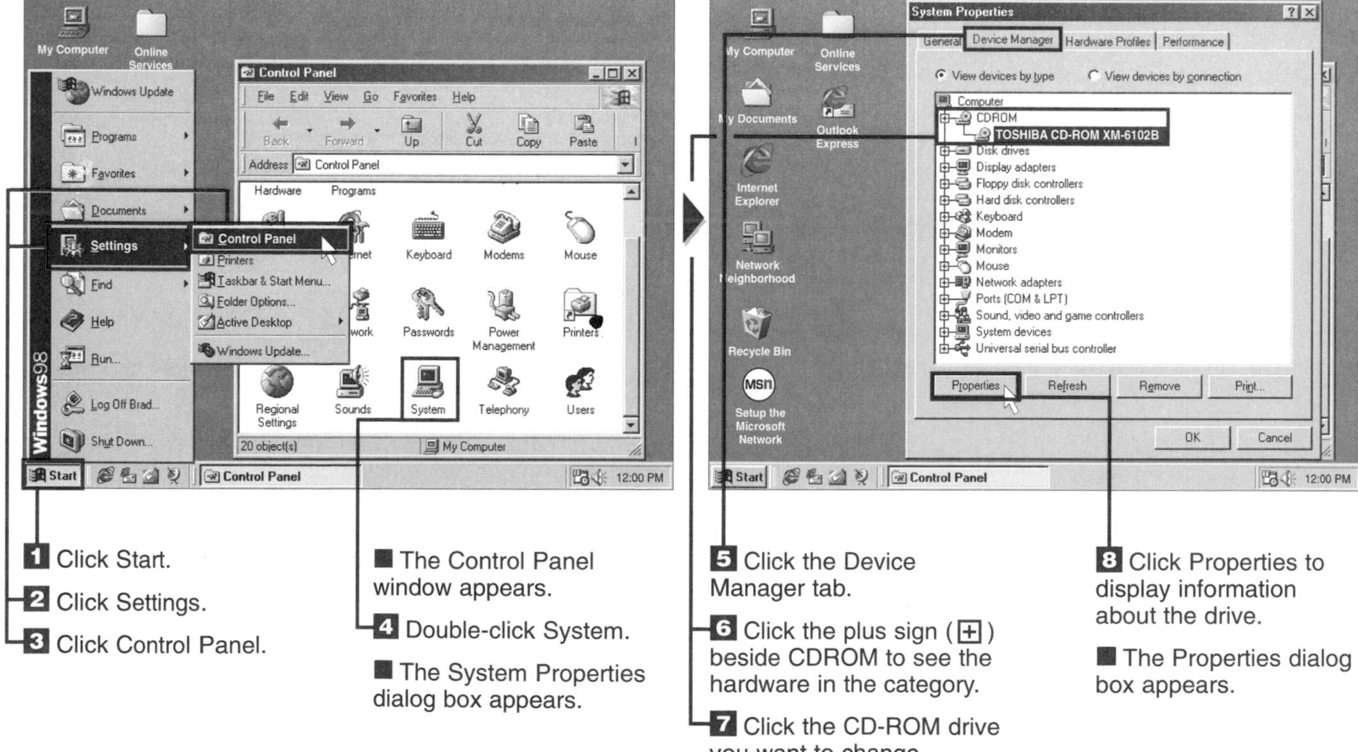

1 Click Start.

2 Click Settings.

3 Click Control Panel.

■ The Control Panel window appears.

4 Double-click System.

■ The System Properties dialog box appears.

5 Click the Device Manager tab.

6 Click the plus sign (⊞) beside CDROM to see the hardware in the category.

7 Click the CD-ROM drive you want to change.

8 Click Properties to display information about the drive.

■ The Properties dialog box appears.

Are there any settings I should change for my DVD drive?

A DVD (Digital Versatile Disc) drive allows you to play DVD discs, software CDs and music CDs. You may need to enable the DMA setting for a DVD drive. Perform steps 1 to 9 below, except select your DVD drive in step 7. On the Settings tab, click the DMA option (☐ changes to ☑).

How do I stop an AutoPlay CD from playing when I put it in the drive?

Hold down the Shift key while you insert the CD you do not want to automatically play. If you do not want any CDs you insert to automatically play, turn off the Auto insert notification option.

Can I add AutoPlay to older CDs?

No. An AutoPlay CD contains an autorun command file. Since you cannot record on a CD-ROM disc, it is not possible to add the autorun command file to older CDs you have purchased.

Can I improve the performance of my older CD-ROM drive?

If you have 16 MB of RAM or more, you should make sure that the CD-ROM's cache is set to the largest setting. The cache stores information from a CD-ROM disc in memory where it can be accessed more quickly than from the disc. In the System Properties dialog box, select the Performance tab and then click the File System button. Then click the CD-ROM tab and adjust the setting.

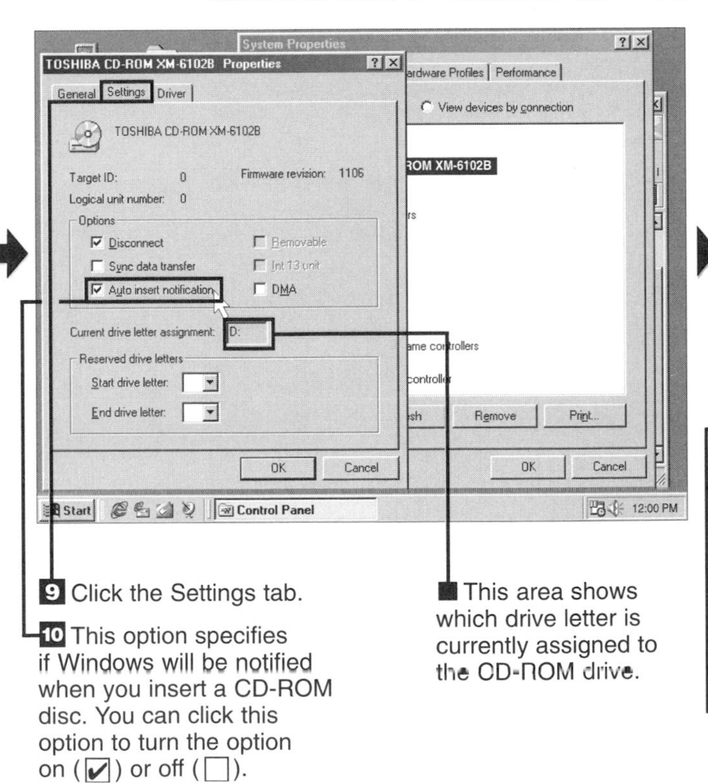

9 Click the Settings tab.

10 This option specifies if Windows will be notified when you insert a CD-ROM disc. You can click this option to turn the option on (☑) or off (☐).

■ This area shows which drive letter is currently assigned to the CD-ROM drive.

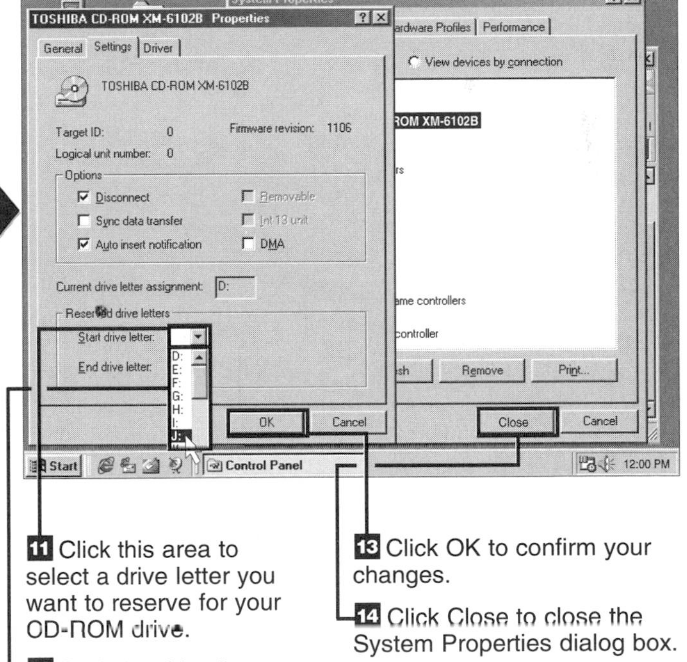

11 Click this area to select a drive letter you want to reserve for your CD-ROM drive.

12 Click the drive letter you want to reserve.

13 Click OK to confirm your changes.

14 Click Close to close the System Properties dialog box.

15 Windows will ask you to restart your computer. Click Yes to restart your computer.

USING MEDIA PLAYER

Play a File

Media Player lets you play sound, video and animation files on your computer. Media Player is a combination VCR and CD player.

Media Player provides several devices you can use to play multimedia files. The ActiveMovie and Video for Windows devices allow you to play video files.

You can use the Sound and MIDI Sequencer devices to play sound files. The CD Audio device allows you to play music CDs.

The setup of your computer determines the types of multimedia files you can play. You need a sound card and speakers to play sound files. You need a CD-ROM drive to play CDs.

Media Player has the same controls you would find on a VCR. These controls allow you to play, stop, rewind or fast forward a file.

A timeline indicates the length of the file. A slider on the timeline indicates your current position in the file. You can use the slider to move through a file.

The Windows 98 CD-ROM disc includes several sample video files you can play. You can also obtain files on the Internet.

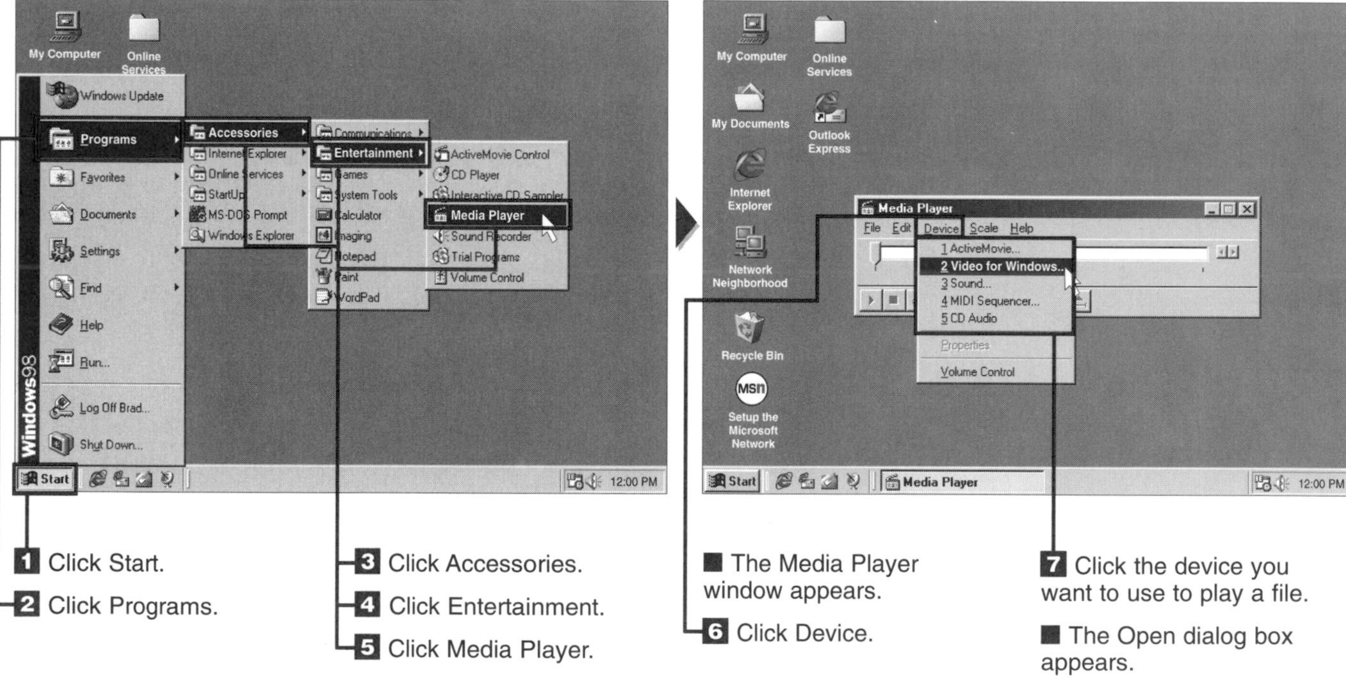

1 Click Start.

2 Click Programs.

3 Click Accessories.

4 Click Entertainment.

5 Click Media Player.

■ The Media Player window appears.

6 Click Device.

7 Click the device you want to use to play a file.

■ The Open dialog box appears.

TIPS

What types of video and sound files can I play?

You can play Video for Windows (.avi), MPEG (.mpg) and most QuickTime (.mov and .qt) video files. You can play many types of sound files, including Wave (.wav) and MIDI (.mid). You can also play sound files associated with ActiveMovie, such as files with the .au and .aif extensions.

Is there another way I can play video files?

You can also play some video files using the ActiveMovie Control program. To open and play your video files, click Start, select Programs and then click Accessories. Choose Entertainment and then select ActiveMovie Control.

The Media Player window is covering the viewing window. Can I combine the windows?

You can double-click the title bar of the Media Player window to combine it with the viewing window. You can double-click the title bar of the viewing window to restore the Media Player window.

How can I tell how long a CD will play?

When using Media Player to play an audio CD, the timeline displays the selections on the CD. From the Scale menu, select the Time option to view the amount of time it will take to play the CD.

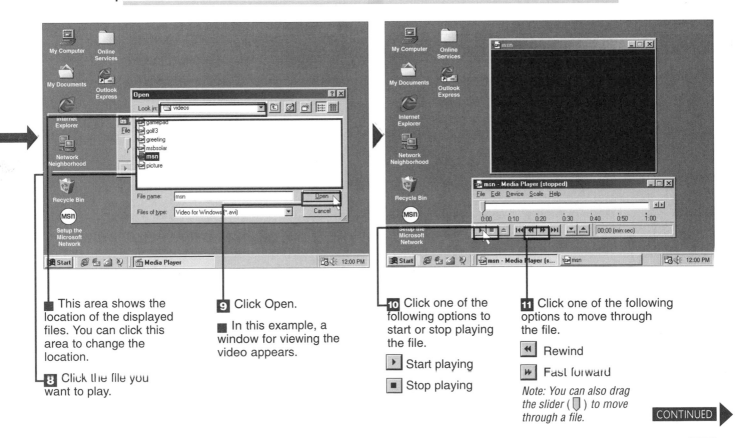

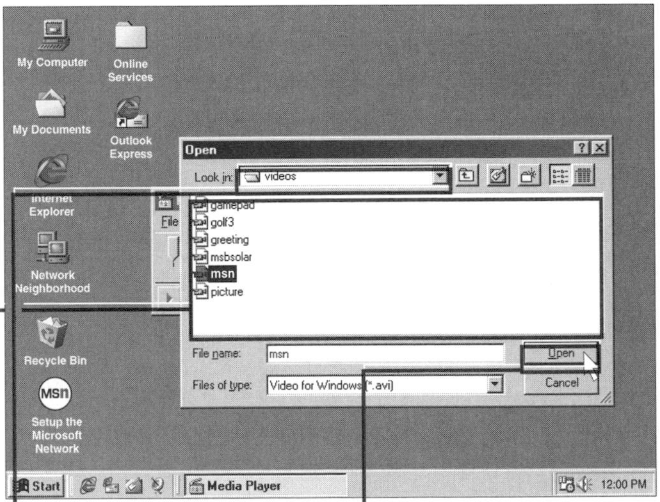

■ This area shows the location of the displayed files. You can click this area to change the location.

8 Click the file you want to play.

9 Click Open.

■ In this example, a window for viewing the video appears.

10 Click one of the following options to start or stop playing the file.

▶ Start playing

■ Stop playing

11 Click one of the following options to move through the file.

◀◀ Rewind

▶▶ Fast forward

Note: You can also drag the slider ( ) to move through a file.

CONTINUED

USING MEDIA PLAYER CONTINUED

Change Play Options

You can change the way Media Player plays certain types of files. When you change the play options for one type of file, Media Player will use the new settings you specify for all files of that type.

You can have a multimedia file automatically rewind when it is finished playing. You can also have a multimedia file play continuously. This is useful if you are using a multimedia file in a demonstration.

A video is designed to play best at its original size. However, you can increase the size of the viewing window or even have a video fill your entire screen.

When you enlarge a video beyond its original size, the quality of the video may be affected. The video may become jerky, appear grainy or display other visual distortions. Reducing the size of the video may help the video run more smoothly and appear more clearly.

If you want to stop playing a video that fills your screen, you can press the Esc key to pause the video and access the Media Player window.

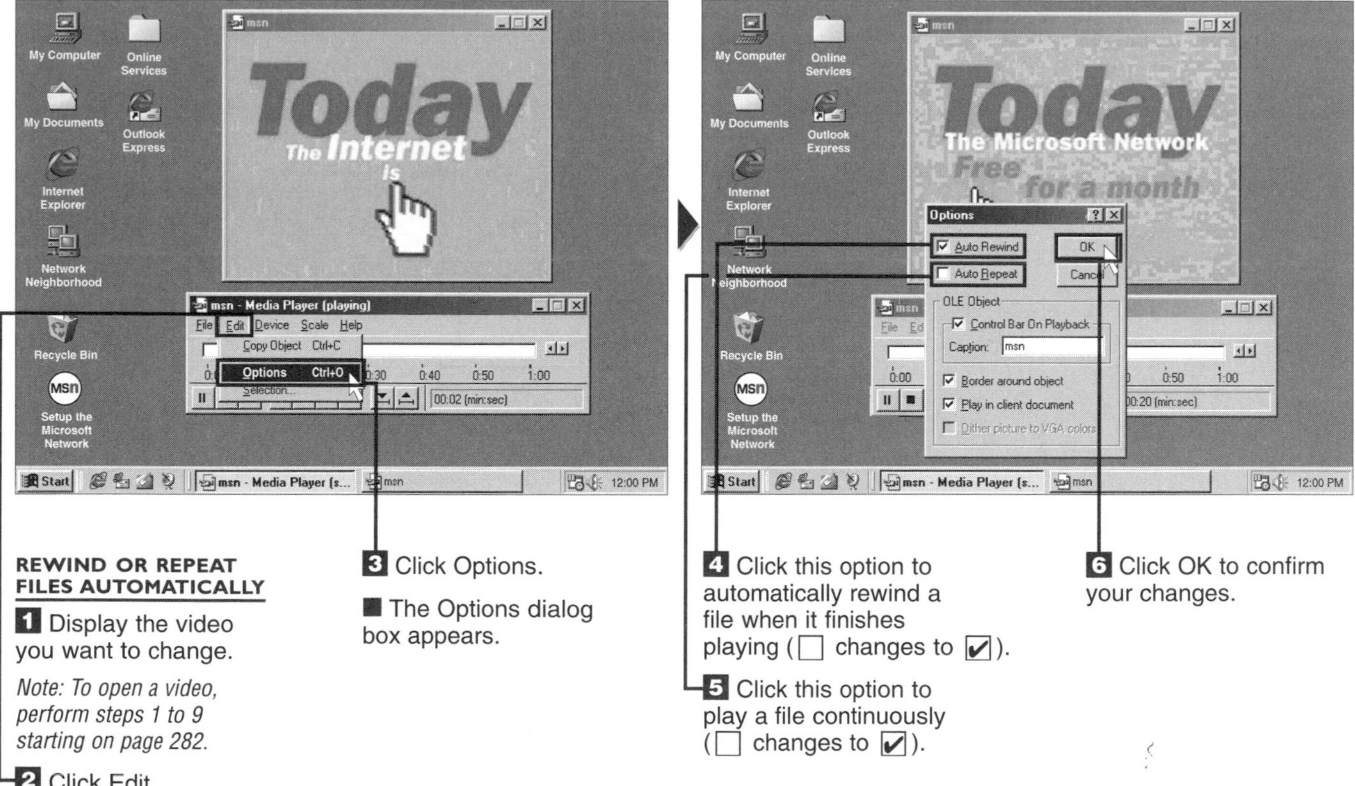

REWIND OR REPEAT FILES AUTOMATICALLY

1 Display the video you want to change.

Note: To open a video, perform steps 1 to 9 starting on page 282.

2 Click Edit.

3 Click Options.

■ The Options dialog box appears.

4 Click this option to automatically rewind a file when it finishes playing (☐ changes to ☑).

5 Click this option to play a file continuously (☐ changes to ☑).

6 Click OK to confirm your changes.

TIPS

Why doesn't Media Player start when I double-click a video?

The default player for video files, including files with the .avi and .mpg extensions, is ActiveMovie. The default player for audio CDs is CD Player. You can change the default action so these types of files always play in Media Player. See page 240.

Can I copy a multimedia file to a word processing document?

You can copy a multimedia file to any program that supports Object Linking and Embedding (OLE). In the Media Player window, click Edit and then select Copy Object. Open the document where you want to place the file and then paste the file into the document. For information on OLE, see pages 126 to 133.

Can I copy only part of a multimedia file?

To copy only part of a multimedia file, you must first select the part you want to copy. In the Media Player window, position the slider (▯) at the beginning of the part you want to copy and then click the Start Selection button (▣). Drag the slider to the end of the part you want to copy and then click the End Selection button (▣).

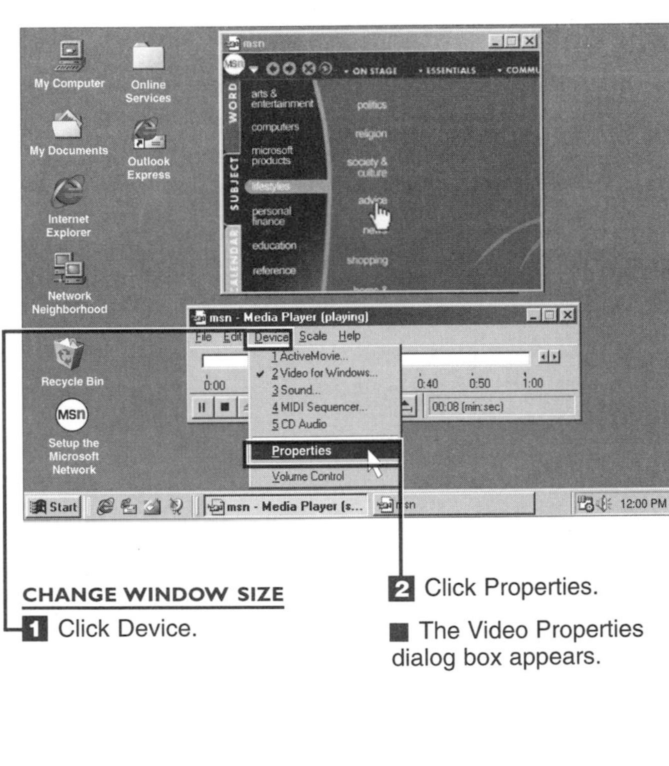

CHANGE WINDOW SIZE

1 Click Device.

2 Click Properties.

■ The Video Properties dialog box appears.

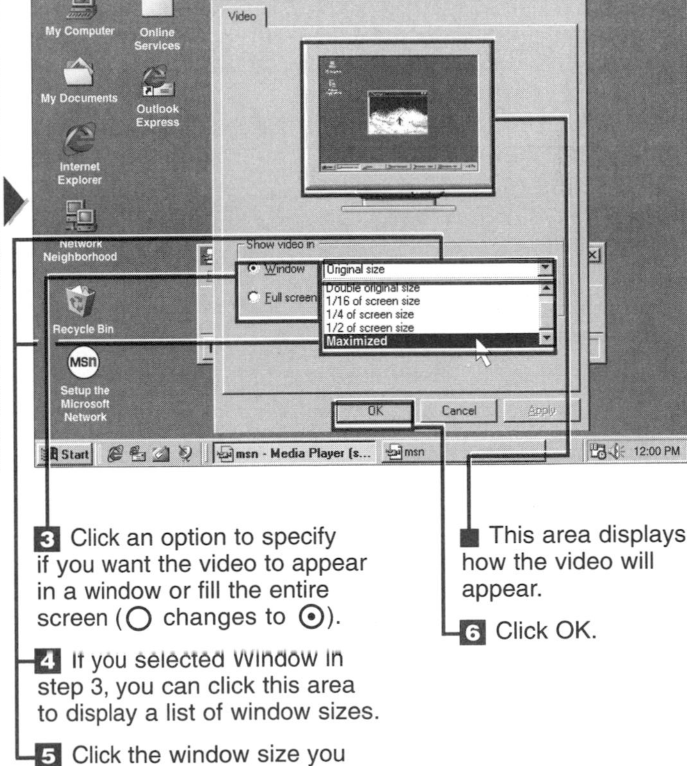

3 Click an option to specify if you want the video to appear in a window or fill the entire screen (○ changes to ⊙).

4 If you selected Window in step 3, you can click this area to display a list of window sizes.

5 Click the window size you want to use.

■ This area displays how the video will appear.

6 Click OK.

USING SOUND RECORDER

You can use Sound Recorder to record, play back and edit sounds from a microphone, CD player, stereo, VCR or any other sound device you connect to your computer.

You need a sound card and speakers to record and play sounds.

You can use recorded sounds to make a document or presentation unique. For example, a presentation at a sales meeting can be more interesting if energetic music is playing while you present the agenda.

You can also record sounds, effects or comments and have them play when specific events occur, such as when you close a program. This can help personalize your computer. To assign sounds to program events, see page 270.

Sound Recorder lets you complete basic work with sound files. There are many other more sophisticated sound recording and editing programs that you can get on the Internet and at computer stores.

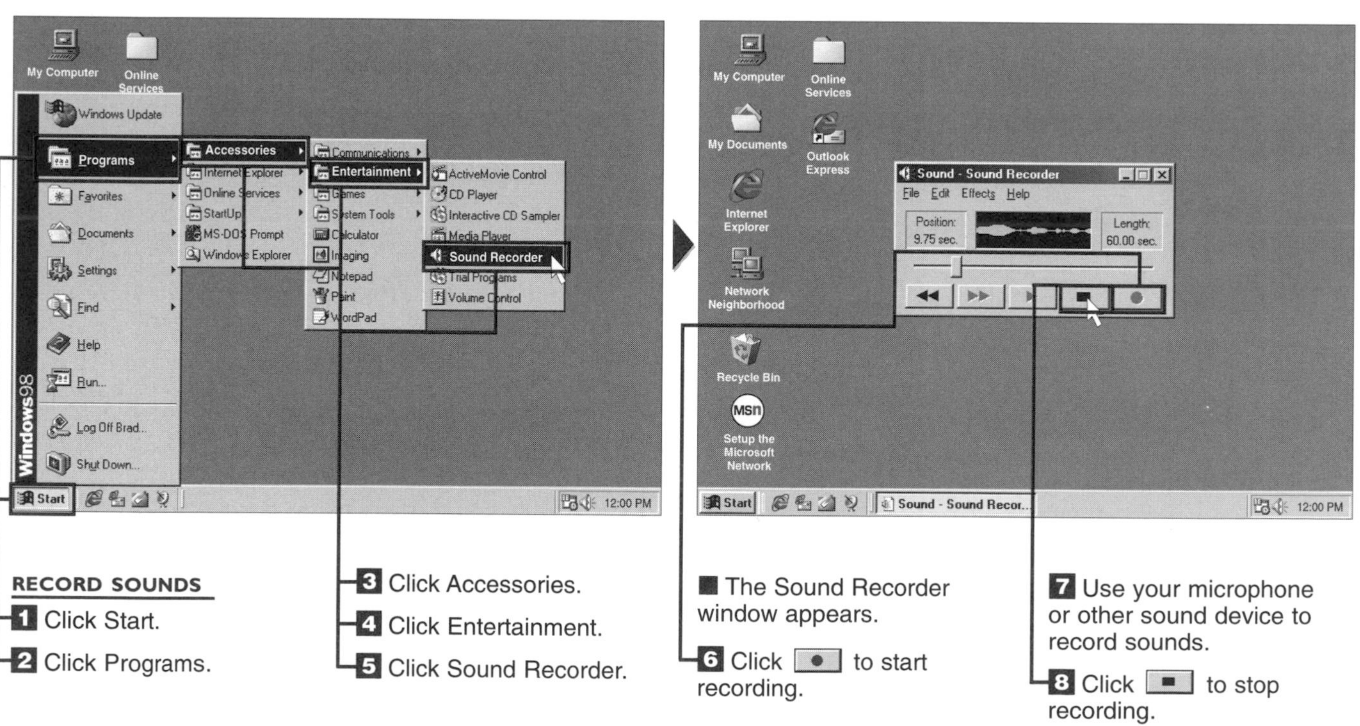

RECORD SOUNDS

1 Click Start.

2 Click Programs.

3 Click Accessories.

4 Click Entertainment.

5 Click Sound Recorder.

■ The Sound Recorder window appears.

6 Click ● to start recording.

7 Use your microphone or other sound device to record sounds.

8 Click ■ to stop recording.

TIPS

The recording is too quiet or too loud and distorted. Can I change the recording volume?

In the Sound Recorder window, the green line shows the level of the volume of your recording. If the green line barely moves, you need to increase the recording volume. If the green line reaches to the top and bottom of the box, you need to decrease the recording volume. To adjust the recording volume, click Edit and then select Audio Properties. Click the icon in the Recording area and then adjust the appropriate volume slider.

How can I begin a new recording?

Choose the File menu and then select New to begin a new recording.

How do I save my recording?

From the File menu, select Save As to save your recording as a file on your computer. To open a file you previously saved, select the File menu and click Open. In the Open dialog box, select the file you want to open and then click Open.

How can I change the volume of the playback?

Use the speaker icon (🔈) on the taskbar to change the volume of the playback. See page 274.

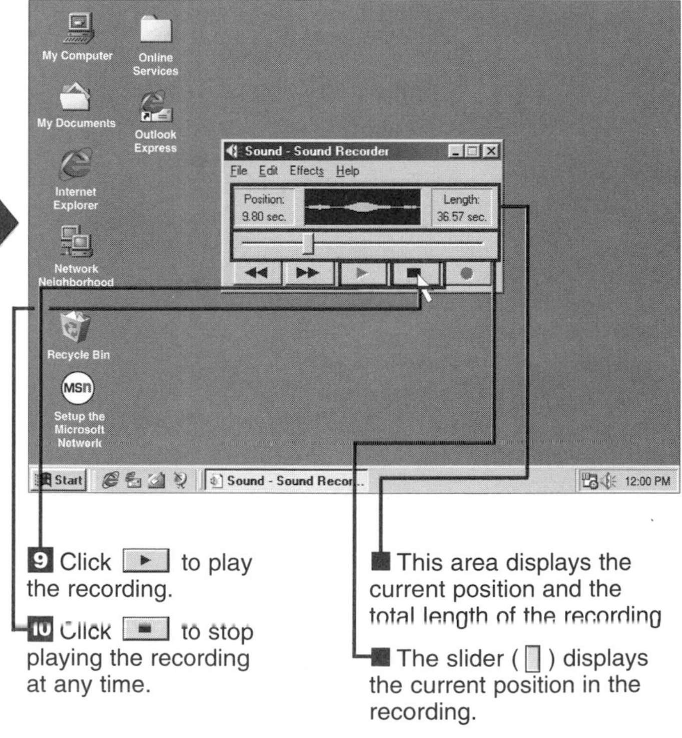

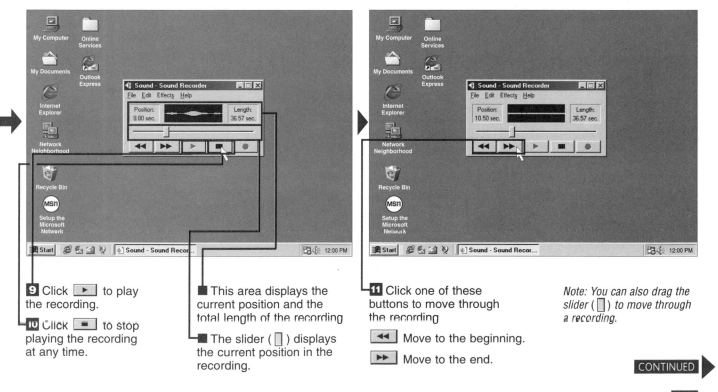

9 Click ▶ to play the recording.

10 Click ■ to stop playing the recording at any time.

■ This area displays the current position and the total length of the recording.

■ The slider (▯) displays the current position in the recording.

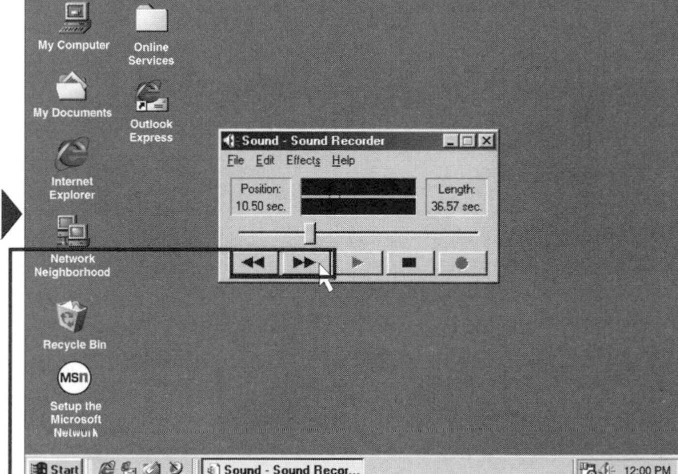

11 Click one of these buttons to move through the recording.

◀◀ Move to the beginning.

▶▶ Move to the end.

Note: You can also drag the slider (▯) to move through a recording.

CONTINUED

USING SOUND RECORDER

CONTINUED

Sound Recorder has several sound effects you can use to change your recording. You can adjust the volume of your recording to make it softer or louder. You can also speed up your recording to create a chipmunk effect or slow it down to create a spooky and mysterious effect. You may also find it entertaining to add an echo to your recording or play the recording backwards.

Sound Recorder allows you to insert another sound file into an existing recording. You can choose the exact position in your recording where you want to insert the other sound file. Inserting a sound file into an existing recording lets you create one sound file containing your favorite sounds. For example, you can create a Halloween sound file by inserting howls and screams into a recording of spooky music.

When you insert a sound file into an existing recording, the file size of the recording increases. The file size of a recording also depends on the quality of the recording.

There are many sound files available on the Internet that you can insert into another recording. Sound Recorder can only work with files in the Windows .wav format.

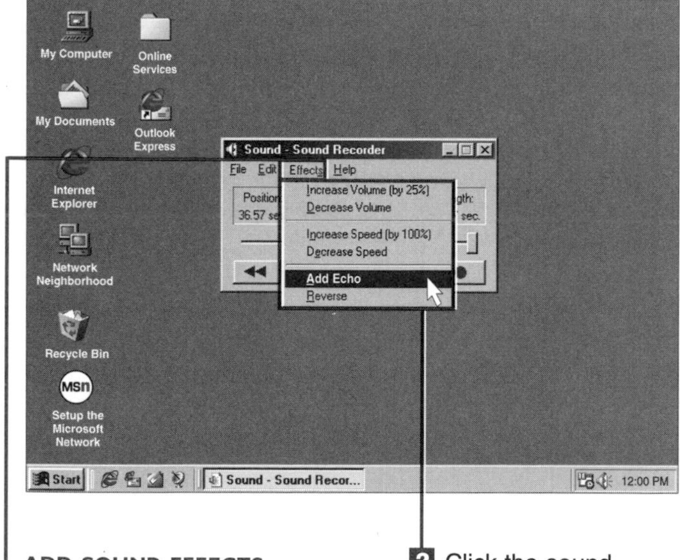

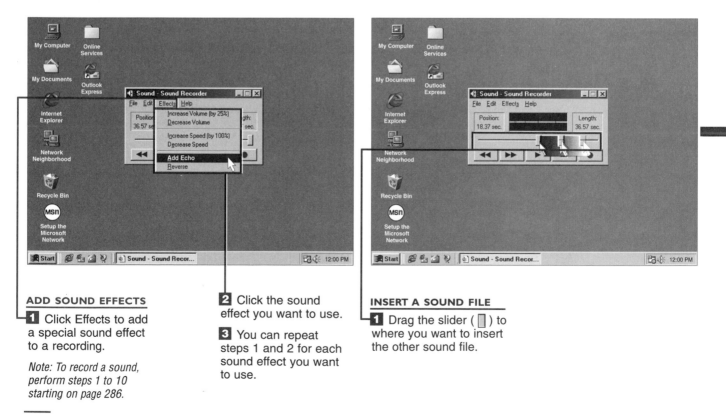

ADD SOUND EFFECTS

1 Click Effects to add a special sound effect to a recording.

Note: To record a sound, perform steps 1 to 10 starting on page 286.

2 Click the sound effect you want to use.

3 You can repeat steps 1 and 2 for each sound effect you want to use.

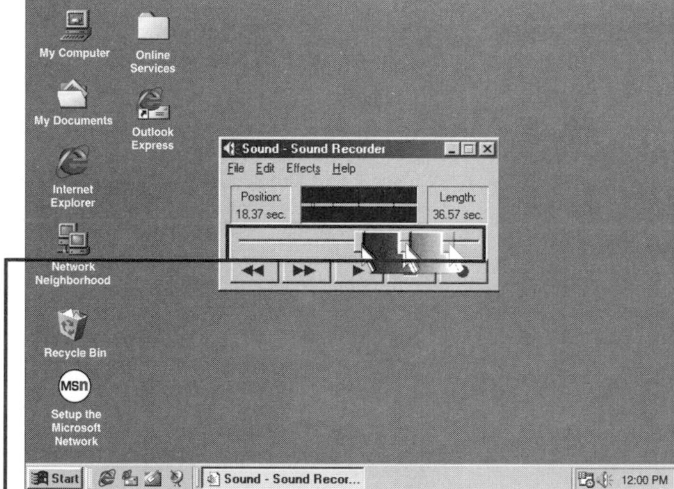

INSERT A SOUND FILE

1 Drag the slider (▯) to where you want to insert the other sound file.

How do I undo a mistake?

On the File menu, click Revert. This command will undo all the changes you made since you last saved the recording. You should save your recording every time you make a successful change.

How can I mix two sound files together so both sounds play at the same time?

Position the slider where you want the second sound file to start playing. On the Edit menu, click Mix with File. Select the sound file you want to mix with your existing recording and then click the Open button. Mixing two sound files is useful if you are adding a music background to a voice recording.

Can I change the quality of my recording?

Sound Recorder normally creates recordings in Radio Quality. To change the quality of a recording, click the File menu and then select Properties. On the Details tab, click the Convert Now button. Click the Name area and then select the quality you want to use. CD Quality is useful if you are recording files to play over a high-quality speaker system. Telephone Quality is useful for files you will transfer over the Internet.

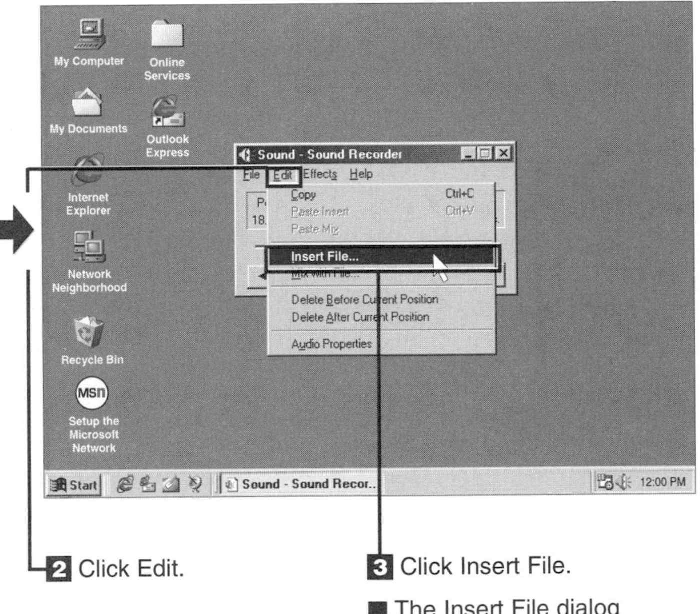

2 Click Edit.

3 Click Insert File.

■ The Insert File dialog box appears.

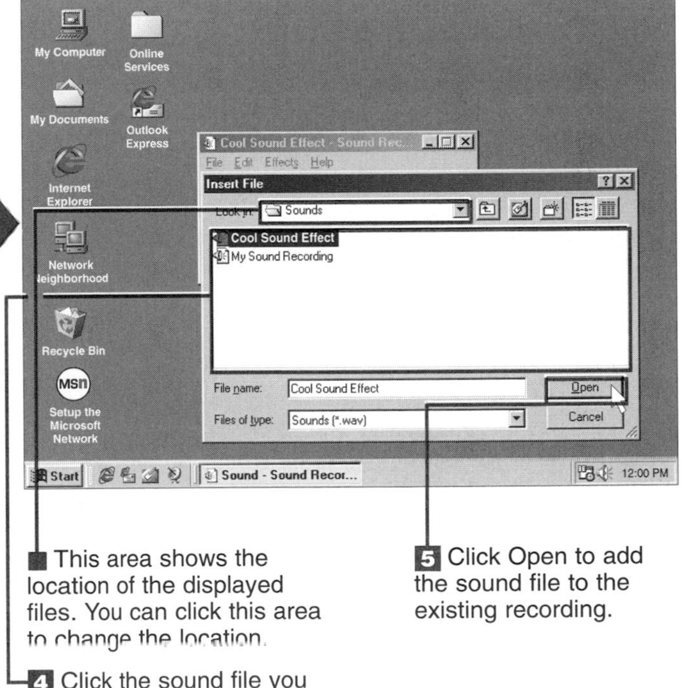

■ This area shows the location of the displayed files. You can click this area to change the location.

4 Click the sound file you want to insert.

5 Click Open to add the sound file to the existing recording.

USING WEBTV

Start WebTV

You can use WebTV to watch television programs on your computer. You need a TV tuner card, such as ATI All-in-Wonder, to use WebTV. You also need a sound card and speakers to hear sounds in the television programs.

The first time you start WebTV, a welcome message appears on your screen and a presentation begins. Make sure your speakers are turned on and the volume is turned up so you can hear the presentation.

Even if you do not have a TV tuner card, you can still use WebTV to view free TV listings on your computer. WebTV will display the TV listings in the Program Guide so you can see when your favorite television programs will play. You need a connection to the Internet to get the listings.

After starting WebTV, you can display the Program Guide to view information about the television programs you can watch.

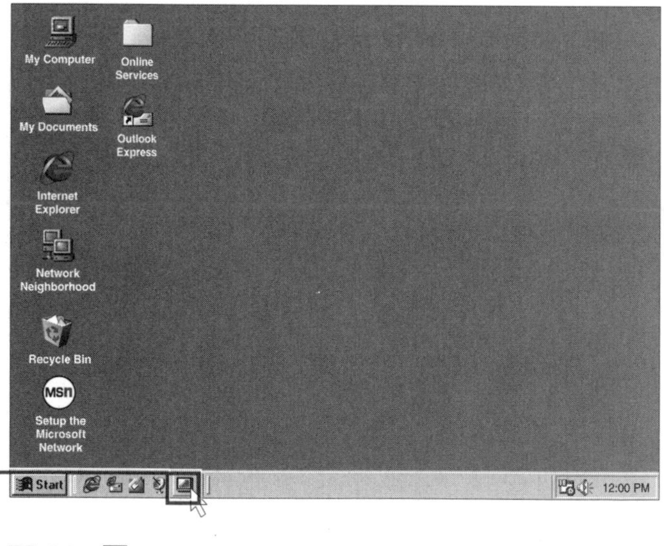

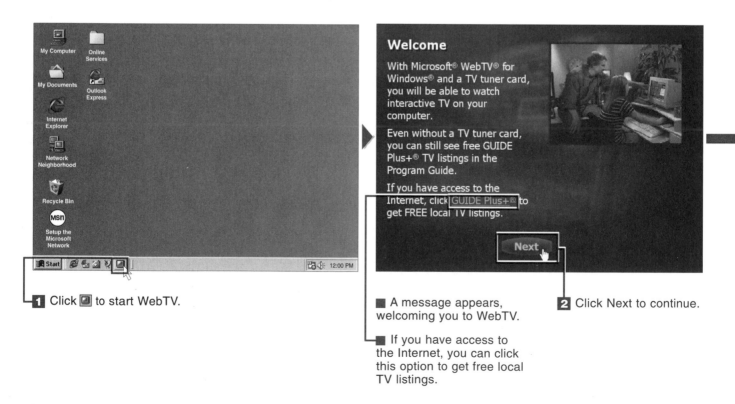

1 Click ▣ to start WebTV.

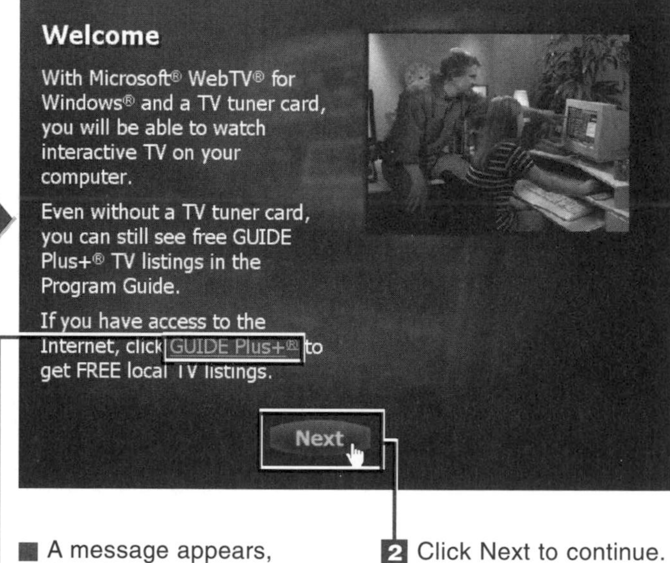

■ A message appears, welcoming you to WebTV.

■ If you have access to the Internet, you can click this option to get free local TV listings.

2 Click Next to continue.

TIPS

There is no WebTV ( ) icon on my taskbar. What is wrong?

The WebTV for Windows component may not be installed on your computer. To install Windows components, see page 610.

Should I get the TV listings?

You need to have WebTV find the channels offered by your local cable provider before you can watch television programs. When you click the GUIDE Plus+ option, Windows connects you to a Web site to get the TV listings. You will be asked to enter your Zip code and select your cable provider or broadcast region. Follow the instructions on your screen to get the TV listings.

Will I be able to watch all the programs offered by my cable provider?

You should be able to watch all the programs offered by your cable provider, except for programs that require an external converter. Programs that require an external converter include pay-per-view programs.

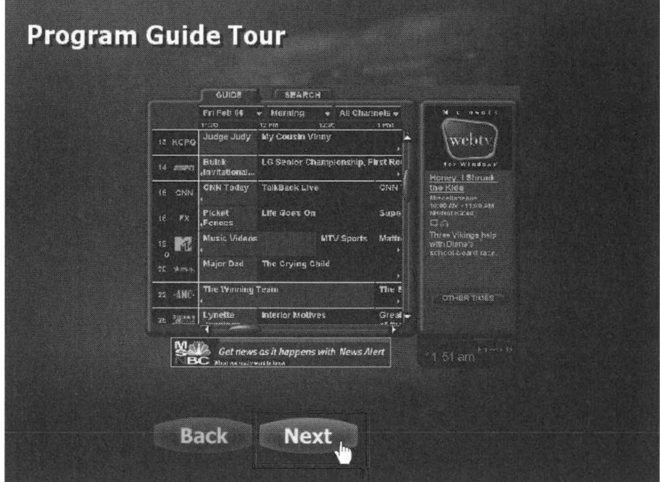
Program Guide Tour
Back
Next

■ A screen appears, providing a tour of the Program Guide.

3 Click Next to continue.

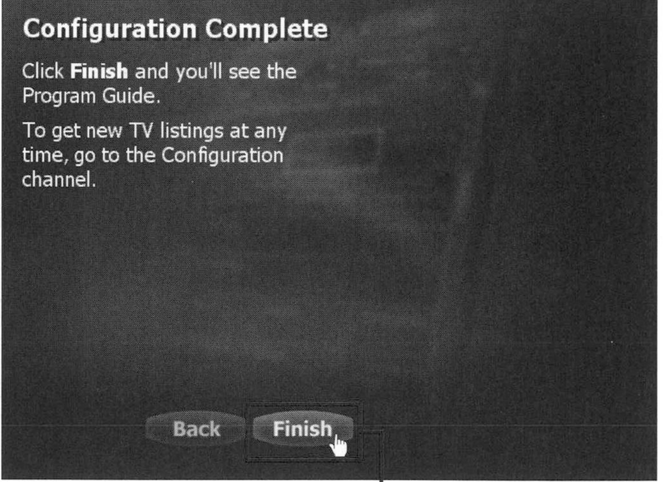
Configuration Complete
Click **Finish** and you'll see the Program Guide.
To get new TV listings at any time, go to the Configuration channel.
Back
Finish

■ A message appears, indicating that the configuration is complete.

4 Click Finish to display the Program Guide.

USING WEBTV

Using the Program Guide

You can use the Program Guide to view information about the television programs available on the channels offered by your cable provider.

The Program Guide displays the channels offered by your cable provider and the names of the programs available on each channel. Programs that are currently playing appear in a different color than programs that will play at another time.

You can select a channel to see a preview of the program that is currently playing on the channel. The Program Guide displays a description of the program. You may be able to view parental rating information or a critic rating for the program. Symbols may also appear, providing you with additional information about the program. The symbol indicates the program is a rerun. When the symbol is displayed, closed captioning is available. When the symbol is displayed, stereo sound is available. The symbol indicates enhancements are available. Enhancements can include background facts about a program or the ability to chat with other viewers.

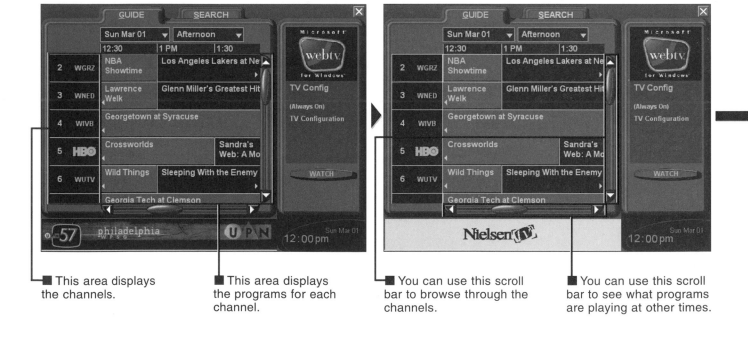

■ This area displays the channels.

■ This area displays the programs for each channel.

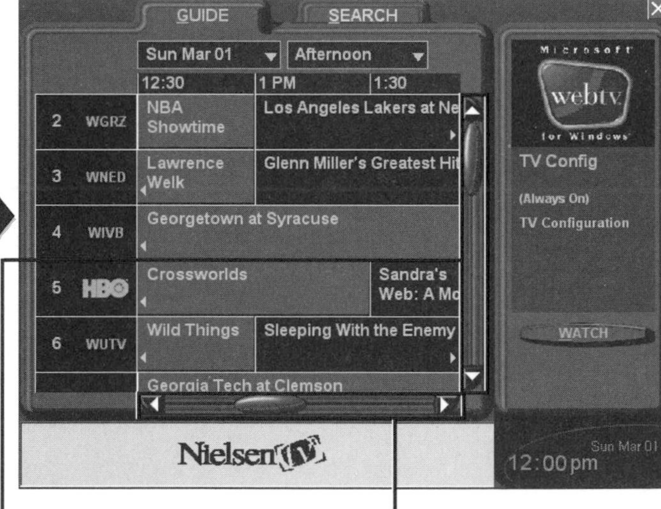

■ You can use this scroll bar to browse through the channels.

■ You can use this scroll bar to see what programs are playing at other times.

TIPS

Why doesn't my Program Guide display any program information?

If you did not get the TV listings when you first started WebTV, the Program Guide will not display any program information. To get the TV listings, double-click the channel named TV C. This is your TV Configuration channel. Click the GUIDE Plus+ option to connect to a Web site to get the TV listings. Follow the instructions on your screen. You can also use this procedure to update the TV listings at any time.

Can I have the Program Guide display only the channels I want to watch?

Yes. Press the F10 key and then click the Settings button. Each channel that displays a check mark (✔) will appear in the Program Guide. You can click the check box beside a channel to add or remove a check mark.

Can I have WebTV display closed captioning?

Yes. Press the F10 key and then click the Settings button. Click the Show closed captioning option (☐ changes to ☑).

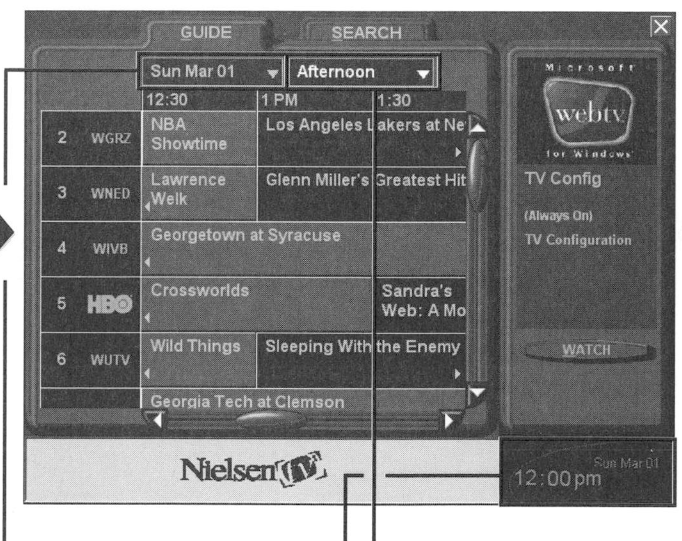

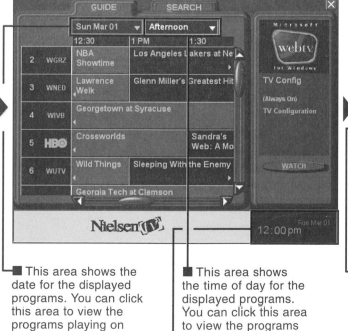

■ This area shows the date for the displayed programs. You can click this area to view the programs playing on another day.

■ This area shows the time of day for the displayed programs. You can click this area to view the programs playing at another time.

■ This area displays the current time and date.

1 To see what is currently playing on a channel, click the channel.

■ This area displays what is playing on the channel and a description of the program.

USING WEBTV

Watch Programs

Once you find a program you want to watch, you can increase your viewing area by using the entire screen to display the program.

If you are using multiple monitors, you will only be able to display the program on the primary monitor. For information on using multiple monitors, see page 244.

When you are watching a program, WebTV allows you to display the TV banner at the top of your screen. The TV banner displays the number of the channel you are viewing and a brief description of the program you are watching. You can use the TV banner to change channels and close WebTV. The TV banner also contains a toolbar that allows you to quickly display the Program Guide, change settings and get help using WebTV. You can add your favorite channels to the toolbar for quick access.

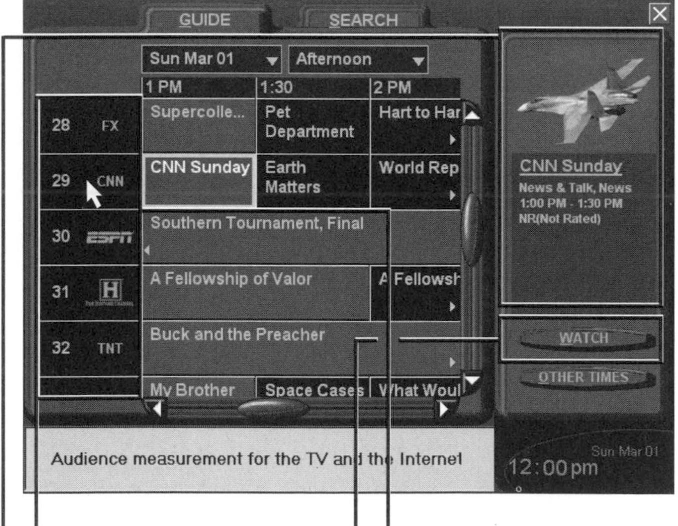

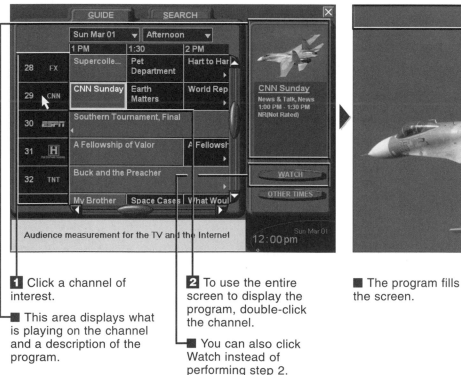

1 Click a channel of interest.

■ This area displays what is playing on the channel and a description of the program.

2 To use the entire screen to display the program, double-click the channel.

■ You can also click Watch instead of performing step 2.

■ The program fills the screen.

3 To view the TV banner, move the mouse over the top of the screen or press the F10 key.

■ The TV banner appears.

TIPS

Can I watch a program in a window?

When you are watching a program using your entire screen, you can press the F6 key to display the program in a window. This allows you to perform other tasks on your computer while you watch the program.

How do I quickly change channels using my keyboard?

You can type the number of the channel you want to view and then press the Enter key.

Can I increase or decrease the volume using my keyboard?

To increase the volume, press the Windows logo ( )+Ctrl+V keys. To decrease the volume, press the Windows logo ( )+Shift+V keys. To mute the sound, press the Windows logo ( )+V keys.

How do I add my favorite channels to the TV banner toolbar?

Display the channel you want to add to the toolbar. Display the TV banner and then click the Add button. You can click a button you have added to the TV banner toolbar to quickly view a channel.

■ This area displays the channel number and a description of the current program.

■ You can click the up ( ) or down ( ) arrow to move through the channels.

Note: You can also press the Page Up and Page Down keys to move through the channels.

4 To return to the Program Guide, click Guide.

■ To remove the TV banner, press the F10 key.

USING WEBTV

Search for Programs

You can use the Program Guide to search for programs of interest. Browsing through the Program Guide to find a specific program can be time consuming. The SEARCH tab allows you to quickly locate the programs you want to watch.

You can search for a program by category. The categories offered in the Program Guide include Action, Comedy and Drama.

You can also find a program by searching for the name of the program or the name of the station the program is broadcast on. If you want to find a program starring a certain actor or actress, you can search for the name of the actor or actress.

The Program Guide displays the names of the programs it finds and information such as which channel the program is on and when the program will play.

You can choose to narrow your search to display only programs that play on a certain day. You can also sort the programs the Program Guide finds by the time the program will play or the name of the program.

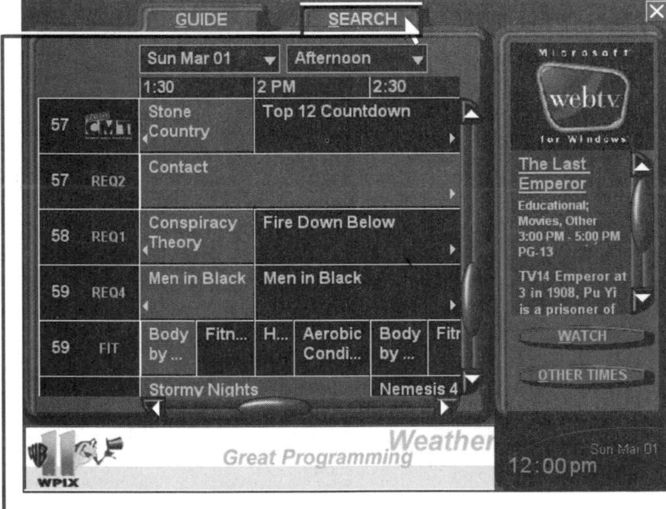

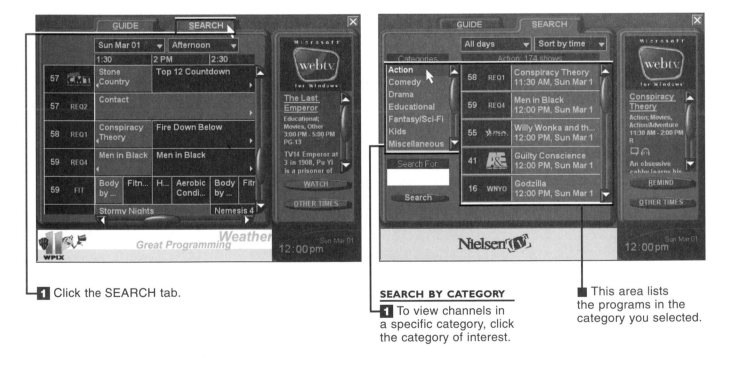

1 Click the SEARCH tab.

SEARCH BY CATEGORY

1 To view channels in a specific category, click the category of interest.

■ This area lists the programs in the category you selected.

TIPS

Do I need to know the exact name of a program, actor or actress?

No. You can type as much of the name as you know and WebTV will attempt to find a match. For example, you can type **Trav** to find movies starring the actor John Travolta.

Can I search for programs based on a specific critic rating?

Yes. Press the Spacebar and then type the number of stars you want to search for. Put square brackets [ ] around each star and then type a closing parenthesis. For example, press the Spacebar and then type [*][*][*][*][*]) to find a program with a five-star rating.

How can I speed up a search?

If you know the exact name of a program, type an equal sign (=) before the name.

How can I find the other times a program will play?

If you click the SEARCH tab while you are previewing a program in the Program Guide, the SEARCH tab will display the other times the program will play. You can also select a program in the Program Guide and then click the Other Times button.

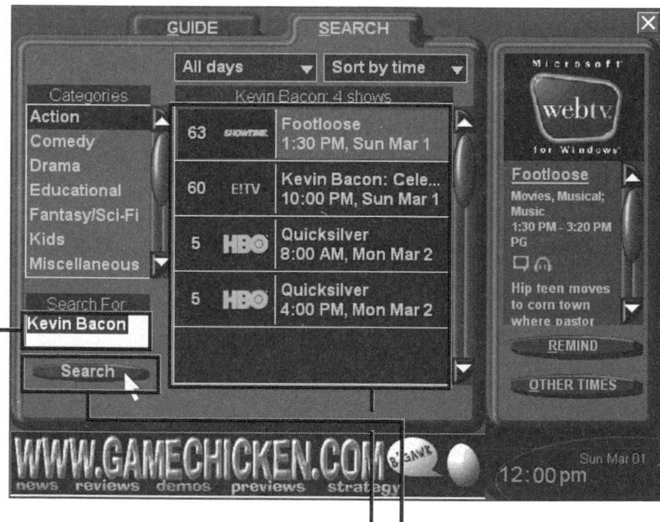

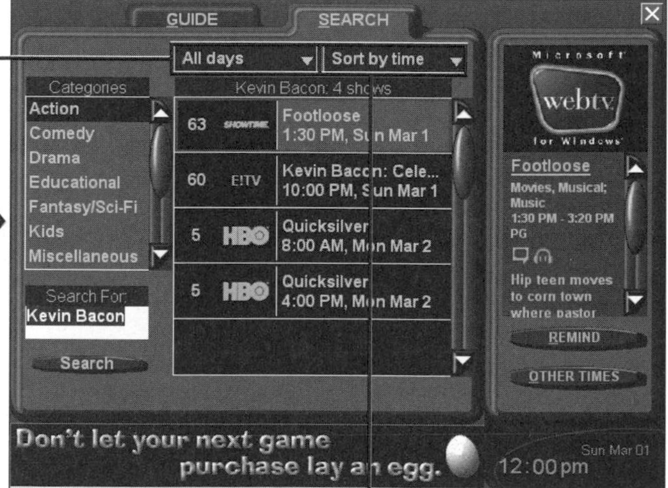

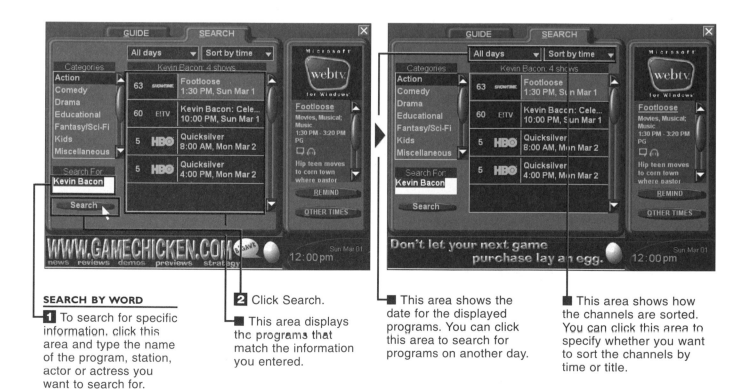

SEARCH BY WORD

1 To search for specific information, click this area and type the name of the program, station, actor or actress you want to search for.

2 Click Search.

■ This area displays the programs that match the information you entered.

■ This area shows the date for the displayed programs. You can click this area to search for programs on another day.

■ This area shows how the channels are sorted. You can click this area to specify whether you want to sort the channels by time or title.

SECTION IV

14) DISK MANAGEMENT

15) COMPRESS A DRIVE

16) BACK UP INFORMATION

WORK WITH DISKS

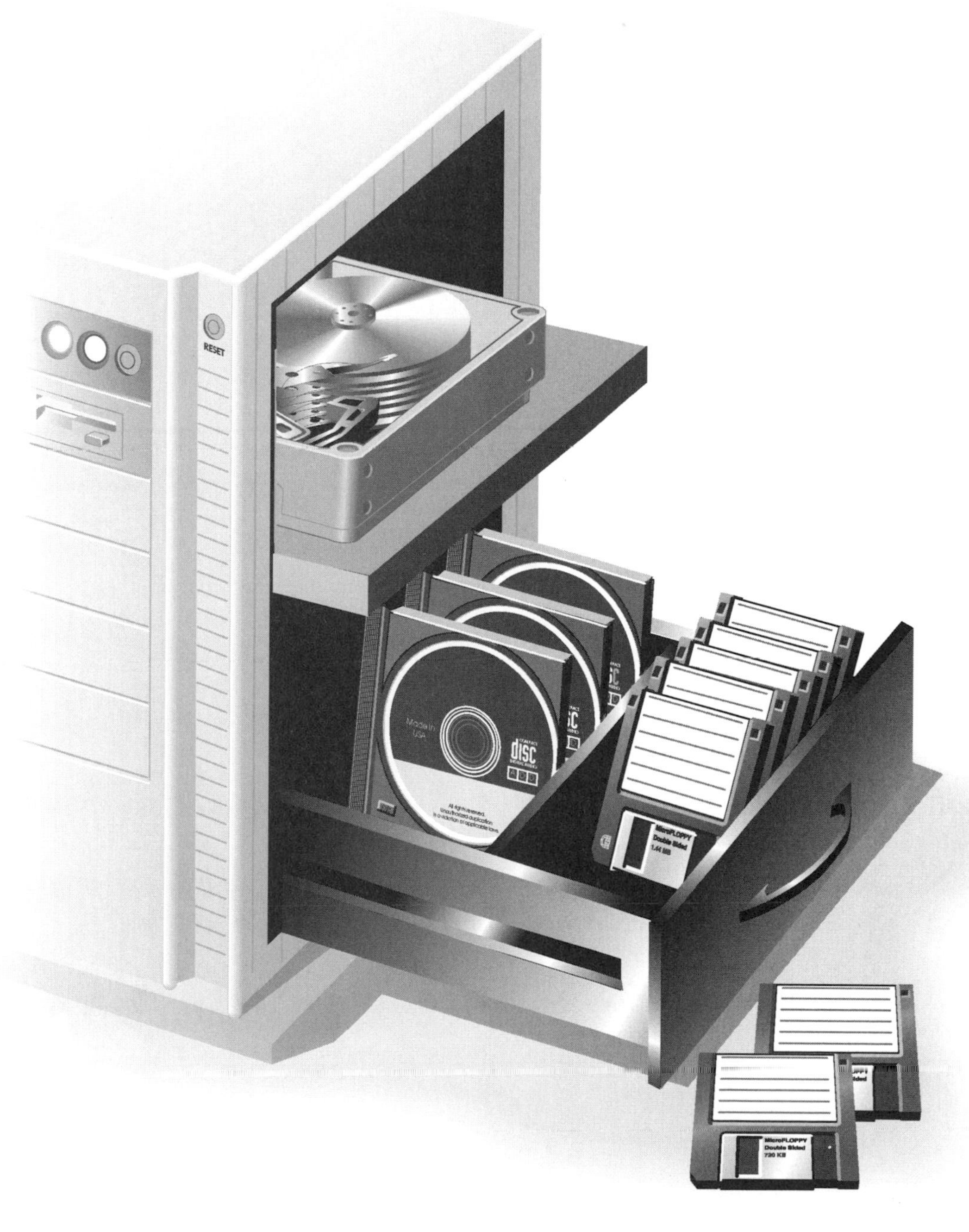

FORMAT FLOPPY DISKS

A floppy disk must be formatted before you can use it to store information.

When you purchase a new box of blank disks, you may need to format the disks so they can be used to store files. You can also buy formatted disks.

If the disk you want to format has already been used, make sure the disk does not contain information you want to keep.

Formatting will remove all the information on a disk.

Disks are available in two capacities. A double-density disk can hold 720 KB of information. A high-density disk can hold twice that amount, or 1.44 MB.

The Quick (erase) format type removes all files but does not check the disk for damaged areas. This type of format is useful for a disk that was previously formatted. You should only use this type of format if you are sure the disk is not damaged.

The Full format type removes all files and checks the disk for damaged areas. If Windows finds bad areas on the disk, the areas are marked so they will not be used to store information.

Windows allows you to label the disk so you can easily identify it later.

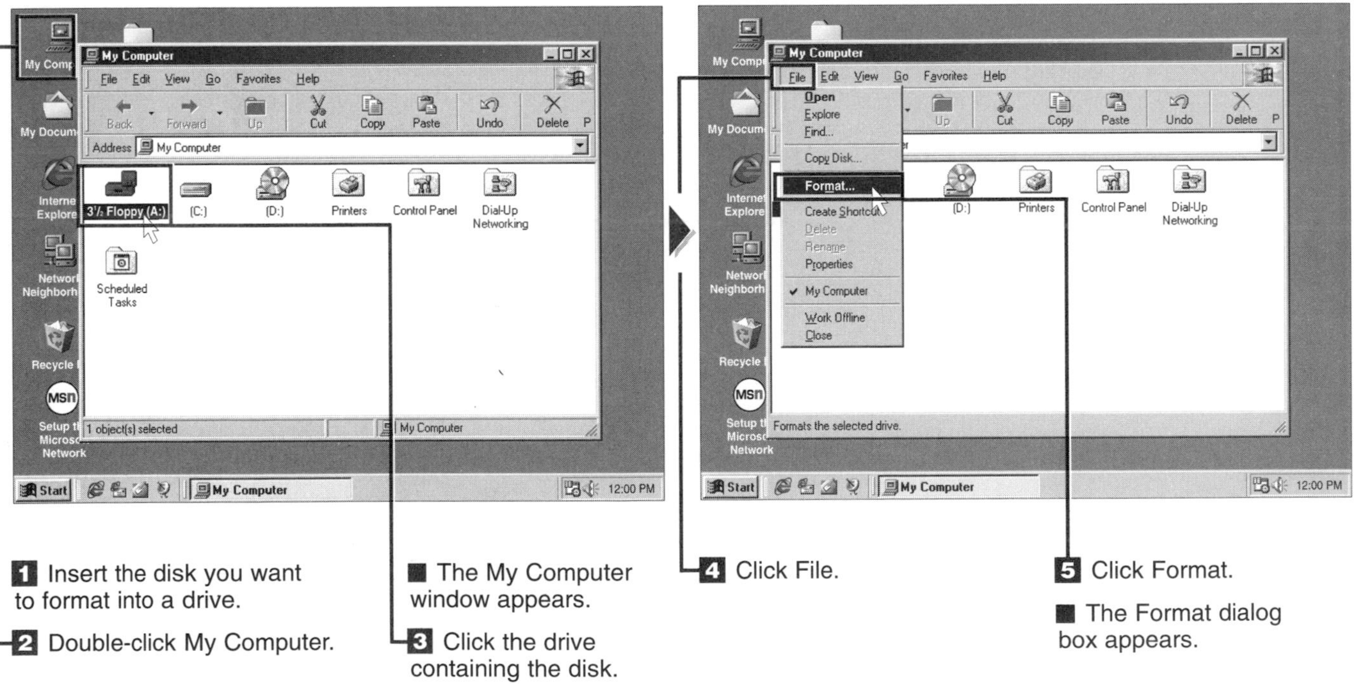

1 Insert the disk you want to format into a drive.

2 Double-click My Computer.

■ The My Computer window appears.

3 Click the drive containing the disk.

4 Click File.

5 Click Format.

■ The Format dialog box appears.

TIPS

How can I tell if a disk is formatted?

Windows will tell you if a disk is not formatted when you try to view the contents of the disk. You cannot tell if a disk is formatted just by looking at it.

A friend gave me a disk with documents on it, but Windows tells me the disk is not formatted. What is wrong with the disk?

Either the disk has been formatted using a different file system, like the system used on Macintosh computers, or the disk has been damaged.

How can I protect my disks from damage?

You can help protect your disks by keeping them away from moisture, heat and magnets.

When should I use the Copy system files only format type?

You can use this type of format if you want to add system files to a disk. This is useful if you want to be able to use the disk to start your computer. This type of format does not format the disk and does not erase any existing files on the disk.

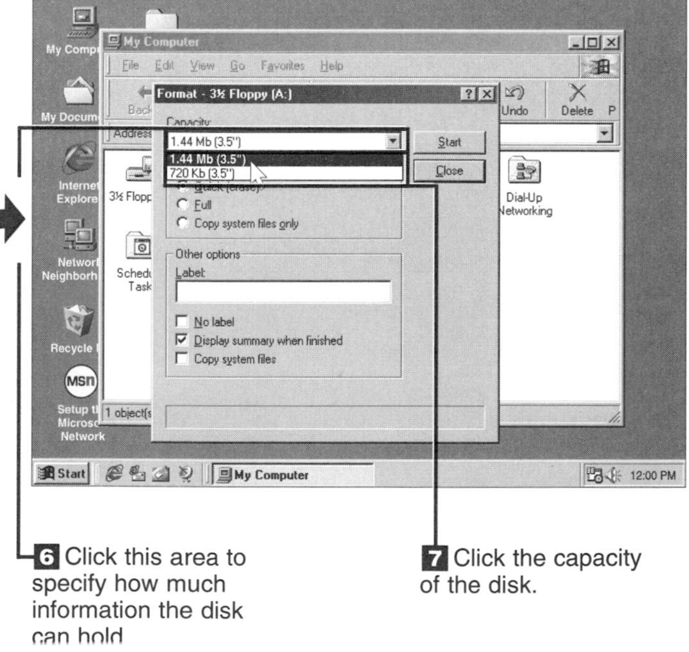

6 Click this area to specify how much information the disk can hold.

7 Click the capacity of the disk.

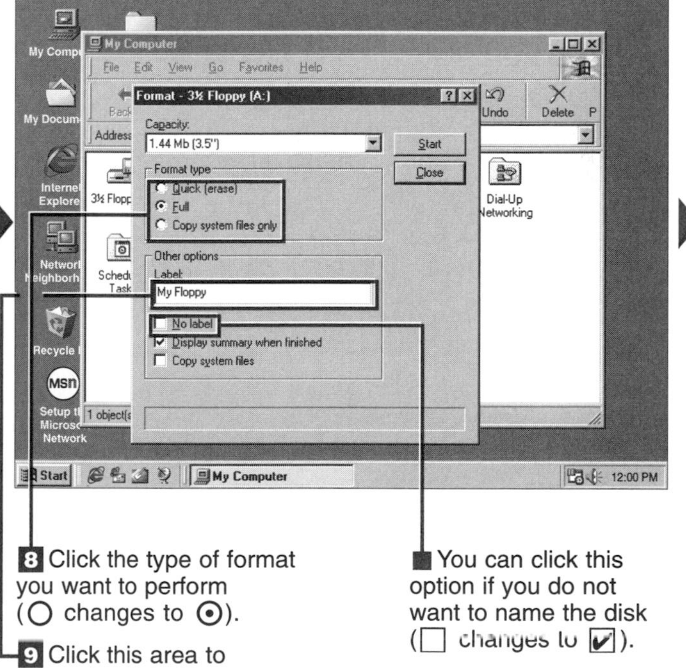

8 Click the type of format you want to perform (○ changes to ⊙).

9 Click this area to name the disk. Then type a name for the disk.

■ You can click this option if you do not want to name the disk (☐ changes to ☑).

CONTINUED

FORMAT FLOPPY DISKS
CONTINUED

You can have Windows display summary information about the disk when the format is complete. The Format Results dialog box contains information about the disk, such as the total amount of disk space, the amount of space used by the system files, the amount of space in bad sectors and the total available space on the disk.

You can have Windows copy system files to the disk you are formatting. A disk with system files can be used to start a computer.

You should not copy the system files to every disk you format. System files take up space on a disk. System files are also often the target of viruses, which can put other files or your computer at risk.

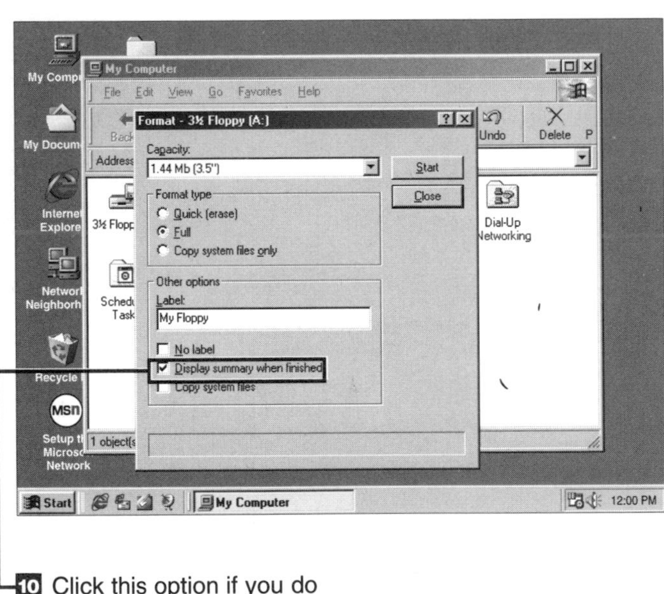

10 Click this option if you do not want to display summary information about the disk when the format is complete (☑ changes to ☐).

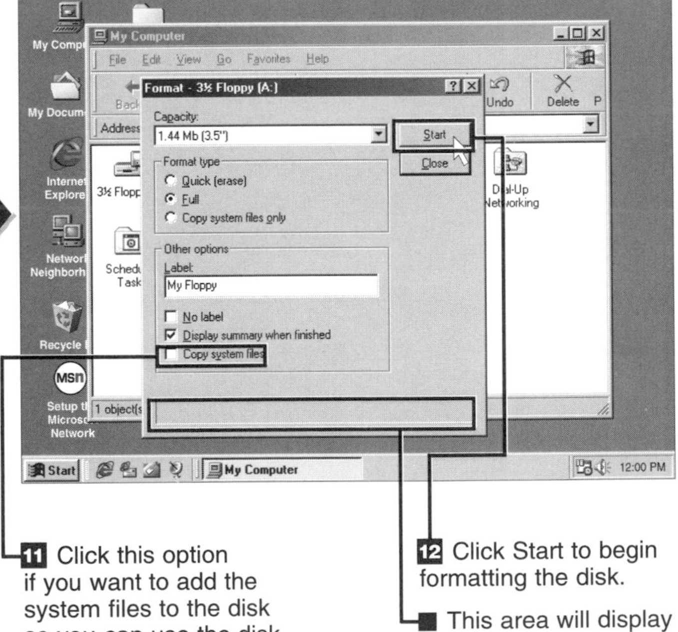

11 Click this option if you want to add the system files to the disk so you can use the disk to start the computer (☐ changes to ☑).

12 Click Start to begin formatting the disk.

■ This area will display the progress of the format.

TIPS

Instead of formatting the disk, I get an error message. What is wrong?

If you get an error message when you try to format a disk, you should check the capacity setting you selected for the disk. A damaged disk may also cause an error message to appear.

Can I format disks from a Windows Explorer window?

You can format a disk from a Windows Explorer window by right-clicking the drive containing the disk and then selecting Format.

What should I do if a disk has bad sectors?

If you have one or two damaged sectors, you can still use the disk to store information. If a new disk has many damaged sectors, you should return the disk to the manufacturer for a replacement. If the disk has many damaged sectors and it is an old disk, throw out the disk.

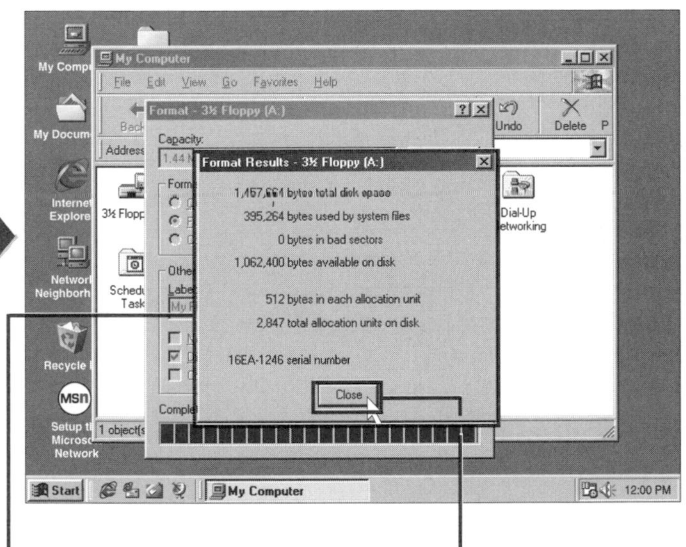

■ The Format Results dialog box appears when the format is complete. The dialog box displays information about the formatted disk.

Note: The dialog box does not appear if you turned off the Display summary option in step 10.

13 Click Close to close the dialog box.

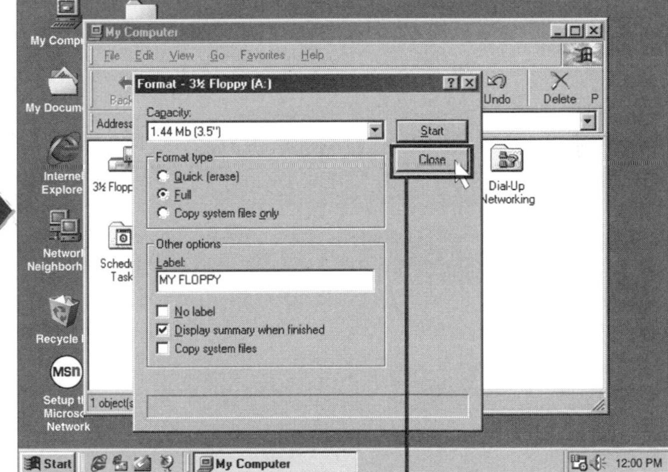

■ To format another disk, insert the disk and then repeat steps 6 to 12 starting on page 301.

14 Click Close to close the Format dialog box.

COPY FLOPPY DISKS

Windows makes it easy to copy a floppy disk. Copying a floppy disk is useful when you want to give a copy of a disk to a friend or colleague. You may also want to copy a floppy disk to make a backup copy of important information.

You can copy floppy disks even if your computer has only one floppy drive. Windows makes a temporary copy of the information from the original disk. When you insert the second disk, Windows copies the information to the disk.

Make sure the floppy disk receiving the copy does not contain information you want to keep. Copying will remove all the old information from the disk.

The original disk and the disk that will receive the copy must be able to store the same amount of information. A double-density disk has one hole and can store 720 KB of information. A high-density disk has two holes and can store 1.44 MB of information. You can copy information from a double-density disk to a high-density disk, but Windows will reformat the second disk as a double-density disk.

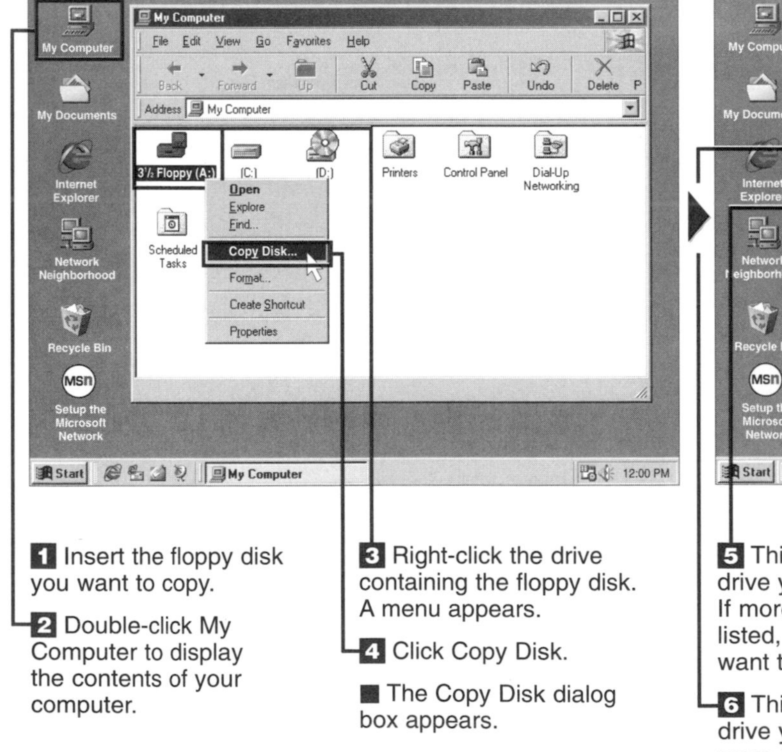

1 Insert the floppy disk you want to copy.

2 Double-click My Computer to display the contents of your computer.

3 Right-click the drive containing the floppy disk. A menu appears.

4 Click Copy Disk.

■ The Copy Disk dialog box appears.

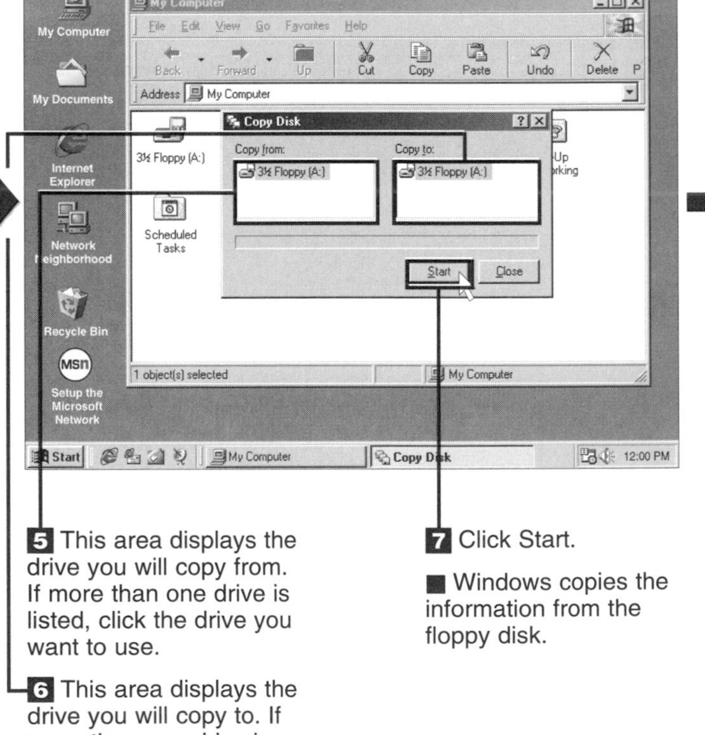

5 This area displays the drive you will copy from. If more than one drive is listed, click the drive you want to use.

6 This area displays the drive you will copy to. If more than one drive is listed, click the drive you want to use.

7 Click Start.

■ Windows copies the information from the floppy disk.

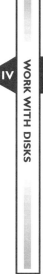

TIPS

Do I need to format the disk I want to receive the copy?

If the disk is unformatted, Windows will format the disk as part of the copy process.

Why did Windows display a message saying the floppy disk could not be formatted?

If the disk is inserted properly, check that the write-protect tab on the disk is closed. An error message also appears if you are copying the contents of a high-density disk onto a double-density disk.

I made a copy from a double-density disk to a high-density disk, but the file names are not displayed correctly in the window. What should I do?

Remove the disk from the drive and then reinsert it. Press the F5 key to refresh the window.

How can I make several copies of a floppy disk without having to reinsert the disk each time?

It may be faster to copy the contents of the disk to a folder on the desktop. Then copy the information onto the disks from the desktop.

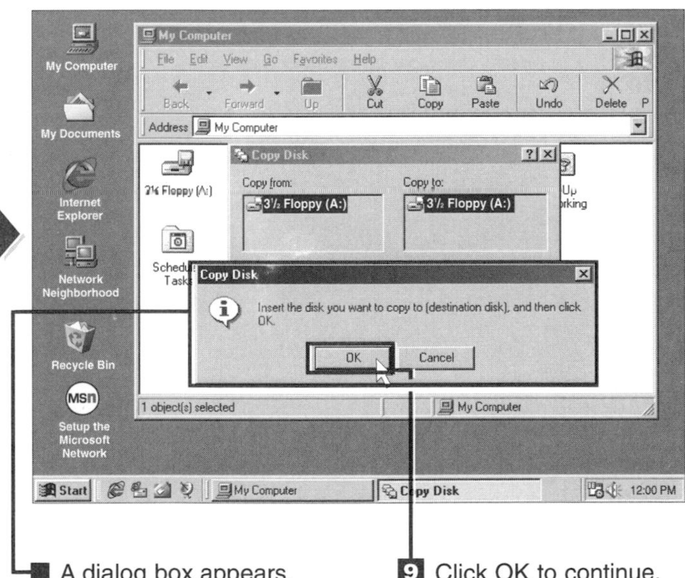

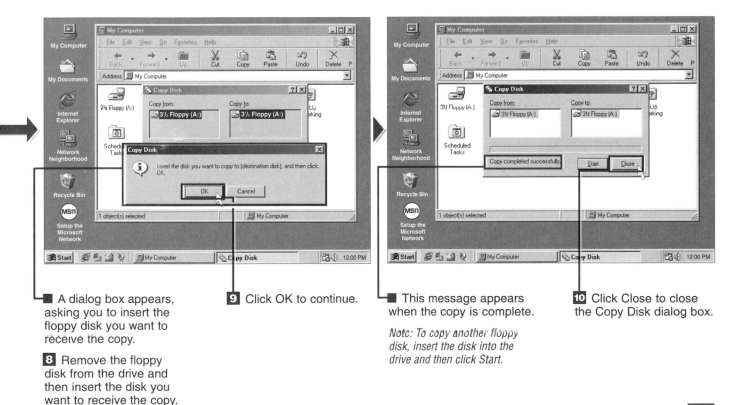

■ A dialog box appears, asking you to insert the floppy disk you want to receive the copy.

8 Remove the floppy disk from the drive and then insert the disk you want to receive the copy.

9 Click OK to continue.

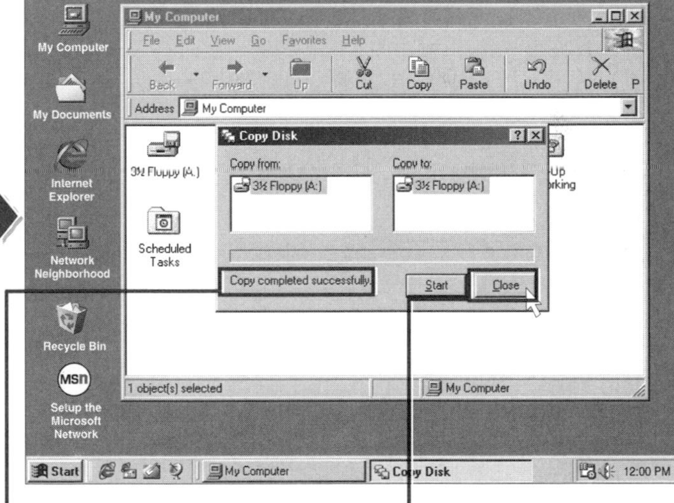

■ This message appears when the copy is complete.

Note: To copy another floppy disk, insert the disk into the drive and then click Start.

10 Click Close to close the Copy Disk dialog box.

DISPLAY VERSION AND REGISTRATION NUMBER

You can find out information about Windows and your computer by displaying the System Properties dialog box.

The System Properties dialog box contains a number that indicates the version of Windows you are using. Over time, Microsoft may make changes and additions to Windows 98. The version number may change to reflect these changes.

You can also find registration information, such as the user name that was entered when Windows 98 was installed on your computer. The last line of the registration area contains the registration number for your copy of Windows. You should record the registration number for future reference in case you must re-install Windows on your computer. You will not be able to re-install Windows without this number.

The System Properties dialog box also displays information about your computer's processor and the amount of memory (RAM) installed in your computer.

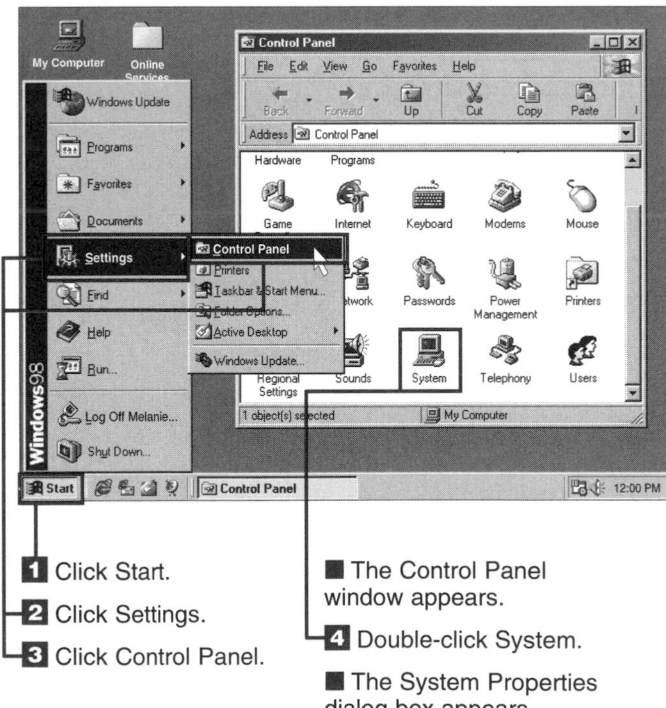

1 Click Start.

2 Click Settings.

3 Click Control Panel.

■ The Control Panel window appears.

4 Double-click System.

■ The System Properties dialog box appears.

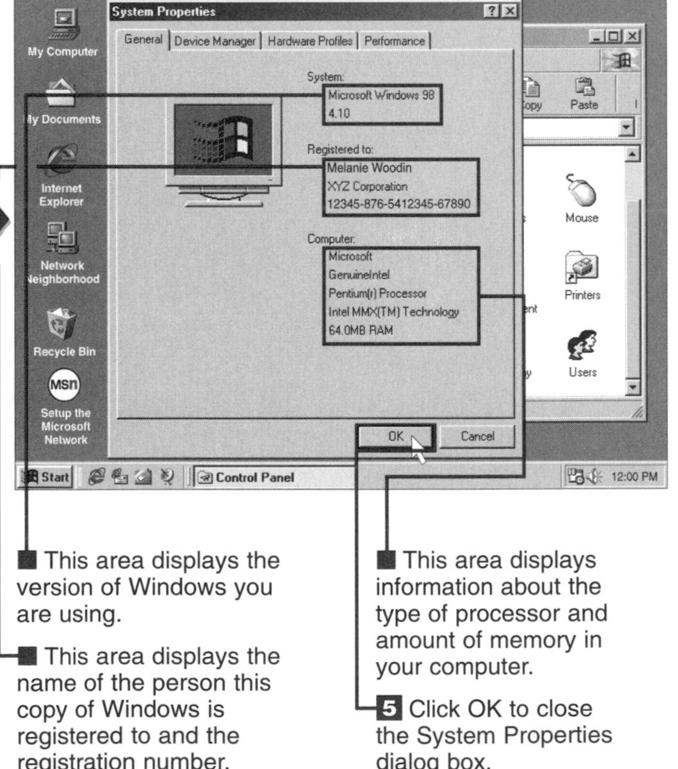

■ This area displays the version of Windows you are using.

■ This area displays the name of the person this copy of Windows is registered to and the registration number.

■ This area displays information about the type of processor and amount of memory in your computer.

5 Click OK to close the System Properties dialog box.

CHECK PERFORMANCE STATUS

You can check the performance of your computer by viewing the six items displayed on the Performance tab in the System Properties dialog box.

The first item, Memory, displays the amount of memory (RAM) in your computer. This amount will not change unless you add or remove memory from your computer. More memory means better performance.

The second item, System Resources, displays a percentage that will change while you are working. When there is less than 30% free, you should close some programs or restart Windows to avoid potential problems.

The third and fourth items, File System and Virtual Memory, should both be set at 32-bit for the best performance. There are a few isolated cases where this might not be true.

The fifth item, Disk Compression, indicates if you have any disk compression software installed on your computer. This may affect system performance, depending on processor speed, disk speed and the amount of memory installed.

PC Cards is the last item and applies to portable computers. This area indicates the type of PC Cards installed on your computer.

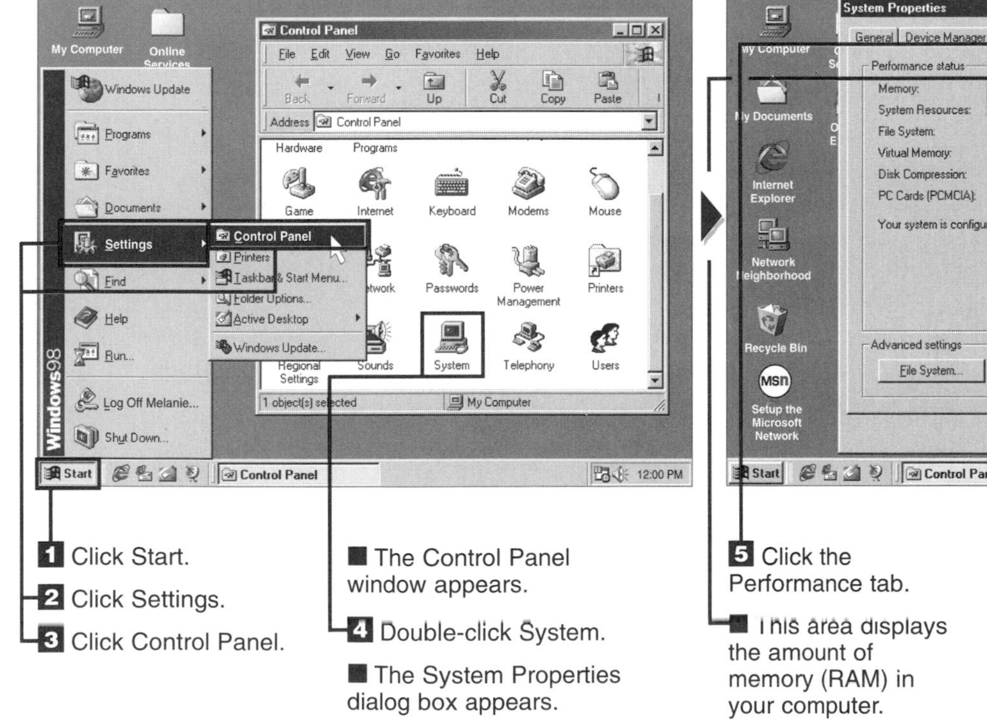

1 Click Start.

2 Click Settings.

3 Click Control Panel.

■ The Control Panel window appears.

4 Double-click System.

■ The System Properties dialog box appears.

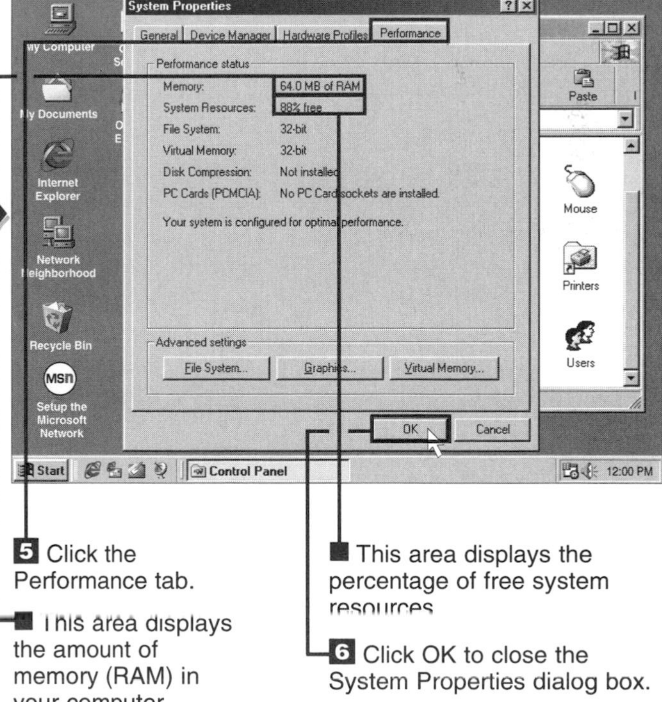

5 Click the Performance tab.

■ This area displays the amount of memory (RAM) in your computer.

■ This area displays the percentage of free system resources.

6 Click OK to close the System Properties dialog box.

RENAME A DISK

You can rename your hard disk, removable disk or floppy disks. Renaming a disk allows you to more easily identify the disk. You cannot rename a CD-ROM disc or network drive.

You can use up to 11 letters or numbers to rename a disk.

The name can contain spaces, but cannot contain the \ / : * ? " < > or | characters.

If you are renaming a floppy disk, you can label the disk by date, project name or whatever other information will help you to identify it quickly.

The new name of the floppy disk will only appear in the Properties dialog box.

The Properties dialog box displays all names in capital letters.

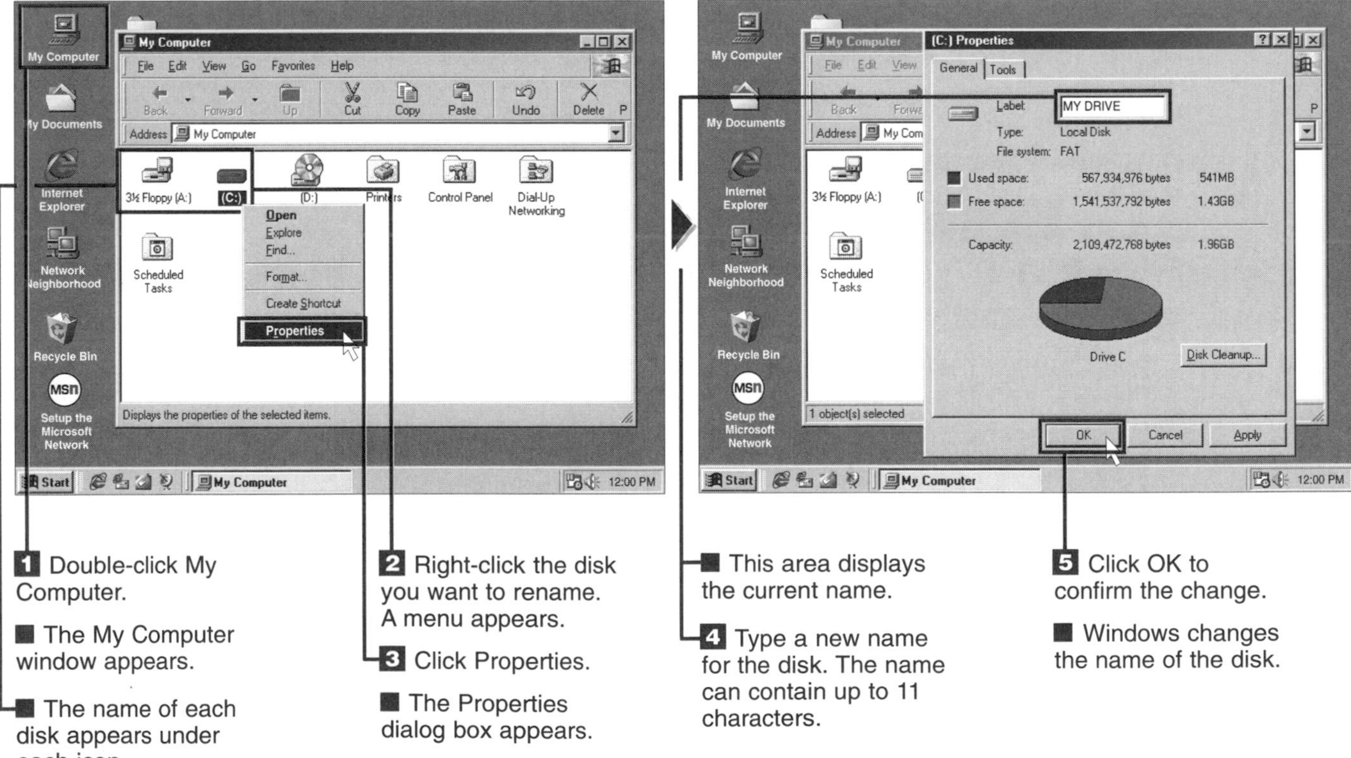

1 Double-click My Computer.

■ The My Computer window appears.

■ The name of each disk appears under each icon.

2 Right-click the disk you want to rename. A menu appears.

3 Click Properties.

■ The Properties dialog box appears.

■ This area displays the current name.

4 Type a new name for the disk. The name can contain up to 11 characters.

5 Click OK to confirm the change.

■ Windows changes the name of the disk.

VIEW AMOUNT OF DISK SPACE

You can view the amount of used and free space on any disk, including hard disks, floppy disks, removable disks and CD-ROM discs.

The amount of space on a disk is measured in bytes, megabytes (MB) and gigabytes (GB). A byte equals one character. One MB equals approximately one million characters. A GB equals approximately one billion characters.

You should check the amount of available disk space on your computer at least once a month. You should also check the amount of available disk space before you install a new program.

You should have at least 10% of your hard disk free. For example, if you have a 2 GB hard disk, make sure you have at least 0.2 GB free. This will help improve virtual memory performance as well as decrease fragmentation of files.

If you want to increase the amount of free space on your hard disk, you have many choices. You can empty the Recycle Bin to free up disk space. You can also save older files you no longer use onto a floppy disk and delete the files from your hard disk. You can also delete programs you no longer use. For information, see page 336.

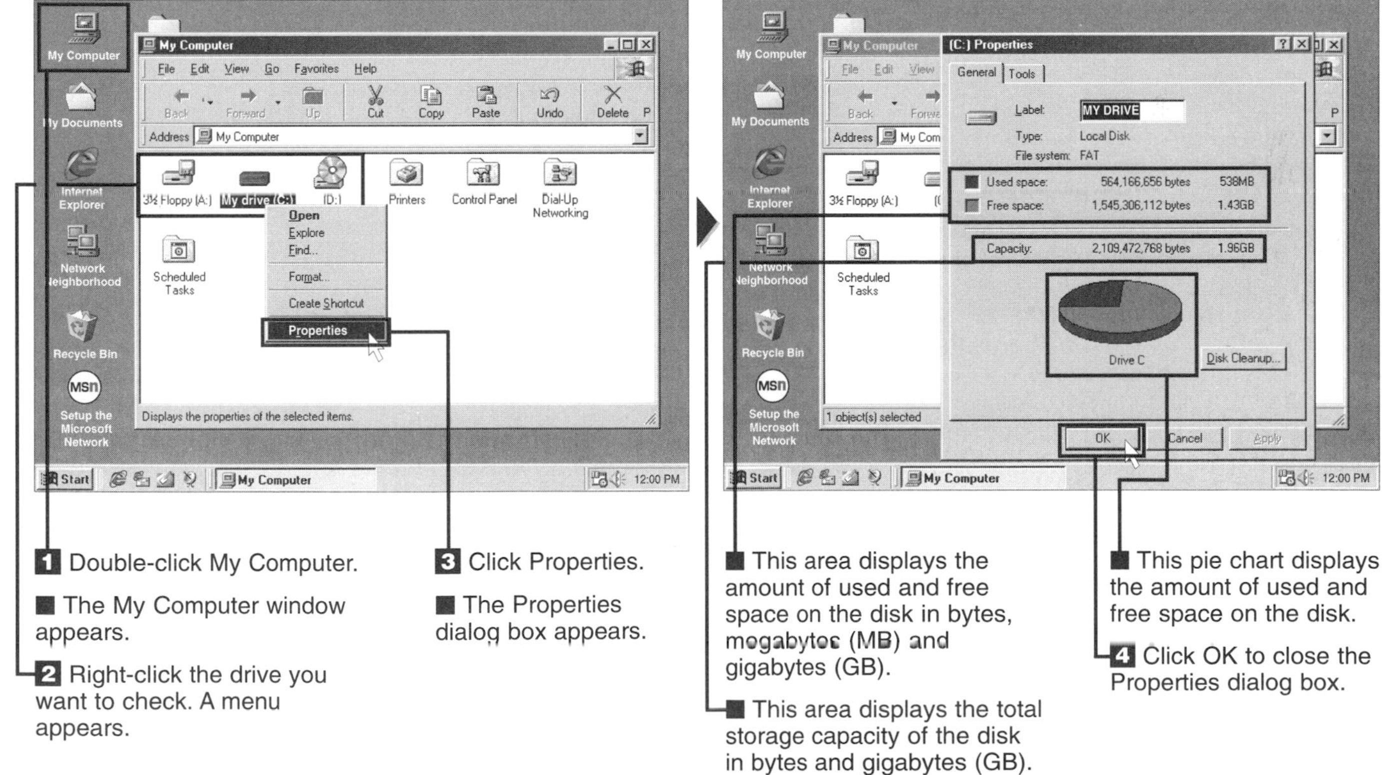

1 Double-click My Computer.

■ The My Computer window appears.

2 Right-click the drive you want to check. A menu appears.

3 Click Properties.

■ The Properties dialog box appears.

■ This area displays the amount of used and free space on the disk in bytes, megabytes (MB) and gigabytes (GB).

■ This area displays the total storage capacity of the disk in bytes and gigabytes (GB).

■ This pie chart displays the amount of used and free space on the disk.

4 Click OK to close the Properties dialog box.

USE DISK CLEANUP TO REMOVE UNNEEDED FILES

You can use Disk Cleanup to find and remove files that are no longer needed. This can increase the amount of available space on your hard disk.

Disk Cleanup can find four types of files. You can select which of the four types of files you want to remove from your disk.

Temporary Internet files are Web pages and images Windows stores on your hard disk while you are browsing the Web. Using temporary Internet files saves Windows from having to transfer the same pages and images to your computer each time you view them.

Downloaded program files are small programs that some Web pages require to display properly or to perform certain functions. These programs are transferred to your hard disk when you visit the Web page.

The Recycle Bin contains files you have deleted. These files are permanently removed from your computer when you empty the Recycle Bin.

While working, some programs store temporary files on your hard disk. If these files are not removed when the program has finished using them, they can take up valuable storage space.

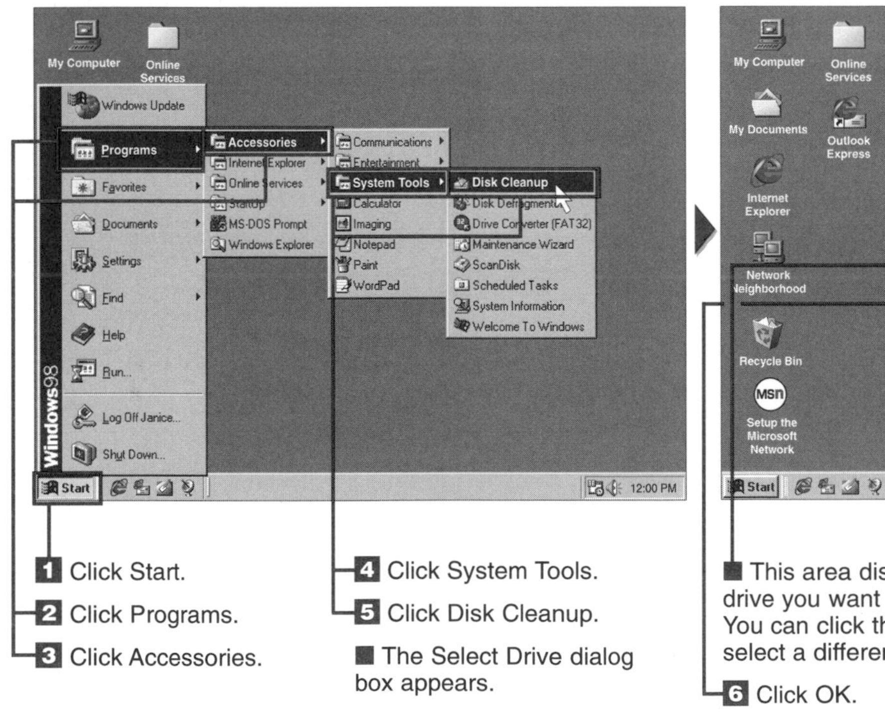

1 Click Start.

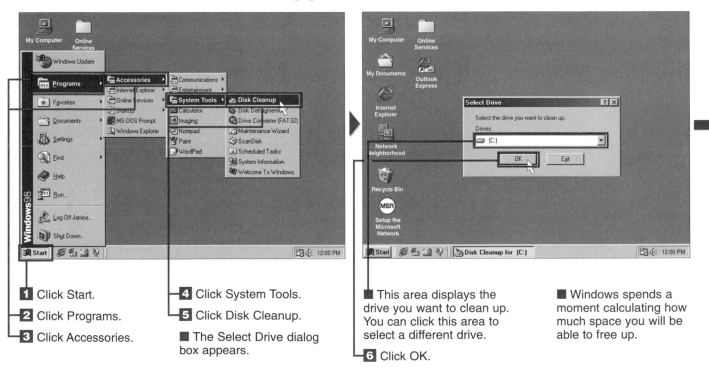

2 Click Programs.

3 Click Accessories.

4 Click System Tools.

5 Click Disk Cleanup.

■ The Select Drive dialog box appears.

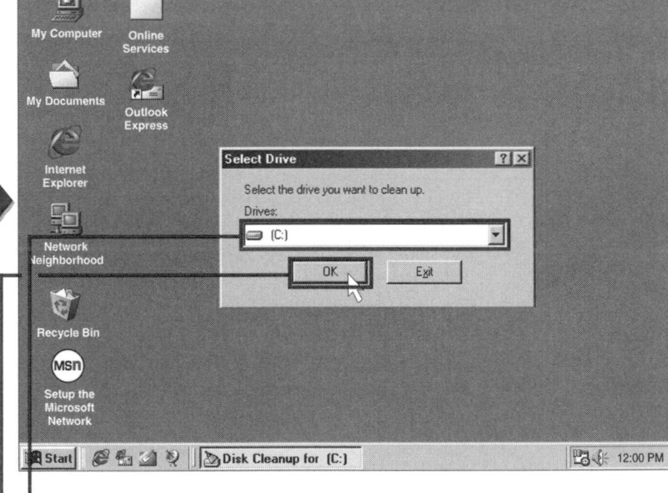

■ This area displays the drive you want to clean up. You can click this area to select a different drive.

6 Click OK.

■ Windows spends a moment calculating how much space you will be able to free up.

How can I see which files will be removed?

Select a file type and then click the View Files button. A window displays the files that will be removed. The View Files button is not available for temporary files.

Can I change how much disk space is used by temporary Internet files or the Recycle Bin?

To adjust the size of the temporary Internet files, right-click the Internet Explorer icon on your desktop and select Properties. On the General tab, in the Temporary Internet Files area, click the Settings button. You can adjust the slider to change the size of temporary Internet files. To set the maximum size of the Recycle Bin, see page 76.

Can Disk Cleanup help me create even more available disk space?

Yes. In the Disk Cleanup dialog box, click the More Options tab. This tab can help you remove Windows components, remove installed programs and convert the disk to the FAT32 file system.

Will Windows notify me when I need to increase the amount of free disk space?

Depending on the size of your disk, when the available space reaches between 25 and 60 MB Windows will prompt you to use Disk Cleanup.

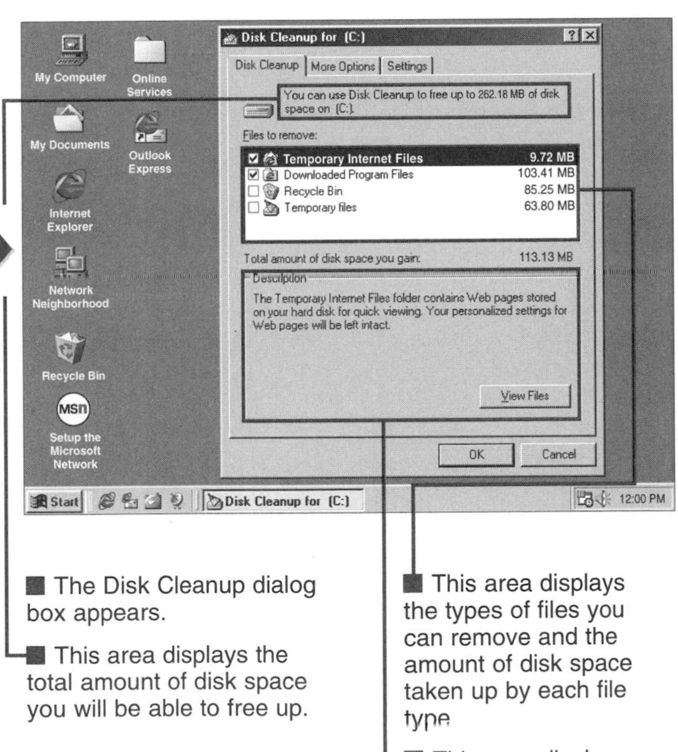

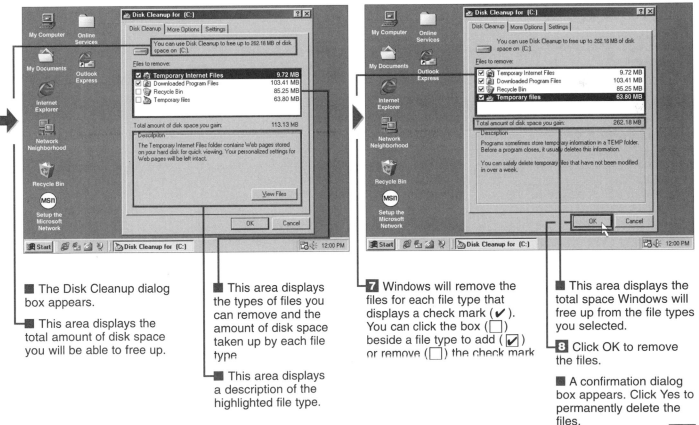

■ The Disk Cleanup dialog box appears.

■ This area displays the total amount of disk space you will be able to free up.

■ This area displays the types of files you can remove and the amount of disk space taken up by each file type.

■ This area displays a description of the highlighted file type.

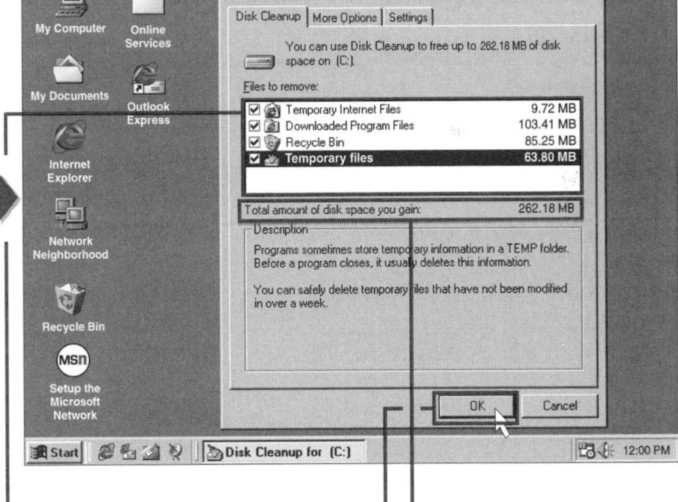

7 Windows will remove the files for each file type that displays a check mark (✔). You can click the box (☐) beside a file type to add (☑) or remove (☐) the check mark.

■ This area displays the total space Windows will free up from the file types you selected.

8 Click OK to remove the files.

■ A confirmation dialog box appears. Click Yes to permanently delete the files.

CHECK FOR DISK ERRORS

ScanDisk is a program included with Windows that detects and repairs disk errors on hard or floppy drives and removable hard drives. ScanDisk cannot check CD-ROM drives or network drives.

The standard test checks for errors in files and folders. The thorough test performs the same check as the standard test and also checks the disk surface for physically damaged areas that can no longer be used to store information.

You can have ScanDisk automatically fix the errors it finds.

When ScanDisk is finished checking a drive, a summary appears, displaying information about the drive. You can have ScanDisk display the summary only when errors are found.

You can save the summary for each check. You can store the summaries in a log to keep track of the errors that occur over time. You will find the log in a file named Scandisk.log.

ScanDisk checks for cross-linked files. Cross-linked files are two or more files stored in the same area of a disk. The data in cross-linked files is often correct for only one of the files. The Make copies setting provides the best chance of recovering information from cross-linked files.

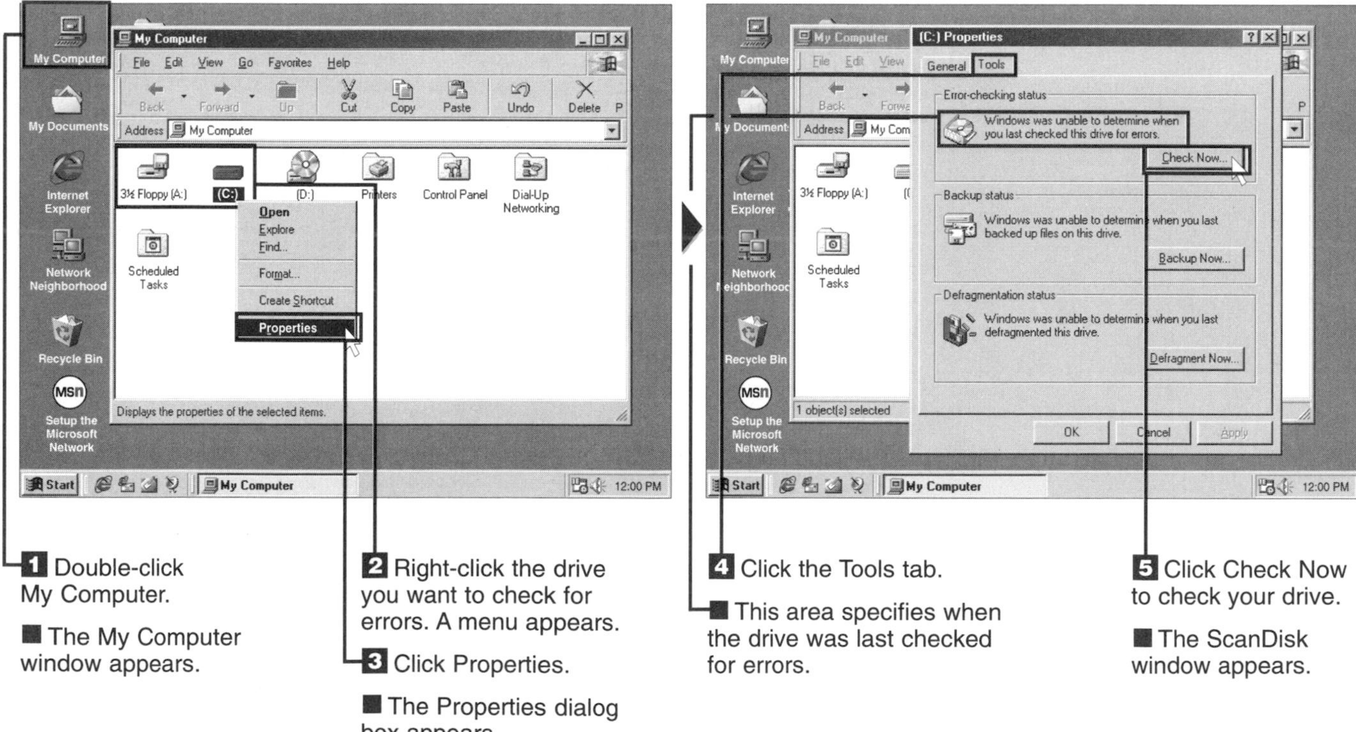

1 Double-click My Computer.

■ The My Computer window appears.

2 Right-click the drive you want to check for errors. A menu appears.

3 Click Properties.

■ The Properties dialog box appears.

4 Click the Tools tab.

■ This area specifies when the drive was last checked for errors.

5 Click Check Now to check your drive.

■ The ScanDisk window appears.

TIPS

How long does the thorough test take?

The thorough test can be time-consuming, especially on large disks. While the standard test takes about a minute, the thorough test may take about twenty minutes on a one gigabyte drive.

Can I speed up the thorough test?

You can click the Options button in the ScanDisk window to change the options for the thorough test to perform the test more quickly. You can specify which areas you want ScanDisk to check—the system and data areas, the system area only or the data area only. ScanDisk can check the system area very quickly.

Will ScanDisk ever run automatically?

If Windows was not shut down properly the last time you used it, Windows will automatically run the command prompt version of ScanDisk to check for errors in your files and folders.

How often should I use ScanDisk?

You should perform the thorough test once a month. If you experience problems opening or saving files, you should perform the test more often. You can perform the standard test as often as you like.

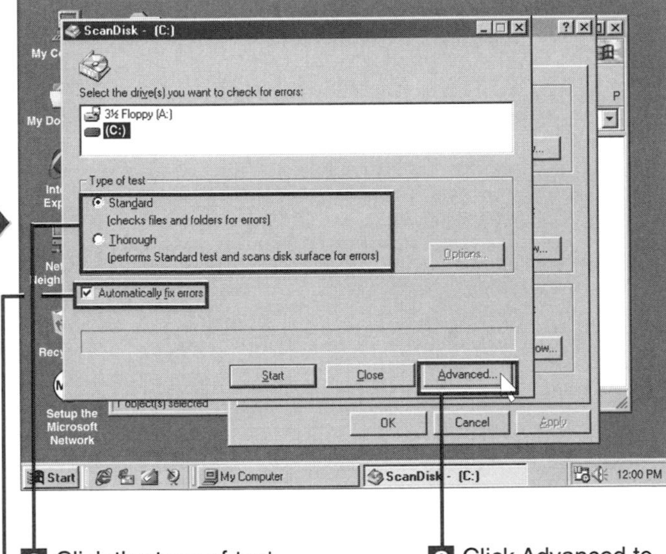

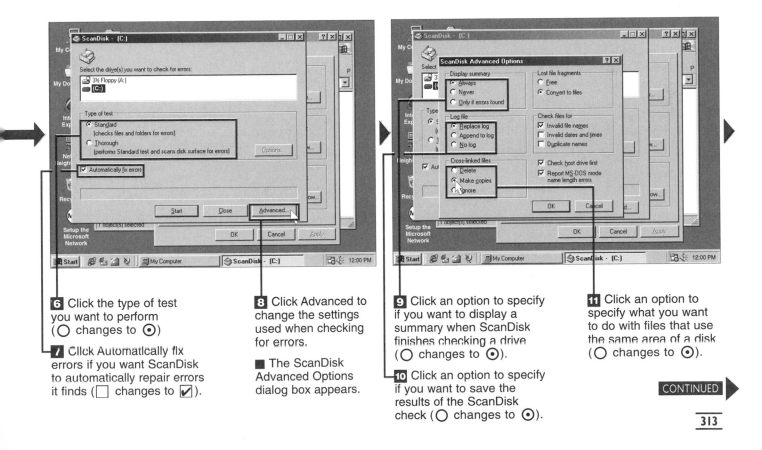

6 Click the type of test you want to perform (○ changes to ⦿)

7 Click Automatically fix errors if you want ScanDisk to automatically repair errors it finds (☐ changes to ☑).

8 Click Advanced to change the settings used when checking for errors.

■ The ScanDisk Advanced Options dialog box appears.

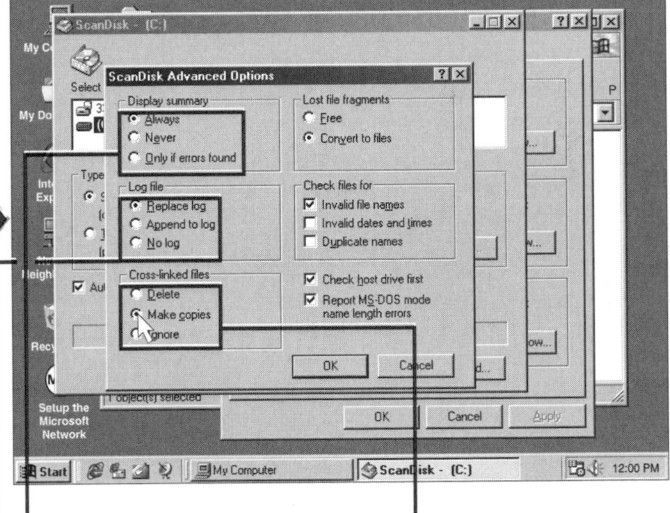

9 Click an option to specify if you want to display a summary when ScanDisk finishes checking a drive (○ changes to ⦿).

10 Click an option to specify if you want to save the results of the ScanDisk check (○ changes to ⦿).

11 Click an option to specify what you want to do with files that use the same area of a disk (○ changes to ⦿).

CONTINUED

CHECK FOR DISK ERRORS
CONTINUED

You can change the settings that ScanDisk uses when checking your files and folders for errors.

ScanDisk checks for lost file fragments. Lost fragments are pieces of data that are no longer associated with a file. The Convert to file setting saves fragments so you can view their contents before you delete them. The files are saved on the c: drive with names such as File0000.

You can check for files with invalid names. You may be unable to work with files with invalid names. You can also check for invalid dates and times. Files with invalid dates and times may not sort correctly.

When file names become corrupted, two files in the same folder may have the same name. You can have ScanDisk locate and fix duplicate file names.

If you compressed the information on your hard drive, you can enable the Check host drive first setting. This setting ensures that the hard drive storing your compressed files contains no errors before ScanDisk tries to detect errors on the compressed files.

If you use your computer to run MS-DOS programs, you can have ScanDisk report any problems with file names that may cause MS-DOS programs to run incorrectly.

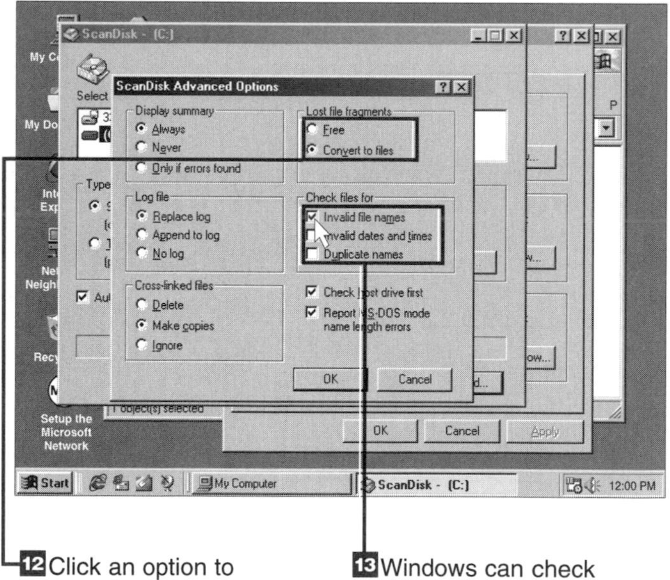

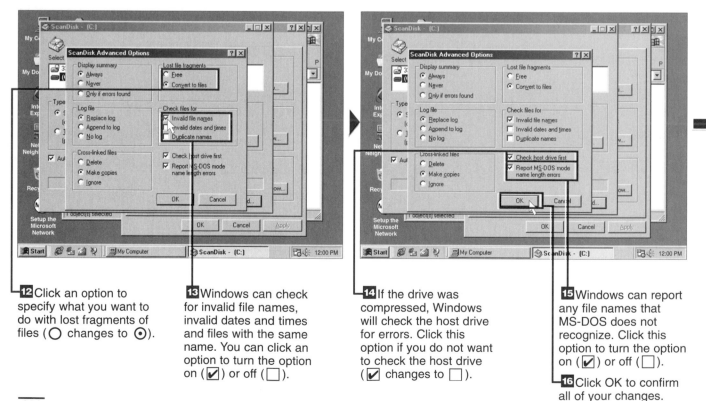

12 Click an option to specify what you want to do with lost fragments of files (○ changes to ⊙).

13 Windows can check for invalid file names, invalid dates and times and files with the same name. You can click an option to turn the option on (☑) or off (☐).

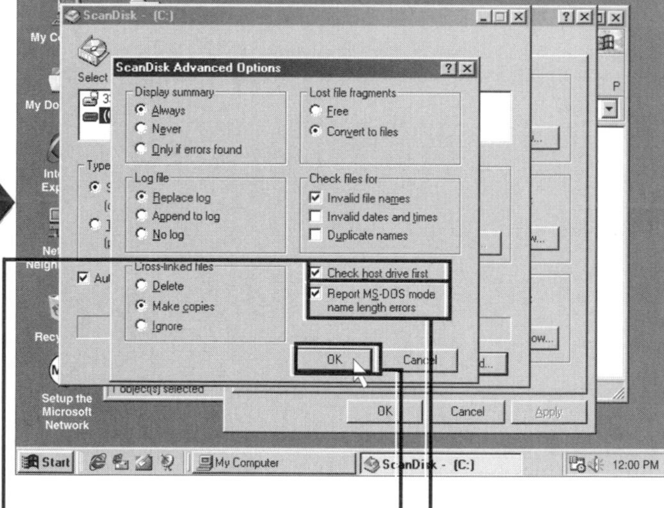

14 If the drive was compressed, Windows will check the host drive for errors. Click this option if you do not want to check the host drive (☑ changes to ☐).

15 Windows can report any file names that MS-DOS does not recognize. Click this option to turn the option on (☑) or off (☐).

16 Click OK to confirm all of your changes.

Can I use ScanDisk on a compressed drive?

ScanDisk can check and repair drives that have been compressed using the compression program included with Windows 98. For information on compressed drives, see pages 344 to 361.

Can I schedule ScanDisk to run at a specified time?

You can use Task Scheduler to start ScanDisk automatically at times and dates you specify. See page 320.

Can I use my computer while ScanDisk is running?

You can use your computer while ScanDisk is running, but the check may slow down. ScanDisk will restart if the disk being checked is accessed. The use of screen savers may also affect a thorough check. You should run ScanDisk when you do not need to use your computer.

Can I stop ScanDisk before it is finished?

You can click the Cancel button to stop ScanDisk at any time.

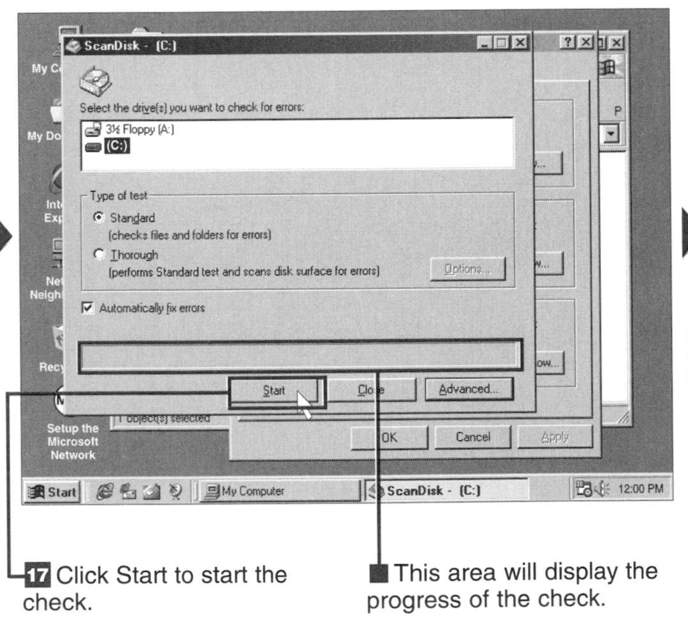

17 Click Start to start the check.

■ This area will display the progress of the check.

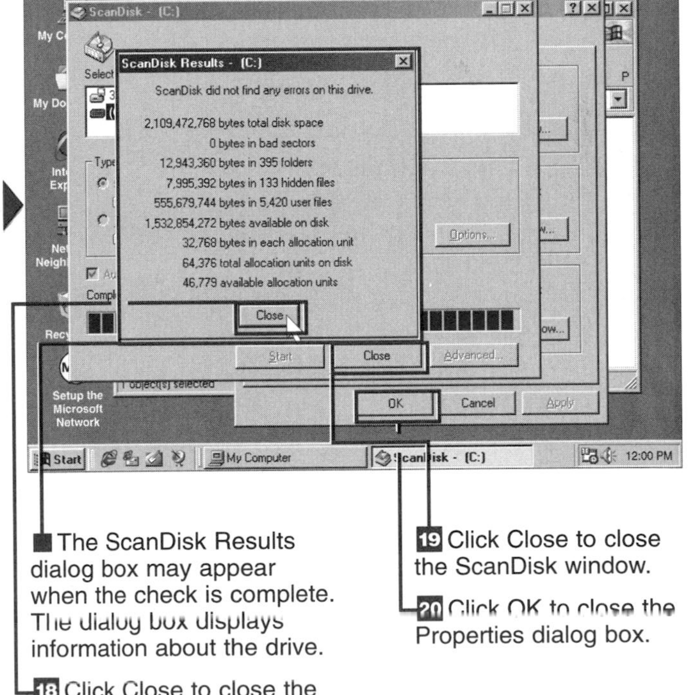

■ The ScanDisk Results dialog box may appear when the check is complete. The dialog box displays information about the drive.

18 Click Close to close the dialog box.

19 Click Close to close the ScanDisk window.

20 Click OK to close the Properties dialog box.

DEFRAGMENT YOUR HARD DRIVE

You can improve the performance of your computer by using Disk Defragmenter.

Over time, the files on a hard drive become more and more fragmented. To retrieve or save a file, the computer must use many different areas on the hard drive. Disk Defragmenter reorganizes your files to reduce fragmentation and improve the performance of your drive.

You can choose which drive you want to defragment. If you have more than one hard drive, you can choose to defragment all of your hard drives at once.

You can change the settings you want to use when defragmenting a drive. You can have Disk Defragmenter rearrange your most frequently used programs so they will start faster. You can also check a drive for errors before defragmenting the drive.

If a drive contains errors, the drive cannot be defragmented.

You can tell Disk Defragmenter whether you want to save the settings you selected for the defragmentation. Saving your settings lets you avoid having to select the same settings the next time you defragment your hard drive.

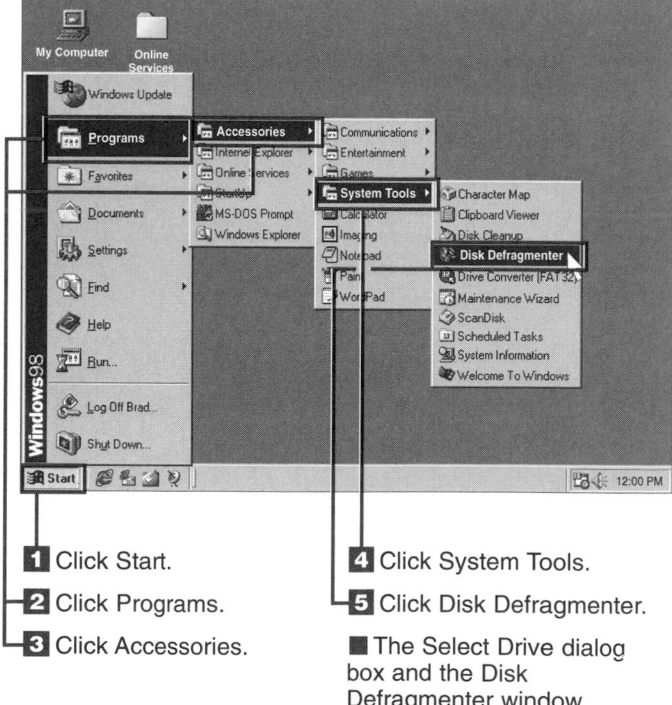

1 Click Start.

2 Click Programs.

3 Click Accessories.

4 Click System Tools.

5 Click Disk Defragmenter.

■ The Select Drive dialog box and the Disk Defragmenter window appear.

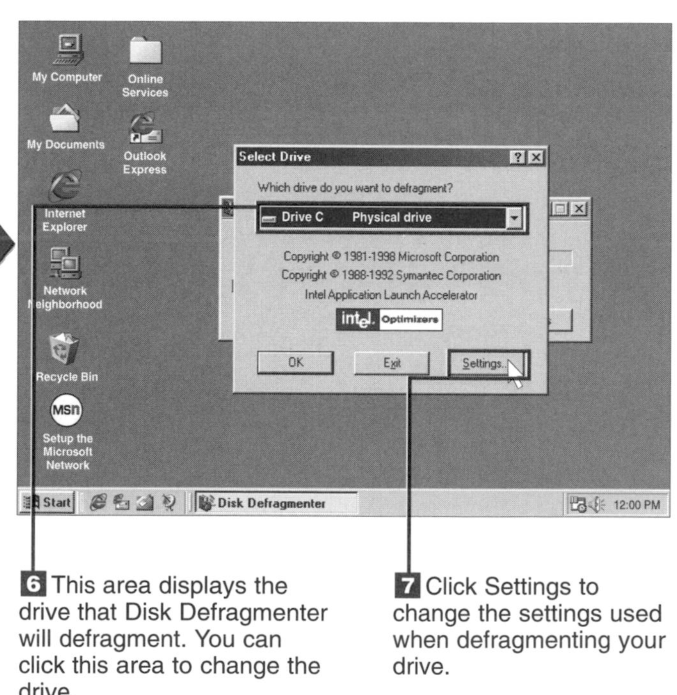

6 This area displays the drive that Disk Defragmenter will defragment. You can click this area to change the drive.

7 Click Settings to change the settings used when defragmenting your drive.

■ The Disk Defragmenter Settings dialog box appears.

TIPS

How long will the defragmentation process take?

The amount of time it takes to defragment a hard drive depends on several factors, including how badly the files are fragmented and the amount of free space on the drive.

What drives cannot be defragmented?

Disk Defragmenter cannot defragment a CD-ROM drive or a network drive. Disk Defragmenter also cannot defragment a hard drive that has been compressed using a compression program Windows does not support.

Are there other defragmentation programs with more features available?

Some defragmentation programs can move specific files to faster areas of the hard drive or defragment files that Disk Defragmenter does not affect.

How can I find out when I last defragmented a drive?

Open the My Computer window and then right-click the drive. On the menu that appears, select Properties. Then click the Tools tab.

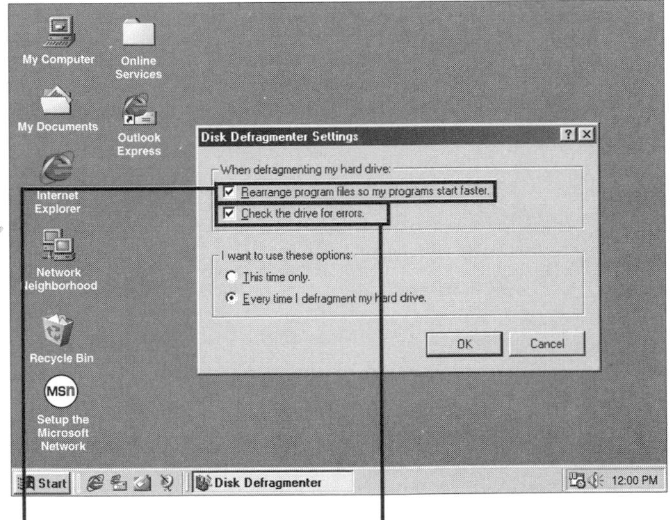

8 This option rearranges your most frequently used program files so they start faster. Click the option to turn the option on (☑) or off (☐).

9 This option checks the files and folders on your drive for errors before defragmenting the drive. Click the option to turn the option on (☑) or off (☐).

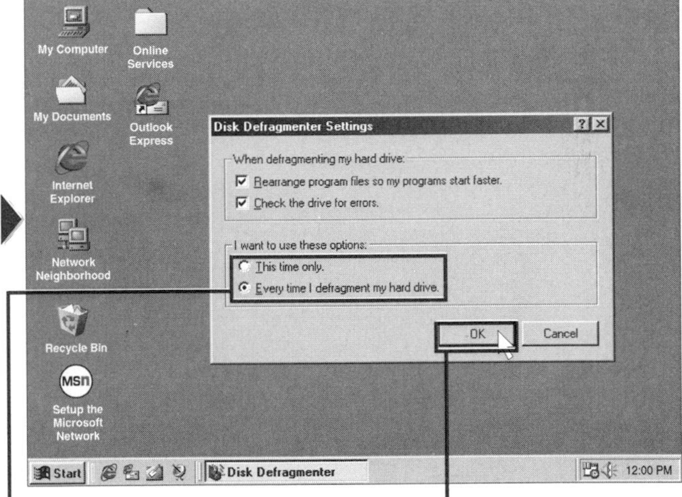

10 Click an option to use the settings you selected only this time or every time you defragment the drive (○ changes to ⊙).

11 Click OK to confirm your changes.

CONTINUED

DEFRAGMENT YOUR HARD DRIVE CONTINUED

When defragmenting a hard drive, Disk Defragmenter displays the progress of the defragmentation. You can also have Disk Defragmenter graphically display the details of the defragmentation process.

You can use your computer to perform tasks while Disk Defragmenter is running, but your computer will operate more slowly. Disk Defragmenter must restart each time another program accesses the drive, so the defragmentation process will take longer. You may want to close other programs before defragmenting a drive.

It is best to defragment at a time when you are not using your computer. You can schedule Disk Defragmenter to run automatically at a time that is convenient for you, such as after work. To schedule events using Task Scheduler, see page 320.

For best performance of your computer, you should defragment your hard drive regularly. Defragmenting a hard drive will not create more free space on the drive. Defragmenting only reorganizes your files to make them easier to find and access.

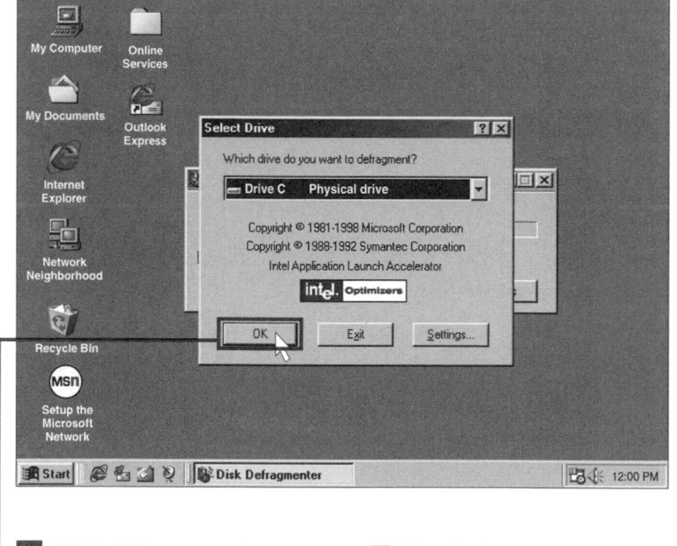

12 Click OK to start the defragmentation process.

■ The Defragmenting Drive window appears.

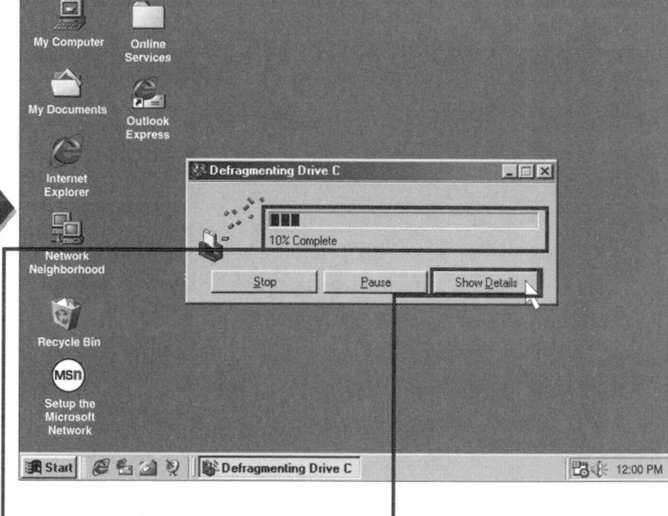

■ This area shows the progress of the defragmentation.

13 Click Show Details to graphically display the defragmentation process.

TIPS

Can I pause the defragmentation?

You can pause the defragmentation by clicking the Pause button. Click the Resume button to continue defragmenting your drive. Pausing is useful if you need to finish another task immediately. The defragmentation will start over if you access the drive while Disk Defragmenter is paused.

Can I stop the defragmentation while it is running?

You can click the Stop button to stop defragmenting your drive. The defragmentation process will not be completed. There will be no effect on your files or their locations on your hard drive.

When viewing the details of the defragmentation process, how can I find out what the colored blocks represent?

After clicking the Show Details button to graphically view the defragmentation process, you can click the Legend button to display a description of what each colored block on your screen represents.

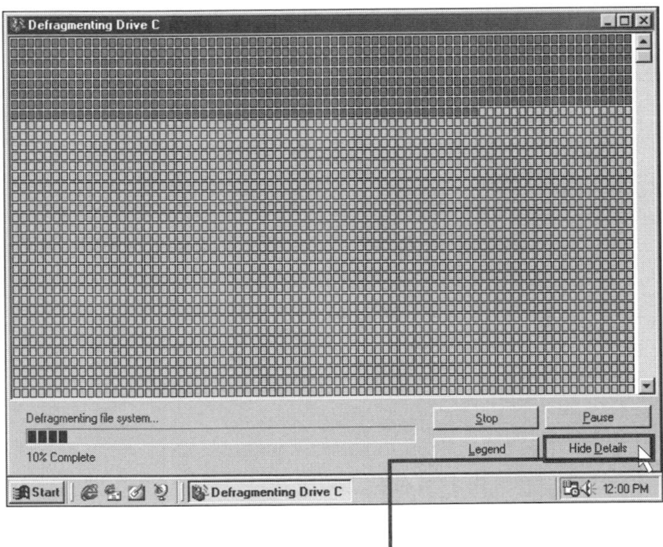

■ A window appears, graphically displaying the defragmentation process.

14 Click Hide Details to close the window.

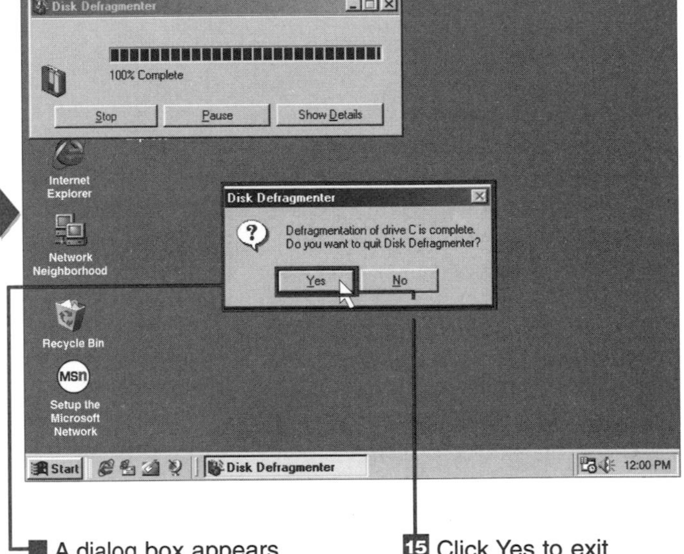

■ A dialog box appears when the defragmentation is complete.

15 Click Yes to exit Disk Defragmenter.

SCHEDULE A NEW TASK

You can use Task Scheduler to automatically start a program at a specific date and time. This allows you to schedule tasks at times that are convenient for you.

The Scheduled Task Wizard takes you step by step through the process of scheduling a new task. You can add any program on your computer to the list of programs that Task Scheduler will automatically start. This allows you to perform tasks such as opening Outlook Express each time you turn on your computer so you can check your e-mail. Scheduling a task is also useful for running computer maintenance programs such as Disk Defragmenter, ScanDisk and Disk Cleanup on a regular basis.

Task Scheduler starts each time you start Windows and operates in the background. The Task Scheduler icon ( ) appears on the right side of the taskbar.

For Task Scheduler to operate properly, your computer's date and time must be set correctly. To set the date and time, see page 200.

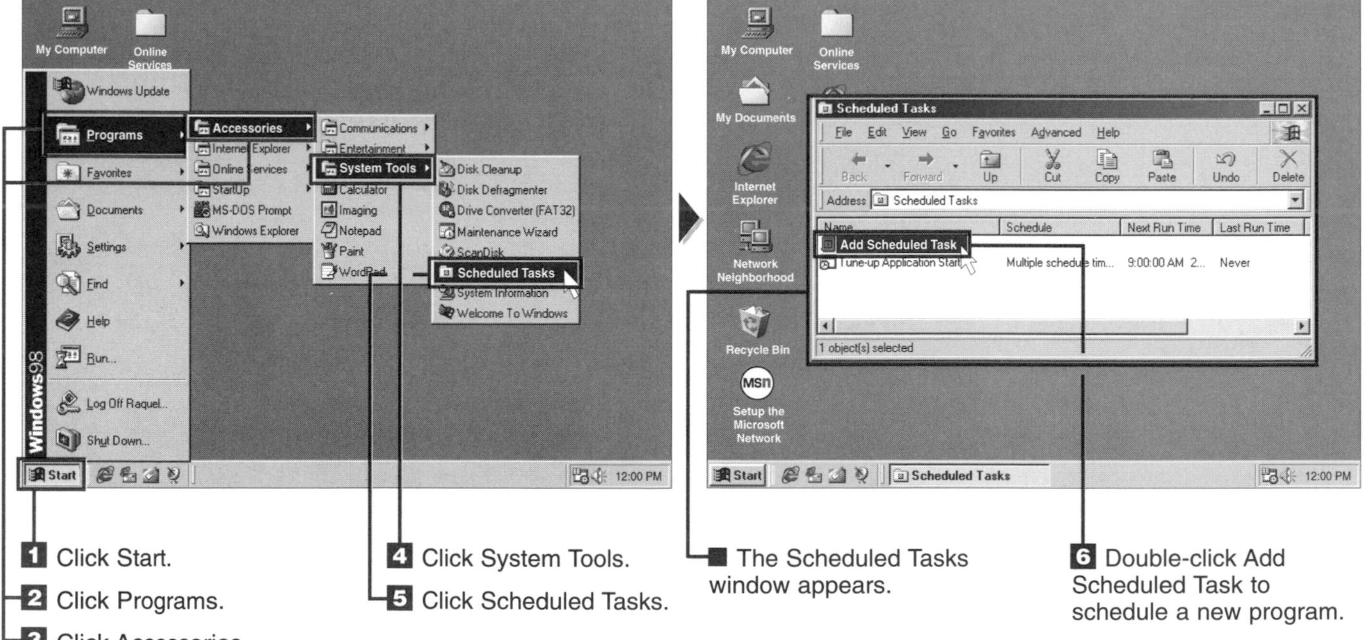

1 Click Start.

2 Click Programs.

3 Click Accessories.

4 Click System Tools.

5 Click Scheduled Tasks.

■ The Scheduled Tasks window appears.

6 Double-click Add Scheduled Task to schedule a new program.

TIPS

The Scheduled Task Wizard does not display the program I want to schedule. What should I do?

You can click the Browse button to search your computer for the program.

How do I turn off Task Scheduler?

In the Scheduled Tasks window, select the Advanced menu and then click the Stop Using Task Scheduler command. Your scheduled tasks will not run and Task Scheduler will not start the next time you start Windows.

How do I reactivate Task Scheduler?

In the Scheduled Tasks window, select the Advanced menu and then click the Start Using Task Scheduler command.

The Scheduled Tasks window displays a task I do not want to start automatically. How can I remove it from Task Scheduler?

Click the task and then press the Delete key. Removing a task from Task Scheduler prevents the program from starting automatically but does not remove the program from your computer.

Is there another way to add tasks to Task Scheduler?

You can use the Maintenance Wizard to add Disk Defragmenter, ScanDisk and Disk Cleanup to Task Scheduler. See page 328.

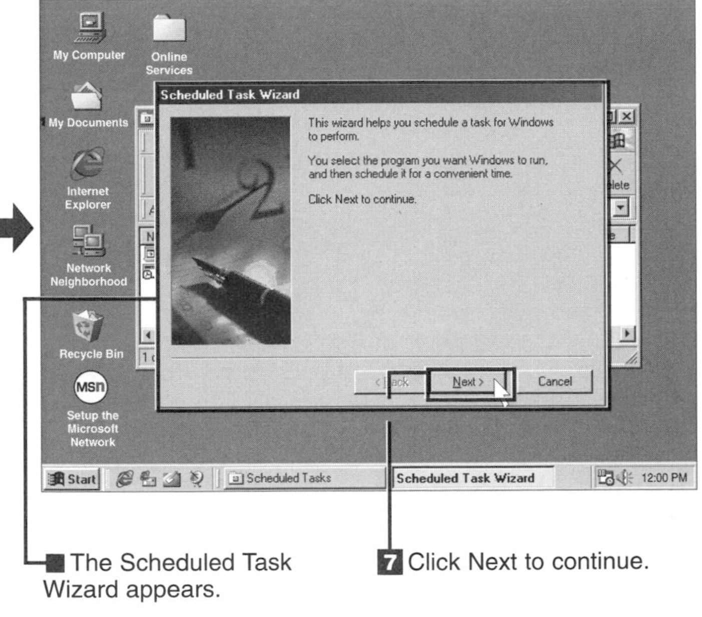

■ The Scheduled Task Wizard appears.

7 Click Next to continue.

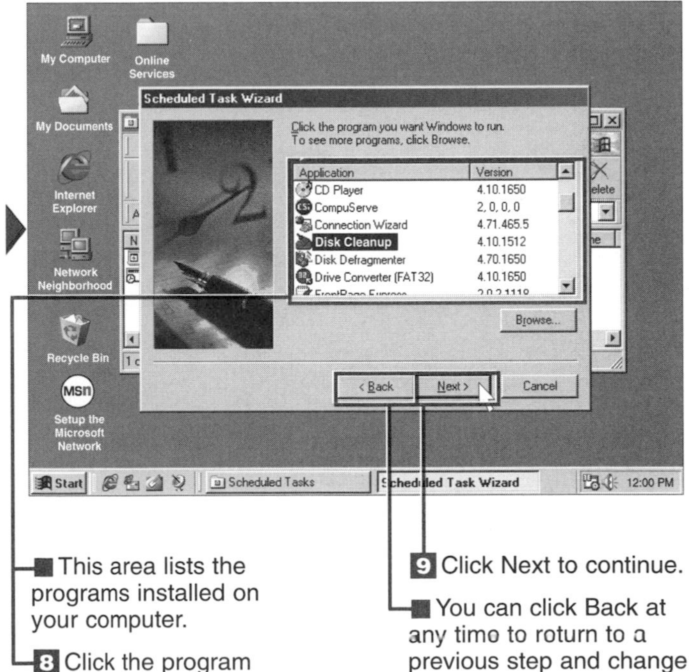

■ This area lists the programs installed on your computer.

8 Click the program you want to schedule.

9 Click Next to continue.

■ You can click Back at any time to return to a previous step and change your answers.

CONTINUED

SCHEDULE A NEW TASK CONTINUED

The Scheduled Task Wizard displays a name for the program you want to start automatically. You can change this name to one that is more descriptive. This can help you more easily identify your scheduled tasks.

You can specify when you want the program to start. You can select a daily, weekly or monthly schedule. The wizard also lets you schedule a program to start only once. You can also have a program start when you start your computer or each time you log on to the network.

Depending on the schedule you choose, additional options may be available. For example, if you select a weekly schedule, you will be asked what days of the week you want to run the program and at what time.

After you schedule the task, the new task appears in the Scheduled Tasks window. The Scheduled Tasks window provides information such as when the task was last run and when it will run next.

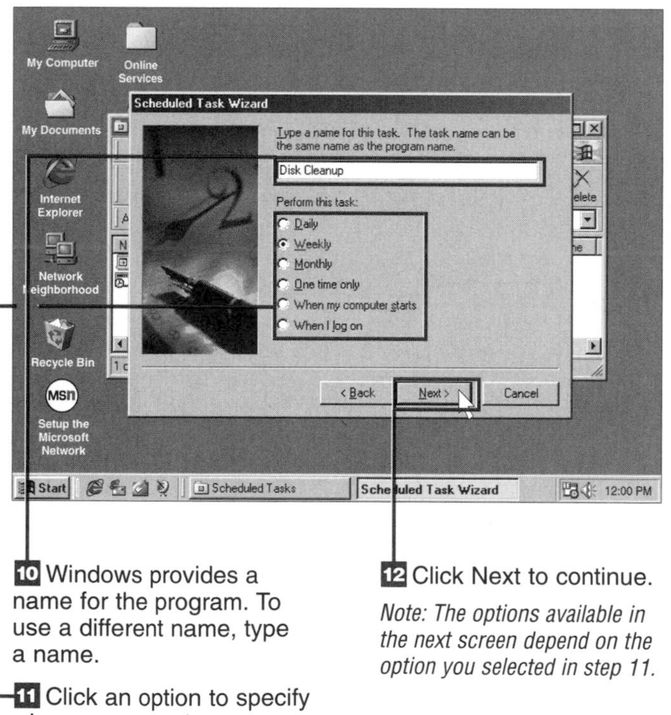

10 Windows provides a name for the program. To use a different name, type a name.

11 Click an option to specify when you want the program to run (○ changes to ⊙).

12 Click Next to continue.

Note: The options available in the next screen depend on the option you selected in step 11.

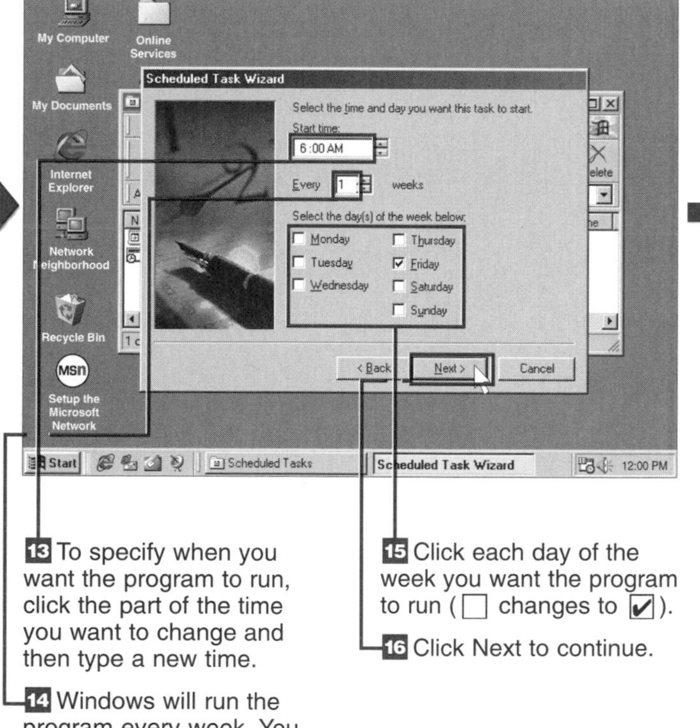

13 To specify when you want the program to run, click the part of the time you want to change and then type a new time.

14 Windows will run the program every week. You can double-click this area and type a new number.

15 Click each day of the week you want the program to run (☐ changes to ☑).

16 Click Next to continue.

How do I change the time and date that a program will run?

In the Scheduled Tasks window, right-click the program you want to change. Select Properties and then click the Schedule tab. You can then change the time and date the program will run.

Can I stop a task while it is running?

If a program begins to run at a time that is not convenient, you can stop the task. In the Scheduled Tasks window, right-click the task you want to stop and then select End Task.

Can I temporarily stop Task Scheduler from running all tasks?

If you do not want to be interrupted while playing a game or performing another task, you can temporarily prevent Task Scheduler from running all tasks. In the Scheduled Tasks window, click the Advanced menu and then select Pause Task Scheduler. To once again have Task Scheduler run all scheduled tasks, click the Advanced menu and then select Continue Task Scheduler.

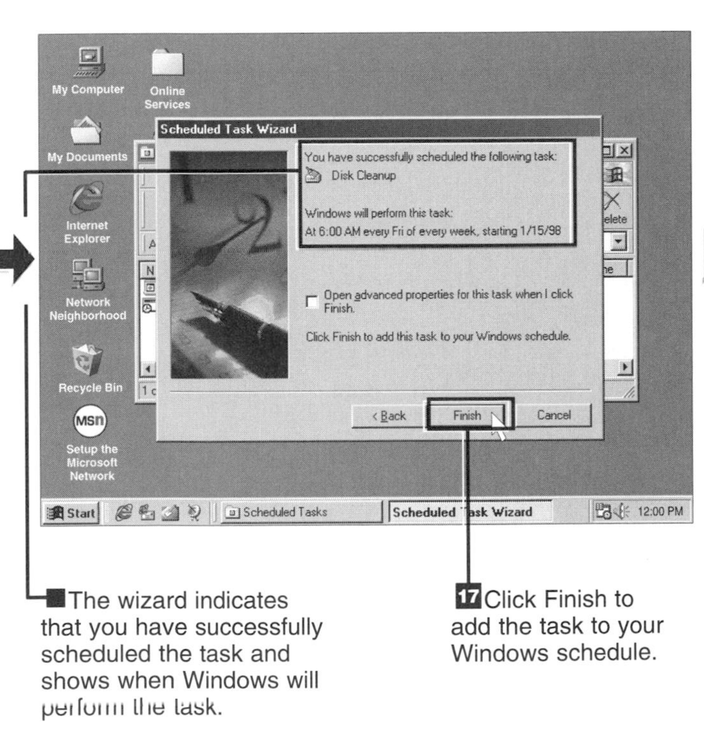

■ The wizard indicates that you have successfully scheduled the task and shows when Windows will perform the task.

17 Click Finish to add the task to your Windows schedule.

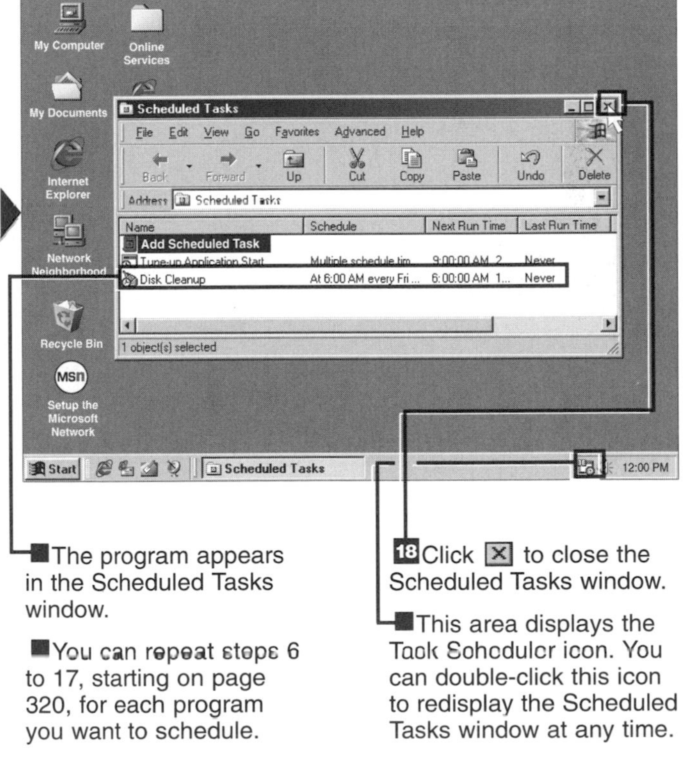

■ The program appears in the Scheduled Tasks window.

■ You can repeat steps 6 to 17, starting on page 320, for each program you want to schedule.

18 Click ☒ to close the Scheduled Tasks window.

■ This area displays the Task Scheduler icon. You can double-click this icon to redisplay the Scheduled Tasks window at any time.

CHANGE A SCHEDULED TASK

You may find that a task you have scheduled does not work the way you expected. For example, the program you scheduled may open, but it may not perform the action you require. You can change the settings for a task you have scheduled to control how and when Task Scheduler performs the task.

Some programs may require extra settings to perform the task you want. The help information for a program may provide details about the additional settings you must enter.

The program that will perform the task may also need to access additional files stored on your computer to perform the task. If necessary, you can specify the location of the folder that contains the required files.

Task Scheduler lets you enter comments about a task you have scheduled. Adding comments and descriptions to your tasks will help you later identify each task.

If you do not want to be interrupted by a task you have scheduled, you can temporarily turn off the task.

Task Scheduler also allows you to change the date and time when a task runs. This is useful if a task runs at an inconvenient time or you want to change how often it runs.

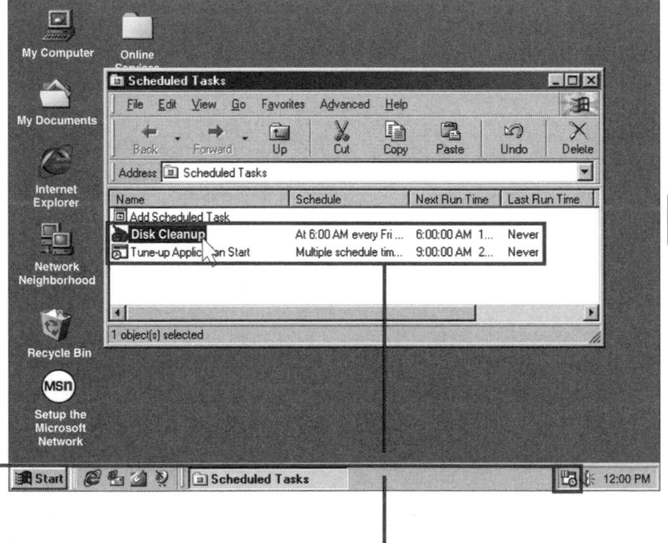

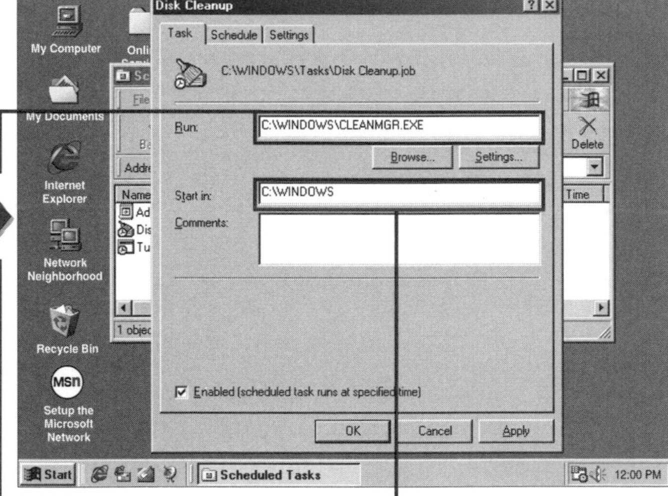

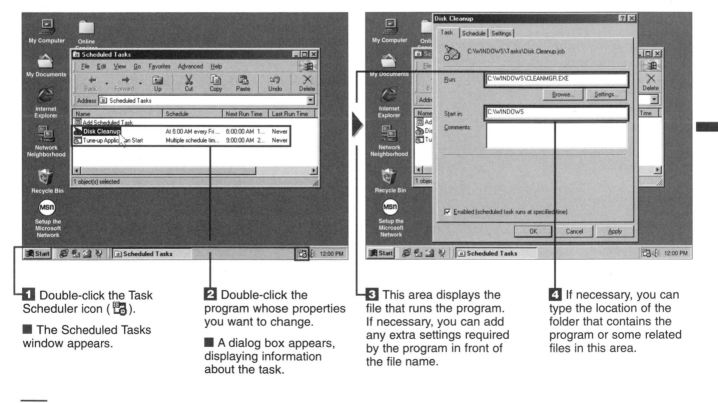

1 Double-click the Task Scheduler icon ( ).

■ The Scheduled Tasks window appears.

2 Double-click the program whose properties you want to change.

■ A dialog box appears, displaying information about the task.

3 This area displays the file that runs the program. If necessary, you can add any extra settings required by the program in front of the file name.

4 If necessary, you can type the location of the folder that contains the program or some related files in this area.

I scheduled a sound file to play every day at noon, but it isn't working. What can I do?

Sound files require specific instructions to play automatically. To add the specific instructions that Windows uses to play sound files, click the Start button, then click Settings and select Folder Options. Display the File Types tab and select Wave Sound in the list of file types. Click the Edit button. In the Actions list, select Play and then click the Edit button. Windows displays the command used to play the sound file, along with the additional settings required. Press Ctrl+C to copy this information. Perform steps 1 and 2 below to display the properties for the task. Click in front of the name of the file in the Run box. Press Ctrl+V to paste the extra settings information and then press the Spacebar.

How can I find out which extra settings a program needs to run?

If the program is stored in the C:\Windows\Command folder, you can click the Start menu and then click Run. Type the program's name followed by a space and /?. For example, type **chkdsk /?** to find the extra settings you can use with the CheckDisk program.

Can I add Microsoft Backup as a scheduled task?

No. You cannot schedule Microsoft Backup to run automatically.

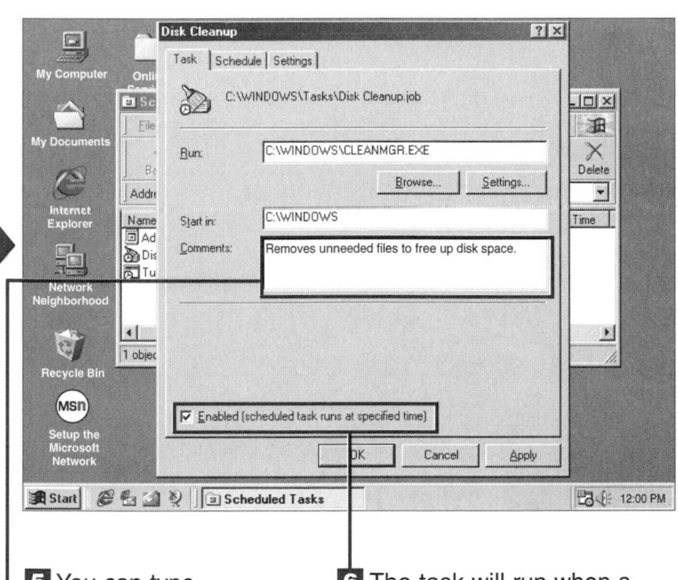

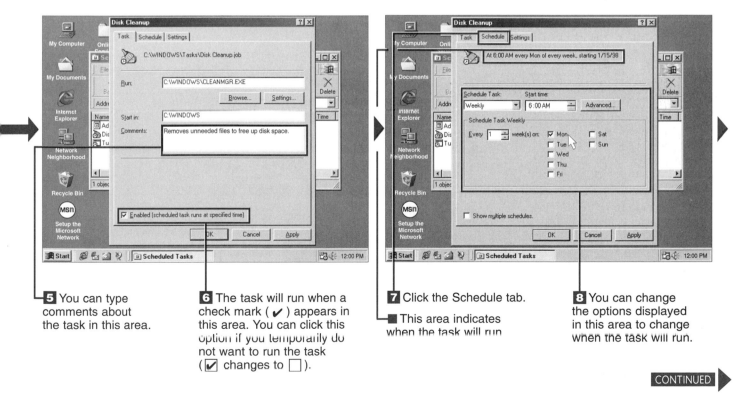

5 You can type comments about the task in this area.

6 The task will run when a check mark (✔) appears in this area. You can click this option if you temporarily do not want to run the task (☑ changes to ☐).

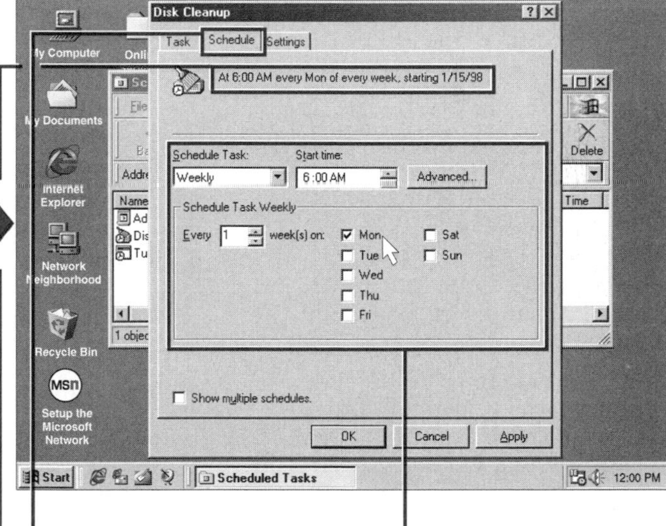

7 Click the Schedule tab.

■ This area indicates when the task will run.

8 You can change the options displayed in this area to change when the task will run.

CONTINUED

CHANGE A SCHEDULED TASK CONTINUED

You can have Task Scheduler delete a task once the task is complete. This is useful if you want a program to run only once.

Task Scheduler lets you stop a program after it has run for a certain length of time. For example, you could have your fax software start receiving faxes at 8:30 a.m. and then stop nine hours and 30 minutes later, at 6:00 p.m.

To prevent Task Scheduler from interrupting your work, you can have a task run only if you are not using your computer at the scheduled time. If you are using your computer, Task Scheduler can monitor your computer for a period of inactivity. If the task starts to run and then you start using your computer again, Task Scheduler can stop running the task.

You may want to avoid performing certain tasks while your computer is running on battery power. You may also want to have Task Scheduler stop a task if your computer switches to battery power while the task is running. These options help avoid running down your batteries.

If your computer uses a sleep mode to conserve power, you can have Task Scheduler wake your computer to perform a task.

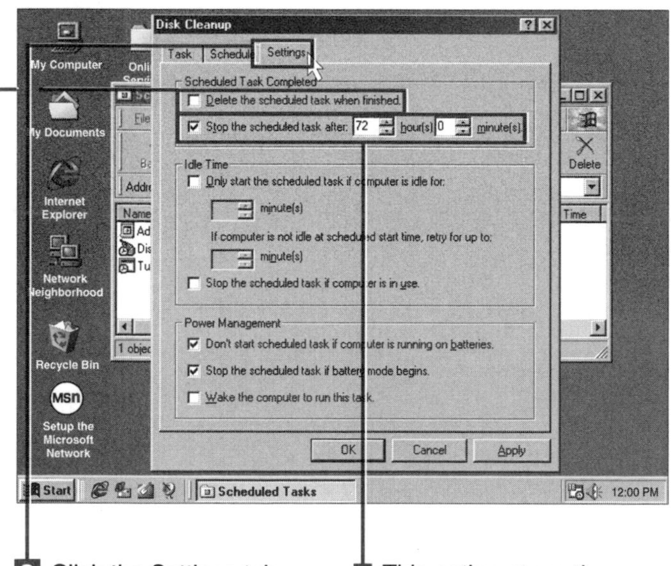

9 Click the Settings tab.

■ This option will delete the scheduled task when the task is complete.

■ This option stops the scheduled task after the task has run for the number of hours and minutes specified. You can change the number of hours and minutes.

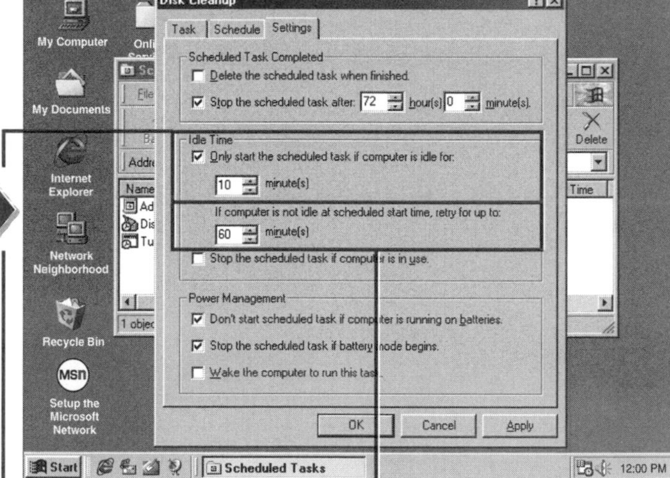

■ This option starts the task only if you do not use your computer for the number of minutes specified. You can change the number of minutes.

■ If you are using your computer when the task first tries to start, Task Scheduler will continue to check if you are using the computer for the number of minutes specified. You can change the number of minutes.

Can I have a program run only between certain dates, such as over a long weekend or while I am on vacation?

Yes. On the Schedule tab, click the Advanced button. You can then select a start date and an end date for the task.

Why would I want to place a time limit on a task?

Some tasks, such as disk defragmenting, may take a long time and interfere with your work schedule. You may also want to use this option to close a task program that does not close automatically when it finishes running.

I chose to delete a task when it was completed, but the task is still listed. What is wrong?

Task Scheduler will delete a task only after all the scheduled occurrences of the task have run. You can click the Advanced button on the Schedule tab to view the end date for the task.

Should I delete all my tasks when they are finished?

When a completed task is deleted, there is no longer any record that the task was completed. You should not delete completed tasks unless you do not require confirmation of the date and time the task was performed.

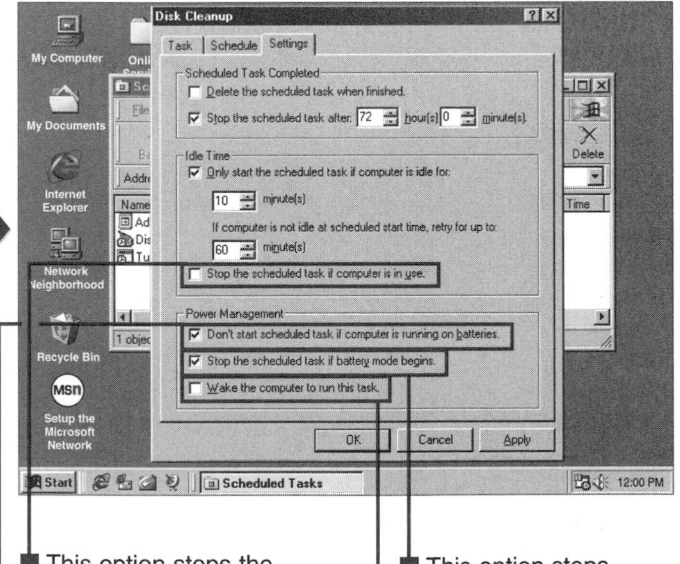

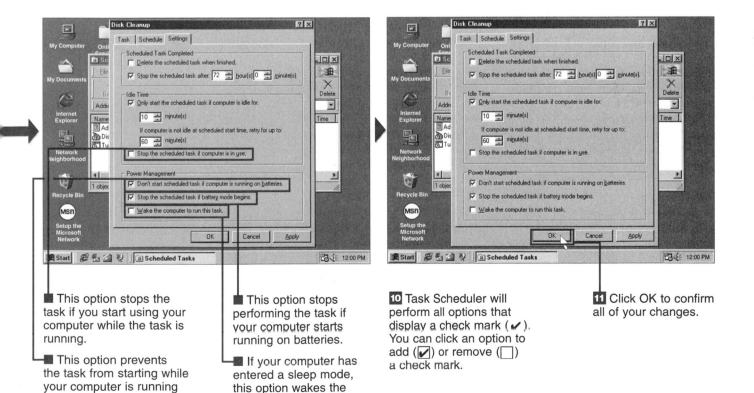

■ This option stops the task if you start using your computer while the task is running.

■ This option prevents the task from starting while your computer is running on batteries.

■ This option stops performing the task if your computer starts running on batteries.

■ If your computer has entered a sleep mode, this option wakes the computer to run the task.

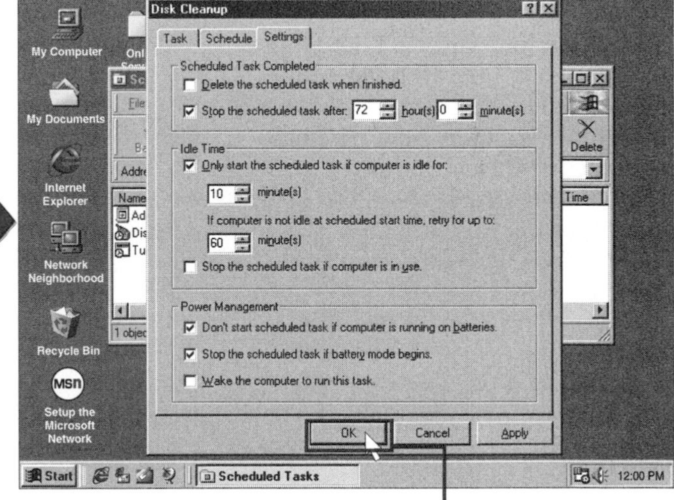

10 Task Scheduler will perform all options that display a check mark (✔). You can click an option to add (☑) or remove (☐) a check mark.

11 Click OK to confirm all of your changes.

USING THE MAINTENANCE WIZARD

You can use the Maintenance Wizard to help optimize the performance of your computer on a regular basis. The wizard can help make your programs run faster, free up space on your hard disk and check your hard disk for errors.

Windows lets you select the maintenance settings you want to use. The Express option uses the most common maintenance settings. The Custom option allows you to choose your own settings.

You can also specify when you want Windows to run the Maintenance Wizard on your computer. You may prefer to schedule maintenance tasks at night so they do not interfere with your work during the day. You must ensure that your computer is turned on at the time the maintenance tasks are scheduled to occur.

Your computer may be set up to automatically open certain programs each time you start Windows. You can decrease the time it takes Windows to start by preventing unnecessary programs from opening automatically.

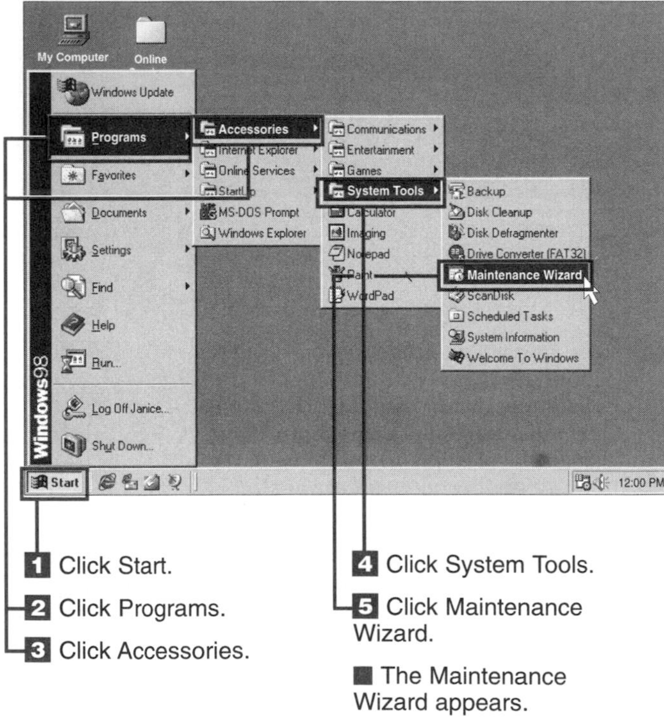

1 Click Start.

2 Click Programs.

3 Click Accessories.

4 Click System Tools.

5 Click Maintenance Wizard.

■ The Maintenance Wizard appears.

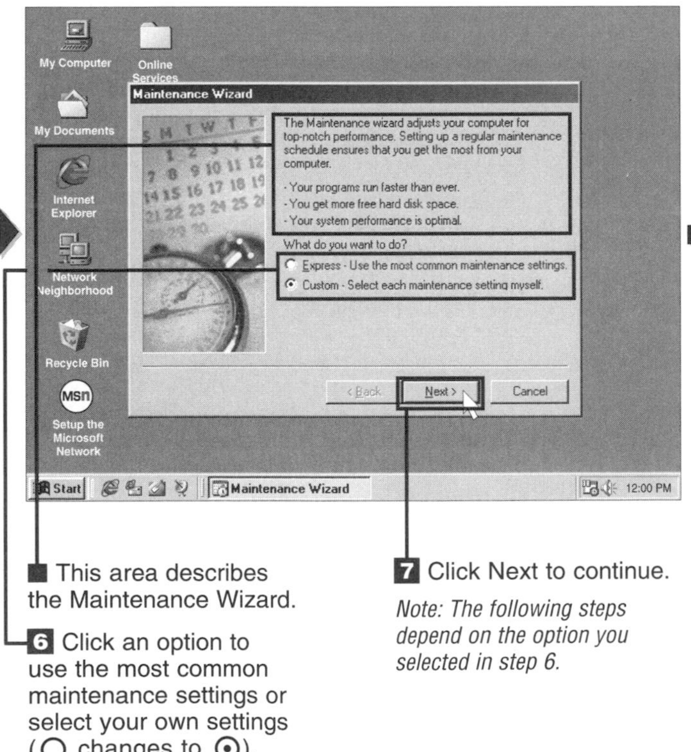

■ This area describes the Maintenance Wizard.

6 Click an option to use the most common maintenance settings or select your own settings (○ changes to ⊙).

7 Click Next to continue.

Note: The following steps depend on the option you selected in step 6.

TIPS

Should I prevent all of my programs from opening automatically?

Opening too many programs automatically can cause your computer to slow down and may place a strain on your computer's resources. You should only automatically open the programs you use frequently. For more information, see page 268.

Can I change the settings for a task without using the wizard?

The tasks that the Maintenance Wizard will perform can be viewed and changed by using Task Scheduler. See page 324.

Why does a different dialog box appear the next time I start the wizard?

After you have set the maintenance settings, a new dialog box appears the next time you start the Maintenance Wizard. To run the maintenance, select the Perform maintenance now option. If you want to review or change your settings, select Change my maintenance settings or schedule.

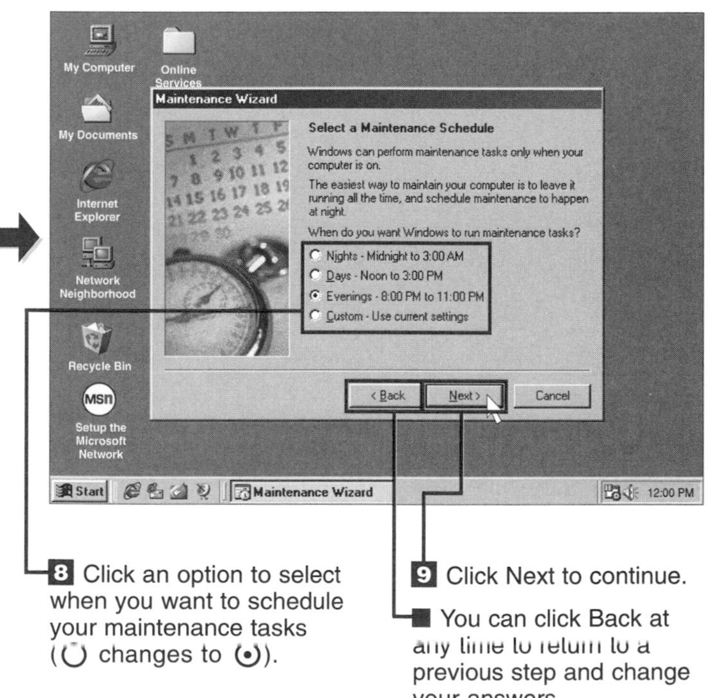

8 Click an option to select when you want to schedule your maintenance tasks (◯ changes to ◉).

9 Click Next to continue.

■ You can click Back at any time to return to a previous step and change your answers.

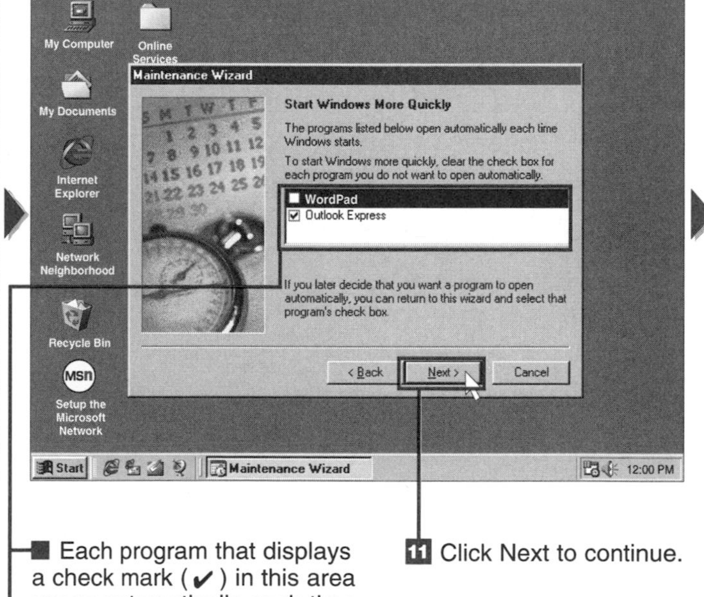

■ Each program that displays a check mark (✔) in this area opens automatically each time you start Windows.

10 Click the box beside a program to add (☑) or remove (☐) a check mark.

11 Click Next to continue.

CONTINUED

USING THE MAINTENANCE WIZARD CONTINUED

The Maintenance Wizard can run Disk Defragmenter to help make your programs operate faster. Over time, the files on a hard disk become more and more fragmented. To access a program file, your computer must use many different areas on the hard disk. Disk Defragmenter reorganizes your program files to reduce fragmentation so the programs operate more quickly.

You can also have the wizard run ScanDisk during the maintenance operation. ScanDisk is a program that detects and repairs errors on your hard disk.

The wizard can run Disk Cleanup to find and remove unneeded files on your hard disk as part of your maintenance. This can help increase the amount of available space on your hard disk. By default, the files the wizard will find and remove include temporary Internet files, files automatically downloaded from the Internet, lost file fragments saved by ScanDisk and temporary files that your programs no longer need.

You can have Windows perform the maintenance tasks you have selected as soon as you finish using the wizard.

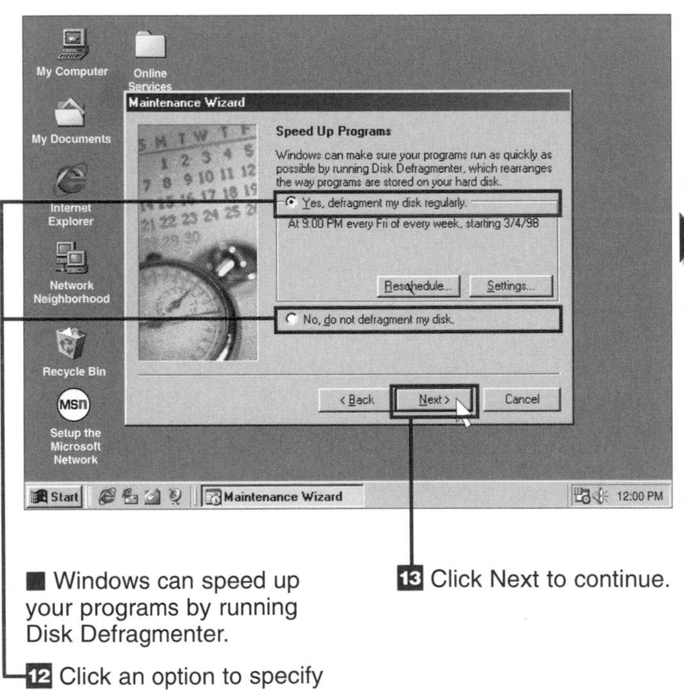

■ Windows can speed up your programs by running Disk Defragmenter.

12 Click an option to specify if you want to defragment your hard disk regularly (○ changes to ⊙).

13 Click Next to continue.

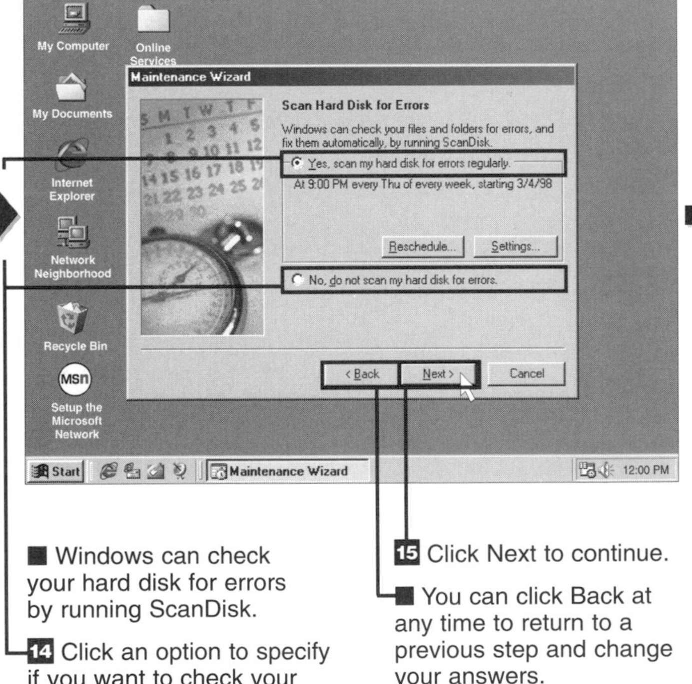

■ Windows can check your hard disk for errors by running ScanDisk.

14 Click an option to specify if you want to check your hard disk for errors regularly (○ changes to ⊙).

15 Click Next to continue.

■ You can click Back at any time to return to a previous step and change your answers.

TIPS

Why did the Maintenance Wizard ask me to convert my drive to FAT32?

FAT32 is a file system that improves the organization of data on a large hard drive. To convert the drive to FAT32, click the Yes button. If you do not want to convert the drive, click the No button. To have Windows ask you again the next time you start your computer, click the Remind me button. For information on FAT32 conversion, see page 332.

Can I run Disk Defragmenter, ScanDisk or Disk Cleanup at any time?

These programs appear on the Start menu and you can run them at any time. For information on Disk Defragmenter, see page 316. For information on ScanDisk, see page 312. For information on Disk Cleanup, see page 310.

Why does Disk Defragmenter keep restarting?

If you have Microsoft Office 95 or 97 installed on your computer, the Find Fast utility that is included with Office may cause Disk Defragmenter to continually restart. You must disable Find Fast when you want to run Disk Defragmenter. To disable Find Fast, open the Control Panel window and then double-click the Find Fast icon. On the Index menu, click Close and Stop.

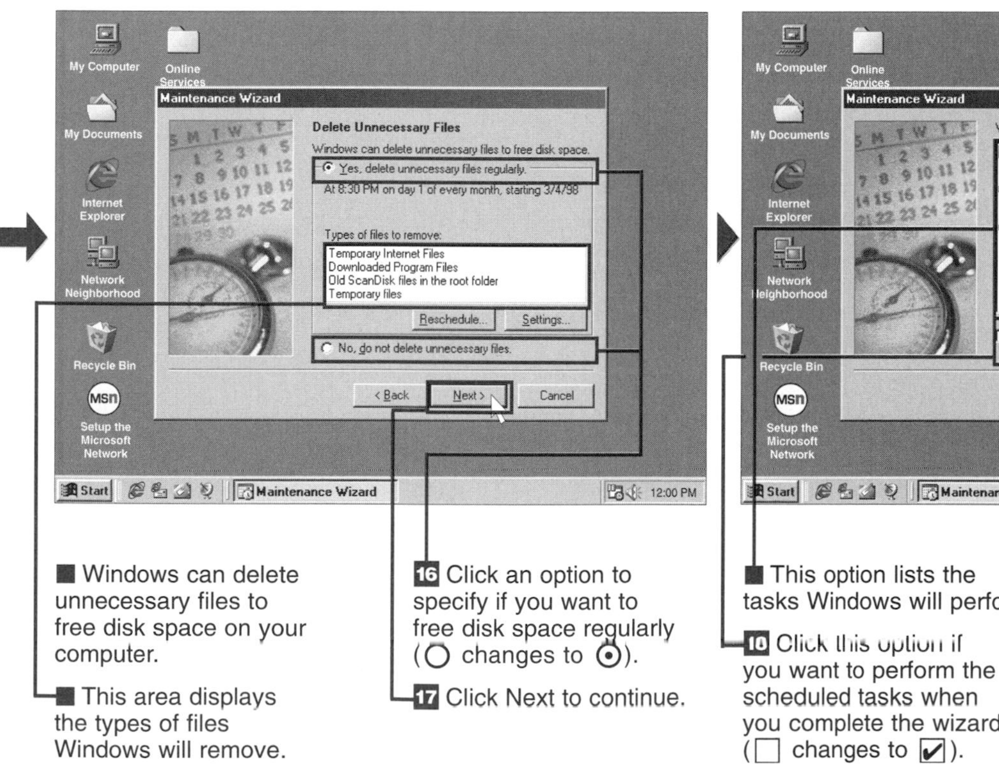

■ Windows can delete unnecessary files to free disk space on your computer.

■ This area displays the types of files Windows will remove.

16 Click an option to specify if you want to free disk space regularly (○ changes to ⊙).

17 Click Next to continue.

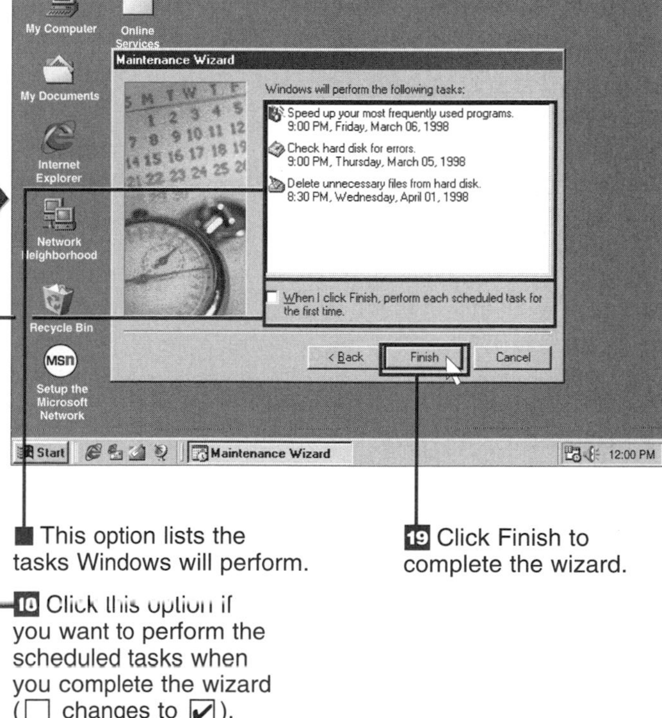

■ This option lists the tasks Windows will perform.

18 Click this option if you want to perform the scheduled tasks when you complete the wizard (☐ changes to ☑).

19 Click Finish to complete the wizard.

CONVERT YOUR DRIVE TO FAT32

You can use the Drive Converter (FAT32) wizard to convert your hard drive from FAT16 to FAT32.

On hard drives larger than 512 MB, the FAT32 file system improves the organization of data by storing data in smaller groups, called clusters. Organizing data in this way helps to reduce wasted space on a hard drive. For example, converting a 1 GB drive to FAT32 may increase the amount of free space on the drive by over 200 MB.

With FAT32, you can also create a single drive larger than 2 GB. This is not possible using the FAT16 file system.

Before you can use the wizard to convert your drive, Windows asks you to remove any anti-virus software that may not be compatible with FAT32.

You should not convert a drive to FAT32 if the drive is compressed or if you plan to compress the drive in the future.

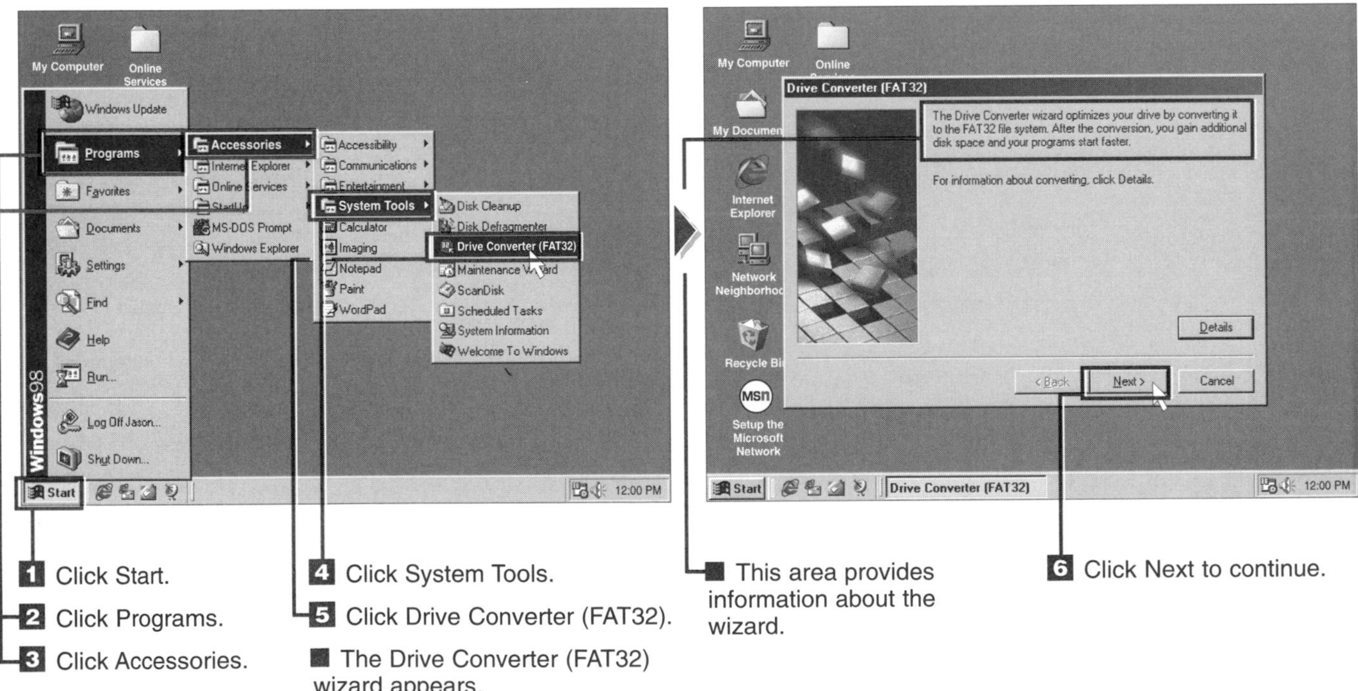

1 Click Start.

2 Click Programs.

3 Click Accessories.

4 Click System Tools.

5 Click Drive Converter (FAT32).

■ The Drive Converter (FAT32) wizard appears.

■ This area provides information about the wizard.

6 Click Next to continue.

TIPS

How can I tell whether a drive on my computer is using FAT16 or FAT32?

To find out which file system is being used on a drive, open the My Computer window. Right-click the drive and then click Properties.

How long will the conversion take?

Converting to FAT32 usually takes only a few minutes, depending on the size and speed of the drive and the number of files the drive contains.

Will converting to FAT32 make my drive faster?

There may be a small change in speed, depending on the type of hard drive. In general, however, you should not notice a difference.

Is there another way to convert a hard drive to FAT32?

You can use a program called FDISK to convert a hard drive to FAT32. FDISK is included with Windows 98. When you use FDISK to convert a drive to FAT32, all of the data on the drive will be erased.

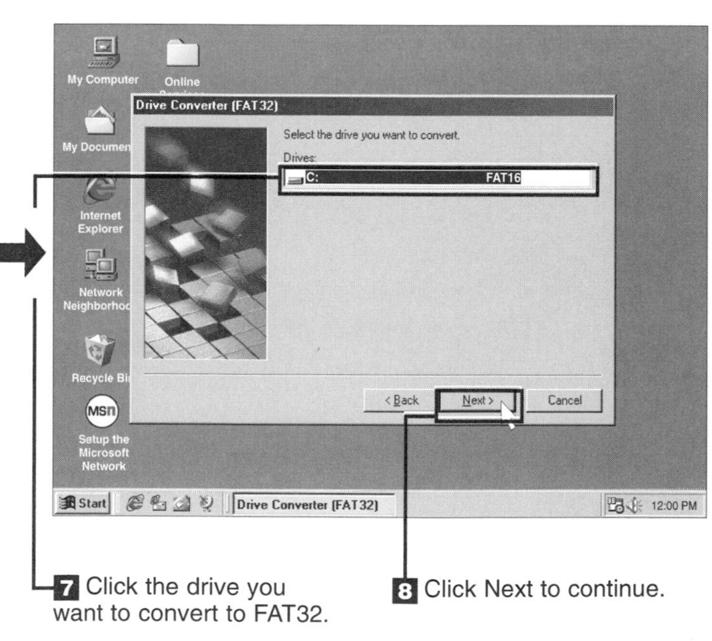

7 Click the drive you want to convert to FAT32.

8 Click Next to continue.

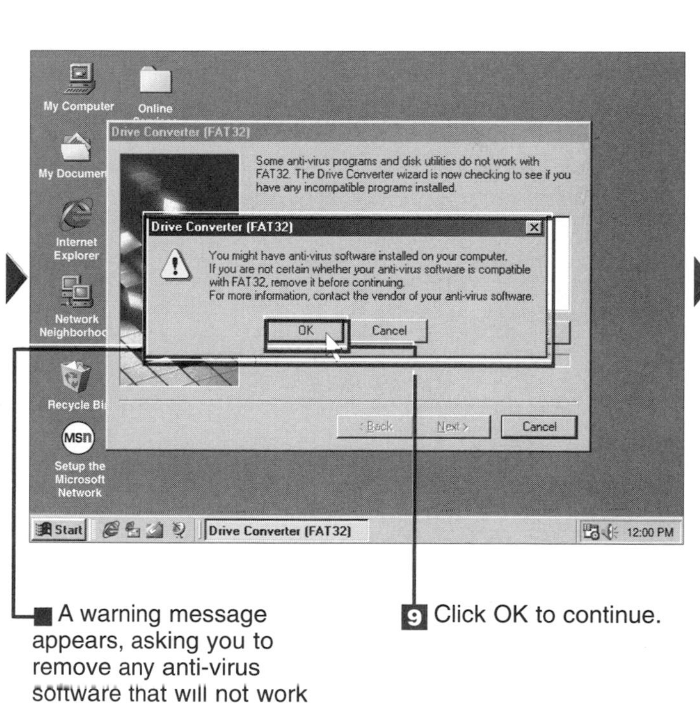

■ A warning message appears, asking you to remove any anti-virus software that will not work with FAT32 before continuing.

9 Click OK to continue.

CONTINUED

CONVERT YOUR DRIVE TO FAT32

CONTINUED

Before converting to FAT32, there are some important points to consider.

Some people divide their hard drive into sections, called partitions, so they can have a different operating system running in each section. You will not be able to access a FAT32 drive from another operating system, such as MS-DOS, a previous version of Windows or Window NT, that is running on another partition on your computer.

The Drive Converter wizard searches the drive for anti-virus and disk utility programs that will not work with FAT32. Some older utility programs, such as defragmenters and unerasers, may not be compatible with FAT32. You should remove all programs that will not work with FAT32 before you convert.

Before the conversion begins, Windows gives you the chance to back up the files on the drive.

Performing a backup is a good idea if the drive stores important information that you do not want to lose.

Windows will automatically defragment the hard drive when the conversion is complete to help improve the performance of the drive. Defragmenting a drive you have converted to FAT32 could take several hours the first time.

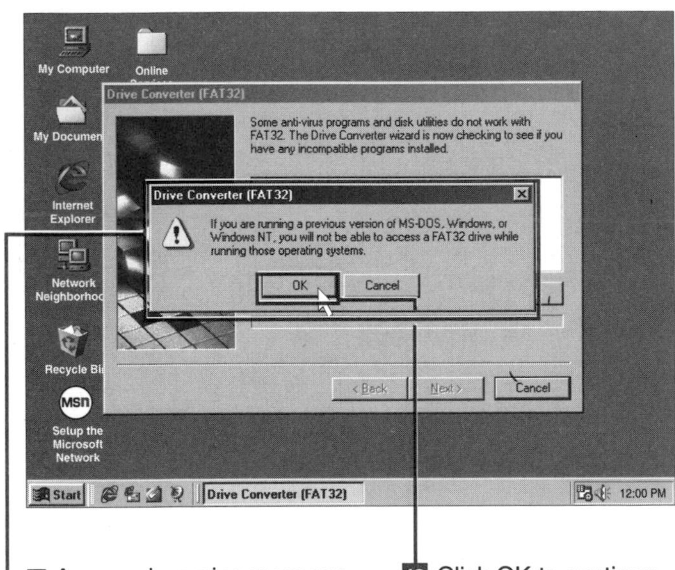

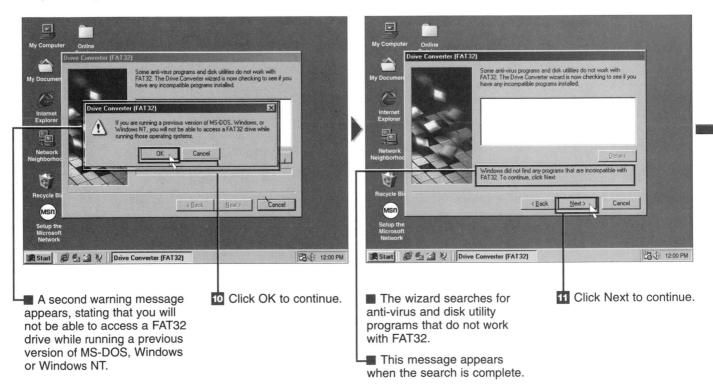

■ A second warning message appears, stating that you will not be able to access a FAT32 drive while running a previous version of MS-DOS, Windows or Windows NT.

10 Click OK to continue.

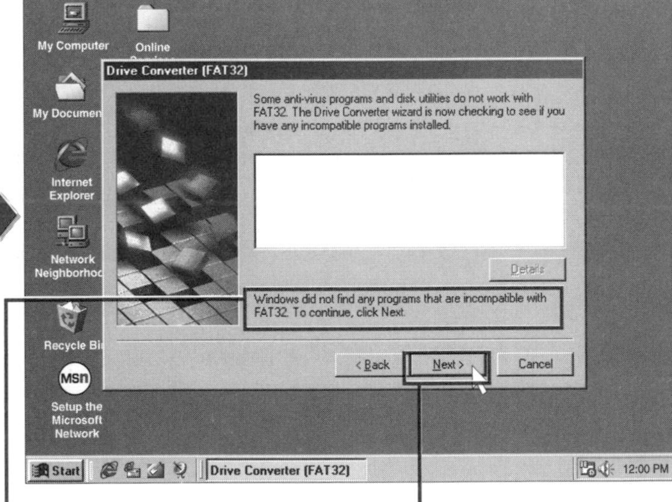

■ The wizard searches for anti-virus and disk utility programs that do not work with FAT32.

■ This message appears when the search is complete.

11 Click Next to continue.

TIPS

Which utility programs are compatible with FAT32?

Microsoft first released FAT32 in September 1996. Utility programs created before that date will not work with FAT32, but most programs have now been upgraded to be fully compatible with FAT32. You can contact the manufacturer of a utility if you are unsure whether the utility will work with FAT32. All the disk utility programs included with Windows 98, except the disk compression utility, will work with FAT32.

Will people on a network still be able to access my shared files after I convert to FAT32?

People on the network will still be able to access files on a shared FAT32 drive, even if they are not using Windows 98.

Can I convert a removable disk to FAT32?

You can use FAT32 on removable disks larger than 512 MB. However, only computers using FAT32 will be able to access the information on the removable disk.

Will FAT32 affect any of my computer's power management features?

After you convert a drive to FAT32, you will no longer be able to use some of your computer's power management features.

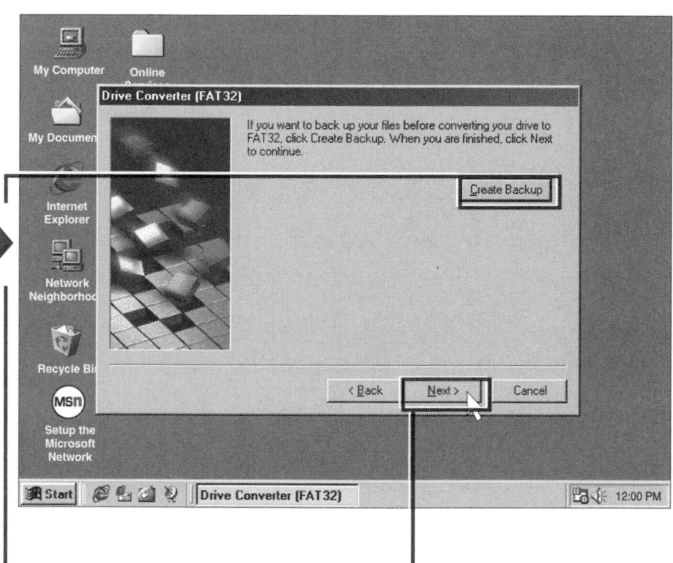

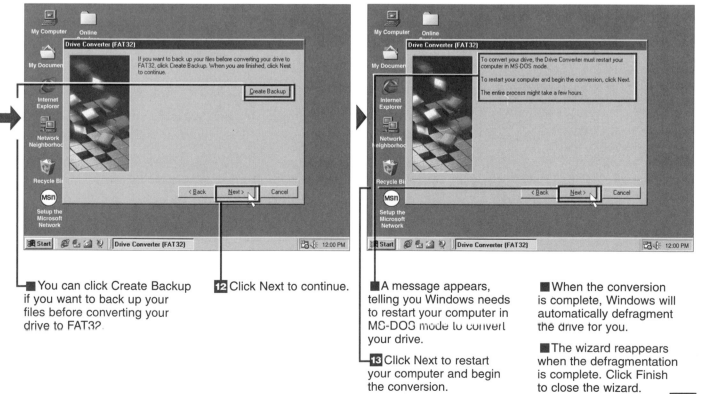

■ You can click Create Backup if you want to back up your files before converting your drive to FAT32.

12 Click Next to continue.

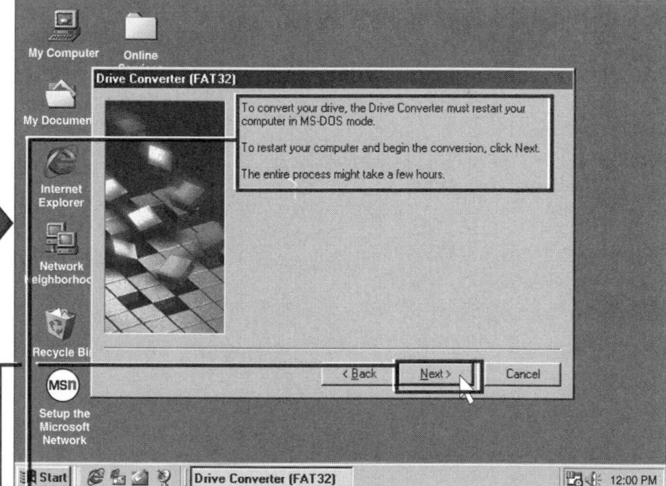

■ A message appears, telling you Windows needs to restart your computer in MS-DOS mode to convert your drive.

13 Click Next to restart your computer and begin the conversion.

■ When the conversion is complete, Windows will automatically defragment the drive for you.

■ The wizard reappears when the defragmentation is complete. Click Finish to close the wizard.

CREATE MORE DISK SPACE

As you create documents and install programs, the available space on your hard drive decreases. You should always have at least 20 MB of available disk space. There are many ways to increase the amount of free space on your hard drive.

When all other options fail, you can add a second hard drive or replace your current drive with a larger one. You may also consider a removable hard drive or a CD-Recordable drive to increase your storage capacity.

ScanDisk

You can run ScanDisk to create more space on your hard drive. ScanDisk locates errors such as lost file fragments on your hard drive. Lost file fragments are saved on your hard drive with a name such as "FILE0000.CHK". You can delete these file fragments.

Upgrade to FAT32

If you do not have the FAT32 file system installed, you can upgrade your hard drive to FAT32. The FAT32 file system provides additional free space on drives larger than 512 MB. On a 1 GB drive, FAT32 may free over 200 MB. Use the FAT32 Converter to upgrade to the FAT32 file system. See page 332.

Compress a Drive

You can use DriveSpace to compress, or squeeze together, the information stored on your hard drive. Compression may be able to double the amount of information the drive can store. Compression is not possible with FAT32.

Delete Unneeded Files

You can delete unneeded files from your computer to create more disk space. You can also use Microsoft Backup to make a backup copy of files you rarely use and then delete those files from your computer as well. For information on Backup, see page 362. Even if you save the backup copy on your hard drive, there will be more space available because the backed up files are compressed.

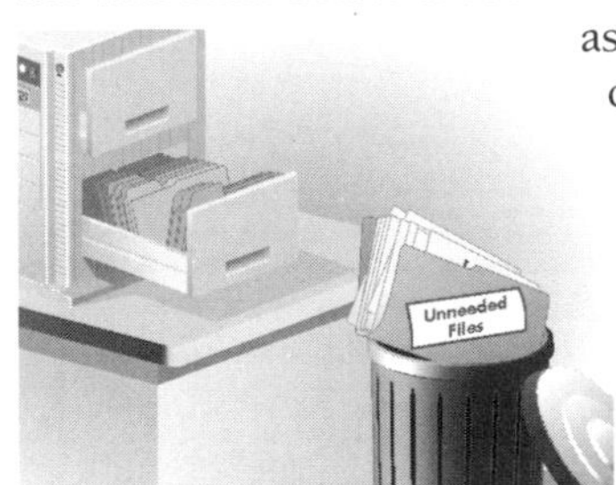

Remove Unused Programs and Components

You can delete programs and components you no longer use to free up space on your hard drive. In the Control Panel, use Add/Remove Programs and select the Install/Uninstall tab to delete programs. Select the Windows Setup tab to remove Windows components.

Delete E-Mail Messages

You can delete e-mail messages you no longer need. Messages with attached files can be particularly large. Once you save the attachment, you probably do not need to keep the message. The disk space recovered by deleted messages may not appear immediately. Outlook Express saves all messages in one file. Outlook Express may take a day or more to adjust the file and remove the messages you deleted.

Delete Temporary Internet Files

Internet Explorer saves Web pages you have viewed in a folder called Temporary Internet Files. Using temporary Internet files saves Explorer from having to transfer the same Web pages to your computer each time you view them. You can delete the temporary Internet files. See page 310. You can also determine the amount of disk space temporary Internet files can use. See the top of page 311.

Delete Temporary and Backup Files

When Windows is not shut down properly, temporary files are not deleted. To remove temporary files, restart Windows and then delete any files in the C:\Windows\Temp folder. You may also find temporary files in other folders. Temporary files usually have the extension .tmp or start with the tilde (~) character.

Many programs automatically save backup files. This allows you to recover a previous version of a file but takes up a lot of space on your hard drive. Backup files usually have the .bak extension or start with "Backup of". You can use the Find feature to look for temporary and backup files.

Empty the Recycle Bin

You can create more space on your computer by permanently removing all the files from the Recycle Bin. See page 75. You can also adjust the Recycle Bin properties so it will use less space. If you have not changed the default settings, the Recycle Bin could be storing as much as 100 MB of files on a 1 GB drive. See page 76 to adjust the properties.

Use Disk Cleanup

You can use Disk Cleanup to find and remove files that are no longer needed. Removing unneeded files can free up disk space. The four types of files Disk Cleanup can find and remove are temporary Internet files, downloaded program files, Recycle Bin files and temporary files. When you select the types of files you want to remove, Disk Cleanup shows you the total amount of space that will be freed up. See page 310.

CHANGE ROLE OF COMPUTER

You can tell Windows how you normally use your computer. This can help Windows use your hard drive more efficiently.

Before you change the role of your computer, you should ensure that the computer meets or exceeds the minimum memory requirements needed to run Windows and the other programs on your computer. If your computer does not meet the minimum memory requirements, changing the role of your computer will be of no benefit.

When Windows retrieves information from your hard drive, the information is stored in an area of your computer's memory, called a cache. When the information is needed again, Windows can quickly retrieve the information from the cache instead of having to look on the hard drive. The role you choose for your computer determines the size of the cache.

The role you specify for your computer controls the number of paths and file names Windows keeps in the cache. The more paths and file names that are kept in the cache, the less time Windows has to spend searching for the paths and file names on your hard drive.

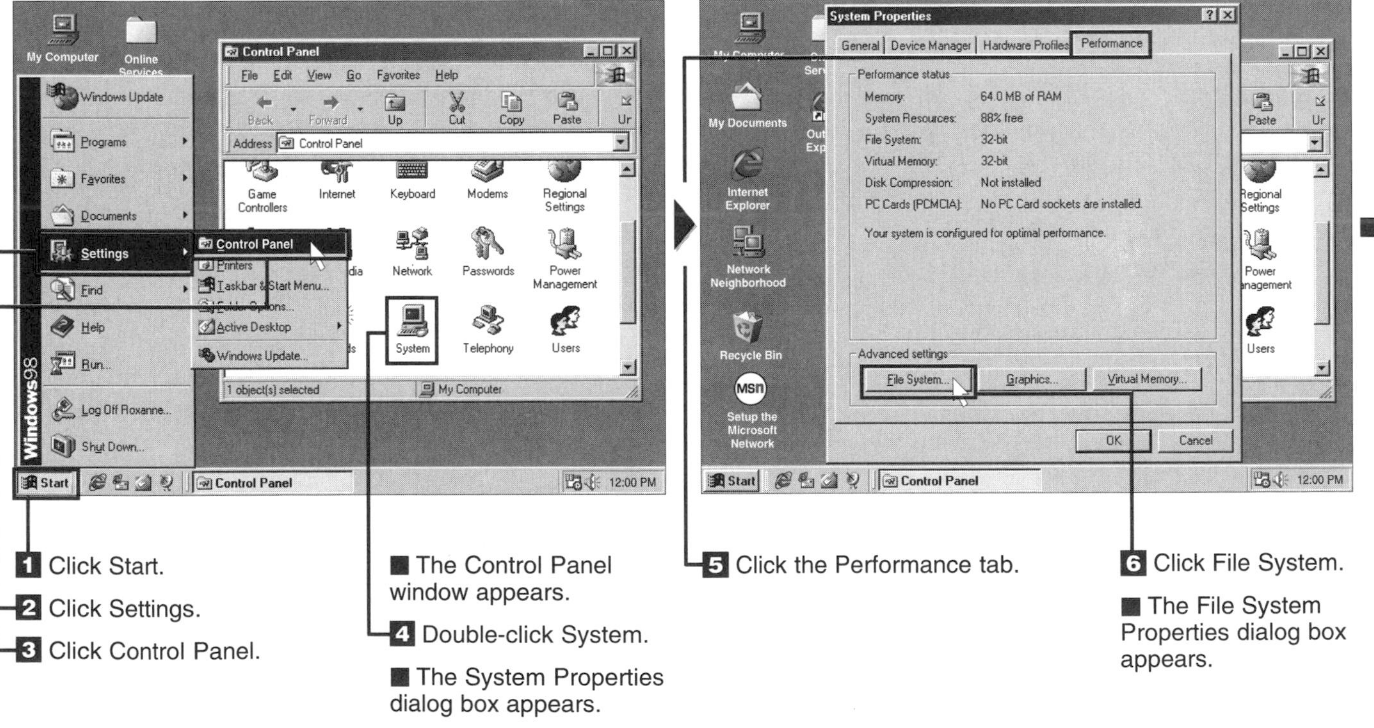

1 Click Start.

2 Click Settings.

3 Click Control Panel.

■ The Control Panel window appears.

4 Double-click System.

■ The System Properties dialog box appears.

5 Click the Performance tab.

6 Click File System.

■ The File System Properties dialog box appears.

When should I choose the Desktop computer setting?

This is the most common setting. You should use this setting when you use a computer that remains on your desk and does not use battery power.

When should I use the Mobile or docking system setting?

You should use this setting when your computer has the minimum amount of memory and uses battery power, such as when you are using a portable computer. The Mobile or docking system setting keeps the smallest number of paths and file names in the cache.

When is the Network server setting appropriate?

You should use this setting when you are connected to a network and share your files with other people. The Network setting retains the largest number of paths and file names in the cache.

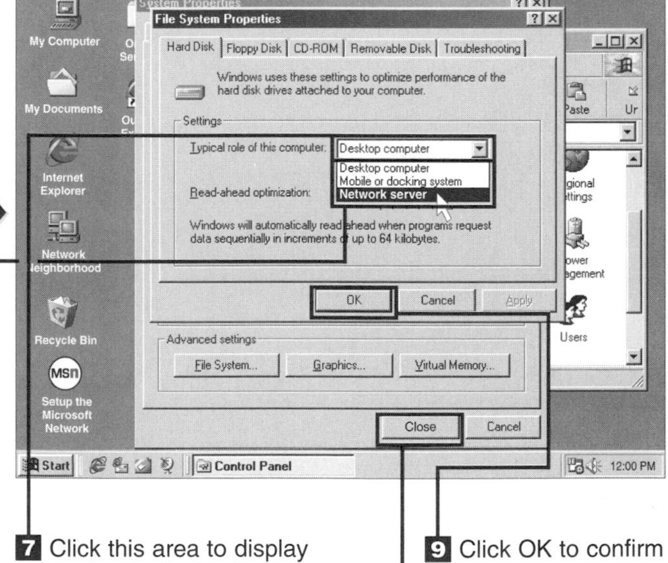

7 Click this area to display a list of typical roles for your computer.

8 Click the most common role for your computer.

9 Click OK to confirm your change.

10 Click Close to close the System Properties dialog box.

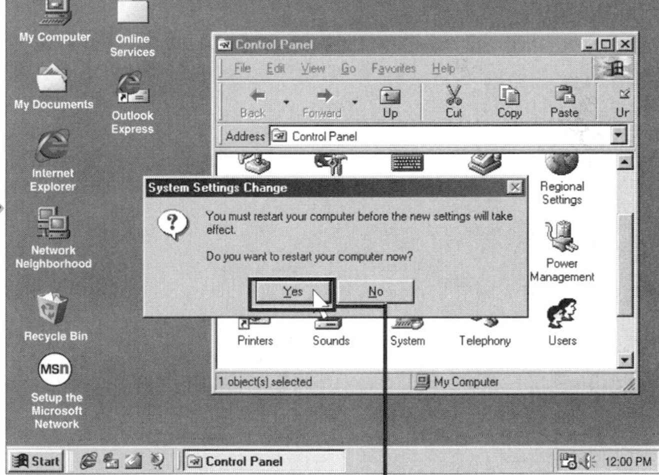

■ A dialog box appears, stating that you must restart your computer before the new settings will take effect.

11 Click Yes to restart your computer now.

CHANGE POWER MANAGEMENT SETTINGS

You can change the power management settings on your computer to reduce the amount of power the computer uses. This is useful if you want to reduce the energy consumption of your desktop computer or increase the battery life of your portable computer.

You can choose the power scheme that best describes the way you use your computer. A power scheme is a collection of settings that manage the power your computer uses.

Windows places your computer on standby when you do not use the computer for a certain length of time. Standby conserves power by turning off items that use power. You can change the amount of time that passes before your computer goes on standby. You can move your mouse or press any key to bring the computer out of standby and resume working where you left off. If a power failure occurs while your computer is on standby, you will lose any unsaved information.

Windows also conserves power by turning off your monitor and hard disks when your computer has been idle for a certain period of time. You can change the amount of time that passes before Windows turns off these items.

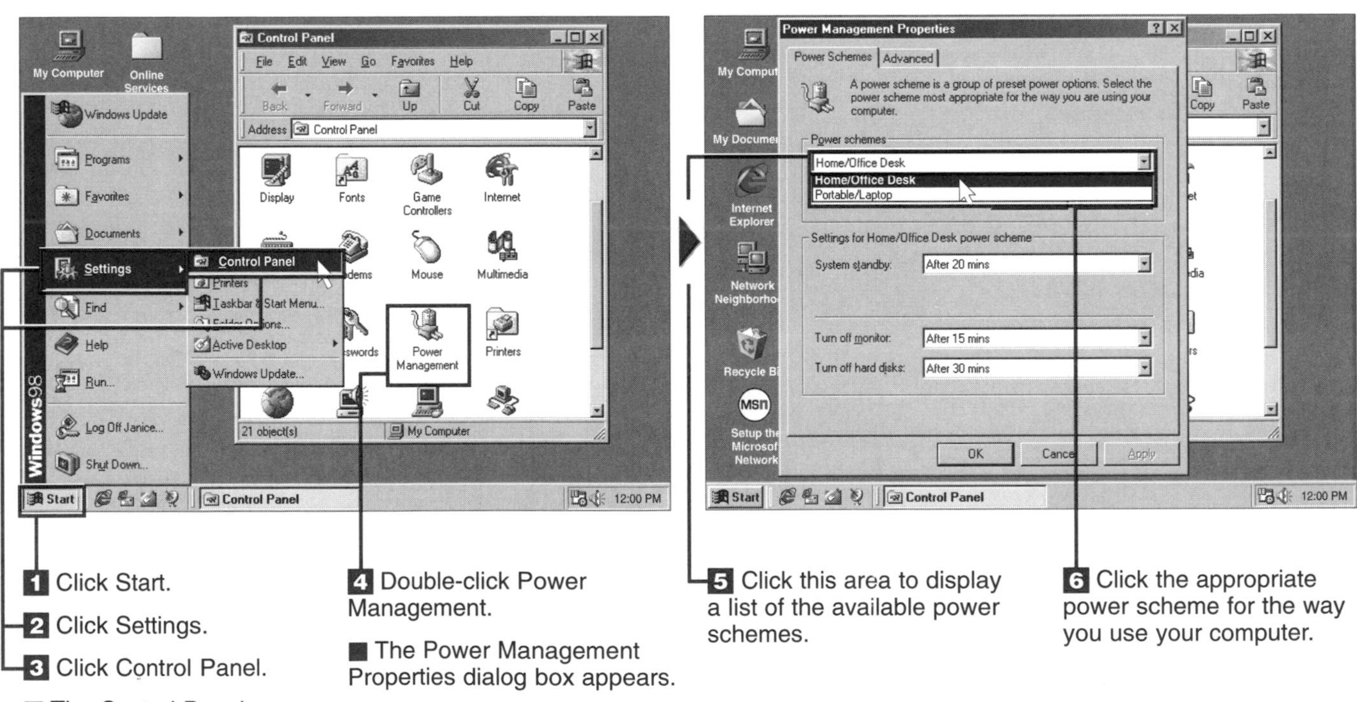

1 Click Start.

2 Click Settings.

3 Click Control Panel.

■ The Control Panel window appears.

4 Double-click Power Management.

■ The Power Management Properties dialog box appears.

5 Click this area to display a list of the available power schemes.

6 Click the appropriate power scheme for the way you use your computer.

TIPS

How can I tell if my computer supports power management?

Your computer must have been set up by the manufacturer to support power management. Display the Control Panel window, double-click System and then select the Device Manager tab. Click the plus sign (⊞) beside System devices. If Advanced Power Management support does not display a yellow warning symbol ( ), your computer supports power management.

Can I create a new power scheme?

You can create a new power scheme that uses the time settings you choose. To save a new power scheme, click the Save As button.

Why aren't all the power management settings available on my computer?

The power management settings displayed in the Power Management Properties dialog box depend on the hardware installed on your computer. Windows only displays the settings your hardware supports.

After Windows turns off my hard disk, I can't resume using my computer by moving the mouse or pressing a key. What should I do?

If your computer does not respond properly after the hard disk is turned off, you should not use this setting. Restart your computer and perform steps 1 to 9 below, selecting Never in the area beside Turn off hard disks.

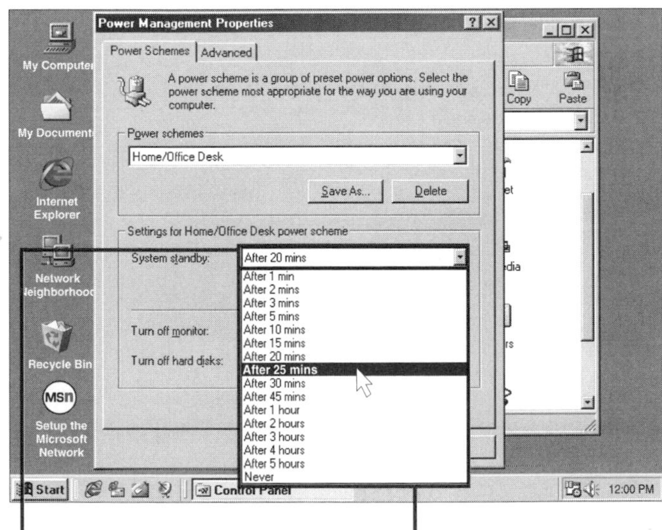

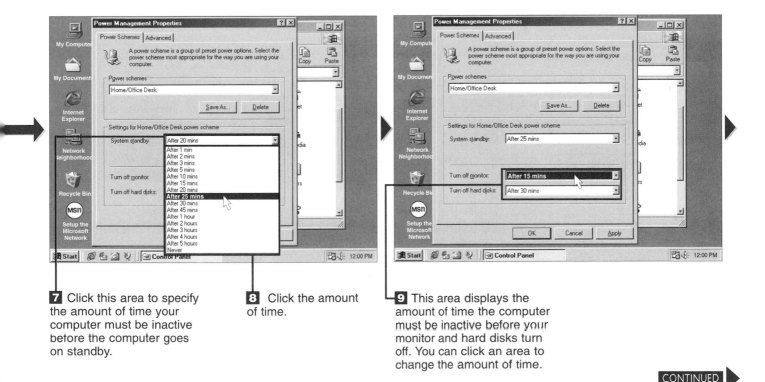

7 Click this area to specify the amount of time your computer must be inactive before the computer goes on standby.

8 Click the amount of time.

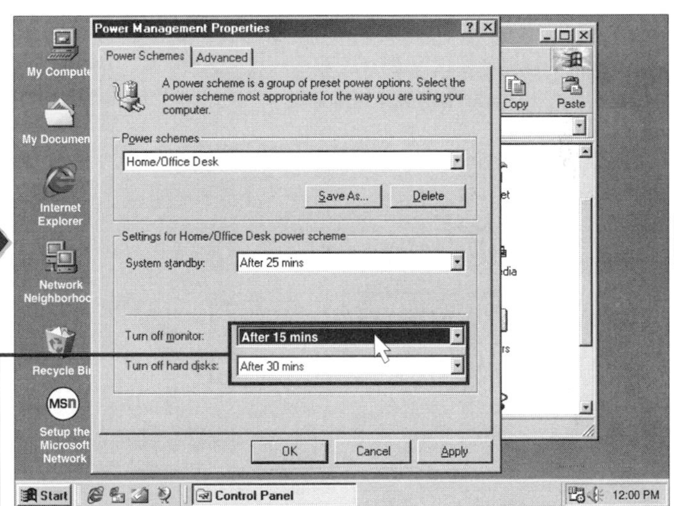

9 This area displays the amount of time the computer must be inactive before your monitor and hard disks turn off. You can click an area to change the amount of time.

CONTINUED

CHANGE POWER MANAGEMENT SETTINGS CONTINUED

You can have Windows display a power icon on the right side of the taskbar. When you double-click the icon, Windows displays the Power Management Properties dialog box so you can adjust your power management settings. If you are using a portable computer running on battery power, you can view the amount of remaining power by positioning the mouse pointer over the icon.

You can also have Windows request a password when the computer comes out of standby. A password prevents unauthorized people from using your computer when it goes on standby while you are away from your desk. The password you enter to bring the computer out of standby is the same password you enter when you start Windows.

You can place your computer on standby at any time. This allows you to conserve power when you know you will not be using the computer for a period of time.

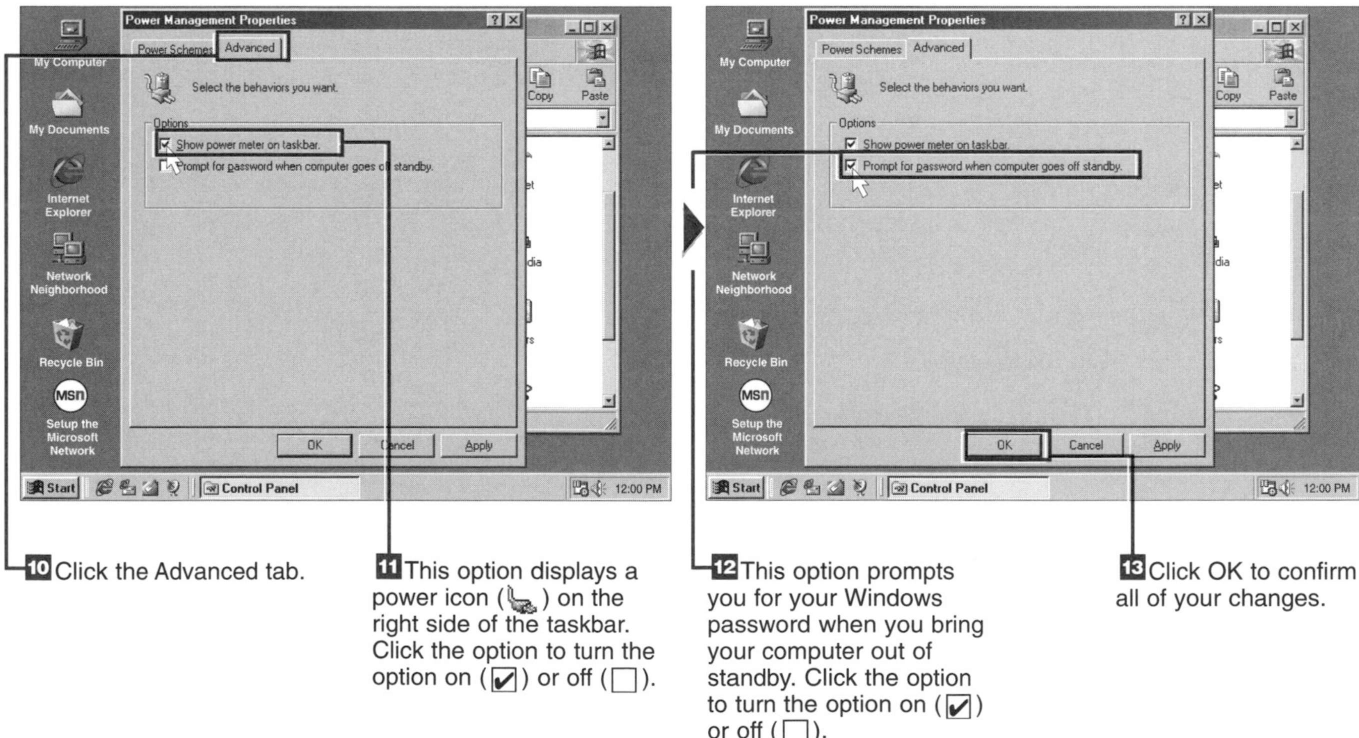

10 Click the Advanced tab.

11 This option displays a power icon ( ) on the right side of the taskbar. Click the option to turn the option on (☑) or off (☐).

12 This option prompts you for your Windows password when you bring your computer out of standby. Click the option to turn the option on (☑) or off (☐).

13 Click OK to confirm all of your changes.

TIPS

How do I change the password required to bring my computer out of standby?

You must change your Windows password. To change your Windows password, display the Control Panel window and then double-click the Passwords icon. Then click the Change Windows Password button.

Will my portable computer warn me when battery power is low?

If the Power Management Properties dialog box displays the Alarms tab, you can select visual or sound alarms that will warn you when battery power is low. You can also choose whether the computer enters standby or shuts down when power is low.

Are there other power management features that my computer may support?

Some computers support the OnNow feature. This feature allows you to continue working where you stopped the last time you turned your computer off. Windows saves your open documents before your computer turns off. When you restart your computer, everything appears as you left it.

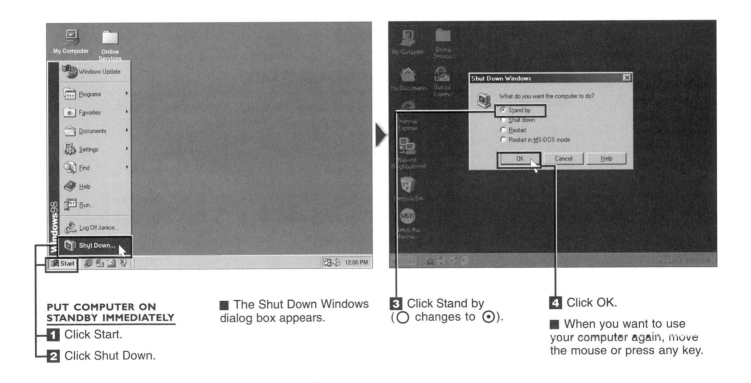

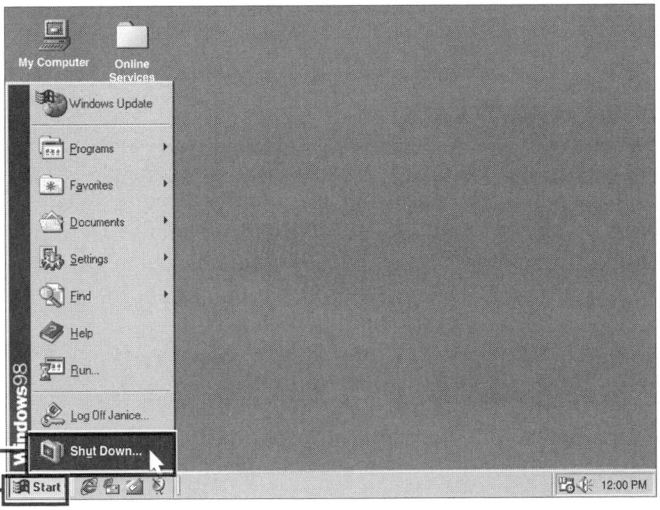

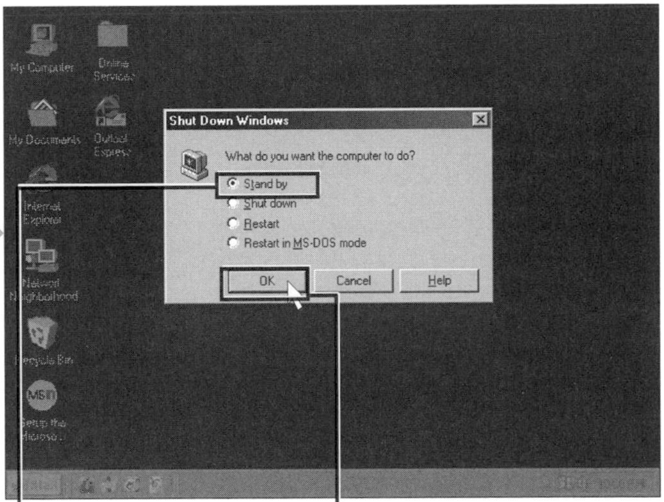

PUT COMPUTER ON STANDBY IMMEDIATELY

1 Click Start.

2 Click Shut Down.

■ The Shut Down Windows dialog box appears.

3 Click Stand by (○ changes to ⦿).

4 Click OK.

■ When you want to use your computer again, move the mouse or press any key.

COMPRESS A DRIVE

You can use DriveSpace to compress, or squeeze together, the information stored on your hard drive.

As you install new programs and create new files, you may find that you need more space on your hard drive. You should first try to create more free space on the drive using methods such as deleting programs and files you no longer use. If you cannot create enough free space, DriveSpace can provide the additional space you need.

DriveSpace estimates that it will increase the amount of information the drive can store by approximately 70 percent. For example, a 1 GB hard drive may be able to hold about 1.7 GB when compressed. The actual amount of free space that will be available on the drive depends on the size of the drive and the types of information stored on the drive. Document files such as spreadsheets and databases compress significantly, whereas program files compress very little.

When DriveSpace is compressing a drive, you cannot use your computer. Because compressing your hard drive may take several hours, you should compress your hard drive when you will not need your computer.

If your computer uses the FAT32 file system, you cannot use DriveSpace to compress your hard drive.

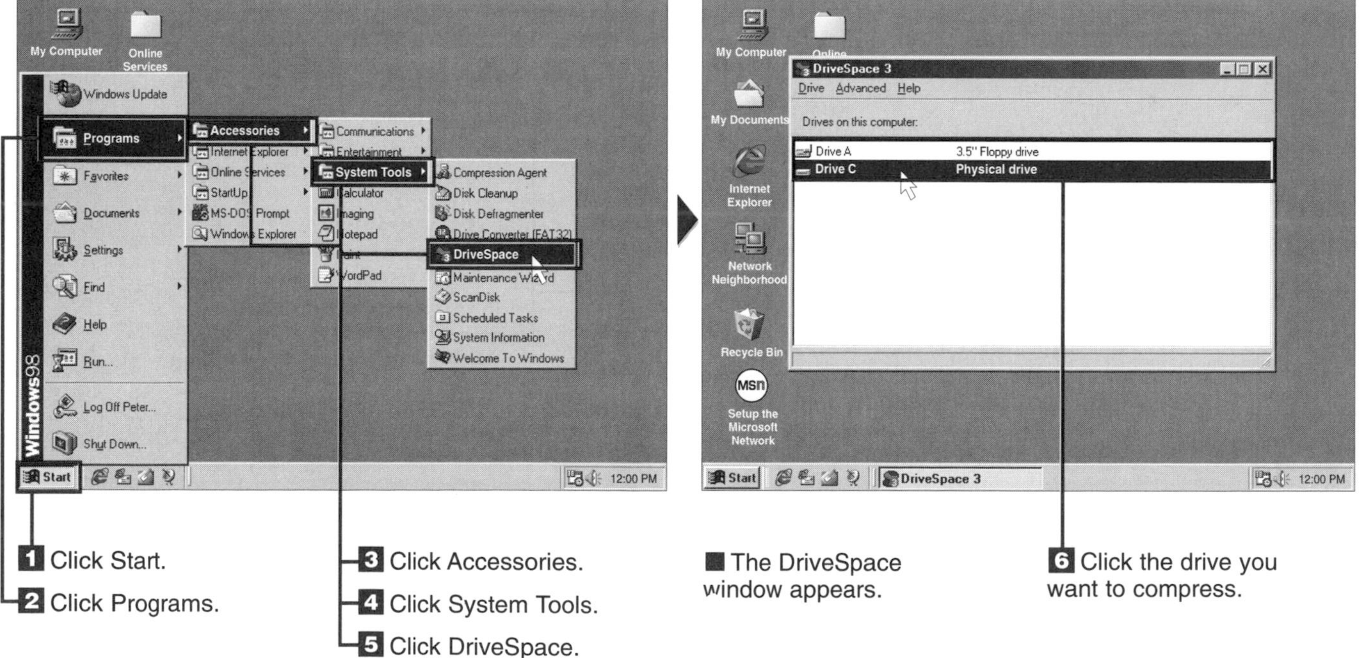

1 Click Start.

2 Click Programs.

3 Click Accessories.

4 Click System Tools.

5 Click DriveSpace.

■ The DriveSpace window appears.

6 Click the drive you want to compress.

TIPS

Why isn't DriveSpace listed on the Start menu?

DriveSpace may not be installed on your computer. Install the Disk compression tools located in the System Tools component. To add Windows components, see page 610.

Can I compress part of the hard drive?

Yes. Compressing part of the hard drive allows you to increase the available space for storing information, such as the document files you create. See page 352.

Can I compress a floppy disk or removable drive?

You can compress any disk or removable drive that appears in the DriveSpace window. You can only compress a floppy disk that has at least 512 K of free space. To access a compressed floppy disk or removable drive on another computer, the other computer must have DriveSpace and either Windows 95 or 98 installed.

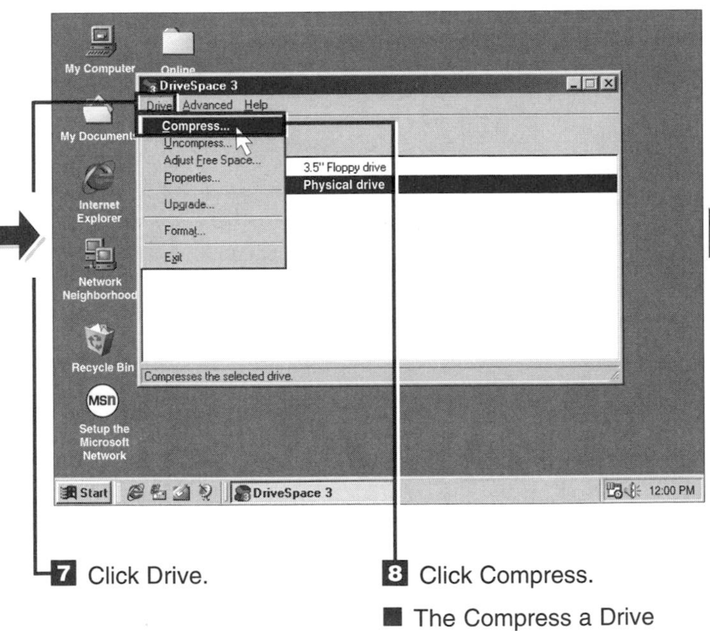

7 Click Drive.

8 Click Compress.

■ The Compress a Drive dialog box appears.

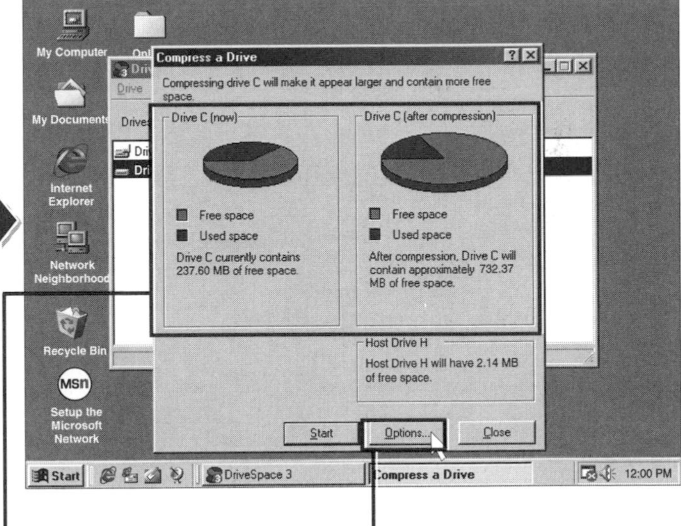

■ This area displays the amount of free and used space before and after you compress the drive.

9 Click Options to change the compression options.

■ The Compression Options dialog box appears.

CONTINUED

COMPRESS A DRIVE CONTINUED

When you compress a drive, DriveSpace stores all of your old files in one large file. DriveSpace also looks for repeated elements in your files. When repeated elements are found, they are replaced with a shorter element.

The compressed drive is called a Compressed Volume File (CVF) and is assigned a drive letter. You can access the compressed drive as you would any other drive on the computer.

The hard drive becomes a host drive and stores the compressed drive. Windows assigns the host drive a new drive letter.

The host drive also contains the software needed to start and access the compressed drive. You can hide the host drive so that the compressed drive cannot be accidentally deleted.

DriveSpace can use up to 1 GB of space to store from 1 to 2 GB worth of files.

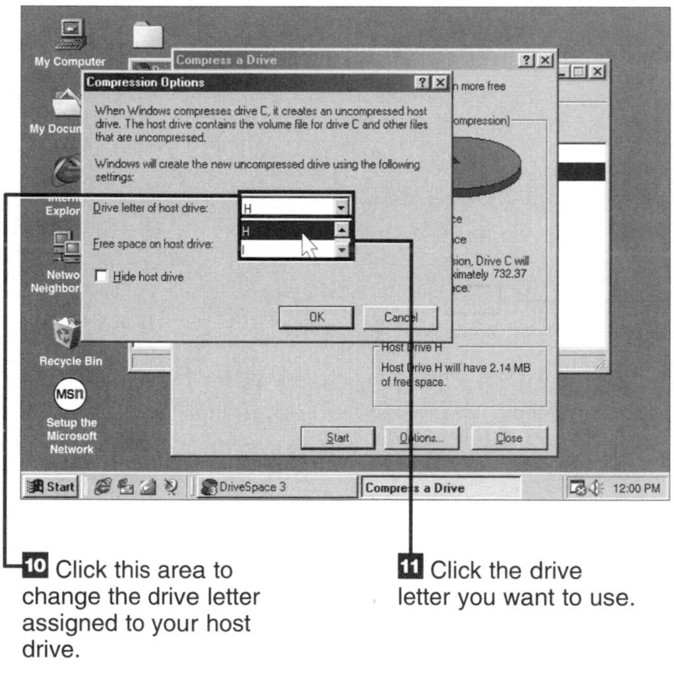

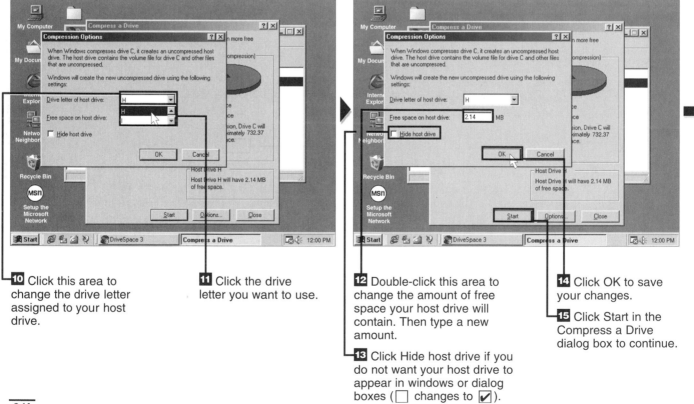

10 Click this area to change the drive letter assigned to your host drive.

11 Click the drive letter you want to use.

12 Double-click this area to change the amount of free space your host drive will contain. Then type a new amount.

13 Click Hide host drive if you do not want your host drive to appear in windows or dialog boxes (☐ changes to ☑).

14 Click OK to save your changes.

15 Click Start in the Compress a Drive dialog box to continue.

TIPS

Why should I create a new startup disk?

If you are having trouble starting Windows, you can use a startup disk to start your computer. You should create a new startup disk if you have installed DriveSpace since the last time you created a startup disk. The updated startup disk will recognize the compressed drive and allow you access to the drive.

My hard drive is larger than 1 GB. How can I compress the drive?

If your drive is larger than the maximum size DriveSpace can compress, you can compress smaller parts of the drive. See page 352.

What letter should I use for the host drive?

The letter DriveSpace suggests should be fine, unless you require that letter for another drive, such as a new hard drive or a mapped network drive.

Can I hide or unhide the host drive later?

In the DriveSpace window, select the Drive menu and then select Properties. Then click Hide this host drive.

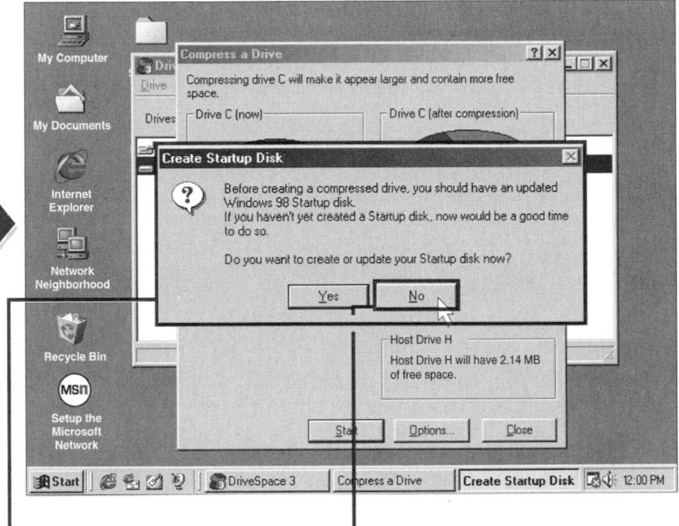

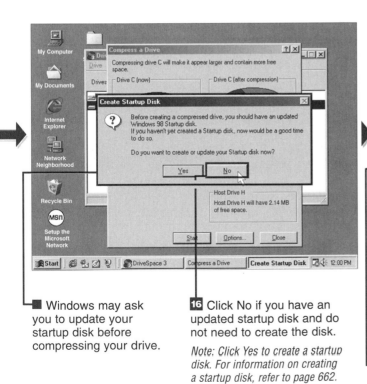

■ Windows may ask you to update your startup disk before compressing your drive.

16 Click No if you have an updated startup disk and do not need to create the disk.

Note: Click Yes to create a startup disk. For information on creating a startup disk, refer to page 662.

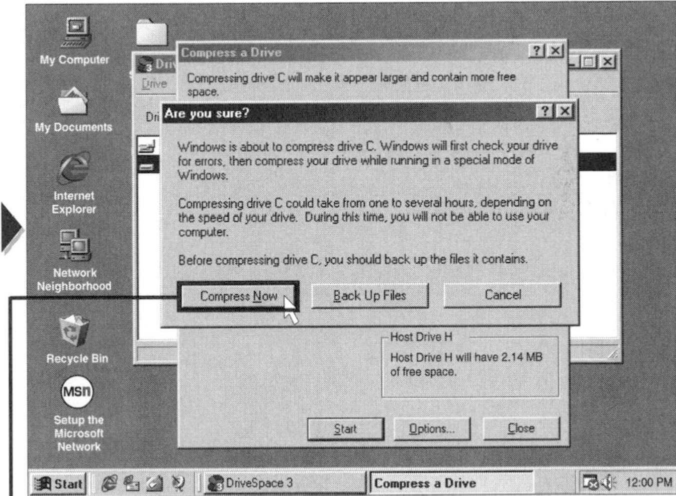

■ Windows is about to compress the drive. Windows asks you to back up your files before compressing your drive.

17 Click Compress Now if you have backed up your files and want to start the compression.

Note: Click Back Up Files if you want to back up your files now. For information on backing up files, refer to page 364.

CONTINUED

COMPRESS A DRIVE CONTINUED

Before compressing a drive, DriveSpace runs ScanDisk. ScanDisk checks for errors on the drive you want to compress.

The DriveSpace setup procedure takes care to protect your files. You will be able to recover your files even if a power outage occurs while DriveSpace is working.

After the compressed drive is created, DriveSpace compresses each file and moves it to the compressed drive.

After compressing the drive, Windows defragments the drive. Defragmentation reorganizes your files to improve the performance of the drive.

When the drive is compressed, DriveSpace estimates the amount of free space available on your drive. DriveSpace may double the amount of information the drive can store.

When you use a file from a compressed drive, the file is retrieved from the drive and uncompressed. When you save a file on a compressed drive, the file is compressed and then saved.

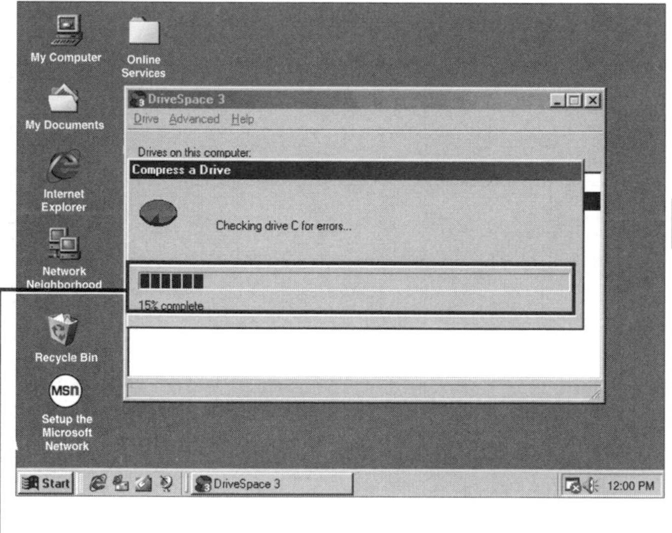

■ The Compress a Drive dialog box shows the progress of the compression.

Note: A dialog box may appear if the drive contains errors. You must correct the errors before you can compress the drive. To run ScanDisk and correct the errors, see page 312.

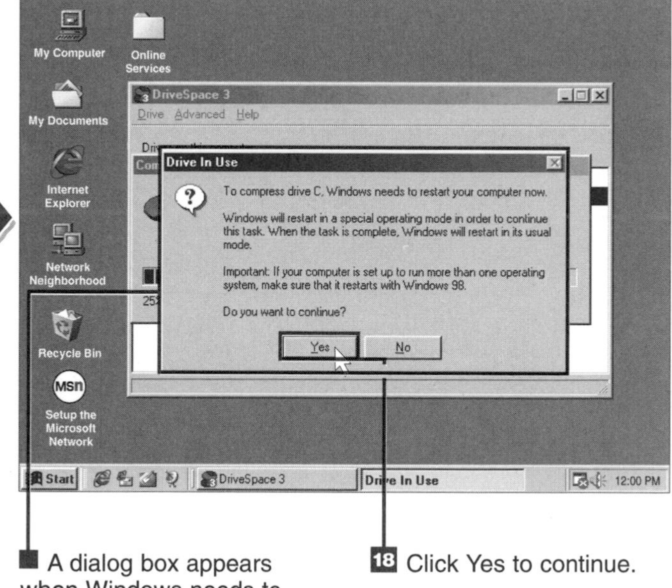

■ A dialog box appears when Windows needs to restart your computer.

18 Click Yes to continue.

TIPS

Where will I find the compressed drive?

Unless the host drive is hidden, you can find the compressed drive on the host drive. Display the Start menu, click Settings and then select Folder Options. Select the View tab and select the Show all files option. Then double-click the host drive in a My Computer or Windows Explorer window. The compressed drive is named Drvspace.000. If you compressed the drive before you installed Windows 98, the name may be Dblspace.000.

Will using compressed files slow down my computer?

As long as you have 8 MB of RAM and your computer is reasonably fast, using compressed files should not affect the speed of your computer. The time required to save or retrieve a file is balanced by the smaller file size. If there is a delay in saving or retrieving files, it should be only a minor delay.

Can I uncompress my drive?

You can undo the compression and return your drive to an uncompressed state. See page 356.

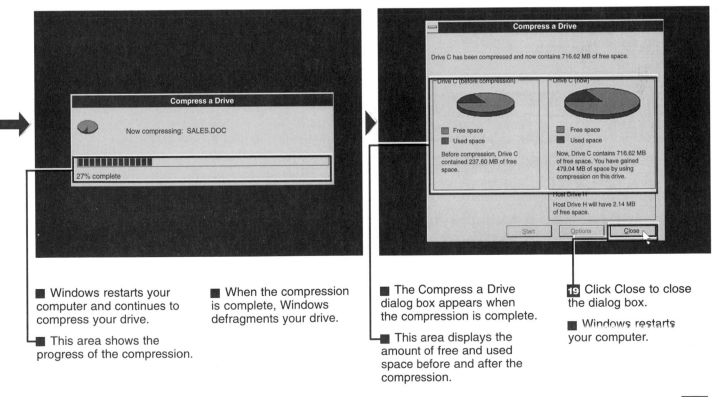

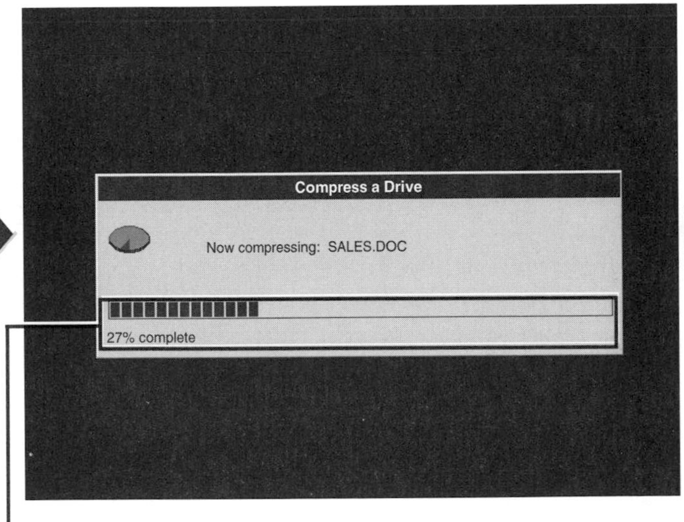

■ Windows restarts your computer and continues to compress your drive.

■ This area shows the progress of the compression.

■ When the compression is complete, Windows defragments your drive.

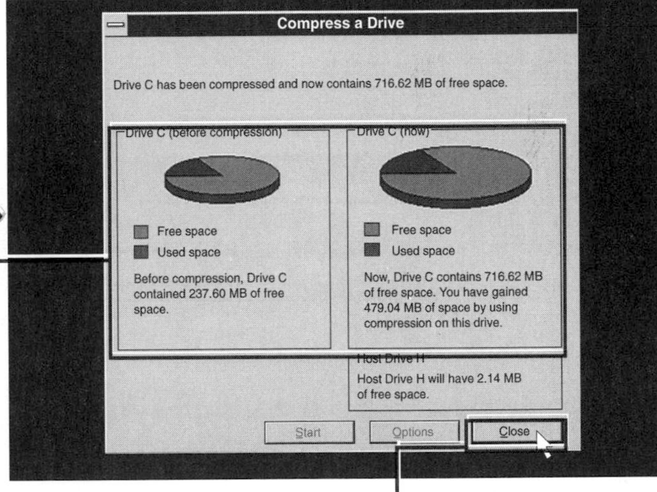

■ The Compress a Drive dialog box appears when the compression is complete.

■ This area displays the amount of free and used space before and after the compression.

19 Click Close to close the dialog box.

■ Windows restarts your computer.

ADJUST FREE SPACE ON A COMPRESSED DRIVE

You can adjust the amount of free disk space for the compressed drive and the host drive. You should save all your files and quit all other programs before you begin to adjust the free space.

You can increase the free space on your compressed drive if there is free space available on your host drive. You can also increase the amount of free space on your host drive if you are not using all the space on your compressed drive.

When you increase the amount of free space on one drive, you decrease the amount of free space on the other drive. The maximum size of a compressed drive is 2 GB.

The larger the adjustment you make to the amount of free space, the longer the resizing process will take.

After you finish adjusting the free space on a compressed drive, Windows restarts the computer.

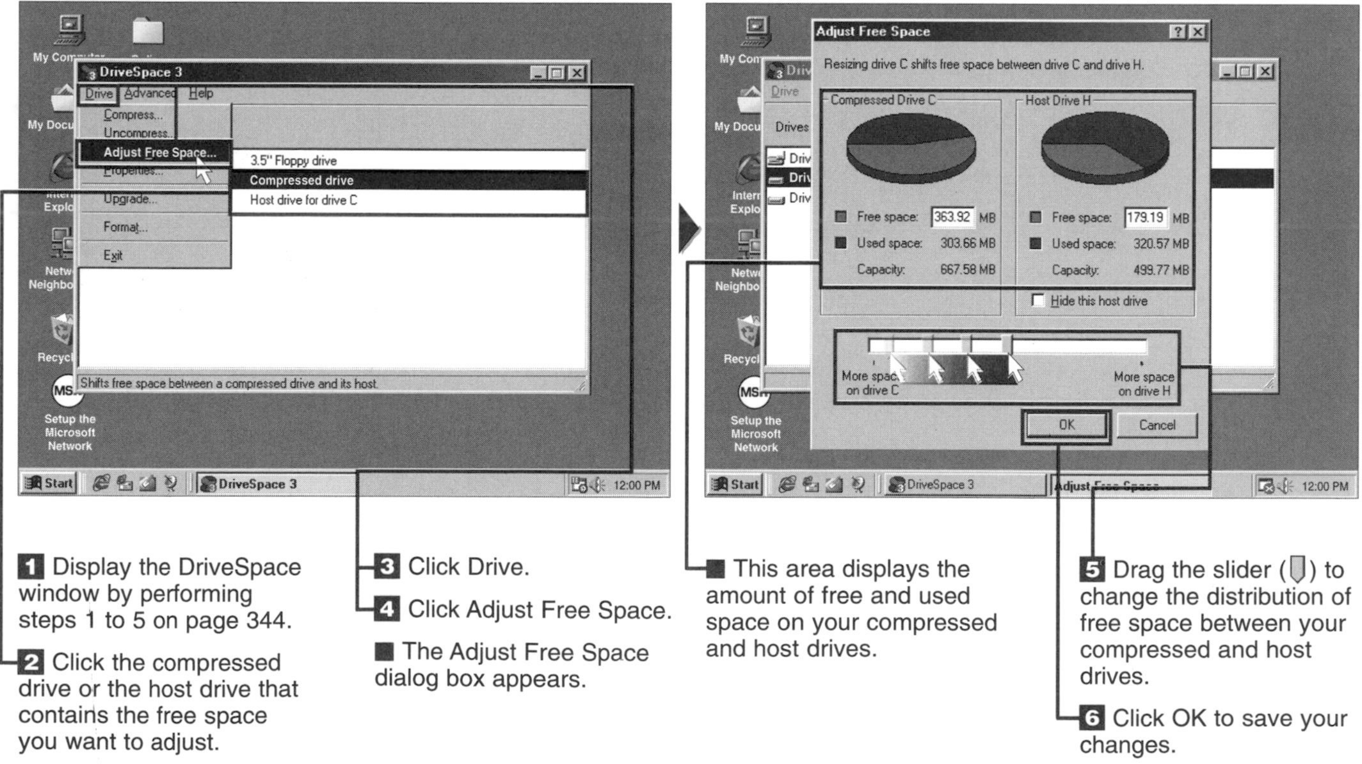

1 Display the DriveSpace window by performing steps 1 to 5 on page 344.

2 Click the compressed drive or the host drive that contains the free space you want to adjust.

3 Click Drive.

4 Click Adjust Free Space.

■ The Adjust Free Space dialog box appears.

■ This area displays the amount of free and used space on your compressed and host drives.

5 Drag the slider (▯) to change the distribution of free space between your compressed and host drives.

6 Click OK to save your changes.

TIPS

Will defragmenting my compressed drive increase available space?

Defragmenting your compressed drive will not increase the amount of free space.

The slider is not very accurate. How can I enter the exact size I want?

You can enter the exact size into the Free space text area for either the compressed or the host drive. You can also place the slider (▯) in approximately the right spot and then use the arrow keys on your keyboard to make more precise adjustments.

I am trying to copy a file to my compressed drive. Why does Windows tell me there is not enough free space?

The amount of free space on a compressed drive is only an estimate, based on files being able to compress to over half of their original size. Some types of files, such as program files, compress less than other types of files. If the file you want to copy to the compressed drive cannot compress enough, the file may not fit on the drive.

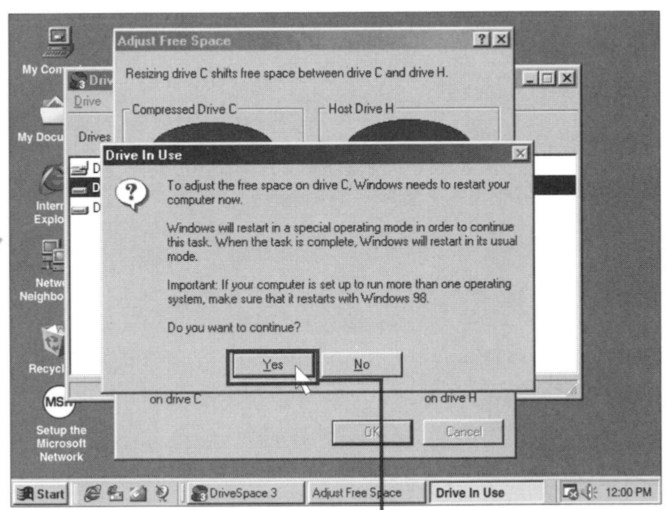

■ Windows needs to restart your computer to adjust the free space on your drives.

7 Click Yes to restart your computer.

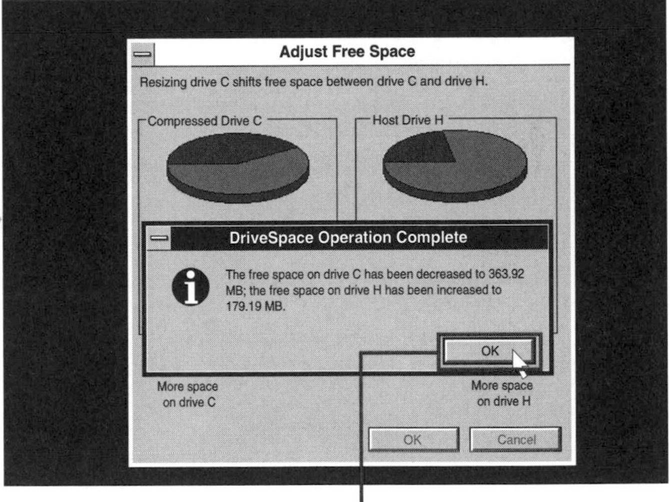

■ The DriveSpace Operation Complete dialog box appears when the operation is complete.

8 Click OK to close the dialog box.

■ Windows restarts your computer.

COMPRESS PART OF A DRIVE

You can use DriveSpace to turn the unused space on your hard drive into a compressed drive. This allows you to increase the available space for storing information by one-and-a-half to two times. Your hard drive and the files on your hard drive are unaffected by the compressed drive.

The compressed drive is actually a file called a Compressed Volume File (CVF). Your hard drive becomes a host drive and stores the compressed drive. DriveSpace assigns the compressed drive a drive letter.

You can specify the amount of space that is used to create the compressed drive. DriveSpace can use up to 1 GB of available space to create a compressed drive.

You should close all of your programs before creating the compressed drive. DriveSpace will need to restart your computer when the compression process is complete.

You cannot compress unused space on a hard drive that is already compressed. You also cannot use DriveSpace to compress any drives that use the FAT32 file system.

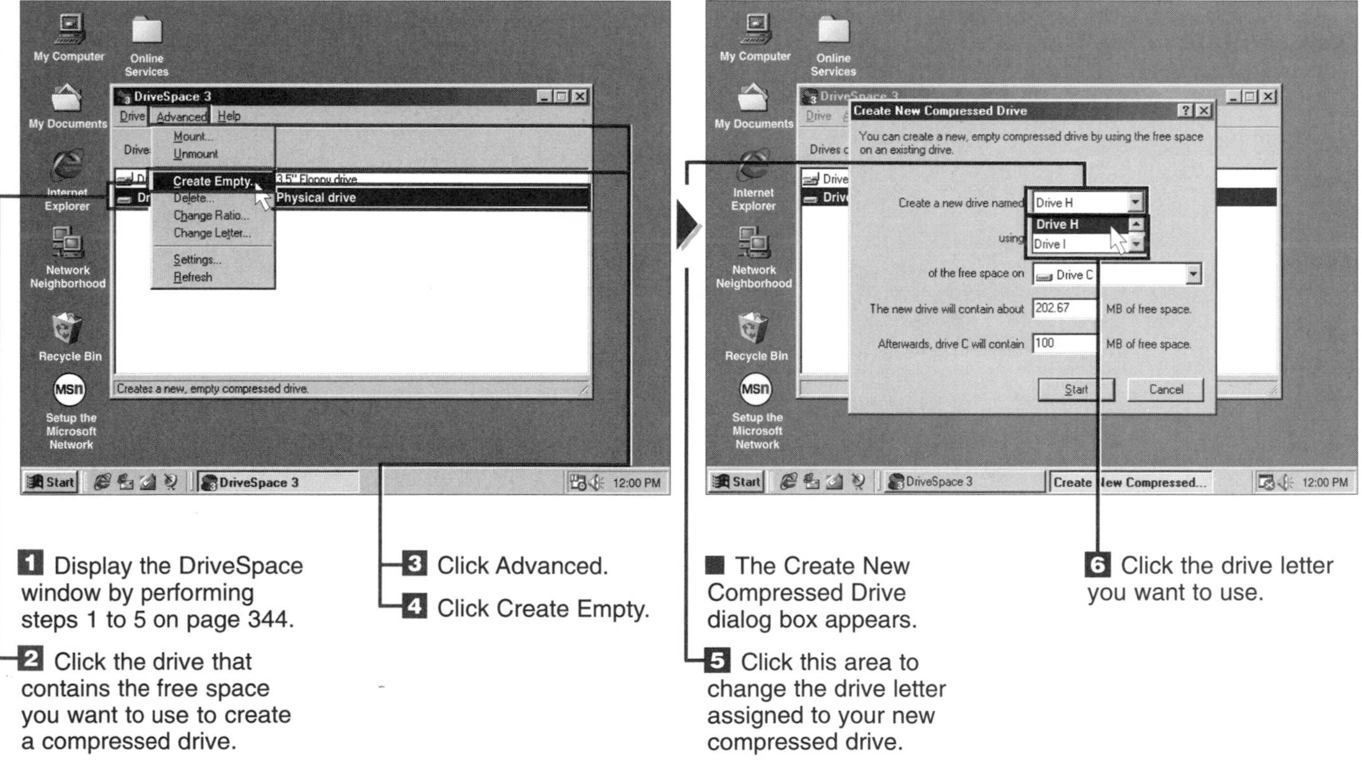

1 Display the DriveSpace window by performing steps 1 to 5 on page 344.

2 Click the drive that contains the free space you want to use to create a compressed drive.

3 Click Advanced.

4 Click Create Empty.

■ The Create New Compressed Drive dialog box appears.

5 Click this area to change the drive letter assigned to your new compressed drive.

6 Click the drive letter you want to use.

TIPS

How does compressing part of a drive differ from compressing an entire drive?

Compressing the unused space on a drive does not compress any of the files that currently exist on the drive. Compressing unused space is often safer because the Windows files are not on a compressed drive. If the files Windows needs to operate are on a compressed drive and the compressed drive fails, Windows will not start.

Can I change the size of the compressed drive after the drive is created?

On the Drive menu, you can use the Adjust Free Space command to make adjustments to the amount of space available on your compressed and host drives. See page 350.

What letter should I use for the new compressed drive?

You should use the letter DriveSpace suggests. The new drive letter should not match any of your current hard drives, CD-ROM drives, removable drives, network drives or any drives you plan to add.

Can I change the drive letter after the compressed drive is created?

On the Advanced menu, you can use the Change Letter command to change the drive letter. You should not change the drive letter if you have installed any programs on the compressed drive.

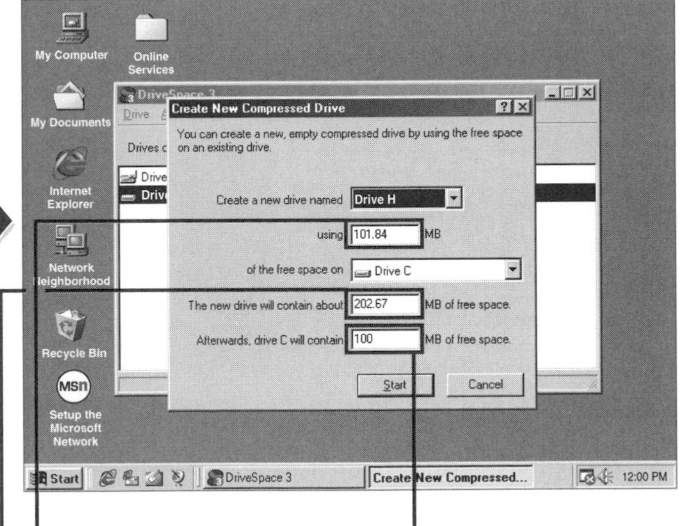

7 Double-click this area to change the amount of free space Windows will use to create your new drive. Then type a new amount.

■ This area displays the approximate amount of free space your new drive will contain.

■ This area displays the amount of free space that will remain on your hard drive.

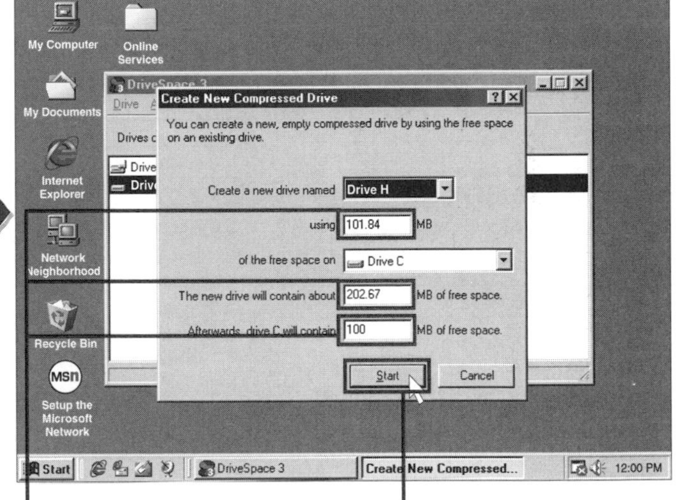

■ When you change the number displayed in one of these areas, Windows updates the numbers in the other two areas.

8 Click Start to start the compression.

CONTINUED

COMPRESS PART OF A DRIVE CONTINUED

Once you have created a compressed drive, you can store files on the compressed drive just as you would on an uncompressed drive. If you have at least 8 MB of RAM, using compressed files should not affect the performance of your computer.

You can create several compressed drives to store different types of files. This is useful if you want to organize your files into specific drives for backup purposes.

When you move or save a file to the compressed drive, DriveSpace compresses the file. When you retrieve a compressed file, DriveSpace uncompresses the file for you. DriveSpace works in the background so you do not notice DriveSpace compressing and uncompressing your files.

A compressed file takes up less space on your drive. Some files compress more than others. For example, document files compress significantly, but program files compress very little. Files that are already compressed, such as files with the .zip extension, may not compress at all.

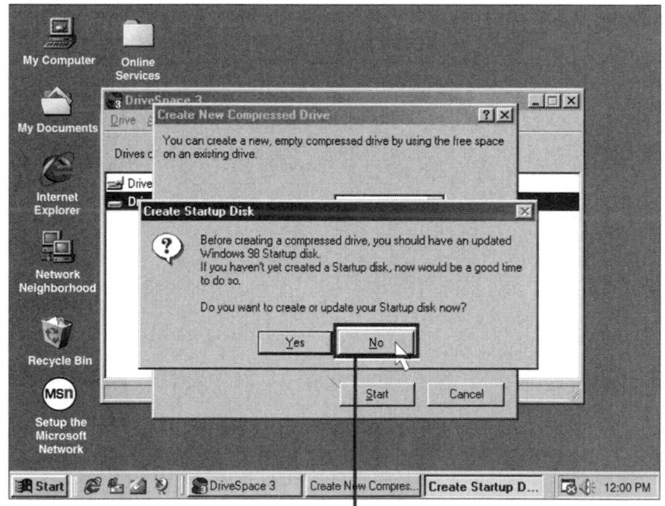

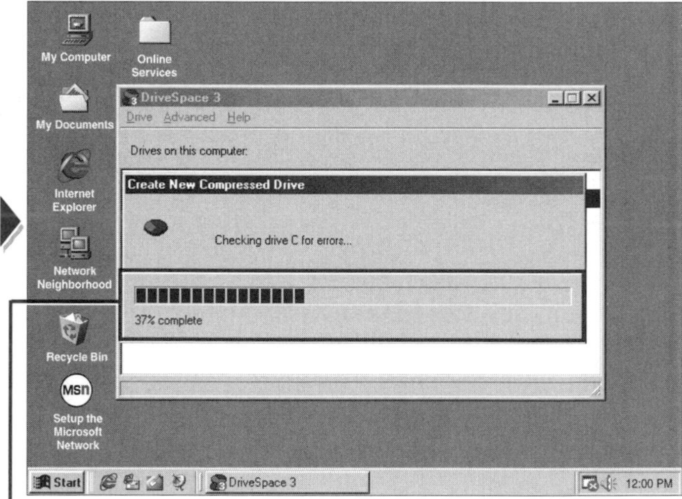

■ Windows may ask you to update your startup disk before creating a compressed drive.

9 Click No if you have an updated startup disk and do not need to create the disk.

Note: Click Yes to create a startup disk. For information on creating a startup disk, refer to page 662.

■ A dialog box appears. This area displays the progress of the compression.

Note: A dialog box may appear if the drive contains errors. You must correct the errors before you can compress the drive. To run ScanDisk and correct the errors, see page 312.

TIPS

Should I create a new startup disk?

A startup disk allows you to start Windows when Windows will not start normally. You should create a new startup disk if you have installed DriveSpace since you created your startup disk.

Can I move my programs to the compressed drive?

Most programs will not work properly if they are moved to a different drive. You should uninstall the program to remove it from the current drive. You can then install the program on the compressed drive.

Why do I have less space available on my compressed drive than I expected?

DriveSpace estimates how much information will fit on a compressed drive. The estimate may not be accurate because some types of files compress more than others. To change the estimate to reflect the type of files you are storing on the compressed drive, choose the Advanced menu in the DriveSpace window and then select the Change Ratio command.

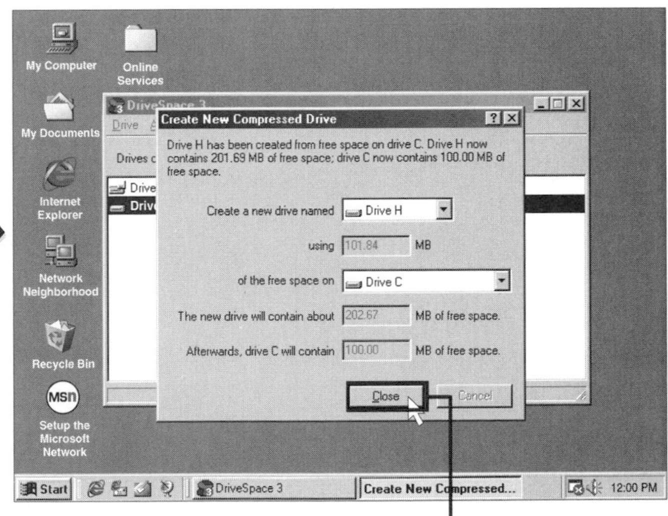

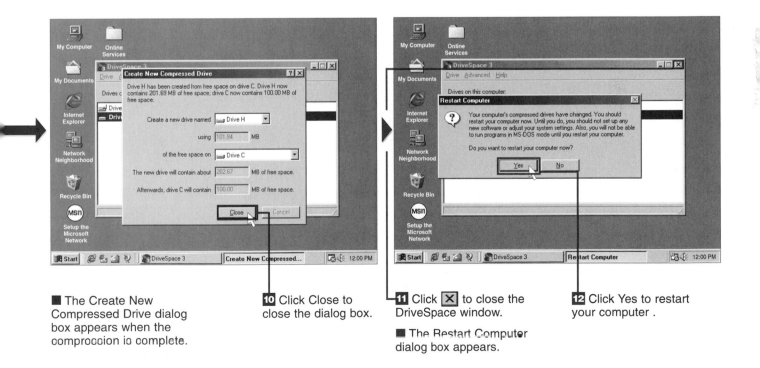

■ The Create New Compressed Drive dialog box appears when the compression is complete.

10 Click Close to close the dialog box.

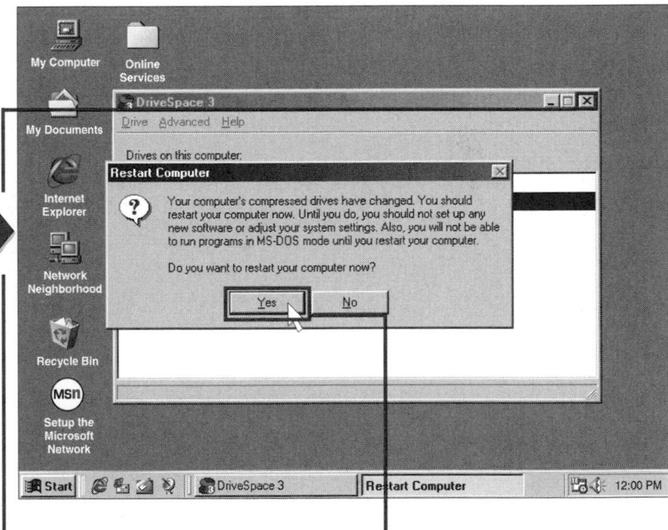

11 Click ☒ to close the DriveSpace window.

■ The Restart Computer dialog box appears.

12 Click Yes to restart your computer .

UNCOMPRESS A DRIVE

When you no longer need a compressed drive, you can uncompress the drive.

DriveSpace verifies that you will have enough space on the drive to store the compressed files when they are uncompressed. If there is not enough space to store the uncompressed files, DriveSpace will warn you and show you how much free space is needed. You can delete files, move them to another drive or archive them in a backup set to make space on the drive.

DriveSpace is careful to protect your files during the uncompression process, but you should make sure you create a backup set of your files before you begin to uncompress a drive.

The uncompression process requires you to restart your computer. You should save all your documents and exit all programs before starting to uncompress a drive.

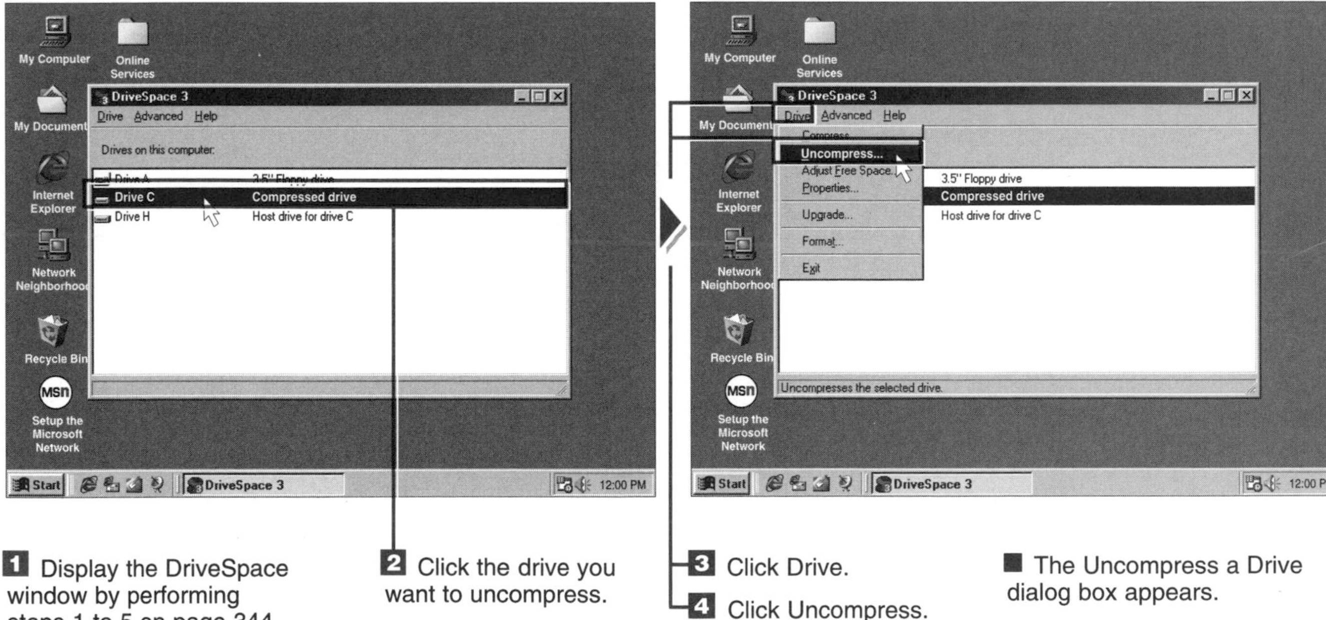

1 Display the DriveSpace window by performing steps 1 to 5 on page 344.

2 Click the drive you want to uncompress.

3 Click Drive.

4 Click Uncompress.

■ The Uncompress a Drive dialog box appears.

Do I need to unhide the host drive before I can uncompress a drive?

DriveSpace will unhide the host drive for you. DriveSpace will also return the host to its original drive letter.

How do I delete all of the files from a compressed drive without deleting the drive?

Choose the Drive menu and then select the Format command to delete all of the files in a compressed drive. You can also open a My Computer or Windows Explorer window for the drive and use Ctrl+A to select all files and folders. Then press the Delete key to move all the files to the Recycle Bin.

Can I reduce the size of a compressed drive without uncompressing it?

In the Drive menu, click the Adjust Free Space command. For information, see page 350.

Can I delete a compressed drive I no longer need?

You can delete a compressed drive and all of the information it contains by choosing the Advanced menu and then selecting the Delete command.

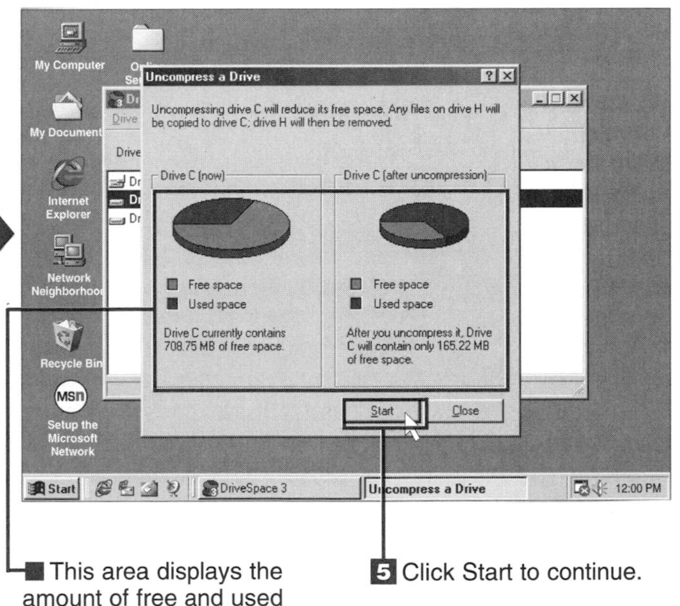

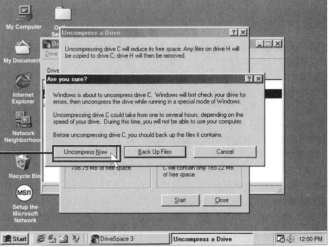

■ This area displays the amount of free and used space before and after you uncompress the drive.

5 Click Start to continue.

■ Windows is about to uncompress the drive. Windows asks you to back up your files before uncompressing the drive.

6 Click Uncompress Now if you have backed up your files and want to start the uncompression.

Note: Click Back Up Files if you want to back up your files now. For information on backing up files, see page 364.

CONTINUED

UNCOMPRESS A DRIVE CONTINUED

When you uncompress a drive, all of the files on the compressed drive are moved back to the uncompressed host drive. DriveSpace removes the compressed drive from your computer and returns the host to its original drive letter.

The uncompression process may take several hours to complete. You will not be able to use your computer while DriveSpace is uncompressing a drive. You may want to wait and uncompress a drive at a time when you will not need your computer, such as after work.

When the last compressed drive is removed from your computer, DriveSpace may ask if you want to remove the software used to access compressed drives, called the compression driver. If you still intend to use compressed floppy or removable disks, do not remove the compression driver.

You cannot uncompress a drive if it will change the letter of the drive that contains Windows. This may happen if you installed Windows on a compressed drive.

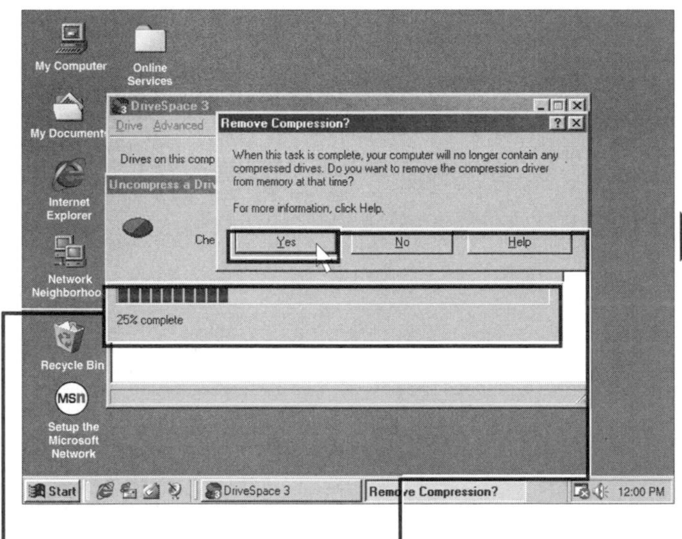

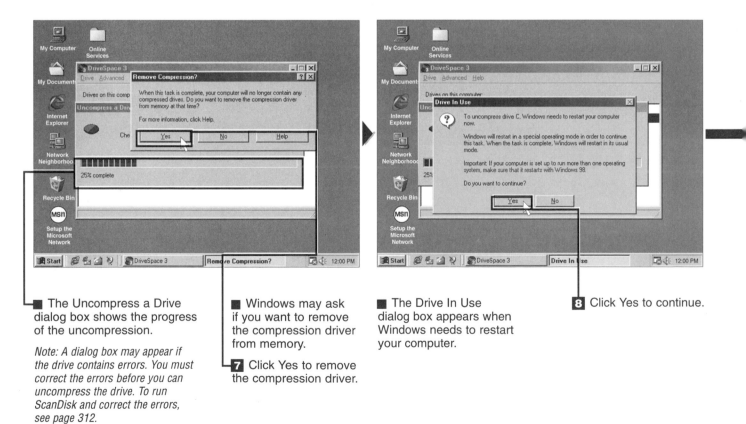

■ The Uncompress a Drive dialog box shows the progress of the uncompression.

Note: A dialog box may appear if the drive contains errors. You must correct the errors before you can uncompress the drive. To run ScanDisk and correct the errors, see page 312.

■ Windows may ask if you want to remove the compression driver from memory.

7 Click Yes to remove the compression driver.

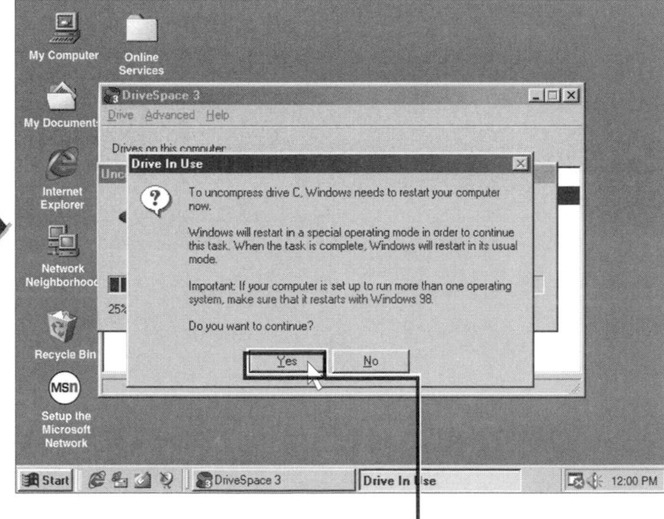

■ The Drive In Use dialog box appears when Windows needs to restart your computer.

8 Click Yes to continue.

TIPS

I uncompressed my hard drive. Why can't I access a compressed floppy disk?

If you removed the compression driver when you uncompressed your hard drive, you will only see a file named Readthis.txt when you try to access a compressed floppy disk. You can open this file to read instructions on how to access the files on a compressed disk.

Should I defragment a drive I uncompressed?

You should defragment a drive after you have uncompressed or deleted a compressed drive. To defragment a drive, see page 316.

Can I uncompress a floppy disk?

You can uncompress a floppy disk as long as there is enough space on the disk to store the files it contains when the files are uncompressed. If you do not have enough space, you can move the files to a folder on your hard drive, uncompress the floppy disk and then move the files you need from your hard drive back to the floppy disk.

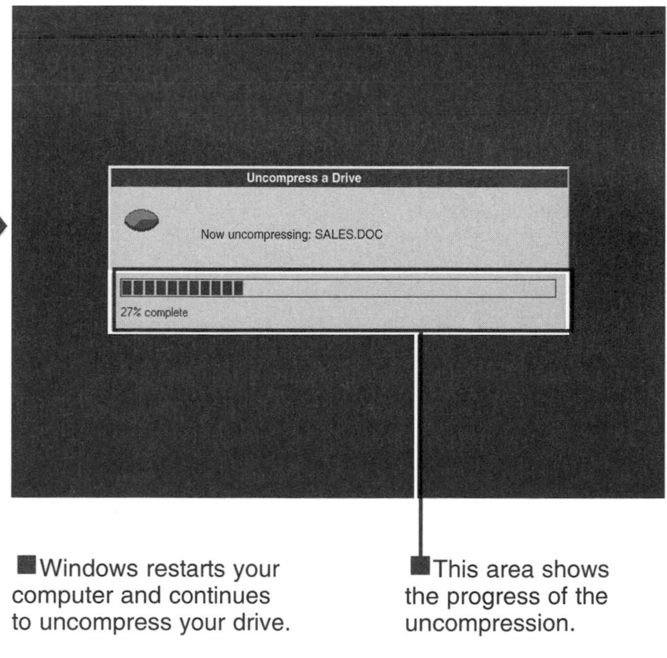

■ Windows restarts your computer and continues to uncompress your drive.

■ This area shows the progress of the uncompression.

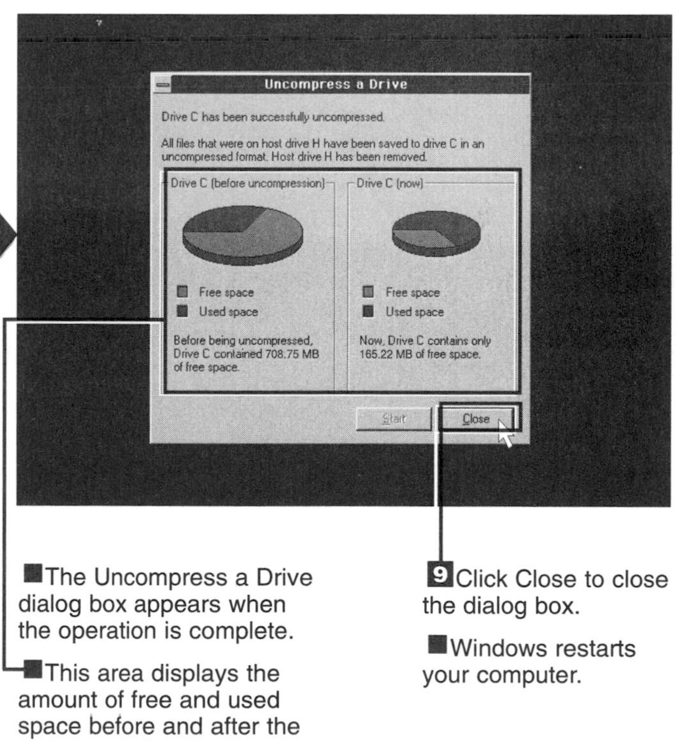

■ The Uncompress a Drive dialog box appears when the operation is complete.

■ This area displays the amount of free and used space before and after the uncompression process.

9 Click Close to close the dialog box.

■ Windows restarts your computer.

USING COMPRESSION AGENT

After using DriveSpace 3 to compress your computer's hard drive, you can use Compression Agent to change the level of compression on your files. Compression Agent optimizes compression and further decreases the space used by files on a compressed drive.

Compression Agent includes two compression formats. HiPack compression improves on the standard DriveSpace 3 compression. UltraPack applies even more compression than HiPack to further reduce the disk space required to store your files.

HiPack and UltraPack reduce the amount of disk space required by your files, but they also increase the amount of time it will take your computer to access and use the compressed files. Files that you have UltraPacked can be slow to access, so you may want to leave recently used files in the HiPack format or without any additional compression.

You can run Compression Agent at regular intervals or whenever you are low on disk space. Compression Agent is a processor-intensive task. You will find other Windows tasks very slow while Compression Agent is running.

You cannot use Compression Agent if your drive uses the FAT32 file system.

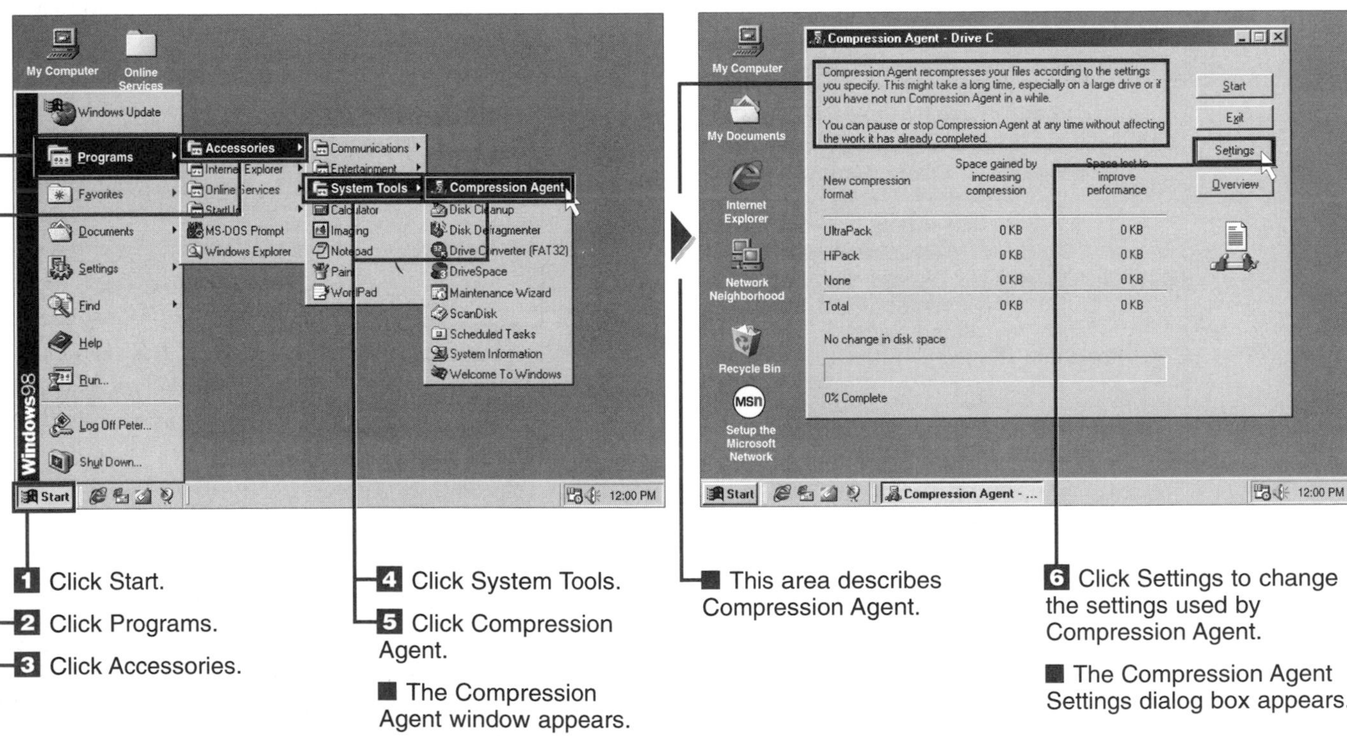

1 Click Start.

2 Click Programs.

3 Click Accessories.

4 Click System Tools.

5 Click Compression Agent.

■ The Compression Agent window appears.

■ This area describes Compression Agent.

6 Click Settings to change the settings used by Compression Agent.

■ The Compression Agent Settings dialog box appears.

TIPS

Why isn't Compression Agent on my Start menu?

Compression Agent may not be installed on your computer. You must add the Disk compression tools located in the System Tools component. To add Windows components, see page 610.

I ran out of disk space when I tried to use a file that I UltraPacked. What can I do?

You can set a minimum amount of free disk space to help avoid running out of disk space when you convert a file from UltraPack. In the Compression Agent Settings window, click the Advanced button to set the minimum amount you want. You should not reduce this setting to less than 20 MB.

Is it safe to pause or stop Compression Agent?

Stopping or pausing does not affect the work that Compression Agent has already completed. You can use the Pause or Stop buttons in the Compression Agent window to pause or stop Compression Agent at any time.

How can I see more information about the files on a compressed drive?

Right-click the drive's icon in the My Computer window and then select Properties. The Compression tab contains information about the drive and the compression status of the files on the drive.

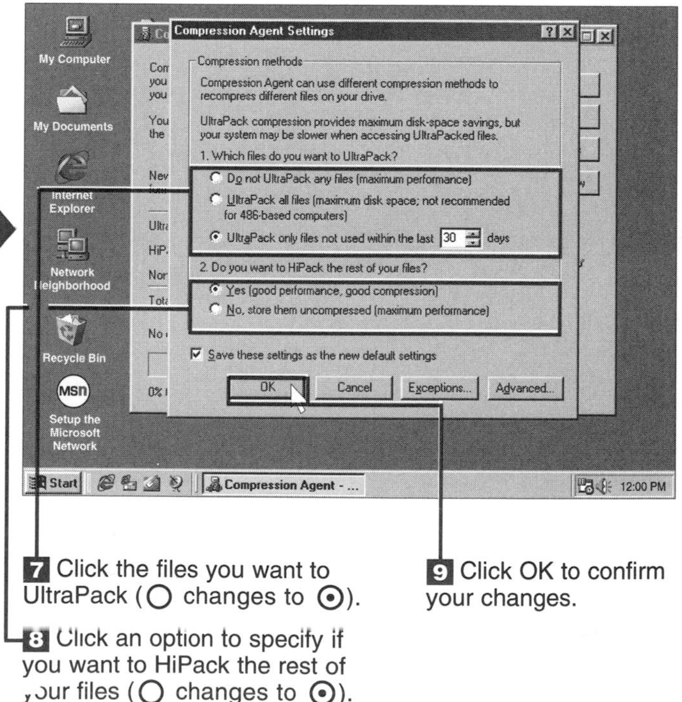

7 Click the files you want to UltraPack (○ changes to ⊙).

8 Click an option to specify if you want to HiPack the rest of your files (○ changes to ⊙).

9 Click OK to confirm your changes.

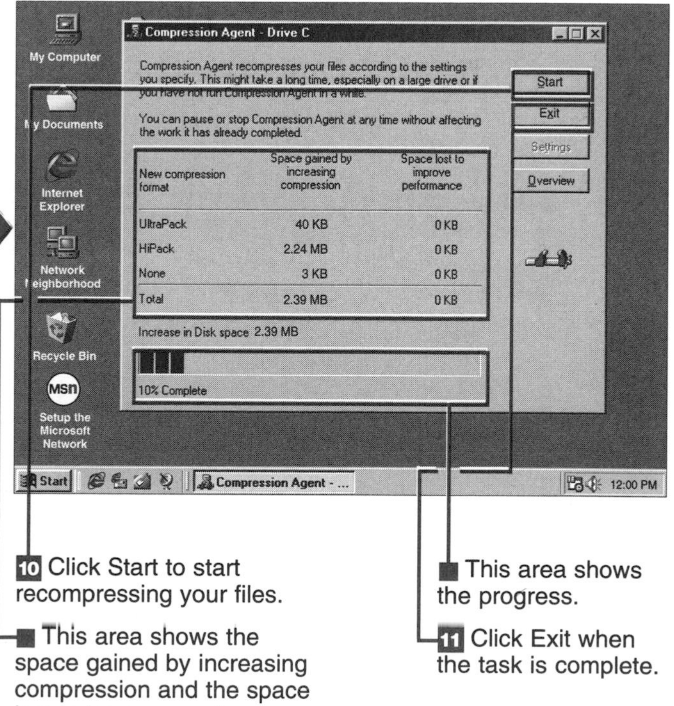

10 Click Start to start recompressing your files.

■ This area shows the space gained by increasing compression and the space lost to improve performance.

■ This area shows the progress.

11 Click Exit when the task is complete.

16

INTRODUCTION TO MICROSOFT BACKUP

You should regularly make backup copies of the files stored on your computer to protect them from theft, computer failure and viruses. To determine how often you should back up your work, consider the time it would take to re-install the software on your computer and recreate your documents. If you cannot afford to lose the work you accomplish in a day, back up your files once a day. If your work does not change much during the week, back up once a week.

You can save your backups on many different types of media, including floppy disks, a second hard drive, a removable disk, a network drive, a recordable CD or a tape cartridge. Using tape cartridges is an inexpensive and fast way to back up a large amount of information, such as all the files on your hard drive.

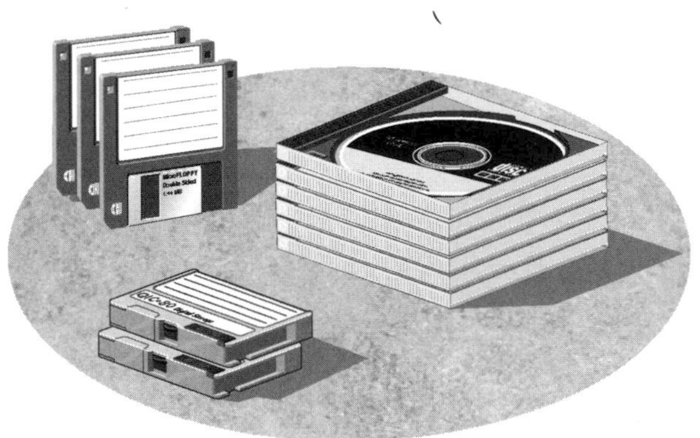

If the backup device you use includes its own software, the software will likely have more features and be better suited to the device than Microsoft Backup. However, Microsoft Backup is useful for transferring files between computers running Windows 98 that do not use compatible backup software.

Microsoft Backup can also use multiple floppy disks. This makes Backup useful for transferring files that will not fit on one disk.

You can also use Backup to compress and store files you seldom use. Once you have a backup copy of the files, you can delete the original files from your computer's hard drive. This creates more storage space on your computer, while allowing you to access the files if necessary.

Types of Backups

You can perform a full backup to back up all the information on your computer. In the event of a hard drive failure, you can use the full backup to restore all the files and folders on your hard drive. A full backup can be very large and time-consuming, but you may want to perform a full backup before you install a new program or change your computer's settings.

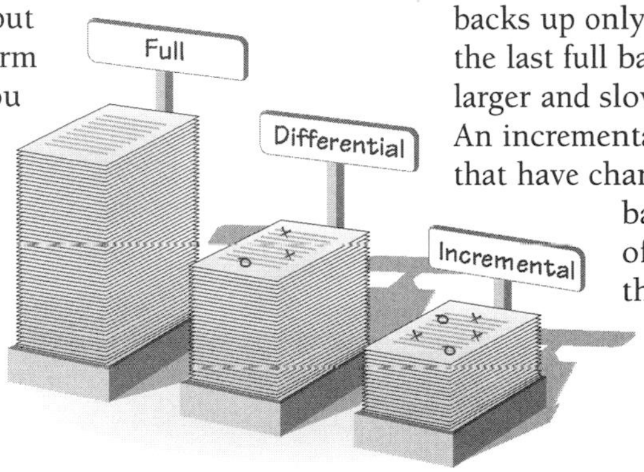

Backup also allows you to back up specific drives, folders and files you select on your computer. You can perform a differential backup or an incremental backup to back up only new or changed files. A differential backup backs up only the files that have changed since the last full backup. This type of backup is larger and slower than an incremental backup. An incremental backup backs up only the files that have changed since the last time you backed up the files. This type of backup is smaller and faster than a differential backup.

Backup Strategies

Hard drive disasters always seem to happen right after you miss a scheduled backup. Create and then strictly follow a backup schedule for full, differential and incremental backups. For example, begin a weekly cycle on a Friday and create a backup job selecting all the files and folders you want to back up. Perform differential or incremental backups Monday through Thursday. On Friday, repeat the cycle with a second set of media.

Using two sets of backup media can help minimize your chances of losing important information. Keep one set near your computer and the second set in another location where it will not be affected by fire or theft.

If your backup requires more than one tape cartridge or disk, you should number and label all the cartridges or disks before you begin the backup.

You may want to perform a full backup of your computer at least once a month.

BACK UP FILES

You can use Microsoft Backup to copy important information from your computer to a storage medium such as a tape cartridge, a removable disk or floppy disks for safekeeping.

If your computer's hard drive fails, you may lose valuable information. If you have backed up the information, you can use the backup copy to restore the information to your computer.

A backup copy also helps minimize loss of information caused by fire or the theft of a computer.

Many people also back up information they do not frequently use, such as large image files. The files can then be deleted from the computer's hard drive to help conserve disk space.

Before you can back up the information on your computer, you must create a backup job. A backup job allows you to specify what information you want to back up and where you want to store the information. When creating a backup job, you can choose to back up all of the information on your computer or just specific files, folders and drives.

It is strongly recommended that you back up all of the information on your computer on a regular basis.

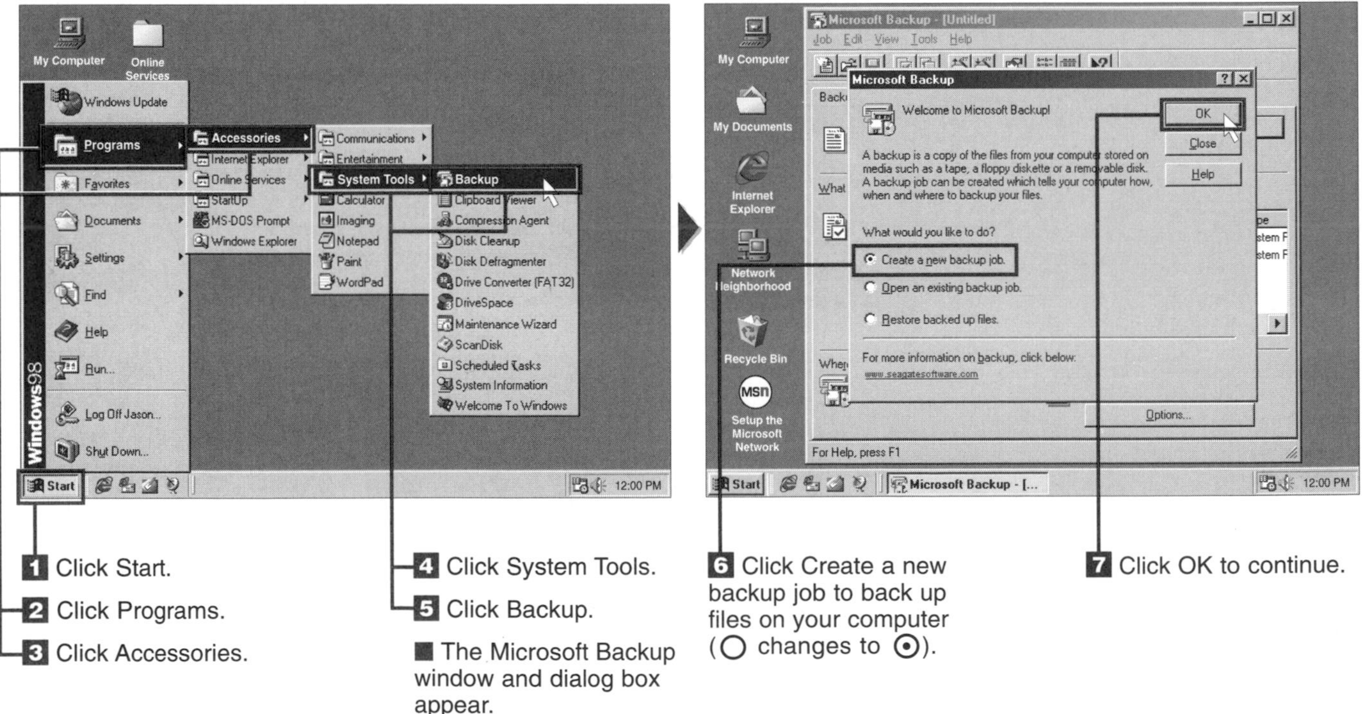

1 Click Start.

2 Click Programs.

3 Click Accessories.

4 Click System Tools.

5 Click Backup.

■ The Microsoft Backup window and dialog box appear.

6 Click Create a new backup job to back up files on your computer (○ changes to ⦿).

7 Click OK to continue.

TIPS

Why isn't Backup on my Start menu?

Microsoft Backup may not be installed on your computer. Backup is located in the System Tools component. To add Windows components, see page 610.

When I start Backup, a dialog box appears, stating that no backup devices were found on my computer. What should I do?

If you are not using a tape drive, click No and continue creating the backup job. If you are using a tape drive, Backup does not recognize the tape drive. Click Yes to install the tape drive so Backup can recognize the drive.

Do I need to format a tape cartridge before using it for a backup?

Many tape cartridges are already formatted when you buy them. To format a tape cartridge, display the Microsoft Backup window and click the Tools menu. Select Media and then select Format.

Do I have to create a new backup job every time I want to back up my files?

You only have to create a backup job once. You can then use the same backup job the next time you want to back up the information. See page 370.

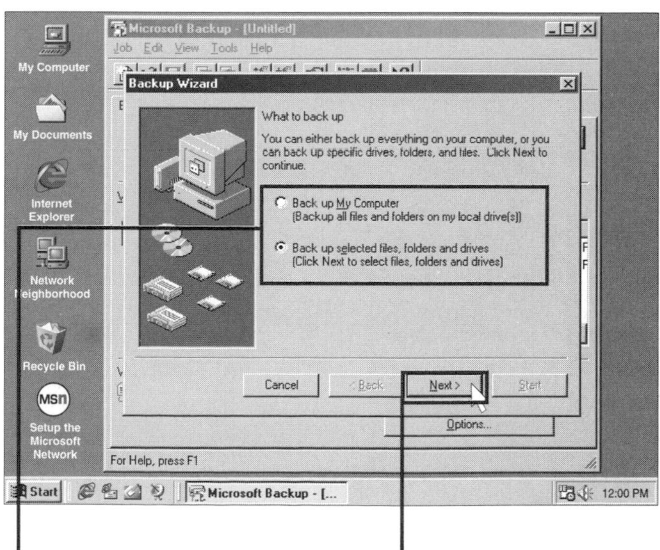

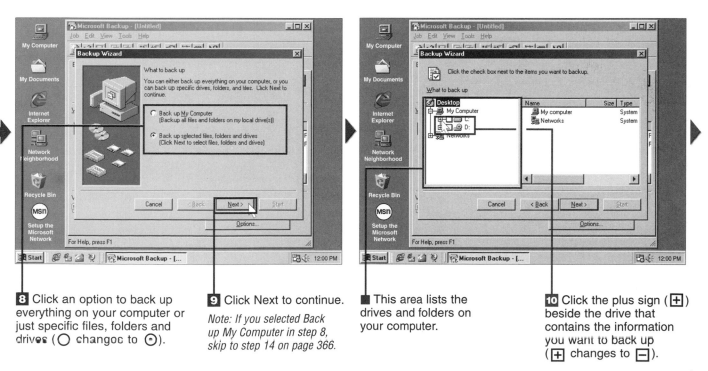

8 Click an option to back up everything on your computer or just specific files, folders and drives (○ changes to ⊙).

9 Click Next to continue.

Note: If you selected Back up My Computer in step 8, skip to step 14 on page 366.

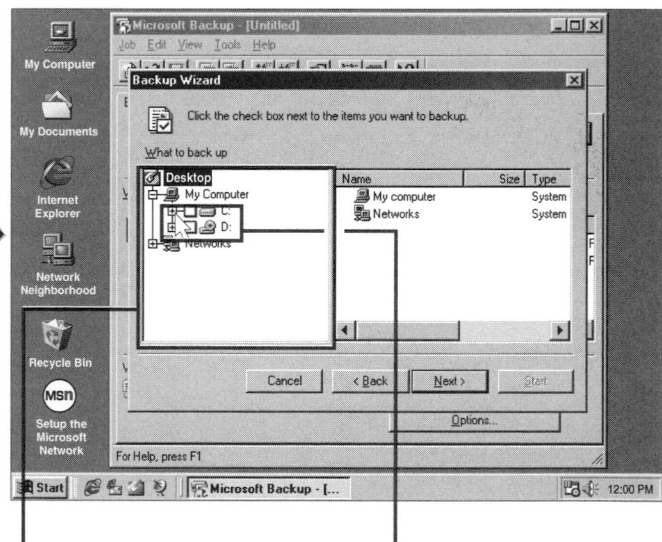

■ This area lists the drives and folders on your computer.

10 Click the plus sign (⊞) beside the drive that contains the information you want to back up (⊞ changes to ⊟).

CONTINUED

BACK UP FILES CONTINUED

You must specify which drives, folders and files on your computer you want to back up. When you select a drive, all of the folders and files on the drive will be backed up. If you select a folder, all of the folders and files within the folder will be backed up. You can also back up individual files.

You can choose to back up all the files you have selected or only the files that are new or have changed since a previous backup. The first time you perform a backup, you should back up all the files you have selected.

You can also specify where you want to store the backed up information. All of the drives, folders and files that you choose will be backed up to the storage medium in the location you select.

When the backup is complete, you can have Backup compare the original files to the backed up files to make sure that all of the information was successfully backed up.

You can also have Backup compress the information so more files will fit on a tape cartridge or disk. Different types of files can be compressed by different amounts.

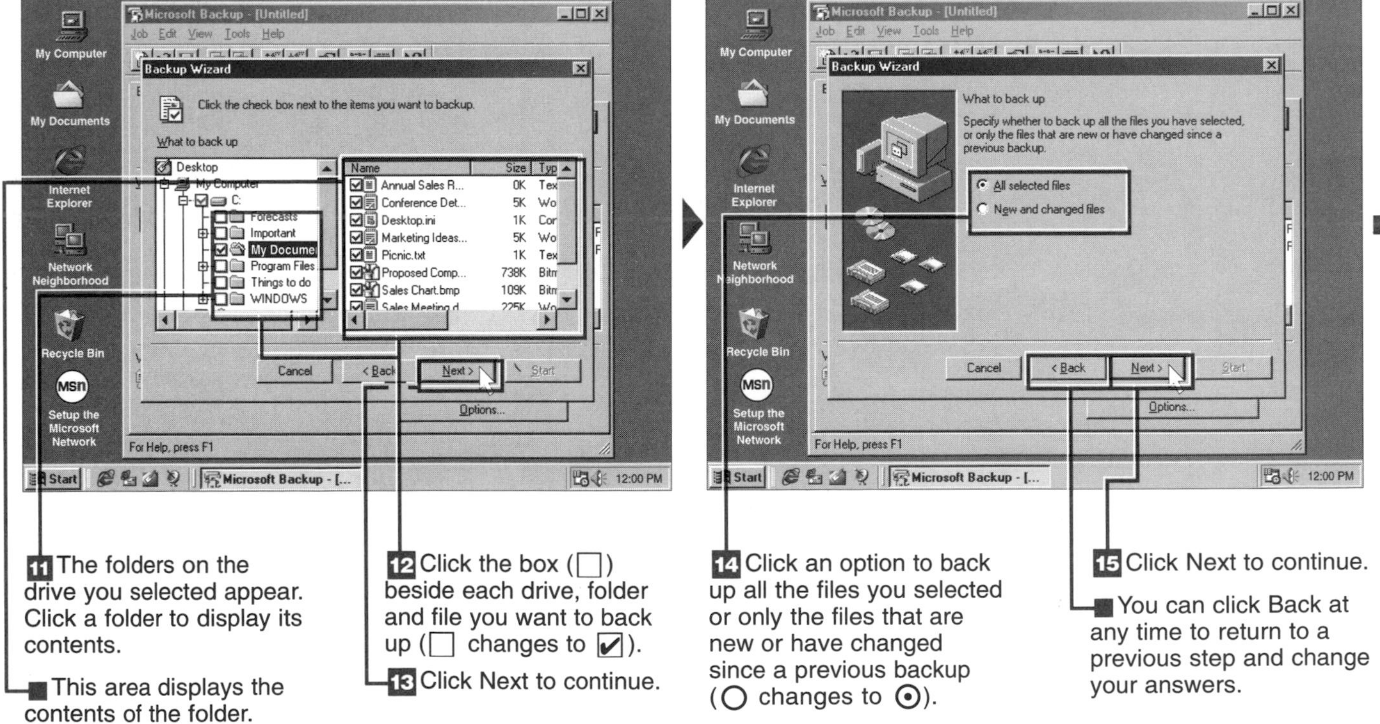

11 The folders on the drive you selected appear. Click a folder to display its contents.

■ This area displays the contents of the folder.

12 Click the box (☐) beside each drive, folder and file you want to back up (☐ changes to ☑).

13 Click Next to continue.

14 Click an option to back up all the files you selected or only the files that are new or have changed since a previous backup (○ changes to ⊙).

15 Click Next to continue.

■ You can click Back at any time to return to a previous step and change your answers.

TIPS

How can I tell what information will be backed up?

A blue check mark beside a drive, folder or file indicates that the entire drive, folder or file will be backed up. A gray check mark beside a drive or folder indicates that some, but not all, of the files or folders within the drive or folder will be backed up.

How can I back up my information to a different location?

You can choose to back up information to a specific location, such as your hard drive, a removable drive, a floppy drive or a network drive. To back up information to one of these locations, select File in step 16 below and then click the Browse button ( ) to select the location you want.

When Windows compared my original files to the files I backed up, errors were found. What causes this?

When errors occur, they are usually caused by faulty disks or tape cartridges. The existence of errors probably means that the disks or tape cartridges you are using are starting to wear out and should be replaced.

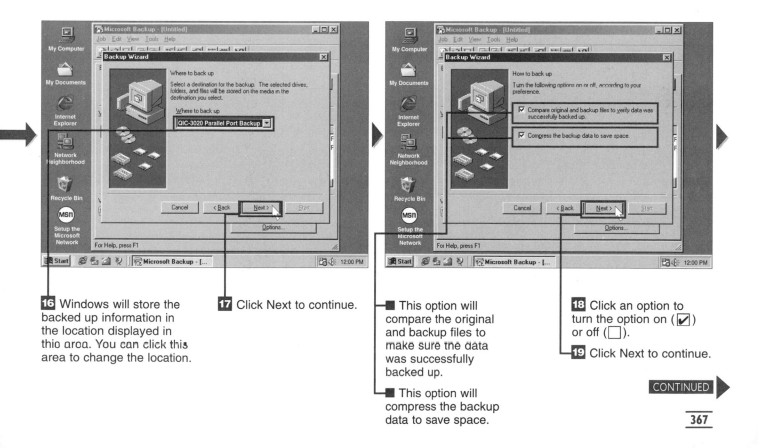

16 Windows will store the backed up information in the location displayed in this area. You can click this area to change the location.

17 Click Next to continue.

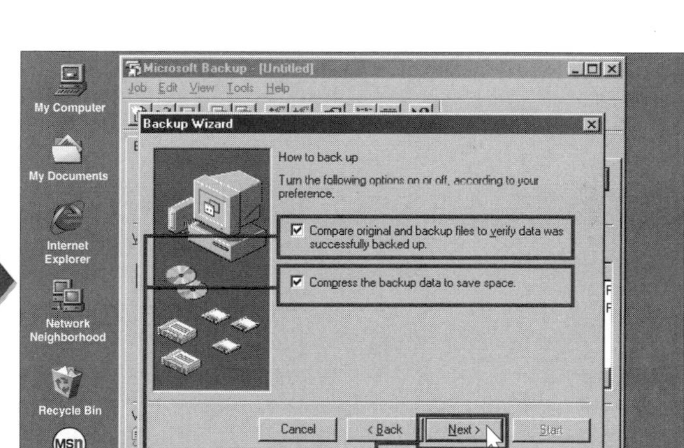

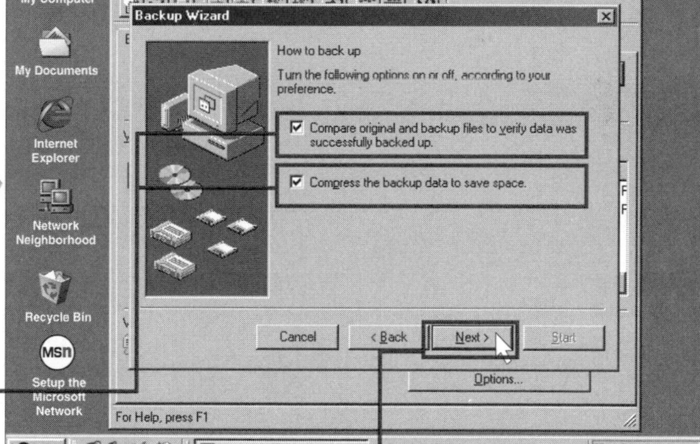

■ This option will compare the original and backup files to make sure the data was successfully backed up.

■ This option will compress the backup data to save space.

18 Click an option to turn the option on (☑) or off (☐).

19 Click Next to continue.

CONTINUED

BACK UP FILES CONTINUED

You must specify a name for the new backup job. You should use a name that describes the files that are being backed up and the backup job type. For example, a backup job called "System Files-All Files" will let you know exactly what type of information the backup job contains.

Once the backup has started, the Backup Progress window appears, displaying the status of the backup. The Backup Progress window also contains information such as the time elapsed and the number of files and bytes processed.

Depending on the type of backup medium you are using, you may need to provide information about the medium. For example, you may be asked to enter a name for the tape cartridge you are using.

You can use your computer while Microsoft Backup is backing up your files, but your computer may operate more slowly than normal. During the backup, if you open or change a file that is part of the backup job, the file may not be properly backed up.

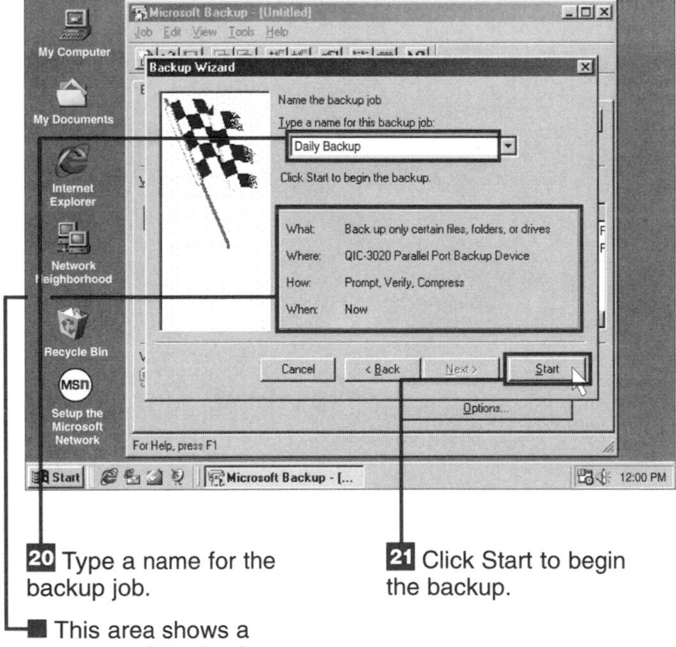

20 Type a name for the backup job.

■ This area shows a summary of the backup options you selected.

21 Click Start to begin the backup.

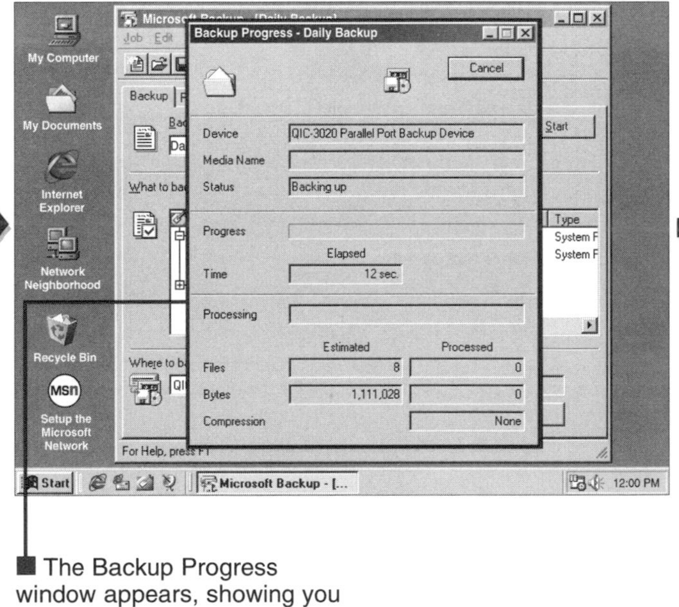

■ The Backup Progress window appears, showing you the progress of the backup.

TIPS

When I start a backup, a dialog box appears, stating that the media contains one or more backup sets. What should I do?

Click Overwrite if you wish to replace the existing backup with the current backup. If you are using a tape cartridge to store your backup, you can add the current backup to the tape cartridge without erasing the other backups on the cartridge. To add the current backup without replacing other backups, click Append.

Can I view information about a backup?

You can view a report at the end of a completed backup. In the Backup Progress window, click the Report button. A Notepad window opens and displays the report.

How do I print a report?

Many people print a copy of the report and keep it with their storage media so they can quickly see information about the backup. To print the report displayed in the Notepad window, click the File menu and then click Print.

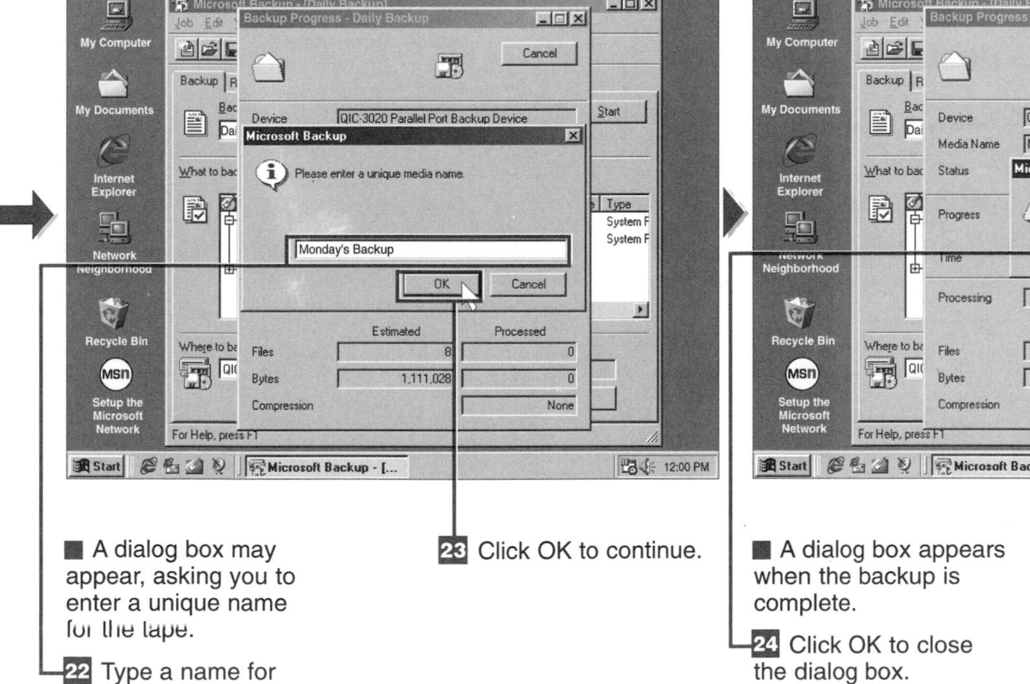

■ A dialog box may appear, asking you to enter a unique name for the tape.

22 Type a name for the tape.

23 Click OK to continue.

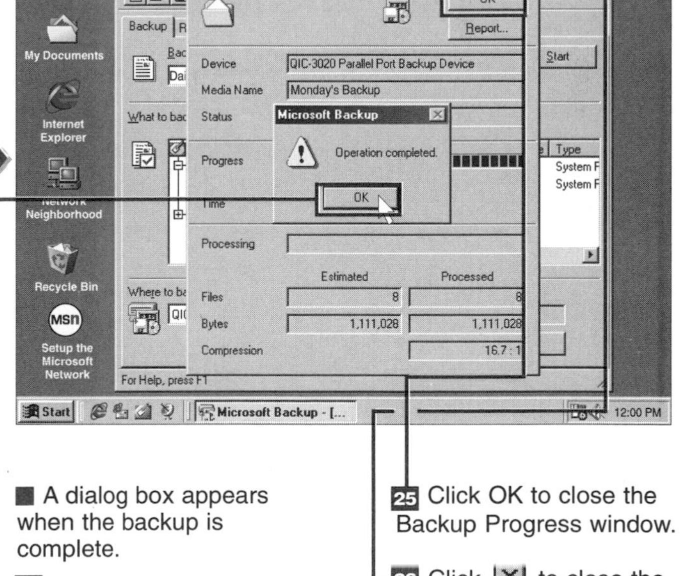

■ A dialog box appears when the backup is complete.

24 Click OK to close the dialog box.

25 Click OK to close the Backup Progress window.

26 Click ☒ to close the Microsoft Backup window.

16

OPEN AN EXISTING BACKUP JOB

A backup job contains all the settings for a backup, such as the drives, folders and files to be backed up, the type of backup to be performed and the backup media you want to use. You can open any backup job you have previously created to perform other backups using the same settings.

Microsoft Backup can store multiple backup jobs. For example, you may have one backup job that you use to back up all of your documents at the end of each week. You may have another backup job that you use once a month to back up the program files on your computer.

When you open an existing backup job, you can make changes to the current settings. You can choose to back up all the files in the backup job or only the files that are new or have changed since the last backup. You can also select new drives, folders or files to be backed up.

When you finish making changes to the backup job, you should save the changes.

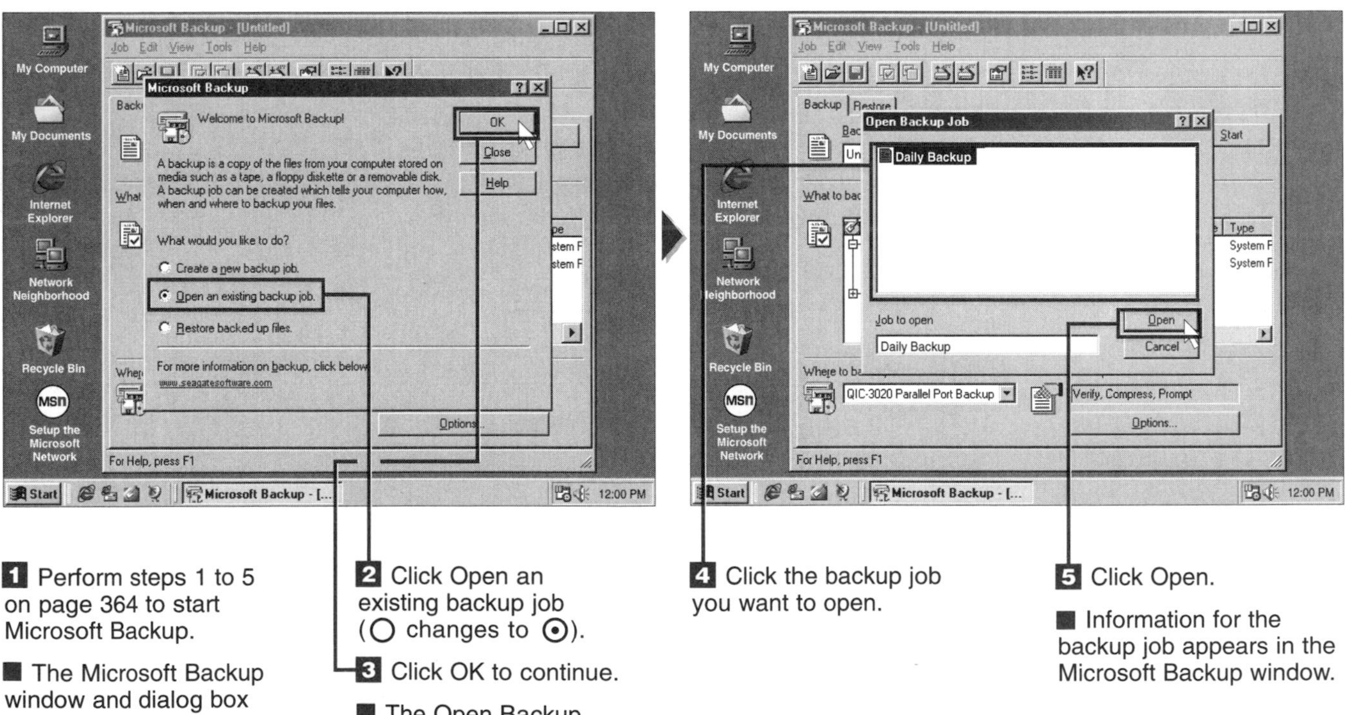

1 Perform steps 1 to 5 on page 364 to start Microsoft Backup.

■ The Microsoft Backup window and dialog box appear.

2 Click Open an existing backup job (○ changes to ⊙).

3 Click OK to continue.

■ The Open Backup Job dialog box appears.

4 Click the backup job you want to open.

5 Click Open.

■ Information for the backup job appears in the Microsoft Backup window.

How do I add folders and files to a backup job?

In the Microsoft Backup window, click the box beside the drive, folder or file that you wish to add to the backup job. A blue check mark (☑) appears beside each item included in the backup job.

How do I view the number of files in a backup job?

In the Microsoft Backup window, click the View menu and then click Selection Information to view the number of files selected for backup and the number of bytes for the selected files.

Can I save the changes to the backup job with a different name?

In the Microsoft Backup window, choose the Job menu and then select Save As. Then type a new name for the backup job and click Save. This gives you two copies of the backup job–the original backup job and the backup job with all your changes.

How do I delete a backup job?

To delete a backup job you no longer need, click the Job menu in the Microsoft Backup window and then select Delete. Then select the backup job you want to remove and click the Delete button.

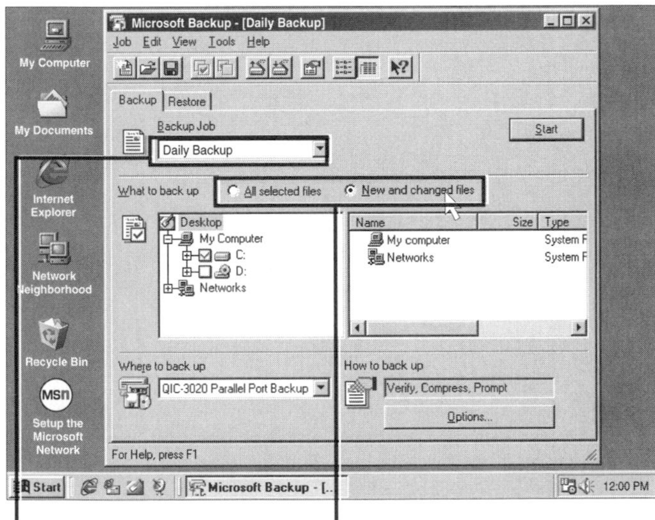

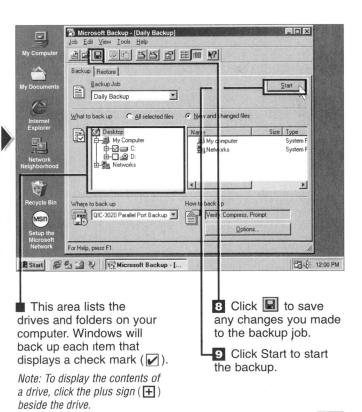

6 This area displays the name of the backup job. You can click this area to display the information for another backup job.

7 Click an option to back up all the files in the backup job or only the files that are new or have changed since a previous backup (○ changes to ⊙).

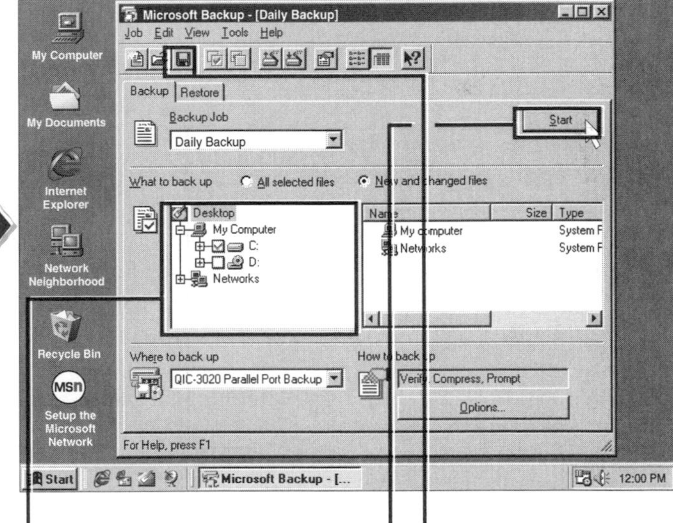

■ This area lists the drives and folders on your computer. Windows will back up each item that displays a check mark (☑).

Note: To display the contents of a drive, click the plus sign (⊞) beside the drive.

8 Click 💾 to save any changes you made to the backup job.

9 Click Start to start the backup.

CHANGE BACKUP JOB OPTIONS

Backup offers several options you can change to simplify and customize your backup. The options you choose will be saved with the backup job and used every time you perform the backup.

You can have Backup compare the files in the backup with the original files on your computer to ensure that the files are identical and the backup was successful.

You can specify whether you want Backup to compress the backed up files. If you choose the fastest way to compress information, the backup will require more space on your storage medium. If you choose to compress information to save space on your storage medium, the backup job will take longer to complete.

When backing up information onto a tape cartridge that already contains backed up information, you can have Backup add the new backup to the tape cartridge or replace the existing backups on the tape cartridge with the new backup.

You can also assign a password to a backup job to help prevent unauthorized people from restoring the backup to another computer. You should carefully note your password. Without it, you will not be able to restore your backed up information.

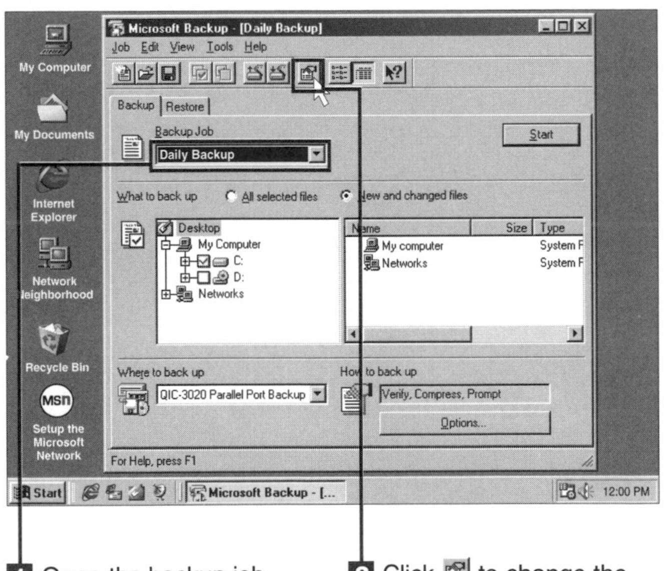

1 Open the backup job you want to change. See page 370 to open an existing backup job.

2 Click to change the options for the backup job.

■ The Backup Job Options dialog box appears.

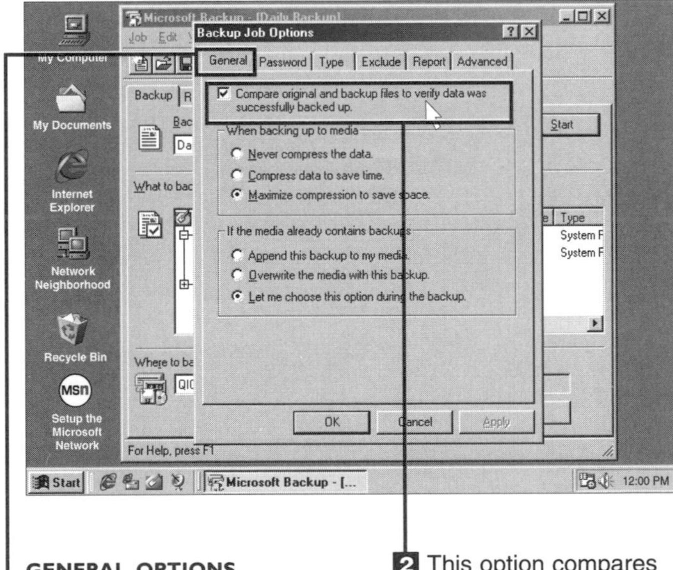

GENERAL OPTIONS

1 Click the General tab.

2 This option compares the original and backup files to verify the data was successfully backed up. Click this option to turn the option on (✔) or off (☐).

TIPS

Should I compress all of my files?

Some file formats, such as those with the .zip or .jpg extension, are already compressed and would not benefit by being compressed further. When backing up files that are already compressed, use the Never compress the data option on the General tab. Using this option will also help to reduce the time it takes to complete the backup.

Should I overwrite the existing backups on my media?

Overwriting will erase any previous backups stored on the storage medium. You should only overwrite previous backups if you have another copy of the information that you are backing up. If the computer fails during the backup, you may not be able to access the files on the computer or use the backup you were making.

What type of password should I use?

You should pick a password that will be difficult for others to guess. Passwords can be up to eight characters in length and are case-sensitive. Ideally, your password should be a mixture of upper and lower case letters combined with numbers and other characters, such as BLue@321.

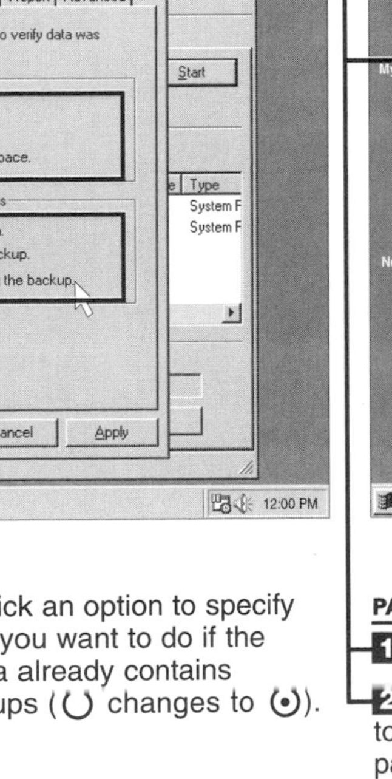

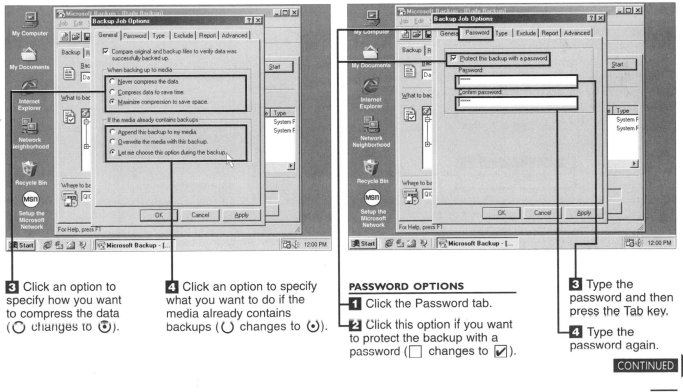

3 Click an option to specify how you want to compress the data (○ changes to ⦿).

4 Click an option to specify what you want to do if the media already contains backups (○ changes to ⦿).

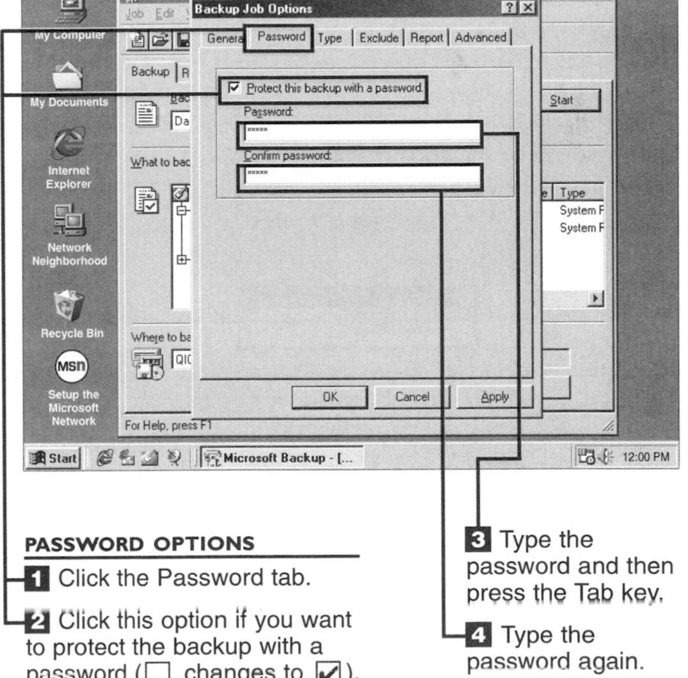

PASSWORD OPTIONS

1 Click the Password tab.

2 Click this option if you want to protect the backup with a password (☐ changes to ☑).

3 Type the password and then press the Tab key.

4 Type the password again.

CONTINUED

CHANGE BACKUP JOB OPTIONS
CONTINUED

When changing the options for a backup job, you can specify which files you want to back up. You can back up all your selected files or only the files that are new or have changed since your last backup.

If you choose to back up only new or changed files, you can select a differential or incremental backup type. The differential type backs up all the selected files that have changed since the last time you backed up all the selected files. The incremental type backs up all the selected files that have changed since the last time you performed any type of backup.

You can also choose to have Windows leave out files with a certain extension from the backup.

Backup generates a report after each backup has been completed. You can select what information you want to appear in the report.

When performing a backup, dialog boxes appear, which pause the backup until a selection is made. If you will not be at your computer when the backup is performed, you can stop Backup from displaying these dialog boxes.

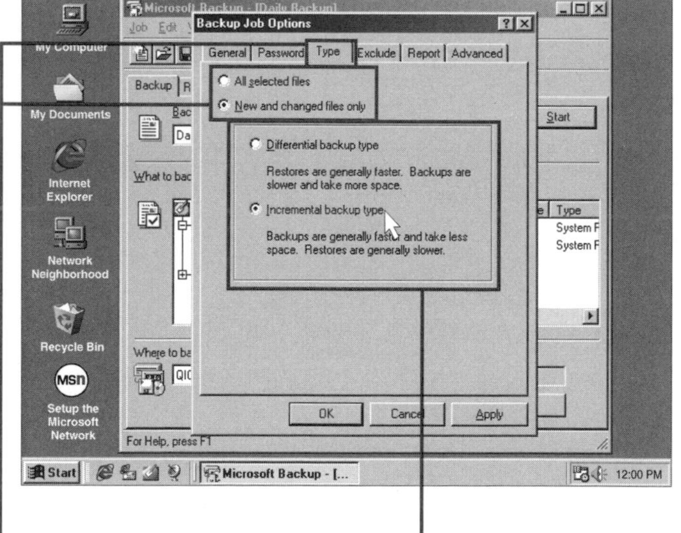

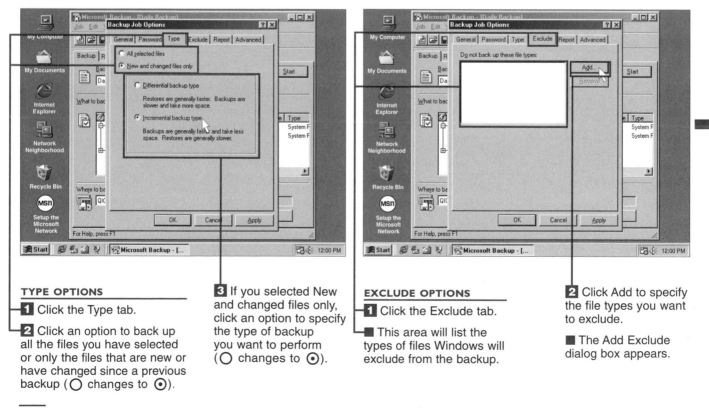

TYPE OPTIONS

1 Click the Type tab.

2 Click an option to back up all the files you have selected or only the files that are new or have changed since a previous backup (○ changes to ⊙).

3 If you selected New and changed files only, click an option to specify the type of backup you want to perform (○ changes to ⊙).

EXCLUDE OPTIONS

1 Click the Exclude tab.

■ This area will list the types of files Windows will exclude from the backup.

2 Click Add to specify the file types you want to exclude.

■ The Add Exclude dialog box appears.

How can I exclude a file type that does not appear in the Registered type list?

In the Add Exclude dialog box, click Custom type (○ changes to ⊙). Type the extension for the file type you want to exclude.

Can I back up the Windows Registry?

The Windows Registry contains information that Windows 98 needs to operate. You should backup the Windows Registry on a regular basis and whenever you back up all the files on your computer. To back up the Windows Registry, click the Advanced tab in the Backup Job Options dialog box and then select the Back up Windows Registry option (☑ changes to ☐).

When I open my backup job, how do I know which files are excluded from the backup job?

When you exclude a file type, a red x (☒) appears beside files of that type in the Microsoft Backup window.

Can I view reports for previous backups that I have performed?

You can look at old reports to view information on backups that you have performed. Reports are automatically saved as text files in the C:\Program Files\Accessories\Backup\reports folder.

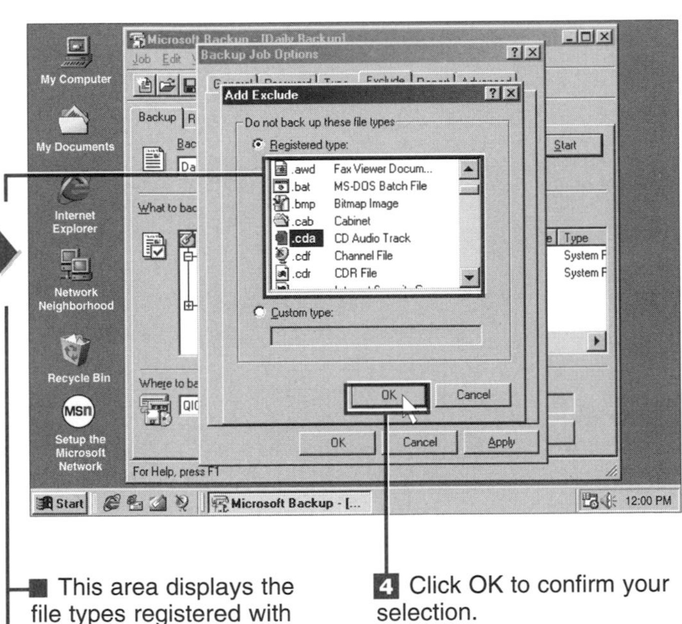

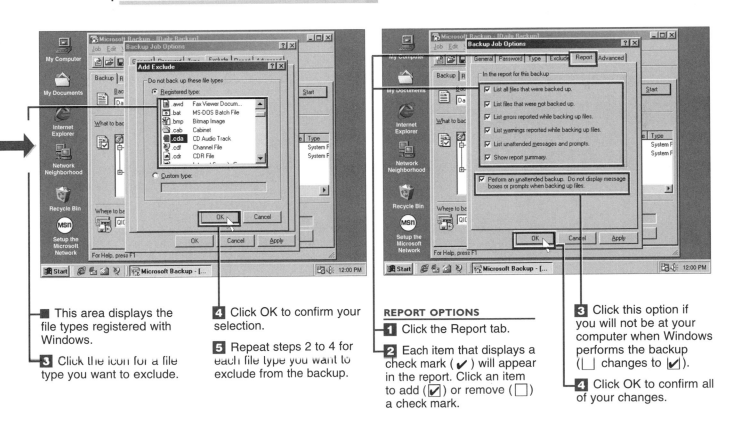

■ This area displays the file types registered with Windows.

3 Click the icon for a file type you want to exclude.

4 Click OK to confirm your selection.

5 Repeat steps 2 to 4 for each file type you want to exclude from the backup.

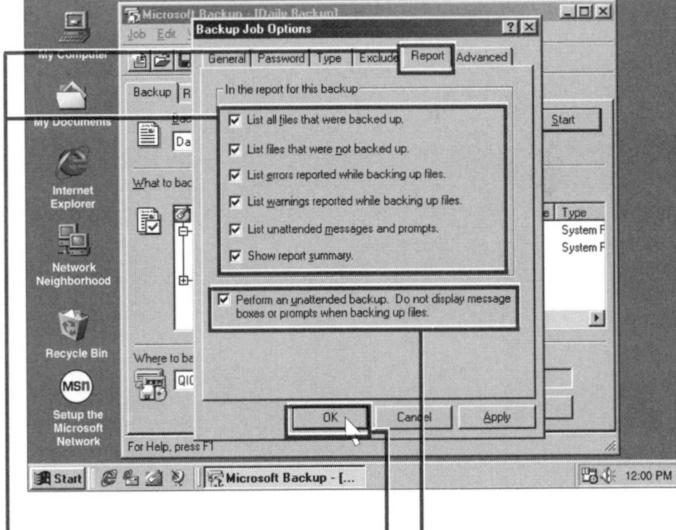

REPORT OPTIONS

1 Click the Report tab.

2 Each item that displays a check mark (✔) will appear in the report. Click an item to add (☑) or remove (☐) a check mark.

3 Click this option if you will not be at your computer when Windows performs the backup (☐ changes to ☑).

4 Click OK to confirm all of your changes.

RESTORE FILES

If files on your computer are lost or damaged, you can use a backup to restore the files to your computer. The Restore Wizard takes you step-by-step through the process of restoring your files.

If the backup is stored on more than one tape cartridge or disk, you must start restoring the files with the first tape cartridge or disk. Files must be restored in the order that they were originally backed up. You should clearly label the order of all your tape cartridges or disks to prevent any confusion when restoring.

If you are restoring a backup from a tape cartridge, you can select the backup job you want to restore from a list of backups on the tape cartridge.

Backup displays all the drives, folders and files in the backup job, so you can select exactly which folders and files you want to restore. This is useful if you do not need to restore all the files.

If your backup contains a copy of the Windows Registry, you should not restore the Registry unless you need to. Restoring the Registry may adversely affect your computer if your hardware or software setup has changed since you last backed up the Registry.

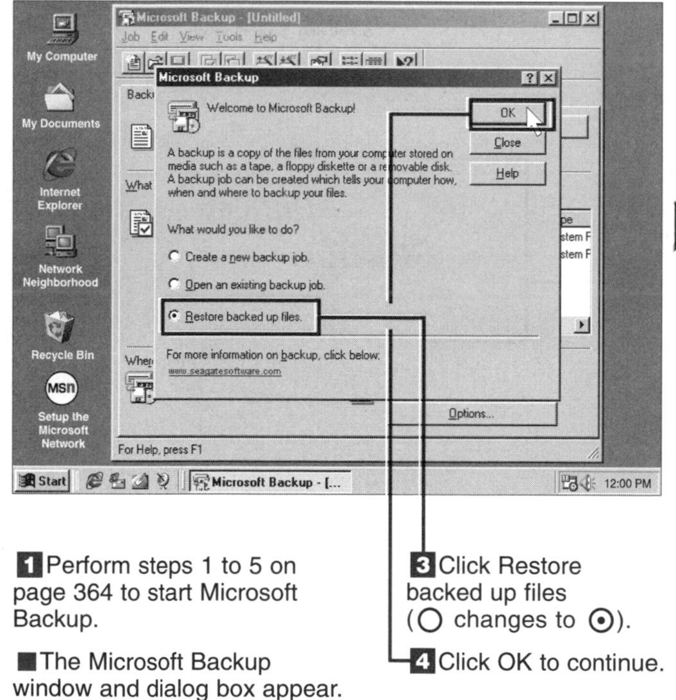

1 Perform steps 1 to 5 on page 364 to start Microsoft Backup.

■ The Microsoft Backup window and dialog box appear.

2 Insert the tape or disk that contains the information you want to restore into the drive.

3 Click Restore backed up files (○ changes to ⊙).

4 Click OK to continue.

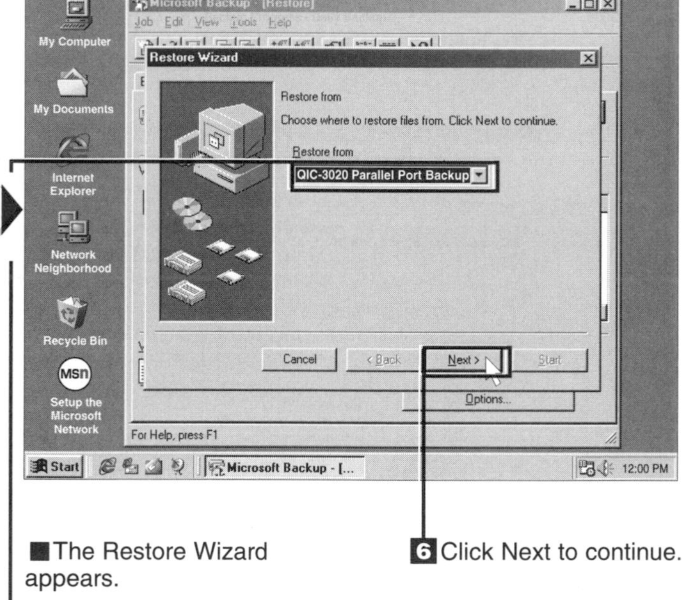

■ The Restore Wizard appears.

5 This area displays where you will restore the files from. You can click this area to change the location.

6 Click Next to continue.

TIPS

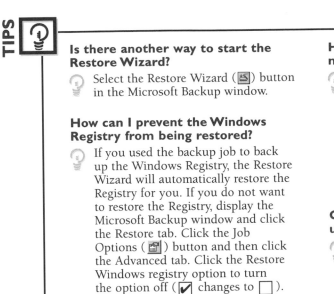

Is there another way to start the Restore Wizard?

Select the Restore Wizard ( ) button in the Microsoft Backup window.

How can I prevent the Windows Registry from being restored?

If you used the backup job to back up the Windows Registry, the Restore Wizard will automatically restore the Registry for you. If you do not want to restore the Registry, display the Microsoft Backup window and click the Restore tab. Click the Job Options ( ) button and then click the Advanced tab. Click the Restore Windows registry option to turn the option off (☑ changes to ☐).

How do I restore information if my hard drive fails?

If your hard drive fails, you can restore your information to a reformatted hard drive. First, you must install Windows 98. See page 624. Then you must install the Microsoft Backup component. See page 610. You can then access and restore the most recent backup of all your files.

Can I restore information without using the Restore Wizard?

Select the Restore tab in the Microsoft Backup window. You can then specify the settings you want to use to restore the information. Click Start to begin restoring the information.

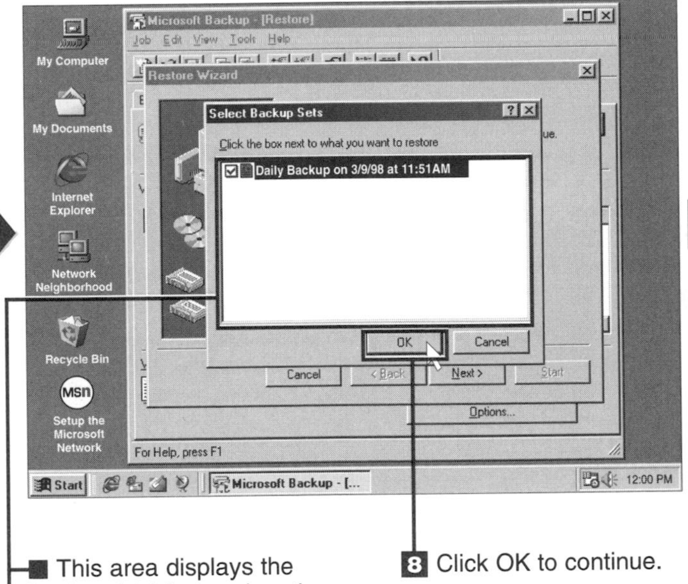

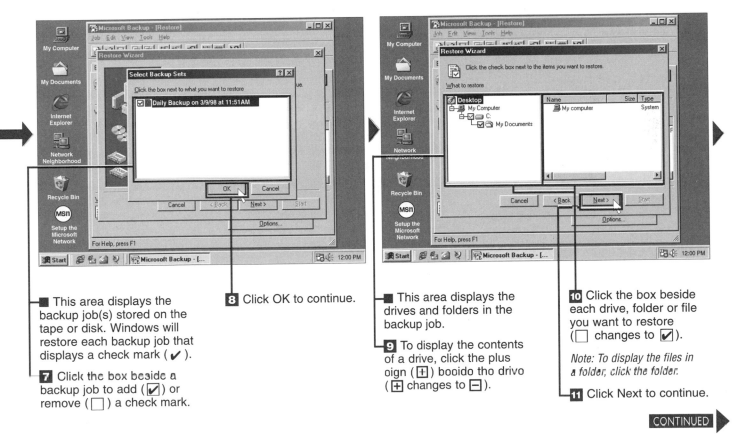

■ This area displays the backup job(s) stored on the tape or disk. Windows will restore each backup job that displays a check mark (✔).

7 Click the box beside a backup job to add (☑) or remove (☐) a check mark.

8 Click OK to continue.

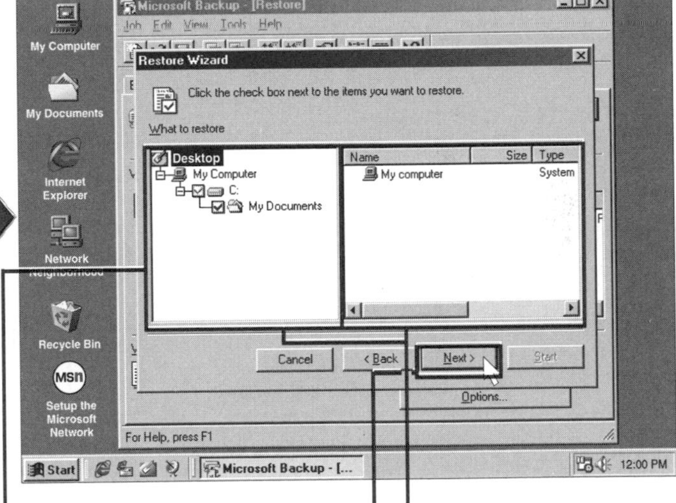

■ This area displays the drives and folders in the backup job.

9 To display the contents of a drive, click the plus sign (⊞) beside the drive (⊞ changes to ⊟).

10 Click the box beside each drive, folder or file you want to restore (☐ changes to ☑).

Note: To display the files in a folder, click the folder.

11 Click Next to continue.

CONTINUED

RESTORE FILES CONTINUED

When restoring files, you can have Backup restore the files to their original location on your computer or to a new location. In most cases, you should restore the files back to the original location.

You can specify how you want Backup to restore your files.

Restoring a file only if a file with the same name does not exist in the same location prevents you from replacing an updated file with an older version of the file. Restoring a file to your computer only if the file on your computer is older than the file in the backup helps ensure that you have all the newest files on your computer. You can also have Backup restore all the files in a backup, regardless of whether a file with the same name exists or newer files exist on your computer. This method ensures all the files in a backup will be restored to your computer.

The Restore Progress window shows you the status of the restore.

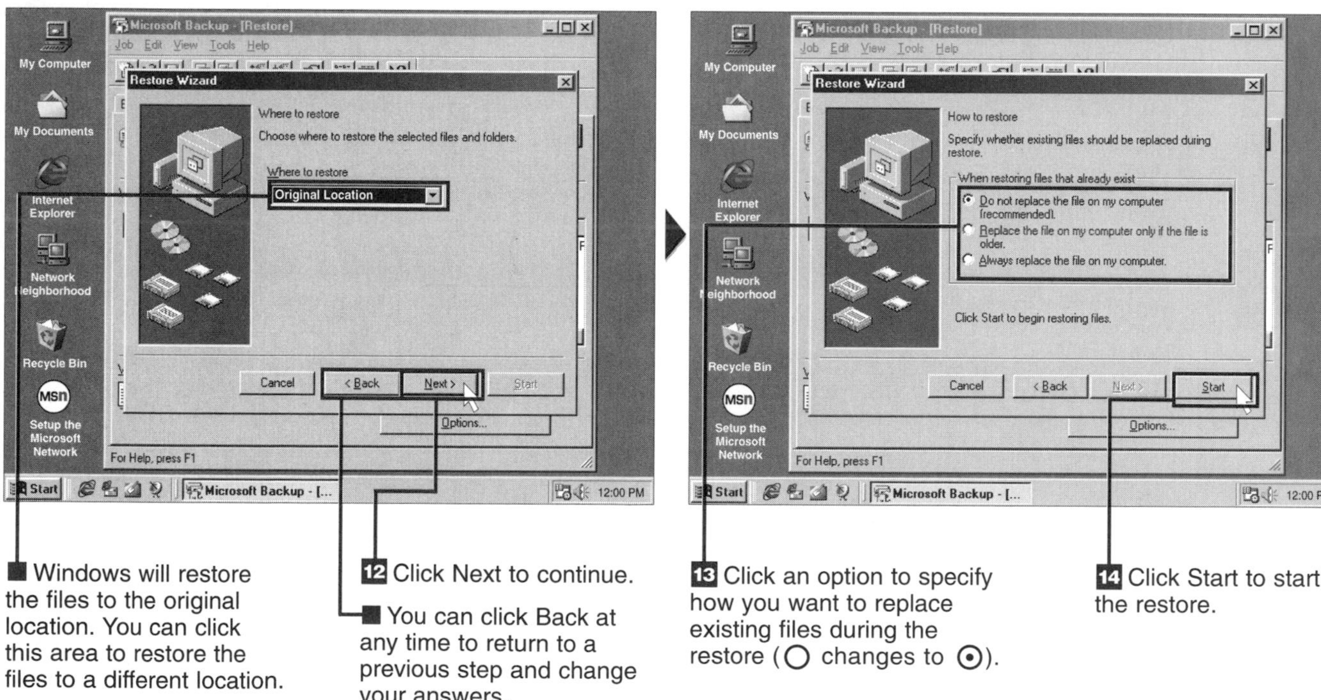

■ Windows will restore the files to the original location. You can click this area to restore the files to a different location.

12 Click Next to continue.

■ You can click Back at any time to return to a previous step and change your answers.

13 Click an option to specify how you want to replace existing files during the restore (○ changes to ⊙).

14 Click Start to start the restore.

TIPS

How do I restore a differential backup?

A differential backup consists of one backup containing all the files and one or more backups containing the files that changed after the full backup was performed. To restore a differential backup, restore the backup containing all the files and then restore the last backup that was performed.

How do I restore an incremental backup?

An incremental backup consists of one backup containing all the files and one or more backups containing files that changed since the previous backup. To restore an incremental backup, restore the backup containing all the files and then restore each of the following backups. You must restore the backups in the order that they were performed.

Can I restore my backup to another computer?

If the computer you want to restore your information to has Backup installed and can access the same type of backup medium, such as a floppy drive, you can restore your information to the computer. When restoring information to another computer, make sure you do not restore configuration files such as the Windows Registry.

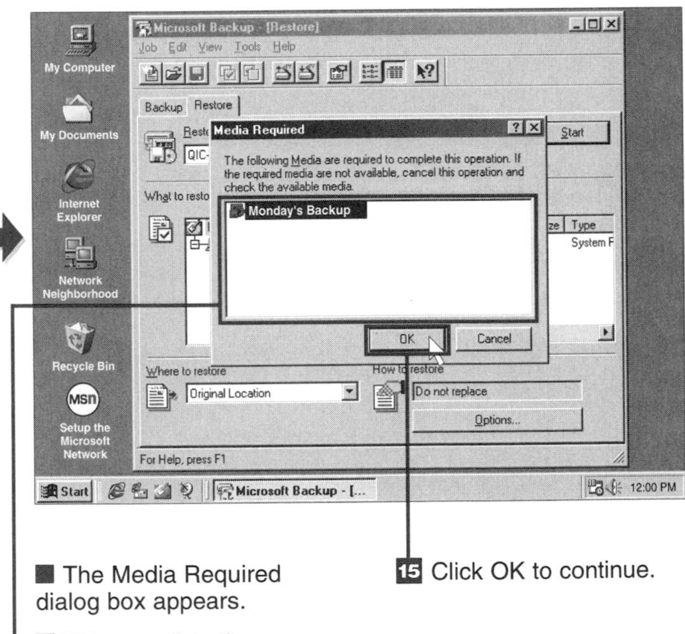

■ The Media Required dialog box appears.

■ This area lists the tape(s) or disk(s) you will need to restore the files.

15 Click OK to continue.

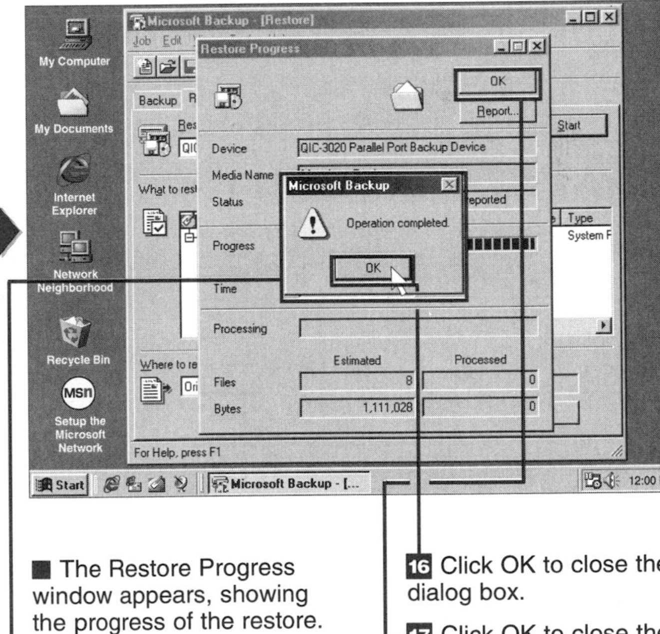

■ The Restore Progress window appears, showing the progress of the restore.

■ A dialog box appears when the restore is complete.

16 Click OK to close the dialog box.

17 Click OK to close the Restore Progress window.

SECTION V

17) MODEMS

18) DIAL-UP NETWORKING

19) HYPERTERMINAL

CONNECT TO OTHER COMPUTERS

20) WORK WITH PORTABLE COMPUTERS

INSTALL A MODEM

You can install a modem on your computer. The Add New Hardware Wizard guides you step by step through the installation process.

A modem is a device that allows computers to exchange information using telephone lines. A modem allows you to connect to the Internet, send and receive e-mail messages and exchange information with another computer.

There are two types of modems. An external modem attaches to a computer using a cable. External modems are portable and easier to fix if a problem arises. An internal modem is installed inside a computer. Internal modems are less expensive than external modems. Both types of modems provide the same features.

When you install a modem, Windows installs the necessary software, called a driver. The driver allows your computer to communicate with the new modem.

Windows searches your computer for a new modem that is Plug and Play compatible. Plug and Play hardware uses technology that allows Windows to automatically detect and install the device without requiring you to adjust any of the settings on the device. Windows can also help you install a modem that is not Plug and Play compatible.

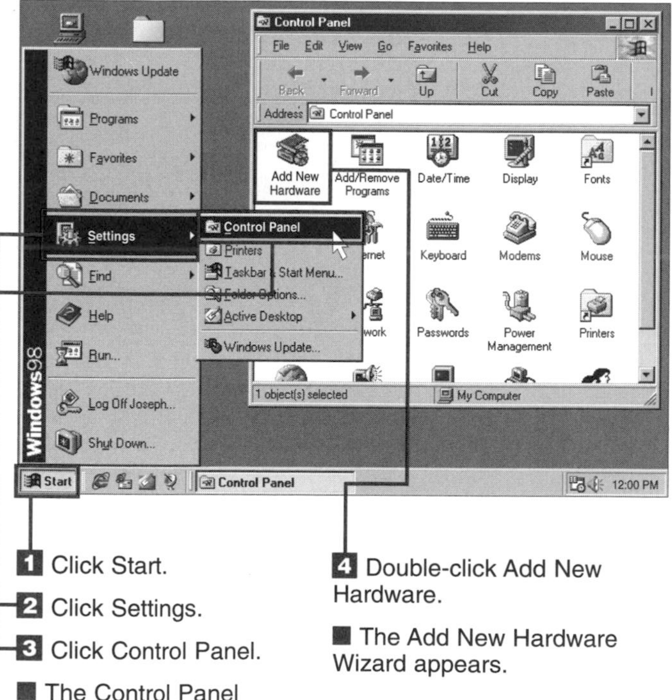

1 Click Start.

2 Click Settings.

3 Click Control Panel.

■ The Control Panel window appears.

4 Double-click Add New Hardware.

■ The Add New Hardware Wizard appears.

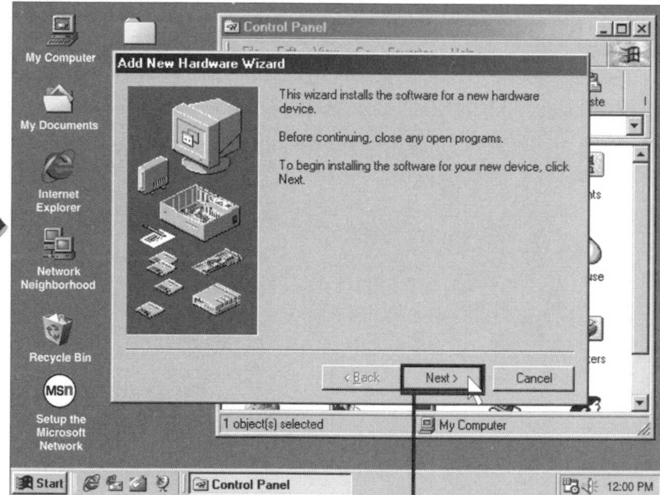

■ The wizard will help you install the necessary software for your modem. Make sure you close any open programs before you continue.

5 Click Next to begin installing the modem.

What happens when Windows finds a Plug and Play device?

If Windows finds a Plug and Play device, a dialog box may appear, displaying the name of the device Windows found. Click the device you want to install and then follow the instructions on your screen. If the device you want to install is not displayed, select No, the device isn't in the list (○ changes to ⊙) and then click Next.

Do I have to use the wizard to install a new Plug and Play modem?

After you physically connect the modem to your computer and turn the computer on, Windows may be able to automatically detect your modem and ask you for the driver for the device.

Why would I install more than one modem?

Windows 98 allows you to use more than one modem to connect to your Internet service provider. This will increase the speed of your connection so information will transfer to your computer more quickly. To use more than one modem, display the Dial-Up Networking window. See page 398. Right-click the icon for the connection to your Internet service provider and select Properties. Click the Multilink tab and then click the Use additional devices option. Click the Add button and then use the drop-down list to select an additional modem. You should check with your Internet service provider to confirm that they allow connections using more than one modem.

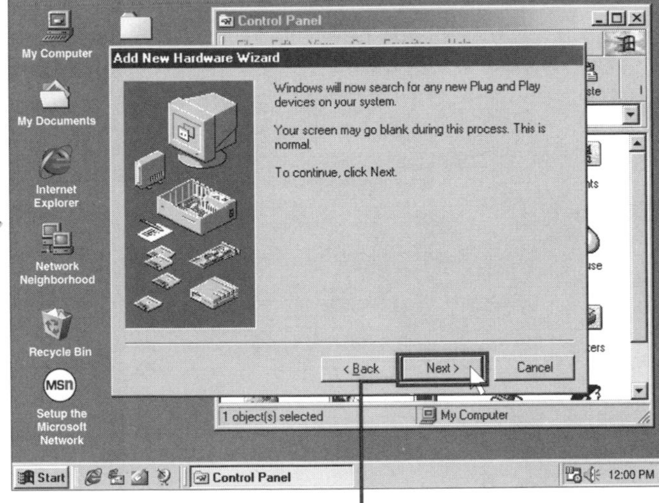

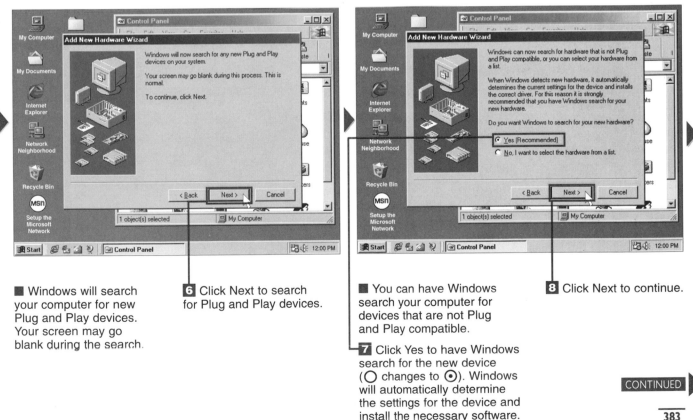

■ Windows will search your computer for new Plug and Play devices. Your screen may go blank during the search.

6 Click Next to search for Plug and Play devices.

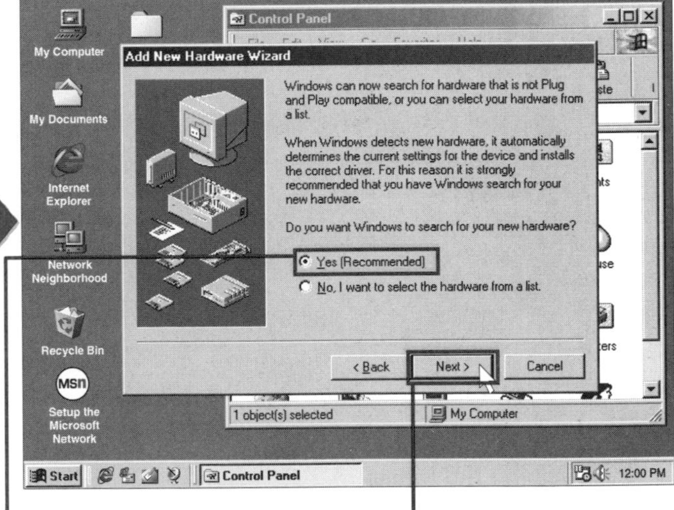

■ You can have Windows search your computer for devices that are not Plug and Play compatible.

7 Click Yes to have Windows search for the new device (○ changes to ⊙). Windows will automatically determine the settings for the device and install the necessary software.

8 Click Next to continue.

CONTINUED

INSTALL A MODEM CONTINUED

Windows may take several minutes to search your computer for a modem that is not Plug and Play compatible. If the progress stops, you should wait three to five minutes and then restart your computer.

A device that is not Plug and Play compatible is sometimes referred to as a legacy device. If your modem is a legacy device, Windows may ask you to provide the driver that came with the modem. This driver is stored on the modem's installation disk.

When installing a modem, Windows determines which port the modem will use. A port is a connector that allows instructions and data to flow between the computer and the modem. Most modems use a COM port.

When you install a modem that is not Plug and Play compatible, you must ensure that the settings Windows suggests for the modem are correct. You may have to adjust the settings on the modem to match the settings suggested by Windows. You can adjust the settings by using the software that came with the modem or by adjusting the jumpers or switches on the modem. Consult the modem's manual before making any adjustments.

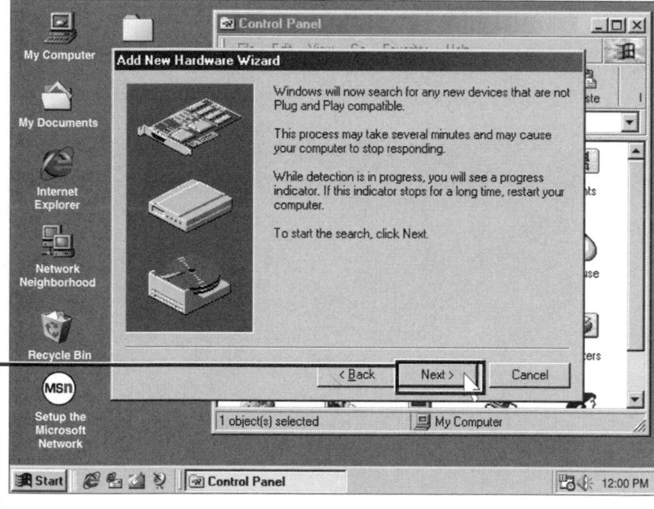

9 Click Next to start searching for new devices that are not Plug and Play compatible.

■ The search may take several minutes.

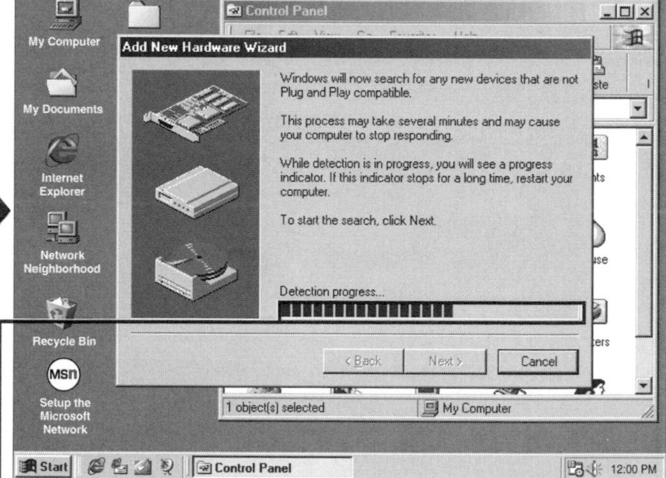

■ This area displays the progress of the search.

Note: You can click Cancel to stop the search at any time.

TIPS

What should I do if Windows does not have the driver I need for my modem and I do not have the modem's installation disk?

You may have to obtain the driver from the manufacturer of the modem. You can call the manufacturer or search the manufacturer's Web site.

What is a USB port?

A USB (Universal Serial Bus) port can be used to connect a wide variety of devices, such as modems and keyboards to a computer. Many new computers have USB ports.

What can I do if the modem does not work after it has been installed?

Click the Start button and then click Help. In the Windows Help window, click the Troubleshooting book and then click Windows 98 Troubleshooters. Select the Modem topic and then follow the instructions on your screen.

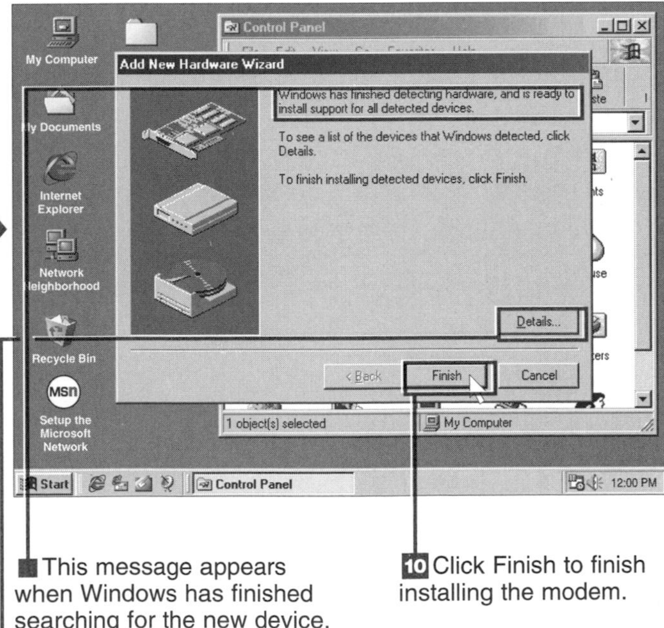

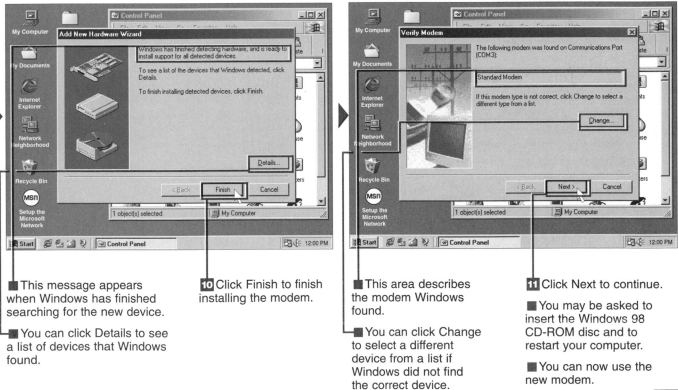

■ This message appears when Windows has finished searching for the new device.

■ You can click Details to see a list of devices that Windows found.

10 Click Finish to finish installing the modem.

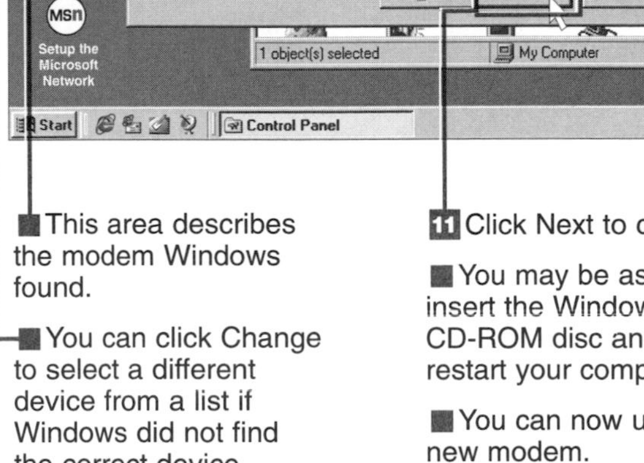

■ This area describes the modem Windows found.

■ You can click Change to select a different device from a list if Windows did not find the correct device.

11 Click Next to continue.

■ You may be asked to insert the Windows 98 CD-ROM disc and to restart your computer.

■ You can now use the new modem.

CHANGE THE MODEM DIALING PROPERTIES

You can change the dialing properties for your modem. Dialing properties are settings that determine how your modem will dial phone numbers. This is helpful when dialing out using a program such as HyperTerminal or when using your modem to connect to an Internet Service Provider (ISP).

Windows sets up your modem dialing properties when you install your modem. These settings are named "New Location".

When changing the modem dialing properties, you can tell Windows which area code and country you are calling from. Your modem may dial a different phone number, depending on whether you are making a local call or a long-distance call.

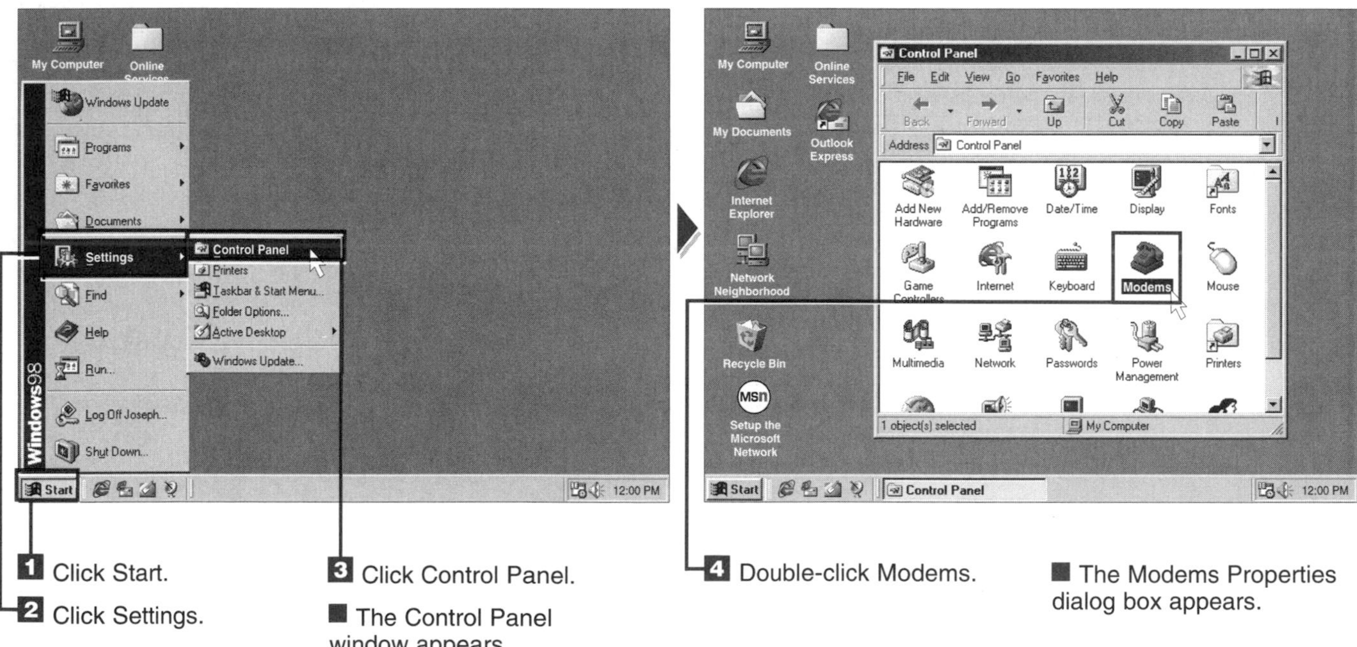

1 Click Start.

2 Click Settings.

3 Click Control Panel.

■ The Control Panel window appears.

4 Double-click Modems.

■ The Modems Properties dialog box appears.

TIPS

Can I set dialing properties for different locations?

Windows allows you to specify different dialing properties for each location where you plan to use your computer. For example, dialing from the office requires different dialing properties than dialing from a hotel room. Click New in the Dialing Properties dialog box. Click OK and then type a name for the new location. You can now enter the properties for the new location.

How can I rename a set of dialing properties?

You can use descriptive names to make it easier to identify your dialing properties. In the Dialing Properties dialog box, click ▼ in the I am dialing from area to display the names of your dialing properties. Click the name you want to change and then type a new name.

How can I tell Windows how to dial long-distance phone numbers within my area code?

Some phone numbers within your area code may be long distance and require you to dial 1 before the number. Phone numbers with other area codes may not be long distance and may not require you to dial 1. You can click the Area Code Rules button and then click the New button to specify which phone numbers you want Windows to dial 1 before.

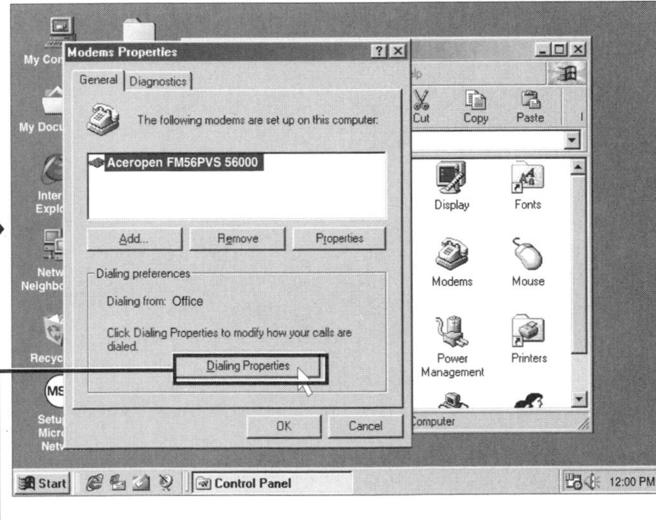

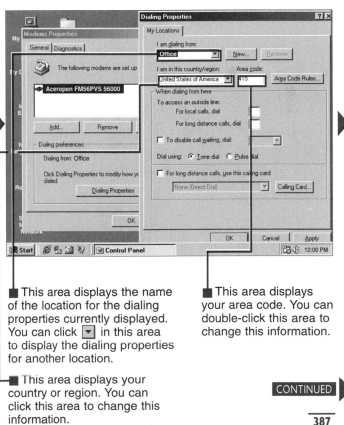

5 Click Dialing Properties to change how your calls are dialed.

■ The Dialing Properties dialog box appears.

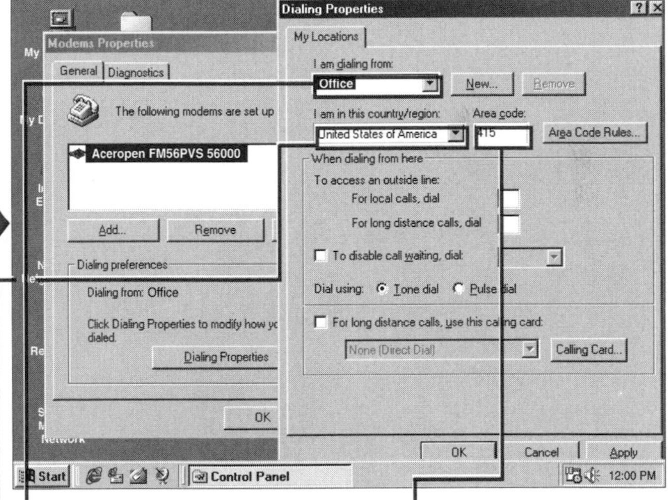

■ This area displays the name of the location for the dialing properties currently displayed. You can click ▼ in this area to display the dialing properties for another location.

■ This area displays your country or region. You can click this area to change this information.

■ This area displays your area code. You can double-click this area to change this information.

CONTINUED

CHANGE THE MODEM DIALING PROPERTIES CONTINUED

When changing the modem dialing properties, you can specify any special numbers you use to dial local or long-distance numbers. This is useful if you will be making calls from a hotel room and you must dial a number to get an outside line.

You can also specify whether you wish to use tone or pulse dialing.

Tone dialing is the most common type of dialing used by phone companies.

If you have the call waiting feature, you can have Windows automatically disable the feature when you use your modem. You should turn off the call waiting feature when using your modem, since this feature could disrupt the modem connection.

You can set up the modem to use a calling card. A calling card is a card that allows you to make long-distance telephone calls and have the charges billed to the owner of the calling card. Calling cards can also be used where toll calls are not permitted.

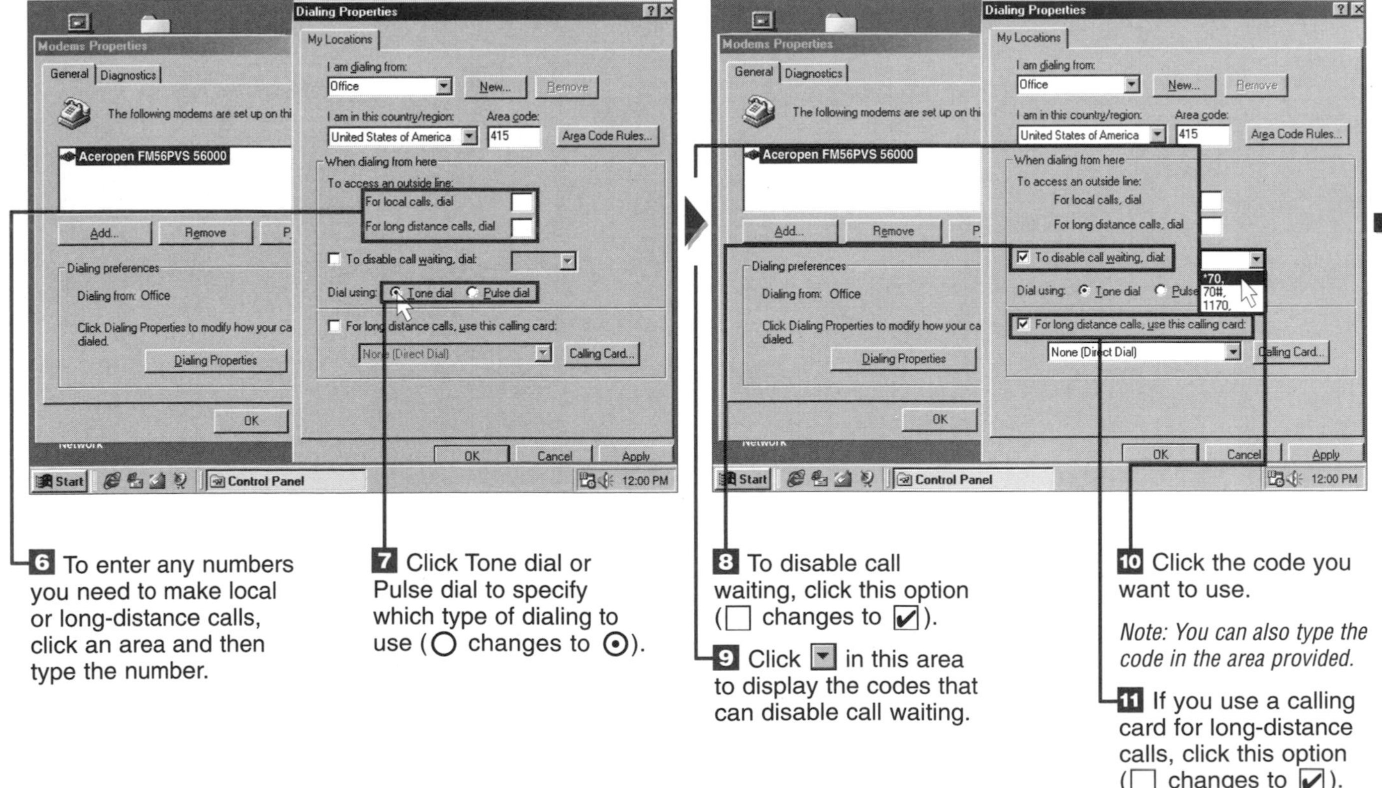

6 To enter any numbers you need to make local or long-distance calls, click an area and then type the number.

7 Click Tone dial or Pulse dial to specify which type of dialing to use (○ changes to ⊙).

8 To disable call waiting, click this option (☐ changes to ☑).

9 Click ▼ in this area to display the codes that can disable call waiting.

10 Click the code you want to use.

Note: You can also type the code in the area provided.

11 If you use a calling card for long-distance calls, click this option (☐ changes to ☑).

TIPS

What code will disable call waiting?

You should check with your local phone company to find out what code you must use to disable call waiting. The most common code used is *70.

Where can I get a calling card?

Most phone companies offer calling cards to their customers. There are many types of calling cards available. Some cards offer incentives, such as discount rates, to attract new customers. Many businesses and organizations use calling cards to track toll calls.

How do I choose the set of dialing properties I want to use?

When you use your modem to communicate with another computer, Windows often provides a dialog box that displays a list of your sets of modem dialing properties. You can select the set of dialing properties you want to use.

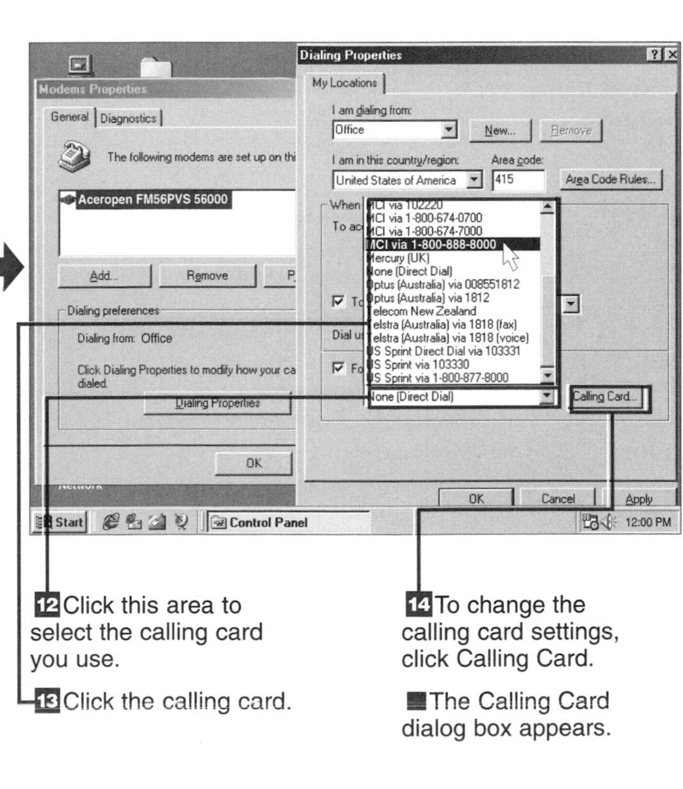

12 Click this area to select the calling card you use.

13 Click the calling card.

14 To change the calling card settings, click Calling Card.

■ The Calling Card dialog box appears.

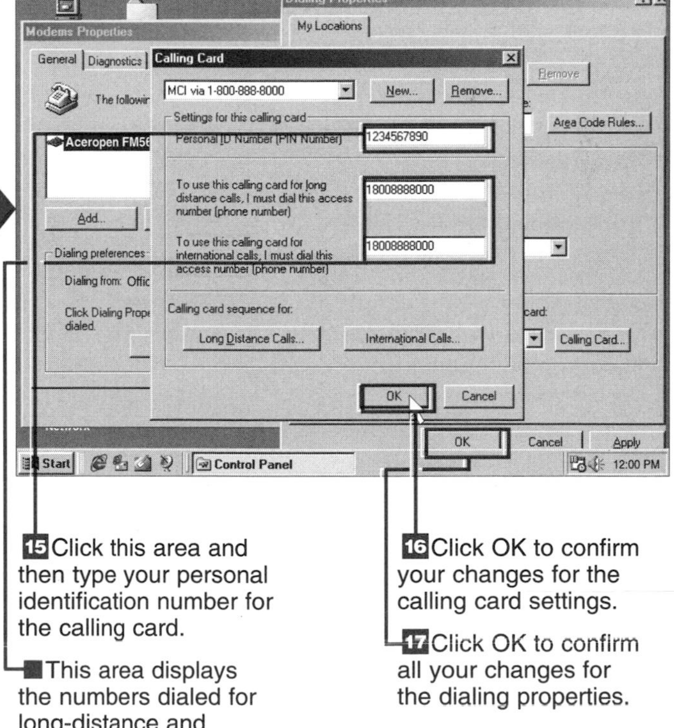

15 Click this area and then type your personal identification number for the calling card.

■ This area displays the numbers dialed for long-distance and international calls.

16 Click OK to confirm your changes for the calling card settings.

17 Click OK to confirm all your changes for the dialing properties.

CHANGE THE MODEM SETTINGS

You can change the settings for a modem installed on your computer. Changing the settings can help a modem operate more efficiently.

A port is a connector that allows instructions and data to flow between the computer and the modem. Most modems connect to a COM port. A COM port is another name for a computer's serial port.

Most modems have a speaker that lets you hear the modem as it dials and connects to another modem. If your modem has a speaker, you may be able to use the modem settings to adjust the speaker volume.

You can specify the maximum speed setting for your modem, which determines how fast your modem can send and receive information. The speed of a modem is measured in Kilobits per second (Kb/s). The maximum speed setting should match the fastest speed setting of your modem. Check your modem's documentation to determine the modem's maximum speed.

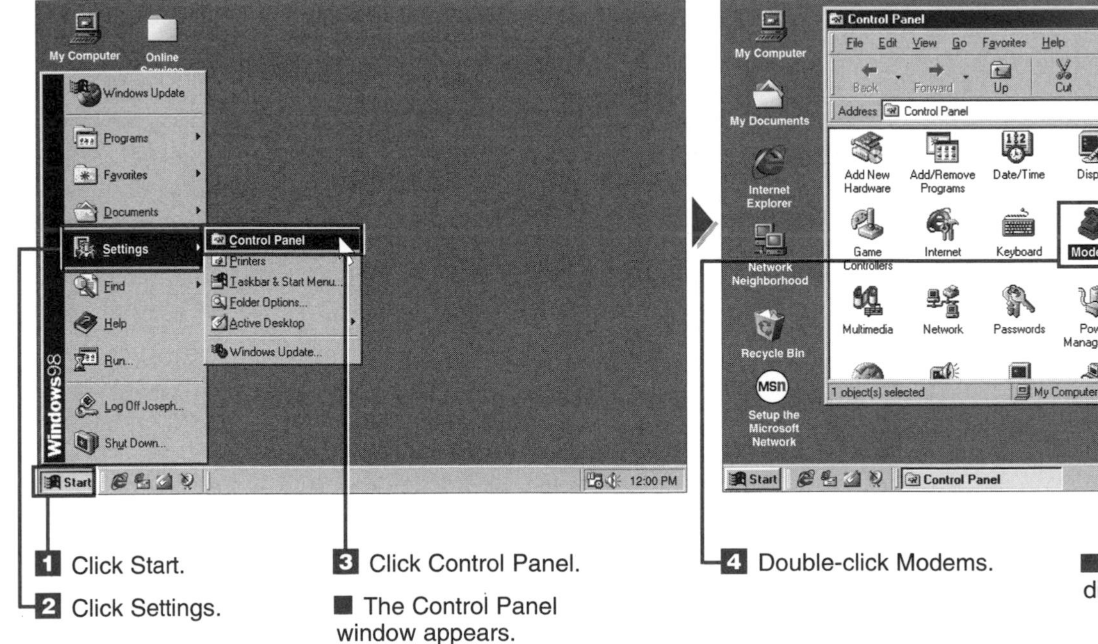

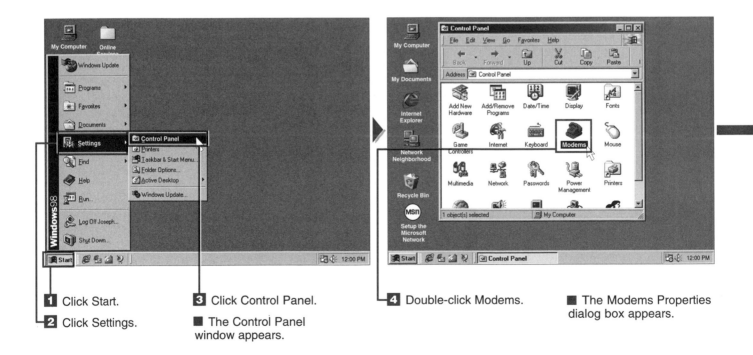

1 Click Start.

2 Click Settings.

3 Click Control Panel.

■ The Control Panel window appears.

4 Double-click Modems.

■ The Modems Properties dialog box appears.

TIPS

Why are some modem settings not available?

The settings you can change depend on the type of modem you are using. One modem may have different features and capabilities than another modem. Also, some settings may not be available if the correct driver is not installed on your computer. A driver is software that allows Windows to communicate with the modem. Installing the correct driver may allow you to change modem settings that are currently not available.

Why is my modem very slow even though I specified a high maximum speed?

Modems must use the same speed when exchanging information. A fast modem can connect to a slower modem, but they will transfer information at the slower speed.

How do I lock the modem speed?

Many phone lines are affected by interference that may result in slow transmission speeds. If you tell Windows to only connect at a specific speed, a connection will not be made with another modem unless Windows can connect at the speed you specified. To lock the modem speed, click the Only connect at this speed option in the Properties dialog box. This option is not available for some modems.

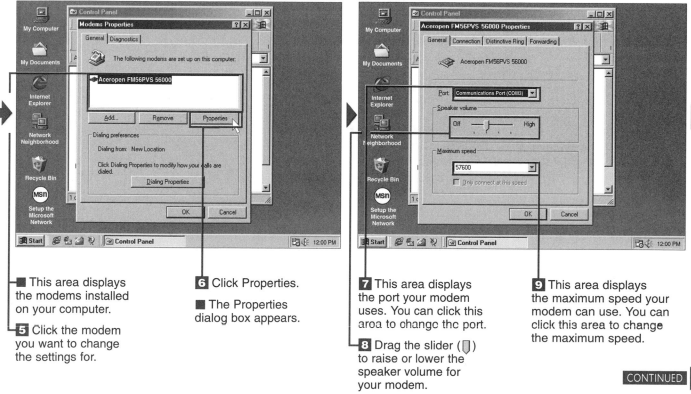

■ This area displays the modems installed on your computer.

5 Click the modem you want to change the settings for.

6 Click Properties.

■ The Properties dialog box appears.

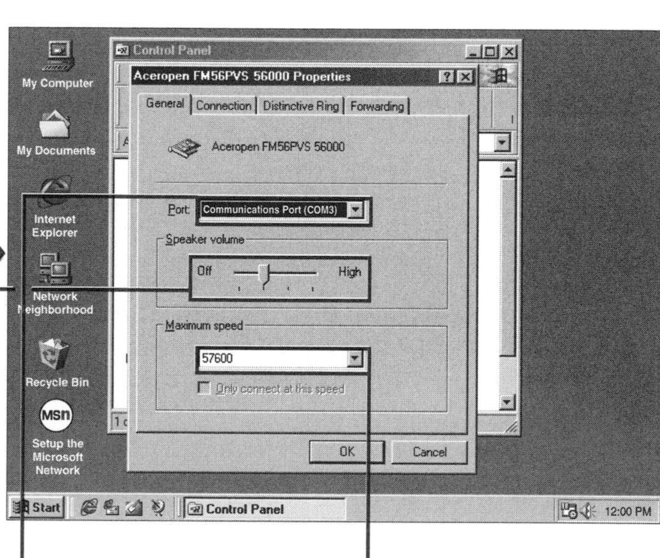

7 This area displays the port your modem uses. You can click this area to change the port.

8 Drag the slider (▯) to raise or lower the speaker volume for your modem.

9 This area displays the maximum speed your modem can use. You can click this area to change the maximum speed.

CONTINUED

CHANGE THE MODEM SETTINGS
CONTINUED

You can change the connection settings for a modem. Changing a modem's connection settings helps the modem better communicate with other modems.

Before two modems can exchange information, the modems must use the same data bits, parity bits and stop bits settings. You will see unreadable text on your screen if the settings are different.

The data bits represent the actual information exchanged between computers. The parity bits determine whether errors occur during the transfer of information. The stop bits indicate when each data bit begins and ends.

You can specify whether you want to wait for a dial tone before the modem starts dialing. You can also tell Windows how long you want to wait before canceling or disconnecting a call. Having Windows disconnect calls when your modem is idle for a period of time can help prevent the accumulation of online charges.

Most modems are already set up to use the most common options, so it is unlikely that you will have to change the connection settings for your modem.

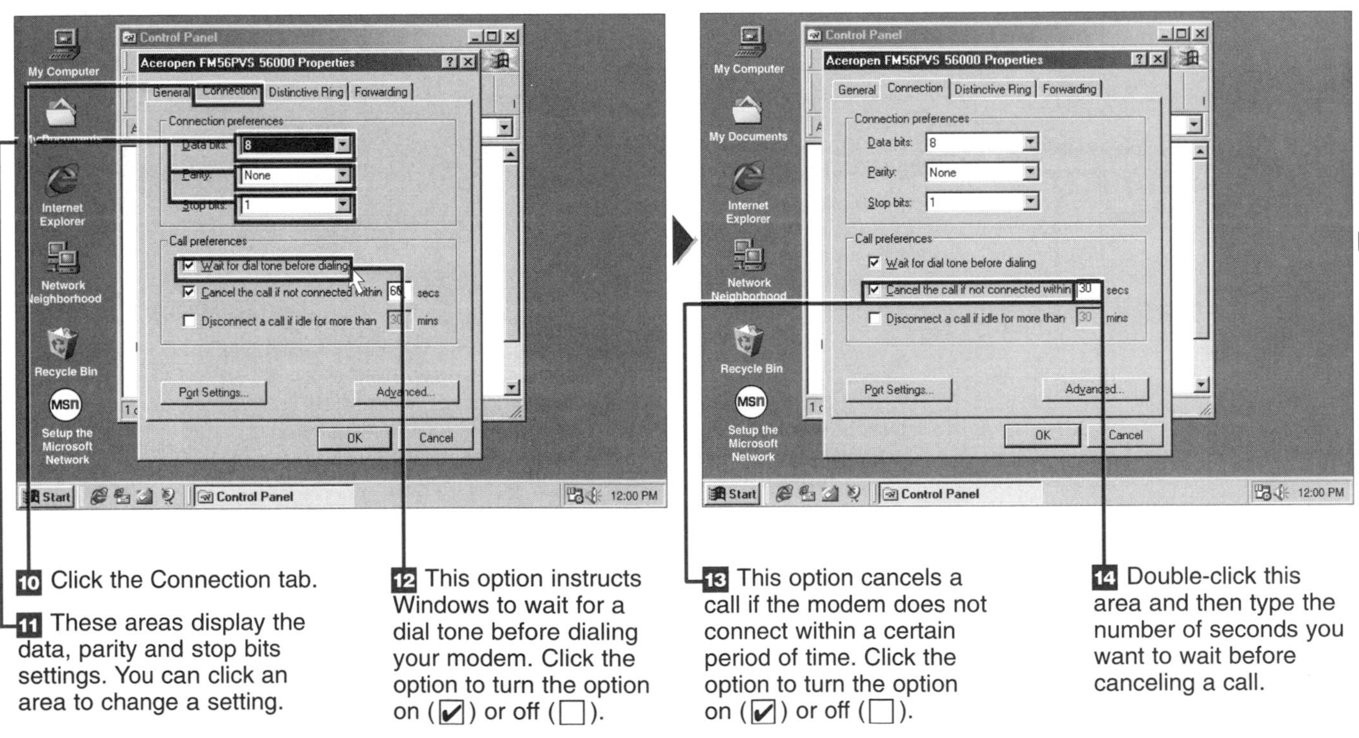

10 Click the Connection tab.

11 These areas display the data, parity and stop bits settings. You can click an area to change a setting.

12 This option instructs Windows to wait for a dial tone before dialing your modem. Click the option to turn the option on (☑) or off (☐).

13 This option cancels a call if the modem does not connect within a certain period of time. Click the option to turn the option on (☑) or off (☐).

14 Double-click this area and then type the number of seconds you want to wait before canceling a call.

TIPS

What are the most common bits settings for modems?

Before modems can communicate with each other, they must be set to use the same number of data, parity and stop bits. The most common settings are 8 data bits, no parity bits and 1 stop bit.

Why should I have my modem wait for a dial tone before dialing?

In many office buildings that use sophisticated phone systems, a modem may not receive a dial tone as soon as it connects to the phone system. Having your modem wait for a dial tone before dialing helps ensure it will be able to dial the number.

Why is my call not connecting?

There are many reasons that a call may not connect. Problems sometimes occur with the phone system or the other modem may not be set to answer calls. Usually, 60 seconds is an adequate length of time to wait before canceling a call.

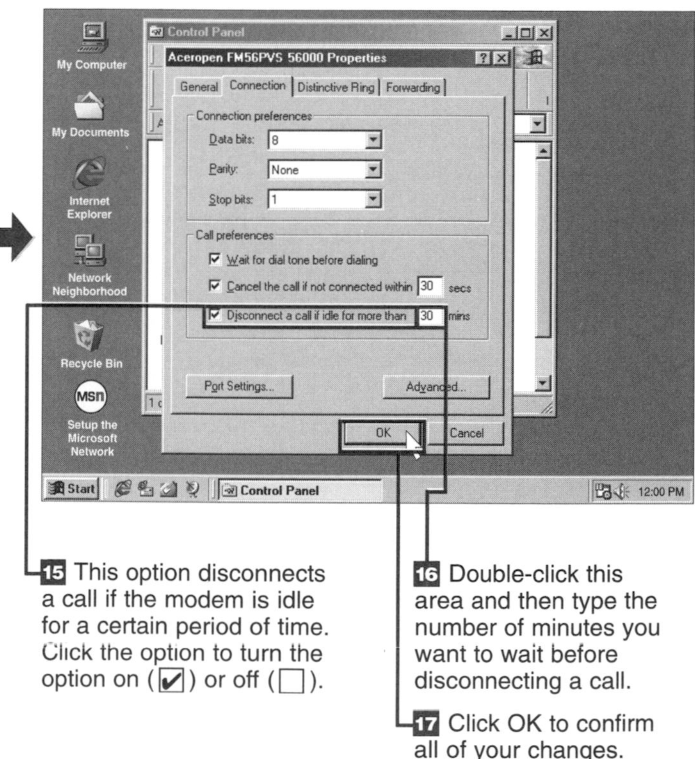

15 This option disconnects a call if the modem is idle for a certain period of time. Click the option to turn the option on (✔) or off (☐).

16 Double-click this area and then type the number of minutes you want to wait before disconnecting a call.

17 Click OK to confirm all of your changes.

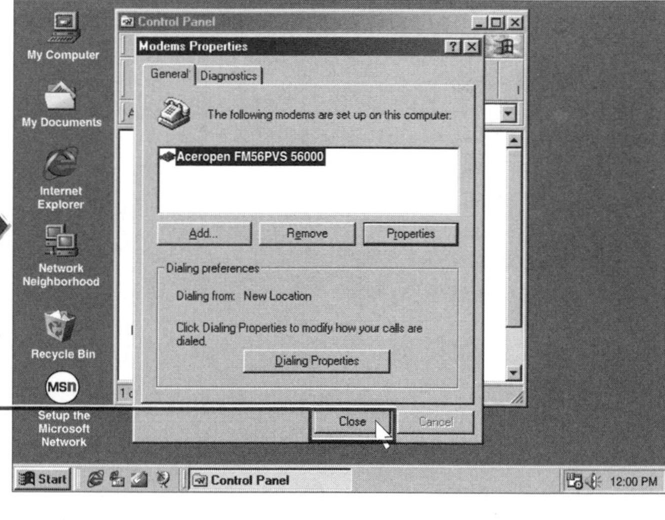

18 Click Close to close the Modems Properties dialog box.

CHANGE THE ADVANCED CONNECTION SETTINGS

Windows allows you to change the advanced connection settings for a modem. Changing the advanced connection settings can help a modem operate more efficiently and exchange information faster.

You may need to adjust the modem's advanced connection settings if you are experiencing problems while using the modem. For example, if you have trouble connecting to other computers or you are losing information when transferring data, adjusting the advanced connection settings may fix the problem.

The hardware and software you use will determine which advanced connection settings you must change. Usually, the advanced connection settings are set properly when a modem is installed.

The advanced connection settings allow you to use error control options to improve the quality of a poor connection between two modems. Both modems must be using error control for the options to take effect. You can have your modem connect to another modem only when the connection is reliable. You can also have Windows compress, or squeeze, the data to increase the speed at which information transfers between the modems. If your modem supports the error control options, you should leave the options turned on.

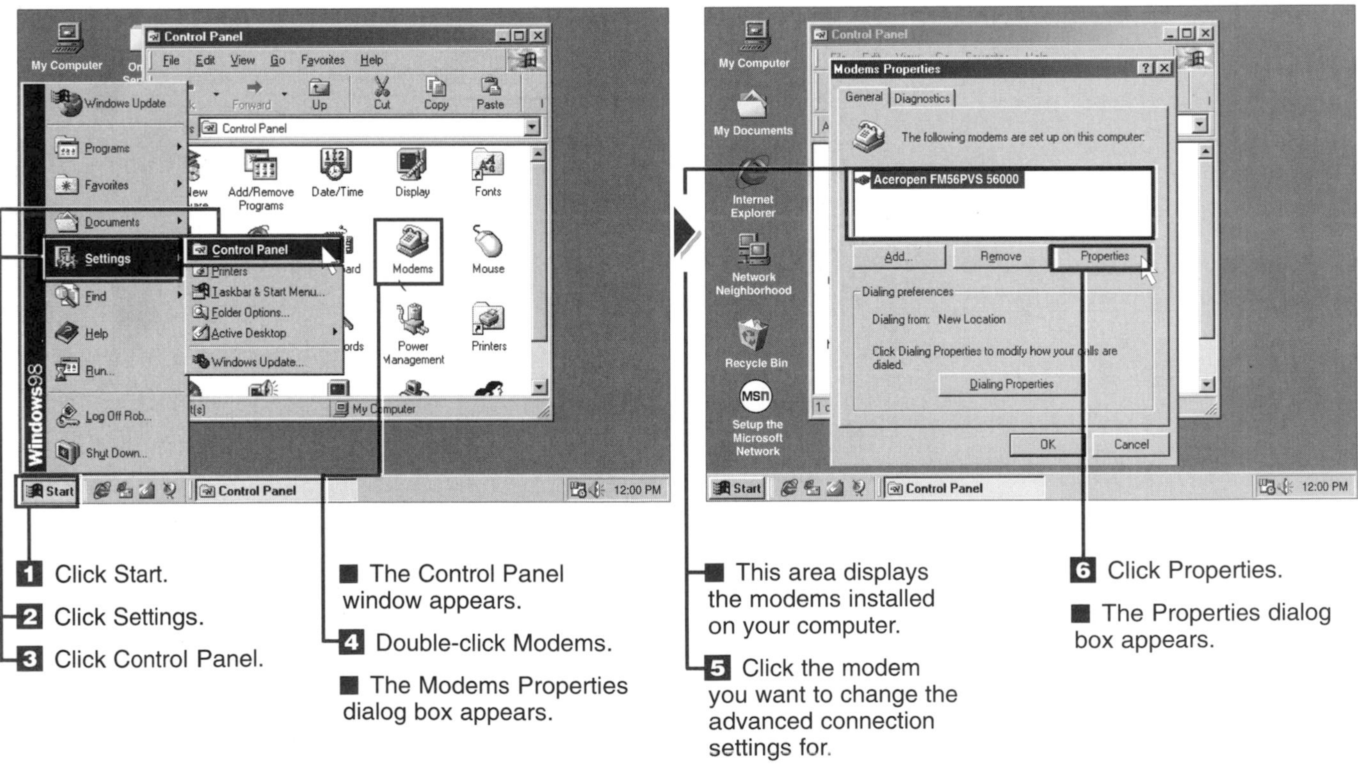

1 Click Start.

2 Click Settings.

3 Click Control Panel.

■ The Control Panel window appears.

4 Double-click Modems.

■ The Modems Properties dialog box appears.

■ This area displays the modems installed on your computer.

5 Click the modem you want to change the advanced connection settings for.

6 Click Properties.

■ The Properties dialog box appears.

Why are some advanced connection settings not available for my modem?

The available advanced connection settings depend on the model and type of modem you are using. Settings that cannot be adjusted have a dimmed appearance in the Advanced Connection Settings dialog box.

What does the Use cellular protocol option do?

Some modems, often those in portable computers, can use cellular telephones to communicate with other modems. Because the cellular phone system is prone to errors, special error correction settings are needed when information is being transferred. If you have a modem that can connect to a cellular telephone, you should turn on the Use cellular protocol option.

The modem I want to change the advanced connection settings for does not appear in the list of modems. Why not?

Your modem may not have been set up for Windows 98. If you want to be able to adjust the advanced settings, you must first set up the modem so the device can communicate with Windows. To install a modem, see page 382.

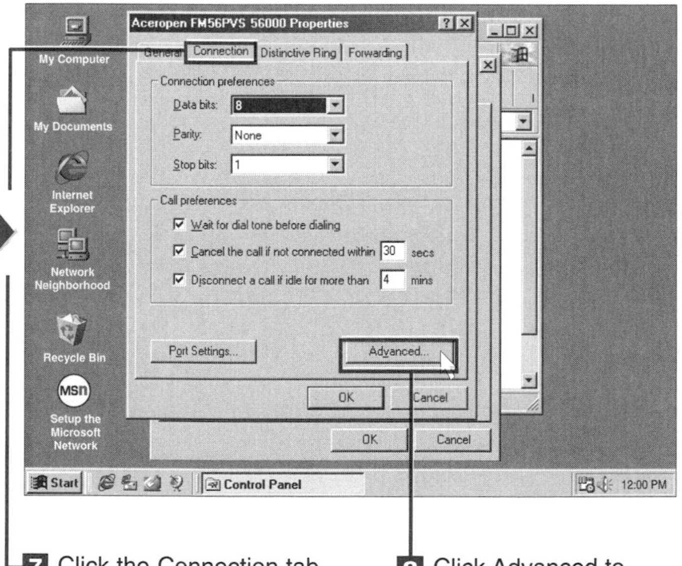

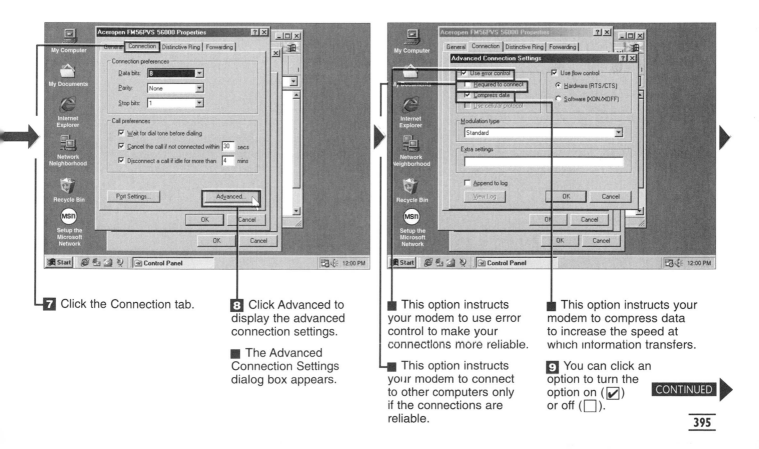

7 Click the Connection tab.

8 Click Advanced to display the advanced connection settings.

■ The Advanced Connection Settings dialog box appears.

■ This option instructs your modem to use error control to make your connections more reliable.

■ This option instructs your modem to connect to other computers only if the connections are reliable.

■ This option instructs your modem to compress data to increase the speed at which information transfers.

9 You can click an option to turn the option on (☑) or off (☐).

CONTINUED

CHANGE THE ADVANCED CONNECTION SETTINGS CONTINUED

You can change the advanced connection settings for a modem to improve the performance of the modem.

The flow control settings determine how data transfers between your computer and the modem. Most modems use hardware flow control.

You can choose a modulation type, which refers to the type of signals sent between modems. Both computers must use the same type of modulation to successfully exchange information. Most modems use the Standard modulation type. It is unlikely that you will have to change the modulation type setting.

You can use extra settings to send special commands to a modem before it starts communicating with another modem. For example, you may be able to type ATM0 to turn the modem speaker off. These extra settings are often referred to as an initialization string. Your modem's manual will explain which extra settings, if any, you can use with your modem.

Windows keeps track of the modem activities for the most recent session in a log file. You can use the Append to log option to have Windows keep a record of all the modem activities.

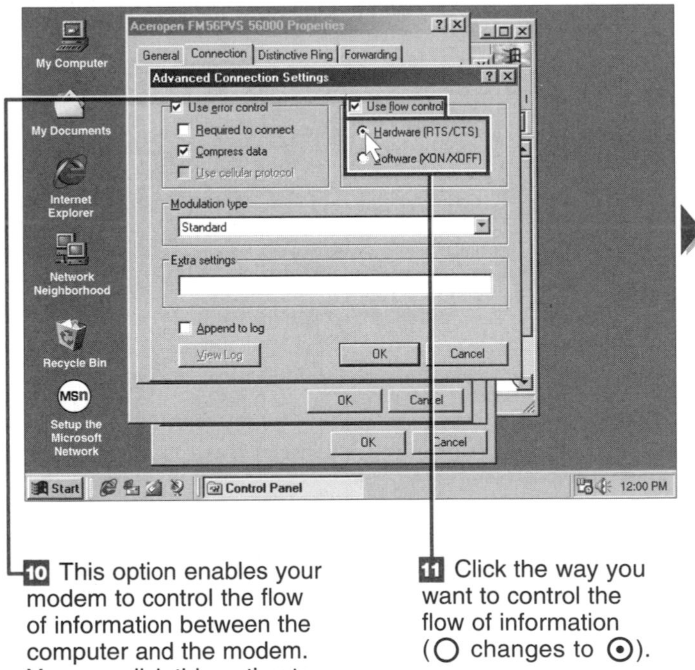

10 This option enables your modem to control the flow of information between the computer and the modem. You can click this option to turn the option on (☑) or off (☐).

11 Click the way you want to control the flow of information (○ changes to ⊙).

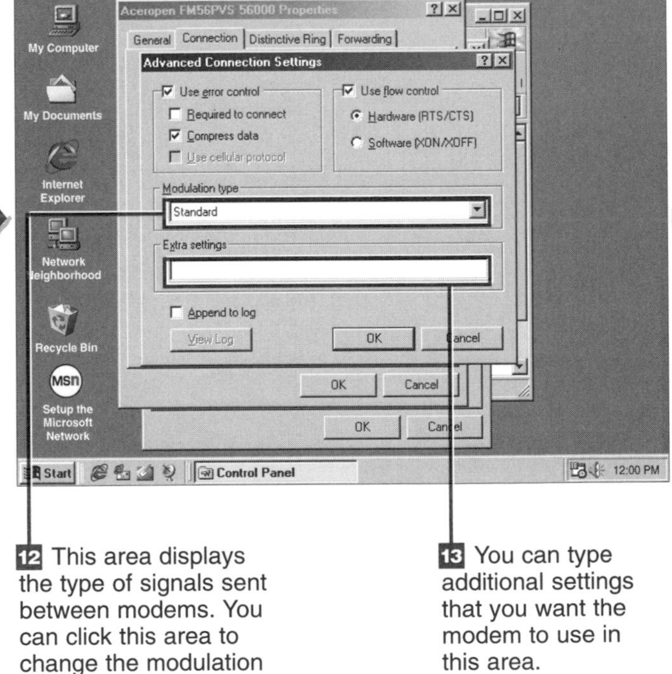

12 This area displays the type of signals sent between modems. You can click this area to change the modulation type to match the modem you are connecting to.

13 You can type additional settings that you want the modem to use in this area.

TIPS

Why should I use the Append to log option?

Keeping a record of all the modem activities can help you keep track of the time you spend connected to other computers. You can also monitor charges you acquire from dialing toll calls or from dialing in to your Internet service provider. The log can also help you fix problems with your modem by showing you which commands are causing errors to occur.

How can I view the log file?

In the Advanced Connection Settings dialog box, click the View Log button. A Notepad window will open, displaying a record of the modem activities.

When would I use extra settings?

Certain modem models may have difficulty making a connection using only their default settings. These connection problems may be fixed by using extra settings. For example, if you have trouble connecting to your Internet service provider, the service provider may be able to tell you which extra settings you need to connect properly.

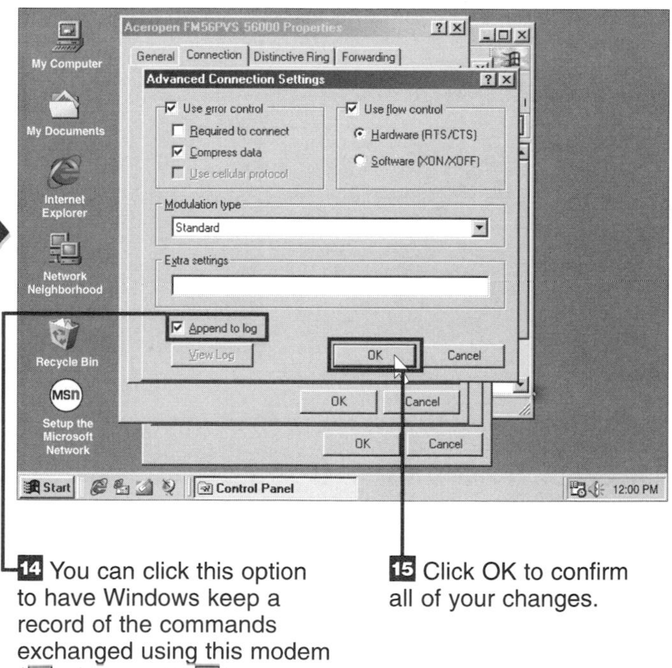

14 You can click this option to have Windows keep a record of the commands exchanged using this modem (☐ changes to ☑).

15 Click OK to confirm all of your changes.

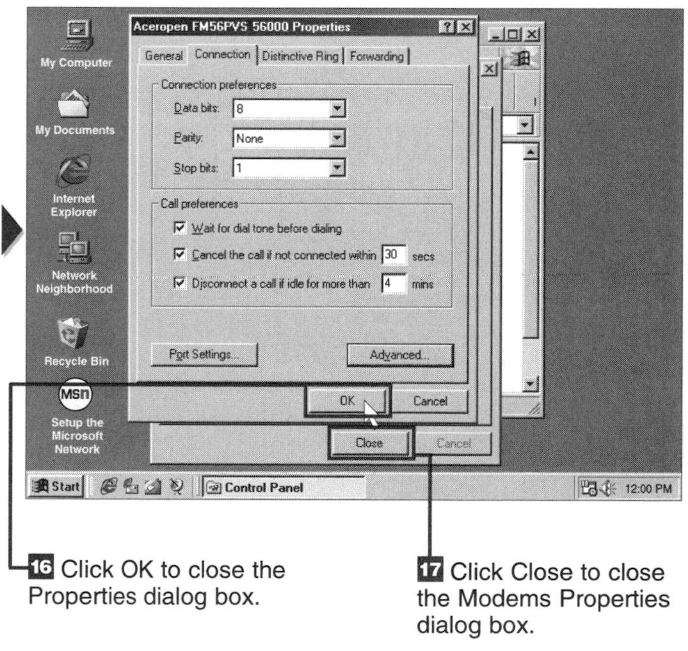

16 Click OK to close the Properties dialog box.

17 Click Close to close the Modems Properties dialog box.

SET UP A CONNECTION TO ANOTHER COMPUTER

You can use Dial-Up Networking to connect to another computer using a modem. When two computers are connected, you can work with files on the other computer as if the files were stored on your own computer. You can also print files and access information on a network.

Connecting to another computer is useful when you are at home or traveling and you need information on your computer at work. The computer you want to contact must be turned on when you want to connect.

Before connecting to another computer, you must tell Windows about the computer you want to contact. Windows will store the information you enter about the other computer. This will help you connect to the computer again.

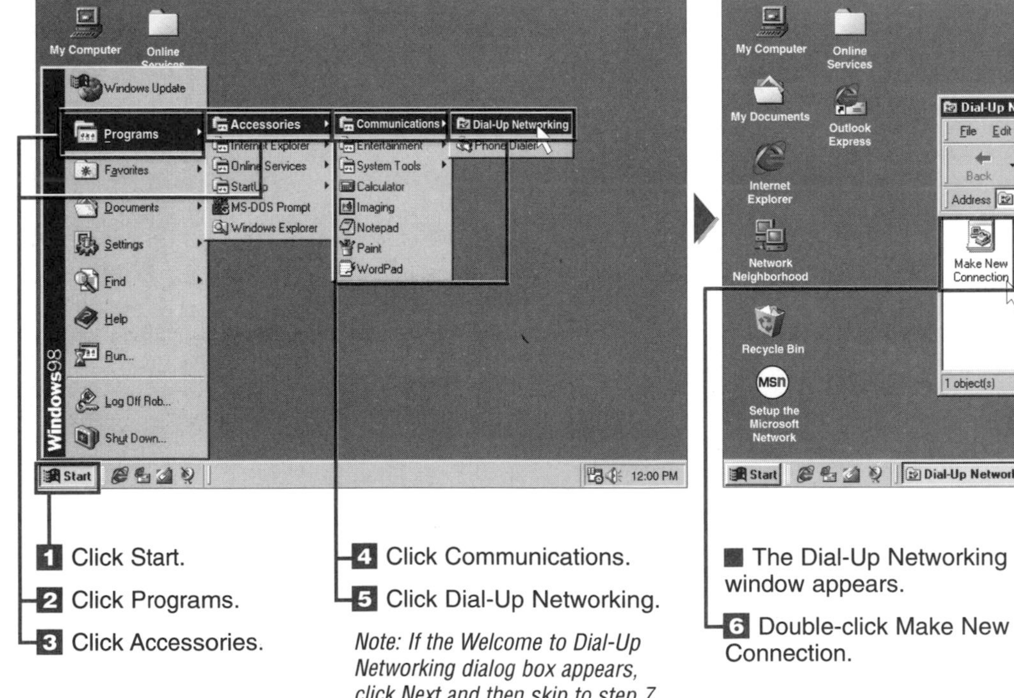

1 Click Start.

2 Click Programs.

3 Click Accessories.

4 Click Communications.

5 Click Dial-Up Networking.

Note: If the Welcome to Dial-Up Networking dialog box appears, click Next and then skip to step 7.

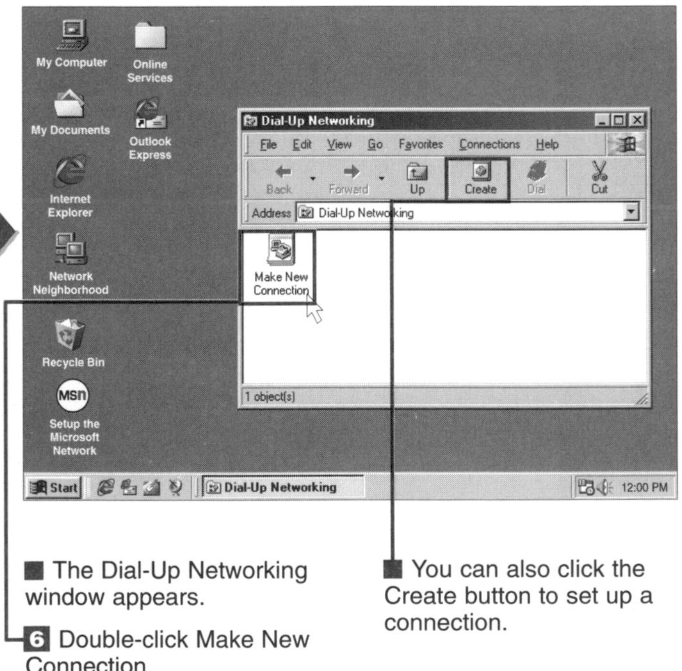

■ The Dial-Up Networking window appears.

6 Double-click Make New Connection.

■ You can also click the Create button to set up a connection.

TIPS

Is there anything I must do before setting up a connection to another computer?

You must have a modem installed before you can use Dial-Up Networking to set up a connection to another computer. To install a modem, see page 382.

Can I set up a Dial-Up Networking connection to the Internet?

You can use the Internet Connection Wizard to set up a connection to your Internet service provider's computer. Once you are connected to the service provider's computer, you can access the resources available on the Internet. See page 498.

Is there another way to open the Dial-Up Networking window?

Double-click My Computer. Then double-click the Dial-Up Networking folder.

Can I set up a secure dial-up connection to another network?

A VPN (Virtual Private Network) adapter is used to connect a computer to a private network using the Internet. When you use a VPN adapter to connect to a private network, other people cannot see the information you transfer. For information on installing a VPN adapter and using it to connect to a network, consult the system administrator of the network you want to connect to.

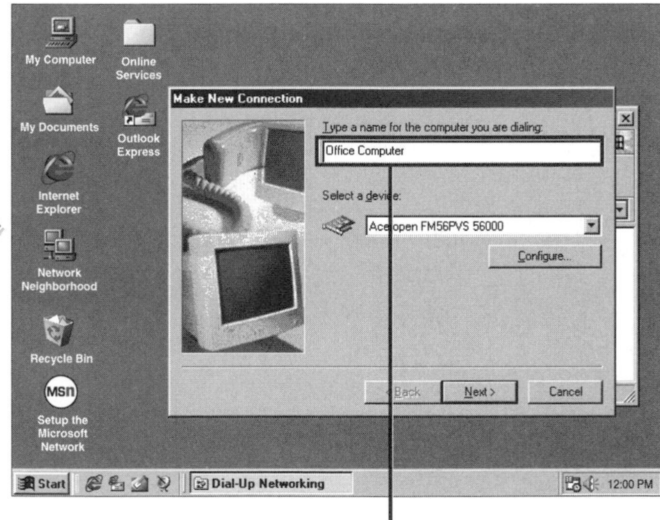

■ The Make New Connection dialog box appears.

7 Type a name for the computer you want to contact.

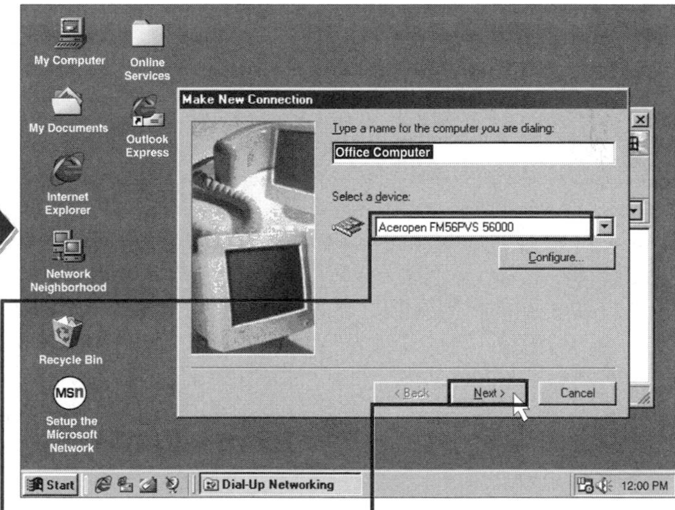

■ This area displays the modem Windows will use to contact the computer.

8 Click Next to continue.

CONTINUED

SET UP A CONNECTION TO ANOTHER COMPUTER CONTINUED

When you set up a connection to another computer using Dial-Up Networking, you must provide Windows with information about the computer you wish to contact, such as the area code and phone number of the computer.

You can specify only one phone number for each dial-up connection you create. If the computer you want to contact has more than one available phone line that you can use to establish a connection, you must set up a separate connection for each phone line.

You only need to set up a connection to another computer once. After the connection is set up, Windows displays an icon for the connection in the Dial-Up Networking window.

Before you can use the dial-up connection to contact the other computer, the computer you wish to connect to must be set up to receive your calls. To set up a dial-up server, see page 406.

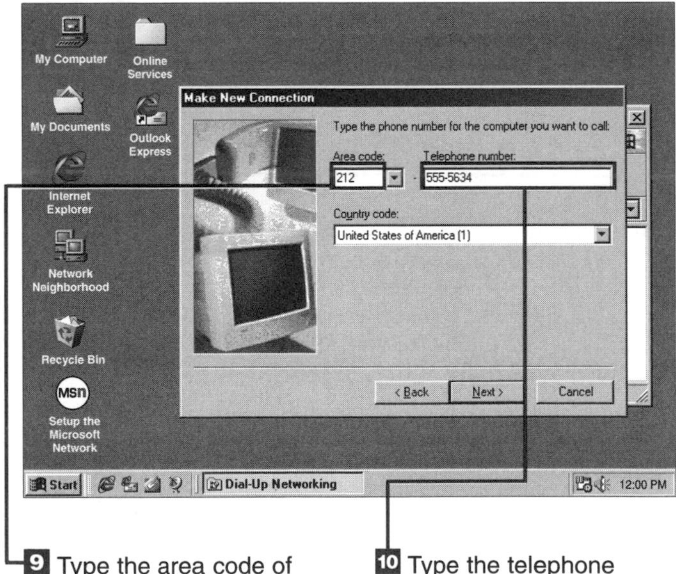

9 Type the area code of the computer you want to contact and then press the Tab key.

10 Type the telephone number of the computer you want to contact.

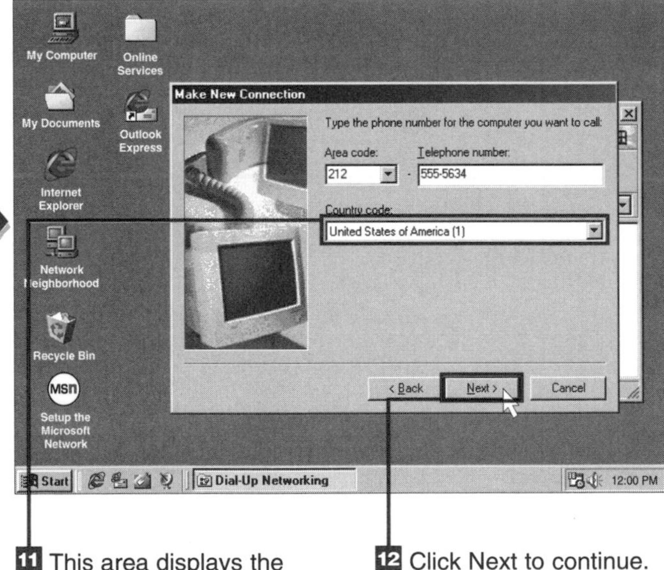

11 This area displays the code for the country you want to contact. You can click this area to change the country code.

12 Click Next to continue.

TIPS

Will I ever need to change the settings for the dial-up connections I create?

You may occasionally need to change the settings for a dial-up connection. If the information required to connect to another computer changes, such as the phone number of the computer, you will have to change the settings. To change the settings for a dial-up connection, display the contents of the Dial-Up Networking window. Right-click the icon for the connection you want to change and then click Properties.

Are there any other settings I must specify before dialing in to the computer?

You may need to change the settings for the dial-up connection to match the settings of the computer you want to connect to. You should contact the administrator of the other computer to find out if there are any special settings you need to change.

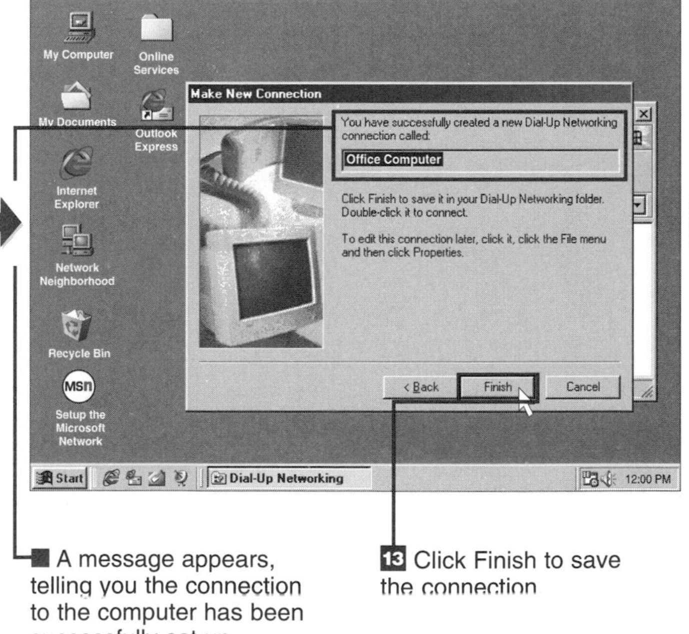

■ A message appears, telling you the connection to the computer has been successfully set up.

13 Click Finish to save the connection.

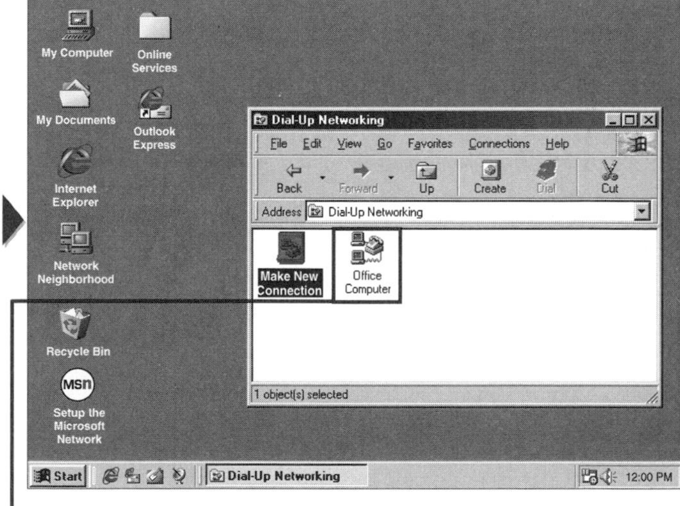

■ An icon for the connection appears in the Dial-Up Networking window.

■ To use this icon to dial in to the other computer, see page 402.

18

DIAL IN TO ANOTHER COMPUTER

After you set up a connection to another computer, you can dial in to the computer to access information. For example, you can dial in to a computer at work to access files you need while you are away from the office. You can access information on a network that the office computer is connected to.

Windows displays an icon in the Dial-Up Networking window for each connection you set up to another computer. To set up a dial-up connection to another computer, see page 398.

When you start to connect to another computer, Windows displays information such as your user name and the telephone number your modem will dial. You may need to enter a password to connect to the other computer.

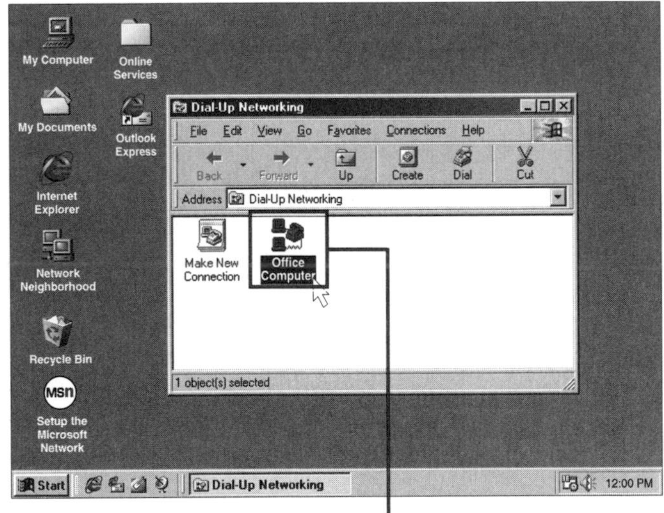

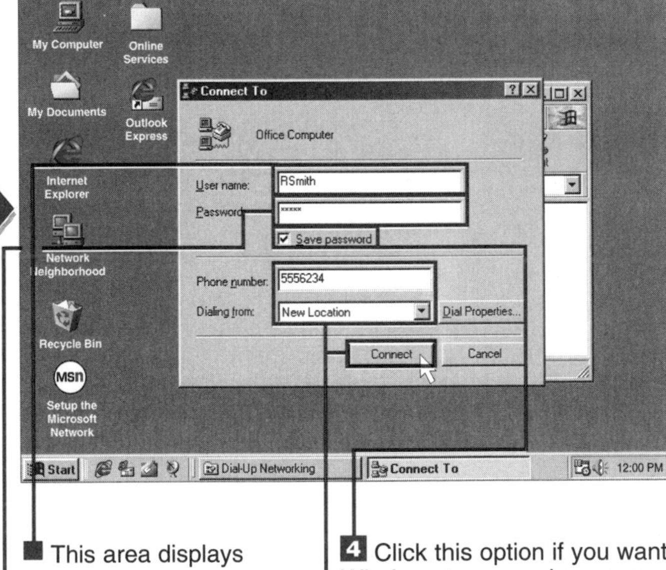

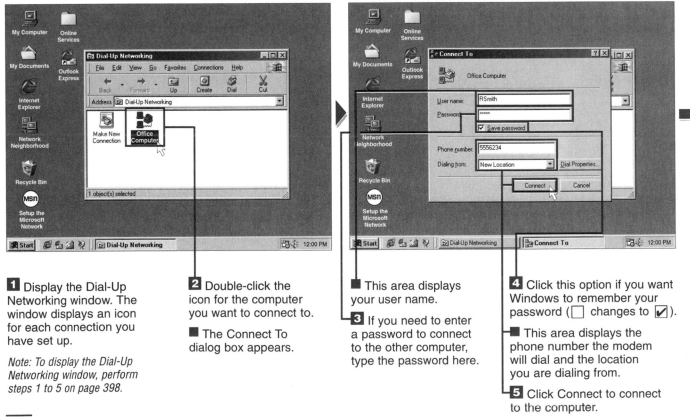

1 Display the Dial-Up Networking window. The window displays an icon for each connection you have set up.

Note: To display the Dial-Up Networking window, perform steps 1 to 5 on page 398.

2 Double-click the icon for the computer you want to connect to.

■ The Connect To dialog box appears.

■ This area displays your user name.

3 If you need to enter a password to connect to the other computer, type the password here.

4 Click this option if you want Windows to remember your password (☐ changes to ☑).

■ This area displays the phone number the modem will dial and the location you are dialing from.

5 Click Connect to connect to the computer.

TIPS

Why did my modem disconnect from the other computer?

There may be interference on the phone line. Although interference may cause only a brief break in a normal telephone call, interference can cause a computer's modem to disconnect from another computer. Try connecting again to get a better phone line connection. Your local phone company may be able to help you eliminate phone line interference. Your modem may also disconnect from another computer if you do not type anything for a long period of time or if the computer you are connected to is turned off.

What will happen if I enter the wrong information when I try to dial in to another computer?

If you enter the wrong information, such as the wrong user name or password, you will not be allowed to connect to the other computer. Some computers may take a few moments before they disconnect you, so it may appear that you are briefly connected before you are disconnected.

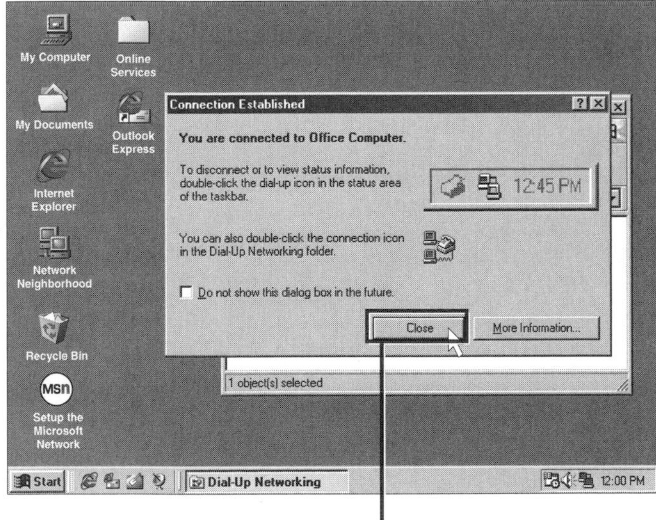

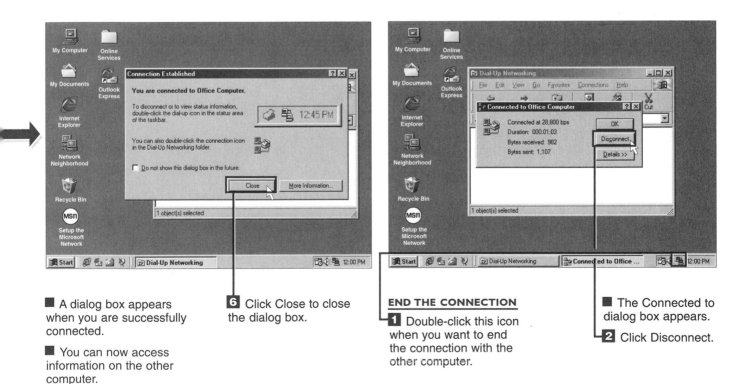

■ A dialog box appears when you are successfully connected.

■ You can now access information on the other computer.

6 Click Close to close the dialog box.

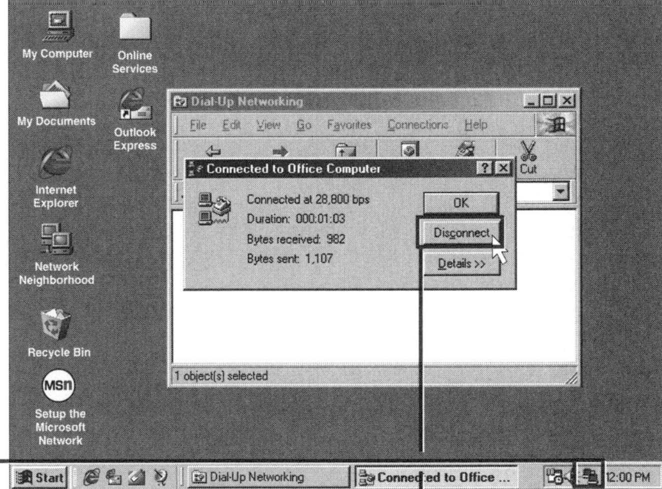

END THE CONNECTION

1 Double-click this icon when you want to end the connection with the other computer.

■ The Connected to dialog box appears.

2 Click Disconnect.

CHANGE SETTINGS FOR DIALING OUT

You can change the way your computer dials in to other computers.

You can display a Dial-Up Networking icon on the taskbar when you are connected to another computer. You can use the icon to view the status of the connection. You can by-pass the Connect To dialog box when you connect to another computer by turning off the Prompt for information before dialing option. You can also have Windows confirm when you have successfully connected to another computer.

When the Redial option is turned on, Windows continues to redial a phone number until it establishes a connection. You can specify how many times Windows should redial the number and the amount of time in minutes and seconds Windows should wait between each redial attempt.

When you are establishing a connection to another computer that is also using Dial-Up Networking, you can have Windows dial and connect to the other computer without prompting you. This is useful if you have mapped the drive of the computer you want to connect to. You can then double-click the mapped drive's icon in a My Computer or Windows Explorer window to establish a connection. For information on mapping a drive, see page 452.

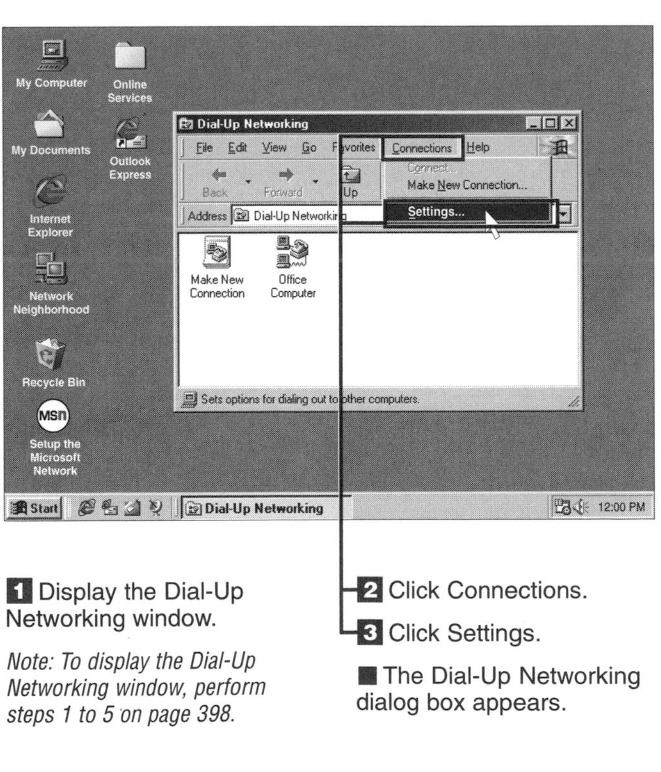

1 Display the Dial-Up Networking window.

Note: To display the Dial-Up Networking window, perform steps 1 to 5 on page 398.

2 Click Connections.

3 Click Settings.

■ The Dial-Up Networking dialog box appears.

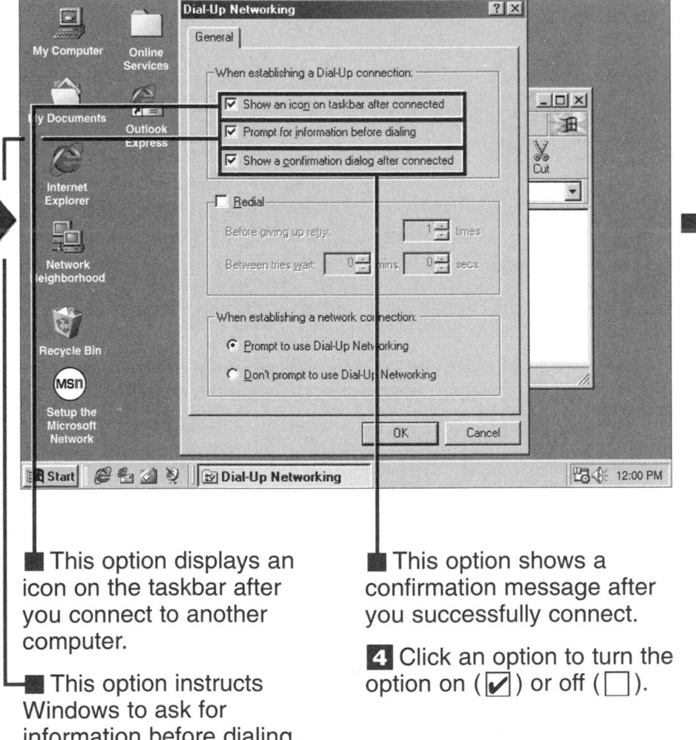

■ This option displays an icon on the taskbar after you connect to another computer.

■ This option instructs Windows to ask for information before dialing.

■ This option shows a confirmation message after you successfully connect.

4 Click an option to turn the option on (☑) or off (☐).

TIPS

How long should I have Windows wait before each redial attempt?

You should set the time between redial attempts as low as possible. When you leave this setting at 0 minutes and 0 seconds, Windows will continuously redial until it connects or reaches the specified number of redials.

Which connections will the new settings affect?

When you change the settings in the Dial-Up Networking dialog box, the new settings take effect immediately and affect all of the connections that you have created.

Why would I want Windows to confirm that I have successfully connected to another computer?

On most computers, the sounds the modem makes while it is connecting to another computer tell you when you have successfully connected. If you have turned off the sound for your modem, you can have Windows tell you when you are connected.

How many times should I have Windows redial?

You should set this option to 100 times so Windows will keep redialing until a connection is made.

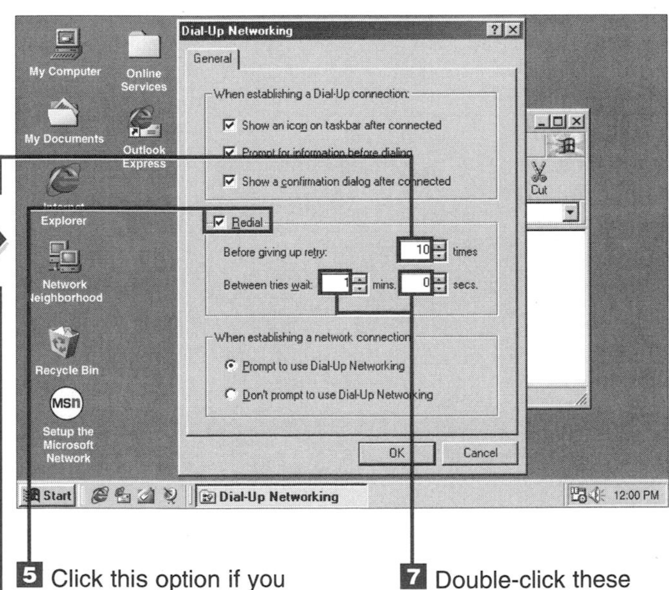

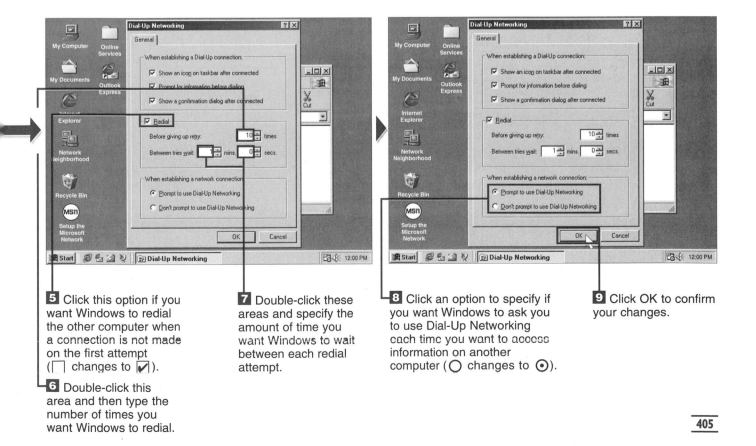

5 Click this option if you want Windows to redial the other computer when a connection is not made on the first attempt (☐ changes to ☑).

6 Double-click this area and then type the number of times you want Windows to redial.

7 Double-click these areas and specify the amount of time you want Windows to wait between each redial attempt.

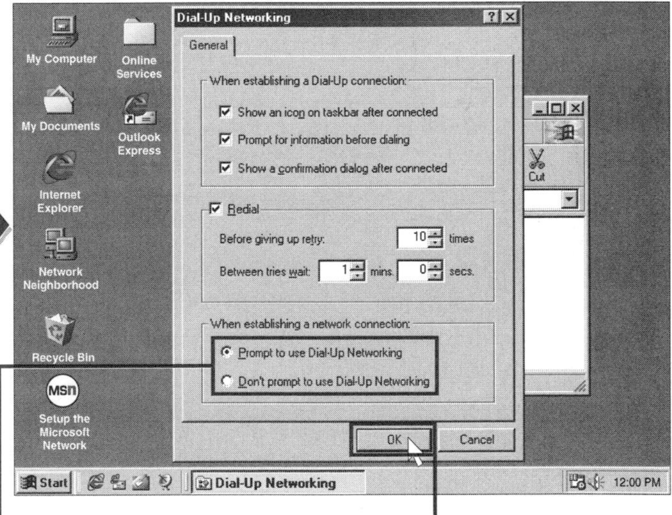

8 Click an option to specify if you want Windows to ask you to use Dial-Up Networking each time you want to access information on another computer (○ changes to ◉).

9 Click OK to confirm your changes.

18

SET UP A DIAL-UP SERVER

You can set up a computer so you can dial in to the computer from another location. Setting up a dial-up server is ideal for someone who uses a laptop computer or a home computer and wants to access information stored on a desktop computer at the office. A modem must be installed on the dial-up server before you can dial in to the computer.

You can dial in to the dial-up server to access information stored on the computer and the network attached to the computer. Connecting to the dial-up server also allows you to print documents on printers located at the office.

You can assign a password so only people who know the password can access the dial-up server.

Many networks have a dedicated dial-up server that accepts calls only from computers that require access to the network. These dedicated dial-up servers are often called remote access servers.

After you set up a dial-up server, you need to set up a connection to the server on your laptop or home computer. See page 398 to set up a connection.

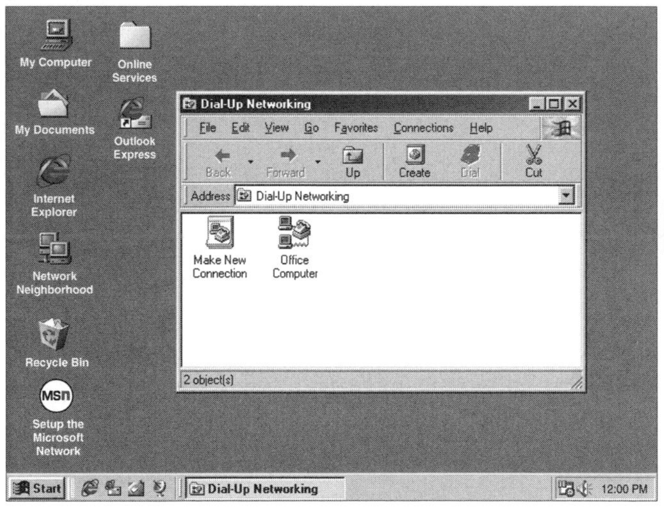

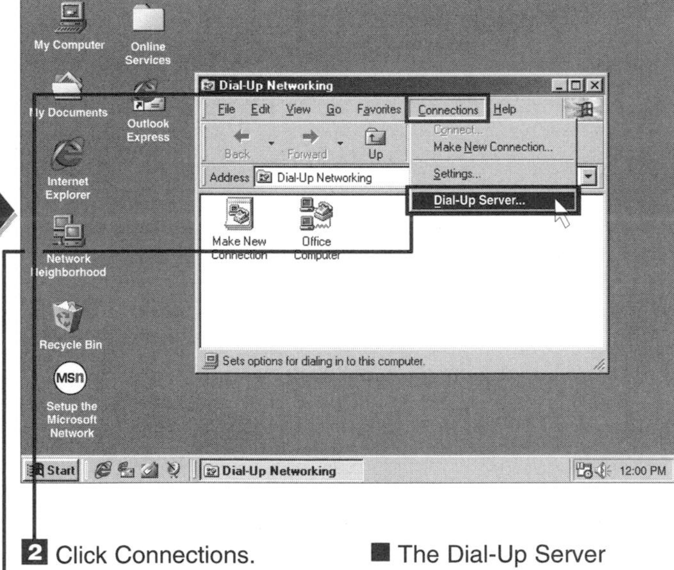

1 Display the Dial-Up Networking window.

Note: To display the Dial-Up Networking window, perform steps 1 to 5 on page 398.

2 Click Connections.

3 Click Dial-Up Server.

■ The Dial-Up Server dialog box appears.

TIPS

Why is the Dial-Up Server option not available on the Connections menu in my Dial-Up Networking window?

Dial-Up Server may not be installed on your computer. Dial-Up Server is part of the Communications component. To add Windows components, see page 610.

What information will be available on the dial-up server?

Before you can use a computer as a dial-up server, you must share the information on the server you want to be able to access from another location. You can share items such as files and printers. See pages 456 to 463 to share information.

Do I need to change the settings on the dial-up server?

If you plan to use a Windows 95 or 98 computer to connect to your dial-up server, you do not need to change the settings on the server. If you plan to connect to your dial-up server using a computer with an older operating system, such as Windows 3.1, you may need to change the settings on the server. To change the settings, click the Server Type button in the Dial-Up Server dialog box. Select the type of dial-up server that matches the operating system on the computer you are going to use to connect to the server.

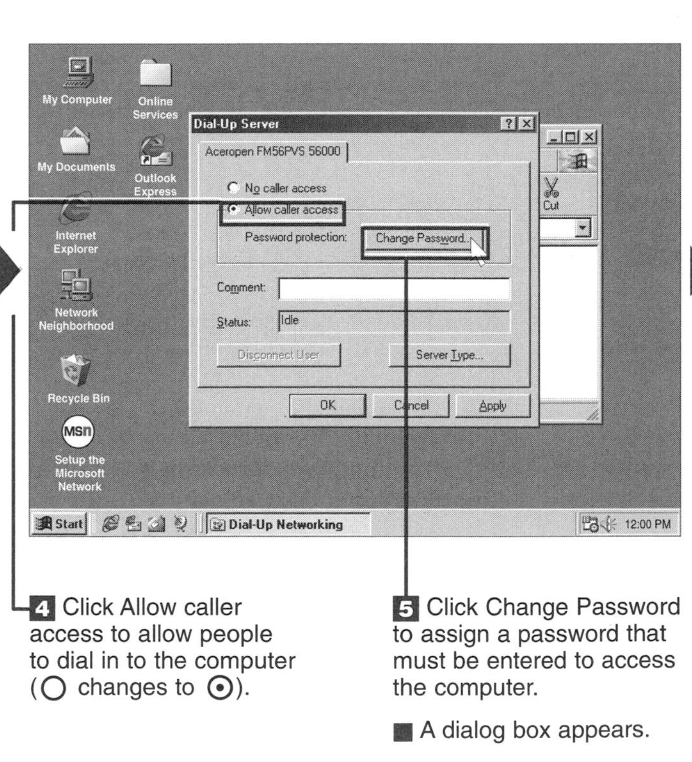

4 Click Allow caller access to allow people to dial in to the computer (○ changes to ⊙).

5 Click Change Password to assign a password that must be entered to access the computer.

■ A dialog box appears.

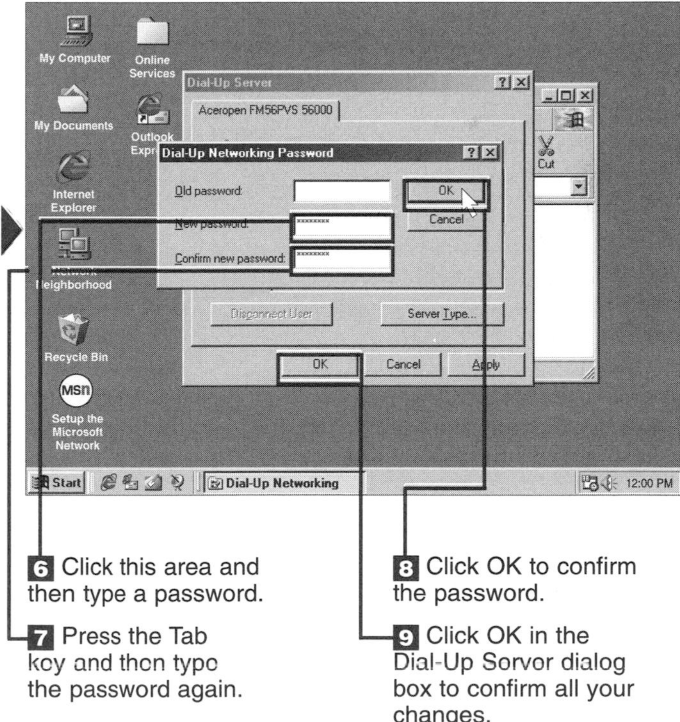

6 Click this area and then type a password.

7 Press the Tab key and then type the password again.

8 Click OK to confirm the password.

9 Click OK in the Dial-Up Server dialog box to confirm all your changes.

CONNECT TO ANOTHER COMPUTER USING HYPERTERMINAL

HyperTerminal is included with Windows 98 and allows you to use a modem to communicate with another computer.

You can use HyperTerminal to connect to a friend's computer, a university, a company, a Bulletin Board Service (BBS) or an online service, such as CompuServe.

Before you can contact another computer, you need to set up a connection to the computer. HyperTerminal will guide you through the process of creating a connection and will ask for information such as the computer's area code and telephone number. After you use HyperTerminal to connect to another computer, you can transfer information between the computers.

HyperTerminal provides connections to popular online services, including AT&T Mail, CompuServe and MCI Mail. You will find these connections in the HyperTerminal window.

If you have not yet set up your modem, HyperTerminal will ask you to set up the modem when you start the program.

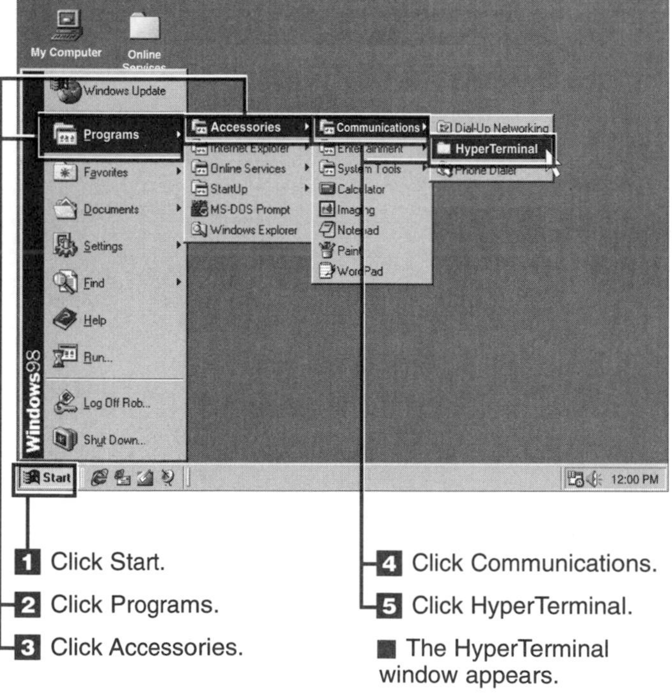

1 Click Start.

2 Click Programs.

3 Click Accessories.

4 Click Communications.

5 Click HyperTerminal.

■ The HyperTerminal window appears.

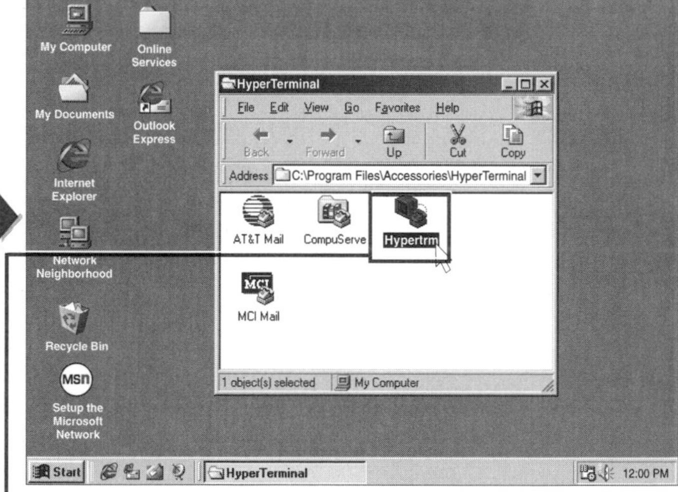

6 Double-click Hypertrm.

■ The New Connection window and the Connection Description dialog box appear.

TIPS

Why doesn't HyperTerminal appear on the Start menu?

HyperTerminal may not be installed on your computer. HyperTerminal is found in the Communications component. To add Windows components, see page 610.

Can I access the Internet using HyperTerminal?

Some computers on the Internet only offer information by telnet. You can use HyperTerminal as a telnet client to connect to another computer on the Internet and access the telnet information. To connect to a telnet site, perform steps 1 to 9 below to display the Connect To dialog box. Click the area beside Connect using and then select TCP/IP (Winsock). Type the telnet address you want to connect to and then press the Enter key. HyperTerminal connects you to the computer. Perform step 14 on page 410 to end the connection.

When shouldn't I use HyperTerminal to connect to another computer?

Most people use HyperTerminal to connect to local bulletin board services. If you want to connect to another computer running Windows, such as your computer at work, you should use Dial-Up Networking instead. See page 398 for information on Dial-Up Networking.

Where can I get the latest version of HyperTerminal?

HyperTerminal is continuously updated to add more features. Windows 98 includes a version of HyperTerminal. You can get the latest version of HyperTerminal or a similar program that offers more features on the Web at www.hilgraeve.com

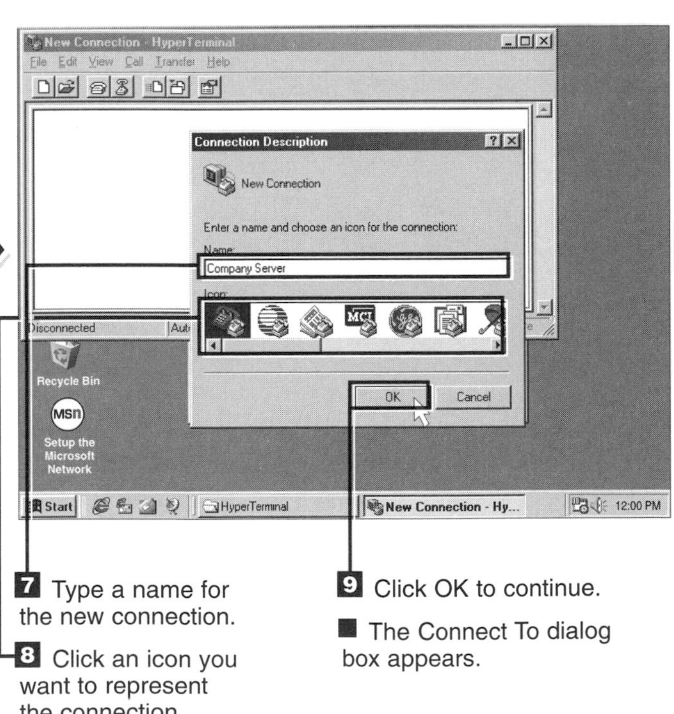

7 Type a name for the new connection.

8 Click an icon you want to represent the connection.

9 Click OK to continue.

■ The Connect To dialog box appears.

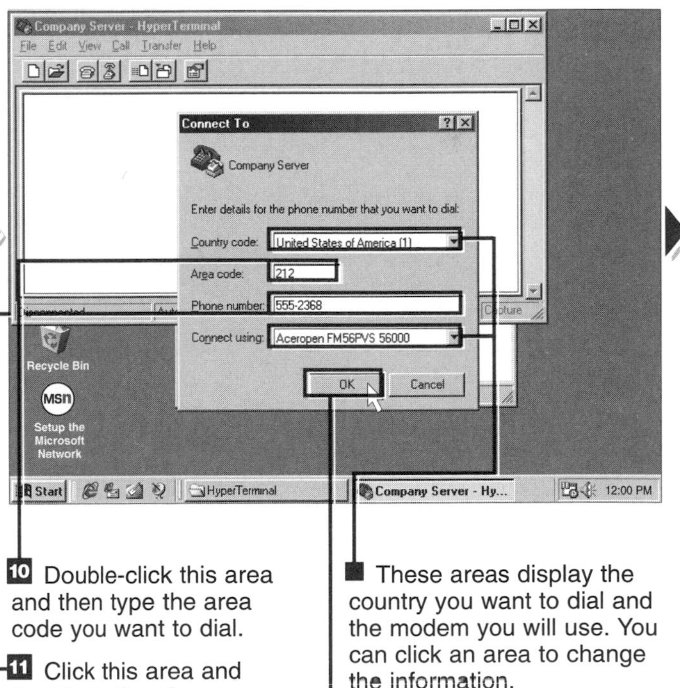

10 Double-click this area and then type the area code you want to dial.

11 Click this area and then type the phone number you want to dial.

■ These areas display the country you want to dial and the modem you will use. You can click an area to change the information.

12 Click OK to continue.

CONTINUED

CONNECT TO ANOTHER COMPUTER USING HYPERTERMINAL CONTINUED

After you connect to another computer using HyperTerminal, you can have Windows save the information you entered about the computer. This prevents you from having to enter the same information each time you want to connect to the computer.

The HyperTerminal window displays an icon for the connection you set up. You can use this icon to connect to the computer at any time.

HyperTerminal can make a computer you connect to believe that your computer is a terminal. This allows your computer to connect to a mainframe computer. Mainframe computers are large computers that are found in banks, schools, universities and large organizations.

There are many different types of terminals and each offers a different set of features. If the computer you connect to can only communicate with a specific type of terminal, HyperTerminal will automatically adjust so you will be able to communicate with the computer.

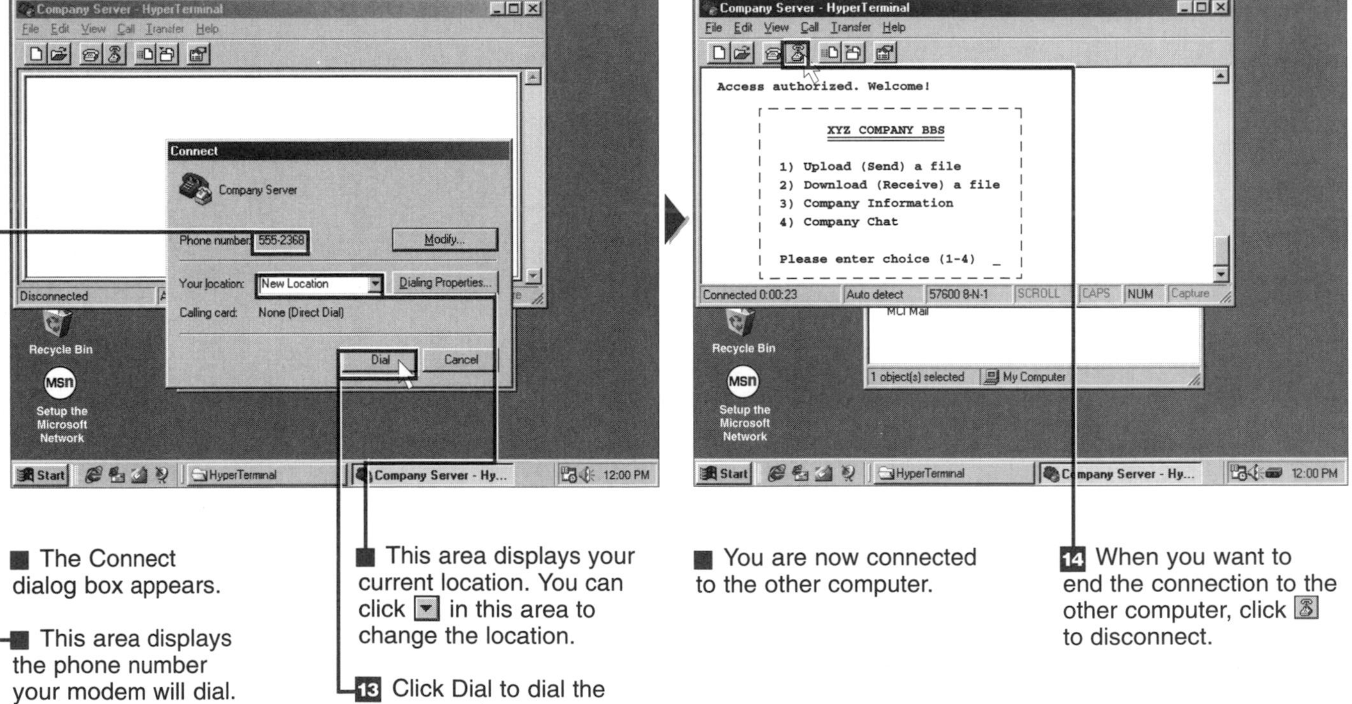

■ The Connect dialog box appears.

■ This area displays the phone number your modem will dial.

■ This area displays your current location. You can click ▼ in this area to change the location.

13 Click Dial to dial the phone number.

■ You are now connected to the other computer.

14 When you want to end the connection to the other computer, click the disconnect button to disconnect.

TIPS

Can I change the phone number for an existing connection?

Most phone numbers for bulletin board services and online services rarely change, but you may have to change the number you dial when calling from a different location, such as when you are traveling. Right-click the connection in the HyperTerminal window and then click Properties. The Connect To tab allows you to change the phone number for the connection.

Can I view images using HyperTerminal?

No. HyperTerminal is only capable of displaying text. You will not be able to view images using HyperTerminal, but you can transfer image files to your computer and then use another program to view the images. See page 416 to receive a file.

Why doesn't anything happen when I connect to another computer?

The computer you connect to must be set up to receive incoming calls. Although a modem may answer your call, the computer connected to the modem may not be properly set up to establish a connection.

How do I delete an existing connection?

Over time, you may find the HyperTerminal window fills up with connections that you create. You may want to remove connections you no longer need to make the window less cluttered. Click a connection you want to delete and then press the Delete key to remove the connection.

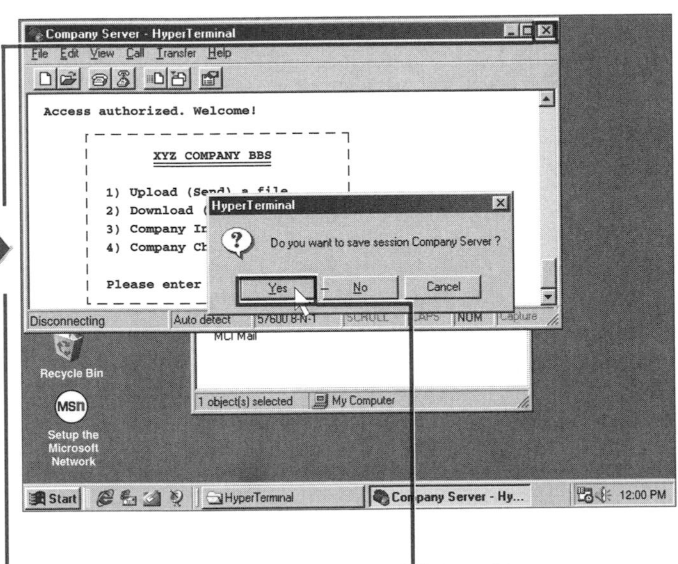

15 Click ☒ to close the HyperTerminal window.

■ A message appears, asking if you want to save the information you entered for the connection.

16 Click Yes to save the connection.

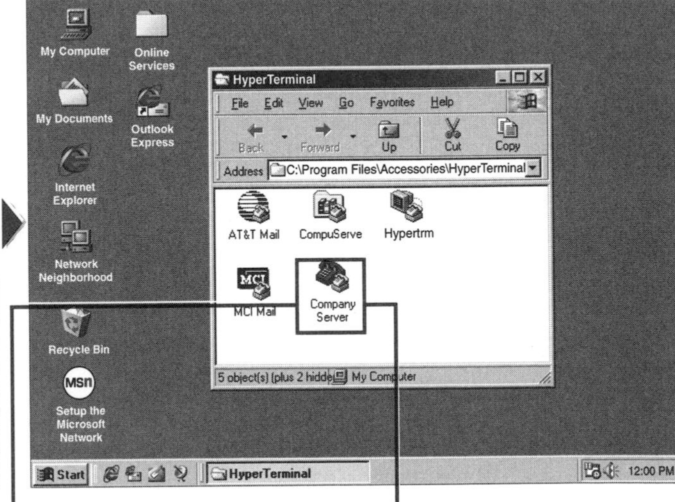

■ The connection you created appears in the HyperTerminal window.

■ You can double-click the connection to reconnect to the computer at any time.

CHANGE FONTS

You can change the font of text displayed in the HyperTerminal window to make the information easier to read. HyperTerminal allows you to change the font, style and size of text.

Some fonts can be difficult to read if you are using HyperTerminal for an extended period of time. When choosing another font, select a font that you find easy to read. You may also want to choose a different font style. HyperTerminal offers regular, italic, bold and bold italic styles.

A smaller font size allows you to fit more information on your screen. A larger font size displays less information on the screen, but the text is easier to see. When you change the font size, HyperTerminal automatically changes the size of the frame that surrounds the text to fit the new font size.

HyperTerminal will remember the font you selected and will use this font the next time you connect to the computer.

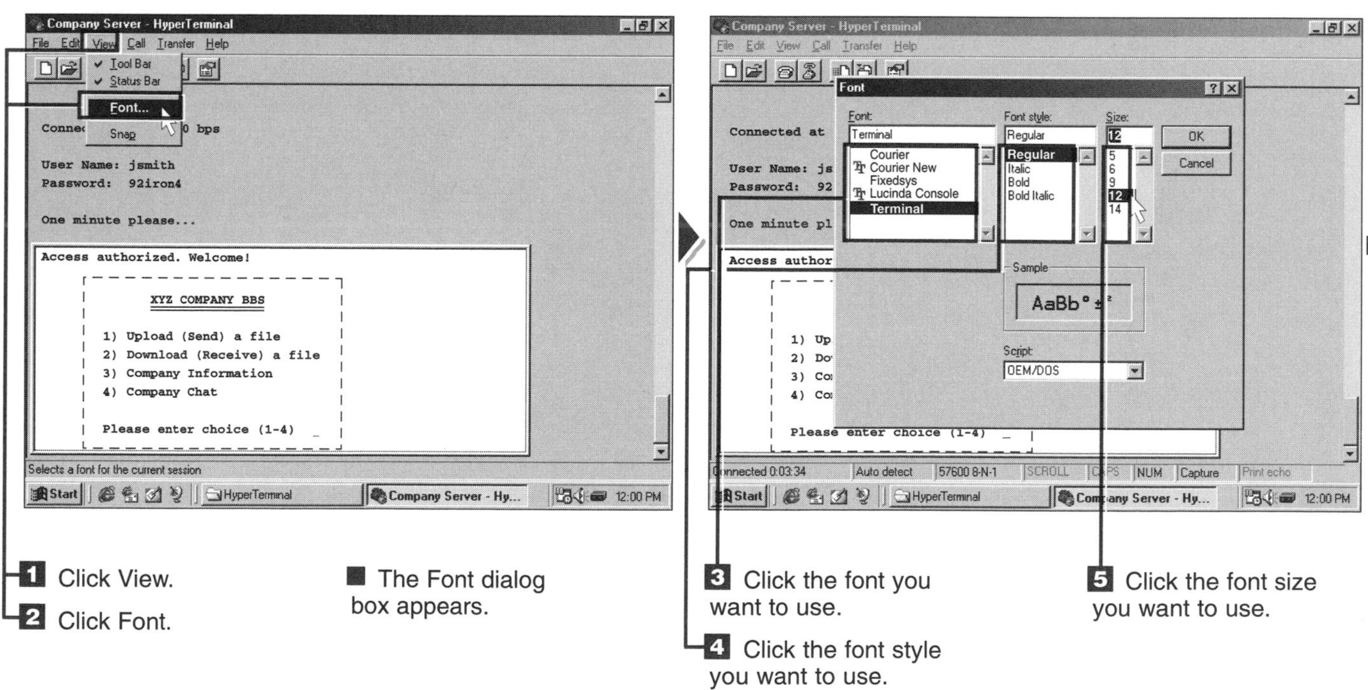

1 Click View.

2 Click Font.

■ The Font dialog box appears.

3 Click the font you want to use.

4 Click the font style you want to use.

5 Click the font size you want to use.

TIPS

Can I change the color of the font?

You cannot change the color of the font by using commands in HyperTerminal, but you can adjust your Windows settings to change the color. Many people find white text on a blue background easier to read. To change the colors displayed, perform steps 1 to 3 on page 208 to open the Display Properties dialog box. Click the Item area and then select Window from the list that appears. Click the Color area and select the background color you want to display in the window. Then click the Color area beside Font and select the color you want to use for the font.

If I change the font, will my captured text be affected?

You can capture text displayed in the HyperTerminal window to send the text to a file or to your printer. Changing the font of text will not affect the way text appears in the captured file or on your printouts. See page 414 to capture text.

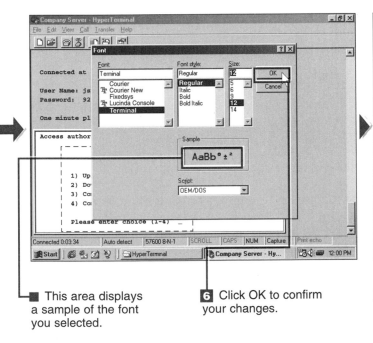

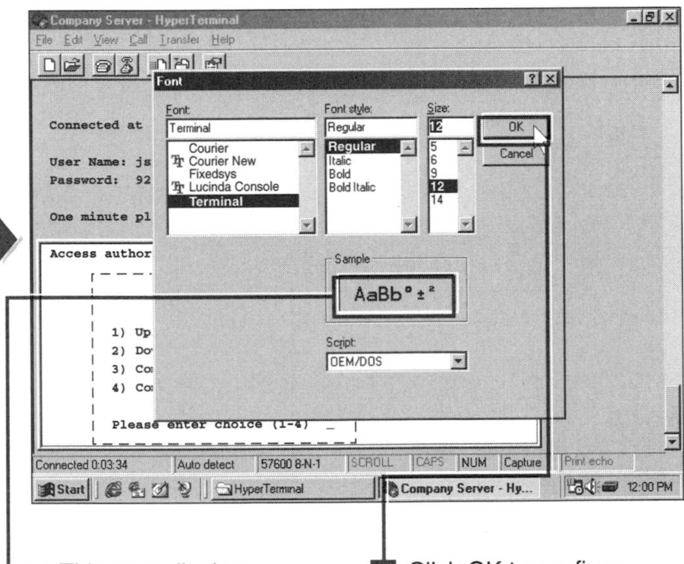

■ This area displays a sample of the font you selected.

6 Click OK to confirm your changes.

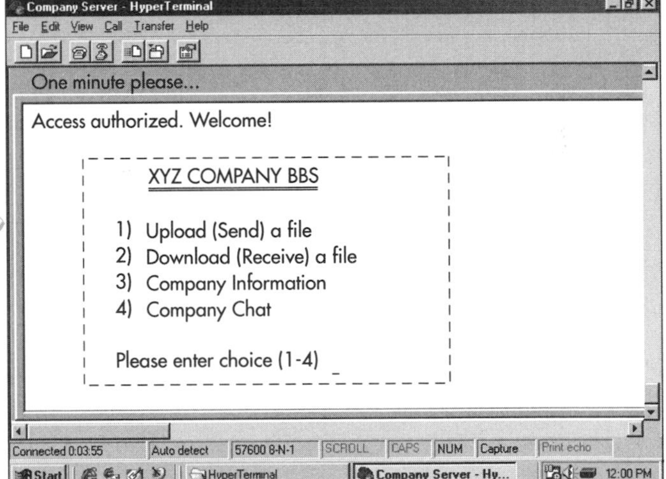

■ The text in the window appears in the new font.

CAPTURE TEXT

Capturing text allows you to send information you see on your screen to a file or to your printer. You can then review and work with the information later.

Capturing information can save you money because some bulletin board services charge you for the time you spend connected to their service.

Instead of reading information while you are connected to the service, you can capture the text and review the information when you are no longer connected.

Information may appear very quickly on your screen. The information at the top of the screen may scroll off before you have time to read the text.

Capturing text is useful since you may not be able to scroll back to text you previously viewed.

You can stop capturing text at any time. If you are capturing text to a file, you can stop or pause the capture when you know the information will be of no interest in the future.

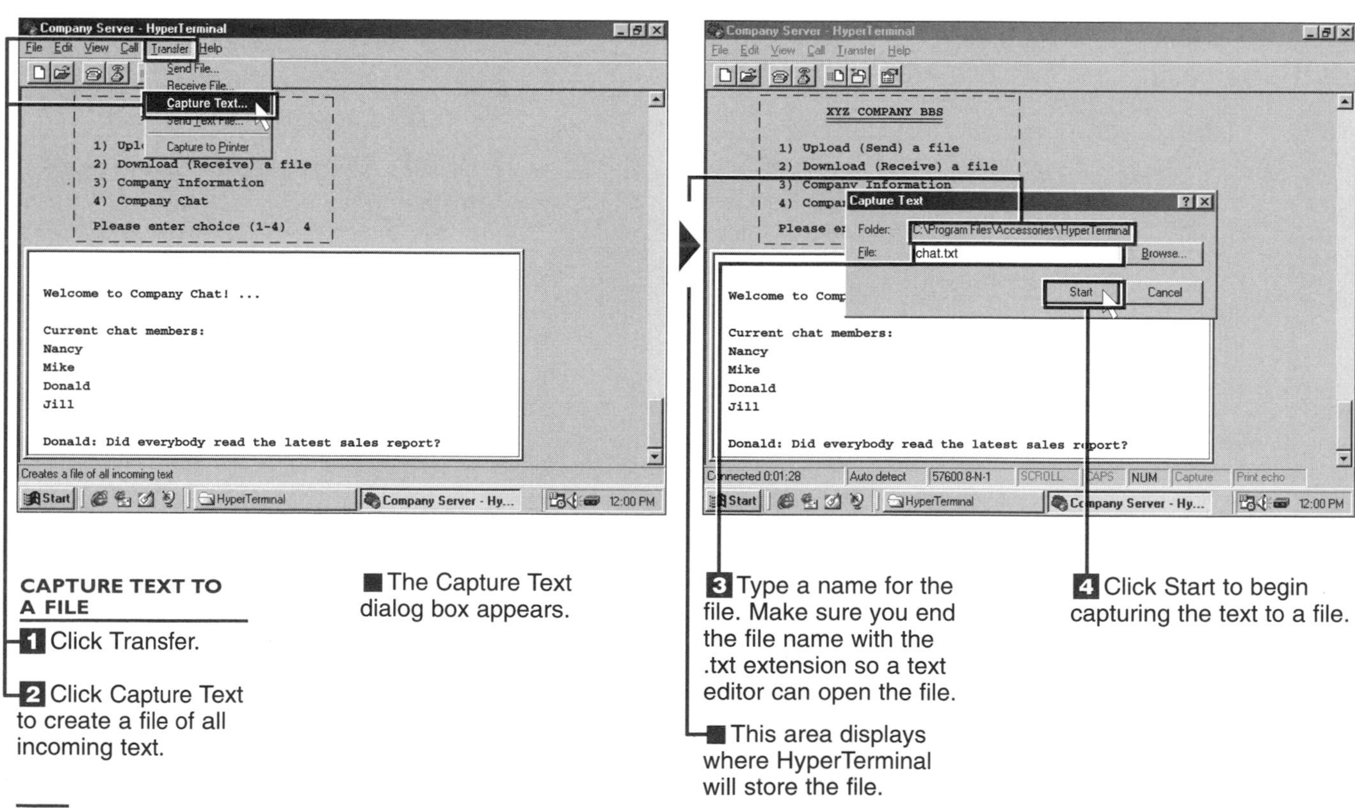

CAPTURE TEXT TO A FILE

1 Click Transfer.

2 Click Capture Text to create a file of all incoming text.

■ The Capture Text dialog box appears.

3 Type a name for the file. Make sure you end the file name with the .txt extension so a text editor can open the file.

■ This area displays where HyperTerminal will store the file.

4 Click Start to begin capturing the text to a file.

How do I view a captured file?

HyperTerminal will save the captured text in a text file so you can use any text editor or word processor to view the file. Even though you can display color and special symbols in HyperTerminal, this information will appear as unreadable text in a text editor or word processor.

How can I stop captured text from printing?

If you want to cancel the printing of captured text, you will have to remove the captured text from the print queue. See page 102.

How else can I capture text?

You can also use the Windows Copy and Paste features to copy information from your HyperTerminal window to another program such as WordPad. This is ideal for small sections of text you want to capture. See page 118.

How much information can I save in a captured file?

There is no limit to the size of your captured files, except the amount of storage space available on your computer. You should only capture information you plan to review later because captured files can take up a lot of storage space.

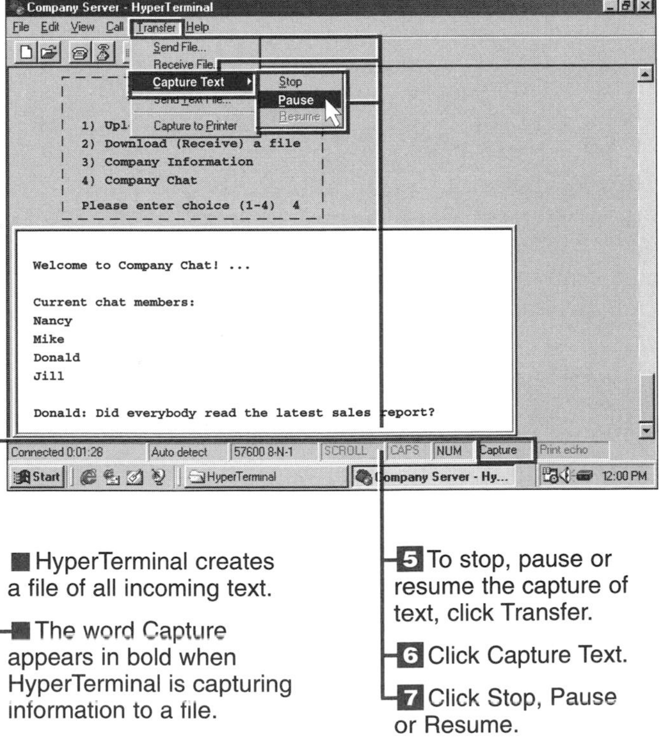

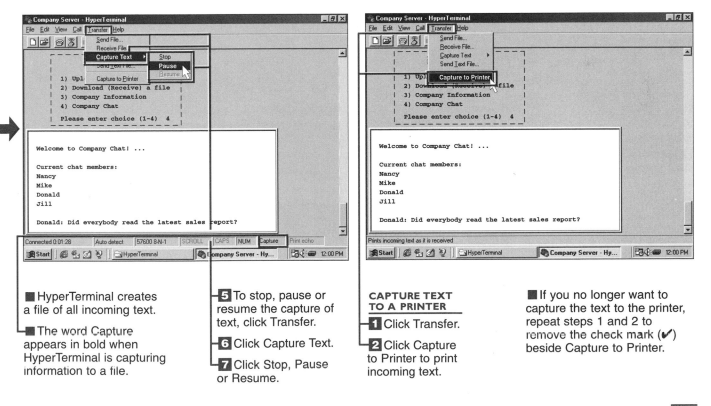

■ HyperTerminal creates a file of all incoming text.

■ The word Capture appears in bold when HyperTerminal is capturing information to a file.

5 To stop, pause or resume the capture of text, click Transfer.

6 Click Capture Text.

7 Click Stop, Pause or Resume.

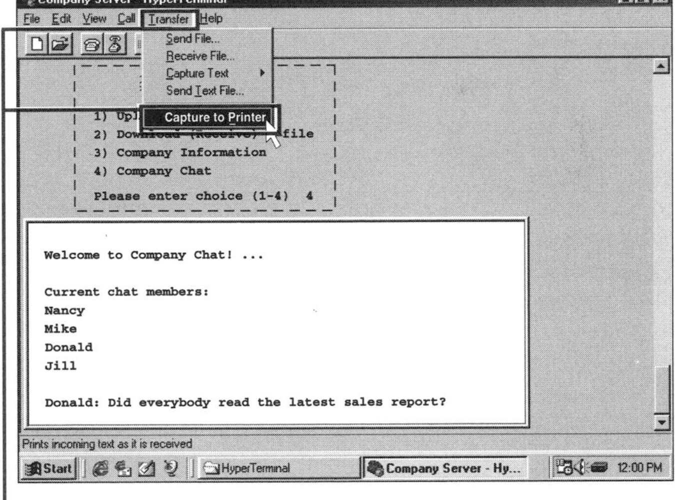

CAPTURE TEXT TO A PRINTER

1 Click Transfer.

2 Click Capture to Printer to print incoming text.

■ If you no longer want to capture the text to the printer, repeat steps 1 and 2 to remove the check mark (✔) beside Capture to Printer.

RECEIVE A FILE

HyperTerminal allows you to receive a file from another computer. One of the primary uses of HyperTerminal is to transfer files from other computers to your computer.

Bulletin board services often have a wide variety of text files, pictures and programs that you can transfer to your computer.

Before you can receive a file from another computer, you need to instruct the other computer to send the file. Each computer you receive files from will have its own preferred method of transferring files. You can usually instruct a computer to send a file by selecting commands from a menu offered by the computer.

When transferring files to your computer, you need to specify which protocol to use. A protocol is a language that computers use to communicate with each other.

Both computers must use the same protocol before they can exchange information. HyperTerminal can use several types of protocols, including Xmodem, Ymodem, Zmodem and Kermit. The most common type of protocol is Zmodem.

The protocol you select determines the information you need to give HyperTerminal before transferring the file. You may not need to perform all the steps below.

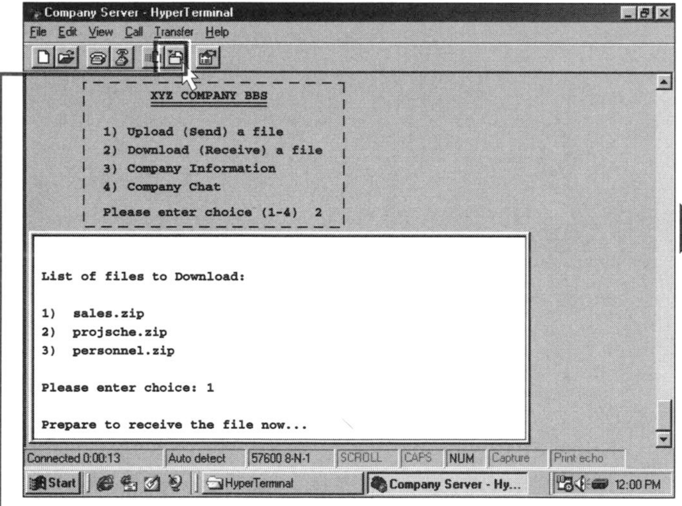

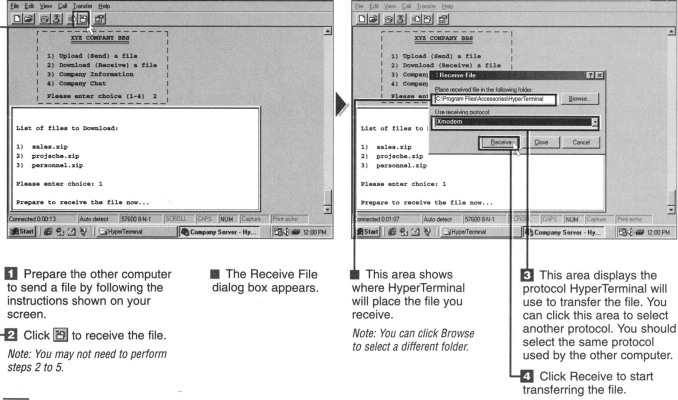

1 Prepare the other computer to send a file by following the instructions shown on your screen.

2 Click to receive the file.

Note: You may not need to perform steps 2 to 5.

■ The Receive File dialog box appears.

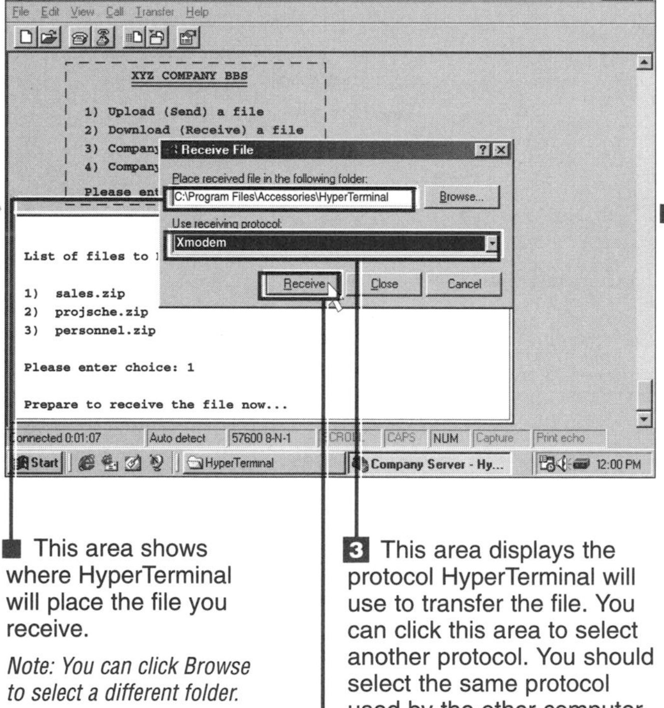

■ This area shows where HyperTerminal will place the file you receive.

Note: You can click Browse to select a different folder.

3 This area displays the protocol HyperTerminal will use to transfer the file. You can click this area to select another protocol. You should select the same protocol used by the other computer.

4 Click Receive to start transferring the file.

TIPS

What does downloading mean?

Transferring a file from another computer to your computer is called downloading. When you are downloading, you are transferring a file "down" to your computer. When you send a file from your computer to another computer, you are uploading the file.

What is throughput?

Throughput measures the speed that information transfers. When you are receiving a file, HyperTerminal displays the throughput of the file. HyperTerminal measures throughput using characters per second (cps).

Should I check programs I receive for viruses?

Programs you get from bulletin board services can contain viruses. Viruses can cause a variety of problems on your computer, such as the appearance of annoying messages on your screen or the destruction of information on your hard drive. You should use anti-virus software to scan any programs you receive before running the programs. Most computer stores offer anti-virus programs. You can also get anti-virus programs on the Internet.

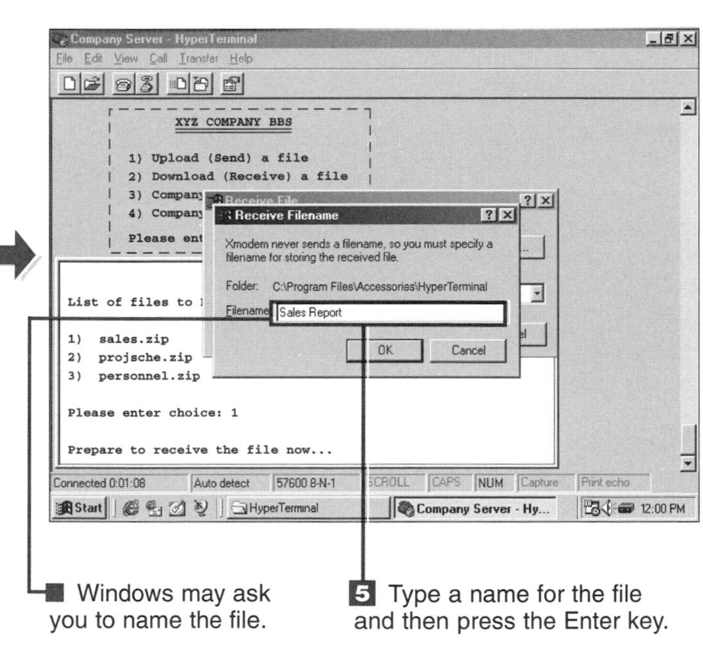

■ Windows may ask you to name the file.

5 Type a name for the file and then press the Enter key.

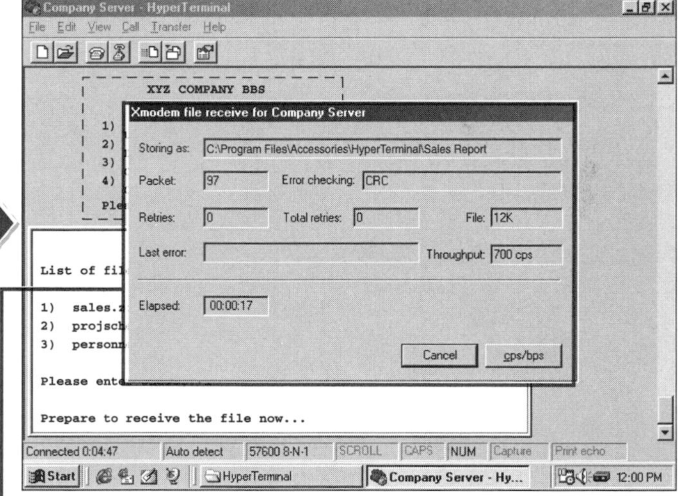

■ A dialog box shows the status of the file transfer. The dialog box that appears depends on the protocol you selected.

SEND A FILE

You can use HyperTerminal to send a file to another computer. You can transfer any type of file stored on your computer, including images, sounds, programs and text files.

The computer you send a file to must use HyperTerminal or a similar communications program to receive files.

When sending a file to another computer, you need to specify which protocol to use. A protocol is a language that computers use to communicate with each other. Both computers must use the same protocol before they can exchange files. Protocols usually compress, or squeeze, the files you send to speed the transfer of information.

The protocol you select determines the information you need to supply before HyperTerminal will transfer a file.

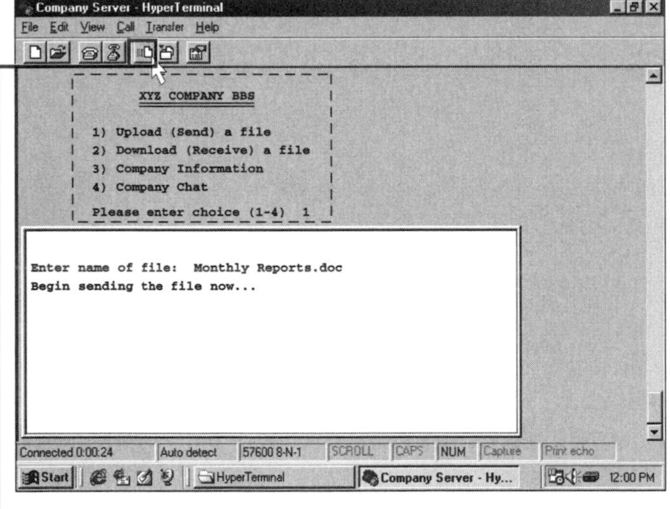

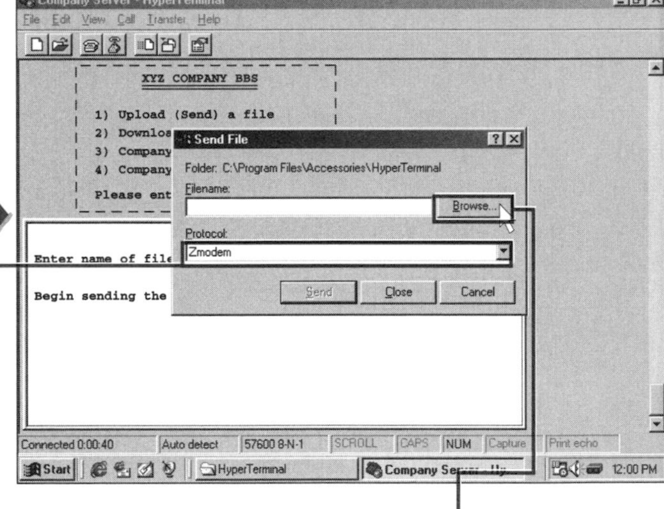

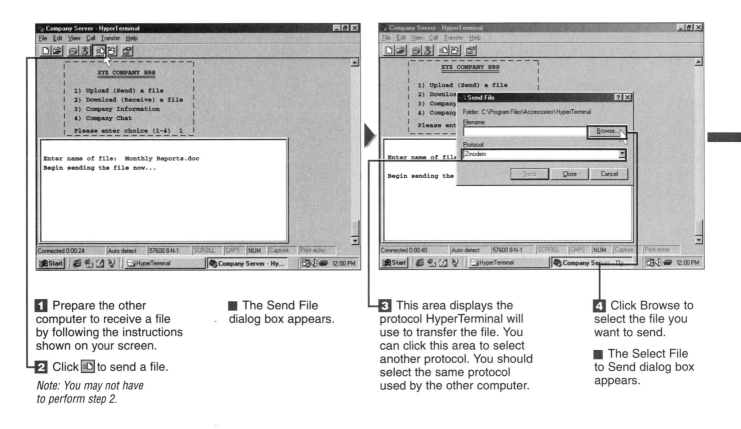

1 Prepare the other computer to receive a file by following the instructions shown on your screen.

2 Click [icon] to send a file.

Note: You may not have to perform step 2.

■ The Send File dialog box appears.

3 This area displays the protocol HyperTerminal will use to transfer the file. You can click this area to select another protocol. You should select the same protocol used by the other computer.

4 Click Browse to select the file you want to send.

■ The Select File to Send dialog box appears.

TIPS

Does HyperTerminal restrict the size of files I can send?

HyperTerminal does not restrict the size of files you can send. However, if you are sending a large file, you should ask the person who operates the computer receiving the file whether there is enough hard drive space to store the file.

Which protocol should I use?

One of the most commonly used protocols is Zmodem. Almost all online services and Bulletin Board Services (BBSs) allow you to transfer files using Zmodem.

What happens if the connection is interrupted while I am transferring a file?

An interruption can occur because of problems with the phone line. The version of HyperTerminal included with Windows 98 uses Zmodem with Crash Recovery. This protocol allows HyperTerminal to automatically recover from a broken connection and continue sending your file.

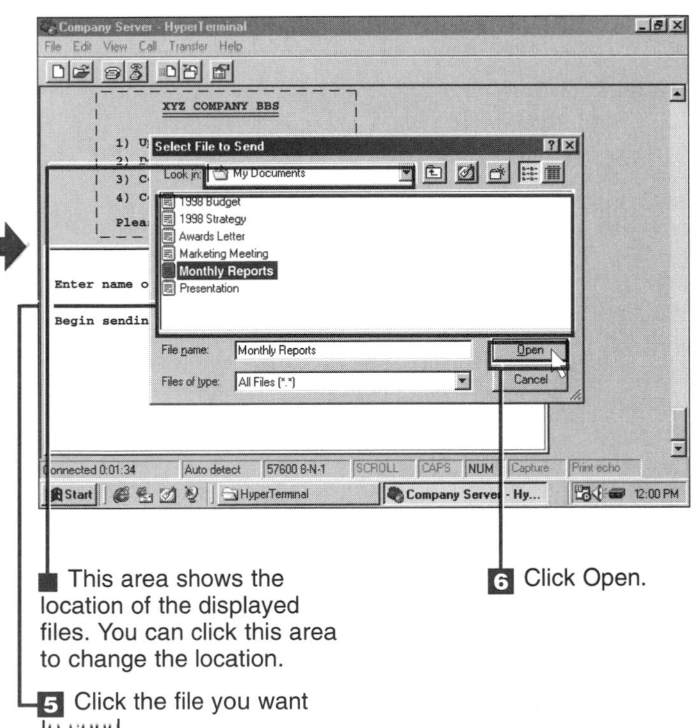

■ This area shows the location of the displayed files. You can click this area to change the location.

5 Click the file you want to send.

6 Click Open.

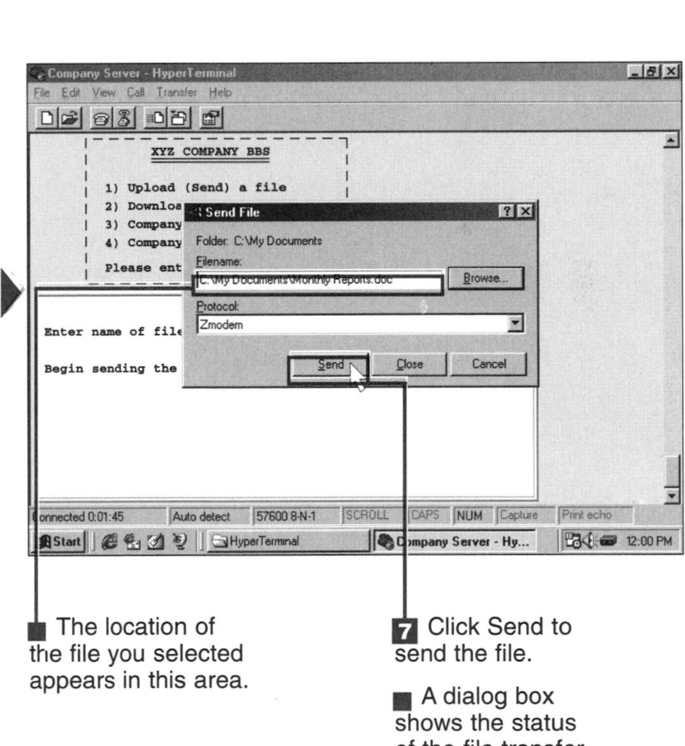

■ The location of the file you selected appears in this area.

7 Click Send to send the file.

■ A dialog box shows the status of the file transfer.

CHANGE SETTINGS FOR A CONNECTION

You can change the settings for any connection you have set up. Changing the settings for a connection gives you more control over how HyperTerminal communicates with another computer.

You can use the Terminal keys option to tell HyperTerminal to send certain keyboard commands to the other computer. You can use the Windows keys option to use these keyboard commands for tasks on your computer. The keyboard commands include the function keys F1 to F12, the arrow keys and the Ctrl keys. For example, F1 will either be sent to the other computer or will display help information on your computer.

You can also specify which command you want to send to the other computer when you press the Backspace key. HyperTerminal will automatically detect and choose which terminal emulation you need to use to communicate with the other computer. Terminal emulation makes the computer you connect to believe that your computer is a terminal. Your computer must use the same type of terminal emulation as the computer you are connecting to.

You can have your computer beep three times to notify you when HyperTerminal connects to or disconnects from the other computer.

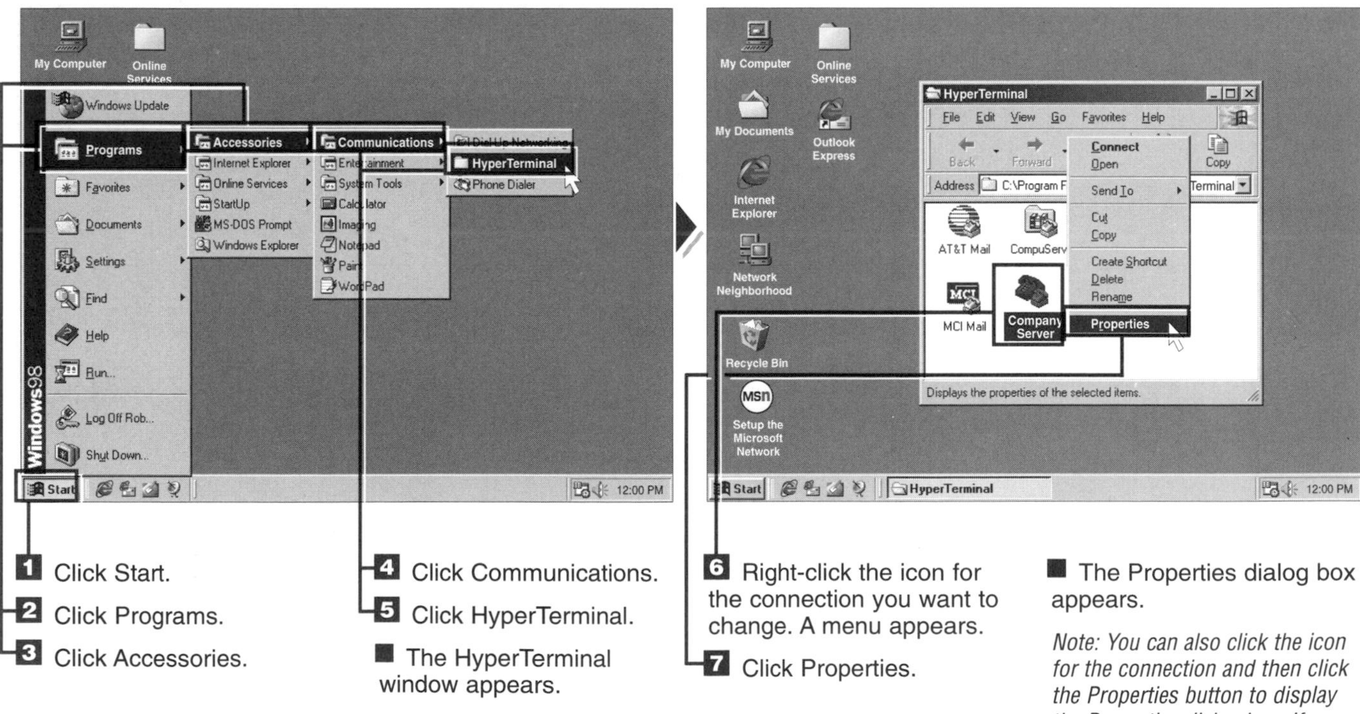

1 Click Start.

2 Click Programs.

3 Click Accessories.

4 Click Communications.

5 Click HyperTerminal.

■ The HyperTerminal window appears.

6 Right-click the icon for the connection you want to change. A menu appears.

7 Click Properties.

■ The Properties dialog box appears.

Note: You can also click the icon for the connection and then click the Properties button to display the Properties dialog box. If you cannot see the Properties button, you can increase the window size. To size a window, see page 21.

TIPS

Is there a way to access the properties for a connection while connected to the other computer?

Click the Properties button ( ) in the HyperTerminal window to display the properties for the connection.

When should I change the terminal emulation used by HyperTerminal?

You may have to choose a different terminal emulation if you have problems displaying information you receive from a computer you connect to. You should contact the administrator of the other computer to determine which type of terminal emulation you should use.

What is the backscroll buffer value?

When connected to another computer, the backscroll buffer stores the information displayed on your screen. The buffer allows you to use the scroll bar or the Page Up key to scroll back through the information that scrolled off the top of your screen. You can specify the number of lines you want to be able to view again.

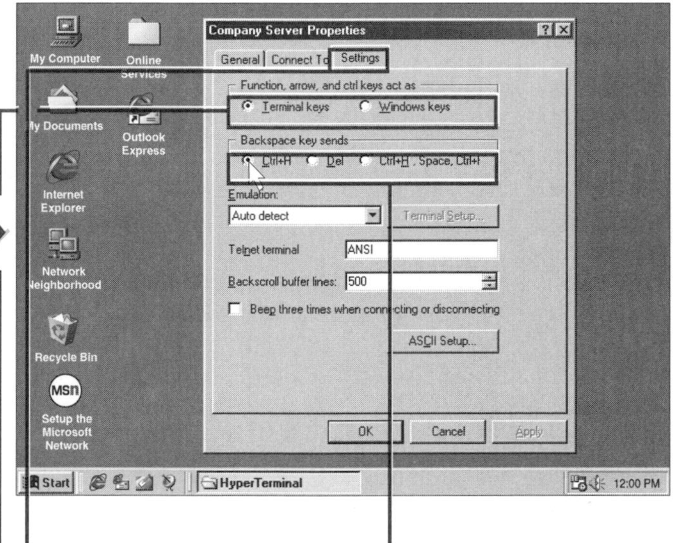

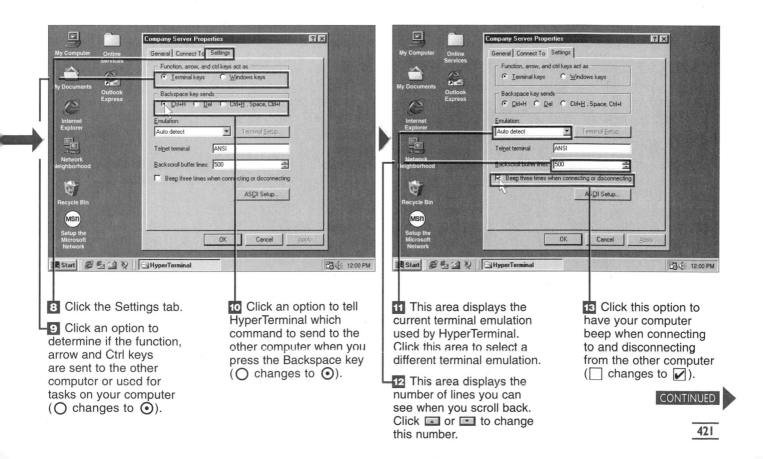

8 Click the Settings tab.

9 Click an option to determine if the function, arrow and Ctrl keys are sent to the other computer or used for tasks on your computer (○ changes to ⊙).

10 Click an option to tell HyperTerminal which command to send to the other computer when you press the Backspace key (○ changes to ⊙).

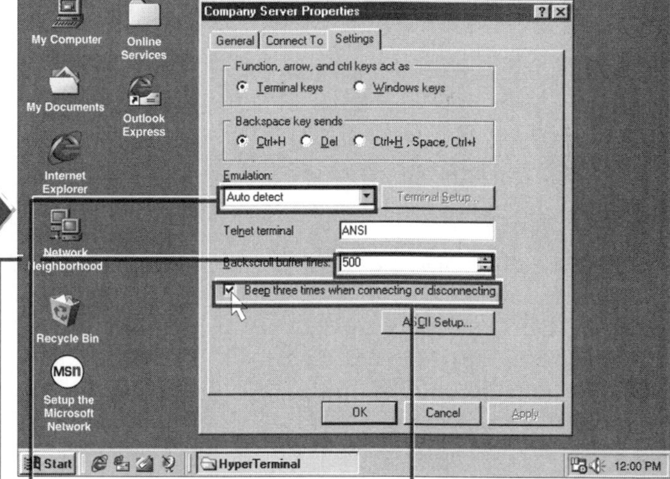

11 This area displays the current terminal emulation used by HyperTerminal. Click this area to select a different terminal emulation.

12 This area displays the number of lines you can see when you scroll back. Click ▲ or ▼ to change this number.

13 Click this option to have your computer beep when connecting to and disconnecting from the other computer (☐ changes to ☑).

CONTINUED

CHANGE SETTINGS FOR A CONNECTION CONTINUED

The ASCII settings in HyperTerminal determine how text transfers between your computer and the computer you are connected to.

You can use the ASCII settings to adjust the way information you enter is sent to the other computer. For example, pressing the Enter key may move you to the beginning of the current line instead of starting a new line. You can use the Send line ends with line feeds option to tell the other computer each time you start a new line. The Echo typed characters locally option is useful if you cannot see the characters you type. You can turn this option off if characters appear twice.

You can tell HyperTerminal how long you want to wait before sending information. If the other computer loses some of the information you send, you can increase the line and character delay settings.

You can also change the ASCII settings to adjust the way your computer receives information. You can include line feeds to ensure each line of text appears on a new line. Using 7-bit ASCII text is helpful if your computer is displaying unreadable characters. You can also wrap the text that appears on your screen so the text will not scroll off the screen.

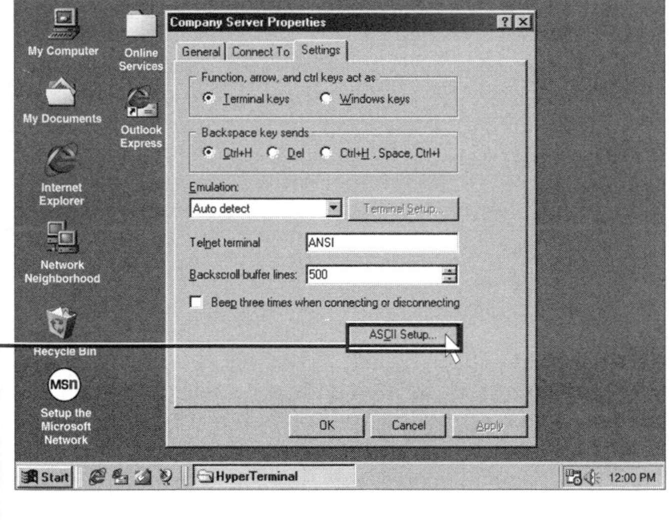

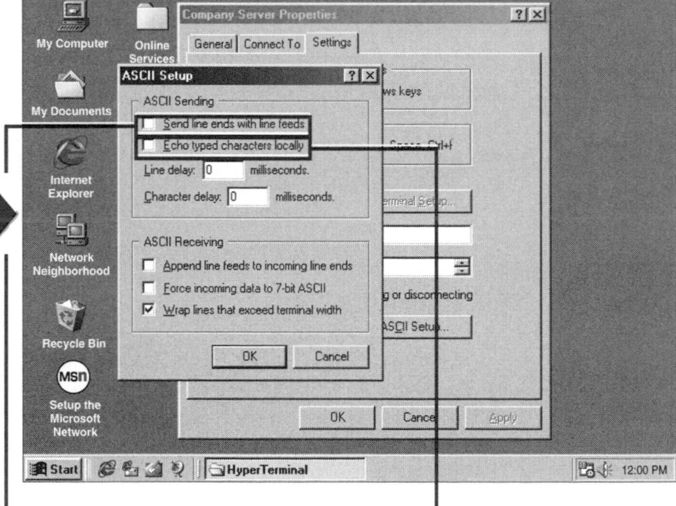

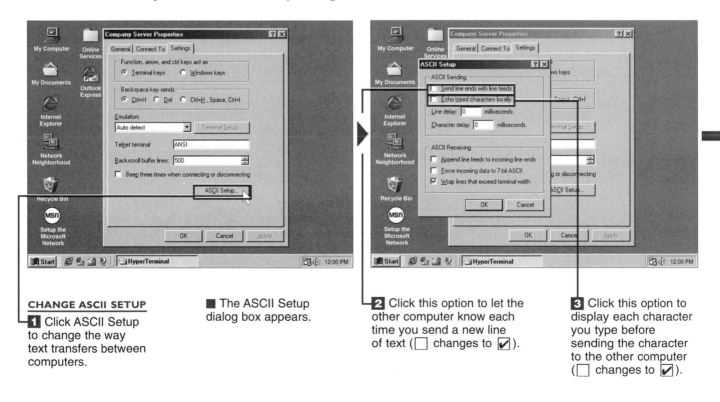

CHANGE ASCII SETUP

1 Click ASCII Setup to change the way text transfers between computers.

■ The ASCII Setup dialog box appears.

2 Click this option to let the other computer know each time you send a new line of text (☐ changes to ☑).

3 Click this option to display each character you type before sending the character to the other computer (☐ changes to ☑).

TIPS

What does ASCII stand for?

ASCII is an acronym for American Standard Code for Information Interchange. ASCII is a code that assigns number values to characters. This helps computers exchange information.

Why am I unable to see what I type?

When you type a character in HyperTerminal, the character is sent to the computer you are connected to and then sent back to HyperTerminal before it is displayed on your screen. If you select the Echo typed characters locally option, HyperTerminal will display each character you type before sending the character to the other computer.

Why does all the text appear on one line at the bottom of my screen?

HyperTerminal may not be able to determine when a new line of text is being displayed. You can select the Append line feeds to incoming line ends option to fix this problem.

What is 7-bit ASCII text?

7-bit ASCII text is a collection of 128 characters that most computers can understand, such as 3, a, B, @ and $. If HyperTerminal is displaying unrecognizable characters, you should select the Force incoming data to 7-bit ASCII option.

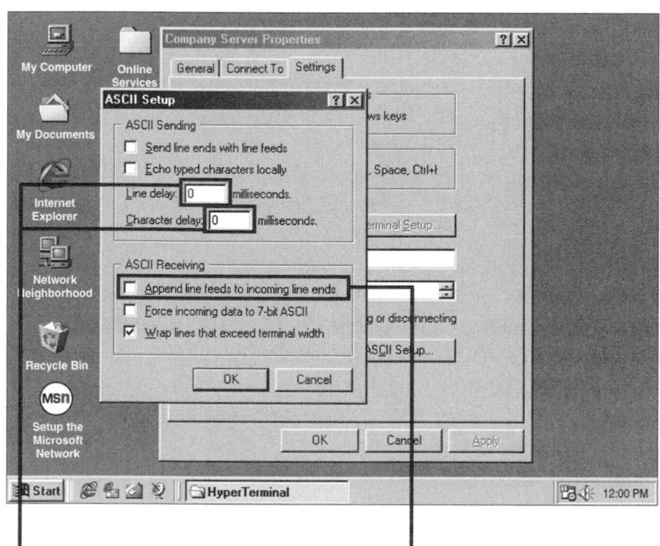

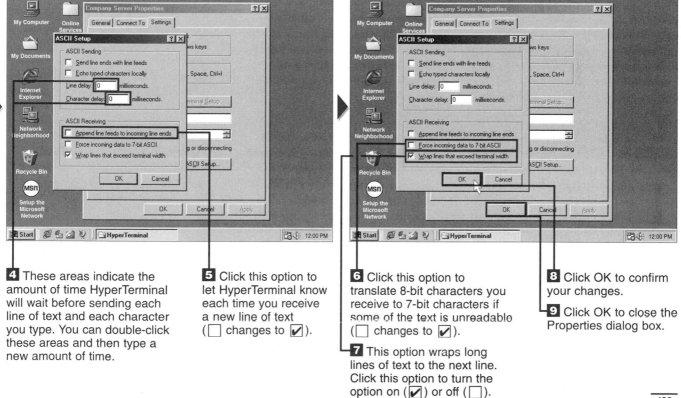

4 These areas indicate the amount of time HyperTerminal will wait before sending each line of text and each character you type. You can double-click these areas and then type a new amount of time.

5 Click this option to let HyperTerminal know each time you receive a new line of text (☐ changes to ☑).

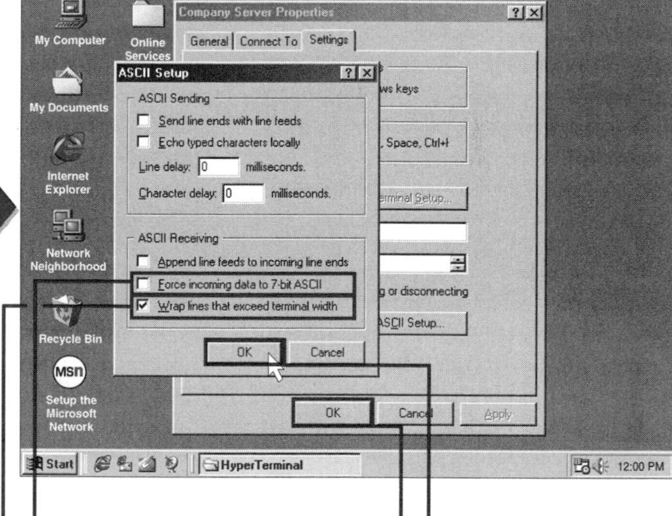

6 Click this option to translate 8-bit characters you receive to 7-bit characters if some of the text is unreadable (☐ changes to ☑).

7 This option wraps long lines of text to the next line. Click this option to turn the option on (☑) or off (☐).

8 Click OK to confirm your changes.

9 Click OK to close the Properties dialog box.

DIRECT CABLE CONNECTION

Set Up Direct Cable Connection

You can use a special cable to connect two computers to share files and resources. This is useful if you want to connect a portable computer to a desktop computer. Unlike a regular network, neither computer needs a network interface card.

You must designate a host computer and a guest computer. The host is the computer that provides the files and resources, such as drives and printers. The guest is a computer that can access files and resources on the host and on the network attached to the host.

Make sure you plug the cable into both computers before you begin. You can choose from two types of cable. A serial cable allows you to connect the computers over a long distance but transfers information slowly. A parallel cable transfers information faster than a serial cable. A parallel cable is the best choice for most direct cable connections.

Before setting up the direct cable connection, you must prepare the host computer to share its files and resources. To turn on sharing, see page 456. To share files, see page 458. To share printers, see page 462.

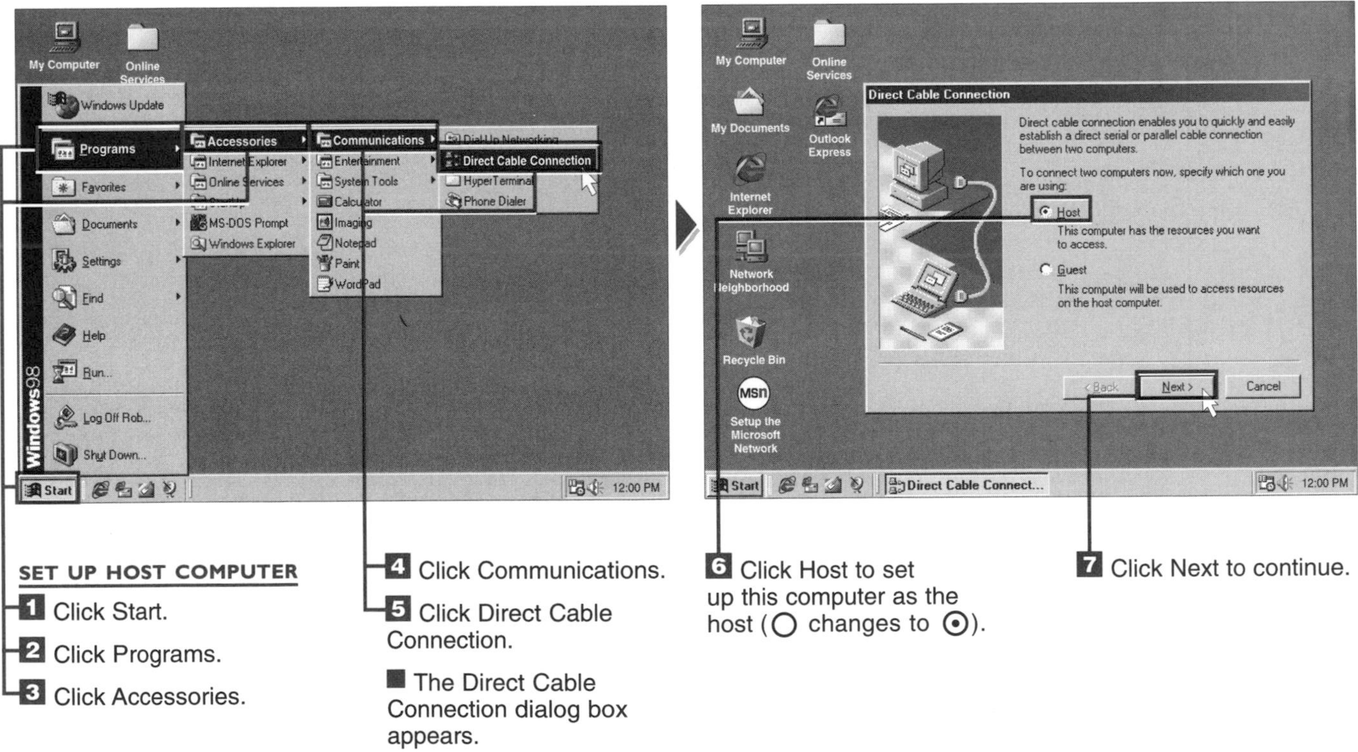

SET UP HOST COMPUTER

1 Click Start.

2 Click Programs.

3 Click Accessories.

4 Click Communications.

5 Click Direct Cable Connection.

■ The Direct Cable Connection dialog box appears.

6 Click Host to set up this computer as the host (○ changes to ⊙).

7 Click Next to continue.

TIPS

Why isn't Direct Cable Connection available on the Start menu?

Direct Cable Connection may not be installed on your computer. Dial-Up Networking will also be added when you install Direct Cable Connection. Direct Cable Connection and Dial-Up Networking are located in the Communications component. To add Windows components, see page 610. When you install Direct Cable Connection, you may be asked to provide a computer and workgroup name. You should use the same workgroup name for the host and guest computers.

Why do I get a dialog box that tells me I cannot connect to the host computer?

You must install the Client for Microsoft Networks to be able to set up a direct cable connection. To install a network client, see page 482. Both computers must also have the same network protocols installed. To install a network protocol, see page 478.

How can I prevent unauthorized people from accessing the host?

You can set a password to prevent unauthorized people from accessing the host. Before selecting Finish in step 10 below, click the Use password protection option. Click Set Password and then specify the password that a guest must enter to access the host.

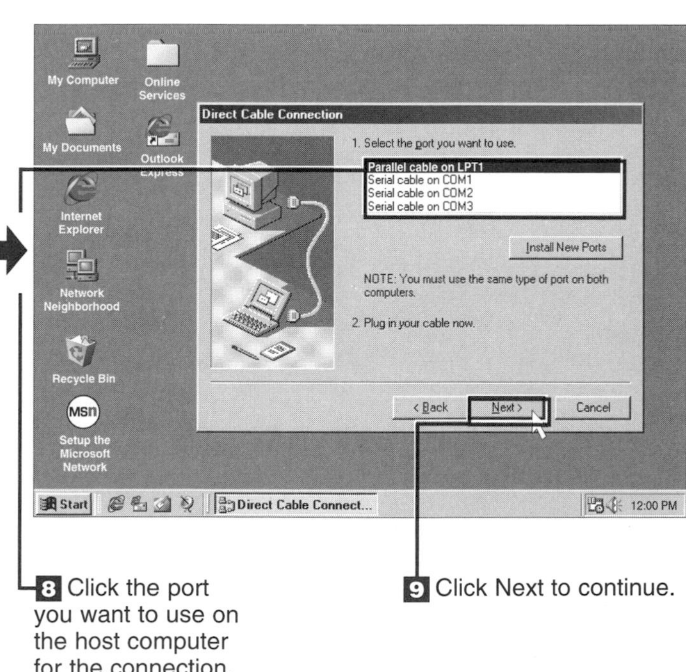

8 Click the port you want to use on the host computer for the connection.

9 Click Next to continue.

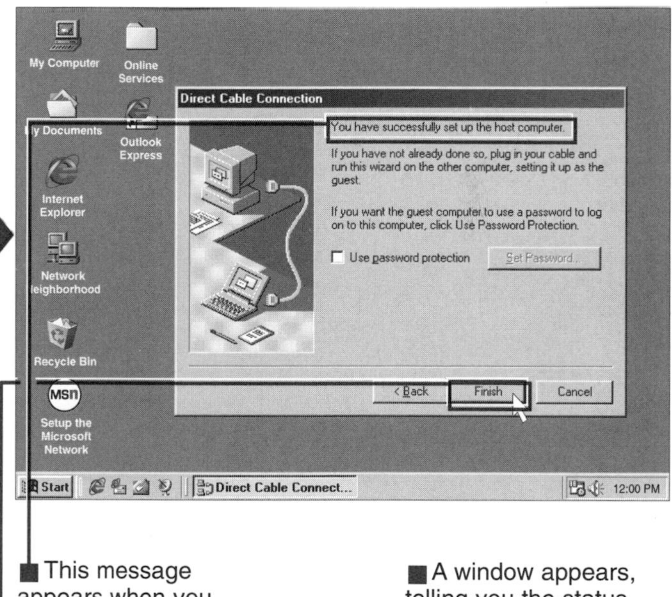

■ This message appears when you have successfully set up the host computer.

10 Click Finish.

■ A window appears, telling you the status of the connection.

■ You are now ready to set up the guest computer.

CONTINUED

DIRECT CABLE CONNECTION

Set Up Direct Cable Connection (Continued)

You must set up the guest computer before using it to access files and resources on the host and on the network attached to the host.

You must specify the port you want to use for the guest computer. You must select the same type of port you chose for the host computer.

Once you set up a direct cable connection between two computers, the host and guest will be able to access each other's shared items. If the host computer is part of a network, the guest will also be able to access the network and all shared items on the network.

If any of the shared files or resources on the host computer are password-protected, you will need to enter a password to access the files or resources.

You cannot use a direct cable connection to share an Internet or any TCP/IP network connection.

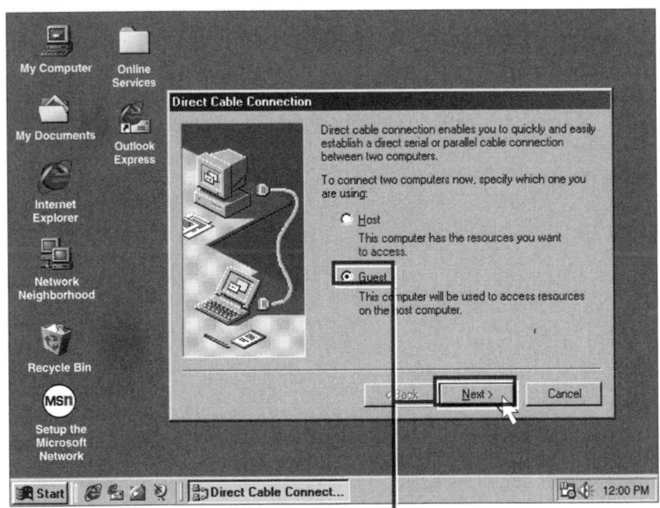

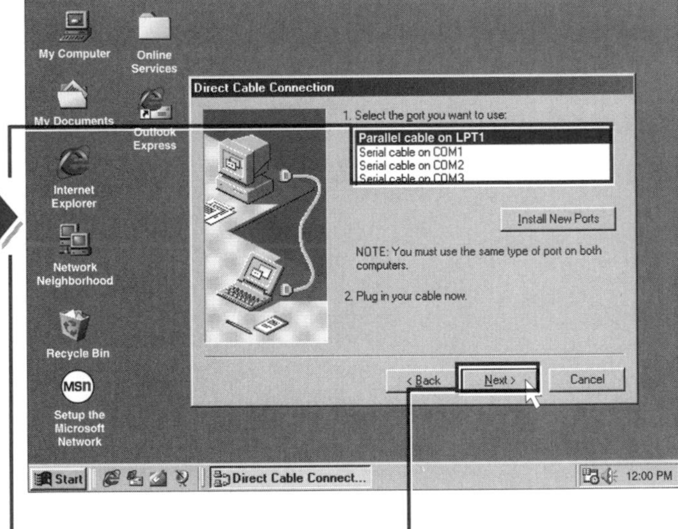

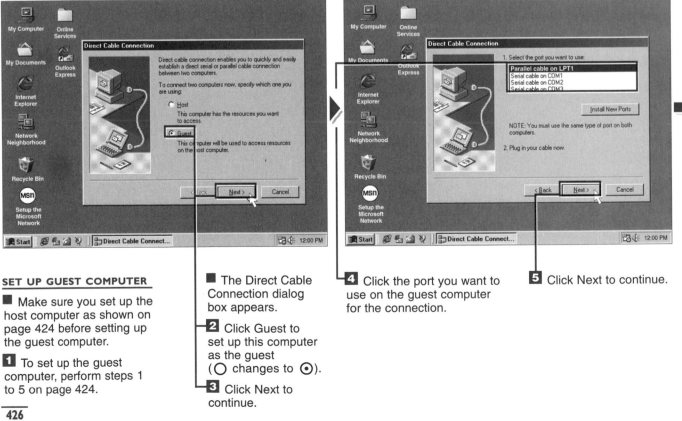

SET UP GUEST COMPUTER

■ Make sure you set up the host computer as shown on page 424 before setting up the guest computer.

1 To set up the guest computer, perform steps 1 to 5 on page 424.

■ The Direct Cable Connection dialog box appears.

2 Click Guest to set up this computer as the guest (○ changes to ⊙).

3 Click Next to continue.

4 Click the port you want to use on the guest computer for the connection.

5 Click Next to continue.

TIPS

Can I use the host computer to access the guest computer?

You can double-click the Network Neighborhood icon on your desktop and then select the guest computer. You can access only the shared items on the guest computer.

How do I print using the host's printer?

Right-click the shared printer in the window that contains the host's shared items. From the menu that appears, select Install to install the printer's software on the guest computer. Then follow the instructions on your screen. When you want to print, choose the shared printer in the program's Print dialog box.

I had to disconnect the printer from the host to plug in the cable for the direct cable connection. How can I print my documents?

From the Control Panel, select the Printers folder and then click the printer you want to use. Choose the File menu and then select Use Printer Offline. Windows will store any documents you send to the printer. When you reconnect to the printer, select the Use Printer Offline command again to print the documents.

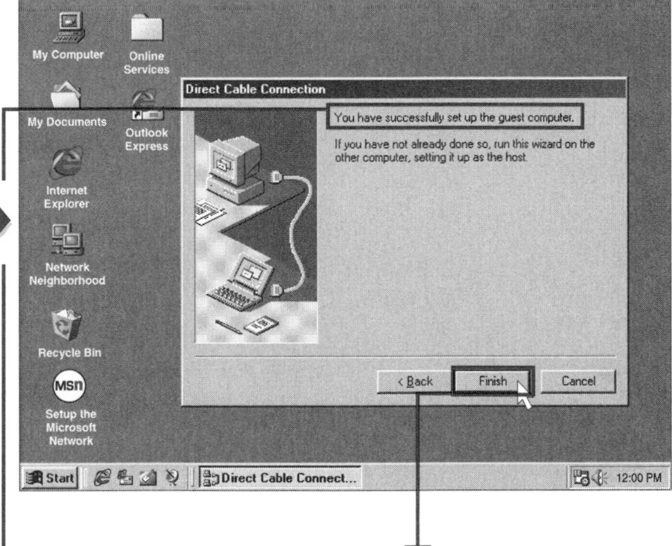

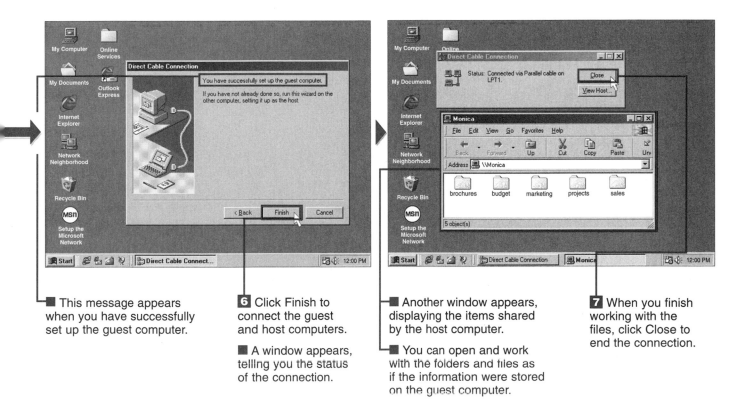

■ This message appears when you have successfully set up the guest computer.

6 Click Finish to connect the guest and host computers.

■ A window appears, telling you the status of the connection.

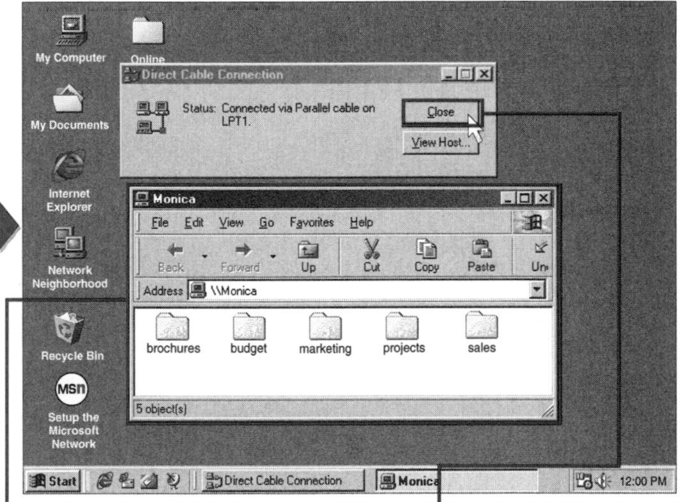

■ Another window appears, displaying the items shared by the host computer.

■ You can open and work with the folders and files as if the information were stored on the guest computer.

7 When you finish working with the files, click Close to end the connection.

DIRECT CABLE CONNECTION

Re-establish Direct Cable Connection

You only need to set up a direct cable connection once. After you set up a connection, you can reconnect the host and guest computers at any time. Windows uses the last successful connection settings to re-establish the connection.

You can leave the cable connected to the host computer all the time.

You can re-attach the cable to the guest computer whenever you need to connect the computers.

You must make sure that the information and resources you want to access on the host computer are still shared. You can open and work with all the shared information and resources as if they were on the guest computer.

Besides opening files and folders, you may be able to run programs that are located on the host computer. You can run programs that do not require special files to be stored on the guest computer.

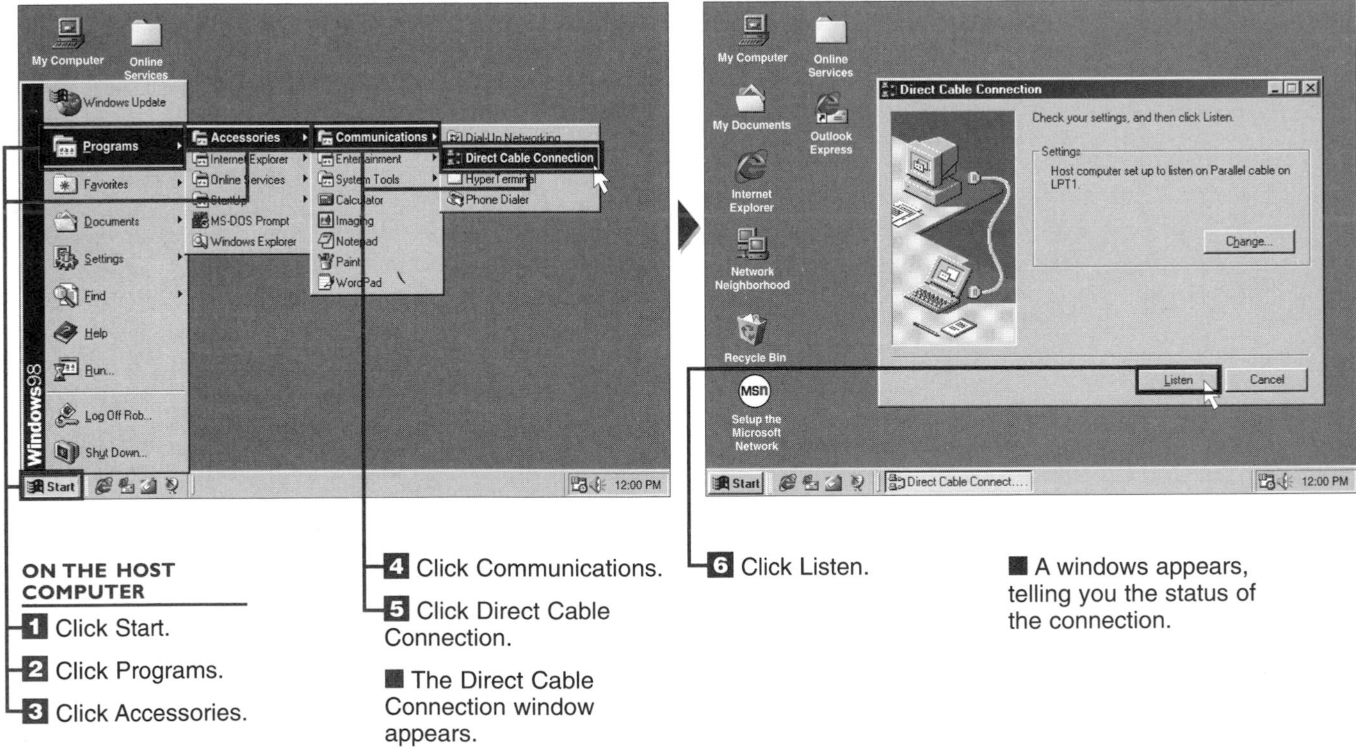

ON THE HOST COMPUTER

1 Click Start.

2 Click Programs.

3 Click Accessories.

4 Click Communications.

5 Click Direct Cable Connection.

■ The Direct Cable Connection window appears.

6 Click Listen.

■ A windows appears, telling you the status of the connection.

TIPS

Can I create a desktop shortcut for the direct cable connection?

Right-click the Start button, select Open, and double-click the Programs folder. Double-click the Accessories folder and then double-click the Communications folder. Use the right mouse button to drag the Direct Cable Connection shortcut icon to the desktop. Select Copy Here from the menu that appears.

How can I change the settings for the direct cable connection?

In the Direct Cable Connection dialog box, click the Change button to make changes to the settings. You can change the ports you are using or the password you set for the host computer.

Why can't I re-establish the connection?

Make sure the cable is plugged in correctly. In Windows Help, click the Contents tab to consult the Troubleshooting book. Select Windows 98 Troubleshooters and then click the "Direct Cable Connection" topic.

Can I have Windows update my files so that both computers have the same information?

You can use the Briefcase feature to update your files. For information on the Briefcase feature, see page 430.

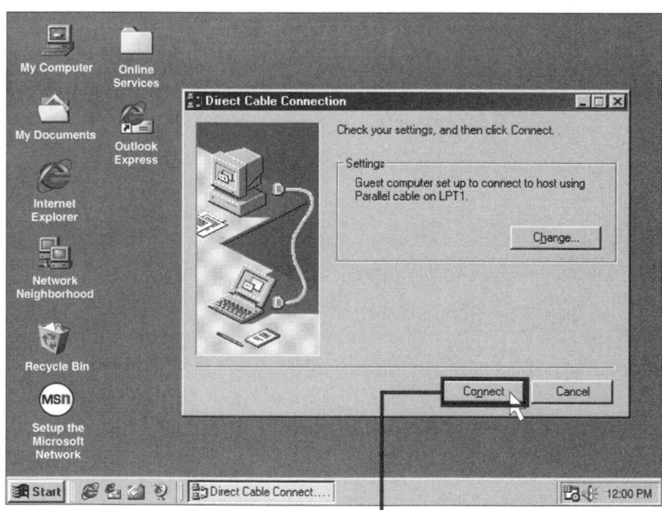

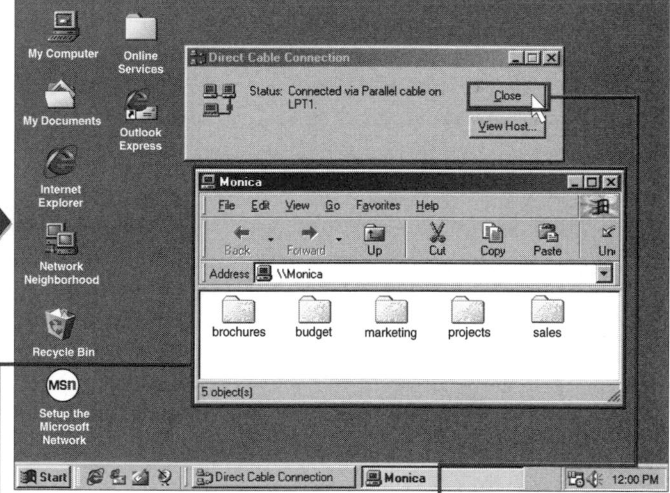

ON THE GUEST COMPUTER

1 Perform steps 1 to 5 on page 428 on the guest computer.

■ The Direct Cable Connection window appears.

2 Click Connect to connect the guest and host computers.

■ A window appears, telling you the status of the connection.

■ Another window appears, displaying the items shared by the host computer.

■ You can open and work with the folders and files as if the information were stored on the guest computer.

3 When you finish working with the files, click Close to end the connection.

USING BRIEFCASE

The computer you use most often to work with documents may be the one in your office, but you may also use a home or portable computer. When you place a document in a Briefcase, you can transport it between computers. Briefcase ensures that you are always working with the most up-to-date version of a document, regardless of the computer you use to edit it.

When you place a folder in a Briefcase, all of the documents in the folder are added to the Briefcase. The Briefcase contains a copy of your document or folder. The original document or folder remains on your main computer.

You can move a Briefcase to a floppy disk so you can transfer the documents you want to work with to another computer. A Briefcase on a floppy disk can contain up to 1.44 MB of information. You can also move a Briefcase to any type of removable or network drive.

When at home or traveling, you can work with Briefcase documents as you would work with any document. Make sure you save and close all Briefcase documents you edited and close the Briefcase window before removing the disk containing the Briefcase from the computer's drive.

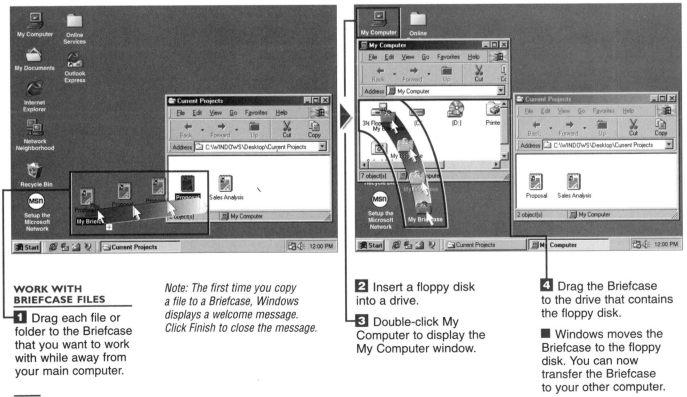

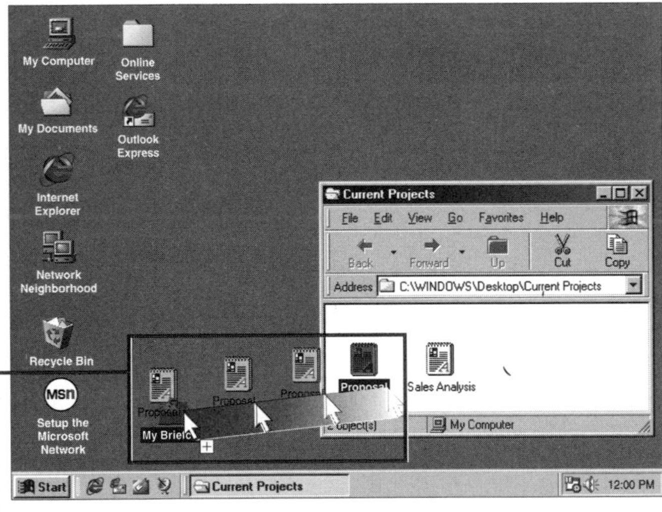

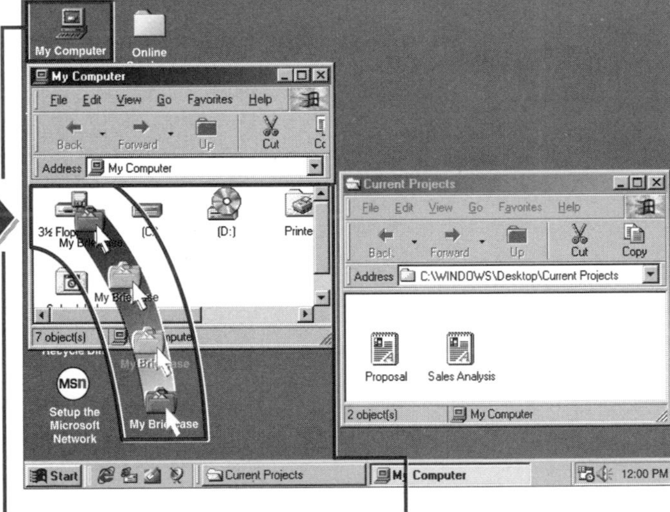

WORK WITH BRIEFCASE FILES

1 Drag each file or folder to the Briefcase that you want to work with while away from your main computer.

Note: The first time you copy a file to a Briefcase, Windows displays a welcome message. Click Finish to close the message.

2 Insert a floppy disk into a drive.

3 Double-click My Computer to display the My Computer window.

4 Drag the Briefcase to the drive that contains the floppy disk.

■ Windows moves the Briefcase to the floppy disk. You can now transfer the Briefcase to your other computer.

Why isn't there a Briefcase icon on my desktop?

Briefcase is only installed automatically on portable computers. You can install Briefcase from the Accessories component. To add Windows components, see page 610.

Why isn't Briefcase listed in the Accessories component?

Briefcase may already be installed on your computer. If you do not see a Briefcase icon, it may have been removed from the desktop. Right-click the desktop, click New and then select Briefcase. You can use this procedure to create as many new Briefcases as you need.

Is there another way to place documents in a Briefcase?

You can right-click a document or folder and select Send To. Then click My Briefcase. If you have more than one Briefcase, you can add each Briefcase to the Send To menu. See page 232.

Is there a faster way to access a Briefcase on a floppy disk?

Double-click the drive that contains the floppy disk to display the Briefcase. Use the right mouse button to drag the Briefcase to the desktop and select Create Shortcut(s) Here from the menu that appears. You will only be able to use the shortcut to access the Briefcase when the disk is in the drive.

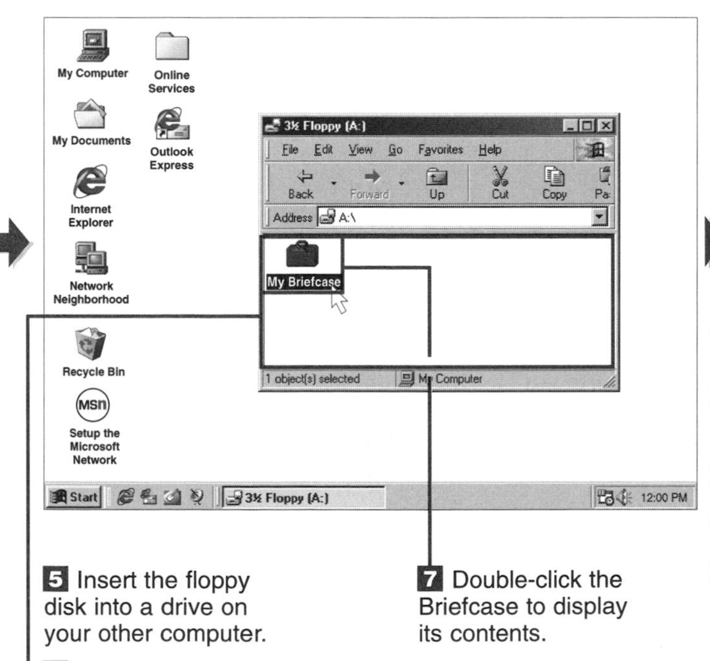

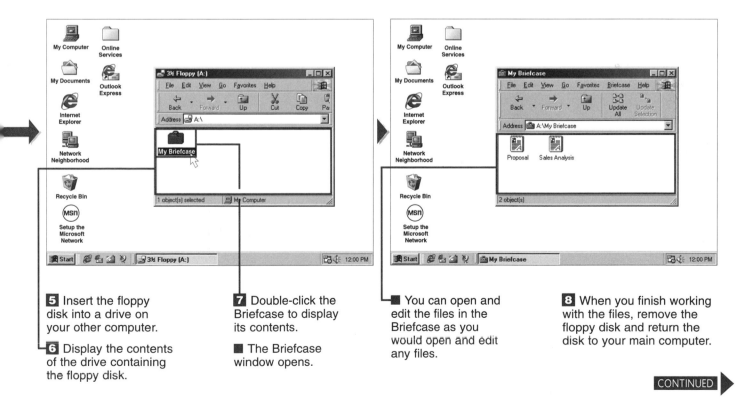

5 Insert the floppy disk into a drive on your other computer.

6 Display the contents of the drive containing the floppy disk.

7 Double-click the Briefcase to display its contents.

■ The Briefcase window opens.

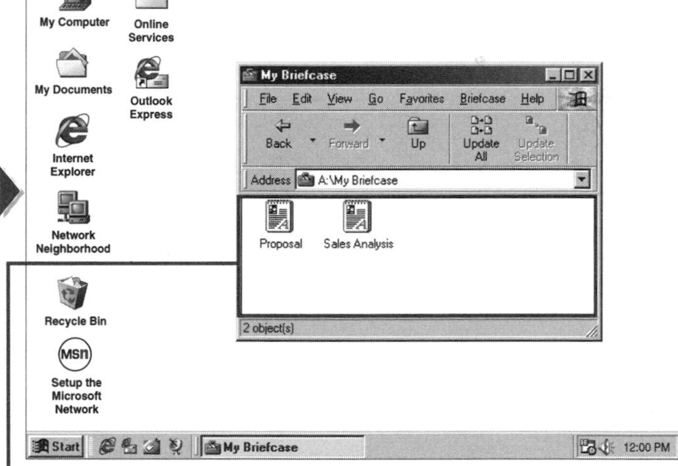

■ You can open and edit the files in the Briefcase as you would open and edit any files.

8 When you finish working with the files, remove the floppy disk and return the disk to your main computer.

CONTINUED

USING BRIEFCASE CONTINUED

Briefcase lets you work with documents while you are away from your main computer. When you change the Briefcase copy of a document, the original document on your main computer becomes out-of-date. Briefcase will update the documents you changed. You can update all documents or only specific documents.

The update process ensures that the original documents and the Briefcase copies are the same. Briefcase compares the documents it contains with the documents on your main computer and shows you which documents need to be updated. You can have Briefcase replace the original document, replace the Briefcase version of the document or skip replacing the document completely.

By default, Briefcase replaces the older version of the document with the newer version of the document.

If both the original and Briefcase copies have been changed, Briefcase will indicate this and will not update the document.

Do not rename or move the original documents on your main computer and do not rename the documents in the Briefcase. If you do, Briefcase will not be able to update the documents.

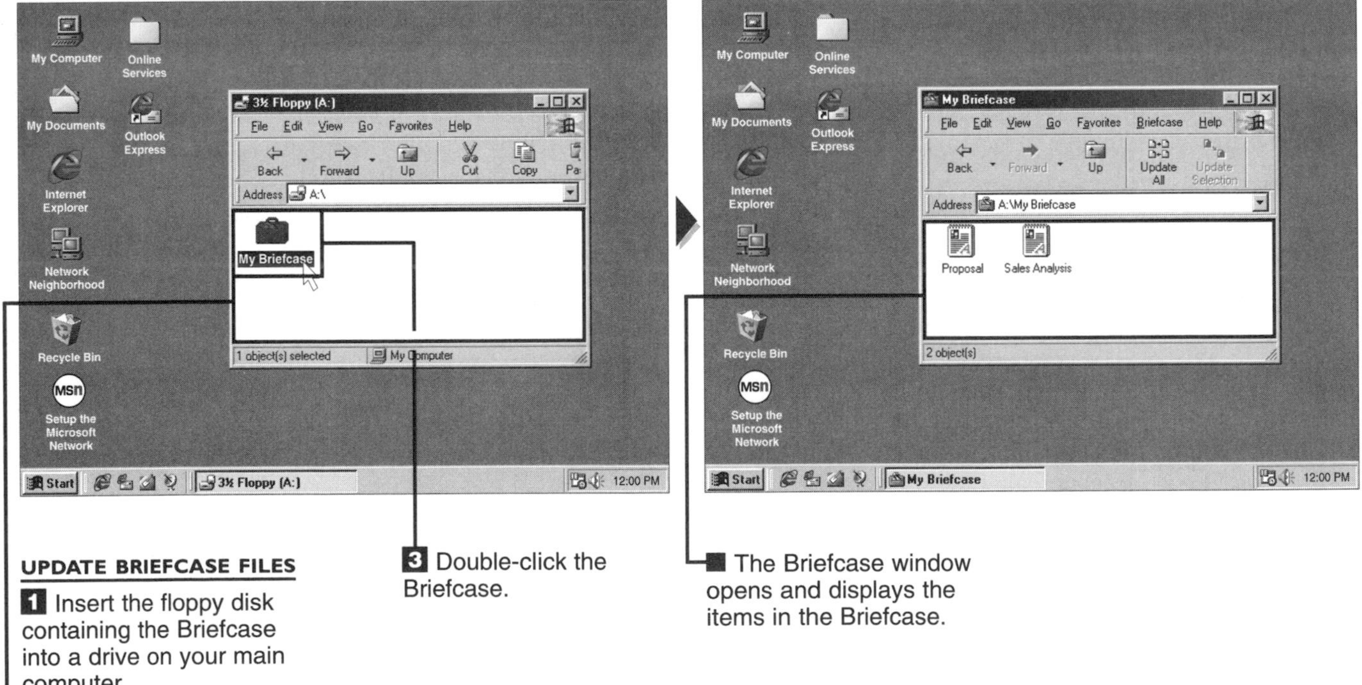

UPDATE BRIEFCASE FILES

1 Insert the floppy disk containing the Briefcase into a drive on your main computer.

2 Display the contents of the drive containing the floppy disk.

3 Double-click the Briefcase.

■ The Briefcase window opens and displays the items in the Briefcase.

TIPS 

Can I add a document to the Briefcase from the other computer?

The document you add will not be updated to the main computer. You may prefer to create a second Briefcase containing the documents that are located on the other computer.

Can I permanently stop a Briefcase document from updating?

In the Briefcase window, select the document you do not want to update. Click the Briefcase menu and then select the Split from Original command. This lets you keep both the original and changed versions of a document.

How do I use Briefcase to update my documents when I have a direct cable connection between my portable and main computers?

To set up a direct cable connection, see page 424. The shared items on your main computer appear in a window on the portable computer. On the portable computer, drag the shared items you want to work with from the window to a Briefcase. You can then work with the documents on the portable when the two computers are not connected. After you reconnect the computers, perform steps 3 to 8 below on the portable computer to update the documents on the main computer.

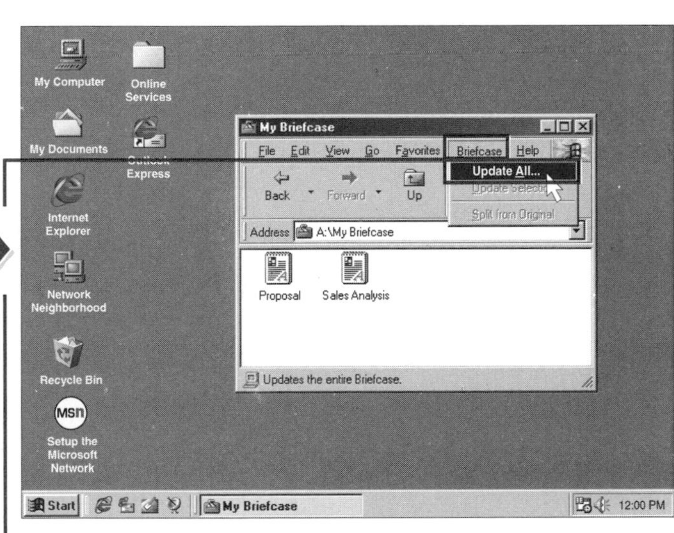

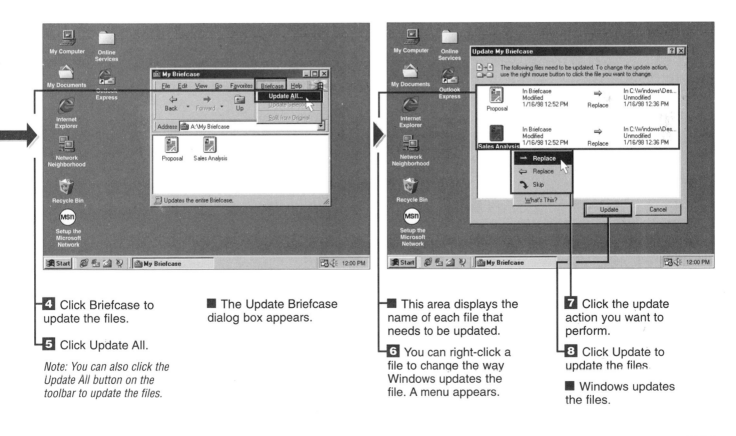

4 Click Briefcase to update the files.

5 Click Update All.

Note: You can also click the Update All button on the toolbar to update the files.

■ The Update Briefcase dialog box appears.

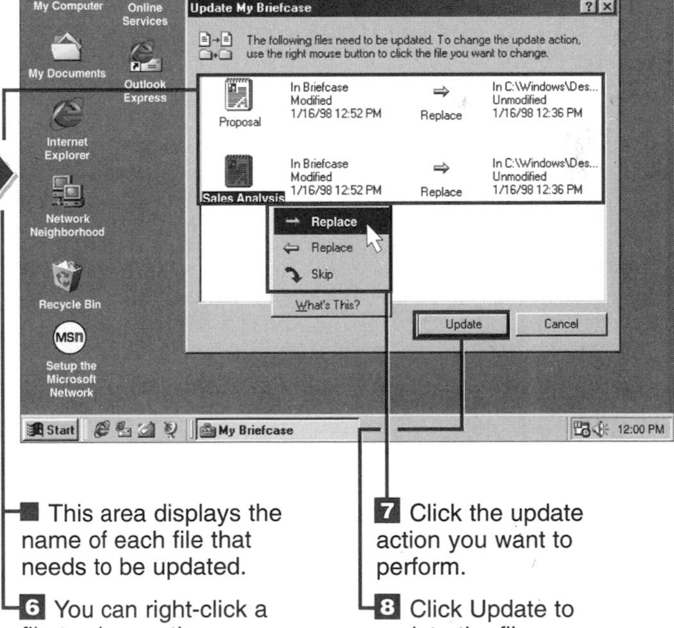

■ This area displays the name of each file that needs to be updated.

6 You can right-click a file to change the way Windows updates the file. A menu appears.

7 Click the update action you want to perform.

8 Click Update to update the files.

■ Windows updates the files.

CREATE HARDWARE PROFILES

You can create a new hardware profile for your portable computer. A profile tells Windows which hardware devices you want to use. To create a new profile, you copy an existing profile and then make changes to the copy.

A portable computer can be used in several different situations. For example, you may use the portable computer at an office where you connect to a docking station to access a network. At home, you may use the portable computer with a printer, monitor, keyboard and mouse. When traveling, you may use the portable computer without additional hardware. Each situation requires a different setup to use the appropriate hardware devices.

To avoid the task of having to set up your computer each time you change locations, you can save the hardware settings for each situation in a profile.

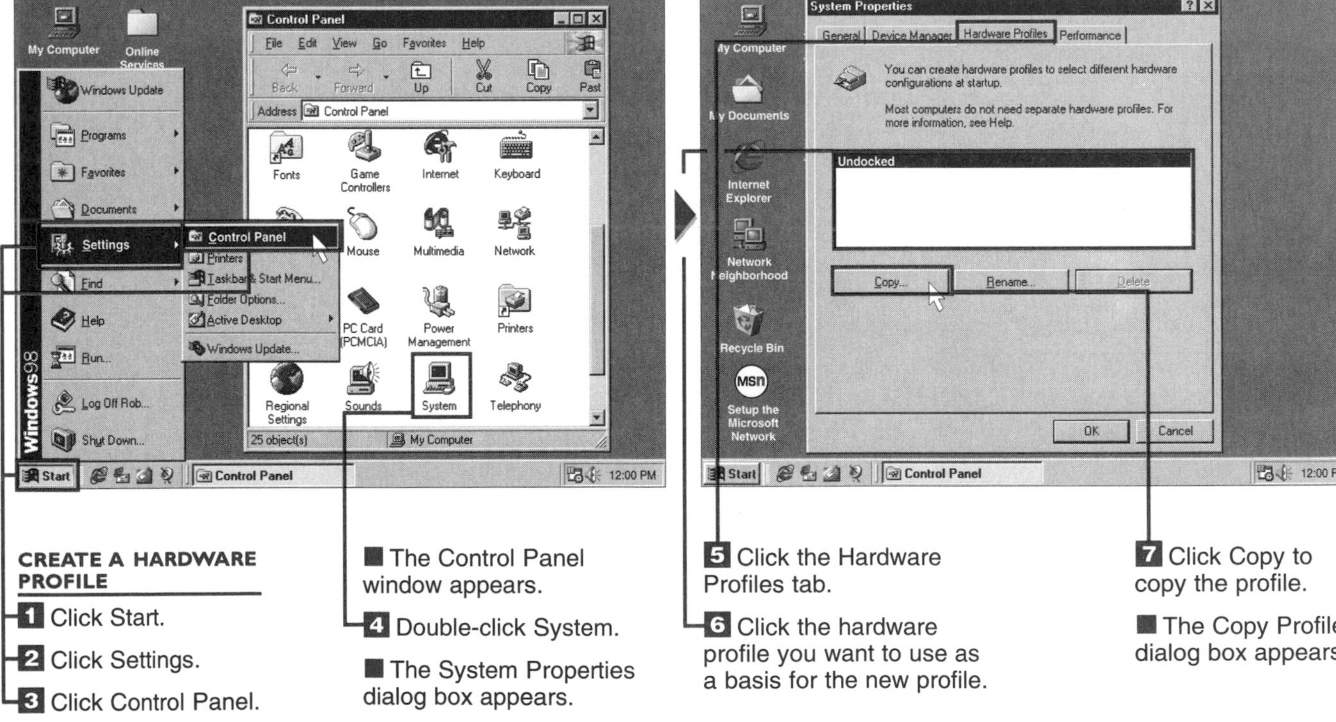

CREATE A HARDWARE PROFILE

1. Click Start.
2. Click Settings.
3. Click Control Panel.

■ The Control Panel window appears.

4. Double-click System.

■ The System Properties dialog box appears.

5. Click the Hardware Profiles tab.
6. Click the hardware profile you want to use as a basis for the new profile.
7. Click Copy to copy the profile.

■ The Copy Profile dialog box appears.

TIPS

Which existing hardware profile should I copy as the basis for my new profile?

You should choose a profile that has a large number of devices already installed, since it is much easier to remove a device than it is to install one. The profile with the most installed devices is probably the profile you use when docked and attached to a network.

Can I rename a profile I created?

On the Hardware Profiles tab, select the profile you want to rename and then click the Rename button. Type a new name for the profile and then click OK.

Will I ever need to use hardware profiles on my desktop computer?

It may sometimes be beneficial for a desktop computer to have different hardware profiles. For example, if your computer does not have enough resources to handle all of your add-in cards, you can use hardware profiles to switch between cards.

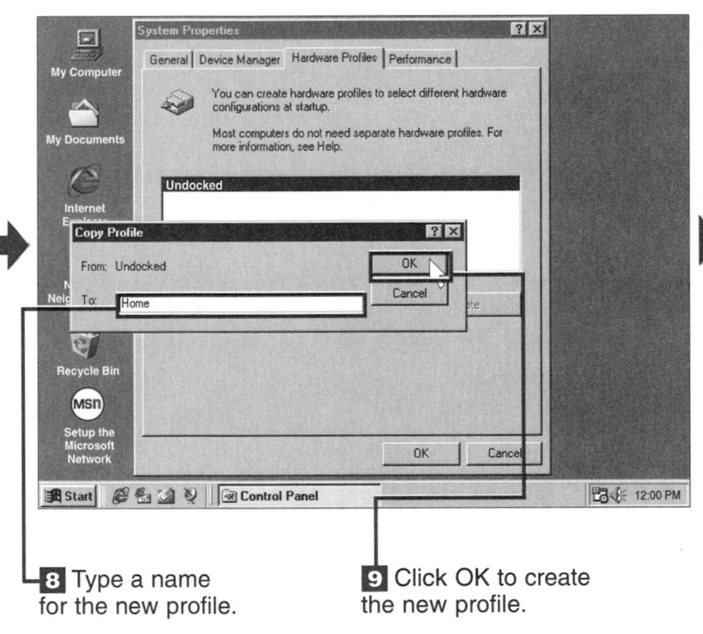

8 Type a name for the new profile.

9 Click OK to create the new profile.

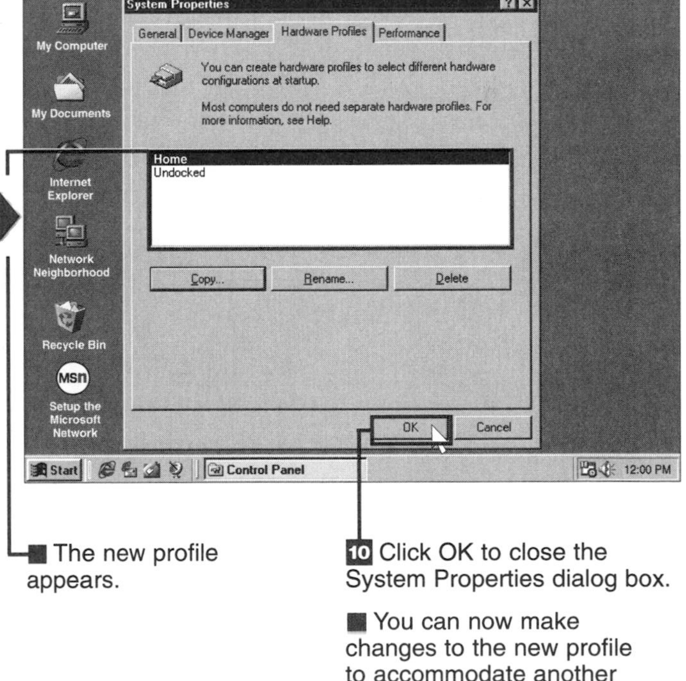

■ The new profile appears.

10 Click OK to close the System Properties dialog box.

■ You can now make changes to the new profile to accommodate another situation.

CONTINUED

CREATE HARDWARE PROFILES
CONTINUED

You create a new hardware profile by copying an existing profile and then changing the copied profile to suit your needs. Changing a copied profile does not affect any of the other profiles on your computer.

When you start your computer, Windows automatically uses the correct profile for the hardware it detects. If Windows does not know which profile to use, you will be asked to choose a profile from a list that appears.

You can only make changes to the profile you used to start the computer.

You can disable or enable devices for a hardware profile. Disabling a device for a profile stops Windows from loading the software needed to communicate with the device. You can disable each device you do not want to use in the profile.

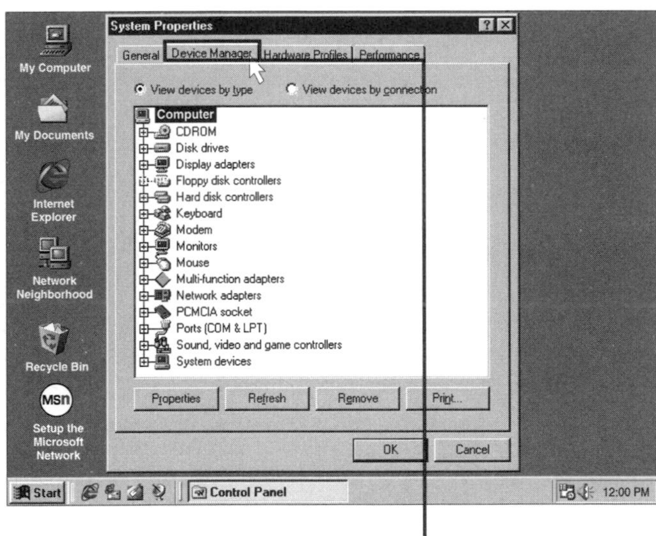

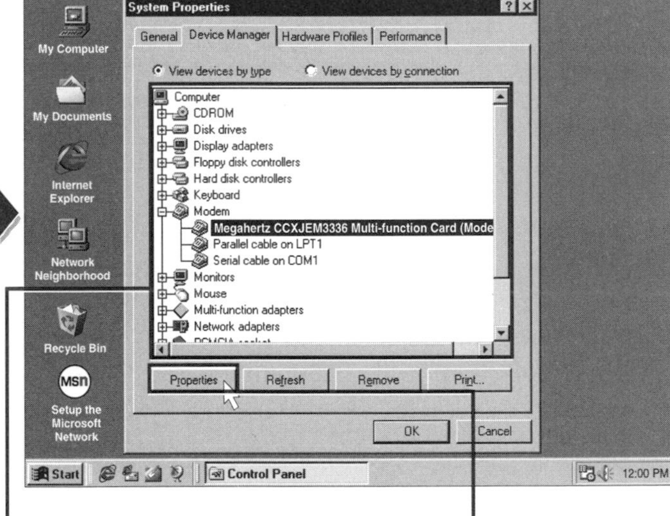

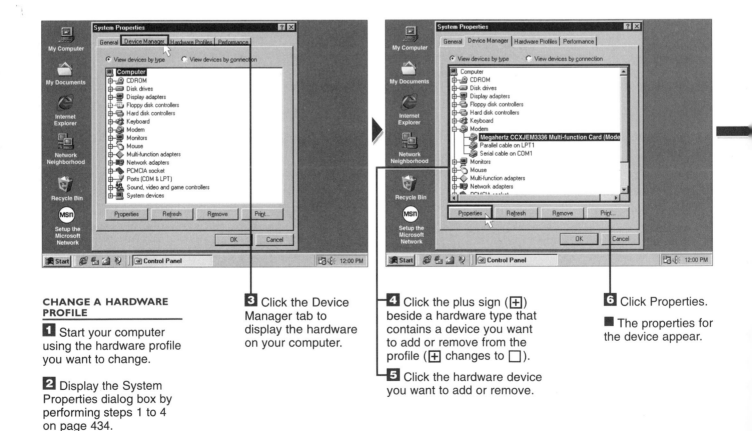

CHANGE A HARDWARE PROFILE

1 Start your computer using the hardware profile you want to change.

2 Display the System Properties dialog box by performing steps 1 to 4 on page 434.

3 Click the Device Manager tab to display the hardware on your computer.

4 Click the plus sign (⊞) beside a hardware type that contains a device you want to add or remove from the profile (⊞ changes to □).

5 Click the hardware device you want to add or remove.

6 Click Properties.

■ The properties for the device appear.

TIPS

Do I have to add my monitor to the new profile?

The first time you use a new profile, Windows detects and automatically sets up the video display and monitor for you.

Do I need to disable the printer?

It is not necessary to disable the printer. If you send documents to a printer that is not currently connected to your computer, Windows stores the print job until you reconnect to the printer. If you will not be using the printer in any of your profiles, you can remove the printer. For information on removing a printer, see page 107.

How do I delete a profile I no longer need?

On the Hardware Profiles tab, click the profile you want to remove and then click the Delete button. Click Yes in the Confirm Profile Delete dialog box to delete the profile.

Can each hardware profile have its own screen resolution?

When you change the screen resolution, it is automatically saved as part of the profile you are currently using. For information on changing your screen resolution, see page 210.

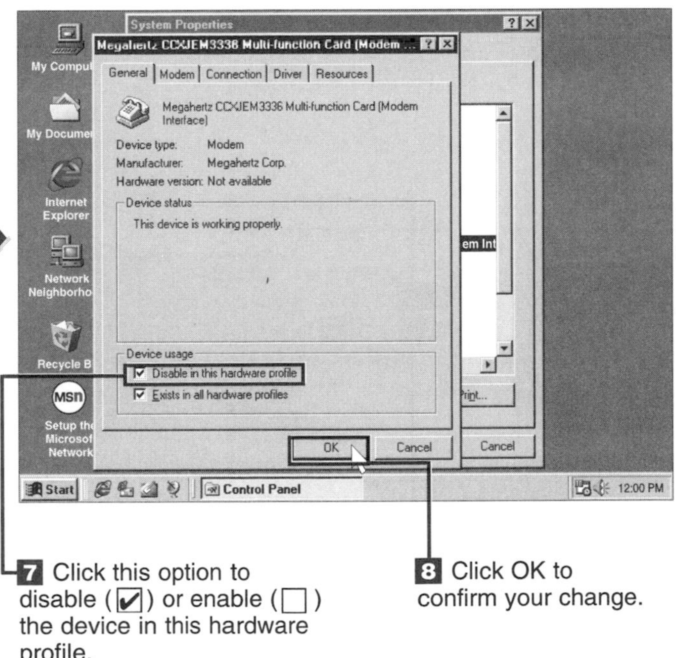

7 Click this option to disable (☑) or enable (☐) the device in this hardware profile.

8 Click OK to confirm your change.

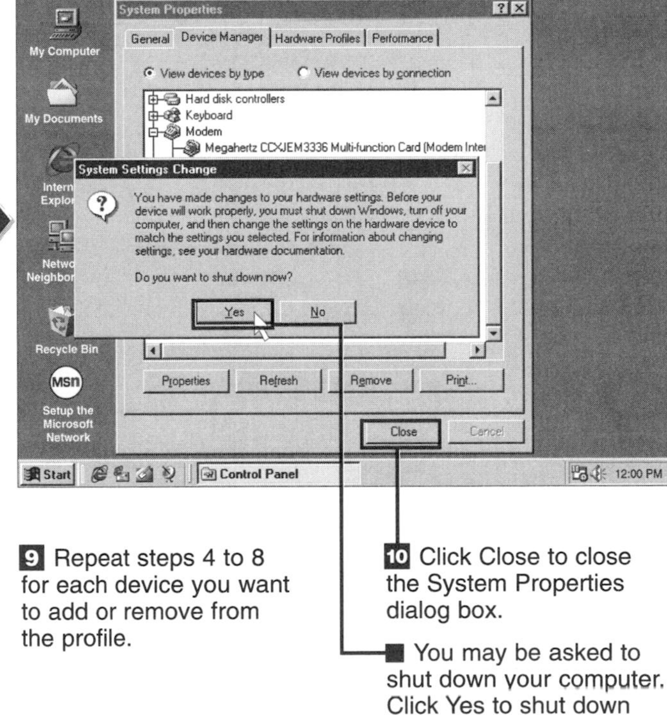

9 Repeat steps 4 to 8 for each device you want to add or remove from the profile.

10 Click Close to close the System Properties dialog box.

■ You may be asked to shut down your computer. Click Yes to shut down the computer.

SECTION VI

21) INTRODUCTION TO NETWORKS

22) SHARE INFORMATION ON A NETWORK

NETWORKING

23) SET UP AND MONITOR A NETWORK

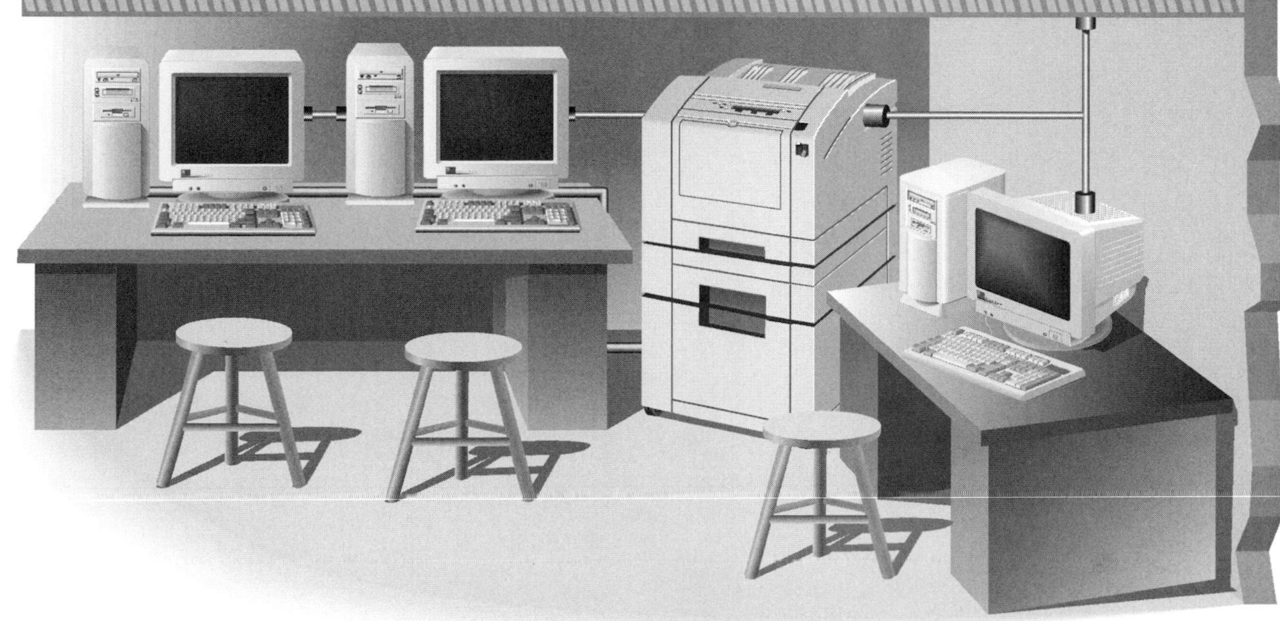

INTRODUCTION TO NETWORKS

A network is a group of connected computers that allow people to share information and equipment.

Before networks, exchanging information between computers was time consuming. The most common way to transfer information from one computer to another was by saving the information on floppy disks and then carrying the disks to the other computer. Physically carrying information from one computer to another is known as sneakernet. Computer networks eliminate the need for sneakernet. When two computers are connected using a network, they can exchange large amounts of information faster and more reliably than when exchanging information using floppy disks.

Networks allow computers to share equipment such as printers. The ability to share equipment reduces the cost of buying computer hardware. For example, instead of having to buy a printer for each computer, a company can buy just one printer and let everyone access the printer from their own computer.

Once networks became more widespread, many companies started allowing employees to access information on the network while at home or traveling. Employees can now use computers with modems to dial in to the network and access company information.

Many companies use networks to back up information stored on their employees' computers. Backing up information using a network is more reliable and secure than performing a backup on each computer.

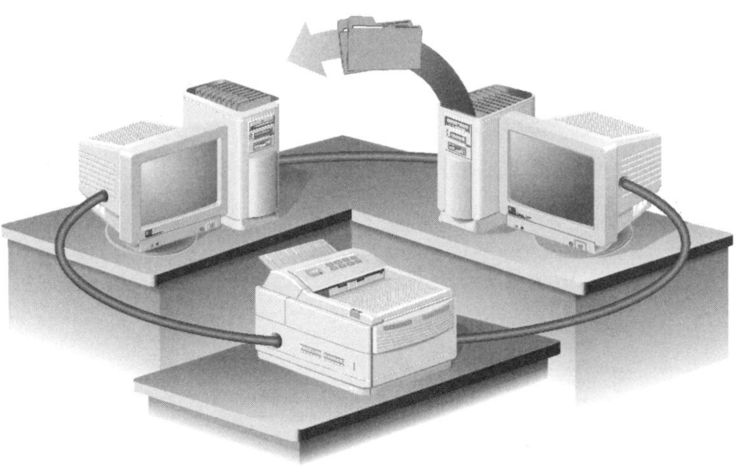

You usually have to enter a user name and password when you want to access information on a network. This ensures that only authorized people can use the information stored on the network.

A system administrator manages the network and makes sure the network functions properly. A system administrator may also be called a network manager, information systems manager or network administrator.

Most businesses and organizations that have computers now use a network to connect the computers. Networks can be used to connect as few as two computers, as in a small business, or millions of computers, as with the world's largest network–the Internet.

TYPES OF NETWORKS

There are many different types of networks used by businesses and organizations. The main types of networks are local area networks, metropolitan area networks and wide area networks.

Just as every business and organization is unique, so is every network. The type of network used by a company or organization depends on where the computers that need to be connected are located. The larger the network, the more costly the network is to build, set up and maintain.

Local Area Network (LAN)

A Local Area Network (LAN) connects computers and devices that are located close to each other, such as in one building. Most computers on a local area network are connected using cables. Local area networks connect from as few as two computers to usually no more than 100 computers. LANs are the most common type of network found in businesses.

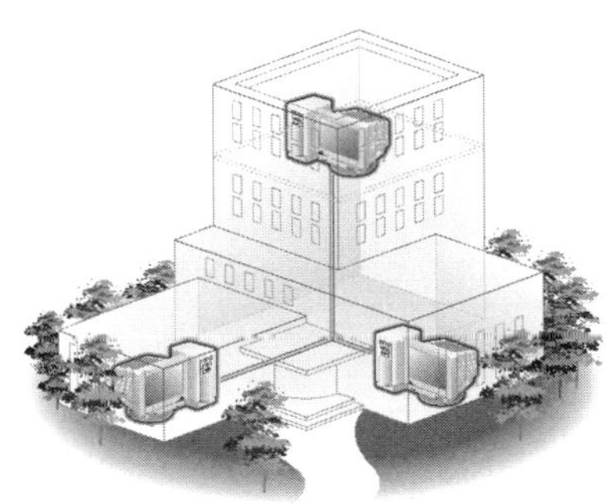

Metropolitan Area Network (MAN)

A Metropolitan Area Network (MAN) is used to connect computers that are located in the same geographic area, such as a town or city. A metropolitan area network is often made up of smaller local area networks that are connected together. For example, a college may use a MAN that connects the local area networks on each campus throughout a city. Networks on a MAN are often connected by radio waves.

Wide Area Network (WAN)

A Wide Area Network (WAN) connects multiple networks together. The networks that make up a wide area network may be located throughout a country or even around the world. Wide area networks are very expensive and complicated to build. Networks in a WAN are often connected by microwave or satellite. A wide area network owned and controlled by one company is often referred to as an enterprise network. The Internet is the largest wide area network in the world.

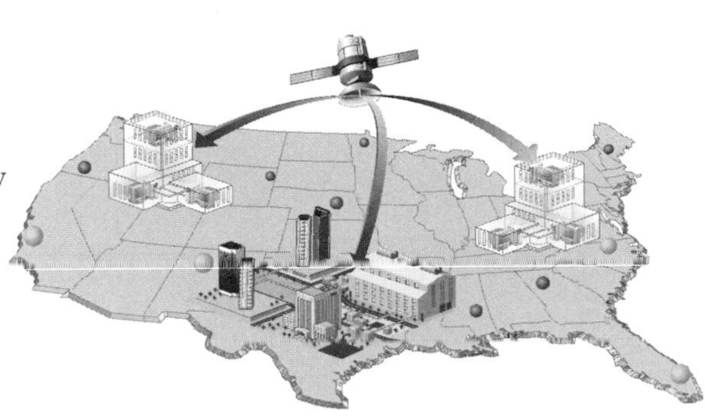

NETWORK HARDWARE

Network hardware is the physical components that make up a network. All networks require special networking equipment.

Computers

The most important job of a network is to link computers together so they can share information. Networks can connect various types of computers, such as IBM-compatible and Macintosh.

Hub

A hub is a device that provides a central location where all the cables on a network come together. All the computers and devices that are connected to a hub can exchange information with each other.

Network Interface Card (NIC)

A Network Interface Card (NIC) physically connects each computer to a network and controls the flow of information between the network and the computer. NICs are installed inside a computer. You can see the edge of the NIC at the back of the computer. An NIC has a port where the network cable plugs in.

Bridge

A bridge is a device that joins two networks together. Both networks can connect to the bridge to allow the computers on each network to exchange information.

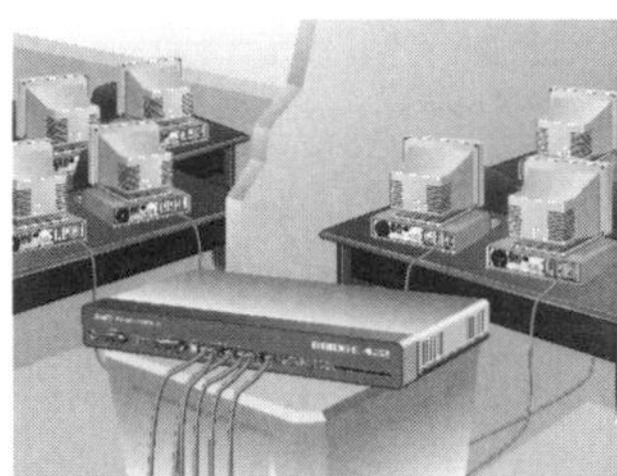

Network Resources

A network resource is a device that computers on a network can use. The most common type of network resource is a printer. All people on a network can send documents to a printer that is connected to the network. Other examples of network resources include hard drives and tape drives.

Transmission Medium

A transmission medium is anything that lets computers exchange information. Cables are the most popular type of transmission medium and are used to connect computers and equipment to a network. There are four main types of cables—coaxial, Unshielded Twisted Pair (UTP), Shielded Twisted Pair (STP) and fiber optic. The type of cable used on a network depends on the type and size of the network. Some newer transmission technologies allow computers to be connected using radio or infrared waves. These networks are called wireless networks.

NETWORK LAYOUT

Peer-to-Peer Networks

Computers on a peer-to-peer network store files and programs on their own hard drives. Each computer that is connected to the peer-to-peer network is used to perform regular tasks, such as word processing.

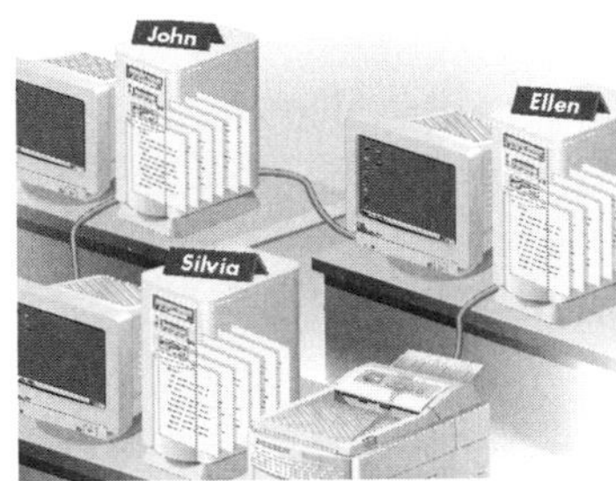

The computers can communicate with other computers to share information or devices. For example, if a person on the peer-to-peer network has a printer attached to their computer, they may share the printer with other people on the network. Peer-to-peer networks are usually used to connect fewer than 10 computers.

Client/Server Networks

Computers on a client/server network store files on a central computer called a server. There are many types of servers. For example, a file server is a computer that stores a large collection of documents. Storing the documents on one computer makes it easy to manage a large collection of information. Backing up files on one server is easier and faster than backing up the files on each person's computer on the network.

A client is a computer that can access information stored on the server. When a computer accesses a server, the computer is acting like the customer, or client, of the server.

Client/server networks can be any size but are usually used when 10 or more computers need to exchange information.

NETWORK ARCHITECTURE

Network architecture is the term used to describe the method of transferring information on a network. Computers and other devices on a network must all use the same method of transmitting information. If devices use different methods to transfer information, the information may become damaged and unreadable.

The most common type of network architecture is Ethernet. An Ethernet network is inexpensive and easy to set up. Other network architecture types include Token-Ring and Arcnet.

The type of network architecture used on a network determines how fast information transfers across the network.

NETWORK COMPONENTS

There are four main components that allow a Windows 98 computer to communicate, share resources and exchange information with other computers and devices on a network. These components are called adapters, services, protocols and clients.

Adapter

A network adapter is a device that physically connects a computer to a network. When you want to send information, such as a document, to another computer on a network, the network adapter converts the document into a format that can transfer over the network's transmission media, such as cables. Most networks connected by cables use Network Interface Cards (NICs) as adapters. Ethernet is a popular type of network adapter.

A modem may also be used as a network adapter since it connects a computer to a network using telephone lines. A modem used as a network adapter is referred to as a dial-up adapter.

Service

A service lets you share and access information and resources on a network. Windows provides services that allow you to share files and printers on Microsoft and Novell networks. There are also services that allow you to connect to Hewlett-Packard printers that are directly attached to a network.

Protocol

A protocol is a language that computers and other devices on a network use to communicate. Computers and devices on a network must use the same protocol before they can exchange information with each other. For example, if you want to print information on a network printer, your computer and the printer must use the same protocol.

Protocols may be used to perform maintenance tasks such as correcting errors in information transmission or redirecting information around broken connections on a network.

Windows 98 supports the most popular protocols used on computer networks, including IPX/SPX, NetBEUI and TCP/IP.

Client

A client is software that lets your computer communicate with other computers on a network. The type of network you want to connect to, such as Microsoft or Novell, determines the client you need. Windows 98 includes client software for the most popular networks.

When you save information, the client software determines whether you are saving the information to your own hard drive or to another computer on the network. Client software is often referred to as a redirector because the client determines where information goes.

THE OSI MODEL

The Open Systems Interconnect (OSI) model is a set of guidelines that companies follow when creating devices and software for networks. Many companies follow the guidelines in the OSI model to make sure all the hardware and software in a network will be able to work together. The OSI model has seven sections, or layers, that describe the tasks that must be performed for information to transfer on a network.

Application Layer

The Application layer is responsible for exchanging information between the programs running on a computer and other services on a network, such as a database or print server.

Presentation Layer

The Presentation layer formats information so that it can be read by an application.

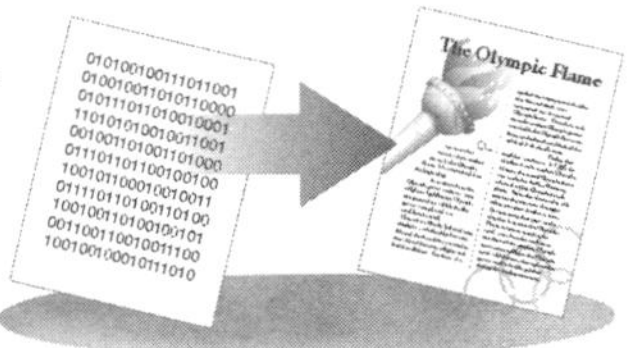

Session Layer

The Session layer determines how two devices communicate. This layer establishes and monitors connections between computers.

Transport Layer

The Transport layer corrects errors in transmission and ensures that the information is delivered reliably.

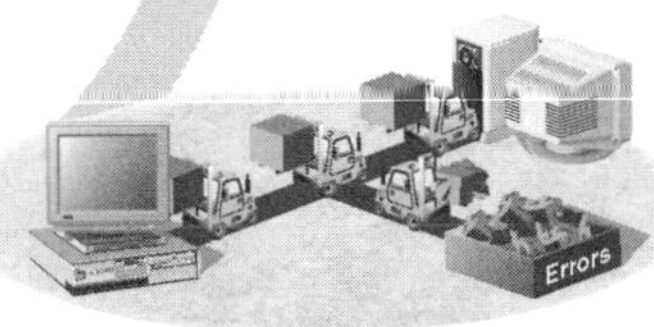

Network Layer

The Network layer identifies computers on a network and determines how to direct information transferring over a network.

Data Link Layer

The Data Link layer groups data into sets to prepare the data for transferring over a network.

Physical Layer

The Physical layer defines how a transmission medium, such as a cable, connects to a computer. This layer also specifies how electrical information transfers through the transmission medium.

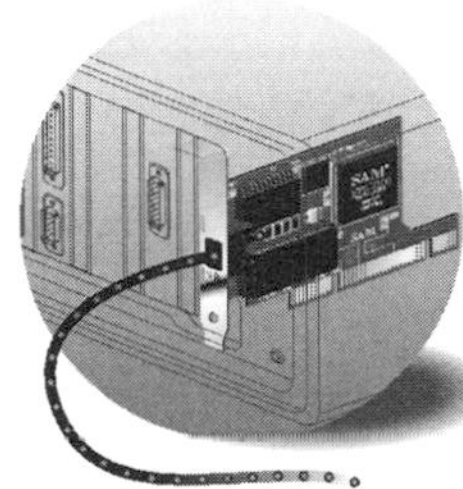

NAME YOUR COMPUTER

You can change the name of your computer on a network. You must name your computer if you want other people to be able to access information or use equipment connected to your computer, such as a printer.

Each computer on a network must have a unique name. A descriptive name such as "Johns_Computer" makes a computer much easier to find and identify than a name such as "Computer-10." A computer name cannot be more than 15 characters in length.

You can change which workgroup your computer belongs to. The workgroup name also cannot be more than 15 characters in length.

You can assign a description to your computer. Assigning a description lets other people know more detailed information about your computer, such as where the computer is located.

You should check with your system administrator before changing your computer or workgroup name.

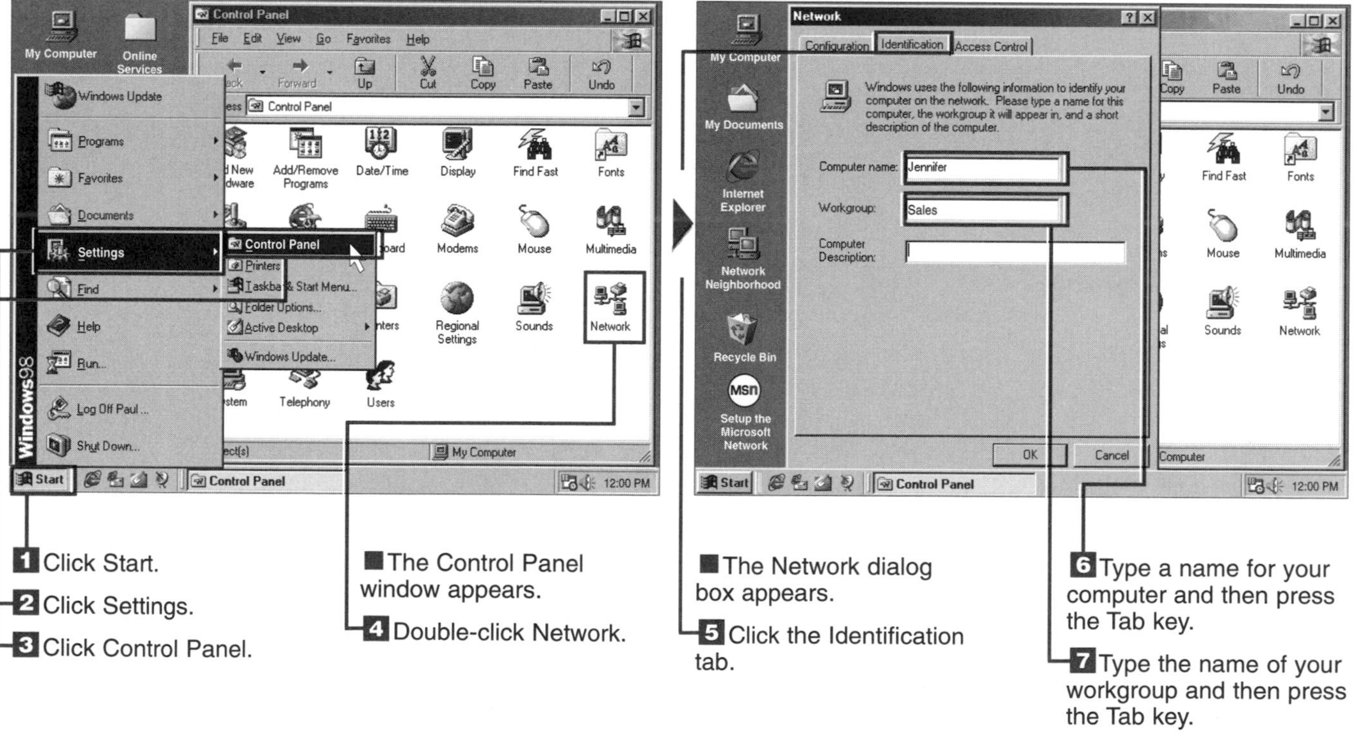

1 Click Start.

2 Click Settings.

3 Click Control Panel.

■ The Control Panel window appears.

4 Double-click Network.

■ The Network dialog box appears.

5 Click the Identification tab.

6 Type a name for your computer and then press the Tab key.

7 Type the name of your workgroup and then press the Tab key.

TIPS

What is a workgroup?

A workgroup is a group of computers on a network that share the same resources, such as printers. A workgroup often consists of computers located close to each other, such as the accounting or sales department of a business. Since all the computers in the department use the same equipment, it makes sense to place the computers in the same workgroup. If you do not know the name of your workgroup, ask your system administrator.

After I change the name of my computer, do I need to inform other individuals on the network?

After you change the name of your computer, you should inform the people who use information or equipment on your computer.

My computer already displays a name and workgroup name. When was this information entered?

The computer name and workgroup name are often entered when Windows is installed on a computer.

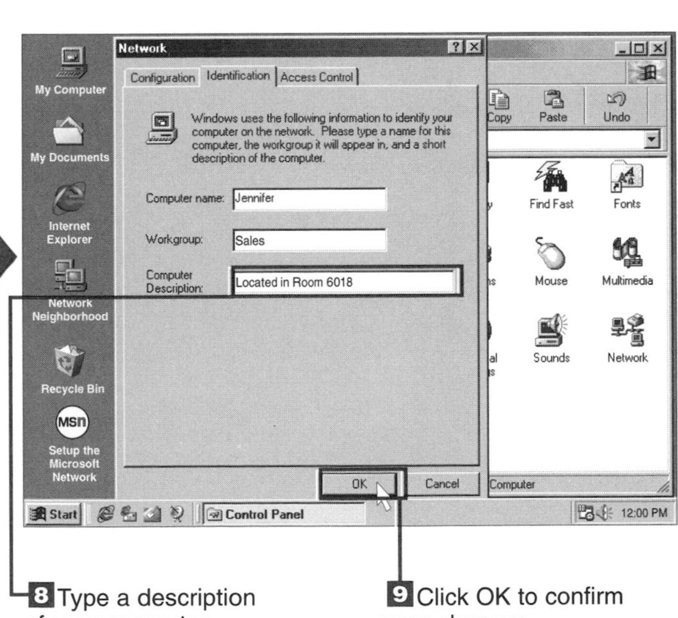

8 Type a description of your computer.

9 Click OK to confirm your changes.

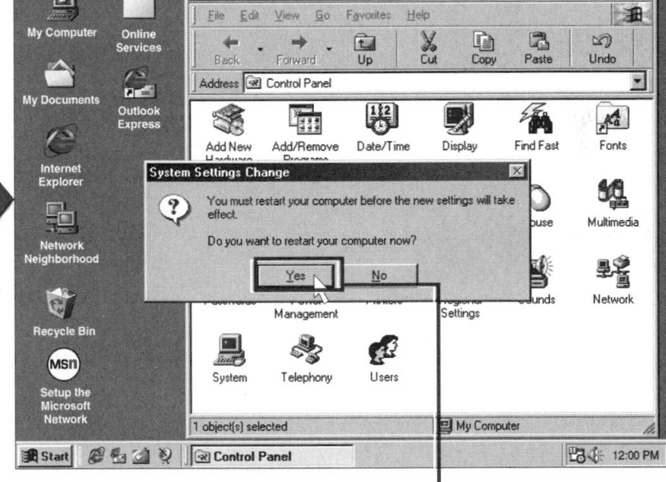

■ The System Settings Change dialog box appears, telling you Windows needs to restart your computer before the new settings will take effect.

10 Click Yes to restart your computer.

BROWSE THROUGH A NETWORK

Network Neighborhood allows you to browse through shared resources available on your network.

The most common types of shared network resources include information such as files, and equipment such as printers and CD-ROM drives.

Windows displays icons to represent network computers and shared network resources. Using Network Neighborhood to locate resources on a network is very similar to using My Computer or Windows Explorer to locate information on your own computer.

Some computers on the network may require you to enter a password before you can access their shared resources. Windows will ask you for the password.

After you find a resource, you can work with the resource as if it were stored on your own computer.

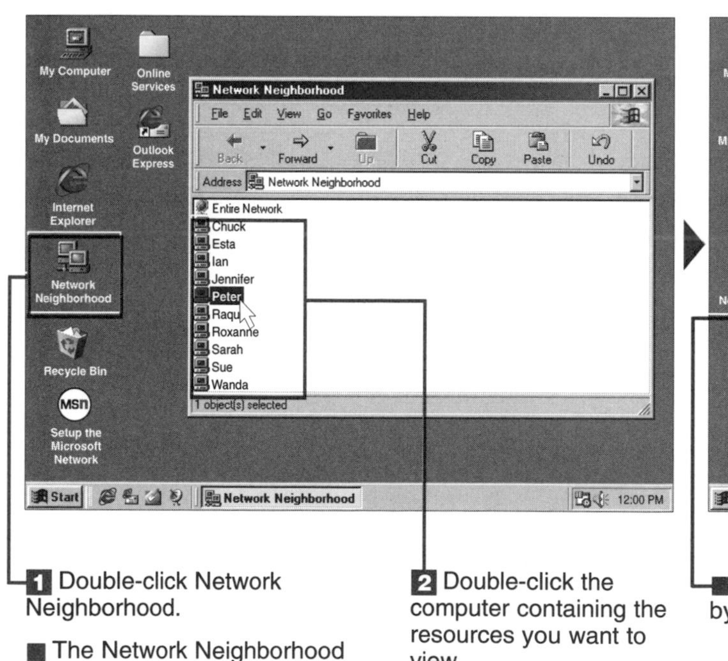

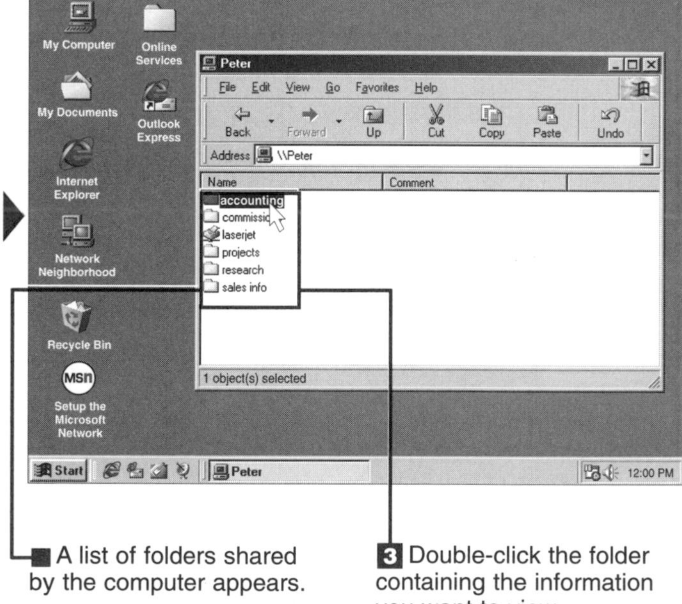

1 Double-click Network Neighborhood.

■ The Network Neighborhood window appears. The window displays the computers in your workgroup.

2 Double-click the computer containing the resources you want to view.

Note: You can double-click Entire Network to view other computers on the network that are not in your workgroup.

■ A list of folders shared by the computer appears.

3 Double-click the folder containing the information you want to view.

TIPS

Why can I no longer access a shared folder on a network?

If the computer that stores the folder is turned off or if the owner of the computer decides to stop sharing the folder, you will no longer be able to access the folder.

How can I quickly access the shared resources on another computer?

You can create shortcuts to shared files, folders, printers and drives. Using the right mouse button, drag the shared item to the location where you want to place a shortcut for the item. From the menu that appears, select Create Shortcut(s) Here. For more information on shortcuts, see page 90.

Can I use Windows Explorer to browse through a network?

In the Windows Explorer window, double-click Network Neighborhood to display a list of computers on the network. The window shows a structural view of the information available on the network. For information on Windows Explorer, see page 60.

Why does the password I use to access a shared folder no longer work?

The person who is sharing the folder you are trying to access may have changed the password. You will need to enter the new password before you can access the folder again.

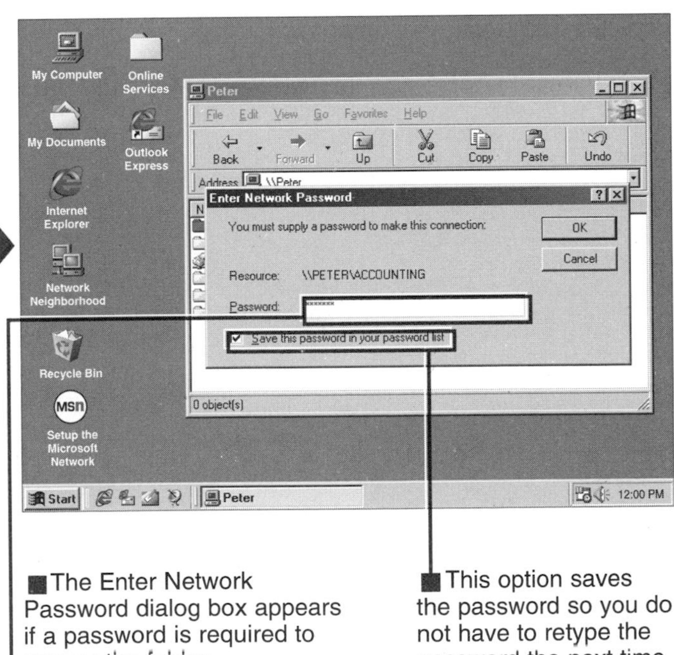

■ The Enter Network Password dialog box appears if a password is required to access the folder.

4 Type the password and then press the Enter key.

■ This option saves the password so you do not have to retype the password the next time you select the folder.

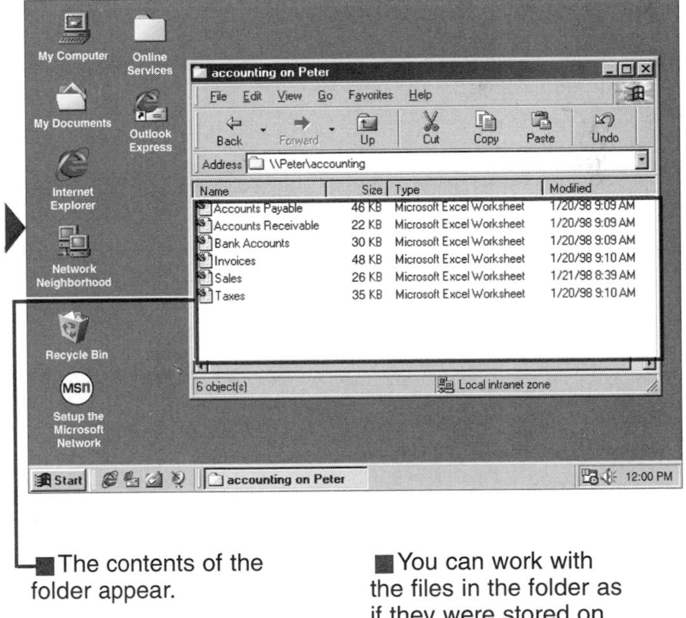

■ The contents of the folder appear.

■ You can work with the files in the folder as if they were stored on your own computer.

FIND A COMPUTER

Windows enables you to find a computer on a network. The ability to locate a computer is especially useful if your network consists of hundreds of computers.

You can enter the entire name of the computer you want to find or just a portion of the name. For example, you can type **Jonathan** or **Jon** to find the computer named Jonathan.

If you are searching for a computer on a large network, Windows may take a while to display the names of any computers it finds. You can cancel the search at any time.

After the search is complete, Windows displays a list of all the computers that match the name you specified. Windows also tells you the location of each computer that was found.

Once you find a computer, you can browse through a list of information and equipment shared by the computer. You can access the information stored on the computer as if it was a folder stored on your own computer. Windows may ask you to enter a password to access some shared items.

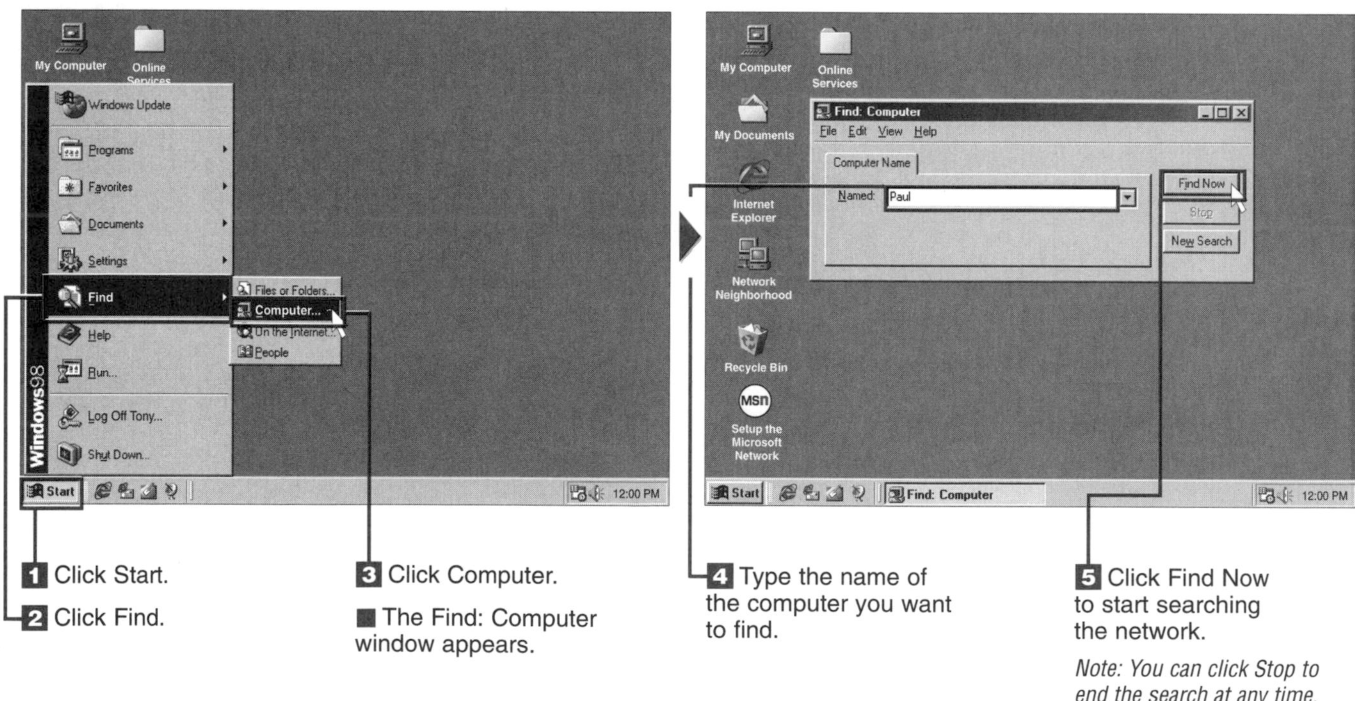

1 Click Start.

2 Click Find.

3 Click Computer.

■ The Find: Computer window appears.

4 Type the name of the computer you want to find.

5 Click Find Now to start searching the network.

Note: You can click Stop to end the search at any time.

TIPS

How can I change the order of the computers that Windows finds?

You can sort the list by name, location or comment. Click the heading of the column you want to sort by. Windows will sort the items alphabetically. You can change the order of the items as often as you want.

Why can't I see a comment for some of the computers Windows found?

Windows will only display a comment for a computer in the Find: Computer window if the person who shared the computer typed a comment.

Can I use wildcards to help me search for a computer?

You can use the asterisk (*) or a question mark (?) to find a computer on the network. The asterisk (*) represents many characters. The question mark (?) represents a single character. For example, you can type **Sale*** to find a computer named Sales&Marketing.

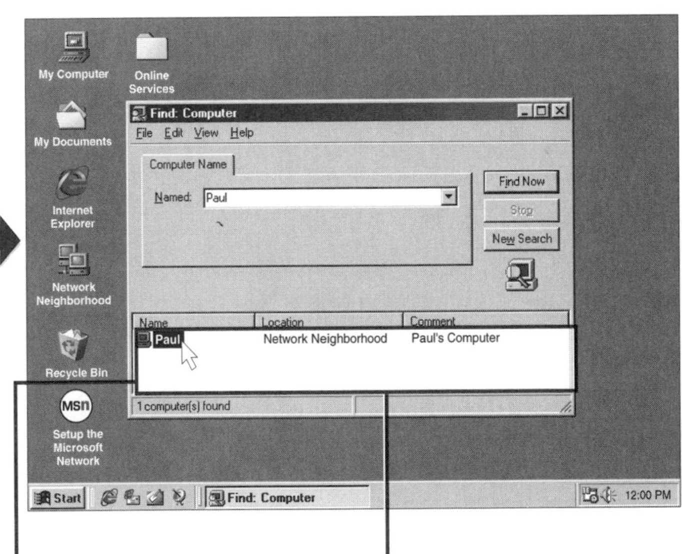

■ This area displays the computer(s) Windows found on the network.

6 To view the information and equipment a computer shares, double-click the computer.

■ A list of the resources shared by the computer appears.

■ You can work with the resources as if they were stored on your own computer.

Note: You may be asked to type a password to access some shared items.

MAP A NETWORK DRIVE

Mapping a network drive provides a quick way to access the information on another computer on a network. You can access a drive or folder on the other computer as if the drive or folder was on your own computer.

If you frequently use information stored on another computer, mapping can save you time. Accessing a drive or folder that has not been mapped may require you to spend a long time searching for the drive or folder. Windows simplifies this process by assigning a single letter to specify the location of a mapped drive.

You can have Windows connect to a mapped network drive each time you log on to the network.

Mapping network drives is also useful if you are working with DOS or older Windows-based programs. Although Windows 98 allows you to use up to 255 characters to name a folder, older programs may not be able to read folder names that contain more than 8 characters. Mapping a network drive uses a shorter name to represent a folder on the network, such as E:, allowing older programs to access the folder.

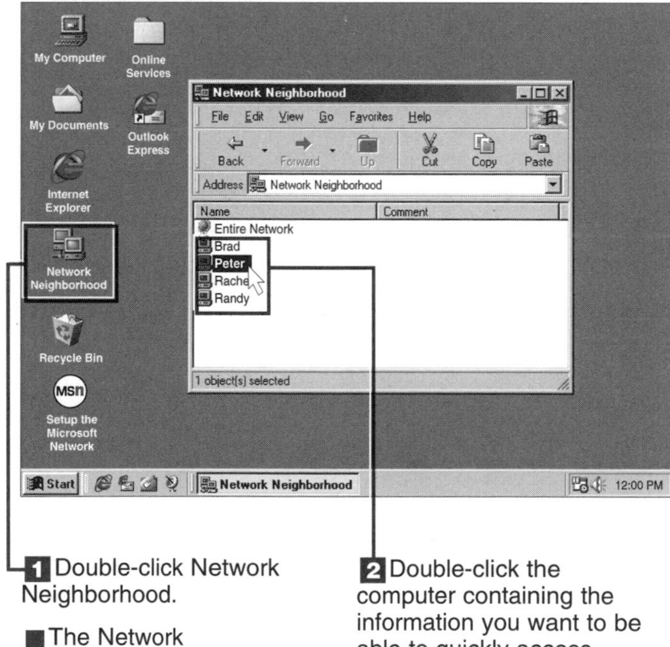

1 Double-click Network Neighborhood.

■ The Network Neighborhood window appears.

2 Double-click the computer containing the information you want to be able to quickly access.

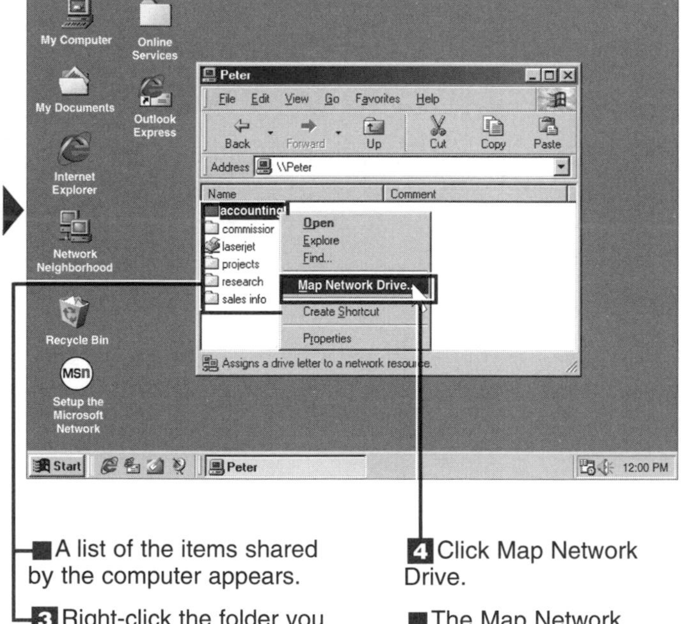

■ A list of the items shared by the computer appears.

3 Right-click the folder you want to be able to quickly access. A menu appears.

4 Click Map Network Drive.

■ The Map Network Drive dialog box appears.

TIPS

Why do I have to enter a password when creating a mapped network drive?

The drives you access on a network are shared by other people. When the owner of a computer turns on sharing for the drive, they may assign a password. Only people who know the password can access the information on the drive.

How do I disconnect a mapped network drive?

In the My Computer window, right-click the mapped network drive you want to disconnect from and then click Disconnect.

Will Windows remember a password needed to create a mapped network drive?

When you create a mapped network drive, you may be asked for a password. Windows will remember the password so you do not have to type it each time you want to connect to the information.

Why does an X appear through a mapped network drive?

An X through the icon of a mapped network drive means the drive is unavailable or the drive has a new password. Windows will notify you of the problem the next time you start Windows.

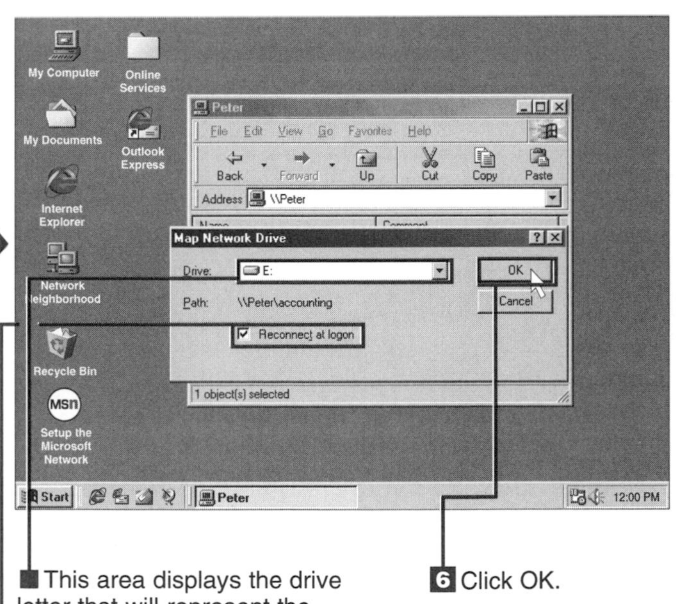

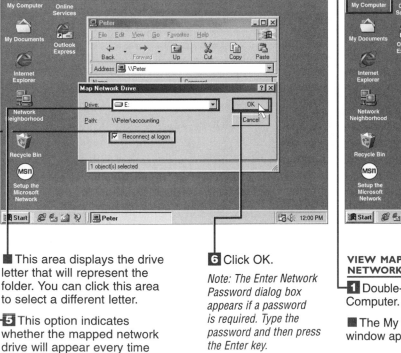

■ This area displays the drive letter that will represent the folder. You can click this area to select a different letter.

5 This option indicates whether the mapped network drive will appear every time you start Windows. Click this option to turn the option on (☑) or off (☐).

6 Click OK.

Note: The Enter Network Password dialog box appears if a password is required. Type the password and then press the Enter key.

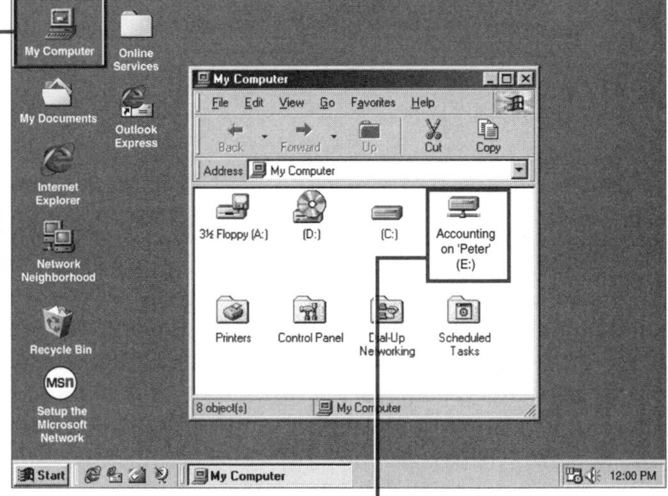

VIEW MAPPED NETWORK DRIVES

1 Double-click My Computer.

■ The My Computer window appears.

■ The icon for the mapped network drive displays a disk attached to a cable. You can double-click the icon to access the contents of the mapped drive.

EXCHANGE MESSAGES WITH WINPOPUP

You can use WinPopup to exchange short messages with other people on your network.

You can send a message to one person or to everyone in a workgroup. The person you send a message to must have their computer turned on and have WinPopup open at the time you send the message.

WinPopup is useful for asking questions, expressing ideas and making short announcements. For example, you can use WinPopup to let all the people in your workgroup know when you are about to stop sharing information or a resource, such as a printer.

The WinPopup button on the taskbar displays the symbol when you receive a message. You can quickly flip through all the messages you receive.

If WinPopup is not installed on your computer, you can install WinPopup from the System Tools component on the Windows 98 CD-ROM. To add Windows components, see page 610.

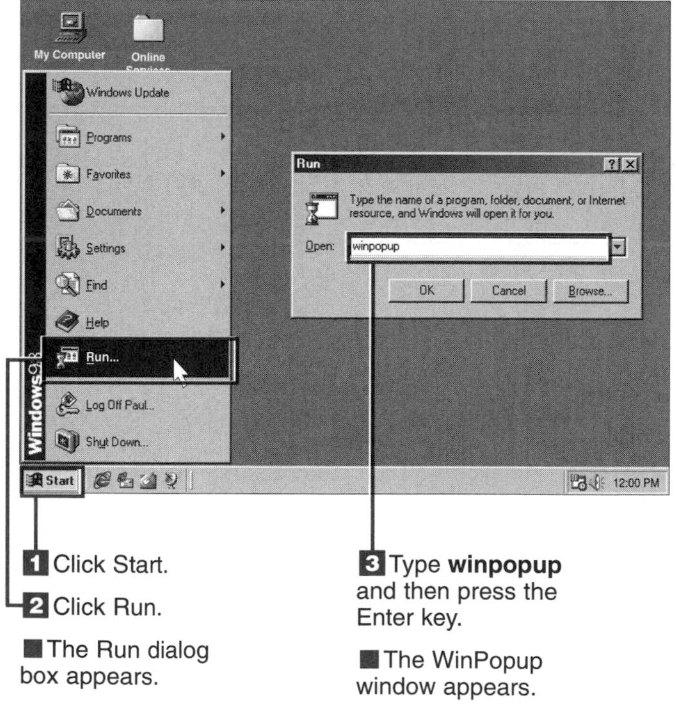

1 Click Start.

2 Click Run.

■ The Run dialog box appears.

3 Type **winpopup** and then press the Enter key.

■ The WinPopup window appears.

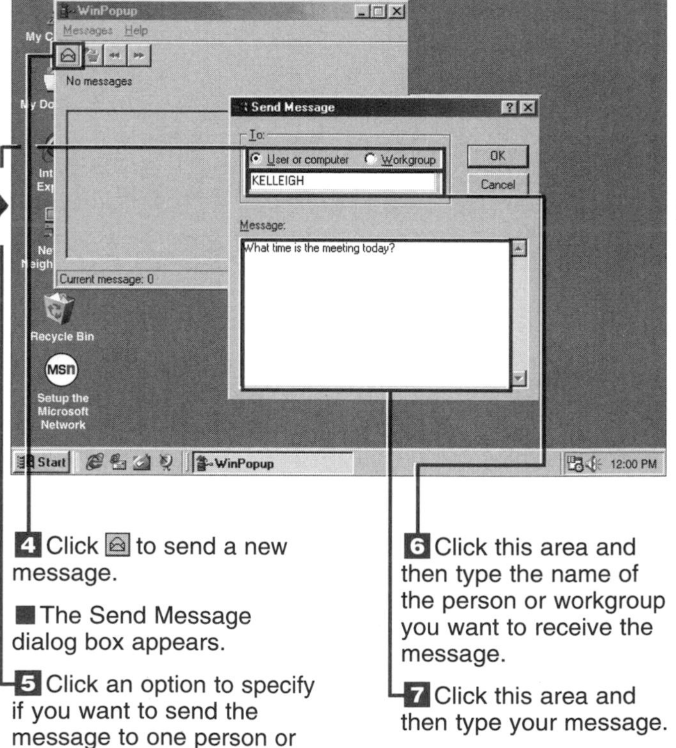

4 Click to send a new message.

■ The Send Message dialog box appears.

5 Click an option to specify if you want to send the message to one person or everyone in the workgroup (○ changes to ⊙).

6 Click this area and then type the name of the person or workgroup you want to receive the message.

7 Click this area and then type your message.

TIPS

Can I have WinPopup open automatically each time I start Windows?

Locate the Winpopup.exe file in the Windows folder and then drag the file to the StartUp folder. See page 268 for more information on starting programs automatically.

Can I save the WinPopup messages I receive?

You cannot save WinPopup messages. If you need to keep a WinPopup message, select the text in the message, right-click the selected text and then click Copy. You can then paste the information into a document in another program.

Can I make the WinPopup window open automatically each time I receive a message?

In the WinPopup window, choose the Messages menu and then select the Options command. In the Options dialog box, click the Pop up dialog on message receipt option (☐ changes to ☑) and then click OK. You can now minimize the WinPopup window. The window will automatically pop up on your screen when you receive a message.

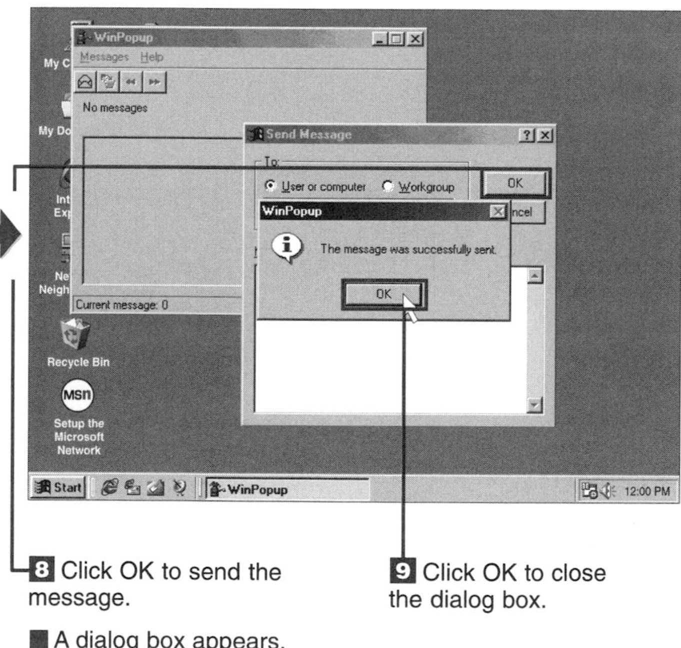

8 Click OK to send the message.

■ A dialog box appears, telling you the message was successfully sent.

9 Click OK to close the dialog box.

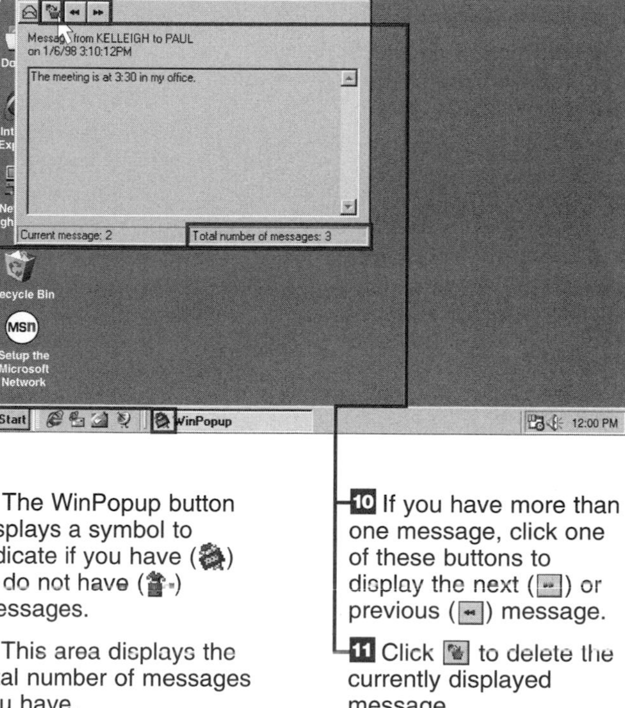

■ The WinPopup button displays a symbol to indicate if you have ( ) or do not have ( ) messages.

■ This area displays the total number of messages you have.

10 If you have more than one message, click one of these buttons to display the next ( ) or previous ( ) message.

11 Click to delete the currently displayed message.

TURN ON SHARING

Before you can share information or a printer with individuals on a network, you must set up your computer to share resources.

You may choose to share files stored on your computer with other people on the network. Sharing files is useful if you want your colleagues to be able to access information on your computer. You can share many types of files, such as programs, documents, videos, sounds and graphics.

You can also share a printer connected to your computer. After you share your printer, people can then send print jobs directly to the printer using the network. When sharing a printer, make sure the printer is turned on and contains paper.

You will have to restart your computer before the new sharing settings will take effect.

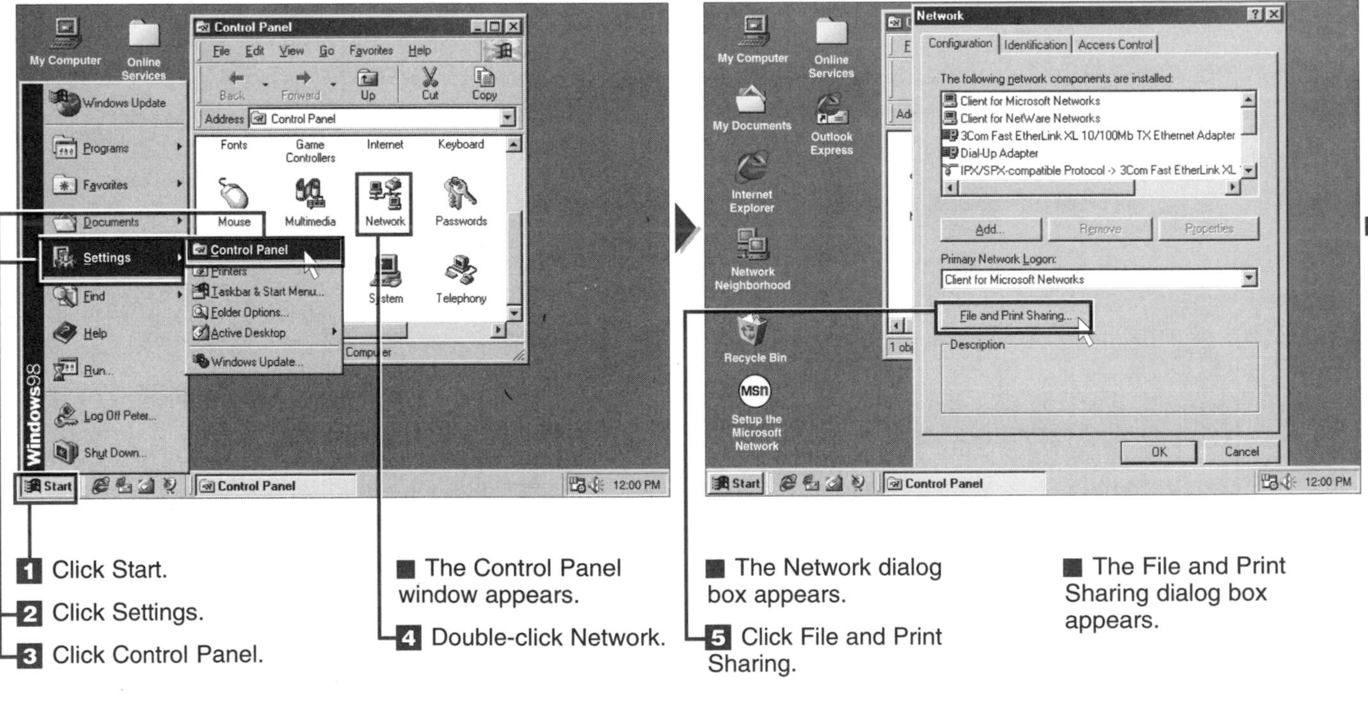

1 Click Start.

2 Click Settings.

3 Click Control Panel.

■ The Control Panel window appears.

4 Double-click Network.

■ The Network dialog box appears.

5 Click File and Print Sharing.

■ The File and Print Sharing dialog box appears.

TIPS

I turned on sharing, but my colleagues still cannot access my files and printer. What is wrong?

Once you turn on sharing, you must specify exactly what you want to share. For information on sharing folders, see page 458. For information on sharing a printer, see page 462.

What happens when I turn off file or print sharing on my computer?

After you turn off file or print sharing, you must restart your computer. Once the computer restarts, other people on the network will no longer be able to access your resources.

If I turn sharing back on, will Windows remember which resources I previously shared?

Windows remembers which resources you were sharing. When you turn on sharing again, all the resources which were previously shared are shared again. To share folders, see page 458. To share a printer, see page 462.

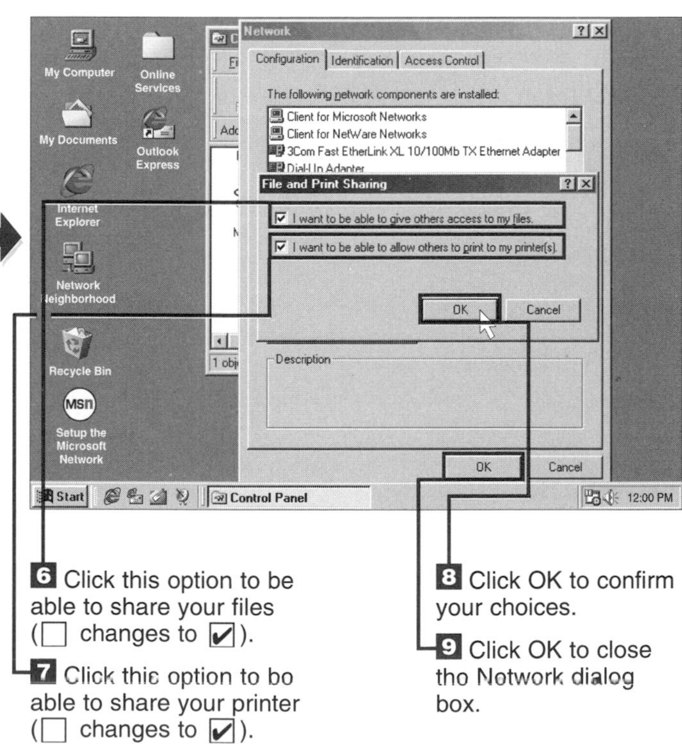

6 Click this option to be able to share your files (☐ changes to ☑).

7 Click this option to be able to share your printer (☐ changes to ☑).

8 Click OK to confirm your choices.

9 Click OK to close the Network dialog box.

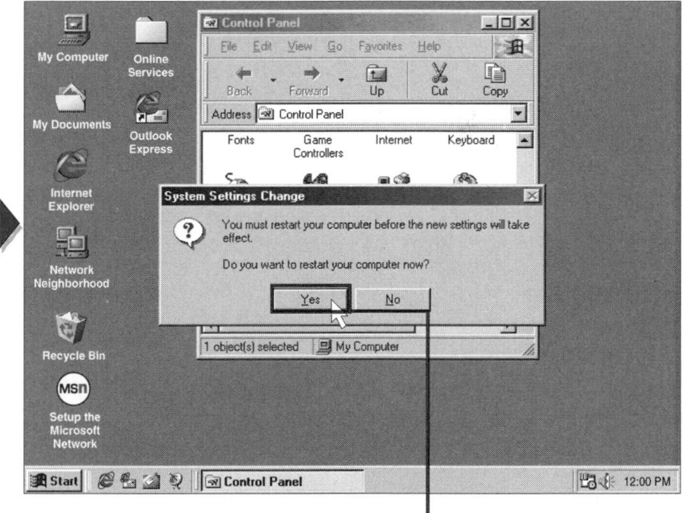

■ Windows may ask you to insert the Windows 98 CD-ROM disc. If so, insert the disc into the drive.

■ The System Settings Change dialog box appears, telling you Windows needs to restart your computer before the new settings will take effect.

10 Click Yes to restart your computer.

Note: To later turn off file and printer sharing, repeat steps 1 to 10 (☑ changes to ☐ in steps 6 and 7).

SHARE INFORMATION

You can specify exactly what information you want to share with individuals on a network. Sharing information is useful if you and your colleagues are working together on a project and need access to the same files.

File sharing is the most common use for a network. You can choose to share your entire hard drive or specific folders on your computer.

Other people can work with your files as if the files were stored on their own computers. You can also let other people access drives that are connected to your computer, such as your floppy drive and CD-ROM drive.

Sharing information on a network is very efficient. Computers can exchange information over a network in a matter of seconds.

Before computer networks, people had to either print a copy of the information or transfer the information using floppy disks when they wanted to share information.

Before you can share information, you must set up your computer to share resources. To turn on file and printer sharing, see page 456.

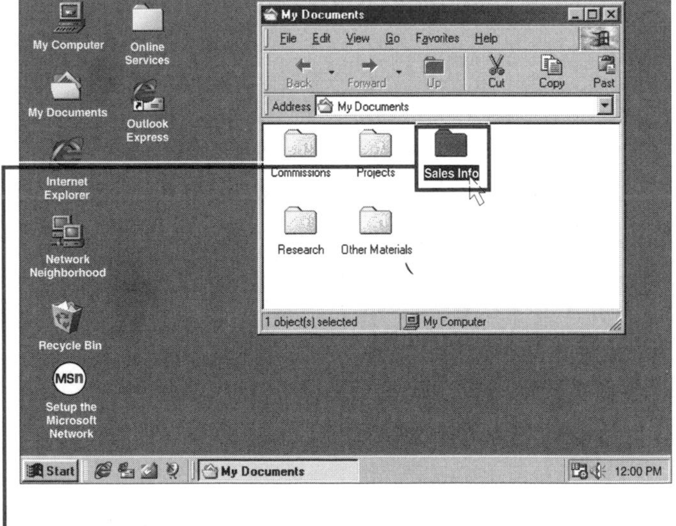

1 Click the folder or drive you want to share.

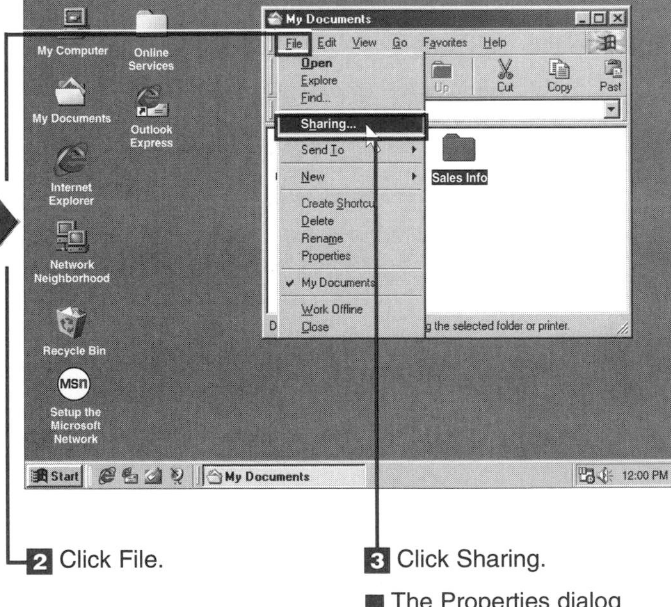

2 Click File.

3 Click Sharing.

■ The Properties dialog box appears.

TIPS

How can I tell which folders and drives on my computer are shared?

You can use My Computer or Windows Explorer to find out which folders and drives on your computer are shared. A hand (☞) appears under the icon for a folder or drive you have shared.

How can I see the folders and drives shared by other computers on the network?

Double-click Network Neighborhood on the desktop to display a list of computers on the network. Double-click the name of a computer of interest to see what information is shared.

What can I do to prevent other people on a network from seeing my shared folder or drive?

In the Properties dialog box, type a dollar sign ($) at the end of the name of the folder or drive. This will ensure that other people on the network will not see the shared folder or drive.

How can I view the comments for shared folders on a network?

In the Network Neighborhood window, you can view the comments entered for shared folders. Click View and then click Details to display information about each shared folder.

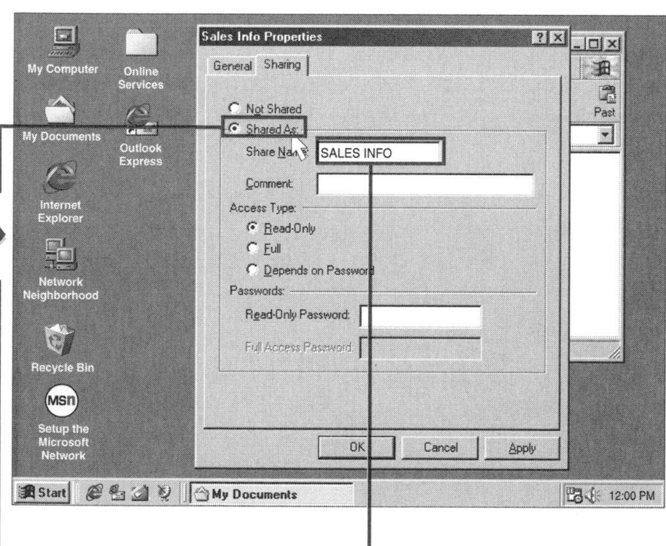

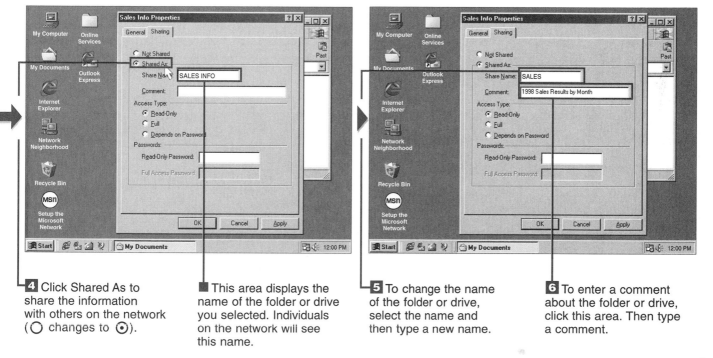

4 Click Shared As to share the information with others on the network (○ changes to ⦿).

■ This area displays the name of the folder or drive you selected. Individuals on the network will see this name.

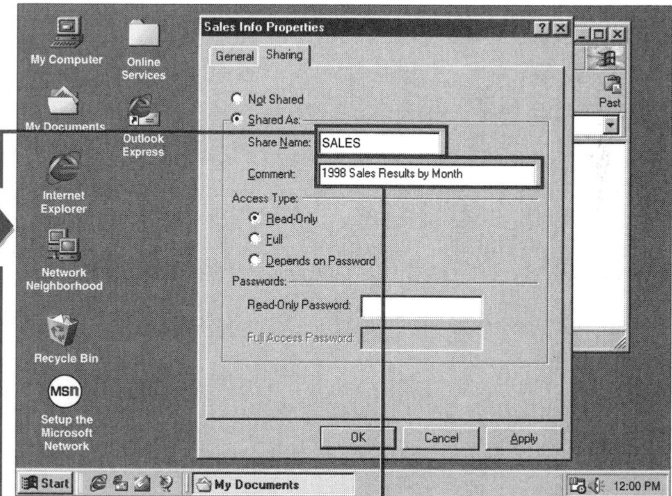

5 To change the name of the folder or drive, select the name and then type a new name.

6 To enter a comment about the folder or drive, click this area. Then type a comment.

CONTINUED

SHARE INFORMATION CONTINUED

You can give individuals on a network one of three types of access to your information.

Read-Only access allows individuals on the network to read, but not change or delete, shared information. People also cannot add files to folders or drives that you have made Read-Only. However, individuals can copy a file with Read-Only access to their own computers and then change the files.

Full access allows individuals on the network to read, change and delete shared information. You should not grant Full access to your main hard drive. If someone erases your computer's system files, you may not be able to use your computer.

Depends on Password access is the best way to share your folders and drives. Windows lets you set two passwords. One password gives Read-Only access to shared files. The other password lets people have Full access to your shared information. Using passwords offers some protection against people changing or erasing your files.

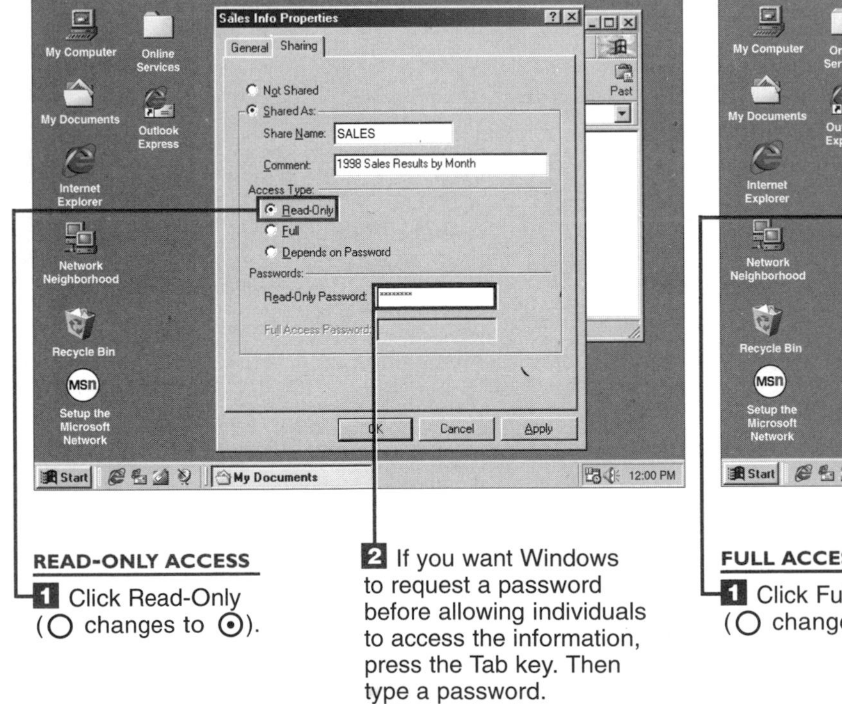

READ-ONLY ACCESS

1 Click Read-Only (○ changes to ⊙).

2 If you want Windows to request a password before allowing individuals to access the information, press the Tab key. Then type a password.

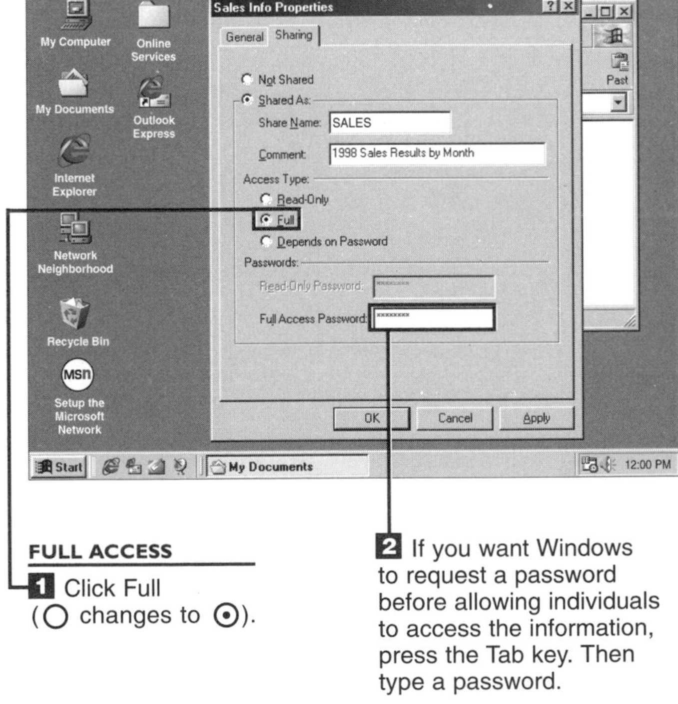

FULL ACCESS

1 Click Full (○ changes to ⊙).

2 If you want Windows to request a password before allowing individuals to access the information, press the Tab key. Then type a password.

TIPS

How do I stop sharing a folder?

When you no longer want individuals on the network to have access to a folder, perform steps 1 to 3 on page 458 and then select Not Shared in step 4.

Why can't I find one of my shared files?

If you gave Full access to the folder that contains the file, another person may have deleted the file. Ask the people with Full access to check their Recycle Bins to see if they can find the file.

How does sharing information affect the performance of my computer?

When another computer accesses your shared information, it uses your computer to retrieve and then transfer the information through the network. Each time someone accesses your shared files, there is less processing power available and your computer operates more slowly.

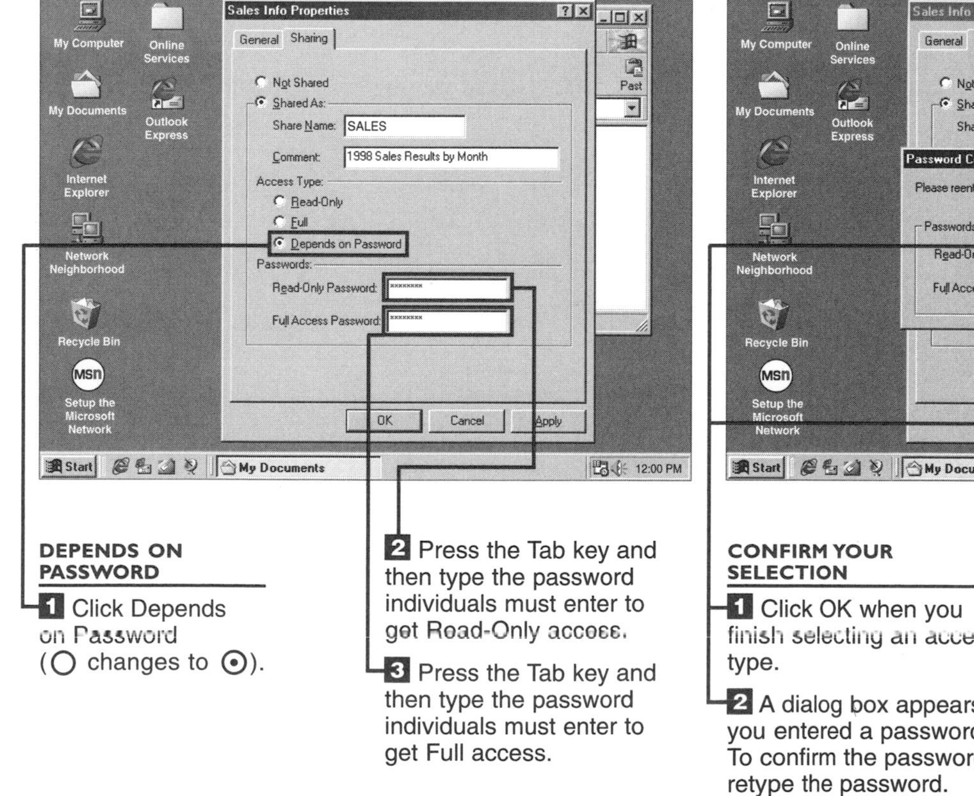

DEPENDS ON PASSWORD

1 Click Depends on Password (○ changes to ⊙).

2 Press the Tab key and then type the password individuals must enter to get Read-Only access.

3 Press the Tab key and then type the password individuals must enter to get Full access.

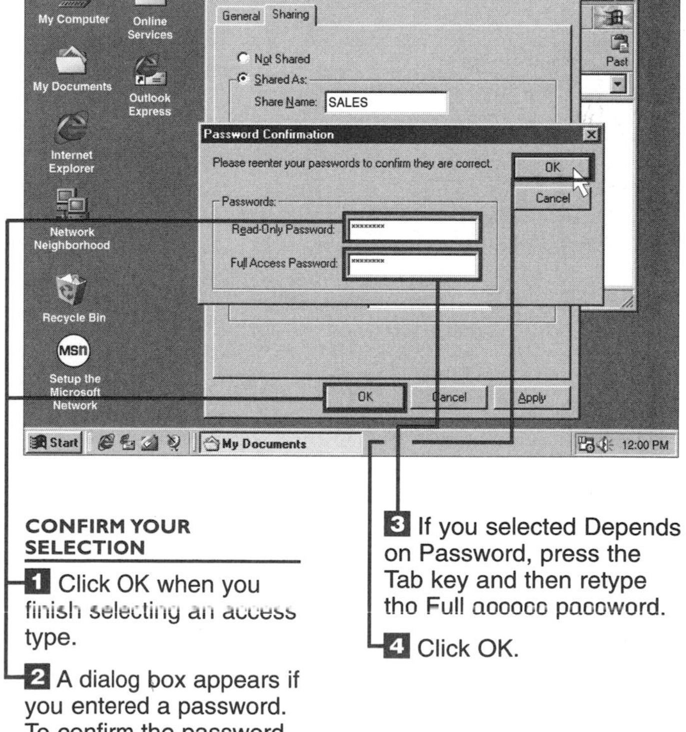

CONFIRM YOUR SELECTION

1 Click OK when you finish selecting an access type.

2 A dialog box appears if you entered a password. To confirm the password, retype the password.

3 If you selected Depends on Password, press the Tab key and then retype the Full access password.

4 Click OK.

SHARE A PRINTER

You can share a printer connected to your computer with other individuals on a network.

Sharing printers allows companies to save money since each person on the network does not need their own printer.

When sharing a printer, you can assign a name, comment and password to the printer. A descriptive name and comment helps to identify your printer if there are several printers available on the network. Other people will be able to see the name and comment when they browse for shared printers on the network.

You should use a printer name that describes where the printer is located, such as “Dan’s Office”. Choosing a descriptive name will help people distinguish your printer from other printers on the network.

When sharing your printer with other people on a network, you must make sure that both your computer and your printer are turned on. You must also make sure your printer is accessible when other people need it. For example, if your printer is located in your office, make sure your office door is not locked when people are using your printer.

Before you can share your printer, you must set up your computer to share resources. To turn on file and printer sharing, see page 456.

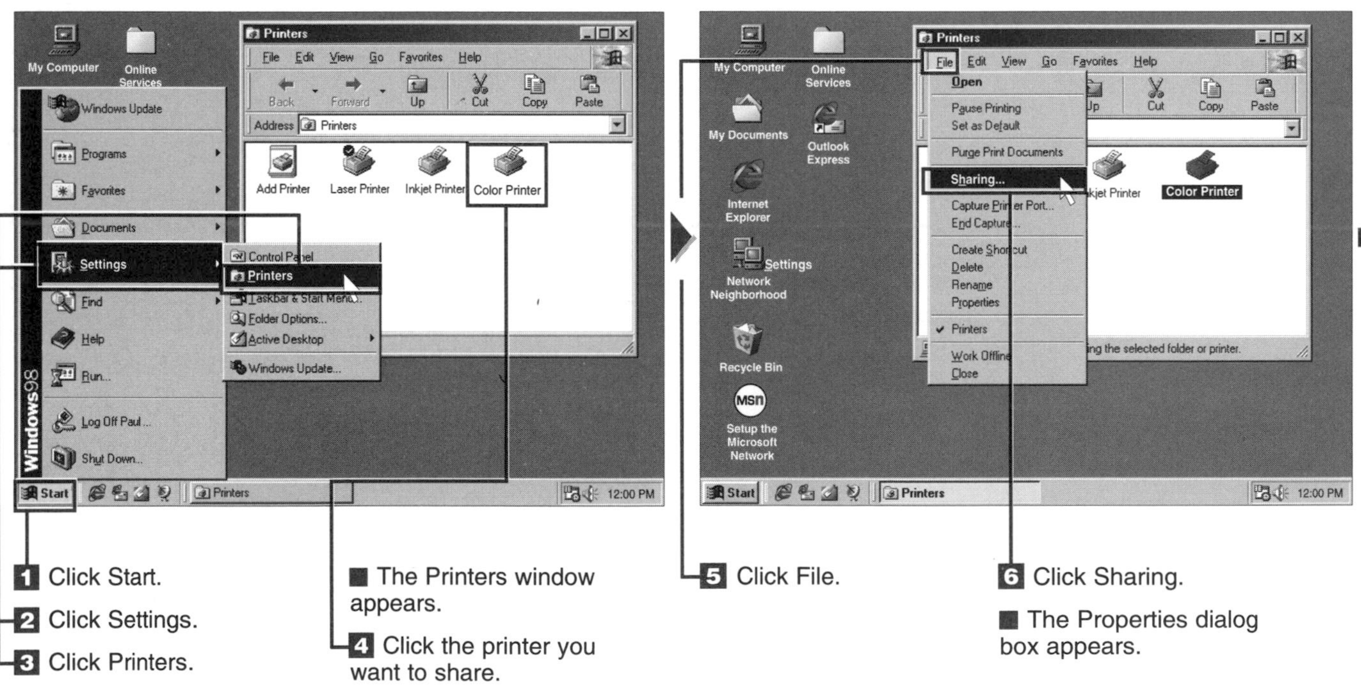

1 Click Start.

2 Click Settings.

3 Click Printers.

■ The Printers window appears.

4 Click the printer you want to share.

5 Click File.

6 Click Sharing.

■ The Properties dialog box appears.

TIPS

How do I restrict access to a printer I am sharing?

You can restrict access by assigning a password that users must enter to send documents to your printer. Only people who know the password will be able to use your printer.

How do I stop sharing a printer?

When you no longer want individuals on the network to use your printer, repeat the steps described below, except click Not Shared in step 7 (○ changes to ⊙).

How do I connect to a shared printer on the network?

If you want to use a printer on the network, you need to install the printer software on your computer. See page 464.

Can I hide my shared printer from other people on the network?

In the Properties dialog box, type a dollar sign ($) at the end of the name of the printer. This ensures that other people on the network will not see your printer when they browse for shared printers.

Will sharing a printer affect my computer's performance?

Your computer stores the files sent by other people and then sends the files to your printer. As a result, your computer operates more slowly while other people are using your printer.

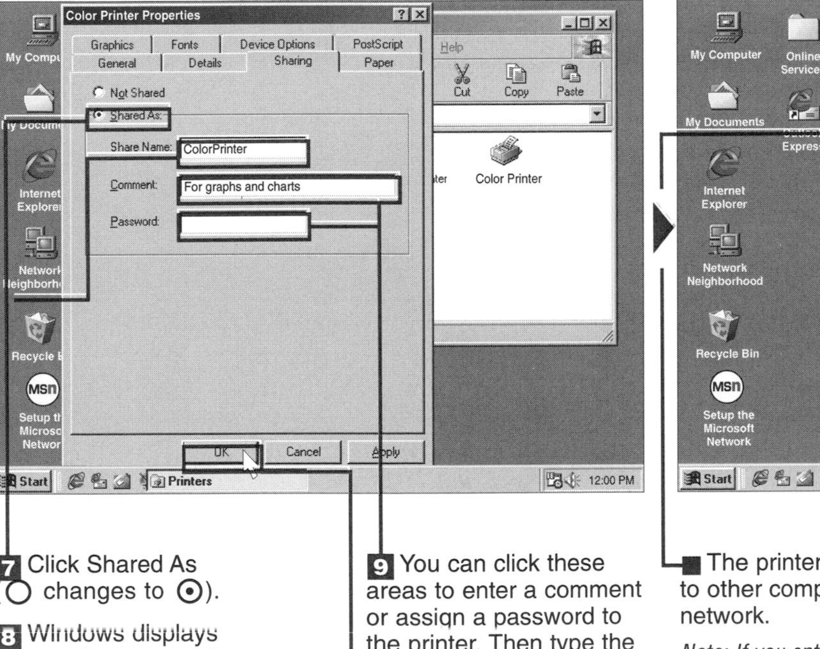

7 Click Shared As (○ changes to ⊙).

8 Windows displays a name for your printer. To give the printer a different name, select the name and then type the new name.

9 You can click these areas to enter a comment or assign a password to the printer. Then type the comment or password.

10 Click OK.

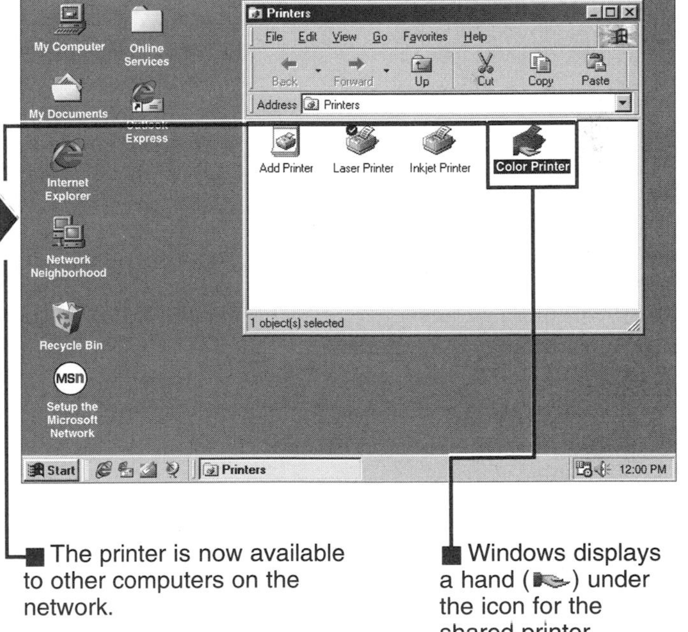

■ The printer is now available to other computers on the network.

Note: If you entered a password, a dialog box appears, asking you to enter the password again.

■ Windows displays a hand (☛) under the icon for the shared printer.

CONNECT TO A SHARED PRINTER

You can connect to a shared printer on your network to produce printed copies of your work.

Companies often connect printers to a network to help reduce printing costs. Everyone can then use the network printer instead of needing a printer connected to each computer.

Some printers on a network are attached to computers whose only function is to process print jobs. This type of printer is called a dedicated network printer.

Dedicated network printers are usually faster and more reliable than standard printers.

Dedicated network printers can be placed in a central part of an office or building to make it easy for people to retrieve the work they have printed. Many dedicated network printers have extra capabilities not available on standard printers, such as job sorting to help organize print jobs that have been printed by many people.

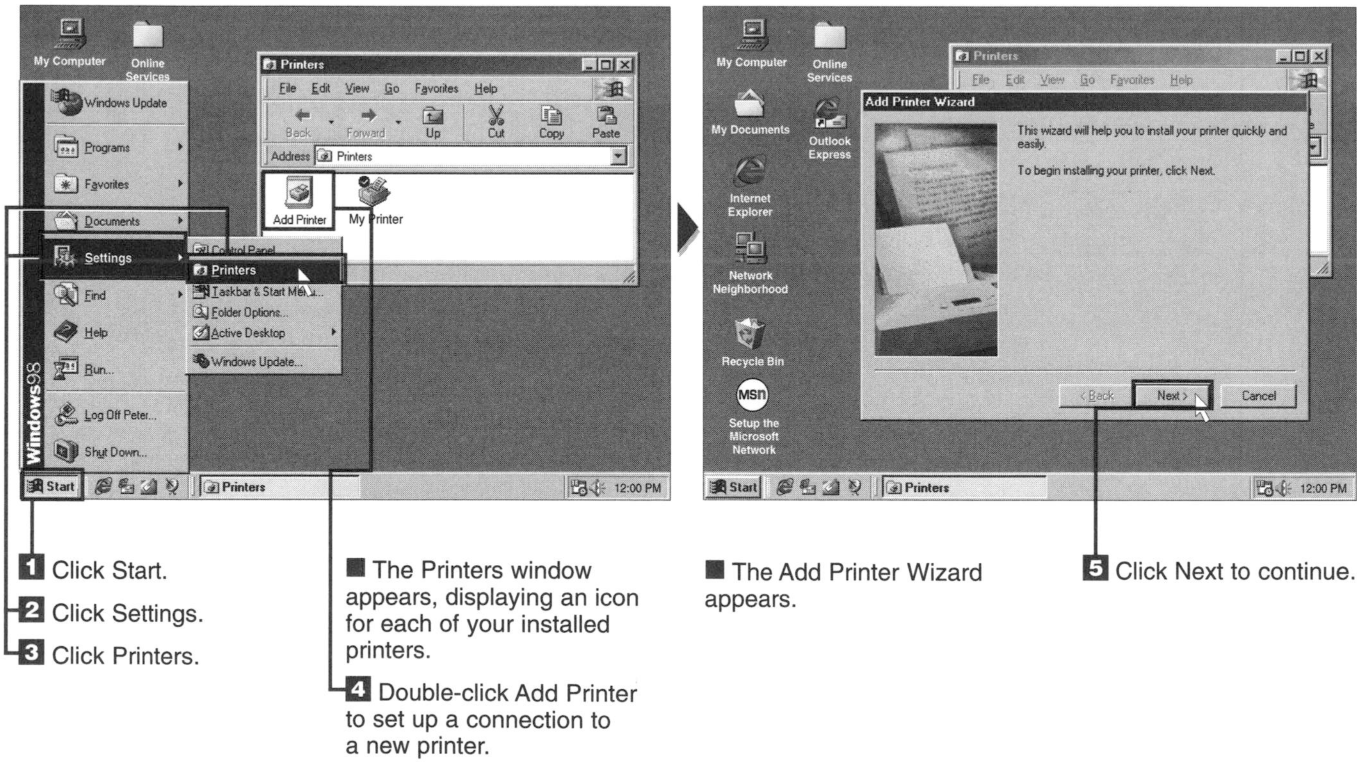

1 Click Start.

2 Click Settings.

3 Click Printers.

■ The Printers window appears, displaying an icon for each of your installed printers.

4 Double-click Add Printer to set up a connection to a new printer.

■ The Add Printer Wizard appears.

5 Click Next to continue.

TIPS

How can I find out which printers on the network are shared?

Double-click Network Neighborhood on your desktop to view a list of the computers in your workgroup or on the network. Double-click a computer to display the printers shared by the computer. For information, see page 448.

Will the wizard require more information if I choose to print from MS-DOS-based programs?

Yes. The wizard will ask you to specify which port you want to use. Many MS-DOS-based programs must send information to a printer port, called an LPT port.

What is a print queue?

A print queue is a location on a computer or printer where files waiting to print are stored. Printers on a network are often busy and new print jobs have to wait for other jobs to finish printing.

What is a print server?

A print server is a computer that has a shared printer attached to it. A computer used for performing regular office tasks with a standard printer attached can be a print server. A print server can also be a computer that is only used for processing print jobs and is connected to several high-speed laser printers.

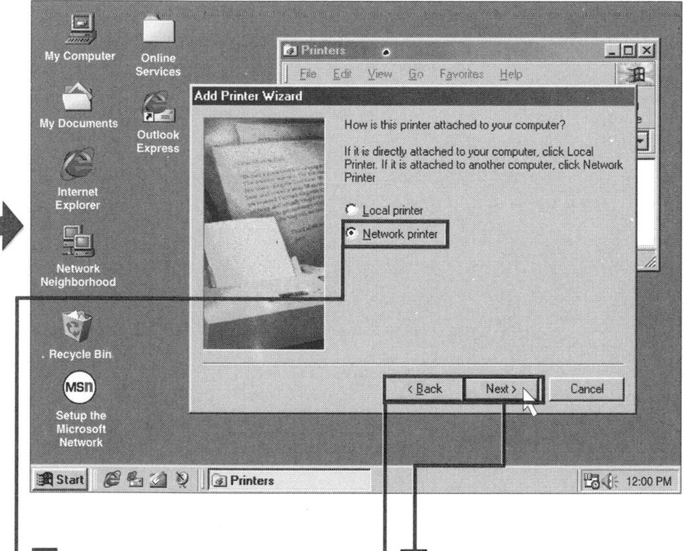

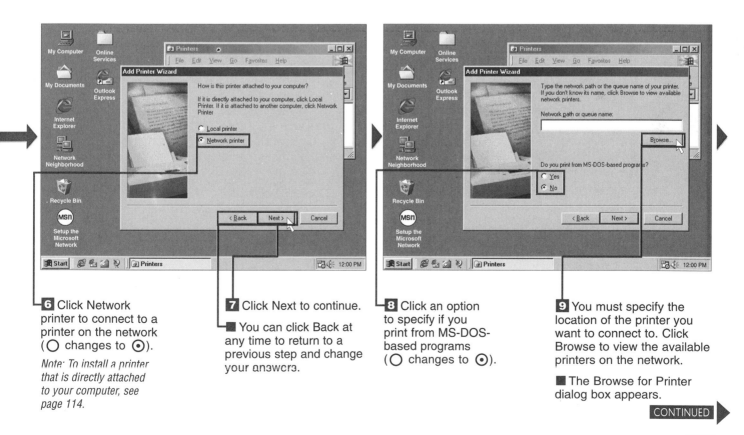

6 Click Network printer to connect to a printer on the network (○ changes to ⊙).

Note: To install a printer that is directly attached to your computer, see page 114.

7 Click Next to continue.

■ You can click Back at any time to return to a previous step and change your answers.

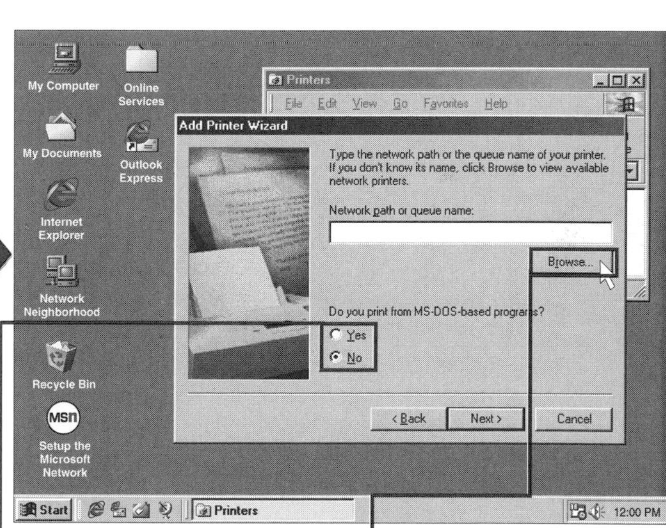

8 Click an option to specify if you print from MS-DOS-based programs (○ changes to ⊙).

9 You must specify the location of the printer you want to connect to. Click Browse to view the available printers on the network.

■ The Browse for Printer dialog box appears.

CONTINUED

CONNECT TO A SHARED PRINTER CONTINUED

When you print a file, the printer must be able to understand the commands your computer is using. A print driver is software that allows Windows to communicate with and send print jobs to a printer. Windows sends the printing instructions to the print driver. The print driver translates the instructions into a format that the printer understands.

Windows includes most of the popular print drivers. If Windows does not have the print driver for your printer, you can obtain the driver from the manufacturer of the printer. You should use the most up-to-date driver you can find for the printer.

When connecting to a shared printer, you can print a test page to confirm everything is working properly. The page contains information about the printer.

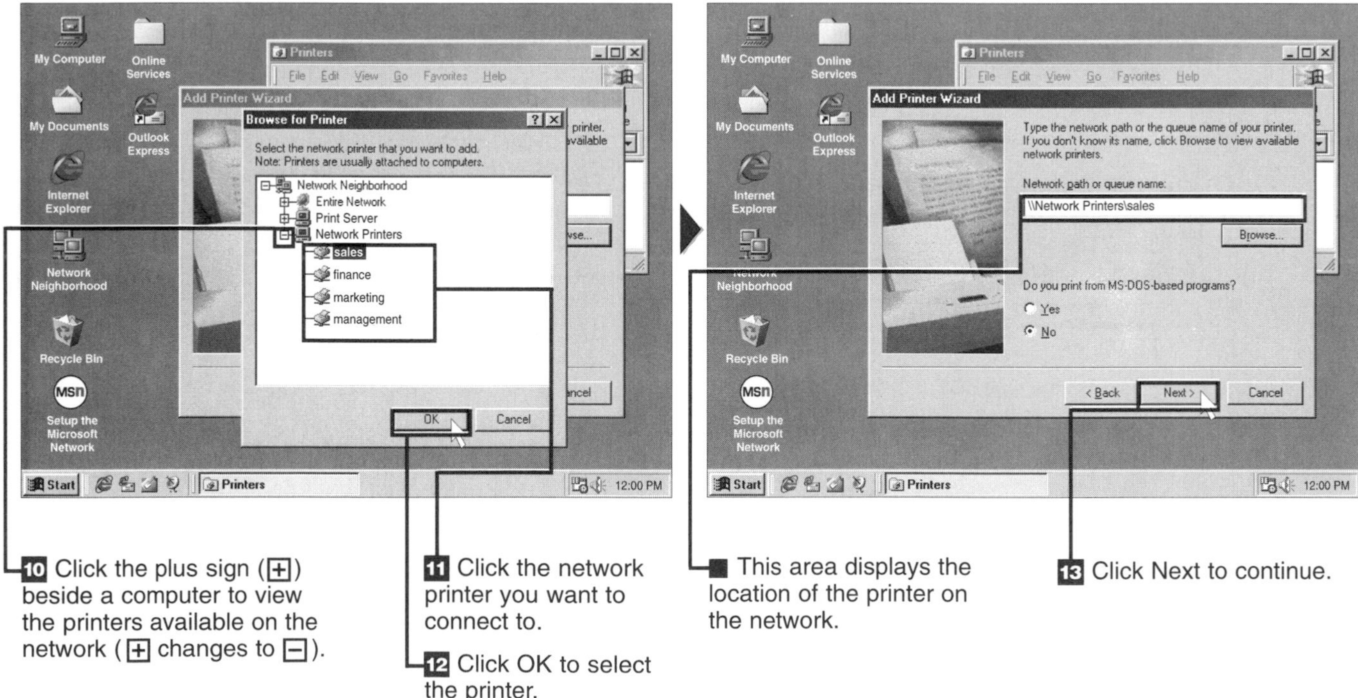

10 Click the plus sign (⊞) beside a computer to view the printers available on the network (⊞ changes to ⊟).

11 Click the network printer you want to connect to.

12 Click OK to select the printer.

■ This area displays the location of the printer on the network.

13 Click Next to continue.

TIPS

Why am I unable to find the printer I want to connect to?

If you want to connect to a printer that is directly connected to the network, you may need to install a network service before you can access the printer. You should check with your system administrator for more information.

Can I connect to more than one network printer?

Windows lets you send print jobs to any shared printer connected to a network, but you can have only one default printer. Windows sends all print jobs to the default printer unless you specify a different printer.

Why does the printer take a long time to print my files?

Most printers on a network are used by many people and may be used to print large print jobs. These factors may be slowing down the printing of your work.

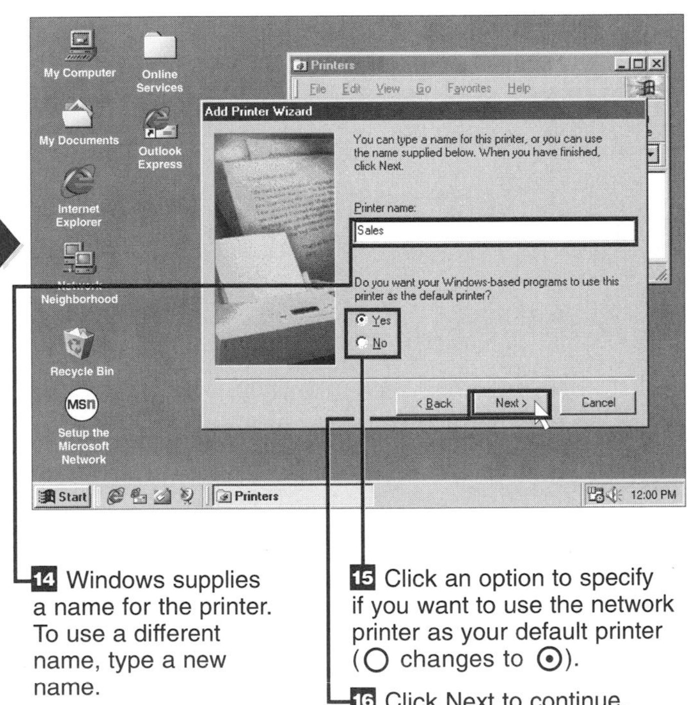

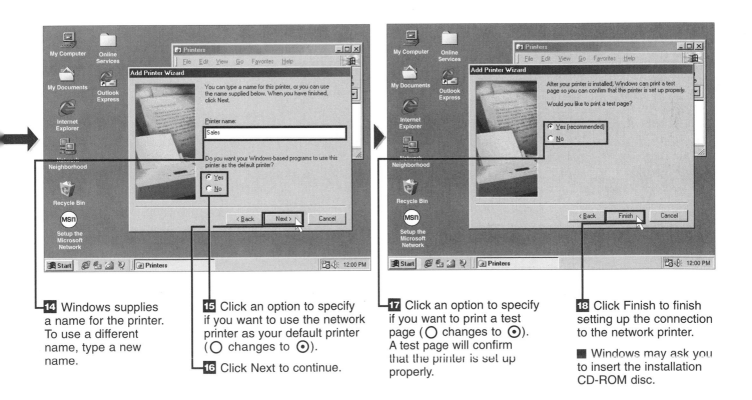

14 Windows supplies a name for the printer. To use a different name, type a new name.

15 Click an option to specify if you want to use the network printer as your default printer (○ changes to ⊙).

16 Click Next to continue.

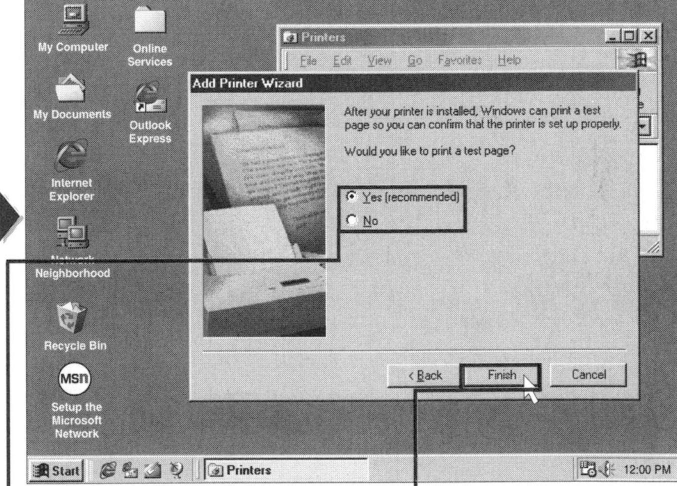

17 Click an option to specify if you want to print a test page (○ changes to ⊙). A test page will confirm that the printer is set up properly.

18 Click Finish to finish setting up the connection to the network printer.

■ Windows may ask you to insert the installation CD-ROM disc.

TURN ON USER-LEVEL ACCESS CONTROL

You can specify which people on a network can have access to your shared resources. Resources you share can include information such as files and folders or devices such as a printer.

There are two ways you can control access to your shared resources–share-level access and user-level access.

Share-level access control allows you to assign a password to each resource and give the password to specific people. Using share-level access control is suitable for small networks but can be unmanageable when there are many people who want to access your shared resources.

User-level access control offers enhanced security on large networks with dedicated servers. The server controls who can access the network and stores a list of people on the network.

You can use the list to determine who you want to be able to access your resources. You can grant access to specific individuals or entire workgroups. The people you select do not need to use a password to access resources you shared.

Contact your network administrator to find out if your network offers user-level access control.

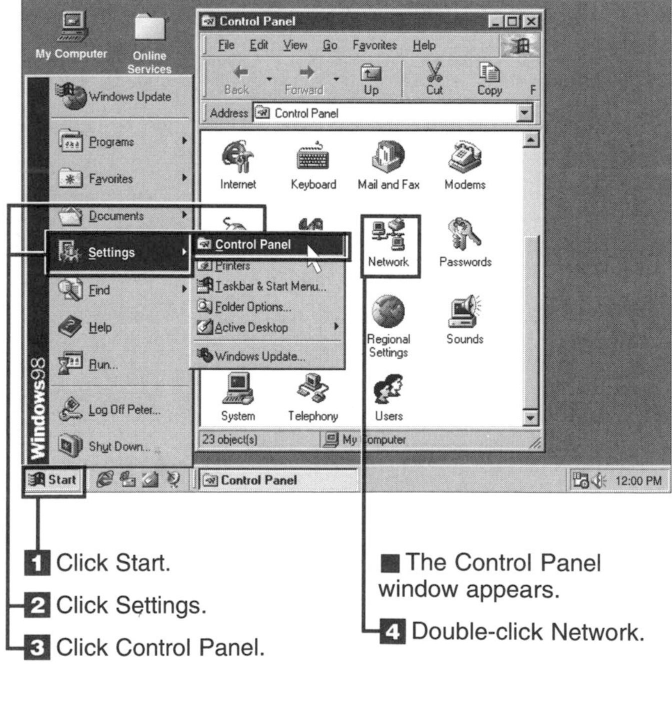

1 Click Start.

2 Click Settings.

3 Click Control Panel.

■ The Control Panel window appears.

4 Double-click Network.

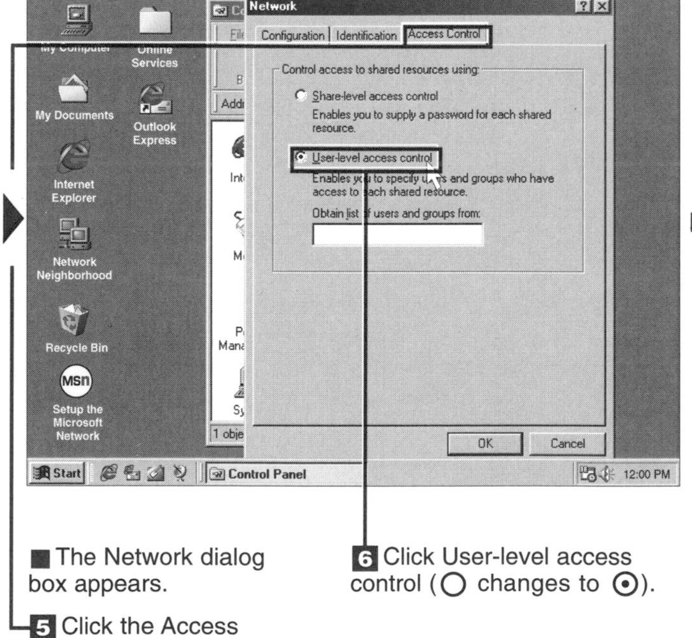

■ The Network dialog box appears.

5 Click the Access Control tab.

6 Click User-level access control (○ changes to ⦿).

TIPS

What is the name of the network that stores the list of users?

Every network has its own unique name. You will need to know the name of your network before you can turn on user-level access control. If you do not know the name, you should contact your system administrator.

What will happen to resources I have already shared after I turn on user-level access control?

When you turn on user-level access control, all the resources that you previously shared will no longer be shared. To continue sharing, you will have to assign access rights for each folder and device you want to share. To assign access rights to your resources, see page 470.

How is the list of users created?

Each large network has a computer that controls who can log on to and use the resources on the network. This computer is called the domain controller. The domain controller maintains a list of all the users on a network. Before someone can access your shared resources, the domain controller checks this list to see if the person is allowed access.

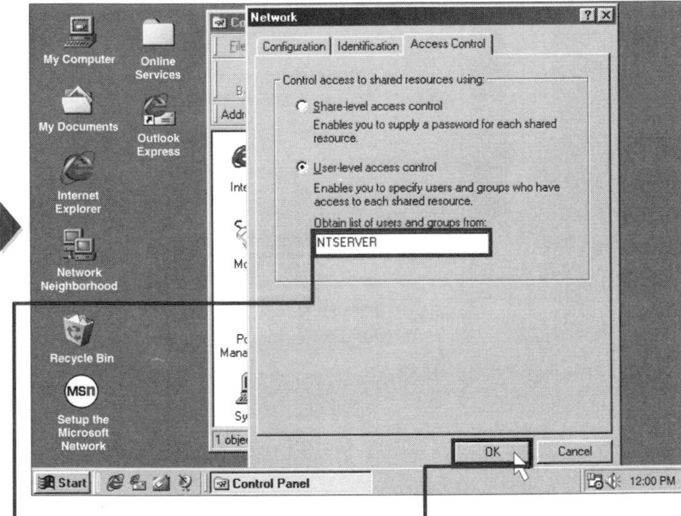

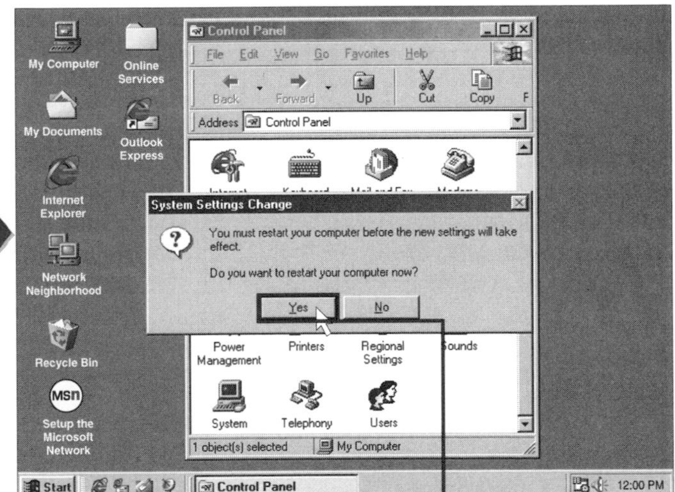

7 Click this area and then type the name of the network or computer that stores the list of users.

Note: The name of the network or computer may already appear in the area.

8 Click OK.

■ A dialog box may appear, telling you that any folders you shared will no longer be shared. Click Yes to continue.

■ The System Settings Change dialog box appears, telling you Windows needs to restart your computer before the new settings will take effect.

9 Click Yes to restart your computer.

ASSIGN ACCESS RIGHTS TO INFORMATION

You can assign access rights to information stored on your computer. Assigning access rights allows you to specify who you want to be able to access your resources and the type of access you want to give. You can change access rights at any time so that only certain people on a network can access and use your resources.

You must be using a client/server network to assign access rights for other people on the network. A client/server network has a central computer, called a server, controlling who may access the network. Windows NT and Novell NetWare networks are popular examples of client/server networks.

The server stores a list of every person on the network. You use this list to determine who you want to be able to access your resources.

You can assign access rights for individuals on the network or every person in a workgroup. A workgroup is a group of computers on a network that frequently share information.

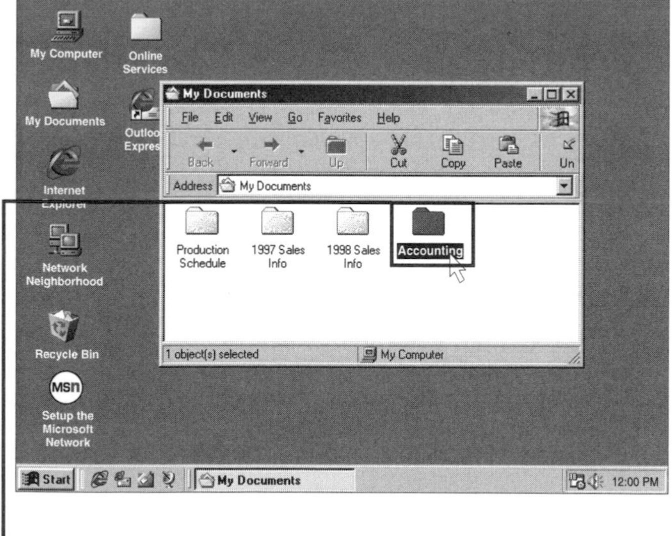

1 Click the folder or drive you want to share.

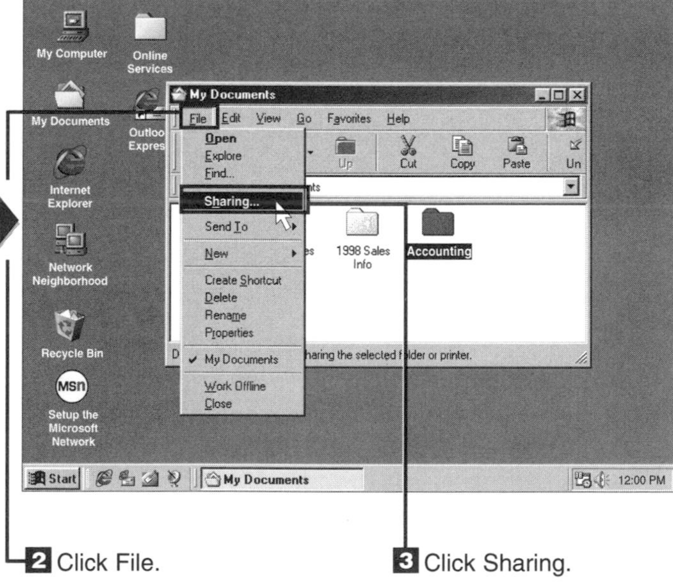

2 Click File.

3 Click Sharing.

■ The Properties dialog box appears.

TIPS

What must I do before I can assign access rights to information on my computer?

Before you can assign access rights for people on your network, you must turn on user-level access control. See page 468.

Which folders and drives on my computer are shared?

In the Network Neighborhood window, double-click your computer to view a list of items on your computer that are shared. You can also use the My Computer or Windows Explorer window to determine which folders and drives on your computer are shared. A hand () appears under the icon for a shared folder or drive.

How do I stop sharing a folder?

When you no longer want to give people on the network access to a folder, perform steps 1 to 3 below. Then select Not Shared in step 4.

How can I view the comments for shared folders on a network?

In the Network Neighborhood window, you can view the comments entered for shared folders. Click View and then click Details to display information about each shared folder.

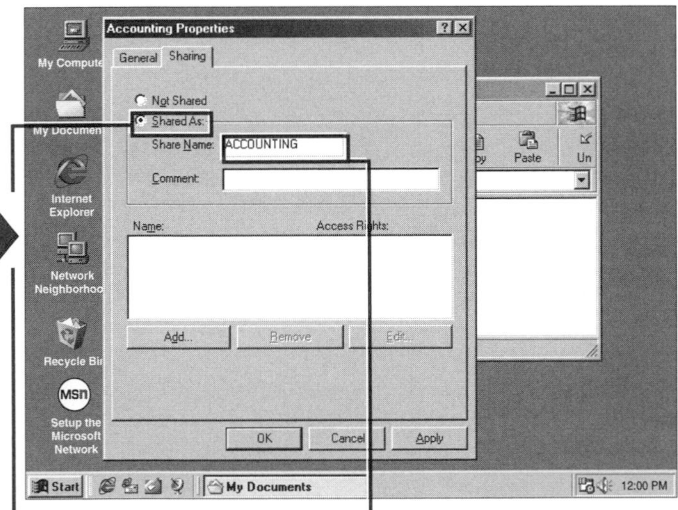

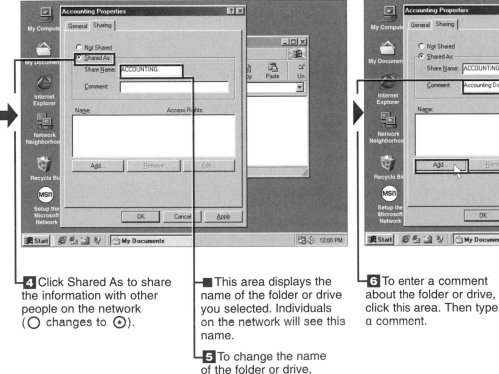

4 Click Shared As to share the information with other people on the network (○ changes to ⊙).

■ This area displays the name of the folder or drive you selected. Individuals on the network will see this name.

5 To change the name of the folder or drive, double-click this area and then type a new name.

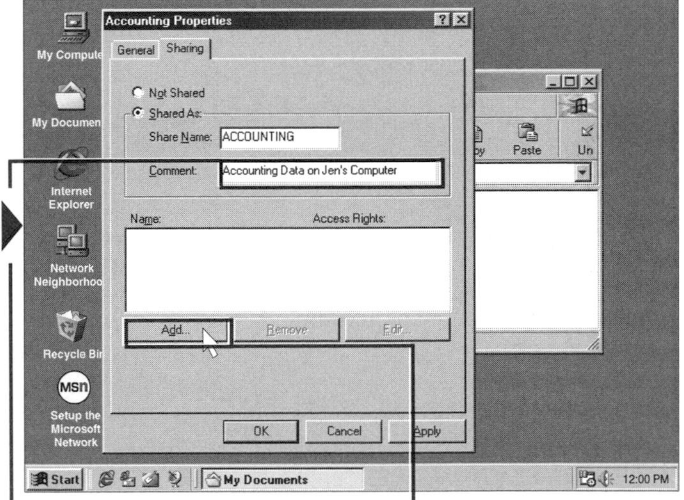

6 To enter a comment about the folder or drive, click this area. Then type a comment.

7 Click Add to specify which people on the network can access the information.

CONTINUED

ASSIGN ACCESS RIGHTS TO INFORMATION CONTINUED

Windows allows you to specify every person and workgroup on the network who you want to be able to access your resources. You can select a person, a workgroup or several people and workgroups all at once.

When assigning access rights for information on your computer, you can choose the type of access you want to assign.

Read-only access allows a person or workgroup to only read the information in a folder. People cannot change the information on your computer, but they can copy the information to their own computers and then change the information.

Full access gives a person or workgroup total control over the information in a folder. Assigning full access rights to information on a computer is very rare because people on the network will be able to change or even delete the information.

There are also several custom access rights you can assign to people on your network. Assigning custom access rights gives you more control over the type of access people have to your resources.

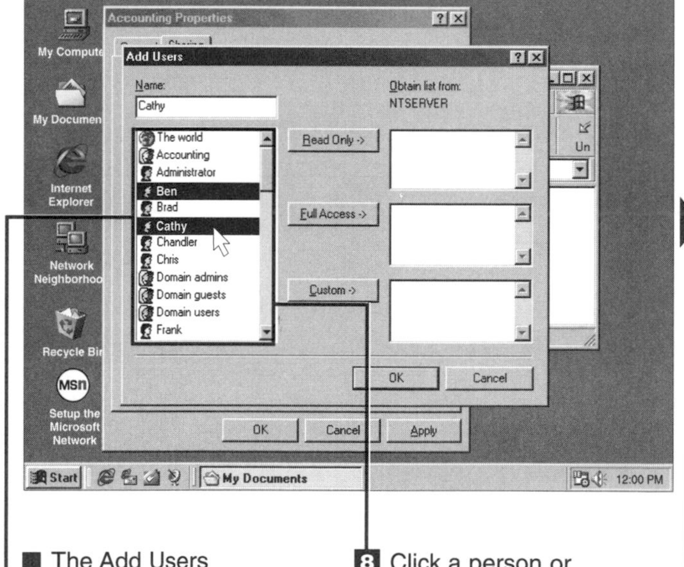

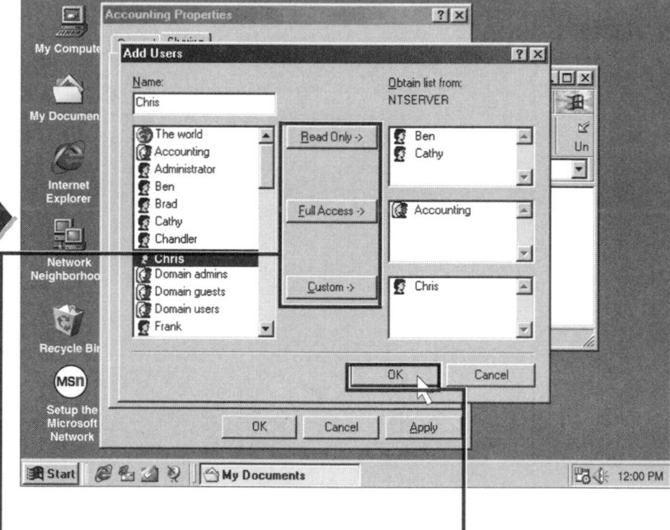

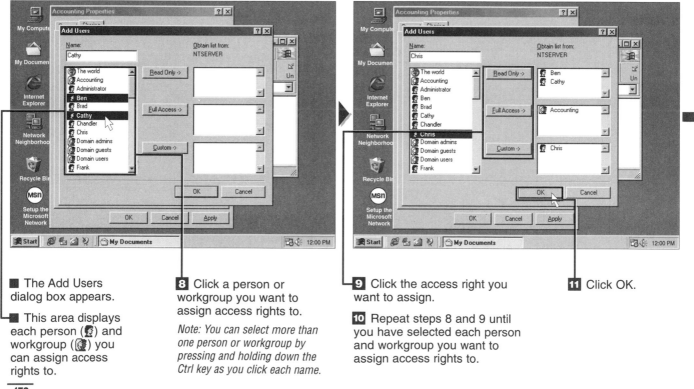

■ The Add Users dialog box appears.

■ This area displays each person (👤) and workgroup (👥) you can assign access rights to.

8 Click a person or workgroup you want to assign access rights to.

Note: You can select more than one person or workgroup by pressing and holding down the Ctrl key as you click each name.

9 Click the access right you want to assign.

10 Repeat steps 8 and 9 until you have selected each person and workgroup you want to assign access rights to.

11 Click OK.

TIPS 

What types of custom access rights can I assign?

Read Files access lets people only read the files in the shared folder. The files cannot be changed.

Write to Files access allows people to make changes to the files in the shared folder.

Create Files and Folders access allows people to create new files and folders in the shared folder.

Delete Files access lets people delete the files from the shared folder. This is a powerful right and should only be given to people you trust.

Change File Attributes access allows people to change the properties of files in the shared folder, such as making a file read-only.

List Files access allows people to view a list of the files in the shared folder.

Change Access Control access lets people change the access rights for the shared folder.

How do I change the access rights I assigned?

Right-click the shared folder or drive and then click the Properties command. On the Sharing tab, click the person or workgroup whose rights you want to change. To assign different access rights, click the Edit button and then select the rights you want. To remove all access rights for the person or workgroup, click the Remove button. A red X appears over the icon for the person or workgroup.

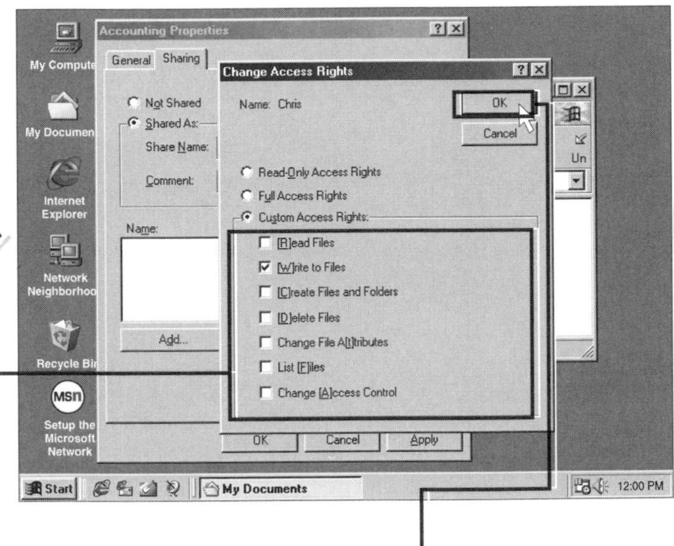

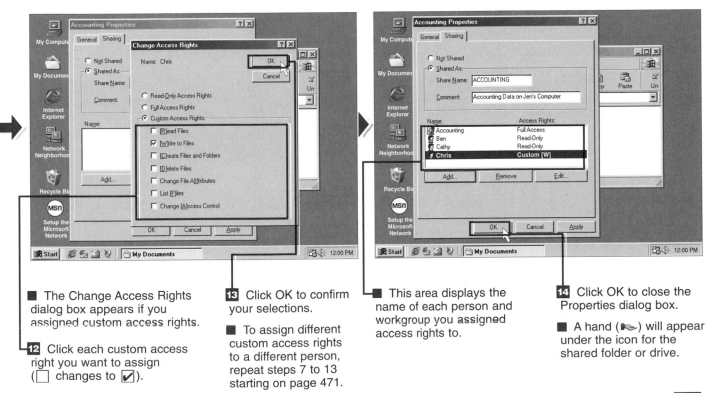

■ The Change Access Rights dialog box appears if you assigned custom access rights.

12 Click each custom access right you want to assign (☐ changes to ☑).

13 Click OK to confirm your selections.

■ To assign different custom access rights to a different person, repeat steps 7 to 13 starting on page 471.

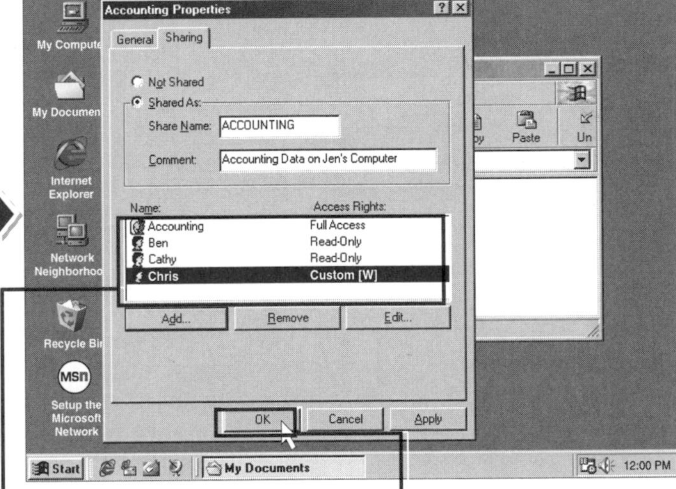

■ This area displays the name of each person and workgroup you assigned access rights to.

14 Click OK to close the Properties dialog box.

■ A hand (hand icon) will appear under the icon for the shared folder or drive.

INSTALL A NETWORK INTERFACE CARD

You can install a Network Interface Card (NIC) on your computer. A network interface card physically connects your computer to a network and controls the flow of information between your computer and the network.

The Add New Hardware Wizard helps you correctly install the network interface card. The wizard will install the necessary software for the card, called a driver. A driver helps the network interface card communicate with your computer.

The type of network interface card you need depends on the type of network you are connected to. You should use a Plug and Play network interface card if possible. A Plug and Play card uses technology that allows Windows to automatically detect and set up the card. When you install a network interface card that is not Plug and Play compatible, the hardware settings Windows suggests for the card and the settings the card actually uses may not be compatible.

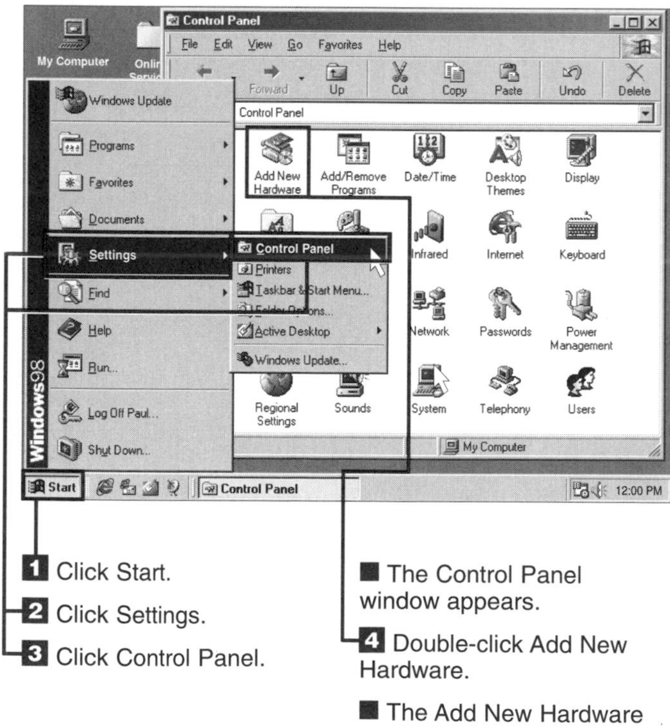

1 Click Start.

2 Click Settings.

3 Click Control Panel.

■ The Control Panel window appears.

4 Double-click Add New Hardware.

■ The Add New Hardware Wizard appears.

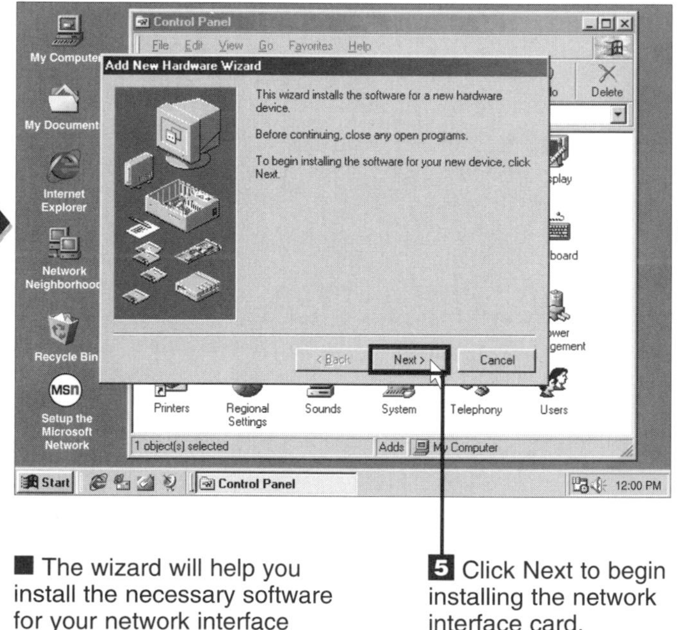

■ The wizard will help you install the necessary software for your network interface card. Make sure you close any open programs before you continue.

5 Click Next to begin installing the network interface card.

TIPS

My network interface card is already set up on my computer. How did this happen?

If the network interface card was in your computer when you installed Windows 98, Windows may have automatically detected and set up the card for you.

Will Windows ever automatically install a Plug and Play network interface card without using the wizard?

Yes. If you add a Plug and Play network interface card to your computer, Windows will usually recognize and set up the card as soon as you turn on your computer.

Can I install a network interface card in my laptop computer?

Laptop computers require a specialized device to connect to a network. Some older laptops use a device that connects the laptop through the computer's printer port, called the LPT port. Today, most laptop computers have a socket that lets you insert a PC card to connect to the network.

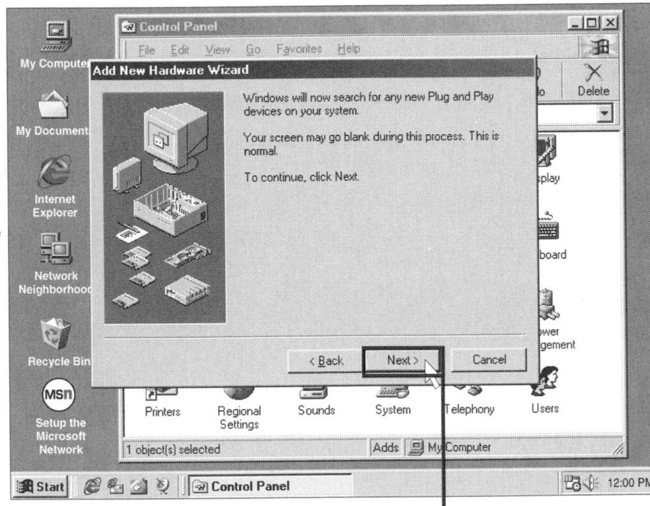

■ Windows will search your computer for new Plug and Play devices. Your screen may go blank during the search.

6 Click Next to search for Plug and Play devices.

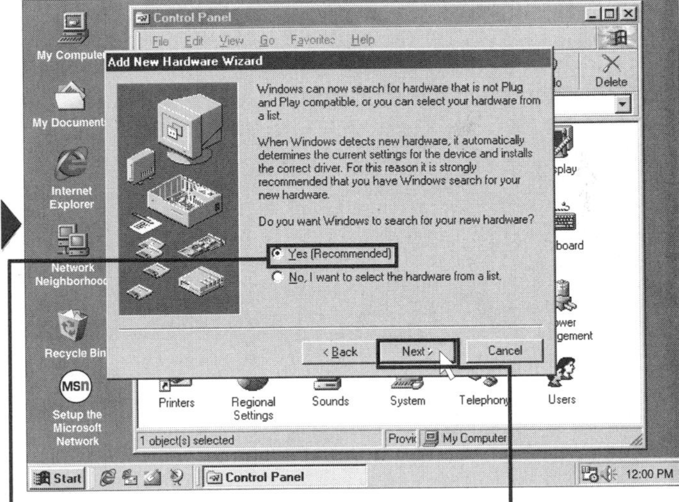

■ You can have Windows search your computer for devices that are not Plug and Play compatible.

7 Click Yes to have Windows search for the network interface card (○ changes to ⊙). Windows will automatically determine the settings for the interface card and install the necessary software.

8 Click Next to continue.

CONTINUED

INSTALL A NETWORK INTERFACE CARD CONTINUED

When installing a network interface card, you can have Windows search your computer for a card that is not Plug and Play compatible. The search may take up to 10 minutes. If the search stops, you should restart your computer and try installing the card again. If the search stops a second time, there may be a problem with the network interface card or the hardware settings used by the card may not work with your computer.

When the search is complete, Windows displays the hardware settings for the network interface card. If you installed a card that is not Plug and Play compatible, you should confirm that these settings are correct. If your network interface card is not set up to use the settings Windows displays, you may need to physically adjust the settings on the card. Most manufacturers of network interface cards supply a program that allows you to view and change the settings for a card. You should consult the manual that came with the network interface card before changing any settings.

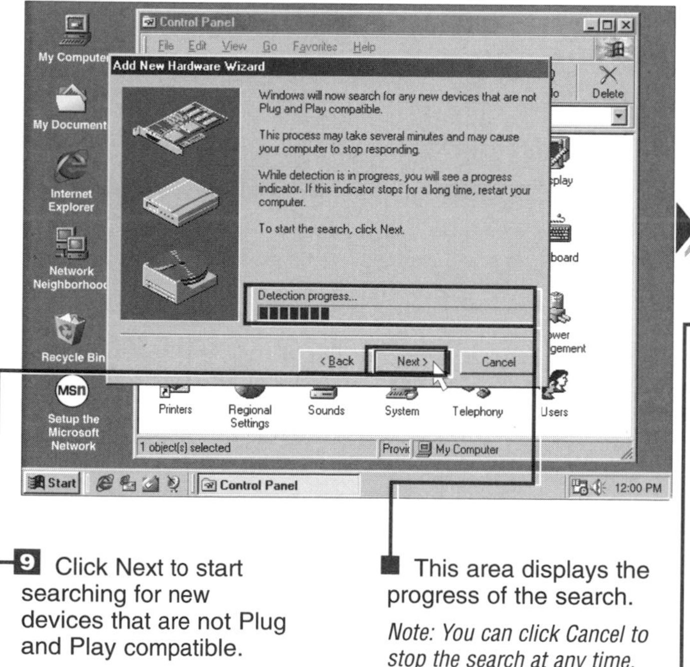

9 Click Next to start searching for new devices that are not Plug and Play compatible.

■ The search may take several minutes.

■ This area displays the progress of the search.

Note: You can click Cancel to stop the search at any time.

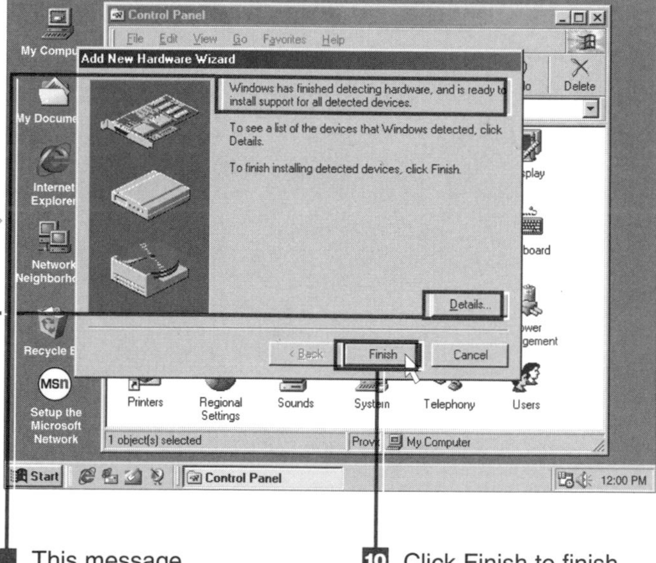

■ This message appears when Windows has finished searching for the new devices.

■ You can click Details to see a list of devices that Windows found.

10 Click Finish to finish installing the network interface card.

Note: If more than one device was detected, a window may appear, listing the devices. Select the device you want to use and then click Next.

TIPS

Why do I need to enter my computer name and workgroup name?

Windows may ask you to enter your computer name and workgroup name if this information was not previously entered on your computer. If you do not know this information, ask your system administrator.

I installed the network interface card, but now my modem does not work. What happened?

If the hardware settings for the network interface card and the modem are the same, a conflict will occur and the devices will not operate properly. Use the Device Manager to examine the settings for the devices so you can resolve the conflict. See page 642.

What should I do if Windows does not detect my network interface card?

If Windows does not detect your network interface card, you will have to install the card manually. Perform steps 1 to 8 starting on page 474, selecting No in step 7. Select Network adapters from the list of hardware types and then click Next. Select the manufacturer and model of the card and then click Next. If the manufacturer or model is not listed, click the Have Disk button and then insert the disk that came with the card into the drive. Follow the instructions on your screen to finish manually installing the card.

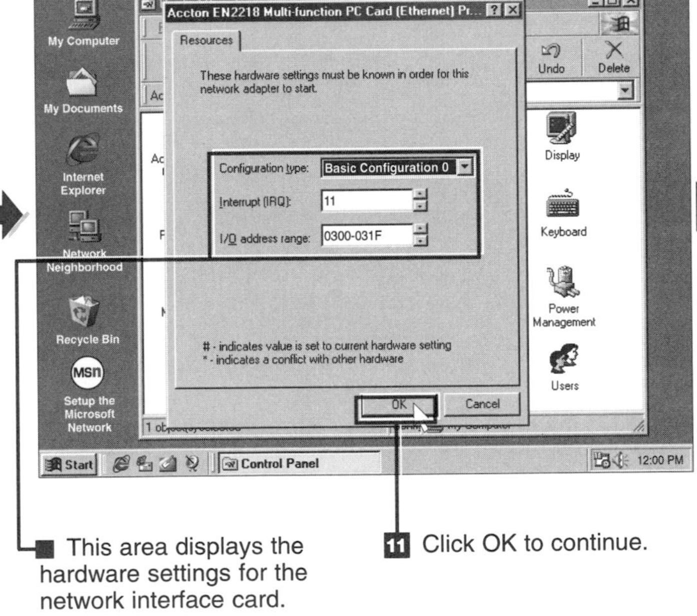

■ This area displays the hardware settings for the network interface card.

11 Click OK to continue.

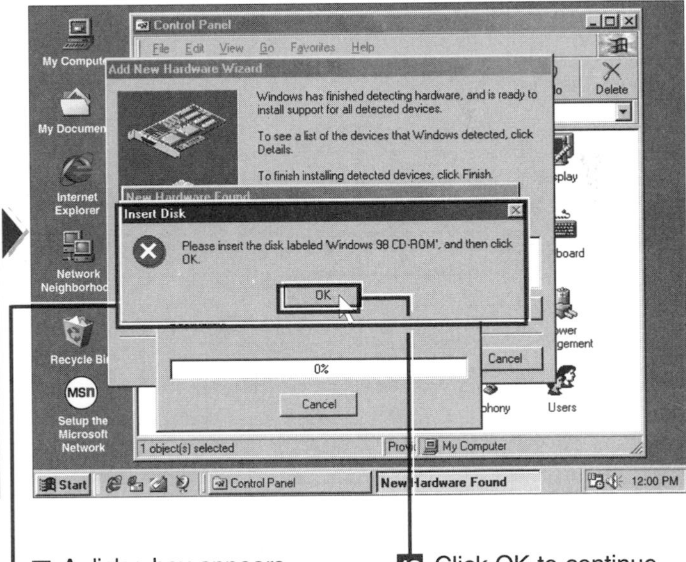

■ A dialog box appears, asking you to insert the Windows 98 CD-ROM disc.

12 Insert the CD-ROM disc into a drive.

13 Click OK to continue.

■ A dialog box will appear, asking you to restart your computer. Click Yes to restart your computer.

INSTALL A NETWORK PROTOCOL

You can install a network protocol to allow your computer to exchange information with other computers and devices on a network. A protocol is a language, or a set of rules, that determines how two computers communicate with each other. A network protocol determines how information transfers from one computer to another on a network.

All computers and devices on a network must use the same protocol before they can communicate with each other. For example, a computer and a network printer must use the same protocol for the computer to successfully send print jobs to the printer.

Many network protocols are designed specifically for use with one type of network. The type of protocol you must install is often determined by the type of network you want to connect to. For example, the protocol you need to connect to a Novell network is different than the protocol you need to connect to the Internet.

When you install Windows, some network protocols will automatically be installed if your computer has a network interface card.

Windows includes support for the most popular types of network protocols, including IPX/SPX, NetBEUI and TCP/IP.

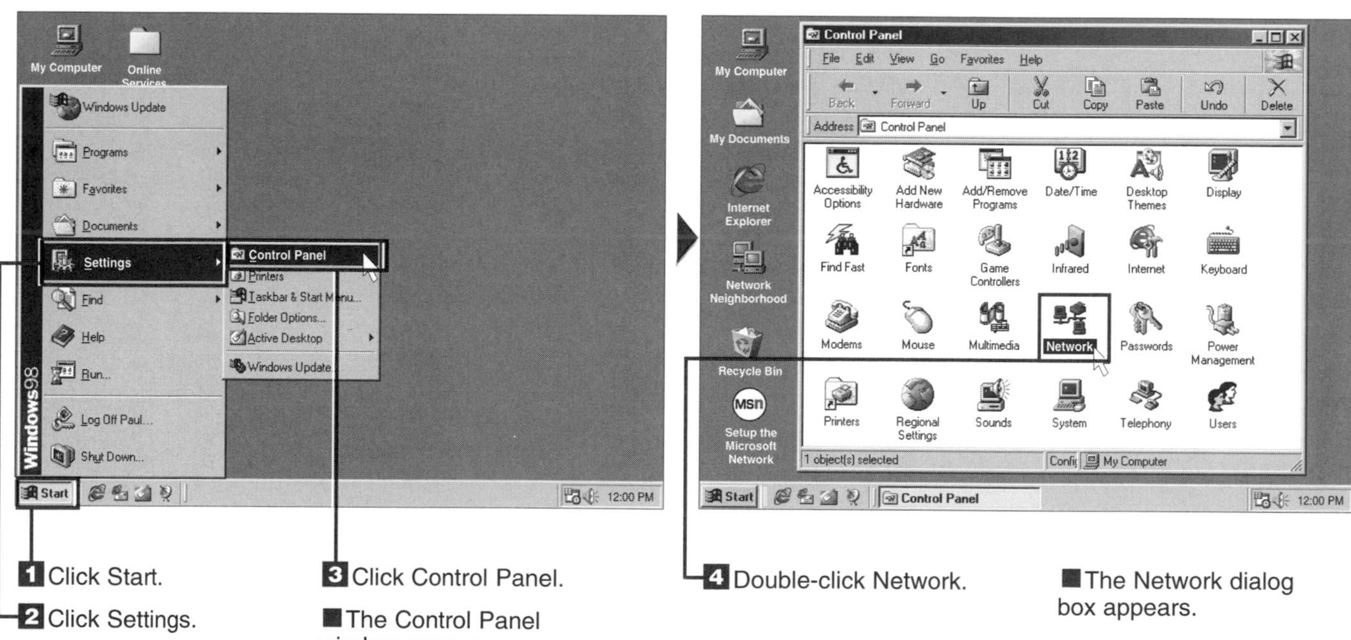

1 Click Start.

2 Click Settings.

3 Click Control Panel.

■ The Control Panel window appears.

4 Double-click Network.

■ The Network dialog box appears.

TIPS

What are the most important features of a protocol?

With error control, a protocol can check for errors in information transferred by a computer on a network. Some protocols try to correct errors by asking the computer to send the information again.

The addressing feature lets a protocol determine where information is to be sent. The addressing feature also makes sure that the information arrives at its intended destination.

Flow control helps regulate the flow of information so slower devices can process information they receive from faster devices on the network.

When do I need to install a network protocol?

If you want to exchange information over the Internet or on a network, you may need to install a protocol. You may also need to install a protocol when the type of network you connect to changes or is upgraded.

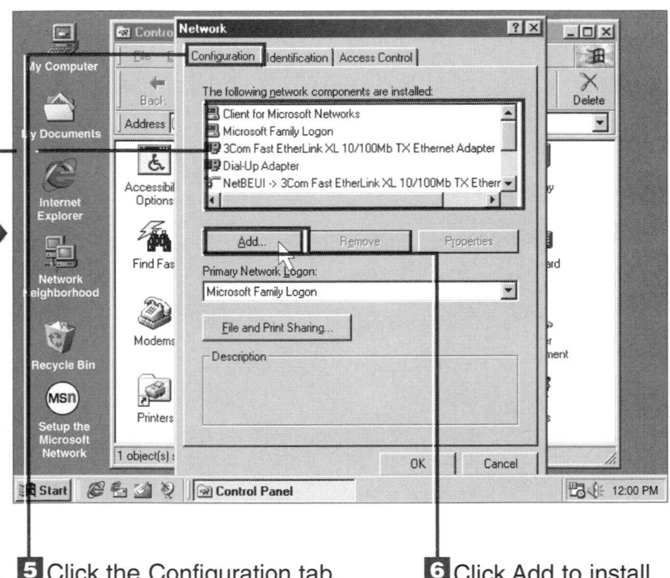

5 Click the Configuration tab.

■ This area lists the network components installed on your computer. Protocols display a cable symbol ( ).

6 Click Add to install a network protocol.

■ The Select Network Component Type dialog box appears.

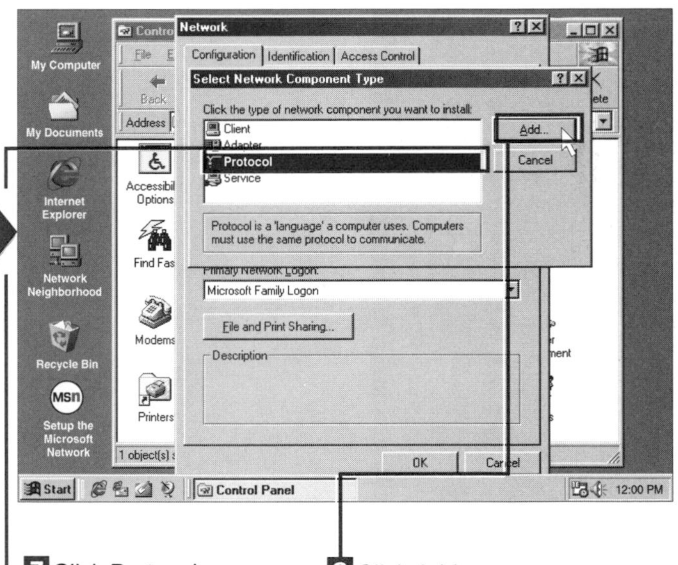

7 Click Protocol.

8 Click Add.

■ The Select Network Protocol dialog box appears.

CONTINUED

INSTALL A NETWORK PROTOCOL
CONTINUED

When installing a network protocol, you must tell Windows the name of the manufacturer and the type of protocol you want to add.

There are many different types of network protocols you can add to a computer. A network can use several different types of protocols at the same time.

Any device that does not understand a protocol used by a computer on the network will simply ignore the information sent using that protocol.

Protocols may be used for specific tasks on a network. For example, the NetBEUI protocol may be used to control all the information transferred between computers on the network. The IPX/SPX protocol may be used to send documents to a network printer.

Windows includes software for the most popular protocols. You need to use your Windows CD-ROM disc to add a network protocol.

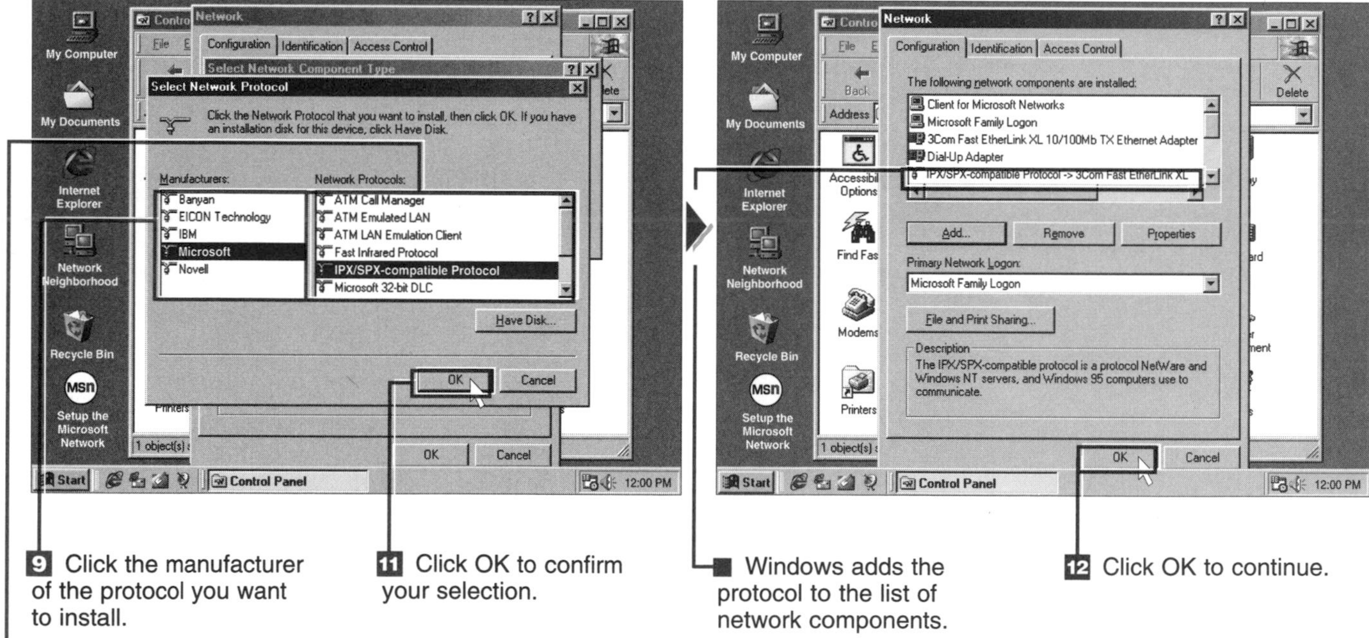

9 Click the manufacturer of the protocol you want to install.

10 Click the type of protocol you want to install.

11 Click OK to confirm your selection.

■ Windows adds the protocol to the list of network components.

12 Click OK to continue.

TIPS

Which network protocols should I install?

Internetwork Packet Exchange/ Sequenced Packet Exchange (IPX/SPX) is a popular network protocol used by Novell networks. Most network devices, such as printers, also use the IPX/SPX protocol.

If you are connecting to a Windows network, you can use the NetBIOS Extended User Interface (NetBEUI) protocol developed by IBM. This protocol is normally used only on small networks.

Transmission Control Protocol/Internet Protocol (TCP/IP) is the protocol needed to connect to the Internet.

What should I do if the network protocol I want to install does not appear in the list of protocols?

If you purchase a new network device that requires a protocol not supported by Windows, you may have to obtain the appropriate software from the manufacturer of the device. Perform steps 1 to 8 starting on page 478 and then click the Have Disk button in the Select Network Protocol dialog box to use the disk included with the device.

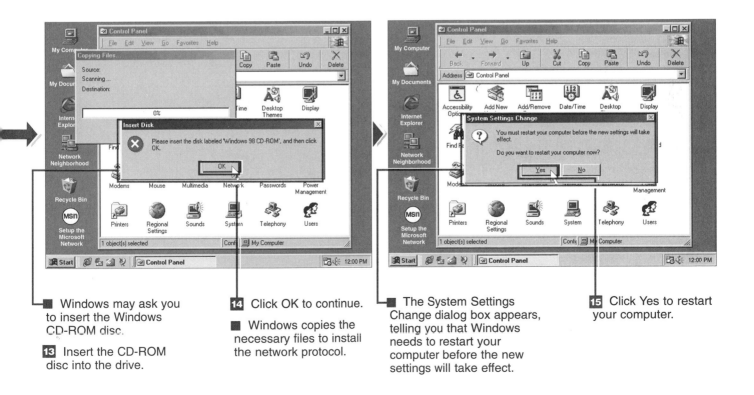

■ Windows may ask you to insert the Windows CD-ROM disc.

13 Insert the CD-ROM disc into the drive.

14 Click OK to continue.

■ Windows copies the necessary files to install the network protocol.

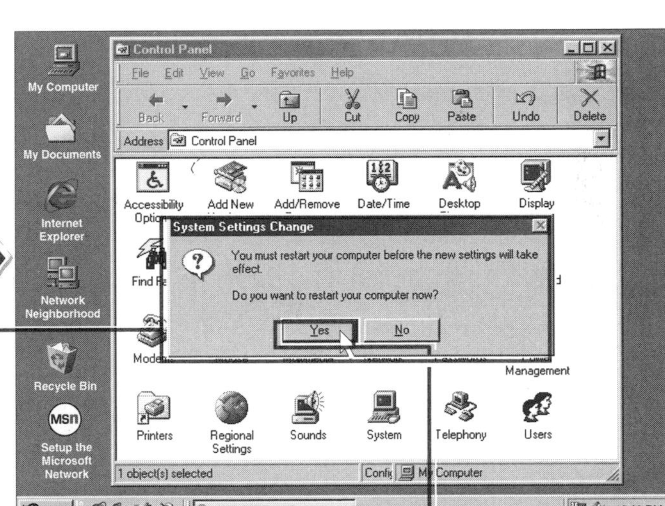

■ The System Settings Change dialog box appears, telling you that Windows needs to restart your computer before the new settings will take effect.

15 Click Yes to restart your computer.

INSTALL A NETWORK CLIENT

A network client is software that lets your computer communicate with other computers on a network. You install a network client to control the flow of information between your computer and other computers.

A network client helps to determine whether information stays on your computer or is sent to a device on the network. For example, when you send a document to a printer, the network client will determine if the document will print on a printer attached to your computer or will be sent to a printer on the network. A network client is often referred to as a redirector because the client determines where information is sent.

A network client also allows a computer using Windows 98 to communicate with a dedicated server on a network. A dedicated server is a computer that supplies information, such as files, to other computers on a network.

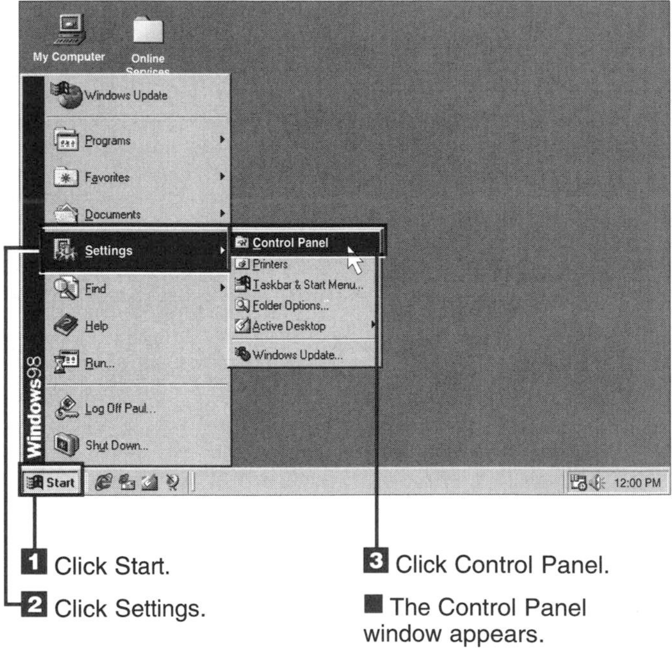

1 Click Start.

2 Click Settings.

3 Click Control Panel.

■ The Control Panel window appears.

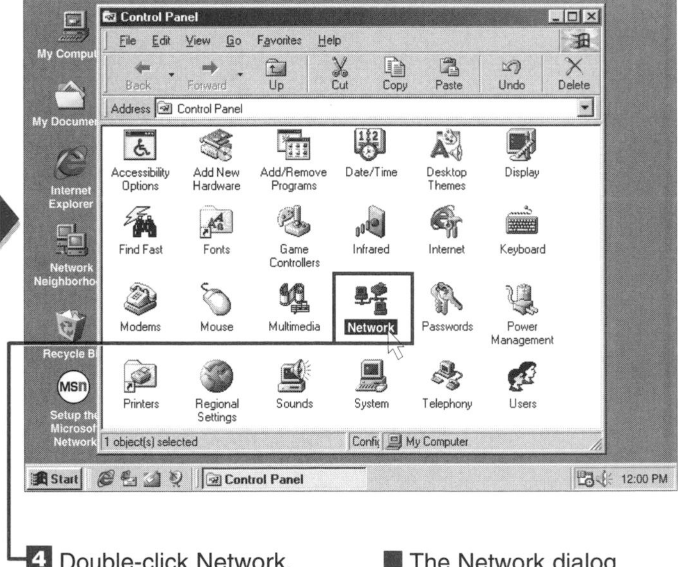

4 Double-click Network.

■ The Network dialog box appears.

TIPS

Why is there a network client already installed on my computer?

If your computer had a network interface card when you installed Windows, the Client for Microsoft Networks was installed automatically. This client lets you connect to networks using Windows NT and to other Windows 98 computers.

Will I ever have to update a network client?

You only need to update a network client when the type of network you connect to changes or is upgraded.

Can I install more than one network client?

Yes. Installing more than one network client allows you to use a wide variety of resources on the network. Many large networks now use more than one type of network to control different resources, such as servers and printers. You can specify a primary client to tell Windows which network client you use most often. See page 490.

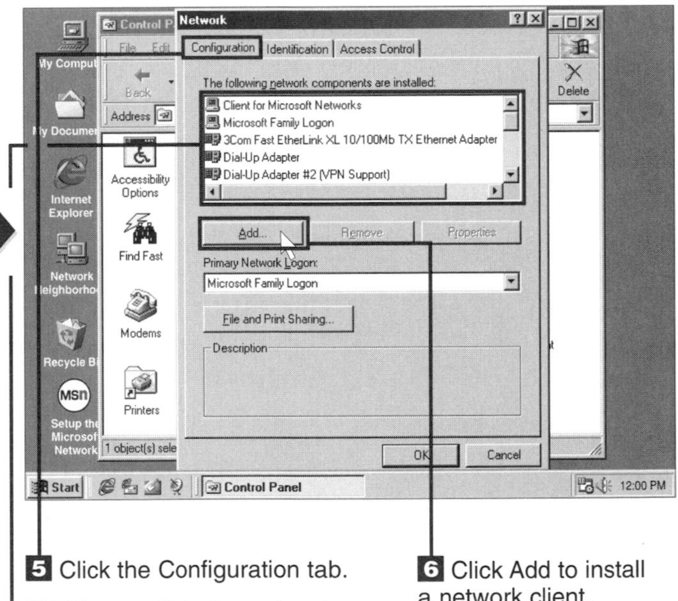

5 Click the Configuration tab.

■ This area lists the network components installed on your computer. Clients display a computer icon ( ).

6 Click Add to install a network client.

■ The Select Network Component Type dialog box appears.

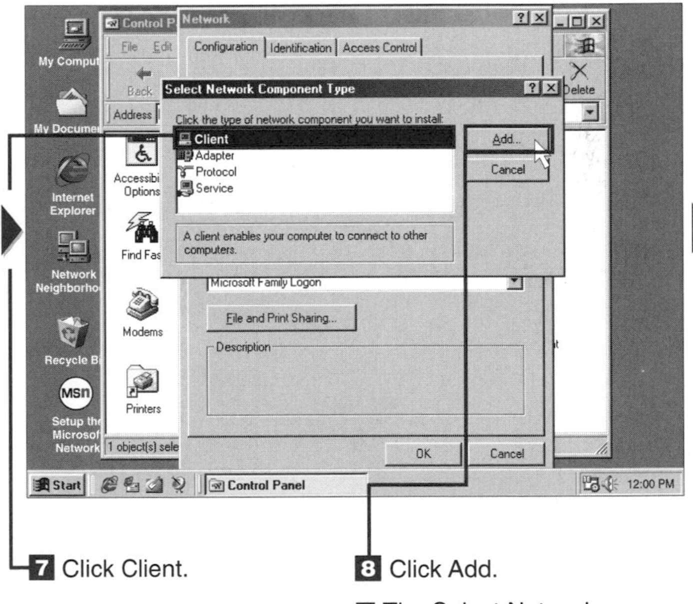

7 Click Client.

8 Click Add.

■ The Select Network Client dialog box appears.

CONTINUED

INSTALL A NETWORK CLIENT
CONTINUED

When installing a network client, you must tell Windows the manufacturer of the network client and the type of client you want to install.

The type of network you want to connect to determines the type of network client you need.

You should check with your system administrator to confirm that any new client software you wish to install will work with your current network.

Windows 98 includes client software for the most popular types of networks, including Microsoft and Novell. You may need to use your Windows 98 CD-ROM disc to install the client software.

After you have installed the network client for each type of network you want to connect to, you can access information and devices on the network.

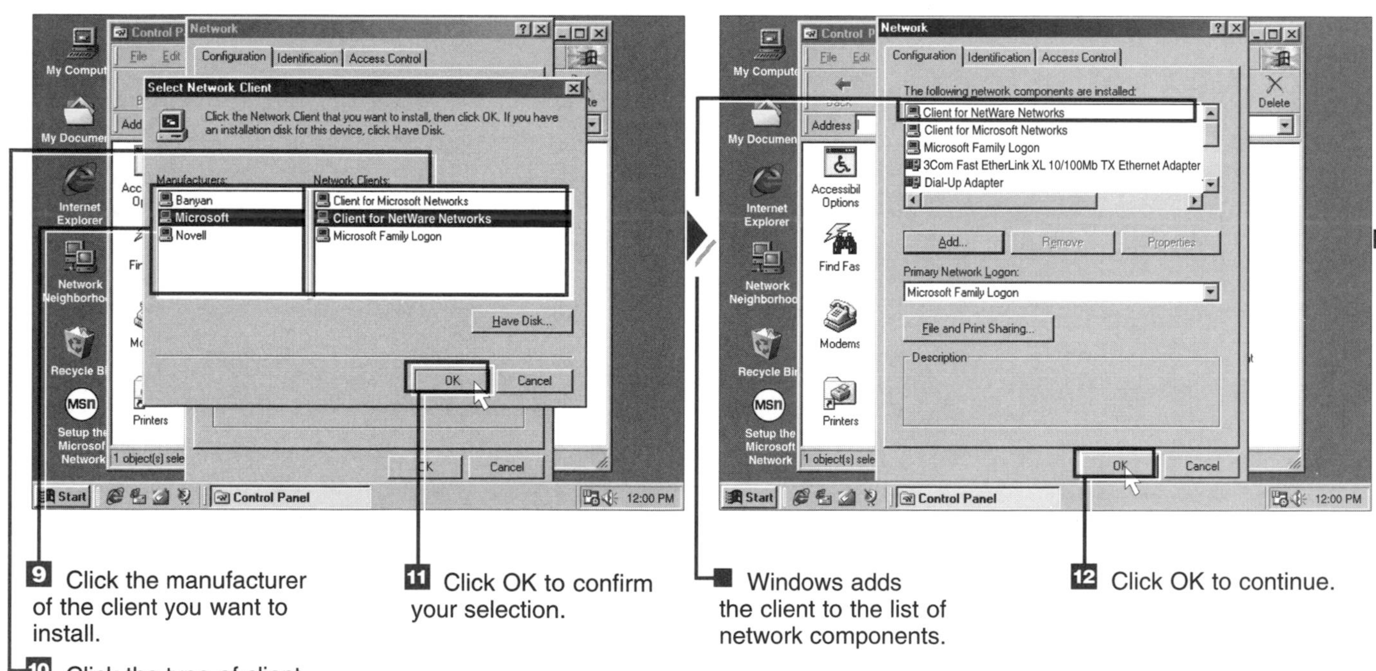

9 Click the manufacturer of the client you want to install.

10 Click the type of client you want to install.

11 Click OK to confirm your selection.

■ Windows adds the client to the list of network components.

12 Click OK to continue.

TIPS

Which network client should I install?

Windows includes several types of Novell NetWare clients. If you are connecting to a Novell NetWare network, you should contact your system administrator to find out which NetWare client to use.

If the network you want to connect to uses Windows NT, you should use the Client for Microsoft Networks.

Windows also includes network clients for Banyan Vines networks.

I have an installation disk for the client. Should I use the disk to install the client?

If the network client you want to install is newer than your version of Windows 98, you should use the network client installation disk to install the client. You can use the method described below to install the client, except use the Have Disk button in the Select Network Client dialog box to copy the files stored on the disk. Using the disk is safer if the information on the disk is more up-to-date than the information supplied by Windows.

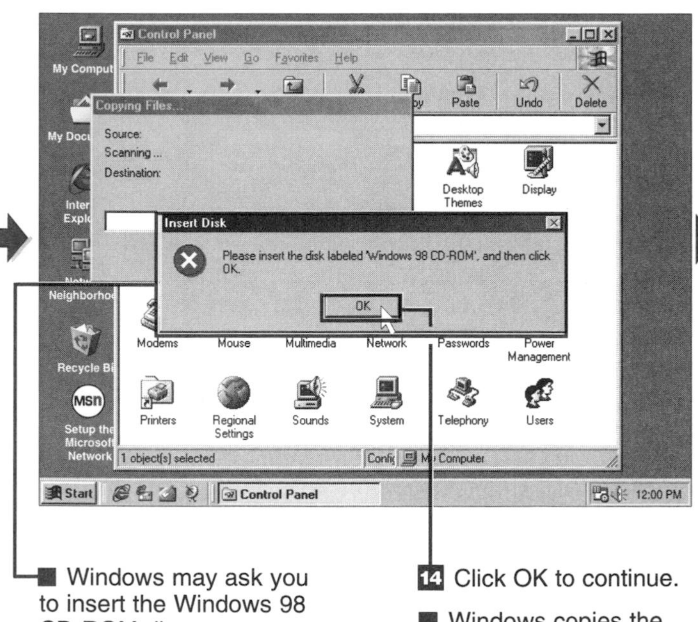

■ Windows may ask you to insert the Windows 98 CD-ROM disc.

13 Insert the CD-ROM disc into the drive.

14 Click OK to continue.

■ Windows copies the necessary files to install the network client.

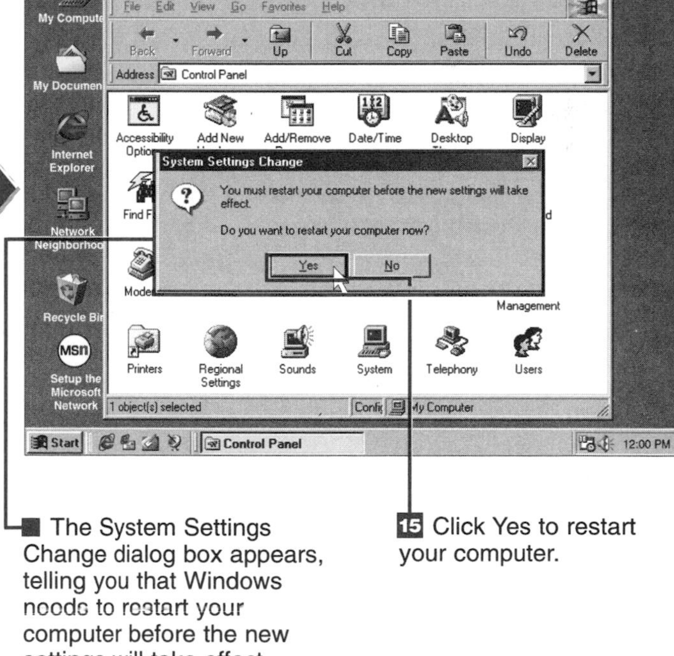

■ The System Settings Change dialog box appears, telling you that Windows needs to restart your computer before the new settings will take effect.

15 Click Yes to restart your computer.

CONFIGURE THE MICROSOFT CLIENT

After you install a network client for a Microsoft network, you can adjust the settings for the client to customize the way your computer connects to the network.

You can have Windows automatically connect to your Windows NT network each time you log on to Windows. You need to tell Windows the name of the server or domain you want to connect to. If you do not know the name of the server or domain, ask your system administrator.

Windows lets you choose between a quick and a regular logon to connect to your network.

Most computers that are always connected to a network use the regular logon option. If you plan to use only a few of the resources on the network, you may want to use the quick logon option.

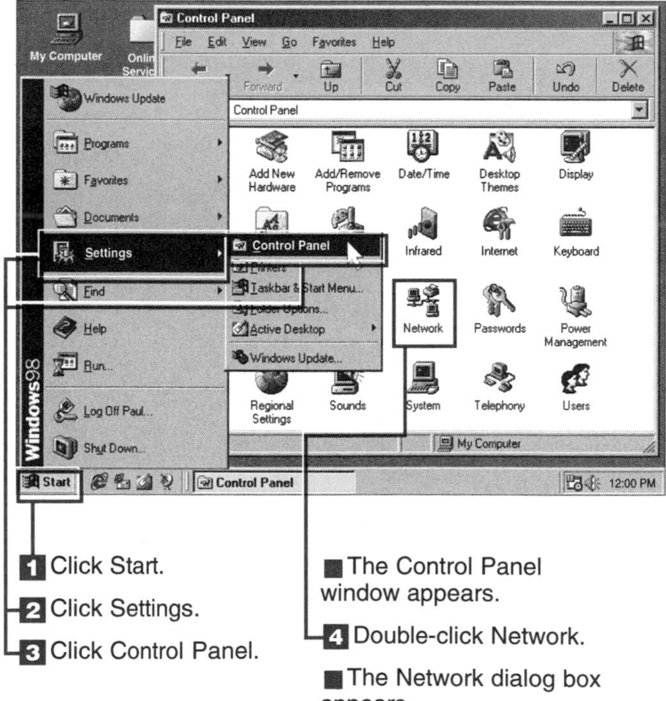

1 Click Start.

2 Click Settings.

3 Click Control Panel.

■ The Control Panel window appears.

4 Double-click Network.

■ The Network dialog box appears.

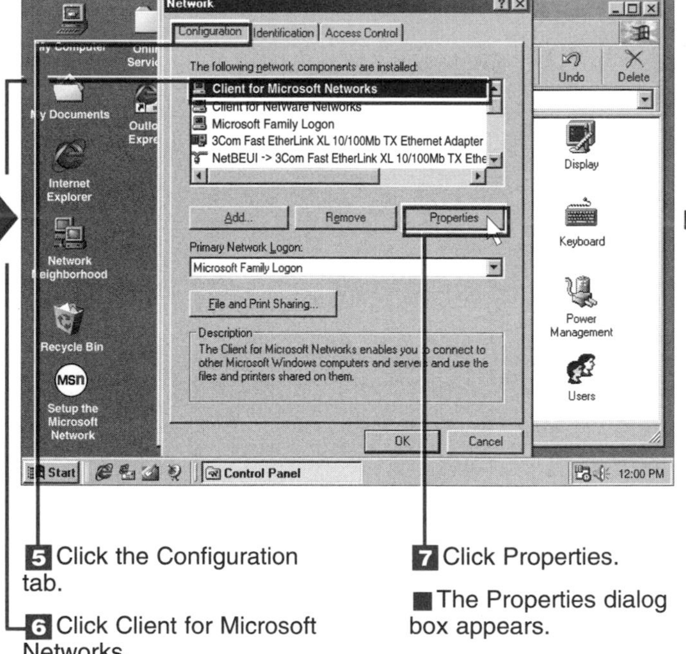

5 Click the Configuration tab.

6 Click Client for Microsoft Networks.

7 Click Properties.

■ The Properties dialog box appears.

TIPS

What is a domain?

A domain is a name given to a collection of related computers on a network. For example, a domain can consist of all computers in a particular department of a business. If a large network consists of many smaller networks connected together, each of the smaller networks is usually a different domain. You need to specify the name of the domain or server if you want Windows to automatically connect you to the network each time you start Windows.

What is the difference between a quick and a regular logon?

If you choose quick logon you will only be connected to resources on the network when you access them. The quick logon feature is useful if you do not plan to use all of the available resources every time you connect to the network. A regular logon connects you to each resource every time you start Windows. You will immediately know if each resource is available, but this option increases the time it takes to log on to the network.

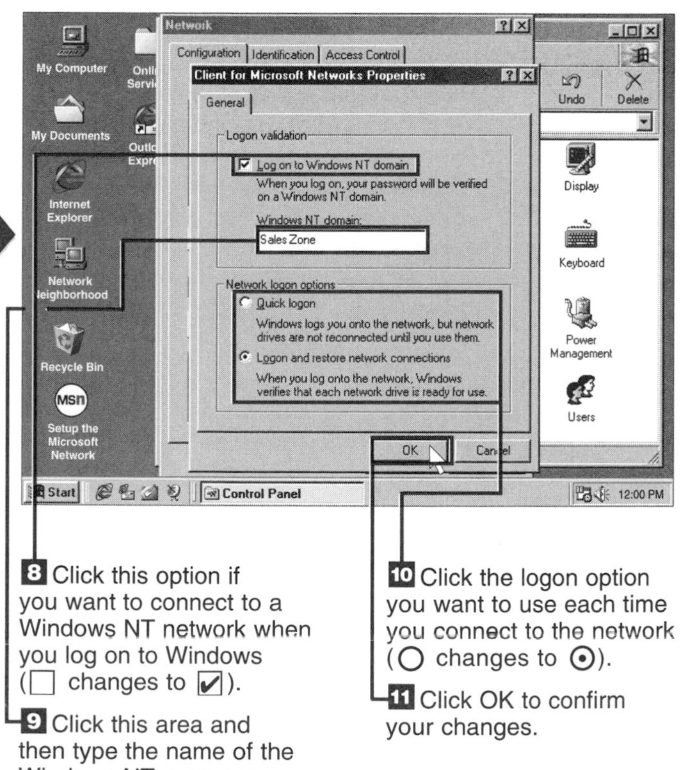

8 Click this option if you want to connect to a Windows NT network when you log on to Windows (☐ changes to ☑).

9 Click this area and then type the name of the Windows NT server or domain.

10 Click the logon option you want to use each time you connect to the network (○ changes to ⊙).

11 Click OK to confirm your changes.

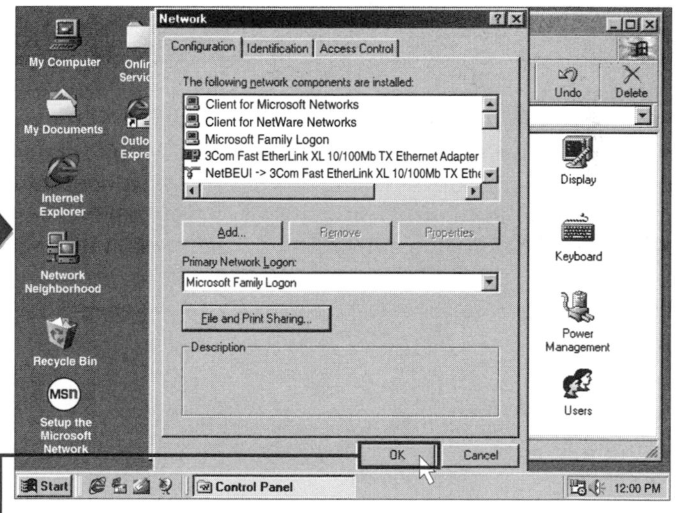

12 Click OK to close the Network dialog box.

■ Windows will ask you to restart your computer. Click Yes to restart your computer.

CONFIGURE THE NETWARE CLIENT

You may need to adjust the settings of your NetWare client to customize the way your computer connects to a Novell network. You must install the NetWare client before you can adjust the settings. To install a client, see page 482.

A Novell NetWare network can consist of many NetWare servers that store information that people on the network can access. When configuring the NetWare client, you need to enter the name of the server you want to connect to each time you log on to the network. This server will give you access to the network. If you do not know the name of the server, ask your system administrator.

You can choose to have Windows automatically run logon scripts. A logon script is a series of instructions that Windows performs when you successfully connect to a NetWare server. The instructions tell Windows what options you want to use. For example, logon scripts often automatically map your network drives.

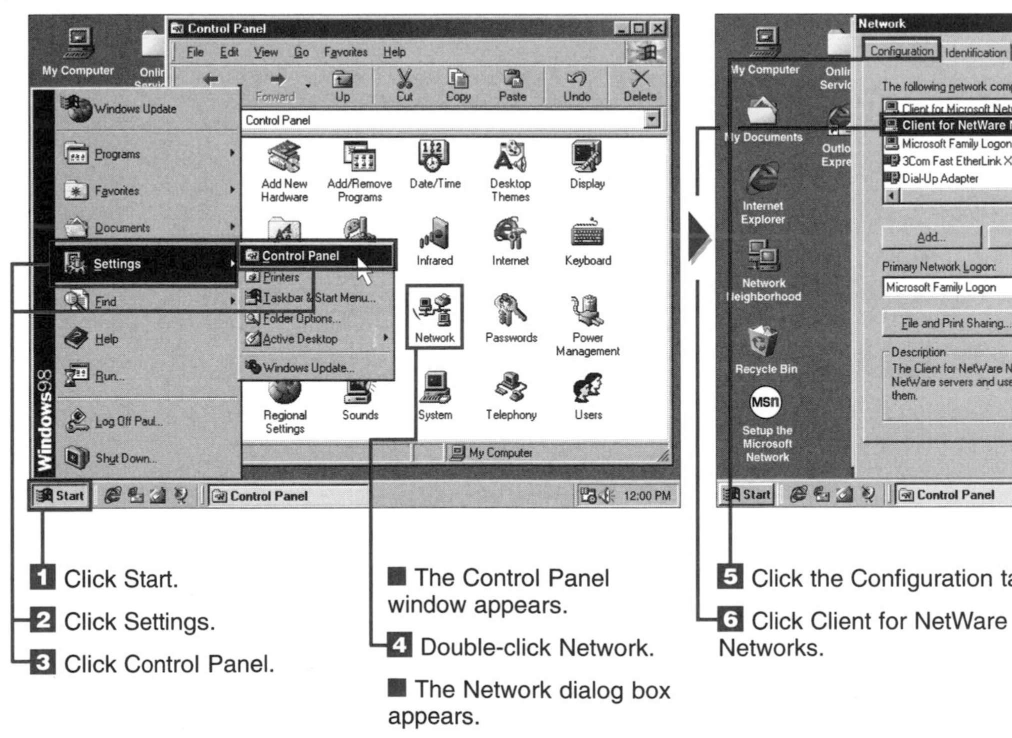

1 Click Start.

2 Click Settings.

3 Click Control Panel.

■ The Control Panel window appears.

4 Double-click Network.

■ The Network dialog box appears.

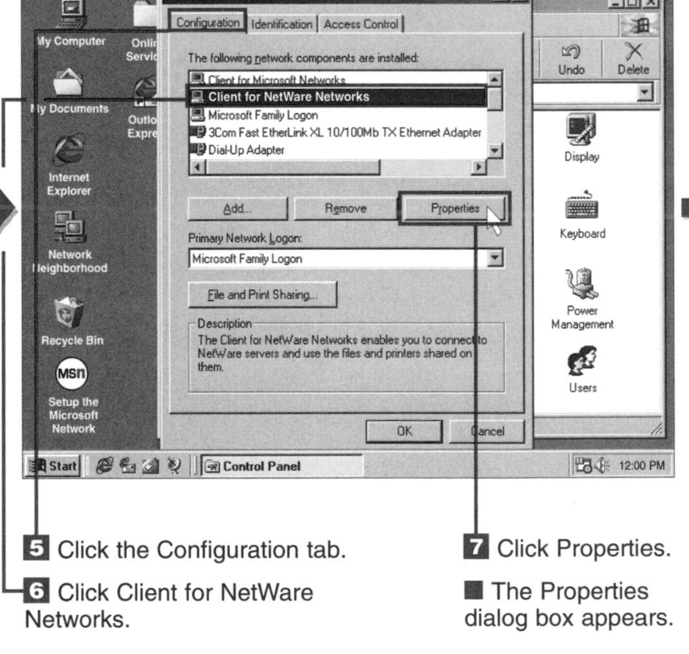

5 Click the Configuration tab.

6 Click Client for NetWare Networks.

7 Click Properties.

■ The Properties dialog box appears.

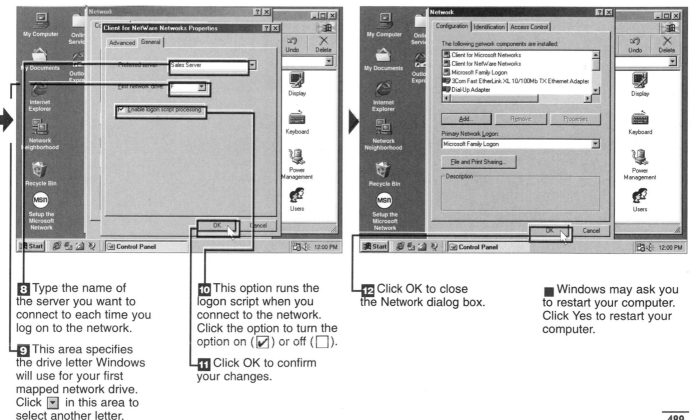

What is a preferred server?

A preferred server is the Novell NetWare server you connect to each time you log on to the network. The preferred server will check your user name and password and allow or deny you access to the network.

What is a mapped network drive?

A mapped network drive provides a quick way to access information stored on a network. Mapping a network drive assigns a drive letter to a resource on the network so you can work with the information as if the information were stored on your own computer. When configuring the NetWare client, you can specify the drive letter you want Windows to use for your first mapped network drive. See page 452 to create a mapped network drive.

Can I change the logon scripts?

Most people will not be able to alter their Novell NetWare logon scripts. The logon scripts are written and installed by the system administrator or by the information systems department responsible for the Novell NetWare server.

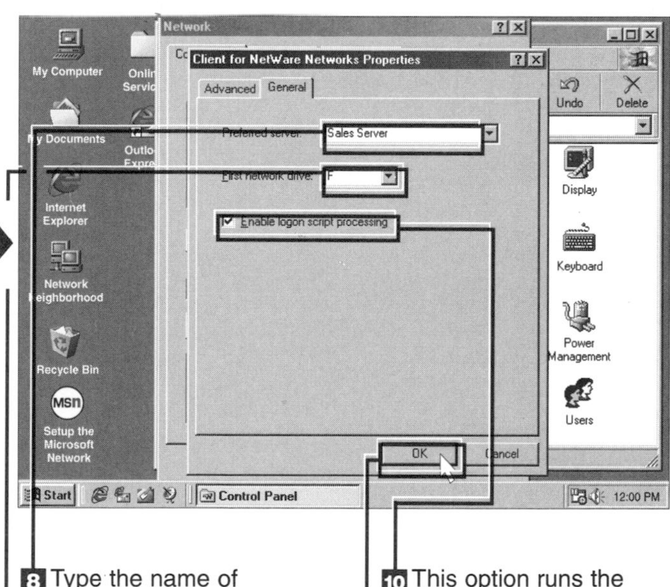

8 Type the name of the server you want to connect to each time you log on to the network.

9 This area specifies the drive letter Windows will use for your first mapped network drive. Click ▼ in this area to select another letter.

10 This option runs the logon script when you connect to the network. Click the option to turn the option on (☑) or off (☐).

11 Click OK to confirm your changes.

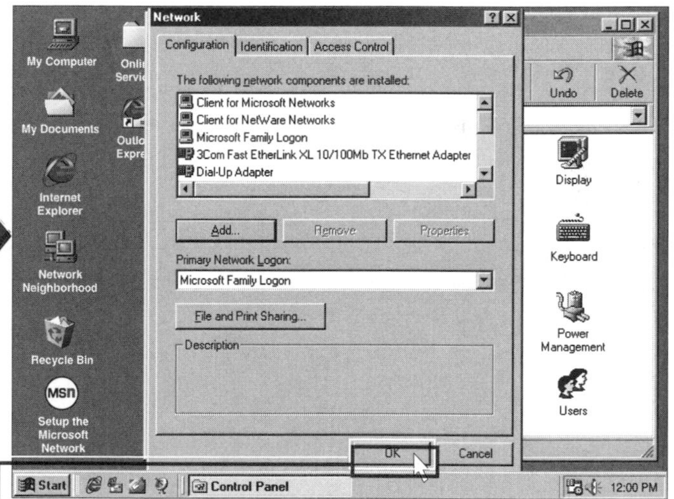

12 Click OK to close the Network dialog box.

■ Windows may ask you to restart your computer. Click Yes to restart your computer.

SELECT A PRIMARY NETWORK CLIENT

Windows lets you choose which network client to use as the primary, or main, network client. A network client is software that allows your computer to communicate with a specific network operating system.

When you start Windows, you need to enter logon information, such as a password. The primary network client determines which network will check your logon information. When entered correctly, this information allows you to use the network.

When selecting the primary network client, you should choose the client for the network you use most often. For example, if you frequently use a Novell NetWare network to access files and printers and you occasionally use a Microsoft network to access a database, you should set the Novell NetWare client as your primary client.

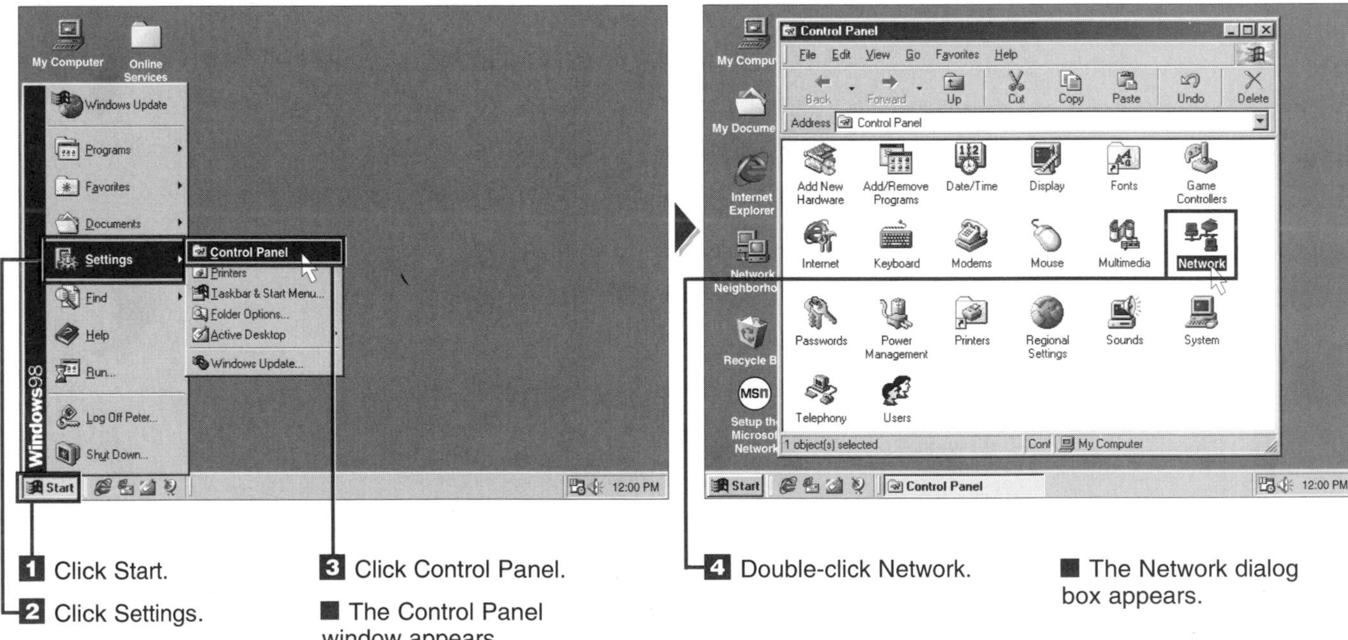

1 Click Start.

2 Click Settings.

3 Click Control Panel.

■ The Control Panel window appears.

4 Double-click Network.

■ The Network dialog box appears.

TIPS

When would I need to change my primary network client?

Once you set your primary network client, you will rarely need to change the client. If the network you usually connect to changes or you will be using another network for more than a few days, you may want to change your primary client.

Why can't I find the client that I want to use as the primary network client?

If the client you want to use as the primary network client is not displayed in the Network dialog box, you must install the client on your computer. To install a network client, see page 482.

Why would I select the Windows Logon option when selecting a primary network client?

The Windows Logon option enables you to log on to Windows 98. Using the Windows Logon option will not log you on to any networks. This option is useful if you are currently using a computer that is not connected to a network, such as when using a portable computer away from the office.

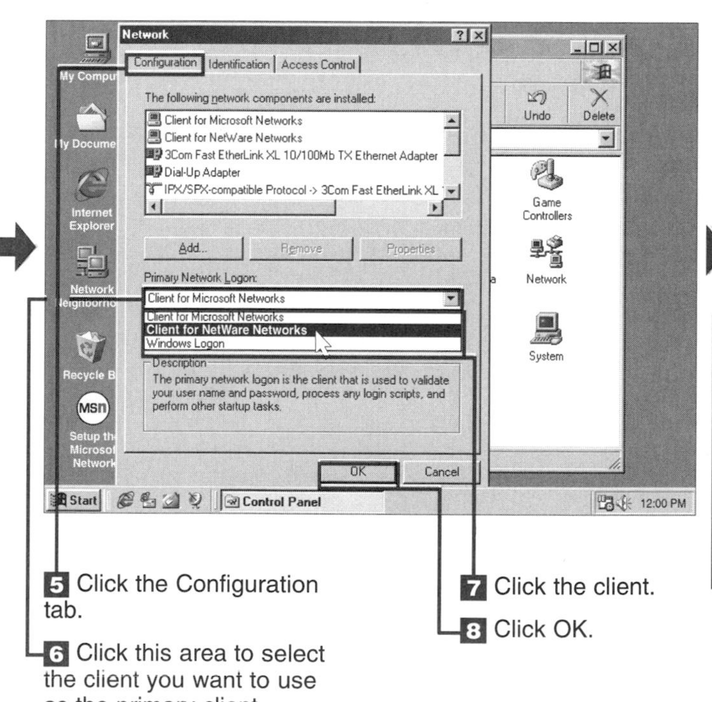

5 Click the Configuration tab.

6 Click this area to select the client you want to use as the primary client.

7 Click the client.

8 Click OK.

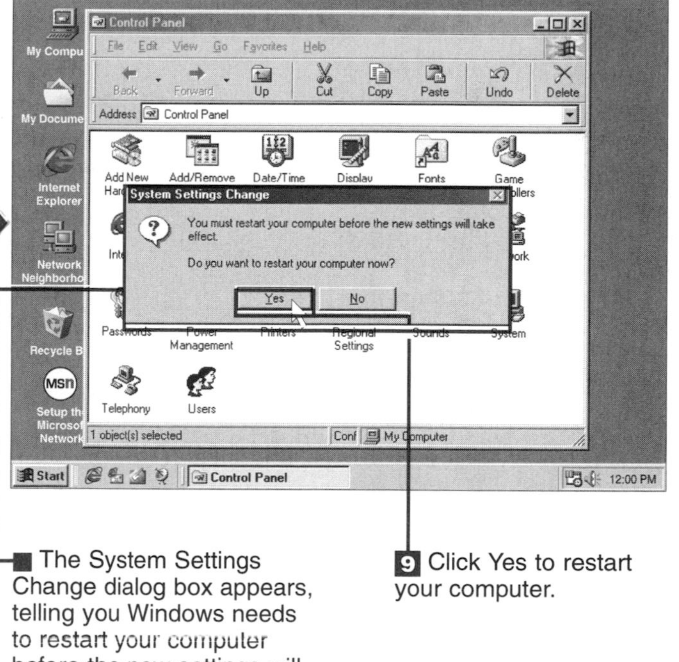

■ The System Settings Change dialog box appears, telling you Windows needs to restart your computer before the new settings will take effect.

9 Click Yes to restart your computer.

MONITOR SHARED RESOURCES USING NET WATCHER

You can use Net Watcher to monitor and manage shared files and folders on your computer.

You can view a list of people who are currently accessing files and folders on your computer to determine how long each person has been accessing your computer and which files they are using. You can also verify that only specific people are using your files. If people you do not want to use your files are accessing files on your computer, you can restrict access to your shared information by using passwords.

Net Watcher can display a list of all the folders for which you have turned on sharing. You can also view details about the folders, such as the type of access for each shared folder. Net Watcher can also display a list of shared files on your computer that are currently being accessed by other people.

Monitoring how many people access your shared folders helps you determine how sharing affects the performance of your computer. If too many people access the information on your computer, your computer will operate slower.

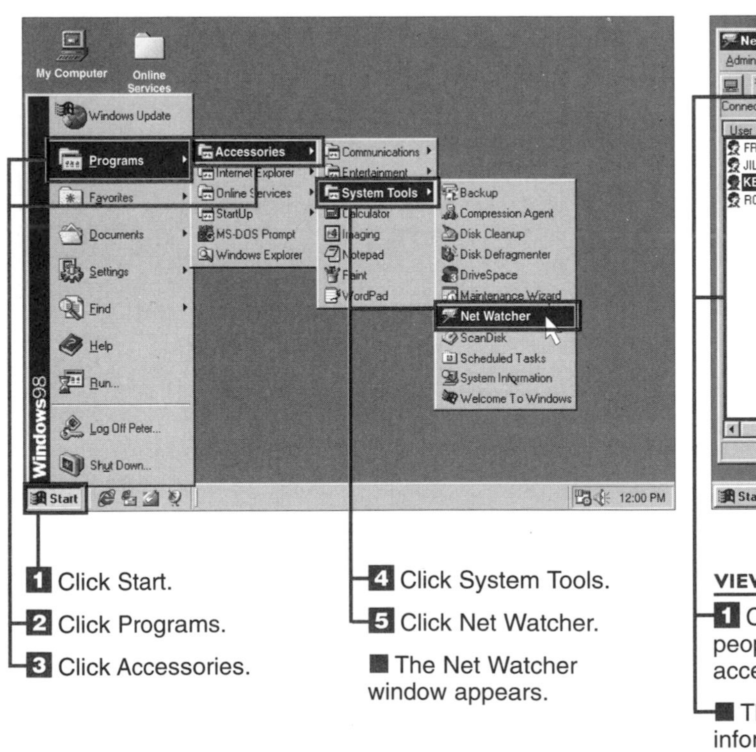

1 Click Start.

2 Click Programs.

3 Click Accessories.

4 Click System Tools.

5 Click Net Watcher.

■ The Net Watcher window appears.

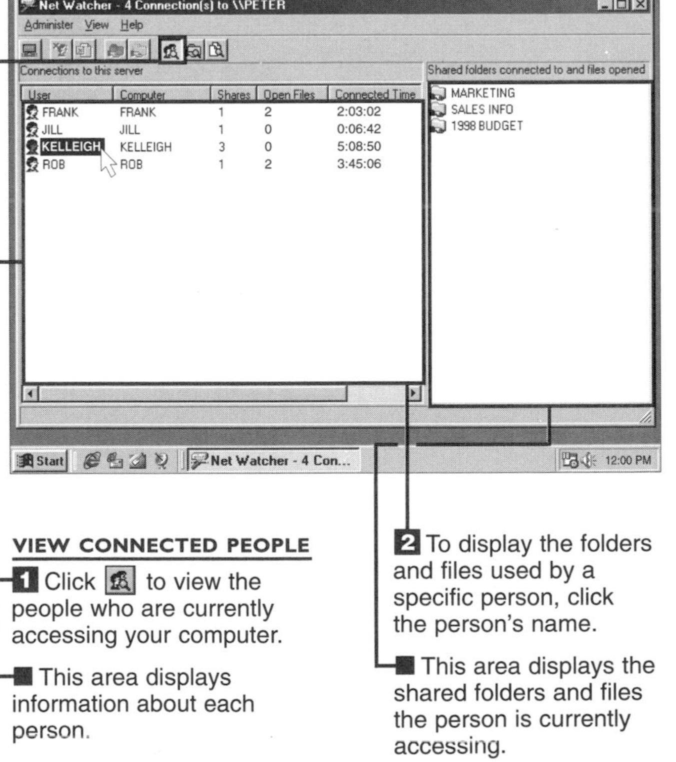

VIEW CONNECTED PEOPLE

1 Click [icon] to view the people who are currently accessing your computer.

■ This area displays information about each person.

2 To display the folders and files used by a specific person, click the person's name.

■ This area displays the shared folders and files the person is currently accessing.

TIPS

Why isn't Net Watcher on my Start menu?

Net Watcher may not be installed on your computer. Net Watcher is found in the System Tools component. To add Windows components, see page 610.

What must I do before I can use Net Watcher?

Before you can use Net Watcher to monitor shared resources, you must install the Client for Microsoft Networks on your computer. To install a network client, see page 482. You must also turn on file sharing on your computer. To turn on file sharing, see page 456.

I want to turn off sharing for a folder. Is there anything I should do first?

You should use Net Watcher to find out whether people are accessing the folder before you turn off sharing. If you turn off sharing for a folder while someone is accessing it, the other person's computer may not work properly. You should warn everyone who is accessing the folder to stop using it before you turn off sharing.

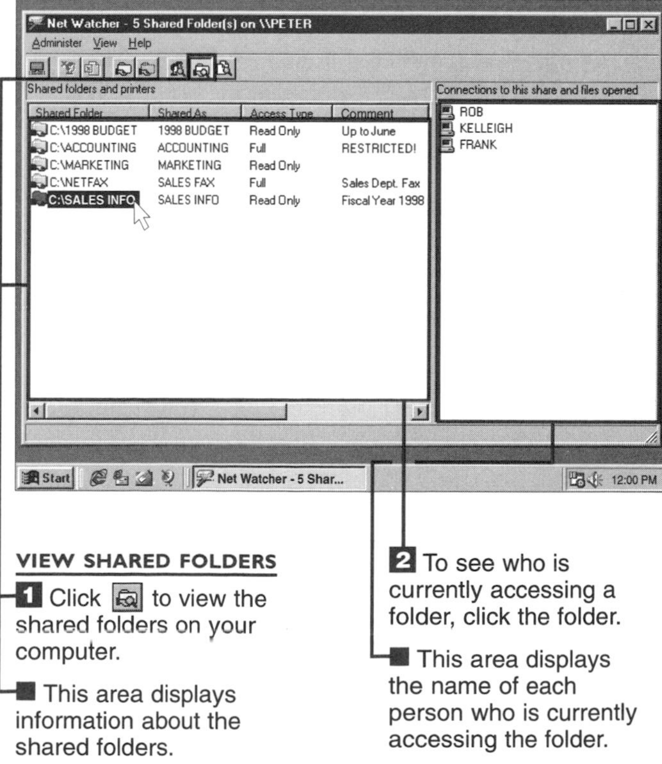

VIEW SHARED FOLDERS

1 Click [icon] to view the shared folders on your computer.

■ This area displays information about the shared folders.

2 To see who is currently accessing a folder, click the folder.

■ This area displays the name of each person who is currently accessing the folder.

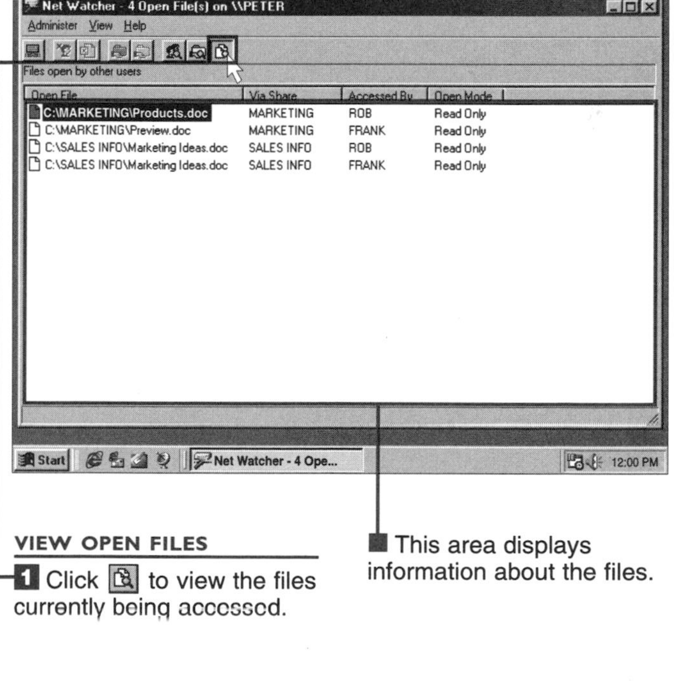

VIEW OPEN FILES

1 Click [icon] to view the files currently being accessed.

■ This area displays information about the files.

SECTION VII

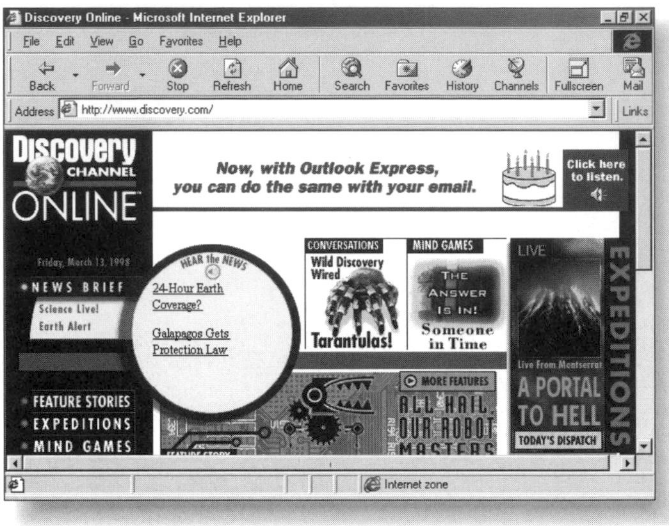

24) GET CONNECTED TO THE INTERNET

25) BROWSING THE WEB

WINDOWS 98 AND THE INTERNET

26) EXCHANGE E-MAIL MESSAGES

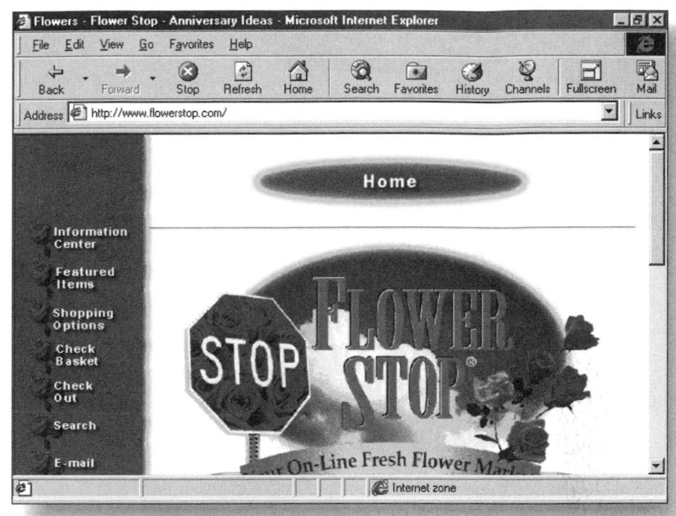

27) READING NEWSGROUP MESSAGES

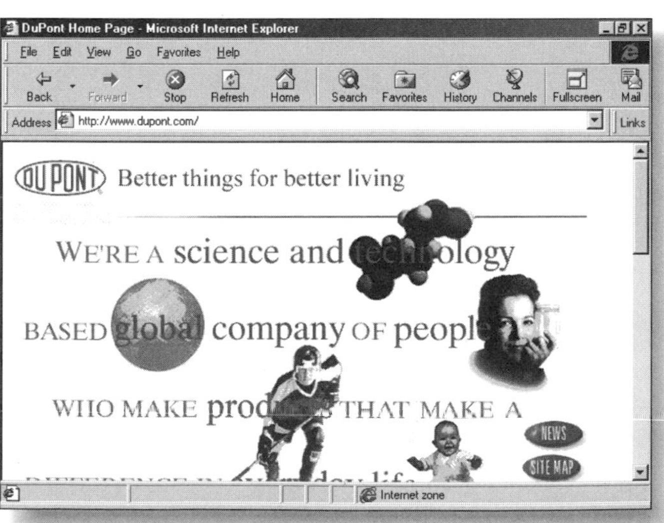

SECTION VII

Movie Critic Being Upgraded. - Microsoft Internet Explorer
File Edit View Go Favorites Help
Back Forward Stop Refresh Home Search Favorites History Channels Fullscreen Mail
Address http://www.moviecritic.com/
Links
Movie Critic
YOU RATE GOOD AND BAD MOVIES YOU'VE SEEN, AND I PREDICT WHICH NEW MOVIES YOU'LL LIKE!
Done
Internet zone

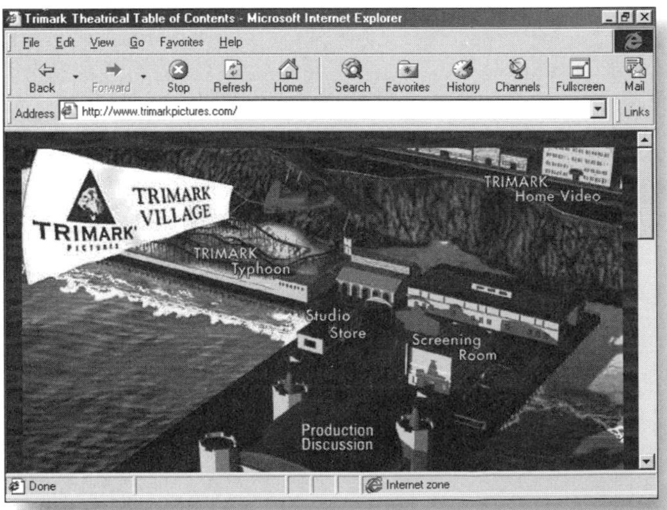
Trimark Theatrical Table of Contents - Microsoft Internet Explorer
File Edit View Go Favorites Help
Back Forward Stop Refresh Home Search Favorites History Channels Fullscreen Mail
Address http://www.trimarkpictures.com/
Links
TRIMARK VILLAGE
TRIMARK PICTURES
TRIMARK Home Video
TRIMARK Typhoon
Studio Store
Screening Room
Production Discussion
Done
Internet zone

WINDOWS 98 AND THE INTERNET

28) VIEWING CHANNELS

29) CREATING WEB PAGES

30) USING MICROSOFT NETMEETING

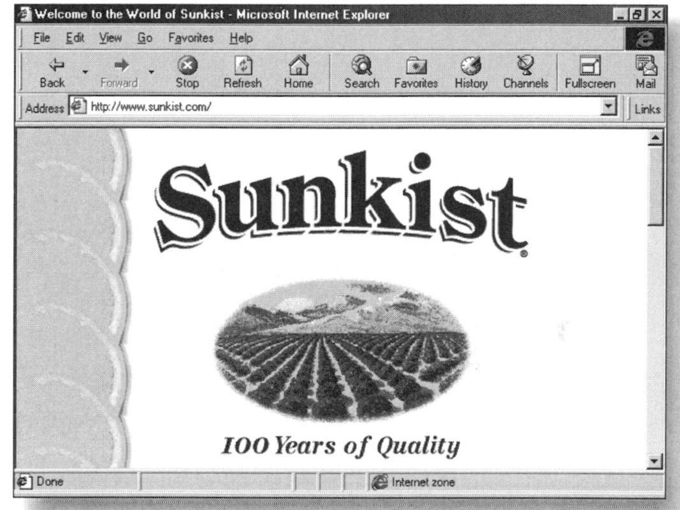

31) USING MICROSOFT CHAT

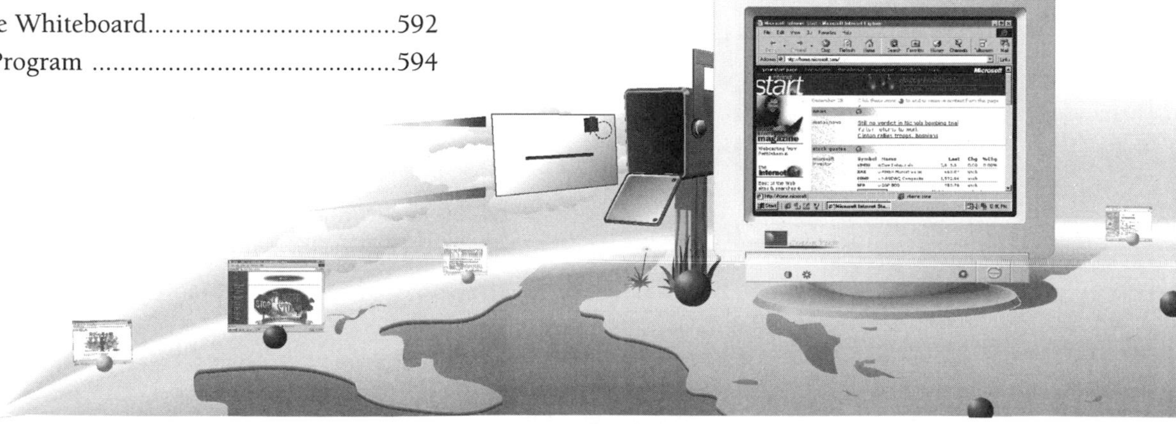

USING THE INTERNET CONNECTION WIZARD

You can use the Internet Connection wizard to set up a connection to the Internet. The wizard helps you find an Internet Service Provider (ISP) in your area and set up an account.

When you select the service provider you want to use, the wizard connects you to the service provider so you can enter information about yourself and the account you want to set up.

Most of the service providers available through the Internet Connection wizard require you to enter your credit card number.

After setting up an account with a service provider, you can access the resources available on the Internet. You will be able to browse through information on the World Wide Web, exchange e-mail and read messages in newsgroups.

You must have a modem installed on your computer to use the wizard to set up a connection to a service provider. See page 382 to install a modem.

After using the Internet Connection wizard to set up a connection to a service provider, you can connect at any time. To connect to your service provider to access the Internet, click on the taskbar.

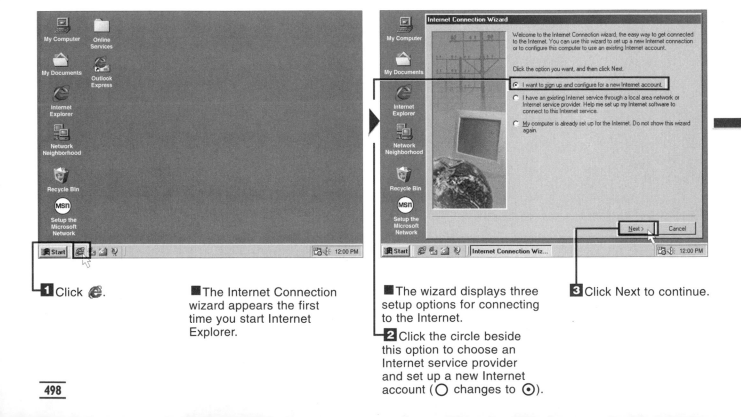

1 Click .

■ The Internet Connection wizard appears the first time you start Internet Explorer.

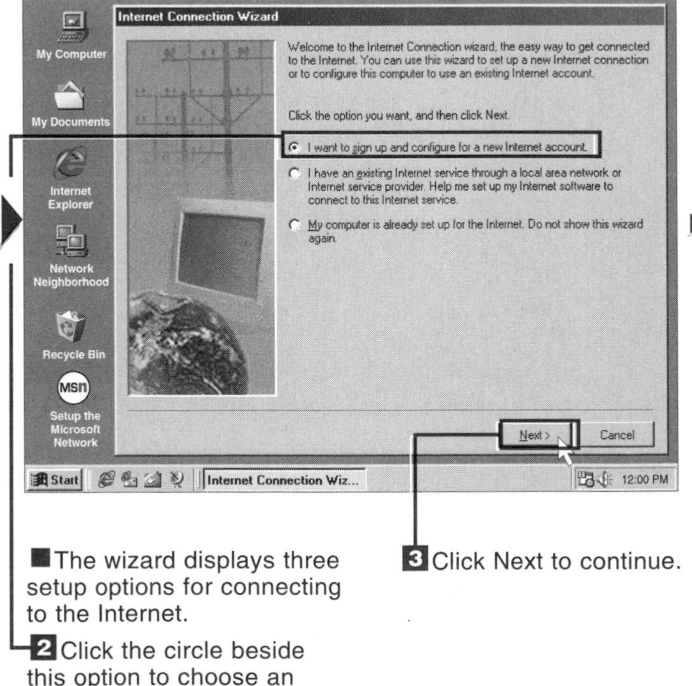

■ The wizard displays three setup options for connecting to the Internet.

2 Click the circle beside this option to choose an Internet service provider and set up a new Internet account (○ changes to ⊙).

3 Click Next to continue.

TIPS

Is there another way to start the Internet Connection wizard?

If you previously started the Internet Connection wizard, clicking on the taskbar may not start the wizard. To start the wizard at any time, click the Start button and then click Programs. Select Internet Explorer and then click Connection Wizard.

I have to enter my credit card number to set up an Internet account. Is this safe?

Yes. When you set up an Internet account, you are directly connected to the service provider. The information you enter is not transmitted over the Internet.

I already have a connection set up, but the wizard starts when I click on the taskbar. What should I do?

Perform steps 1 to 3 below, except select the "My computer is already set up for the Internet. Do not show this wizard again" option in step 2.

Can I set up a connection without having the wizard find a provider for me?

The Internet Connection wizard will let you specify information about your service provider and the connection you want to set up. Perform steps 1 to 3 below, except select the "I have an existing Internet service through a local area network or Internet service provider. Help me set up my Internet software to connect to this Internet service" option in step 2.

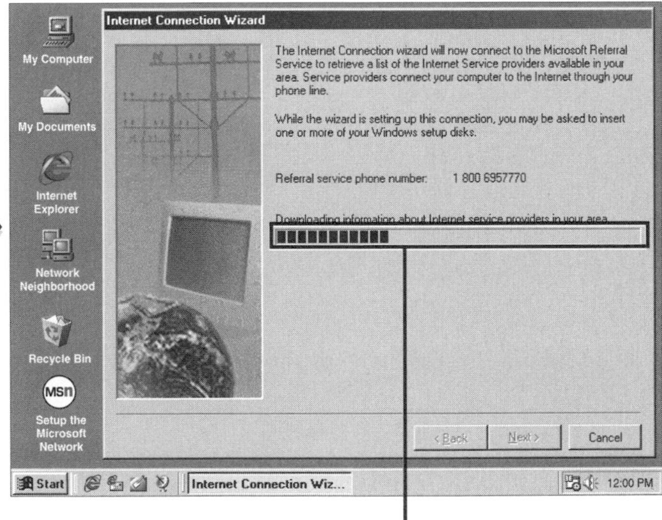

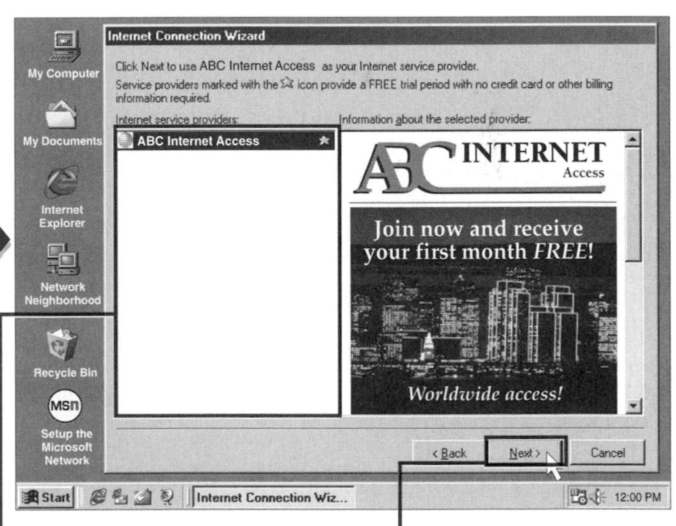

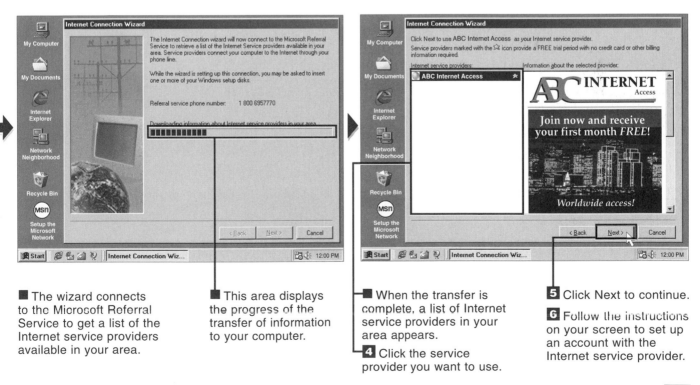

■ The wizard connects to the Microsoft Referral Service to get a list of the Internet service providers available in your area.

■ This area displays the progress of the transfer of information to your computer.

■ When the transfer is complete, a list of Internet service providers in your area appears.

4 Click the service provider you want to use.

5 Click Next to continue.

6 Follow the instructions on your screen to set up an account with the Internet service provider.

DIAL IN TO A SERVICE PROVIDER

After you set up a connection to a computer at your Internet Service Provider (ISP), you can dial in to the computer to access the Internet. Windows displays an icon in the Dial-Up Networking window for each connection you have set up. To use the Internet Connection Wizard to set up a connection to a service provider, see page 498.

Windows needs to know your user name and password to dial in to your ISP. Your service provider should have provided you with this information when you set up your account.

Dialing in to an Internet service provider allows you to access the wide range of resources available on the Internet. You can browse through documents on various subjects, exchange electronic mail with friends and colleagues and read messages in newsgroups.

Before you can access information on the Internet, you need a program, such as Internet Explorer, that allows you to use the services available.

You may not always have to perform the steps below to dial in to your service provider. Most programs used to access information on the Internet will automatically dial in to your service provider when you start the program.

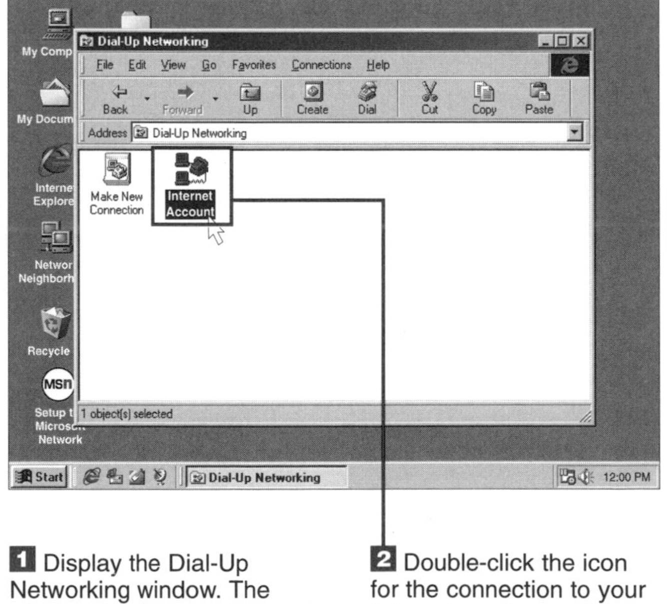

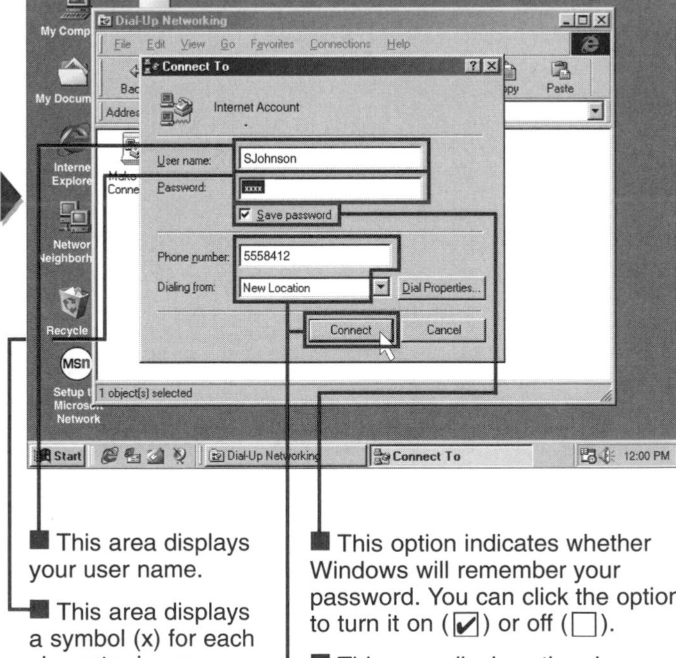

1 Display the Dial-Up Networking window. The window displays an icon for each connection you have set up.

Note: To display the Dial-Up Networking window, perform steps 1 to 5 on page 398.

2 Double-click the icon for the connection to your Internet service provider.

■ The Connect To dialog box appears.

■ This area displays your user name.

■ This area displays a symbol (x) for each character in your password.

■ This option indicates whether Windows will remember your password. You can click the option to turn it on (☑) or off (☐).

■ This area displays the phone number the modem will dial and the location you are dialing from.

3 Click Connect.

TIPS

Why do I keep getting disconnected when I dial in to my Internet service provider?

Check your service provider's setup information. Although you can connect to most ISPs with the name and password settings provided in the Connect To dialog box, some service providers may require you to enter your name, password and other information in a terminal window to complete the connection. If you want Windows to display a terminal window after dialing the ISP, right-click the icon for the connection in the Dial-Up Networking window and then click Properties. Click the Configure button and then click the Options tab. Select the Bring up terminal window after dialing option (☐ changes to ☑).

How can I test my connection to the Internet?

Windows includes a program called PING that you can use to test a connection with another computer on the Internet. In the MS-DOS Prompt window, type **ping** followed by a space and the name (**www.maran.com**) or IP number (**207.136.66.25**) of the computer you want to communicate with. Then press the Enter key. PING will report how long it takes to send and receive a signal between your computer and the other computer. If PING displays a message stating that the request timed out, the connection is not working. See page 134 to open the MS-DOS Prompt window.

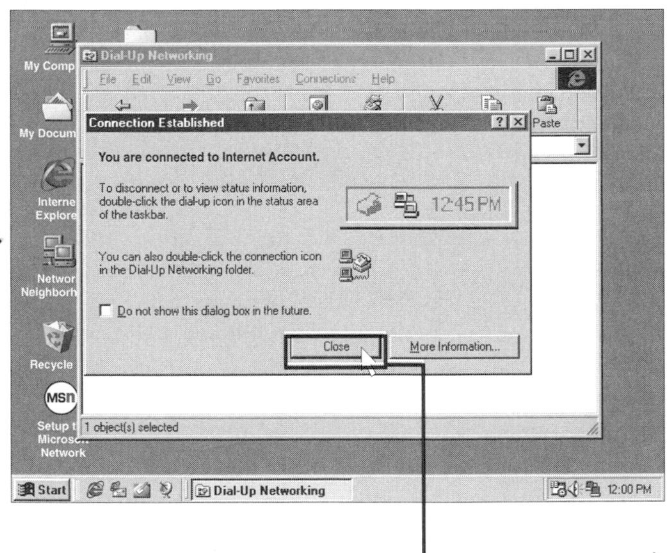

■ A dialog box appears when you are successfully connected.

4 Click Close to close the dialog box.

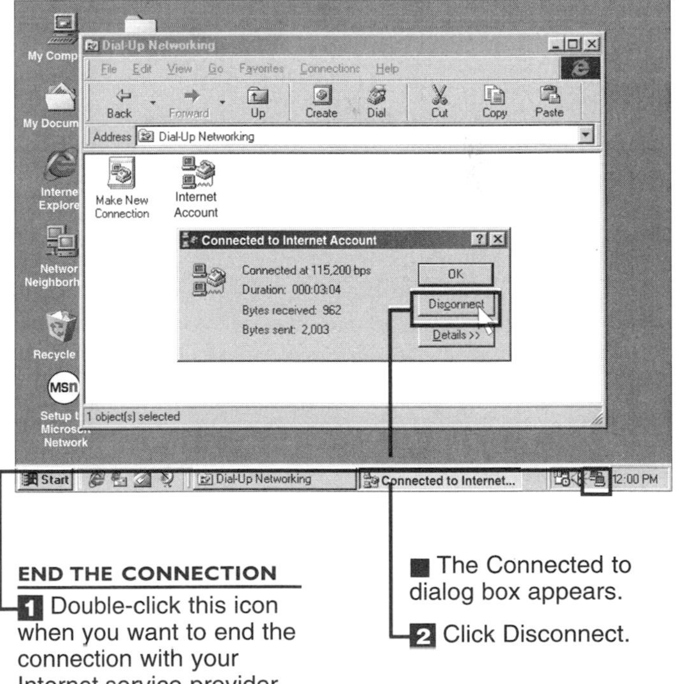

END THE CONNECTION

1 Double-click this icon when you want to end the connection with your Internet service provider.

■ The Connected to dialog box appears.

2 Click Disconnect.

DISPLAY WEB PAGES

You can use Internet Explorer to browse through information on the World Wide Web. The Web is part of the Internet and consists of a huge collection of documents, called Web pages, stored on computers around the world.

Web pages contain highlighted text or images, called links, that connect to other pages on the Web. Links allow you to easily move through a vast amount of information by jumping from one Web page to another. The Web pages you display may be located on the same Web site or another Web site on the World Wide Web.

You can also display a specific Web page that you have heard or read about if you know the address of the Web page. Each page on the Web has a unique address, called a Uniform Resource Locator (URL).

When you display a Web page, the text on the page transfers to your computer quickly so you can start reading the text right away. Images transfer more slowly, so you may have to wait a moment to clearly view the images.

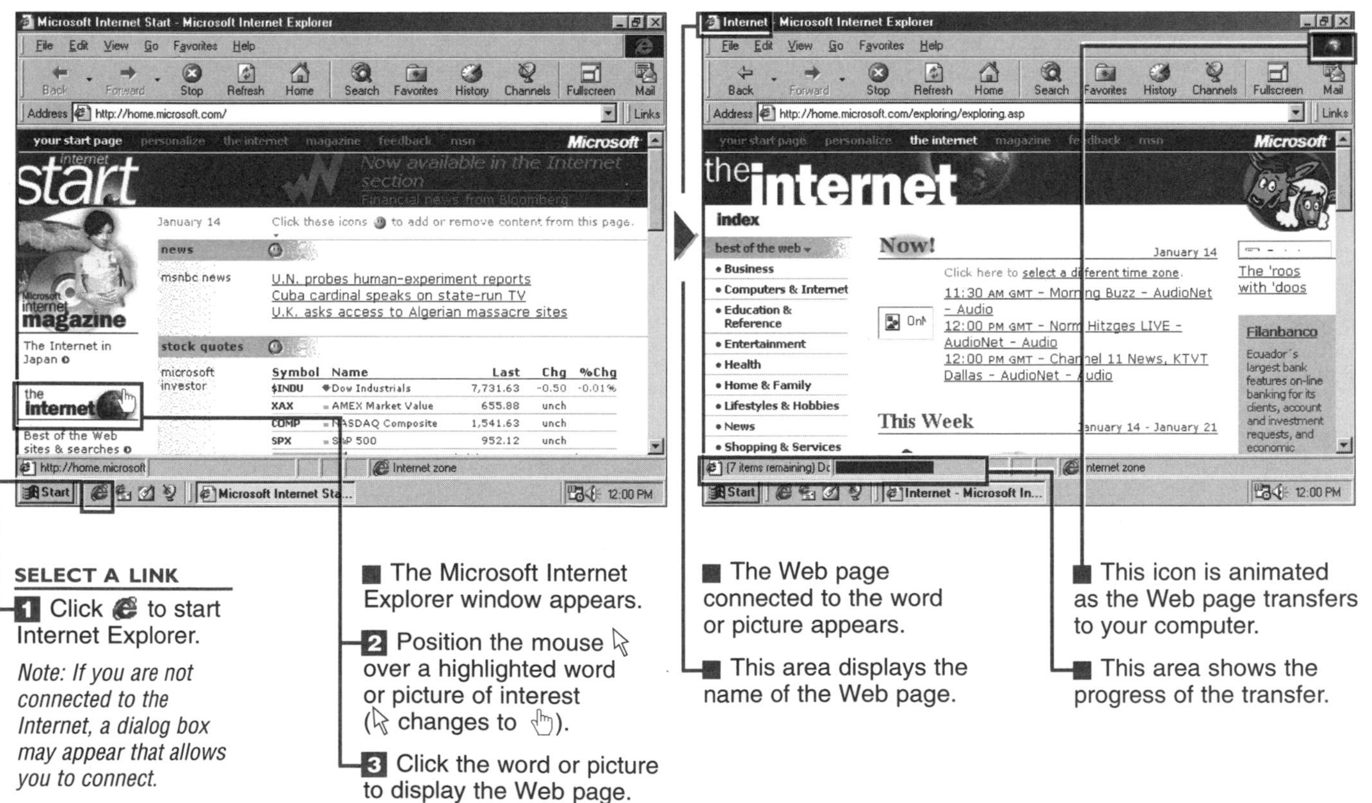

SELECT A LINK

1 Click to start Internet Explorer.

Note: If you are not connected to the Internet, a dialog box may appear that allows you to connect.

■ The Microsoft Internet Explorer window appears.

2 Position the mouse over a highlighted word or picture of interest (changes to).

3 Click the word or picture to display the Web page.

■ The Web page connected to the word or picture appears.

■ This area displays the name of the Web page.

■ This icon is animated as the Web page transfers to your computer.

■ This area shows the progress of the transfer.

TIPS

Why does the Internet Connection Wizard appear when I start Internet Explorer?

The first time you start Internet Explorer, the Internet Connection Wizard appears and helps you get connected to the Internet. See page 498 for more information.

How can I save time when typing Web page addresses?

You can have Internet Explorer fill in parts of the address, such as http:// and .com, for you. Type a partial address and then press Ctrl+Enter. For example, if you type **abc**, Internet Explorer attempts to connect to a Web site at http://www.abc.com

Can I have more than one Internet Explorer window open at a time?

If a Web page is taking a long time to transfer, you can open another window to view other Web pages while you wait. From the File menu, select New and then choose Window.

Can I change the font size and font used to display Web pages?

From the View menu, select Fonts and then choose the font size and font you want to use. The current font size and font display a check mark (✔).

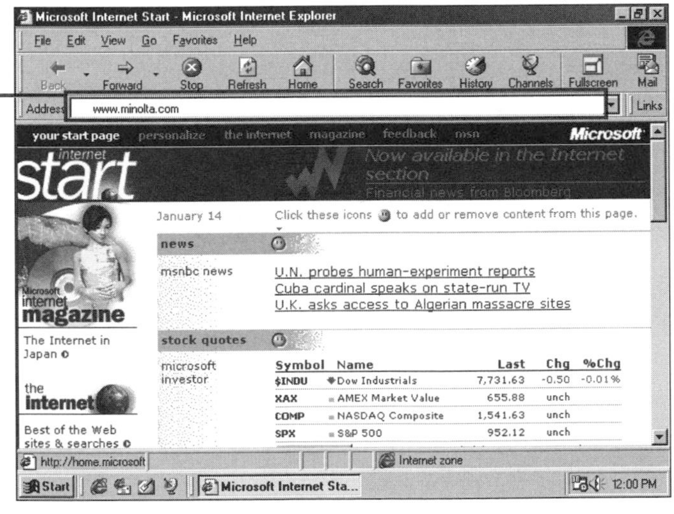

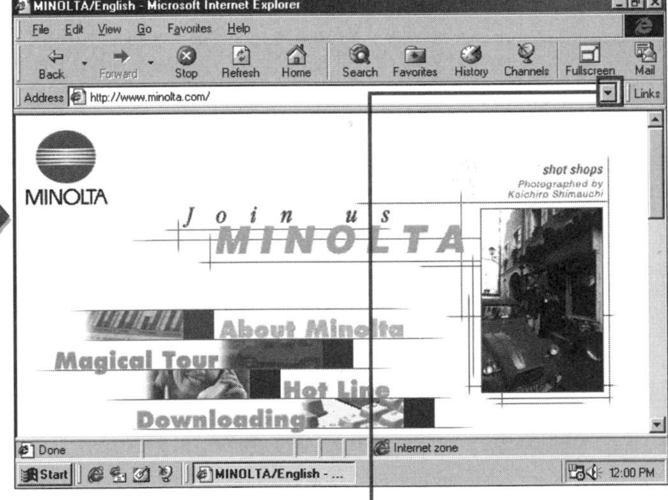

DISPLAY A SPECIFIC WEB PAGE

1 Click this area to highlight the current Web page address.

2 Type the address of the Web page you want to view and then press the Enter key.

■ When you start typing the address of a Web page you have previously entered, Internet Explorer completes the address for you.

■ The Web page appears on your screen.

■ You can click ▾ in this area to display a list of Web page addresses you recently typed. You can then click an address to once again view a Web page.

WORK WITH WEB PAGES

Internet Explorer provides several toolbar buttons that help you view and work with Web pages.

If a Web page is taking a long time to appear on your screen or is the wrong page, you can stop the transfer of information.

You can move back or forward through the Web pages you have viewed since you last started Internet Explorer.

Many Web pages contain information that is constantly being updated, such as news, sports scores or stock market data. Some Web pages also contain frequently changing images from a live camera. You can transfer a fresh copy of a Web page at any time to view the most up-to-date information or images.

You can display your home page at any time. The home page appears each time you start Internet Explorer.

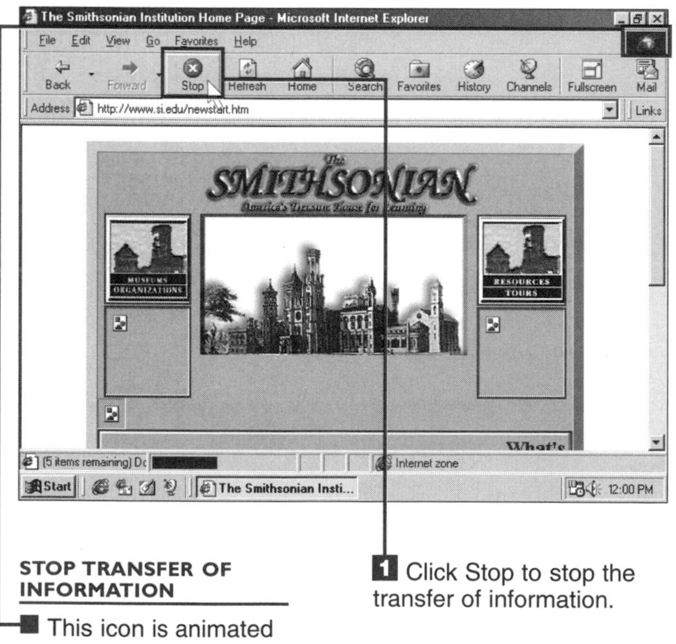

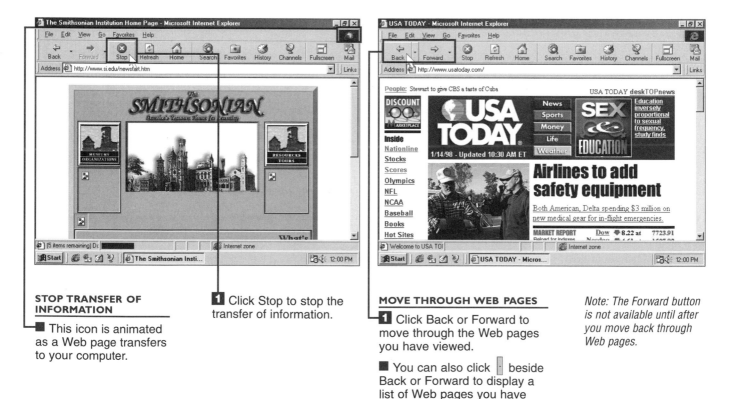

STOP TRANSFER OF INFORMATION

■ This icon is animated as a Web page transfers to your computer.

1 Click Stop to stop the transfer of information.

MOVE THROUGH WEB PAGES

1 Click Back or Forward to move through the Web pages you have viewed.

■ You can also click ▾ beside Back or Forward to display a list of Web pages you have viewed. Then click the Web page you want to view again.

Note: The Forward button is not available until after you move back through Web pages.

TIPS

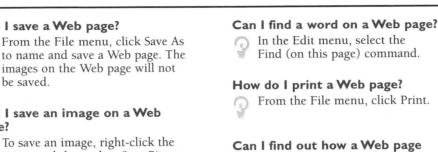

Can I save a Web page?

From the File menu, click Save As to name and save a Web page. The images on the Web page will not be saved.

Can I save an image on a Web page?

To save an image, right-click the image and then select Save Picture As. Type a name for the image and then click Save.

How do I open a Web page or image I saved?

To open a saved Web page or image, select the File menu and then choose Open. Click the Browse button to find the Web page or image on your computer.

Can I find a word on a Web page?

In the Edit menu, select the Find (on this page) command.

How do I print a Web page?

From the File menu, click Print.

Can I find out how a Web page was created?

Viewing the HTML code used to create a Web page is useful if you want to find out how the effects on a Web page were created. From the View menu, choose the Source option.

REFRESH A WEB PAGE

1 Click Refresh to transfer a fresh copy of the displayed Web page to your computer.

DISPLAY THE HOME PAGE

1 Click Home to display your home page.

■ The Internet Start Web page appears.

Note: Your home page may be different.

■ To change your home page, see page 514.

SEARCH THE WEB

You can use the search services on the World Wide Web to locate Web pages of interest. Internet Explorer provides an easily accessible list of popular search services such as Excite, Infoseek, Yahoo! and Lycos.

You can enter a word or phrase in a search service to display a list of Web pages containing the word or phrase you specified. The other available search capabilities depend on the search service you use.

Search services often use software programs called robots to search the World Wide Web and catalog new Web pages. Many search services also have people who review cataloged Web pages and place them in appropriate categories. When you use a search service to find Web pages about a specific topic, the search service searches its catalog for matching or related items.

Searching for information will give you a good starting point but will not find every page on the Web that discusses the topic. It is almost impossible to catalog every Web page because Web pages change frequently and new Web pages are created every day.

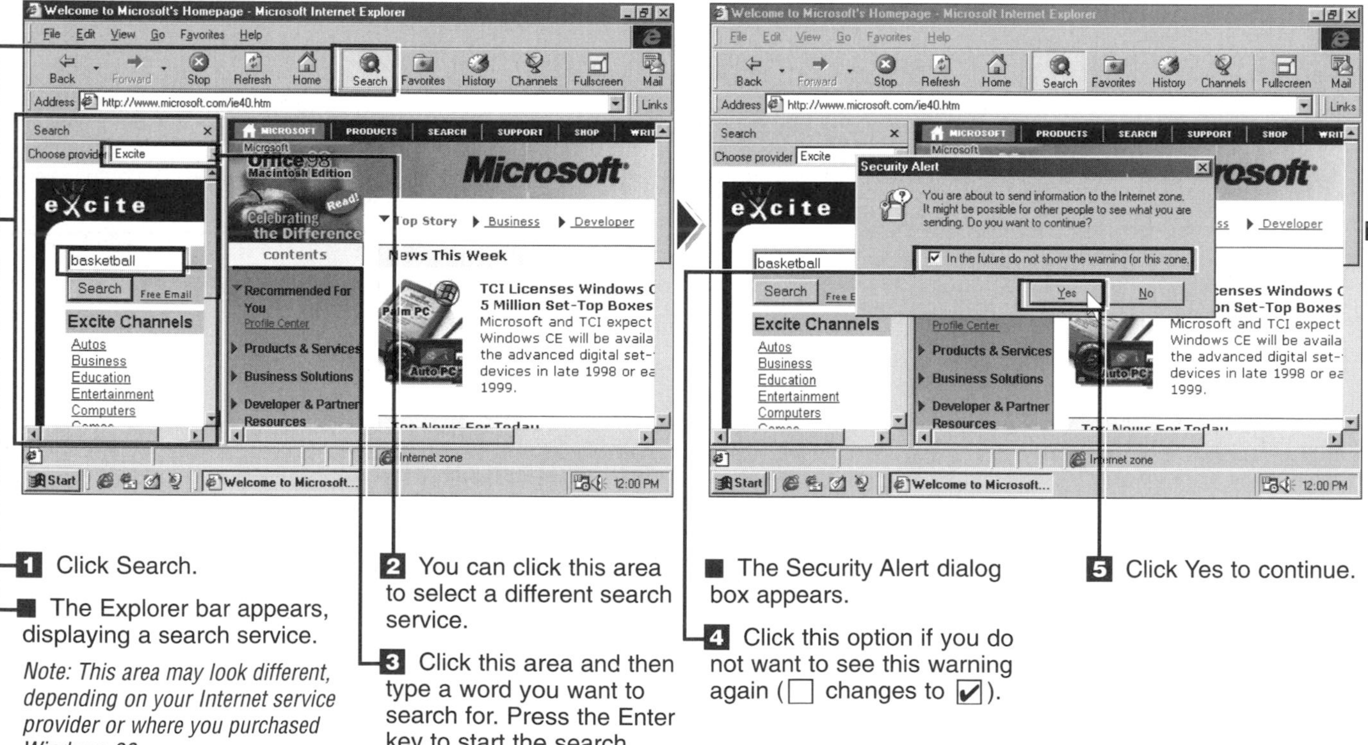

1 Click Search.

■ The Explorer bar appears, displaying a search service.

Note: This area may look different, depending on your Internet service provider or where you purchased Windows 98.

2 You can click this area to select a different search service.

3 Click this area and then type a word you want to search for. Press the Enter key to start the search.

■ The Security Alert dialog box appears.

4 Click this option if you do not want to see this warning again (☐ changes to ☑).

5 Click Yes to continue.

TIPS

Is there a quicker way to search for Web pages?

In the Address bar of the Internet Explorer window, type a question mark (?) followed by a space and the word or phrase you want to search for. Then press the Enter key. Internet Explorer will use a search service to locate Web pages containing the word or phrase you specified.

How else can I search for a Web page?

You can browse through categories such as arts, health and sports to find information that interests you. Most search services provide categories that you can search through.

Can I add my Web page to a search service?

Most search services let people add their own Web pages. Each search service requires you to enter specific information about the Web page you are submitting. Once you have submitted your Web page to a search service, it may take a few weeks for the search service to add it to their listings.

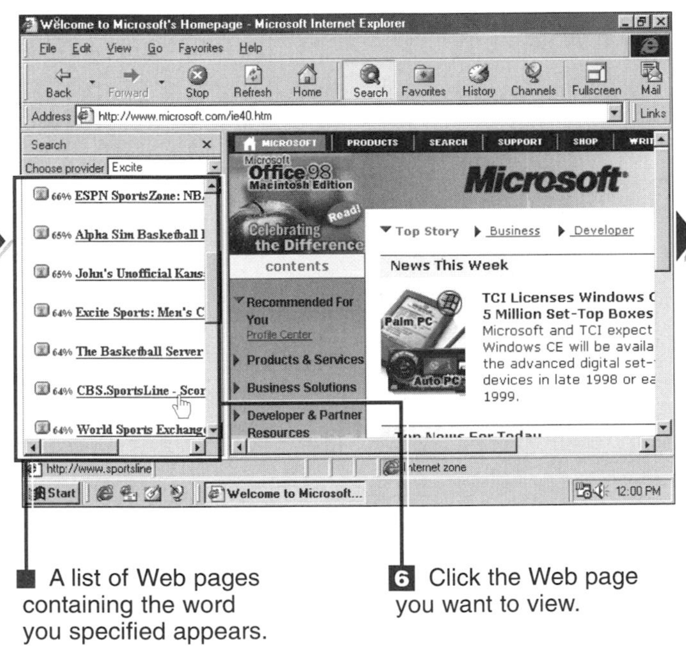

■ A list of Web pages containing the word you specified appears.

6 Click the Web page you want to view.

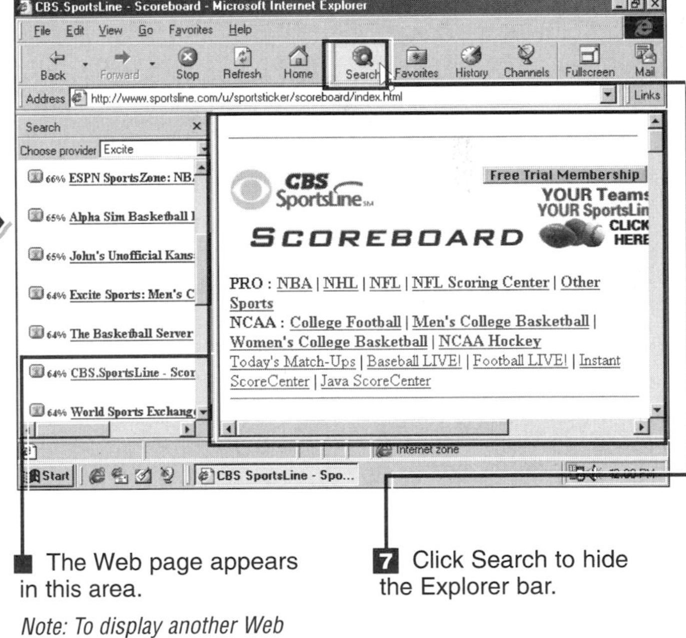

■ The Web page appears in this area.

Note: To display another Web page, click the page you want to view.

7 Click Search to hide the Explorer bar.

ADD WEB PAGES TO FAVORITES

The Favorites feature allows you to store the addresses of Web pages you frequently visit. When you know that you will be returning to a Web page, you can add the page to the Favorites list. You may return to the same Web page several times to investigate the page further or to check for new or updated information.

When you add a Web page to the Favorites list, you should give the page a meaningful name that clearly indicates its contents. Choose a name that will help you remember why you think the page is significant.

You can quickly access Web pages in the Favorites list. Selecting Web pages from the Favorites list saves you from having to remember and retype the same addresses over and over. Using the Favorites list also eliminates the possibility that you will not be able to access a Web page because you have made a typing mistake in the address.

The Favorites list includes the Links folder. The Links folder contains important Web pages that you can visit. Internet Explorer adds certain pages, such as Best of the Web, to the Links folder for you.

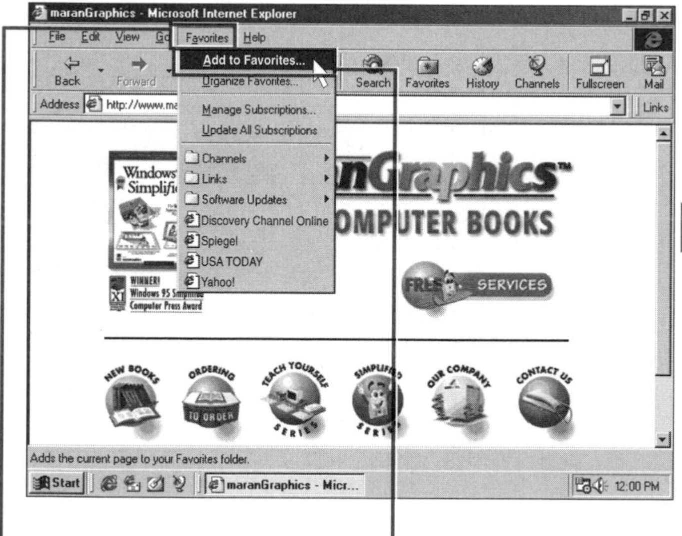

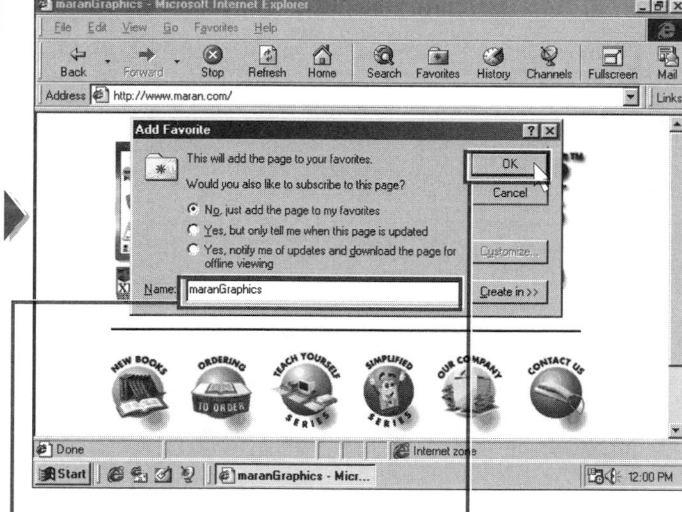

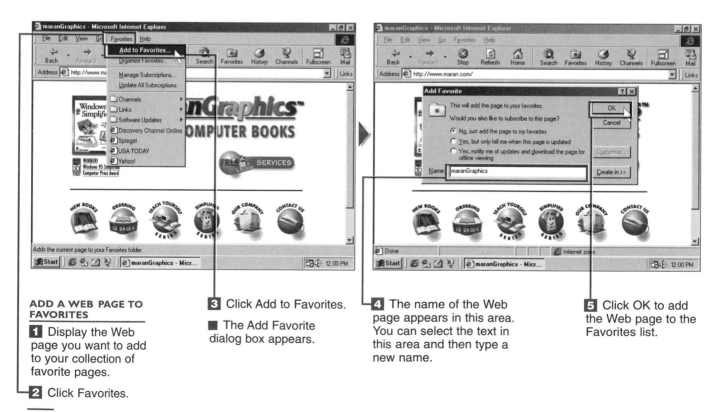

ADD A WEB PAGE TO FAVORITES

1 Display the Web page you want to add to your collection of favorite pages.

2 Click Favorites.

3 Click Add to Favorites.

■ The Add Favorite dialog box appears.

4 The name of the Web page appears in this area. You can select the text in this area and then type a new name.

5 Click OK to add the Web page to the Favorites list.

TIPS

Should I subscribe to a Web page when I add the Web page to the Favorites list?

You can subscribe to a Web page if you want Internet Explorer to automatically notify you when the content of the Web page changes. You can choose to have Internet Explorer also automatically update the Web page on your computer. For information on subscribing, see page 564.

Are there any other ways to access the Favorites list?

You can select the Favorites menu to display the list of your favorite Web pages. To access the Favorites list from the Start menu, click the Start button and then select Favorites.

How do I add a Web page to the Links folder?

To add a Web page to the Links folder, drag the Web page icon (🌐) from the Address bar to the Links folder in the Favorites list. Any Web pages you add to the Links folder are also added to the Links toolbar.

How do I display the Links toolbar?

Double-click the Links button to the right of the Address bar.

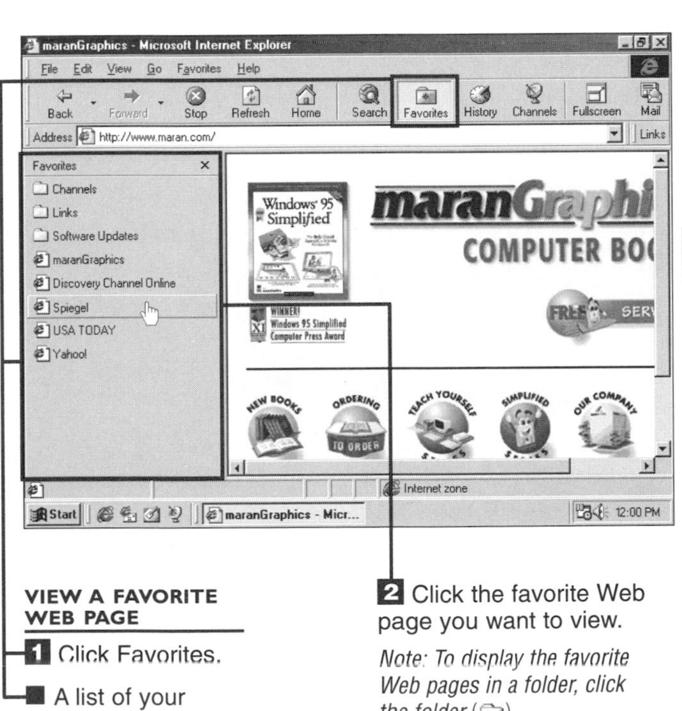

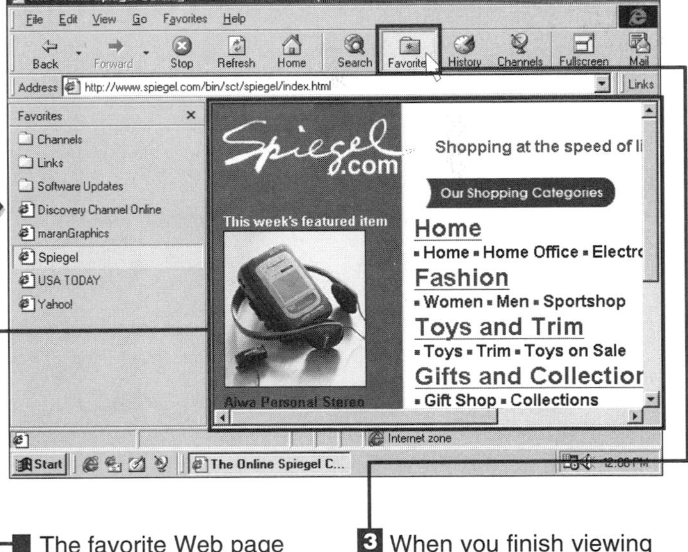

VIEW A FAVORITE WEB PAGE

1 Click Favorites.

■ A list of your favorite Web pages appears in this area.

2 Click the favorite Web page you want to view.

Note: To display the favorite Web pages in a folder, click the folder (📁).

■ The favorite Web page you selected appears in this area.

■ You can repeat step 2 to view another favorite Web page.

3 When you finish viewing your favorite Web pages, click Favorites to hide the Favorites list.

ORGANIZE FAVORITE WEB PAGES

You can organize the items in the Favorites list to help make the list easier to use.

You can create new folders to organize your favorite Web pages. For example, you can create a folder called Entertainment to keep all your favorite entertainment Web pages together. Web pages organized into folders are easier to find. To further organize your favorite Web pages, you can create a new folder within an existing folder. A folder within another folder is called a sub-folder.

You can move your favorite Web pages to a new location in the Favorites list. This is useful if you want to organize your favorite Web pages by topic. For example, you can move Web pages that cover topics such as music and movies to the Entertainment folder you created.

Eventually, your list of favorite Web pages may become large and unmanageable. To keep your Favorites list organized, you should delete the Web pages that you no longer visit or that no longer exist.

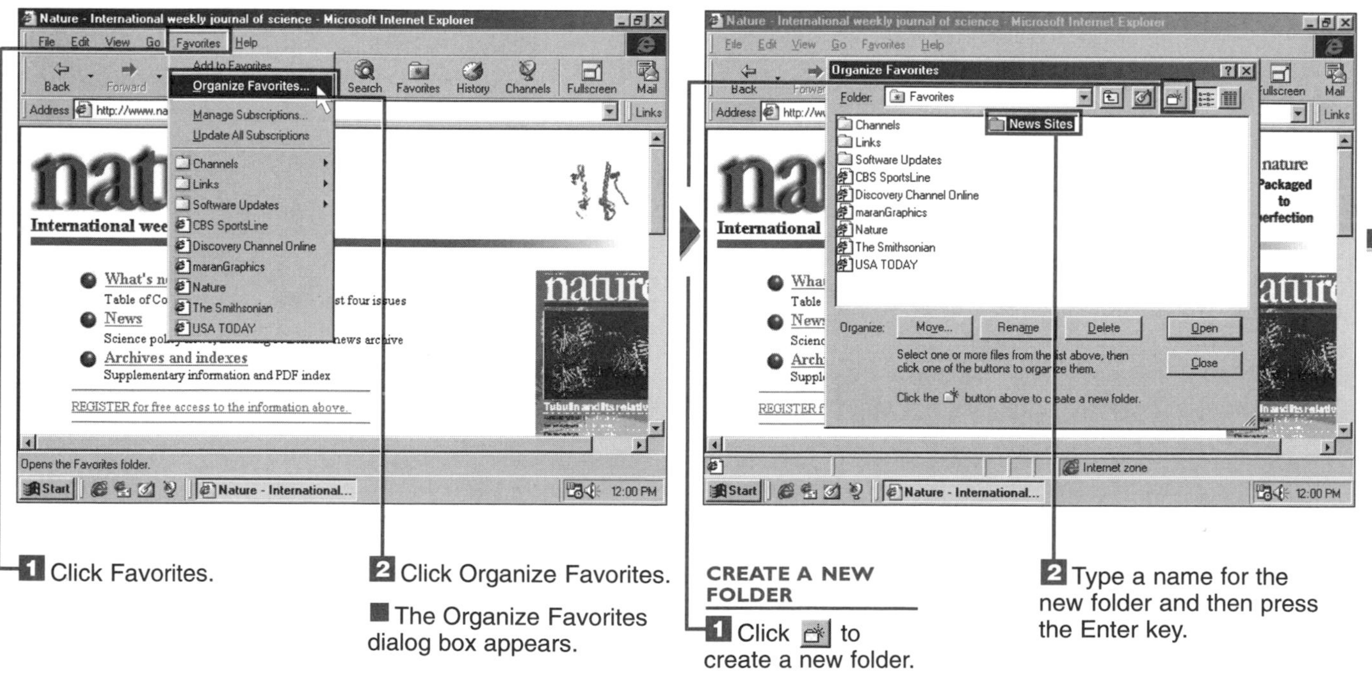

1 Click Favorites.

2 Click Organize Favorites.

■ The Organize Favorites dialog box appears.

CREATE A NEW FOLDER

1 Click [new folder button] to create a new folder.

2 Type a name for the new folder and then press the Enter key.

TIPS

Can I change the name of a favorite Web page?

You may want to change the name of a favorite Web page to better describe its contents. In the Organize Favorites dialog box, click the favorite Web page you want to rename and then select the Rename button. Type a new name for the Web page and then press the Enter key.

Is there another way to rearrange the items on the Favorites list?

When the Favorites list is displayed, you can drag and drop the items to a new location in the list.

Can I work with more than one favorite Web page at a time?

Working with favorite Web pages in the Organize Favorites dialog box is similar to working with files in a My Computer or Windows Explorer window. To select multiple favorite Web pages, hold down the Ctrl key as you click each page you want to work with. This allows you to move or delete many favorite Web pages at once.

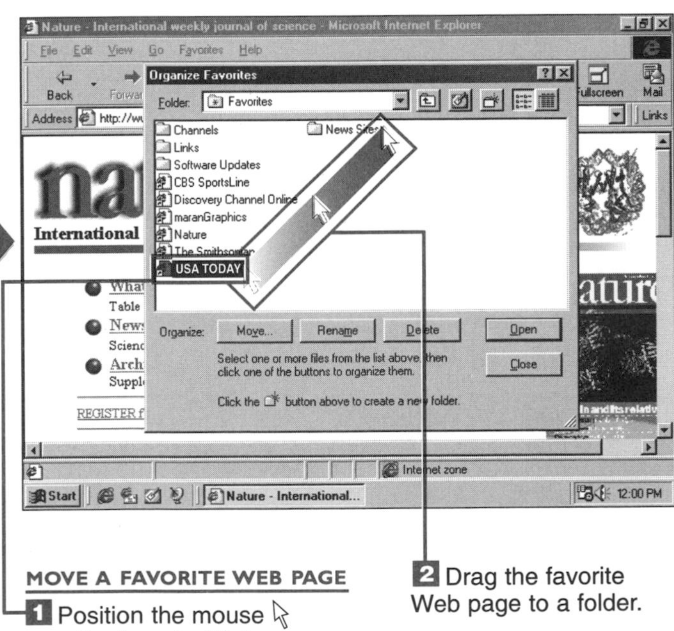

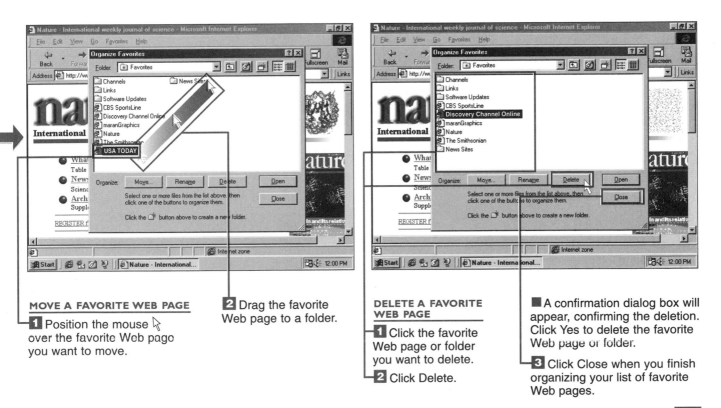

MOVE A FAVORITE WEB PAGE

1 Position the mouse over the favorite Web page you want to move.

2 Drag the favorite Web page to a folder.

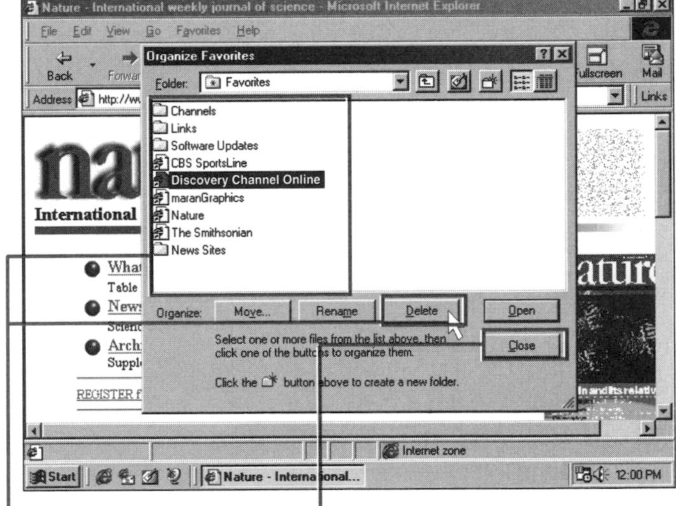

DELETE A FAVORITE WEB PAGE

1 Click the favorite Web page or folder you want to delete.

2 Click Delete.

■ A confirmation dialog box will appear, confirming the deletion. Click Yes to delete the favorite Web page or folder.

3 Click Close when you finish organizing your list of favorite Web pages.

DISPLAY HISTORY OF VIEWED WEB PAGES

The History list keeps track of the Web pages you have recently viewed. You can select a Web page from the History list to easily return to the page.

The History list keeps track of the Web pages you have recently viewed even when you close Internet Explorer. The list is organized into weeks and days so you can quickly find a Web page you viewed on a specific day. Each day contains an alphabetical listing of the Web sites you visited that day. When you select a Web site, a list of all the Web pages you visited at that site appear.

Your History list can grow quite large and may contain hundreds of Web pages. When the History list contains a large number of Web pages, Internet Explorer allows you to scroll through the list.

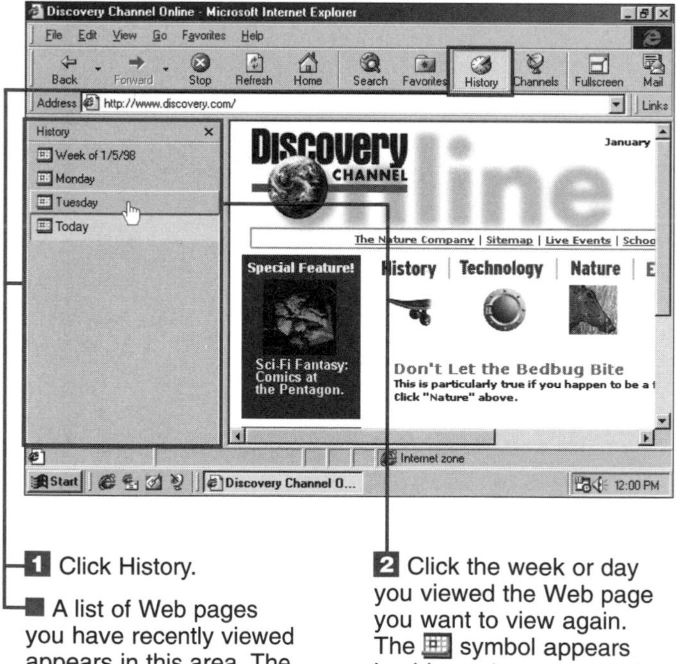

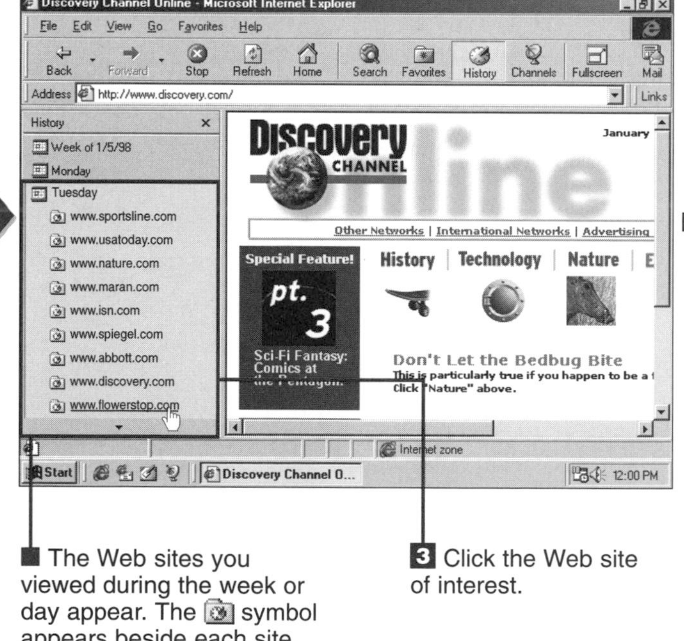

1 Click History.

■ A list of Web pages you have recently viewed appears in this area. The list is organized by week and day.

2 Click the week or day you viewed the Web page you want to view again. The ▦ symbol appears beside each week and day.

■ The Web sites you viewed during the week or day appear. The ◙ symbol appears beside each site.

3 Click the Web site of interest.

TIPS

How long does the History list keep recently viewed Web pages?

The History list keeps track of the Web pages you have viewed over the last 20 days. You can change the number of days by choosing the View menu and then selecting Internet Options. In the History area, double-click the box beside Days to keep pages in history and then type a new number.

Can I clear the History list?

Select the View menu and then click Internet Options. In the History area, click the Clear History button. Clearing the History list frees up space on your computer.

Are there other ways to display recently viewed Web pages?

The File menu contains a short list of Web pages you have recently viewed. Internet Explorer starts a new list on the File menu each time you start the program. Click File and then click the Web page you want to view. You can also display Web pages you viewed since you last started Internet Explorer by clicking the arrow (▾) beside the Back and Forward buttons.

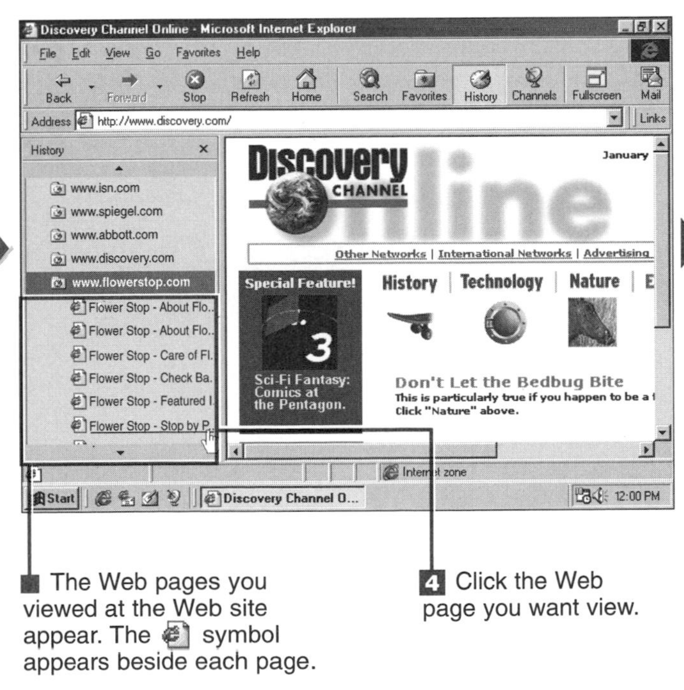

■ The Web pages you viewed at the Web site appear. The symbol appears beside each page.

4 Click the Web page you want view.

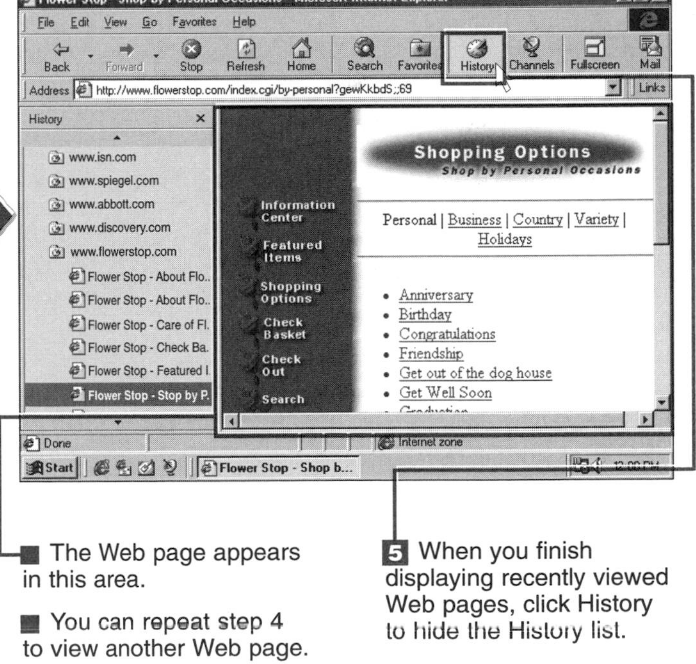

■ The Web page appears in this area.

■ You can repeat step 4 to view another Web page.

5 When you finish displaying recently viewed Web pages, click History to hide the History list.

CHANGE YOUR HOME PAGE

You can specify which Web page you want to appear each time you start Internet Explorer. This Web page is called your home page. While browsing the Web, you can click the Home button at any time to display your home page.

You can use any page on the Web as your home page. You can choose a Web page with news and information related to your personal interests or your work. You may want to use a Web page that provides a good starting point for exploring the Web, such as www.yahoo.com or www.infoseek.com. Your home page can be any Web page you frequently visit.

You can design and create your own home page using a Web page creation program such as FrontPage Express. For information on using FrontPage Express to create Web pages, see pages 570 to 587.

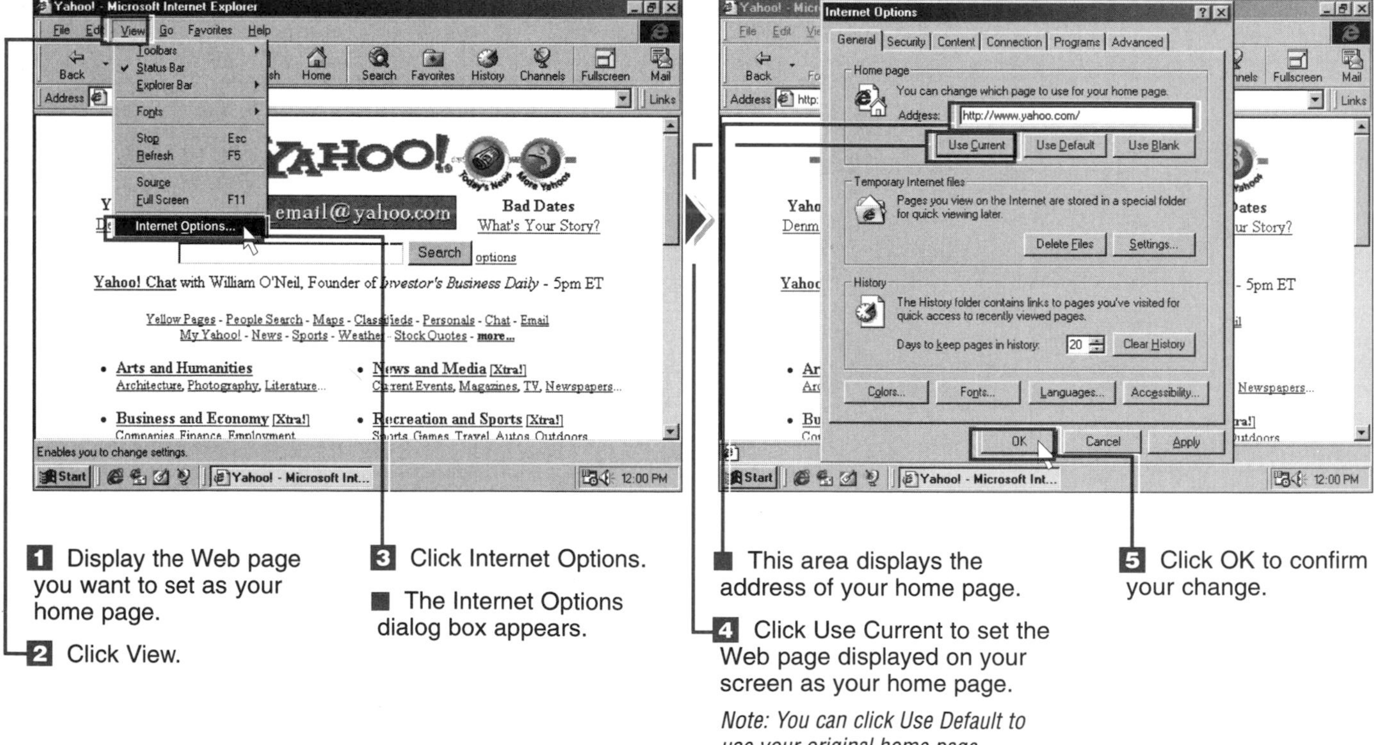

1 Display the Web page you want to set as your home page.

2 Click View.

3 Click Internet Options.

■ The Internet Options dialog box appears.

■ This area displays the address of your home page.

4 Click Use Current to set the Web page displayed on your screen as your home page.

Note: You can click Use Default to use your original home page.

5 Click OK to confirm your change.

DELETE TEMPORARY INTERNET FILES

You can delete temporary Internet files from your hard drive. Temporary Internet files are Web pages Internet Explorer stores on your hard drive while you are browsing the Web.

Before transferring a Web page to your computer, Internet Explorer checks to see if the page is stored in the temporary Internet files. If the Web page is stored in the temporary Internet files, Internet Explorer displays the stored page rather than transferring the page to your computer from the Internet. Using temporary Internet files saves Internet Explorer from having to transfer the same pages to your computer over and over.

Temporary Internet files can take up a lot of space on your hard drive. You can delete these files to free up space on your computer.

You can also delete copies of the Web pages you are subscribed to from your computer. This does not cancel your subscription, but you will not be able to view the subscribed Web pages until Internet Explorer transfers the pages to your computer again. Internet Explorer will transfer the pages to your computer according to the schedule you have specified. For information on subscribing, see page 564.

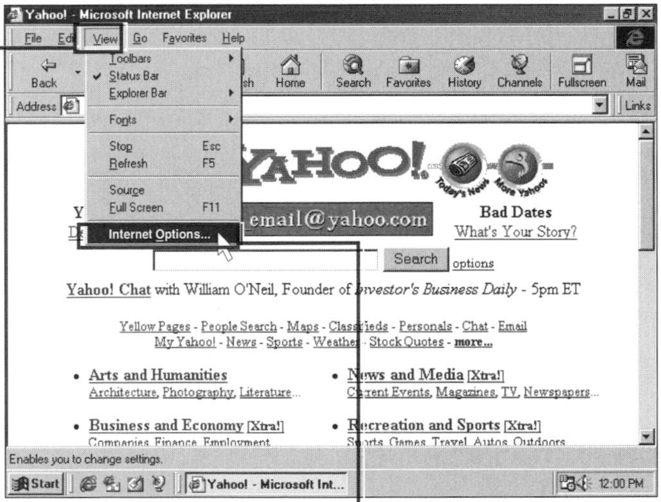

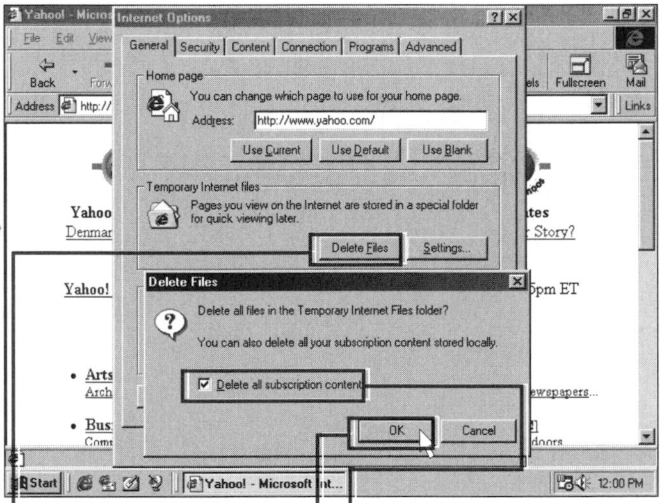

1 Click View.

2 Click Internet Options.

■ The Internet Options dialog box appears.

3 Click Delete Files.

■ A confirmation dialog box appears.

4 Click this option if you want to delete all the subscribed Web pages that are stored on your computer (☐ changes to ☑).

5 Click OK.

VIEW SECURITY LEVELS FOR ZONES

You can assign Web sites available on the Internet and on an intranet to different zones.

The security level of the zone a Web site is assigned to determines the type of content that can be downloaded from the Web site. Some Web sites contain programs that may cause Internet Explorer to malfunction and may damage the information on your computer.

The Local intranet zone contains Web sites on your intranet and has a medium security level. Internet Explorer will warn you before downloading any potentially damaging content from Web sites with the medium security level.

The Trusted sites zone contains Web sites you do not believe will damage the information on your computer and has a low security level. Internet Explorer will not warn you before downloading content from sites with the low security level.

The Restricted sites zone contains Web sites that may include items that could damage the information on your computer. This zone is set to a high security level. Internet Explorer will not download any content that may pose a security problem from Web sites with the high security level.

The Internet zone consists of all the Web sites not in other zones and has a medium security level.

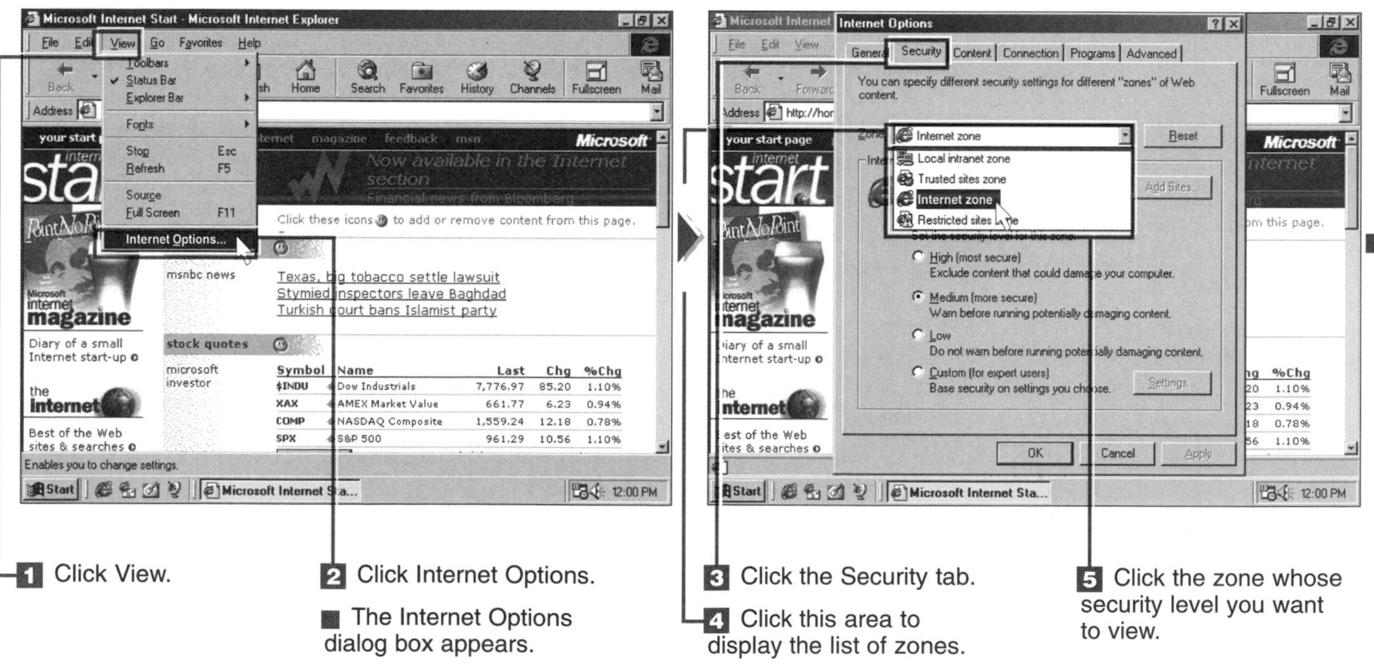

1 Click View.

2 Click Internet Options.

■ The Internet Options dialog box appears.

3 Click the Security tab.

4 Click this area to display the list of zones.

5 Click the zone whose security level you want to view.

TIPS

How do I assign a Web site to a zone?

Web sites can be assigned to the Restricted sites or Trusted sites zones. Select the zone you want to assign a Web site to and then click the Add Sites button. Type the full address of the Web site you want to assign to the zone and then click the Add button. When you are assigning a Web site to the Trusted sites zone, click the Require server verification (https:) for all sites in this zone option (☑ changes to ☐).

Can I assign Web pages stored on my computer to a zone?

No. Internet Explorer assumes that Web pages stored on your computer are secure and will not assign these pages to a zone.

I changed the security level for a zone. How do I once again use the default security level for the zone?

To use the default security level for a zone, select the zone and then click the Reset button.

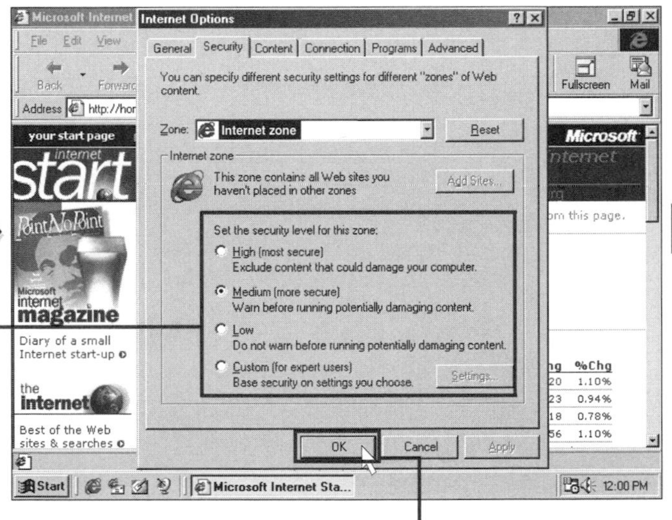

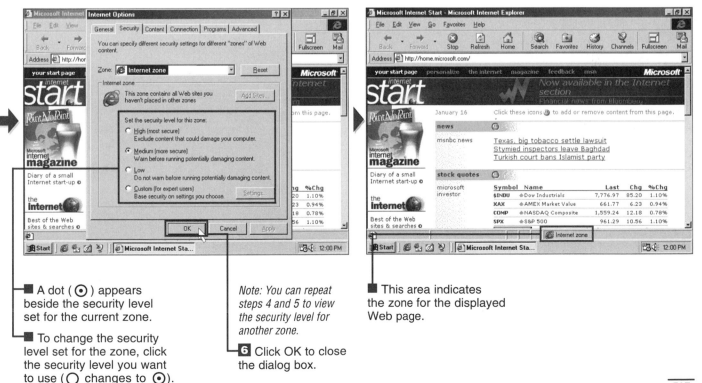

■ A dot (⊙) appears beside the security level set for the current zone.

■ To change the security level set for the zone, click the security level you want to use (○ changes to ⊙).

Note: You can repeat steps 4 and 5 to view the security level for another zone.

6 Click OK to close the dialog box.

■ This area indicates the zone for the displayed Web page.

WORK WITH SECURE WEB CONTENT

Internet Explorer offers many features that can make exchanging information and browsing the World Wide Web more secure. Some people feel it is unsafe to send confidential information such as credit card numbers over the Internet. However, the security features offered by Internet Explorer make it almost impossible for unauthorized people to access your confidential information.

Internet Explorer allows you to connect to secure Web sites to create an almost unbreakable security system. When you connect to a secure Web site, other people on the Internet cannot view the information you transfer.

Addresses of secure Web sites start with "https" instead of "http". Internet Explorer may display a message when you are about to access or leave a secure Web site. Internet Explorer also displays a lock icon (🔒) on the status bar when you are connected to a secure Web site.

Internet Explorer also includes features such as the Content Advisor, Certificates, the Microsoft Profile Assistant and Microsoft Wallet to help meet your specific security needs.

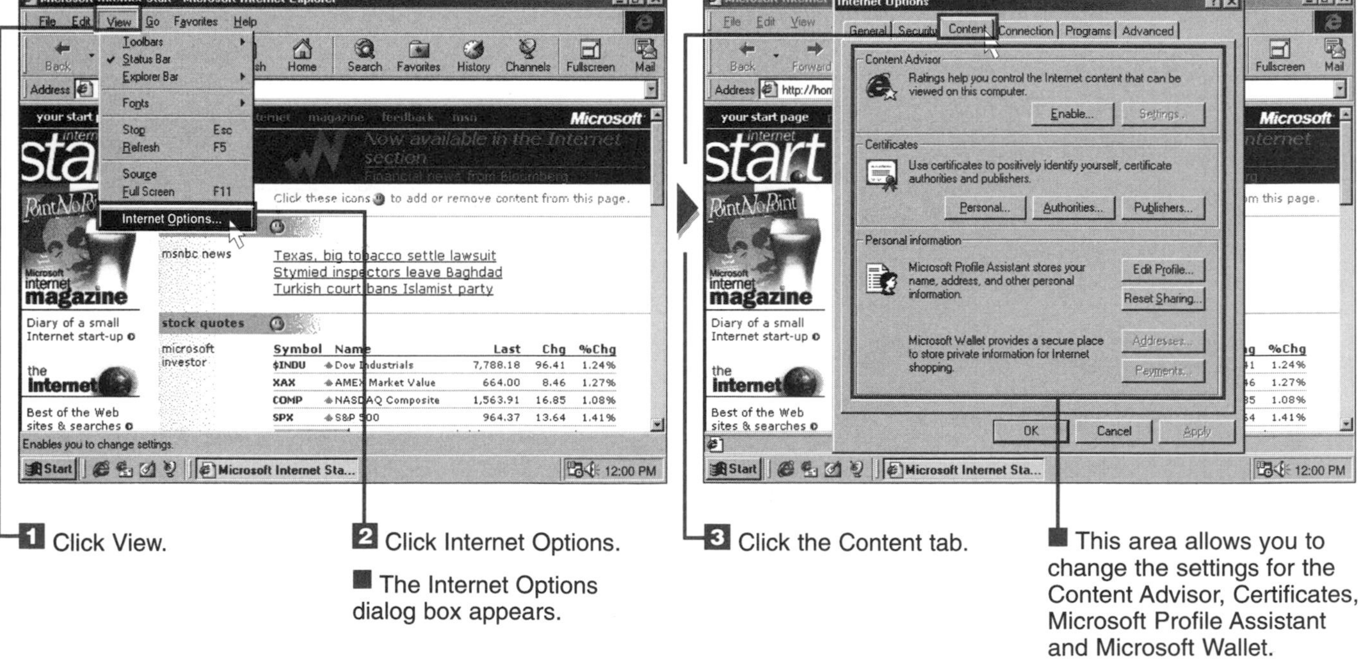

1 Click View.

2 Click Internet Options.

■ The Internet Options dialog box appears.

3 Click the Content tab.

■ This area allows you to change the settings for the Content Advisor, Certificates, Microsoft Profile Assistant and Microsoft Wallet.

Content Advisor

The Content Advisor allows you to restrict access to Web sites depending on the content of the site. This is useful if you want to allow children to browse the World Wide Web while restricting their access to offensive material.

The Content Advisor lets you rate Web site content according to four categories: language, nudity, sex and violence. You can set a supervisor password to help prevent other people from changing the Content Advisor settings.

Although this rating system is gaining in popularity, many Web sites do not yet use the rating system. You can specify whether you want to be able to access Web sites that are not rated.

Certificates

A certificate is similar to an identification card. Personal certificates guarantee the identity of a person and can only be obtained from specific companies. For information on personal certificates, see page 548. Web site certificates ensure that Web sites are genuine. Web site certificates are often used to verify a program manufacturer's identity before you download a program from the Web site.

Microsoft Profile Assistant

The Profile Assistant lets you use an electronic business card, or profile, to share personal information on the Internet. Profiles can contain information such as your e-mail address, phone number, where you work and if you can be contacted using Microsoft NetMeeting.

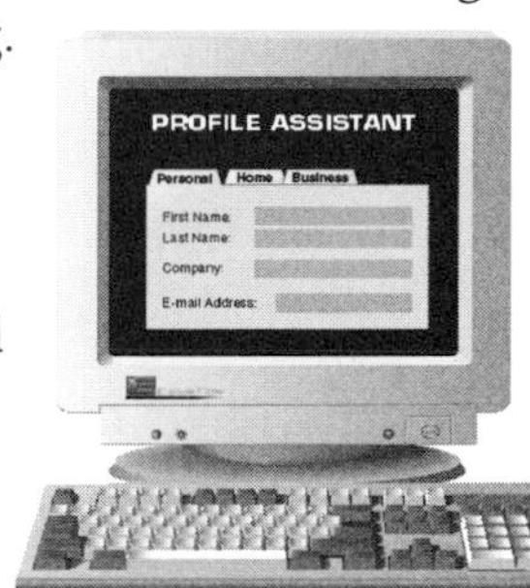

Sending your profile to other people or to a Web site saves you from typing the same information over and over. Many Web sites use profiles to track visits from users.

Microsoft Wallet

Microsoft Wallet is a secure place to store information such as shipping addresses and credit card numbers for shopping on the Internet. You can safely transfer the information stored in Microsoft Wallet to online merchants who support this feature. You must have a major credit card in order to use Microsoft Wallet. If Microsoft Wallet is not installed, you can easily add it to your computer. Microsoft Wallet is located in the Internet Tools component. To add Windows components, see page 610.

READ MESSAGES

You can use Outlook Express to open your messages and read their contents.

The name of a folder containing unread messages appears in bold type. A number in brackets beside a folder indicates how many unread messages the folder contains. Each unread message in a folder displays a closed envelope and appears in bold type. When you read a message, it displays an open envelope and appears in regular type.

Outlook Express has five folders to store your messages. The Inbox folder contains new messages you receive. Messages waiting to be sent are held in the Outbox folder. Messages that have been sent are saved in the Sent Items folder. The Deleted Items folder contains any messages you have deleted. Messages you have not yet completed are stored in the Drafts folder.

Outlook Express automatically checks for new messages every 30 minutes, but you can check for new messages as often as you like.

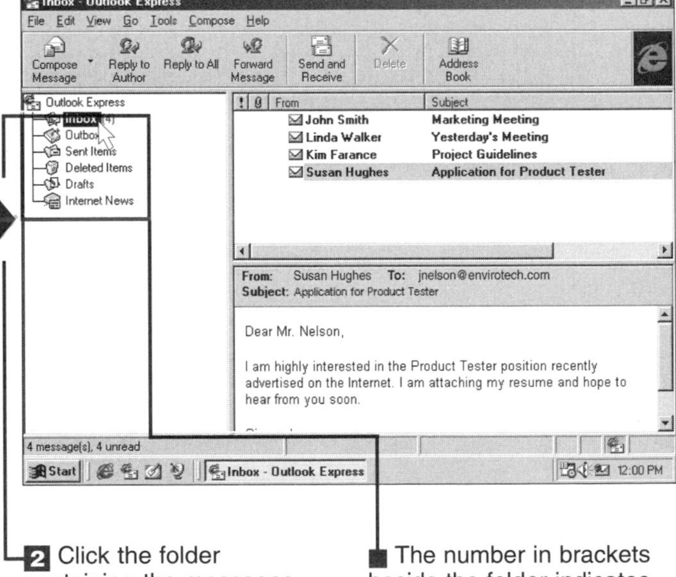

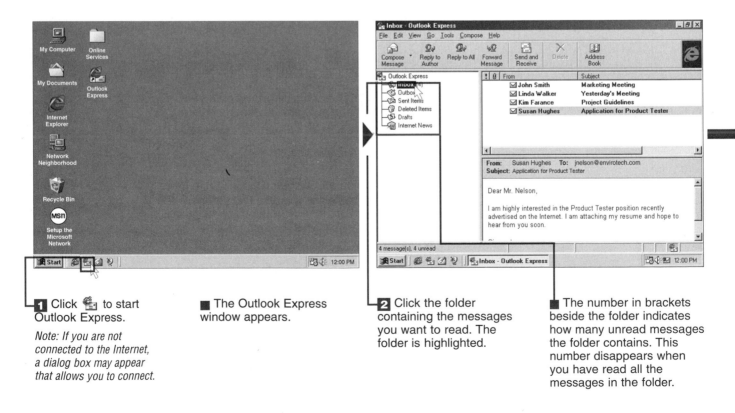

1 Click [icon] to start Outlook Express.

Note: If you are not connected to the Internet, a dialog box may appear that allows you to connect.

■ The Outlook Express window appears.

2 Click the folder containing the messages you want to read. The folder is highlighted.

■ The number in brackets beside the folder indicates how many unread messages the folder contains. This number disappears when you have read all the messages in the folder.

TIPS

Is it possible to view the contents of the message in a larger area?

You can change the size of the three parts of the Outlook Express window. To change the size of the parts of the window, position the mouse over the vertical or horizontal line separating the parts (changes to ↔ or ↕). Drag the line to a new location. You can also double-click a message to view its contents in a separate window.

Can I make a message appear as if I have not read it?

Yes. This is useful if you want to remind yourself to review the message at a later time. Click the message you want to appear as unread. From the Edit menu, select Mark as Unread.

Can I change the font and font size used to display my messages?

Some fonts are easier to read than others. Smaller font sizes let you view more text in a message at once. You can choose the font and font size that are best for you. From the Tools menu, select Options and then click the Read tab. Select the Fonts button and then choose the font and font size you want to use.

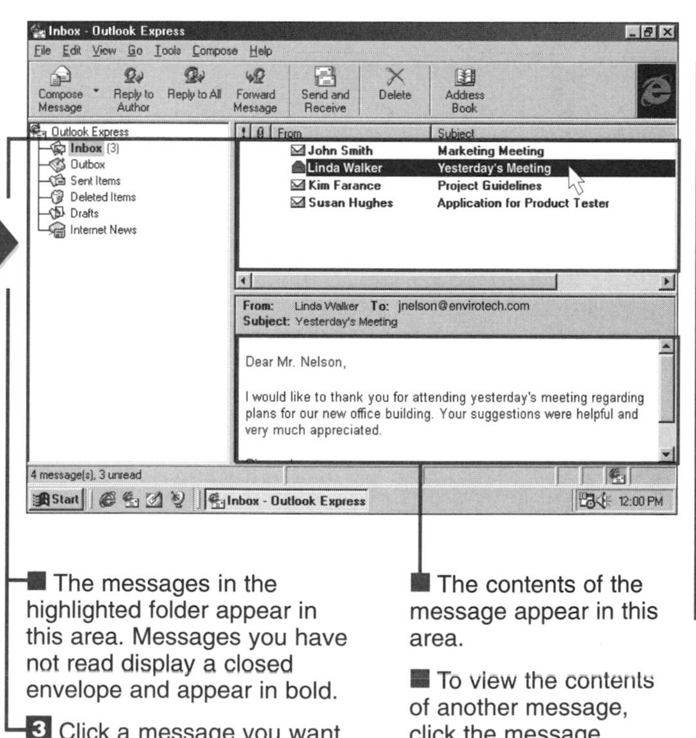

■ The messages in the highlighted folder appear in this area. Messages you have not read display a closed envelope and appear in bold.

3 Click a message you want to read.

■ The contents of the message appear in this area.

■ To view the contents of another message, click the message.

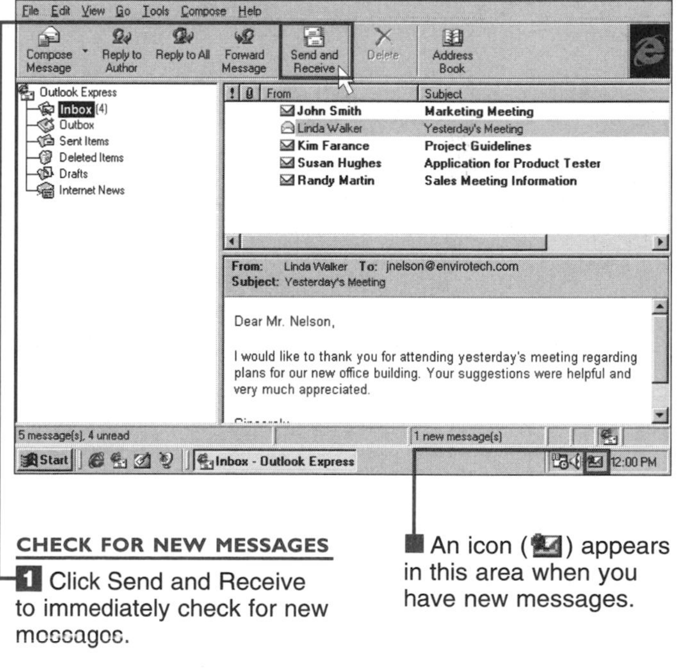

CHECK FOR NEW MESSAGES

1 Click Send and Receive to immediately check for new messages.

■ An icon ( ) appears in this area when you have new messages.

REPLY TO OR FORWARD A MESSAGE

You can reply to a message to answer a question, express an opinion or supply additional information.

You can send your reply to just the person who sent the message or to the sender and everyone who received the original message. When you reply to a message, a new window appears, displaying the name of the recipients and the subject of the message you are replying to.

The reply includes the contents of the original message. This is called quoting. Including the contents of the original message helps the reader identify which message you are replying to. To save the reader time, make sure you delete all parts of the original message that do not directly relate to your reply.

You can also forward a message to another person. When you forward the message, you can add your own comments to the original message. Forwarding a message is useful if you know that another person would be interested in the contents of the message.

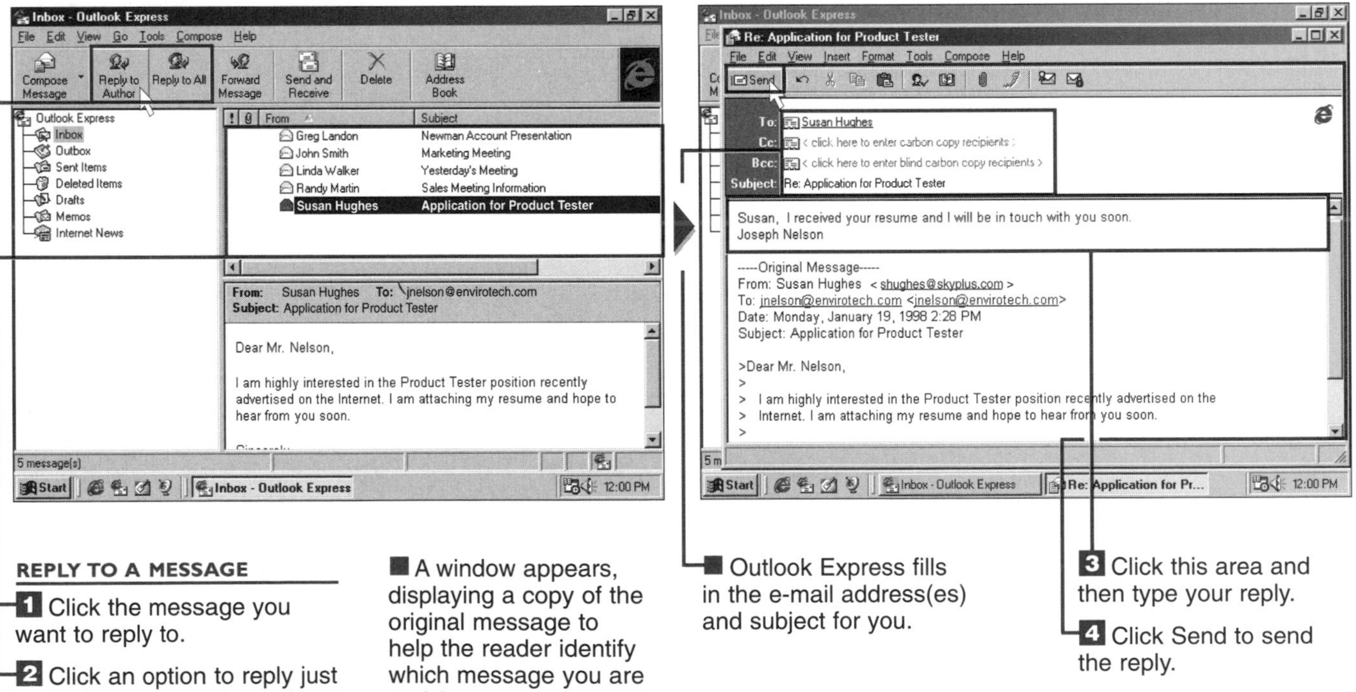

REPLY TO A MESSAGE

1 Click the message you want to reply to.

2 Click an option to reply just to the author or to the author and everyone who received the original message.

■ A window appears, displaying a copy of the original message to help the reader identify which message you are replying to.

■ Outlook Express fills in the e-mail address(es) and subject for you.

3 Click this area and then type your reply.

4 Click Send to send the reply.

Can I stop Outlook Express from including the original message in my replies?

If you do not want to include the original message in your replies, choose the Tools menu and then select Options. Select the Send tab and click the Include message in reply option (☑ changes to ☐).

How do I forward a message to more than one person?

To forward a message to more than one person, repeat steps 1 to 3 on this page. In step 3, separate each e-mail address with a semicolon (;) or a comma (,).

Can I forward a message as an attached file?

You can forward a message as an attached file instead of displaying the contents of the message. The attached file appears as an icon in the message. Click the message you want to forward as an attached file. From the Compose menu, select Forward as Attachment.

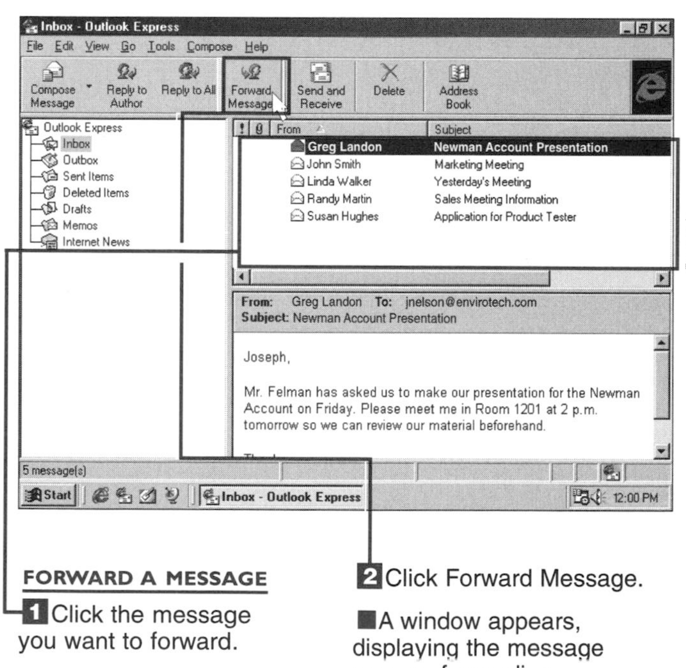

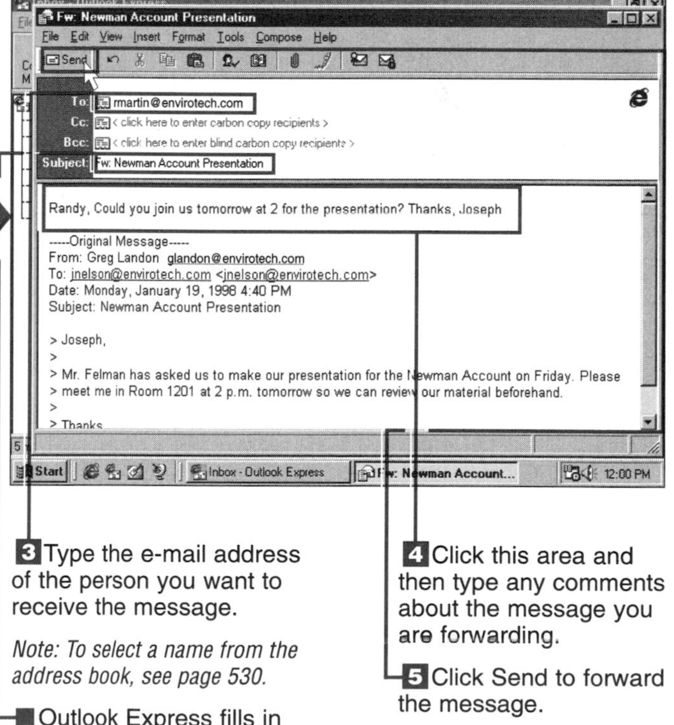

FORWARD A MESSAGE

1 Click the message you want to forward.

2 Click Forward Message.

■ A window appears, displaying the message you are forwarding.

3 Type the e-mail address of the person you want to receive the message.

Note: To select a name from the address book, see page 530.

■ Outlook Express fills in the subject for you.

4 Click this area and then type any comments about the message you are forwarding.

5 Click Send to forward the message.

COMPOSE A MESSAGE

You can compose and send an e-mail message to exchange ideas or request information. To practice sending a message, you can send a message to yourself.

You can address a message to more than one person. You can enter the address of each person you want to receive the original message in the To: area. You can use the Cc: area if you want to send a copy of a message to a person who would be interested in the message, but is not directly involved. By entering an address in the Bcc: area, you can send a copy of the message to a person without anyone else knowing that the person received the message.

When you compose a message, you should enter a subject that will help the reader quickly identify the contents of your message.

Outlook Express allows you to use stationery to send messages with attractive background designs and unique fonts. There are several kinds of stationery available, including designs for birthdays, announcements and invitations.

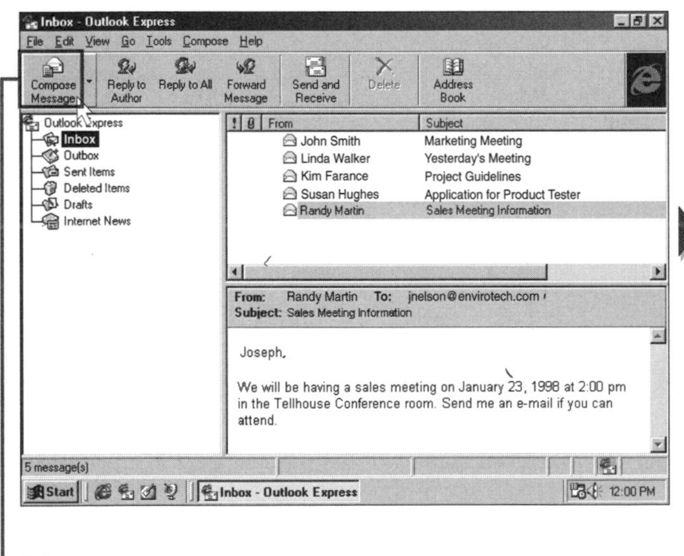

1 Click Compose Message to create a new message.

■ The New Message window appears.

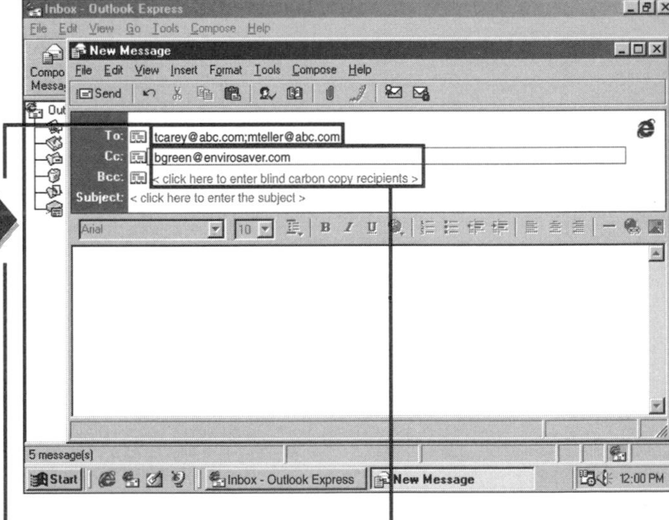

2 Type the e-mail address of the person you want to receive the message.

■ To send the message to more than one person, separate each address with a semicolon (;) or a comma (,).

3 To send a copy of the message to another person, click one of these areas and then type the e-mail address.

Note: To select names from the address book, see page 530.

TIPS

How can I indicate the importance of a message?

You can change the priority of a message to indicate its importance. In the New Message window, display the Tools menu and then select Set Priority. You can choose a high, normal or low priority for the message. The recipient sees an exclamation mark (!) for high priority messages and an arrow (↓) for low priority messages.

How can I find an e-mail address I do not have?

Click the Start button, click Find and then click People. The Find People dialog box allows you to search directories such as Four11 and Bigfoot for e-mail addresses on the Internet.

Can I spell check my messages?

Outlook Express does not include a spell checker, but it can use the spell checker from other Microsoft programs, such as Excel or Word, on your computer. To spell check a message, click the Tools menu in the New Message window and then select Spelling.

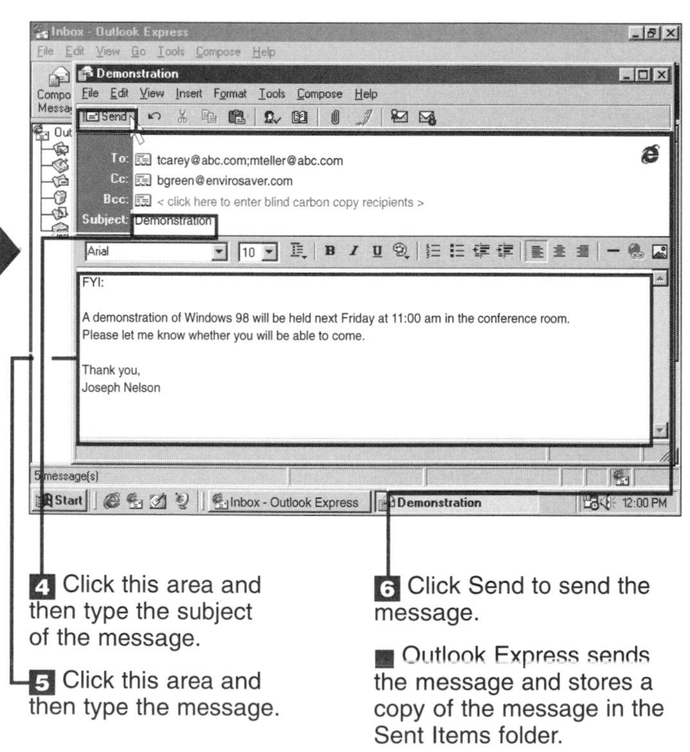

4 Click this area and then type the subject of the message.

5 Click this area and then type the message.

6 Click Send to send the message.

■ Outlook Express sends the message and stores a copy of the message in the Sent Items folder.

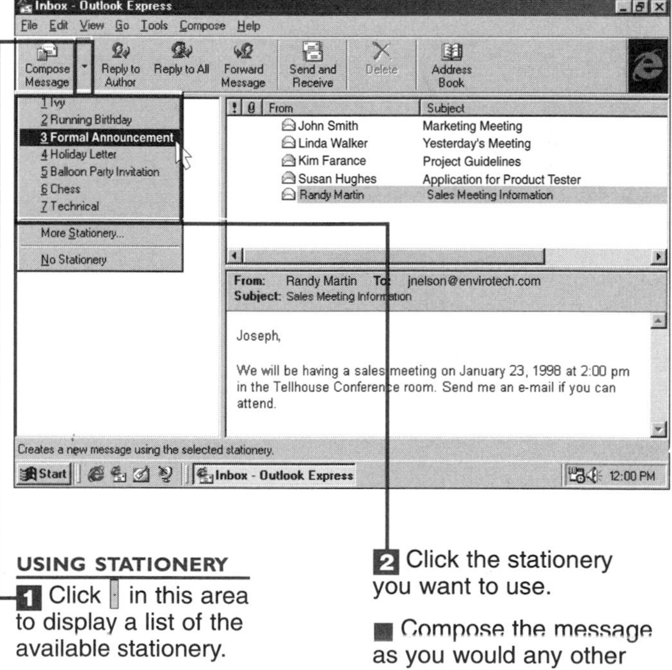

USING STATIONERY

1 Click ▾ in this area to display a list of the available stationery.

2 Click the stationery you want to use.

■ Compose the message as you would any other message.

ADD A NAME TO THE ADDRESS BOOK

You can store the names and e-mail addresses of people you frequently send messages to in the address book.

When you add a new name to the address book, you can enter the person's first, middle and last name. Outlook Express also gives you the option of entering a nickname for the person. A nickname is a name or word that describes the person. You must also enter the person's e-mail address.

When you send a message, you can select an e-mail address from the address book. You can also quickly address the message by typing the person's nickname. Outlook Express will automatically fill in the e-mail address of the person for you.

Using the address book to automatically enter e-mail addresses saves you from having to type the same addresses over and over. Using the address book also helps prevent typing mistakes in an address. Typing mistakes can result in a message being delivered to the wrong person or being returned to you.

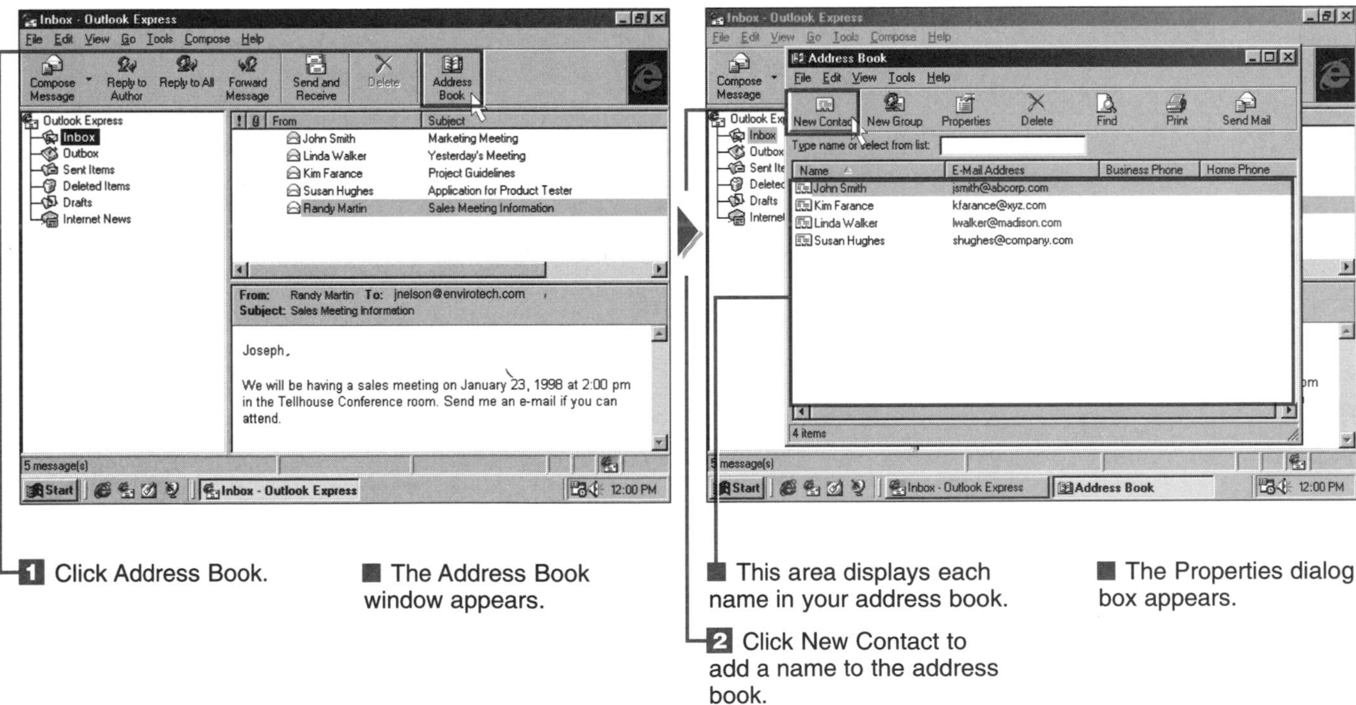

1 Click Address Book.

■ The Address Book window appears.

■ This area displays each name in your address book.

2 Click New Contact to add a name to the address book.

■ The Properties dialog box appears.

TIPS

Can I quickly add the addresses of people I exchange messages with to the address book?

When you receive a message, you can quickly add the person's name to the address book. Double-click the message to display the message in its own window. Right-click the name you want to add to the address book and then click Add To Address Book. You can also have Outlook Express automatically enter the addresses of people you send replies to in the address book. In the Outlook Express window, select the Tools menu and then click Options. On the General tab select the Automatically put people I reply to in my Address Book option (☐ changes to ☑).

How do I change the information for a person in the address book?

In the Address Book window, double-click the person's name to display the information for the person and then make the changes. To delete a person from the address book, click the person's name and then press the Delete key.

Can I send the same message to many people at the same time?

You can add a group to the address book to be able to send the same message to many people at the same time. See page 528.

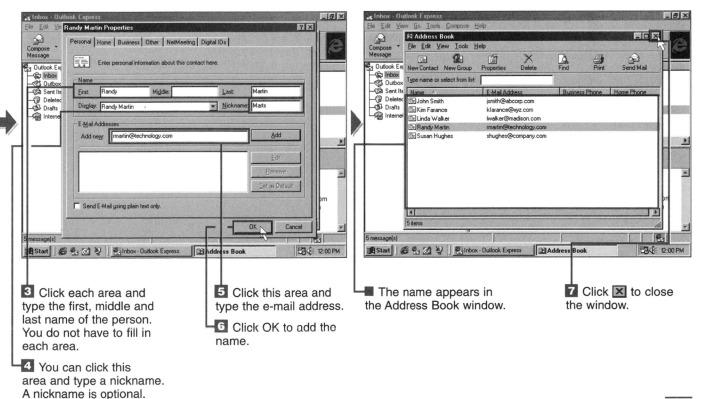

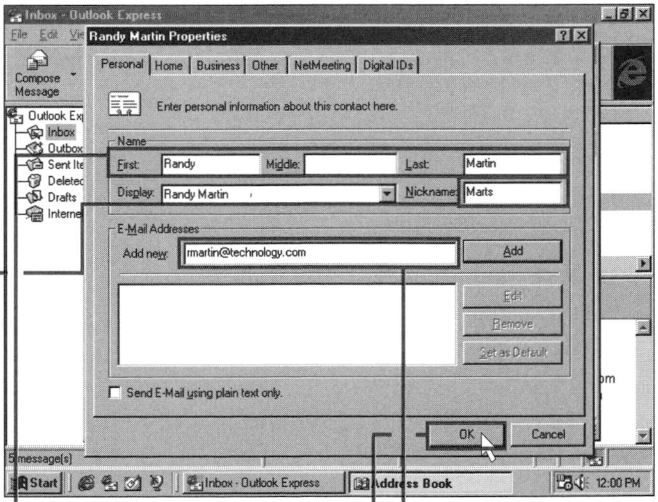

3 Click each area and type the first, middle and last name of the person. You do not have to fill in each area.

4 You can click this area and type a nickname. A nickname is optional.

5 Click this area and type the e-mail address.

6 Click OK to add the name.

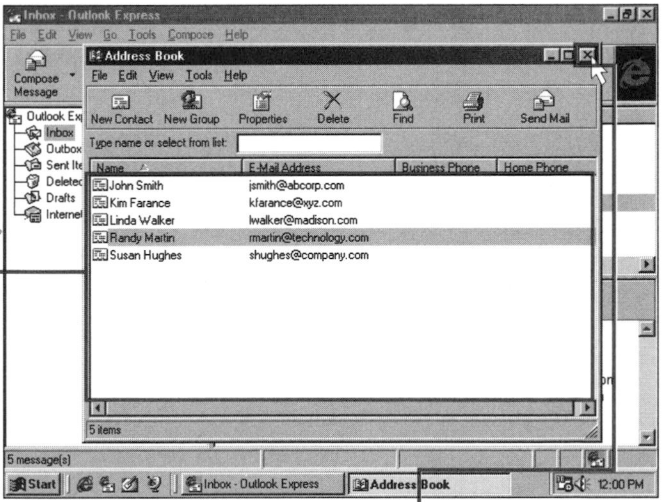

■ The name appears in the Address Book window.

7 Click ☒ to close the window.

CREATE A GROUP IN THE ADDRESS BOOK

You can create a group in the address book to send the same message to many people at once. Creating a group saves you the time of having to enter each person's address into a message. For example, if you are planning to send a message to your customers advising them of your monthly specials, you can create a group to send the message to all your customers at once.

You can use the addresses in your address book to create the new group. Each group appears as a name in the address book. You can create as many groups as you need.

When composing a message you want to send to a group, you can select the name of the group from the address book. You can also type the name of the group in the New Message window. Outlook Express will send the message to everyone in the group.

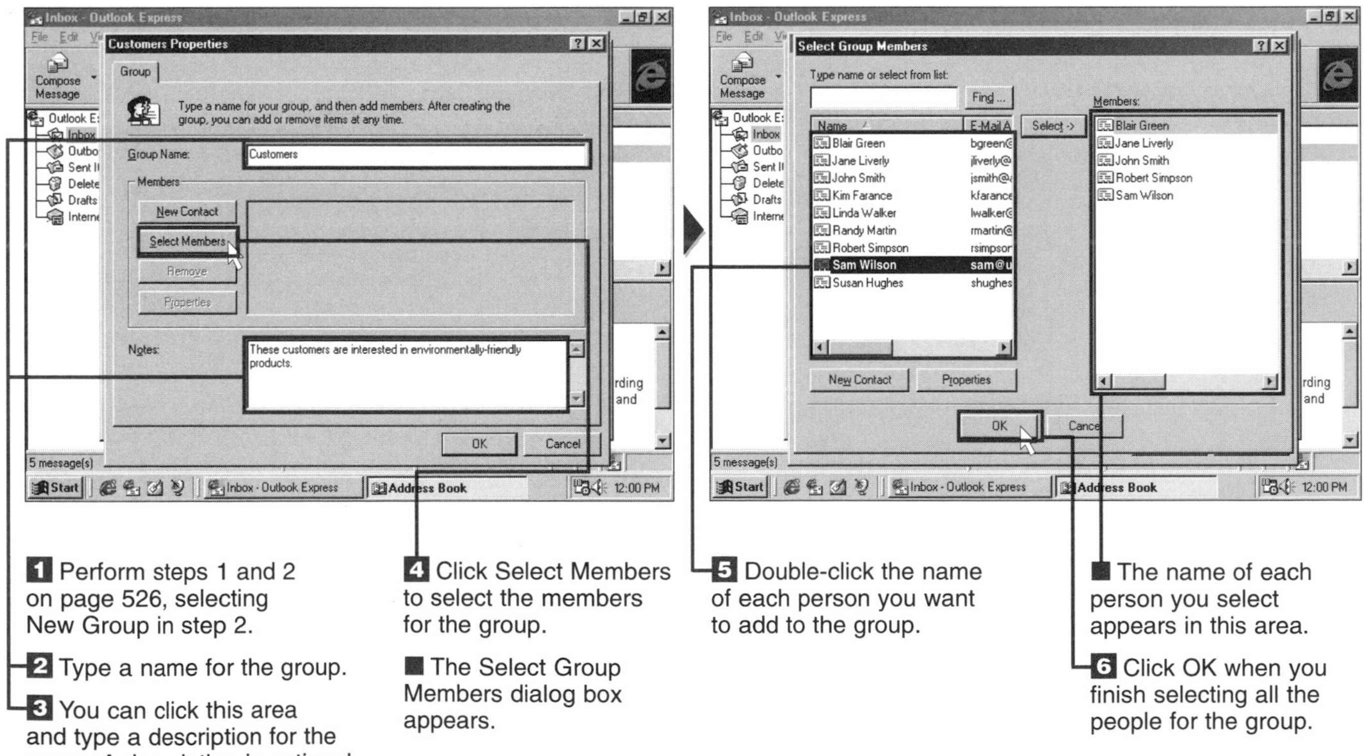

1 Perform steps 1 and 2 on page 526, selecting New Group in step 2.

2 Type a name for the group.

3 You can click this area and type a description for the group. A description is optional.

4 Click Select Members to select the members for the group.

■ The Select Group Members dialog box appears.

5 Double-click the name of each person you want to add to the group.

■ The name of each person you select appears in this area.

6 Click OK when you finish selecting all the people for the group.

TIPS

How do I remove a name from a group?

In the Address Book window, double-click the group to display the list of names in the group. Select the name you want to remove from the group and then press the Delete key. You can also remove a name from a group by deleting the name from the address book. This will remove the name from all the groups it was in.

How do I remove an entire group from my address book?

In the Address Book window, click the name of the group you want to remove and then press the Delete key.

Can I add a name that is not in the address book to a group?

You must add a name to the address book before you can include the name in a group. In the Select Group Members dialog box, click the New Contact button to add the name to the address book. See page 526 for more information.

How do I know if all of the messages have been sent?

Outlook Express places the messages that have been sent in the Sent Items folder. If Outlook Express cannot deliver a message, you may receive a message informing you which people did not receive the message.

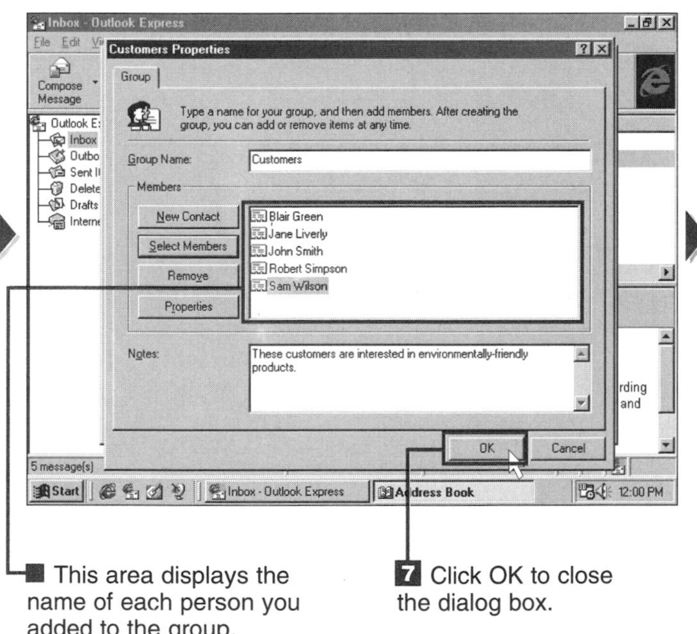

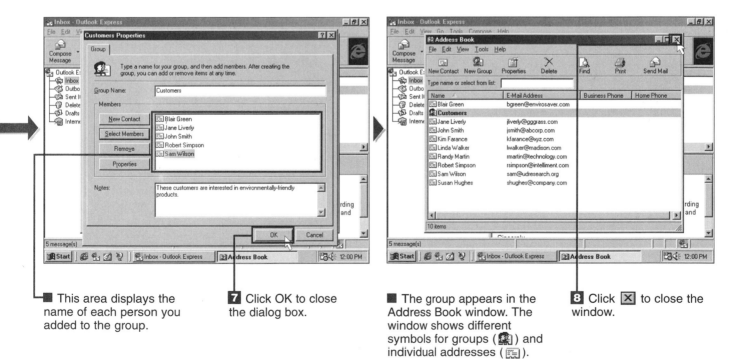

■ This area displays the name of each person you added to the group.

7 Click OK to close the dialog box.

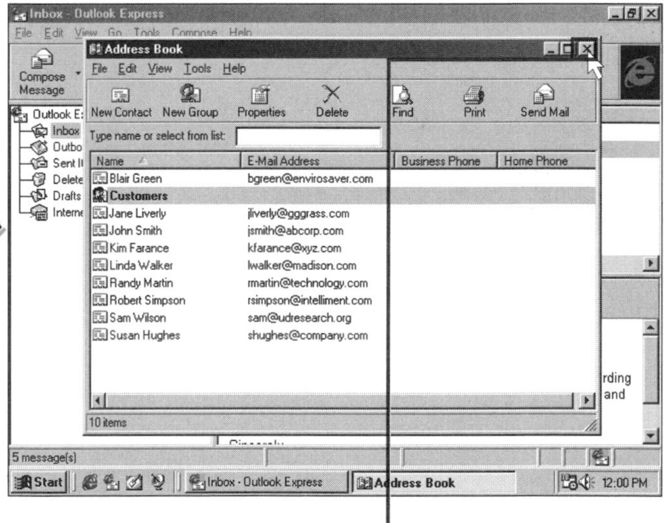

■ The group appears in the Address Book window. The window shows different symbols for groups ( ) and individual addresses ( ).

8 Click ☒ to close the window.

SELECT A NAME FROM THE ADDRESS BOOK

When sending a message, you can select the name of the person you want to receive the message from the address book. Selecting names from the address book saves you from having to remember and type addresses you use often.

The address book makes it easy to send a message when you do not remember the exact spelling of the recipient's address. The address book also reduces the possibility that the message will be undeliverable because of a typing mistake in the address.

The address book makes it easy to address a message to more than one person. You can specify the people you want to receive the original message. You can also send a copy of a message, called a carbon copy (Cc), to another person. This is useful if you want to send a copy of the message to someone who is not directly involved, but would be interested in the message. The address book also allows you to send a blind carbon copy (Bcc) of the message. A blind carbon copy is useful if you want to send a copy of the message to a person without anyone else knowing that the person received the message.

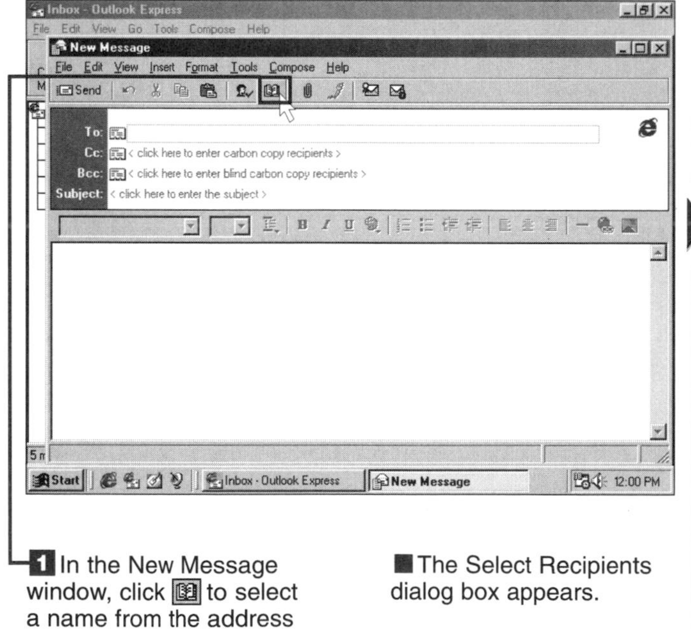

1 In the New Message window, click [address book icon] to select a name from the address book.

Note: To display the New Message window, perform step 1 on page 524.

■ The Select Recipients dialog box appears.

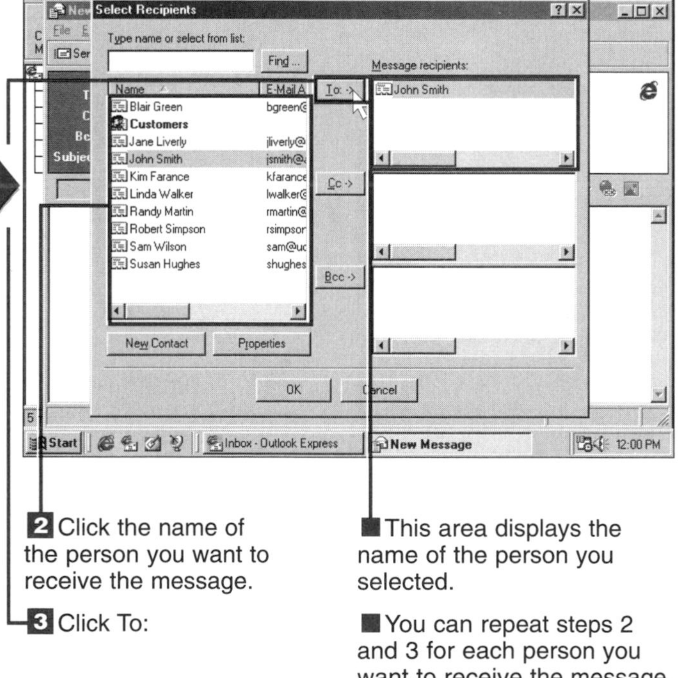

2 Click the name of the person you want to receive the message.

3 Click To:

■ This area displays the name of the person you selected.

■ You can repeat steps 2 and 3 for each person you want to receive the message.

TIPS

Is there a faster way to select a name from the address book?

You can quickly enter names from the address book by typing the first few letters of a person's nickname, name or e-mail address in the To:, Cc: or Bcc: areas in the New Message window. If the person is listed in your address book, Outlook Express will automatically complete the name for you.

I know a person is in the address book, but I can't remember their name. What can I do?

Type as much of the name as you know in the To: area and then click the Check Names button ( ). Outlook Express will either complete the name for you or allow you to choose the name from a list of possible matches.

How do I add names to the address book?

To add names to the address book, see page 526.

Can I mix names selected from the address book with names I type?

You can use names from the address book and names you type to send a message. When you type names in the New Message window, you must separate the names with a comma (,) or a semicolon (;).

How do I remove a name from the To, Cc or Bcc area in the Select Recipients dialog box?

To remove a name, click the name and then press the Delete key.

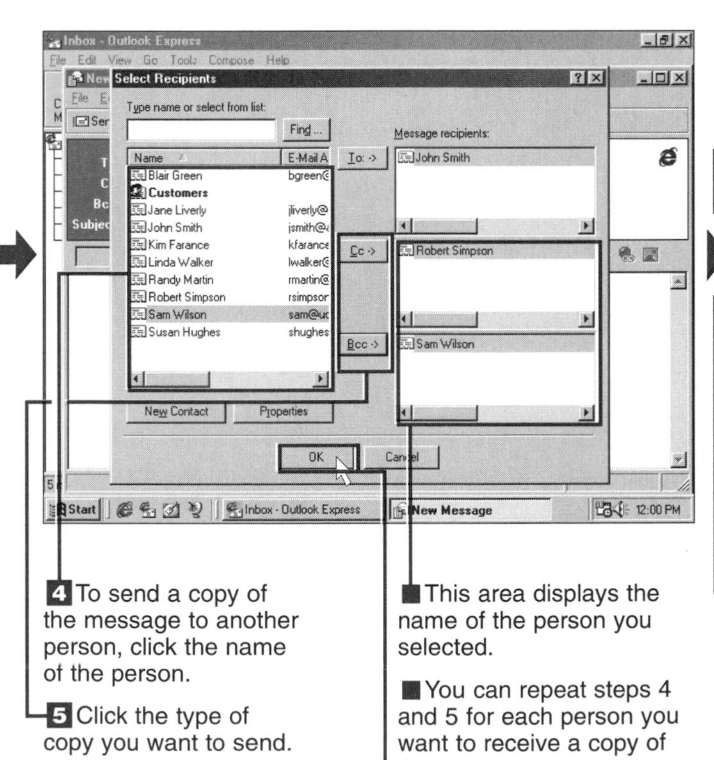

4 To send a copy of the message to another person, click the name of the person.

5 Click the type of copy you want to send.

■ This area displays the name of the person you selected.

■ You can repeat steps 4 and 5 for each person you want to receive a copy of the message.

6 Click OK.

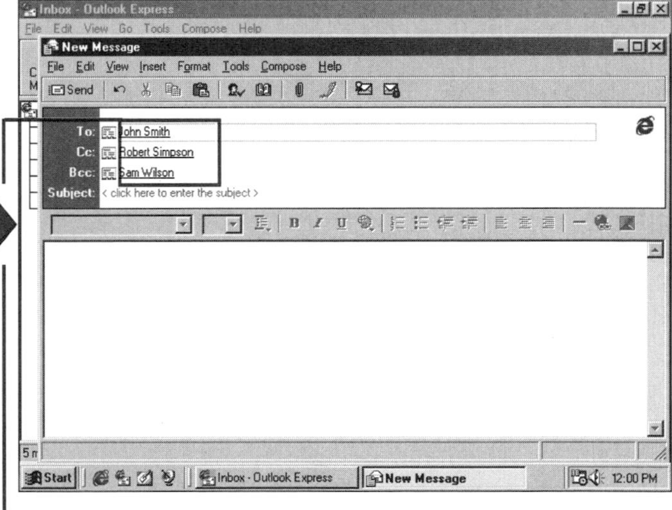

■ This area displays the name of each person you selected from the address book.

■ You can now finish composing the message.

FORMAT MESSAGES

You can format the text in a message you are composing. The formatting features found in Outlook Express are similar to those found in most word processing programs.

You can change the design and size of the text in a message. Changing the design and size of text allows you to make your messages more interesting and can help make long messages easier to read. You can use the bold, italic and underline styles to emphasize information. Changing the color of the text helps to draw attention to important information and can make a message more attractive.

Outlook Express uses HyperText Markup Language (HTML) to format messages. HTML is the code used to display pages on the World Wide Web. Most new e-mail programs use HTML to format messages.

If the recipient of the message uses an e-mail program that cannot display HTML formatted text, the message will appear as plain text with no formatting.

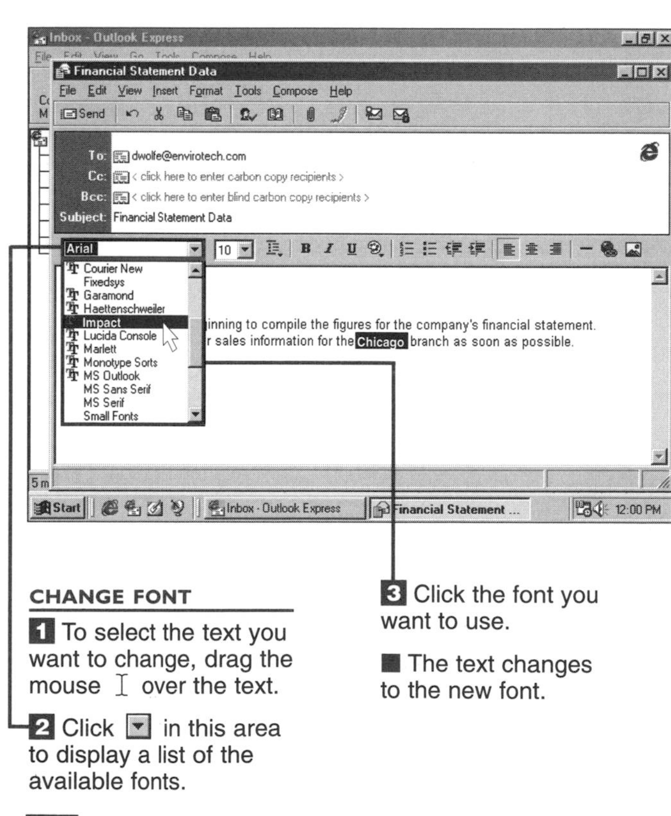

CHANGE FONT

1 To select the text you want to change, drag the mouse over the text.

2 Click ▾ in this area to display a list of the available fonts.

3 Click the font you want to use.

■ The text changes to the new font.

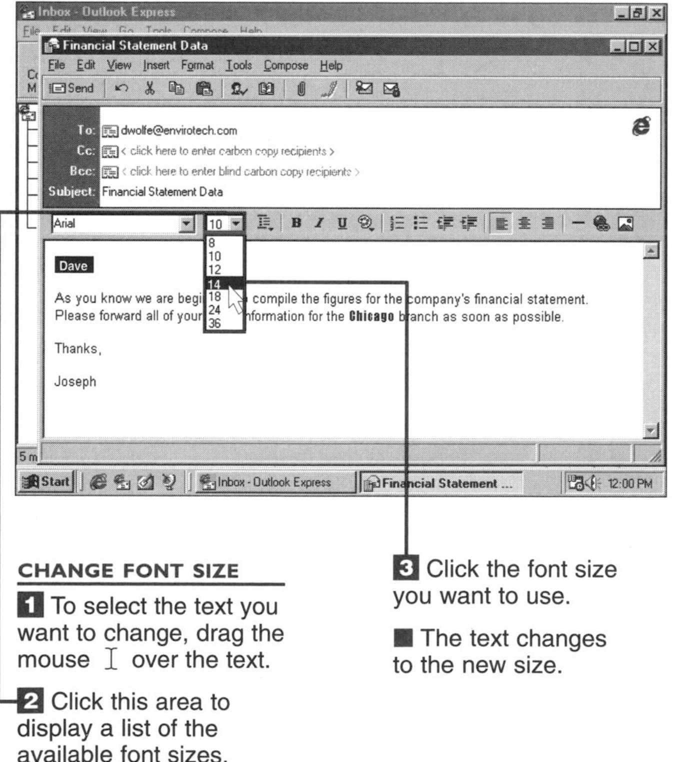

CHANGE FONT SIZE

1 To select the text you want to change, drag the mouse over the text.

2 Click this area to display a list of the available font sizes.

3 Click the font size you want to use.

■ The text changes to the new size.

TIPS

Why does Outlook Express underline the e-mail and Web page addresses I type in a message?

Outlook Express automatically converts any e-mail and Web page addresses you type into a link. If the person who receives your message has a an e-mail program that can work with links, they will be able to select the link to send a message or connect to the Web page.

Can I change the background color of a message?

To change the background color of a message you are sending, choose the Format menu then select Background. Click Color and then select the background color you want to use. Make sure you use text and background colors that work well together. For example, red text on a blue background can be difficult to read.

Can I remove the formatting from a message?

You may want to remove the formatting from a message when you know the recipient of the message uses an e-mail program that cannot display HTML formatted text. In the New Message window, select the Format menu and then click Plain Text. Removing the formatting also reduces the size of the message.

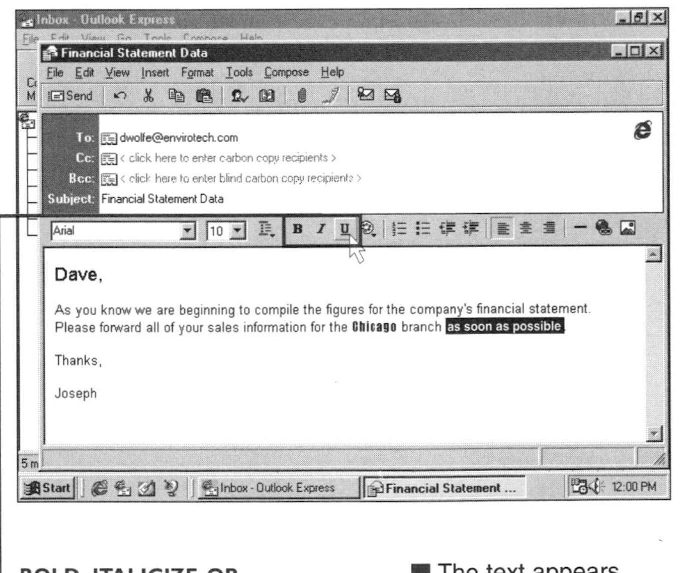

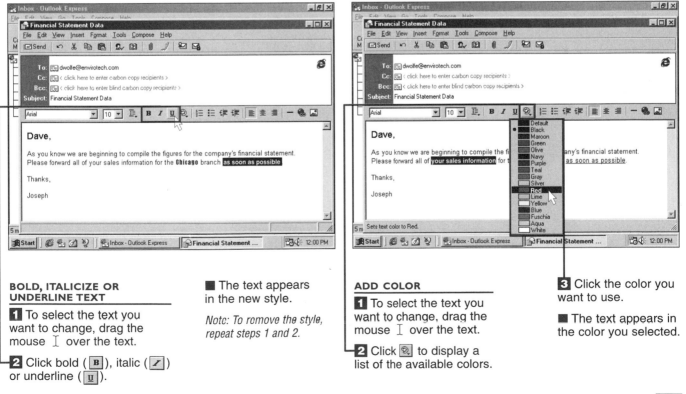

BOLD, ITALICIZE OR UNDERLINE TEXT

1 To select the text you want to change, drag the mouse I over the text.

2 Click bold (B), italic (I) or underline (U).

■ The text appears in the new style.

Note: To remove the style, repeat steps 1 and 2.

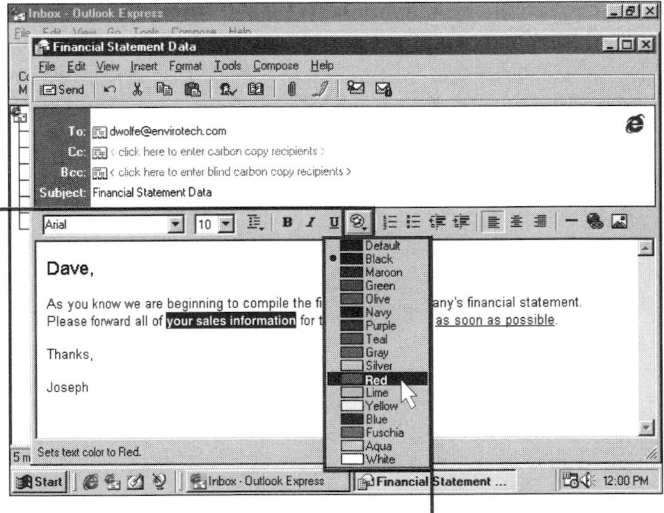

ADD COLOR

1 To select the text you want to change, drag the mouse I over the text.

2 Click the color button to display a list of the available colors.

3 Click the color you want to use.

■ The text appears in the color you selected.

ATTACH A FILE TO A MESSAGE

You can attach a file to a message. This is useful when you want to include additional information with a message.

You can attach many different types of files to your messages. You can attach images, documents, video or sound recordings and even program files. The computer receiving the message must have the necessary hardware and software to display or play the file you attach.

When you receive a message with an attached file, you can easily open and view the file. Some files, such as program files, can contain viruses. If you open and run a program file that contains a virus, the virus could be transferred to your computer. Therefore, it is important to make sure the files you receive are from reliable sources. When you select a file you want to view, Outlook Express asks if you want to open or save the file. You should save the file to a folder on your computer and run an anti-virus program on the file before you open it.

Some pictures, such as those in the .bmp, .jpg and .gif formats, are displayed in the body of the message, as well as in the list of attached files.

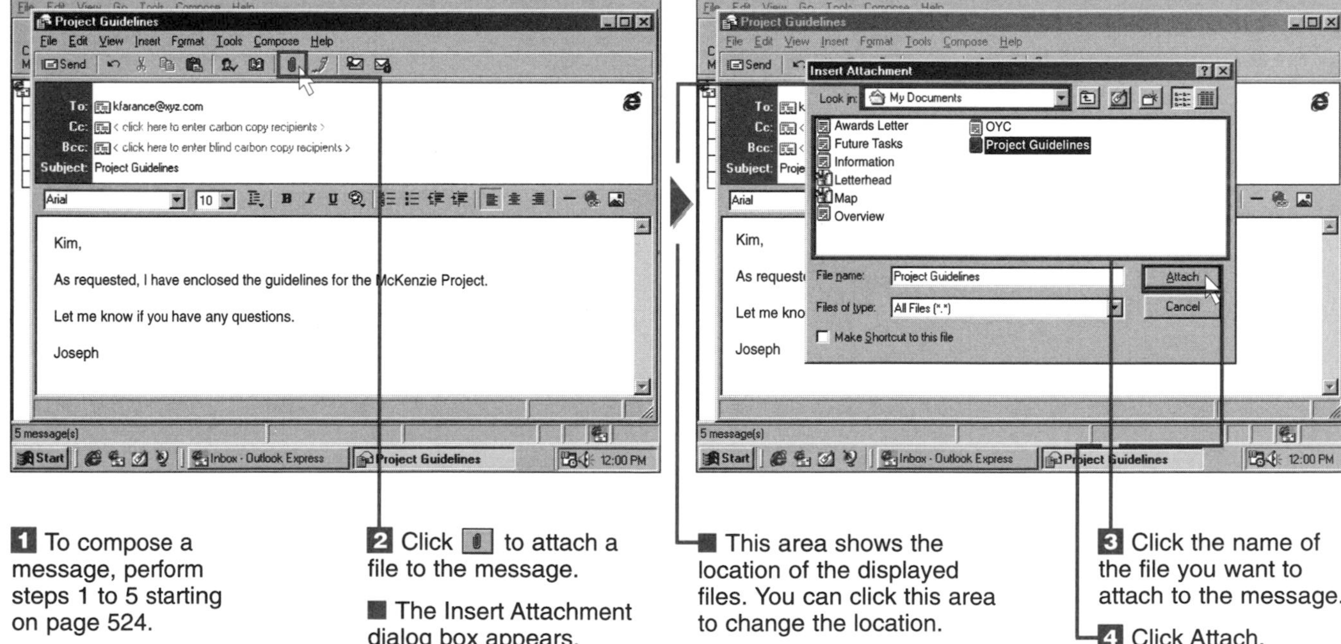

1 To compose a message, perform steps 1 to 5 starting on page 524.

2 Click [attach icon] to attach a file to the message.

■ The Insert Attachment dialog box appears.

■ This area shows the location of the displayed files. You can click this area to change the location.

3 Click the name of the file you want to attach to the message.

4 Click Attach.

TIPS

Can I drag and drop a file into a message?

You can drag and drop a file into a message from the desktop or any open window. An icon appears in the message. This is the easiest way to insert many files into a message.

Can I send a large message with many attachments?

Many mail servers will not transfer messages larger than 1 MB. To send a large message, you can break the message into several small messages. In the Outlook Express window, select the Tools menu and then click Accounts. Select the Mail tab, click the Properties button and then click the Advanced tab. Select the Break apart messages larger than option and then specify the maximum file size you can send.

Why does the program I sent not work on the other computer?

The program may not be compatible with the operating system on the other computer. Also, Outlook Express has to encode the program file before it can send the program. The recipient's e-mail program may not be able to decode the program file properly.

Can I prevent Outlook Express from saving copies of the messages and attached files I send in the Sent Items folder?

In the Outlook Express window, display the Tools menu, click Options and then select the Send tab. Click the Save copy of sent messages in the Sent Items folder option (☑ changes to ☐).

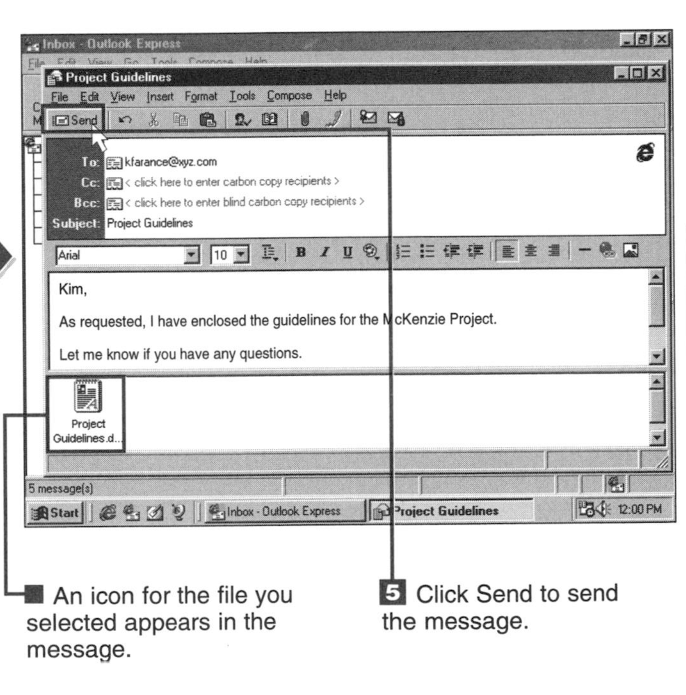

■ An icon for the file you selected appears in the message.

5 Click Send to send the message.

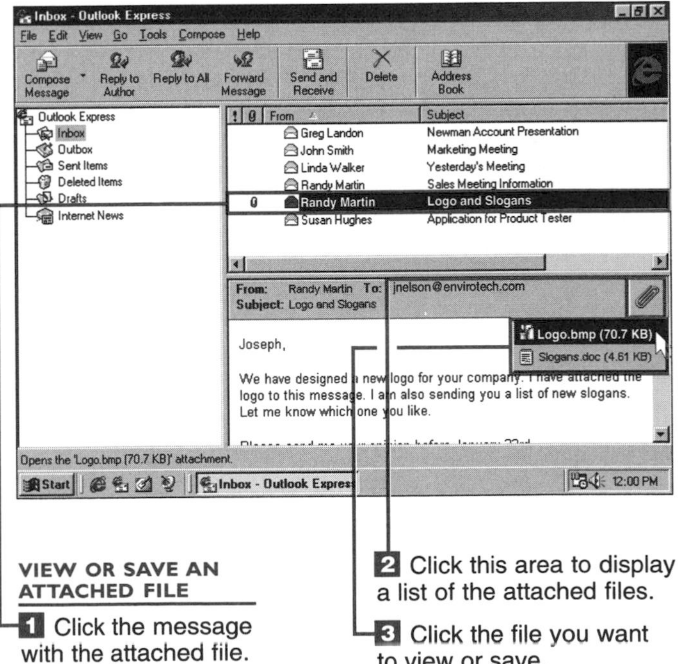

VIEW OR SAVE AN ATTACHED FILE

1 Click the message with the attached file.

A message with an attached file displays a paper clip icon ( ).

2 Click this area to display a list of the attached files.

3 Click the file you want to view or save.

■ Outlook Express will ask if you want to open or save the file.

ADD A SIGNATURE TO MESSAGES

You can have Outlook Express add information about yourself to the bottom of every message you send. This information is called a signature. A signature saves you from having to type the same information every time you send a message.

A signature can include information such as your name, e-mail address, occupation or Web page address. If you wish, you can use plain characters to display simple pictures in your signature. Many people use a signature to display their favorite humorous or inspirational quote.

You should leave a blank line at the beginning of your signature to separate it from the body of your message. As a courtesy to people who will be reading your messages, you should limit your signature to 4 or 5 lines.

You can have Outlook Express add your signature to all the messages you send, reply to and forward.

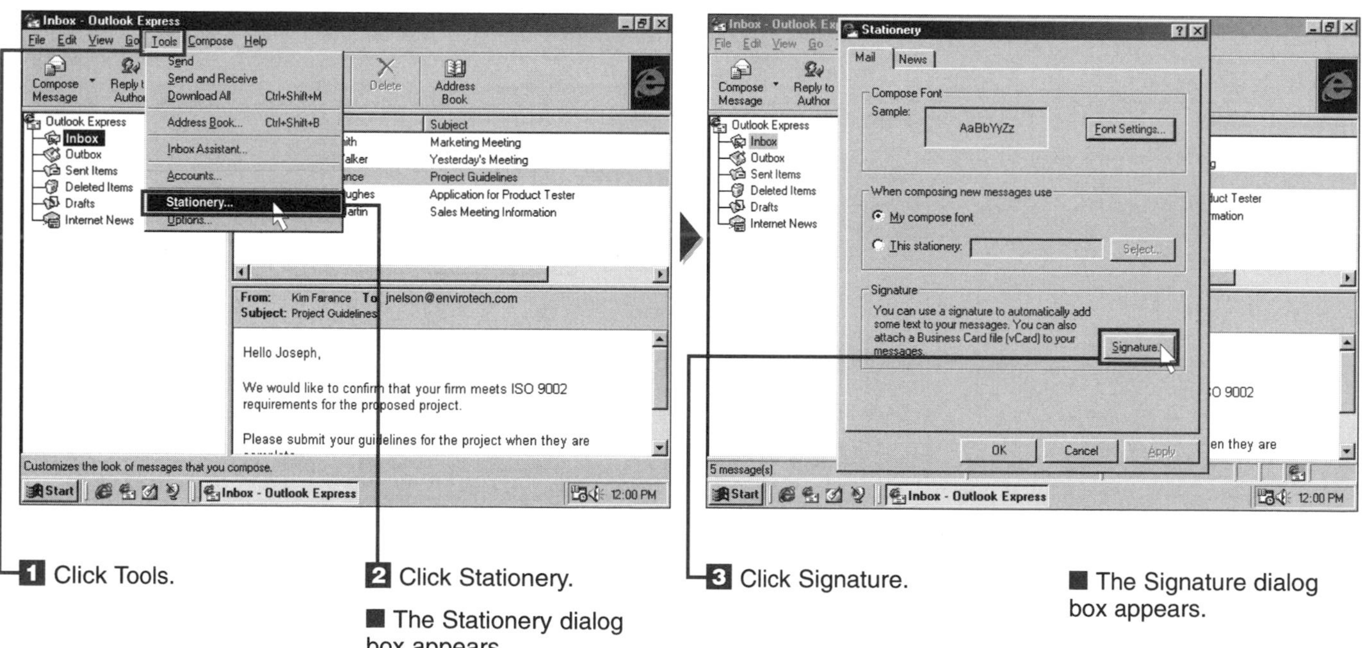

1 Click Tools.

2 Click Stationery.

■ The Stationery dialog box appears.

3 Click Signature.

■ The Signature dialog box appears.

TIPS

Can I stop adding a signature to all my messages?

If you no longer want to add a signature to all your messages, perform steps 1 to 4 below (☑ changes to ☐ in step 4). You can add a signature to a single message at any time by selecting the Insert Signature button (✎) when you are composing the message.

Can I use a file on my computer as my signature?

Yes. Use a text editor such as Notepad to create the file you want to use as your signature. Then perform steps 1 to 5 below, selecting File in step 5. Click the Browse button to find the file on your computer.

Can I attach additional information to my messages?

You can use a Business Card to send contact information, such as your phone number and address, to other people. You must first click the New button in the Signature dialog box to add your personal information to the address book. In the Signature dialog box, click the Card area and select your name. Then click the Attach card to all outgoing messages option. If the recipient's e-mail program supports Business Cards, the recipient can click the Business Card (▦) symbol in your message to read your contact information.

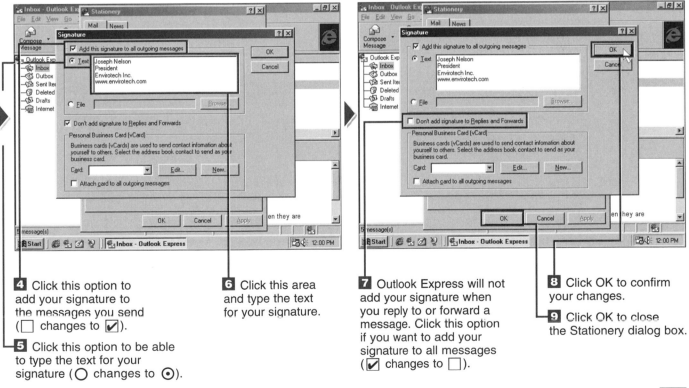

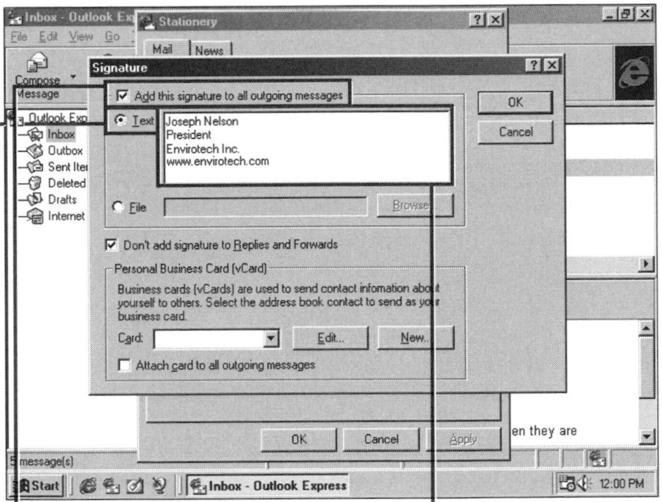

4 Click this option to add your signature to the messages you send (☐ changes to ☑).

5 Click this option to be able to type the text for your signature (○ changes to ⦿).

6 Click this area and type the text for your signature.

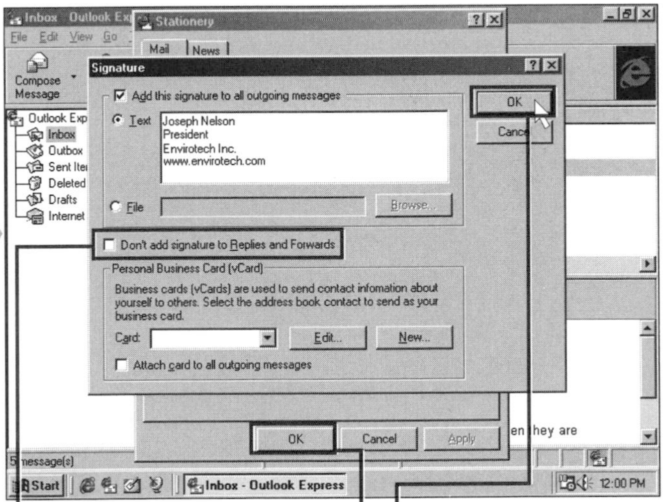

7 Outlook Express will not add your signature when you reply to or forward a message. Click this option if you want to add your signature to all messages (☑ changes to ☐).

8 Click OK to confirm your changes.

9 Click OK to close the Stationery dialog box.

SAVE A DRAFT

You can save a draft of a message you are unable to finish composing. Saving a draft allows you to complete the message at a later time. When you save a draft, Outlook Express stores the message in the Drafts folder until you are ready to complete and send the message.

When you want to complete a message you have saved as a draft, display the contents of the Drafts folder and double-click the message you want to complete. When you send the message, Outlook Express removes the message from the Drafts folder and places it in the Sent Items folder.

If you no longer want to complete and send a message you have saved, you can delete the message from the Drafts folder as you would delete any message. To delete a message, see page 540.

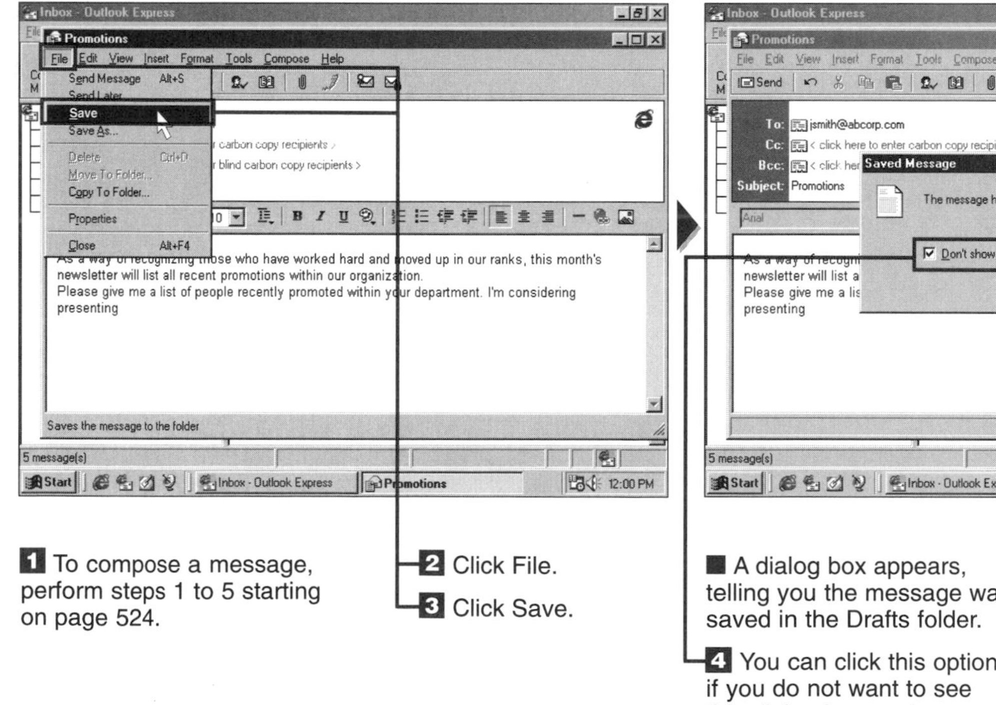

1 To compose a message, perform steps 1 to 5 starting on page 524.

2 Click File.

3 Click Save.

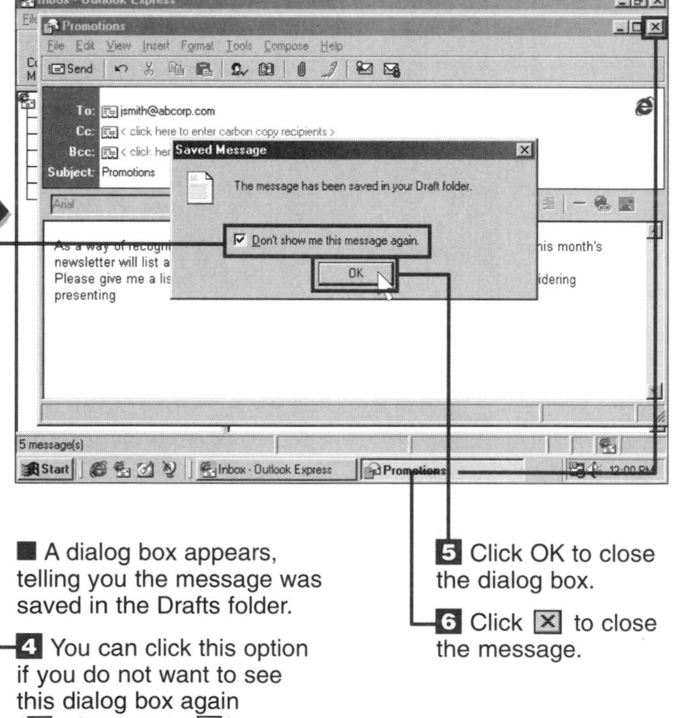

■ A dialog box appears, telling you the message was saved in the Drafts folder.

4 You can click this option if you do not want to see this dialog box again (☐ changes to ☑).

5 Click OK to close the dialog box.

6 Click ☒ to close the message.

CHECK FOR NEW MESSAGES AUTOMATICALLY

You can change how often Outlook Express checks for new messages. When Outlook Express checks for new messages, the new messages are transferred from the mail server at your Internet service provider to your computer.

If you have a constant connection to the Internet, such as at work, you may want to have Outlook Express check for new messages as often as every few minutes. If you connect to the Internet using a modem, such as at home, you may only want to have Outlook Express check for new messages once every hour. Checking for messages frequently can slow down other tasks you are performing, such as Web browsing.

When Outlook Express is set up to check for new messages, it automatically checks for messages each time you start the program.

You can click the Send and Receive button to check for new messages at any time. Clicking the Send and Receive button also immediately sends any messages stored in the Outbox folder.

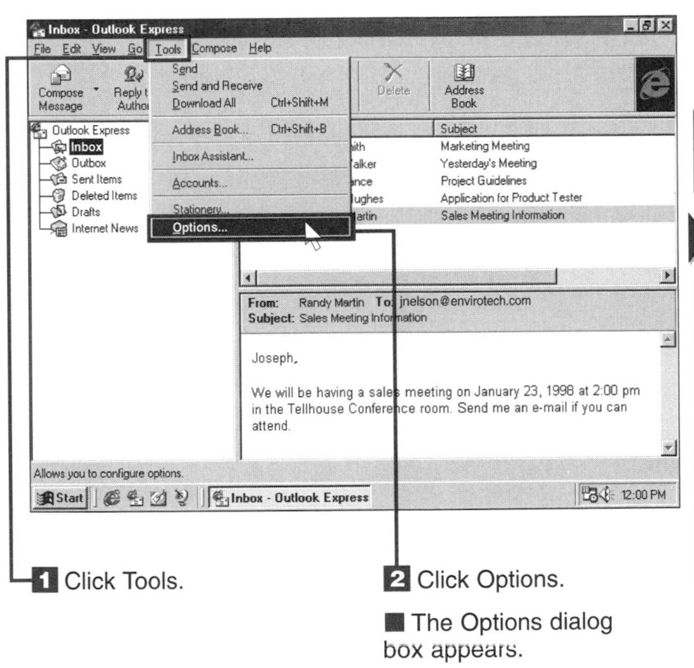

1 Click Tools.

2 Click Options.

■ The Options dialog box appears.

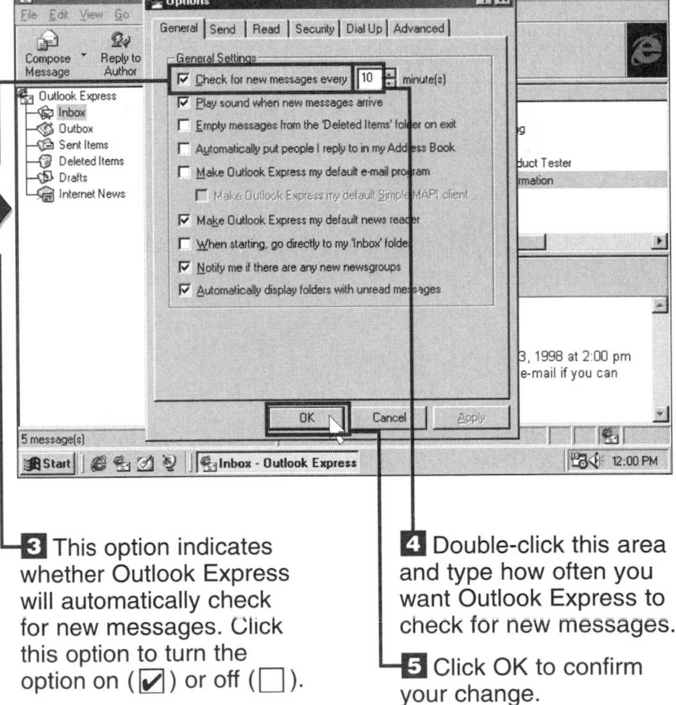

3 This option indicates whether Outlook Express will automatically check for new messages. Click this option to turn the option on (☑) or off (☐).

4 Double-click this area and type how often you want Outlook Express to check for new messages.

5 Click OK to confirm your change.

WORK WITH E-MAIL MESSAGES

You can sort messages in Outlook Express so they are easier to find. You can sort by the name of the person who sent or received the message, the subject of the message or the date the message was sent or received. Messages can be sorted in ascending or descending order. Messages are usually sorted by the date they were sent or received, in descending order.

You can delete a message you no longer need. Deleting messages prevents your folders from becoming cluttered with messages. When you delete a message, Outlook Express places the deleted message in the Deleted Items folder.

You can produce a paper copy of a message. A printed message is useful when you need a reference copy of the message. Outlook Express prints the page number at the top of each page and the current date at the bottom of each page of the message.

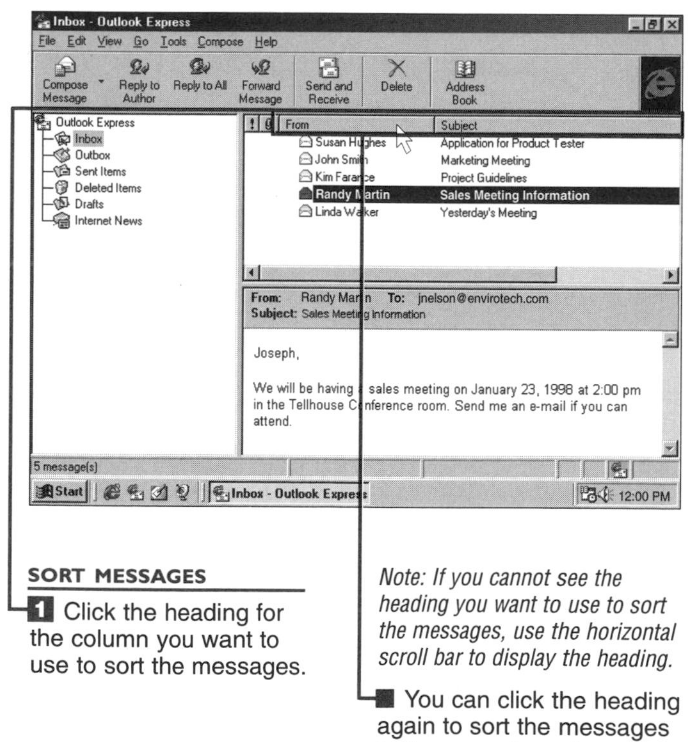

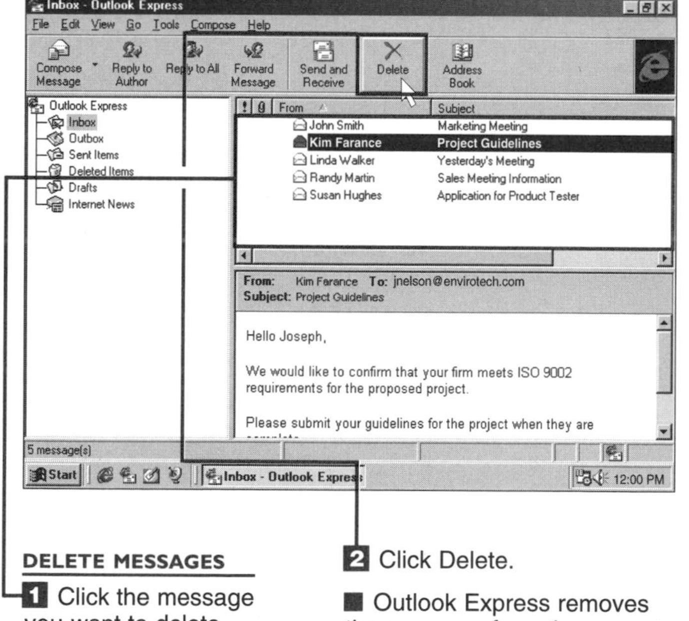

SORT MESSAGES

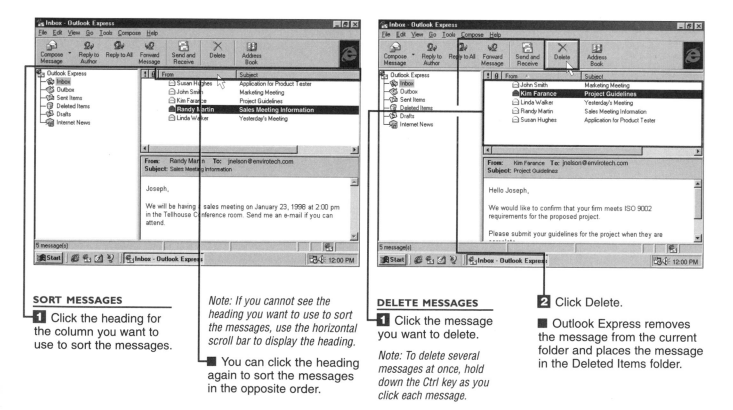

1 Click the heading for the column you want to use to sort the messages.

Note: If you cannot see the heading you want to use to sort the messages, use the horizontal scroll bar to display the heading.

■ You can click the heading again to sort the messages in the opposite order.

DELETE MESSAGES

1 Click the message you want to delete.

Note: To delete several messages at once, hold down the Ctrl key as you click each message.

2 Click Delete.

■ Outlook Express removes the message from the current folder and places the message in the Deleted Items folder.

TIPS

Can I change the width of a column?

Place the mouse pointer on the right edge of the column heading you want to change. The mouse pointer changes to a double-headed arrow (✛). Drag the edge of the column until it displays the size you want. You can also double-click the right edge of a column to make the column fit the longest item.

Can I work with a message in another program?

You can save a message as a file so you can work with the message in another program, such as a word processor. From the File menu, select Save As to save the message as a file.

Can I empty the Deleted Items folder?

You can empty the Deleted Items folder to permanently remove deleted messages from your computer. Emptying the Deleted Items folder saves space on your computer. Right-click the Deleted Items folder and select Empty Folder. If you want the Deleted Items folder to automatically empty each time you close Outlook Express, choose the Tools menu and then click the Options command. Select the General tab and click the Empty messages from the 'Deleted Items' folder on exit option (☐ changes to ☑).

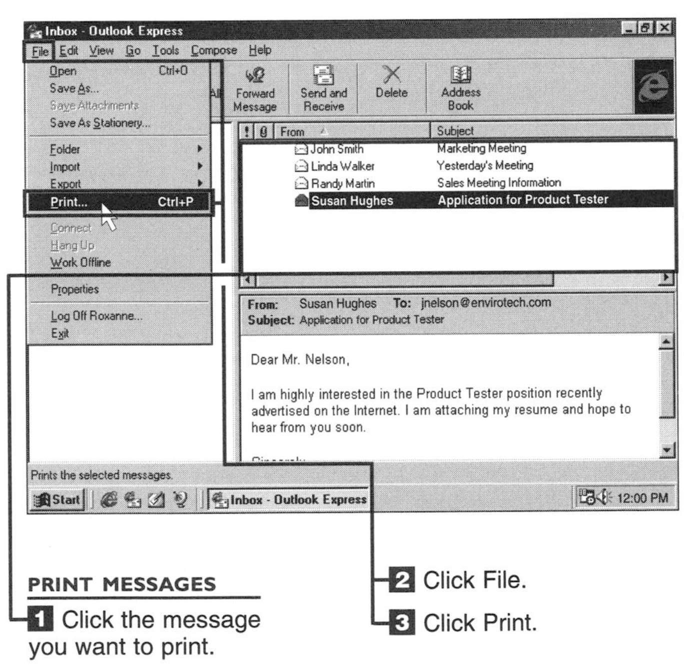

PRINT MESSAGES

1 Click the message you want to print.

2 Click File.

3 Click Print.

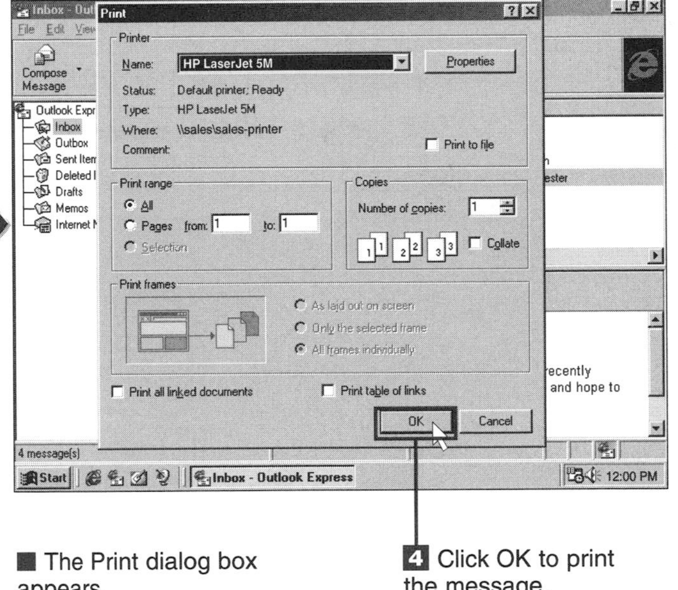

■ The Print dialog box appears.

4 Click OK to print the message.

CREATE A NEW FOLDER

You can create folders in Outlook Express to keep related messages together and make your messages easier to find. For example, if you have many messages related to a specific project or client, you can use a folder to organize the messages and keep them together.

You can create a new folder within an existing folder, such as the Inbox folder, to better organize your messages.

You can use descriptive names to label the folders you create, but you should try to keep the names short. Long names may not be fully displayed in the Outlook Express window. When you can see the full name of a folder in the Outlook Express window, you will be able to work with the folder more easily.

After you create a folder, you can move messages into the folder.

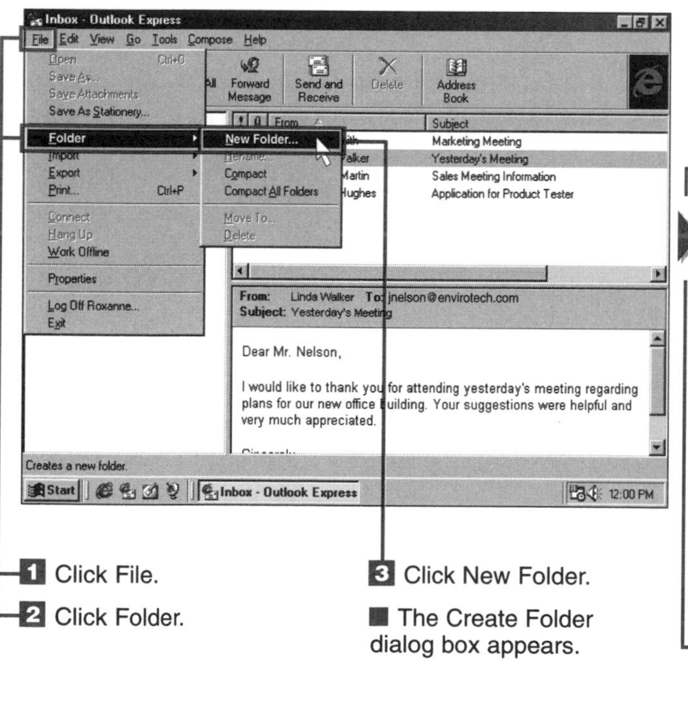

1 Click File.

2 Click Folder.

3 Click New Folder.

■ The Create Folder dialog box appears.

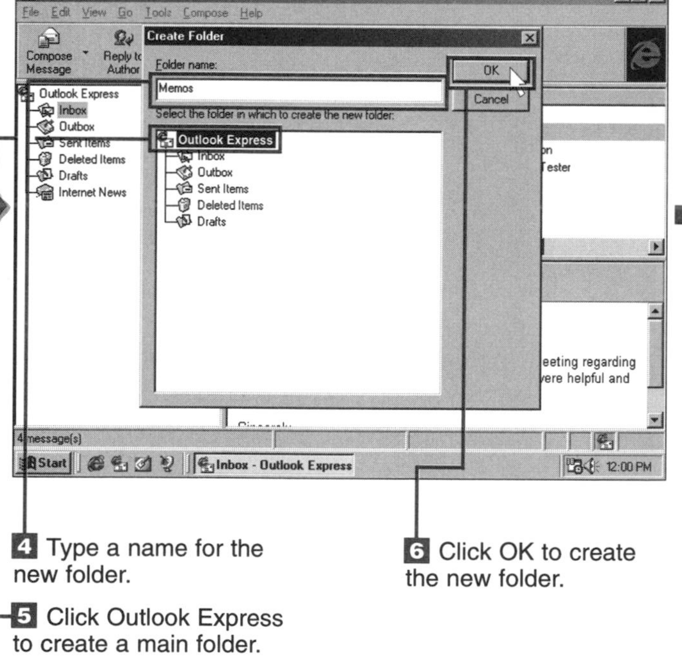

4 Type a name for the new folder.

5 Click Outlook Express to create a main folder.

Note: To create a new folder within another folder, click the folder.

6 Click OK to create the new folder.

TIPS

Why can't I see the new folder I created?

If you create a folder within another folder, the folder you created may be hidden. Click the plus sign (+) beside the folder that contains the folder you created.

How do I rename a folder?

Right-click the folder whose name you want to change and select Rename from the menu that appears. Type the new name and press the Enter key. You cannot rename the Inbox, Outbox, Sent Items, Deleted Items or Drafts folders.

Can I rearrange the folders I created?

You can drag and drop the folders you created to a new location.

How do I delete a folder I no longer need?

Select the folder you want to delete and press the Delete key. You cannot delete the Inbox, Outbox, Deleted Items, Sent Items or Drafts folders. If you delete a folder that contains messages, the messages will also be deleted.

Can I change the columns displayed in a folder?

When you create a new folder, the new folder displays the same column headings as the Inbox. From the View menu, select Columns to change which columns appear in a folder.

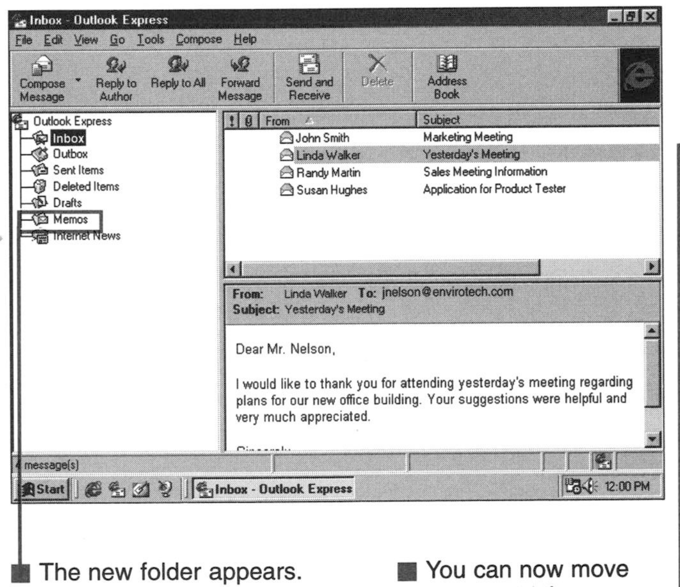

■ The new folder appears.

■ You can now move messages to the new folder.

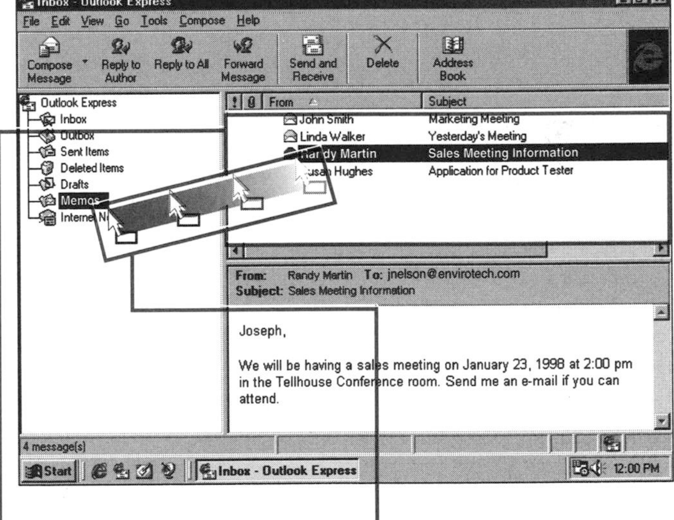

MOVE MESSAGES TO OTHER FOLDERS

1 Click the message you want to move to another folder.

2 Position the mouse over the message.

3 Drag the message to the folder you want to store the message.

■ Outlook Express moves the message to the folder.

FIND MESSAGES

If you cannot find a message you want to review, you can have Outlook Express search for the message. You should provide Outlook Express with as much information about the message as possible to narrow your search.

Outlook Express can search for a message you have received. This is useful if you are looking for a message from a specific person. Outlook Express can also find a message you have sent to a certain person.

If you can only remember a word from the subject of the message you want to find, you can have Outlook Express search the subject areas of your messages. You can also search for messages with specific text in the body of the message.

You may also want to search for messages with attached files or messages received after or before a certain date.

If you know which folder contains the message, it may be helpful to search a specific folder.

When the search is complete, Outlook Express will display a list of messages that match all of the information you specified. You can open and read the messages.

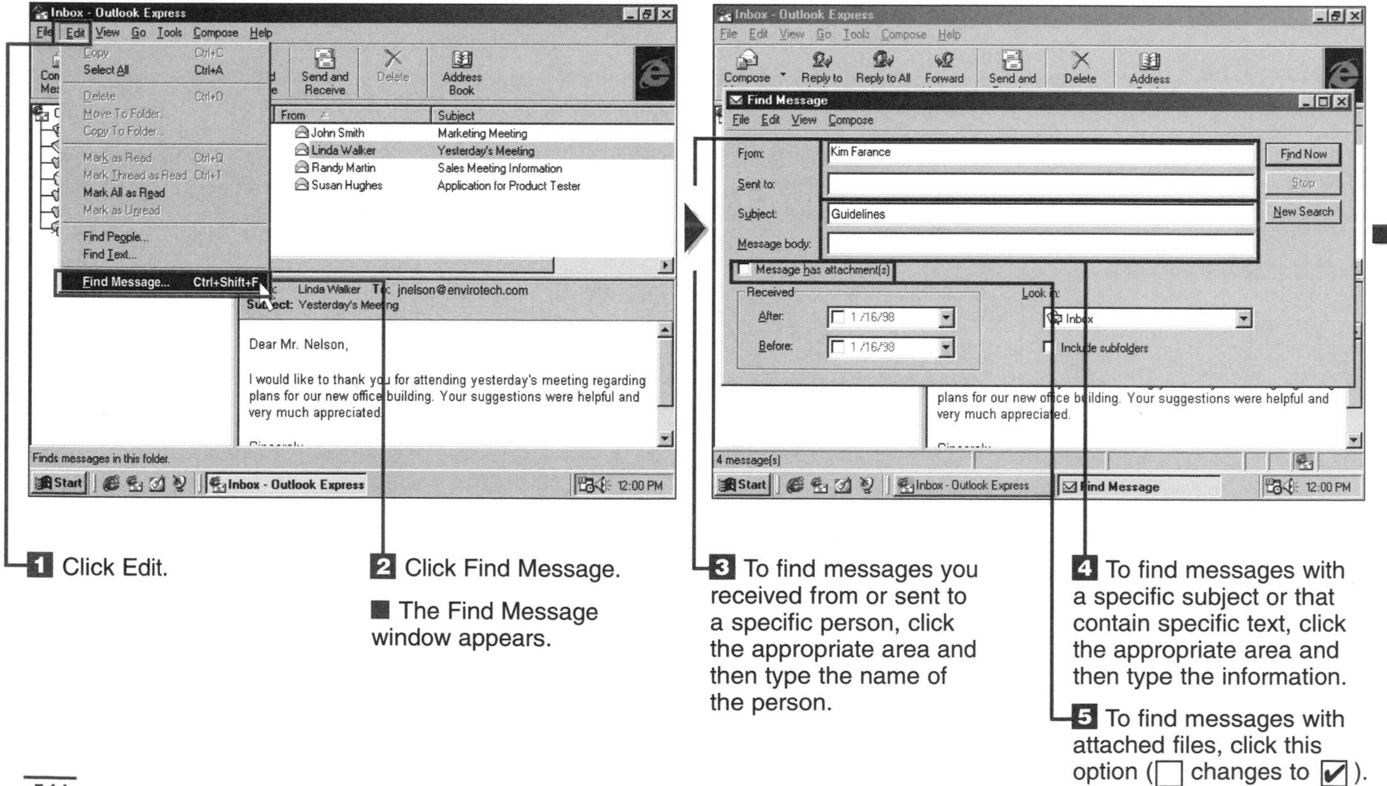

1 Click Edit.

2 Click Find Message.

■ The Find Message window appears.

3 To find messages you received from or sent to a specific person, click the appropriate area and then type the name of the person.

4 To find messages with a specific subject or that contain specific text, click the appropriate area and then type the information.

5 To find messages with attached files, click this option (☐ changes to ☑).

TIPS

Will Outlook Express find messages in the subfolders I created?

Your subfolders are automatically searched when you select Outlook Express in the Look in area. To search the subfolders within a specific folder, select the folder in the Look in area and then click the Include subfolders option (☐ changes to ☑).

Can I find text in one message?

If you are reviewing a message that contains a lot of text, you can use the Find feature to quickly locate a word in the message. Click the message you want to search. From the Edit menu, select Find Text. Type the text you want to find and then click Find Next.

Outlook Express didn't find the message I was looking for. What can I do?

If the search did not provide the results you were expecting, you may not have provided Outlook Express with enough information or you may have specified incorrect information. Click the New Search button in the Find Message window to clear the contents of the window and start a new search.

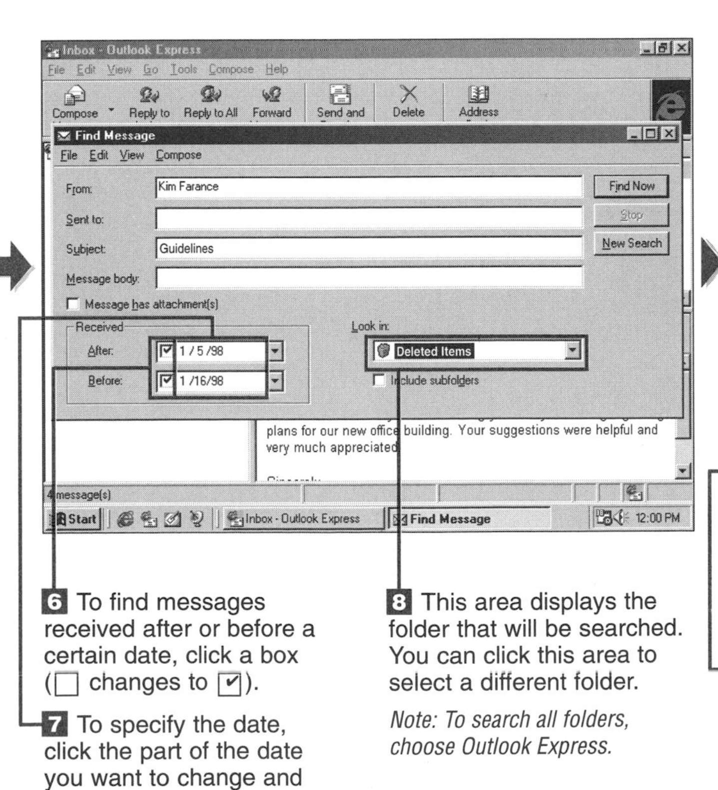

6 To find messages received after or before a certain date, click a box (☐ changes to ☑).

7 To specify the date, click the part of the date you want to change and then type a new date.

8 This area displays the folder that will be searched. You can click this area to select a different folder.

Note: To search all folders, choose Outlook Express.

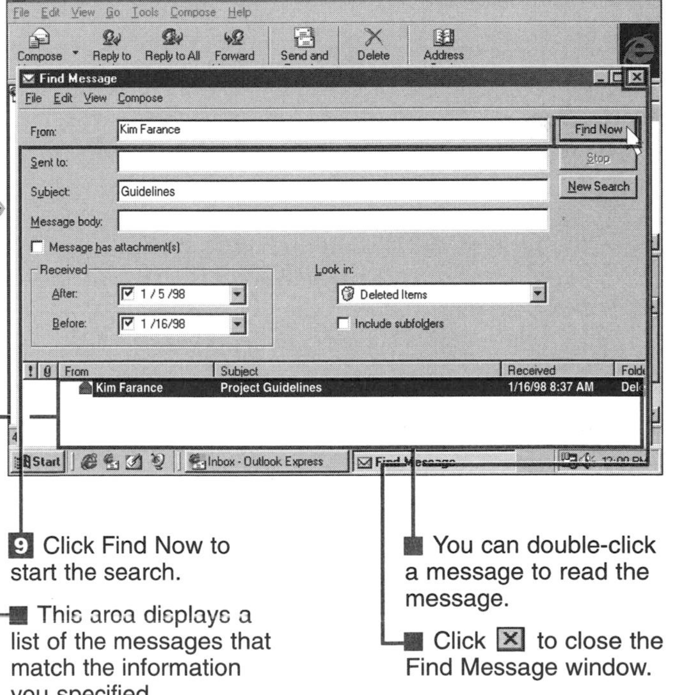

9 Click Find Now to start the search.

■ This area displays a list of the messages that match the information you specified.

■ You can double-click a message to read the message.

■ Click ☒ to close the Find Message window.

SORT MESSAGES YOU RECEIVE

Outlook Express can sort your incoming messages before you read them. This is useful if you want to organize the messages you receive from mailing lists or avoid unsolicited commercial messages.

You can set up rules to tell Outlook Express how you want to sort the messages you receive. You can sort incoming messages by the e-mail address they are sent to. This is useful if you have more than one e-mail address. Outlook Express also allows you to sort messages by the address the message was carbon copied to or sent from. If you are waiting for a message on a particular topic, you can sort messages by specific text in the subject.

You can specify the actions you want Outlook Express to perform on your incoming messages. Outlook Express can automatically move or copy messages to specific folders, forward messages to another address and delete messages you do not want to read from your mail server. You can even instruct Outlook Express to automatically reply to messages. Many people use automatic replies to inform other people that they are on vacation or that their e-mail address is changing.

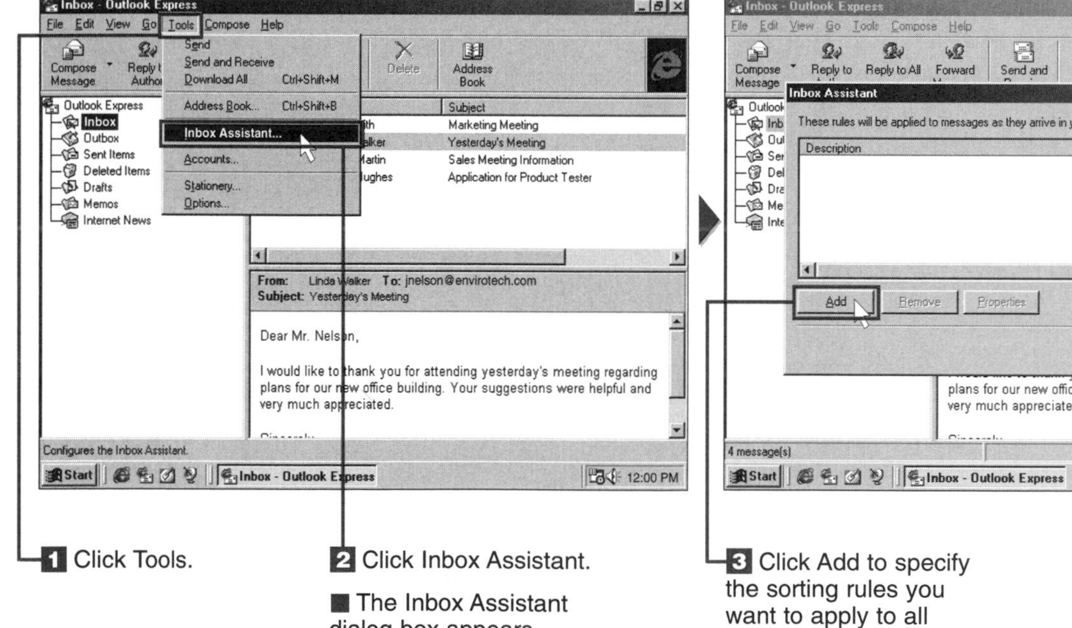

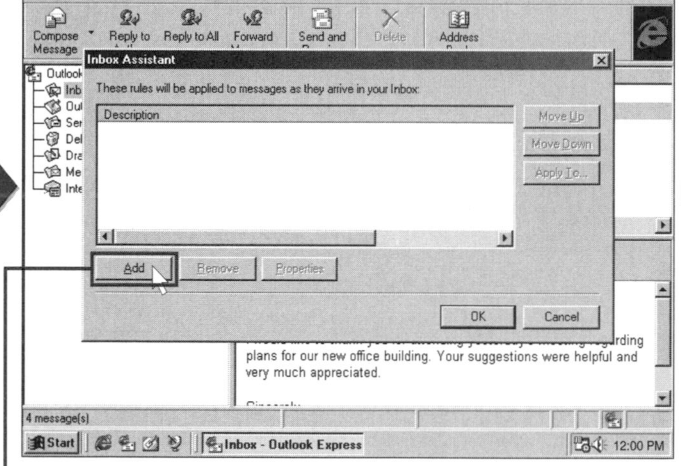

1 Click Tools.

2 Click Inbox Assistant.

■ The Inbox Assistant dialog box appears.

3 Click Add to specify the sorting rules you want to apply to all incoming messages.

■ The Properties dialog box appears.

TIPS

Why are my messages not being sorted properly?

If you are using more than one sorting rule, the rules may not be affecting your messages in the proper order. The rule at the top of the Inbox Assistant dialog box affects your messages first. Use the Move Up and Move Down buttons to adjust the order in which the sorting rules affect your messages.

Can I remove a sorting rule I no longer need?

In the Inbox Assistant dialog box, select the rule you no longer want to use and then click the Remove button.

Large messages take too long to transfer to my computer. How can I avoid receiving large messages?

When setting your sorting rules, click the Larger than option (☐ changes to ☑). Double-click the box beside the option and type the message size you want to sort by. Then specify the action you want to perform for large messages.

How can I create a message I want to use as an automatic reply?

Compose your reply in Outlook Express leaving the To:, Cc: and Bcc: areas blank. From the File menu, select Save As to save the reply as a file on your computer.

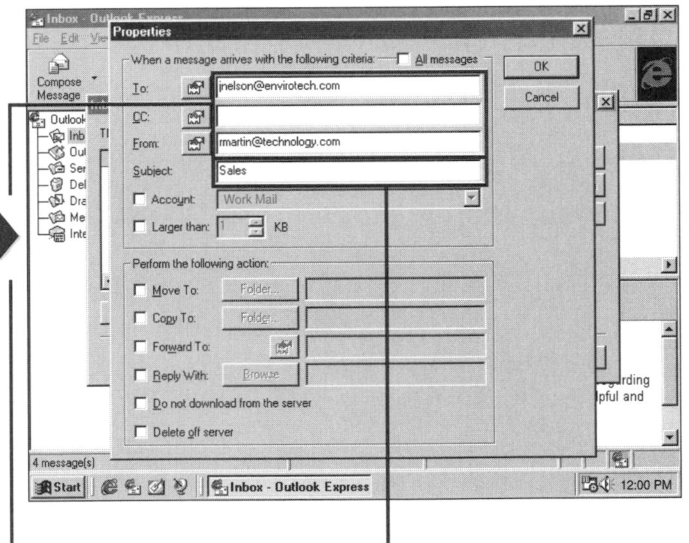

4 To sort messages addressed to or sent from a specific person, click an area and then type their e-mail address.

5 To sort messages that contain specific text in the subject, click this area and then type the text.

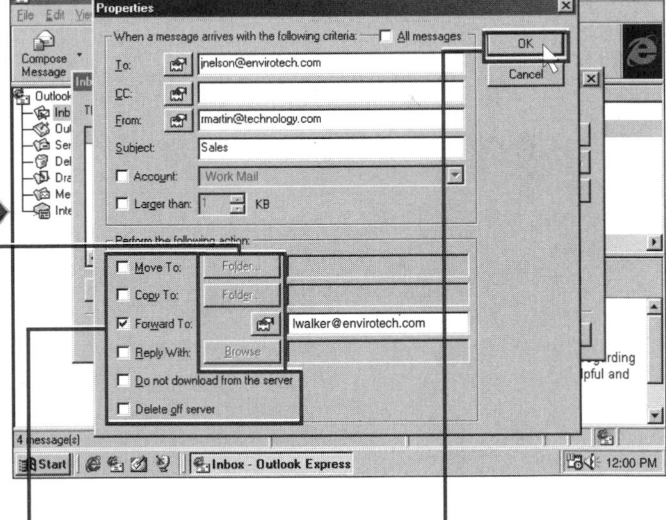

6 Click the action you want Outlook Express to perform when a message matches the information you specified (☐ changes to ☑).

7 Click the button beside the option you selected to choose the folder, person or file involved in the action which will be performed.

8 Click OK.

■ A description of the sorting rules appears in the Inbox Assistant dialog box.

SEND SECURE MESSAGES

You can use Outlook Express to send secure messages. Many businesses send secure messages to prevent corporate information, such as sales reports, from being monitored by unauthorized people. Many individuals send secure messages so that they can include personal information, such as credit card numbers, in their messages without fear of a security breach.

You must obtain a digital ID and set up your e-mail account to use the digital ID before you can send secure messages. Only approved companies, such as VeriSign, can issue digital IDs. You can visit VeriSign's Web site at www.verisign.com for more information about obtaining a digital ID.

A digital ID allows you to send two types of secure messages–signed and encrypted. You can send a signed message if you want the recipient of the message to know the message was not created or altered by anyone other than you. You can send an encrypted message to scramble the contents of a message. Encryption prevents the message from being read by anyone except the intended recipient of the message.

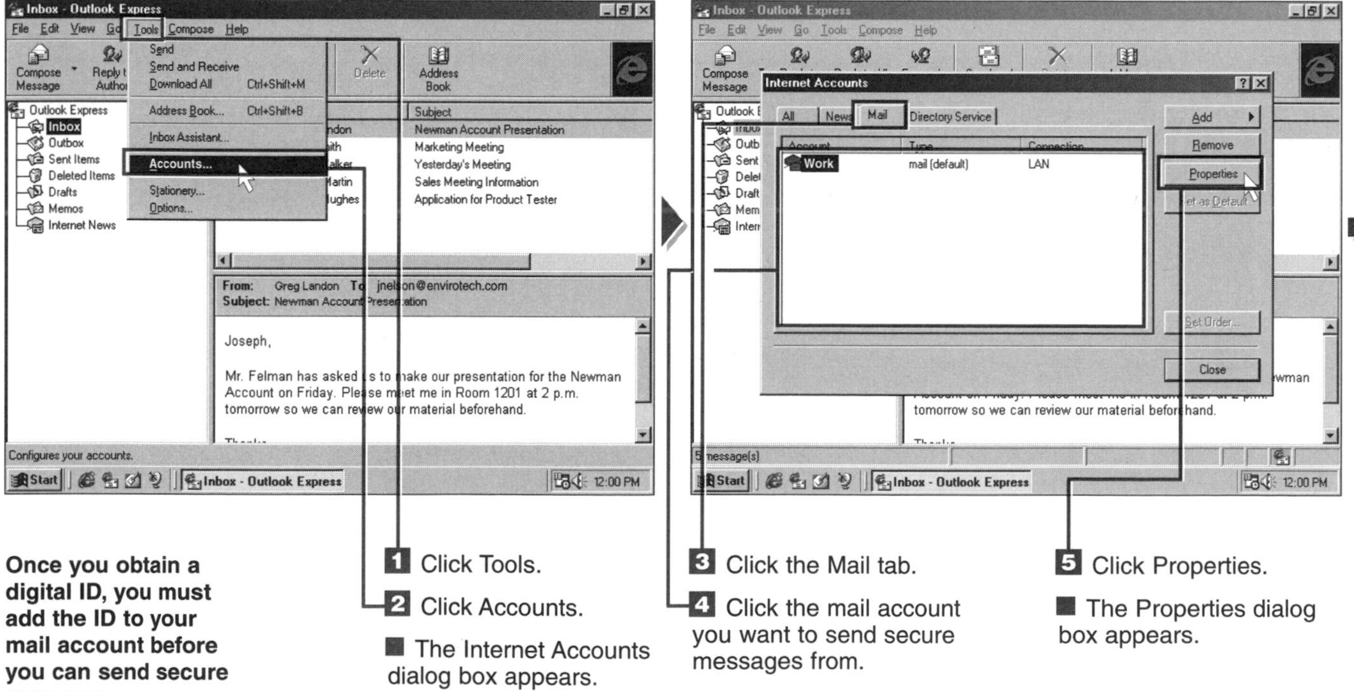

Once you obtain a digital ID, you must add the ID to your mail account before you can send secure messages.

1 Click Tools.

2 Click Accounts.

■ The Internet Accounts dialog box appears.

3 Click the Mail tab.

4 Click the mail account you want to send secure messages from.

5 Click Properties.

■ The Properties dialog box appears.

TIPS

How do I send a signed message?

When you are composing a message, click the Digitally sign message button ( ) at the top of the window before you send the message. A badge ( ) will appear across from the subject of the message.

In the Outlook Express window, right-click the signed message you received and then click Properties. Select the Security tab and then click the Add Digital ID to Address Book button. Click OK to close the dialog box that appears.

How do I send an encrypted message?

You must first receive a signed message from the person you want to send an encrypted message to. When you receive the signed message, you must add the person's digital ID to your address book.

Once you have added the person's digital ID to your address book, you can send them encrypted messages. When you are composing a message, click the Encrypt message button ( ) at the top of the window before you send the message. A lock ( ) will appear across from the subject of the message.

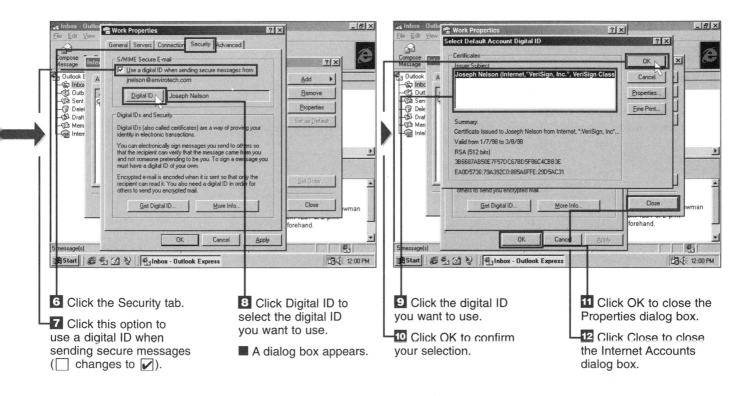

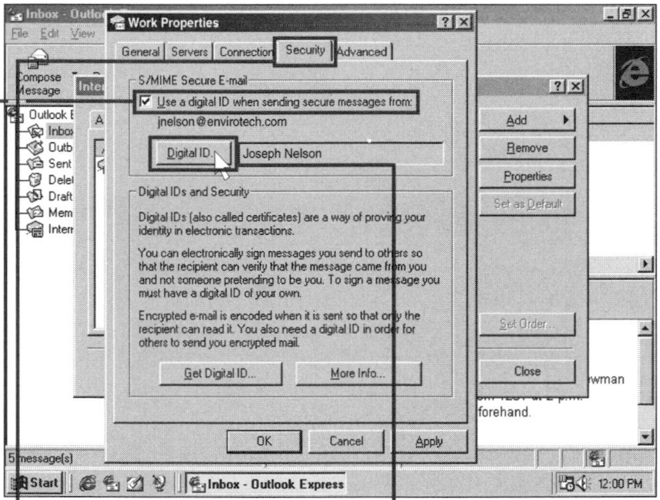

6 Click the Security tab.

7 Click this option to use a digital ID when sending secure messages (☐ changes to ☑).

8 Click Digital ID to select the digital ID you want to use.

■ A dialog box appears.

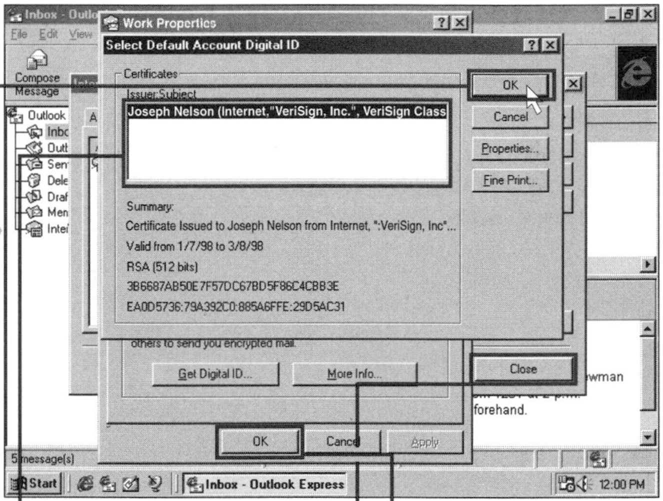

9 Click the digital ID you want to use.

10 Click OK to confirm your selection.

11 Click OK to close the Properties dialog box.

12 Click Close to close the Internet Accounts dialog box.

SUBSCRIBE TO NEWSGROUPS

You can use Outlook Express to subscribe to newsgroups. Newsgroups allow people with common interests to communicate with each other. You can subscribe to a newsgroup you want to read on a regular basis.

Newsgroups are stored on computers called news servers, which are run and maintained by Internet service providers. The newsgroups available to you depend on your news server.

You can have Outlook Express display a list of all the newsgroups available to you.

There are thousands of newsgroups on every subject imaginable. The name of a newsgroup describes the type of information discussed in the newsgroup. A newsgroup name consists of two or more words, separated by dots (.). The first word describes the main topic of the newsgroup. Each of the following words narrows the topic.

For example, the rec.music.folk newsgroup contains messages from folk music enthusiasts.

The main newsgroup categories include alt (alternative), biz (business), comp (computers), k12 (kindergarten to grade 12 or education related), misc (miscellaneous), news, rec (recreation), sci (science), soc (social) and talk.

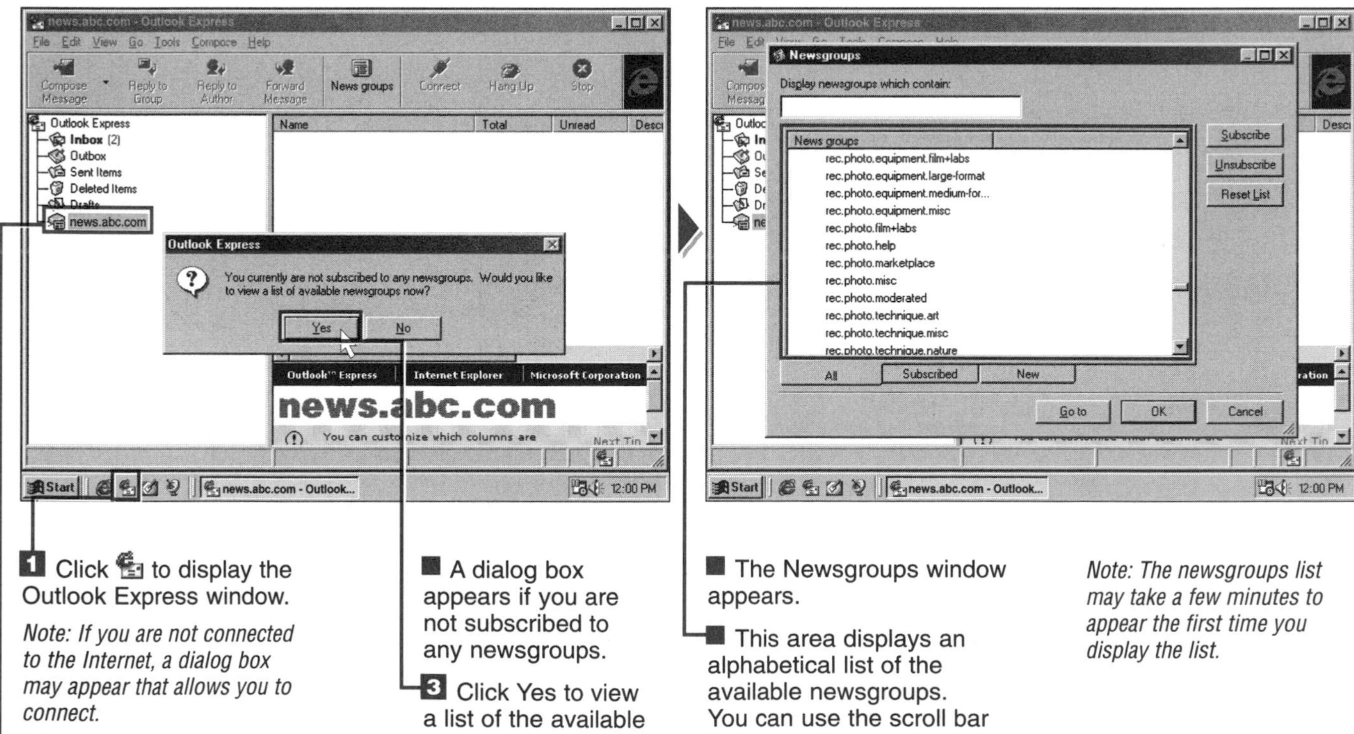

1 Click to display the Outlook Express window.

Note: If you are not connected to the Internet, a dialog box may appear that allows you to connect.

2 Click your news server.

■ A dialog box appears if you are not subscribed to any newsgroups.

3 Click Yes to view a list of the available newsgroups.

■ The Newsgroups window appears.

■ This area displays an alphabetical list of the available newsgroups. You can use the scroll bar to browse through the list.

Note: The newsgroups list may take a few minutes to appear the first time you display the list.

Are there any newsgroups designed for beginners?

There are several newsgroups that are useful for beginners. The news.announce.newusers and news.newusers.questions newsgroups provide useful information and let you ask questions about newsgroups.

How do I see a list of only new newsgroups?

The Newsgroups window has three tabs. Clicking the New tab displays new newsgroups. You can click the Subscribed tab to view newsgroups you are subscribed to. Click the All tab to view all the available newsgroups.

Can I view the messages in a newsgroup without subscribing to the newsgroup?

Yes. In the Newsgroups window, click the newsgroup you want to read the messages for and then click Go to.

How do I unsubscribe from a newsgroup?

In the Outlook Express window, click the plus sign (⊞) beside your news server. Right-click the newsgroup you want to unsubscribe from and then click Unsubscribe from this newsgroup. You can unsubscribe from a newsgroup at any time if the material no longer interests you.

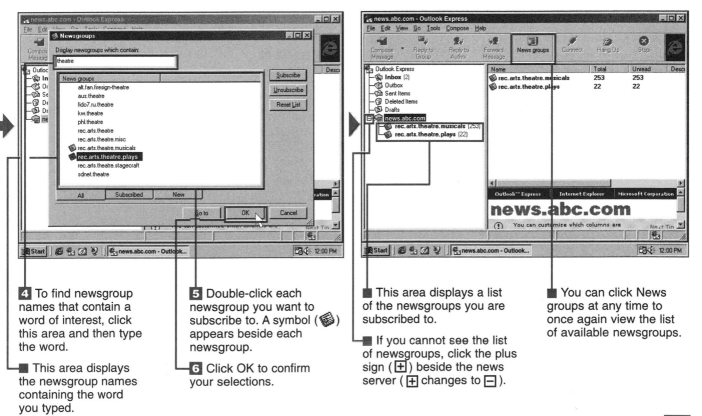

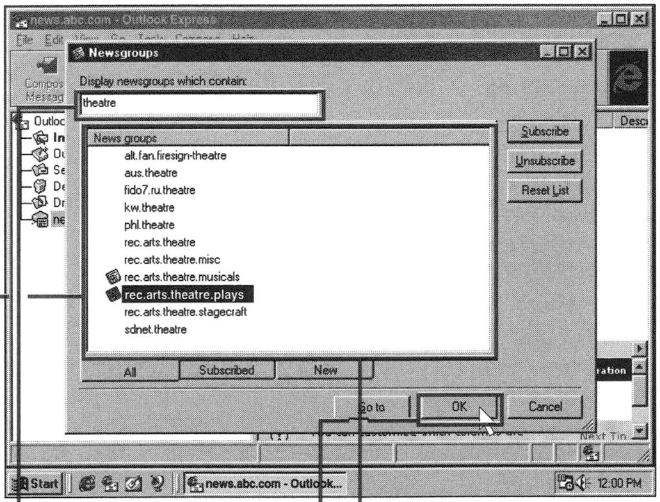

4 To find newsgroup names that contain a word of interest, click this area and then type the word.

■ This area displays the newsgroup names containing the word you typed.

5 Double-click each newsgroup you want to subscribe to. A symbol ( ) appears beside each newsgroup.

6 Click OK to confirm your selections.

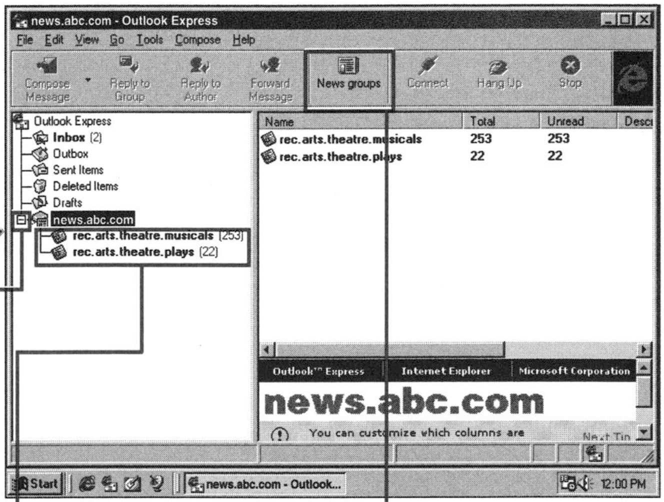

■ This area displays a list of the newsgroups you are subscribed to.

■ If you cannot see the list of newsgroups, click the plus sign (⊞) beside the news server (⊞ changes to ⊟).

■ You can click News groups at any time to once again view the list of available newsgroups.

READ NEWSGROUP MESSAGES

You can read the messages in a newsgroup to learn the opinions and ideas of thousands of people around the world.

Newsgroup messages that display a plus sign (⊞) are called threads. Threads consist of an initial message and related comments and replies. Threads can help you easily keep track of all the replies to a message. Outlook Express groups all of the messages in a thread with the initial message. For example, a message with the title "Tips for Windows 98" would be grouped with replies titled "Re: Tips for Windows 98".

Many newsgroups include a message called a FAQ (Frequently Asked Questions). A FAQ normally contains a list of questions and answers that regularly appear in a newsgroup. A FAQ helps prevent new readers from posting questions to newsgroups that have already been answered. The news.answers newsgroup provides FAQs for a wide variety of newsgroups.

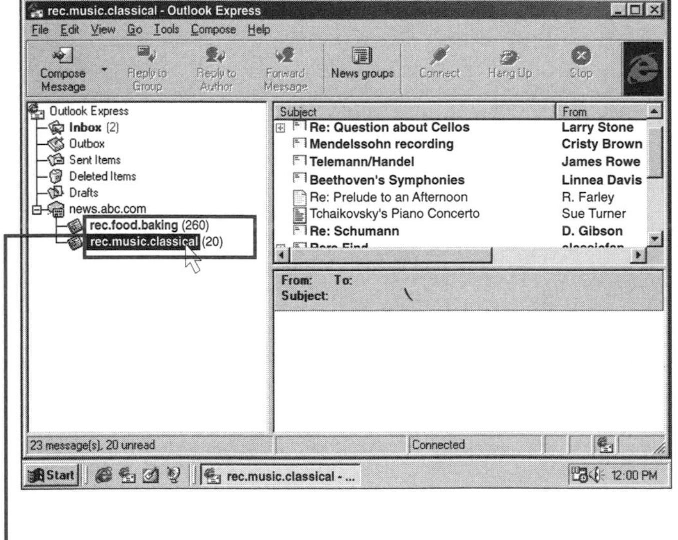

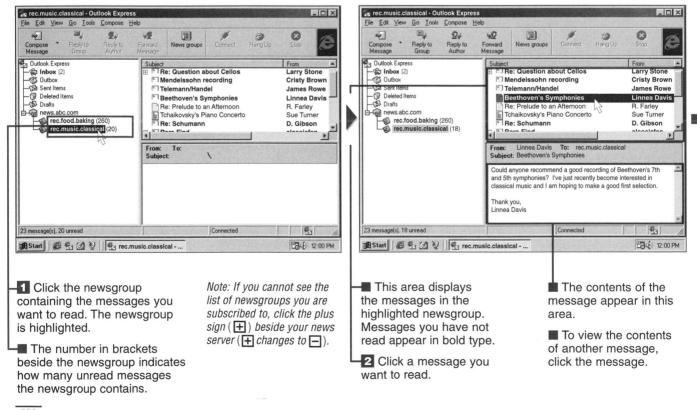

1 Click the newsgroup containing the messages you want to read. The newsgroup is highlighted.

■ The number in brackets beside the newsgroup indicates how many unread messages the newsgroup contains.

Note: If you cannot see the list of newsgroups you are subscribed to, click the plus sign (⊞) beside your news server (⊞ changes to ⊟).

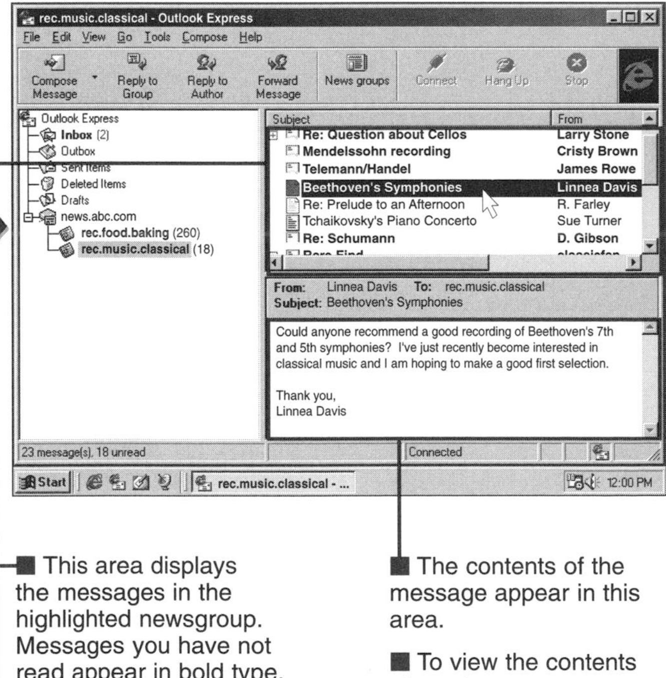

■ This area displays the messages in the highlighted newsgroup. Messages you have not read appear in bold type.

2 Click a message you want to read.

■ The contents of the message appear in this area.

■ To view the contents of another message, click the message.

TIPS

Can I change the font size displayed in my messages?

Choose the View menu, click Fonts and then select the font size you want to use. The current font size displays a bullet (●).

Outlook Express didn't download all of the messages in the newsgroup. Why?

Outlook Express automatically downloads only the first 300 messages in a newsgroup. To always download all of the messages, click the Tools menu and then click Options. Click the Read tab and then click the box (☑) beside the Download 300 headers at a time option (☑ changes to ☐).

Can I view the contents of a message in a separate window?

To view a message in a separate window, double-click the message.

Can I expand all the threads in a newsgroup at once?

You can have Outlook Express automatically expand all the threads every time you read a newsgroup. From the Tools menu, select the Options command. On the Read tab, click the Automatically expand conversation threads option (☐ changes to ☑).

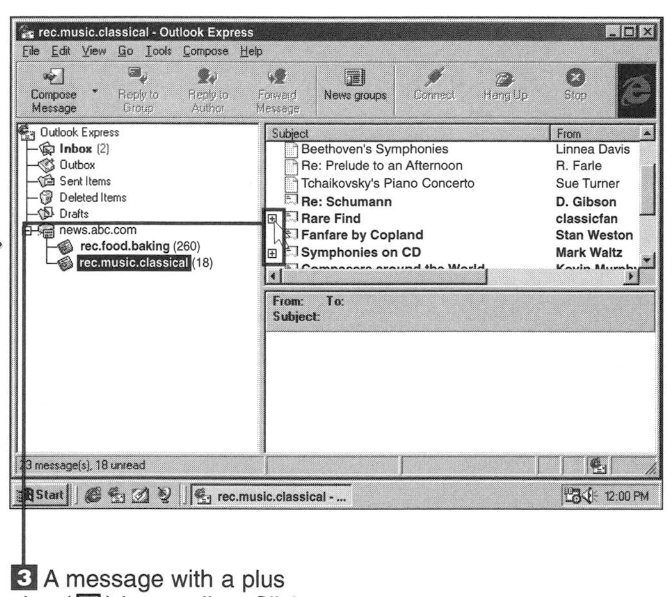

3 A message with a plus sign (⊞) has replies. Click the plus sign to display the replies to the message (⊞ changes to ⊟).

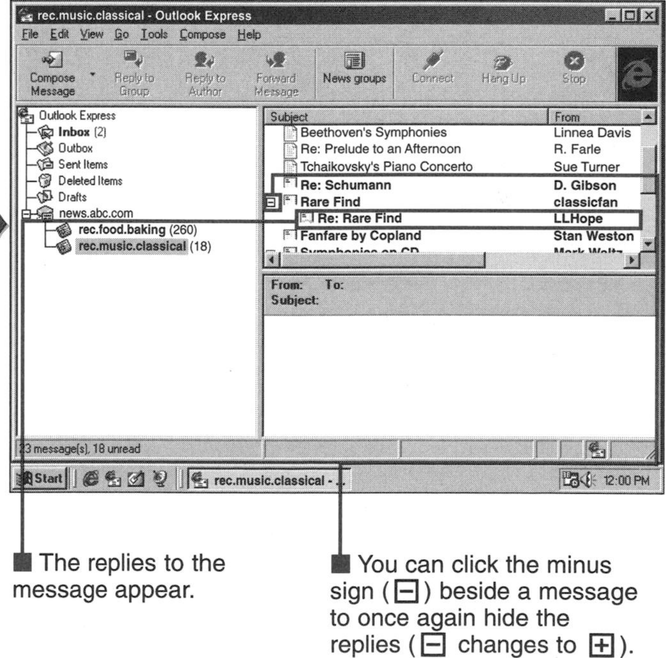

■ The replies to the message appear.

■ You can click the minus sign (⊟) beside a message to once again hide the replies (⊟ changes to ⊞).

WORK WITH NEWSGROUP MESSAGES

You can work with newsgroup messages to make it easier for you to focus on messages of interest.

Messages posted to newsgroups are stored on the news server only for a limited amount of time. If you want to read a message later or keep a message for future reference, you can copy a newsgroup message to a folder in Outlook Express. If the message has an attachment, such as an image file, the attachment will also be copied to the folder.

You can choose to display all the messages in a newsgroup or only the messages that you have not yet read. Displaying only messages you have not yet read can help speed up your search for messages that interest you.

Once you have viewed a message in a newsgroup, it will be marked as read. You can also mark messages as read without viewing them. Marking a message as read takes the focus away from messages which have subjects you are not interested in. You can mark a single message, an entire thread or all the messages in a newsgroup as read.

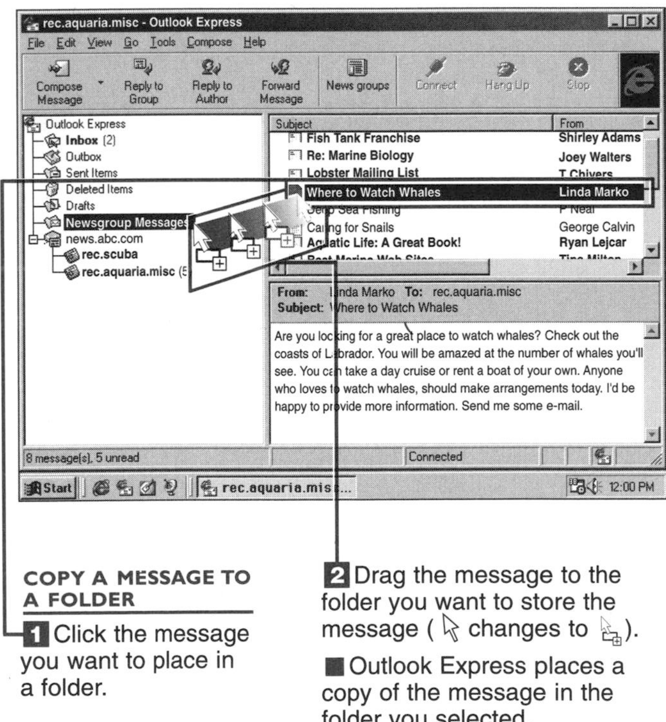

COPY A MESSAGE TO A FOLDER

1 Click the message you want to place in a folder.

2 Drag the message to the folder you want to store the message (↖ changes to ↖⊞).

■ Outlook Express places a copy of the message in the folder you selected.

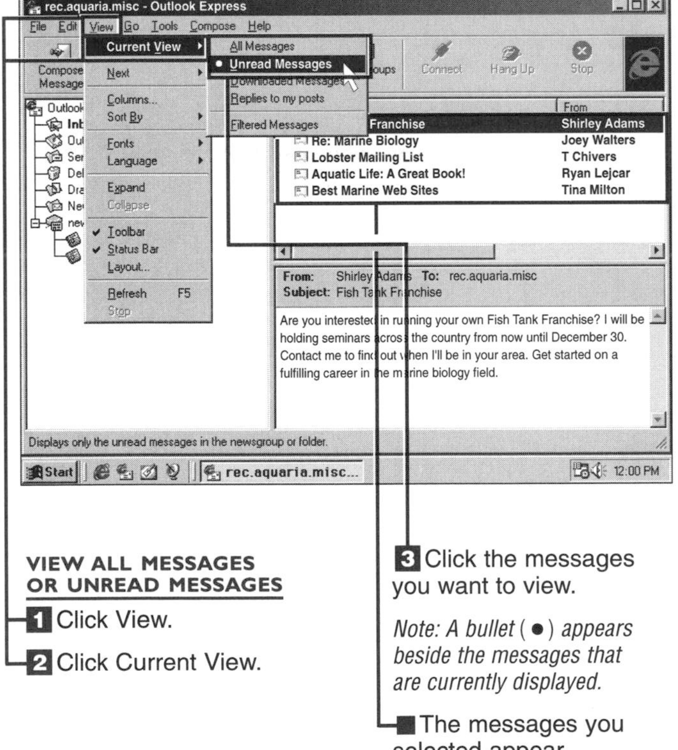

VIEW ALL MESSAGES OR UNREAD MESSAGES

1 Click View.

2 Click Current View.

3 Click the messages you want to view.

Note: A bullet (●) appears beside the messages that are currently displayed.

■ The messages you selected appear.

TIPS

Can I mark all messages as read when I leave a newsgroup?

You can have Outlook Express automatically mark all messages as read every time you leave a newsgroup. Select the Tools menu and then click Options. On the Read tab, select Mark all messages as read when exiting a newsgroup (☐ changes to ☑).

How can I copy only one message in a thread?

A thread is an initial message and all replies to the message. A thread displays a plus sign (⊞). To copy only one message in a thread to a folder, click the plus sign (⊞) beside the thread. Click the message you want to copy and then drag the message to a folder.

Can I sort newsgroup messages?

Sorting messages can help you find messages on a certain subject or written by a particular person. To sort messages, click the heading for the column you want to use to sort the messages. You can sort messages in reverse order by clicking the column heading again.

Can I print newsgroup messages?

Yes. Click the message you want to print. Select the File menu and then click Print.

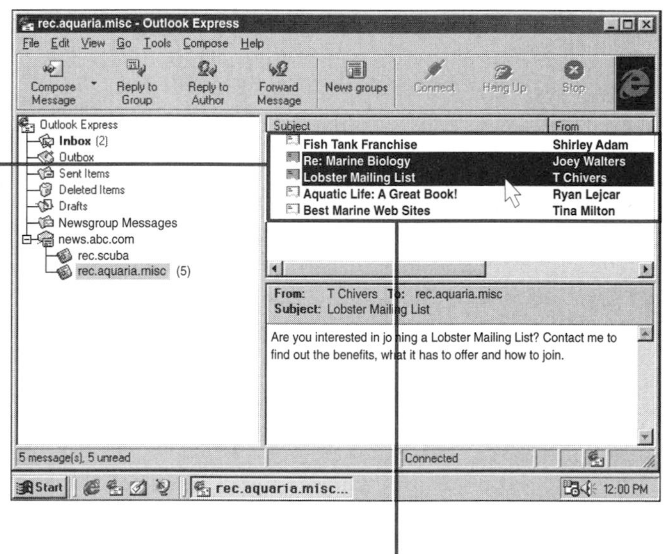

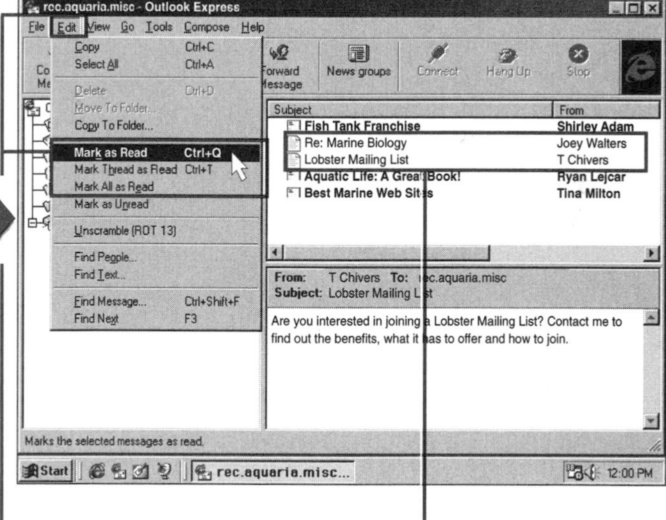

MARK MESSAGES AS READ

■ Messages you have not read appear in bold type.

1 Click a message you want to mark as read.

■ To mark more than one message as read, hold down the Ctrl key as you click each message.

Note: If you want to mark all messages as read, you do not need to select any messages.

2 Click Edit.

3 Click the messages you want to mark as read.

■ The messages you marked as read appear in regular type.

REPLY TO AND COMPOSE A MESSAGE

You can reply to a newsgroup message to answer a question or supply information. You can send a reply to the entire newsgroup. If your reply would not be of interest to other readers, or if you want to send a private response, send the reply directly to the author of the message.

When you reply to a message, Outlook Express includes a copy of the original message to help readers follow the ongoing discussion. This is called quoting. The > symbol appears in front of each quoted line.

You can also compose and send, or post, a new message to a newsgroup if you want to ask a question or express an opinion. Thousands of people around the world may read a message you post.

Make sure the subject of the message clearly identifies its contents. For example, a subject that says "Read this now" is not very informative. Also, make sure the message is clear, concise and contains no spelling or grammar errors.

To practice sending a message, send a message to the misc.test newsgroup. If you send a test message to other newsgroups, you may receive unwanted replies or flames.

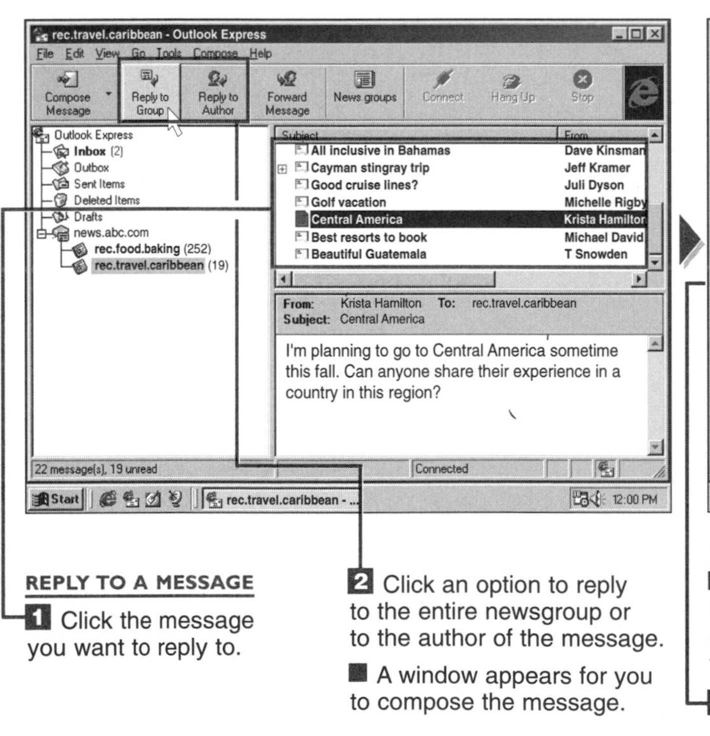

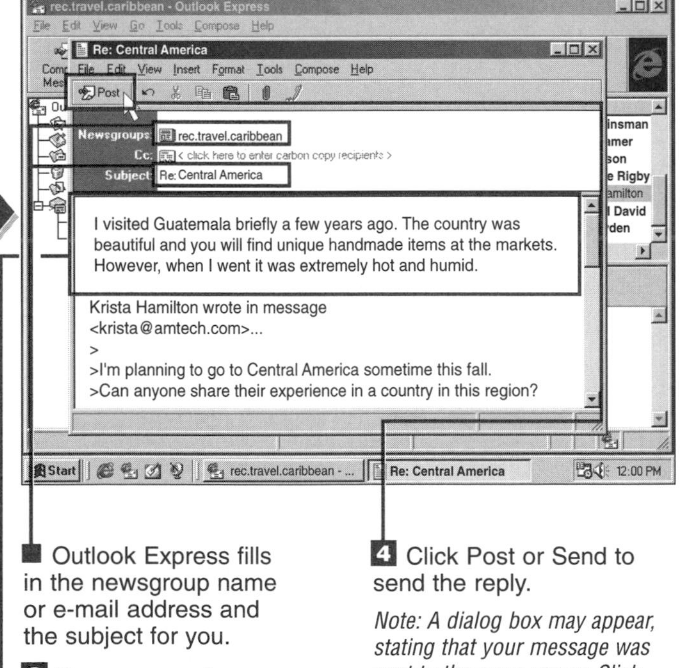

REPLY TO A MESSAGE

1 Click the message you want to reply to.

2 Click an option to reply to the entire newsgroup or to the author of the message.

■ A window appears for you to compose the message.

■ Outlook Express fills in the newsgroup name or e-mail address and the subject for you.

3 Type your reply.

4 Click Post or Send to send the reply.

Note: A dialog box may appear, stating that your message was sent to the news server. Click OK to close the dialog box.

Can I cancel a message I sent to a newsgroup?

Select the newsgroup you posted the message to and click the message you want to cancel. Choose the Compose menu and then click the Cancel Message command. If someone downloaded the message before you canceled it, the message will not be removed from that person's computer.

What is a flame?

When another reader does not like your opinion, they may reply to your message in a negative or hostile manner. These rude messages are called flames. You should ignore flames.

Can I forward an interesting message?

Yes. Select the message you want to send to a friend or colleague who might be interested and then click the Forward Message button.

Do I have to use my real name in my messages?

No. Choose the Tools menu and then click the Accounts command. Select the Properties button to change the name and e-mail address that appear in your messages. Changing your e-mail address prevents junk mailers from sending you automatic messages. Remember to include your real e-mail address in the body of your message so other readers can contact you if they wish.

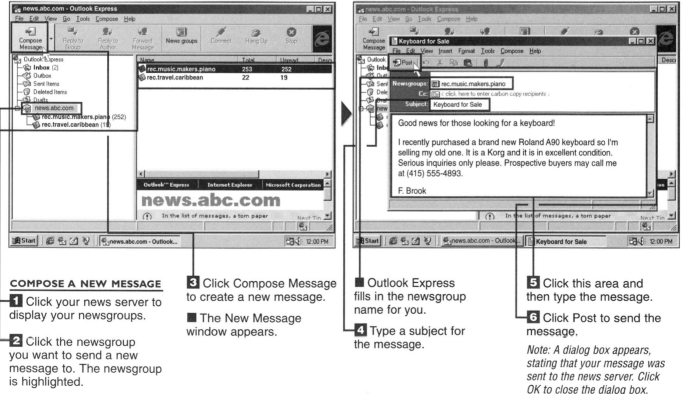

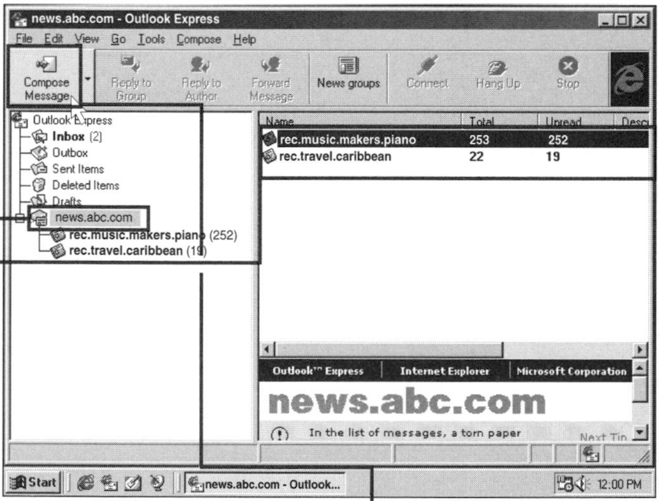

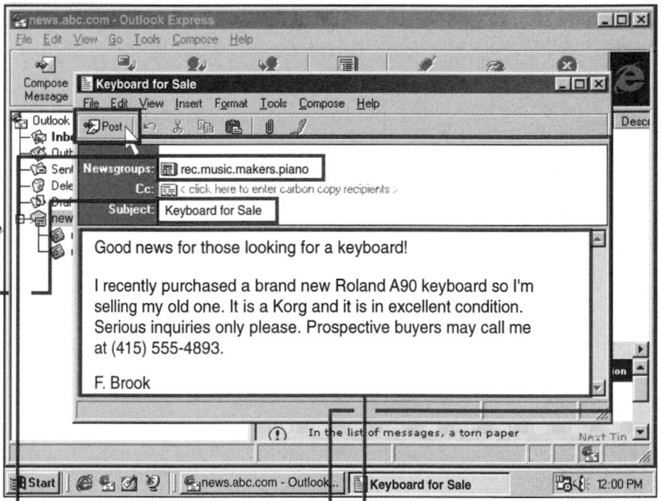

COMPOSE A NEW MESSAGE

1 Click your news server to display your newsgroups.

2 Click the newsgroup you want to send a new message to. The newsgroup is highlighted.

3 Click Compose Message to create a new message.

■ The New Message window appears.

■ Outlook Express fills in the newsgroup name for you.

4 Type a subject for the message.

5 Click this area and then type the message.

6 Click Post to send the message.

Note: A dialog box appears, stating that your message was sent to the news server. Click OK to close the dialog box.

FILTER NEWSGROUP MESSAGES

You can use a filter to specify which messages you do not want to read. The messages you filter will not appear in the list of messages in the newsgroup.

Some newsgroups contain hundreds of messages, so filtering the messages you do not want to read can save you time. You can create as many filters as you need.

You can apply a filter to the messages you receive from all news servers. This is useful if you subscribe to newsgroups from more than one news server. You can also apply a filter to the messages you receive from one news server or from one individual newsgroup.

You can filter messages based on the name of the person who wrote the message, the subject of the message, the number of lines in the message and the date the message was posted to the newsgroup.

Most people filter messages based on the text in the subject of the message. For example, filtering messages that contain text such as "Make money fast" in the subject can help you avoid receiving junk mail messages that contain nothing more than get-rich-quick schemes.

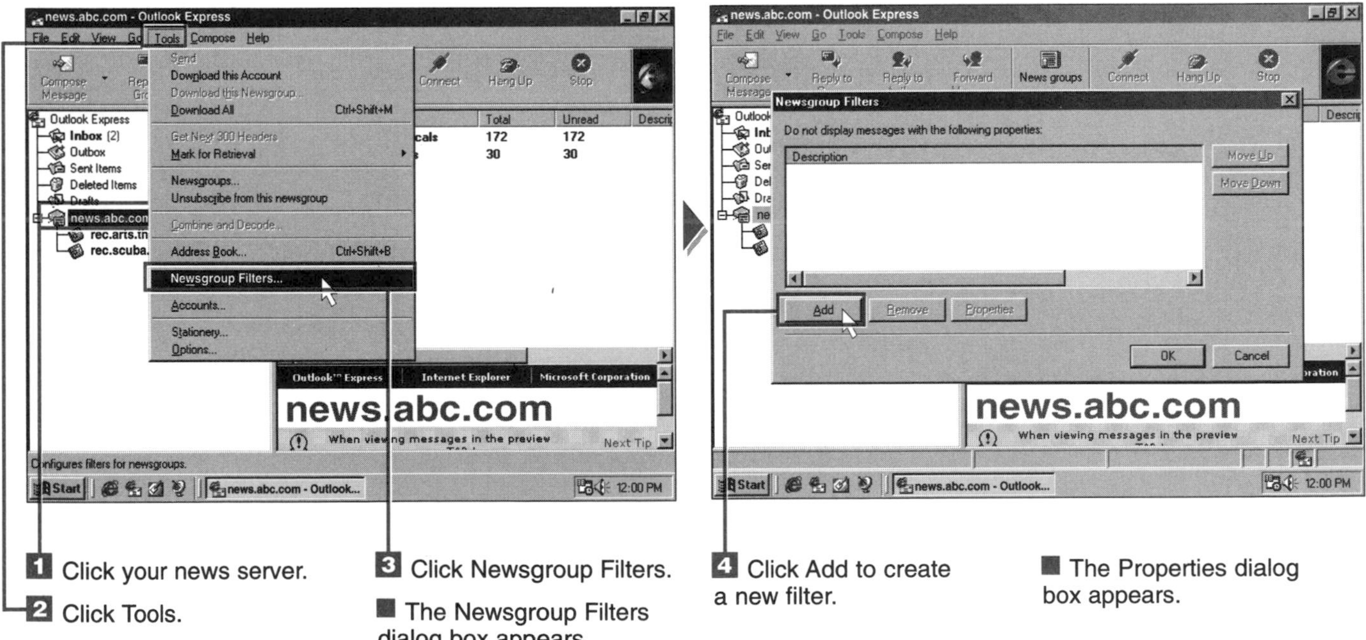

1 Click your news server.

2 Click Tools.

3 Click Newsgroup Filters.

■ The Newsgroup Filters dialog box appears.

4 Click Add to create a new filter.

■ The Properties dialog box appears.

TIPS

How do I remove a filter?

When you create a filter, a description of the filter appears in the Newsgroup Filters dialog box. Display the Newsgroup Filters dialog box, select the filter you want to remove and then click the Remove button. You cannot restore a filter you have removed. You must create a new filter.

Can I temporarily turn off a filter?

Yes. To temporarily turn off a filter, display the Newsgroup Filters dialog box and then click the box beside the filter you wish to turn off (☑ changes to ☐). You can repeat this procedure to turn the filter on again (☐ changes to ☑).

Why are messages I want to read being filtered?

When you filter messages by the subject of the message, all messages containing the text you specify are filtered. For example, when filtering messages containing "file" in the subject, messages with subjects containing text such as "Profile" and "filename" are also filtered.

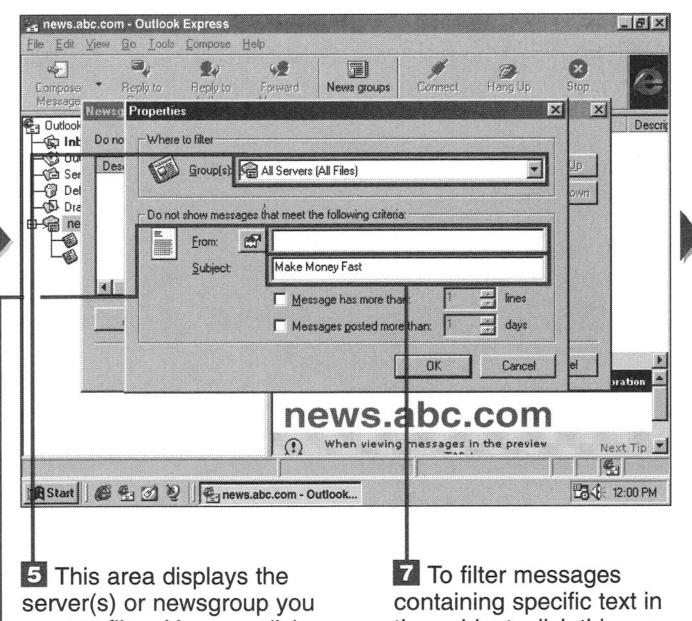

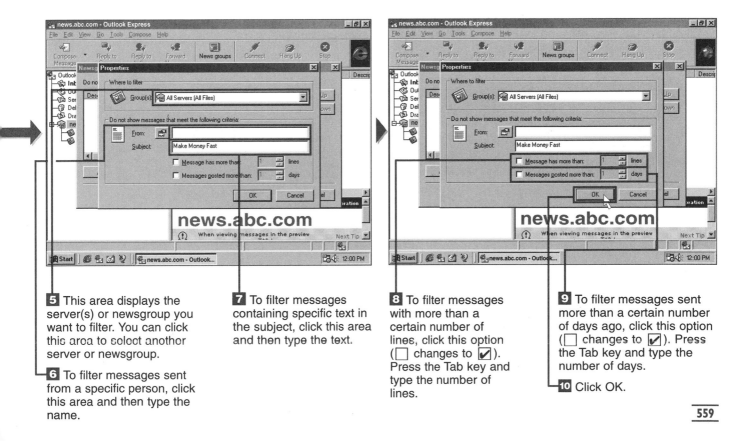

5 This area displays the server(s) or newsgroup you want to filter. You can click this area to select another server or newsgroup.

6 To filter messages sent from a specific person, click this area and then type the name.

7 To filter messages containing specific text in the subject, click this area and then type the text.

8 To filter messages with more than a certain number of lines, click this option (☐ changes to ☑). Press the Tab key and type the number of lines.

9 To filter messages sent more than a certain number of days ago, click this option (☐ changes to ☑). Press the Tab key and type the number of days.

10 Click OK.

ADD AN ACTIVE DESKTOP ITEM

You can add pieces of Web pages, called Active Desktop items, to your desktop to display information that is continuously changing, such as a stock ticker or a weather map. This lets you display items you need to refer to on a regular basis on your desktop for easy access.

Microsoft's Active Desktop Gallery provides a variety of items you can use to customize your desktop. The Active Desktop items are organized into different categories, such as news, sports and entertainment. Each category contains related Active Desktop items. For example, the entertainment category contains items such as movie and music news.

There are many interesting Active Desktop items you can add to your desktop. For example, you can personalize your desktop with a comic strip or with a search service component that allows you to quickly find information on the Web. Some Active Desktop items contain sounds or videos.

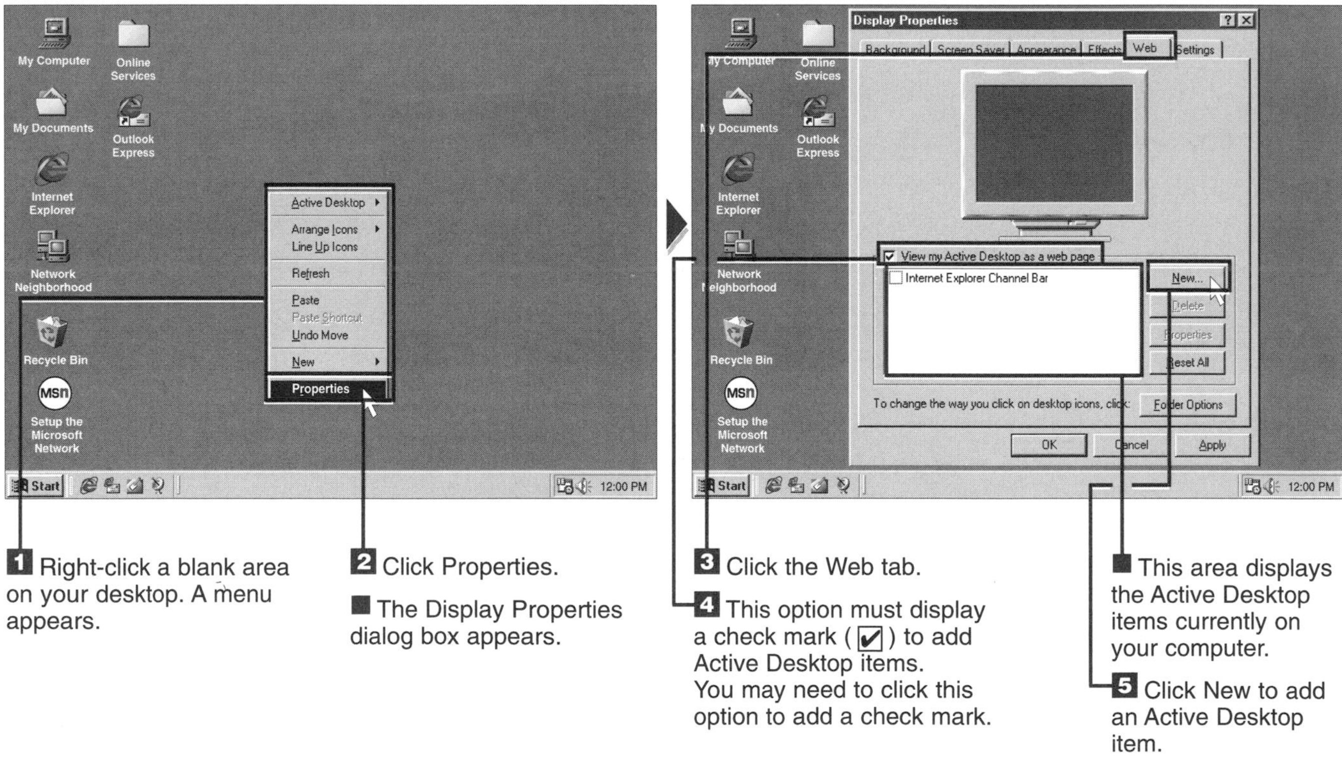

1 Right-click a blank area on your desktop. A menu appears.

2 Click Properties.

■ The Display Properties dialog box appears.

3 Click the Web tab.

4 This option must display a check mark (✔) to add Active Desktop items. You may need to click this option to add a check mark.

■ This area displays the Active Desktop items currently on your computer.

5 Click New to add an Active Desktop item.

TIPS

Why does the Security Warning dialog box appear when I display the gallery?

If the Security Warning dialog box appears when you visit the Active Desktop Gallery, Microsoft needs to transfer information to your computer. Click Yes to transfer the information to your computer.

How do I add an entire Web page to my desktop?

When using Internet Explorer to view a Web page, use the right mouse button to drag the Web page icon ( ) from the Address bar to your desktop. Then select the Create Active Desktop item(s) Here option.

What is the Internet Explorer Channel Bar option in the Display Properties dialog box?

The Internet Explorer Channel Bar is an Active Desktop item that automatically appears on your desktop the first time you start Windows. The Channel Bar allows you to quickly access specially designed Web sites called channels. If the Channel Bar is not displayed on your screen, perform steps 1 to 4 below and then click the box beside the Channel Bar option (☐ changes to ☑).

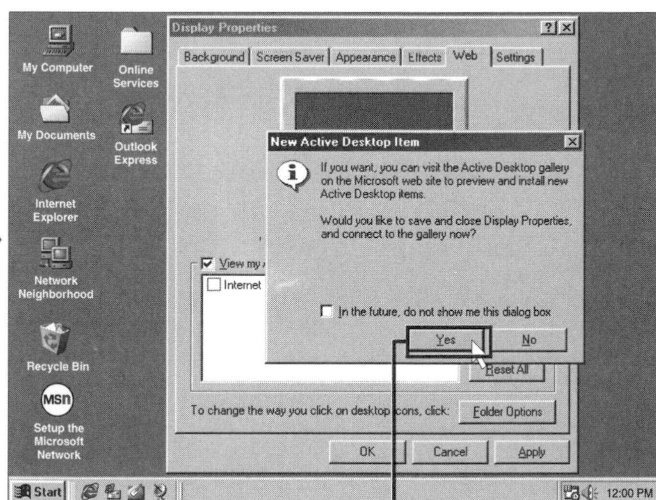

■ A dialog box appears, asking if you want to visit the gallery where you can see a list of Active Desktop items.

6 Click Yes to visit the gallery.

Note: If you are not connected to the Internet, a dialog box may appear that allows you to connect.

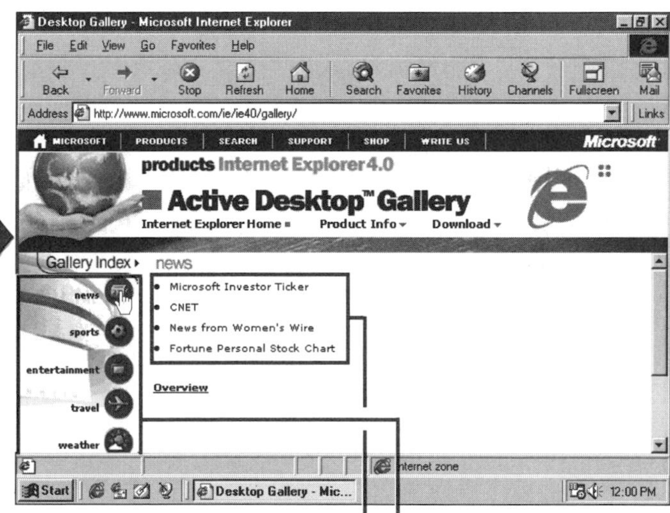

■ The Internet Explorer Web browser opens and the Active Desktop Gallery appears.

Note: To maximize the window to fill your screen, click ☐ in the top right corner of the window.

7 Click a category to display Active Desktop items of interest.

■ This area displays the Active Desktop items in the category you selected.

CONTINUED

ADD AN ACTIVE DESKTOP ITEM
CONTINUED

After selecting the category that interests you, you can view information about any Active Desktop item in the category. This helps you decide which items you want to add to your desktop.

When you add an item to the desktop, you must subscribe to the Active Desktop item. An item that you are subscribed to will be updated on a regular basis. Most of the Active Desktop items contain information that must be updated to continue being useful, such as a weather map. Active Desktop items automatically update at times that have been preset by the item's designer.

When you add an Active Desktop item to your desktop, it is copied to your computer and automatically appears on the desktop. You can move the Active Desktop item to any position on your desktop.

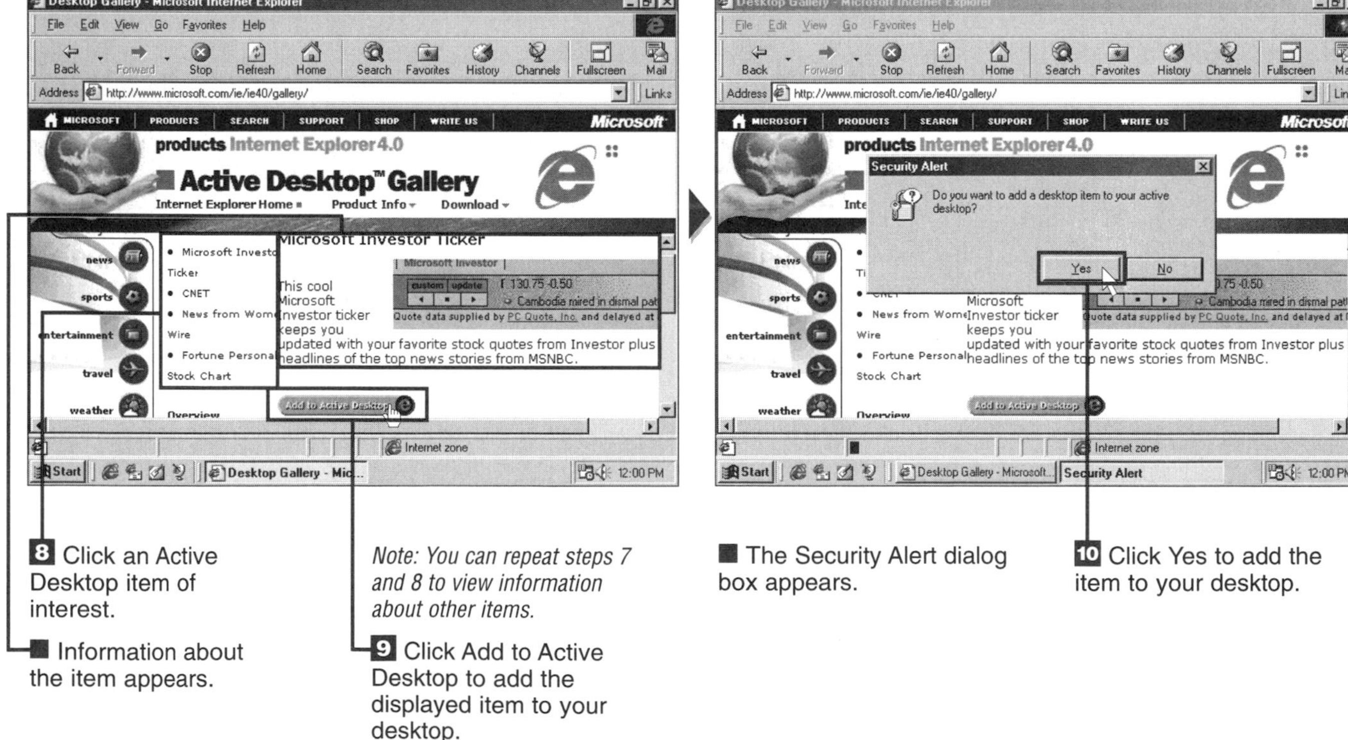

8 Click an Active Desktop item of interest.

■ Information about the item appears.

Note: You can repeat steps 7 and 8 to view information about other items.

9 Click Add to Active Desktop to add the displayed item to your desktop.

■ The Security Alert dialog box appears.

10 Click Yes to add the item to your desktop.

TIPS

Can I change the size of my Active Desktop items?

To change the size of an Active Desktop item, position the mouse pointer over the edge of the item (↖ changes to ↕ or ↔). Then drag the item to a new size. Some Active Desktop items cannot be sized.

Can I remove a single Active Desktop item?

Display the Web tab in the Display Properties dialog box and then click the box beside the item you want to remove (☑ changes to ☐). Repeat this procedure to redisplay the item at any time (☐ changes to ☑).

Can I remove all the currently displayed Active Desktop items?

To remove all the currently displayed Active Desktop items, right-click a blank area on the desktop. Click Active Desktop and then select View As Web Page. Repeat this procedure to redisplay these items at any time.

What can I do if an Active Desktop item does not transfer completely to my desktop?

Right-click a blank area on the desktop and then click Refresh.

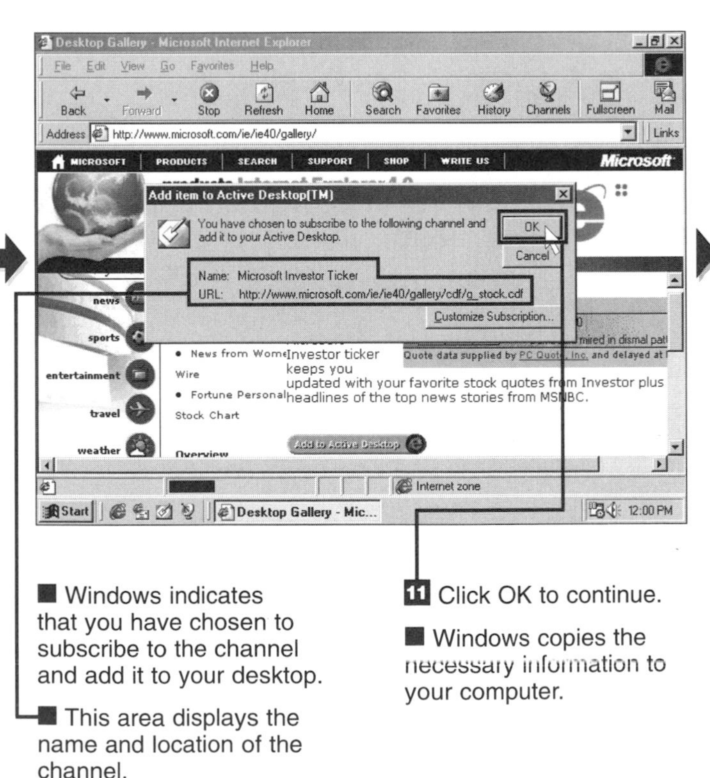

■ Windows indicates that you have chosen to subscribe to the channel and add it to your desktop.

■ This area displays the name and location of the channel.

11 Click OK to continue.

■ Windows copies the necessary information to your computer.

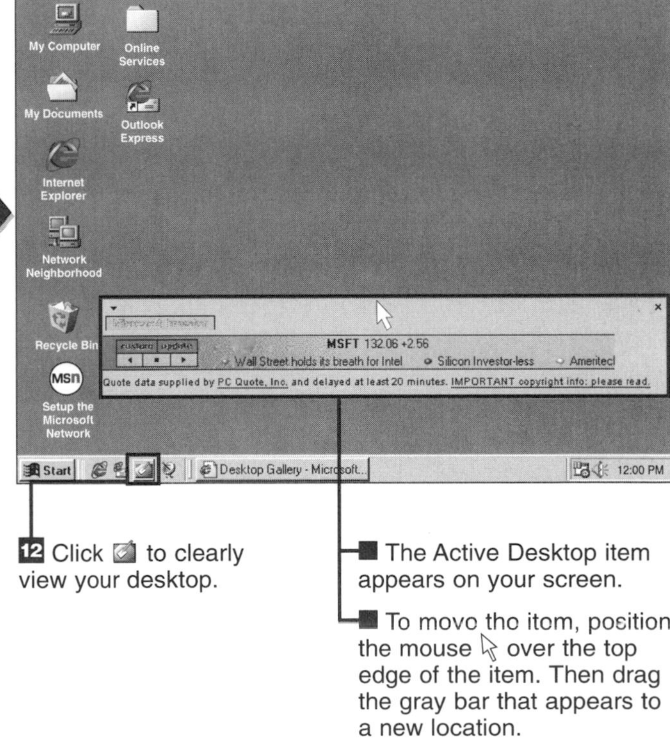

12 Click the desktop icon to clearly view your desktop.

■ The Active Desktop item appears on your screen.

■ To move the item, position the mouse ↖ over the top edge of the item. Then drag the gray bar that appears to a new location.

ADD A CHANNEL

A channel is a specially designed Web site that you can have Windows automatically deliver from the Internet to your computer.

When you add a channel, you can specify how you want the information from the channel to be delivered to your computer. You can simply add the channel to your Channel Bar or you can subscribe to the channel.

Subscribing is useful if you want Internet Explorer to notify you whenever the content of the channel changes. This makes it possible for you to keep up to date and ensure you always have access to the latest information. You can also choose to have the channel copied to your computer each time it is updated. If you choose to have the channel copied to your computer, you can view the channel when you are not connected to the Internet.

You can use some channels as screen savers. A channel screen saver is an active channel with moving patterns or pictures that appears on your screen when you do not use your computer for a period of time.

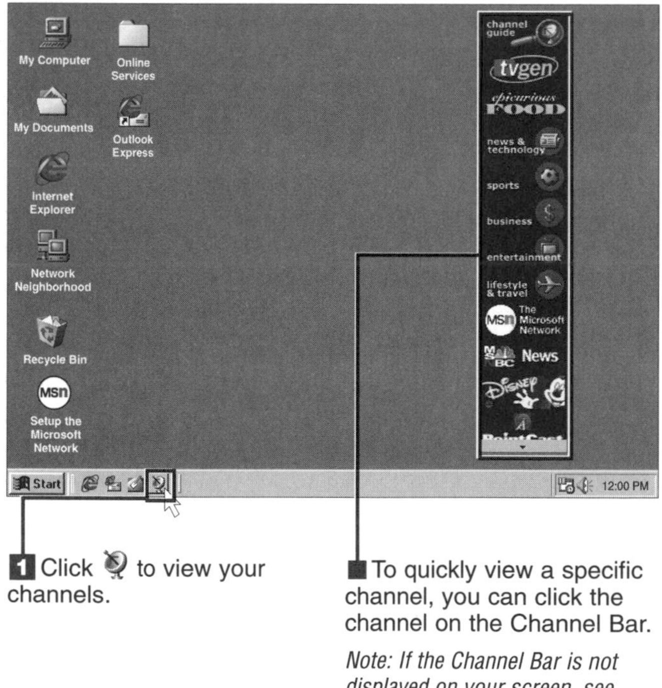

1 Click to view your channels.

■ To quickly view a specific channel, you can click the channel on the Channel Bar.

Note: If the Channel Bar is not displayed on your screen, see the top of page 561 to display the Channel Bar.

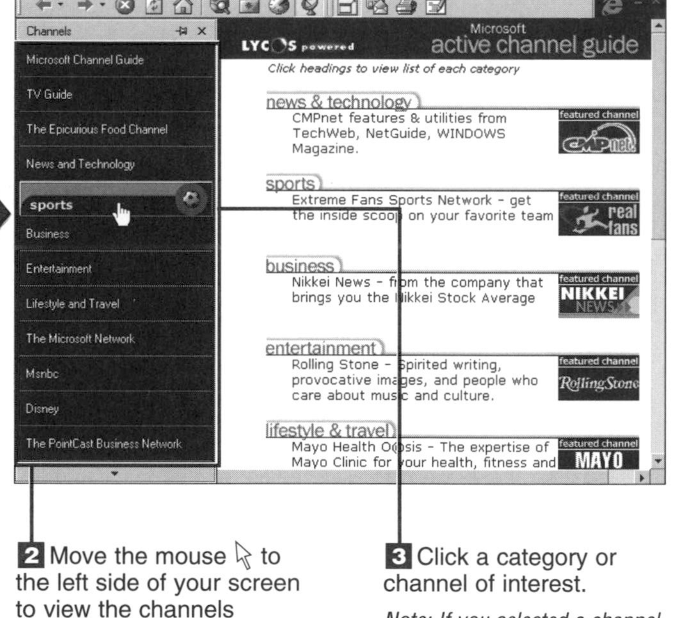

2 Move the mouse to the left side of your screen to view the channels (changes to).

3 Click a category or channel of interest.

Note: If you selected a channel in step 3, skip to step 5.

TIPS

Can I decide to use a channel as a screen saver later on?

Yes. To later use a channel as a screen saver, right-click a blank area on the desktop and then click Properties. Choose the Screen Saver tab and then click ▼ beside the Screen Saver box. Select the Channel Screen Saver option from the drop-down list that appears and then click the Settings button. Click the channel you want to use as a screen saver (☐ changes to ☑).

Can I rearrange the items in the Channel Bar?

To move an item in the Channel Bar, drag the item to a new location.

How can I display a channel in the Internet Explorer window?

Channels are automatically displayed in the full-screen view. You can click ▣ to display the channel in the Internet Explorer window. Click Fullscreen in the Internet Explorer window to return to the full-screen view.

Where can I find other channels to add to the Channel Bar?

You can use the Microsoft Channel Guide to locate new channels. For more information, see page 566.

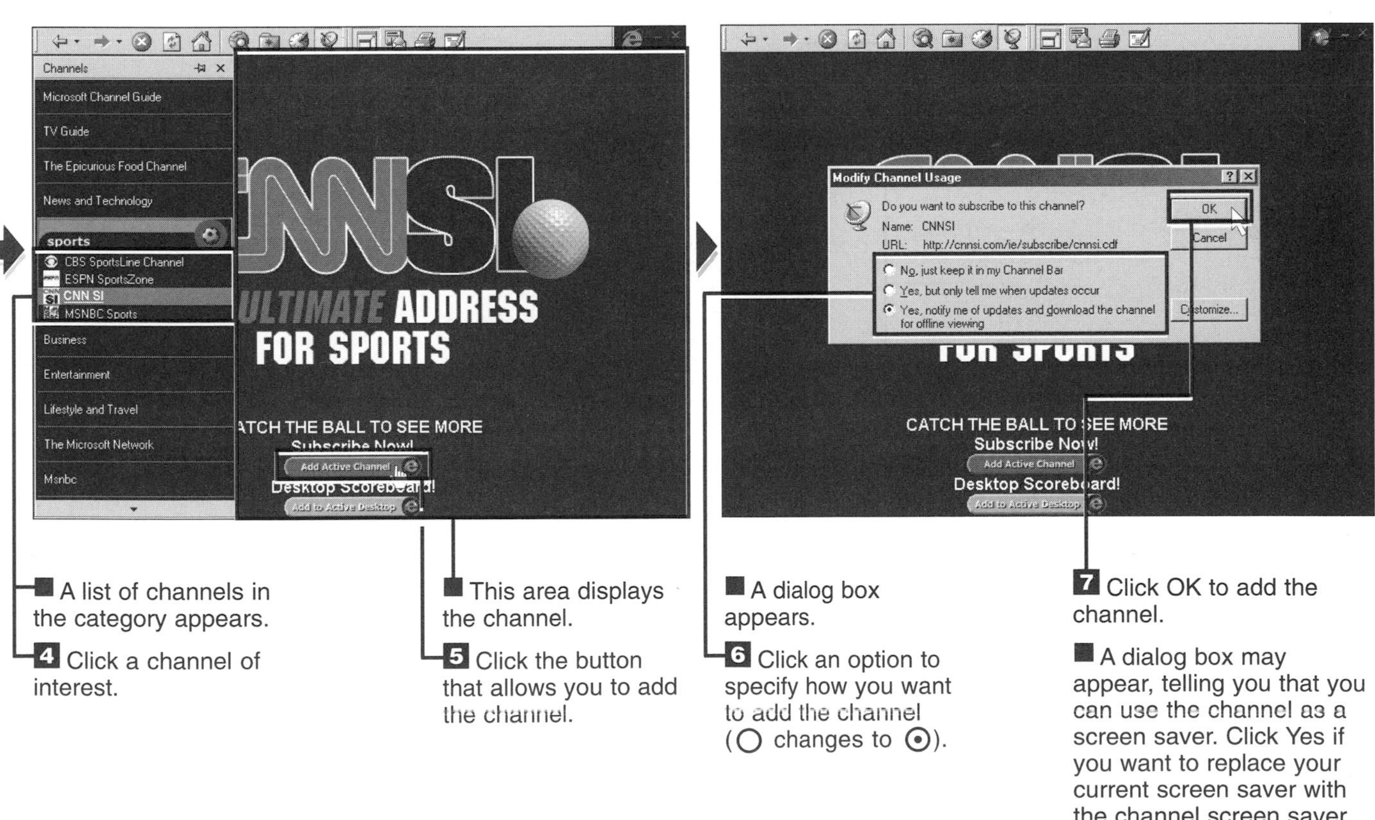

■ A list of channels in the category appears.

4 Click a channel of interest.

■ This area displays the channel.

5 Click the button that allows you to add the channel.

■ A dialog box appears.

6 Click an option to specify how you want to add the channel (○ changes to ⊙).

7 Click OK to add the channel.

■ A dialog box may appear, telling you that you can use the channel as a screen saver. Click Yes if you want to replace your current screen saver with the channel screen saver.

USING THE MICROSOFT CHANNEL GUIDE

You can use the Microsoft Channel Guide to find and preview channels of interest. The Channel Guide is frequently updated to provide you with the latest channels.

You can browse through categories of channels, such as news & technology, sports, business, entertainment and lifestyle & travel. When you select a category, you can view many channels related to the category. For example, you can choose the business category to browse through channels that provide information about stock markets or the latest business news.

You can also enter a specific topic of interest and have Internet Explorer search for channels related to the topic. Internet Explorer then displays a list of all the matching channels it found.

After you find a channel of interest, you can display a description of the channel, preview the channel and even add the channel to your computer directly from the Channel Guide.

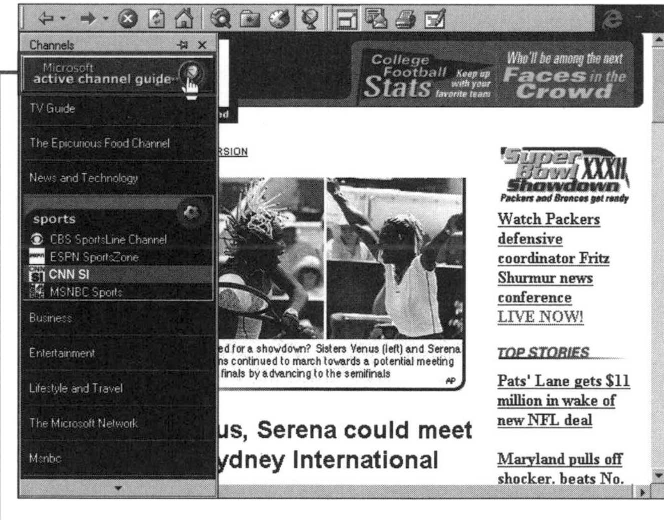

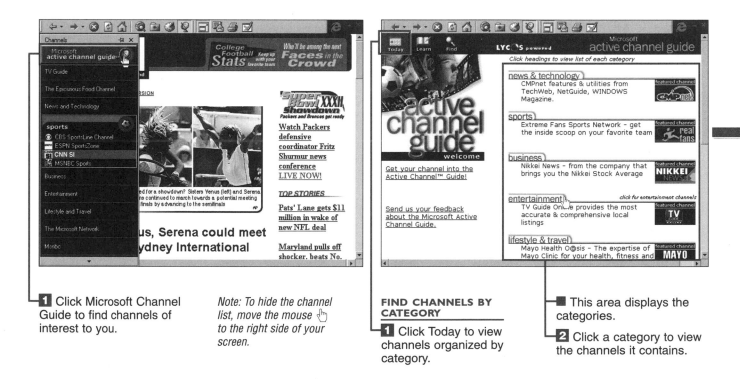

1 Click Microsoft Channel Guide to find channels of interest to you.

Note: To hide the channel list, move the mouse to the right side of your screen.

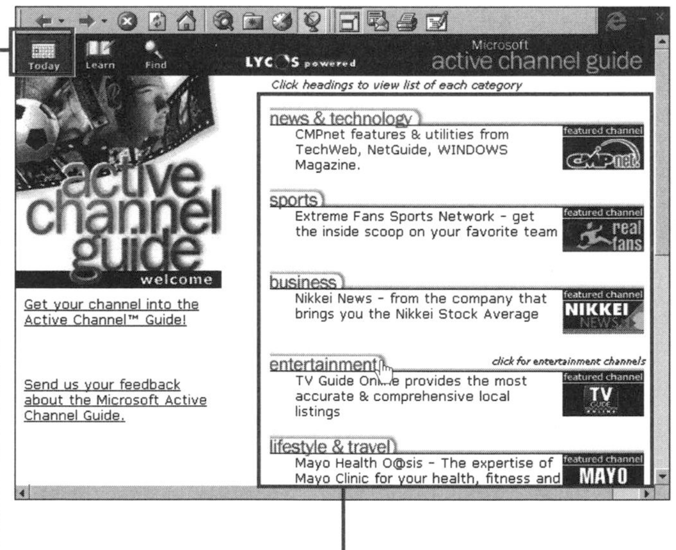

FIND CHANNELS BY CATEGORY

1 Click Today to view channels organized by category.

■ This area displays the categories.

2 Click a category to view the channels it contains.

TIPS

How can I display the channel list to access the Microsoft Channel Guide?

To display the channel list, click on your taskbar and then move your mouse to the left side of your screen.

How do I add a channel from the Microsoft Channel Guide?

When you have found a channel you want to add, click the Add Active Channel button in the preview area of your screen. A dialog box will appear, allowing you to choose how you want to add the channel. For information on adding a channel, see page 564.

Is there another way to access the Microsoft Channel Guide?

You can access the Microsoft Channel Guide by selecting it from the Channel Bar on your desktop. If the Channel Bar is not displayed, right-click the desktop. Click Properties and then select the Web tab. Click View my Active Desktop as a Web page (☐ changes to ☑). Then click the box (☐) beside the Internet Explorer Channel Bar option (☐ changes to ☑).

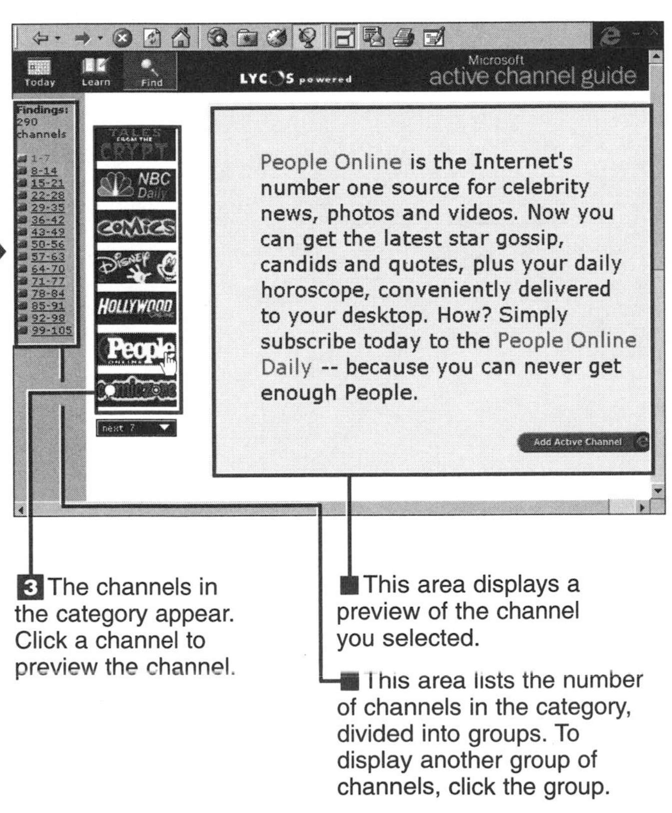

3 The channels in the category appear. Click a channel to preview the channel.

■ This area displays a preview of the channel you selected.

■ This area lists the number of channels in the category, divided into groups. To display another group of channels, click the group.

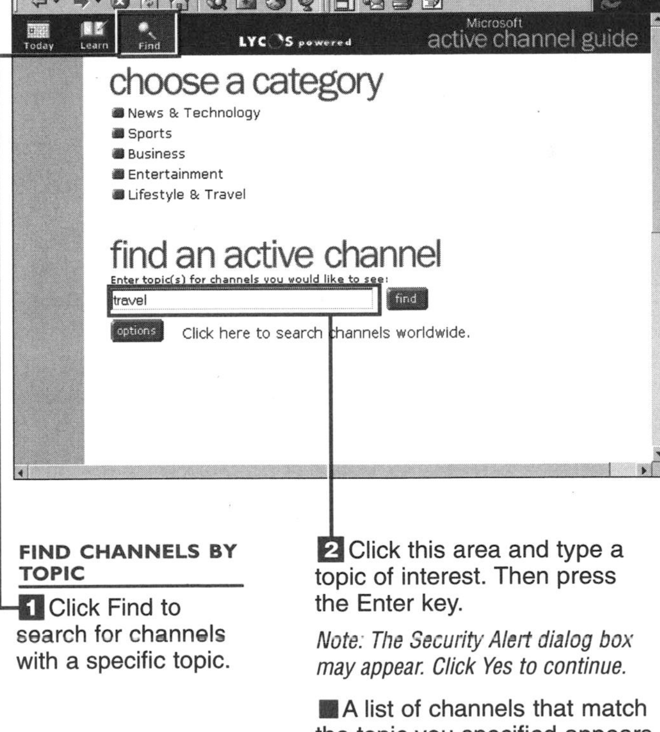

FIND CHANNELS BY TOPIC

1 Click Find to search for channels with a specific topic.

2 Click this area and type a topic of interest. Then press the Enter key.

Note: The Security Alert dialog box may appear. Click Yes to continue.

■ A list of channels that match the topic you specified appears.

CHANGE CHANNEL PROPERTIES

You can change the settings that Internet Explorer uses to monitor and update the channels you have added to your computer.

You can have Internet Explorer notify you when the contents of a channel change or you can choose to be notified and have Internet Explorer automatically transfer a copy of the updated channel to your computer. Transferring a copy of the updated channel allows you to later view the channel without having to be connected to the Internet.

You can also have Internet Explorer send you an e-mail message to notify you when the contents of a channel change.

You can specify when you want Internet Explorer to check for updates to a channel. Internet Explorer automatically updates the channel according to the publisher's recommended schedule. You can choose to update a channel once a day, once a week or once a month, if you wish.

If you use a modem to connect to the Internet, you can have Internet Explorer automatically connect to the Internet at the scheduled time to find out whether the contents of the channel have changed.

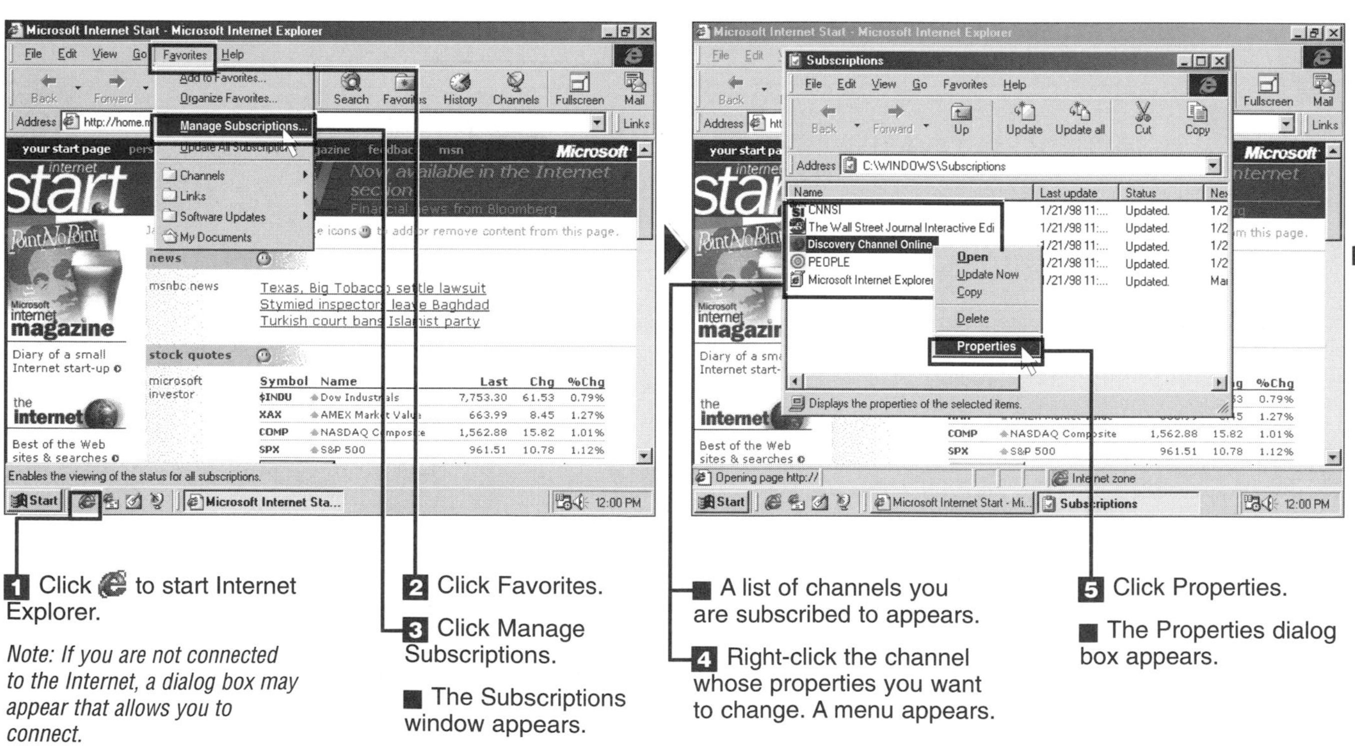

1 Click [icon] to start Internet Explorer.

Note: If you are not connected to the Internet, a dialog box may appear that allows you to connect.

2 Click Favorites.

3 Click Manage Subscriptions.

■ The Subscriptions window appears.

■ A list of channels you are subscribed to appears.

4 Right-click the channel whose properties you want to change. A menu appears.

5 Click Properties.

■ The Properties dialog box appears.

TIPS

Can I update a channel immediately?

Yes. You can update a channel at any time. In the Subscriptions window, click the channel you want to update and then click the Update button. To update all your channels at once, click the Update all button.

How do I unsubscribe from a channel?

Display the Subscriptions window and then click the channel you want to unsubscribe from. Then press the Delete key. The channel still appears on the Channel Bar, but the contents of the channel will no longer be updated automatically.

I chose to have Internet Explorer automatically connect to the Internet to update a channel, but it is not working. What is wrong?

Before you can use the automatic dialing feature, you must set up your computer to use the feature. In the Control Panel window, double-click the Internet icon. Select the Connection tab and then click the Settings button. Click the Connect automatically to update subscriptions option (☐ changes to ☑).

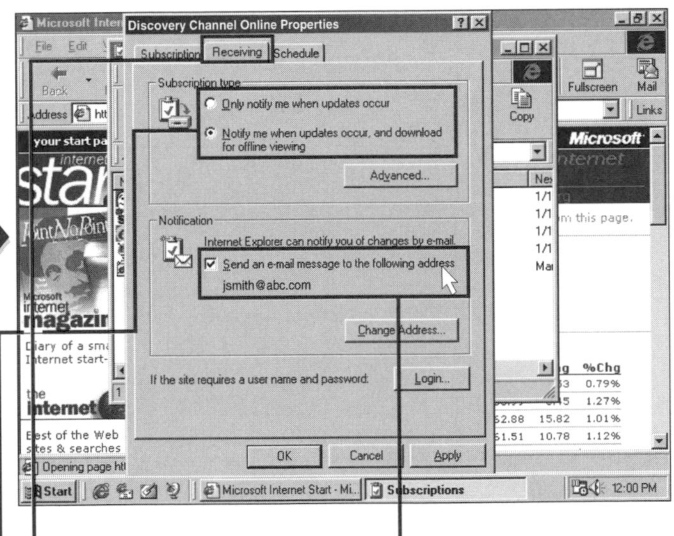

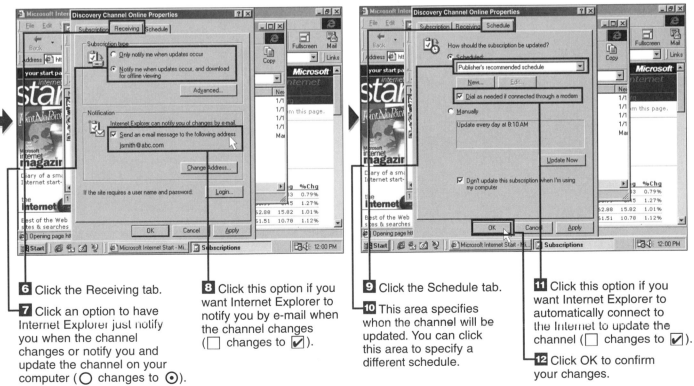

6 Click the Receiving tab.

7 Click an option to have Internet Explorer just notify you when the channel changes or notify you and update the channel on your computer (○ changes to ⊙).

8 Click this option if you want Internet Explorer to notify you by e-mail when the channel changes (☐ changes to ☑).

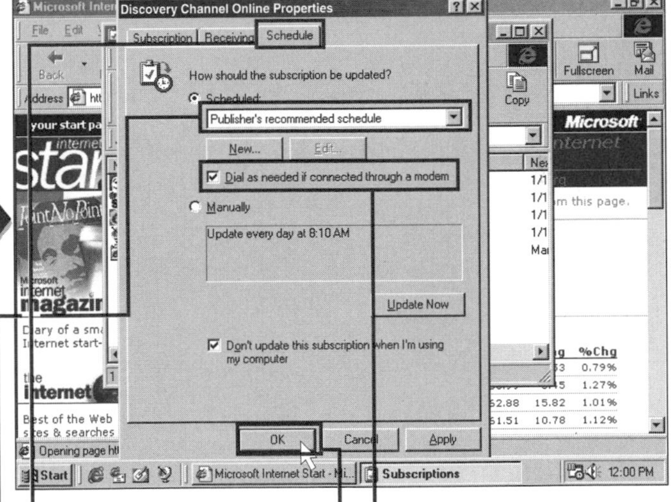

9 Click the Schedule tab.

10 This area specifies when the channel will be updated. You can click this area to specify a different schedule.

11 Click this option if you want Internet Explorer to automatically connect to the Internet to update the channel (☐ changes to ☑).

12 Click OK to confirm your changes.

CREATE AND SAVE A WEB PAGE

FrontPage Express allows you to create your own Web pages without having to learn HTML (HyperText Markup Language). HTML is the code used to construct Web pages. FrontPage Express enters the HTML code for you and keeps it hidden from view so you can concentrate on the content of the page.

Many people use the Web to share information about a topic that interests them, such as a favorite celebrity or a hobby. Companies often place pages on the Web to provide the public with information about the company and to allow people to place orders for products and services.

If you publish your Web page on the World Wide Web, the page will be available to everyone on the Web. If you are connected to a corporate intranet, you can share your Web page with other users on the intranet. An intranet is a small version of the Internet within a company or organization.

You should save a Web page you create to store the page for future use. This lets you later review and update the page. When you save a page, you must specify a title and a file name for the page.

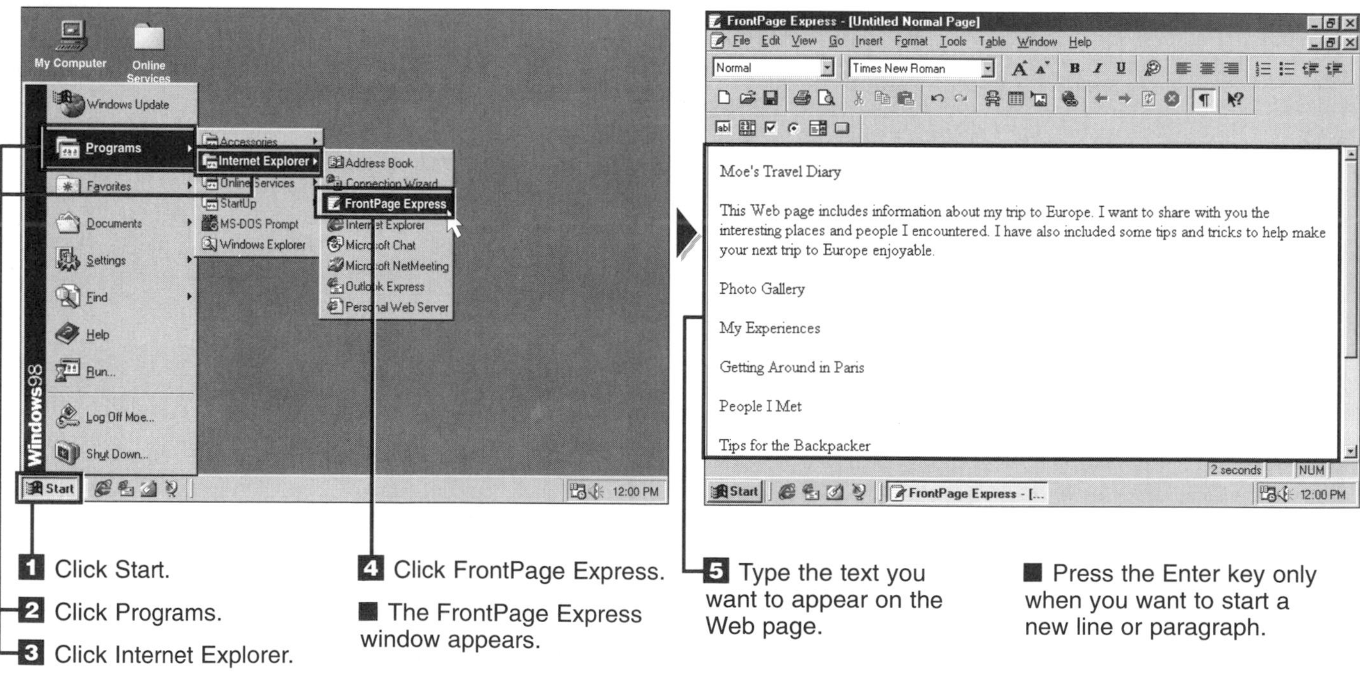

1 Click Start.

2 Click Programs.

3 Click Internet Explorer.

4 Click FrontPage Express.

■ The FrontPage Express window appears.

5 Type the text you want to appear on the Web page.

■ Press the Enter key only when you want to start a new line or paragraph.

TIPS

What is the difference between the title and file name of a Web page?

The title provides a brief description of the information on the page and appears at the top of the screen when the page is viewed in a Web browser. The file name is the name given to the saved Web page. You must know the file name in order to later find and open the Web page on your computer.

How do I open a Web page I have previously saved?

In the FrontPage Express window, click [open icon] and then select the Browse button to find the page on your computer. Double-click the Web page you want to open.

How do I change the title of my Web page?

To later change the title of your Web page, choose the File menu and then select Page Properties. On the General tab, type a new title for the Web page in the Title area.

Can I display the HTML code for my Web page?

Yes. From the View menu, select the HTML command.

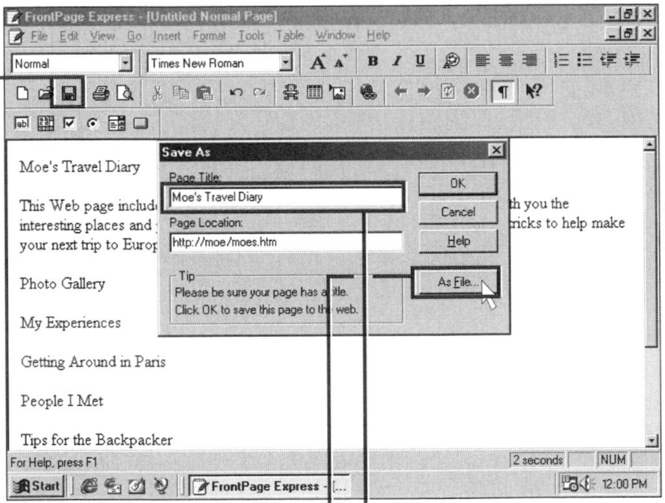

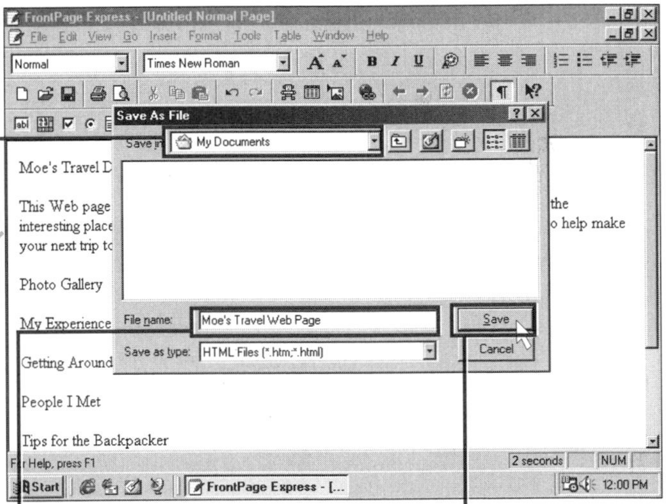

SAVE THE WEB PAGE

1 Click [save icon] to save the Web page.

■ The Save As dialog box appears.

2 Type a title for the Web page.

3 Click As File to save the Web page on your computer.

■ The Save As File dialog box appears.

4 Type a name for the Web page.

■ This area shows where FrontPage Express will store the page. You can click this area to change the location.

5 Click Save.

FORMAT TEXT

You can format or change the appearance of text on a Web page. Formatting can make your Web page look more attractive.

You can change the design of the text, as well as increase or decrease the size of the text on your Web page. A larger text size makes the information on your Web page easier to read. A smaller text size lets you fit more information on a single screen.

FrontPage Express can also help you draw attention to important information on your Web page. You can color the text to enhance the appearance of the information. The bold, italic and underline commands are also helpful for emphasizing important areas on your Web page. You should use underlines only when necessary, since underlined text may be confused with links by people visiting your Web page.

When formatting text on your Web page, keep in mind that Web browsers can be set to override the formatting defined for a Web page. This allows readers to display all Web pages with the text styles and colors they prefer. Therefore, the formatting you choose for your Web page may not appear the way you expect on some computers.

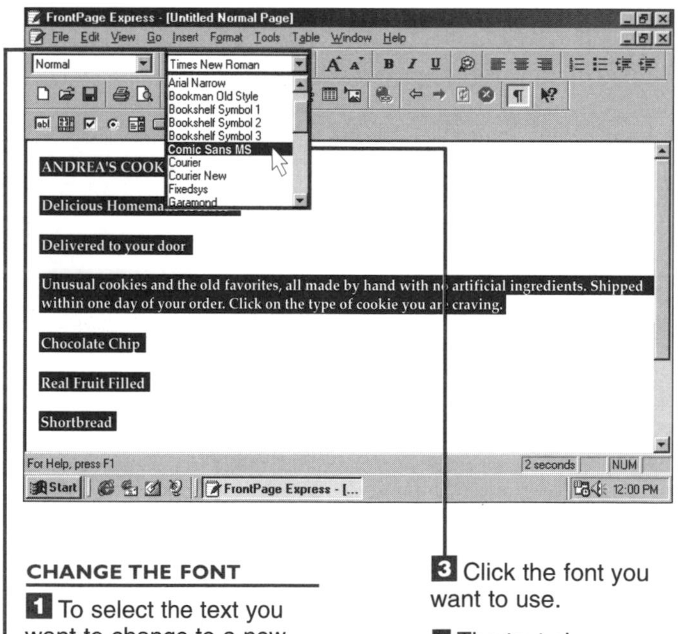

CHANGE THE FONT

1 To select the text you want to change to a new font, drag the mouse over the text.

2 Click this area to display a list of the available fonts.

3 Click the font you want to use.

■ The text changes to the new font.

CHANGE THE TEXT SIZE

1 To select the text you want to change to a new size, drag the mouse over the text.

2 Click one of the following options.

A Increase the text size

A Decrease the text size

TIPS

Can I change the font, size, style and color of text at the same time?

Yes. Select the text you want to change. Then choose the Format menu and select Font. The Font dialog box appears, allowing you to select many options at once and also preview how the text will look once the formatting is applied.

Can I remove the formatting from text?

You can remove the formatting from any of the text on your Web page. Select the text displaying the formatting you want to remove. Choose the Format menu and then select Remove Formatting.

Is there a faster way to select text in my Web page?

When you format text, you may want to format more than a few words at a time. To quickly select an entire line of text, move the mouse pointer (I) to the left of the line (I changes to ). Click once to select the line of text. You can double-click to select the entire paragraph.

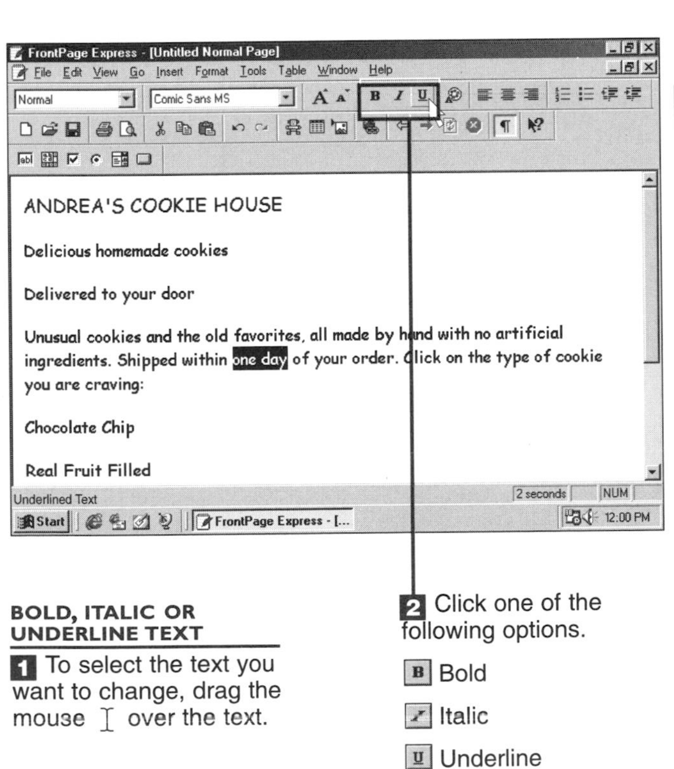

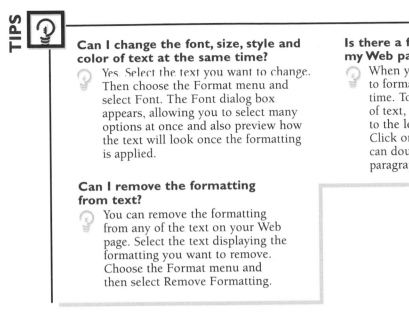

BOLD, ITALIC OR UNDERLINE TEXT

1 To select the text you want to change, drag the mouse I over the text.

2 Click one of the following options.

B Bold

I Italic

U Underline

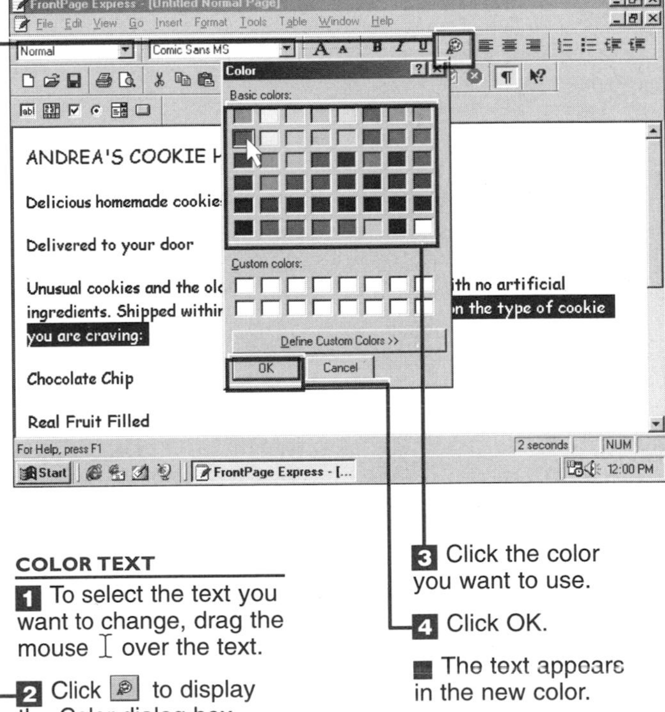

COLOR TEXT

1 To select the text you want to change, drag the mouse I over the text.

2 Click to display the Color dialog box.

3 Click the color you want to use.

4 Click OK.

■ The text appears in the new color.

CONTINUED

FORMAT TEXT CONTINUED

You can format the paragraphs on your Web page to organize the page and make it easier to read.

FrontPage Express automatically left aligns the text on your Web page, but you may find changing the alignment useful for tasks such as centering a title or right aligning a column of text.

Indents can help you emphasize where the content of your Web page changes. For example, you may want to indent your copyright information to separate it from the rest of the text on your Web page.

You can separate items in a list by beginning each item with a number or a bullet. A numbered list is useful for items in a specific order, such as a set of instructions or a table of contents. A bulleted list is useful for items in no particular order, such as a list of products.

You can use headings to separate the text in a Web page into smaller sections. There are six heading levels, ranging in size from very large to very small. You can use headings to provide an outline of your Web page for your readers.

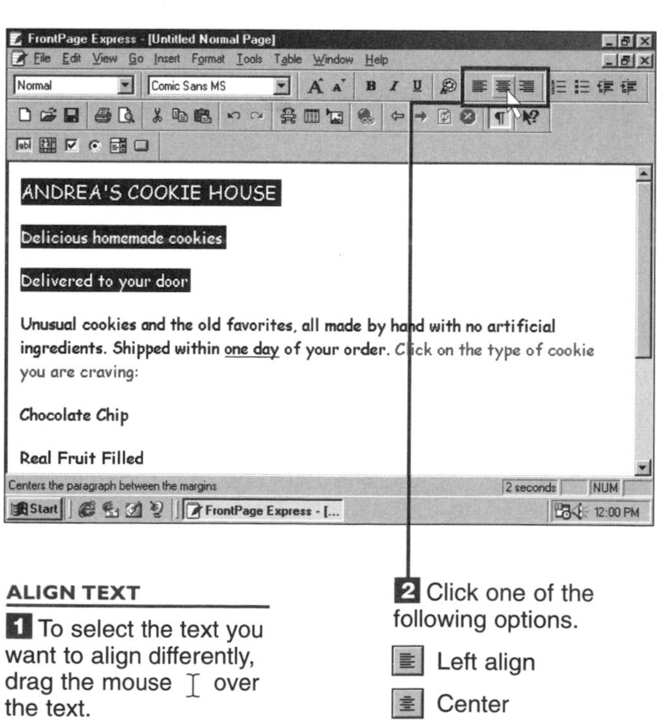

ALIGN TEXT

1 To select the text you want to align differently, drag the mouse over the text.

2 Click one of the following options.

- Left align
- Center
- Right align

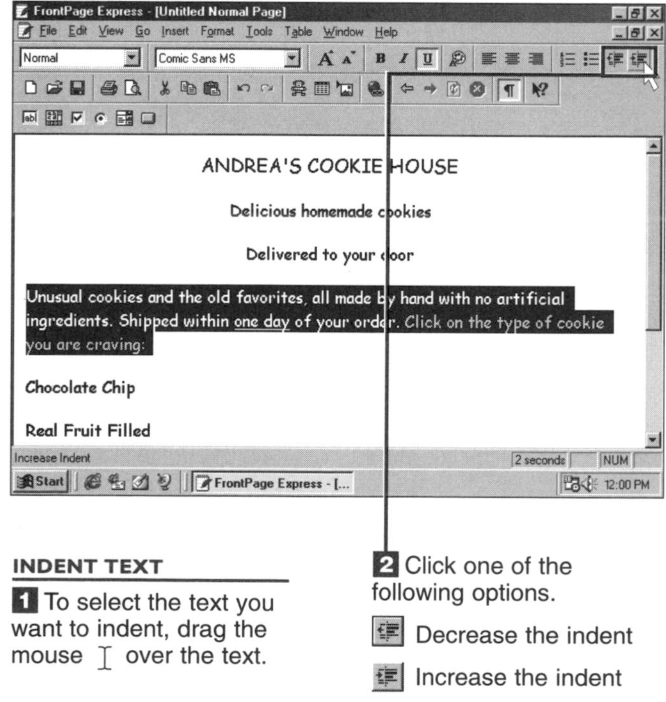

INDENT TEXT

1 To select the text you want to indent, drag the mouse over the text.

2 Click one of the following options.

- Decrease the indent
- Increase the indent

TIPS

How do I change the type of bullet or number used in a list?

Select the list you want to change. Choose the Format menu and then select Bullets and Numbering. Click the Bulleted or Numbered tab and then click the type of bullets or numbers you want to use.

How can I make the sections of my Web page more distinct?

You can insert a horizontal line to visually separate the sections of your Web page. Position the insertion point where you want to add the horizontal line. From the Insert menu, click Horizontal Line.

Can I change the margins on my Web page?

You can change the top and left margins to help make your Web page easier to read. From the Format menu, select Background and then choose the Margins tab. Click the margin you want to change (☐ changes to ☑). Double-click the box below the margin and type a margin size you want to use.

Can I add items to a bulleted or numbered list?

Yes. When you add an item to a numbered list, FrontPage Express will automatically renumber the items in the list.

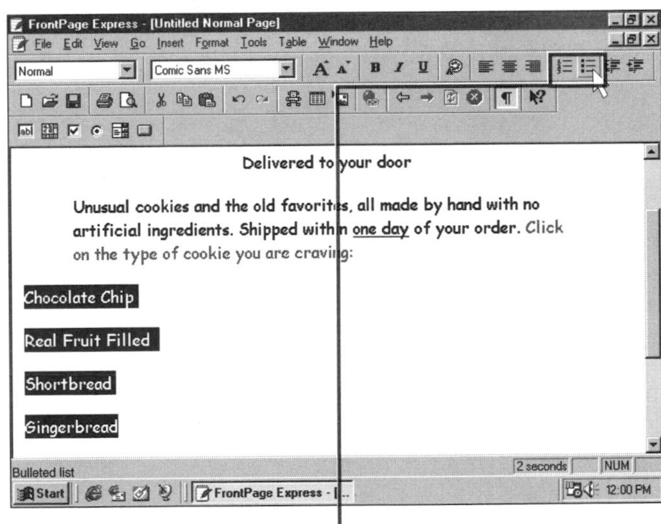

CREATE A LIST

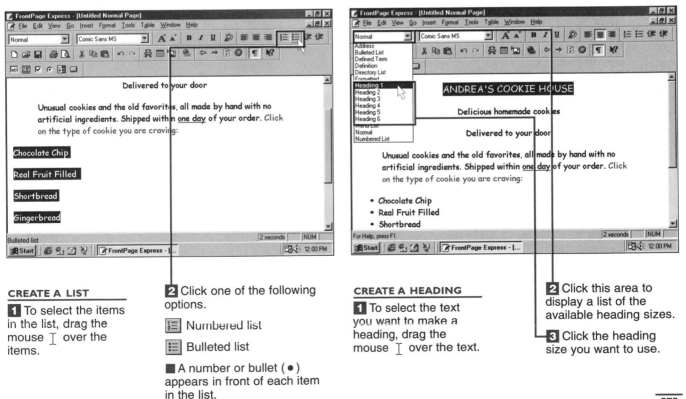

1 To select the items in the list, drag the mouse over the items.

2 Click one of the following options.

Numbered list

Bulleted list

■ A number or bullet (•) appears in front of each item in the list.

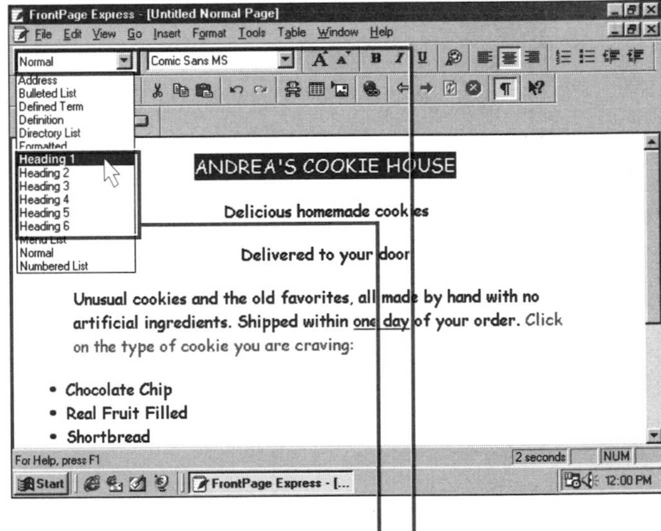

CREATE A HEADING

1 To select the text you want to make a heading, drag the mouse over the text.

2 Click this area to display a list of the available heading sizes.

3 Click the heading size you want to use.

INSERT AN IMAGE

You can add images to your Web pages to make the pages more interesting and attractive. An image that appears on a Web page is called an inline image.

Many pages on the Web offer images you can use for free. You can buy a collection of ready-made images, called clip art, at most computer stores or use a scanner to scan images into your computer. You can also use a drawing program to create your own images. Make sure you have permission to use any images you did not create yourself.

Images increase the time it takes for a Web page to appear on a screen. Whenever possible, use small images rather than large images, since large images take longer to transfer.

When adding images to your Web pages, you must use image files with the .gif or .jpg extension. These file types are supported in all Web browsers. Most image editing programs and utilities can convert an image to the .gif or .jpg file type.

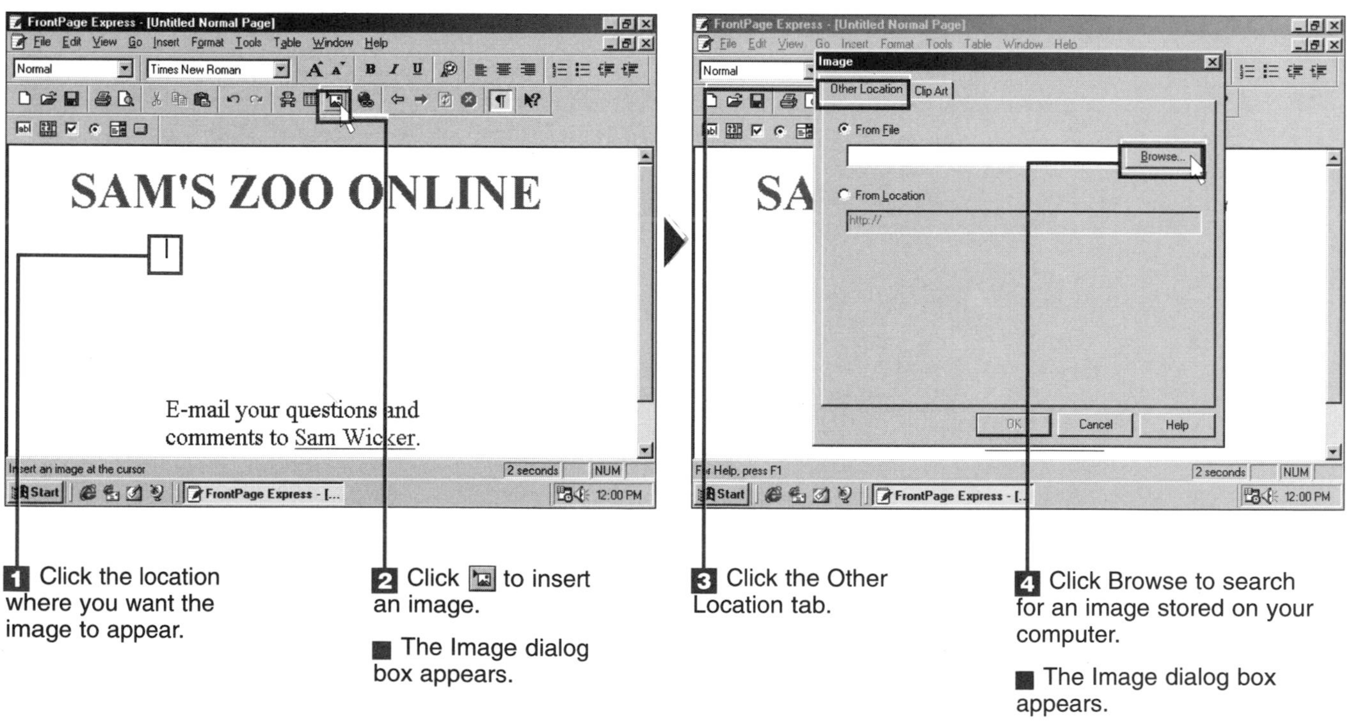

1 Click the location where you want the image to appear.

2 Click the image button to insert an image.

■ The Image dialog box appears.

3 Click the Other Location tab.

4 Click Browse to search for an image stored on your computer.

■ The Image dialog box appears.

TIPS

Can I center an image on my Web page?

You can align an image on a Web page the same way you align text in a word processor. To center an image on your Web page, click the image and then click ☰. To right align an image, click the image and then click ☰. To left align an image, click the image and then click ☰.

Can I specify the exact size of an image?

Double-click the image you want to size. The Image Properties dialog box appears. Select the Appearance tab and click the Specify Size option (☐ changes to ☑). Then specify a new width and height for the image.

How do I move an image on my Web page to a new location?

Click the image and then drag the image to the new location.

Will everyone see my images?

Some people use Web browsers that cannot display images, while other people turn off the display of images to browse more quickly. To have the Web page display text when the image is not displayed, double-click the image. On the General tab of the Image Properties dialog box, click the area beside Text and then type the text you want to display.

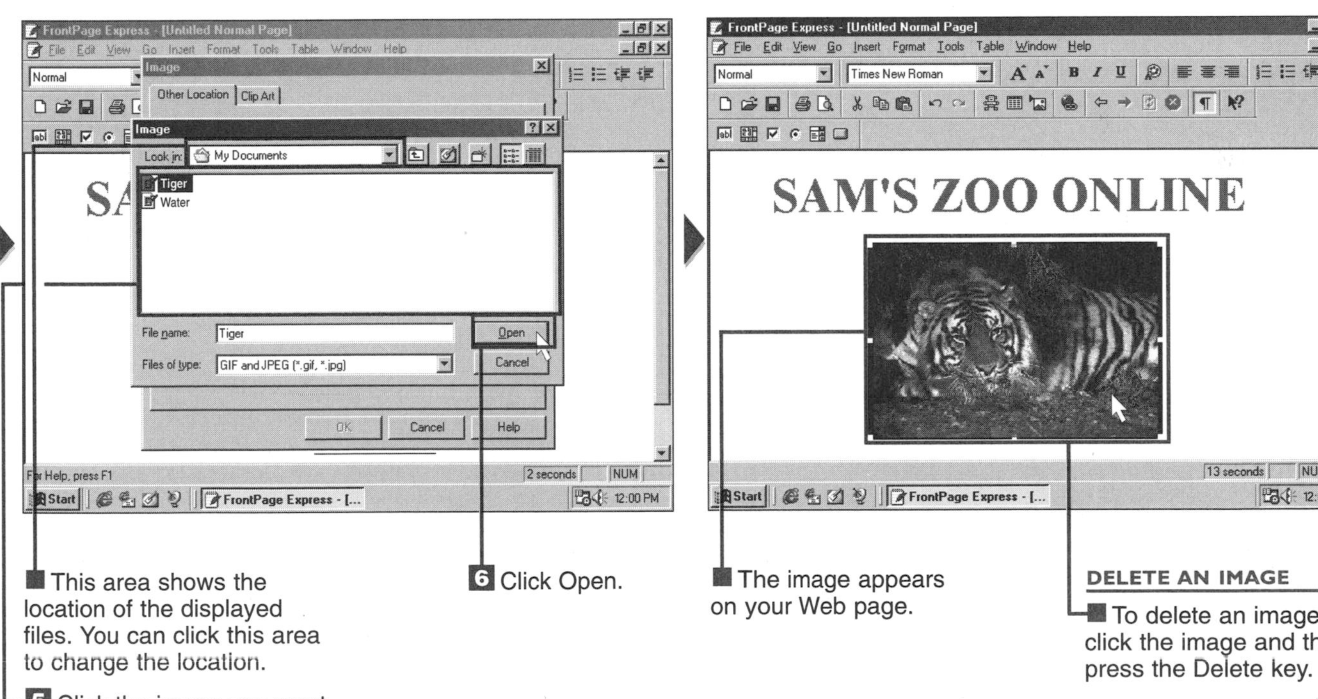

■ This area shows the location of the displayed files. You can click this area to change the location.

5 Click the image you want to add to your Web page.

6 Click Open.

■ The image appears on your Web page.

DELETE AN IMAGE

■ To delete an image, click the image and then press the Delete key.

ADD A BACKGROUND IMAGE

You can have an image repeat to fill an entire Web page. This can add an interesting background texture. Background images can make your Web page more attractive and give your Web page a distinctive look.

You can create your own background images using a paint program or you can find background images on the World Wide Web. In order to be compatible with most Web browsers, a background image should be in the .gif format.

A good background image should have invisible edges. When the images repeat to fill the Web page, you should not be able to tell where the edges of the images meet.

You should choose an image that creates an interesting background design without overwhelming your Web page. Since background images increase the time it takes for a page to appear on a screen, choose a background image with a small file size.

You should also make sure the background image you choose does not affect the readability of your Web page. You may need to change the color of the text on the page to make the page easier to read. To change text color, see page 573.

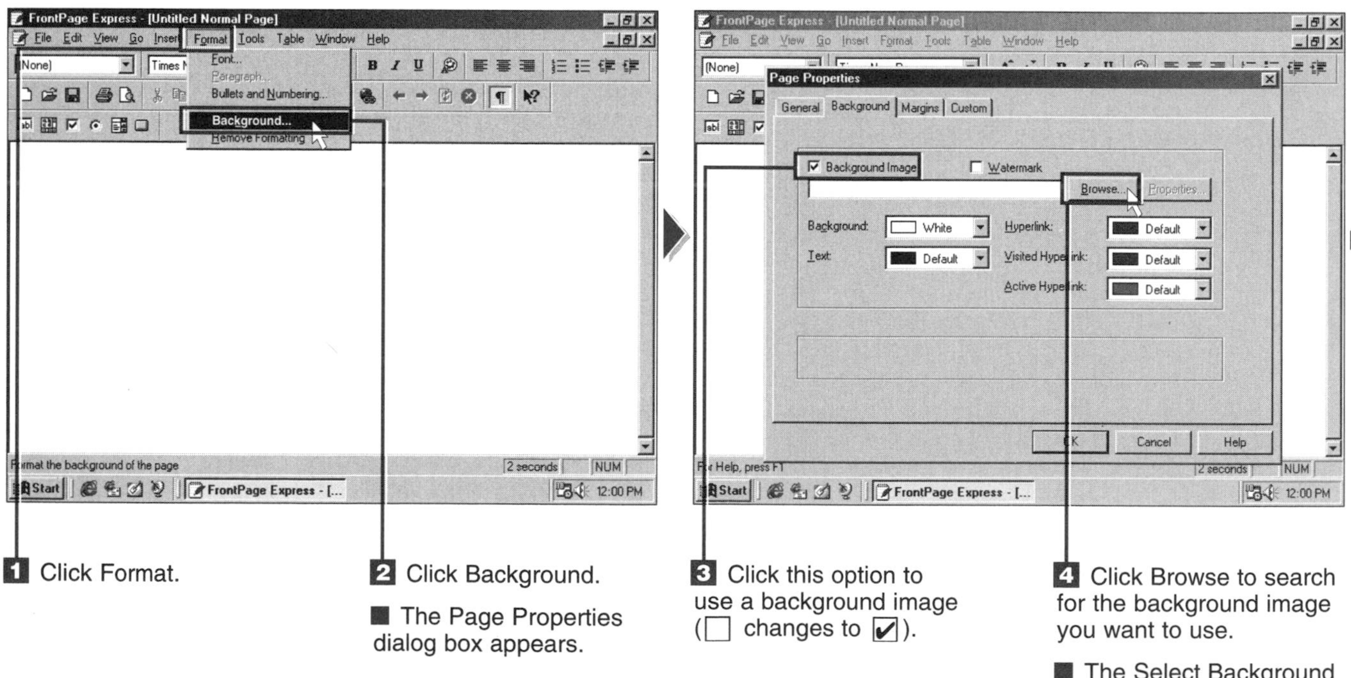

1 Click Format.

2 Click Background.

■ The Page Properties dialog box appears.

3 Click this option to use a background image (☐ changes to ☑).

4 Click Browse to search for the background image you want to use.

■ The Select Background Image dialog box appears.

TIPS

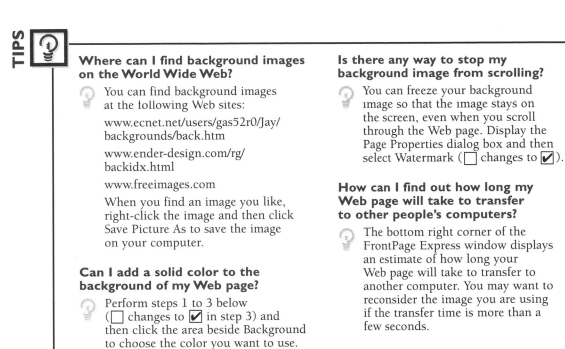

Where can I find background images on the World Wide Web?

You can find background images at the following Web sites:

www.ecnet.net/users/gas52r0/Jay/backgrounds/back.htm

www.ender-design.com/rg/backidx.html

www.freeimages.com

When you find an image you like, right-click the image and then click Save Picture As to save the image on your computer.

Can I add a solid color to the background of my Web page?

Perform steps 1 to 3 below (☐ changes to ☑ in step 3) and then click the area beside Background to choose the color you want to use.

Is there any way to stop my background image from scrolling?

You can freeze your background image so that the image stays on the screen, even when you scroll through the Web page. Display the Page Properties dialog box and then select Watermark (☐ changes to ☑).

How can I find out how long my Web page will take to transfer to other people's computers?

The bottom right corner of the FrontPage Express window displays an estimate of how long your Web page will take to transfer to another computer. You may want to reconsider the image you are using if the transfer time is more than a few seconds.

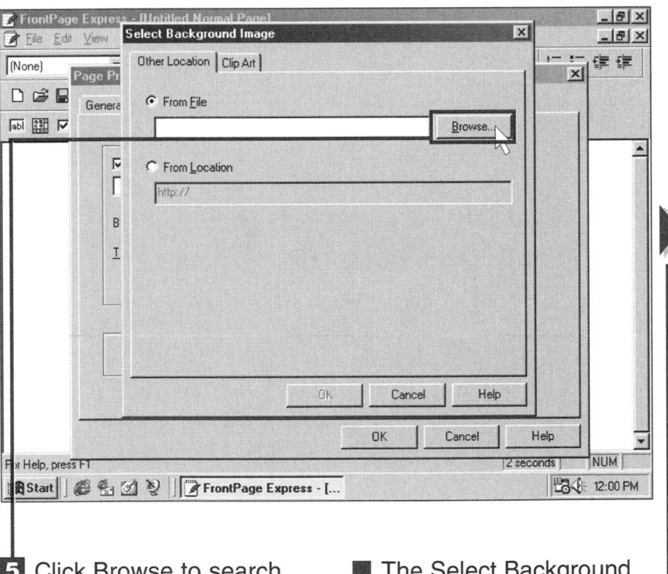

5 Click Browse to search for a background image stored on your computer.

■ The Select Background Image dialog box appears.

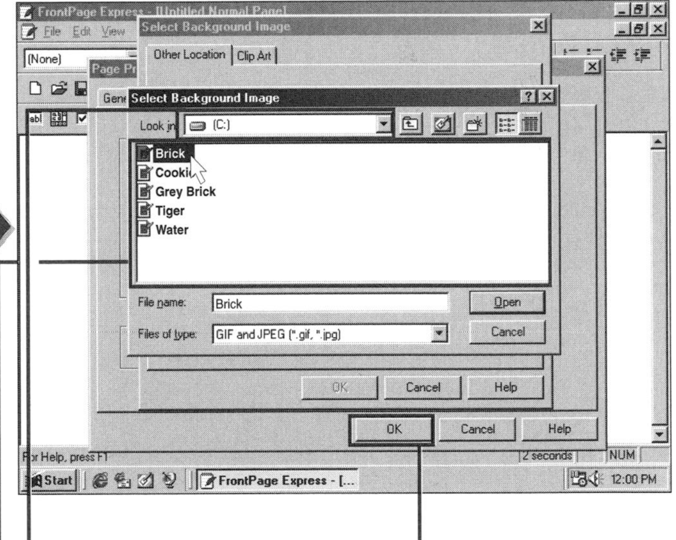

■ This area shows the location of the displayed files. You can click this area to change the location.

6 Double-click the image you want to use as the background image.

7 Click OK in the Page Properties dialog box.

■ The background image appears on your Web page.

INSERT A LINK

You can link a word, phrase or image in your Web page to related information on the Web. When other people select the word, phrase or image, the other Web page appears. Linking is what makes the Web such a powerful tool. Adding links to your Web page gives readers quick access to Web pages that relate to your document.

Each Web page on the World Wide Web has a unique address called a Uniform Resource Locator (URL). You need to specify the address of the Web page you want the text or image to link to.

You can use any text or image on your page as a link. Make sure the text or image you choose clearly indicates where the link will take the reader. Avoid using the phrase "click here," since this phrase is not very informative.

After you publish your Web page, you should visit the links on a regular basis. If a reader selects a link that no longer contains relevant information or displays an error message, the reader may assume that all the information on your Web page is out of date.

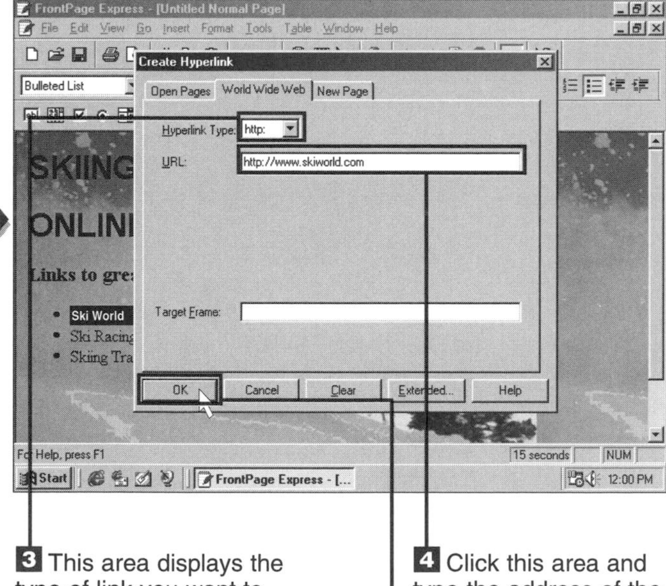

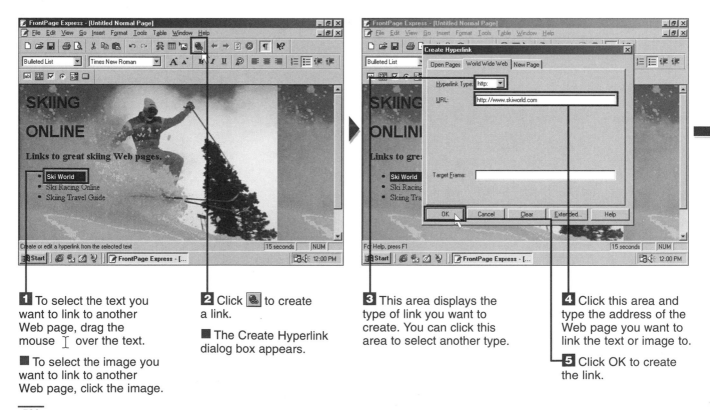

1 To select the text you want to link to another Web page, drag the mouse I over the text.

■ To select the image you want to link to another Web page, click the image.

2 Click [icon] to create a link.

■ The Create Hyperlink dialog box appears.

3 This area displays the type of link you want to create. You can click this area to select another type.

4 Click this area and type the address of the Web page you want to link the text or image to.

5 Click OK to create the link.

TIPS

How do I remove a link?

Select the text or image that is linked and then click . Click the Clear button and then click OK. Removing a link will not remove the text or image from the Web page.

Can I change the color of the text links on my Web page?

Yes. Choose the Format menu and then select Background. Click ▼ beside Hyperlink or Visited Hyperlink to select the color you want to use. Make sure the colors you choose for unvisited and visited links are different and the colors are easy to see on your Web page background.

What other types of links can I create?

In the Create Hyperlink dialog box, you can select mailto: to create a link to an e-mail address. This is useful when you want people reading your page to be able to easily contact you. You can select news: to link text or an image to a newsgroup related to the information on your Web page. Newsgroups allow people with common interests to communicate with each other.

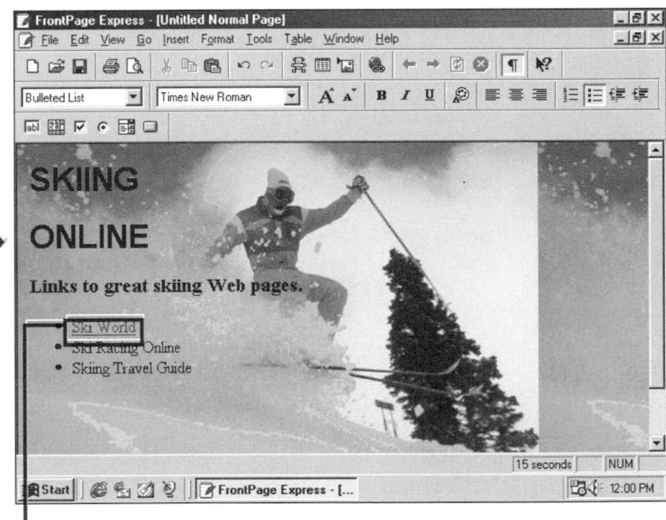

■ FrontPage Express creates the link. Text links appear underlined and in color.

■ When you click the text or image in a Web browser, the Web page connected to the link will appear.

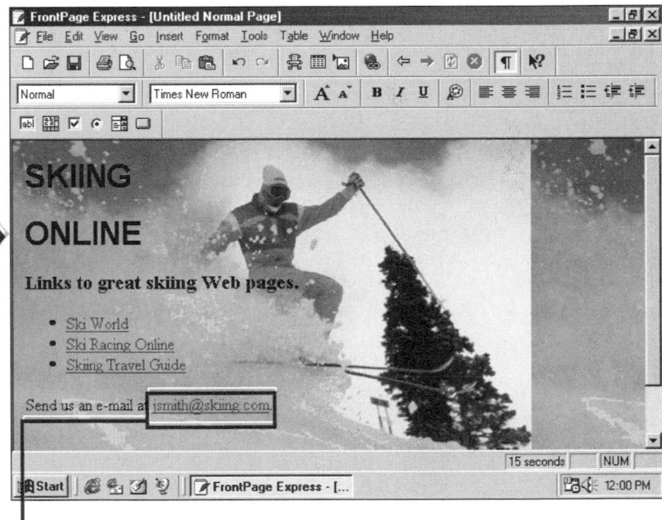

■ When you type a Web page address, e-mail address or FTP address and press the Spacebar or Enter key, FrontPage Express automatically converts the address to a link for you.

INSERT A TABLE

FrontPage Express allows you to create tables on your Web page. Tables allow you to control the placement of text and images on a Web page.

A table consists of rows, columns and cells. A row is a horizontal line of data. A column is a vertical line of data. A cell is the area where a row and column intersect. You can insert text or an image into any cell in a table.

Tables help you neatly present lists of information, such as financial data and product lists. For example, you can present information in newspaper-style columns by using a table that contains one row with three cells.

FrontPage Express automatically left aligns the data in each cell of a table. You can center or right align the data in each cell. This is useful for lining up a column of numbers. Aligning information can help make your table more organized and easier to read. You cannot align information that fills the entire width of a cell.

After you create a table, you can add rows and columns if you want to display additional information.

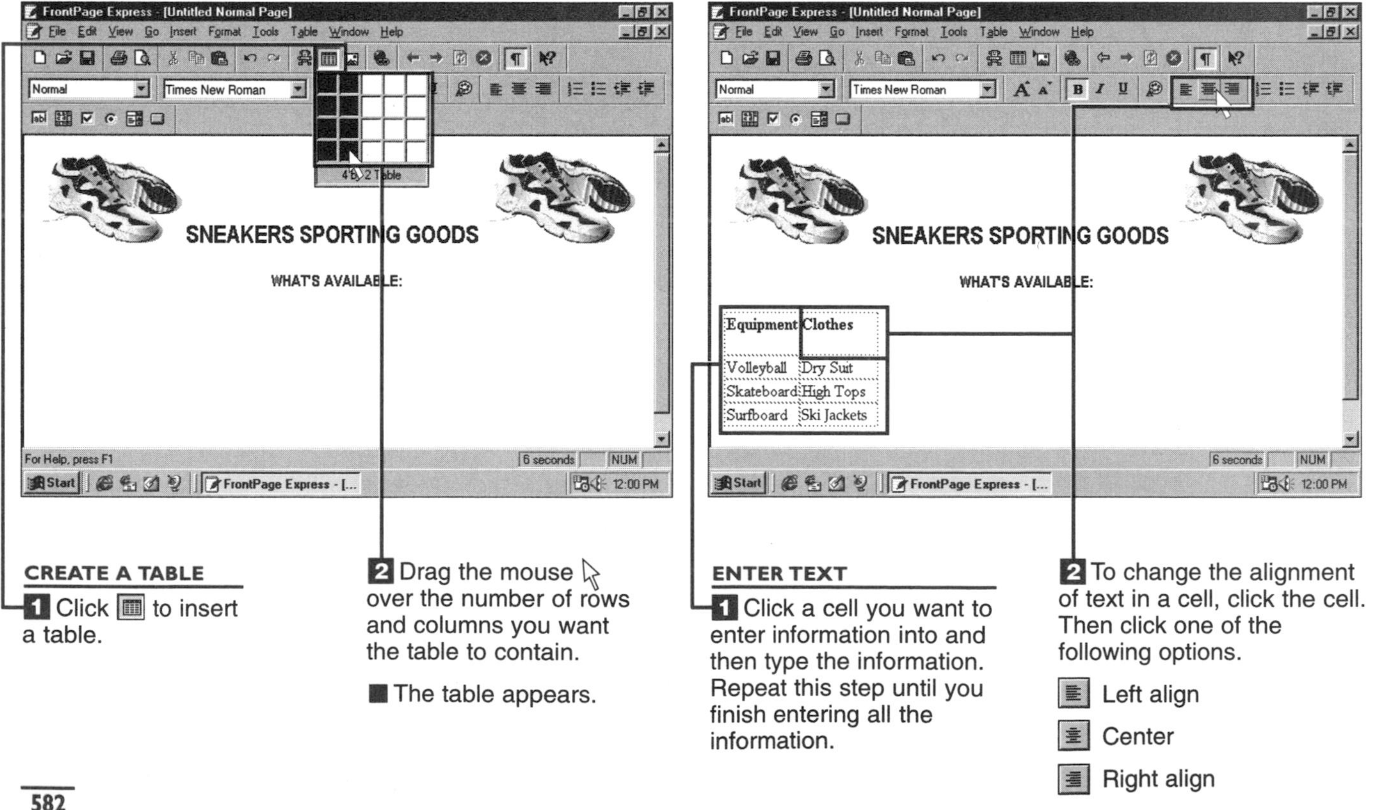

CREATE A TABLE

1 Click ▦ to insert a table.

2 Drag the mouse over the number of rows and columns you want the table to contain.

■ The table appears.

ENTER TEXT

1 Click a cell you want to enter information into and then type the information. Repeat this step until you finish entering all the information.

2 To change the alignment of text in a cell, click the cell. Then click one of the following options.

- Left align
- Center
- Right align

TIPS

Can I make the outline of a table appear in a Web browser?

The outline of a table will not automatically appear when your Web page is displayed in a Web browser. To add a three-dimensional border around the table, right-click the table and then select the Table Properties command. Double-click the area beside Border Size and then type the width you want the border of the table to be.

Can I change the color of a table?

Yes. Right-click the table and then select the Table Properties command. Click the area beside Background Color and select a background color for your table.

Can I make the width of the table fit my screen?

Yes. Right-click the table and then select the Table Properties command. Click Specify Width (☐ changes to ☑).

How can I preview my table in my Web browser?

Save the Web page. See page 571. In the Internet Explorer window, click the File menu and then click Open. Click the Browse button to find the Web page on your computer. Double-click the Web page you want to view and then click OK. For information on starting Internet Explorer, see page 502.

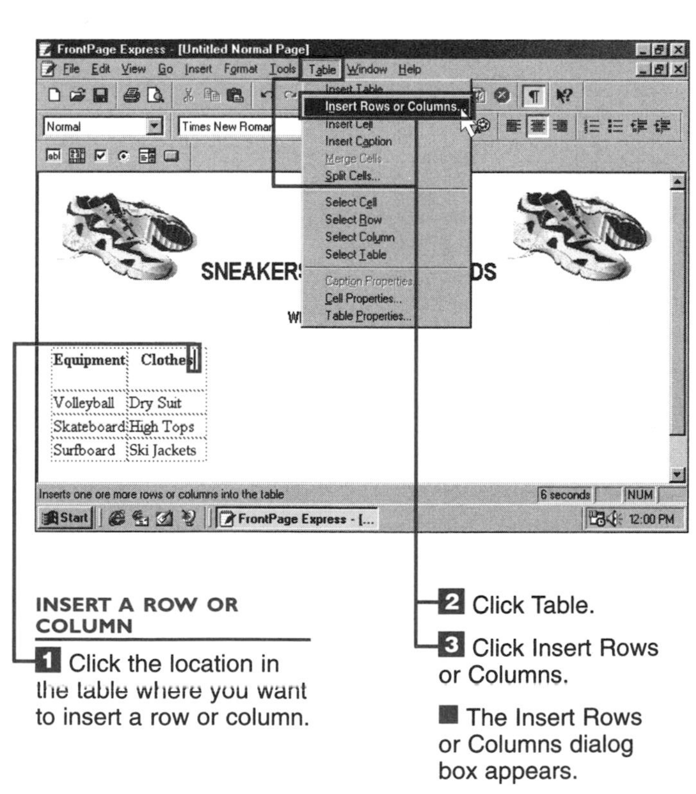

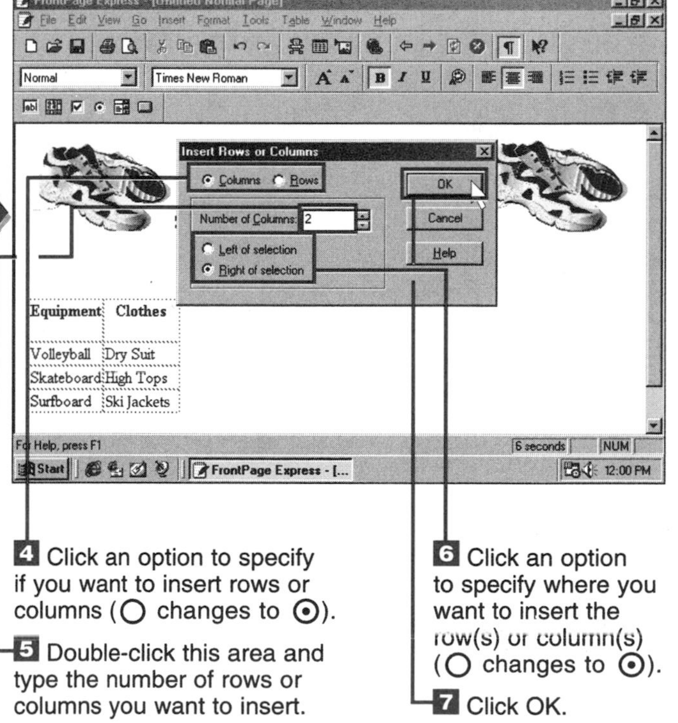

INSERT A ROW OR COLUMN

1 Click the location in the table where you want to insert a row or column.

2 Click Table.

3 Click Insert Rows or Columns.

■ The Insert Rows or Columns dialog box appears.

4 Click an option to specify if you want to insert rows or columns (○ changes to ⊙).

5 Double-click this area and type the number of rows or columns you want to insert.

6 Click an option to specify where you want to insert the row(s) or column(s) (○ changes to ⊙).

7 Click OK.

PUBLISH WEB PAGES

When you finish creating your Web page, you can transfer the Web page to a Web server. Once the Web page is on the server, your page will be available for other people to view.

A Web server is a computer that can store thousands of Web pages. Web servers monitor and control access to your Web page.

The company that gives you access to the Internet usually offers space on its Web server where you can publish your Web pages. There are also places on the Internet that will publish your Web page for free, such as GeoCities (www.geocities.com).

The Web Publishing Wizard makes it easy for you to publish your Web page on a Web server.

The wizard helps you transfer any files that you need for your Web page, such as image files, to the Web server. If a Web page contains links to image files or other Web pages you have created, you must ensure that those items are also transferred to the Web server.

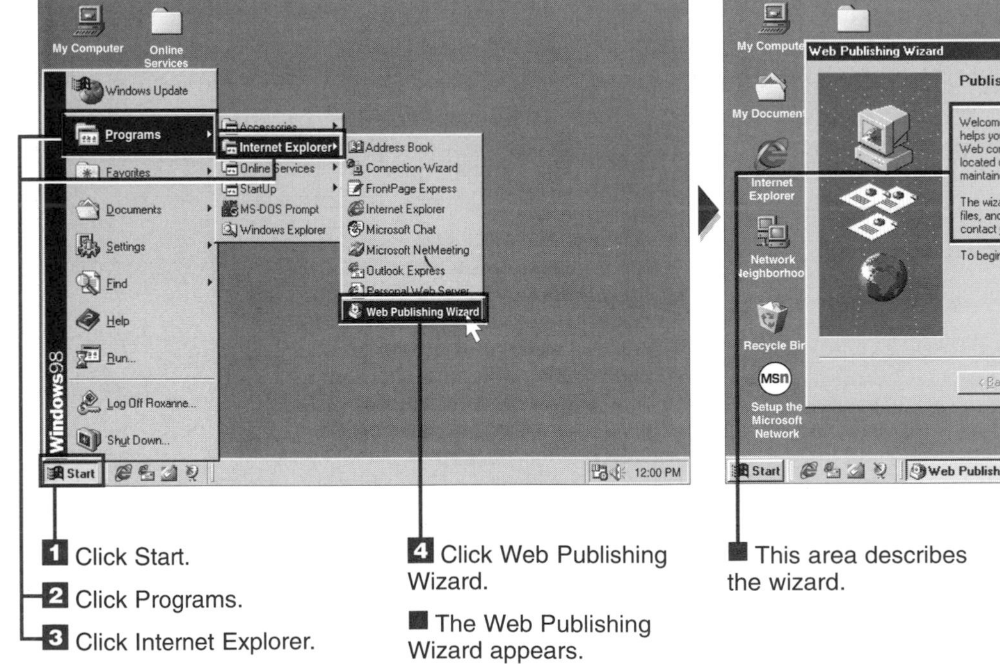

1 Click Start.

2 Click Programs.

3 Click Internet Explorer.

4 Click Web Publishing Wizard.

■ The Web Publishing Wizard appears.

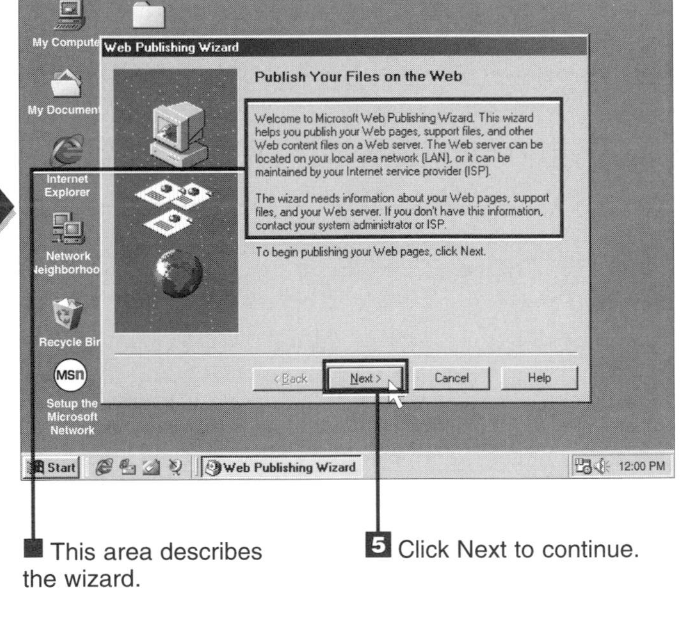

■ This area describes the wizard.

5 Click Next to continue.

TIPS

Why isn't the Web Publishing Wizard on my Start menu?

The Web Publishing Wizard may not be installed on your computer. The Web Publishing Wizard is located in the Internet Tools component. To add Windows components, see page 610.

Can I use the Web Publishing Wizard to publish my Web page on my company's intranet?

Yes. You can publish your Web page on your company's intranet Web server. An intranet is a small version of the Internet within a company or organization. Ask your system administrator for details.

Can I publish more than one Web page?

If you have created more than one Web page, you can transfer all the pages to the Web server at once. Place all of your Web pages in a folder on your computer. Perform steps 1 to 17 starting on page 584, selecting Browse Folders in step 6. Then select the folder where your Web pages are stored and click OK. Skip to step 9 to continue publishing the Web pages.

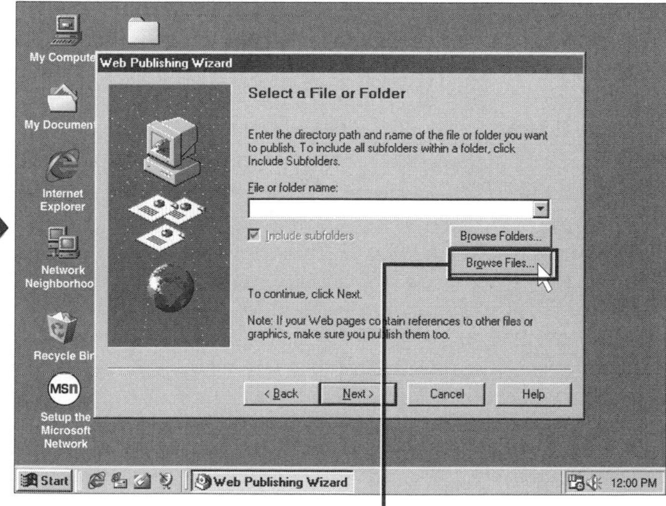

■ The wizard asks you to enter the name of the file you want to publish.

6 Click Browse Files to locate the file on your computer that you want to publish.

■ The Browse dialog box appears.

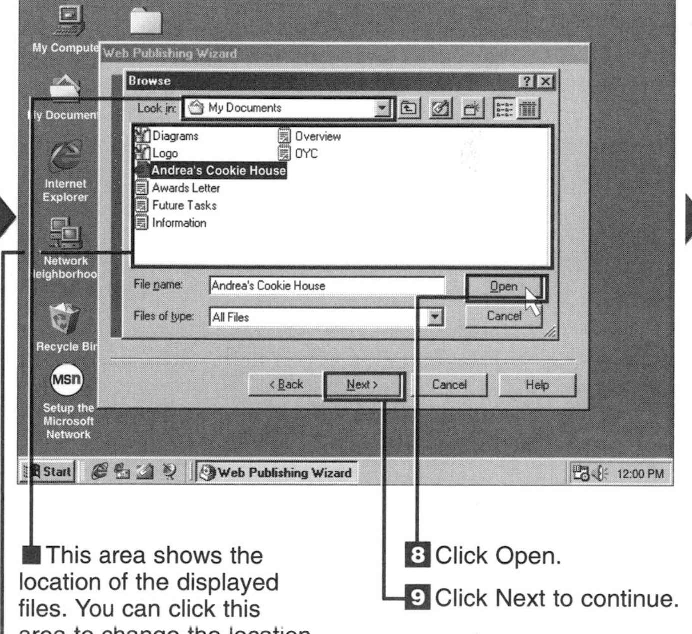

■ This area shows the location of the displayed files. You can click this area to change the location.

7 Click the file you want to publish.

8 Click Open.

9 Click Next to continue.

CONTINUED

PUBLISH WEB PAGES CONTINUED

When publishing a Web page, you must type a name for the Web server. You can choose any name you want. You will use this name to select the Web server each time you publish a Web page.

You must also tell the Web Publishing Wizard the Internet address, also called a Uniform Resource Locator (URL), that you use to access the Web server where you want to publish your Web page. If you do not know this address, you can ask your system administrator or Internet Service Provider (ISP).

Before you can publish your Web page, the Web Publishing Wizard will ask you to enter the user name and password for the Web server. If you do not have the user name and password, you should contact your system administrator or Internet service provider. You can have the wizard save the user name and password so you do not have to enter this information each time you publish a Web page.

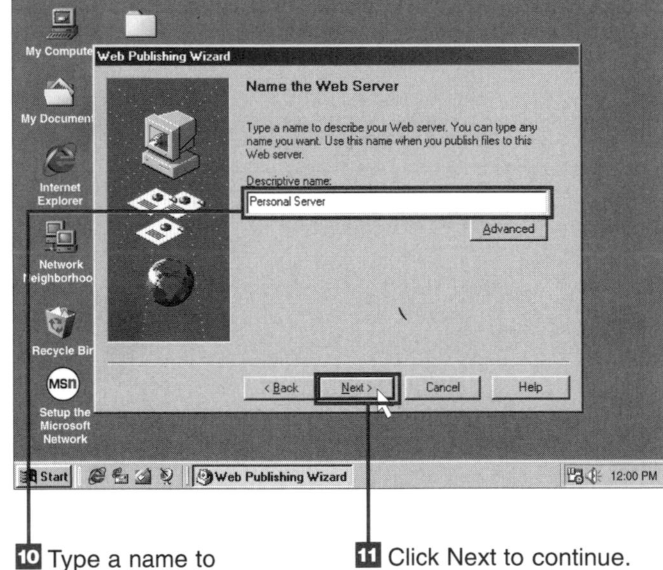

10 Type a name to describe your Web server.

Note: If you have published Web pages before, the wizard fills in the name of the Web server for you.

11 Click Next to continue.

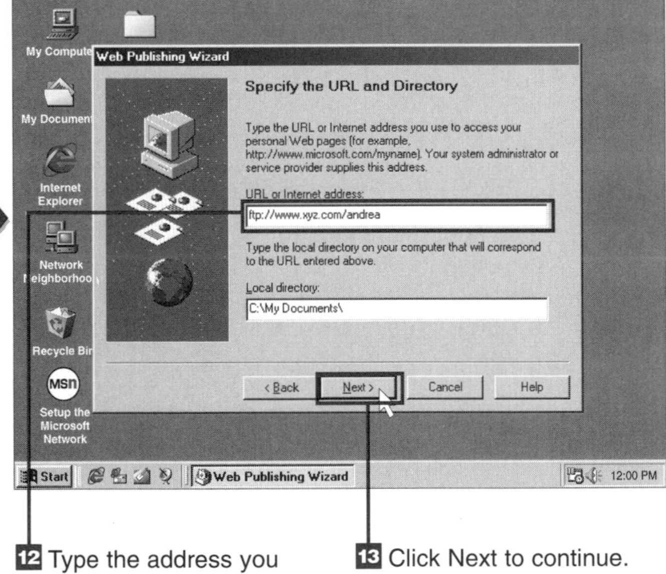

12 Type the address you use to access your personal Web pages.

Note: If you have published Web pages before, this dialog box does not appear.

13 Click Next to continue.

TIPS

Can I set up my own Web server?

If you have access to a company network, you can use Microsoft's Personal Web Server to set up your own Web server and make your Web page available to other people on the network. You can also set up your own Web server to preview and test your Web page before publishing it on the World Wide Web. If Personal Web Server is not installed on your computer, you can install the program. Personal Web Server is located in the Internet Tools component. To install Windows components, see page 610.

What should I name the Web server?

When you type a name for the Web server in the Web Publishing Wizard, you should try to use a descriptive name. You should choose a name such as "Personal Web Site" or "Business Web Site," as opposed to "Web Site 1." If you publish Web pages on different servers, a descriptive name will help prevent confusion the next time you publish a Web page.

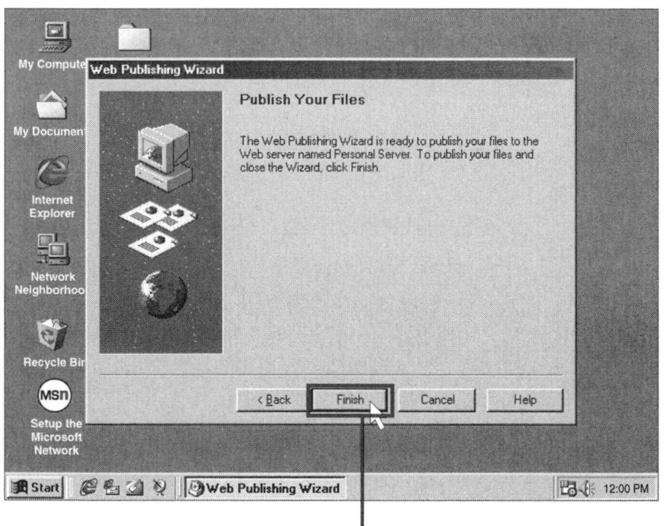

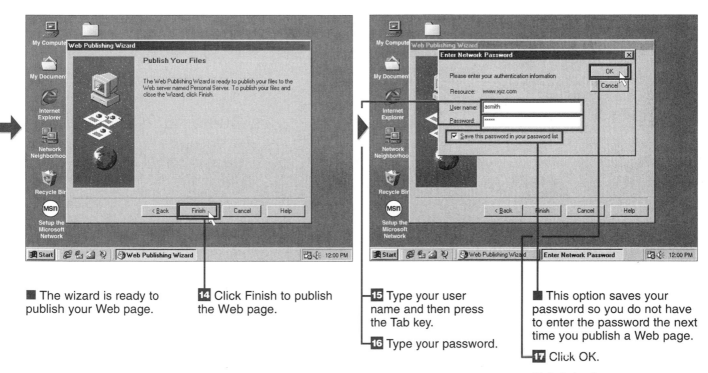

■ The wizard is ready to publish your Web page.

14 Click Finish to publish the Web page.

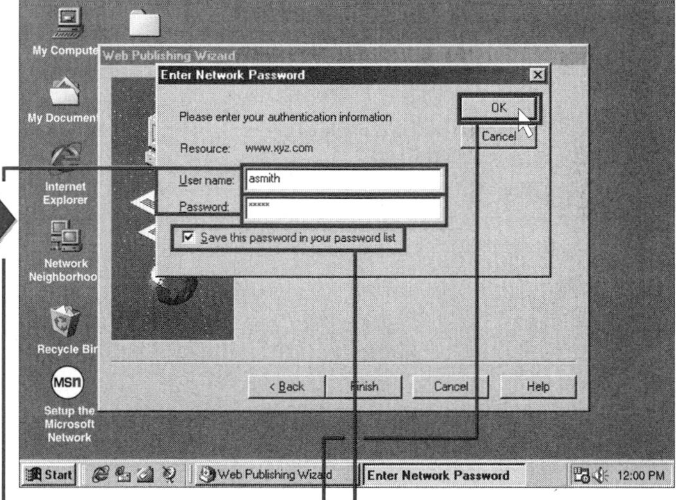

15 Type your user name and then press the Tab key.

16 Type your password.

■ This option saves your password so you do not have to enter the password the next time you publish a Web page.

17 Click OK.

■ A dialog box appears, confirming that the Web page was successfully published.

PLACE A CALL

NetMeeting lets you use a network connection to work with other people. A NetMeeting session can consist of only two people or can be a conference with many participants working together at the same time.

You can connect to people who have Netmeeting open on their computer.

Microsoft has several servers you can use to locate other NetMeeting users. If you are planning a NetMeeting session, you and the other participants should agree on which server you will use.

After you connect to a server, you can use the directory to display a list of people you can call. You can narrow the list by selecting a different category in the list, such as Business or Personal.

When you place a call, a message is sent and the person you are calling can either accept or ignore the call.

Two people in a NetMeeting session can use voice and video communication if both participants have sound cards, speakers, microphones and video cameras. Additional participants cannot use voice or video communication.

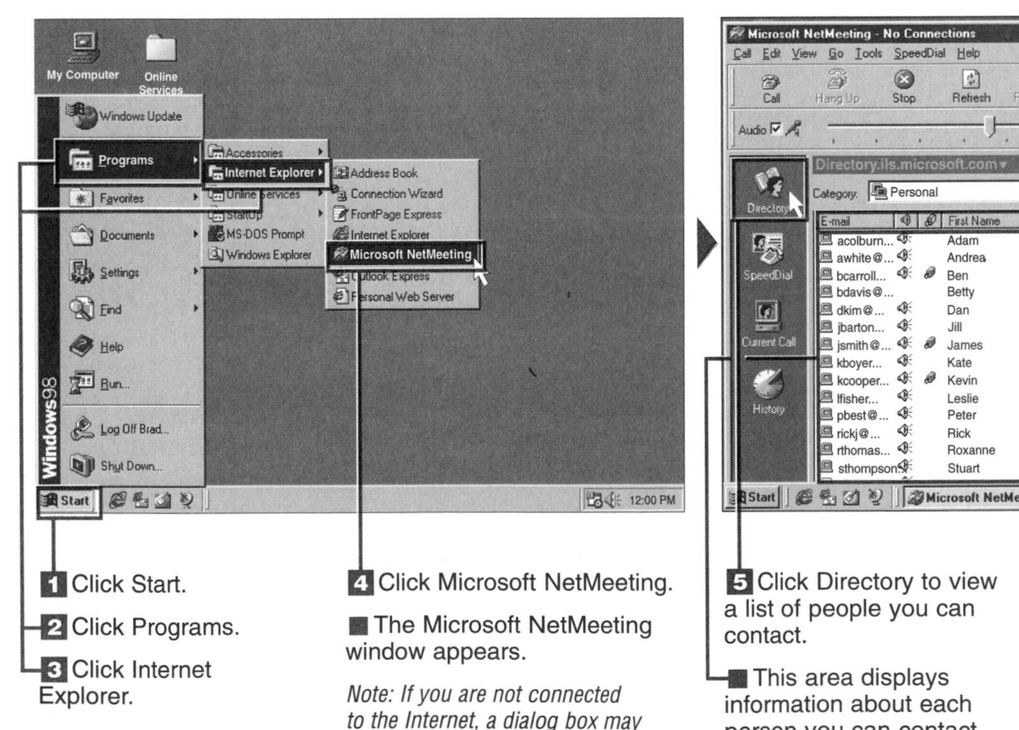

1 Click Start.

2 Click Programs.

3 Click Internet Explorer.

4 Click Microsoft NetMeeting.

■ The Microsoft NetMeeting window appears.

Note: If you are not connected to the Internet, a dialog box may appear that allows you to connect.

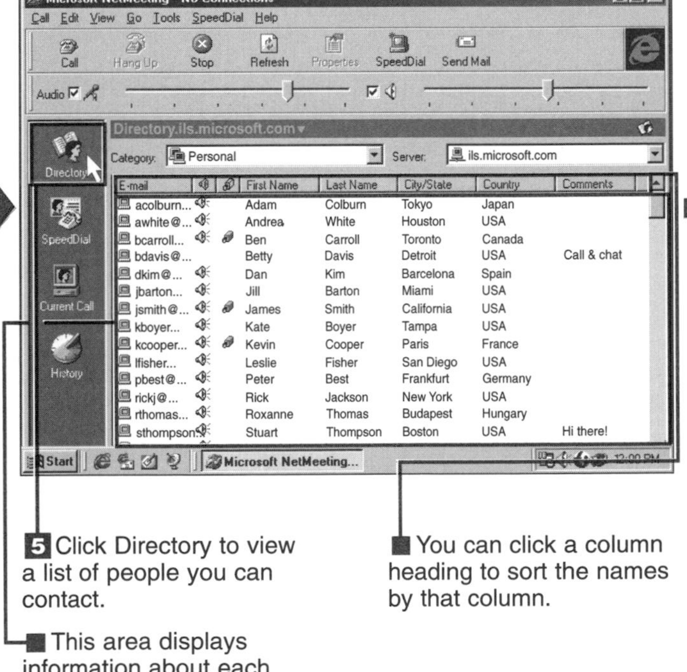

5 Click Directory to view a list of people you can contact.

■ This area displays information about each person you can contact.

■ You can click a column heading to sort the names by that column.

TIPS

How do I set up NetMeeting?

The first time you start the program, you will be asked to provide information such as the name and e-mail address you want people to use to contact you. You can also specify the server you want to be listed on and how you want to categorize your information. If you have a sound card, NetMeeting will ask you to perform a sound test.

What do the symbols beside the names in the directory mean?

The symbol indicates that the person is not in a call. The symbol indicates that the person is already in a call. The symbol shows that the person has a microphone and speakers. The symbol shows that the person has a video camera.

Is there an easier way to find the person I want to call?

When the directory is displayed, you can click a column heading to sort the information in the column.

Can I remove my name from the server?

When your information is listed on the server, you may receive unwanted calls. To avoid this, choose the Tools menu and then select the Options command. Click the Calling tab and then select the Do not list my name in the directory option (☐ changes to ☑).

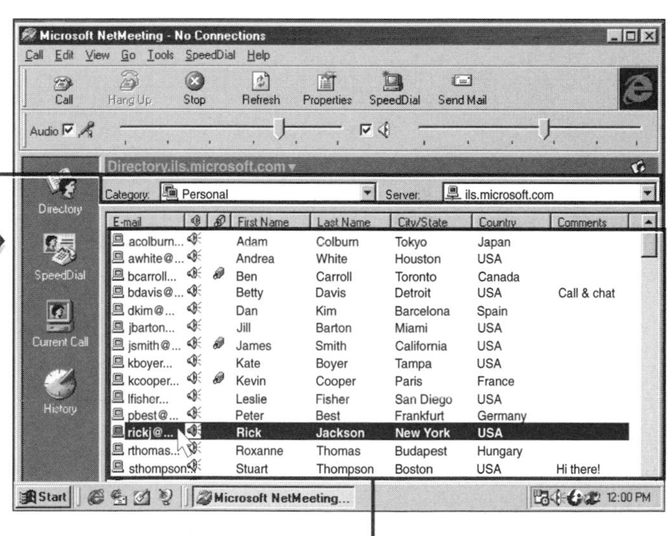

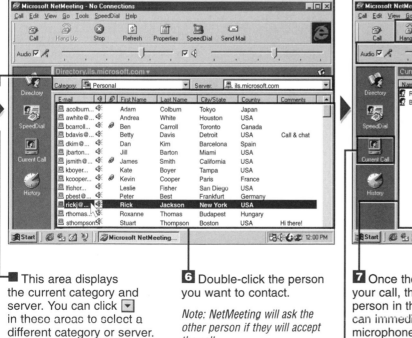

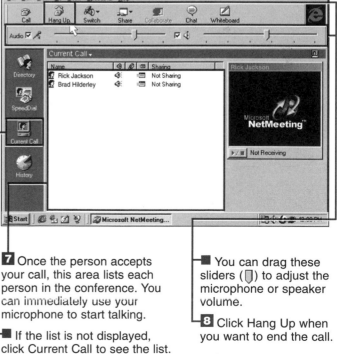

■ This area displays the current category and server. You can click ▾ in these areas to select a different category or server.

6 Double-click the person you want to contact.

Note: NetMeeting will ask the other person if they will accept the call.

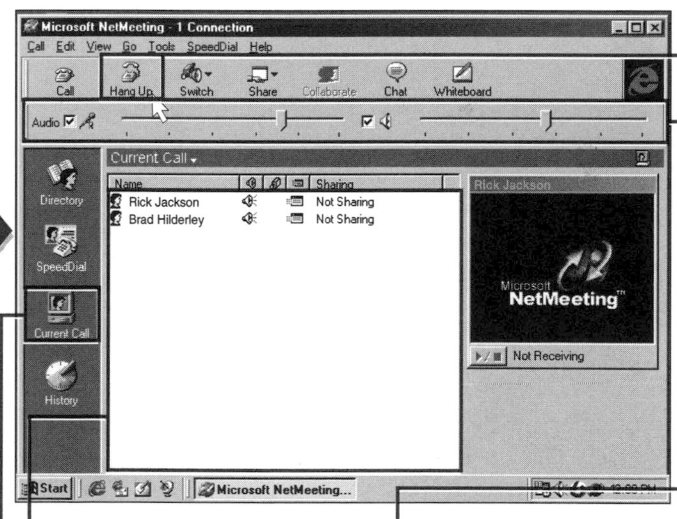

7 Once the person accepts your call, this area lists each person in the conference. You can immediately use your microphone to start talking.

■ If the list is not displayed, click Current Call to see the list.

■ You can drag these sliders (▯) to adjust the microphone or speaker volume.

8 Click Hang Up when you want to end the call.

30

USING CHAT

You can use Chat to send typed messages to the participants in a NetMeeting conference.

When one participant starts Chat, the Chat window appears on each participant's screen. You can choose to send a message to everyone in the conference. You can also choose to send a private message to a person you specify.

The text you type will not appear on the screens of the other participants until you press the Enter key. This lets you prepare your comments or questions before sending them to the conference. Each line in the Chat window is preceded by the name of the participant who entered the comment. In a large conference, it may be useful to have a moderator or one participant who controls the flow of the chat.

When you close the Chat window, NetMeeting asks if you want to save the chat as a file. Saving a chat is useful when you want to make a copy of the chat session so that it can be shared with the participants or read by other people.

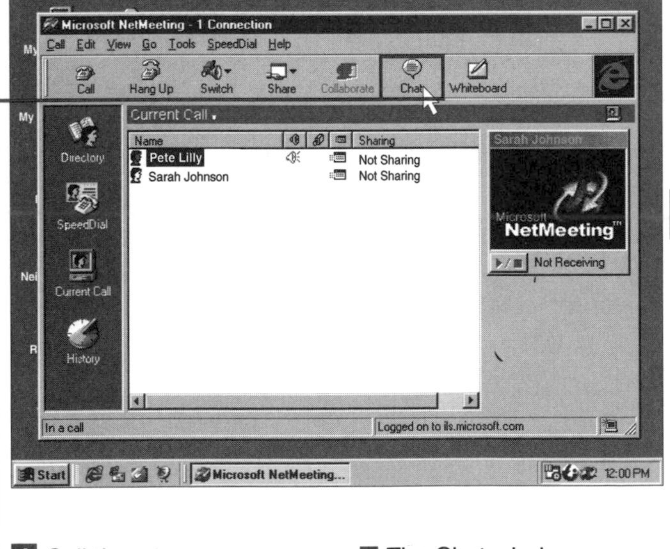

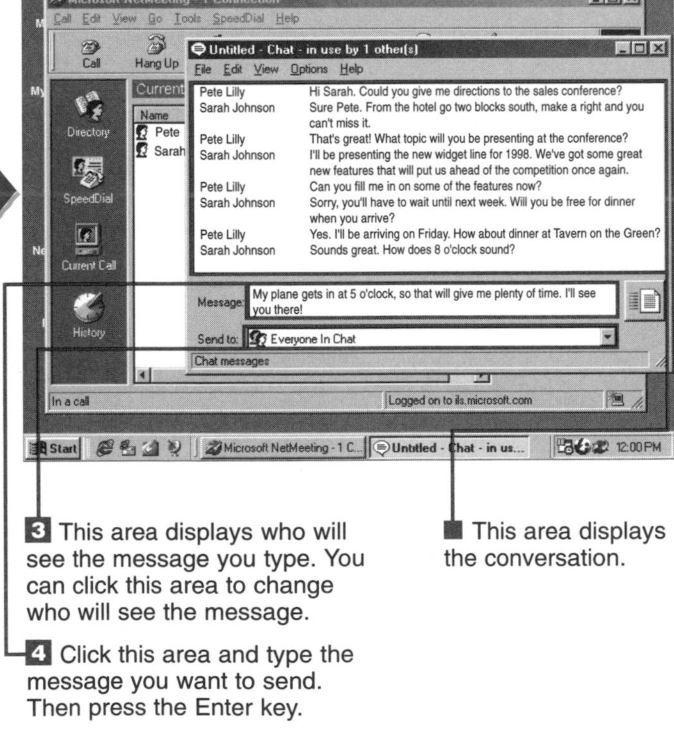

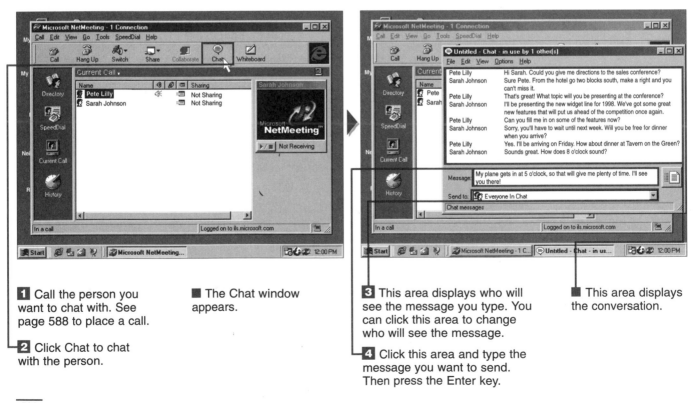

1 Call the person you want to chat with. See page 588 to place a call.

2 Click Chat to chat with the person.

■ The Chat window appears.

3 This area displays who will see the message you type. You can click this area to change who will see the message.

4 Click this area and type the message you want to send. Then press the Enter key.

■ This area displays the conversation.

SEND A FILE

You can send a file to the participants in a NetMeeting conference. You can send any type of file, including a document you want to present, a font needed to display a document or a program upgrade.

When you send a file, the file transfers in the background while you continue to work or chat.

When you send a file, each participant will see a dialog box indicating that the file is being transferred. Each participant can decide whether to keep the file or delete it.

Any files you keep will be saved in the NetMeeting folder, in a subfolder called Received Files.

You should be very cautious of files you receive from NetMeeting participants you do not know. If you accept a program file, check it with an anti-virus program. You should also use an anti-virus program to check documents with extensions used by Microsoft Word (.doc) and Excel (.xls). These types of documents may contain macro viruses.

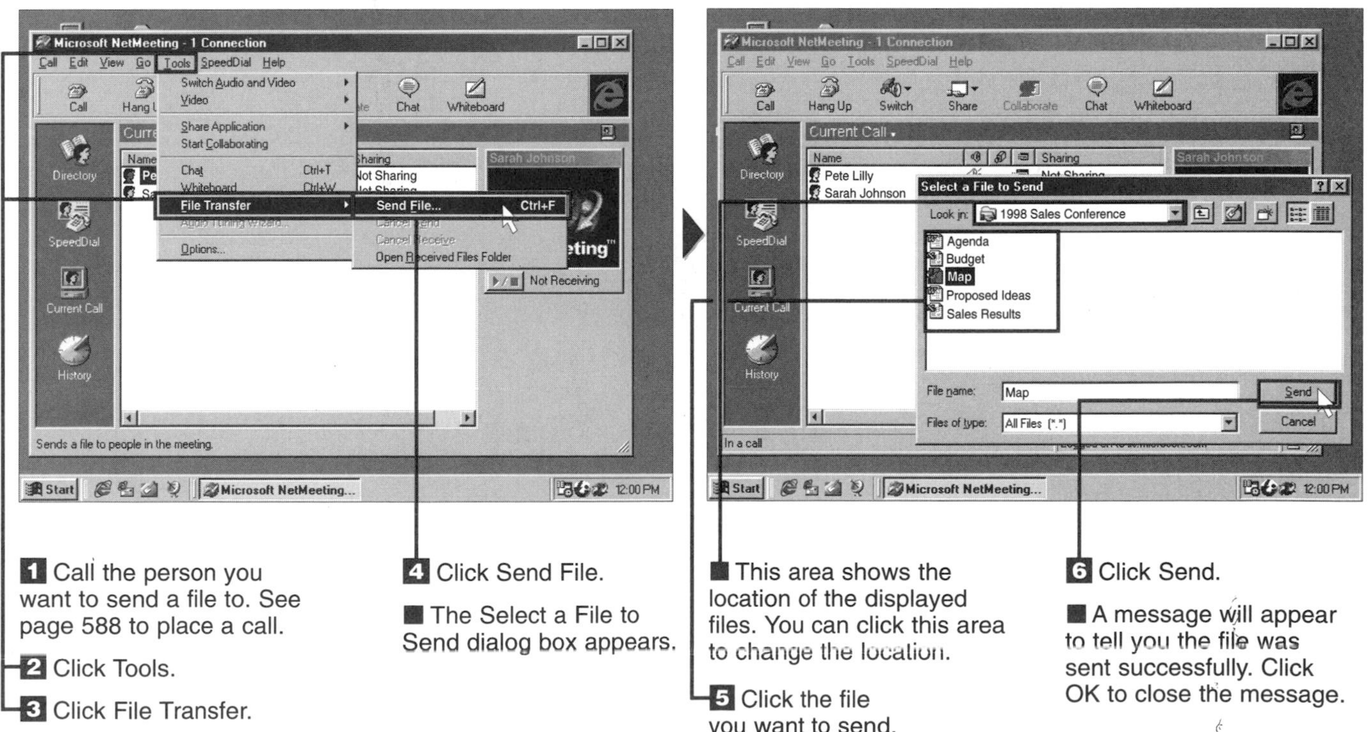

1 Call the person you want to send a file to. See page 588 to place a call.

2 Click Tools.

3 Click File Transfer.

4 Click Send File.

■ The Select a File to Send dialog box appears.

■ This area shows the location of the displayed files. You can click this area to change the location.

5 Click the file you want to send.

6 Click Send.

■ A message will appear to tell you the file was sent successfully. Click OK to close the message.

USING THE WHITEBOARD

The NetMeeting Whiteboard gives all conference participants the opportunity to share and comment on information or pictures on a page. All the participants can see all of the comments and marks that are being made on the Whiteboard page. The Whiteboard is useful for helping participants describe, create, edit and correct many types of projects.

The Whiteboard is especially useful for displaying and discussing images and designs. The Whiteboard tools are similar to the tools found in Paint. Participants can use the Whiteboard tools to create lines and other basic shapes, such as rectangles and ellipses. Each participant can also use the tools to type text on the page and highlight or underline the text.

The Whiteboard also provides a hand tool that can be used to point out objects on the page. This makes it easy for a participant to draw attention to an object or area of the page.

There is no way to tell who is making the changes to the page when there are several participants in a NetMeeting conference.

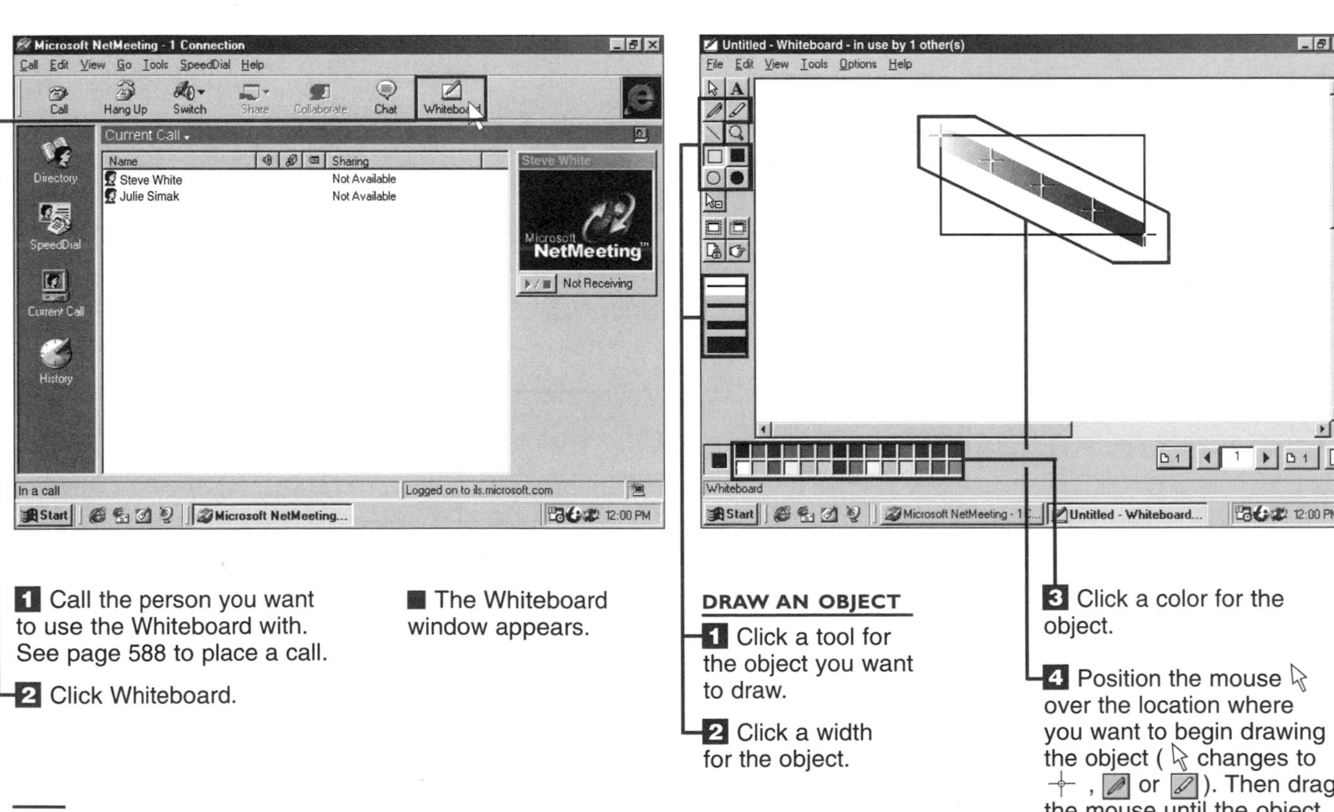

1 Call the person you want to use the Whiteboard with. See page 588 to place a call.

2 Click Whiteboard.

■ The Whiteboard window appears.

DRAW AN OBJECT

1 Click a tool for the object you want to draw.

2 Click a width for the object.

3 Click a color for the object.

4 Position the mouse over the location where you want to begin drawing the object (changes to , or). Then drag the mouse until the object appears the way you want.

TIPS

Can I add a new page to the Whiteboard?

You can click [new page] at the bottom of the Whiteboard window to insert a new page. You can then click the arrows (◀ or ▶) to move through the pages. When one participant changes the page, it changes for all participants.

Can I rearrange the objects on the Whiteboard?

Click the Select tool ([select]) and then drag the object you want to move to the new location.

Can I place a document on the Whiteboard so all the conference participants can see it and make suggestions?

Make the document you want to place on the Whiteboard the active window. Maximize the Whiteboard window and click [select window]. In the dialog box that appears, click OK. Then click the document you want to display in the Whiteboard.

How do I delete an object on the Whiteboard?

Click the Eraser tool ([eraser]) and then click the object or text you want to delete.

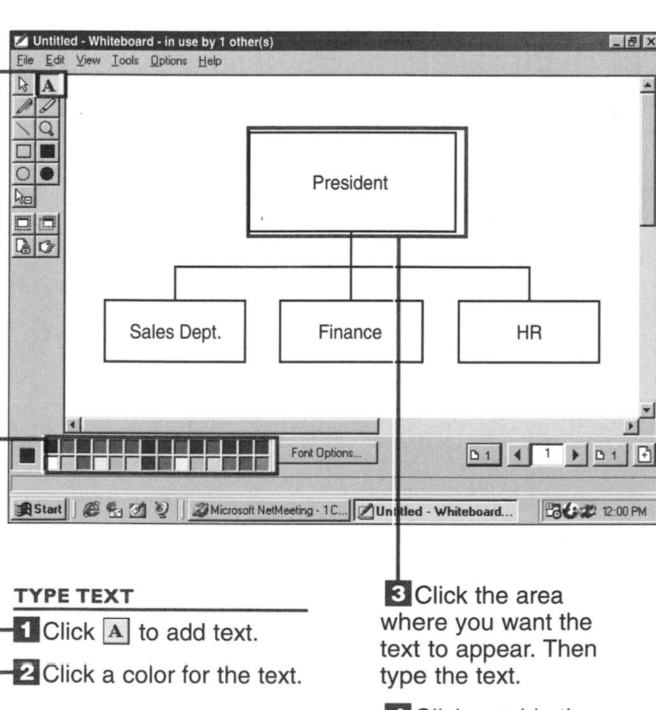

TYPE TEXT

1. Click [A] to add text.
2. Click a color for the text.
3. Click the area where you want the text to appear. Then type the text.
4. Click outside the text area.

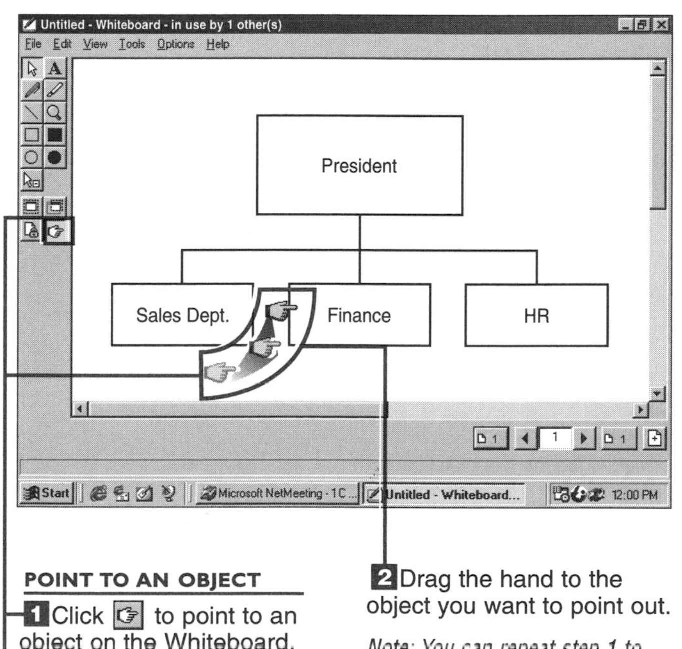

POINT TO AN OBJECT

1. Click [hand] to point to an object on the Whiteboard.

- A hand ([hand]) appears on the Whiteboard.

2. Drag the hand to the object you want to point out.

Note: You can repeat step 1 to hide the hand.

SHARE A PROGRAM

You can use NetMeeting to work interactively and cooperatively with other participants on the same document. When you share a program, every participant in a NetMeeting conference can use the program, even if they do not have the program installed on their computer.

Sharing a program makes it easy to present a demonstration while the other participants watch you work. You can also allow the other participants to work with you in the shared program. This is called collaborating.

When the other conference participants are collaborating with you, any of the participants can take control of the program. The participant who controls the shared program can use the program's menus and commands. They can also move the program's window to another location on the screen and resize the window.

The other participants cannot save or print information in a program you have shared. If you want the other participants to have a copy of the information, you must send them the file. To send a file using NetMeeting, see page 591.

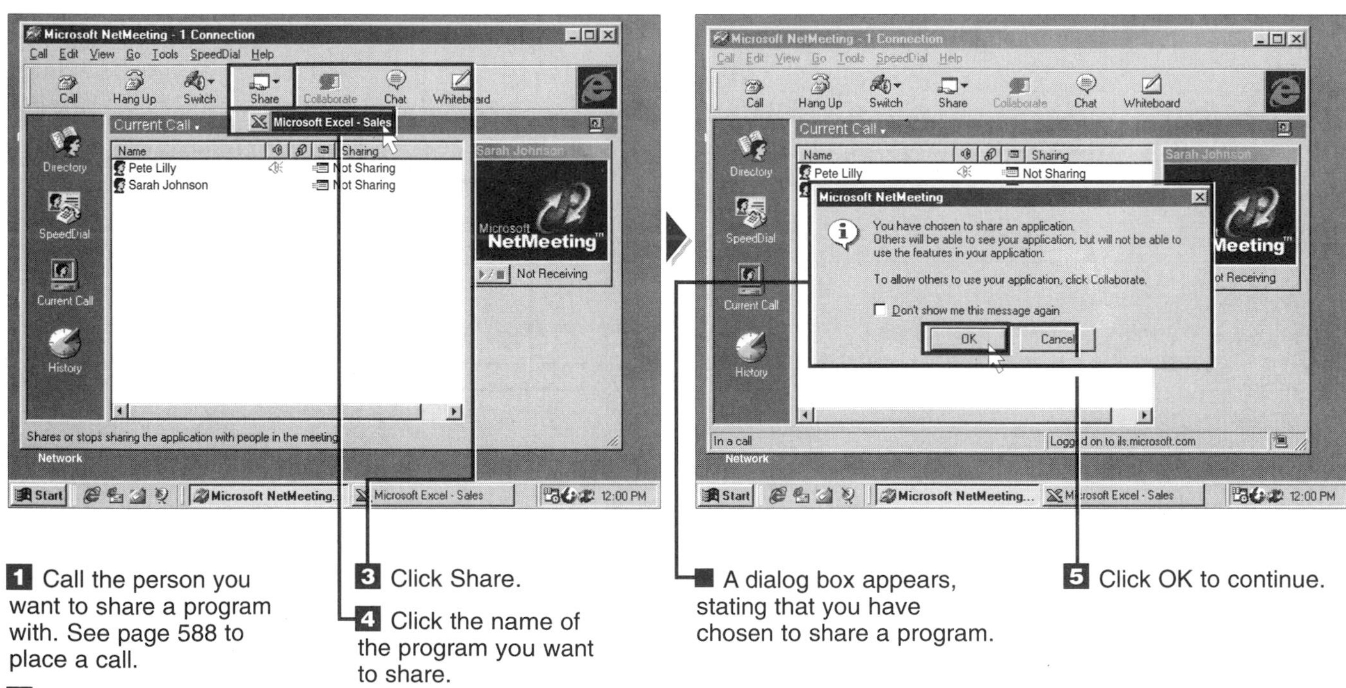

1 Call the person you want to share a program with. See page 588 to place a call.

2 Start the program you want to share.

3 Click Share.

4 Click the name of the program you want to share.

■ A dialog box appears, stating that you have chosen to share a program.

5 Click OK to continue.

TIPS

How can I tell who is using the program?

A small box appears above the upper right corner of the program. The box contains the name of the person who is controlling the program.

How do I take control of a shared program?

You must double-click to take control of a shared program for the first time. If you have already used the shared program, you only need to click once to take control again. The initials of the person who currently has control of a program appear as part of the mouse pointer.

How do I work alone again?

To turn off collaboration, press the Esc key.

The shared program is covered with a pattern of colored triangles. Why am I unable to see and use the shared program?

The person who is sharing the program is currently using another program. You will only be able to see and use the shared program when it is the active window.

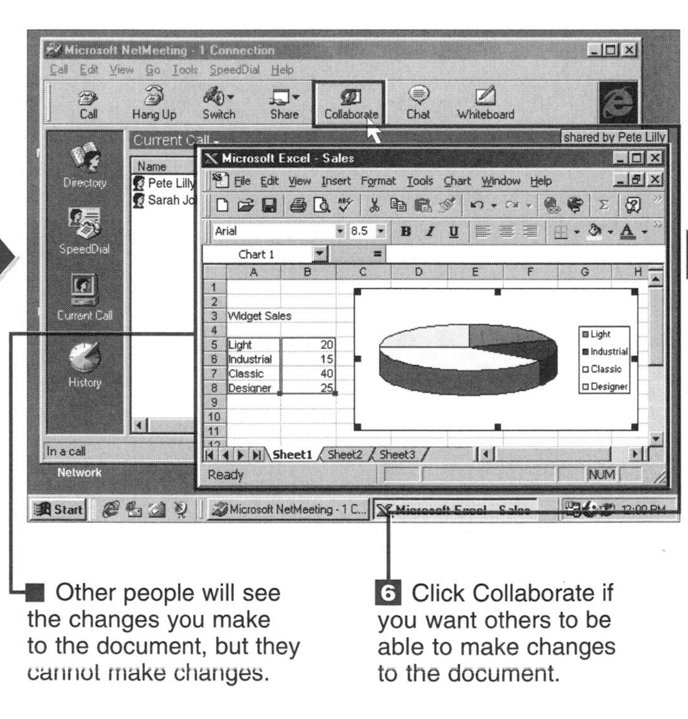

■ Other people will see the changes you make to the document, but they cannot make changes.

6 Click Collaborate if you want others to be able to make changes to the document.

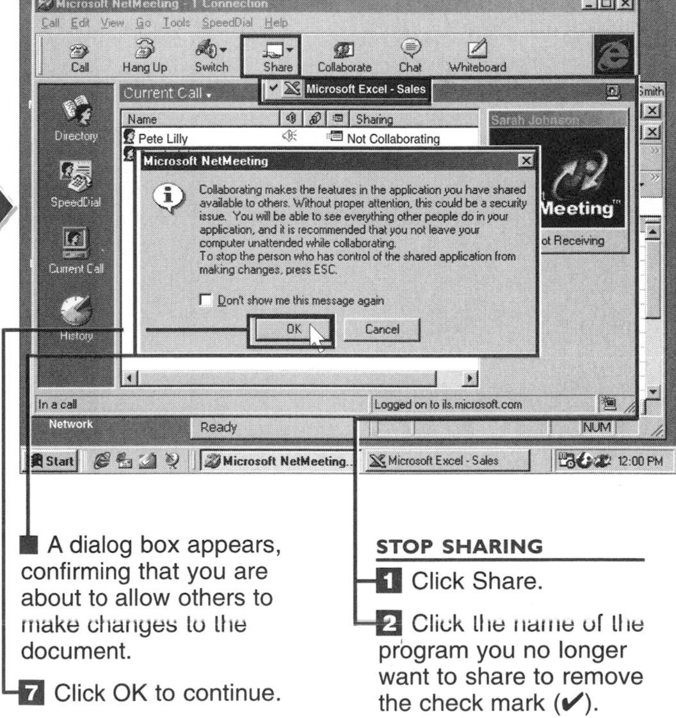

■ A dialog box appears, confirming that you are about to allow others to make changes to the document.

7 Click OK to continue.

STOP SHARING

1 Click Share.

2 Click the name of the program you no longer want to share to remove the check mark (✔).

ENTER A CHAT ROOM

Microsoft Chat allows you to conduct a two-way conversation with other people on the Internet. Unlike e-mail, Microsoft Chat allows you to have a real-time conversation with someone as opposed to waiting for a response by e-mail.

There are several Microsoft chat servers you can connect to. A chat server hosts chat rooms on the Internet. You can display a list of chat rooms on the server. Each chat room discusses a topic, such as politics, humor or music. You can quickly find a chat room of interest by displaying a list of chat rooms that contain a specific word.

Each person participating in a chat room is represented by a cartoon character. Microsoft Chat displays text in a bubble above the character who is speaking so you can view what other people type. The entire conversation in a chat room is represented by a comic strip so everyone can easily read and participate in the conversation.

The Microsoft Chat window is made up of several parts. You can view the conversation, a list of the people who are participating in the conversation, your character and the emotions your character can display.

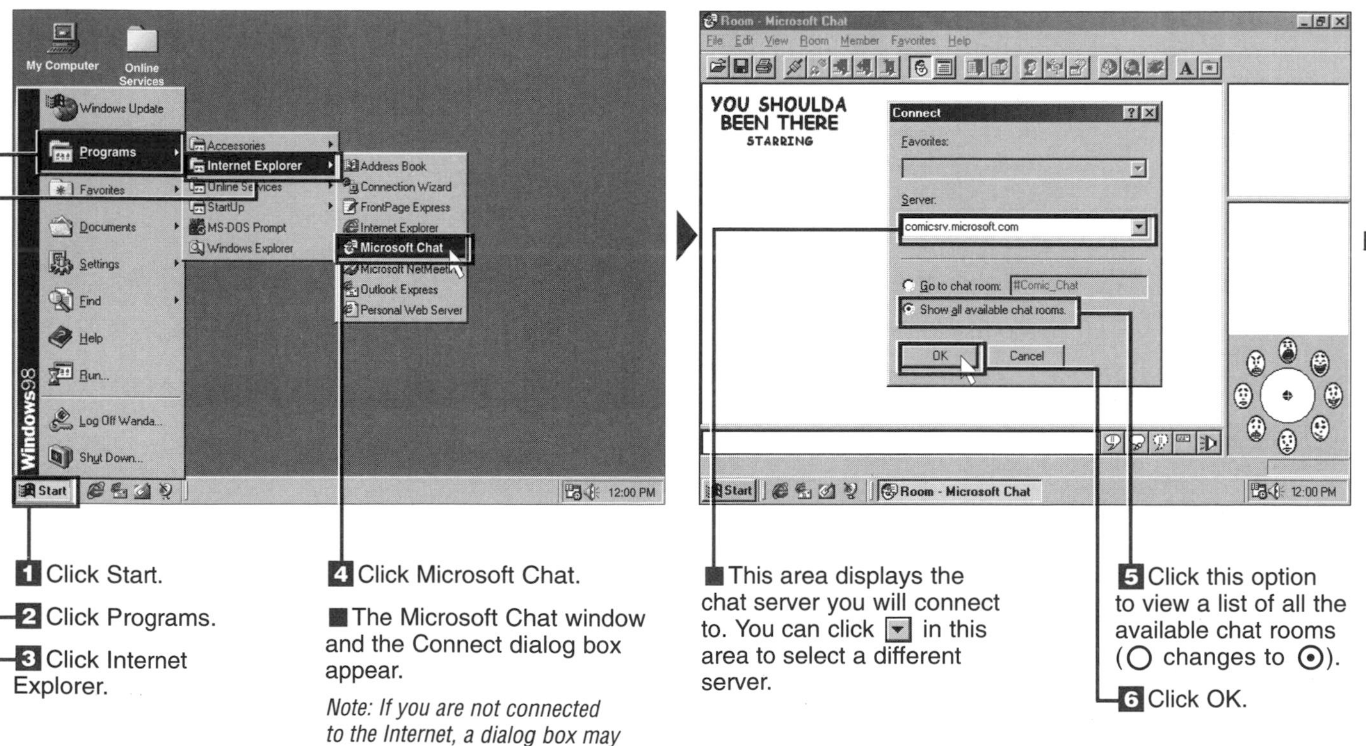

1 Click Start.

2 Click Programs.

3 Click Internet Explorer.

4 Click Microsoft Chat.

■ The Microsoft Chat window and the Connect dialog box appear.

Note: If you are not connected to the Internet, a dialog box may appear that allows you to connect.

■ This area displays the chat server you will connect to. You can click ▼ in this area to select a different server.

5 Click this option to view a list of all the available chat rooms (○ changes to ⦿).

6 Click OK.

TIPS

Why isn't Microsoft Chat listed on my Start menu?

Microsoft Chat may not be installed on your computer. Microsoft Chat is located in the Communications component. To add Windows components, see page 610.

What are registered chat rooms?

You can choose to display only rooms that are registered by the administrator of the chat server or the Internet service provider. Administrators can choose not to register rooms that contain objectionable or offensive material. To display only registered chat rooms, click the Show only registered rooms option in the Chat Room List window (☐ changes to ☑).

What is a nickname?

A nickname is the name you use to identify yourself to other people in a chat room. Microsoft Chat asks you to enter a nickname the first time you start the program. To change your nickname, see page 598.

How can I go to another chat room?

You can visit another chat room at any time. Click the Chat Room List button (▣). You can then select another chat room you want to visit.

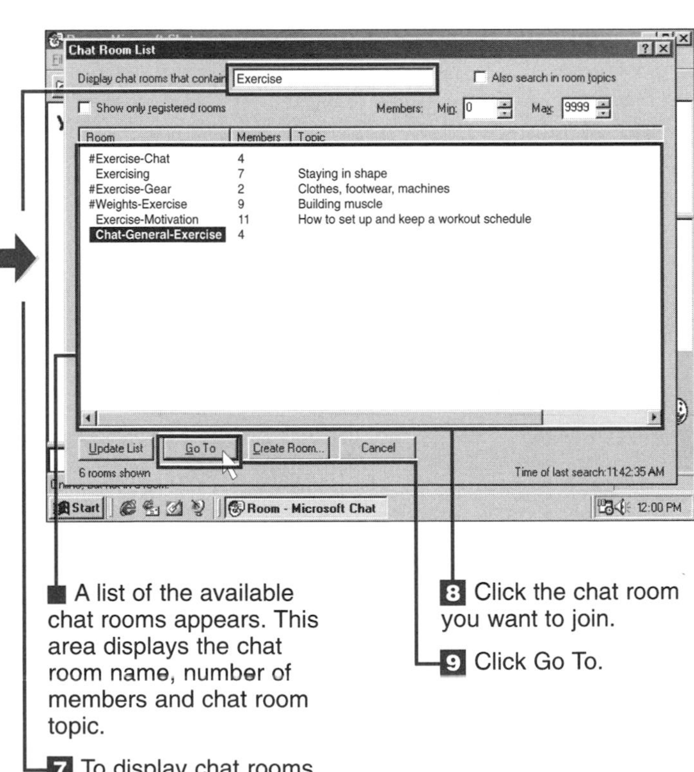

■ A list of the available chat rooms appears. This area displays the chat room name, number of members and chat room topic.

7 To display chat rooms containing a specific word, click this area and then type the word.

8 Click the chat room you want to join.

9 Click Go To.

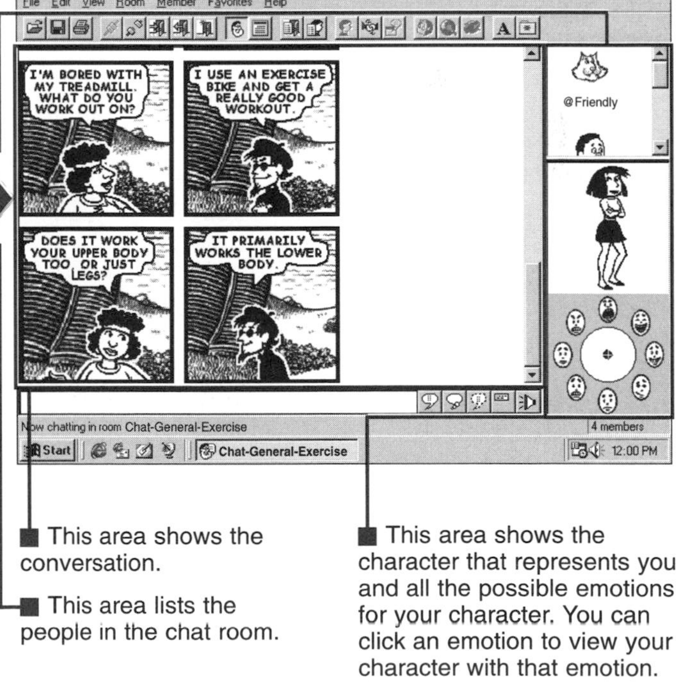

■ This area shows the conversation.

■ This area lists the people in the chat room.

■ This area shows the character that represents you and all the possible emotions for your character. You can click an emotion to view your character with that emotion.

SET UP YOUR CHARACTER

You can choose the cartoon character you want to represent you in Microsoft Chat.

Once you choose a character, you can select the emotion you want your character to display. Having your character display an emotion may help prevent people from misinterpreting what you are saying. For example, if your character is laughing, people can see that what you are saying is meant to be humorous.

Microsoft Chat offers three different backgrounds, including a field, a pastoral setting and a room. You can choose the background you want to display in the comic strip panels.

You can enter personal information about yourself, such as your name, e-mail address, Web page address or a brief description of yourself. You can also enter a new nickname. The information you enter can be viewed by the other people in the chat room. If you are concerned about your privacy, enter only a nickname and leave the other areas blank.

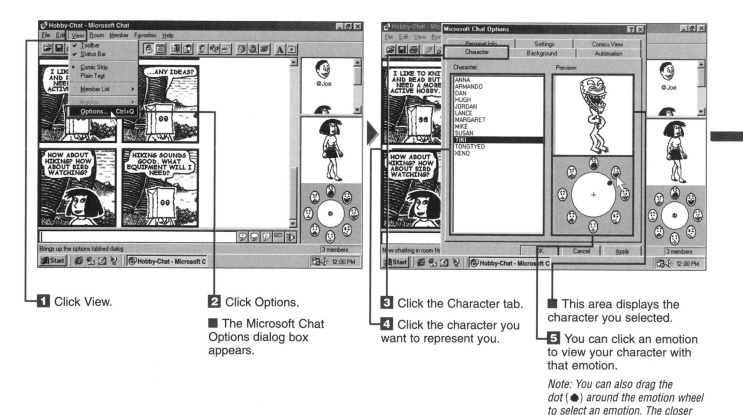

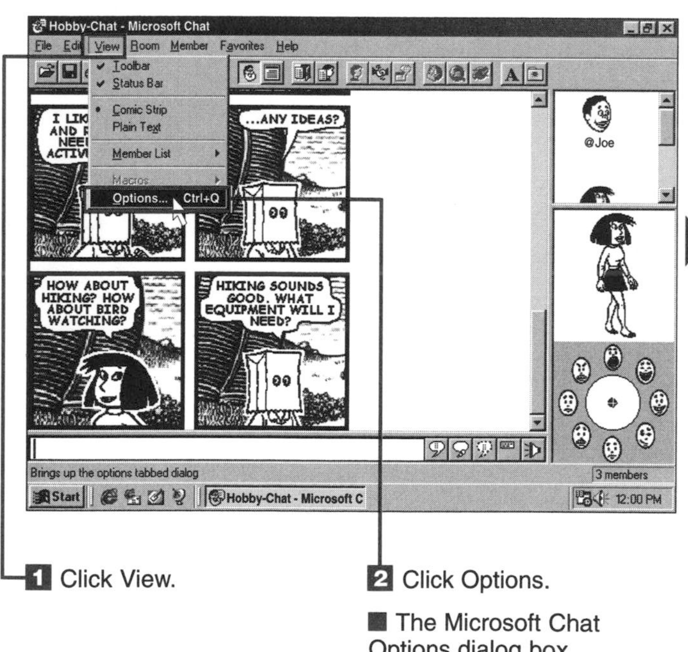

1 Click View.

2 Click Options.

■ The Microsoft Chat Options dialog box appears.

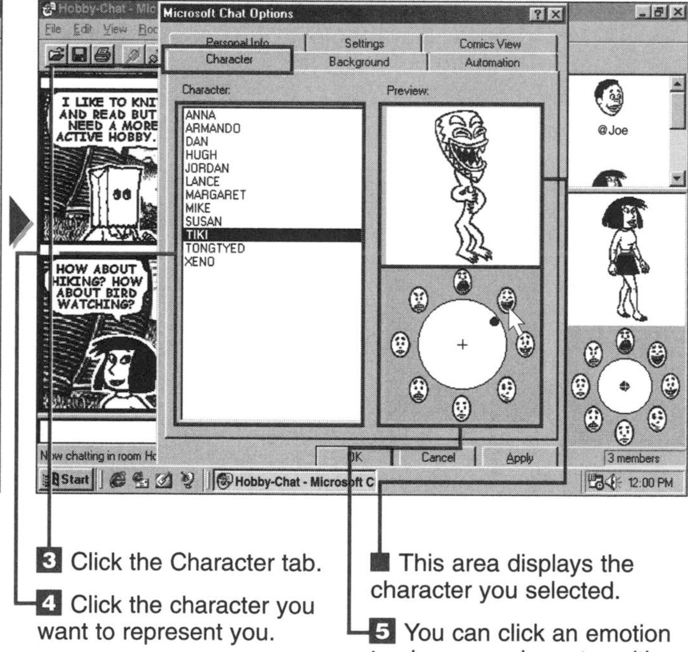

3 Click the Character tab.

4 Click the character you want to represent you.

■ This area displays the character you selected.

5 You can click an emotion to view your character with that emotion.

Note: You can also drag the dot (●) around the emotion wheel to select an emotion. The closer the dot appears to the edge of the wheel, the stronger the emotion.

TIPS

How do I view the description of a person in a chat room?

To display a person's description, double-click the person in the list of people in the chat room. The person's description appears in a comic strip panel.

Can I send an e-mail message to a person in a chat room?

You can send an e-mail message to anyone who makes their e-mail address available. Select the person in the list of people in the chat room and then click the Send E-mail button.

How do I view a person's Web page?

Many people now have their own personal Web pages on the World Wide Web. If a person makes the address of their Web page available, you can view the Web page by selecting the person in the list of people in the chat room and then clicking the Visit HomePage () button.

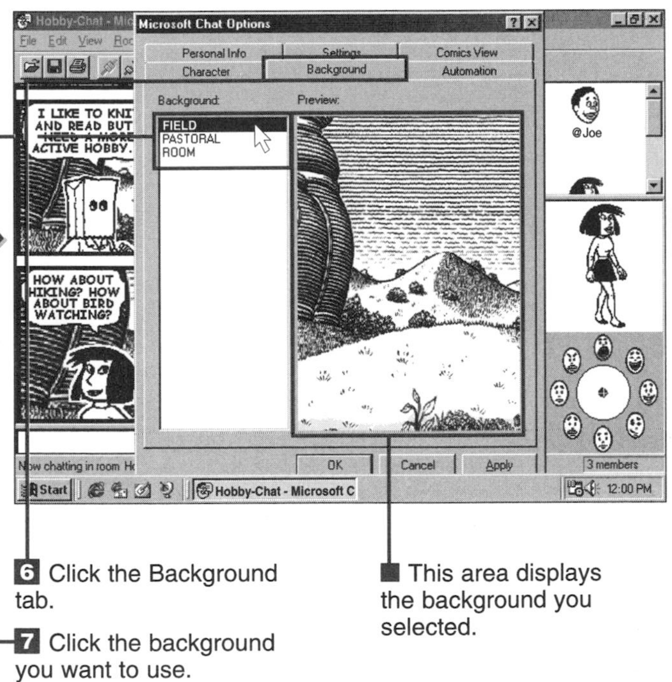

6 Click the Background tab.

7 Click the background you want to use.

■ This area displays the background you selected.

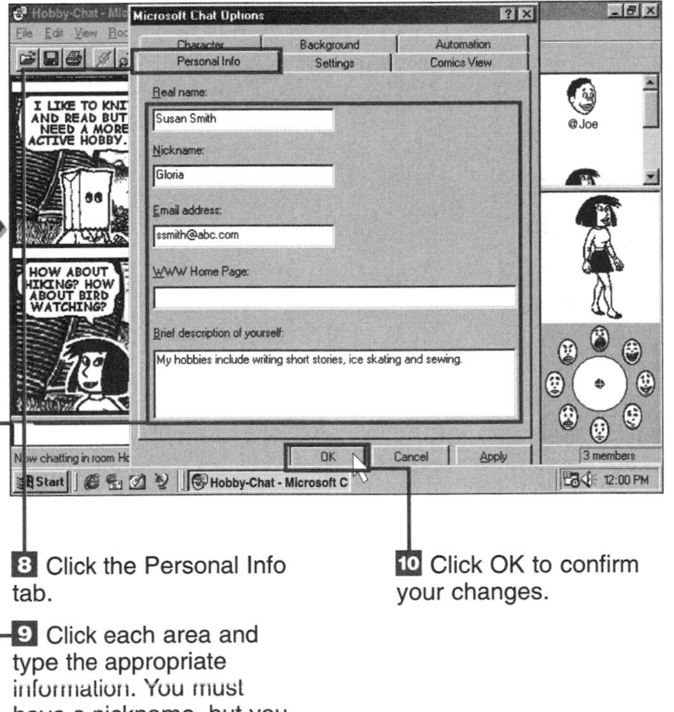

8 Click the Personal Info tab.

9 Click each area and type the appropriate information. You must have a nickname, but you can leave the other areas blank if you wish.

10 Click OK to confirm your changes.

JOIN THE CONVERSATION

When you join a chat room, you can start chatting with other people in the room immediately.

Microsoft Chat shows you what your character looks like and displays the various emotions your character can display. Before participating in a conversation, you should choose an appropriate emotion for your character. You can choose from eight different emotions including angry, sad, happy, bored, shout, laugh, coy and scared. Not all characters can display a full range of emotions.

There are four ways you can make conversation in a chat room. You can "say" text to talk to everyone in the chat room at once. You can have the text you type appear as a thought. You can also whisper so only the character you select from the list of people in the chat room can see what you type. Sending an action message places the text you type in a caption. Action messages automatically begin with your nickname.

You can also enter Web page and e-mail addresses in your conversation. When chatting, people can click any address you enter, such as http://www.abc.com or mailto:johns@abc.com, to display the Web page or send an e-mail message.

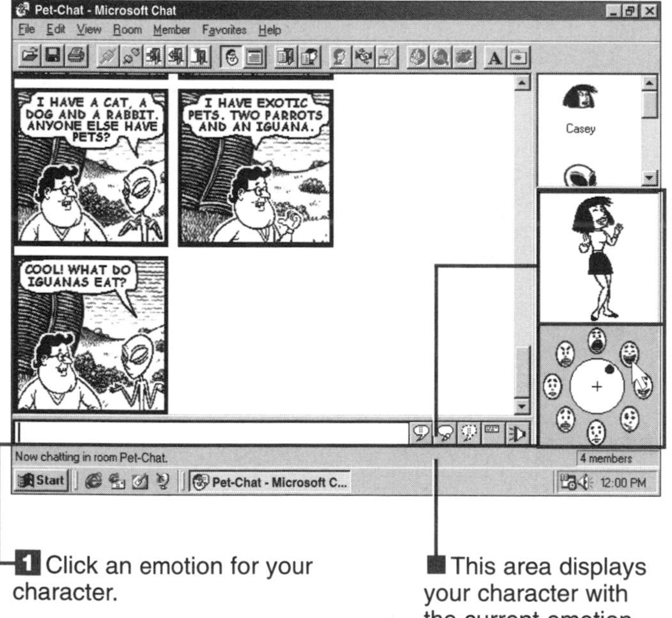

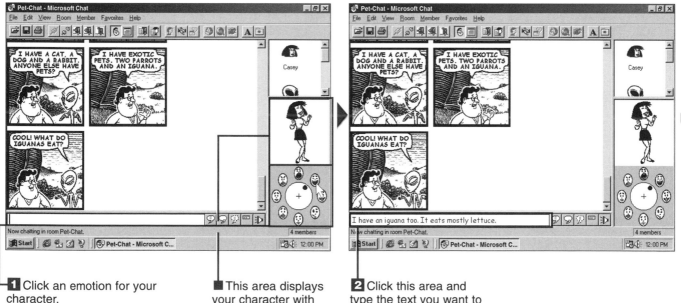

1 Click an emotion for your character.

Note: You can also drag the dot (●) around the emotion wheel to select an emotion. The closer the dot appears to the edge of the wheel, the stronger the emotion.

■ This area displays your character with the current emotion.

2 Click this area and type the text you want to add to the conversation.

TIPS

Why is my character waving?

Your character will perform certain actions depending on what you are saying. For example, when you type "hello," your character will wave. When you type text in uppercase, your character will shout.

Can I change the number of comic strip panels displayed?

Yes. Click the View menu and then click Options. Select the Comics View tab. In the Page Layout drop-down list, select the number of comic strip panels you want to display across the window.

Can I send sounds to others in a chat room?

You can send sounds to other people in a chat room, but other people will only be able to hear the sounds if they have the sound files on their computers. Click the Play sound (▷) button and then click the sound file you want other people to hear. Click the Accompanying message area and type the message you want to send with the sound file.

Can I talk to only one person?

If you select a person from the list of people in the chat room before clicking the Say (💬) button, your character will appear to talk directly to that person.

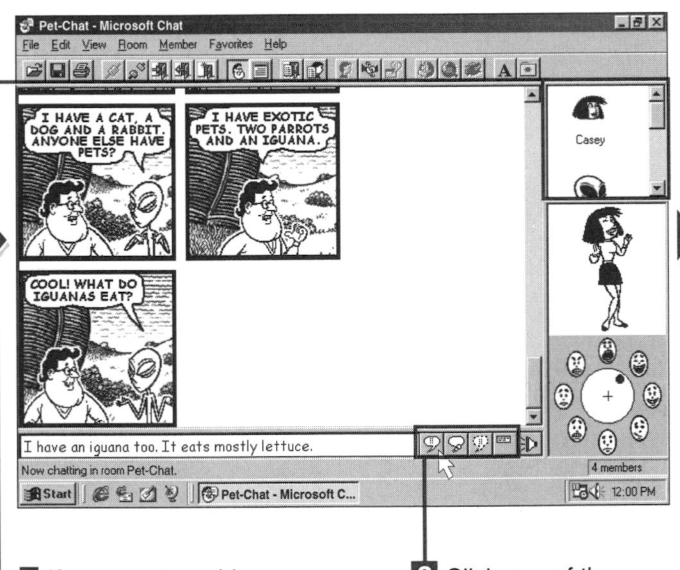

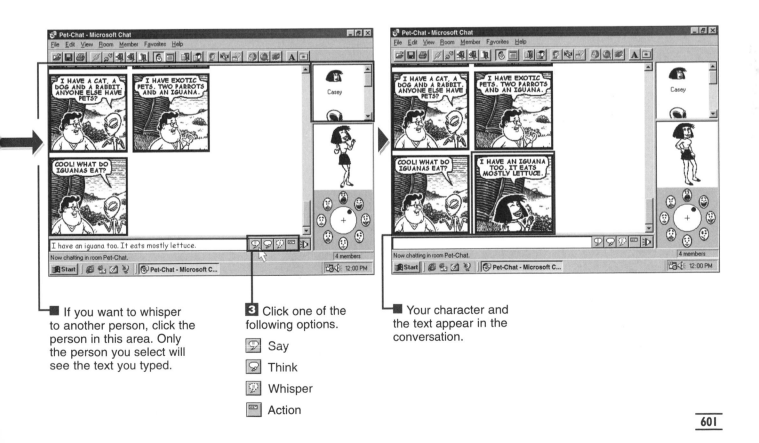

■ If you want to whisper to another person, click the person in this area. Only the person you select will see the text you typed.

3 Click one of the following options.

- Say
- Think
- Whisper
- Action

■ Your character and the text appear in the conversation.

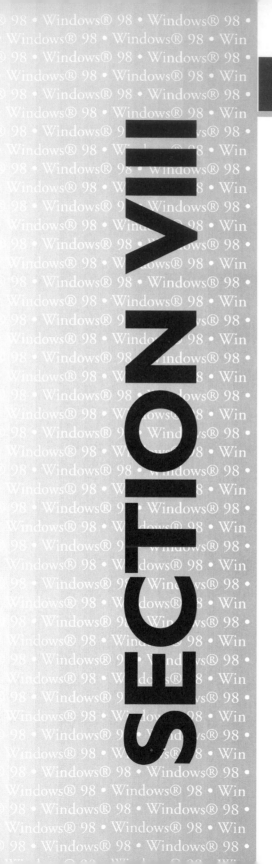

SECTION VIII

INSTALLING AND TROUBLESHOOTING

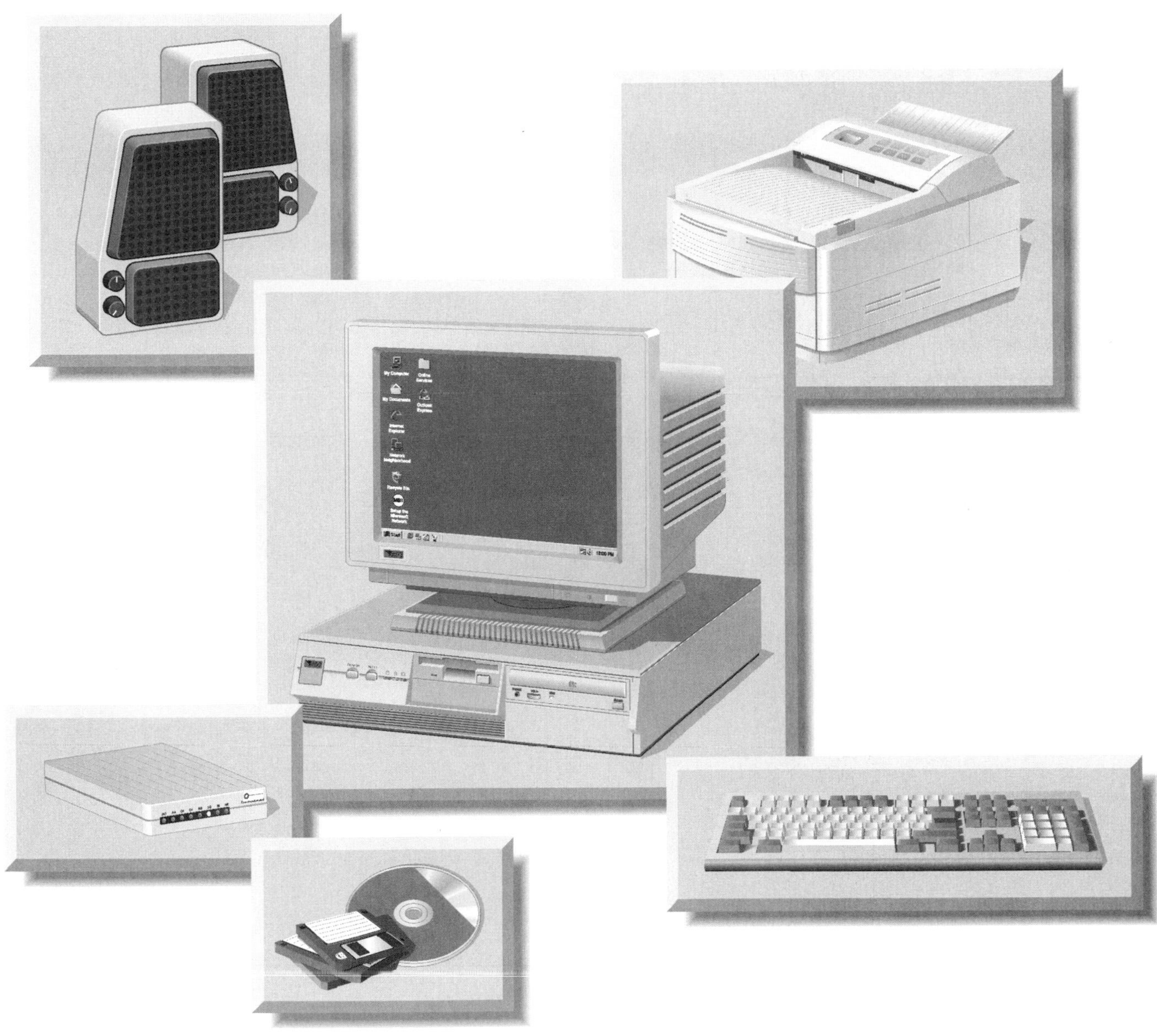

VIEW FONTS ON YOUR COMPUTER

You can view the fonts on your computer to see what they look like before using the fonts in your documents.

A font is a set of characters with a particular design and size. There are a wide variety of fonts you can use. Fonts can be serious and corporate or fancy and funny.

Viewing the fonts on your computer allows you to choose the right font for a document.

Most of the fonts included with Windows are TrueType fonts. A TrueType font generates characters using mathematical formulas. You can change the size of a TrueType font without distorting the font.

A TrueType font will print exactly as it appears on the screen.

Windows displays information about each font on your computer as well as samples of each font in various sizes. You can print a copy of this font information and save it for later reference.

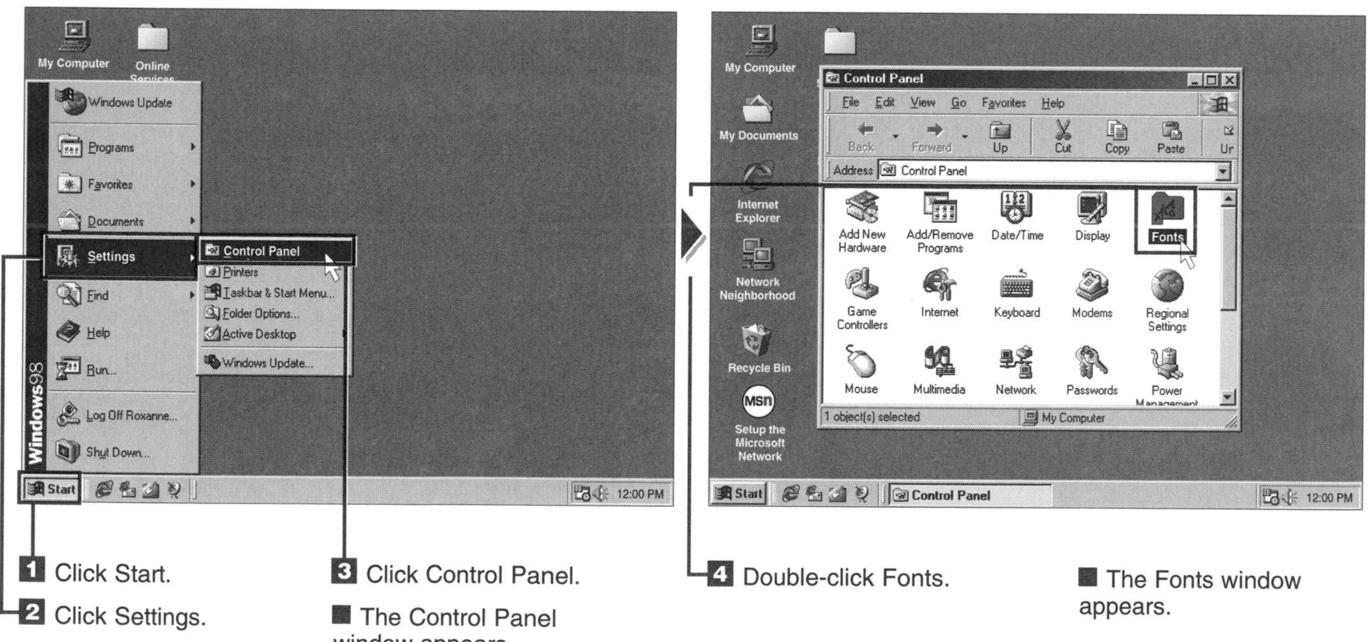

1 Click Start.

2 Click Settings.

3 Click Control Panel.

■ The Control Panel window appears.

4 Double-click Fonts.

■ The Fonts window appears.

TIPS

What are printer fonts?

Printer fonts are fonts stored in a printer's memory. Nearly all printers include printer fonts. Unlike TrueType fonts, printer fonts may not be accurately represented on your screen. Printer fonts are not displayed in the Fonts window. This type of font may appear in a program's font list and is indicated by a printer icon.

Why do some fonts in the Fonts window display a red A?

Fonts displaying a red A are system fonts. Windows uses system fonts to display text in menus and dialog boxes. These fonts are only available in specific sizes. Although system fonts may appear in a program's font list, they are not suitable for most printing tasks.

Why do many font names appear more than once in the Fonts window?

Windows displays variations of many fonts, such as bold and italic versions of a font. In the View menu, click Hide Variations to remove the variations and display only the basic style for each font in the window.

How can I change the way Windows displays items in the Fonts window?

In the Fonts window, click the Large Icons button to display items as large icons. Click the List button to display items as small icons in a list. Click the Similarity button to have Windows display how similar each font is to the selected font. Click the Details button to view file information for each item.

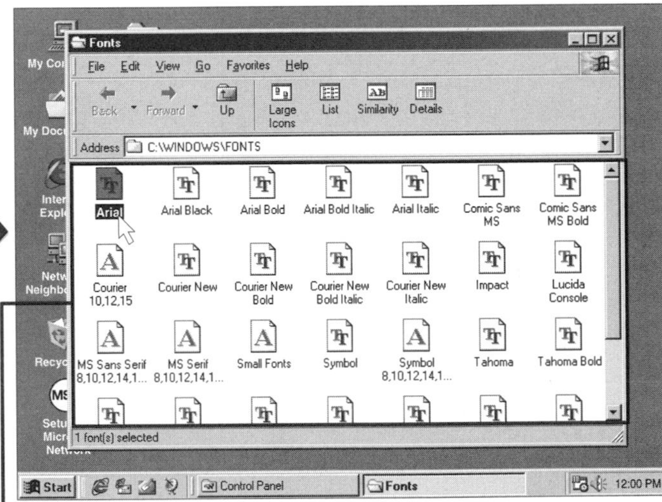

■ Each icon in the Fonts window represents a font installed on your computer. The icon for a TrueType font displays two letter Ts.

5 Double-click a font you want to view.

■ A window appears.

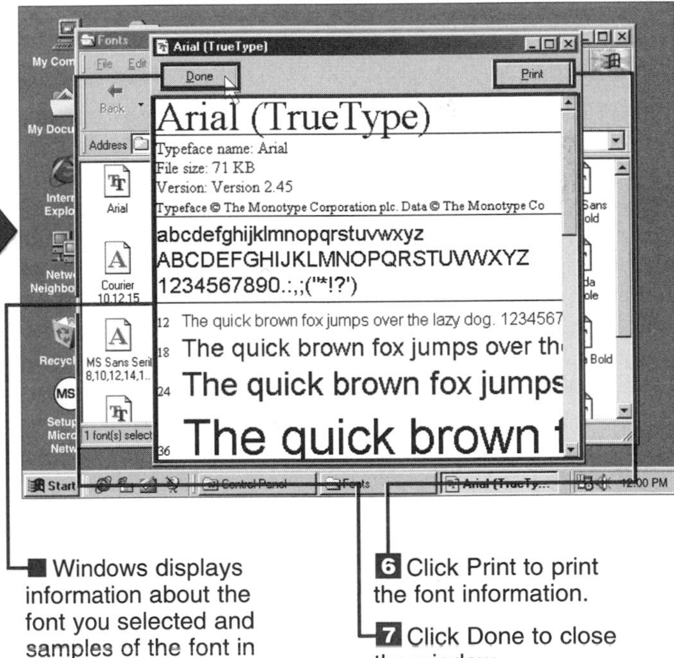

■ Windows displays information about the font you selected and samples of the font in various sizes.

6 Click Print to print the font information.

7 Click Done to close the window.

ADD AND DELETE FONTS

You can add fonts to your computer to give you more choices when creating documents.

Windows includes a few standard fonts. The standard Windows fonts and any other fonts you install can be used in all programs on your computer.

There are thousands of fonts available. You can buy fonts wherever software is sold. You can also search for free fonts on the Internet. Simply search for "TrueType fonts."

When you buy or download fonts, choose the Windows version of TrueType fonts.

A TrueType font generates characters using mathematical formulas. This type of font will print exactly as it appears on your screen.

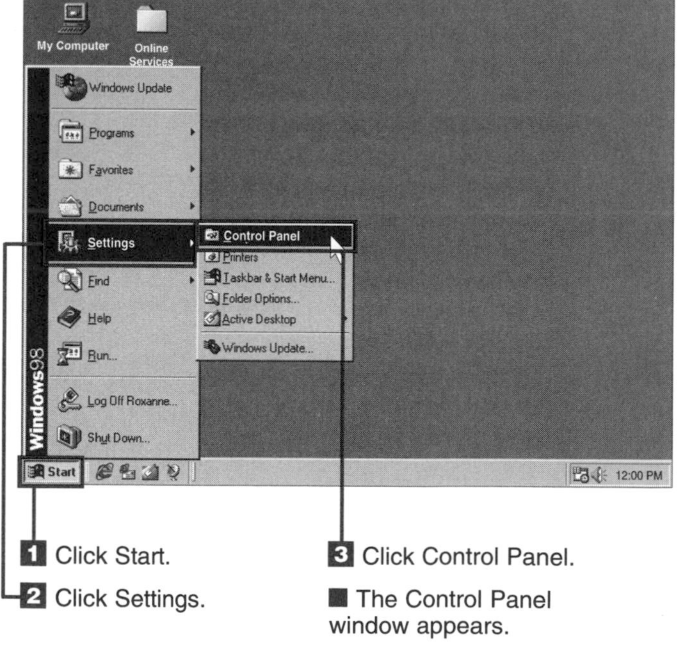

1 Click Start.

2 Click Settings.

3 Click Control Panel.

■ The Control Panel window appears.

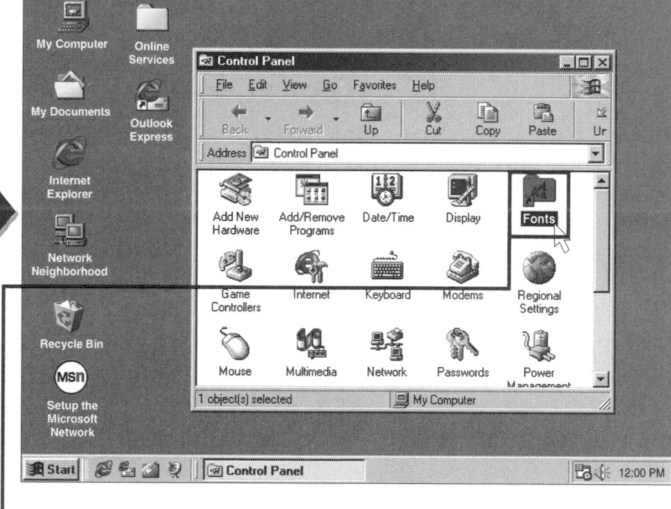

4 Double-click the Fonts folder.

■ The Fonts window appears.

TIPS

How many fonts can I install?

There is no limit to the number of fonts you can install, but keep in mind that fonts take up storage space on your computer. You may also find a long list of fonts becomes cluttered and difficult to use.

Is there a faster way to install a TrueType font?

When the Fonts window is open on your screen, you can drag and drop the icon for a new TrueType font from another window or your desktop into the Fonts window.

Can I move any file into the Fonts folder?

You can only place font files in the Fonts folder. If you try to place another type of file in the Fonts folder, Windows will display an error message.

Is there an easy way to manage fonts?

There are several programs, such as Adobe Type Manager, that can arrange fonts in groups. The fonts can then be installed and used as a group on your computer. You may want to group fonts that you only use for specific projects.

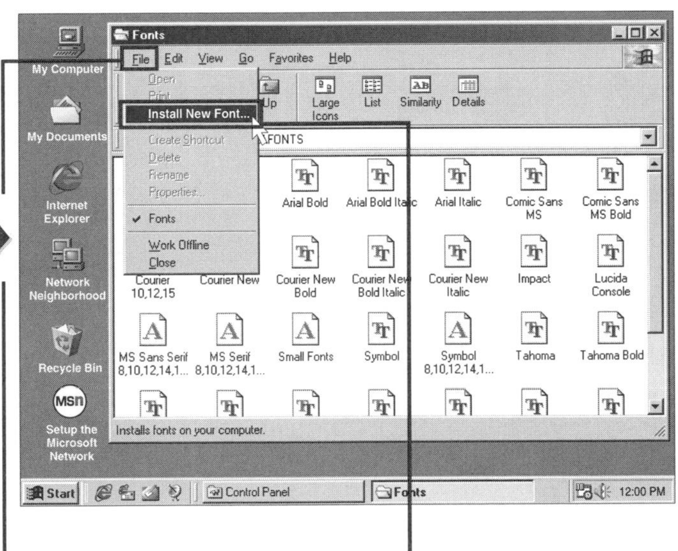

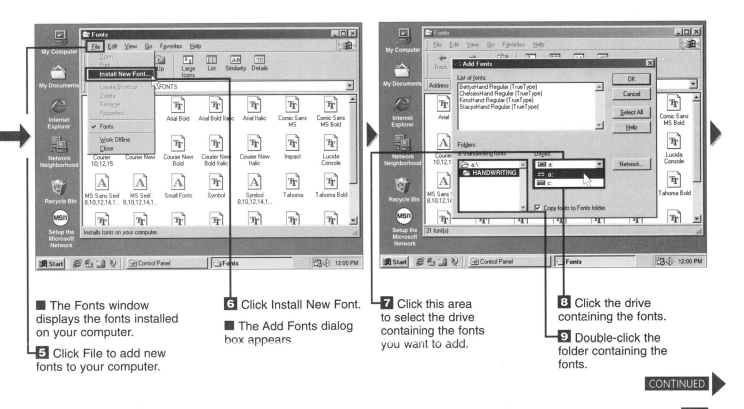

■ The Fonts window displays the fonts installed on your computer.

5 Click File to add new fonts to your computer.

6 Click Install New Font.

■ The Add Fonts dialog box appears.

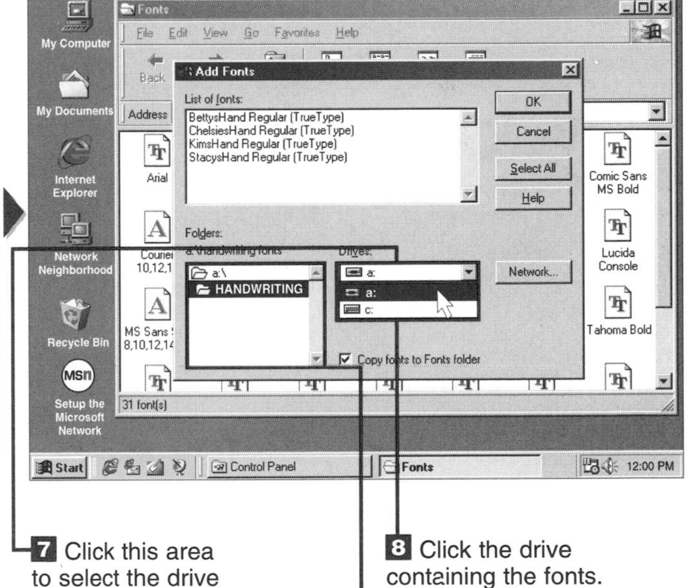

7 Click this area to select the drive containing the fonts you want to add.

8 Click the drive containing the fonts.

9 Double-click the folder containing the fonts.

CONTINUED

ADD AND DELETE FONTS
CONTINUED

When adding fonts, you can select one font or all the available fonts in the folder.

You can organize your fonts and store them in the Fonts folder or other folders on your computer.

You can remove fonts you no longer use from your computer.

Any font that is required by Windows displays a red A on its icon. You should not delete these fonts.

Many programs install their own special fonts. Before you delete a font you do not recognize, make sure the font is not required by a program.

If you delete a font that is used by Windows or a Windows program, a different font will be used to replace the one you deleted. You may not like the substitution Windows makes.

Deleted fonts are sent to your Recycle Bin. To be safe, you may want to make a backup copy of the font before you delete it.

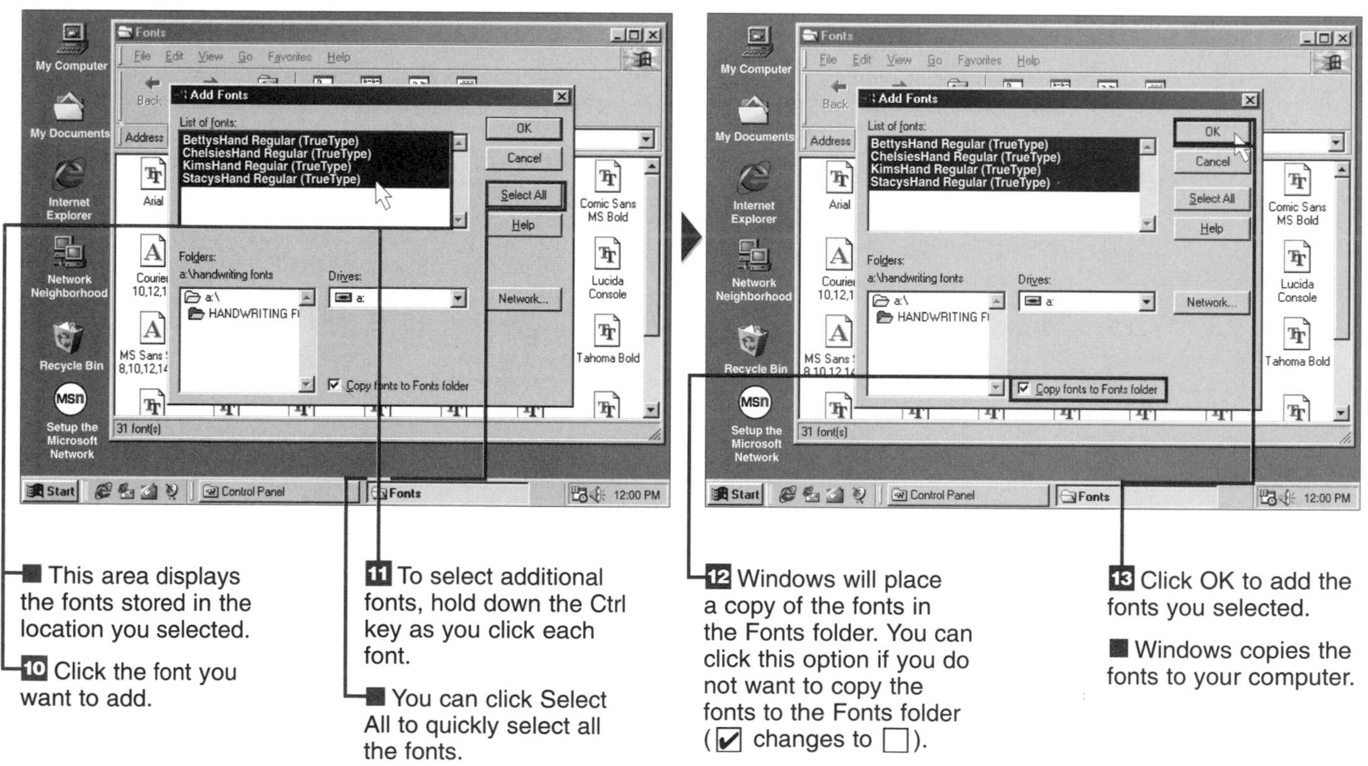

■ This area displays the fonts stored in the location you selected.

10 Click the font you want to add.

11 To select additional fonts, hold down the Ctrl key as you click each font.

■ You can click Select All to quickly select all the fonts.

12 Windows will place a copy of the fonts in the Fonts folder. You can click this option if you do not want to copy the fonts to the Fonts folder (☑ changes to ☐).

13 Click OK to add the fonts you selected.

■ Windows copies the fonts to your computer.

TIPS

I added some fonts to the Fonts folder. Why are the fonts still in the original folder?

When you drag and drop a font file into the Fonts folder, Windows places a copy of the file in the Fonts folder. The original file stays in its location on your computer.

Can I delete several fonts at once?

You can select several fonts and delete them at the same time. To select several fonts, hold down the Ctrl key as you click each font you want to delete. Then perform steps 2 and 3 below.

Is there another way to delete fonts?

You can drag and drop a font's icon to your Recycle Bin.

How can I get a font back that I accidentally deleted?

You can open your Recycle Bin to retrieve a font you deleted by mistake. Right-click the font you want to retrieve and click Restore from the menu that appears. See page 74.

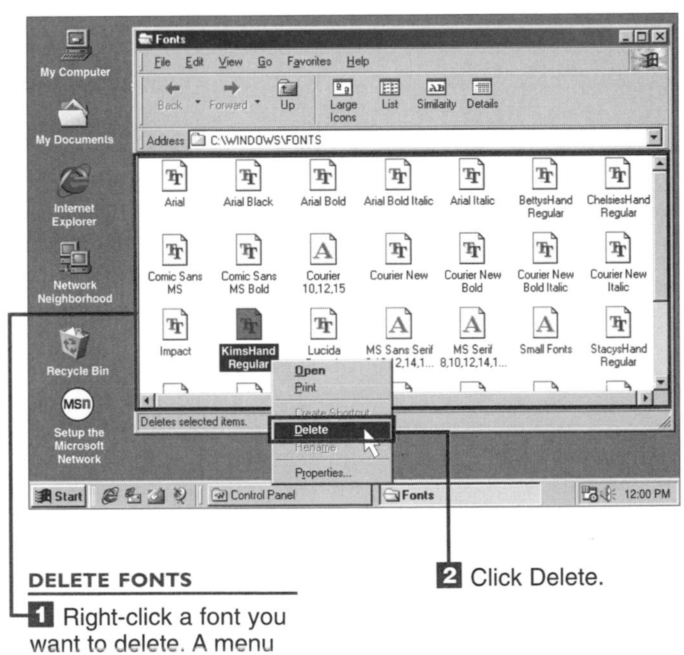

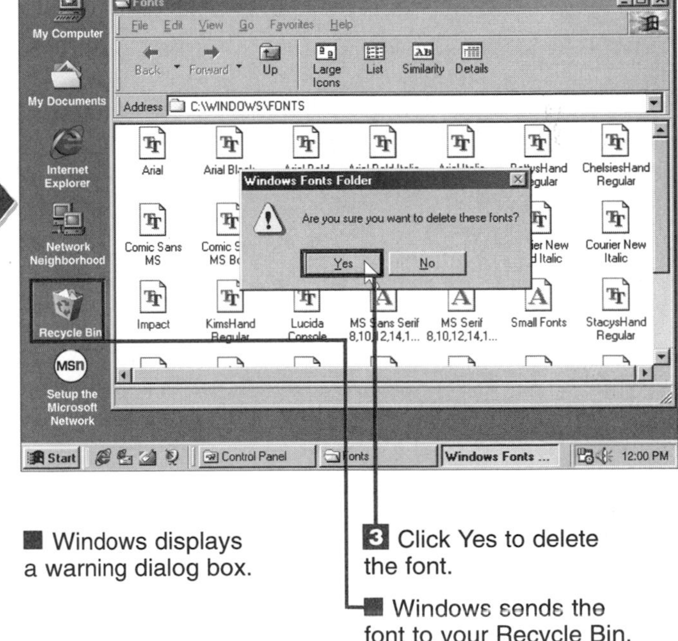

DELETE FONTS

1 Right-click a font you want to delete. A menu appears.

Note: To display the Fonts window, perform steps 1 to 4 on page 604.

2 Click Delete.

■ Windows displays a warning dialog box.

3 Click Yes to delete the font.

■ Windows sends the font to your Recycle Bin.

ADD OR REMOVE WINDOWS COMPONENTS

You can use the Windows 98 CD-ROM disc to add parts of your Windows operating system. You can install components to add additional capabilities and enhancements to your computer. You can also remove components you do not use to free up storage space on your computer.

When setting up Windows for the first time, most people do not install all the components included with the program. This avoids taking up storage space with unnecessary components.

Windows displays a list of all the components and indicates which components are not yet installed on your computer. Windows provides you with a brief description of each component.

Windows groups similar types of components together. For example, Desktop Wallpaper and Screen Savers are parts of the Accessories component. Windows uses check boxes to indicate whether all, none or some of the parts of a component are installed.

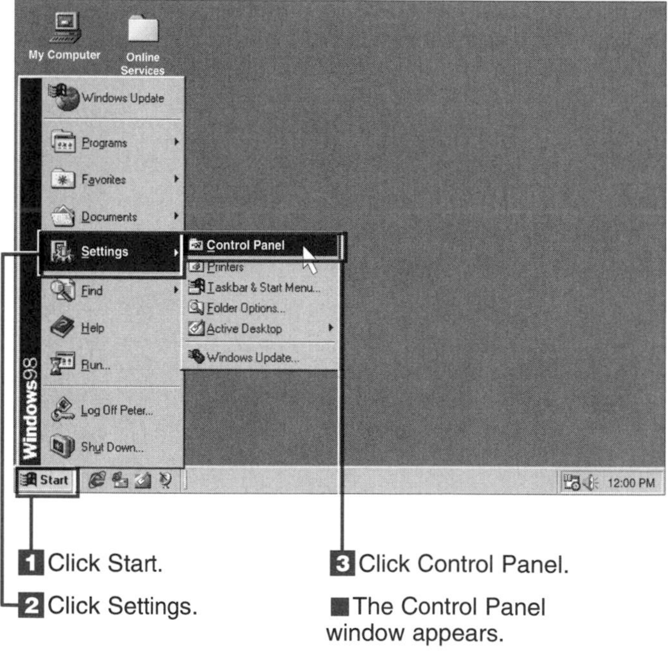

1 Click Start.

2 Click Settings.

3 Click Control Panel.

■ The Control Panel window appears.

4 Double-click Add/Remove Programs.

■ The Add/Remove Programs Properties dialog box appears.

TIPS

I did not receive a Windows 98 CD-ROM disc when I bought my computer. How can I add the extra components?

Many computer manufacturers store the contents of the Windows 98 CD-ROM disc on the hard drive of a new computer. You can check the instructions that came with the computer or ask the computer vendor to determine if the disc was copied to your hard drive.

When I installed Windows, why weren't all the components installed?

A typical installation does not install components that are rarely used or are of special interest, like Multilanguage Support.

When would I use the Have Disk button?

You use the Have Disk button to install a Windows component that is not listed on the Windows Setup tab. For example, if you download a Windows component from the Internet, you can use the Have Disk button to install the component.

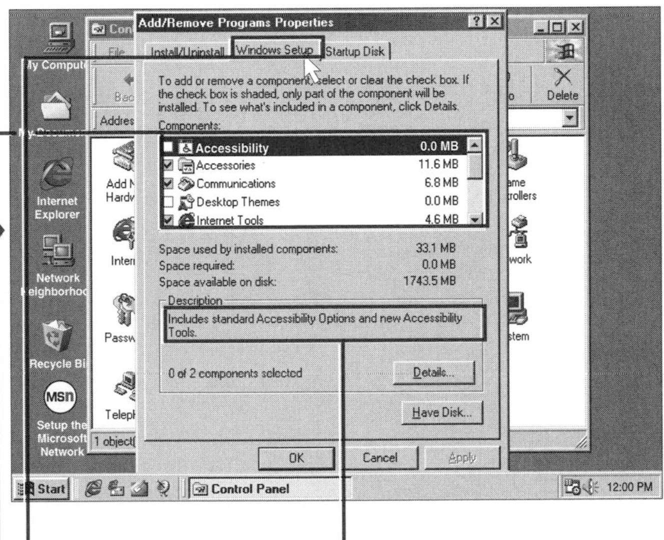

5 Click the Windows Setup tab.

■ This area displays the components you can add or remove from your computer.

■ This area displays a description of the highlighted component.

Note: You can click the name of another component to display its description.

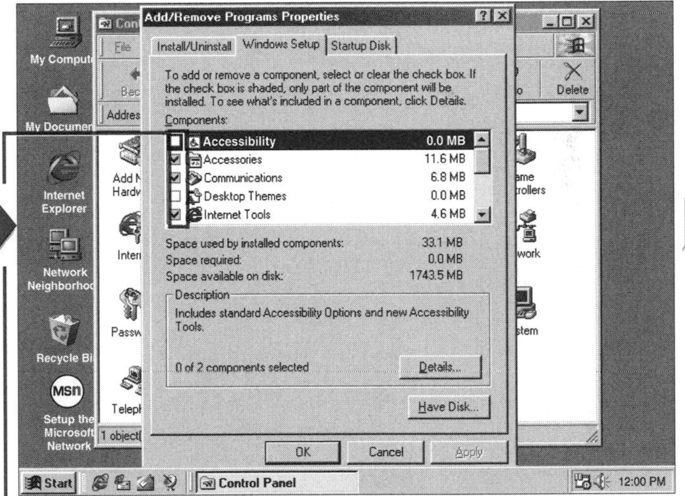

■ The box beside each component tells you how much of the component is installed.

☑ All parts of the component are installed.

☑ Some parts of the component are installed.

☐ No parts of the component are installed.

CONTINUED

ADD OR REMOVE WINDOWS COMPONENTS CONTINUED

There are many useful components that are not part of the typical Windows installation. You can add the components you want with the Windows 98 CD-ROM disc.

The Accessories component has several useful options. Quick View lets you preview the contents of files before you open them. You will also find games, desktop wallpaper and screen savers in the Accessories component.

The Communications component contains Direct Cable Connection to allow you to create a simple network by attaching two computers with a cable.

The System Tools component contains tools that allow you to optimize the performance of your computer. For example, the Backup program helps you save copies of your data and files to floppy and tape drives. The Character Map is invaluable when you need to find a special character that is not available on the keyboard. Disk compression tools are helpful when you need to increase the amount of free space on your hard drive.

You can view all the parts of each component and select the parts you want to add or remove.

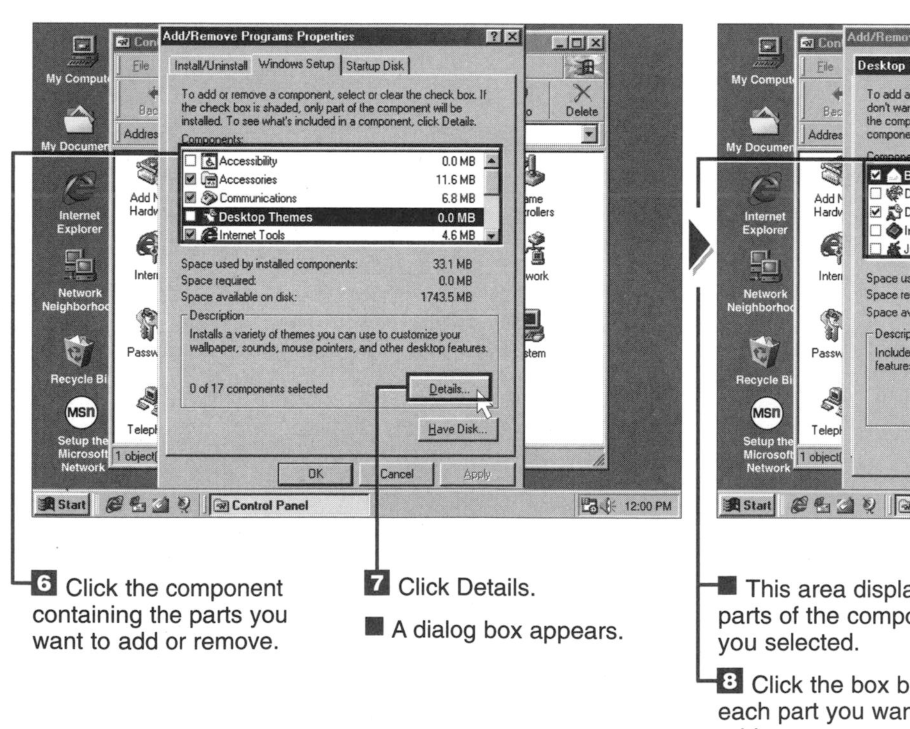

6 Click the component containing the parts you want to add or remove.

7 Click Details.

■ A dialog box appears.

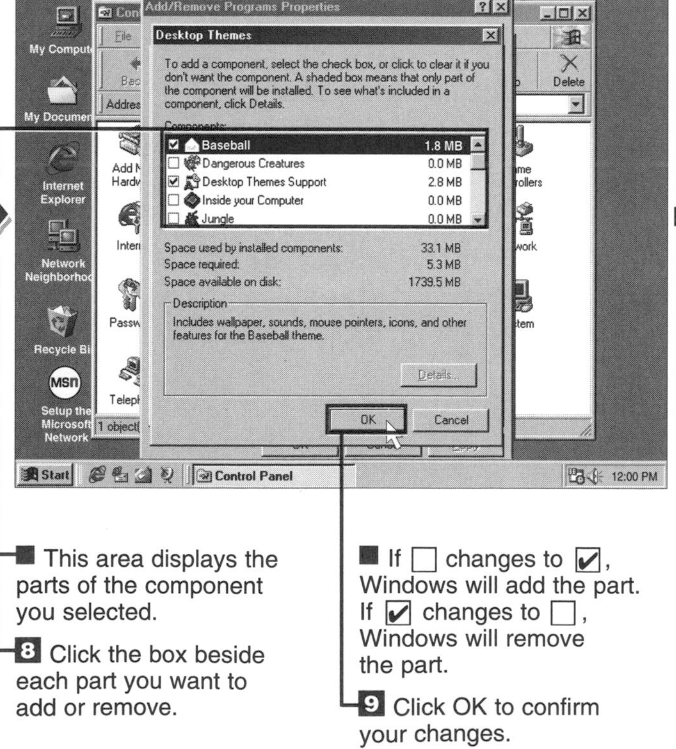

■ This area displays the parts of the component you selected.

8 Click the box beside each part you want to add or remove.

■ If ☐ changes to ☑, Windows will add the part. If ☑ changes to ☐, Windows will remove the part.

9 Click OK to confirm your changes.

TIPS

Can I add components to my computer without using the CD-ROM disc every time?

You can copy all the files from the Win98 directory on the CD-ROM disc to a folder on your hard drive. When Windows asks for the CD-ROM disc, click OK. Then click the Browse button in the Copying Files dialog box and select the folder containing the files.

How can I remove the Briefcase?

Once you install the Briefcase from the Accessories component, it cannot be removed.

I wanted to install one component. Why were other parts also installed?

Some components require parts of other components to work properly. Windows will automatically install all the parts that are needed.

What does the Multilanguage Support component do?

Multilanguage Support installs the specific files needed to allow you to work with and create documents in several non-Western languages, including Greek, Polish and Ukrainian. There are five language groups you can choose from.

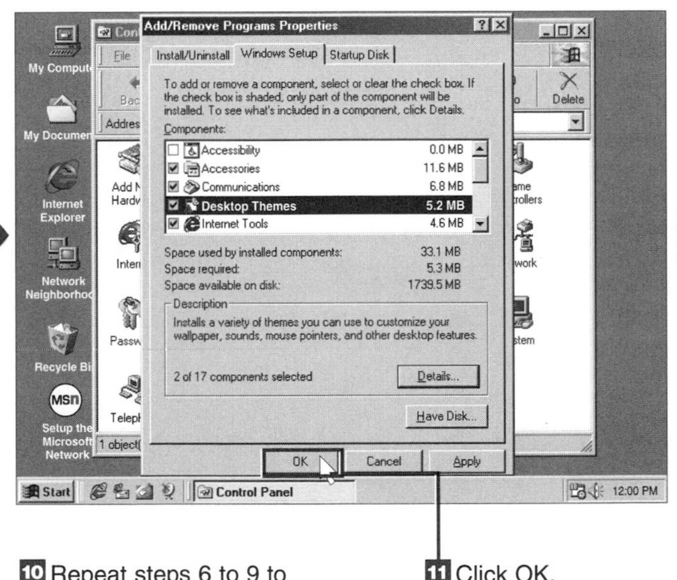

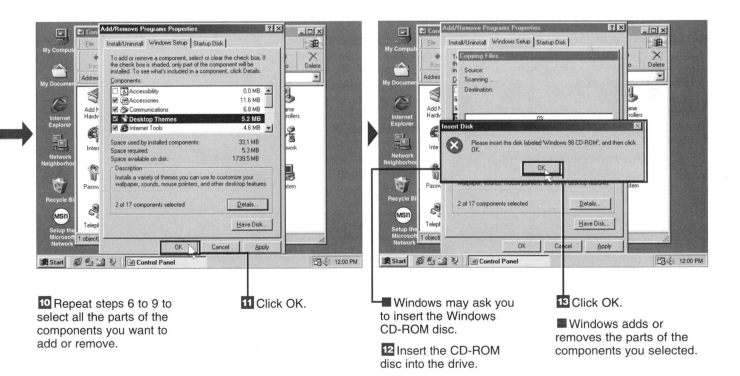

10 Repeat steps 6 to 9 to select all the parts of the components you want to add or remove.

11 Click OK.

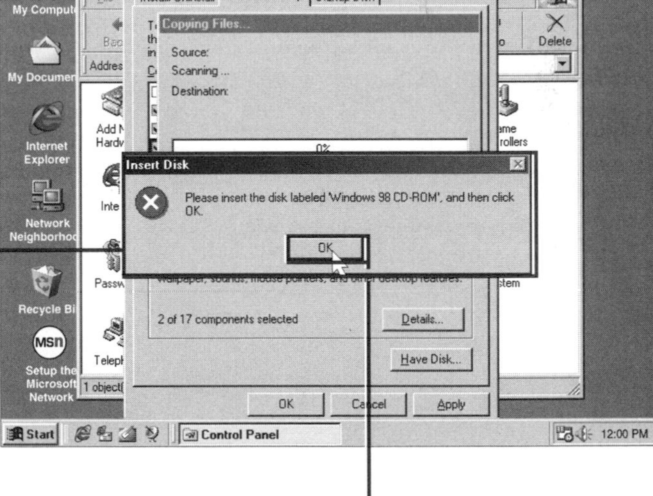

■ Windows may ask you to insert the Windows CD-ROM disc.

12 Insert the CD-ROM disc into the drive.

13 Click OK.

■ Windows adds or removes the parts of the components you selected.

INSTALL A PROGRAM

You can use a CD-ROM disc or floppy disks to add a new program to your computer.

Most Windows programs available on a CD-ROM disc will automatically start an installation program when the CD-ROM disc is inserted. If the installation program does not start automatically, you can have Windows start the installation process.

The installation program asks you questions about your computer and how you would like to have the program installed. There are three common types of installations. A typical installation sets up the program as recommended for most people. A custom installation allows you to customize the program to suit your specific needs. A minimum installation sets up the minimum amount of the program needed.

When you finish installing a program, make sure you keep the CD-ROM disc or floppy disks in a safe place. If your computer fails or if you accidentally erase the program files, you may need to install the program again.

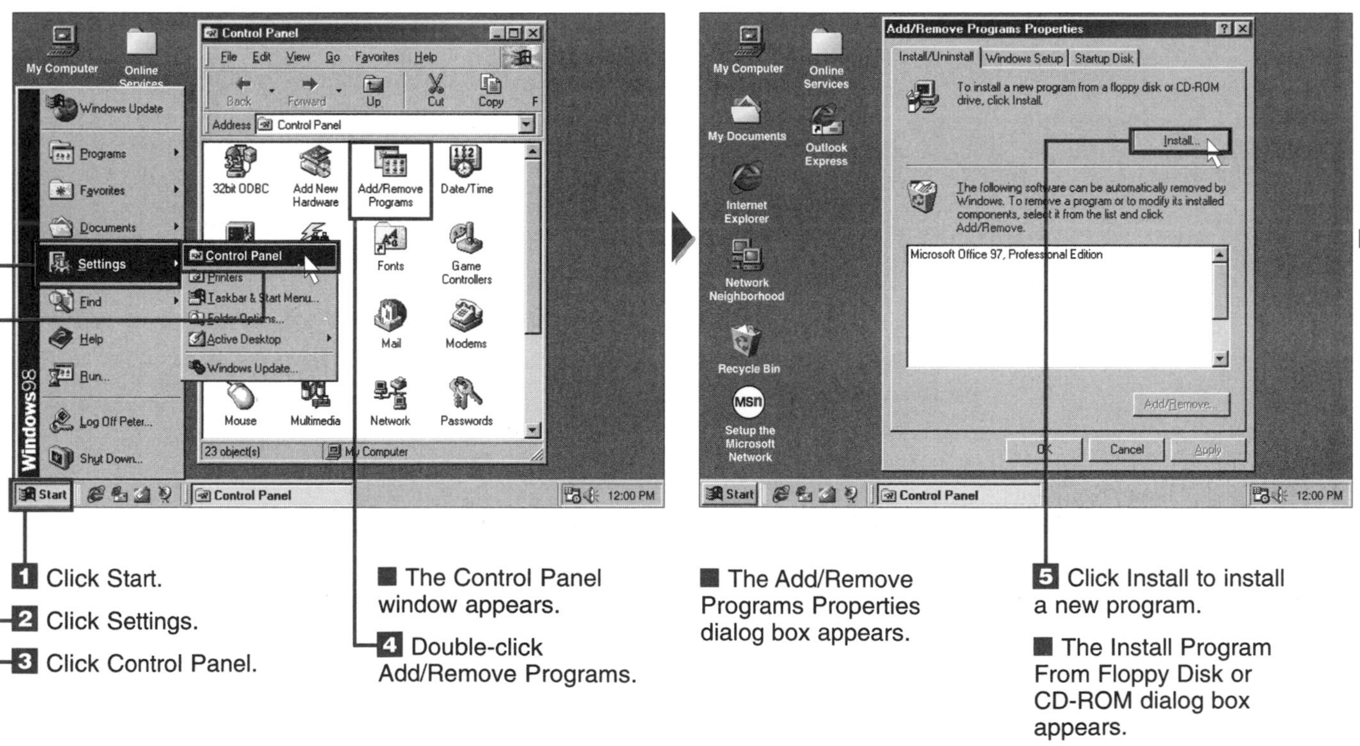

1 Click Start.

2 Click Settings.

3 Click Control Panel.

■ The Control Panel window appears.

4 Double-click Add/Remove Programs.

■ The Add/Remove Programs Properties dialog box appears.

5 Click Install to install a new program.

■ The Install Program From Floppy Disk or CD-ROM dialog box appears.

TIPS

How can I install a program if it does not have an installation program?

If you are installing an older program that does not have an installation program, create a new folder on your computer. Then copy all the files from the installation disk to the new folder. You can run the program from the folder.

I already installed a program for Windows 3.1. Do I need to install it again?

If you upgraded to Windows 98 from a previous version of Windows, you do not have to re-install the program. If you currently have both Windows 3.1 and Windows 98 installed on your computer, you must re-install the program for Windows 98.

What is a readme file?

A readme file is a file usually found on the installation disk or CD-ROM disc. This file may contain the latest information about the product or information to help you install the program.

Windows did not find an installation program. What can I do?

If Windows did not find an installation program, you can search for the program using the Browse button. Display the contents of the drive containing the installation disk and look for a file named "setup" or "install."

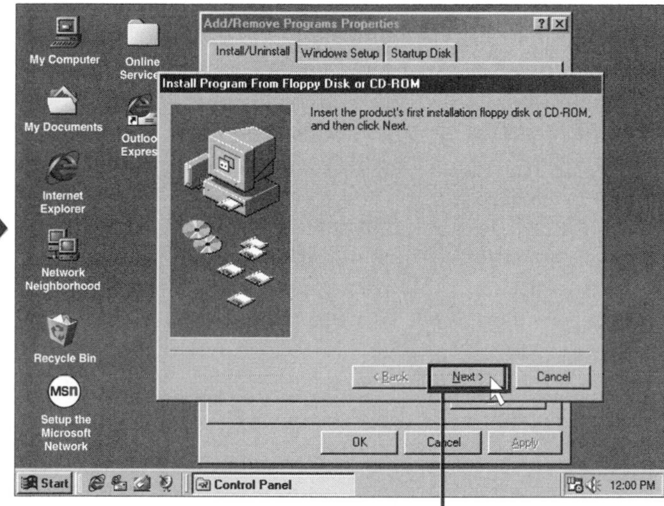

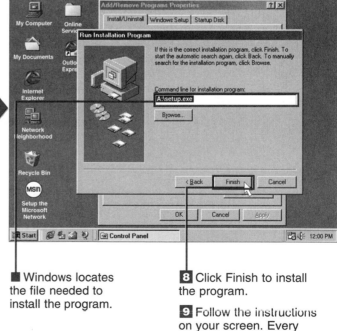

6 Insert the program's first installation floppy disk or CD-ROM disc into a drive.

7 Click Next to continue.

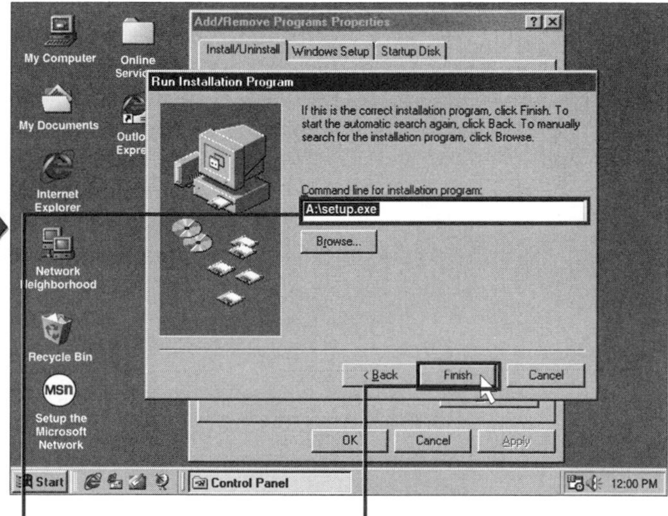

■ Windows locates the file needed to install the program.

8 Click Finish to install the program.

9 Follow the instructions on your screen. Every program will ask you a different set of questions.

REMOVE A PROGRAM

You can remove a program you no longer use from your computer. Removing programs will free up space on your hard drive and allow you to install newer or more useful programs.

Most programs installed on your computer appear in a list. You can select the program you want to remove in the list and have Windows remove the program from your computer.

Windows deletes the files and may reverse the settings that were changed when the program was installed. To avoid affecting other programs, Windows may leave some of the files related to the program on your computer.

When you remove a program, Windows may ask you for the original floppy disks or CD-ROM disc you used to install the program.

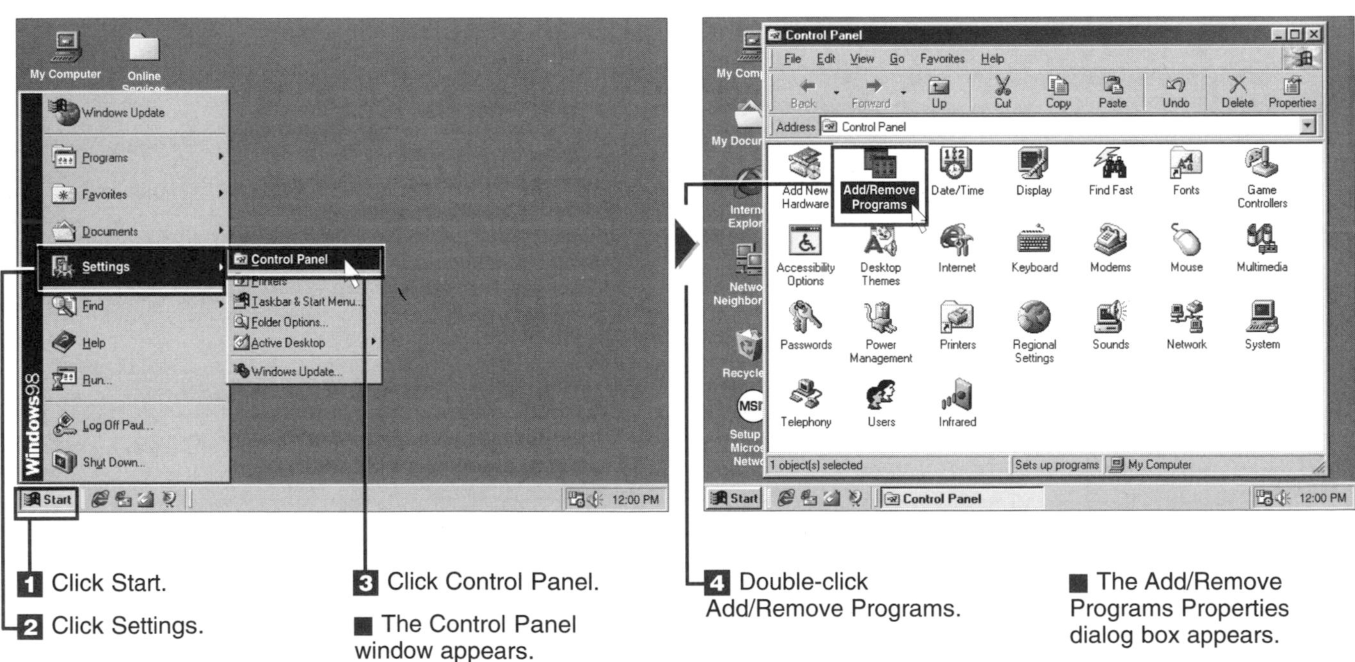

1 Click Start.

2 Click Settings.

3 Click Control Panel.

■ The Control Panel window appears.

4 Double-click Add/Remove Programs.

■ The Add/Remove Programs Properties dialog box appears.

TIPS

How can I remove a program that Windows cannot automatically remove?

Older programs, such as those created before Windows 95, may not appear in the Add/Remove Programs list. You can delete most program files yourself. You must be careful to delete only the files for the program you want to remove. Check the documentation supplied with the program for more information. There are also many commercial uninstall programs that you can purchase to delete a program's files.

How do I delete the program's shortcut from my desktop?

After deleting a program, you can drag any shortcuts you no longer need to the Recycle Bin.

I removed a program from my computer but the Start menu still displays the program. How do I remove a program from the Start menu?

To remove a program from the Start menu, see page 264.

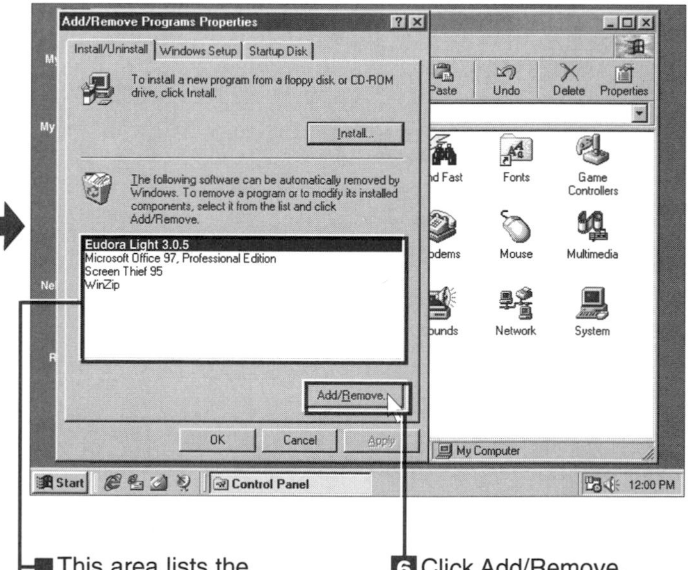

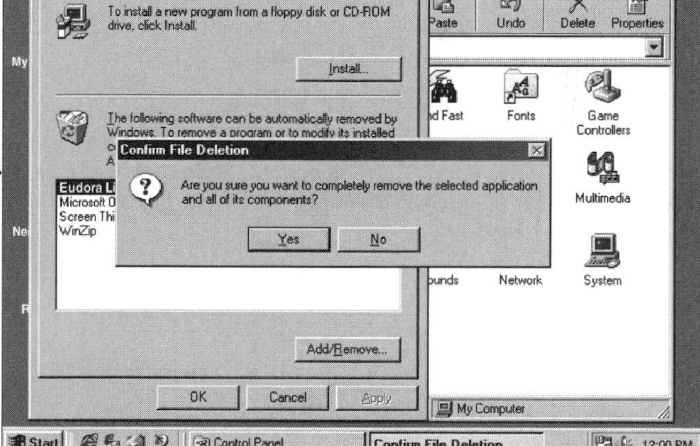

■ This area lists the programs Windows can automatically remove.

5 Click the program you want to remove.

6 Click Add/Remove.

■ Windows runs the setup program.

7 Follow the instructions on your screen. Every program will take you through different steps to remove the program.

INSTALL NEW HARDWARE

You can install new hardware on your computer, such as a CD-ROM drive, network interface card, modem or printer. The Add New Hardware Wizard guides you step-by-step through the process and completes most of the work for you.

Before beginning, you should locate your Windows 98 CD-ROM disc and any materials that were included with the hardware. You should also read the hardware manufacturer's instructions and exit all open programs on your computer.

During the installation, Windows will install the necessary software, called a driver, for the new hardware device. The driver allows your computer to communicate with the new device.

Windows searches your computer for Plug and Play hardware. Plug and Play hardware uses technology that allows Windows to automatically detect the hardware settings for the device. Your computer and the device you are installing must both support Plug and Play.

You can also have Windows search your computer for new hardware that is not Plug and Play compatible.

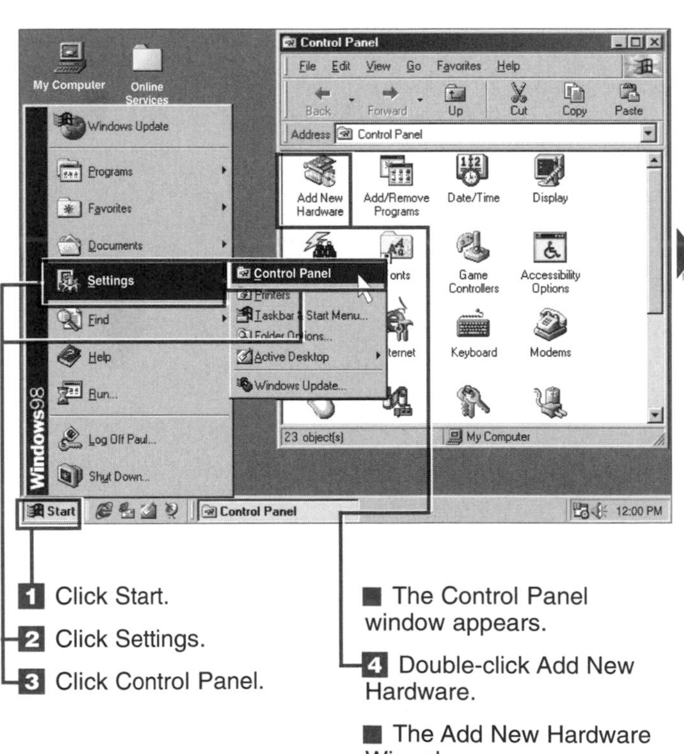

1 Click Start.

2 Click Settings.

3 Click Control Panel.

■ The Control Panel window appears.

4 Double-click Add New Hardware.

■ The Add New Hardware Wizard appears.

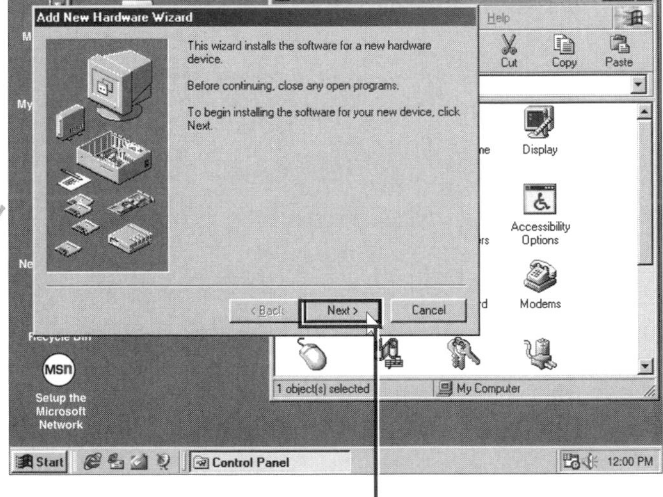

■ The wizard will help you install the necessary software for your new hardware. Make sure you close any open programs before you continue.

5 Click Next to begin installing the new hardware.

TIPS

Do I have to use the wizard to install new Plug and Play hardware?

You may not always have to use the wizard to install Plug and Play hardware. After you physically connect the device to your computer and turn the computer on, Windows may automatically detect the device and ask you for the driver for the device.

Should I use the wizard even if I know the details about the device and have the installation disk?

Yes. The wizard may simplify the procedure and will install the Windows 98 version of the driver. This is particularly important for devices you purchased before Windows 98 was released. Older drivers may not use the full potential of Windows 98.

How can I tell if my computer supports Plug and Play?

In the Control Panel window, double-click System. Select the Device Manager tab and then click the plus sign (⊞) beside System devices to expand the list. If your system has a Plug and Play BIOS, your computer supports Plug and Play.

What happens when Windows finds a Plug and Play device?

If Windows finds a Plug and Play device, a dialog box may appear, displaying the name of the device Windows found. Click the device you want to install and then follow the instructions on your screen. If the device you want to install is not listed, select No, the device isn't in the list (○ changes to ⊙) and then click Next.

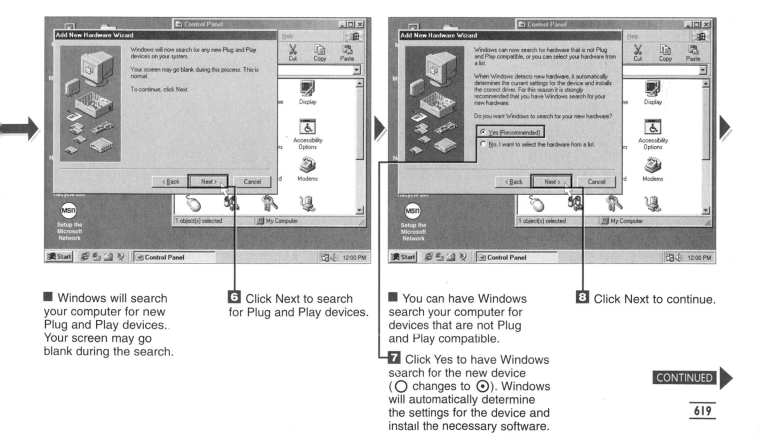

■ Windows will search your computer for new Plug and Play devices. Your screen may go blank during the search.

6 Click Next to search for Plug and Play devices.

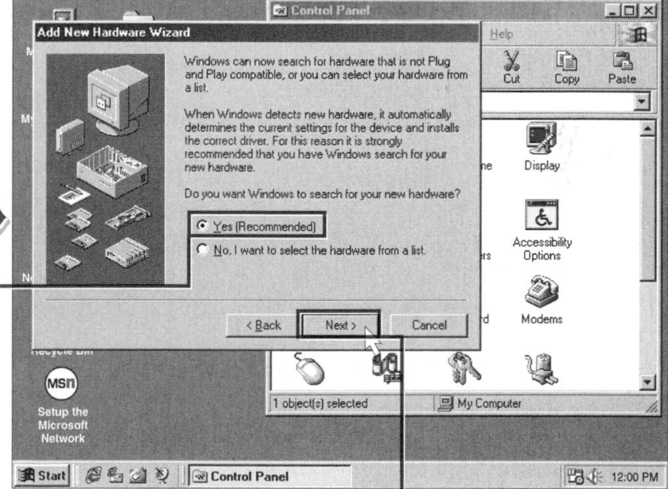

■ You can have Windows search your computer for devices that are not Plug and Play compatible.

7 Click Yes to have Windows search for the new device (○ changes to ⊙). Windows will automatically determine the settings for the device and install the necessary software.

8 Click Next to continue.

CONTINUED

INSTALL NEW HARDWARE
CONTINUED

When installing new hardware, Windows may take several minutes to search your computer for hardware that is not Plug and Play compatible. If the progress stops, you should wait five minutes and then restart your computer. You can then try installing the new hardware again.

A hardware device that is not Plug and Play compatible is sometimes referred to as a legacy device. Windows may ask you to provide the driver that came with a legacy device. This driver is stored on the device's installation disk.

You must ensure that the hardware settings Windows suggests for a legacy device are correct. You may have to adjust the settings on the device to match the settings suggested by Windows. You can adjust the settings by using the software that came with the device or by adjusting the jumpers and switches on the device. Consult the device's manual before making any adjustments.

If you want to install a printer, see page 114 to use the Add Printer Wizard. You can find more information on installing a modem on page 382. Installing a network interface card is discussed in detail on page 474.

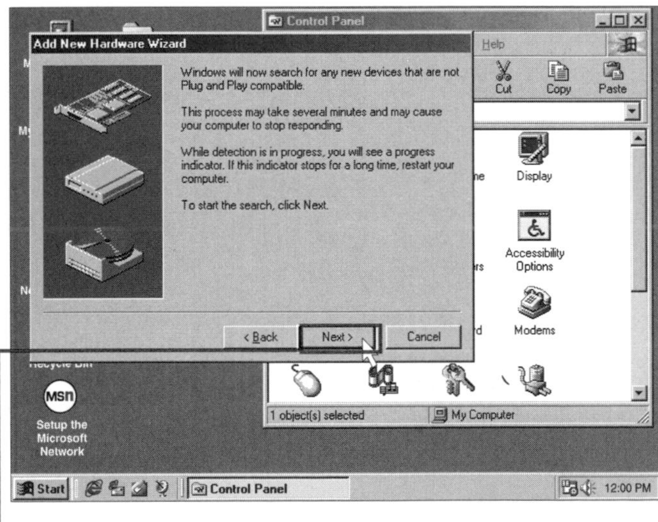

9 Click Next to start searching for new devices that are not Plug and Play compatible.

■ The search may take several minutes.

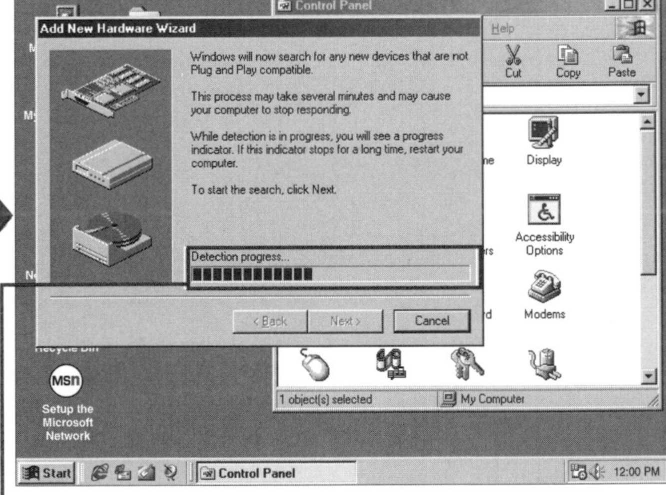

■ This area displays the progress of the search.

Note: You can click Cancel to stop the search at any time.

TIPS

What should I do if Windows did not find any new hardware?

Windows will allow you to select your hardware device from a list. If you cannot find the type of device you are installing, select Other devices from the Hardware types list. This option provides you with a list of computer product manufacturers to help you find the device.

What should I do if I cannot find the driver for an older device?

Call the manufacturer or search the manufacturer's Web site. You can also search the Internet. Even if you have the driver for a device, you should determine if there is a newer version available.

Where can I find out which hardware settings are available before I start installing a new device?

You can find this information in the Device Manager. See page 642.

What can I do if the device does not work after it has been installed?

In the Windows Help window, click the Troubleshooting book and then click Windows 98 Troubleshooters. Select the Hardware Conflict topic and then follow the instructions on your screen.

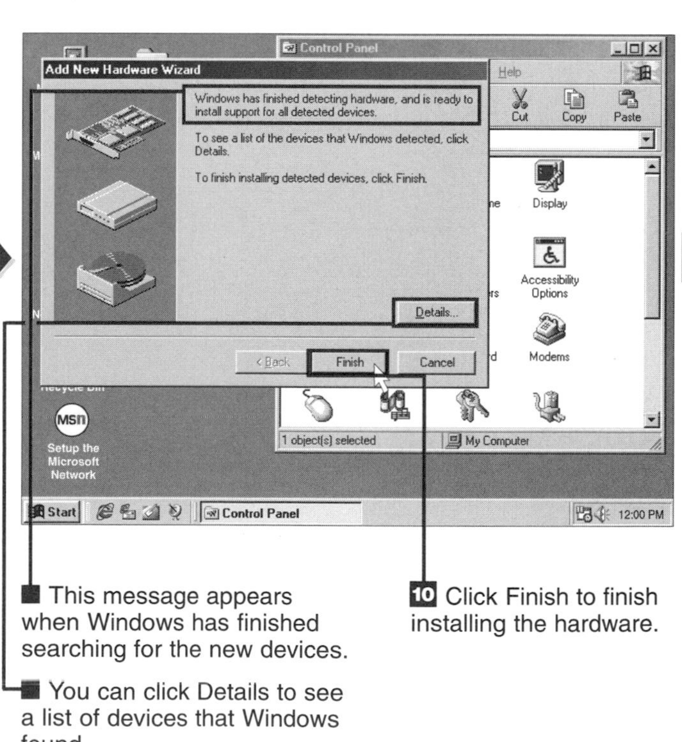

■ This message appears when Windows has finished searching for the new devices.

■ You can click Details to see a list of devices that Windows found.

10 Click Finish to finish installing the hardware.

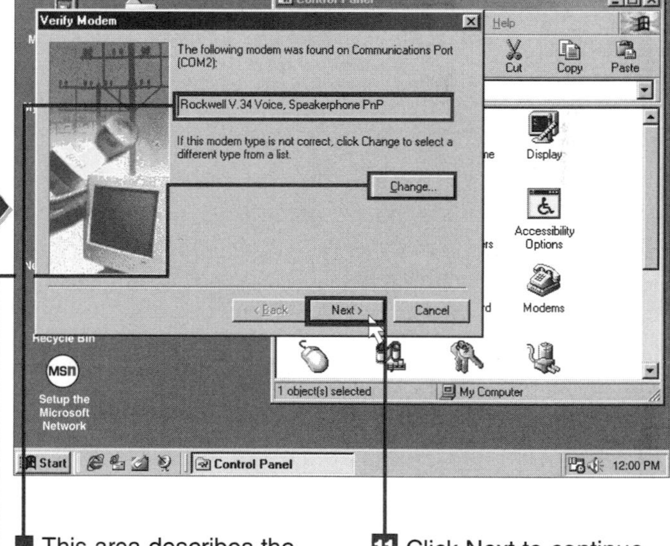

■ This area describes the device Windows found.

■ You can click Change to select a different device from a list if Windows did not find the correct device.

11 Click Next to continue.

■ You may be asked to insert the Windows 98 CD-ROM disc and to restart your computer.

■ You can now use your new hardware.

FORMAT A HARD DRIVE

You can format a hard drive on your computer to remove all the files the drive contains. This is useful if you plan to give your hard drive to someone and do not want the drive to contain any of your information. You can also format your hard drive when you want to re-install Windows 98 on your computer.

Formatting a hard drive organizes the space available on the drive so Windows can save and read files from the drive. A hard drive must be formatted before Windows can use it.

When the format is complete, you can name the hard drive. A hard drive name can be up to 11 characters long.

Your screen displays information about the drive you formatted, such as the total disk space and the total amount of space available on the drive.

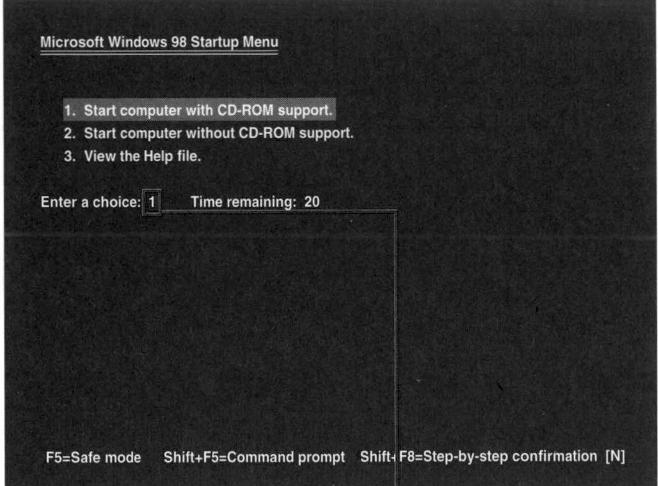
Microsoft Windows 98 Startup Menu
1. Start computer with CD-ROM support.
2. Start computer without CD-ROM support.
3. View the Help file.
Enter a choice: 1 Time remaining: 20
F5=Safe mode Shift+F5=Command prompt Shift+F8=Step-by-step confirmation [N]

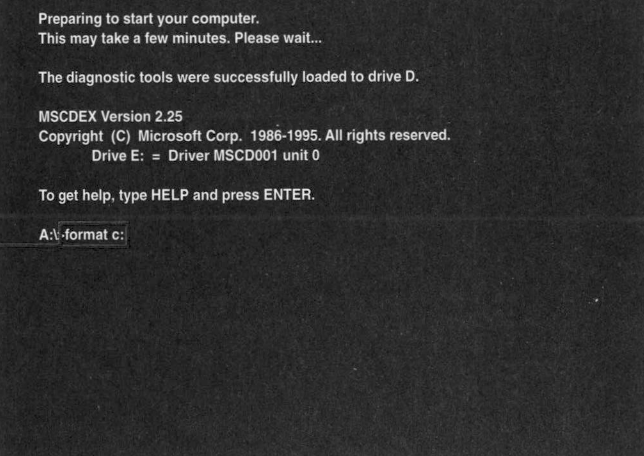
Preparing to start your computer.
This may take a few minutes. Please wait...
The diagnostic tools were successfully loaded to drive D.
MSCDEX Version 2.25
Copyright (C) Microsoft Corp. 1986-1995. All rights reserved.
Drive E: = Driver MSCD001 unit 0
To get help, type HELP and press ENTER.
A:\>format c:

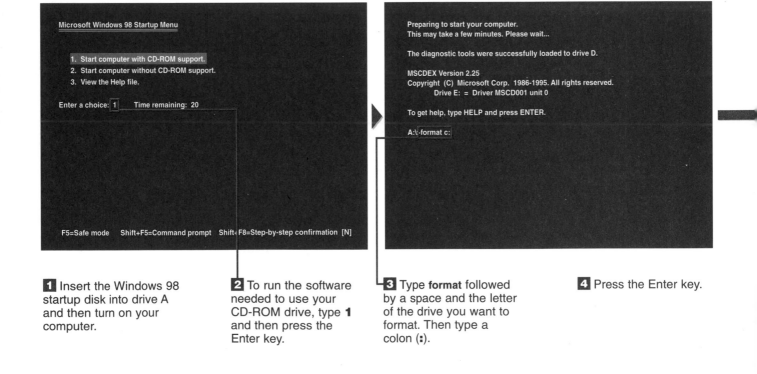

1 Insert the Windows 98 startup disk into drive A and then turn on your computer.

2 To run the software needed to use your CD-ROM drive, type **1** and then press the Enter key.

3 Type **format** followed by a space and the letter of the drive you want to format. Then type a colon (**:**).

4 Press the Enter key.

TIPS

Is formatting the hard drive a secure way to remove confidential information?

No. There are programs and drive recovery companies that determined people can use to recover information from a formatted drive.

How long will it take to format my hard drive?

It will take approximately 15 minutes to format a 2 GB drive.

I do not have a Windows 98 startup disk. How can I get one?

You can create a startup disk on any computer running Windows 98. To create a startup disk, see page 662.

I do not want to name my hard drive. What should I do?

If you do not want to name the formatted hard drive, simply press the Enter key when prompted for a name.

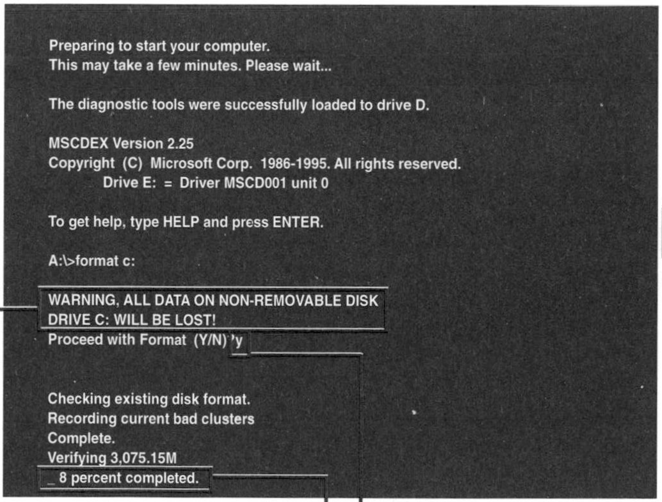

```
Preparing to start your computer.
This may take a few minutes. Please wait...

The diagnostic tools were successfully loaded to drive D.

MSCDEX Version 2.25
Copyright (C) Microsoft Corp. 1986-1995. All rights reserved.
        Drive E: = Driver MSCD001 unit 0

To get help, type HELP and press ENTER.

A:\>format c:

WARNING, ALL DATA ON NON-REMOVABLE DISK
DRIVE C: WILL BE LOST!
Proceed with Format (Y/N)?y


Checking existing disk format.
Recording current bad clusters
Complete.
Verifying 3,075.15M
_ 8 percent completed.
```

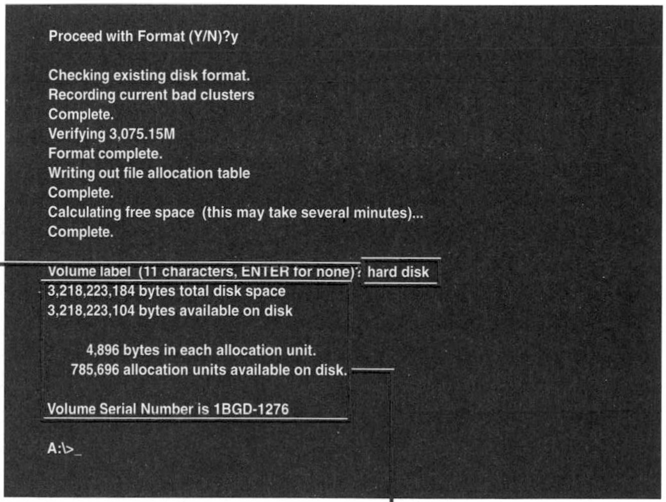

■ A message appears, warning that you will lose the data on the drive.

5 Type **Y** (for Yes) to format the drive and then press the Enter key.

■ This area displays the progress of the format.

```
Proceed with Format (Y/N)?y

Checking existing disk format.
Recording current bad clusters
Complete.
Verifying 3,075.15M
Format complete.
Writing out file allocation table
Complete.
Calculating free space (this may take several minutes)...
Complete.

Volume label (11 characters, ENTER for none)? hard disk
3,218,223,184 bytes total disk space
3,218,223,104 bytes available on disk

      4,896 bytes in each allocation unit.
    785,696 allocation units available on disk.

Volume Serial Number is 1BGD-1276

A:\>_
```

6 When the format is complete, you are asked to name the drive. Type a name for the drive and then press the Enter key.

■ Information about the drive appears, such as the total disk space.

■ You can now store data on the drive.

INSTALL WINDOWS 98

You can install Windows 98 to upgrade your computer's operating system from a previous version of Windows. Upgrading from Windows 95 can enhance Windows 98 by allowing you to continue using components that are not offered in Windows 98, such as Microsoft Fax and Microsoft Exchange.

You should set aside 30 to 60 minutes to install Windows 98. After you insert the Windows 98 installation CD-ROM disc into your drive, the Windows 98 Setup Wizard will guide you step by step through the installation.

The Windows 98 Setup Wizard displays the Microsoft License Agreement. To continue with the installation, you must accept the terms of the license agreement.

You can save your existing operating system files, which will enable you to later uninstall Windows 98 and return to your old operating system if you wish.

If you want more information about installing Windows 98, you can check the Windows 98 installation CD-ROM disc for a readme file.

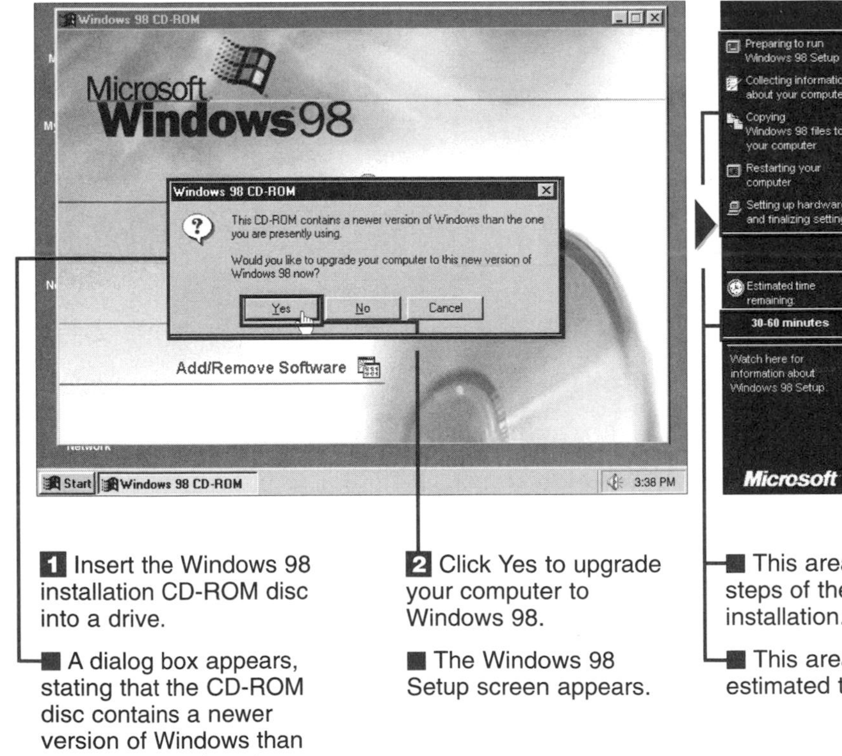

1 Insert the Windows 98 installation CD-ROM disc into a drive.

■ A dialog box appears, stating that the CD-ROM disc contains a newer version of Windows than you are currently using.

2 Click Yes to upgrade your computer to Windows 98.

■ The Windows 98 Setup screen appears.

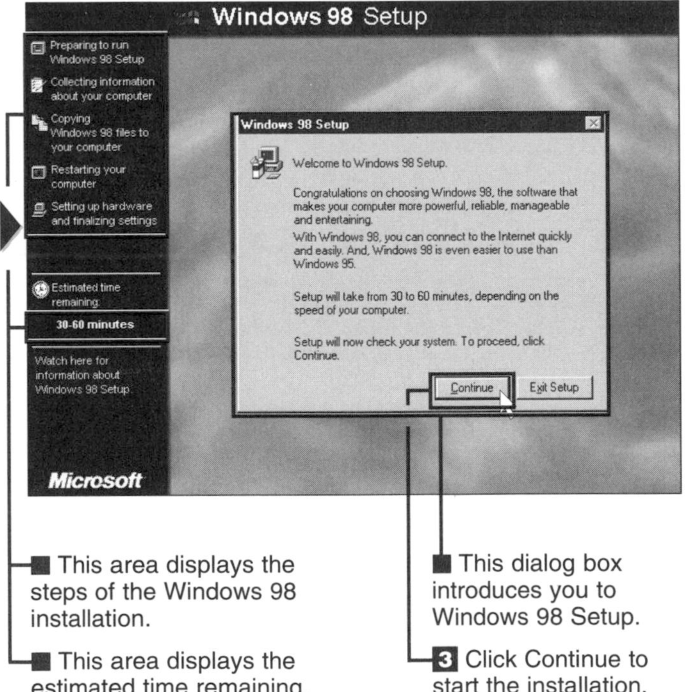

■ This area displays the steps of the Windows 98 installation.

■ This area displays the estimated time remaining.

■ This dialog box introduces you to Windows 98 Setup.

3 Click Continue to start the installation.

TIPS

The first dialog box did not appear. What should I do?

Display the contents of the drive containing the CD-ROM disc and double-click the Setup.exe file. Then follow the steps below.

The wizard is asking for a serial number. What should I do?

You may be required to enter a serial number for your Windows 98 CD-ROM disc. You can find the serial number on the disc's packaging or on the license certificate included with the disc's documentation.

How do I install Windows on a computer that does not have an operating system currently installed?

You can use the Windows 98 startup disk that came with your software to install Windows. Insert the startup disk, turn on your computer and then insert the Windows 98 installation CD-ROM disc. Follow the instructions on your screen to start the setup program.

Why didn't I get a startup disk with my Windows 98 software?

There are two versions of Windows 98 for sale. The upgrade version is designed for people who are upgrading to Windows 98 from a previous release of Windows. The full version of Windows 98 is designed for people who do not have a previous release of Windows on their computers. Only the full version of Windows 98 comes with a startup disk.

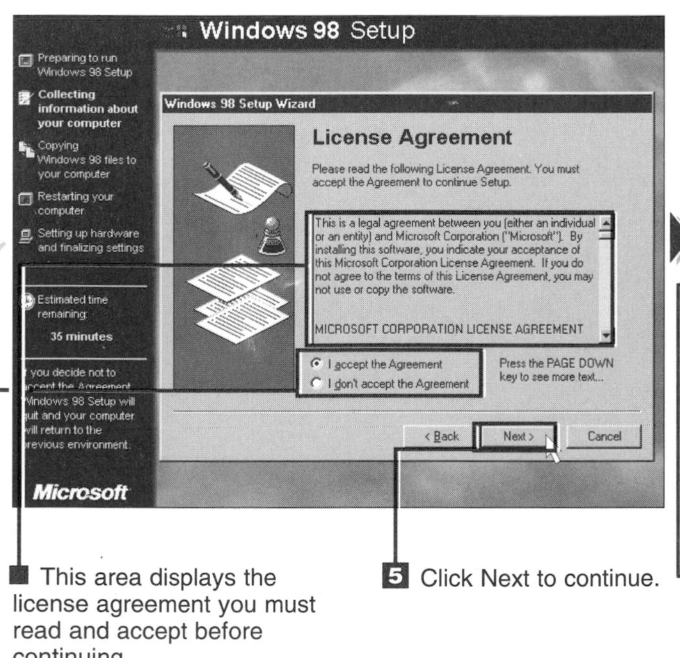

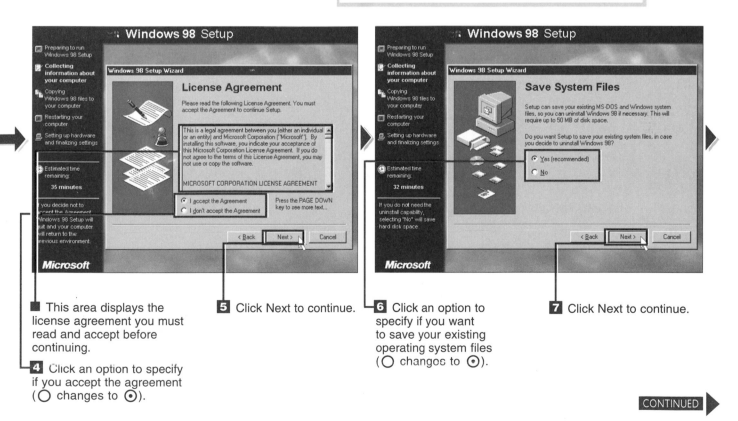

■ This area displays the license agreement you must read and accept before continuing.

4 Click an option to specify if you accept the agreement (○ changes to ⊙).

5 Click Next to continue.

6 Click an option to specify if you want to save your existing operating system files (○ changes to ⊙).

7 Click Next to continue.

CONTINUED

INSTALL WINDOWS 98 CONTINUED

During installation, the Windows 98 Setup Wizard asks you to select your country from a list. The wizard will use this information to provide you with channels it considers to be of interest to people in your country. Channels are specially designed Web sites that Windows can automatically deliver to your computer. The channels that appear in the Channel Bar on your desktop when you first start Windows 98 depend on the country you select during the installation.

The Windows 98 Setup Wizard also creates a startup disk during the installation process. This disk will help you later start Windows 98 if the operating system will not start normally. The floppy disk you use to create the startup disk must be able to store at least 1.2 MB of information. If your computer has more than one floppy disk drive, you should insert the disk into the A: drive. The A: drive is used to start the computer when the hard drive cannot.

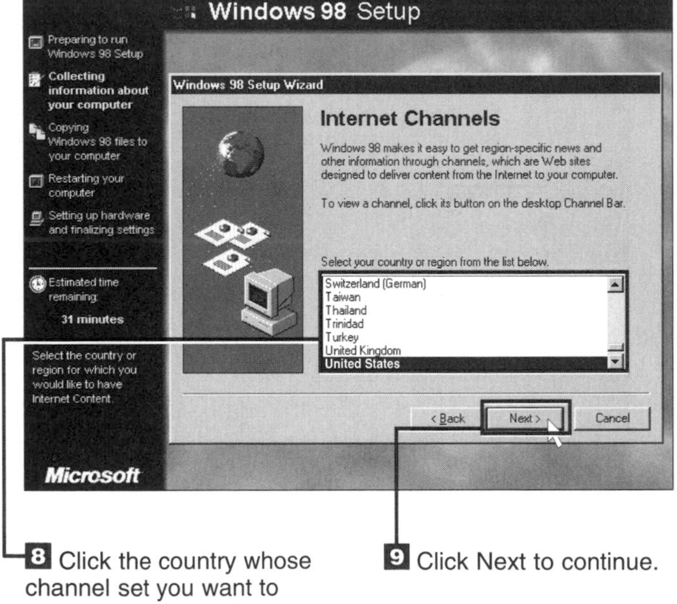

8 Click the country whose channel set you want to see on your computer.

9 Click Next to continue.

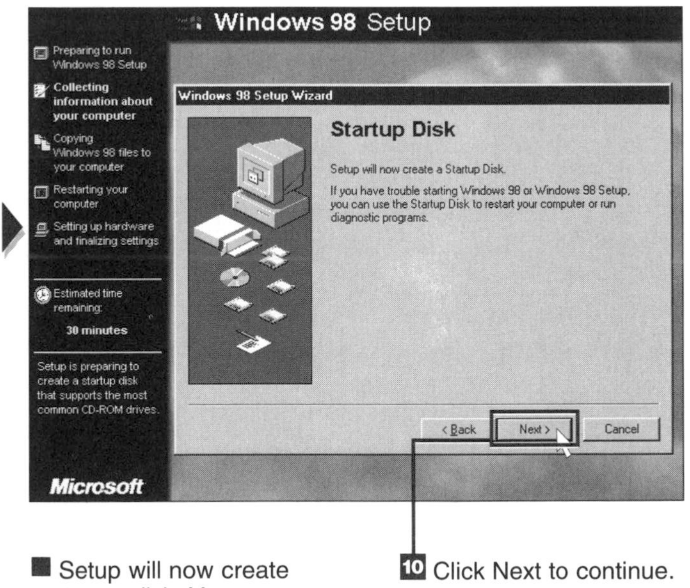

■ Setup will now create a startup disk. You can use the disk if you have trouble starting Windows 98.

10 Click Next to continue.

TIPS

Will I be able to change my list of channels later?

After you install Windows 98, you will be able to customize your channel list at any time. To add a channel, see page 564.

What is on the startup disk?

The startup disk contains basic operating system files that will allow you to start Windows 98 if Windows will not start normally. The startup disk also contains generic CD-ROM drivers that let you access the CD-ROM drive. Several utility programs are also found on the startup disk. ScanDisk checks and repairs hard disk errors. FDISK allows you to partition your hard disk. Format allows you to format your hard disk.

Can I create a startup disk later?

Yes. You can create a startup disk at any time after Windows 98 is installed. See page 662.

Why did the wizard ask me to select a setup option?

If you are installing Windows 98 on a computer that does not currently have an operating system installed, you must select the type of setup you want to use. The setup you select will determine which components are installed with Windows 98. You can later add or remove components. See page 610.

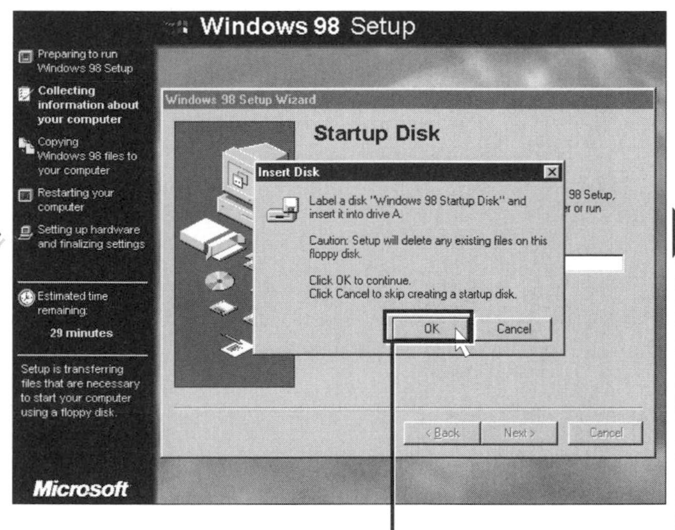

11 Label a floppy disk "Windows 98 Startup Disk."

12 Insert the floppy disk into drive A.

13 Click OK to continue.

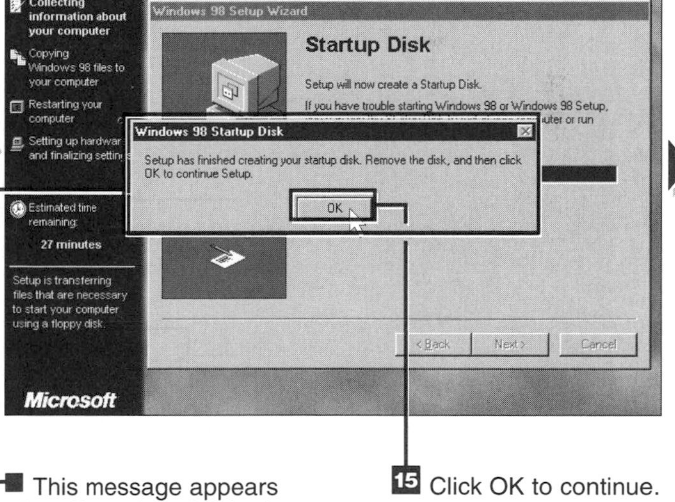

■ This message appears when Setup has finished creating your startup disk.

14 Remove the floppy disk from the drive.

15 Click OK to continue.

CONTINUED

INSTALL WINDOWS 98 CONTINUED

When the Windows 98 Setup Wizard has finished collecting information about your computer, it copies the Windows operating system files to your computer from the Windows 98 CD-ROM disc. It will take several minutes to copy all the Windows files to your computer. The wizard takes this opportunity to tell you about the features and benefits of Windows 98.

When all the files have been transferred to your computer, the wizard restarts your computer to begin the final part of the installation process.

The wizard will set up any hardware devices and Plug and Play devices it finds on your computer. If you have new devices or devices that were not properly installed before, the wizard may install or correct the software for the devices.

If your computer has a network card, you may be asked to enter a password. If you used a password with your previous version of Windows, you can continue to use the password with Windows 98.

When the installation process is complete, Windows 98 will start and display the Welcome to Windows 98 dialog box.

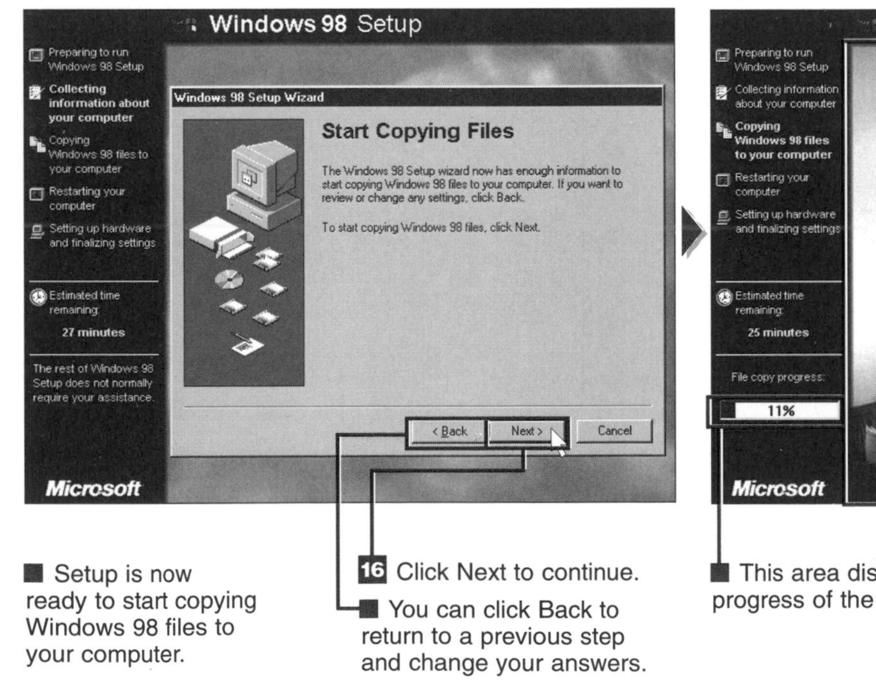

■ Setup is now ready to start copying Windows 98 files to your computer.

16 Click Next to continue.

■ You can click Back to return to a previous step and change your answers.

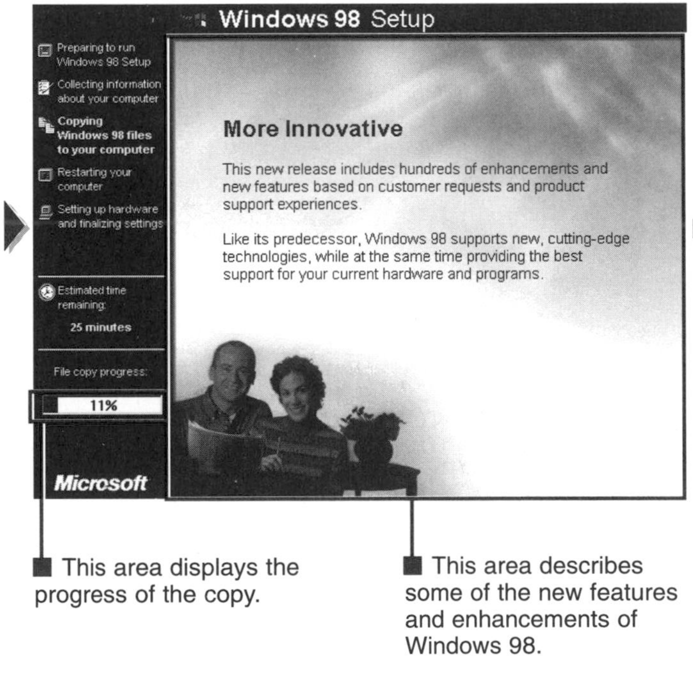

■ This area displays the progress of the copy.

■ This area describes some of the new features and enhancements of Windows 98.

TIPS

I upgraded from Windows 3.1. How can I get my Program Manager groups back?

Display the Start menu and then click Run. Type **grpconv /m**. A dialog box displays the Program Manager groups. Select the group you want to convert to a folder. You can then save the folder on your desktop for easy access.

Can I uninstall Windows 98 after upgrading from a previous version?

If you have not converted your hard drive to FAT32 and have not installed the disk compression component for Windows 98, you can uninstall the operating system. In the Control Panel window, double-click the Add/Remove Programs icon and then click the Install/Uninstall tab. Select Uninstall Windows 98 and then click the Add/Remove button.

Can I remove the files for my old operating system?

If you are sure you will not want to later uninstall Windows 98, display the Control Panel window and double-click the Add/Remove Programs icon. Select the Install/Uninstall tab, click Delete Windows 98 uninstall information and then click the Add/Remove button. Windows automatically removes these files for you when you convert your hard drive to FAT32 or when you install the disk compression component.

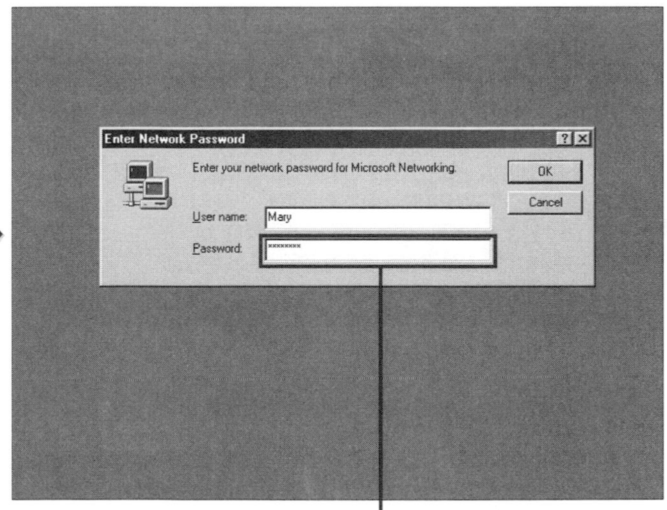

■ When the setup is complete, the Enter Network Password dialog box may appear.

17 Type your password and then press the Enter key.

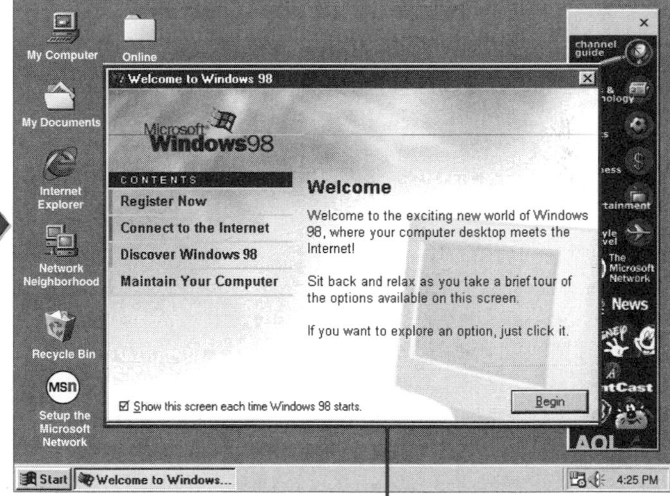

■ Windows 98 starts.

■ The Welcome to Windows 98 dialog box appears, welcoming you to Windows 98.

UPDATE WINDOWS 98

You can use the Windows Update feature to automatically connect to the Windows Update page on the World Wide Web.

The Windows Update Web page lets you access the Update Wizard to add new capabilities to your computer, fix bugs and install components to improve computer performance. The wizard uses the latest information available from Microsoft to check for outdated software on your computer. You can then choose from a list of updates that may be useful for your computer. If you later decide that the update was not useful, you can use the wizard to remove the update and restore your computer to its previous state.

Some updates may require you to restart your computer. You should close your documents and programs before using the Update Wizard.

You can also use the Windows Update feature to access technical support information available from Microsoft's Web site. You can type a question or keyword to search Microsoft's Knowledge Base, Troubleshooting Wizards and downloadable files for information on a topic of interest.

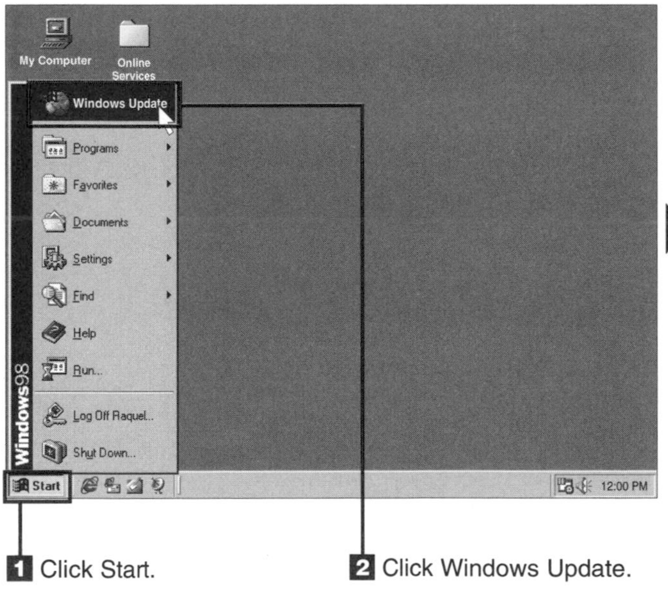

1 Click Start.

2 Click Windows Update.

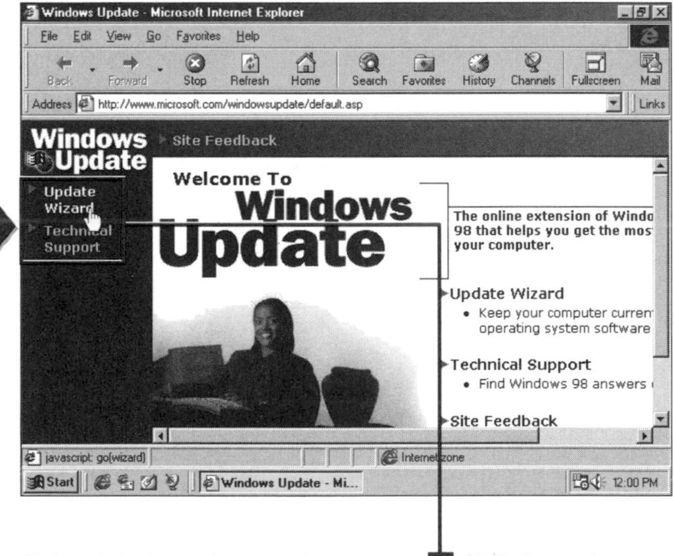

■ The Windows Update Web page appears. You can use this page to update Windows 98.

Note: If you are not connected to the Internet, a dialog box may appear that allows you to connect.

3 Click the task you want to perform.

TIPS

Do I need to initialize ActiveX objects to use the Update Wizard?

Yes. ActiveX objects are small programs that the Update Wizard needs to run. Windows asks permission before transferring these programs to your computer.

When I started the Update Wizard, I was asked if I wanted to register. Should I register?

If you have not registered your copy of Windows 98, you must do so before you can use the Update Wizard or the Technical Support feature. When you are asked to register, click Yes and then follow the instructions on your screen.

Are other updates for Windows 98 available?

Microsoft may occasionally make other Windows 98 updates or utilities available. For more information, check the Microsoft Web site at www.microsoft.com/windows98

Are there other sources for updates?

Manufacturers of devices such as sound cards and video adapters often offer software driver updates at their Web sites. The manufacturers of some Windows components also provide updates at their Web sites. For example, you may be able to find updates for HyperTerminal at www.hilgraeve.com and updates for the Imaging component at www.eastmansoftware.com

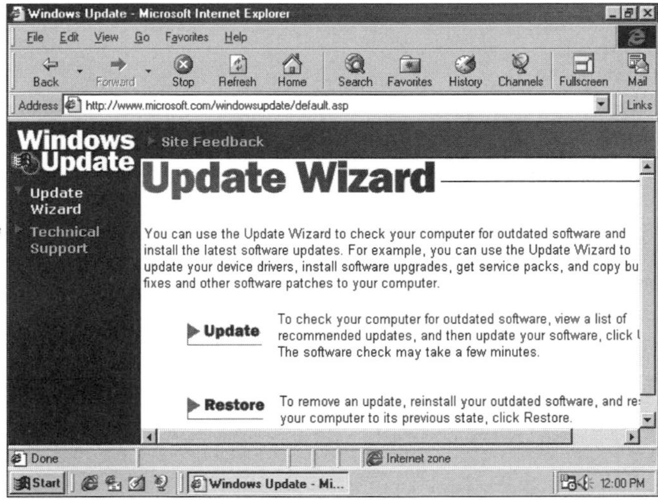

UPDATE WIZARD

■ You can use the Update Wizard to check your computer for outdated software and install the latest software updates.

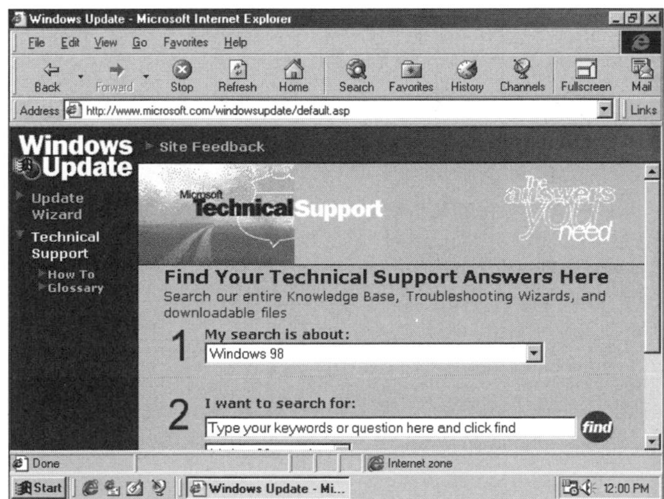

TECHNICAL SUPPORT

■ You can search the Microsoft Technical Support Web site to quickly find answers to your questions.

UTILITIES YOU CAN USE WITH WINDOWS 98

There are many utility programs available that you can use with Windows 98. You can obtain programs that make computer maintenance tasks easier, protect your computer from viruses and enhance Windows features.

Adobe Acrobat and Acrobat Reader

Adobe Systems Incorporated at www.adobe.com

You can use Adobe Acrobat to create Portable Document Format (.pdf) files. These files allow you to display documents such as books and magazines on the screen exactly as they appear in printed form. A .pdf file stores all of the font and formatting information with the document. The user does not need to have the program or fonts used to create the document installed on their computer. Acrobat can create .pdf files from any program.

The Acrobat Reader is a program used to view .pdf files. The Acrobat Reader includes the ability to view and print .pdf files directly from a Web browser. There are versions of the Acrobat Reader for many different operating systems. This program is free and is available from Adobe's Web site.

Norton Utilities

Symantec Corporation at www.symantec.com

Norton Utilities includes several components to help you with computer maintenance tasks. The Norton System Doctor monitors your computer for potential problems. Norton CrashGuard will try to intercept a potential crash so you can save your work before the program freezes.

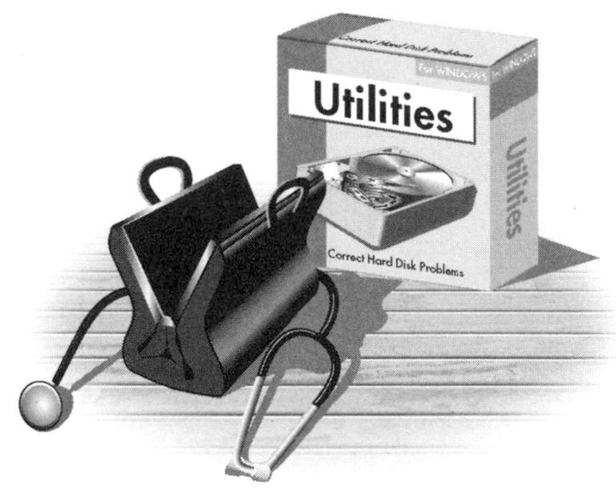

Norton Utilities also provides advanced tools you can use to optimize the performance of your computer. Speed Disk is a disk defragmenter. Norton SpeedStart makes your programs start faster. The Norton Optimization Wizard includes several tools you can use, such as Registry Optimization.

You can use the LiveUpdate Pro feature to automatically update Norton Utilities and other programs on your computer from the Internet.

Paint Shop Pro

Jasc Software Inc. at www.jasc.com

Paint Shop Pro is an inexpensive and easy-to-use graphics program you can use to view, edit and convert images from over 30 image formats. The supported formats include vector image formats and bitmap image formats.

You can use Paint Shop Pro's selection of drawing and painting tools to manipulate and create pictures. Paint Shop Pro also has the tools you need to create images for Web pages, retouch photos and add special effects, such as embossing, chisel effects and drop shadows.

Paint Shop Pro allows you to display multiple images at once and supports the TWAIN standard to work with scanners. The program also includes a screen capture feature which allows you to select specific areas of the screen and include the mouse pointer.

You can download a shareware version of Paint Shop Pro from the Jasc Web site.

PowerDesk

Mijenix Corporation at www.mijenix.com

PowerDesk includes utility programs that can help make Windows 98 easier to use.

PowerDesk ExplorerPlus replaces Windows Explorer and has the ability to display, open and manage files in .zip and other archive formats. To simplify drag and drop operations, the ExplorerPlus window displays multiple panes. ExplorerPlus also offers a built-in file viewer.

The PowerDesk File Finder can make searching for files easier. The File Finder offers the ability to refine your search, view the contents of the files you have found and print a list of all the files found.

There is a time-limited evaluation version of PowerDesk available at Mijenix's Web site.

CONTINUED

UTILITIES YOU CAN USE WITH WINDOWS 98 CONTINUED

Quick View Plus

Inso Corporation at www.inso.com

Windows 98 includes Quick View, which allows you to preview a file before you open it. You can extend Quick View's capabilities with Quick View Plus. Quick View Plus accurately displays the fonts, tables, headers, footers, page numbers and embedded graphics in a document. You can preview a document even if you do not have the program used to create the document installed on your computer.

Quick View Plus enables you to preview more file types than Quick View. You can preview graphic file types like those created in CorelDRAW and Micrografx Designer and image file types such as .jpg, .gif and .tiff. You can also use Quick View Plus to work with many compressed file types, including .zip files.

Quick View Plus can print the documents it displays. You can use the Quick View Plus window to cut and paste items between any of the supported file types.

There is a time-limited trial version of Quick View Plus available at Inso's Web site.

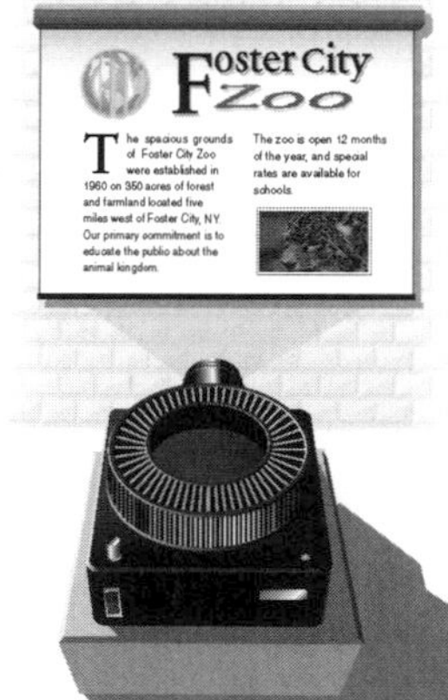

VirusScan Security Suite

McAfee Associates at www.mcafeemall.com

You can reduce the risk of a virus infecting your computer by using an anti-virus program. A virus is a program that can cause problems ranging from displaying annoying messages on your screen to erasing all the information on your hard drive.

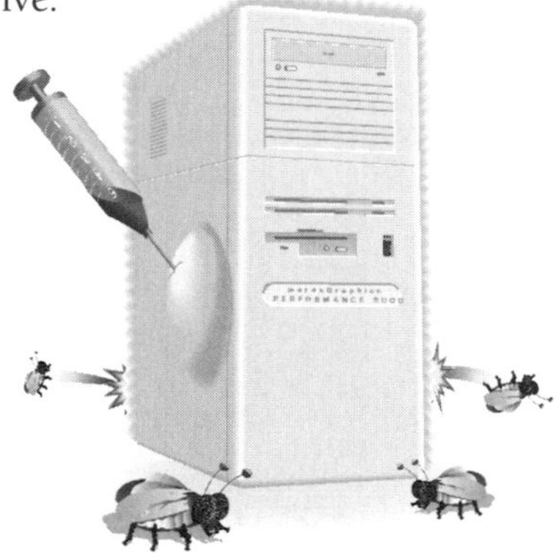

McAfee offers the VirusScan Security Suite which contains anti-virus programs, such as VirusScan and WebScanX. VirusScan checks for and removes viruses that are already on your computer. WebScanX provides virus protection for files you download from the Web and for e-mail attachments.

The VirusScan Security Suite also provides the SecureCast feature, which automatically delivers new versions of the VirusScan Security Suite to your computer.

WinFax PRO

Symantec Corporation at www.symantec.com

With WinFax PRO, you can use your computer's fax modem to send and receive faxes. WinFax PRO sends and receives faxes in the background so you can continue your work uninterrupted.

You can use WinFax PRO's drag and drop feature to customize your phone books and fax cover pages.

You can have WinFax PRO answer all incoming calls to automatically receive faxes. If you use one phone line for both fax and voice calls, you can also activate WinFax PRO manually to receive faxes.

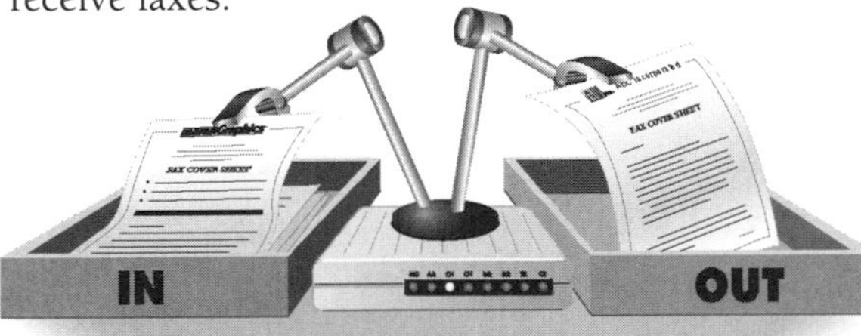

You can use WinFax PRO's Optical Character Recognition capabilities to convert the faxes you receive into documents that can be edited using a word processor or spreadsheet.

There is a time-limited trial version of WinFax PRO available at Symantec's Web site.

WinZip

Nico Mak Computing, Inc. at www.winzip.com

WinZip compresses files to make it easier and faster to transfer information from one computer to another. Many of the files you transfer to your computer from online services or the Internet are in the .zip format.

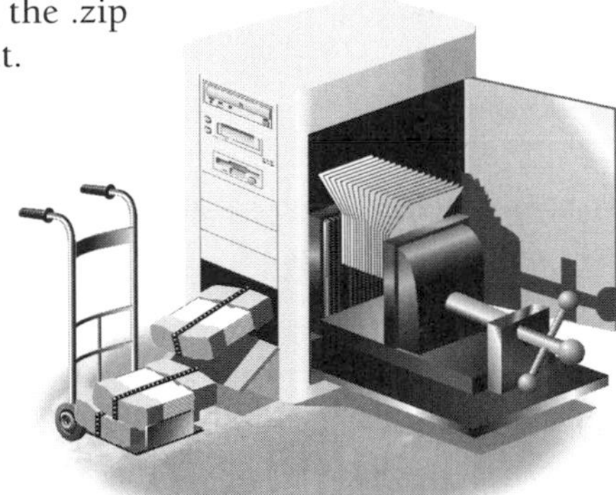

WinZip allows you to point and click or drag and drop to view, extract, add, delete and test .zip files.

The Install/Try/Uninstall feature makes it easy to evaluate programs in the .zip format. WinZip lets you try the program. When you are done, WinZip can uninstall the program.

WinZip also supports many other compressed and encoded file formats.

There is an evaluation version of WinZip available at the WinZip Web site. For information on using WinZip, see pages 636 to 639.

USING WINZIP TO WORK WITH COMPRESSED FILES

WinZip compresses, or squeezes, files to make it easier and faster to transfer information from one computer to another. Although WinZip is not included with Windows 98, you will find it essential once you start transferring files from online services or the Internet. Many of the files that you transfer, or download, to your computer will be in the .zip format.

Groups of files are often compressed and then packaged into a single .zip file. This saves you from having to transfer each file to your computer individually.

Before you can use a compressed file, you have to unzip, or separate and decompress, the files.

There are two ways you can use WinZip to work with compressed files. The WinZip Wizard takes you through the unzipping process step by step. WinZip Classic displays the files in a window and provides additional capabilities for advanced users.

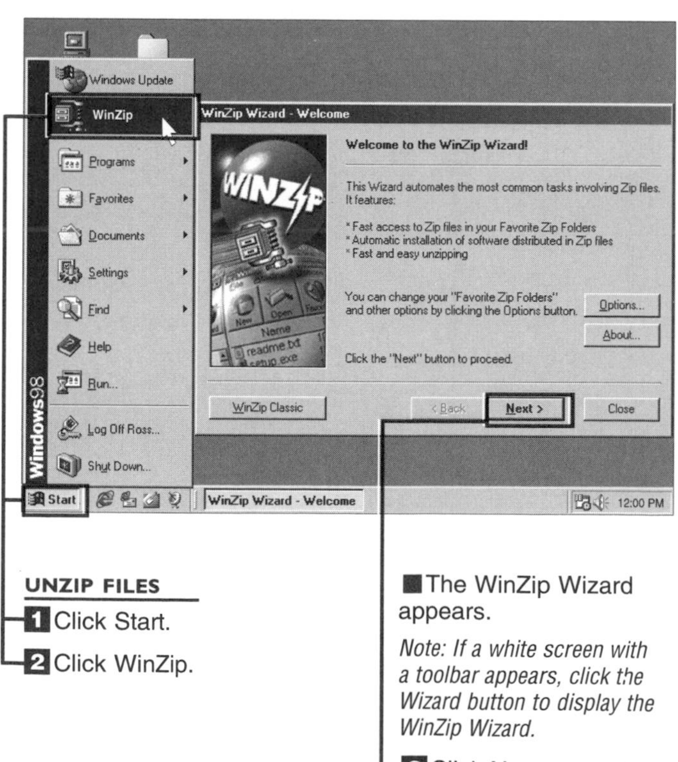

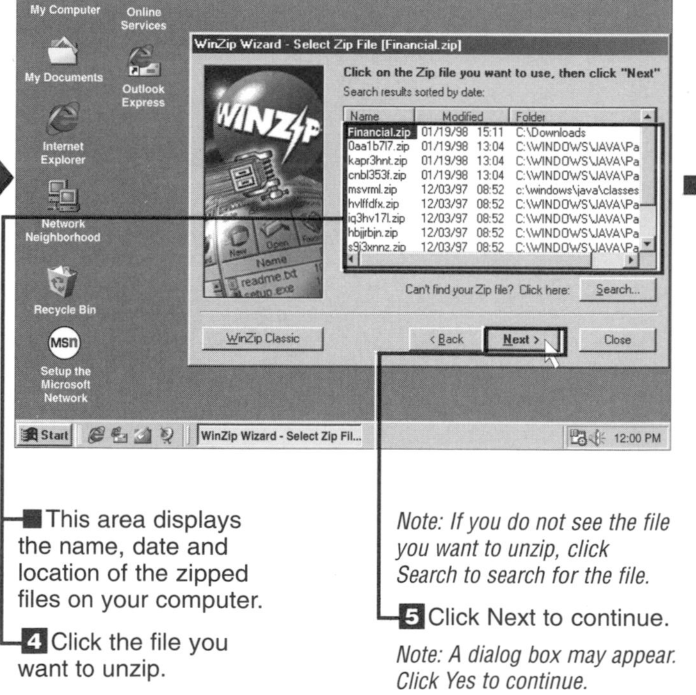

UNZIP FILES

1. Click Start.
2. Click WinZip.

■ The WinZip Wizard appears.

Note: If a white screen with a toolbar appears, click the Wizard button to display the WinZip Wizard.

3. Click Next to continue.

■ This area displays the name, date and location of the zipped files on your computer.

4. Click the file you want to unzip.

Note: If you do not see the file you want to unzip, click Search to search for the file.

5. Click Next to continue.

Note: A dialog box may appear. Click Yes to continue.

TIPS

How do I get WinZip?

WinZip is available on the Web at www.winzip.com. Select to download the evaluation version of WinZip and then select the 32-bit version. You can save the file to a disk. WinZip will take a few minutes to transfer to your computer. When the transfer is complete, double-click the WinZip icon to start installing WinZip and then follow the instructions on your screen.

Can I unzip a file from a My Computer or Windows Explorer window?

Once WinZip is installed, the program will open when you double-click a file with the .zip extension. In a My Computer or Windows Explorer window, .zip files display the or icon.

Are there other programs that work with .zip files?

Mijenix PowerDesk and Inso Quick View Plus are two other programs that work with .zip files. For information about these and other utility programs, see pages 632 to 635.

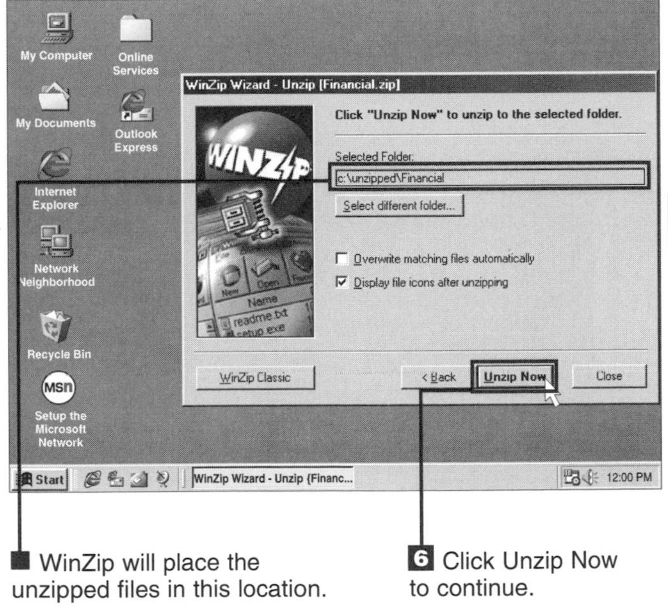

■ WinZip will place the unzipped files in this location.

Note: You can click Select different folder to place the unzipped files in a different location.

6 Click Unzip Now to continue.

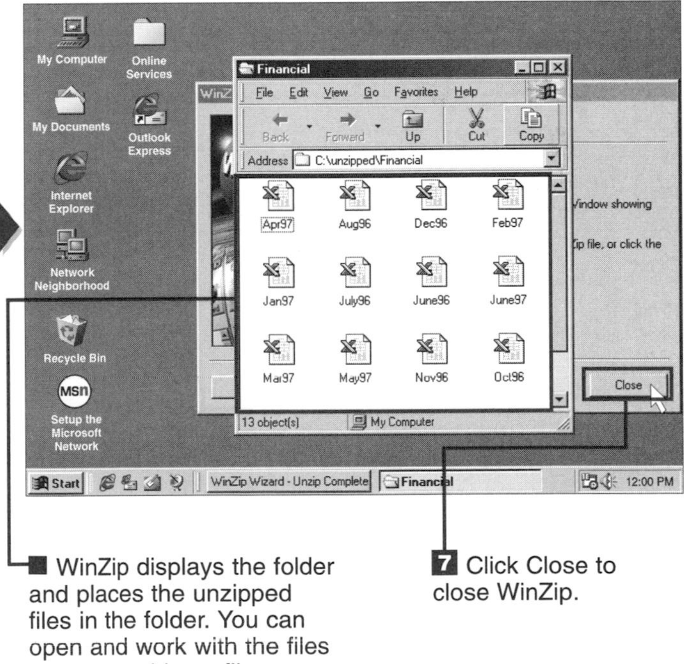

■ WinZip displays the folder and places the unzipped files in the folder. You can open and work with the files as you would any file on your computer.

7 Click Close to close WinZip.

CONTINUED

USING WINZIP TO WORK WITH COMPRESSED FILES CONTINUED

You can combine several files into one compressed .zip file. The .zip file acts like a folder that contains the files you want to send. Zipped files take up less space and are easier to transfer than the original files.

The .zip format is widely used. WinZip is not the only program that allows you to work with .zip files. There are many other programs available for MS-DOS and previous versions of Windows that allow you to open and manage .zip files. When creating a .zip file that will be used on a computer that does not use Windows 95 or 98, remember that some operating systems cannot use long file names.

You can create a .zip file to store files on a floppy disk. You can also use WinZip to compress and save documents that you do not often need in an archive. This enables you to keep the files on your hard drive, but the files will take up less space.

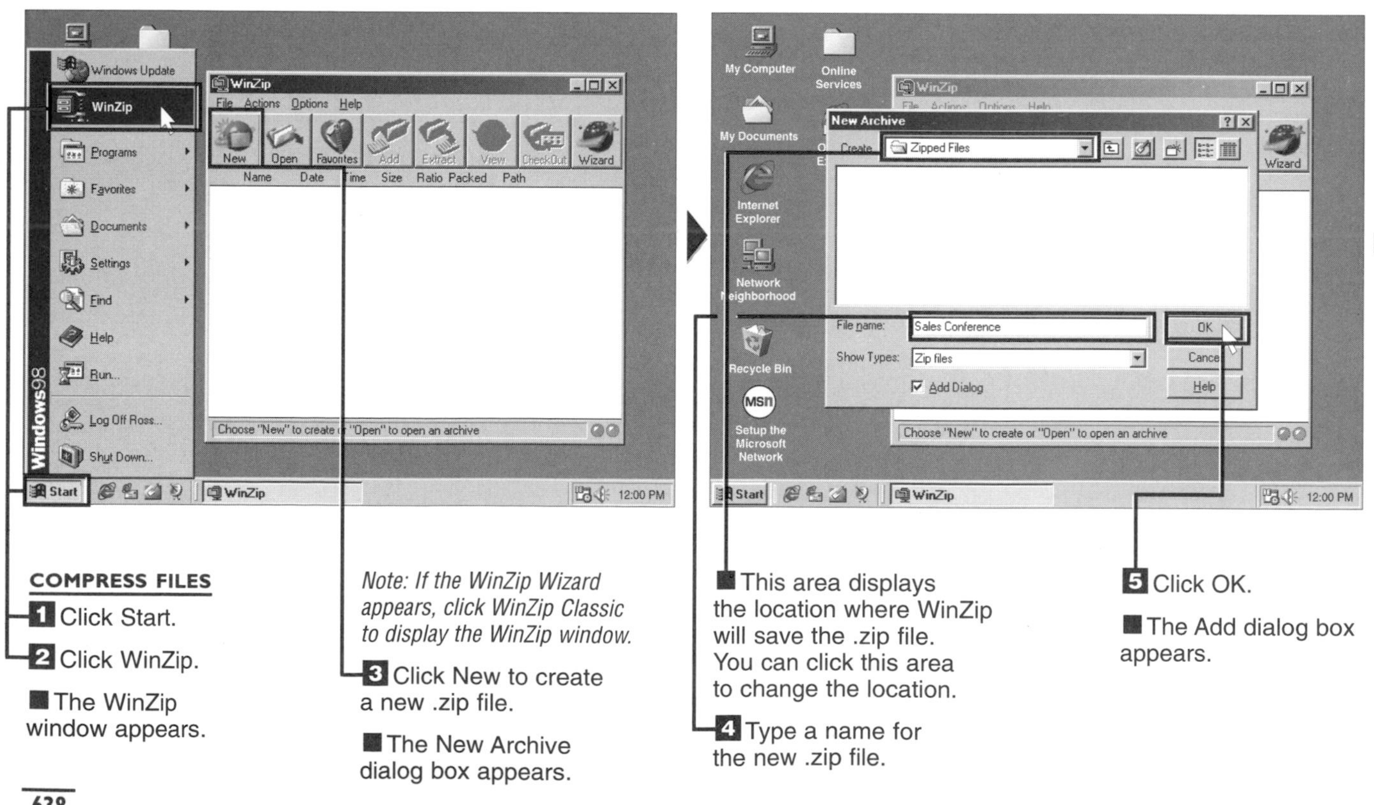

COMPRESS FILES

1 Click Start.

2 Click WinZip.

■ The WinZip window appears.

Note: If the WinZip Wizard appears, click WinZip Classic to display the WinZip window.

3 Click New to create a new .zip file.

■ The New Archive dialog box appears.

■ This area displays the location where WinZip will save the .zip file. You can click this area to change the location.

4 Type a name for the new .zip file.

5 Click OK.

■ The Add dialog box appears.

Is there another way to add more files to a .zip file?

You can drag and drop any file onto the icon for a .zip file or into the open WinZip window.

How do I update the files contained in a .zip file?

In the WinZip window, use the Open button to display the contents of the .zip file that needs to be updated. Click Add and use the Action list to select Freshen Existing Files. Then select the files you want to update and click Freshen.

Can I uncompress only one file from a .zip file?

If a .zip file contains several files, you can uncompress a single file from the .zip file. In the WinZip window, select the file you want to uncompress and then click the Extract button.

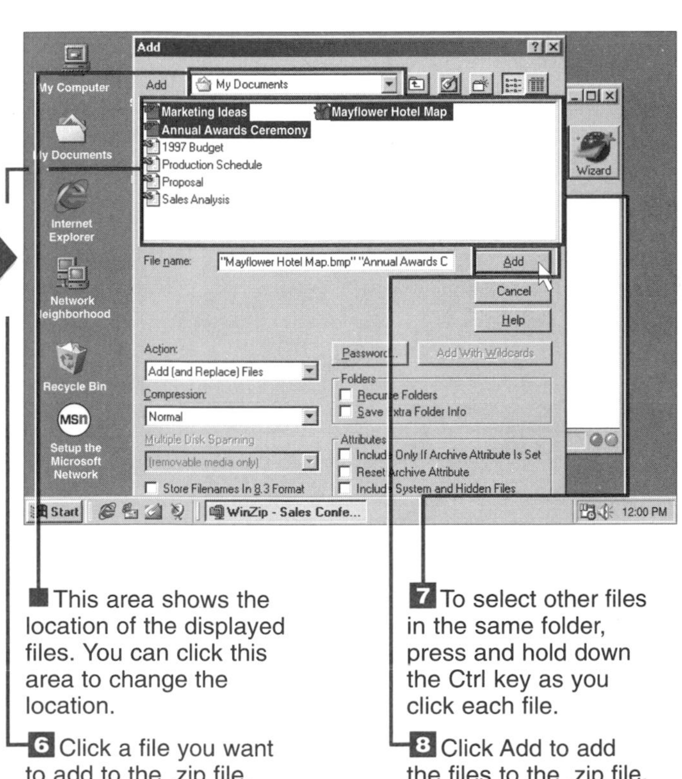

■ This area shows the location of the displayed files. You can click this area to change the location.

6 Click a file you want to add to the .zip file.

7 To select other files in the same folder, press and hold down the Ctrl key as you click each file.

8 Click Add to add the files to the .zip file.

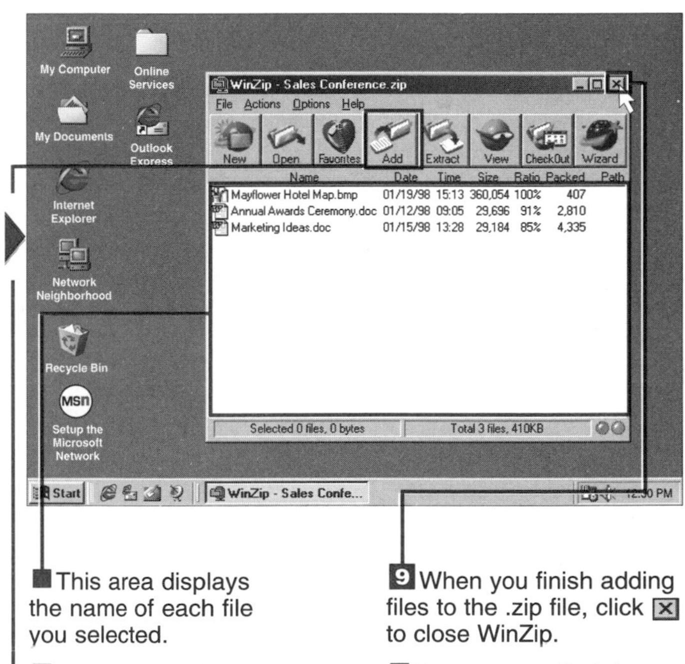

■ This area displays the name of each file you selected.

■ To add more files to the .zip file, click Add to once again display the Add dialog box.

9 When you finish adding files to the .zip file, click ☒ to close WinZip.

■ You can now find the .zip file on your computer.

VIEW HARDWARE INFORMATION

If you are having problems with your computer, the Device Manager can often help you identify the problem and find a solution.

The Device Manager organizes hardware devices into categories, such as disk drives and monitors. Each category lists the specific hardware devices installed on your computer.

If there is a problem with a hardware device, the Device Manager displays a symbol, such as an X or an exclamation mark (!), with the icon for the hardware device. These symbols can simplify the task of identifying and solving problems with your hardware.

The Device Manager information can be helpful when adding a new hardware device to your computer. You can quickly view which hardware devices are already installed on your computer.

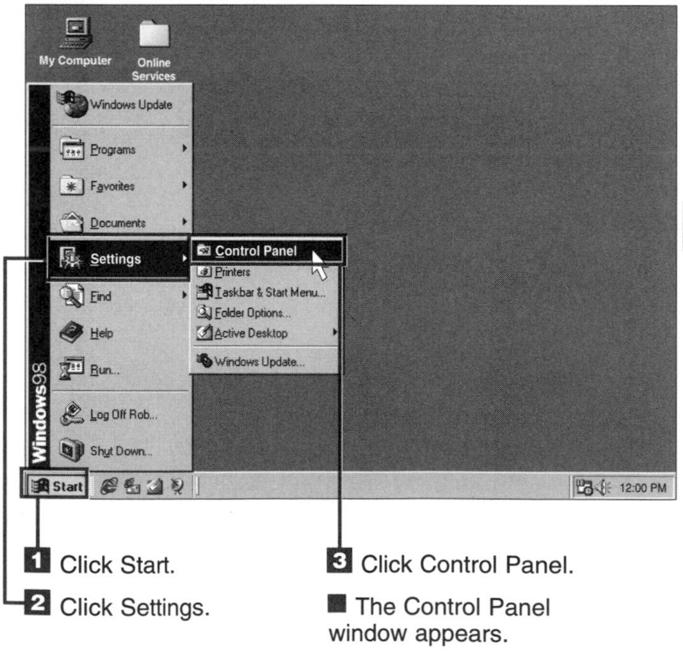

1 Click Start.

2 Click Settings.

3 Click Control Panel.

■ The Control Panel window appears.

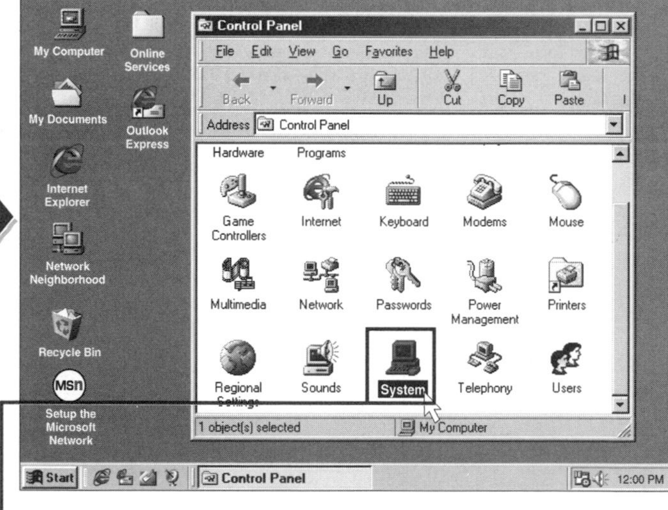

4 Double-click System.

■ The System Properties dialog box appears.

Note: You can also right-click My Computer and select Properties to display the System Properties dialog box .

TIPS

What do the symbols displayed with hardware devices in the Device Manager mean?

A hardware device icon displaying a red X indicates the hardware will not work. This may occur if two devices are trying to use the same hardware settings. An icon with a yellow exclamation mark (!) indicates the hardware may not work. For example, the hardware may not have been properly installed.

Can I use the Device Manager in safe mode?

If there is a problem with your computer and you must start it in safe mode, you can open the System Properties dialog box and display the Device Manager to find out whether the problem is being caused by a malfunctioning hardware device. For information on safe mode, see page 664.

How do I remove a hardware device from my computer?

You may want to remove a hardware device when you are upgrading a device or when the device is outdated. To remove a device, you must first physically remove the device from your computer. To remove the device from the Device Manager, select the device you want to delete and then click the Remove button. When you remove a hardware device, all related files are deleted.

How do I re-install a hardware device on my computer?

To re-install a hardware device, use the Add New Hardware icon in the Control Panel. See page 618.

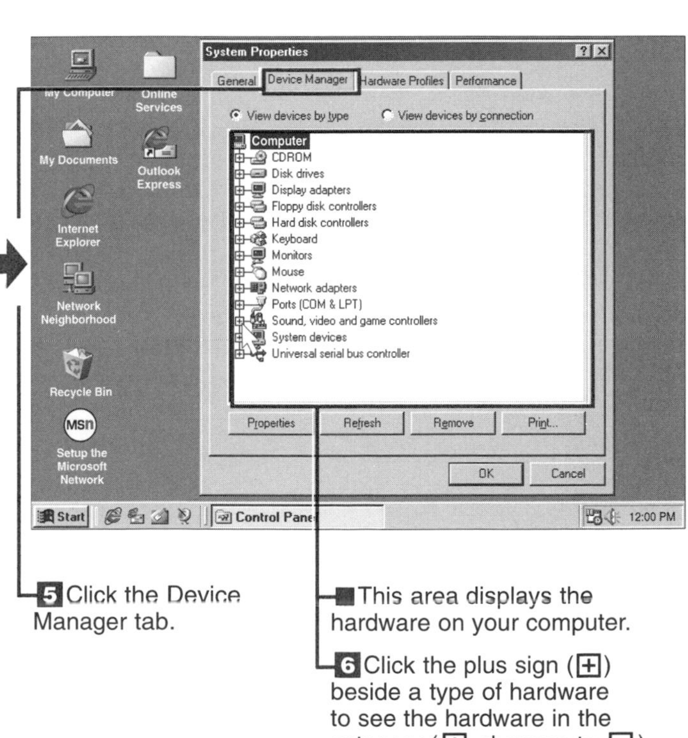

5 Click the Device Manager tab.

■ This area displays the hardware on your computer.

6 Click the plus sign (⊞) beside a type of hardware to see the hardware in the category (⊞ changes to ⊟).

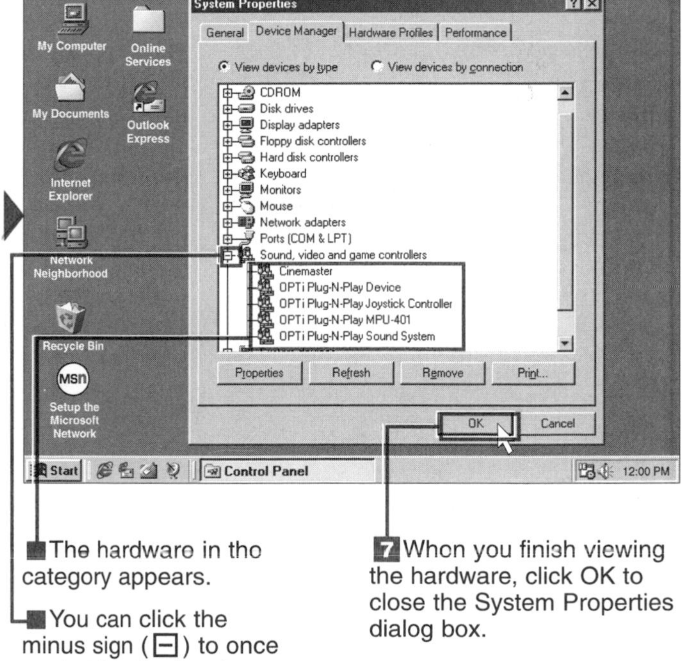

■ The hardware in the category appears.

■ You can click the minus sign (⊟) to once again hide the hardware in the category.

7 When you finish viewing the hardware, click OK to close the System Properties dialog box.

VIEW OR CHANGE RESOURCES FOR HARDWARE

You can use the Device Manager to identify which resources on your computer are available to use with new hardware.

There are four main types of resources on your computer including Interrupt Requests (IRQ), Direct Memory Access (DMA) channels, Input/Output (I/O) ports and Memory. Some hardware devices require several resources to run properly.

An IRQ tells the computer that the device needs attention. The DMA channel lets a device communicate directly with your computer's memory to speed up the processing of information. The I/O address specifies which area of memory a device uses to communicate with the computer.

The Memory resource displays the memory used by each device on your computer.

If the resource settings conflict with the settings for another device, the devices may not work properly. You can view the resources used by a hardware device and find out if there are any conflicts with the device.

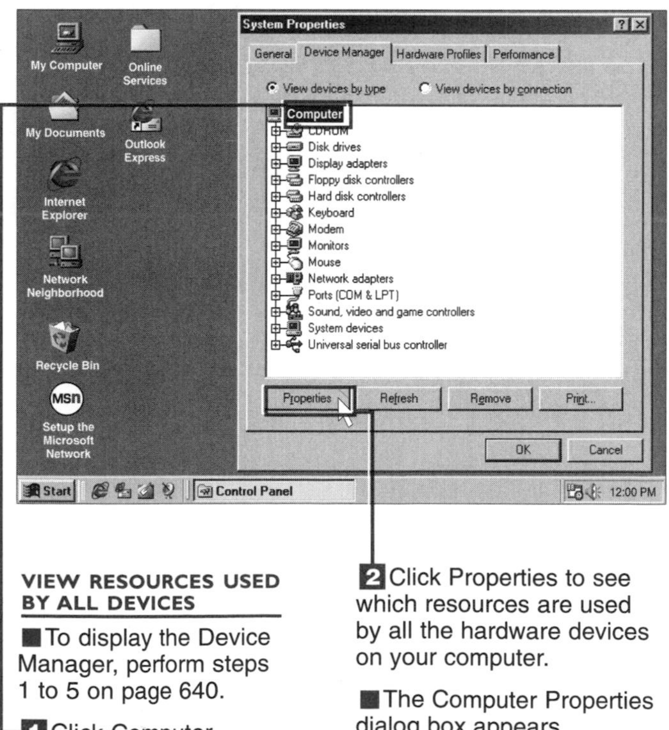

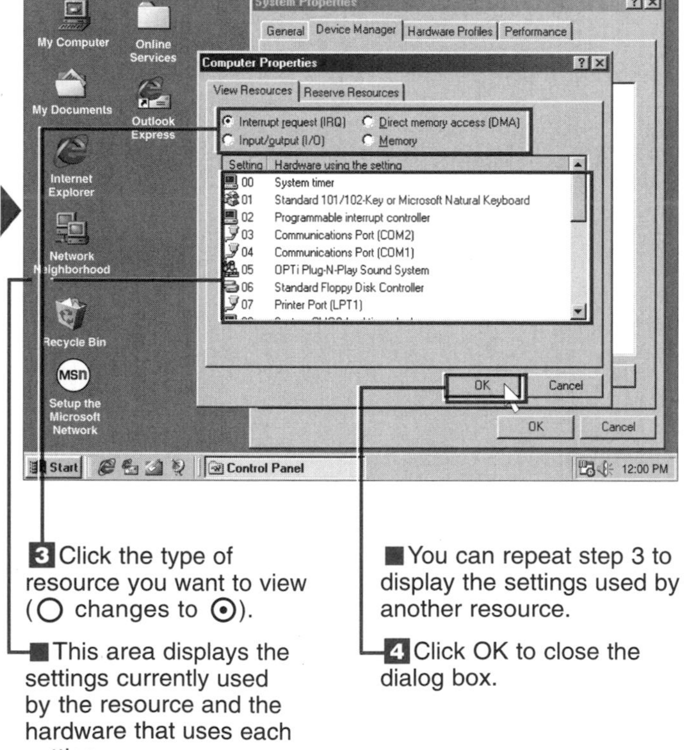

VIEW RESOURCES USED BY ALL DEVICES

■ To display the Device Manager, perform steps 1 to 5 on page 640.

1 Click Computer.

2 Click Properties to see which resources are used by all the hardware devices on your computer.

■ The Computer Properties dialog box appears.

3 Click the type of resource you want to view (○ changes to ⊙).

■ This area displays the settings currently used by the resource and the hardware that uses each setting.

■ You can repeat step 3 to display the settings used by another resource.

4 Click OK to close the dialog box.

TIPS

What is the best way to resolve hardware conflicts?

On the Start menu, select Help. Click the Contents tab and then click Troubleshooting. Click Windows 98 Troubleshooters and then select the Hardware Conflict topic. Windows Help will ask you questions to help resolve the hardware conflict.

Can I print my hardware information?

You can use the Print button in the System Properties dialog box to print the information you want. The System summary option prints the information displayed in the Computer Properties dialog box. The Selected class or device option prints the resource information for the device you selected. The All devices and system summary option prints detailed information about all the hardware devices and the versions of the drivers being used.

I just installed a device in my computer. Why doesn't the device appear in the System Properties dialog box?

Many devices, such as PC cards for laptop computers and devices that connect to a universal serial bus, can be attached to or disconnected from a computer while the computer is running. You do not need to restart your computer for these devices to work. After installing or removing a device, you can use the Refresh button in the System Properties dialog box to update the list of devices and view the new settings.

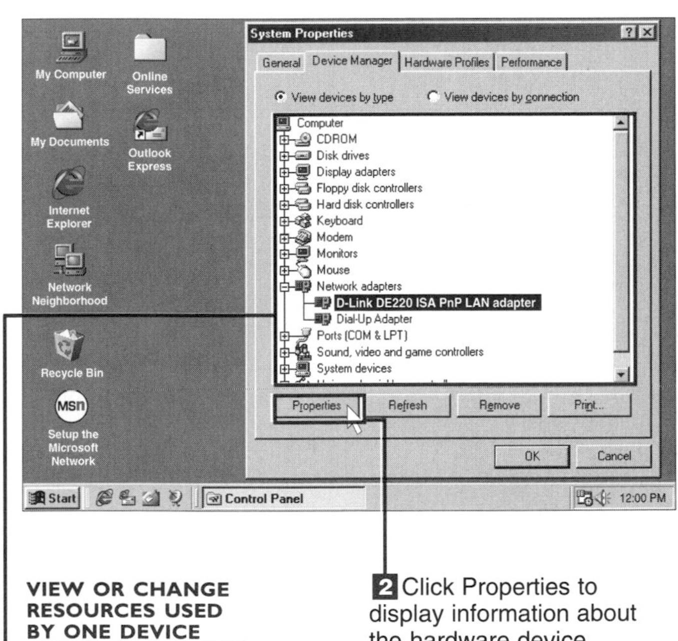

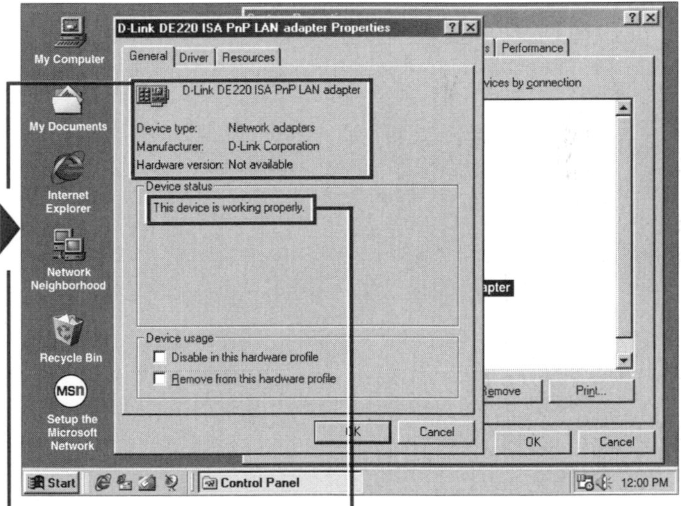

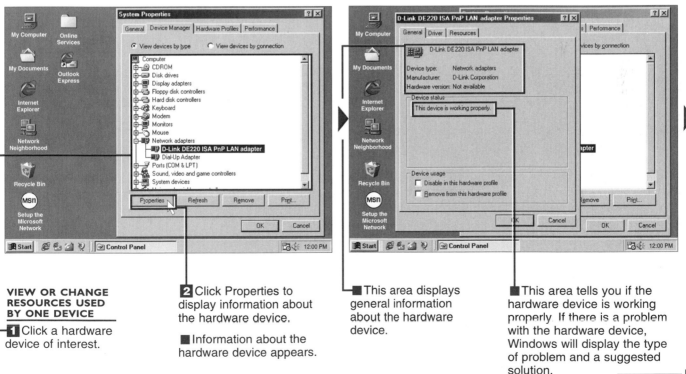

VIEW OR CHANGE RESOURCES USED BY ONE DEVICE

1 Click a hardware device of interest.

2 Click Properties to display information about the hardware device.

■ Information about the hardware device appears.

■ This area displays general information about the hardware device.

■ This area tells you if the hardware device is working properly. If there is a problem with the hardware device, Windows will display the type of problem and a suggested solution.

CONTINUED

VIEW OR CHANGE RESOURCES FOR HARDWARE CONTINUED

If you have conflicts between your hardware devices, you may need to change some of the resource settings the hardware devices use. The resource settings control the communication between the computer and its hardware devices. Making unnecessary changes to resource settings may create very complicated problems.

Windows can help you find the correct resource settings, but you need to install the hardware device so the computer can detect the device. You may have to use the configuration software or read the documentation that came with the hardware device to install the device properly.

When trying to fix hardware conflicts, it is best to change only one resource setting at a time. If the problem is not fixed when you change a resource setting, return to the original resource setting before making more changes.

You should print the current resource settings before making any changes and take careful notes when you do make changes. These notes will be a useful reference for future use or when seeking technical support.

You should not have to change the resources for hardware with Plug and Play or self-configuring capabilities.

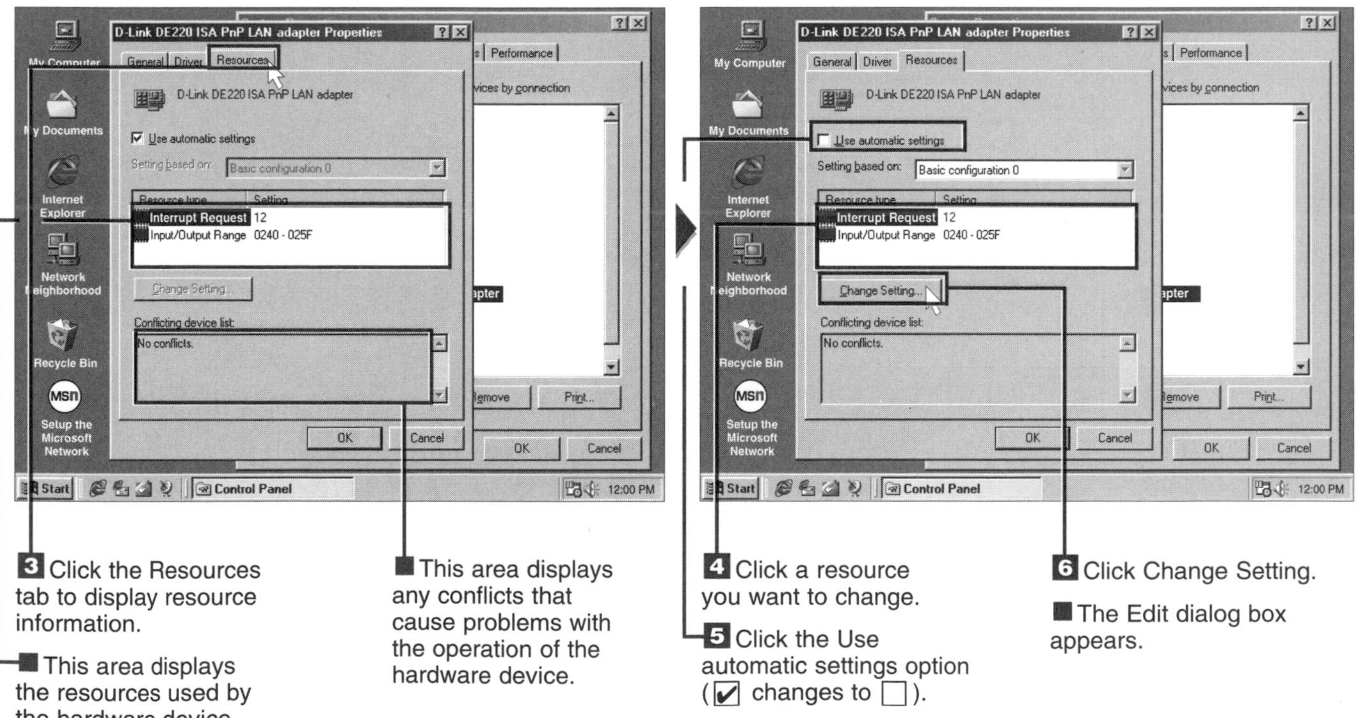

3 Click the Resources tab to display resource information.

■ This area displays the resources used by the hardware device.

■ This area displays any conflicts that cause problems with the operation of the hardware device.

4 Click a resource you want to change.

5 Click the Use automatic settings option (☑ changes to ☐).

6 Click Change Setting.

■ The Edit dialog box appears.

TIPS

Why don't all devices have a Resources tab?

Not all devices use resources directly. For example, the resources for a CD-ROM drive are usually set by the disk controller.

Why does my sound card use two DMA channels?

Your sound card uses two DMA channels to enable your computer to playback and record sound at the same time. This capability is called "duplex" and allows voice communication over the Internet to sound more like a real telephone call.

What can I do if I get an error message saying a resource cannot be modified?

Many devices, such as disk controllers and display adapters, have resource settings that cannot be changed. If you are trying to change a resource setting to fix a conflict, you must resolve it by changing the resource settings for another device.

What can I do if there are no resources available?

You must analyze which devices are using the resources you need. You can then decide if you are able to remove any of those devices to free up the resources you need.

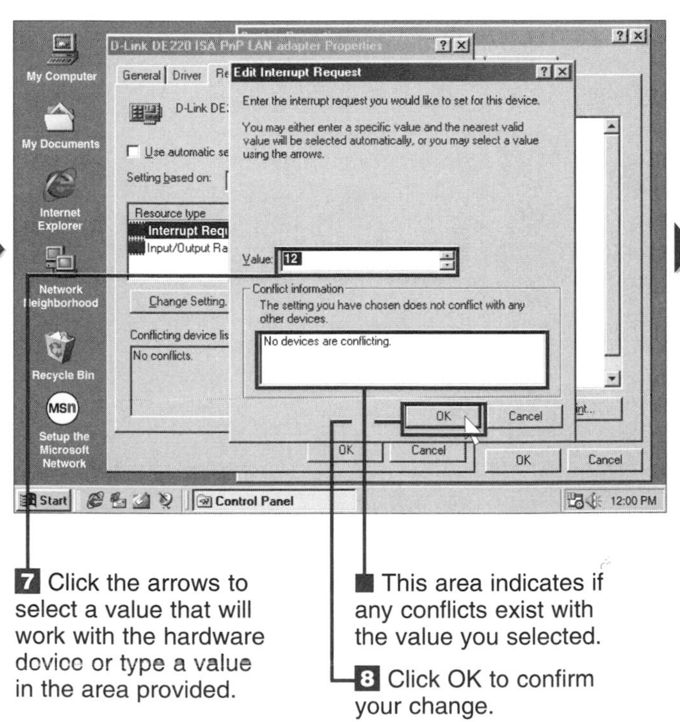

7 Click the arrows to select a value that will work with the hardware device or type a value in the area provided.

■ This area indicates if any conflicts exist with the value you selected.

8 Click OK to confirm your change.

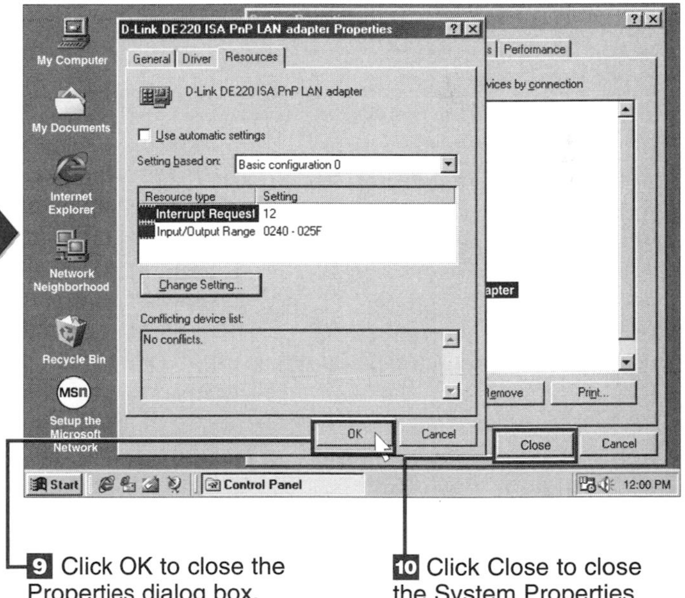

9 Click OK to close the Properties dialog box.

■ A dialog box may appear, warning you Windows will no longer be able to automatically adjust the resource setting. Click Yes to continue.

10 Click Close to close the System Properties dialog box.

■ You may need to restart Windows before the new setting takes effect.

UPDATE DEVICE DRIVERS

Your hardware may work better if you are using the latest version of the software it needs to operate. Hardware devices ranging from your mouse to your modem are all controlled by specific software, called drivers. A driver allows the computer to communicate with and control the device.

When you install a device, Windows checks for the hardware and then installs the appropriate driver. Windows does not include all possible device drivers. If the correct driver is not installed, the device may not work properly.

Even Plug and Play devices may not install correctly. Again, you may have to update the device driver for the hardware to work. The Update Device Driver Wizard helps you update the drivers for your hardware devices.

When you purchase a device, the manufacturer may include drivers on a floppy disk or CD-ROM disc. You should insert the disk before performing the steps described below.

You can also obtain new drivers directly from the manufacturer. Most manufacturers provide the latest drivers in the support area of their Web site. You should particularly check for newer drivers for your video display adapter card. These drivers are frequently updated and improved. The latest driver may be faster and offer more features.

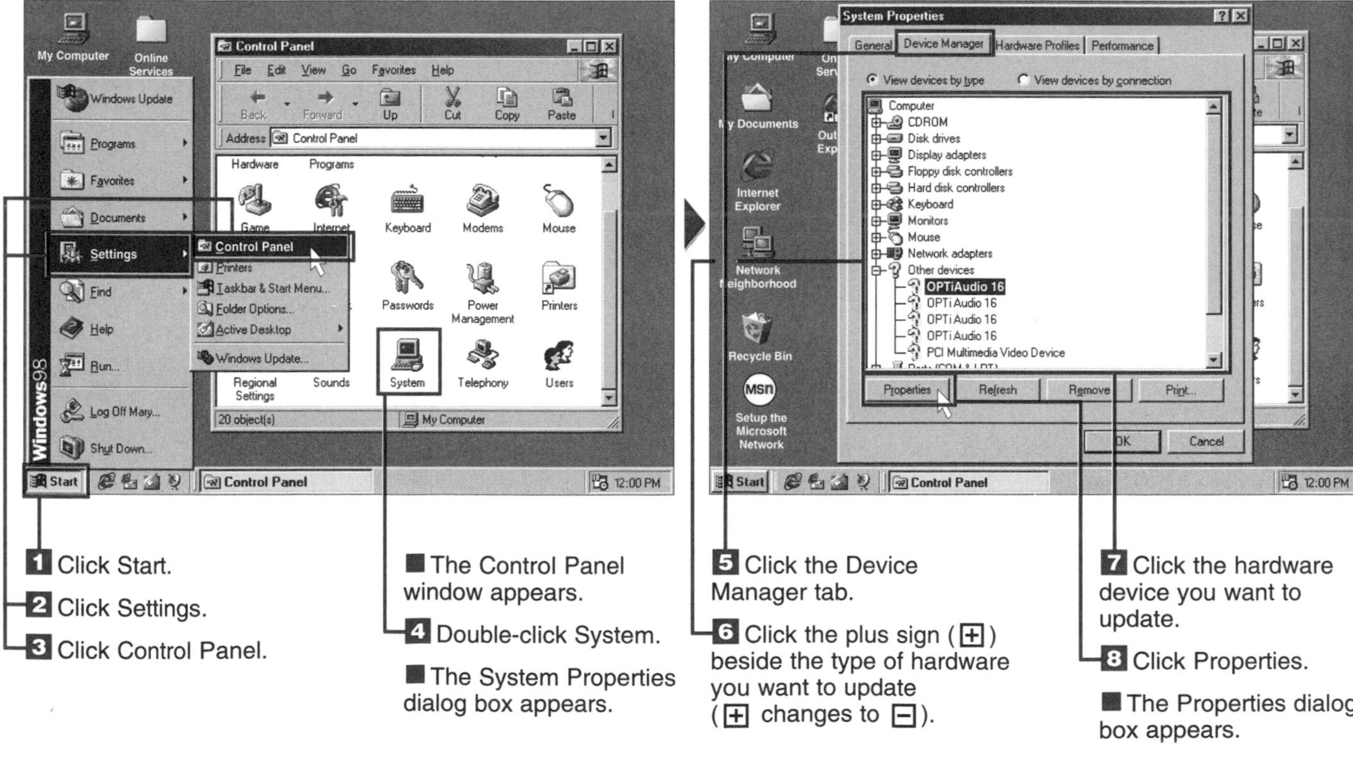

1 Click Start.

2 Click Settings.

3 Click Control Panel.

■ The Control Panel window appears.

4 Double-click System.

■ The System Properties dialog box appears.

5 Click the Device Manager tab.

6 Click the plus sign (⊞) beside the type of hardware you want to update (⊞ changes to ⊟).

7 Click the hardware device you want to update.

8 Click Properties.

■ The Properties dialog box appears.

TIPS

What can I do if the device does not have a Driver tab?

Some devices, such as modems and monitors, may not have a Driver tab. You can change the settings for many of these devices in the Control Panel. For example, to change the driver for a monitor, double-click Display, select the Settings tab and then click the Advanced button. In the dialog box that appears, click the Adapter tab. To change the driver for a modem, you must remove the modem and then re-install it using a new driver.

How can I tell what driver files a device is using?

To view a list of driver files being used by a device, click the Driver File Details button on the Driver tab. A device may use several driver files to operate. You should never delete files that are currently being used by a device because Windows 98 may no longer operate properly.

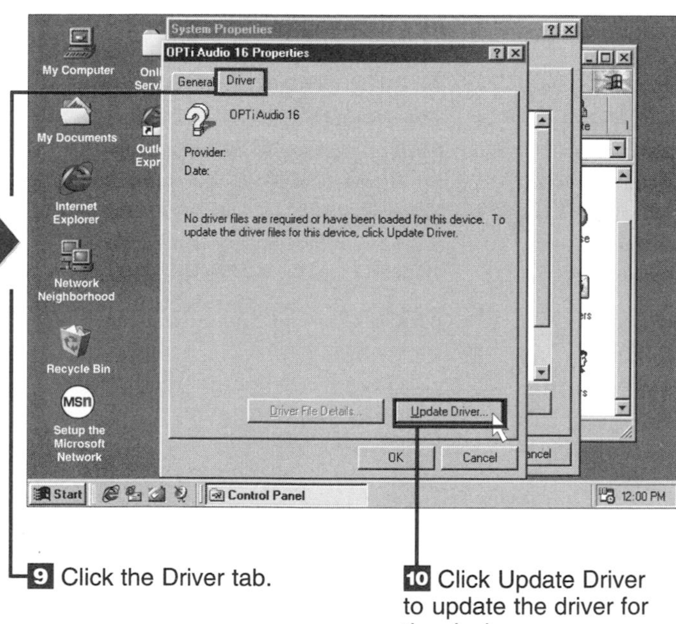

9 Click the Driver tab.

10 Click Update Driver to update the driver for the device.

■ The Update Device Driver Wizard appears.

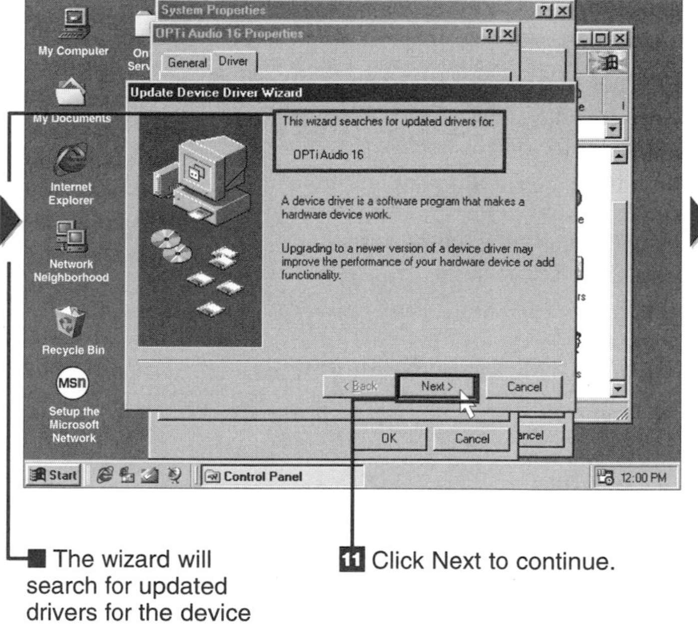

■ The wizard will search for updated drivers for the device shown in this area.

11 Click Next to continue.

CONTINUED

UPDATE DEVICE DRIVERS CONTINUED

You can have Windows search for a better driver or display a list of all the drivers in a specific location on your computer. Displaying a list of all the available drivers lets you choose the driver you want to use.

Windows will search the driver database on your hard drive for updated drivers. If you inserted a floppy disk or CD-ROM disc into a drive, you can have Windows search the drive. You can also specify another location on your computer you want Windows to search. The Microsoft Windows Update option searches an online collection of updated drivers. If you are not already registered for Windows 98, follow the instructions on your screen to register and use the Microsoft Windows Update option.

When searching for updated drivers, the wizard always looks for a file with the .inf extension. The .inf file contains information that tells Windows how to install the driver. After the wizard reads the .inf file, it will copy the files Windows needs and adjust any settings that are required by the device. In addition to the .inf file, the wizard may need files from the Windows 98 CD-ROM disc.

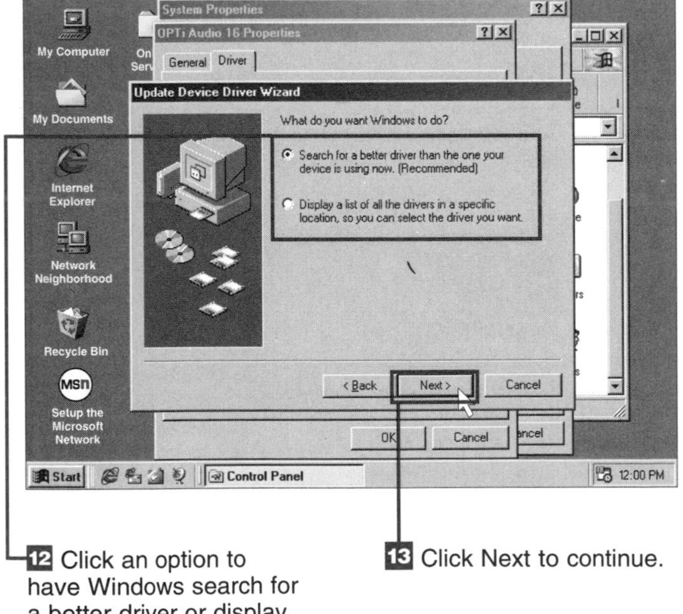

12 Click an option to have Windows search for a better driver or display a list of all the drivers in a specific location (○ changes to ⊙).

13 Click Next to continue.

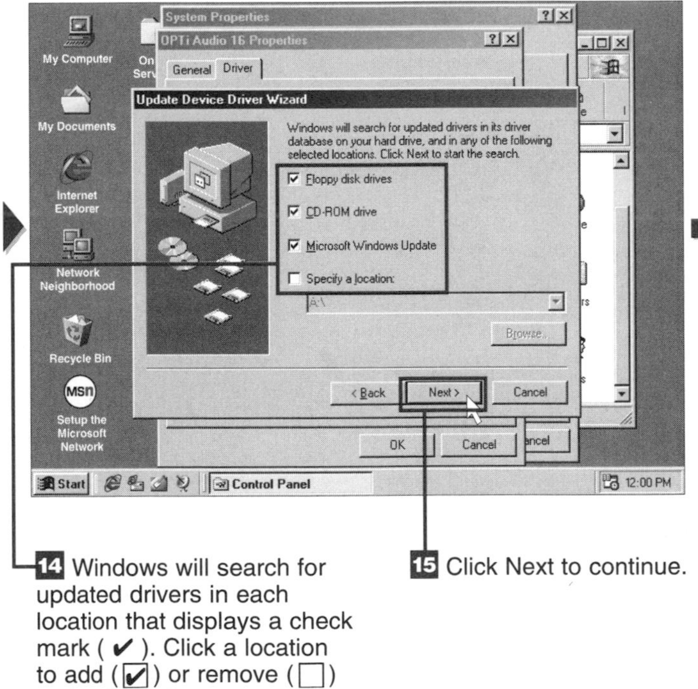

14 Windows will search for updated drivers in each location that displays a check mark (✔). Click a location to add (☑) or remove (☐) a check mark.

15 Click Next to continue.

TIPS

The floppy disk is inserted, so why is Windows still asking me to insert the disk?

The .inf file may refer to folders that Windows cannot locate on the floppy disk. If this happens, click OK to display the Copying Files dialog box and then select the Browse button. The Open dialog box displays the name of the file Windows is looking for. To help locate the driver, first try changing the drive letter to A. If this does not work, browse through the folders.

What are my options if the driver does not work? Also, what if the new driver does not work as well as the previous version?

It may be as easy as re-installing the previous driver you were using. In some cases, it may be necessary to remove the hardware and re-install it. To return to the previous driver, you may be able to use System File Checker. See page 656. Before changing anything, always check the information supplied by the manufacturer of the device.

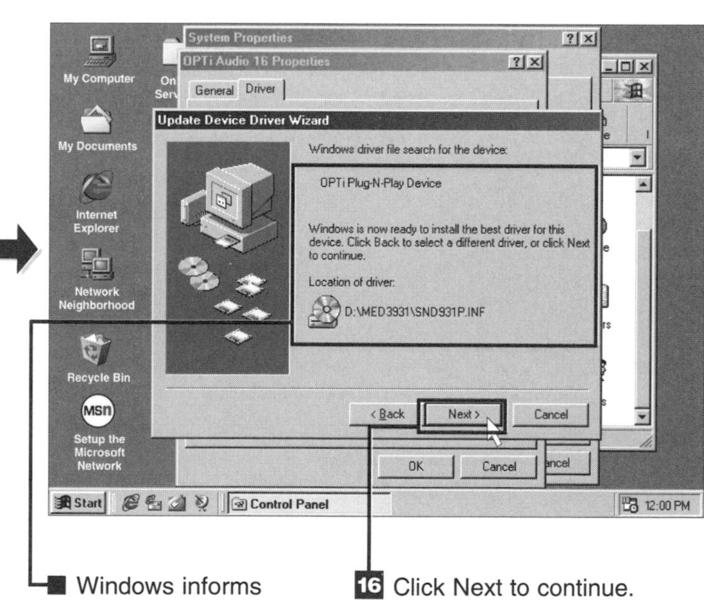

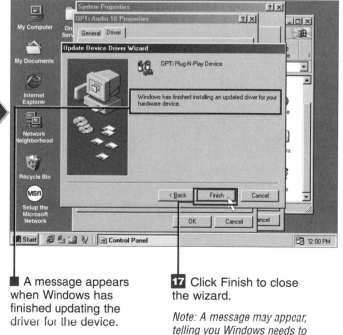

■ Windows informs you that it located a better driver for the device and is ready to install the driver.

16 Click Next to continue.

■ Windows copies the driver files to your computer.

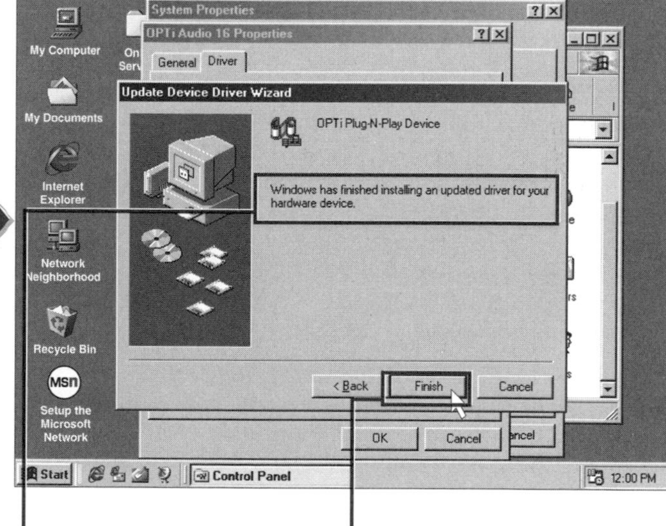

■ A message appears when Windows has finished updating the driver for the device.

17 Click Finish to close the wizard.

Note: A message may appear, telling you Windows needs to restart your computer. Click Yes to restart the computer.

USING MICROSOFT SYSTEM INFORMATION

Display System Data

You can use Microsoft System Information to display information about your computer and how it is set up. You can use this information to learn more about your computer or troubleshoot a problem you are experiencing. The information provided may also help a support technician identify the cause of a problem and suggest a solution.

Microsoft System Information is organized into three categories. The Hardware Resources category contains information about the hardware resources offered by your computer and how these resources are being used by the hardware devices installed on your computer.

The Components category contains information about your Windows setup and the hardware devices on your computer. You can use the Components category to determine the driver for a specific device. In this category, you can choose to display Basic Information, Advanced Information and a History for most items.

The Software Environment category contains details about the software that is currently installed on and being used by your computer.

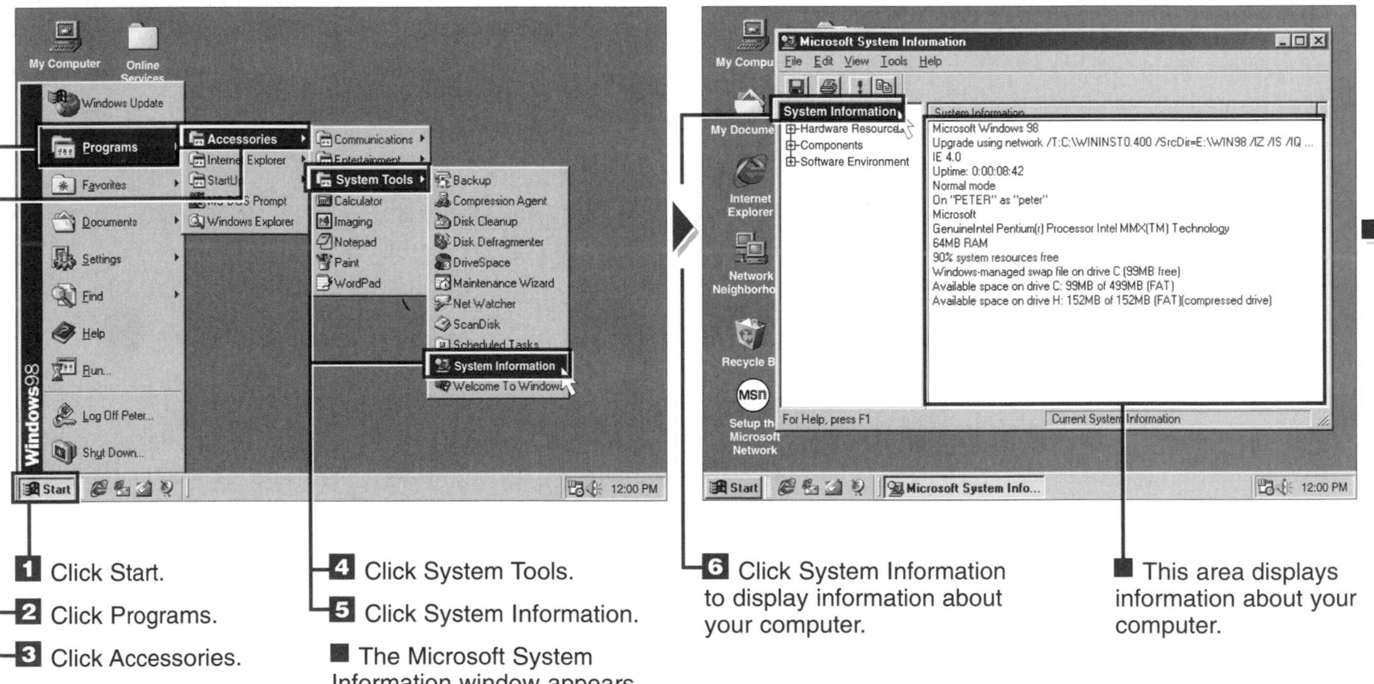

1 Click Start.

2 Click Programs.

3 Click Accessories.

4 Click System Tools.

5 Click System Information.

■ The Microsoft System Information window appears.

6 Click System Information to display information about your computer.

■ This area displays information about your computer.

TIPS

Why does it take so long for Windows to display the information?

It may take Windows a few moments to collect the information. If you want to stop the collection process, select the View menu and then click Cancel Update.

How do I print the information from Microsoft System Information?

Select the File menu and then click Print.

I made a change on my computer. How do I display the updated information?

To update the information displayed in the Microsoft System Information window, select the View menu and then click Refresh.

Can I save the information from Microsoft System Information?

Yes. Select the File menu and then click Save. To later view the saved information, you must open the Microsoft System Information window, select the File menu and then click Open.

How do I save the information so I can open it with a text editor?

Select the File menu and then click Export. Saving the information in a text file allows you to send the information to others via e-mail.

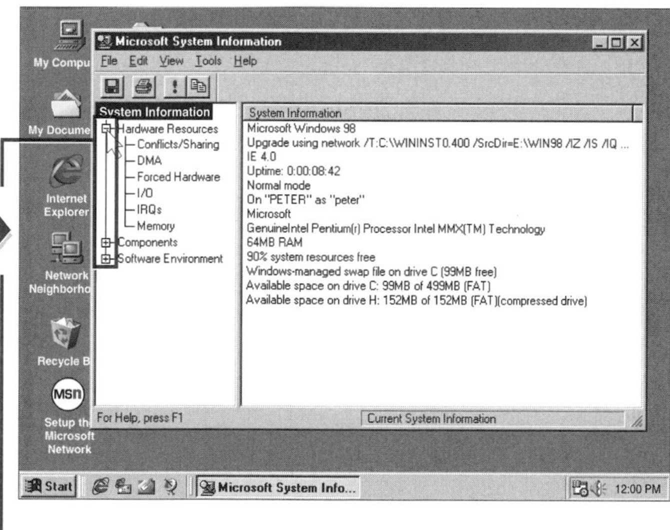

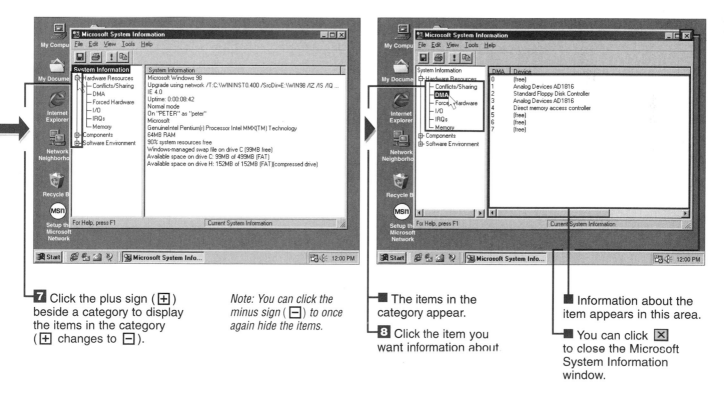

7 Click the plus sign (⊞) beside a category to display the items in the category (⊞ changes to ⊟).

Note: You can click the minus sign (⊟) to once again hide the items.

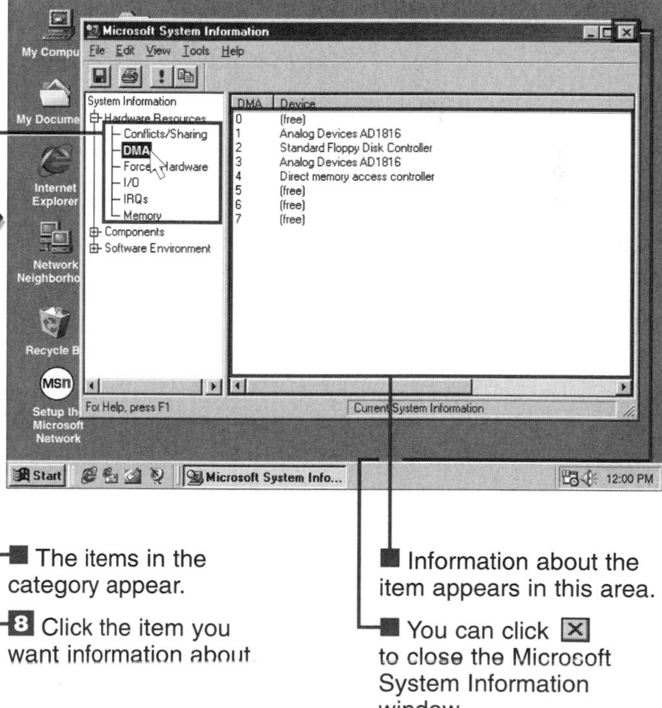

■ The items in the category appear.

8 Click the item you want information about.

■ Information about the item appears in this area.

■ You can click ☒ to close the Microsoft System Information window.

USING MICROSOFT SYSTEM INFORMATION

Run a System Tool

Microsoft System Information contains several tools you can use to help identify and solve your computer problems. These tools include the Windows Report Tool, Update Wizard Uninstall, System File Checker, Signature Verification Tool, Registry Checker, Automatic Skip Driver Agent, Dr. Watson, System Configuration Utility, ScanDisk and Version Conflict Manager. Support technicians may ask you to run one or more of these tools when they are trying to find the cause of a specific problem you are experiencing with your computer.

Although these tools were originally designed to be used when you are working with a support technician, you may want to try running some of these tools on your own. These tools may help you troubleshoot and resolve a problem before calling for technical support.

Advanced users may want to use these tools even when they are not experiencing problems with their computer. The tools can help you learn more about the technical aspects of your computer, such as its capabilities and setup.

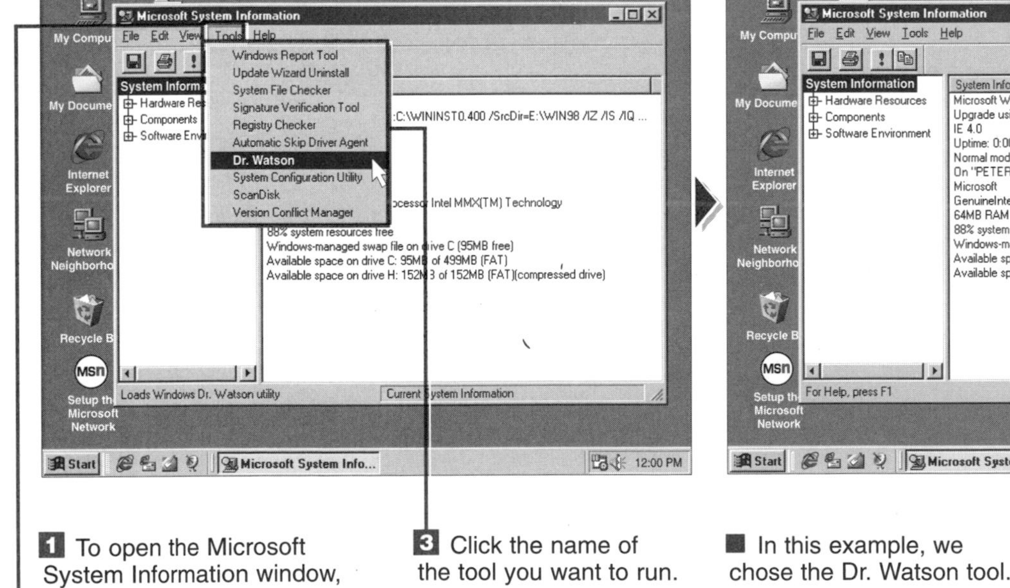

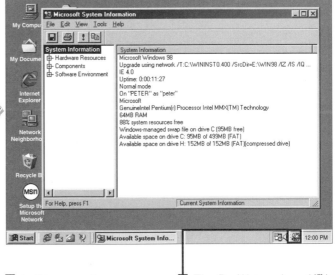

1 To open the Microsoft System Information window, perform steps 1 to 5 on page 650.

2 Click Tools.

3 Click the name of the tool you want to run.

■ In this example, we chose the Dr. Watson tool.

■ The Dr. Watson icon appears on the taskbar. You can double-click the icon to run Dr. Watson.

Windows Report Tool

This tool allows you to report information about your computer problems to Microsoft. When you describe the problem you are having, the tool will collect the necessary information about your computer and then send the information to Microsoft over the Internet. Microsoft can then review your report and offer advice on how to correct the problem.

Update Wizard Uninstall

This tool lets you view a list of updates that you have installed from the Windows Update Web site. You can use this tool to remove some or all of the updates and restore your system to its previous configuration without having to connect to the Web site again.

System File Checker

System File Checker verifies that your system files have not been damaged. If this tool finds a problem with one of your system files, you can restore the original system file. For information on System File Checker, see page 656.

Signature Verification Tool

You can use the Signature Verification Tool to search for files that have been digitally signed. This helps you verify that a file on your computer is the authentic file provided by the developer.

Registry Checker

Registry Checker scans the contents of your Registry for problems and errors. Registry Checker runs each time you start Windows and creates a backup copy of the Registry each day. If Registry Checker finds a serious problem, it may suggest that you restore the Registry from the backup.

Automatic Skip Driver Agent

This tool checks for devices that do not respond properly when you start Windows. If a device does not respond properly, this tool prevents Windows from loading the driver for the device.

Dr. Watson

When your computer crashes, Dr. Watson records what your computer was doing at the time of the crash. This tool may be able to identify the cause of a problem and offer suggestions to help you fix the problem.

System Configuration Utility

This tool allows you to create and test different system configuration settings to help you determine the cause of a problem. Advanced users may also want to use this tool to change their system files. For information on System Configuration Utility, see page 654.

ScanDisk

ScanDisk checks for and repairs errors on your hard disk. For information on ScanDisk, see page 312.

Version Conflict Manager

This tool keeps track of system files that are replaced with different versions when a program or a hardware device is installed. Both versions of the system files are saved. You can switch between the versions whenever you choose.

USING MICROSOFT SYSTEM INFORMATION

Using the System Configuration Utility

You can use the System Configuration Utility to find the cause of a problem you are experiencing with your computer.

You can specify how you want Windows to start. The Normal startup option starts Windows in the regular way and loads all the device drivers and software. When you choose the Diagnostic startup option, a menu will appear when you start Windows. You can then select the Step-by-step confirmation option to specify which drivers and software you want to load. The Selective startup option allows you to choose the items you want to load when Windows starts from a list in the System Configuration Utility window.

You can also use the System Configuration Utility to change your Config.sys, Autoexec.bat, System.ini and Win.ini files. Only advanced users should attempt to change these system files. Conflicts or errors in the system files are often the cause of problems. To attempt to determine the cause of the problem, you can turn off an item in the system files to prevent the item from loading and then restart your computer.

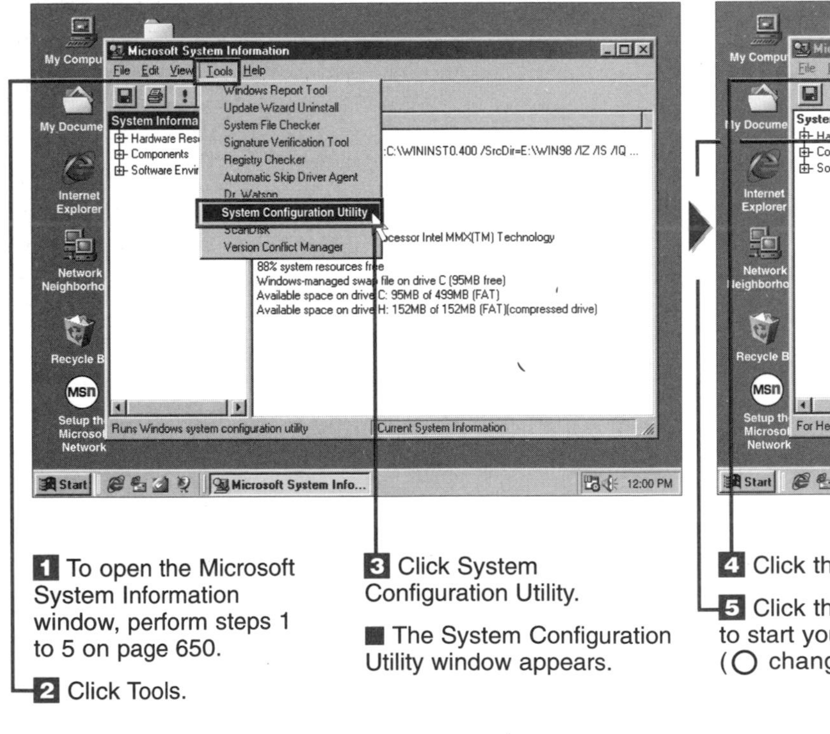

1 To open the Microsoft System Information window, perform steps 1 to 5 on page 650.

2 Click Tools.

3 Click System Configuration Utility.

■ The System Configuration Utility window appears.

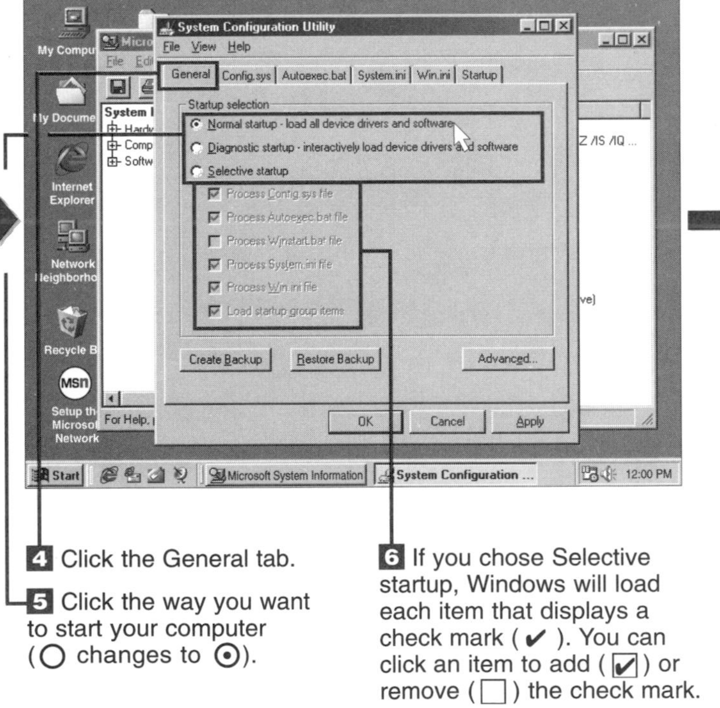

4 Click the General tab.

5 Click the way you want to start your computer (○ changes to ⊙).

6 If you chose Selective startup, Windows will load each item that displays a check mark (✔). You can click an item to add (☑) or remove (☐) the check mark.

TIPS

What items does the Startup tab contain?

The Startup tab contains a list of the programs and other items that run automatically each time you start Windows. To determine if one of these programs is causing a problem, click the check box beside a program (☑ changes to ☐). Then restart your computer.

Can I edit the system files?

Yes. Click the tab for the system file you want to edit. Click the item you want to edit and then select the Edit button.

Should I back up my system files before making changes?

You should always back up your system files before making any changes. Display the General tab in the System Configuration Utility window and then click the Create Backup button. Each time you click the Create Backup button, Windows saves the current version of your system files.

If the changes you make do not resolve the problem, you can restore the most recent version of the system files from the backup copy. On the General tab, click the Restore Backup button.

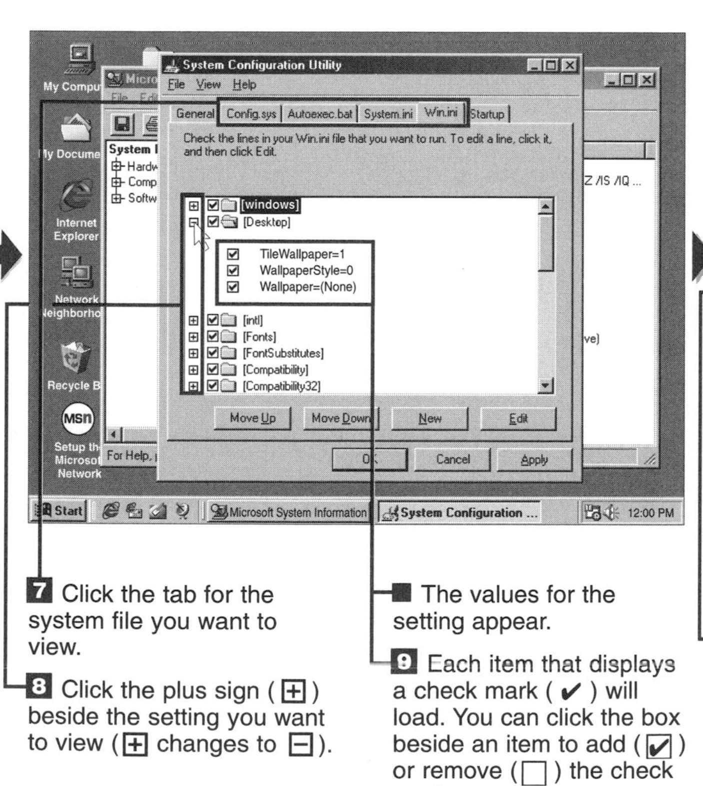

7 Click the tab for the system file you want to view.

8 Click the plus sign (⊞) beside the setting you want to view (⊞ changes to ⊟).

■ The values for the setting appear.

9 Each item that displays a check mark (✔) will load. You can click the box beside an item to add (☑) or remove (☐) the check mark.

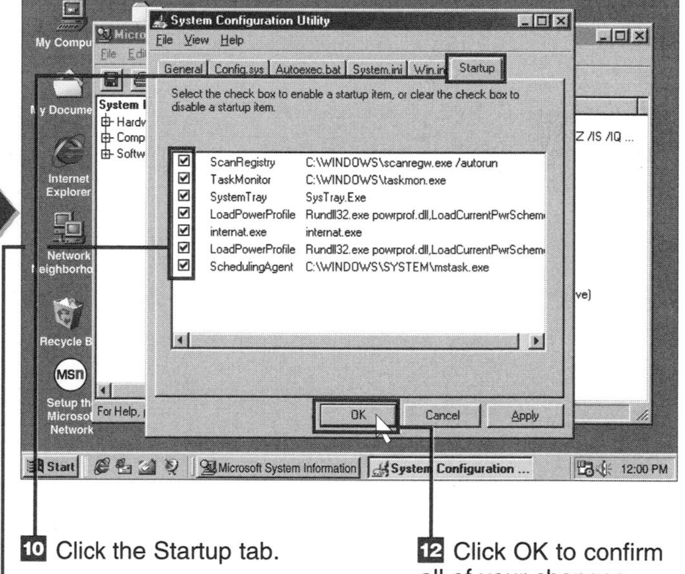

10 Click the Startup tab.

11 Each item that displays a check mark (✔) will run automatically each time you start Windows. You can click the box beside an item to add (☑) or remove (☐) the check mark.

12 Click OK to confirm all of your changes.

Note: Windows may ask you to restart your computer. Click Yes to restart your computer.

USING MICROSOFT SYSTEM INFORMATION

Using System File Checker

System File Checker can check the system files stored on your computer and notify you if any of these files have been damaged. System files store information such as fonts and configuration settings that your computer needs to run Windows 98. If these files have been damaged, Windows 98 may not run properly.

Although you do not have to use System File Checker on a regular basis, you should run the program if your computer begins to operate improperly. You may also want to run System File Checker after you install a new program on your computer.

System File Checker checks your system files against verification files that are included with Windows 98. When System File Checker finds a problem with a system file, the program allows you to restore the file to its original settings. Before restoring a file, you can save a backup copy of the current file. You can later return to the backup copy of the file if you see no improvement in the operation of your computer.

System File Checker keeps a record of its activities in a log file.

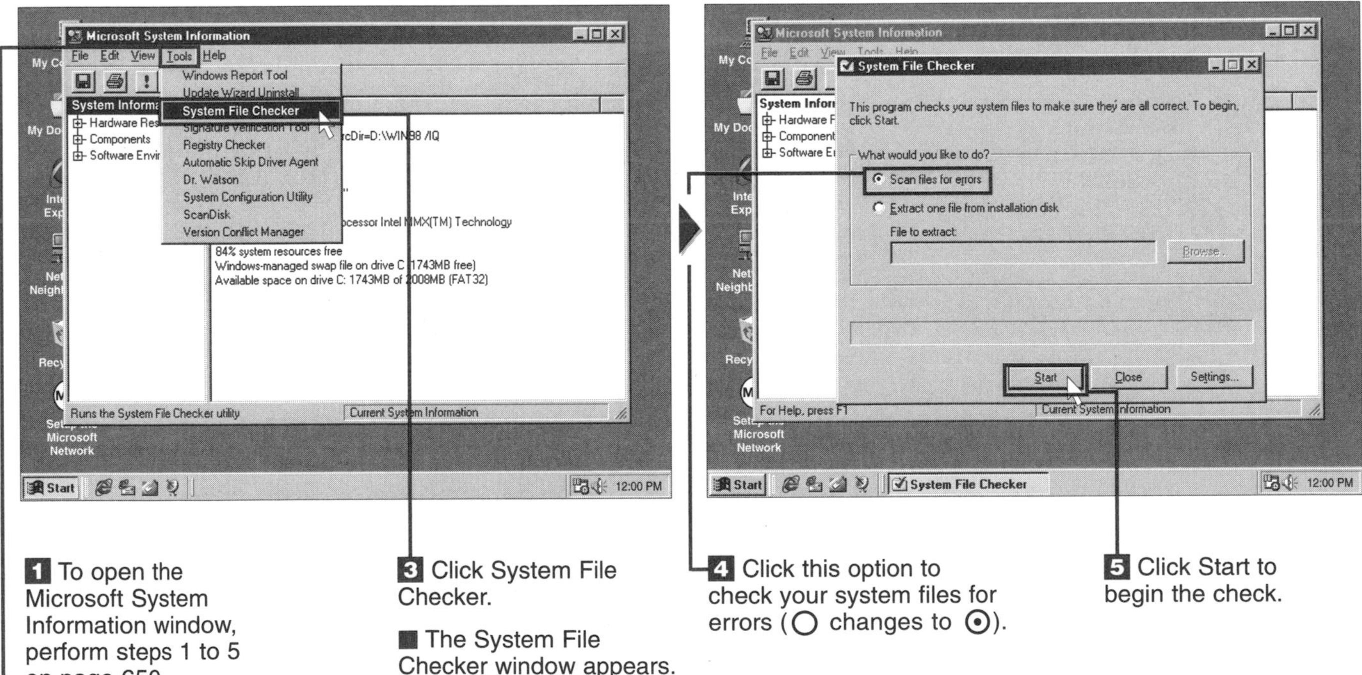

1 To open the Microsoft System Information window, perform steps 1 to 5 on page 650.

2 Click Tools.

3 Click System File Checker.

■ The System File Checker window appears.

4 Click this option to check your system files for errors (○ changes to ⊙).

5 Click Start to begin the check.

TIPS

What is the Extract one file from installation disk option used for?

System File Checker can copy a specific file from the Windows 98 CD-ROM disc to your computer. This is useful if you know the file, such as a driver, you want to use. Click the Extract one file from installation disk option (○ changes to ⦿). Use the Browse button to find the file you want to extract from the CD-ROM disc and then click the Start button. In the Extract File dialog box, click the Restore from area and then type the location of the file on the Windows 98 CD-ROM disc. In the Save file in area, type the location where you want to store the file on your computer.

How do I view the log file created by System File Checker?

On the Start menu, click Run. Type **sfclog.txt** and then press the Enter key.

Can I have System File Checker also check for changed or deleted system files?

Yes. In the System File Checker window, click the Settings button. Click the Check for changed files option (☐ changes to ☑). Then click the Check for deleted files option (☐ changes to ☑).

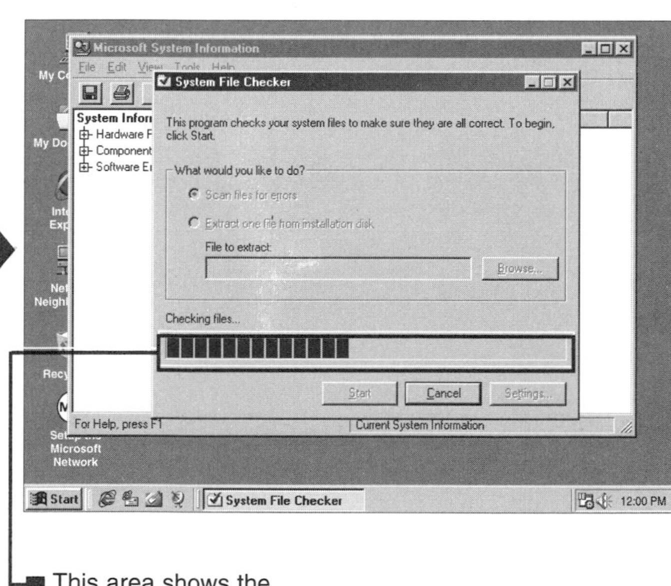

■ This area shows the progress of the check.

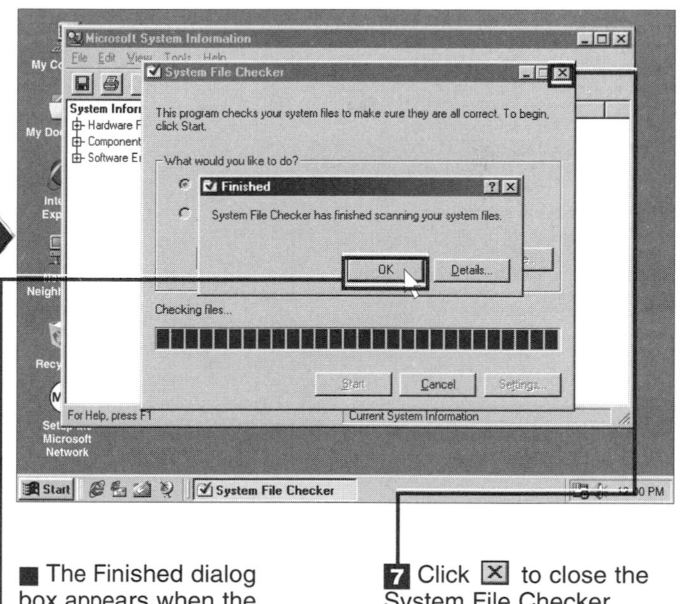

■ The Finished dialog box appears when the check is complete.

6 Click OK to close the dialog box.

7 Click ☒ to close the System File Checker window.

MONITOR COMPUTER PERFORMANCE USING SYSTEM MONITOR

You can use System Monitor to view information about how your computer is performing.

System Monitor is often used to monitor the speed at which parts of a computer process information. This information may help you determine the cause of a problem your computer is having. System Monitor can also help you decide whether you need to upgrade your computer hardware.

You may want to observe and keep records of how your computer performs when there are no problems. You can use this information in a comparison later on if your computer's performance starts to deteriorate. You should monitor your computer's performance over an extended period of time to get a better estimate of what normal performance is. A good way to determine if your computer is running properly is to compare it with another computer that is set up in a similar way.

System Monitor remembers which resources you selected to monitor. The next time you open System Monitor, it will display information about those resources.

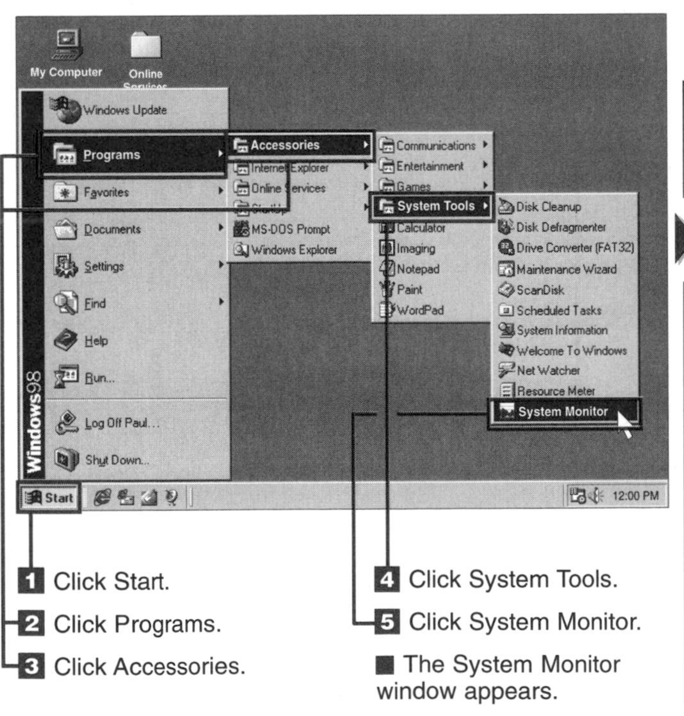

1 Click Start.

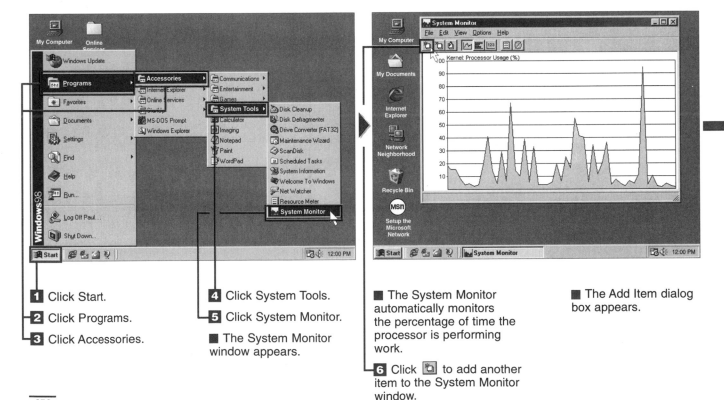

2 Click Programs.

3 Click Accessories.

4 Click System Tools.

5 Click System Monitor.

■ The System Monitor window appears.

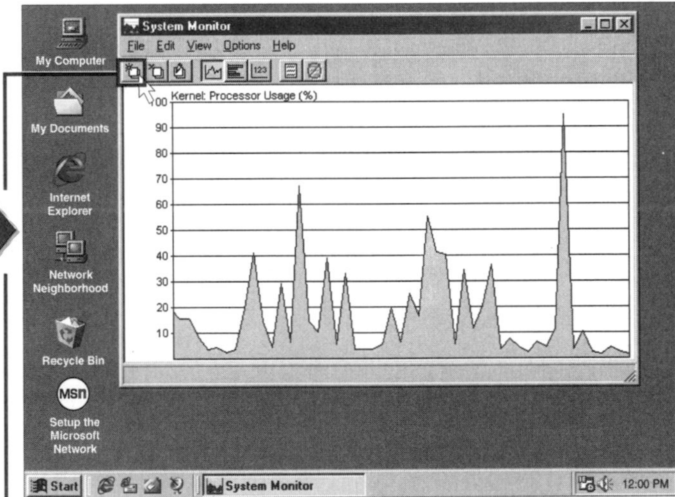

■ The System Monitor automatically monitors the percentage of time the processor is performing work.

6 Click to add another item to the System Monitor window.

■ The Add Item dialog box appears.

TIPS

Why isn't System Monitor on the Start menu?

System Monitor may not be installed on your computer. System Monitor is located in the System Tools component. To add Windows components, see page 610.

Can I save and print the information displayed by System Monitor?

You can save the information displayed by System Monitor in a text file. Click File and then select Start Logging. You can then open and print the text file from any word processing program, such as WordPad.

How do I remove an item from the System Monitor window?

When you no longer want to monitor an item, click the Remove button ( ) to display a list of items currently shown in the window. Click the item you want to remove and then click OK.

Is there another way to view information about my computer's performance?

You can use Resource Meter to monitor how your computer's resources are being used. If Resource Meter is not installed on your computer, you can install it from the System Tools component. To add Windows components, see page 610.

To start Resource Meter, perform steps 1 to 5 below, selecting Resource Meter in step 5. When Resource Meter is running, an icon ( ) appears on your taskbar. You can double-click the icon to display the Resource Meter window and view the information.

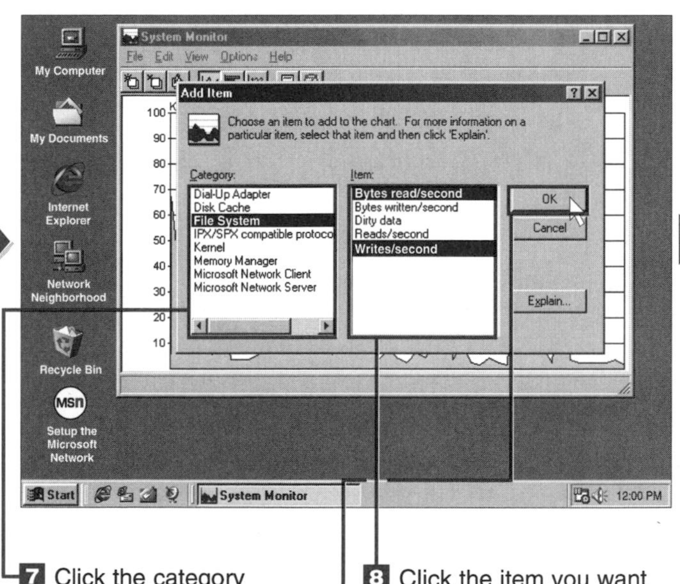

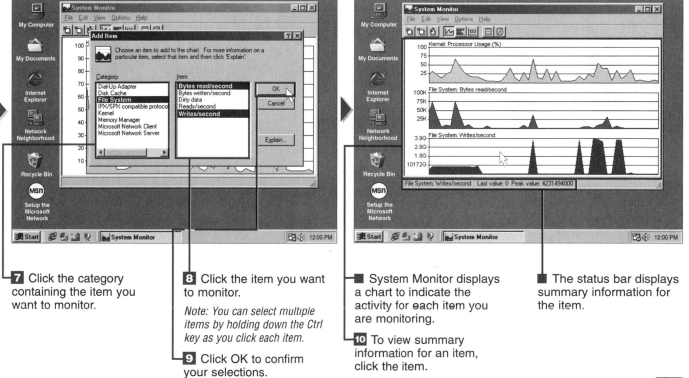

7 Click the category containing the item you want to monitor.

8 Click the item you want to monitor.

Note: You can select multiple items by holding down the Ctrl key as you click each item.

9 Click OK to confirm your selections.

■ System Monitor displays a chart to indicate the activity for each item you are monitoring.

10 To view summary information for an item, click the item.

■ The status bar displays summary information for the item.

VIRTUAL MEMORY SETTINGS

Virtual memory improves the operation of computers that do not have large amounts of memory, or RAM.

If your computer exceeds the minimum memory requirements for Windows 98, Windows will be able to operate faster and run more programs at the same time. When your computer runs out of RAM, Windows uses part of your hard disk as RAM. This borrowed storage space is called virtual memory. The hard disk space that Windows uses as virtual memory is also called a swap file.

Windows is always busy managing your computer's memory. Whenever you choose a different font, open a new window or begin a task like printing, RAM is required. When your computer runs out of RAM, Windows frees up some RAM by placing some of the information in virtual memory. When that information is required, Windows retrieves the information from virtual memory.

When Windows is using virtual memory, you may notice that your hard drive is accessed more often.

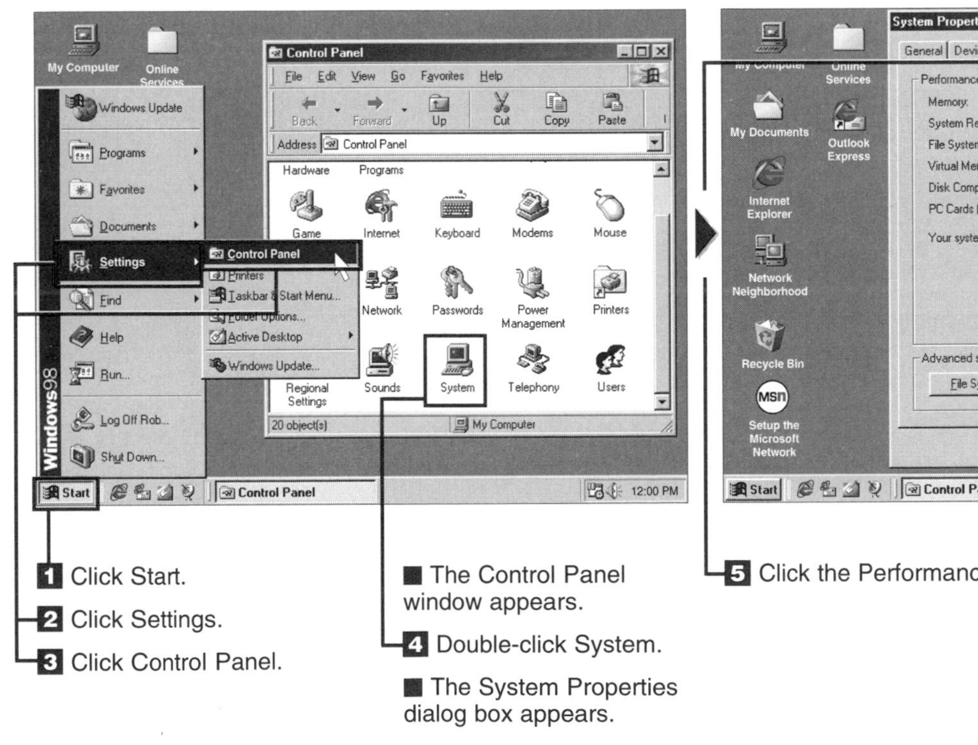

1 Click Start.

2 Click Settings.

3 Click Control Panel.

■ The Control Panel window appears.

4 Double-click System.

■ The System Properties dialog box appears.

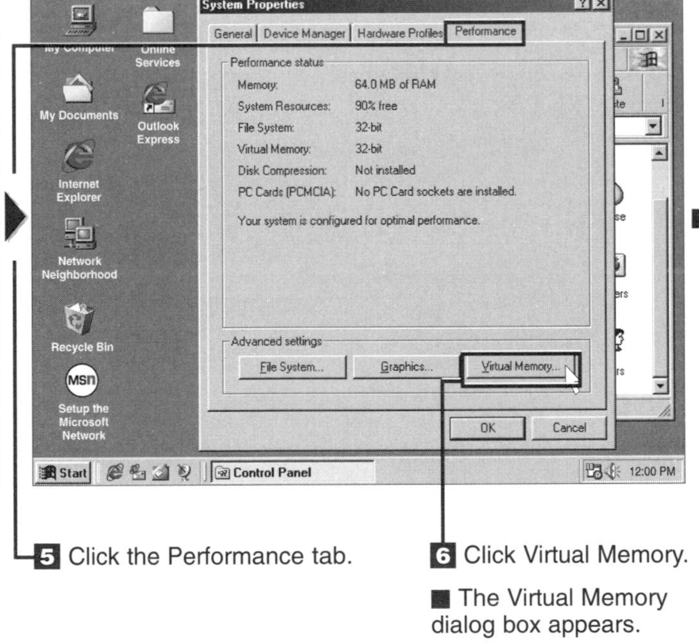

5 Click the Performance tab.

6 Click Virtual Memory.

■ The Virtual Memory dialog box appears.

TIPS

Should I change the virtual memory settings?

In general, you should not change the virtual memory settings. However, if you must change the settings, you may find that Windows spends less time using the hard drive if you use the same number for the minimum and maximum amount of hard disk space reserved for virtual memory.

When would I move the virtual memory to a different hard drive?

If you have more than one hard drive, you could move the virtual memory to the fastest drive or to the drive with the most free space.

How much virtual memory do I need?

The amount of virtual memory you need depends on the amount of RAM you have and the number of programs you want to use at one time. If you have 32 MB or more of RAM, try setting the minimum and maximum amount of hard disk space you want to use for virtual memory to 32 MB. If "out of memory" messages start to appear, change the settings to 64 MB.

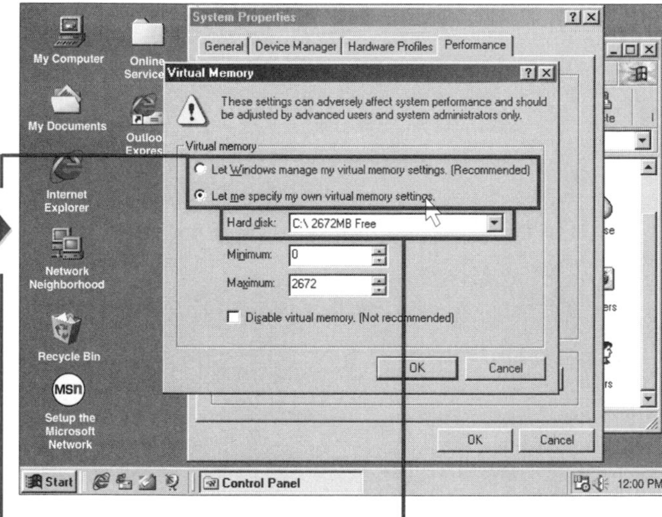

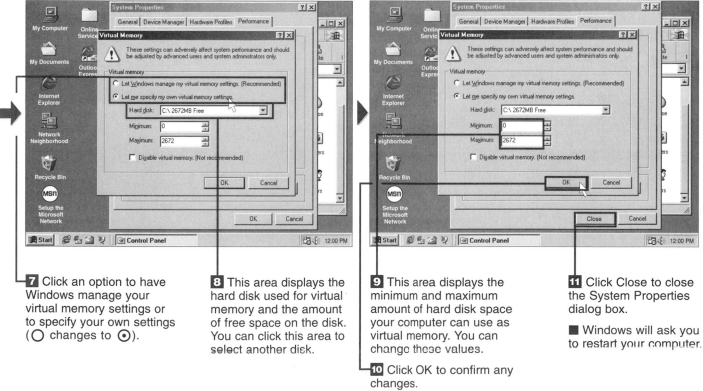

7 Click an option to have Windows manage your virtual memory settings or to specify your own settings (○ changes to ⊙).

8 This area displays the hard disk used for virtual memory and the amount of free space on the disk. You can click this area to select another disk.

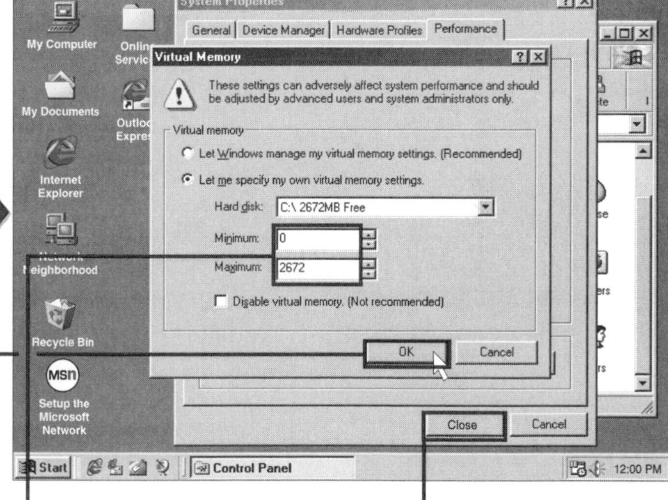

9 This area displays the minimum and maximum amount of hard disk space your computer can use as virtual memory. You can change these values.

10 Click OK to confirm any changes.

Note: If a confirmation dialog box appears, click Yes.

11 Click Close to close the System Properties dialog box.

■ Windows will ask you to restart your computer.

CREATE A STARTUP DISK

You should create a startup disk and keep it on hand in case you have trouble starting Windows. When you cannot start Windows normally, you can insert the startup disk into your floppy drive to start your computer.

When you use a startup disk to start your computer, a command prompt similar to MS-DOS appears on your screen. You can access several utility programs to try to solve the problem that prevents Windows from starting properly. You may not be able to access your CD-ROM drive. You will not be able to log on to the network.

The floppy disk you use to create the startup disk must be able to store at least 1.2 MB of information. All files currently stored on the floppy disk will be erased when you create a startup disk.

After you have created the startup disk, open the write-protect tab on the disk so you do not accidentally delete any files stored on the disk. Make sure you label your startup disk and keep it with your Windows 98 installation CD-ROM disc.

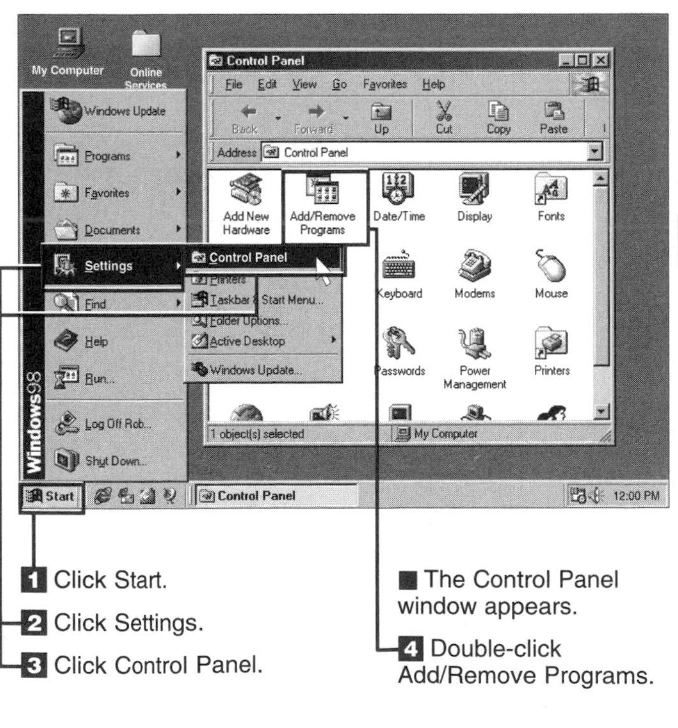

1 Click Start.

2 Click Settings.

3 Click Control Panel.

■ The Control Panel window appears.

4 Double-click Add/Remove Programs.

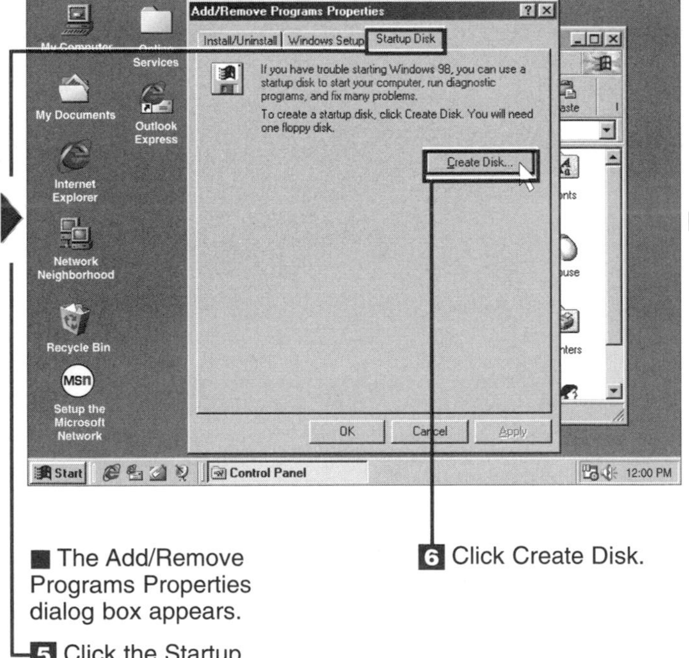

■ The Add/Remove Programs Properties dialog box appears.

5 Click the Startup Disk tab.

6 Click Create Disk.

TIPS

Which floppy drive should I use when I create my startup disk?

If your computer has more than one floppy drive, you should use the A: drive to create your startup disk.

What is on the startup disk?

In addition to the system files needed to start a command prompt, the startup disk contains several utility programs. ScanDisk checks and repairs hard disk errors. FDISK allows you to partition your hard disk. Format allows you to format your hard disk. Edit is a text editor that lets you make changes to text configuration files.

I inserted the floppy disk, but my computer is still trying to start from the hard drive. What can I do?

If your computer does not start from the floppy drive containing the startup disk, consult your system documentation, or contact the manufacturer of your computer to find out which settings must be adjusted to start from a floppy disk.

Can I create a startup disk using another Windows 98 computer?

If you have a problem starting Windows and have not created a startup disk, you can create a startup disk using another Windows 98 computer.

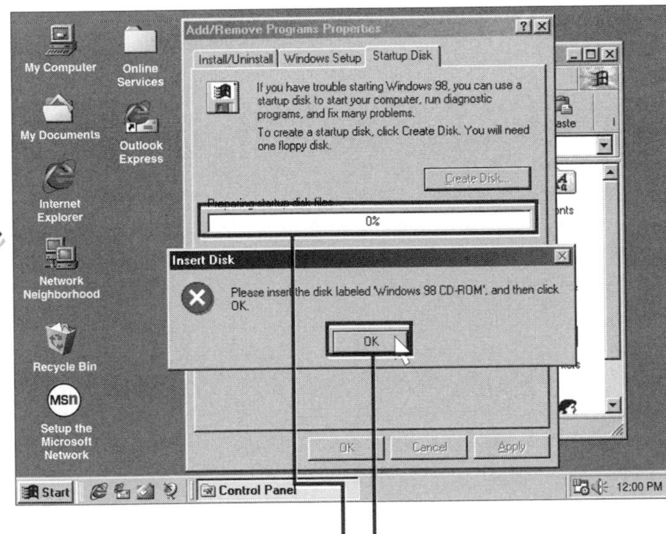

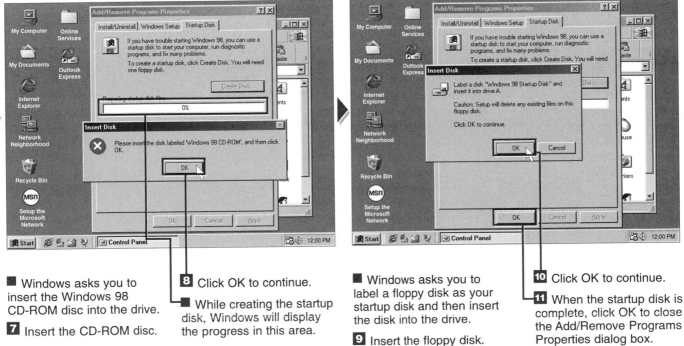

■ Windows asks you to insert the Windows 98 CD-ROM disc into the drive.

7 Insert the CD-ROM disc.

8 Click OK to continue.

■ While creating the startup disk, Windows will display the progress in this area.

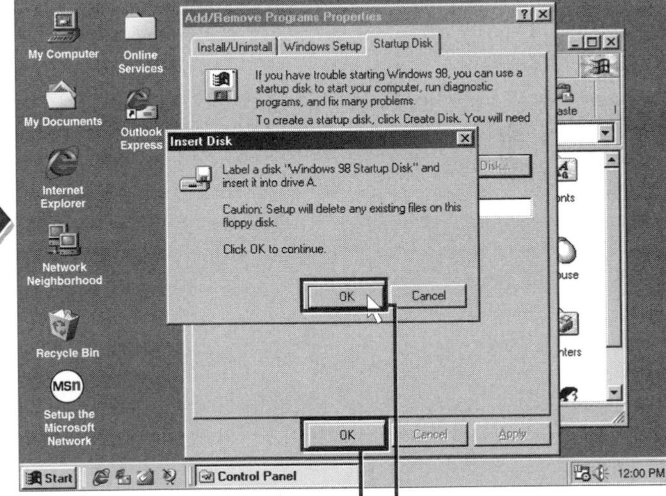

■ Windows asks you to label a floppy disk as your startup disk and then insert the disk into the drive.

9 Insert the floppy disk.

10 Click OK to continue.

11 When the startup disk is complete, click OK to close the Add/Remove Programs Properties dialog box.

START WINDOWS IN SAFE MODE

If Windows does not start properly, you can start Windows in safe mode. Safe mode is a limited version of Windows.

Windows may not start properly if you have made inappropriate changes to your computer's setup. For example, you may have incorrectly installed a new device or accidentally changed important Windows settings. In safe mode, you may be able to correct the problem that prevents Windows from starting normally.

Safe mode uses the minimum capabilities required to run Windows. When you use safe mode, you cannot access CD-ROM drives, tape drives, SCSI devices, printers and devices such as sound cards or modems.

Safe mode will not start any of the items in your StartUp folder.

Windows may automatically start in safe mode if it cannot start properly.

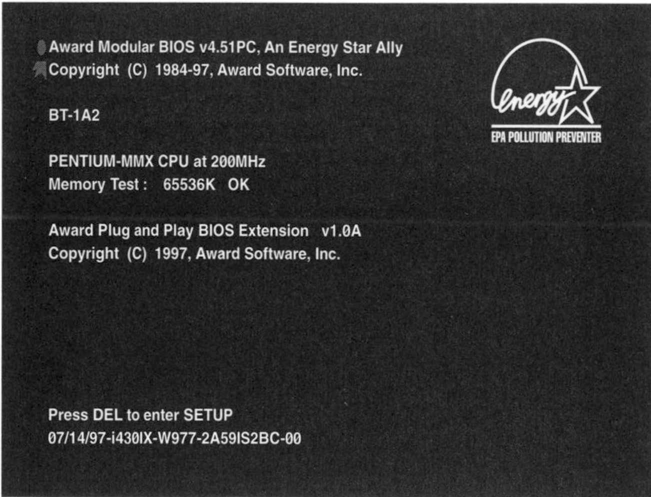

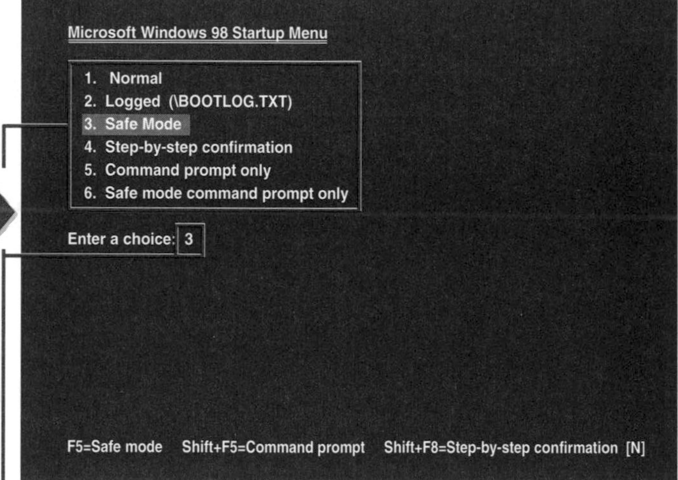

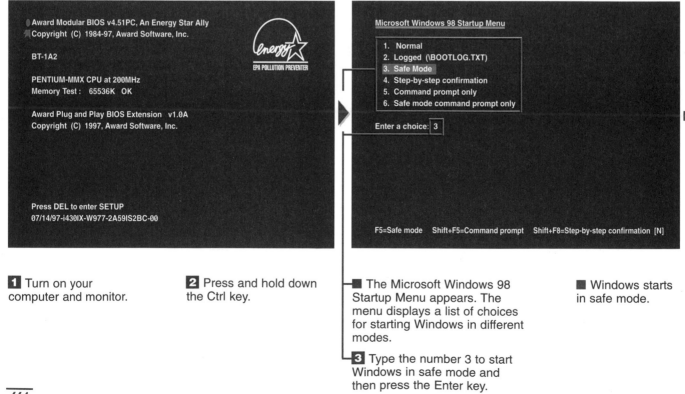

1 Turn on your computer and monitor.

2 Press and hold down the Ctrl key.

■ The Microsoft Windows 98 Startup Menu appears. The menu displays a list of choices for starting Windows in different modes.

3 Type the number 3 to start Windows in safe mode and then press the Enter key.

■ Windows starts in safe mode.

TIPS

When Windows is in safe mode, where should I start looking for the problem?

In the Windows Help window, click the Contents tab and then click the Troubleshooting book. Click Windows 98 Troubleshooters and then select the Hardware Conflict topic. To use Windows Help, see page 34.

What are the other options for starting my computer?

A Logged start creates a file on your hard drive that documents the entire startup procedure. This file may allow you to see where a problem is occurring in startup. The Step-by-step confirmation lets you choose which devices to load to start Windows and see where a problem may be occurring. The Command prompt only and Safe mode command prompt only options start MS-DOS.

How do I quickly select an alternative startup option?

Instead of pressing the Ctrl key to display the Windows Startup Menu, you can access some alternative startup options by using keyboard shortcuts. For example, you can press the F5 key to start Safe mode. You can use Shift+F5 to activate the Command prompt.

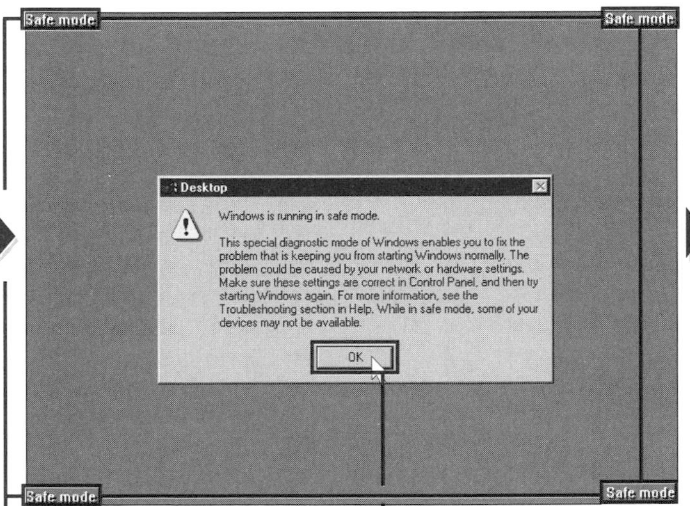

■ A message appears, telling you that Windows is running in safe mode and that some of your devices may not be available.

■ Windows displays the words "Safe mode" in each corner of your screen.

4 Click OK to continue.

■ You can now try to fix the problem that is keeping Windows from starting normally.

■ When you finish fixing the problem, restart your computer. You should now be able to use your computer as usual.

START THE REGISTRY EDITOR

The Registry Editor is an advanced tool you can use to view and edit the Registry. The Registry contains information needed to run Windows 98 with your hardware and software.

The contents of the Registry are complex, so you should only use the Registry Editor when absolutely necessary. Before making any changes to the Registry, you should create a backup copy of the Registry and make sure you understand how to restore it.

Each branch of the Registry is called a key. Each key can contain other keys, as well as pieces of information called values. Each value has a name and data.

The Registry contains six main keys, or branches, including two master keys. HKEY_LOCAL_MACHINE contains information about your hardware and software. HKEY_USERS contains information about desktop settings and network connections.

There are also three keys that contain copies of sections of the master keys. HKEY_CLASSES_ROOT contains information about the associations between your programs and documents. HKEY_CURRENT_USER contains information specific to the current user. HKEY_CURRENT_CONFIG contains information about display and printer settings.

The final main key, HKEY_DYN_DATA, stores data from the computer's memory, including Plug and Play information.

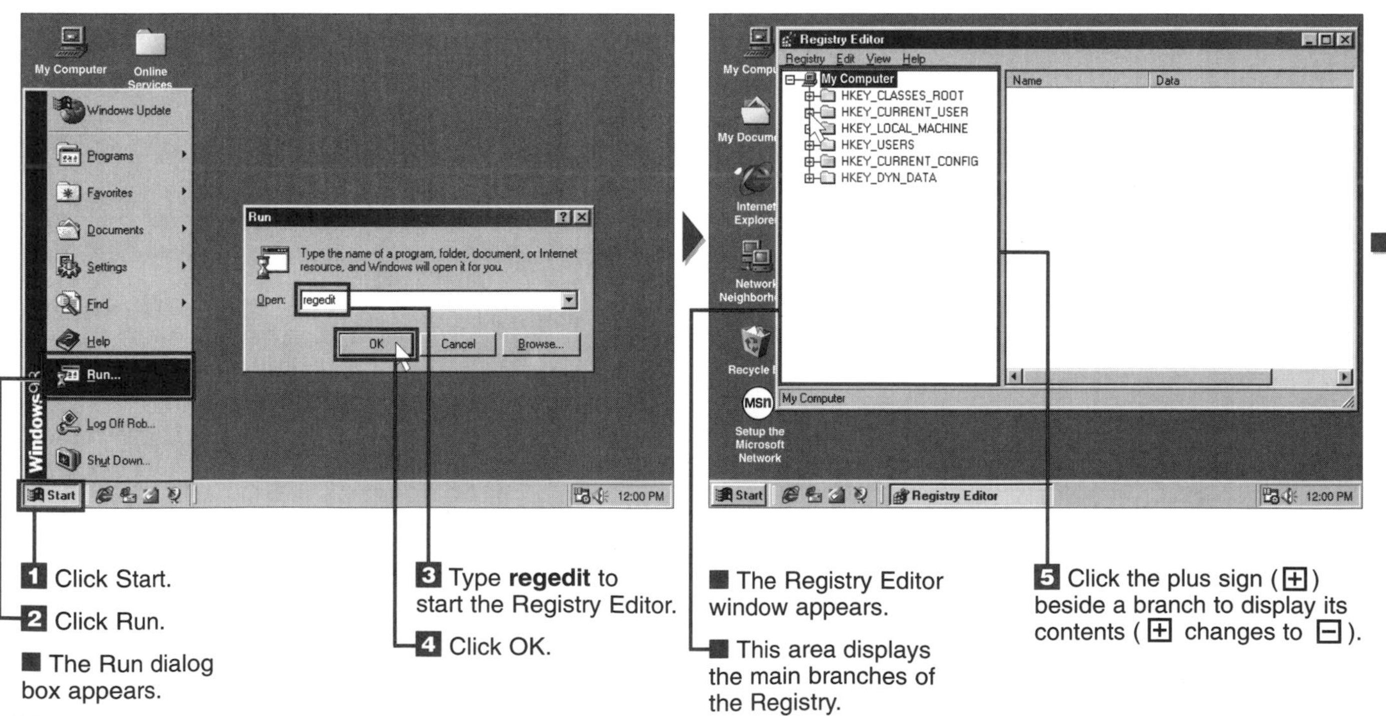

1 Click Start.

2 Click Run.

■ The Run dialog box appears.

3 Type **regedit** to start the Registry Editor.

4 Click OK.

■ The Registry Editor window appears.

■ This area displays the main branches of the Registry.

5 Click the plus sign (⊞) beside a branch to display its contents (⊞ changes to ⊟).

TIPS

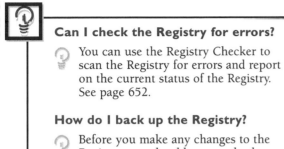

Can I check the Registry for errors?

You can use the Registry Checker to scan the Registry for errors and report on the current status of the Registry. See page 652.

How do I back up the Registry?

Before you make any changes to the Registry, you should create a backup copy of the Registry. You can use Microsoft Backup to back up the Registry. See the top of page 375.

I forgot to back up the Registry! Can I still restore the settings?

If you made changes to the Registry and Windows will not start properly, restart the computer and press the Ctrl key. When the Windows 98 Startup Menu appears, select the Command prompt only option. At the C:\> prompt, type **scanreg /restore**. The Microsoft Registry Checker appears, displaying one or more previous settings. Select the setting that was used the last time Windows started successfully.

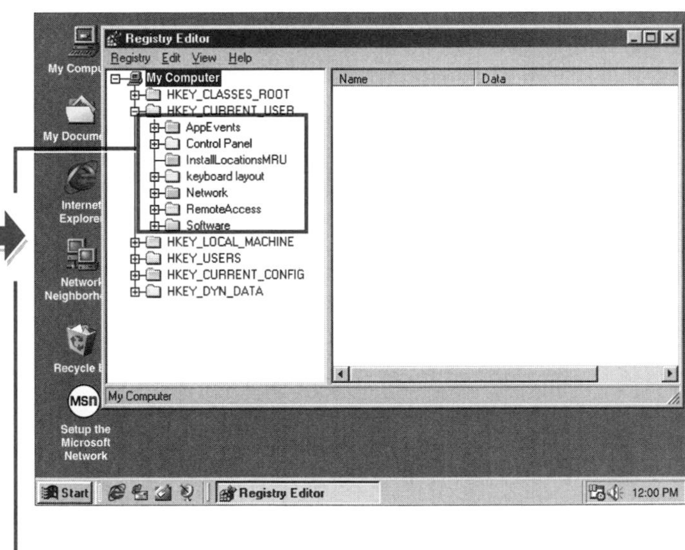

■ The contents of the branch appear.

Note: You can click the minus sign (⊟) to once again hide the contents of the branch.

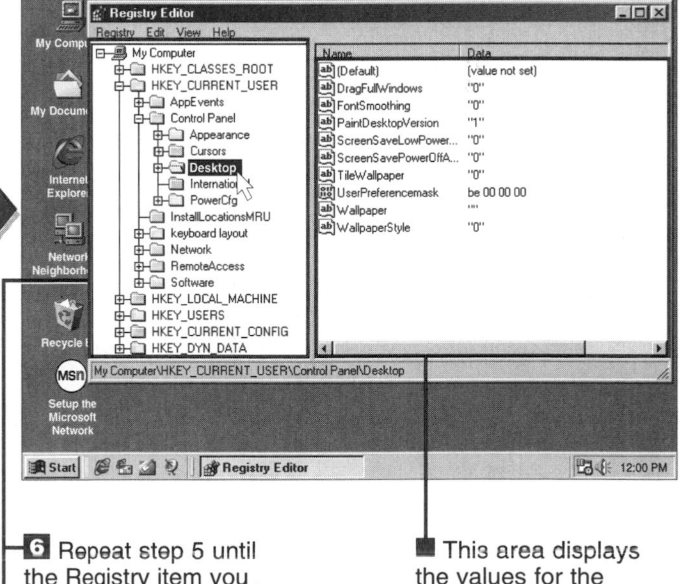

6 Repeat step 5 until the Registry item you want to view appears.

7 Click the Registry item to display its values.

■ This area displays the values for the Registry item.

SEARCH THE REGISTRY

You can search for a specific key in the Registry.

The Registry Editor window has two panes, similar to Windows Explorer. The left pane displays the list of keys contained in the Registry. The right pane displays the values, or information, stored in the currently selected key.

Looking for a specific key by browsing through the Registry Editor window can be time-consuming and difficult. The Find feature can help you quickly find information in the Registry.

When you use the Find feature to find a key, you must search for specific information. For example, if you want to find your screen appearance settings so you can copy them to another computer, search for the name of one of the appearance schemes, such as eggplant.

Windows will search the keys, values and data in the Registry for matching information.

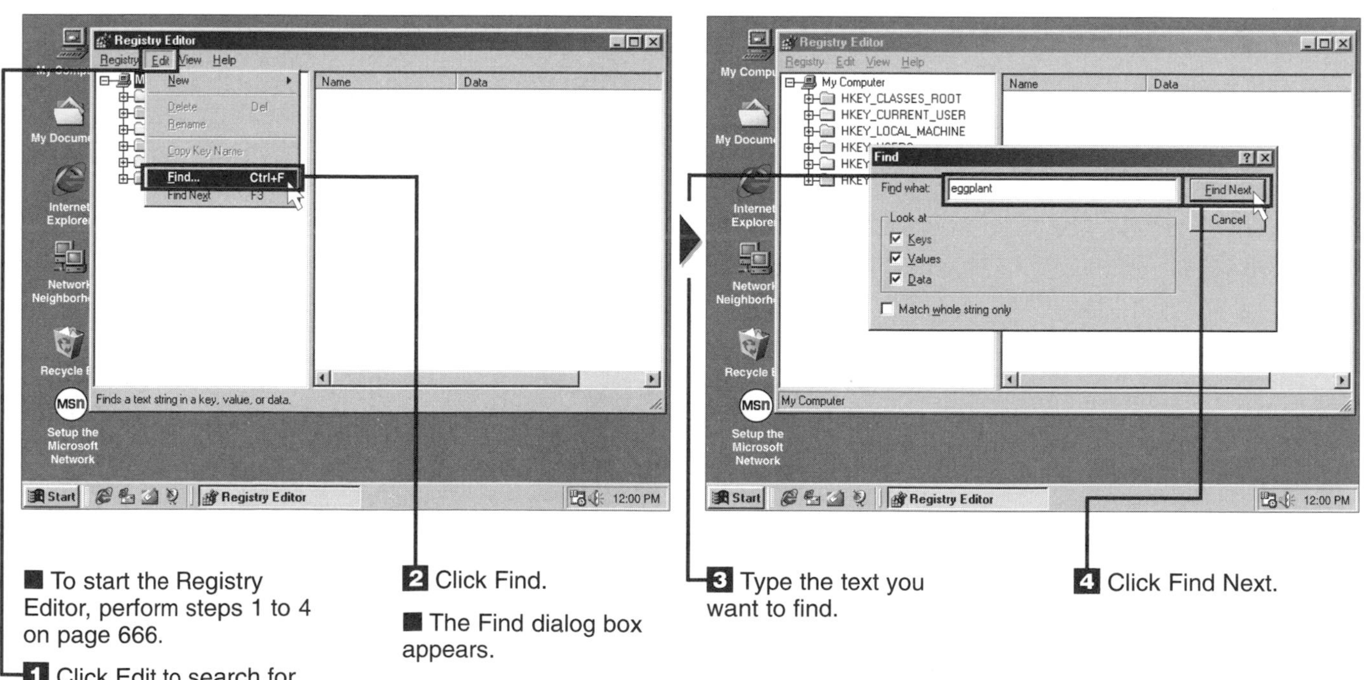

■ To start the Registry Editor, perform steps 1 to 4 on page 666.

1 Click Edit to search for information in the Registry.

2 Click Find.

■ The Find dialog box appears.

3 Type the text you want to find.

4 Click Find Next.

TIPS

What type of data can I search for?

The Find feature can only search for string data. You will not be able to search for binary or DWORD data. String data appears in quotation marks. Binary data is presented in hexadecimal (hex) format, or pairs of characters and numbers. DWORD data displays 0x followed by 8 characters and a number in parentheses.

The Registry Editor's Find feature is slow. How can I perform faster searches?

You can choose to search only keys, values or data to speed up the Find feature. Click each option in the Find dialog box that you do not want to search for (☑ changes to ☐). You can also export the Registry to a text file and then use a word processor, such as WordPad, to search the Registry. To export the Registry to a text file, see page 672.

I found the key I was searching for. How do I transfer the key's settings to another computer?

Export the key to a text file and place the file on a floppy disk. To export part of the Registry to a text file, see page 672. Insert the floppy disk into the other computer and then double-click the file you exported to merge the settings into the Registry of the other computer.

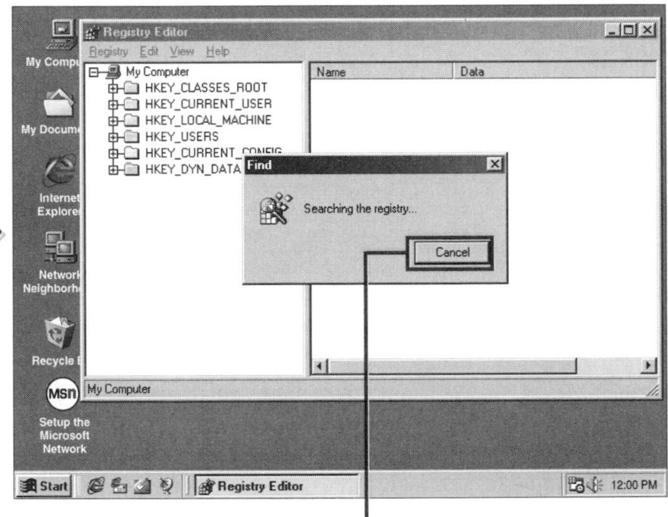

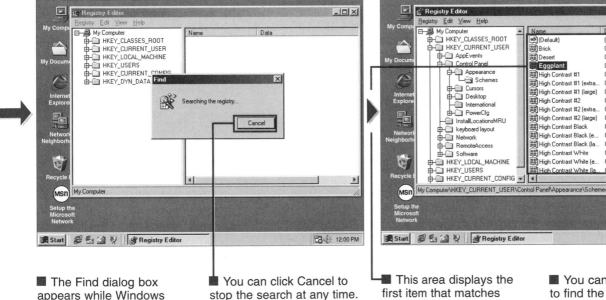

■ The Find dialog box appears while Windows searches the Registry.

■ You can click Cancel to stop the search at any time.

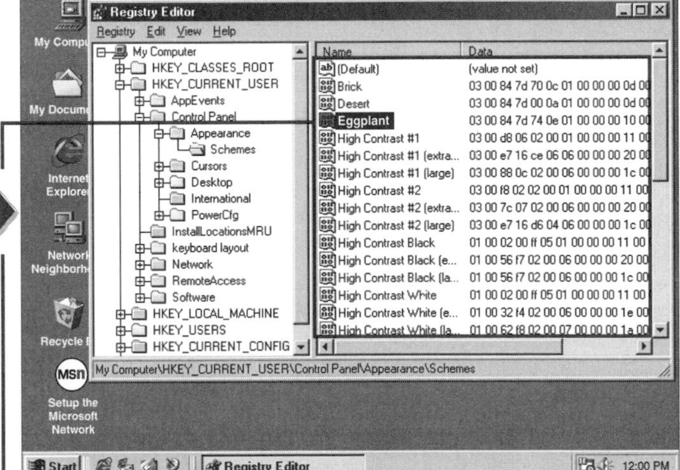

■ This area displays the first item that matches the text you typed.

■ You can press the F3 key to find the next instance of the text in the Registry.

EDIT THE REGISTRY

You can use the Registry Editor to add or change information in the Registry. The Registry Editor does not have an Undo feature and changes to the Registry are made immediately. If you make a mistake while editing the Registry, Windows may not start. Before making any changes, you should create a backup copy of the Registry.

You can add information to the Registry. For example, you can have a program start automatically without placing it in the StartUp folder. This is useful if you want to make sure a program runs every time you start your computer.

You can change the information in the Registry. You can change the data in an existing value or in a value you have added. This is useful if you want to change the behavior of your programs. For example, you can prevent ActiveMovie from closing when it has finished playing an .avi video file.

Any changes you make to the Registry should be based on tested information from reliable sources. Many computer magazines contain articles about editing the Registry and the changes that are possible. You can also find Web sites and newsgroups containing information about changing the Registry.

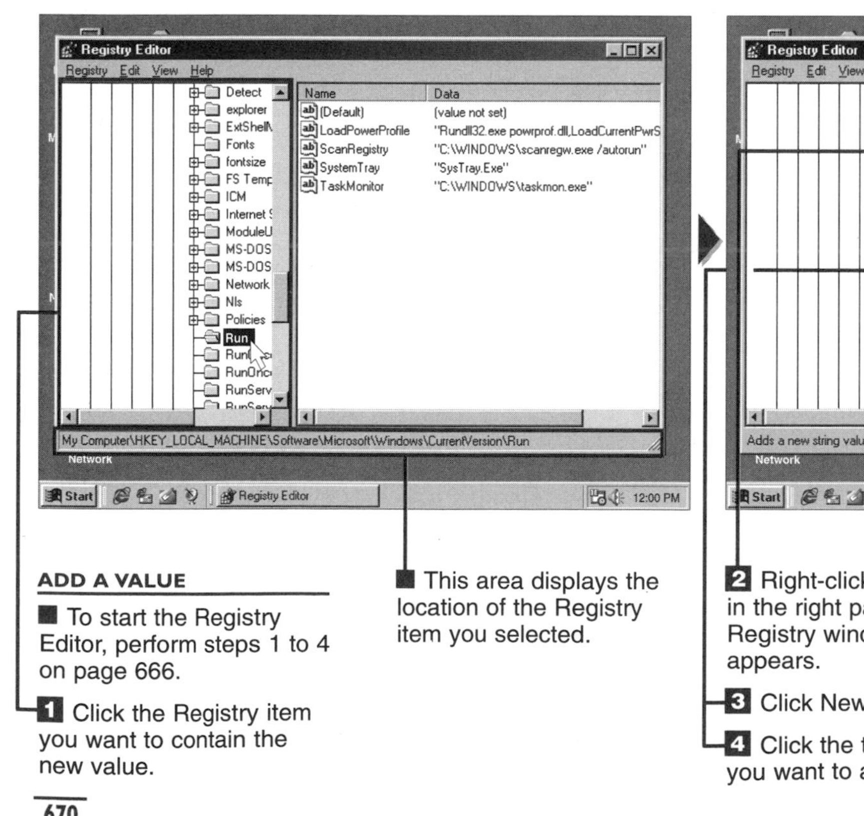

ADD A VALUE

■ To start the Registry Editor, perform steps 1 to 4 on page 666.

1 Click the Registry item you want to contain the new value.

■ This area displays the location of the Registry item you selected.

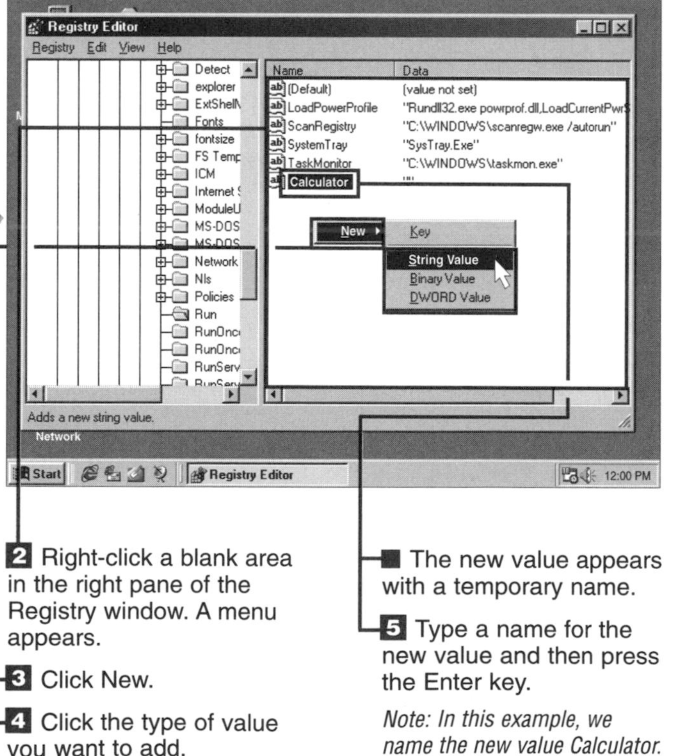

2 Right-click a blank area in the right pane of the Registry window. A menu appears.

3 Click New.

4 Click the type of value you want to add.

■ The new value appears with a temporary name.

5 Type a name for the new value and then press the Enter key.

Note: In this example, we name the new value Calculator.

TIPS

Is there another way to make changes to the Registry?

Whenever possible, you should use the Control Panel to make changes to the Registry. When you adjust settings in the Control Panel, Windows makes changes to the Registry for you.

How do I delete a key or value?

Click the key or value you want to remove and then press the Delete key. This is useful if you have removed a program from your computer but it is still listed in the Control Panel's Add/Remove Programs dialog box. To remove the program from the dialog box, delete the program's key from HKEY_LOCAL_MACHINE\Software\Microsoft\Windows\CurrentVersion\Uninstall.

How do I edit the Registry to prevent ActiveMovie from closing when it has finished playing an .avi file?

In the HKEY_CLASSES_ROOT\avifile\Shell\Play\Command key, double-click the (Default) value and remove **/close**.

How else can I change a value?

When the data for a value is "0" or "1" with no other letters or numbers, you can turn the value on or off by changing the data. In the data column, a "0" means the value is off and a "1" means the value is on.

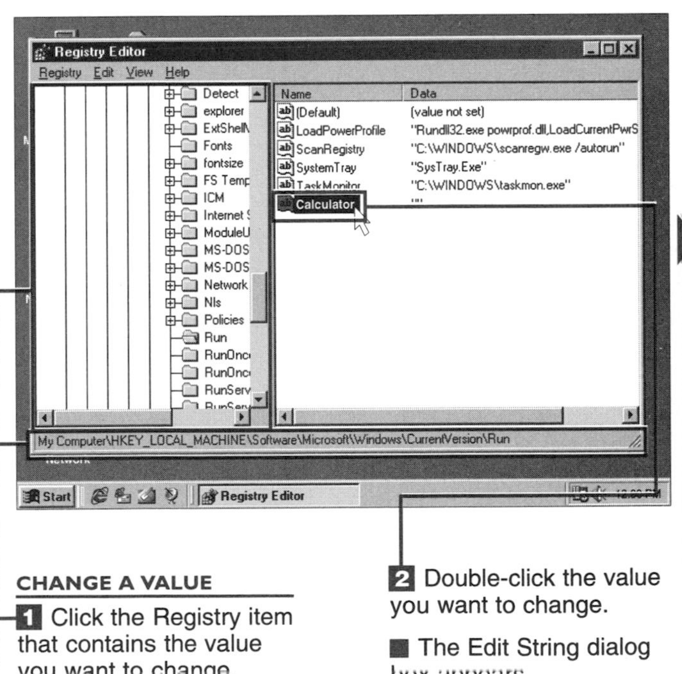

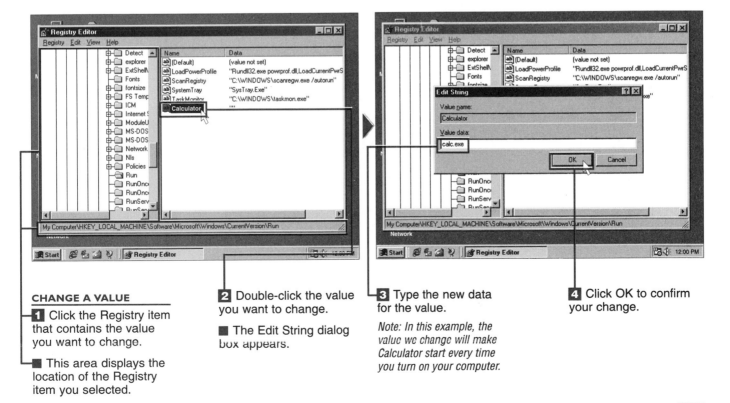

CHANGE A VALUE

1 Click the Registry item that contains the value you want to change.

■ This area displays the location of the Registry item you selected.

2 Double-click the value you want to change.

■ The Edit String dialog box appears.

3 Type the new data for the value.

Note: In this example, the value we change will make Calculator start every time you turn on your computer.

4 Click OK to confirm your change.

EXPORT THE REGISTRY TO A TEXT FILE

You can copy registry settings into a file that can be saved and edited with a word processor. You can copy the entire Registry or just one branch.

You may prefer to use a word processor to edit the Registry since the Registry Editor has a slow Find feature and does not support Find and Replace. When editing the Registry, keep in mind that the structure of the Registry is complex and its rules for punctuation are complicated. It is easier to make an editing mistake when you use a word processor than when you use the Registry Editor. When you finish editing the Registry, you can merge the exported file back into the Registry.

You can create a copy of all the registry settings and use the copy as a backup in case there is ever a problem with your settings.

You can also transfer copied registry settings to another computer. For example, you can export your customized screen color settings to a file. You can then share your screen color settings with a coworker or use them on your home or portable computer.

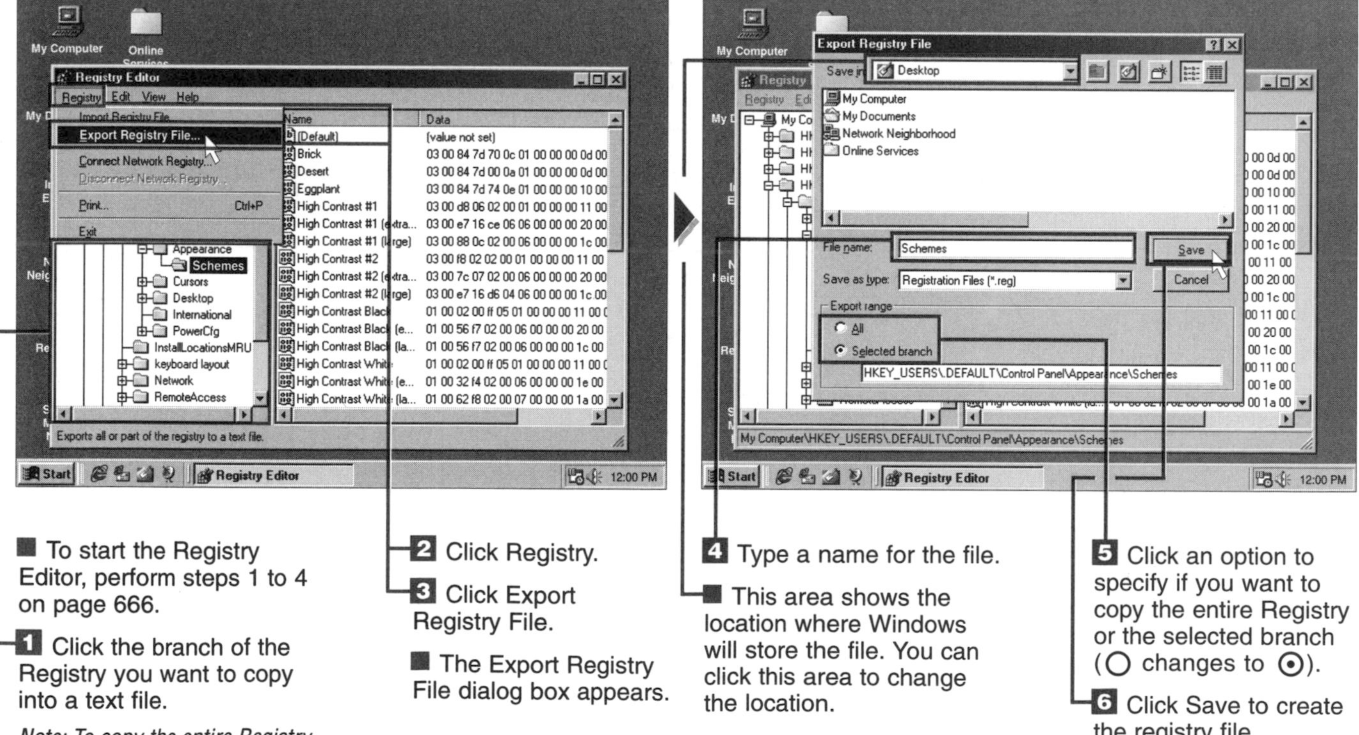

■ To start the Registry Editor, perform steps 1 to 4 on page 666.

1 Click the branch of the Registry you want to copy into a text file.

Note: To copy the entire Registry, you do not need to click a branch.

2 Click Registry.

3 Click Export Registry File.

■ The Export Registry File dialog box appears.

4 Type a name for the file.

■ This area shows the location where Windows will store the file. You can click this area to change the location.

5 Click an option to specify if you want to copy the entire Registry or the selected branch (○ changes to ⊙).

6 Click Save to create the registry file.

TIPS

How do I merge the exported file into the Registry?

If the file has the .reg extension, you can copy the contents of the exported file into the Registry by double-clicking the file. You can also open the Registry Editor, choose the Registry menu and select the Import Registry File command. In the Import Registry File dialog box, click the file you want to import and click the Open button.

What will happen to my current registry settings when I merge the exported file into the Registry?

The contents of the file will overwrite the current registry settings. If the settings in the file do not exist in the Registry, they will be added. If settings exist in the Registry and not in the file, the settings in the Registry will not be affected.

When I double-click an exported registry file, I want to be able to edit it. How do I change the default action for the file?

Click Start, select Settings and then choose the Folder Options command. Click the File Types tab. In the Registered file types list, select Registration Entries and then click the Edit button. Select the Edit action and then click the Set Default button.

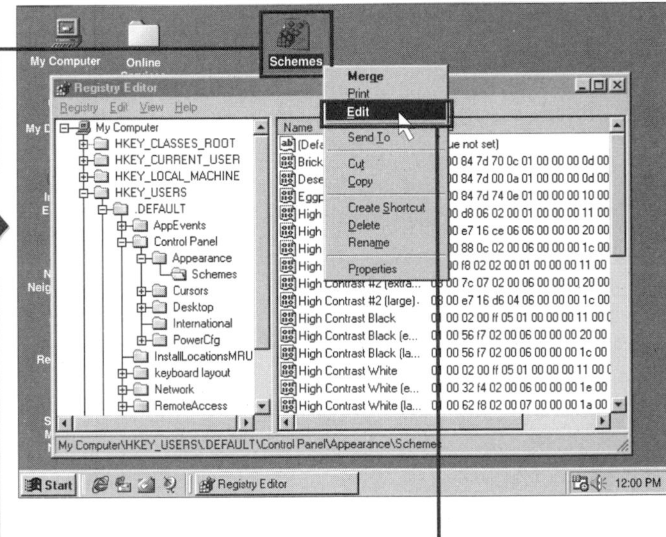

■ Windows creates the registry file.

7 Right-click the registry file. A menu appears.

8 Click Edit to edit the file.

Note: Do not double-click the file since this will merge the information back into the Registry.

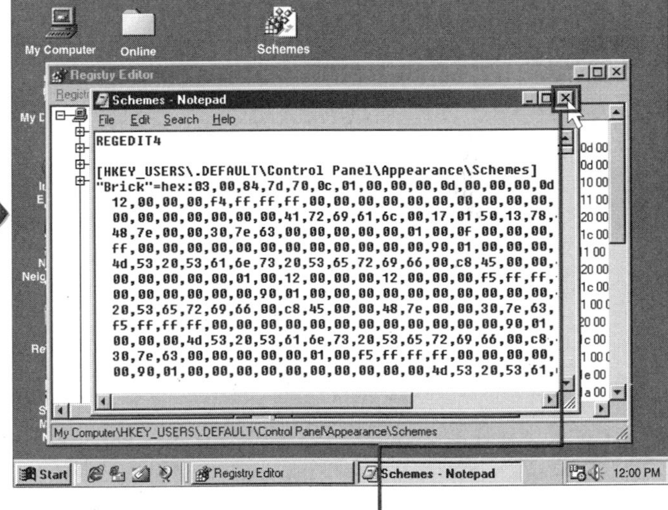

■ The registry file opens in Notepad.

Note: A message appears if the file is too large for Notepad to open. Click Yes to use WordPad to open the file.

9 Click ☒ to close Notepad when you finish viewing the file.

WHAT'S ON THE CD-ROM

The CD-ROM included in this book contains many useful files and programs. You will find a Web page providing one-click access to all the Internet links mentioned in the book. The disc also includes a version of the book that you can view and search using Adobe Acrobat Reader, as well as Netscape 4.0 and a special Internet sign up offer. There are also several utility programs and viewers for documents created in Microsoft Word, Excel and PowerPoint.

System Requirements

You can use this disc on any computer running Windows that has a CD-ROM drive. To get the most out of the items on the disc, you should have a 486 or Pentium computer with at least 16 MB of RAM. You should have at least 40 MB of free hard disk space and your system should be able to display at least 256 colors.

Use the My Computer or Windows Explorer window to display the contents of the CD-ROM.

Note: If you have trouble viewing the directory structure of the CD-ROM, or if the directory names are truncated (example: \directo~), your CD-ROM drive is currently using 16-bit drivers instead of the necessary 32-bit drivers. Please contact your CD-ROM drive vendor for information on upgrading the CD-ROM drivers.

Web Links

The CD-ROM contains a Web page that provides one-click access to all the Web pages and Internet references in the book. To use these links, you must have an Internet connection and a Web browser such as Internet Explorer installed. For more information about using Internet Explorer, see pages 502 to 519.

To display the Web links page, open the Web Links folder on the CD-ROM and then double-click Web Links.html. Your Web browser opens and displays the page.

Master Windows 98 VISUALLY

The CD-ROM contains a version of this book that you can view and search using Adobe Acrobat Reader. You cannot print the pages or copy text from the Acrobat files. A full and free version of Adobe Acrobat Reader 3.01 is also included on the disc. For more information about Adobe Acrobat Reader, see page 632. For information on how to install Acrobat Reader and use the book on the CD-ROM, see page 676.

EarthLink Network® Internet Sign Up Offer

If you are not yet connected to the Internet, you can use the CD-ROM to set up an account and start using the *EarthLink Network®* Internet service. This package also contains Netscape 4.0 browser software.

Open the EarthLink Setup folder on the CD-ROM. To set up an Internet account and install Netscape 4.0, double-click Setup.exe and then follow the instructions on your screen.

Utility Programs

The Utilities folder on the CD-ROM contains eight utility programs. The first four utilities mentioned below are also discussed on pages 632 to 635.

Before installing a utility from the CD-ROM, you should exit all other programs. In order to use most of the utilities, you must accept the license agreement provided with the utility. Make sure you read any Readme files provided with each utility.

For information on removing utilities you have installed, see page 616.

Adobe Acrobat Reader

The disc contains a full version of Acrobat Reader 3.01. For more information on using Acrobat Reader, see page 676.

In the Utilities folder, open the Acrobat Reader with Search folder. To install the utility, double-click rs32e301(1).exe and then follow the instructions on your screen.

Jasc Paint Shop Pro

The disc contains version 4.14 of Paint Shop Pro. You may use the program for free for 30 days. If you wish to continue using the program, you must then purchase the licensed version.

In the Utilities folder, open the Paint Shop Pro folder. To install the utility, double-click psp414.exe and then follow the instructions on your screen.

WinFax PRO

The disc contains version 8.0 of WinFax PRO. You may use the program for free for 45 days. If you wish to continue using the program, you must then purchase the licensed version.

In the Utilities folder, open the WinFax Pro folder. To install the utility, double-click setup.exe and then follow the instructions on your screen.

Nico Mak WinZip

The disc contains version 6.3 of WinZip. You may use the program for free for 21 days. If you wish to continue using the program, you must pay a registration fee. For more information on using WinZip, see page 636.

In the Utilities folder, open the WinZip folder. To install the utility, double-click winzip95.exe and then follow the instructions on your screen.

CyberMedia Oil Change

You can have Oil Change find program updates on the Internet and install them on your computer.

The disc contains a trial version of Oil Change. You must have an Internet connection to run Oil Change. During the setup process, you must register with CyberMedia. If you do not register, you will not be able to run Oil Change.

In the Utilities folder, open the Oil Change folder. To install the utility, double-click ocsetup.exe and then follow the instructions on your screen.

CyberMedia First Aid

You can use First Aid to identify and solve problems with your computer.

The disc contains a time-limited trial version of First Aid.

In the Utilities folder, open the First Aid folder. To install the utility, double-click fasetup.exe and then follow the instructions on your screen.

Quarterdeck CleanSweep Deluxe

CleanSweep Deluxe finds files that can be removed to free up space on your hard drive.

The disc contains a demonstration version of CleanSweep Deluxe. You may use the program for free for 15 days. If you wish to continue using the program, you must then purchase the licensed version.

In the Utilities folder, open the CleanSweep Deluxe folder. To install the utility, double click csdtrial.exe and then follow the instructions on your screen.

Microsoft Viewers

If you do not have Microsoft Office 97 installed on your computer, you can use the Microsoft viewers to display documents created in Microsoft Word, Excel or PowerPoint.

Each viewer must be installed separately. In the Utilities folder, open the Microsoft Viewers folder. To install the Word 97 viewer, double-click wd97vwr32.exe. To install the Excel Viewer, double-click Excel97Viewer.exe. To install the PowerPoint viewer, double-click PPView97.exe. Follow the instructions on your screen to set up each viewer.

MASTER WINDOWS 98 VISUALLY ON CD

You can view Master Windows 98 VISUALLY on your screen using the CD included at the back of this book. The CD allows you to search the contents of the book for a specific word or phrase. The CD also provides a convenient way of keeping the book handy while traveling.

You must install Acrobat Reader on your computer before you can view the information on the CD. This program is also provided on the CD. Acrobat Reader allows you to view Portable Document Format (.pdf) files. These files can display books and magazines on your screen exactly as they appear in printed form.

To install Acrobat Reader, open the Utilities folder on the CD and then open the Acrobat Reader with Search folder. Double-click the rs32e301(1).exe file and then follow the instructions on your screen.

After Acrobat Reader is installed, you can view the contents of the book, found on the CD in the folder called Master Windows 98 VISUALLY Acrobat Files. The contents are divided into eight sections that correspond to the sections of this book. To view the contents of a section, double-click the section.

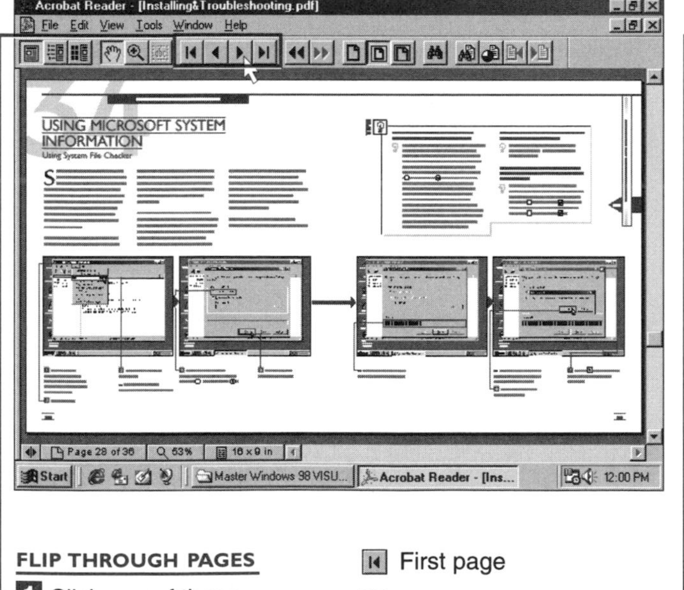

FLIP THROUGH PAGES

1 Click one of these options to flip through the pages of a section.

- First page
- Previous page
- Next page
- Last page

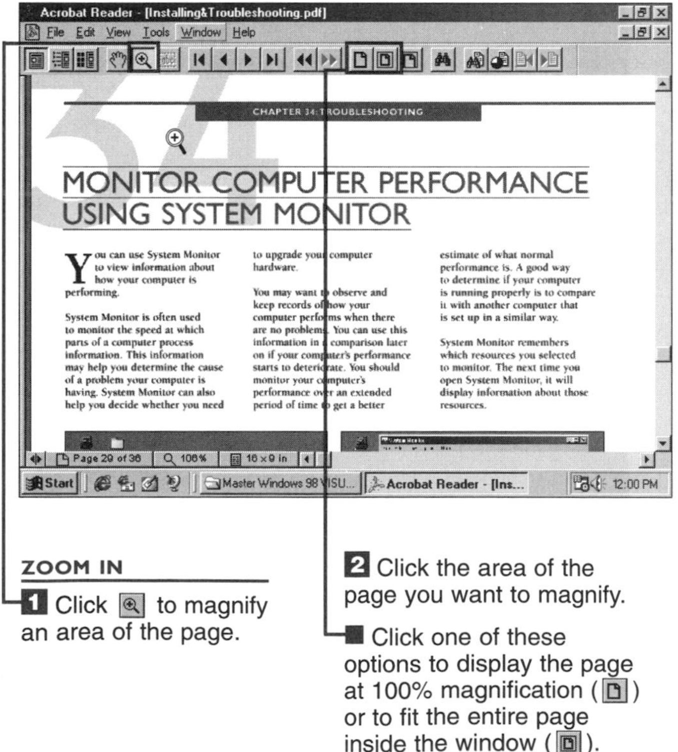

ZOOM IN

1 Click to magnify an area of the page.

2 Click the area of the page you want to magnify.

■ Click one of these options to display the page at 100% magnification ( ) or to fit the entire page inside the window ( ).

TIPS

Can I use an older version of Acrobat Reader to view the information on the CD?

Yes, but the latest version of Acrobat Reader offers more features, such as the ability to search all the sections at once.

How do I search all the sections on the CD at once?

You must first locate the index. While viewing the contents of the book, click [icon] in the Acrobat Reader window. Click Indexes and then click Add. Click index.pdx, click Open and then click OK. You only need to locate the index once. After locating the index, you can click [icon] to search all the sections.

How can I speed up access to the information?

Copy the Master Windows 98 VISUALLY Acrobat Files folder from the CD to your hard drive. Copying the folder to your hard drive will help speed up your searches.

Can I use Acrobat Reader for anything else?

Acrobat Reader is a popular and useful program. There are many files available on the Web that are designed to be viewed using Acrobat Reader. Look for files with the .pdf extension.

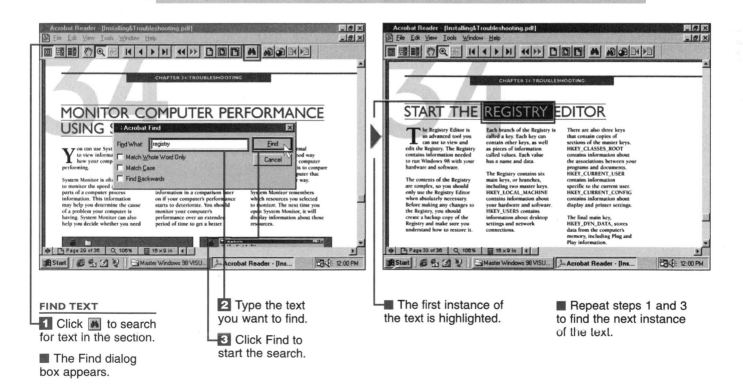

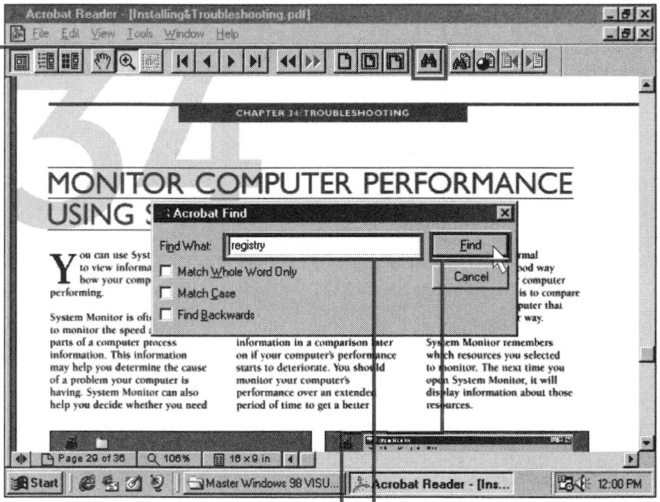

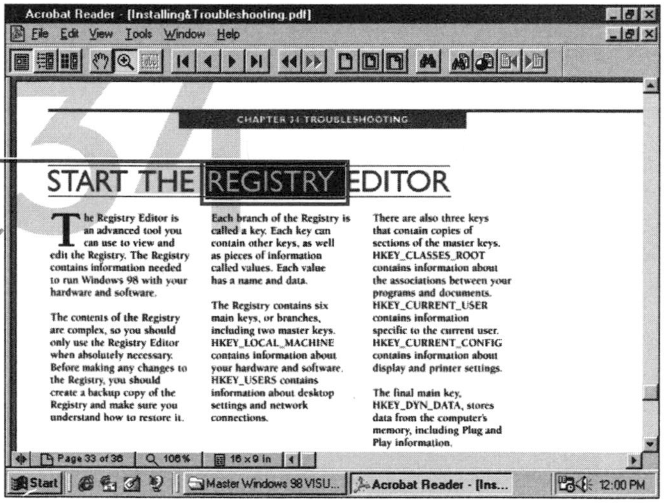

FIND TEXT

1 Click [icon] to search for text in the section.

■ The Find dialog box appears.

2 Type the text you want to find.

3 Click Find to start the search.

■ The first instance of the text is highlighted.

■ Repeat steps 1 and 3 to find the next instance of the text.

IDG BOOKS WORLDWIDE, INC.
END-USER LICENSE AGREEMENT

Read This. You should carefully read these terms and conditions before opening the software packet(s) included with this book ("Book"). This is a license agreement ("Agreement") between you and IDG Books Worldwide, Inc. ("IDGB"). By opening the accompanying software packet(s), you acknowledge that you have read and accept the following terms and conditions. If you do not agree and do not want to be bound by such terms and conditions, promptly return the Book and the unopened software packet(s) to the place you obtained them for a full refund.

1. License Grant. IDGB grants to you (either an individual or entity) a nonexclusive license to use one copy of the enclosed software program(s) (collectively, the "Software") solely for your own personal or business purposes on a single computer (whether a standard computer or a workstation component of a multi-user network). The Software is in use on a computer when it is loaded into temporary memory (i.e., RAM) or installed into permanent memory (e.g., hard disk, CD-ROM or other storage device). IDGB reserves all rights not expressly granted herein.

2. Ownership. IDGB is the owner of all right, title and interest, including copyright, in and to the compilation of the Software recorded on the CD-ROM. Copyright to the individual programs on the CD-ROM is owned by the author or other authorized copyright owner of each program. Ownership of the Software and all proprietary rights relating thereto remain with IDGB and its licensors.

3. Restrictions On Use and Transfer.

(a) You may only (i) make one copy of the Software for backup or archival purposes, or (ii) transfer the Software to a single hard disk, provided that you keep the original for backup or archival purposes. You may not (i) rent or lease the Software, (ii) copy or reproduce the Software through a LAN or other network system or through any computer subscriber system or bulletin-board system, or (iii) modify, adapt or create derivative works based on the Software.

(b) You may not reverse engineer, decompile, or disassemble the Software. You may transfer the Software and user documentation on a permanent basis, provided that the transferee agrees to accept the terms and conditions of this Agreement and you retain no copies. If the Software is an update or has been updated, any transfer must include the most recent update and all prior versions.

4. Restrictions on Use of Individual Programs. You must follow the individual requirements and restrictions detailed for each individual program. These limitations are contained in the individual license agreements recorded on the CD-ROM. These restrictions include a requirement that after using the program for the period of time specified in its text, the user must pay a registration fee or discontinue use. By opening the Software packet(s), you will be agreeing to abide by the licenses and restrictions for these individual programs. None of the material on this disk(s) or listed in this Book may ever be distributed, in original or modified form, for commercial purposes.

5. Limited Warranty.

(a) IDGB warrants that the Software and CD-ROM are free from defects in materials and workmanship under normal use for a period of sixty (60) days from the date of purchase of this Book. If IDGB receives notification within the warranty period of defects in materials or workmanship, IDGB will replace the defective CD-ROM.

(b) IDGB AND THE AUTHOR OF THE BOOK DISCLAIM ALL OTHER WARRANTIES, EXPRESS OR IMPLIED, INCLUDING WITHOUT LIMITATION IMPLIED WARRANTIES OF MERCHANTABILITY AND FITNESS FOR A PARTICULAR PURPOSE, WITH RESPECT TO THE SOFTWARE, THE PROGRAMS, THE SOURCE CODE CONTAINED THEREIN, AND/OR THE TECHNIQUES DESCRIBED IN THIS BOOK. IDGB DOES NOT WARRANT THAT THE FUNCTIONS CONTAINED IN THE SOFTWARE WILL MEET YOUR REQUIREMENTS OR THAT THE OPERATION OF THE SOFTWARE WILL BE ERROR FREE.

(c) This limited warranty gives you specific legal rights, and you may have other rights which vary from jurisdiction to jurisdiction.

6. Remedies.

(a) IDGB's entire liability and your exclusive remedy for defects in materials and workmanship shall be limited to replacement of the Software, which is returned to IDGB at the address set forth below with a copy of your receipt. This Limited Warranty is void if failure of the Software has resulted from accident, abuse, or misapplication. Any replacement Software will be warranted for the remainder of the original warranty period or thirty (30) days, whichever is longer.

(b) In no event shall IDGB or the author be liable for any damages whatsoever (including without limitation damages for loss of business profits, business interruption, loss of business information, or any other pecuniary loss) arising out of the use of or inability to use the Book or the Software, even if IDGB has been advised of the possibility of such damages.

(c) Because some jurisdictions do not allow the exclusion or limitation of liability for consequential or incidental damages, the above limitation or exclusion may not apply to you.

7. U.S. Government Restricted Rights. Use, duplication, or disclosure of the Software by the U.S. Government is subject to restrictions stated in paragraph (c) (1) (ii) of the Rights in Technical Data and Computer Software clause of DFARS 252.227-7013, and in subparagraphs (a) through (d) of the Commercial Computer—Restricted Rights clause at FAR 52.227-19, and in similar clauses in the NASA FAR supplement, when applicable.

8. General. This Agreement constitutes the entire understanding of the parties, and revokes and supersedes all prior agreements, oral or written, between them and may not be modified or amended except in a writing signed by both parties hereto which specifically refers to this Agreement. This Agreement shall take precedence over any other documents that may be in conflict herewith. If any one or more provisions contained in this Agreement are held by any court or tribunal to be invalid, illegal or otherwise unenforceable, each and every other provision shall remain in full force and effect.

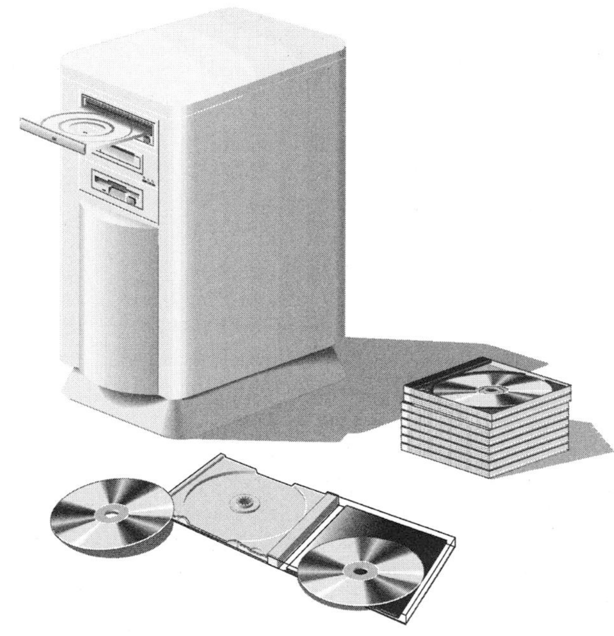

INDEX

A

B

C

INDEX

INDEX

D

INDEX

F

INDEX

I

INDEX

J

K

L

M

O

P

Q

R

S

T

U

V

W

X

Y

Z

OVER 5 MILLION

OTHER 3-D Visual SERIES

SIMPLIFIED BOOKS

Windows 95 Simplified
ISBN 1-56884-662-2
$19.99 USA/£18.99 UK

More Windows 95 Simplified
ISBN 1-56884-689-4
$19.99 USA/£18.99 UK

Windows 3.1 Simplified
ISBN 1-56884-654-1
$19.99 USA/£18.99 UK

Excel 97 Simplified
ISBN 0-7645-6022-0
$24.99 USA/£23.99 UK

Excel For Windows 95 Simplified
ISBN 1-56884-682-7
$19.99 USA/£18.99 UK

Word 97 Simplified
ISBN 0-7645-6011-5
$24.99 USA/£23.99 UK

Word For Windows 95 Simplified
ISBN 1-56884-681-9
$19.99 USA/£18.99 UK

Office 97 Simplified
ISBN 0-7645-6009-3
$29.99 USA/£28.99 UK

Creating Web Pages Simplified
ISBN 0-7645-6007-7
$24.99 USA/£23.99 UK

Internet and World Wide Web Simplified 2nd Edition
ISBN 0-7645-6029-8
$24.99 USA/£23.99 UK

Computers Simplified, Third Edition
ISBN 0-7645-6008-5
$24.99 USA/£23.99 UK

The 3-D Visual Dictionary of Computing
ISBN 1-56884-678-9
$19.99 USA/£18.99 UK

WordPerfect 6.1 For Windows Simplified
ISBN 1-56884-665-7
$19.99 USA/£18.99 UK

Lotus 1-2-3 R5 For Windows Simplified
ISBN 1-56884-670-3
$19.99 USA/£18.99 UK

FOR CORPORATE ORDERS, PLEASE CALL: 800-469-6616

ORDER FORM

TRADE & INDIVIDUAL ORDERS

Phone: **(800) 762-2974**
or **(317) 895-5200**
(8 a.m.–6 p.m., CST, weekdays)
FAX : **(317) 895-5298**

EDUCATIONAL ORDERS & DISCOUNTS

Phone: **(800) 434-2086**
(8:30 a.m.–5:00 p.m., CST, weekdays)
FAX : **(817) 251-8174**

CORPORATE ORDERS FOR 3-D VISUAL™ SERIES

Phone: **(800) 469-6616**
(8 a.m.–5 p.m., EST, weekdays)
FAX : **(905) 890-9434**

Qty	ISBN	Title	Price	Total

Shipping & Handling Charges

	Description	First book	Each add'l. book	Total
Domestic	Normal	$4.50	$1.50	$
	Two Day Air	$8.50	$2.50	$
	Overnight	$18.00	$3.00	$
International	Surface	$8.00	$8.00	$
	Airmail	$16.00	$16.00	$
	DHL Air	$17.00	$17.00	$

Subtotal ______________

CA residents add applicable sales tax ______________

IN, MA and MD residents add 5% sales tax ______________

IL residents add 6.25% sales tax ______________

RI residents add 7% sales tax ______________

TX residents add 8.25% sales tax ______________

Shipping ______________

Total ______________

Ship to:

Name ______________

Address ______________

Company ______________

City/State/Zip ______________

Daytime Phone ______________

Payment: ☐ Check to IDG Books (US Funds Only)
☐ Visa ☐ Mastercard ☐ American Express

Card # ______________ Exp. ______________ Signature ______________